Frommer's

F

from $70 a Day

5th Edition

by Lesley Abravanel

with Laura Lea Miller

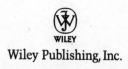

WILEY

Wiley Publishing, Inc.

Published by:

Wiley Publishing, Inc.

111 River St.
Hoboken, NJ 07030-5774

ISBN 0-7645-7795-6

Editor: Kendra L. Falkenstein
Production Editor: Ian Skinnari
Cartographer: Elizabeth Puhl
Photo Editor: Richard Fox
Production by Wiley Indianapolis Composition Services

Front cover photo: Closeup of a woman floating in a pool
Back cover photo: The Canopy Room at Behind the Fence Bed & Breakfast in Brandon, Florida

For information on our other products and services or to obtain technical support, please contact our Customer Care Department within the U.S. at 800/762-2974, outside the U.S. at 317/572-3993 or fax 317/572-4002.

Wiley also publishes its books in a variety of electronic formats. Some content that appears in print may not be available in electronic formats.

Manufactured in the United States of America

5 4 3 2 1

Contents

(12) Northeast Florida   466

(13) Northwest Florida: The Panhandle   521

Index   581

List of Maps

About the Authors

Lesley Abravanel is a freelance journalist and a graduate of the University of Miami School of Communication. When she isn't combing South Florida for the latest hotels, restaurants, and attractions, she is on the lookout for vacationing celebrities, about whom she writes in her weekly nightlife and gossip column, "Velvet Underground," for the *Miami Herald.* She is a contributor to *Condé Nast Traveller, Time Out,* all three illustrious supermarket tabloids, reviews restaurants for AOL/Digital City South Florida, is the Miami correspondent for *Black Book Magazine,* and is the author of *Frommer's South Florida* and *Frommer's Portable Miami.*

*To Mommy, Daddy, Mags, Winston, and the so-called Peanut Gang,
you know who you are.*

Laura Lea Miller is a freelance writer based in Buffalo, New York, though she's spent countless hours scouring Central Florida's theme parks over the years—both with and without her husband and five kids. A family-travel expert who religiously makes an annual pilgrimage to the Land the Mouse built, she is currently researching and writing a guide to Florida for families.

Acknowledgments

To my mother and father, without whose influence, encouragement, and support I would never have ended up in Miami doing what I'm doing.

To all the publicists and proprietors for putting up with the endless e-mails, inquiries, and spur-of-the-moment visits, I thank you for your cooperation and eagerness to answer pressing questions about hair dryers, irons, hours, and credit cards.

Thanks to Kendra Falkenstein, my fabulous editor, for being on the same page as me, "getting it," and, most especially, for being so, ahem, Internet savvy.

Thanks to Gabe Berman and Ronna Gradus. Your help is most appreciated, even though I know you still want to kill me.

Thanks to all my friends and colleagues who know that I'm much more than a party girl and accept my quirkiness, compulsive behavior, and genuine penchant for all things bizarre.

Thank you, Mrs. Ritchie, for inspiring me to express myself and aspire to greatness.

And, last but not at all least, thanks to my Swede for putting up with me and my inanity and my insanity. Mwah!

—Lesley Abravanel

An Invitation to the Reader

In researching this book, we discovered many wonderful places—hotels, restaurants, shops, and more. We're sure you'll find others. Please tell us about them, so we can share the information with your fellow travelers in upcoming editions. If you were disappointed with a recommendation, we'd love to know that, too. Please write to:

Frommer's Florida from $70 a Day, 5th Edition
Wiley Publishing, Inc. • 111 River St. • Hoboken, NJ 07030-5774

An Additional Note

Please be advised that travel information is subject to change at any time—and this is especially true of prices. We therefore suggest that you write or call ahead for confirmation when making your travel plans. The authors, editors, and publisher cannot be held responsible for the experiences of readers while traveling. Your safety is important to us, however, so we encourage you to stay alert and be aware of your surroundings. Keep a close eye on cameras, purses, and wallets, all favorite targets of thieves and pickpockets.

Other Great Guides for Your Trip:

Frommer's Florida

Frommer's South Florida

Frommer's Walt Disney World® & Orlando

Frommer's Caribbean Cruises & Ports of Call

Frommer's Florida's Best-Loved Driving Tour

Frommer's Irreverent Guide to Walt Disney World®

The Unofficial Guide to Florida with Kids

The Unofficial Guide to Walt Disney World®

The Unofficial Guide to Walt Disney World® with Kids

The Unofficial Guide to Walt Disney World® for Grown-Ups

The Unofficial Guide to the Best RV & Tent Campgrounds in Florida & the Southeast

Frommer's Portable Miami

Frommer's Portable Tampa & St. Petersburg

Frommer's Star Ratings, Icons & Abbreviations

Every hotel, restaurant, and attraction listing in this guide has been ranked for quality, value, service, amenities, and special features using a **star-rating system.** In country, state, and regional guides, we also rate towns and regions to help you narrow down your choices and budget your time accordingly. Hotels and restaurants are rated on a scale of zero (recommended) to three stars (exceptional). Attractions, shopping, nightlife, towns, and regions are rated according to the following scale: zero stars (recommended), one star (highly recommended), two stars (very highly recommended), and three stars (must-see).

In addition to the star-rating system, we also use **seven feature icons** that point you to the great deals, in-the-know advice, and unique experiences that separate travelers from tourists. Throughout the book, look for:

Finds	Special finds—those places only insiders know about
Fun Fact	Fun facts—details that make travelers more informed and their trips more fun
Kids	Best bets for kids and advice for the whole family
Moments	Special moments—those experiences that memories are made of
Overrated	Places or experiences not worth your time or money
Tips	Insider tips—great ways to save time and money
Value	Great values—where to get the best deals

The following **abbreviations** are used for credit cards:

AE	American Express	DISC	Discover	V	Visa
DC	Diners Club	MC	MasterCard		

Frommers.com

Now that you have the guidebook to a great trip, visit our website at **www.frommers.com** for travel information on more than 3,000 destinations. With features updated regularly, we give you instant access to the most current trip-planning information available. At Frommers.com, you'll also find the best prices on airfares, accommodations, and car rentals—and you can even book travel online through our travel booking partners. At Frommers.com, you'll also find the following:

- Online updates to our most popular guidebooks
- Vacation sweepstakes and contest giveaways
- Newsletter highlighting the hottest travel trends
- Online travel message boards with featured travel discussion

What's New in Florida

After being unmercifully hit by four hurricanes during the summer and fall of 2004, the Southwest Florida areas of Punta Gorda and Port Charlotte experienced the most damage. While the areas of Captiva and Sanibel Islands also experienced damage, most of the hotels there have already been repaired and thanks to FEMA, the damage caused by beach erosion in those areas as well as the Daytona Beach area, are also in the process of repair. Thankfully, while many major tourist attractions may have been closed immediately after the storms hit, by the time this book is in your hands, everything will have been restored to its original, if not better, condition.

MIAMI While a plethora of hotels and restaurants have opened recently in Miami, unfortunately for the budget-conscious traveler, most of them fall into the expensive category. For complete information on Miami, see chapter 4.

Dining **Bayside Marketplace,** (401 Biscayne Blvd., Miami; ✆ **305/577-3344**), has reintroduced a group dine-around program, featuring group dining options at fixed prices, allowing you the flexibility of enjoying the various restaurants and meals at affordable prices. A new 200-seat **Chili's** restaurant opened at Bayside as well, featuring the restaurant's new concept, **Chili's Margarita Bar.**

Attractions The city of Coral Gables now offers the **Coral Gables Trolley** (www.coralgables.com/r1_trolley.htm), a free service running Monday through Friday on three different shifts around the city's most popular shopping and sightseeing routes.

After Dark At press time, the hottest nightspots are located on the still sizzling South Beach. However, over the causeway, a burgeoning nocturnal buzz is emanating from the once desolate area of **downtown Miami,** off of Biscayne Boulevard, thanks to cheaper rents and 24-hour liquor licenses. Among them, **I/O** (30 NE 14th St.; ✆ **305/358-8007**), a dance club where indie music fanatics hang out; and **Grass Restaurant and Lounge** (12 NE 40th St.; ✆ **305/573-3355**) brings a taste of Tiki-chic to the Design District with thatched-roof banquettes and a decidedly artsy crowd. Back on South Beach, Mötley Crüe–man Tommy Lee opened **Rok Bar** (1905 Collins Ave.; ✆ **305/538-7171**) in May of 2004, a rock 'n' roll themed bar where Lee will make surprise appearances as guest DJ and musician.

THE GOLD COAST While the Gold Coast's beaches remain less congested than those in Miami, the area isn't impervious to development—especially when it comes to resorts, restaurants, and nightlife. Whereas the Gold Coast used to be a sleepy beachfront, today it's slowly en route to rivaling the liveliness of a big city like Miami. For complete information on this region, see chapter 7.

Accommodations Opened in the summer of 2004, the $200 million **Seminole Hard Rock Hotel &**

Casino, 1 Seminole Rd., Hollywood (© **954/327-7625**), offers 500 luxury rooms as well as a lakeside beach club, 130,000-square-foot casino, and European Health Spa. It's sort of just like the Hard Rock in Vegas, only without blackjack, slots, and all other forms of "bet against the house" gambling. Well, there's always bingo.

Attractions Hooray for Hollywood—Beach, Florida, that is, where **The Reel Hollywood Entertainment Museum** (101 N. Ocean Drive, Hollywood; © **954-925-6109**) is slated to open in the winter of 2005, featuring 50,000 square feet of exhibitions, interactive displays, movie and television sets, and countless videos and films on the history and technology of the film and TV industry. Over at the pricey Westin Diplomat Resort & Spa (3555 S. Ocean Dr., Hollywood; © **954/602-6000**), **Adventure World** (www.abcadventureworld. com), opened at the hotel's Diplomat Landing complex, featuring air cat excursions; kayak, canoe, and jet ski trips; fishing; and Segway human transporters.

Shopping The Mall at **Wellington Green** (10300 W. Forest Hill Blvd., Wellington; © **561/227-6900**) is Palm Beach's newest shopping center, featuring 140 specialty stores and department stores. **Sawgrass Mills** (12801 West Sunrise Blvd., Sunrise; © **954/846-2300**), the monstrous outlet mall in Sunrise, is adding the Colonnade Outlets at Sawgrass, which will include 110,000 square feet of new retail space featuring high end, but deeply discounted, fashion and gourmet dining. The Colonnade is slated to open at the end of 2005. Also at Sawgrass, **Wannado City** (www. wannadocity.com), the size of three football fields, is an interactive entertainment experience for kids featuring 140,000 square feet of a "city" that will imaginatively transport kids to a world of their own, where they can transform into firefighter, archaeologist, actor, TV news reporter, chef, judge, airplane pilot, doctor, and a slew of other professions.

SOUTHWEST FLORIDA All telephone numbers in Fort Myers, Fort Myers Beach, Sanibel and Captiva islands, Naples, and Marco Island are now in **area code 239.** Boca Grande and Charlotte County remain in area code 941.

For complete information on this region, see chapter 9.

Fort Meyers, Sanibel & Captiva Islands The beaches of Fort Myers and Sanibel have rolled out the **Great Calusa Blueway** (© **800/296-0249**), over 40 miles of a new paddling trail for kayakers and canoers covering the waters of Lovers Key State Recreation Area, Mound Key State Archaeological Site, Koreshan State Historic Site, Fort Myers Beach, Sanibel, Captiva, and Pine islands, ending at Cayo Costa. Even cooler, the Blueway utilizes Global Positioning System (GPS) technology, marking key points along the trail to aid in navigation. **Dolphin Watch and Wildlife Adventure Cruise** (© **239/472-5300**), offered by Captiva Cruises, is a 90-minute tour by boat that leaves daily at 4pm from South Seas Resort on Captiva Island. Explore the wildlife in and around picturesque Pine Island Sound, which is home to birds, dolphins, manatees, and more. The cost is $20 for adults and $10 for children ages 3 through 10. Reservations required; group outings and private charters also are available.

THE TAMPA BAY AREA For complete information on this region, see chapter 10.

Tampa Busch Gardens Tampa Bay (© **888/800-5447** or 813/987-5283; www.buschgardens.com) premiered KaTonga, a 40-minute musical tribute to animal folklore featuring African-inspired dance, music, and puppetry taking place at the park's Moroccan Palace Theater. Also at Busch Gardens, a five-story family roller coaster, Cheetah Chase, featuring 1,200 feet of track, speeds up to 22 mph, drops, turns, and corkscrews. Downtown, the **Florida Aquarium** (© 813/273-4000; www.flaquarium.net) added **Explore a Shore,** a 2.2-acre outdoor aquatic discovery zone for kids featuring sea life models, a pirate ship, water slide, water cannons, and live animals. The two-story, 24-foot-long pirate ship will allow kids to fire water cannons from the deck, climb across cargo nets, view a shipwreck through a telescope, and take the helm to follow a map to buried treasure. Kids can also climb on a 10-foot eel reef rock structure, slide through tunnels, and crawl through an 8-by-4-foot wave in the Surf's Up Wave Tunnel.

Sarasota/Clearwater The **Philadelphia Phillies** (© 727/442-8496 or 215/436-1000; www.phillies.mlb.com) moved to new spring training digs in Clearwater—**Bright House Networks Field** (601 Old Coachman Rd.; © 727/442-8496).

WALT DISNEY WORLD & ORLANDO For complete information on this region, see chapter 11.

Accommodations Disney's **Pop Century Resort** (© 407/938-4000 or 407/939-6000; disneyworld.com), opened in December 2003, is Mickey's newest budget property and features themed buildings decorated with larger-than-life memorabilia from the past 50 years.

Exploring Walt Disney World In the theme parks, Disney raised ticket prices $2 to $55 for adults. Epcot's new out-of-this-world (literally) attraction, **Mission: Space,** opened in August 2003 to great acclaim—even NASA astronauts have voiced approval of this simulator.

Universal Studios Florida (© 800/837-2273; www.universalorlando.com) welcomed two new attractions. **Shrek 4-D** is a 20-minute show that can be seen, heard, felt, and smelled thanks to film and motion simulators, OgreVision glasses, and other special effects, including water spritzers. **Jimmy Neutron's Nicktoon Blast** lets riders board a spinning, careening adventure that includes a battle against Yokians—evil, egg-shaped aliens. And **The Revenge of the Mummy** is an indoor screamer that combines roller-coaster technology with space age robotics and pyrotechnics.

SeaWorld (© 800/327-2424 or 407/351-3600; www.seaworld.com) is diving deeper into the restaurant game with **Dine with Shamu,** a reservations-only seafood buffet served poolside with Shamu as a special guest and **Sharks Underwater Grill,** where diners can dig into Florida and Caribbean treats while watching denizens of the deep swim by in the Terrors of the Deep exhibit. SeaWorld also has added a new shark encounter that lets snorkelers and divers have limited contact with some of the 58 sharks in its Terrors of the Deep area ($125).

Universal and SeaWorld also raised their ticket prices ($54 adults at SeaWorld and $55 at Universal Orlando).

NORTHEAST FLORIDA For complete information on this region, see chapter 12.

Daytona Beach Believe it or not, there is something scarier in Daytona than half-naked, mullet-sporting/bikini-wearing teenagers. **Haunts of Daytona** (© 386/253-6034; www.hauntsofdaytona.com) is the only ghost tour in Florida that is owned and operated by a certified ghost hunter and active certified paranormal researcher. Tours begin at 7:30pm. Tickets are $8 per person; children under 6 are free.

NORTHWEST FLORIDA: THE PANHANDLE   For complete information on this region, see chapter 13.

Pensacola   In July 2003, Pensacola Beach received a $16 million, 6-month beach nourishment project, restoring 200 feet of beach along an 8-mile stretch of coastline. With special attention paid to matching the new sand's color and grain size to the area's existing trademark sugar-white sand, the project brought sand from an off-shore borrow site, along with enough shells to keep beachcombers busy for quite some time.

In 2004, Pensacola was named as the site for the decommissioned aircraft carrier USS *Oriskany* to be used as an artificial reef in the Gulf of Mexico 22½ miles southeast of Pensacola Pass. The Navy committed $2.8 million for its preparation and deployment as a reef. For more information on the project, call ⓒ **850/595-3476.**

1

The Best of Florida from $70 a Day

The moniker "Sunshine State," does no justice to the state of Florida. It's just too obvious. You already know to leave the snow boots at home and to pack the sunscreen. It's also common knowledge that a separate state within the state, known as Disney, attracts throngs of visitors every day. But did you also know that the so-called Sunshine State has castles that aren't made of sand, an all-psychic town that would even stump *Crossing Over*'s John Edwards, and a restaurant where clothing is optional? There's a lot more than rays of sun in this delightfully wacky state.

Here you can choose from a wide array of accommodations, from deluxe resorts, chichi boutiques, and theme hotels to down home-away-from-home mom-and-pop motels. You can visit remote little towns like Apalachicola or a megalopolis like Miami. Devour fresh seafood, from amberjack to oysters—and work off those calories by doing whichever activities you like best: bicycling, golfing, kayaking, or—yes, it's a sport, especially in South Beach—clubbing. Despite overdevelopment in many parts of the state, Floridians have maintained thousands of acres of wilderness areas, from the little respite of Clam Pass County Park in downtown Naples to the magnificent, mysterious, and mystical Everglades National Park, which stretches across the state's southern tip.

Choosing the "best" of all this is a daunting task, and the selections in this chapter are only a rundown on some of the affordable highlights. You'll find numerous other outstanding resorts, hotels, destinations, activities, and attractions—all described in the pages of this book. With a bit of serendipity you'll come up with some bests of your own.

And the real best of Florida: You can see it, do it, and eat it on a budget. Really. We swear. Mouseketeer's honor.

1 The Best Beaches

Many of Florida's best beaches are in its state parks and recreation areas. Admission to most of them is $4 per vehicle with up to eight occupants, $2 for a vehicle with one occupant, or $1 per pedestrian or bicyclist. Given the quality of what you'll see, that's one of Florida's best bargains.

- **Virginia Key** (Key Biscayne): The producers of *Survivor* could feasibly shoot their show on this ultra-secluded, picturesque, and deserted key, where people go purposely not to be found. See p. 122.

- **Bill Baggs Cape Florida State Park** (Key Biscayne): The pot of gold at the end of the rainbow, Bill Baggs Cape Florida State Park radiates serenity with 1¼ miles of sandy beach, nature trails, and even a historic lighthouse that recalls an era before pristine places like this one gave way to avaricious developers and pollutants. See p. 132.

- **Lummus Park Beach** (South Beach): This beach is world renowned, not necessarily for its pristine sands, but for its more common name of **South Beach,** on which seeing, being seen, and, at times, the obscene, go hand in hand with the sunscreen and beach towels. The 12th Street section of this beach is the beach of choice for gay residents and travelers who come to show off just how much time they've spent in the gym and, of course, catch up on the latest gossip and upcoming must-attend parties and events. Oftentimes, this beach is the venue for some of the liveliest parties South Beach has ever seen. See p. 122.

- **Haulover Beach** (Miami Beach): Nestled between the Intracoastal Waterway and the ocean, especially at the north end, is the place to be for that all-over tan: Haulover is the city's only clothing-optional—aka nude—beach. See p. 125.

- **Bahia Honda State Park** (Bahia Honda Key): One of the nicest and most peaceful beaches in Florida, located amidst 635 acres of nature trails and even a portion of Henry Flagler's railroad. See p. 183.

- **John U. Lloyd Beach State Park** (Dania Beach): Unfettered by high-rise condominiums, T-shirt shops, and hotels, this wonderful beach boasts an untouched shoreline surrounded by a canopy of Australian pine to ensure complete seclusion. See p. 233.

- **Lover's Key State Park** (Fort Myers Beach): You'll have to walk or take a tram through a bird-filled forest of mangroves to this gorgeous, unspoiled beach just a few miles south of busy Fort Myers Beach. Although Sanibel Island gets all the accolades, the shelling here is just as good, if not better. See p. 309.

- **Cayo Costa State Park** (off Captiva Island): These days, deserted tropical islands with great beaches are scarce in Florida, but this 2,132-acre barrier strip of sand, pine forests, mangrove swamps, oak hammocks, and grasslands provides a genuine get-away-from-it-all experience. Access is only by boat from nearby Gasparilla, Pine, and Captiva islands. See p. 328.

- **Naples Beach** (Naples): Many Florida cities and towns have beaches, but few are as lovely as the gorgeous strip that runs in front of Naples' famous Millionaires' Row. You don't have to be rich to wander its length, peer at the mansions, and stroll on historic Naples Pier to catch a sunset over the Gulf. See p. 332.

- **Caladesi Island State Park** (Clearwater Beach): Even though 3½-mile-long Caladesi Island is in the heavily developed Tampa Bay area, it has a lovely, relatively secluded beach with soft sand edged in sea grass and palmettos. Dolphins cavort in offshore waters. In the park itself, there's a nature trail, and you might see one of the rattlesnakes, black racers, raccoons, armadillos, or rabbits that live here. The park is accessible only by ferry from Honeymoon Island State Recreation Area off Dunedin. See p. 381.

- **Fort DeSoto Park** (St. Petersburg): Where else can you get a good tan *and* a history lesson? At Fort DeSoto Park, you not only have 1,136 acres of five interconnected islands and 3 miles of unfettered beaches, but a fort, for which the park was named, that's listed on the National Register of Historic Places, nature trails, fishing piers, a 2¼-mile canoe trail, and spectacular views of Tampa Bay and the Gulf. See p. 382.

- **Canaveral National Seashore** (Cape Canaveral): Midway between the crowded attractions at Daytona Beach and the Kennedy Space Center is a protected stretch of coastline 13 miles long, backed by cabbage palms, sea grapes, and palmettos. See p. 472.

- **Gulf Islands National Seashore** (Pensacola): You could argue that all of Northwest Florida's Gulf shore is one of America's great beaches—an almost-uninterrupted stretch of pure white sand that runs the entire length of the Panhandle, from Perdido Key to St. George Island. The Gulf Islands National Seashore preserves much of this natural wonder in its undeveloped state. Countless terns, snowy plovers, black skimmers, and other birds nest along the dunes topped with sea oats. East of the national seashore and equally beautiful are **Grayton Beach State Park** near Destin and **St. George Island State Park** off Apalachicola. See p. 528.

- **St. Andrews State Park** (Panama City Beach): With more than 1,000 acres of dazzling white sand and dunes, this preserved wilderness demonstrates what Panama City Beach looked like before motels and condominiums lined its shore, with lacy, golden sea oats swaying in Gulf breezes and fragrant rosemary growing wild. The area is also home to foxes, coyotes, and a herd of deer. See p. 554.

2 The Best Destinations for Low-Cost Vacations

- **The Middle & Lower Keys:** With all the hype over Key West, the other keys are often neglected by tourists who race through en route to the wild tip of the continental United States. But that's a good thing. The string of islands that are far enough from Miami to dissuade day-trippers are a virtual treasure trove for active travelers who enjoy biking, boating, fishing, bird-watching, snorkeling, or just plain old relaxing and doing nothing—the cheapest activity of them all. Areas like Conch Key, Grassy Key, Marathon, Big Pine Key, and Sugarloaf are dotted with lush parks, simple fish houses, and modest accommodations. There is the National Key Deer Refuge, home to hundreds of nearly extinct miniature golden deer, and Bahia Honda State Park, where Florida's unusual plant and animal life thrive for all to see. And of course, these keys are surrounded by some of the country's most incredible underwater attractions, including a living reef system that divers flock to from all over the world. See chapter 5.

- **Hollywood:** For about half what you'd spend in trendy South Beach, nearby Hollywood (whose most recent ad campaign strangely promoted itself as "Vintage South Florida") offers wide beaches, plenty of outdoor activities, a few funky nightspots, and some real bargain hotels. Plus, you can drive half an hour in either direction to visit Fort Lauderdale's elegant restaurants and tourist attractions, or head south to Miami Beach to partake in some of its outrageous activity. See "Broward County: Hallandale & Hollywood to Fort Lauderdale" in chapter 7, beginning on p. 229.

- **Lake Okeechobee:** Head inland to Clewiston on Lake Okeechobee for a real feel of Old Florida. This is a popular spot for RVs and anglers. Everything from food to lodging is reasonably priced. You can stay in the nicest spot in town for about $40 a person. And while you're on the lake, why not catch your own dinner? See p. 291.

- **Fort Myers Beach:** Just a few miles from trendy Sanibel and Captiva islands and ritzy Naples, Fort Myers Beach offers just as much sun, sand, and shells—and at much less expensive prices—as its more affluent neighbors. Its busy "Times Square" and the rest of Estero Island offer some very comfortable accommodations at reasonable rates, even in the winter high season. And the gorgeous Lovers Key State Park is just across the bridge. See "Fort Myers Beach" in chapter 9.

- **Naples:** For a town with residents possessing industrial-strength money, charming and friendly Naples offers some surprisingly affordable accommodations and dining. And admission to Naples's great beach and historic pier is free. See "Naples" in chapter 9.

- **Anna Maria Island:** Although it sits next door to affluent Sarasota and expensive Longboat Key, Anna Maria Island is down-to-earth in both lifestyle and prices. It has fine beaches and a host of cost-conscious activities—and you only have to drive a few miles south to dine and shop on St. Armands Key, or to enjoy Sarasota's fine performing arts scene. See "Sarasota" in chapter 10.

- **The St. Pete & Clearwater Beaches:** The 20 miles of sand between St. Pete Beach and Clearwater Beach have been a vacation mecca for a century now, and they attract vacationers across the economic spectrum. Here is one of Florida's finest and most expensive grand old resorts, but you can also choose from many comfortable and inexpensive motels and condos, too. Granted, some four million guests a year can crowd this area at times, but there's a multitude of activities to keep them—and you—busy without breaking the bank. See "St. Pete & Clearwater Beaches" in chapter 10.

- **Daytona Beach:** Like the Panhandle, Daytona Beach attracts a working-class clientele—not to mention stock-car fans and bikers who make pilgrimages to this "World Center of Racing." Accordingly, you'll find many low-cost places to stay and dine here. In addition to its famous racetrack, the area sports a beach so hard-packed that you can drive on it. See "Daytona Beach" in chapter 12.

- **The Beaches of Northwest Florida:** Many visitors to Pensacola Beach, Fort Walton Beach, Destin, and Panama City Beach are working-class families, couples, and singles from Alabama and Georgia. They don't have all the money in the world to spend. As a result, the Panhandle has a multitude of inexpensive accommodations and restaurants. And there's plenty to keep everyone busy here, from touring historic Pensacola to trying your luck in Destin, "The World's Luckiest Fishing Village." The only problem: The Panhandle can get cold in winter. See chapter 13.

3 The Best Experiences You Can Have for Free (or Almost Free)

- **See the Boys of Spring** (Statewide): Although Florida has the big-league Florida Marlins in Miami and the Tampa Bay Devil Rays in St. Petersburg, the whole state goes baseball crazy during spring training from mid-February through March. Great seats close to the action are a bargain compared to what you'll pay when the Boys of Spring get home. See the box, "The Boys of Spring," in chapter 2.

- **Experience Cuba on U.S. Soil** (Miami): Stroll down Little Havana's Calle Ocho, 8th Street, to get a flavor of Hispanic culture. Stop at Versailles, an iconoclastic, gaudy Cuban diner humming with old-timers reminiscing about pre-Castro Cuba, local politicos trying to appease them, and a slew of detached people only there for the fantastically cheap and authentic Cuban fare. Watch expert cigar rollers make handmade stogies at one of the many cigar factories. Overlook the purely American fast-food joints in favor of a much more flavorful Little Havana bodega. See chapter 4.

- **Relish the View from Bill Baggs Cape Florida State Park:** You haven't truly seen South Florida until you've checked out the view from the southern point of Key Biscayne. Whether it's the turquoise water or the sight of Stiltsville—seven still-inhabited aquatic cabins dating back to the 1930s, perched smack in the middle of the Biscayne Channel—it may take a little coercing to get you to leave. See "Nature Preserves, Parks & Gardens" in chapter 4.

- **Everglades National Park:** Unfettered by jet skis, cruise ships, and neon thong bikinis, the Everglades are Florida's outback, resplendent in its swampy nature, which is best explored via an airboat that can navigate its way through the most stubborn of saw grass, providing you with an up-close and personal view of the land's inhabitants, from alligators and manatees to raccoons and Florida panthers. See "A Glimpse of Everglades National Park" in chapter 6.

- **Drive along A1A:** This ocean-front route, which runs north up from Miami Beach, through Sunny Isles and Hollywood, and on along the entire eastern edge of Florida, embodies the essence of the state. Especially in South Florida, where you'll discover time-warped hotels steeped in Art Deco kitsch alongside multi-million-dollar modern high-rises, A1A is one of the most scenic, albeit heavily trafficked, roads in all of Florida.

- **Eye the Estates on Palm Beach:** The winter playground for the *Lifestyles of the Rich and Famous* set, Palm Beach is lined with jaw-dropping palatial estates, including the biggest one, which belongs to—who else—Donald "You're Fired" Trump. While many of them are hidden behind towering shrubbery, head south on South County Road, from Brazilian Avenue, where you will see some of the most opulent homes ever built. Make sure someone holds the steering wheel if you're driving, because you *will* do a double-take. See "Palm Beach & West Palm Beach" in chapter 7.

- **Catch the "Green Flash" at Sunset** (Key West & the Gulf Coast Beaches): Key West and the beaches of Southwest Florida and the Tampa Bay area face due west, thus providing glorious sunsets over the Gulf of Mexico and a chance to see the elusive "green flash"—a quick burst of green light just as the top of the sun dips below the horizon. It costs not a cent to wander down to the shore and keep a sharp eye peeled. Or for a few bucks, grab a drink from a beachside restaurant or

Gulf-front bar. See chapters 5, 9, and 10.

- **Walk or Ride Along Wildlife Drive** (Sanibel Island): The mangrove swamps, winding waterways, and uplands of Sanibel Island's **J. N. "Ding" Darling National Wildlife Refuge** (© **239/472-1100**) are great places to see alligators, raccoons, otters, and hundreds of species of birds. You can see many of the creatures from the 5-mile, one-way Wildlife Drive, which costs $5 per vehicle or $1 per pedestrian or biker. A naturalist will explain what you're seeing on a 2-hour narrated tram tour—a very good value at $8 for adults, $4 for children 12 and under. See "Sanibel & Captiva Islands" in chapter 9.

- **Stoop for Shells** (Sanibel Island): Okay, you'll have to pay a $3 toll to get here and a small fee to park your car (or lock your bike to a tree for nothing), but you can stroll Sanibel Island's world-famous shelling beaches as long as you want for free. After a few hours hunched over in the "Sanibel stoop," you're sure to go home with a prize find or two. See "Sanibel & Captiva Islands" in chapter 9.

- **Stroll Among the Millionaires** (Naples): Olde Naples residents love to stroll out on their ancient city pier to fish, catch a sunset, or look at Millionaires' Row, a string of magnificent mansions along the town's lovely beach. Now a state historic site, the pier is open 24 hours a day and is free, although it will cost you a few quarters to park in the nearby municipal lots. When you're done ogling the wealthy from the Naples Pier, you can walk among them while window-shopping in the ritzy 3rd Street district nearby. Naples is so Midwestern-friendly that nobody

will care if you maxed out your credit cards just to get here. See "Naples" in chapter 9.

- **Walk, Jog, Bike, or Blade Along Bayshore Boulevard** (Tampa): A 7-mile promenade with an unmatched view across the bay to Tampa's downtown skyline, Bayshore Boulevard reputedly has the world's longest continuous sidewalk. It's a favorite for runners, joggers, walkers, and in-line skaters. The route passes stately old homes of Hyde Park, a few high-rise condos, retirement communities, and houses of worship before ending at Ballast Point Park. See "Tampa" in chapter 10.

- **Trip Out in Sideshow and Psychic Towns** (Gibsonton and Cassadaga): Who needs $10 a minute 1-900 numbers when you can walk around Cassadaga for free and get a look into the past and future? The small town near Orlando is a throwback in time but also a look ahead into your future if you encounter one of the many psychic mediums who live and work in this tiny 'psychic' town. Although private readings with psychics cost big bucks, there's always someone roaming the streets or hanging out in the general store who will be happy to give you a thought or two for free or for a penny. It's all definitely freaky. In Gibsonton, you'll see a freak show of a literal nature, as it's the home to many a retired circus acts and carnies, including the late Lobster Boy, and a living bearded lady or two. See p. 358 and 480 respectively.

- **See What Circus Money Bought** (Sarasota): Adults pay $9 or $10 to get in, but you'll have three "rings" to visit at the **FSU Ringling Center for the Cultural Arts** in Sarasota (© **941/359-5700,** or · 941/351-1660 for recorded information), which houses the phenomenal collections of circus master John Ringling. A pink Italian Renaissance villa is filled with over 500 years of European and American art, including one of the world's most important collections of grand 17th-century baroque paintings. The Ringling's 30-room winter residence displays their personal mementos. And the Circus Galleries are devoted to memorabilia from The Greatest Show on Earth. See p. 395.

- **Visit a Virtual Stepford Town** (Celebration): There was no need for a remake of the '70s classic, *The Stepford Wives,* especially considering that there's a similarly eerie town in Orlando known as Celebration. A planned community to the max, this pristine, picket fenced in Victorian-style utopian town has rules on everything from proper porch decor to car etiquette. Enter at your own risk. See p. 413.

- **Search for the Fountain of Youth** (St. Augustine): Ponce de León never found it and some say that today, Botox is the real fountain of youth, but a stroll through the nation's oldest town may give you new perspective on the inevitable and positive effects of aging. You'll have to pay a few dollars to enter sites such as the oldest store and the oldest jail, but you can freely stroll these narrow streets for hours. Poke your head into antiques shops, peer into lush yards surrounding ancient buildings, and watch the boats out on the Matanzas River. See "St. Augustine: America's First City" in chapter 12.

- **Visit a New Breed of National Park** (Jacksonville): The **Timucuan Ecological and Historic Preserve** isn't one chunk of land; instead, it's a vast, intriguing system of sites on both sides of the St. Johns River. The prime attraction is the Fort Carolina National Memorial (© **904/641-7155**), the site of a 16th-century French Huguenot settlement. It's on the edge of the 600-acre Theodore **Roosevelt Area,** a beautiful, undisturbed wood- and marshland rich in history and wildlife. On the north side of the river, the Zephaniah Kingsley Plantation (© **904/251-3537**) was an early 19th-century manse owned by Zephaniah Kingsley, a white man who married one of his slaves and then moved her and his family to Haiti to escape racism at home. Admission is free to all the park's attractions. See "Jacksonville" in chapter 12.

- **Walk the Streets of a Charming Victorian Town** (Fernandina Beach, Amelia Island): Amelia Island might be an exclusive, money-on-the-hoof kind of place, but you need not a penny to stroll around the gorgeous 50-block area of bayside **Fernandina Beach.** This charming small town is filled with so many Victorian and Queen Anne homes that it's listed in the National Register of Historic Places. See "Amelia Island" in chapter 12.

- **Massage your Feet on a Talcum-Like Beach** (Northwest Florida): Admission is free to most of 100-plus miles of powdery, snow-white beaches that make the Panhandle special. And just a few bucks will let you into the Gulf Islands National Seashore at Pensacola, the Henderson Beach and Grayton Beach state recreation areas at Destin, the St. Andrews State Recreation Area at Panama City Beach, and St. George Island State Park near Apalachicola. You won't soon forget the time you spend on these protected sands and dunes, all consistently ranked among the nation's finest beaches. See chapter 13.

- **Imagine Yourself Under Five Flags** (Pensacola): You'll have to pay to go into its homes and museums, but there's no admission to walk the streets of **Historic Pensacola Village** (© 850/595-5985). The original part of Pensacola resembles a shady English colonial community, but America's second oldest city saw the flags of five nations fly over its quaint streets. Some of Florida's oldest homes are here, along with charming boutiques and interesting restaurants. During summer, costumed characters go about their daily chores and demonstrate old crafts, and archaeologists unearth the old Spanish commanding officer's compound. See p. 531.

- **Visit the Blue Angels & Top Guns** (Pensacola and Fort Walton Beach): Next to the Smithsonian Institute's National Air and Space Museum in Washington, D.C., the next best places to see our nation's warplanes on display are at the **National Museum of Naval Aviation** in Pensacola (© 850/452-3604) and at the **U.S. Air Force Armament Museum** in Fort Walton Beach (© 850/882-4062). Admission to both is free. They cost a few dollars, but the naval museum's IMAX films will make you believe you're flying in a Blue Angel's cockpit. See p. 532 and 544 respectively.

- **See Where Johnny Weissmuller Played Tarzan** (Tallahassee): Wakulla Springs, 15 miles south of Tallahassee, is so jungly that some of the 1930s Tarzan movies starring Johnny Weissmuller were filmed here. Today they are within the 2,860 acres of **Edward W. Ball Wakulla Springs State Park** (© 850/224-5950), which means you'll have to pay a few dollars to get in. You can also pay $4.50 for adults, half price for children, to take glass-bottom-boat sightseeing and wildlife-observation tours. You can swim in the lake formed by the springs, but watch for alligators! See "Tallahassee" in chapter 13.

4 The Best Family Attractions

- **Miami Seaquarium** (Key Biscayne; © 305/361-5705): Kids seem to love the splashy and dramatic performances by killer whales and dolphins. Come early and get a very wet look at some of the biggest hams of marine life. See p. 135.

- **Parrot Jungle Island** (Miami): Settled into its new swanky $47 million digs on Watson Island as of June 2003, Parrot Jungle Island is a revamped version of the original in South Miami. You'll still need to watch your head, however, since flying above are hundreds of parrots, macaws, peacocks, cockatoos, and flamingos. Continuous suitable but cheesy shows star roller-skating cockatoos, card-playing macaws, and numerous stunt-happy parrots. There are also tortoises, iguanas, and a rare albino alligator on exhibit.

- **Miami Metrozoo** (Miami; © 305/251-0400): This completely cageless (but safe!) zoo offers a horde of animals with much personality all ready for their close-ups. See p. 135.

- **Mel Fisher Maritime Heritage Museum** (Key West; © 305/294-2633): Because it's human nature to have somewhat of a morbid curiosity about disasters and wrecks, this museum full of doubloons, pieces of eight, emeralds, and solid-gold bars has fascinated visitors intrigued with shipwrecks. See p. 193.

- **Key West Aquarium** (Key West; © **305/296-2051**): The oldest attraction on the island, this modest but fascinating exhibit is a great place for children who are accustomed to only animals of the animated kind. Touch tanks and feeding exhibitions get kids involved. See p. 192.

- **Playmobil Fun Park** (Palm Beach Gardens; © **800/351-8697**): It's the only Playmobil park outside of Germany, it's free, and it's a ball. This indoor fantasy world offers more than 17,000 square feet filled with thousands of toys. *Warning:* All toys are also for sale. See p. 260.

- **Edison and Ford Winter Estates** (Fort Myers; © **239/334-3614**): Inventor Thomas Alva Edison and his friend, automobile magnate Henry Ford, built side-by-side winter homes on the banks of the Caloosahatchee River in Fort Myers. Today these Victorian cottages serve as memorials to the two men, and especially to Edison. The museum will show the kids how we got the lightbulb, the phonograph, and hundreds of other Edison inventions. See p. 298.

- **Caribbean Gardens** (Naples; © **239/262-5409**): Owned and operated by the family of noted animal trainer Larry Tetzlaff, this zoo features a variety of animals and birds, including a fascinating community of primates living free on their own island. Larry's son, David Tetzlaff, himself a talented trainer, puts lions and tigers through their paces in his Big Cat Show. For kids, there's a Petting Farm, elephant rides, and a

playground. You can easily spend a day here. See p. 335.

- **Busch Gardens Tampa Bay** (Tampa; © **888/800-5447**): Although the thrill rides, live entertainment, shops, restaurants, and games get most of the ink at this 335-acre family theme park, Busch Gardens ranks among the top zoos in the country, with several thousand animals living in naturalistic environments. If you can get them off the roller coasters, the kids can find out what all those wild beasts they've seen on the Discovery Channel look like in person. You can save a few bucks off admission by buying your tickets outside the main gate. See p. 349.

- **Florida Aquarium** (Tampa; © **813/273-4000**): This major aquarium will introduce you and the kids to more than 5,300 aquatic animals and plants that call Florida home. There's an Explore a Shore playground to educate the kids, a deep-water exhibit, and a tank housing moray eels. See p. 359.

- **MOSI (Museum of Science and Industry)** (Tampa; © **813/987-6100**): One of the largest educational science centers in the Southeast, MOSI has more than 450 interactive exhibits in which the kids can experience hurricane-force winds, defy the laws of gravity, cruise the mysterious world of microbes, explore the human body, and much more. They can also watch stunning movies in MOSIMAX, Florida's first IMAX dome theater. Admission includes IMAX movies. See p. 360.

- **The Magic Kingdom & Disney– MGM Studios** (Orlando; © **407/824-4321**): Of the four Disney parks, these two are the most fun for families. Young ones will be thrilled to meet and greet the famed characters, and rides will delight young and old alike. Yes, admission is expensive, but with a little know-how and a lot of planning, you can have a memorable Disney experience without breaking the bank. See chapter 11.

• **Universal Orlando** (Orlando; © **800/837-2273**): Even with fast-paced, grown-up rides, Universal still is a ton of fun for kids (there's even a youngster-size roller coaster). And it's a working motion-picture and TV-production studio, so occasionally there's some live filming done in the park, especially at the Nickelodeon soundstage. The little ones can spend the whole day exploring the whimsical Seuss Landing and meeting MGM's cartoon characters such as Woody Woodpecker, Yogi, BooBoo, Scooby Doo, Fred, Barney, Fievel, and Elroy Jetson. See chapter 11.

• **SeaWorld** (Orlando; © **800/327-2424**): Beautifully landscaped grounds, centering on a 17-acre lagoon, include flamingo and pelican ponds and a lush tropical rainforest. Shamu, a killer whale, is the star of the park along with his expanding family, which includes several baby whales. The newest addition is Journey to Atlantis, a flume coaster with plenty of twists and turns. See chapter 11.

• **Daytona USA** (Daytona Beach; © **386/947-6800**): Opened in late 1996 on Daytona International Speedway grounds, this huge state-of-the-art interactive attraction is an exciting and fast-paced stop even for non–race fans. Kids can see real stock cars, go-carts, and motorcycles, and even participate in a pit stop on a NASCAR Winston Cup race car. See p. 480.

• **ZooWorld Zoological & Botanical Park** (Panama City Beach; © **850/230-1243**): "Mr. Bubba," the largest captive alligator in Florida, lives in a re-created pine forest habitat at this educational and entertaining zoo, an active participant in the Species Survival Plan, which helps protect endangered species with specific breeding and housing programs. Other guests include rare and endangered animals as well as orangutans and other primates, big cats, and more reptiles. Also included are a walk-through aviary, a bat exhibit, and a petting zoo. See p. 556.

5 The Best Golf Courses with Greens Fees That Won't Break Your Budget

• **Crandon Park Golf Course** (Key Biscayne, Miami): Formerly known as the Links of Key Biscayne, this stunning and famous course was ranked the number-one municipal course in the state and one of the top five in the country. Located on a posh residential island, it's one of the few courses remaining in South Florida not surrounded by development. Golfers enjoy pristine vistas of hammocks and stretches of water, with a glimpse of Miami's dramatic skyline to the north. See "Affordable Outdoor Pursuits" in chapter 4.

• **Miami's Biltmore Golf Course, Biltmore Hotel** (Coral Gables): If it's good enough for former President Clinton, it's good enough for those of you who don't travel with a bevy of Secret Service agents. But the real question is: Are *you* good enough for the course? The 6th hole is notoriously difficult, with distracting water hazards among other difficulties. Nonetheless, it's an excellent course with a picture postcard setting. See "Affordable Outdoor Pursuits" in chapter 4.

- **Doral Golf Resort and Spa** (Miami): There are four championship courses here, including the famous Blue Monster, which is the site of the annual Doral-Ryder Open. The Gold Course, recently restored by golf great Raymond Floyd, has water on every hole. Look in the *Miami Herald* sports section for special discounts and coupons or call for twilight specials starting at $25 per person. See "Affordable Outdoor Pursuits" in chapter 4.

- **Haulover Beach Park** (Miami): The longest hole on this par-27 course is 125 yards in a pretty bayside location. Golfers here are patient with beginners, and greens fees start at a remarkable $6 per person in winter. See "Affordable Outdoor Pursuits" in chapter 4.

- **The Boca Raton Municipal Golf Course** (Boca Raton): This 18-hole, par-72 course covers approximately 6,200 yards. With greens fees starting at $11 for 9 holes, this is a superior deal. See "Boca Raton & Delray Beach" in chapter 7.

- **Emerald Dunes Golf Course** (West Palm Beach): This beautiful Tom Fazio championship course features 60 acres of water, including a waterfall, and great views of the Atlantic. Prime weekend times are pricey, but it is one of the only great courses open to the public in this area of ritzy resorts. Twilight prices from Monday through Thursday are a mere $45. See "Palm Beach & West Palm Beach" in chapter 7.

- **"Golf-A-Round"** (Gold Coast): From May to October or November, about a dozen private courses open their greens to visitors staying in Palm Beach County hotels. This "Golf-A-Round" program is free or severely discounted (carts are additional), and reservations can be made through most major hotels. Or contact the **Palm Beach County Convention and Visitors Bureau** (☎ 561/471-3995). See chapter 7.

- **Orangebrook Golf Course** (Hollywood): Built in 1937, this 18-holer is one of the state's oldest courses and one of the area's best bargains. Morning and noon rates range from $15 to $20. After 3pm, prices go down to about $13. See "Broward County: Hallandale & Hollywood to Fort Lauderdale" in chapter 7.

- **Fort Myers Country Club** (Fort Myers; ☎ 239/936-2457): Designed in 1917 by Donald Ross, this municipal course is flat and uninteresting by today's standards, but it's right in town and looks like an exclusive private enclave. Fort Myers's other municipal course, Eastwood Golf Club (☎ 239/275-4848), is more challenging. Greens fees at both range from about $20 in summer to $50 during winter. See "Fort Myers" in chapter 9.

- **Babe Zaharias, Rocky Point, & Rogers Park Courses** (Tampa): With three fine municipal courses charging about $25 to $40, Tampa is a great place for affordable golf. The Babe Zaharias Municipal Golf Course (☎ 813/631-4374) is the shortest, but small greens and narrow fairways present ample challenges. Water presents obstacles on 12 of the 18 holes at Rocky Point Golf Course

(© **813/673-4316**). On the Hillsborough River, the Rogers Park Golf Course (© **813/673-4396**) has a lighted driving and practice range. Lessons and club rentals are available. See "Tampa" in chapter 10.

- **Mangrove Bay Golf Course** (St. Petersburg; © **727/893-7800**): One of the nation's top 50 municipal courses, these 18-hole, par-72 links hug the inlets of Old Tampa Bay. Facilities include a driving range; lessons and golf-club rental are also available. Fees are about $20, $30 including a cart in winter, slightly lower off season. The city also operates the challenging, par-3 **Twin Brooks Golf Course,** 3800 22nd Ave. S. (© **727/893-7445**), charging the same fees. See "St. Petersburg" in chapter 10.

- **Bobby Jones Golf Complex** (Sarasota; © **941/365-4653**): Sarasota's municipal facility has two 18-hole championship layouts—the American (par-71) and British (par-72) courses—and a 9-hole executive course (par-30). Greens fees range from $5 to $25, including cart rental, a bargain in this affluent area. See "Sarasota" in chapter 10.

- **Buffalo Creek Golf Course** (Bradenton; © **941/776-2611**): Locals love to play this 18-hole, par-72 municipal course on the north side of the Bradenton River. At well over 7,000 yards, it's the longest in the area, and lots of water and alligators will keep you entertained. Wintertime greens fees are about $49 with cart, $39 without. They drop to about $22 and $20, respectively, during

summer. See "Sarasota & Bradenton" in chapter 10.

- **Cocoa Beach Country Club** (Cocoa Beach; © **321/868-3351**): This fine municipal course has 27 holes of championship golf and 10 lighted tennis courts set on acres of natural woodland, rivers, and lakes. Greens fees are about $45 in winter, dropping to about $40 in summer, including cart. Nearby, The Savannahs at Sykes Creek (© **321/455-1377**) has 18 holes over 6,636 yards bordered by hardwood forests, lakes, and savannahs inhabited by a host of wildlife. You'll have to hit over a lake to reach the 7th hole. Fees with cart are about $40 in winter, less in summer. See "Cocoa Beach, Cape Canaveral, the Kennedy Space Center & Melbourne" in chapter 12.

- **Pelican Bay Country Club** (Daytona Beach; © **386/756-0034**): The South Course of this semiprivate club is one of the area's favorites, with fast greens to test your putting skills. With-cart fees are about $40 in winter, less in summer (no walking allowed). See "Daytona Beach" in chapter 12.

- **The Moors** (Pensacola; © **800/727-1010** or 850/995-4653): Pot bunkers make you think you're playing in Scotland at this course, which has greeted the Nike Tour and is home to the Emerald Coast Classic, a PGA seniors' event. Greens fees here are about $15 to $30 without cart. The Moors also has a lodge with eight luxury rooms. See "Pensacola" in chapter 13.

6 The Best of Natural Florida

- **National Key Deer Refuge** (Big Pine Key): With lots of patience (bring a book) and a bit of luck you may catch a glimpse of these

delicate creatures in their natural habitat; with the country's largest herd (only about 300), the tiny, protected island of Big Pine Key is worth a stop. See "The Lower Keys: Big Pine Key to Coppitt Key" in chapter 5.

- **Exploring the Everglades:** The supermodel of swamps, the Everglades in all its marshy glory is absolutely stunning, full of lush greenery and beautiful wildlife. From egrets and orchids to gators and frogs, these quiet grounds are peaceful and intriguing. See "A Glimpse of Everglades National Park" in chapter 6.

- **Lover's Key State Park** (Fort Myers Beach; © **239/463-4588**): Just south of Fort Myers Beach, this gorgeous state preserve provides respite from the hustle and bustle of its busy neighbor. A highway runs the length of the island, but otherwise Lover's Key is totally undeveloped. Access through a mangrove forest to a truly fine beach is by foot or by a tractor-pulled tram driven by park rangers, who take a dim view of anyone leaving trash behind. See "Fort Myers Beach" in chapter 9.

- **J. N. ("Ding") Darling National Wildlife Refuge** (Sanibel Island; © **239/472-1100**): Preserving most of the mangrove forests and winding waterways on Sanibel Island's north side, this famous 5,000-acre refuge is rich in such barrier-island wildlife as roseate spoonbills, ospreys, shorebirds, white pelicans, ducks, loons, and mangrove cuckoos. Visitors can hike, bike, or canoe on their own or be escorted by experts such as former Sanibel Mayor Mark "Bird" Westall. See "Sanibel & Captiva Islands" in chapter 9.

- **Cayo Costa State Park** (off Captiva Island; © **941/964-0375**): A huge variety of sea- and shorebirds congregate on this state preserve, which encompasses one of the northernmost of Southwest Florida's Ten Thousand Islands.

This uninhabited island is only accessible via boat. See "Sanibel & Captiva Islands" in chapter 9.

- **Briggs Nature Center** (Marco Island; © **239/775-8569**): Operated by The Nature Conservancy and part of the Rookery Bay National Estuarine Research Reserve, this refuge is a pristine example of Florida's disappearing scrublands, home to the threatened scrub jays and gopher tortoises. There's a self-guided canoe trail and canoes for rent during winter. You can also canoe through The Conservancy's smaller Naples Nature Center in Naples. See "Marco Island" in chapter 9.

- **Canaveral National Seashore/ Merritt Island National Wildlife Refuge** (Cape Canaveral; © **321/ 867-4077** or 321/867-0677): When the federal government set up the national space center at Cape Canaveral, it bought a lot more land than it needed to shoot rockets at the moon. The unneeded acres are now preserved in Canaveral National Seashore and the adjacent Merritt Island National Wildlife Refuge. The seashore's undeveloped Playalinda Beach is one of America's most beautiful stretches of sand. See "Cocoa Beach, Cape Canaveral, the Kennedy Space Center & Melbourne" in chapter 12.

- **St. Vincent National Wildlife Refuge** (Apalachicola; © **850/ 653-8808**): There are no facilities whatsoever on this 12,358-acre barrier island, which has been left in its natural state by the U.S. Fish and Wildlife Service. The local chamber of commerce will arrange a boat to get you here. Then you can walk through pine forests, marshlands, ponds, dunes, and beaches. In addition to native species like the bald eagle and alligators, the island is home to a small herd of sambar deer from Southeast Asia, and red wolves are bred here for reintroduction to other wildlife areas. See "Apalachicola" in chapter 13.

- **St. Marks Lighthouse and National Wildlife Refuge** (Tallahassee; © 850/925-6121): On the Gulf, due south of Tallahassee, this 65,000-acre preserve is home

to more species of birds than anyplace else in Florida except the Everglades. Built of limestone blocks 4 feet thick at the base, the 80-foot-tall St. Marks Lighthouse has marked the harbor entrance since 1842. The nearby Apalachicola National Forest is another good spot. See "Tallahassee" in chapter 13.

7 The Best Affordable Accommodations

- **The Lily Leon Hotel** (South Beach, Miami; © 305/673-3767): This classy little hotel in the very hippest part of South Beach is beautifully maintained and fantastically practical. Although there are no fancy grounds or facilities, this has to be one of the best deals on the beach. See p. 91.
- **Aqua** (South Beach, Miami; © 305/538-4361): The Jetsons meet the fabulous '50s at this retro-hip 50-room motel that's very high-tech, very European and, most importantly, a real bargain. See p. 88.
- **The Creek** (South Beach, © 305/538-1951): Part Playboy's Penthouse and part Jetsons, The Creek Hotel is a kitschy, 81-room haven for hipsters who don't feel the need to spend $400 a night for a hip hotel. Of the three types of rooms—shared, Cabana, and Waterway Standard, the latter is the way to go, with 18 signature rooms designed by local artists and designers. An 8,000-square-foot pool deck with a 40-foot fully stocked bar, outdoor BBQs, Ms. Pacman, pool tables, and theater, The Creek is somewhere you wouldn't mind being stuck without a paddle. See p.90.
- **Indian Creek Hotel** (Miami Beach; © 800/491-2772 or 305/531-2727): A charming Key

West–style hotel that's full of character, the Indian Creek Hotel takes you back in time, with period furnishings, attitude-free service, and a quaint pool and garden, completely lacking water slides, Tiki huts, or calypso bands. See p. 92.
- **Conch Key Cottages** (Marathon; © 800/330-1577 or 305/289-1377): This oceanfront hideaway offers rustic but immaculate and well-outfitted cottages that are especially popular with families. Each has a hammock, barbecue grill, and kitchen. See p. 178.
- **The Grand** (Key West; © 888/947-2630): There's no better value than this little hotel that is slightly out of the way, but still within walking distance of Duval Street. All of the clean and quaint rooms have private bathrooms, air-conditioning, and private entrances starting at $98 during season and $78 off season. Suites are slightly more expensive but worth it if you want to save some money on food; the large two-room units come with kitchens. See p. 201.
- **Hotel Biba** (West Palm Beach; © 561/832-0094): West Palm Beach's first boutique hotel proves that it's hip to be square with this single-floor, 43-room property that has been renovated and redesigned in a remarkably retro-modern

fashion. An enormous pool, Asian gardens, and requisite hipster bar make Biba a hotspot for those whose budgets aren't necessarily in the rock-star category, even if their tastes are. See p. 263.

- **Palm Beach Hotel** (Palm Beach; © 561/659-7794): The best deal in town for those who want the convenience of a private apartment and don't need all the fancy extras of a full-service resort. A well-outfitted kitchenette means you don't have to rely on overpriced room service; you can always have milk, juice, and snacks on hand. A pool and sun deck, plus a coin laundry, all for less than the price of most Holiday Inns, make this a real steal. See p. 262.

- **Harborfront Inn Bed & Breakfast** (Stuart; © 800/294-1703): Located riverfront and within walking distance of the restaurants and shops of downtown Stuart, this handsome, highly recommended B&B offers private rooms with their own entrances. See p. 279.

- **Island House Motel** (Fort Myers Beach; © 800/951-9975): Sitting on stilts in the Old Florida fashion, but with modern furnishings, this clapboard-sided establishment enjoys a quiet location across the street from the beach and within walking distance of busy Times Square. You'll have screened porches, kitchens, ceiling fans, an open-air lounge with a small library, a small pool and sun-deck area, a guest laundry, beach chairs, and free local calls. See p. 309.

- **Tarpon Tale Inn** (Sanibel Island; © 888/345-0939): The Tarpon Tale Inn tells many stories of great catches on Sanibel's north shore, but the biggest score of them all is the Inn itself, located in Sanibel's

Old Town, consisting of five attached, yet completely private, bungalows hidden amidst palms, bougainvillea, hibiscus, ferns, sea grapes, gumbo limbos, and Key limes. See p. 320.

- **Cabbage Key Inn** (Cabbage Key, off Sanibel and Captiva islands; © 239/283-2278): You never know who's going to get off a boat on this 100-acre islet and walk unannounced into the funky, rustic house built in 1938 by the son and daughter-in-law of mystery novelist Mary Roberts Rinehart. Singer and avid yachtie Jimmy Buffett likes Cabbage Key so much that it inspired his hit song "Cheeseburger in Paradise." The inn has six rooms and six cottages, all with original 1920s furnishings, private bathrooms, and airconditioners. Four of the cottages have kitchens, and one room reputedly has its own ghost. See p. 327.

- **Lighthouse Inn Motel** (Naples; © 239/597-3345): A relic from decades gone by, Judy and Buzz Dugan's no-frills but spotlessly clean motel sits across the street from other more expensive Gulfside properties on Vanderbilt Beach and within walking distance of The Ritz-Carlton, Naples. The efficiencies and apartments are simple, but you can't beat the proximity to the beach. See p. 338.

- **Best Western All Suites Hotel Near USF Behind Busch Gardens** (Tampa; © 800/786-7446): This all-suite hacienda-style building (each unit can accommodate up to four persons) is the most beachlike vacation venue close to Busch Gardens Tampa Bay. Great for kids, "family suites" have over-and-under bunk beds in addition to a queen-size bed for parents. The three-story complex surrounds a lush, tropical court-yard with heated pool, hot tub, covered games area, and lively, sports-oriented Tiki bar. You won't have kitchens in your suites (they do have microwave ovens), but you can graze at a complimentary full-breakfast buffet, and the bar serves inexpensive chargrilled ribs, burgers, fish, and chicken for dinner. See p. 364.

- **Beach Haven** (St. Pete Beach; © 727/367-8642): These low-slung, pink-with-white-trim structures were built in the 1950s but were gutted and completely rebuilt. Today they have bright tile floors, vertical blinds, pastel tropical furniture, and many modern amenities, including TVs, VCRs, refrigerators, and coffeemakers. There's an outdoor heated pool surrounded by a white picket fence, plus a sunning deck with lounge furniture by the beach. It's in the heart of the hotel district, so lots of restaurants are just steps away. See p. 384.

- **Island's End Resort** (St. Pete Beach; © 727/360-5023): A wonderful respite from the madding crowd, and a great bargain to boot, this little all-cottage hideaway sits right on the southern tip of St. Pete Beach, smack-dab on Pass-a-Grille, where the Gulf of Mexico meets Tampa Bay. You can step from the six contemporary cottages right onto the beach. One unit even has its own private swimming pool. See p. 384.

- **Captiva Beach Resort** (Siesta Key, Sarasota; © 800/349-4131 or 941/349-4131): Owners Robert and Jane Ispaso have done a terrific job updating this older motel about a half block from the beach on Siesta Key. Every one of their comfortable, sparkling-clean units has cooking facilities, and some

have separate living rooms with sleeper sofas. Units go for $135 to $235 single or double in winter, but fall to $90 to $160 off season. See p. 400.

- **Disney's All-Star Resorts** (Orlando; © 407/934-7639). There are three All-Star resorts in the Disney complex, with Movie, Sports, and Music themes. The newest addition to these value resorts is the **Pop Century Resort,** which pays homage to pop culture with '50s to '90s kitsch including a giant Play Doh container and Rubik's cube. The rooms may be small, but at $77 to $124 a night, it's the least expensive way to take advantage of all the perks of being a Disney resort guest. Food courts serve pizza, pasta, sandwiches, and family dinner platters. There's also a full-size pool. See p. 420.

- **Monterey Inn** (St. Augustine; © 904/824-4482): A great choice for the price, this family-operated, wrought-iron-trimmed motel overlooks the Matanzas Bay from a location in St. Augustine's historic district. Three generations of the Six family have kept the 1960s building and grounds clean and comfortable. A small swimming pool, pleasant staff, and free coffee each morning are just some of the extras. See p. 500.

- **Kenwood Inn** (St. Augustine; © 800/824-8151 or 904/824-2116): Rooms in this Victorian wood-frame house with graceful verandas are larger and more private than most other accommodations in converted single-family homes. Everything from the carpeting to the linens to the china is first-class. There's an outdoor swimming pool, a lushly landscaped sun deck, and a secluded garden courtyard complete with a fish pond and neat flower bed under a sprawling pecan tree. See p. 500.

- **Florida House Inn** (Amelia Island; © **800/258-3301**): Built by a railroad in 1857, this clapboard Victorian building is Florida's oldest operating hotel. You can rock on the gingerbread-trimmed front veranda, from which President Ulysses S. Grant once made a speech. Although modernized, most rooms still have working fireplaces, and some have claw-foot tubs. Rates include breakfast in the boardinghouse-style dining room, which still provides family-style, all-you-can-eat Southern fare. See p. 518.

- **Five Flags Inn** (Pensacola Beach; © **850/932-3586**): This friendly motel looks like a jail from the road, but big picture windows look out to the swimming pool and gorgeous white-sand beach, which comes right up to the property. Although the accommodations are small, the rates are a bargain for well-furnished, Gulf-front rooms. See p. 536.

- **Gibson Inn** (Apalachicola; © **850/653-2191**): Built in 1907 as a seaman's hotel, this brilliant, cupola-topped example of Victorian architecture is listed on the National Register of Historic Inns. No two guest rooms are alike—some still have the original sinks in the sleeping area—but all are richly furnished with period reproductions. Grab a drink from the oak bar and relax in one of the high-back rockers on the old-fashioned veranda. See p. 565.

8 The Best Places to Stay on a Shoestring

- **Clay Hotel & International Hostel** (South Beach, Miami; © **800/379-2529** or 305/534-2988): Housed in a gorgeous Mediterranean building at the corner of bustling and historic Española Way, this is South Beach's best budget find. See p. 89.

- **Key West International Hostel** (Key West; © **800/51-HOSTEL**): Whether you are renting a bed in one of the supercheap dorm rooms or a pricier, private motel room, if you can get a spot at this well-run hostel you have found one of the best deals in Key West. Motel rooms come with cooking facilities, a real plus in a town where overpriced tourist restaurants dominate the scene. Cheap eats are also prepared on the premises. See p. 202.

- **Sea Downs (and the Bougainvillea)** (Hollywood; © **954/923-4968**): On a relatively quiet but convenient stretch of Hollywood beach, these oceanside properties offer a heated pool, barbecue grills, a picnic area, laundry facilities, a sun deck, and many units with kitchens for very reasonable rates. See p. 240.

- **Clearwater Beach International Hostel** (Clearwater Beach; © **727/443-1211**): In a predominantly residential neighborhood a short walk north of Clearwater Beach's busy commercial area, this official youth hostel has a swimming pool, communal kitchen, TV lounge, canoes and other toys to borrow, and bicycles to rent. See p. 385.

- **Days Inn Eastgate** (Kissimmee; © **800/423-3864**): Families like the picnic tables and play area on the lawn. The rooms are nicely decorated and range from $30 to $89. There's a restaurant (kids eat free), a sports lounge, a video-game room, coin-op washers/dryers, and a gift shop. Guest services sells tickets to the surrounding theme parks and offers rides to and from them (free for Disney). See p. 424.

- **Pirate Haus Inn & Hostel** (St. Augustine; ✆ **904/808-1999**): You won't find a more convenient base for seeing St. Augustine's sites than this youth hostel in the heart of the historic district. It has five private units (three with their own bathrooms), equipped with either a queen or double bed plus one or two bunk beds. Two other units have dormitory-style bunk beds. See p. 499.

9 The Best Camping

Florida's state parks offer a variety of camping facilities, from primitive sites without even running water to full hookups for RVs. The sites cost between $10 and $20 a night, depending on the season, and all state parks accept camping reservations up to 11 months in advance.

- **Everglades National Park:** Although the National Park Service recently instituted a $10 fee for backcountry permits, the Everglades still has some of the most affordable and scenic campsites around. Choose from beachfront sites, rough ground sites inland, or *chickee huts*, large wooden platforms built over water. The *chickees*, which have toilets, are the most civilized and unusual. Be prepared for the bugs! See "A Glimpse of Everglades National Park" in chapter 6.

- **Boca Chita Key** (Biscayne National Park): After a thorough cleanup, Boca Chita, the former Gilligan's Island of the monied set, shines in its rustic glory, with somewhat primitive campsites accessible only by boat. Enjoy the calm and quiet with no noisy generators to drown out the gentle sound of waves lapping against the shore. See "Biscayne National Park" in chapter 6.

- **Koreshan State Historic Site** (Fort Myers; ✆ **239/992-0311**): The shady sites here are near the gardens and some of the buildings erected by the Koreshan Unity Movement, a sect that believed that humans lived *inside* the earth and established a self-sufficient settlement on these 300 acres on the narrow Estero River in 1894. Nature and canoe trails (rentals available) wind downriver to Mound Key, an islet made of the shells discarded by the Calusa Indians. See p. 300.

- **Fort DeSoto Park** (St. Pete Beach; ✆ **727/582-2267**): The 230 sites in this 900-acre bird, animal, and plant sanctuary sit on an island by themselves, and all have water and electricity hook-ups. The bayside sites are some of Florida's best, but they're sold out, especially on weekends. There's one major drawback: Unless you get lucky and arrive when there's a vacancy, you must appear *in person* and pay for your site no more than 30 days in advance. See p. 382.

- **Disney's Fort Wilderness Resort & Campground** (Orlando; ✆ **407/934-7639**): This woodsy 780-acre camping resort offers real life, not animatronic, fish-filled lakes and streams. It also has a lot of facilities to keep you busy, and you're close to the Magic Kingdom. Secluded campsites offer 110/220-volt outlets, barbecue grills, picnic tables, and children's play areas. See p. 419.

- **Anastasia State Park** (St. Augustine; ☎ **904/461-2033**): You'll be near 4 miles of sandy beach bordered by picturesque dunes, as well as a lagoon flanked by tidal marshes, at this urban park. Anastasia is one of Florida's most popular state facilities for camping, with its 139 wooded sites in high demand all year. They have picnic tables, grills, and electricity. Campsite reservations are required. See p. 496.
- **Fort Pickens Area, Gulf Islands National Seashore** (Pensacola; ☎ **800/365-2267**): You'll be near one of Florida's finest beaches at these 200 sites (135 with electricity) in a pine forest beside Santa Rosa Sound. Nature trails lead from the camp through Blackbird Marsh and to the beach. A small store sells provisions. You can make reservations up to 5 months in advance here. See "Pensacola" in chapter 13.
- **St. Andrews State Park** (Panama City Beach; ☎ **800/326-3521**): This preserve of dazzling white sand and dunes has RV and tent sites beautifully situated in a pine forest right on the shores of Grand Lagoon. See "Panama City Beach" in chapter 13.

10 The Best Affordable Restaurants

- **Shells** (Statewide): You'll see Shells restaurants all over Florida, but don't confuse it with Red Lobster: this casual, award-winning chain consistently provides excellent value *and* fresh seafood, especially if you have a family to feed. Starting at under $7, main courses range from the usual fried-seafood platters to pastas and chargrilled shrimp, fish, steaks, and chicken. They all have the same prices and menu, including a children's menu.
- **Grillfish** (South Beach, Miami; ☎ **305/538-9908**): A limited menu of only the freshest and simplest seafood is served in a relaxed but upscale atmosphere. It's remained popular in an area where many others have failed because of its excellent food and trendy atmosphere but reasonable prices. See p. 103.
- **Latin American Cafeteria** (Miami; ☎ **305/226-2393**): Hands down, this place serves the best Cuban sandwich north of Havana. Not only cheap, it's so big, you'll have leftovers for a subsequent snack, meal, or craving. See p. 113.
- **Versailles** (Miami; ☎ **305/444-0240**): This is the place where Miami's Cuban power brokers meet over *café con leche* and pastries. The homey food is plentiful and cheap, if not always gourmet quality. See p. 116.
- **El Toro Taco Family Restaurant** (Homestead, near Miami; ☎ **305/245-8182**): It's worth the price in gas to schlep down to Homestead for the most fantastic, homemade Mexican food in Miami. See p. 121.
- **Tom's Place** (Boca Raton; ☎ **561/997-0920**): An institution in otherwise exorbitantly priced Boca Raton, this successful barbecue joint offers expertly grilled meats paired with well-spiced sauces. See p. 253.
- **Alabama Jack's** (Key Largo; ☎ **305/248-8741**) The favorite waterfront honky-tonk of locals

and travelers en route to and back from the Keys, Alabama Jack's has killer conch chowder, peel-and-eat shrimp, and other fresh seafood at bargain basement prices. Live entertainment and Harley types are added bonuses. See p. 169.

- **Banana Café** (Key West; ℂ 305/ 294-7227): For fabulous French food, three meals a day, Banana Café is the place to indulge without breaking the bank. Their crepes are phenomenal. See p. 203.
- **Farmers Market Restaurant** (Fort Myers; ℂ 239/334-1687): The retail Farmers Market next door may be tiny, but the best of the cabbage, okra, green beans, and tomatoes end up here at this simple eatery, frequented by everyone from business executives to truck drivers. The specialties of the house are Southern favorites like smoked ham hocks with a bowl of black-eyed peas. See p. 305.
- **The Fish House** (Fort Myers Beach; ℂ 239/765-6766): You'll find the beach's least-expensive outdoor dining at the dockside tables of this no-frills friendly pub. You'll also see charter-boat skippers slaking their thirst at a large wooden bar occupying about half the open-air but screened dining room. Go for the fried or grilled grouper and other fish the captains have just landed. Sandwiches are available all day, including a tasty grouper version. See p. 312.
- **Hungry Heron** (Sanibel Island; ℂ 239/395-2300): There's something for everyone on the huge, tabloid-size menu at Sanibel's most popular family restaurant— from hot and cold "appiteezers" and overstuffed "seawiches" to pasta and steamed shellfish. And even though this is an affluent island, main courses start at just

$9. To keep the kids occupied, video cartoons run all the time. An all-you-can-eat breakfast buffet on Saturday and Sunday is an excellent value. See p. 322.

- **Sanibel Cafe** (Sanibel Island; ℂ 239/472-5323): Be sure to call for preferred seating at Sanibel's most popular breakfast spot, whose tables are museumlike glass cases containing delicate fossilized specimens from the Miocene and Pliocene epochs. Fresh-squeezed orange and grapefruit juice, Danish Havarti omelets, and homemade muffins and biscuits highlight the breakfast menu, while lunch features specialty sandwiches; shrimp, Greek, and chicken-and-grape salads made with a very light, fat-free dressing; and a limited list of main courses such as grilled or blackened chicken breast. See p. 323.
- **R. C. Otter's Island Eats** (Captiva Island; ℂ 239/395-1142): You can spend a fortune at Captiva Island's haute-cuisine restaurants, but not at this friendly, Key West–style cottage a block from the beach. Bare feet and bathing suits are welcome. The wide-ranging menu includes the island's best breakfasts, from bacon-and-eggs to house-smoked salmon. Musicians perform out in the yard every day. See p. 325.
- **Old Naples Pub** (Naples; ℂ 239/ 649-8200): You would never guess that the person sitting next to you at the bar here is very, very rich, so relaxed is this small, intimate pub. The fare is extraordinarily inexpensive, given the location in the center of Naples's high-end 3rd Street South shopping district. Best bets are the chicken salad with grapes and walnuts and the burgers, steaks, and fish from the grill. There's live entertainment nightly during

winter, Wednesday to Saturday nights off season. See p. 339.

- **First Watch** (Naples, ℭ 239/434-0005; and Sarasota, ℭ 941/954-1395): These little restaurants are everyone's favorite spots for breakfast, late brunch, or a midday meal in Naples and Sarasota. They are anything but diners: You get classical music and widely spaced tables topped with pitchers of lemon-tinged ice water. The identical menus lean heavily on healthy selections, but you can get your cholesterol from a sizzling skillet of fried eggs served over layers of potatoes, vegetables, and melted cheese. Lunch features large salads, sandwiches, and quesadillas. See p. 340.

- **The Dock at Crayton Cove** (Naples; ℭ 239/263-9940): Located right on the City Dock, this locals hangout is the best place in town for a supercasual open-air meal or a cool drink while watching the boats go back and forth across Naples Bay. Servers are friendly and conversational, which, depending on how you look at it, can be a good or not so good thing. The chow ranges from hearty chowders by the mug to seafood with a Floribbean fare, with Jamaican-style jerk shrimp thrown in for spice; main courses are moderately priced. See p. 339.

- **Mel's Hot Dogs** (Tampa; ℭ 813/985-8000): Just outside Busch Gardens, Tampa Bay, this red-and-white cottage offers everything from "bagel-dogs" and corndogs to a bacon/cheddar Reuben. Even the decor is dedicated to wieners: The walls and windows are lined with hot-dog memorabilia. See p. 365.

- **Carmine's Restaurant & Bar** (Tampa; ℭ 813/248-3834): Bright blue poles hold up an ancient pressed-tin ceiling above this noisy corner cafe. It's not the cleanest joint in town, but a great variety of loyal local patrons gather here for genuine Cuban sandwiches—smoked ham, roast pork, Genoa salami, Swiss cheese, pickles, salad dressing, mustard, lettuce, and tomato on crispy Cuban bread. The combination half-sandwich and choice of black beans and rice or a bowl of Spanish soup made with sausages, potatoes, and garbanzo beans all make a hearty meal for just $7 at lunch, $8 at dinner.

- **Fourth Street Shrimp Store** (St. Petersburg; ℭ 727/822-0325): The outside of this place looks like it's covered with graffiti, but it's actually a gigantic drawing of people eating. Inside, murals on two walls seem to look out on an early 19th-century seaport (one painted sailor permanently peers in to see what you're eating). This is the best and certainly the most interesting bargain in St. Petersburg. See p. 377.

- **Yoder's** (Sarasota; ℭ 941/955-7771): It's worth driving about 3 miles east of downtown Sarasota to this award-winning, Amish restaurant evoking the Pennsylvania Dutch country. The simple dining room displays handcrafts, photos, and paintings celebrating the Amish way. You'll get plain, made-from-scratch   meatloaf, baked and Southern fried chicken, country-smoked ham, and fried filet of flounder. Burgers, salads, soups, and sandwiches are also available. Leave room for traditional shoofly pie. See p. 402.

- **Gulf Drive Café** (Bradenton Beach; ℭ 941/778-1919): The coral and green dining room of this inexpensive gem opens to a beachside patio with tables shaded by a trellis. The breakfast fare is led by sweet Belgian waffles, which are available all day. You can also order salads, sandwiches, and burgers anytime here, with quiche du jour, Mediterranean seafood pasta, and regular seafood platters coming on line after 4pm. See p. 406.

- **Le Cellier Steakhouse** (Epcot; ✆ **407/939-3463**): Meet what is arguably one of the best menus in the theme parks' moderate class, featuring the usual cuts of beef in the $15 to $26 range and a good list of Canadian wine and Canadian beer. See p. 428.

- **Pebbles** (Orlando, Lake Buena Vista; ✆ **407/827-1111**): Pebbles is one of Orlando's most popular restaurants, especially with yuppies. It offers the option of a casual meal, perhaps a cheddar burger on toasted brioche, honey-roasted spare ribs, or a Caesar salad with grilled chicken. See p. 434.

- **The Bunnery Bakery & Café** (St. Augustine; ✆ **904/829-6166**): Alluring aromas waft from this bakery and cafe in the heart of St. Augustine's historic district. It's a great spot for breakfast before you start sightseeing, or for a fresh pastry and hot latte, cappuccino, or espresso any time you need a break. Lunch features soup, salads, burgers, panini, and croissants stuffed with walnut-and-pineapple chicken salad. See p. 502.

- **Biscottis** (Jacksonville; ✆ **904/387-2060**): This brick-walled little neighborhood gem might have come out of New York's East Village, San Francisco's downtown, or Washington's Georgetown. A young and hip waitstaff is pleasant and well-informed. Daily specials, like pan-seared salmon or pork loin, are always fresh and beautifully presented, and huge and inventive salads are especially good. See p. 511.

11 The Best Deals for Serious Shoppers

- **Prime Outlets at Florida City** (in the Upper Keys; ✆ **305/248-4727**): This outlet mall has a manageable 60 or so stores including Nike Factory Store, Bass Co. Store, Levi's, OshKosh B'Gosh, and Izod. Although it is not well publicized, any customer at the mall is welcome to pick up a valuable "Come Back Pack" from the customer service desk. The square red packet contains dozens of coupons good for significant discounts. See p. 177.

- **Half Buck Freddie's** (Key West; ✆ **305/294-2007**): Here, they stock out-of-season bargains and "rejected" clothing from the main store. See p. 199.

- **Sawgrass Mills** (Sunrise, Fort Lauderdale; ✆ **800-FL-MILLS**): The monster of all outlet malls has more than 300 shops, kiosks, and restaurants in nearly 2.3 million square feet covering 50 acres. Look for discount coupon books at the information booth. They are good for substantial savings at dozens of mall stores. See p. 238.

- **Fleamasters** (Fort Myers; ✆ **239/334-7001**): This is one of the largest of Florida's numerous flea markets. The weekend Fleamasters has more than 800 busy booths offering bargains on antiques, crafts, fashions, and fresh produce. It has snack bars and entertainment, too. See p. 296.

- **Orlando Outlets** (Orlando): **Belz Factory Outlet World,** 5401 W. Oak Ridge Rd. (at the north end of International Dr.; ✆ **407/354-0126**), and **Orlando Premium Outlets,** 8200 Vineland Ave. (✆ **407/238-7787**), are two of the better outlet malls in the area, if not the entire state. I've driven up from Miami just to shop here. See p. 462 and p. 462 respectively.

- **Ron Jon Surf Shop** (Cocoa Beach; © **321/799-8888**): Hundreds of billboards will lure you to this glaring, 24-hour surf shop, where you'll find a lot more than boards, wax, and everything else you need to look like a surfer. The shelves and racks hold souvenirs of every description and a wide array of beachwear. See p. 474.

- **Silver Sands Factory Stores** (Destin; © **800/510-6255** or 850/864-9771): The third largest designer outlet center in the United States sports the upscale likes of Anne Klein, Donna Karan, J. Crew, Jones New York, Brooks Brothers, Hartman Luggage, Coach leathers, and Bose electronics. There are so many you'll have to drive from one end to the other to spot your favorite brands. See p. 545.

12 The Best Bars & Nightspots Outside of Miami

- **Duval Street** (Key West): The partying-est strip this side of Bourbon Street is home to literally dozens of bars and dance spots. Explore them for yourself. See p. 188.

- **Woody's Saloon and Restaurant** (Islamorada; © **305/664-4335**): This raunchy bar has live bands almost every night, but it is the house band you want to see. Big Dick and the Extenders is headed by a 300-pound Native American who does a lewd, rude, and crude routine of jokes and songs guaranteed to offend everyone in the house. Despite a small cover charge, drink specials, contests, and the legendary Big Dick keep this place packed until 4am almost every night. See p. 182.

- **Clematis Street** (West Palm Beach): This newly gentrified area has some of the area's best (and only) nightlife. Just over the bridge from stodgy Palm Beach, this 5-block area, from Flagler Drive to Rosemary Avenue, has everything from late-night bookshops and wine bars to dance clubs and outdoor cafes. See p. 265.

- **O'Hara's** (Hollywood/Fort Lauderdale; © **954/925-2555**): Kitty Ryan owns two of South Florida's best spots for live music. On Las Olas Boulevard in Fort Lauderdale, there is always a crowd enjoying smoking music. The newer Hollywood spot is swinging every night with live jazz and blues and good food, too. See p. 245.

- **Las Olas Boulevard** (Fort Lauderdale): This wide, scenic street, dotted with good clubs and late-night shopping, is especially popular with a more mature local crowd and European visitors. See p. 238.

- **The Leopard Lounge in the Chesterfield Hotel** (Palm Beach; © **561/659-5800**): This is a popular hangout, especially for older locals who come for live music, a great happy hour, and no cover charge. A generous spread of hot and cold appetizers, plus two-for-one drink specials, keep the blue-blazer crowd happy every evening starting at 5pm. See p. 266.

- **E. R. Bradley's** (Palm Beach; © **561/833-3520**): This big, old bar attracts a fun, loud crowd of young professionals and serious older drinkers. Come for the generous happy-hour buffets. See p. 265.

- **The Dock at Crayton Cove** (Naples; © **239/263-9940**): Right on the City Dock, this lively pub is a perfect place for an open-air meal or a libation while watching the action on Naples Bay. It's the best place in town to meet the locals; in fact, you're almost guaranteed to get into a conversation at the friendly bar. See p. 339.

- **Downtown Disney West Side** (Lake Buena Vista; © **407/824-4321**): The happening hotspots here include Bongo's Cuban Café, House of Blues, and Planet Hollywood as part of a district that also includes shops and restaurants. See p. 464.
- **CityWalk** (Orlando; © **407/363-8000**): Universal Orlando's nighttime entertainment district showcases several popular clubs, from the more laid-back pace of City-Jazz, Motown Café, and Bob Marley—A Tribute to Freedom to the giddy-up and go of the Latin Quarter, the groove, Pat O'Brien's, and a Hard Rock Live concert venue. See p. 464.
- **Ocean Deck Restaurant & Beach Club** (Daytona Beach; © **386/253-5224**): Generations of spring breakers, bikers, and other beachgoers know the Ocean Deck as Daytona's best "beach pub." Opening to the sand and surf, the sweaty, noisy downstairs bar is always packed, especially when the reggae bands crank up after 9:30pm nightly. The upstairs dining room can be noisy, too, but both you and the kids can come

here for some very good chow, reasonable prices, and great views out the big window walls facing the ocean. See p. 487.

- **Seville Quarter** (Pensacola; © **850/434-6211**): In Pensacola's Seville Historic District, this restored antique brick complex with New Orleans–style wrought-iron balconies contains pubs and restaurants whose names capture the ambience: Rosie O'Grady's Goodtime Emporium; Lili Marlene's Aviator's Pub; Apple Annie's Courtyard; End o' the Alley Bar; Phineas Phogg's Balloon Works (a dance hall, not a balloon shop); and Fast Eddie's Billiard Parlor (which has electronic games for kids, too). Live entertainment ranges from Dixieland jazz to country and western. See p. 538.
- **Flora-Bama Lounge** (Perdido Key, near Pensacola; © **850/492-0611**): Billing itself as the last great roadhouse, this slapped-together Gulf-side pub is almost a shrine to country music, with jam sessions from noon until way past midnight on Saturday and Sunday. Flora-Bama is the prime sponsor and a key venue for the Frank Brown International Songwriters' Festival during the first week of November. Take in the great Gulf views from the Deck Bar. See p. 539.

2

Planning an Affordable Trip
to Florida

Contrary to popular belief, Florida is not one huge beach or theme park. Sure, there are 800 miles of beaches, and as for the theme parks, need we say more? But beyond that, Florida is a big, diverse state with all sorts of people, places, and things to see. There are also many discounts in the state, some of which are obvious and others which have to be dug up.

We have scoured the state to come up with the great money-saving tips in this chapter, which will tell you where and how to look for the best deals. Also here is information and our advice about transportation, seasons and special events, taking care of your special needs, and picking among the myriad types of accommodations—always with an eye on saving you money.

Don't just rely on this chapter, however. We've captured Florida's many personalities, attractions, and specific bargains in the chapters that follow. Peruse each one to see which destinations offer the activities you're looking for and the prices that fit your budget. If you pick the right place and go at the right time of year, you can have a terrific trip to Florida without feeling forced into bankruptcy.

THE $70-A-DAY PREMISE

With careful planning, two people *can* travel in Florida from $70 a day, combining their money for accommodations and at least two meals a day. That is, we assume you have at least $140 a day between the two of you for room and board, less drinks and tip. The costs of sightseeing, outdoor activities, transportation, and entertainment are all extras, but don't worry: We'll provide tips on saving money in those areas as well.

1 50 Money-Saving Tips

IN GENERAL

1. Avoid traveling during the high seasons, especially in southern Florida where hotel rates can more than double from mid-December to April. Also keep in mind that many airlines have deep-discount promotional fares to Florida during the off season. Central Florida sees less seasonal difference in prices, given its somewhat cooler winters and the year-round clientele visiting its theme parks. You can survive on $70 a day in northern Florida even during its high-summer season.

2. Always ask about discounts: corporate, student, military, auto club, senior citizen, and so on. Most airlines, car-rental firms, accommodations, attractions, and even some restaurants offer such price breaks but don't necessarily volunteer the information. Be sure to bring identification or your group membership card with you.

Florida

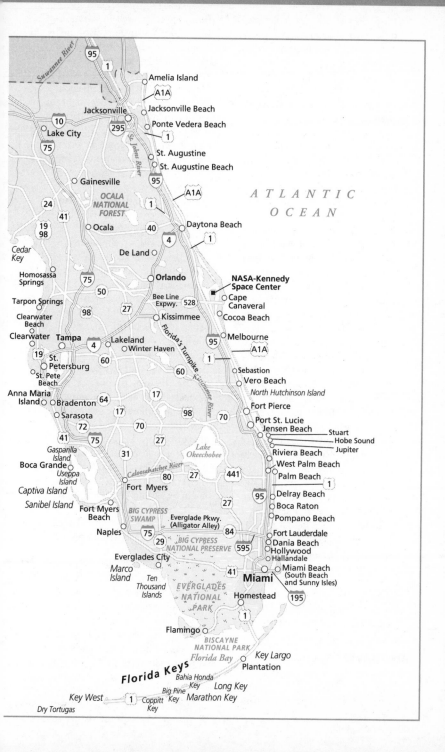

Most Florida activities and attractions offer discounts, but you'll need a valid ID to qualify for the bargain rates.

3. Use any coupons you can get your hands on. The ubiquitous giveaway booklets (such as *Florida on the Go*) you'll see in racks at the tourist information offices and elsewhere may look like junk mail, but they're loaded with discount coupons you can use at hotels, motels, restaurants, and attractions throughout the state. Other, more comprehensive coupon books are for sale. In business since 1961, the *Entertainment* publications (℗ **800/374-4464**) offer particularly well-stocked versions for Miami, the Keys, and Orlando. Its books usually cost between $28 and $48, depending on the locale. Over at the St. Pete and Clearwater beaches, the **Gulf Beaches of Tampa Bay Chamber of Commerce** (℗ **800/944-1847** or 727/360-6957) sells a book with discounts at many area restaurants, attractions, and other establishments for about $30. You can recoup more than the cost of these books if you use them religiously. In Orlando, call the **Orlando/Orange County Convention & Visitors Bureau** (℗ **800/643-9492**) and ask for a "Magicard" providing up to $500 in discounts on meals, some lodging, and at the smaller attractions. Also look for the free *Where Orlando* in restaurants and hotel lobbies; it contains discount coupons, and its website (www. travelfacts.com) has links to hot deals.

AIR TRAVEL

4. Ask for the cheapest airfare, not just the coach fare. As the tips below illustrate, there are many options.

5. Buy your ticket well in advance. Most airlines offer deep discounts on tickets purchased 7, 14, or 21 days before the departure date— and the cheap seats sell out first. Always ask about restrictions such as staying over a Saturday night. Tickets are usually nonrefundable if you must cancel your trip, but even if you have to pay an extra fee if you alter your plans later, you'll get substantial savings over the regular fare.

6. On the other hand, you can often benefit by buying at the last minute. You do run the risk of being stuck with a really expensive ticket—or no ticket at all—but when a flight is only half-sold, the airlines may offer deep, deep discounts to fill seats that aren't sold 72 hours before takeoff. This is a better strategy in the off season, when flights are more likely to have empty seats.

7. Be flexible in your schedule. Flying on Tuesday, Wednesday, or Thursday can save you money with some airlines; the prime Friday, Sunday, and Monday flights are often priced higher. Also inquire about night flights; the red-eye may leave you bleary, but if it's substantially cheaper, it might be worth it—you can make up the sleep later.

8. Surf the Internet and save. There are lots of Web pages and online services designed to clue you in on discounted airfares, accommodations, and car rentals. And the airlines often sell last-minute unused seats on their websites.

9. If you don't have access to the Internet, consult a travel agent. They can find you the cheapest airfares, room rates, package deals, and other travel bargains that you could never find. You're under no obligation to buy, although most agents now charge a fee for airline

tickets, since most airlines have all but eliminated commissions in recent years. On the other hand, agents still work for commissions when selling hotels, car-rental companies, and tour operators.

10. Ask a travel agent about charter flights. Several airlines, such as the Canadian carrier Air Transat, have charter flights to Florida during winter. They can offer great savings over commercial airline fares, but make sure you book with a reputable firm and inquire about all restrictions before you pay.

11. Check out consolidators (also known as "bucket shops"). These wholesalers buy tickets directly from the airlines in bulk at heavy discounts, and then resell them. Many consolidators also book charter as well as commercial flights. The tickets are usually heavily restricted (ask about all the details), but you may save a bundle—usually 20% to 35%. See "Getting There," later in this chapter, for the names of reputable consolidators.

12. Check the travel ads in your local newspaper. Airlines, consolidators, and charter and tour companies love to advertise package deals and promotions in weekend travel sections around the country. *Just remember:* If you're dealing with a new company, or one that you're unfamiliar with, it's a good idea to check with the Better Business Bureau to make sure it's legit.

13. Take local shuttle services to and from the airports. Unless you're a family or group, they usually are less expensive than taxis. Some hotels will even pick you up at the airport for free, so be sure to ask if they have airport transportation when you book your room.

CAR RENTALS

14. Reserve your rental in advance, especially during the high seasons when cars, particularly the small, least expensive models, can be in heavy demand. Not only will you have a car waiting, you'll avoid paying top dollar for a vehicle that's larger than you need.

15. Call all the major car-rental firms, or check their websites, and compare rates (see "Getting Around," later in this chapter, for their toll-free numbers). Always ask for their cheapest rates. Even after you've made your reservations, call again and check rates a few days or weeks later—you may stumble upon a cheaper rate.

16. If you'll be visiting for a week or more, ask for a long-term rate. Most Florida firms offer substantial discounts for weekly rentals, especially during the off season.

17. Be sure to ask for discounts if you belong to a national organization such as AAA, AARP, Costco Wholesale, or USAA, which negotiate special rates for their members. But be wary: Some of these specials may be more expensive than the rental companies' weekly rates or promotional deals, so ask about all possibilities.

18. Keep in mind that Florida has a $2.05-per-day state highway fund surcharge, that state and local sales taxes will be added to your bill, and that many airports tack on another fee. The car-rental companies don't include these taxes when they quote rates, so before you hang up, be sure to ask how much your entire bill will be.

19. If there are only one or two of you traveling, reserve the least expensive subcompact or compact (sometimes called economy) cars. You'll also save money on fuel and have an easier time parking. But be careful: Some reservations agents may tell you that all their least expensive cars are booked; this may be a ploy to get you to

upgrade, so thank them and call another company. On the other hand, if you arrive with a valid reservation with a confirmation number, the agents are obligated to honor the rate you were quoted, even if they have to give you an upgrade. Make them stick to their original quote.

20. Never agree to buy gasoline from a car-rental company. It will always be less expensive at a station in town, so fill up just before returning the vehicle.

21. If you don't mind driving to Florida, ask about "drive out" programs that some firms use to reposition their fleets. Major companies like Avis, Budget, Hertz, and National sometimes move their cars from northern cities to southern Florida for the winter season, and you could get a ridiculously cheap rate if you'll drive the vehicles south (or back north in the warmer months).

ACCOMMODATIONS

22. Book early to get the least expensive room, and shop around. Use the toll-free numbers as well as the direct numbers; at some chains, only the reservation clerks at the national number know about package deals that can save you money. At other places you'll often get a better deal by calling the individual hotel's reservation desk rather than the chain's main number. Some major chains also post deals on their websites.

23. Don't just accept the "rack" or published rate—there's almost always a lower price available. Ask for the cheapest rate and about discounts for seniors, families, or any national organizations that you might belong to (especially AAA and AARP). Ask about special promotions and discounts for stays of a week or more.

24. Inquire about golf, tennis, and other packages. Many Florida establishments offer them, and you will pay less than if you ante up separately for the room and activities. Sometimes you can even get a rental car thrown in. We've mentioned the hotels and resorts that regularly offer package deals in the accommodations listings in this book. Their offers change frequently, however, so you'll have to ask.

25. Choose a hotel or motel that offers free continental breakfasts. The savings could enable you to afford better meals at lunch and dinner. The accommodations listings in this book indicate the properties that offer free breakfasts.

26. Stay a block or more from the beach, since hotels and motels not directly on the water usually are less expensive than those directly facing the sand. And in places where the prime resorts are on islands, mainland hotels and motels usually cost less than their offshore brethren (they also are more likely to offer discounted weekday or weekend rates). And even if you elect a beachfront hotel, rooms with bay or garden views normally are less expensive than those directly facing the ocean or gulf.

27. If you're traveling with children, check to see if they can stay in your room for free. Or better yet, consider getting a one-bedroom suite with a pullout sofa in the living room; one suite is usually cheaper than two hotel rooms, and you'll still have privacy.

28. Get a room with cooking facilities. Many Florida establishments have units with at least kitchenettes. They cost a bit more than regular rooms, but preparing your own breakfast and lunch could

slash your food costs in half. And it makes life a lot easier, especially if you're traveling with kids.

29. If you're staying for a week or more, consider a condominium unit, apartment, or cottage, especially if you're traveling with children. Condos usually have a sleeper sofa as extra bedding, a kitchen that lets you prepare some of your own meals, and the complexes usually have a pool and often tennis courts and other recreational facilities. Most have weekly rates that are less than paying by the night at hotels. Do note, however, that you'll usually have to pay extra for daily maid service.

30. Choose a hotel or motel that lets you make local calls for free. Most charge 50¢ or more per local phone call, and some even hit you with a fee on credit card calls. Use your cellphone or the pay phone down in the lobby instead. Many hotels also tack on hefty surcharges for laundry, dry cleaning, and other services. You can cut these costs by choosing one with a guest laundry and washing your own clothes, and you can easily find dry cleaners on your own.

31. If you show up without a reservation, bargain at the front desk. This usually won't work during the high seasons, when most hotels are nearly full, but you might be able to strike a very favorable off-season deal. If you try this, arrive in late afternoon or early evening, when the majority of the guests with reservations have already checked in, and rooms that aren't yet occupied are likely to stay empty for the night. If the front-desk clerk is unhelpful, ask to speak to the hotel manager, who may be the only employee who can discount rooms.

DINING

32. Take advantage of Florida's usually fine weather by planning daytime and romantic sunset picnics. Many towns and cities have shops purveying gourmet picnic fare, and most of the large supermarkets such as Publix, Albertson's, and Winn-Dixie have deli sections with good selections of meats, cheeses, breads, and salads.

33. Ask the staff at your hotel or motel which local restaurants and cocktail lounges have happy-hour specials. They signal reduced prices on drinks, and sometimes appetizers.

34. If you don't mind dining before 6pm, take advantage of the early-bird specials offered by many restaurants. The selections may be limited, but they are a less-expensive way to sample the fine fare at otherwise expensive establishments. We've pointed out many of them in the dining listings in this book.

35. If you're traveling with the kids, inquire about children's menus or discounts. Most restaurants in Florida offer them—and at resort-restaurant prices, they can be a real boon to your budget.

36. Look for fixed-price menus at the pricier restaurants, or splurge on a special meal at lunch rather than dinner. In general, you'll pay half (and sometimes even less than that) as much for a lunchtime main course as you will at dinner. You may not get the attentive service, but you'll be surprised at the quality, even at some of the pricier restaurants.

37. The Friday Calendar section of *The Orlando Sentinel* sometimes includes two-for-one dinner special coupons and other discounts on entertainment. It also lists cultural events and concerts throughout Central Florida, some of them free or for a small admission.

GOLF

38. Bring your own golf clubs, tennis rackets, snorkeling and scuba gear, and other equipment. In addition to saving the rental costs, your gear will fit correctly and be in top condition.

39. Before booking a tee time, check with the agencies that represent many Florida golf courses (see "Special-Interest Trips," later in this chapter). Some of them offer discounted fees and golf-travel packages. The best way to find a good deal for Orlando's many golf courses is to look in the sports section of the local newspaper, *The Orlando Sentinel,* for discount coupons and otherwise unadvertised specials.

THE MAJOR THEME PARKS

40. Visitors who stay at WDW for a few days get better deals than those who come for just a day. **1-day/1-park tickets** cost $59.75 for adults, $48 for children 3 to 9. A 7-day **multiday ticket** costs $199 for adults, $160 for kids. **Premium Passes** that allow visitors admission to other attractions range from $139.95 for a 1-day adult pass to $268 for a 7-day pass. Purchase them in advance and you'll save up to $11 per person. See p. 438 for details.

41. Buy a combined pass to Universal Studios Florida, SeaWorld, Wet 'n Wild in Orlando, and Busch Gardens Tampa. You pay one price to get into all three over either a 7- or a 10-day period. The combined passes cost more up front, but you'll save in the long run. You can also save 10% if you purchase tickets on the Internet at Universal's site (www.uescape.com).

42. Look for discount tickets to Sea-World and Universal Studios Florida on 2-liter bottles of Pepsi products. These discounts are usually available during Halloween Horror Night at Universal.

43. You can save 10% by purchasing your SeaWorld tickets through its website (www.SeaWorld.com).

44. Take food and drink with you into the parks. Grocery stores and discount drugstores tend to be a little more expensive in tourist areas, but filling coolers in your car or bringing backpacks into the parks with snacks, lunch basics, sodas, bottled water, juices, and other drinks will save you a bundle over the cost inside the parks.

45. Invest in inexpensive plastic rain ponchos for the entire family before you leave home. Many major parks include water rides, and it's miserable to walk around wet all day, even in the summer. Plus, they will come in handy during summer storms, which can come up quickly. In the parks, they cost twice what you'll pay at home.

46. If you have young children, bring lightweight, easy-to-carry strollers, since rentals inside the parks can add up. Don't bring your Cadillac of kiddie carriers: It could be stolen.

47. Think twice about items such as souvenir cups or fanny packs that some hotels leave in your room. These are not complimentary: If you use them, you will be charged.

48. The Disney parks have outdoor carts selling things such as turkey legs, baked potatoes, and fresh fruit. These can easily make a simple meal and are cheaper than any restaurant food.

49. Buy your tickets to Busch Gardens Tampa Bay at Tampa Bay Visitor Information Center, across the street from the main entrance (© **813/985-3601**). You'll save a few dollars, and the staff is expert at advising you on how to maximize your time in the park. Many

area hotels and motels have packages that include free or discounted admission.

NIGHTLIFE

50. Check out the local newspapers for free concerts and other entertainment in municipal parks. The Friday newspapers usually have entertainment sections listing activities for the upcoming weekend. And be sure to pick up copies of the local "alternative" tabloid newspapers; they're free and are packed with entertainment ideas.

2 The Regions in Brief

The first decision you'll have to make is where to go in Florida. Contrary to popular belief, it's not all sun, sand, and hanging chads—there are countless cultural, culinary, and nocturnal diversions as well. Of course, you will find ample sun, sea, and sand all along the 800 miles of shoreline here, but not every place in the Sunshine State is warm all the time. Many Florida beaches are lined with flashy hotels and condominiums, whereas others are pristinely preserved in their natural states. You can spend your days in busy cosmopolitan cities or while them away in picturesque small towns steeped in history. You can take the kids to see Mickey Mouse, or you can find a romantic retreat far from the maddening crowds. The choice is yours.

Here is a brief rundown of the state's regions to help get you started.

MIAMI & MIAMI BEACH Sprawling across the southeastern corner of the state, metropolitan Miami is a city that prides itself on benefiting from its multiple, vibrant personalities, and its no-passport-necessary international flair. Here you will hear a cacophony of Spanish and many other languages, not to mention accents, spoken all around you, for this cosmopolitan area is a melting pot of immigrants from Latin America, the Caribbean, and, undeniably, the northeastern United States in particular. Cross the causeways and you'll come to the sands of Miami Beach, long a resort mecca and home to the hypertrendy South Beach, famous for its Art Deco architecture, electric nightlife, and celebrity sightings. See chapter 4 for more on the Miami area and p. 79 for descriptions of the different districts within Miami.

THE KEYS From the southern tip of the Florida mainland, U.S. 1 travels through a 100-mile-long string of islands stretching from Key Largo to the famous and funky yet laid-back "Conch Republic" of Key West, only 90 miles from Cuba and the southernmost point in the United States (it's always warm down here). While some of the islands are crammed with strip malls and tourist traps, most are dense with unusual species of tropical flora and fauna. The Keys don't have the best beaches in Florida, but the waters here—all in a vast marine preserve—offer the state's best scuba diving and snorkeling and some of its best deep-sea fishing. See chapter 5, "The Keys," for more information on this region.

THE EVERGLADES & BISCAYNE NATIONAL PARK This is not your B-movie swamp. In fact, no excessive Hollywood studio budget could afford to replicate the stunning beauty found in this national landmark. Encompassing more than 2,000 square miles and 1.5 million acres, Everglades National Park covers the entire southern tip of Florida. The park, along with nearby Big Cypress National Preserve, protects a unique and fragile "River of Grass" ecosystem teeming with wildlife that is best seen by canoe, by boat, or on long or short hikes. To the east of the Everglades is Biscayne National Park, preserving the northernmost living-coral reefs in the continental United States. See chapter 6 for more information on these parks.

THE GOLD COAST North of Miami, the Gold Coast is aptly named, for here are booming Hollywood and Fort Lauderdale and ritzy Boca Raton and Palm Beach—sun-kissed, glitzy, glammy, and sandy playgrounds of the rich and famous. Beyond its dozens of gorgeous beaches, the area offers fantastic shopping, entertainment, dining, boating, golfing, tennis, and many places to relax in beautiful settings. With some of the country's most famous golf courses and even more tennis courts, this area also attracts big-name tournaments. See chapter 7 to learn more about the Gold Coast.

THE TREASURE COAST Despite gaining unprecedented numbers of new residents in recent years, the beach communities running from Hobe Sound north to Sebastian Inlet have successfully and blissfully managed to retain their small-town feel. In addition to a vast array of wildlife (not to be mistaken with nightlife, which is intentionally absent from these parts), the area has a rich and colorful history. Its name stems from a violent 1715 hurricane that sunk an entire fleet of treasure-laden Spanish ships. The sea around Sebastian Inlet draws surfers to the largest swells in the state, and the area has some great fishing as well. See chapter 8 for more information on the Treasure Coast.

SOUTHWEST FLORIDA Ever since inventor Thomas Alva Edison built a home here in 1885, some of America's wealthiest families have spent their winters along Florida's southwest coast. They are attracted by the area's subtropical climate, shell-strewn beaches, and intricate waterways winding among 10,000-plus islands. Many charming remnants of Old Florida coexist with modern resorts in the sophisticated riverfront towns of Fort Myers and Naples and on islands like Gasparilla, Useppa, Sanibel, Captiva, and Marco. And thanks to some timely preservation, the area has many wildlife refuges, including the "backdoor" entrance to Everglades National Park. See chapter 9, "Southwest Florida."

THE TAMPA BAY AREA Halfway down the west coast of Florida lies Tampa Bay, one of the state's most densely populated areas. A busy seaport and commercial center, the city of Tampa is home to Busch Gardens Tampa Bay, which is both a major theme park and one of the country's largest zoos. Boasting a unique pier and fine museums, St. Petersburg's waterfront downtown is one of Florida's most pleasant. Most visitors elect to stay near the beaches skirting the narrow barrier islands running some 25 miles between St. Pete Beach and Clearwater Beach. Across the bay to the south lies Sarasota, one of Florida's prime performing-arts venues, the riverfront town of Bradenton, and another string of barrier islands with great beaches and resorts spanning every price range. See chapter 10 for more information.

WALT DISNEY WORLD & ORLANDO Walt Disney announced plans to build the Magic Kingdom in 1965, a year before his death and 6 years before the theme park opened, changing forever what was then a sleepy Southern town. Walt Disney World claims four distinct parks, two entertainment districts, enough hotels and restaurants to fill a small city, and several smaller attractions including water parks and miniature-golf courses. And then there are the rapidly expanding Universal Studios Orlando and SeaWorld, as well as many more non-Disney attractions. Orlando is Florida's most popular tourist destination thanks not only to an animated rodent but also to those enterprising entertainment venues that have risen to the mouse's challenge. See chapter 11.

NORTHEAST FLORIDA The northeast section of the state contains the oldest permanent settlement in America—St. Augustine, where Spanish colonists arrived and settled more than 4 centuries ago. Today, its history comes to life in a quaint historic district. St. Augustine is bordered to the north by Jacksonville, an up-and-coming Sunbelt metropolis with miles of oceanfront beach and beautiful marine views along the St. Johns River. Up on the Georgia border, Amelia Island has two of Florida's finest resorts and its own historic town of Fernandina Beach. To the south of St. Augustine, Daytona Beach is the home of the Daytona International Speedway and is a maddening, spring-break mecca for the MTV generation. Another brand of excitement is offered down at Cape Canaveral, where the Kennedy Space Center launches all manned U.S. space missions. See chapter 12.

NORTHWEST FLORIDA: THE PANHANDLE Historic roots run deep in Florida's narrow northwest extremity; and Pensacola's historic district, which blends Spanish, French, and British cultures, is a highlight of any visit to today's Panhandle. Despite that, however, the accents here are decidedly Deep South. So, too, are the powdery, dazzlingly white beaches that stretch for more than 80 miles past the resorts of Pensacola Beach, Fort Walton Beach, Destin, and Panama City Beach. The Gulf Islands National Seashore has preserved much of this beach and its wildlife, and inland are state parks that offer some of the state's best canoeing adventures. All this makes the area a favorite summertime vacation destination for residents of neighboring Georgia and Alabama, with whom Northwest Floridians share many Deep South traditions. Sitting in a pine and oak forest just 30 miles from the Georgia line, the state capital of Tallahassee has a moss-draped, football-loving charm all its own. See chapter 13 for more information.

3 Visitor Information

Your best sources for detailed information about a specific destination in Florida are the **local visitor information offices.** They're listed under "Orientation" or "Essentials" in the following chapters.

Contact **Visit Florida,** P.O. Box 1100, Tallahassee, FL 32302-1100 (© **888/7-FLA-USA;** www.flausa. com), the state's official tourism marketing agent, for a free comprehensive guide to the state. Florida State Parks have a new website at www.florida stateparks.org. Visit Florida also operates **welcome centers** 16 miles west of Pensacola on I-10, 4 miles north of Jennings on I-75, 7 miles north of Yulee on I-95, and 3 miles north of Campbellton on U.S. 231. There's also a walk-in information office in the west foyer of the New Capitol Building in Tallahassee (see chapter 13).

4 Money

How much money you spend on your Florida vacation will depend on your own desires and choices, when you go, and most definitely *where* you go.

The state has a wide range of accommodations, from some of the country's most luxurious and expensive beachfront resorts to no-frills but friendly mom-and-pop motels sitting right by the beach. If you can do without the luxuries, you needn't spend a fortune.

Tourism is Florida's biggest industry, and the economic law of supply and demand dictates that the prices of hotel rooms are highest during the seasons when tourists invade Florida: the winter months in the southern half of the state and during summertime up north.

See "When to Go," below, for details about Florida's high, low, and in-between seasons.

CREDIT CARDS & ATMS

The easiest way to pay for almost everything in Florida is with a credit card. MasterCard and Visa credit and debit cards are accepted almost everywhere. American Express, Diner's Club, and Discover cards also are accepted, although not as widely as MasterCard and Visa.

The best way to get cash while you're traveling in Florida is to use your debit or credit cards at **ATMs.** Of the big national banks, **First Union Bank** and **Bank of America** have offices with ATMs throughout Florida.

Most ATMs are linked to a national network that most likely includes your bank at home. **Cirrus** (℡ 800/424-7787; www.mastercard.com/atm locator) and **PLUS** (℡ 800/843-7587; www.visa.com/atms) are the two most popular networks; check the back of your ATM card to see which network your bank belongs to. Use the toll-free numbers or check online to locate ATMs in your destination. Be sure to check your bank's daily withdrawal limit and your credit limits before leaving home.

Also be sure to have your personal identification number (PIN), which you will need to activate the cash withdrawal functions at all ATMs.

5 When to Go

To a large extent, the timing of your visit will determine how much you'll spend—and how much company you'll have—once you get to Florida. That's because room rates can more than double during the high seasons, when countless visitors migrate to Florida.

The weather determines the high seasons (see "Climate," below). In subtropical Southern Florida, it's during the winter, from mid-December to mid-April. On the other hand, you'll be rewarded with incredible bargains if you can stand the heat and humidity of a South Florida summer between June and early September. In North Florida, the reverse is true: Tourists flock here during the summer, from Memorial Day to Labor Day.

Presidents' Day weekend in February, Easter week, Memorial Day weekend at the end of May, the Fourth of July, Labor Day weekend at the start of September, Thanksgiving, Christmas, and New Year's are busy throughout the state, and especially at Walt Disney World and the other Orlando area attractions, which can be packed anytime school's out (see chapter 11 for more information on these areas).

Northern and Southern Florida share the same "shoulder seasons": April and May and from September to November, when the weather is pleasant throughout Florida and hotel rates are considerably less than during the high seasons. If price is a consideration, these months of pleasant temperatures and fewer tourists are the best times to visit.

See the accommodations sections in the chapters that follow for specifics about the local high, shoulder, and off seasons.

CLIMATE   Northern Florida has a temperate climate, and even in the warmer southern third of the state, it's subtropical, not tropical. Accordingly, Florida sees more extremes of temperatures than, say, the Caribbean islands.

Spring (late Mar–May) sees warm temperatures throughout Florida, but it also brings tropical showers.

Summer runs from May to September in Florida, when it's hot and very humid throughout the state. If you're in an inland city during these months, you may not want to do anything too taxing when the sun is at its peak. Coastal areas, however, reap the benefits of sea breezes. Severe afternoon thunderstorms are prevalent during the summer heat (there aren't professional sports teams here named *Lightning* and *Thunder* for nothing), so schedule your activities for earlier in the day, and take precautions to avoid being hit by lightning during the storms.

Autumn (from about Sept–Nov) is a great time to visit—the hottest days are gone, and the crowds have thinned out. Unless a hurricane blows through, November usually is Florida's driest month. August through November is hurricane season here, but even if one threatens, the National Weather Service closely tracks the storms and gives ample warning if there's need to evacuate coastal areas.

Winter (roughly Nov–Mar) can get a bit nippy throughout the state, and sometimes downright cold in Northern Florida. Although snow is rare, a flake or two has been known to fall as far south as Miami. The "cold snaps" usually last only a few days in the southern half of the state, however, and daytime temperatures quickly return to the 70s.

For up-to-the-minute weather info, tune in to cable TV's Weather Channel, or click onto its website: www. weather.com.

Average Temperatures in Selected Florida Cities (°F/°C)

	Jan	Feb	Mar	Apr	May	June	July	Aug	Sept	Oct	Nov	Dec
Key West	69/21	72/22	74/23	77/25	80/27	82/28	85/29	85/29	84/29	80/27	74/23	72/22
Miami	69/21	70/21	71/22	74/23	78/26	81/27	82/28	84/29	81/27	78/26	73/23	70/21
Tampa	60/16	61/16	66/19	72/22	77/25	81/27	82/28	82/28	81/27	75/24	67/19	62/17
Orlando	60/16	63/17	66/19	71/22	78/26	82/28	82/28	82/28	81/27	75/24	67/19	61/16
Tallahassee	53/12	56/13	63/17	68/20	72/22	78/26	81/27	81/27	77/25	74/23	66/19	59/15

FLORIDA CALENDAR OF EVENTS

January

FedEx Orange Bowl Classic, Miami. Football fanatics flock down to the big Orange Bowl game (oddly taking place not at the Orange Bowl in seedy downtown, but at the much more savory Pro Player Stadium) on New Year's Day, featuring two of the year's best college football teams. Call © **305/ 341-4700** for tickets, but call early as they sell out quickly.

Key West Literary Seminar, Key West. Literary types get a good reason to put down the books and head to Key West. This annual 3-day event features a different theme every year, and a roster of incredible authors, writers, and other literary types. The event is so popular it sells out well in advance, so call early for tickets (available for individual lectures or events, or the entire 3-day conference). For information call © **888/293-9291** or visit www.key westliteraryseminar.org.

February

Gasparilla Pirate Fest, Tampa. Hundreds of boats and rowdy "pirates" invade the city and then parade along Bayshore Boulevard, showering crowds with beads

The Boys of Spring

Major-league baseball fans can watch the Florida Marlins in Miami and the Tampa Bay Devil Rays in St. Petersburg throughout their seasons, April through September, but the entire state is a baseball hotbed from late February to the end of March, when many other teams tune up for the regular season with "Grapefruit League" exhibition games.

Most of Florida's spring-training stadiums are relatively small, so fans can see their favorite players up close, maybe even get a handshake or an autograph. Also, tickets are priced from $5 to $12, a bargain when compared with admission for regular-season games. Many games sell out by early March, so don't wait until you're in Florida to buy tickets.

The teams can move from year to year, so contact the **Florida Sports Foundation**, 2390 Kerry Forest Pkwy., Suite 101, Tallahassee, FL 32309 (© **850/488-8347**; fax 850/922-0482; www.flasports.com), which usually posts the Grapefruit League schedules on its website late in January. The main office of **Major League Baseball,** 350 Park Ave., New York, NY 10022 (www.mlb.com), is another place to find out where your favorite teams will be playing.

Here's where the teams played in 2004. See the outdoor activities sections in subsequent chapters for specifics.

Atlanta Braves, Lake Buena Vista, near Orlando (© **407/939-GAME**; www.braves.mlb.com); **Baltimore Orioles,** Fort Lauderdale (© 954/

and coins (© **813/353-8108**; www.gasparillapiratefest.com). Early February.

Everglades Seafood Festival, Florida City. What seems like schools of fish-loving people flock down to Florida City for a 2-day feeding frenzy, in which Florida delicacies from stone crab to gator tails are served from shacks and booths on the outskirts of this quaint Old Florida town. Free admission, but you pay for the food you eat, booth by booth (© **239/ 695-2561**; www.evergladesseafood festival.com). First full weekend in February.

Miami Film Festival. Though not exactly Cannes, the Miami Film Festival, sponsored by the Film Society of America, is an impressive 10-day celluloid celebration, featuring world premieres of Latin American, domestic, and other foreign and independent films. Actors, producers, and directors show up to plug their films and participate in Q and A sessions with the audiences. Call © **877/888-MIFF** or visit www.miamifilmfestival.com. Early to mid-February.

Speedweeks, Daytona. Nineteen days of events with a series of races that draw the top names in NASCAR stock car racing, all culminating in the Daytona 500. All events take place at the Daytona International Speedway. Especially for the **Daytona 500,** tickets must be purchased even a year in advance (© **386/254-2700**; www.daytona intlspeedway.com). They go on sale January 1 of the prior year. First 3 weeks of February.

Miami International Boat Show, Miami Beach. If you don't like crowds, beware, as this show draws a quarter of a million boat

776-1921; www.orioles.mlb.com); **Boston Red Sox,** Fort Myers (© **877/ 733-7699;** www.redsox.mlb.com); **Cincinnati Reds,** Sarasota (© **941/954- 4464;** www.reds.mlb.com); **Cleveland Indians,** Winter Haven (© **863/ 293-3900;** www.indians.mlb.com); **Detroit Tigers,** Lakeland (© **813/ 287-8844** or 407/839-3900; www.tigers.mlb.com); **Florida Marlins,** Jupiter (© 561/966-3309; www.marlins.mlb.com); **Houston Astros,** Kissimmee, near Orlando (© **407/839-3900;** www.astros.mlb.com); **Kansas City Royals,** Davenport (© **800/326-4000;** www.royals.mlb.com); **Los Angeles Dodgers,** Vero Beach (© **772/569-6858;** www.dodgers. mlb.com); **Minnesota Twins,** Fort Myers (© **800/338-9467;** www.twins. mlb.com); **Montreal Expos,** Melbourne (© **321/633-4487;** www. expos.mlb.com); **New York Mets,** Port St. Lucie (© **772/871-2115;** www.mets.mlb.com); **New York Yankees,** Tampa (© **813/879-2244;** www.yankees.mlb.com); **Philadelphia Phillies,** Clearwater (© **727/442- 8496;** www.phillies.mlb.com); **Pittsburgh Pirates,** Bradenton (© **941/ 748-4610;** www.pirates.mlb.com); **St. Louis Cardinals,** Jupiter (© **561/ 775-1818,** ext. 7; www.cardinals.mlb.com); **Tampa Bay Devil Rays,** St. Petersburg (© **888/FAN-RAYS** or 727/825-3250; www.devilrays.mlb. com); **Texas Rangers,** Port Charlotte (© **800/326-4000;** www.rangers. mlb.com); **Toronto Blue Jays,** Dunedin (© **800/707-8269;** www.bluejays. mlb.com).

enthusiasts to the Miami Beach Convention Center. Some of the world's priciest megayachts, speedboats, sailboats, and schooners are displayed for purchase or for gawking. Call © **954/441-3231** or visit www.discoverboating.com. Mid-February.

March

Bike Week, Daytona Beach. An international gathering of motorcycle enthusiasts draws a crowd of more than 200,000. In addition to major races held at Daytona International Speedway (featuring the world's best road racers, motorcrossers, and dirt trackers), there are motorcycle shows, beach parties, and the Annual Motorcycle Parade, with thousands of riders (© **800/ 854-1234;** www.officialbikeweek. com). First week in March.

Spring Break, Daytona Beach, Miami Beach, Panama City Beach, Key West, and other beaches. College students from all over the United States and Canada flock to Florida for endless partying, wet-T-shirt and bikini contests, free concerts, volleyball tournaments, and more. Three weeks in March.

Calle Ocho Festival, Little Havana. What Carnivale is to Rio, the Calle Ocho Festival is to Miami. This 10-day extravaganza, also called Carnival Miami, features a lengthy block party spanning 23 blocks, live salsa music, parades, and, of course, tons of savory Cuban delicacies. Those afraid of mob scenes should avoid this party at all costs (© **305/644-8888**). Mid-March.

Winter Party, Miami Beach. Gays and lesbians from around the world book trips to Miami as far as a year in advance to attend this weekend-long series of parties and events benefiting mostly local gay and lesbian organizations now run by the National Gay and Lesbian Task Force Foundation (© 202/393-5177; www.thetaskforce.org). Travel arrangements can be made through Different Roads Travel, the event's official travel company, by calling © 888/ROADS-55, ext. 510. For information on the specific events and prices, call © 305/571-1924 or visit www.winterparty.org. Early March.

April

Black College Reunion, Daytona Beach. Some 75,000 students from 115 predominantly African-American universities bring a sometimes-rowdy end to the spring-break season (© 800/854-1234; www.daytonabeach.com). Mid-April.

PGA Seniors Golf Championship, Palm Beach Gardens. This is the oldest and most prestigious of the senior golf tournaments in which aging swingers prove they've still got spunk in their swing (© 561/624-8400). Mid-April.

July

World's Richest Tarpon Tournament, Boca Grande. Some $175,000 is at stake in the great tarpon waters off Southwest Florida (© 941/964-0568; www.bocagrandechamber.com). Second Wednesday and Thursday in July.

Lower Keys Underwater Music Fest, Looe Key. When you hear the phrase "the music and the madness," you may want to think of this amusing aural aquatic event in which boaters head out to the underwater reef at the Looe Key Marine Sanctuary, drop speakers into the water, and pipe in all sorts of music, creating a disco-diving spectacular. Considering the heat at this time of year, underwater is probably the coolest place for a

concert. Call © 800/872-3722. Early July.

Blue Angels Air Show, Pensacola. World-famous navy pilots do their aerial acrobatics just 100 yards off Pensacola Beach (© 800/874-1234 or 850/434-1234; www.visitpensacola.com or www.blueangels.navy.mil). Early July.

September

Labor Day Pro-Am Surfing Festival, Cocoa Beach. One of the largest surfing events on the East Coast draws pros and amateurs from around the country. There are also rock 'n' roll bands and swimsuit contests (© 321/459-2200; www.space-coast.com). Labor Day weekend.

October

Biketoberfest, Daytona. Road-racing stars compete at the CCS Motorcycle Championship at Daytona International Speedway. There are also parties, parades, concerts, and more (© 386/253-RACE; www.biketoberfest.org). Mid-October.

Clearwater Jazz Holiday, Clearwater. Top jazz musicians play for 4 days and nights at bayfront Coachman Park in this free musical extravaganza (© 727/461-5200; www.clearwaterjazz.com). Mid-October.

Columbus Day Regatta, Miami. On the day that Columbus discovered America, the party-hearty discover their fellow Americans' birthday suits, as this bacchanalia in the middle of Biscayne Bay encourages participants in this so-called regatta (there is a boat race at some point during the day, but most people are too preoccupied to notice) to strip down to their bare necessities and party at the sandbar in the middle of the bay. You may not need a bathing suit, but you will need a boat to get out to where all the action is. Consider renting one on Key Biscayne, which is the closest to the sandbar.

Halloween Horror Nights, Orlando. Universal Studios transforms its grounds for 19 nights into haunted attractions with live bands, a psychopath's maze, special shows, and hundreds of ghouls and goblins roaming the streets. The studio closes at dusk, reopening in a new macabre form at 7pm. Full admission is charged for the event, which is geared toward adults (© **800/837-2273** or 407/363-8000; www.universalorlando.com). Mid-October through Halloween.

Mickey's Not-So-Scary Halloween Party, Orlando. At Walt Disney World, guests are invited to trick or treat in the Magic Kingdom, starting at 7pm. The party includes parades, storytelling, live music, and a bewitching fireworks display. Call © **407/934-7639** for information; www.disneyworld. com. End of October.

Fantasy Fest, Key West. Mardi Gras takes a Floridian holiday as the streets of Key West are overtaken by wildly costumed revelers who have no shame and no parental guidance. This weeklong, hedonistic, X-rated Halloween party is not for children under 18. Make reservations in Key West early, as hotels tend to book up quickly during this event. Call © **305/296-1817.** Last week of October.

November

Miami Bookfair International, downtown Miami. Bibliophiles, literati, and some of the world's most prestigious and prolific authors descend upon downtown Miami for a weeklong homage to the written word, which also happens to be the largest book fair in

the United States. The weekend street fair is the best attended of the entire event, in which regular folk mix with wordsmiths such as Tom Wolfe and Jane Smiley while indulging in snacks, antiquarian books, and literary gossip. All lectures are free, but they fill up quickly, so get there early. Call © **305/237-3258** for lecture schedules. Mid-November.

Blue Angels Homecoming Air Show, Pensacola. World-famous navy pilots do their aerial acrobatics just 100 yards off the beach (© **800/874-1234** or 850/434-1234; www.visitpensacola.com or www.blueangels.navy.mil). Second weekend in November.

American Sandsculpting Festival, Fort Myers Beach. Some 50,000 gather to sculpt or see the world's finest sand castles (© **239/454-7500;** www.fmbchamber.com). First weekend in November.

White Party Week, Miami and Fort Lauderdale. This weeklong series of parties to benefit AIDS research is built around the main event, the White Party, which takes place at Villa Vizcaya and sells out as early as a year in advance. Philanthropists and celebrities such as Calvin Klein and David Geffen join thousands of white-clad mostly gay men (and some women) in what has become one of the world's hottest and hardest-to-score party tickets. Visit www.whitepartyweek. com for a schedule of parties and events. Thanksgiving week.

December

Edison/Ford Winter Homes Holiday House, Fort Myers. Christmas music and thousands of lights hail the holiday season here. At the same time, candles create a spectacular Luminary Trail along the full length of Sanibel Island's Periwinkle Way

(© **239/334-7419;** www.edison-ford-estate.com). First week of December.

Christmas at Walt Disney World, Orlando. As you would imagine, all of the Disney properties get into the holiday spirit. In the Magic Kingdom, Main Street is lavishly decked out with lights and holly and an 80-foot glistening tree. Call © **407/824-4321** for holiday events, or 407/934-7639 for special travel packages, or visit www. disneyworld.com. Throughout December.

British Night Watch & Grand Illumination Ceremony, St. Augustine. A torchlight procession through the Spanish Quarter kicks off a month of Christmas festivities and the "Nights of Lights," in which 1.25 million twinkling bulbs bathe the Old City (© **800/OLD-CITY;** www.visitoldcity.com). First Saturday in December; Nights of Lights to January 31.

Winterfest Boat Parade, Fort Lauderdale. People who complain that the holiday season just isn't as festive in South Florida as it is in colder parts of the world haven't been to this spectacular boat parade along the Intracoastal Waterway. Forget decking the halls. At this parade, the decks are decked out in magnificent holiday regalia as they gracefully—and boastfully—glide up and down the water. If you're not on a boat, the best views are from waterfront restaurants or anywhere you can squeeze in along the water. Call © **954/767-0686.** Mid-December.

6 Health & Safety

THE HEALTHY TRAVELER

Florida doesn't present any unusual health hazards for most people. Folks with certain medical conditions such as liver disease, diabetes, and stomach ailments, however, should avoid eating raw **oysters,** which can carry a natural bacterium linked to severe diarrhea, vomiting, and even fatal blood poisoning. Cooking kills the bacteria, so, if in doubt, order your oysters steamed, broiled, or fried.

Florida has millions of **mosquitoes** and invisible biting **sand flies** (known as "no-see-ums"), especially in the coastal and marshy areas. Fortunately, neither insect carries malaria or other diseases (though there were a few cases of mosquitoes carrying West Nile virus in the Panhandle, it's really not a problem in Florida). Keep these pests at bay with a good insect repellent.

It's especially important to protect yourself against **sunburn.** Don't underestimate the strength of the sun's rays down here, even in the middle of winter. Use a sunscreen with a high protection factor and apply it liberally.

WHAT TO DO IF YOU GET SICK AWAY FROM HOME

In most cases, your existing health plan will provide the coverage you need. But double-check; you may want to buy **travel medical insurance** instead. Always bring your insurance ID card with you when you travel.

Pack **prescription medications** in your carry-on luggage, and carry prescription medications in their original containers, with pharmacy labels—otherwise they won't make it through airport security. Also bring along copies of your prescriptions in case you lose your pills or run out. And don't forget sunglasses and an extra pair of contact lenses or prescription glasses.

If you get sick, consider asking your hotel concierge to recommend a local doctor—even his or her own. You can also try the emergency room at a local hospital; many have walk-in clinics for emergency cases that are not life threatening. You may not get immediate attention, but you won't pay the high price of an emergency room visit.

THE SAFE TRAVELER

While tourist areas in Florida are generally safe, you should always stay alert. This is particularly true in the large cities such as Miami, Orlando, Tampa, and St. Petersburg. It is wise to ask your hotel's front-desk staff or the city's or area's tourist office if you're in doubt about which neighborhoods are safe.

Remember also that hotels are open to the public, and in a large hotel, security may not be able to screen everyone entering. Always lock your room door. Don't assume that once you are inside your hotel you are automatically safe and no longer need to be aware of your surroundings.

7 Specialized Travel Resources

FOR GAY & LESBIAN TRAVELERS

Florida is not without its intolerant contingent, but there are active gay and lesbian groups in most cities here. In fact, the editors of *Out and About,* a gay and lesbian newsletter, have described Miami's **South Beach** as the "hippest, hottest, most happening gay travel destination in the world." For many years that could also be said of **Key West,** which still is one of the country's most popular destinations for gays. **Fort Lauderdale**—where gays own more than 20 motels, 40 bars, and numerous other businesses—is definitely also on the gay-friendly map.

You can contact the **Gay, Lesbian & Bisexual Community Services of Central Florida,** 946 N. Mills Ave., Orlando, FL 32803 (© **407/228-8272;** www.glbcc.org), whose welcome packets usually include the latest issue of the *Triangle,* a quarterly newsletter dedicated to gay and lesbian issues, and a calendar of events pertaining to the gay and lesbian community. Although not a tourist-specific packet, it includes information and ads for the area's gay and lesbian clubs.

Watermark, P.O. Box 533655, Orlando, FL 32853 (© **407/481-2243;** fax 407/481-2246; www.watermarkonline.com), is a biweekly tabloid newspaper covering the gay and lesbian scene, including dining and entertainment options, in Orlando, the Tampa Bay area, and Daytona Beach.

SENIOR TRAVEL

With one of the largest retired populations of any state, Florida offers a wide array of activities and benefits for seniors. Don't be shy about asking for discounts, but always carry some kind of identification, such as a driver's license, that shows your age/date of birth. Mention the fact that you're a senior when you make your travel reservations. In most cities, people over the age of 60 qualify for reduced admission to theaters, museums, and other attractions, as well as discounted fares on public transportation.

Members of **AARP** (formerly known as the American Association of Retired Persons), 601 E St. NW, Washington, DC 20049 (© **888/687-2277** or 202/434-2277; www.aarp.org), get discounts on hotels, airfares, and car rentals. AARP offers members a wide range of benefits, including *AARP: The Magazine* and a monthly newsletter. Anyone over 50 can join.

The **U.S. National Park Service (NPS)** offers a **Golden Age Passport** that gives seniors 62 years or older lifetime entrance to all properties administered by the National Park Service—national parks, monuments, historic sites, recreation areas, and national wildlife refuges—for a one-time processing fee of $10, which must be purchased in person at any NPS facility that charges an entrance fee. For more information, go to www.nps.gov/fees_ passes.htm or call © **888/467-2757.**

FAMILY TRAVEL

Florida is a great family destination, with Walt Disney World leading the list of theme parks geared to young and old alike. Consequently, most Florida hotels and restaurants are willing if not eager to cater to families traveling with children. Many hotels and motels let children 17 and under stay free in their parent's room (be sure to ask when you reserve).

At the beaches, it's the exception rather than the rule for a resort not to have a children's activities program (some will even mind the youngsters while the parents enjoy a night off!). Even if they don't have a children's program of their own, most will arrange babysitting services.

You may also want to consult *The Unofficial Guide to Florida with Kids* (Wiley Publishing, Inc.) as well as *The Unofficial Guide to Walt Disney World with Kids* (Wiley Publishing, Inc.). Additionally, *How to Take Great Trips with Your Kids* (The Harvard Common Press) is full of good general advice that can apply to travel anywhere.

8 Getting There

BY PLANE

Most major domestic airlines fly to and from many Florida cities. Choose from **American** (© 800/433-7300; www.aa.com), **Continental** (© 800/ 525-0280; www.continental.com), **Delta** (© 800/221-1212; www.delta. com), **Northwest/KLM** (© 800/ 225-2525; www.nwa.com), **United** (© 800/241-6522; www.united.com), and **US Airways** (© 800/428-4322; www.usairways.com).

Of these, Delta and US Airways have the most extensive network of commuter connections within Florida (see "Getting Around," later in this chapter).

Several so-called no-frills airlines— low fares but few if any amenities— also fly to Florida. The biggest and best is **Southwest Airlines** (© 800/ 435-9792; www.southwest.com), which has flights from many U.S. cities to Fort Lauderdale, Jacksonville, Orlando, and Tampa.

Others flying to Florida include **AirTran** (© 800/AIR-TRAN; www. airtran.com); **American Trans Air** (© 800/435-9282; www.ata.com); **Carnival Air** (© 800/824-7386), an arm of the popular cruise line; **JetBlue** (© 800/538-2583; www.jetblue.com); **Midwest Express** (© 800/452-2022; www.midwestexpress.com); **PanAm** (© 800/FLY-PANAM; www.flypan am.com); and **Spirit** (© 800/722- 7117; www.spiritair.com).

Internet resources such as **Travelo-city** (www.travelocity.com) and **Micro-soft Expedia** (www.expedia. com) make it relatively easy to compare prices and even purchase tickets.

FLYING FOR LESS: TIPS FOR GETTING THE BEST AIRFARE

Passengers sharing the same airplane cabin rarely pay the same fare. Travelers who need to purchase tickets at the last minute, change their itinerary at a moment's notice, or fly one-way often get stuck paying the premium rate. Here are some ways to keep your airfare costs down.

- Passengers who can book their ticket **long in advance,** who can **stay over Saturday night,** or who **fly midweek** or **at less-trafficked hours** may pay a fraction of the full fare. If your schedule is flexible, say so, and ask if you can secure a cheaper fare by changing your flight plans.

- You can also save on airfares by keeping an eye out in local newspapers for **promotional specials** or **fare wars,** when airlines lower prices on their most popular routes. You rarely see fare wars offered for peak travel times, but if you can travel in the off months, you may snag a bargain.

- Search **the Internet** for cheap fares (see "Planning Your Trip Online").

- **Consolidators,** also known as bucket shops, are great sources for international tickets, although they usually can't beat the Internet on fares within North America. Start by looking in Sunday newspaper travel sections; U.S. travelers should focus on the *New York Times, Los Angeles Times,* and *Miami Herald.* For less-developed destinations, small travel agents who cater to immigrant communities in large cities often have the best deals. *Beware:* Bucket shop tickets are usually nonrefundable or rigged with stiff cancellation penalties, often as high as 50% to 75% of the ticket price, and some put you on charter airlines, which may leave at inconvenient times and experience delays. Several reliable consolidators are worldwide and available on the Net. **STA Travel** is now the world's leader in student travel, thanks to their purchase of Council Travel. They also offer good fares for travelers of all ages. **FlyCheap** (© **800/FLY-CHEAP;** www.1800flycheap.com) is owned by package-holiday megalith MyTravel and so has especially good access to fares for sunny destinations.

- Join **frequent-flier clubs.** Accrue enough miles, and you'll be rewarded with free flights and elite status. It's free, and you'll get the best choice of seats, faster response to phone inquiries, and prompter service if your luggage is stolen, your flight is canceled or delayed, or if you want to change your seat. You don't need to fly to build frequent-flier miles—**frequent-flier credit cards** can provide thousands of miles for doing your everyday shopping.

- For many more tips about air travel, including a rundown of the major frequent-flier credit cards, pick up a copy of *Frommer's Fly Safe, Fly Smart* (Wiley Publishing, Inc.).

BY CAR

Florida is reached by **I-95** along the east coast, **I-75** from the central states, and **I-10** from the west. **The Florida Turnpike,** a toll road, links Orlando, West Palm Beach, Fort Lauderdale, and Miami (it's a shortcut from Wildwood on I-75 north of Orlando to Miami). **I-4** cuts across the state from Cape Canaveral through Orlando to Tampa.

See "Getting Around," later in this chapter, for more information about driving in Florida and the car-rental firms operating here.

If you're a member, your local branch of the **American Automobile Association (AAA)** will provide a free trip-routing plan. AAA also has nationwide emergency road service for its members (© **800/AAA-HELP;** www.aaa.com).

BY TRAIN

Amtrak (© **800/USA-RAIL;** www. amtrak.com) offers train service to Florida from both the East and West Coasts. It takes some 26 hours from New York to Miami, 68 hours from Los Angeles to Miami, and Amtrak's fares aren't much less—if not more—than many of the airlines' lowest fares.

Amtrak's *Silver Meteor* and *Silver Star* both run twice daily between New York and either Miami or Tampa, with intermediate stops along the East Coast and in Florida. Amtrak's Thruway Bus Connections are available from the Fort Lauderdale Amtrak station and Miami International Airport to Key West; from Tampa to St. Petersburg, Treasure Island, Clearwater, Sarasota, Bradenton, and Fort Myers; and from Deland to Daytona Beach. From the West Coast, the *Sunset Limited* runs three times weekly between Los Angeles and Orlando. It stops in Pensacola, Crestview (north of Fort Walton Beach and Destin), Chipley (north of Panama City Beach), and Tallahassee. Sleeping accommodations are available for an extra charge.

If you intend to stop off along the way, you can save money with Amtrak's **Explore America** (or All Aboard America) fares, which are based on three regions of the country.

Amtrak's **Auto Train** runs daily from Lorton, Virginia (12 miles south of Washington, D.C.), to Sanford, Florida (just northeast of Orlando). You ride in a coach while your car is secured in an enclosed vehicle carrier. You should make your train reservations as far in advance as possible.

9 Planning Your Trip Online

SURFING FOR AIRFARES

The "big three" online travel agencies, **Expedia.com**, **Travelocity.com**, and **Orbitz.com** sell most of the air tickets bought on the Internet. (Canadian travelers should try expedia.ca and Travelocity.ca; U.K. residents can go for expedia.co.uk and opodo.co.uk.). Each has different business deals with the airlines and may offer different fares on the same flights, so it's wise to shop around. Expedia and Travelocity will also send you **e-mail notification** when a cheap fare becomes available to your favorite destination. Of the smaller travel agency websites, **SideStep** (www.sidestep.com) has gotten the best reviews from Frommer's authors. It's a browser add-on that purports to "search 140 sites at once," but in reality only beats competitors' fares as often as other sites do.

Also remember to check **airline websites,** especially those for low-fare carriers such as Southwest, JetBlue, AirTran, WestJet, or Ryanair, whose fares are often misreported or simply missing from travel agency websites. Even with major airlines, you can often shave a few bucks from a fare by booking directly through the airline and avoiding a travel agency's transaction fee. But you'll get these discounts only by **booking online:** Most airlines now offer online-only fares that even their phone agents know nothing about. For the websites of airlines that fly to and from your destination, see "Getting There," on p. 48.

Great **last-minute deals** are available through free weekly e-mail services provided directly by the airlines. Most of these are announced on Tuesday or Wednesday and must be purchased online. Most are only valid for travel that weekend, but some (such as Southwest's) can be booked weeks or months in advance. Sign up for weekly e-mail alerts at airline websites or check mega-sites that compile comprehensive lists of last-minute specials, such as **Smarter Living** (www.smarter living.com). For last-minute trips, **site59.com** and **lastminutetravel. com** in the U.S. and **lastminute.com** in Europe often have better air-and-hotel package deals than the major-label sites. A website listing numerous bargain sites and airlines around the world is **www.itravelnet.com**.

If you're willing to give up some control over your flight details, use what is called an **"opaque" fare service** like **Priceline** (www.priceline.com; www.priceline.co.uk for Europeans) or its smaller competitor **Hotwire** (www.hotwire.com). Both offer rock-bottom prices in exchange for travel on a "mystery airline" at a mysterious time of day, often with a mysterious change of planes en route. The mystery airlines are all major, well-known carriers—and the possibility of being sent from Philadelphia to Tampa via Chicago is remote; the airlines' routing computers have gotten a lot better than they used to be. But your chances of getting a 6am or 11pm flight are pretty high. Hotwire tells you flight prices before you buy; Priceline usually has better deals than Hotwire, but you have to play their "name our price" game. If you're new at this, the helpful folks at **BiddingForTravel** (www.biddingfortravel.com) do a good job of demystifying Priceline's prices and strategies. Priceline and Hotwire are great for flights within North America and between the U.S. and Europe. But for flights to other parts of the world, consolidators will almost always beat their fares. *Note:* In 2004 Priceline added non-opaque service to its roster. You now have the option to pick exact flights, times, and airlines from a list of offers—or opt to bid on opaque fares as before.

For much more about airfares and savvy air-travel tips and advice, pick up a copy of *Frommer's Fly Safe, Fly Smart* (Wiley Publishing, Inc.).

SURFING FOR HOTELS

Shopping online for hotels is generally done one of two ways: by booking through the hotel's own website or through an independent booking agency (or a fare-service agency like Priceline; see below). These Internet hotel agencies have multiplied in mind-boggling numbers of late, competing for the business of millions of consumers surfing for accommodations around the world. This competitiveness can be a boon to consumers who have the patience and time to shop and compare the online sites for good deals—but shop they must, for prices can vary considerably from site to site. And keep in mind that hotels at the top of a site's listing may be there for no other reason than that they paid money to get the placement.

Of the "big three" sites, **Expedia** offers a long list of special deals and "virtual tours" or photos of available rooms so you can see what you're paying for (a feature that helps counter the claims that the best rooms are often held back from bargain booking websites). **Travelocity** posts unvarnished customer reviews and ranks its properties according to the AAA rating system. Also reliable are **Hotels. com** and **Quikbook.com**. An excellent free program, **TravelAxe** (www. travelaxe.net), can help you search multiple hotel sites at once, even ones you may never have heard of—and conveniently lists the total price of the room, including the taxes and service charges. Another booking site, **Travel-web** (www.travelweb.com), is partly owned by the hotels it represents (including the Hilton, Hyatt, and Starwood chains) and is therefore plugged directly into the hotels' reservations systems—unlike independent online agencies, which have to fax or e-mail reservation requests to the hotel, a good portion of which get misplaced in the shuffle. More than once, travelers have arrived at the hotel, only to be told that they have no reservation. To be fair, many of the major sites are undergoing improvements in service and ease of use, and Expedia will soon be able to plug directly into the reservations systems of many hotel chains—none of which can be bad news for consumers. In the meantime, it's a good idea to **get a confirmation number** and **make a printout** of any online booking transaction.

In the opaque website category, **Priceline** and **Hotwire** are even better for hotels than for airfares; with both, you're allowed to pick the neighborhood and quality level of your hotel before offering up your money. Priceline's hotel product even covers Europe and Asia, though it's much better at getting five-star lodging for three-star prices than at finding anything at the bottom of the scale. On the down side, many hotels stick Priceline guests in their least desirable rooms. Be sure to go to the BiddingforTravel website (see above) before bidding on a hotel room on Priceline; it features a fairly up-to-date list of hotels that Priceline uses in major cities. For both Priceline and Hotwire, you pay up front, and the fee is nonrefundable. *Note:* Some hotels do not provide loyalty program credits or points or other frequent-stay amenities when you book a room through opaque online services.

Some hotels in Florida offer deep discounts if you book rooms on their websites. Other hotels are dodgy online, in that they may deceive you into thinking you are booking a luxe suite for a deal when, in fact, you're really getting a cramped efficiency. Pictures are lovely, but make sure to ask if you're getting what's in the picture before booking.

SURFING FOR RENTAL CARS

For booking rental cars online, the best deals are usually found at car-rental company websites, although all the major online travel agencies also offer car-rental reservations services. Priceline and Hotwire work well for car rental, too; the only "mystery" is which major rental company you get, and for most travelers the difference between Hertz, Avis, and Budget is negligible.

10 Packages for the Independent Traveler

More than 120 travel companies offer hundreds of package tour options to the Sunshine State, particularly to Orlando and Miami. Quite often these deals will result in savings not just on airfares but on hotels and other activities as well. You pay one price for a package that varies from one tour operator to the next. Airfare, transfers, and accommodations are always covered, and sometimes meals and specific activities are thrown in.

Before you start your search for the lowest airfare, therefore, you may want to consider booking your flight as part of a travel package, such as an escorted tour or a package tour. What you lose in adventure, you could gain in time and money saved when you book accommodations, and maybe even food and entertainment, along with your flight—but not necessarily.

Package tours are not the same thing as escorted tours. Package tours are simply a way to buy the airfare, accommodations, and other elements of your trip (such as car rentals, airport transfers, and sometimes even activities) at the same time and often at discounted prices—kind of like one-stop shopping. Packages are sold in bulk to tour operators—who resell them to the public at a cost that usually undercuts standard rates.

One good source of package deals is the airlines themselves. Most major airlines offer air/land packages, including **American Airlines Vacations** (© 800/321-2121; www.aavacations. com), **Delta Vacations** (© 800/221-6666; www.deltavacations.com), **Continental Airlines Vacations** (© 800/301-3800; www.covacations. com), and **United Vacations** (© 888/854-3899; www.unitedvacations.

Tips   Saving with Golf & Tennis Packages

Many Florida hotels and resorts and even some motels offer **golf and tennis packages,** which bundle the cost of room, greens and court fees, and sometimes equipment, into one price. These deals usually don't include airfare, but they do represent savings over paying for the room and golf or tennis separately. See the accommodations sections in the following chapters for hostelries offering special packages to their guests.

Summer, early fall, and the first 3 weeks of December are good times to search for discounted deals in Southern Florida. For example, the Naples Beach Hotel & Golf Club in Naples has offered bed-and-breakfast specials for about $125 a night per room, including a full breakfast buffet, during September and December. Regular autumn room rates are more than twice that amount, without breakfast.

com). Several big **online travel agencies**—Expedia, Travelocity, Orbitz, Site59, and Lastminute.com—also do a brisk business in packages. If you're unsure about the pedigree of a smaller packager, check with the Better Business Bureau in the city where the company is based, or go online at www.bbb.org. If a packager won't tell you where they're based, don't fly with them.

Travel packages are also listed in the travel section of your local Sunday newspaper. Or check ads in the national travel magazines such as *Arthur Frommer's Budget Travel Magazine, Travel & Leisure, National Geographic Traveler,* and *Condé Nast Traveler.*

Package tours can vary by leaps and bounds. Some offer a better class of hotels than others. Some offer the same hotels for lower prices. Some offer flights on scheduled airlines, while others book charters. Some limit your choice of accommodations and travel days. You are often required to

make a large payment up front. On the plus side, packages can save you money, offering group prices but allowing for independent travel. Some even let you add on a few guided excursions or escorted day trips (also at prices lower than if you booked them yourself) without booking an entirely escorted tour.

Before you invest in a package tour, get some answers. Ask about the **accommodations choices** and prices for each. Then look up the hotels' reviews in a Frommer's guide and check their rates online for your specific dates of travel. You'll also want to find out what **type of room** you get. If you need a certain type of room, ask for it; don't take whatever is thrown your way. Request a nonsmoking room, a quiet room, a room with a view, or whatever you fancy.

Finally, look for **hidden expenses.** Ask whether airport departure fees and taxes, for example, are included in the total cost.

11 Special-Interest Trips

Bird-watching, eco-tourism, boating and sailing, camping, canoeing and kayaking, fishing, diving, golfing, tennis—you name it, the Sunshine State has it. In fact, you'll find these

activities almost everywhere you go in Florida. Of course, beach lovers and watersports enthusiasts can indulge their passions almost anywhere along the state's lengthy coastlines. Merely head east or west, and you'll easily find plenty to do—or viewed another way, Florida's multitudinous watersports operators will find you.

These and other activities are described in the outdoor activities sections of the following chapters, but here's a brief overview of some of the best places to move your muscles, with tips on how to get more detailed information.

The **Florida Sports Foundation,** 2390 Kerry Forest Pkwy., Suite 101, Tallahassee, FL 32309 (© **850/488-8347;** fax 850/922-0482; www.fla sports.com), publishes free brochures, calendars, schedules, and guides to outdoor pursuits and spectator sports throughout Florida. I've noted some of its specific publications in the sections below.

For excellent color maps of state parks, campgrounds, canoe trails, aquatic preserves, caverns, and more, contact the **Florida Department of Environmental Protection,** Office of Communications, 3900 Commonwealth Blvd., Tallahassee, FL 32399 (© **850/245-2118;** www.dep.state.fl. us). Some of the department's publications are mentioned below.

ACTIVITIES A TO Z
BIKING & IN-LINE SKATING
Florida's relatively flat terrain makes it ideal for riding bikes and in-line skating. You can bike right into the **Everglades National Park** along the 38-mile-long Main Park Road, for example, and bike or skate from St. Petersburg to Tarpon Springs on the 47-mile-long converted railroad bed known as the **Pinellas Trail.** Many towns and cities have designated routes for cyclists, skaters, joggers, and walkers, such as the paved pathways running the length of Sanibel Island, the lovely Bayshore Boulevard in **Tampa,** and the bike lanes from downtown **Sarasota** out to St. Armands, Lido, and Longboat Keys.

We've detailed all the many options in the following chapters.

BIRD-WATCHING With hundreds of both land- and sea-based species, Florida is one of America's best places for bird-watching—if you're not careful, pelicans will even steal your picnic lunch on the historic **Naples Pier.** The **J. N. ("Ding") Darling National Wildlife Refuge** is great for watching, and it shares Sanibel Island with luxury resorts and fine restaurants.

With its Northeast Florida section now open, the **Great Florida Birding Trail** will eventually cover some 2,000 miles throughout the state. Fort Clinch State Park on Amelia Island and Merritt Island National Wildlife Refuge in Cape Canaveral are gateways to the northeast trail. Information is available from the Birding Trail Coordinator, Florida Fish & Wildlife Conservation Commission, 620 S. Meridian St., Tallahassee, FL 32399-1600 (© **850/922-0664;** fax 850/ 488-1961; www.floridabirdingtrail. com). You can download trail maps from their website.

Many of the state's wildlife preserves have gift shops that carry books about Florida's birds, including the *Florida Wildlife Viewing Guide,* in which authors Susan Cerulean and Ann Morrow profile 96 great parks, refuges, and preserves throughout the state. The guide is also available directly from the publisher, Falcon Press, at © **888/922-0789** or www. falcbooks.com.

BOATING & SAILING With some 1,350 miles of shoreline, it's not surprising that Florida is a boating and sailing mecca. In fact, you won't be anyplace near the water very long before you see flyers and other advertisements for rental boats and for cruises on sailboats. Many of them are mentioned in the following chapters.

The Moorings, the worldwide sailboat charter company, has its headquarters in Clearwater and its Florida yacht base nearby in St. Petersburg (© **888/952-8420** or 727/530-5651; www.moorings.com). From St. Pete, experienced sailors can take its bareboats as far as the Keys and the Dry Tortugas, out in the Gulf of Mexico.

Key West keeps gaining prominence as a world sailing capital. *Yachting* magazine sponsors the largest winter regatta in America here each January, and smaller events take place regularly.

Even if you've never hauled on a halyard, you can learn the art of sailing at **Steve and Doris Colgate's Offshore Sailing School,** headquartered at the South Seas Plantation Resort & Yacht Harbour on Captiva Island, with an outpost in St. Petersburg (www.offshore-sailing.com). The prestigious **Annapolis Sailing** has bases in St. Petersburg and on Marathon in the Keys (http://annapolissailing.com).

The free *Florida Boating & Fishing,* which has tips about safe boating in the state and is available from the **Florida Sports Foundation** (see the introduction to this section, above), is a treasure trove of regulations; locations of marinas, hotels, and resorts; marine products and services; and more, in magazine format.

CAMPING   Florida is literally dotted with RV parks (if you own such a vehicle, it's the least expensive way to spend your winters here). But for the best tent camping, look to Florida's national preserves and 110 state parks and recreation areas. Options range from luxury sites with hot-water showers and cable TV hookups to primitive island and beach camping with no facilities whatsoever.

Regular and primitive camping in **St. George Island State Park** near Apalachicola, in fact, is a birdwatcher's dream, and you'll be on one of the nation's most magnificent beaches. Equally great are the sands at **St. Andrews State Park** in Panama City Beach (with sites right beside the bay). Other top spots are **Fort DeSoto Park** in St. Pete Beach (more gorgeous bayside sites), the remarkably preserved **Cayo Costa Island State Park** between Boca Grande and Captiva Island in Southwest Florida, **Canaveral National Seashore** near the Kennedy Space Center, **Anastasia State Park** in St. Augustine, **Fort Clinch State Park** on Amelia Island, and **Bill Baggs Cape Florida State Park** on Key Biscayne in Miami. Down in the Keys, the oceanside sites in **Long Key State Park** are about as nice as it gets.

In all these popular campgrounds, reservations are essential, especially in the high seasons. All of Florida's state parks take bookings up to 11 months in advance.

The **Florida Department of Environmental Protection,** Division of Recreation and Parks, Mail Station 535, 3900 Commonwealth Blvd., Tallahassee, FL 32399-3000 (© **850/ 245-2118;** www.dep.state.fl.us), publishes an annual guide of tent and RV sites in Florida's state parks and recreation areas.

Pet owners note: Pets are permitted at some—but not all—state park beaches, campgrounds, and food service areas. Before bringing your animal, check with the department or with the individual parks to see if your pet will be allowed. And bring your pet's rabies certificate, which is required.

For private campgrounds, the **Florida Association of RV Parks & Campgrounds,** 1340 Vickers Dr., Tallahassee, FL 32303 (© **850/562- 7151;** fax 850/562-7179; www.florida camping.com), issues an annual *Camp Florida* directory with locator maps and details about its member establishments throughout the state.

CANOEING   &   KAYAKING Canoers and kayakers have almost limitless options here: picturesque rivers, sandy coastlines, marshes, mangroves, and gigantic Lake Okeechobee. Exceptional trails run through several parks and wildlife preserves, including **Everglades National Park,** the **J. N. ("Ding") Darling National Wildlife Refuge** on Sanibel Island, and the **Briggs Nature Center,** on the edge of the Everglades near Marco Island.

According to the Florida state legislature, however, the state's official "Canoe Capital" is the Panhandle town of **Milton,** on U.S. 90 near Pensacola. Up there, Blackwater River, Coldwater River, Sweetwater Creek, and Juniper Creek are perfect for tubing, rafting, and paddleboating, as well as canoeing and kayaking.

Another good venue is the waterway winding through the marshes between **Amelia Island** and the mainland.

Many conservation groups throughout the state offer half-day, full-day, and overnight canoe trips. For example, **The Conservancy of Naples** (© 239/262-0304; www. conservancy.org) has a popular series of moonlight canoe trips through the mangroves, among other programs.

Based during the winter at Everglades City, on the park's western border, **North American Canoe Tours, Inc.** (© 239/695-3299; www. evergladesadventures.com), offers weeklong, guided canoe expeditions through the Everglades.

Thirty-six creek and river trails, covering 950 miles altogether, are itemized in the excellent free *Canoe Trails* booklet published by the **Florida Department of Environmental Protection,** Office of Communications, 3900 Commonwealth Blvd., Tallahassee, FL 32399 (© 850/245-2118; www.dep.state. fl.us).

Specialized guidebooks include *A Canoeing and Kayaking Guide to the Streams of Florida:* Volume 1, *North Central Florida and Panhandle,* by Elizabeth F. Carter and John L. Eearch, and Volume 2, *Central and Southern Peninsula,* by Lou Glaros and Dough Sphar. Both are published by Menasha Ridge Press (www.menasha ridge.com).

ECOADVENTURES If you don't want to do it yourself, you can observe Florida's flora and fauna on guided field expeditions—and contribute to conservation efforts while you're at it.

The **Sierra Club,** America's oldest and largest grassroots environmental organization, offers ecoadventures through its Florida chapters. Recent outings have included canoeing or kayaking through the Everglades, hiking the Florida Trail in America's southernmost national forest, camping on a barrier island, and exploring the sinkhole phenomenon in North Central Florida. You do have to be a Sierra Club member, but you can join at the time of the trip. Contact the club's national outings office at 85 Second St., Second Floor, San Francisco, CA 94105-3441 (© 415/977-5500; www.sierraclub.org).

The Florida chapter of **The Nature Conservancy** has protected 578,000 acres of natural lands in Florida and presently owns and manages 36 preserves. For a small fee, you can join one of its field trips or work parties that take place periodically throughout the year; fees vary from year to year, event to event, so call for more information. Participants get a chance to learn about and even participate in the preservation of the ecosystem. For details of all the preserves and adventures, contact The Nature Conservancy, Florida Chapter, 222 S. Westmonte Dr., Suite 300, Altamonte Springs, FL 32714 (© 407/682-3664; fax 407/682-3077; http:// nature.org).

A nonprofit organization dedicated to environmental research, the **Earthwatch Institute,** 3 Clocktower Place,

Suite 100 (P.O. Box 75), Maynard, MA 01754 (© **800/776-0188** or 978/461-0081; www.earthwatch.org), has excursions to survey dolphins and manatees around Sarasota and to monitor the well-being of the captive-raised whooping cranes that have been released in the wilds of Central Florida. Another research group, the **Oceanic Society,** Fort Mason Center, Building E, San Francisco, CA 94123 (© **800/326-7491** or 415/441-1106; fax 415/474-3395; www.oceanic-society.org), also has Florida trips among its expeditions, including manatee monitoring in the Crystal River area north of Tampa.

You should also check out the following two websites: www.ecotour directory.com and www.floridasmart. com/attractions/outdoors_ecotour. htm.

FISHING   In addition to the amberjack, bonito, grouper, mackerel, mahimahi, marlin, pompano, redfish, sailfish, snapper, snook, tarpon, tuna, and wahoo running offshore and in its inlets, Florida has countless miles of rivers and streams, plus about 30,000 lakes and springs stocked with more than 100 species of freshwater fish. Indeed, Floridians seem to fish everywhere: off canal banks and old bridges, from fishing piers and fishing fleets. You'll even see them standing alongside the Tamiami Trail (U.S. 41) that cuts across the Everglades—one eye on their line, the other watching for alligators.

Anglers age 16 and older need fishing licenses for any kind of saltwater or freshwater fishing, including lobstering and spearfishing. Licenses are sold at bait-and-tackle shops around the state or online at www.wildlife license.com/fl.

The **Florida Department of Environmental Protection,** 3900 Commonwealth Blvd., Tallahassee, FL 32399-3000 (© **850/245-2118;** www.dep.state.fl.us), publishes the annual *Fishing Lines,* a free magazine with a wealth of information about fishing in Florida, including regulations and licensing requirements. It also distributes free brochures with annual freshwater and saltwater limits. And the **Florida Sports Foundation** (see the introduction to this section, above) publishes *Florida Fishing & Boating,* another treasure trove of information.

GOLF   Florida is the unofficial golf capital of the United States—some would say the world—since the **World Golf Hall of Fame** is located near St. Augustine. This state-of-the-art museum and shrine is worth a brief visit even if you're not in love with the game.

One thing's for certain: Florida has more golf courses than any other state—more than 1,150 at last count and growing. We picked the best in chapter 1, but suffice it to say that you can tee off almost anytime there's daylight. The highest concentrations of excellent courses are in Southwest Florida around Naples and Fort Myers (more than 1,000 holes!), in the Orlando area (Disney alone has 99 holes open to the public), and in the Panhandle around Destin and Panama City Beach. It's a rare town in Florida that doesn't have a municipal golf course—even Key West has 18 great holes.

Greens fees are usually much lower at the municipal courses than at privately owned clubs. Whether public or private, greens fees tend to vary greatly depending on the time of year. You could pay $150 or more at a private course during the high season, but less than half that when the tourists are gone. The fee structures vary so much that it's best to call ahead and ask, and always reserve a tee time as far in advance as possible.

You can learn the game or hone your strokes at one of several excellent golf schools in the state. **David**

Ledbetter has teaching facilities in Orlando and Naples, **Fred Griffin** is in charge of the Grand Cypress Academy of Golf at Grand Cypress Resort in Orlando, and you'll find **Jimmy Ballard**'s school at the Ocean Reef Club on Key Largo. The Westin Innisbrook Resort at Tarpon Springs has its **Innisbrook Golf Institute.** Amelia Island (near Jacksonville) is home to **Amelia Island Plantation Golf School.**

You can get information about most Florida courses, including current greens fees, and reserve tee times through **Tee Times USA,** P.O. Box 641, Flagler Beach, FL 32136 (© **888/GOLF-FLO** or 386/439-0001; www.teetimesusa.com). This company also publishes a vacation guide that includes many stay-and-play golf packages.

Florida Golf, published by the **Florida Sports Foundation** (see the introduction to this section), lists every course in Florida. It's the state's official golf guide and is available from Visit Florida (see the "Visitor Information" section, earlier in this chapter).

Golfer's Guide magazine publishes monthly editions covering most regions of Florida; it is available free at all the local visitor centers and hotel lobbies, or you can contact the magazine at 2 Park Lane, Suite E, Hilton Head Island, SC 29928 (© **800/864-6101** or 843/842-7878; fax 843/842-5743; www.golfersguide.com). Northwest Florida is covered by *South Coast Golf Guide,* published by Tee and J's Ent. LLC, P.O. Box 11278, Pensacola, FL 32524-1278 (© **850/505-7553;** fax 850/505-0057; www.southcoast golfguide.com).

You can also get more information from the **Professional Golfers' Association (PGA),** 400 Ave. of the Champions, Palm Beach Gardens, FL 33418 (© **800/633-9150;** www.pga.com), or the **Ladies Professional**

Golf Association (LPGA), 100 International Golf Dr., Daytona Beach, FL 32124 (© **904/254-6200;** www.lpga.com).

More than 700 courses are profiled in *Florida Golf Guide* by Jimmy Shacky (Open Roads Publishing; $20), available at bookstores.

HIKING   Although you won't be climbing any mountains in this relatively flat state, there are thousands of beautiful hiking trails in Florida. The ideal hiking months are October through April, when the weather is cool and dry and mosquitoes are less prominent. Like anywhere else, you'll find trails that are gentle and short and others that are challenging—some trails in the Everglades require you to wade waist-deep in water!

If you're venturing into the backcountry, watch out for gators, and don't ever try to feed them (or any wild animal). You risk getting bitten (they can't tell the difference between the food and your hand). You're also upsetting the balance of nature, since animals fed by humans lose their ability to find their own food. Most Florida snakes are harmless, but a few have deadly bites, so it's a good idea to avoid them all.

The **Florida Trail Association,** 5415 SW 13th St., Gainesville, FL 32608 (© **877/HIKE-FLA** or 352/378-8823;   www.florida-trail.org), maintains a large percentage of the public trails in the state and puts out an excellent book packed with maps, details, and color photos.

For a copy of *Florida Trails,* which outlines the many options, contact Visit Florida (see "Visitor Information," earlier in this chapter). Another resource is *A Guide to Your National Scenic Trails,* Office of Greenways and Trails, Department of Environmental Protection, 3900 Commonwealth Blvd., Tallahassee, FL 32399 (© **850/245-2118;** www.dep.state. fl.us/gwt). You can also contact the office of **National Forests in Florida,** Woodcrest Office Park, 325 John Knox Rd., Suite F-100, Tallahassee, FL 32303 (© **850/523-8500;** www.southernregion.fs.fed.us/florida). And *Hiking Florida,* by M. Timothy O'Keefe (Falcon Press; www.falc books.com), details 132 hikes throughout the state, with maps and photos.

SCUBA DIVING & SNORKEL- ING Divers love the Keys, where you can see magnificent formations of tree-size elkhorn coral and giant brain coral, as well as colorful sea fans and dozens of other varieties, sharing space with 300 or more species of rainbow-hued fish. Reef diving is good all the way from Key Largo to Key West, with plenty of tour operators, outfitters, and dive shops along the way. Particularly worthy are **John Pennekamp Coral Reef State Park** in Key Largo and **Looe Key National Marine Sanctuary** off Big Pine Key. *Skin Diver* magazine picked Looe Key as the number-one dive spot in North America. Also, the clearest waters in which to view some of the 4,000 sunken ships along Florida's coast are in the Middle Keys and the waters between Key West and the Dry Tortugas. Snorkeling in the Keys is particularly fine between Islamorada and Marathon.

In Northwest Florida, the 100-fathom curve draws closer to the white, sandy Panhandle beaches than to any other spot on the Gulf of Mexico. It's too far north here for coral, but you can see brilliantly colored sponges and fish and, in Timber Hole, discover an undersea "petrified forest" of sunken planes, ships, and even a railroad car. And the battleship USS *Massachusetts* lies in 30 feet of water just 3 miles off Pensacola. Every beach town in Northwest Florida has dive shops to outfit, tour, or certify visitors.

In the Crystal River area, north of the St. Petersburg and Clearwater beaches, you can snorkel with the manatees as they bask in the warm spring waters of Kings Bay.

You may also want to check out www.southfloridadiving.com.

If you want to keep up with what's going on statewide, you can subscribe to *Florida Scuba News,* a monthly magazine published in Jacksonville (© **904/783-1610;** www.scubanews. com). You might also want to pick up a specialized guidebook. Some good ones include *Coral Reefs of Florida,* by Gilbert L. Voss (Pineapple Press; www.pineapplepress.com), and *The Diver's Guide to Florida and the Florida Keys,* by Jim Stachowicz (Windward Publishing).

TENNIS Year-round sunshine makes Florida great for tennis. There are some 7,700 places to play throughout the state, from municipal courts to exclusive resorts. Even some of the municipal facilities—Cambier Park Tennis Center in Naples leaps to mind—are equal to those at expensive resorts, and they're either free or close to it.

If you can afford it, you can learn from the best in Florida. **Nick Bollettieri** has sports academies in Bradenton. Safety Harbor Resort and Spa near St. Petersburg hosts the **Phil Green Tennis Program.** Amateurs can hobnob with the superstars at **ATP Tour International Headquarters** in Ponte Vedra Beach, near Jacksonville. **Mary Jo Fernandez** is affiliated with the **Arthur Ashe Tennis Center** at the Doral Golf Resort & Spa in Miami. And **Chris Evert, Robert Seguso,** and **Carling Basset** have their own center in Boca Raton.

The three hard courts and seven clay courts at the Key Biscayne Tennis Association, 6702 Crandon Blvd. (© **305/361-5263**), get crowded on weekends, since they're some of Miami's most beautiful. You'll play on the same courts as Lendl, Graf, Evert, McEnroe, and other greats; this is the venue for one of the world's biggest annual tennis events, the Nasdaq 100 Open. There's a pleasant, if limited, pro shop, plus many good pros. Only four courts are lit at night, but if you reserve at least 48 hours in advance, you can usually take your pick. They cost $6 per person per hour. The courts are open daily from 8am to 9pm.

Famous as the spot where Chris Evert got in her early serves, the **Jimmy Evert Tennis Center,** 701 NE 12th Ave. (off Sunrise Blvd.), Fort Lauderdale (© **954/828-5378**), has 18 clay and 3 hard courts (15 lighted). Her coach and father, James Evert, still teaches young players here, though he is very picky about whom he'll accept. Nonresidents of Fort Lauderdale pay $3.50 (singles) to $4.50 (doubles) per hour. Reservations are accepted after 2pm for the following day but cost an extra $3. Lights are also an extra $3 per hour and are available only for the clay courts.

Other top places to learn and play are **Amelia Island Plantation** on Amelia Island; **Colony Beach and Tennis Resort** on Longboat Key off Sarasota (which *Tennis* magazine picked as the number-two tennis resort in the nation); **Sanibel Harbour Resort & Spa** in Fort Myers, whose 5,500-seat stadium has hosted Davis Cup matches; **South Seas Plantation Resort & Yacht Harbour** on Captiva Island; and **The Registry Resort** in Naples.

12 Getting Around

Having a car is the best and easiest way to see Florida's sights, or just to get to and from the beach. Public transportation is available only in the cities and larger towns, and even there it may provide infrequent or even inadequate service. When it comes to getting from one city to another, cars and planes are the ways to go.

BY PLANE

The commuter arms of **Continental** (© **800/525-0280;** www.fly continental.com), **Delta** (© **800/ 221-1212;** www.delta.com), and **US Airways** (© **800/428-4322;** www. usairways.com) provide extensive service between Florida's major cities and towns. Fares for these short hops tend to be reasonable.

Cape Air (© **800/352-0714;** www. flycapeair.com) flies between Key West, Fort Myers, and Naples, which means you can avoid backtracking to Miami from Key West if you're touring the state. (You can also take a boat between Key West and Fort Myers Beach, Naples, or Marco Island during the winter months; see p. 342.)

Paradise Aviation (© **305/743-4222;** www.flyparadiseair.com) connects Fort Lauderdale with Marathon.

BY CAR

Jacksonville is about 350 miles north of Miami and 500 miles north of Key West, so don't underestimate how long it will take you to drive all the way down the state. The speed limit is either 65 mph or 70 mph on the rural interstate highways, so you can make good time between cities. Not so on U.S. 1, U.S. 17, U.S. 19, U.S. 41, and U.S. 301; although most have four lanes, these older highways tend to be heavily congested, especially in built-up areas.

CAR RENTALS

Every major car-rental company is represented here, including **Alamo** (© **800/327-9633;** www.goalamo. com), **Avis** (© **800/331-1212;** www. avis.com), **Budget** (© **800/527-0700;** www.budgetrentacar.com), **Dollar** (© **800/800-4000;** www. dollarcar.com), **Enterprise** (© **800/ 325-8007;** pickenterprise.com),

Hertz (© **800/654-3131;** www.hertz. com), **National** (© **800/227-7368;** www.nationalcar.com), and **Thrifty** (© **800/367-2277;** www.thrifty. com).

If you decide to rent a car, shop around and ask a lot of questions. Reservations clerks are used to being asked for the lowest rate available, and most will find it in order to get your business. You may have to try different dates, different pickup and drop-off points, and different discount offers to find the best deal. It changes constantly. Also, if you're a member of any organization (AARP, Costco, or AAA, for example), be sure to ask if you're entitled to discounts.

Check the rental firms' websites. Most will automatically bring up the lowest available rate, and there are boxes to click if you are an association member or have a discount coupon or ID number. You can comparison shop on Internet sites such as **Travelocity** (www.travelocity.com) and **Expedia** (www.expedia.com), which will make reservations for you once you've found the best deal.

State and local **taxes** will add as much as 20% to your final bill. You'll pay an additional $2.05 per day in statewide use tax, and local sales taxes will tack on at least 6% to the total, including the statewide use tax (the state is being sued over this tax-on-a-tax practice). Some airports add another 35¢ per day and as much as 10% in "recovery" fees. You can avoid the recovery fee by picking up your car in town rather than at the airport. Budget and Enterprise both have numerous rental locations away from the airports. But be sure to weigh the cost of transportation to and from your hotel against the amount of the fee.

Competition is so fierce among Florida rental firms that most have now stopped charging **drop-off fees** if you pick up a car at one place and leave it at another. For example, I recently picked up a car at Tampa and dropped it off at Fort Myers for the same price I would have paid had I returned it to Tampa. Be sure to ask if there's a drop-off fee.

You must have a **valid credit card** (not a debit or check card) in your name, and most companies require you to be at least 25 years old to rent a car. Some also set maximum ages and may deny cars to anyone with a bad driving record. Ask about rental requirements and restrictions when you book in order to avoid problems when you get there.

BY TRAIN & BY BUS

You'll find that train travel isn't terribly feasible within Florida, and it's not much less expensive than flying, if at all. See "Getting There," earlier in this chapter, for Florida towns served by **Amtrak** (© **800/USA-RAIL;** www. amtrak.com). For bus travel, see the "Essentials" and "Getting There" sections in the following chapters.

13 Tips on Accommodations

Florida has such a vast array of accommodations—from rock-bottom roadside motels to some of the nation's finest resorts—that we can cover only the tip of the iceberg in this book. Whether you'll spend a pittance or a bundle depends on your budget and your tastes. But, to repeat a well-worn phrase, you can enjoy "champagne on a beer budget"—if you plan carefully.

The annual trip-planning guide published by the state's tourism promotion agency, **Visit Florida** (see "Visitor Information," earlier in this chapter), lists most hotels and motels in the state. It's particularly handy if you're taking your animal along, since it tells whether they accept pets.

Another excellent source is **Superior Small Lodgings** ★, a national organization of quality hotels, motels, and inns. None of these properties has more than 75 rooms, and all have been inspected for cleanliness, quality, comfort, privacy, and safety. Contact the local tourist information offices for lists of members in their areas, or the **Florida Superior Small Lodging Association,** 1809 Silver Valley Court, Apopka, FL 32712 (© **407/ 880-1707;** fax 407/884-1301; www. SuperiorSmallLodging.com). Many hotels and motels recommended in this book are members.

Inn Route, P.O. Box 6187, Palm Harbor, FL 34684 (© **800/524-1880;** fax 281/403-9335; www. florida-inns.com), publishes the *Inns of Florida,* which lists inns and bed-and-breakfasts throughout the state. Inn Route also inspects each property, thus ensuring the quality and cleanliness of its members.

At the inexpensive end, **Hostelling International/American Youth Hostels,** 8401 Colesville Rd., Suite 600, Silver Spring, MD 20910 (© **301/ 495-1240;** www.hiayh.org), offers low-cost accommodations in Miami Beach, Key West, Florida City, Orlando, St. Augustine, and Clearwater Beach.

Some of the resorts listed in this book actually are condominium complexes operated as full-service hotels, but usually you'll have to do without such hotel amenities as on-site restaurants, room service, and even daily maid service. On the other hand, almost every condominium, home, and cottage has a fully equipped kitchen, and many have washers, dryers, and other such niceties of home, which means they can represent significant savings, especially if you're traveling with children or are sharing with another couple or family.

We have pointed out a few of the best condominium complexes in the "Accommodations You Can Afford" sections of the following chapters, and

we have named some of the **reputable real estate agencies** that have inventories of condominiums, private homes, and cottages to rent.

If you think a condominium will meet your needs, your best bet is to contact the rental agencies well in advance and request a brochure describing all the properties they represent, and their rates.

SAVING ON YOUR HOTEL ROOM

The **rack rate** is the maximum rate that a hotel charges for a room. Hardly anybody pays this price, however, except in high season or on holidays. To lower the cost of your room:

- **Ask about special rates or other discounts.** Always ask whether a room less expensive than the first one quoted is available, or whether any special rates apply to you. You may qualify for corporate, student, military, senior, or other discounts. Mention membership in AAA, AARP, frequent-flier programs, or trade unions, which may entitle you to special deals as well. Find out the hotel policy on children—do kids stay free in the room or is there a special rate?

- **Dial direct.** When booking a room in a chain hotel, you'll often get a better deal by calling the individual hotel's reservation desk rather than the chain's main number.

- **Book online.** Many hotels offer Internet-only discounts, or supply rooms to Priceline, Hotwire, or Expedia at rates much lower than the ones you can get through the hotel itself. Shop around. And if you have special needs—a quiet room, a room with a view—call the hotel directly and make your needs known after you've booked online.

- **Remember the law of supply and demand.** Resort hotels are most crowded and therefore most expensive on weekends, so discounts are usually available for midweek stays. Business hotels in downtown locations are busiest during the week, so you can expect big discounts over the weekend. Many hotels have high-season and low-season prices, and booking the day after high season ends can mean big discounts.
- **Look into group or long-stay discounts.** If you come as part of a large group, you should be able to negotiate a bargain rate, since the hotel can then guarantee occupancy in a number of rooms. Likewise, if you're planning a long stay (at least 5 days), you might qualify for a discount. As a general rule, expect 1 night free after a 7-night stay.
- **Avoid excess charges and hidden costs.** When you book a room, ask whether the hotel charges for parking. Use your own cellphone, pay phones, or prepaid phone cards instead of dialing direct from hotel phones, which usually have exorbitant rates. And don't be tempted by the room's minibar offerings: Most hotels charge through the nose for water, soda, and snacks. Finally, ask about local taxes and service charges, which can increase the cost of a room by 15% or more. If a hotel insists upon tacking on a surprise "energy surcharge" that wasn't mentioned at check-in or a "resort fee" for amenities you didn't use, you can often make a case for getting it removed.
- Consider the pros and cons of **all-inclusive** resorts and hotels. The term "all-inclusive" means different things at different hotels. Many all-inclusive hotels will include three meals daily, sports equipment, spa entry, and other amenities; others may include all or most drinks. In general, you'll save money going the "all-inclusive" way—as long as you use the facilities provided. The down side is that your choices are limited and you're stuck eating and playing in one place for the duration of your vacation.
- **Book an efficiency.** A room with a kitchenette allows you to shop for groceries and cook your own meals. This is a big money saver, especially for families on long stays.
- **What's the view like?** Cost-conscious travelers may be willing to pay less for a back room facing the parking lot, especially if they don't plan to spend much time in their room.
- **What's included in the price?** Your room may be moderately priced, but if you're charged for beach chairs, towels, sports equipment, and other amenities, you could end up spending more than you bargained for.

14 Recommended Books

Get psyched for your trip to Florida by reading *Miami Herald* columnist and novelist Carl Hiaasen's hilarious *Basket Case* (Knopf, 2002), about Jack Tagger, a journalist at a small South Florida daily newspaper. Go on an adventure from Miami to Key West in *Bone Key* (Putnam, 2002), author Les Standiford's seventh in his renowned John Deal series, where Deal's convoluted family ties take him to the southernmost point to talk with a developer friend of his father's. Zora Neale Hurston's *Their Eyes Were Watching God* (Perennial, 1998) takes you to an all-black town in Florida during the era of the Harlem Renaissance. Frank Oppel's *Tales of Old Florida* (Castle, 1991) is a fascinating collection of newspaper articles about Florida from the last century. Historian and preservationist Marjorie Stoneman Douglas's *The Everglades: River of Grass*, is an engaging look into one of America's most pristine ecosystems. *And* finally, a must read is Joan Didion's *Miami* (Vintage, 1998), about Cubans in the Magic City.

FAST FACTS: Florida

American Express There are a number of American Express offices in Florida. Call Cardmember Services (ⓒ **800/528-4800;** www.american express.com) for the location nearest you.

ATM Networks ATMs are as ubiquitous in Florida as the palm trees. Machines are found on nearly every street corner, in main shopping areas, and, in most cases, in supermarkets, and even in convenience stores.

Banks Banks are usually open Monday through Friday from 9am to 3 or 4pm, and most have automated teller machines (ATMs) for 24-hour banking. You won't have a problem finding a Cirrus or PLUS machine. See "Money," earlier in this chapter, for more information.

Car Rentals See "Getting Around," earlier in this chapter.

Emergencies To reach the police, ambulance, or fire department, dial ⓒ **911** from any phone. No coins are needed. Emergency hot lines include **Crisis Intervention** (ⓒ **305/358-HELP** or 305/358-4357) and the **Poison Information Center** (ⓒ **800/222-1222**).

Liquor Laws You must be 21 to purchase or consume alcohol in Florida. This law is strictly enforced, so if you look young, carry some photo identification that gives your date of birth. Minors can usually enter bars where food is served but are not allowed to drink alcohol.

Newspapers/Magazines Most cities of any size have a local daily paper. The well-respected *Miami Herald* is generally available all over the state, with regional editions available in many areas. In the major cities, you can also find coin-operated boxes for *USA Today,* the *Wall Street Journal,* and the *New York Times.*

Safety Whenever you're traveling in an unfamiliar city, stay alert. Be aware of your immediate surroundings. Always lock your car doors and the trunk when your vehicle is unattended, and don't leave any valuables in sight. See "Health & Safety," earlier in this chapter, for more information.

Taxes The Florida state sales tax is 6%. Many municipalities add 1% or more to that, and most levy a special tax on hotel and restaurant bills. In general, expect at least 9% to be added to your final hotel bill. There are also hefty taxes on rental cars here (see "Getting Around," above).

Time Zones The Florida peninsula observes Eastern Standard Time (EST), but most of the Panhandle, west of the Apalachicola River, is on Central Standard Time (CST), 1 hour behind the rest of the state.

Weather Hurricane season runs August through November. For an up-to-date recording of current weather conditions and forecast reports, call ⓒ **305/229-4522**. Online, you can check www.intellicast.com or www. weather.com.

3

For International Visitors

Whether it's your first visit or your 10th, a trip to the United States may require an additional degree of planning. This chapter will provide you with essential information, helpful tips, and advice for the more common problems that some visitors encounter.

1 Preparing for Your Trip

ENTRY REQUIREMENTS

Check at any U.S. embassy or consulate for current information and requirements. You can also obtain a visa application and other information online at the **U.S. State Department**'s website, at **www.travel.state.gov**.

VISAS The U.S. State Department has a **Visa Waiver Program** allowing citizens of certain countries (information is available from any U.S. embassy or consulate) to enter the United States without a visa for stays of up to 90 days. Citizens of these countries need only a valid passport and a round-trip air or cruise ticket in their possession upon arrival. Canadian citizens may enter the United States without visas; they need only proof of residence.

Citizens of all other countries must have (1) a valid passport that expires at least 6 months later than the scheduled end of their visit to the United States, and (2) a tourist visa, which may be obtained without charge from any U.S. consulate.

To obtain a visa, the traveler must submit a completed application form (either in person or by mail) with a 1½-inch-square photo, and must demonstrate binding ties to a residence abroad. Usually you can obtain a visa at once or within 24 hours, but it may take longer during the summer

rush June through August. If you cannot go in person, contact the nearest U.S. embassy or consulate for directions on applying by mail. Your travel agent or airline office may also be able to provide you with visa applications and instructions. The U.S. consulate or embassy that issues your visa will determine whether you will be issued a multiple- or single-entry visa and any restrictions regarding the length of your stay.

British subjects can obtain up-to-date visa information by calling the **U.S. Embassy Visa Information Line** (© 0891/200-290) or by contacting the U.K. Passport Service (© 0870/521-0410; www.passport.gov.uk).

Irish citizens can obtain up-to-date passport and visa information through the **Embassy of USA Dublin,** 42 Elgin Rd., Dublin 4, Ireland (© 353/1-668-8777), or by checking the visa page on the website at www.usembassy.ie.

Australian citizens can obtain up-to-date visa information by contacting the **U.S. Embassy Canberra,** Moonah Place, Yarralumla, ACT 2600 (© 02/6214-5600) or by checking the embassy's website at http://usembassy-australia.state.gov.

Citizens of **New Zealand** can obtain up-to-date visa information by contacting the **U.S. Embassy New**

Zealand, 29 Fitzherbert Terrace, Thorndon, Wellington (© 644/462-6000), or get the information directly from the "Services to New Zealanders" section of the website at http://usembassy.org.nz.

MEDICAL   REQUIREMENTS
Unless you're arriving from an area known to be suffering from an epidemic (particularly cholera or yellow fever), inoculations or vaccinations are not required for entry into the United States. If you have a medical condition that requires **syringe-administered medications,** carry a valid signed prescription from your physician—the Federal Aviation Administration (FAA) no longer allows airline passengers to pack syringes in their carry-on baggage without documented proof of medical need. If you have a disease that requires treatment with **narcotics,** you should also carry documented proof with you—smuggling narcotics aboard a plane is a serious offense that carries severe penalties in the U.S.

DRIVER'S   LICENSES   Foreign driver's licenses are mostly recognized in the U.S., although you may want to get an international driver's license if your home license is not written in English.

PASSPORT INFORMATION
Safeguard your passport in an inconspicuous, inaccessible place like a money belt. Make a copy of the critical pages, including the passport number, and store it in a safe place, separate from the passport itself. If you lose your passport, visit the nearest consulate of your native country as soon as possible for a replacement. Passport applications are downloadable from the Internet sites listed below.

Note that the International Civil Aviation Organization (ICAO) has recommended a policy requiring that *every* individual who travels by air

have his or her own passport. In response, many countries are now requiring that children must be issued their own passport to travel internationally, where before those under 16 or so may have been allowed to travel on a parent or guardian's passport.

CUSTOMS
WHAT YOU CAN BRING IN
Every visitor more than 21 years of age may bring in, free of duty, the following: (1) 1 liter of wine or hard liquor; (2) 200 cigarettes, 100 cigars (but not from Cuba), or 3 pounds of smoking tobacco; and (3) $100 worth of gifts. These exemptions are offered to travelers who spend at least 72 hours in the United States and who have not claimed them within the preceding 6 months. It is altogether forbidden to bring into the country foodstuffs (particularly fruit, cooked meats, and canned goods) and plants (vegetables, seeds, tropical plants, and the like). Foreign tourists may bring in or take out up to $10,000 in U.S. dollars or the equivalent in foreign currency with no formalities; larger sums must be declared to U.S. Customs on entering or leaving, which includes filing form CM 4790. For more specific information regarding U.S. Customs and Border Protection, contact your nearest U.S. embassy or consulate, or the **U.S. Customs** office (© 202/927-1770 or www.customs.ustreas.gov).

WHAT YOU CAN TAKE HOME
U.K. citizens should contact HM Customs & Excise at © 0845/010-9000 (from outside the U.K., 020/8929-0152), or consult their website at www.hmce.gov.uk for more information. **Canadian citizens** can contact the **Canada Customs and Revenue Agency** (© 800/461-9999 in Canada, or 204/983-3500; www.ccra-adrc.gc.ca). **Australians** should call the **Australian Customs Service**

at ℡ **1300/363-263,** or log on to www.customs.gov.au. Those from **New Zealand** can get more information from **New Zealand Customs,** The Customhouse, 17–21 Whitmore St., Box 2218, Wellington (℡ **0800/ 428-786** or 04/473-6099; www. customs.govt.nz).

HEALTH INSURANCE

Although it's not required of travelers, health insurance is highly recommended. Unlike many European countries, the United States does not usually offer free or low-cost medical care to its citizens or visitors. Doctors and hospitals are expensive, and in most cases will require advance payment or proof of coverage before they render their services. Policies can cover everything from the loss or theft of your baggage and trip cancellation to the guarantee of bail in case you're arrested. Good policies will also cover the costs of an accident, repatriation, or death. Packages such as **Europ Assistance's "Worldwide Healthcare Plan"** are sold by European automobile clubs and travel agencies at attractive rates. **Worldwide Assistance Services, Inc.** (℡ **800/777-8710;** www.worldwideassistance.com) is the agent for Europ Assistance in the United States.

Though lack of health insurance may prevent you from being admitted to a hospital in nonemergencies, don't worry about being left on a street corner to die: The American way is to fix you now and bill the living daylights out of you later.

MONEY

CURRENCY The U.S. monetary system is very simple: The most common **bills** are the $1 (colloquially, a "buck"), $5, $10, and $20 denominations. There are also $2 bills (seldom encountered), $50 bills, and $100 bills (the last two are usually not welcome as payment for small purchases). All the paper money was recently redesigned, making the famous faces adorning them disproportionately large. The old-style bills are still legal tender.

There are seven denominations of coins: 1¢ (1 cent, or a penny); 5¢ (5 cents, or a nickel); 10¢ (10 cents, or a dime); 25¢ (25 cents, or a quarter); 50¢ (50 cents, or a half dollar); the new gold "Sacagawea" coin worth $1; and, prized by collectors, the rare, older silver dollar.

Note: The "foreign-exchange bureaus" so common in Europe are rare even at airports in the United States, and nonexistent outside major cities. It's best not to change foreign money (or traveler's checks denominated in a currency other than U.S. dollars) at a small-town bank, or even a branch in a big city; in fact, leave any currency other than U.S. dollars at home—it may prove a greater nuisance to you than it's worth.

TRAVELER'S CHECKS Though traveler's checks are widely accepted, make sure that they're denominated in U.S. dollars, as foreign-currency checks are often difficult to exchange. The three traveler's checks that are most widely recognized—and least likely to be denied—are **Visa, American Express,** and **Thomas Cook.** Be sure to record the numbers of the checks, and keep that information in a separate place in case they get lost or stolen. Most businesses are pretty good about taking traveler's checks, but you're better off cashing them in at a bank (in small amounts, of course) and paying in cash. *Remember:* You'll need identification, such as a driver's license or passport, to change a traveler's check.

CREDIT CARDS & ATMs Credit cards are the most widely used form of payment in the United States: **Visa** (Barclaycard in Britain), **MasterCard** (EuroCard in Europe, Access in Britain, Chargex in Canada), **American Express, Diners Club,** and

Discover. There are, however, a handful of stores and restaurants that do not take credit cards, so be sure to ask in advance. Most businesses display a sticker near their entrance to let you know which cards they accept. (**Note:** Businesses may require a minimum purchase, usually around $10, to use a credit card.)

It is strongly recommended that you bring at least one major credit card. You must have a credit or charge card to rent a car. Hotels and airlines usually require a credit card imprint as a deposit against expenses, and in an emergency a credit card can be priceless.

You'll find **automated teller machines (ATMs)** on just about every block—at least in almost every town—across the country. Some ATMs will allow you to draw U.S. currency against your bank and credit cards. Check with your bank before leaving home, and remember that you will need your personal identification number (PIN) to do so. Most accept Visa, MasterCard, and American Express, as well as ATM cards from other U.S. banks. Expect to be charged up to $3 per transaction, however, if you're not using your own bank's ATM.

One way around these fees is to ask for cash back at grocery stores that accept ATM cards and don't charge usage fees. Of course, you'll have to purchase something first.

ATM cards with major credit card backing, known as "debit cards," are now a commonly acceptable form of payment in most stores and restaurants. Debit cards draw money directly from your checking account. Some stores enable you to receive "cash back" on your debit card purchases as well.

SAFETY
GENERAL   SUGGESTIONS
Although tourist areas are generally safe, U.S. urban areas tend to be less safe than those in Europe or Japan. You should always stay alert. This is particularly true of large American cities. If you're in doubt about which neighborhoods are safe, don't hesitate to make inquiries with the hotel front desk staff or the local tourist office.

Avoid deserted areas, especially at night, and don't go into public parks after dark unless there's a concert or similar occasion that will attract a crowd.

Avoid carrying valuables with you on the street, and keep expensive cameras or electronic equipment bagged up or covered when not in use. If you're using a map, try to consult it inconspicuously—or better yet, study it before you leave your room. Hold onto your pocketbook, and place your billfold in an inside pocket. In theaters, restaurants, and other public places, keep your possessions in sight.

Always lock your room door—don't assume that once you're inside the hotel you are automatically safe and no longer need to be aware of your surroundings. Hotels are open to the public, and in a large hotel, security may not be able to screen everyone who enters.

DRIVING SAFETY   Driving safety is important, too, especially given the highly publicized carjackings of foreign tourists in Florida. Question your rental agency about personal safety and ask for a traveler-safety brochure when you pick up your car. Obtain written directions—or a map with the route clearly marked—from the agency showing how to get to your destination. (Many agencies now offer the option of renting a cellular phone for the duration of your car rental; check with the rental agent when you pick up the car.) And, if possible, arrive and depart during daylight hours.

If you drive off a highway and end up in a dodgy-looking neighborhood, leave the area as quickly as possible. If you have an accident, even on the highway, stay in your car with the doors locked until you assess the situation or until the police arrive. If you're bumped from behind on the street or are involved in a minor accident with no injuries, and the situation appears to be suspicious, motion to the other driver to follow you. Never get out of your car in such situations. Go directly to the nearest police precinct, well-lit service station, or 24-hour store. You may want to look into renting a cellphone on a short-term basis. One recommended wireless rental company is **In Touch USA** (✆ **800/872-7626;** www.in touchusa.com).

Park in well-lit and well-traveled areas whenever possible. Always keep your car doors locked, whether the vehicle is attended or unattended. Never leave any packages or valuables in sight. If someone attempts to rob you or steal your car, don't try to resist the thief/carjacker. Report the incident to the police department immediately by calling ✆ **911.**

2 Getting to the U.S.

A number of U.S. airlines offer service from Europe and Latin America to Florida, including American, Delta, Northwest, and United (see "Getting There," in chapter 2). Many of the major international airlines, such as **British Airways** (www.british airways.com), **KLM Royal Dutch Airlines** (www.klm.com), and **Lufthansa** (www.lufthansa.com), also have direct flights from Europe to various Florida cities, either in their own planes or in conjunction with an American "partner" airline (Northwest/KLM, to name one such partnership). You can get here from Australia and New Zealand via **Air New Zealand** (www.airnz.com), **Qantas** (www.qantas.com), **American** (www. aa.com), and **United** (www.ual.com), with a change of planes in Los Angeles. Call the airlines' local offices or contact your travel agent, and be sure to ask about promotional fares and discounts.

From Great Britain, **Virgin Atlantic Airways** (✆ **800/862-8621** in the U.S., or 08/703-80-20-07 in the U.K.; www.virgin-atlantic.com) has attractive deals on its flights from London and Manchester to Miami and Orlando. From Germany, **LTU International Airways** (✆ **866/266-5588** in the U.S., or 941-8888 in Germany; www.ltu.com) frequently has reduced fares to Miami, Orlando, and Fort Myers from Frankfurt, Munich, and Düsseldorf. From Johannesburg and Cape Town, **South African Airways** and **Delta Airlines** (www.delta.com) fly to Fort Lauderdale.

Canadians should check with **Air Canada** (✆ **888-247-2262;** www. aircanada.ca), which offers service from Toronto and Montreal to Miami, Tampa, West Palm Beach, Fort Lauderdale, and Fort Myers. Also ask your travel agent about **Air Transat** (✆ **866/847-1112;** www.airtransat. com), which has wintertime charter flights to several Florida destinations.

AIRFARES Whichever airline you choose, always ask about **advance purchase excursion (APEX)** fares, which represent substantial savings over regular fares. Most require tickets to be bought 21 days prior to departure.

On the Web, the European Travel Network (ETN) operates a site at **www.discount-tickets.com**, which offers cut-rate prices on international airfares to the United States, accommodations, car rentals, and tours. Another site to check for current discount fares worldwide is **www.etn.nl/ discount.htm#disco**.

> **Tips Prepare to Be Fingerprinted**
>
> Since January 2004, many international visitors traveling on visas to the United States are being photographed and fingerprinted at Customs in a new program created by the Department of Homeland Security called **US-VISIT.** Non–U.S. citizens arriving at airports and on cruise ships must undergo an instant background check as part of the government's ongoing efforts to deter terrorism by verifying the identity of incoming and outgoing visitors. Exempt from the extra scrutiny are visitors entering by land or those from 28 countries (mostly in Europe) that don't require a visa for short-term visits. For more information, go to the Homeland Security website at **www.dhs.gov/dhspublic**.

AIRLINE DISCOUNTS The smart traveler can find numerable ways to reduce the price of a plane ticket simply by taking time to shop around. For example, overseas visitors can take advantage of the APEX (Advance Purchase Excursion) reductions offered by all major U.S. and European carriers. For more money-saving airline advice, see "Getting There," in chapter 2, beginning on p. 48. For the best rates, compare fares and be flexible with the dates and times of travel.

IMMIGRATION AND CUSTOMS CLEARANCE Visitors arriving by air, no matter what the port of entry, should cultivate patience and resignation before setting foot on U.S. soil. Getting through immigration control can take as long as 2 hours on some days, especially on summer weekends, so be sure to carry this guidebook or something else to read. This is especially true in the aftermath of the September 11, 2001, terrorist attacks, when security clearances were considerably beefed up at U.S. airports.

3 Getting Around the U.S.

The United States is one of the world's largest countries, with vast distances separating many of its key sights. If you fly from Europe to New York, for example, you still have a trip of more than 1,350 miles to Miami. Accordingly, flying is the quickest and most comfortable way to get around the country.

BY PLANE Some large airlines (for example, Northwest and Delta) offer travelers on their transatlantic or transpacific flights special discount tickets under the name **Visit USA,** allowing mostly one-way travel from one U.S. destination to another at very low prices. These discount tickets are not on sale in the United States and must be purchased abroad in conjunction with your international

ticket. This system is the best, easiest, and fastest way to see the United States at low cost. You should obtain information well in advance from your travel agent or the office of the airline concerned, since the conditions attached to these discount tickets can be changed without advance notice.

BY TRAIN International visitors (excluding Canada) can also buy a **USA Rail Pass,** good for 15 or 30 days of unlimited travel on Amtrak (© **800/USA-RAIL;** www.amtrak.com). The pass is available through many foreign travel agents. Prices in 2004 for a 15-day pass were $295 off-peak, $440 peak; a 30-day pass costs $385 off-peak, $550 peak. With a foreign passport, you can also buy passes at some Amtrak offices in the United

States, including locations in San Francisco, Los Angeles, Chicago, New York, Miami, Boston, and Washington, D.C. Reservations are generally required and should be made for each part of your trip as early as possible. Regional rail passes are also available.

BY BUS Although bus travel is often the most economical form of public transit for short hops between U.S. cities, it can also be slow and uncomfortable—certainly not an option for everyone (particularly when Amtrak, which is far more luxurious, offers similar rates). **Greyhound/ Trailways** (② 800/231-2222; www. greyhound.com), the sole nationwide bus line, offers an **International Ameripass** that must be purchased before coming to the United States, or by phone through the Greyhound International Office at the Port Authority Bus Terminal in New York City (② 212/971-0492). The pass can be obtained from foreign travel agents or through Greyhound's website (order at least 21 days before your departure to the U.S.) and costs less than the domestic version. Passes for 2004 cost as follows: 7 days $209, 10 days $259, 15 days $309, 21 days $359, 30 days $399, 45 days $459, or 60 days $569. You can get more info about the pass at the website, or by calling ② 800/231-2222 or 402/330-8552 (for international callers who don't have toll-free access). In addition, special rates are available for seniors and students.

BY CAR Unless you plan to spend the bulk of your vacation time in a city where walking is the best and easiest way to get around (read: New York City or New Orleans), the most cost-effective, convenient, and comfortable way to travel around the United States is by car. The interstate highway system connects cities and towns all over the country; in addition to these high-speed, limited-access roadways, there's an extensive network of federal, state, and local highways and roads. Some of the national car-rental companies include **Alamo** (② 800/462-5266; www.alamo.com), **Avis** (② 800/230-4898; www.avis. com), **Budget** (② 800/527-0700; www.budget.com), **Dollar** (② 800/ 800-3665; www.dollar.com), **Hertz** (② 800/654-3131; www.hertz.com), **National** (② 800/227-7368; www. nationalcar.com), and **Thrifty** (② 800/ 847-4389; www.thrifty.com).

If you plan to rent a car in the United States, you probably won't need the services of an additional automobile organization. If you're planning to buy or borrow a car, automobile-association membership is recommended. **AAA, the American Automobile Association** (② 800/ AAA-HELP or 800/222-1134; www. aaa.com), is the country's largest auto club and supplies its members with maps, insurance, and, most important, emergency road service. The cost of joining runs from $60 for singles, add another for $30, but if you're a member of a foreign auto club with reciprocal arrangements, you can enjoy free AAA service in America.

FAST FACTS: For the International Traveler

Business Hours Offices are usually open weekdays from 9am to 5pm. Banks are open weekdays from 9am to 3pm or later and sometimes Saturday mornings. Stores typically open between 9 and 10am and close between 5 and 6pm from Monday through Saturday. Stores in shopping complexes or malls tend to stay open late: until about 9pm on weekdays and weekends, and many malls and larger department stores are open on Sundays.

Electricity Like Canada, the United States uses 110 to 120 volts AC (60 cycles), compared to 220 to 240 volts AC (50 cycles) in most of Europe, Australia, and New Zealand. If your small appliances use 220 to 240 volts, you'll need a 110-volt transformer and a plug adapter with two flat parallel pins to operate them here. Downward converters that change 220 to 240 volts to 110 to 120 volts are difficult to find in the United States, so bring one with you.

Embassies & Consulates All embassies are located in the nation's capital, Washington, D.C. Some consulates are located in major U.S. cities, and most nations have a mission to the United Nations in New York City. If your country isn't listed below, call for directory information in Washington, D.C. (© 202/555-1212) or log on to **www.embassy.org/embassies**.

In South Florida, the **Canadian Consulate** is located at 200 S. Bayshore Dr., Miami, FL 33131 (© **305/579-1600**). The **British Consulate** is located at the Brickell Bay Tower, Suite 2110, 1001 S. Bayshore Dr., Coconut Grove, FL 33131 (© **305/374-1522**). The **French Consulate** is located at 1 Biscayne Tower, Suite 1710, Miami, FL 33131 (© **305/372-9799**); the **Italian Consulate** is located at 1200 Brickell Ave., Miami, FL 33131 (© **305/374-6322**); the **Israeli Consulate** is located at 100 N. Biscayne Blvd., Miami, FL 33132 (© **305/925-9400**); the **German Consulate** is located at 100 N. Biscayne Blvd., Suite 2200, Miami, FL 33132 (© **305/358-0290**); the **Australian Consulate** is located at 2525 SW Third Ave., Suite 208, Miami, FL 33129 (© **305/858-7633**); and **Brazil's Consulate General** is located at 2601 S. Bayshore Dr., Suite 800, Coconut Grove, FL 33133 (© **305/285-6200**).

Emergencies Call © **911** to report a fire, call the police, or get an ambulance anywhere in the United States. This is a toll-free call. (No coins are required at public telephones.)

If you encounter serious problems, contact the **Traveler's Aid Society International** (© **202/546-1127**; www.travelersaid.org) to help direct you to a local branch. This nationwide, nonprofit, social-service organization geared to helping travelers in difficult straits offers services that might include reuniting families separated while traveling, providing food and/or shelter to people stranded without cash, or even emotional counseling. If you're in trouble, seek them out.

Gasoline (Petrol) Petrol is known as gasoline (or simply "gas") in the United States, and petrol stations are known as both gas stations and service stations. Gasoline costs about half as much here as it does in Europe (though, at around $2 per gallon at press time, prices are steeply rising), and taxes are already included in the printed price. One U.S. gallon equals 3.8 liters or .85 imperial gallons. A majority of gas stations in Florida are now actually convenience grocery stores with gas pumps outside. They do not service your automobile for you; all but a very few stations have self-service gas pumps.

Holidays Banks, government offices, post offices, and many stores, restaurants, and museums are closed on the following legal national holidays: January 1 (New Year's Day), the third Monday in January (Martin Luther King Jr. Day), the third Monday in February (Presidents' Day, Washington's Birthday), the last Monday in May (Memorial Day), July 4 (Independence Day), the first Monday in September (Labor Day), the second Monday in October (Columbus Day), November 11 (Veterans' Day/Armistice Day), the fourth Thursday in November (Thanksgiving Day), and December 25 (Christmas). Also, the Tuesday following the first Monday in November is Election Day and is a federal government holiday in presidential-election years (held every 4 years, and next in 2008).

Mail If you aren't sure what your address will be in the United States, mail can be sent to you, in your name, c/o General Delivery at the main post office of the city or region where you expect to be. (Call ⓒ **800/ 275-8777** for information on the nearest post office.) The addressee must pick up mail in person and must produce proof of identity (driver's license, passport, and so on.). Most post offices will hold your mail for up to 1 month, and are open Monday through Friday from 8am to 6pm, and Saturday from 9am to 3pm.

At press time, domestic postage rates were 23¢ for a postcard and 37¢ for a letter. For international mail, a first-class letter of up to ½ ounce costs 80¢ (60¢ to Canada and Mexico); a first-class postcard costs 70¢ (50¢ to Canada and Mexico); and a preprinted postal aerogramme costs 70¢.

Taxes The United States has no value-added tax (VAT) or other indirect tax at the national level. Every state, county, and city has the right to levy its own local tax on all purchases, including hotel and restaurant checks, airline tickets, and so on. For Florida's sales taxes, see "Fast Facts: Florida," in chapter 2.

Telephone, Telegraph, Telex & Fax The telephone system in the United States is run by private corporations, so rates, especially for long-distance service and operator-assisted calls, can vary widely. Generally, hotel surcharges on long-distance and local calls are astronomical, so you're usually better off using a **public pay telephone**, which you'll find clearly marked in most public buildings and private establishments as well as on the street. Convenience grocery stores and gas stations always have them. Many convenience groceries and packaging services sell **prepaid calling cards;** these can be the least expensive way to call home. **Local calls** made from public pay phones in Florida cost 35¢. Pay phones do not accept pennies, and few will take anything larger than a quarter.

Most long-distance and international calls can be dialed directly from any phone. **For calls within the United States and to Canada,** dial 1 followed by the area code and the seven-digit number. **For other international calls,** dial 011 followed by the country code, city code, and the telephone number of the person you are calling.

Calls to area codes **800, 888, 866,** and **877** are toll-free. However, calls to numbers in area codes **700** and **900** (chat lines, bulletin boards, "dating" services, and so on) can be very expensive—usually a charge of 95¢ to $3 or more per minute, and they sometimes have minimum charges that can run as high as $15 or more.

For **reversed-charge or collect calls,** and for person-to-person calls, dial 0 (zero, not the letter O) followed by the area code and number you want; an operator will then come on the line, and you should specify that you are calling collect, or person-to-person, or both. If your operator-assisted call is international, ask for the overseas operator.

For **local directory assistance** ("information"), dial ⓒ 411; for long-distance information, dial 1, then the appropriate area code and 555-1212.

Most hotels have **fax machines** available for guest use (be sure to ask about the charge to use it). Many hotel rooms are even wired for guests' fax machines. A less expensive way to send and receive faxes may be at stores such as The UPS Store/Mail Boxes Etc., a national chain of packing service shops. (Look in the Yellow Pages directory under "Packing Services.")

Time The continental United States is divided into **four time zones:** Eastern Standard Time (EST), Central Standard Time (CST), Mountain Standard Time (MST), and Pacific Standard Time (PST). Alaska and Hawaii have their own zones. For example, noon in Miami (EST) is 11am in Pensacola (CST), 10am in Denver (MST), 9am in Los Angeles (PST), 8am in Anchorage (AST), and 7am in Honolulu (HST). Most of Florida observes Eastern Standard Time, though the Panhandle west of the Apalachicola River is on Central Standard Time (1 hr. earlier than Tallahassee, Orlando, and Miami).

Daylight saving time is in effect from 1am on the first Sunday in April through 1am on the last Sunday in October, except in Arizona, Hawaii, part of Indiana, and Puerto Rico. Daylight saving time moves the clock 1 hour ahead of standard time.

Tipping Tips are a very important part of certain workers' salaries, so it's necessary to leave appropriate gratuities.

Here are some rules of thumb:

In hotels, tip **bellhops** at least $1 per bag ($2–$3 if you have a lot of luggage) and tip the **chamber staff** $3 per day (more if you've left a disaster area for him or her to clean up, or if you're traveling with kids and/or pets). Tip the **doorman** or **concierge** only if he or she has provided you with some specific service (for example, calling a cab for you or obtaining difficult-to-get theater tickets). Tip the **valet parking attendant** $1 every time you get your car.

In restaurants, bars, and nightclubs, tip **service staff** 15% to 20% of the check, tip **bartenders** 10% to 15%, tip **checkroom attendants** $1 per garment, and tip **valet-parking attendants** $1 per vehicle. Tip the **doorman** only if he has provided you with some specific service (such as calling a cab for you).

As for other service personnel, tip **cab drivers** 15% of the fare; tip **skycaps** at airports at least $1 per bag ($2–$3 if you have a lot of luggage); and tip **hairdressers** and **barbers** 15% to 20%.

4

Miami

A week in Miami is not unlike watching an episode of, say, *Access Hollywood* with a little CNN thrown in for good measure. What used to be a relatively sleepy beach vacation destination has awakened from its humid slumber, upped its tempo, and finally earned its place in the Palm Pilots of cutting-edge jet-setters worldwide. But don't be fooled by the hipper-than-thou, celebrity-drenched playground known as South Beach. While the chic elite do, indeed, flock to Miami's coolest enclave, it is surprisingly accessible to the average Joe, Jane, or José. For every Philippe Starck–designed, bank-account-busting boutique hotel on South Beach, there's a kitschy, candy-coated Art Deco one that's much less taxing on the pockets. For each Pan-Mediterranean-Asian haute cuisinerie, there's always the down-home, no-nonsense Cuban bodega offering hearty food at ridiculously cheap prices.

Beyond the whole glitzy, *Entertainment Tonight*-meets-beach-blanket-bacchanalia-as-seen-on-TV, Miami has an endless number of sporting, cultural, and recreational activities to keep you entertained. Our sparkling beaches are beyond compare. Plus, there's excellent shopping and nightlife activities that include ballet, theater, and opera (as well as all the celebrity-saturated hotels, restaurants, bars, and clubs that have helped to make Miami so famous).

If there's one thing Miami doesn't have, it's an identity crisis. In fact, it's the city's vibrant, multifaceted personality that attracts millions each year, from all over the world. South Beach may be on the top of many Miami to-do lists, but the rest of the city, a fascinating assemblage of multicultural neighborhoods, should not be overlooked or neglected. Once considered "God's Waiting Room," the magic city now attracts an eclectic mix of old and young, celebs and plebes, American and international, and geek and chic with an equally varied roster of activities.

For starters, Miami boasts some of the most natural beauty there is, with blinding blue waters, fine, sandy beaches, and lush tropical parks. The city's man-made brilliance, in the form of Crayola-colored architecture, never seems to fade in Miami's unique Art Deco District. For cultural variation, you can also experience the tastes, sounds, and rhythms of Cuba in Little Havana.

As in any metropolis, however, there are areas that aren't as great as others. Downtown Miami, for instance, is in the throes of a major, albeit slow, renaissance, in which the sketchier, warehouse sections of the city are being transformed into hubs of all things hip. In contrast to this development, however, are the still poverty-stricken areas of downtown such as Overtown, Liberty City, and Little Haiti (though Overtown is striving to transform itself into the Overtown Historic Village, showcasing its landmarks such as the famous Lyric Theater and the home of DA Dorsey, Miami's first African-American millionaire). While it's obvious to advise you to exercise caution when exploring the less-traveled parts of the city, we would also be remiss in telling you to bypass them completely.

Lose yourself in the city's nature and its neighborhoods, and, best of all, its people—a sassy collection of artists and intellectuals, beach bums and international transplants, dolled-up drag queens and bodies beautiful.

No wonder celebrities love to vacation here—the spotlight is on the city and its residents. And unlike most stars, Miami is always ready for its close-up. With so much to do and see, Miami is a virtual amusement park that's bound to entertain all those who pass through its palm-lined gates.

1 Orientation

ARRIVING

Originally carved out of scrub-land in 1928 by Pan American Airlines, **Miami International Airport (MIA)** has become second in the United States for international passenger traffic and 10th in the world for total passengers. Despite the heavy traffic, the airport is quite user-friendly and not as much of a hassle as you'd think. You can change money or use your ATM card at Nation's Bank of South Florida, located near the exit. Visitor information is available 24 hours a day at the **Miami International Airport Main Visitor Counter,** Concourse E, second level (© 305/876-7000). Information is also available at **www.miami-airport.com.** Because MIA is the busiest airport in South Florida, travelers may want to consider flying into the less crowded **Fort Lauderdale–Hollywood International Airport (FLL)** (© 954/359-1200), which is closer to north Miami than MIA, or the **Palm Beach International Airport (PBI)** (© 561/471-7420), which is about 1½ hours from Miami.

GETTING INTO TOWN

Miami International Airport is located about 6 miles west of downtown and about 10 miles from the beaches, so it's likely you can get from the plane to your hotel room in less than half an hour. Of course, if you're arriving from an international destination, it will take more time to go through Customs and Immigration.

BY CAR   All the major car-rental firms operate off-site branches reached via shuttles from the airline terminals. See the "Rentals" section, under "Getting Around," on p. 82 for a list of major rental companies in Miami. Signs at the airport's exit clearly point the way to various parts of the city, but the car-rental firm should also give you directions to your destination. If you're arriving late at night, you might want to take a taxi to your hotel and have the car delivered to you the next day.

BY TAXI   Taxis line up in front of a dispatcher's desk outside the airport's arrivals terminals. Most cabs are metered, though some have flat rates to popular destinations. The fare should be about $20 to Coral Gables, $18 to downtown, and $24 to South Beach, plus tip, which should be about 15% (add more for each bag the driver handles). Depending on traffic, the ride to Coral Gables or downtown takes about 15 to 20 minutes, and to South Beach, 20 to 25 minutes.

BY VAN   Group limousines (multipassenger vans) circle the arrivals area looking for fares. Destinations are posted on the front of each van, and a flat rate is charged for door-to-door service to the area marked.

SuperShuttle (© 305/871-2000; www.supershuttle.com) is one of the largest airport operators, charging between $9 and $40 per person for a ride

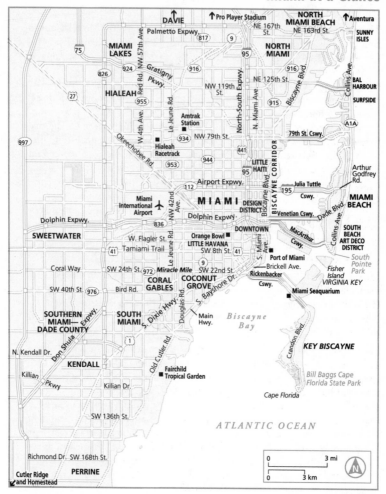

within the county. Its vans operate 24 hours a day and accept American Express, MasterCard, and Visa. This is a cheaper alternative to a cab (if you are traveling alone or with one other person), but be prepared to be in the van for quite a while, as you may have to make several stops to drop passengers off before you reach your own destination. SuperShuttle also has begun service from Palm Beach International Airport to the surrounding communities. The door-to-door, shared-ride service operates from the airport to Stuart, Fort Pierce, Palm Beach, and Broward counties.

BY PUBLIC TRANSPORTATION   Public transportation in South Florida is a major hassle bordering on a nightmare. Painfully slow and unreliable, buses heading downtown leave the airport only once per hour (from the arrivals level), and connections are spotty at best. It could take about an hour and a half to get to South Beach via public transportation. Journeys to downtown and Coral Gables, however, are more direct. The fare is $1.25, plus an additional 25¢ for a transfer.

VISITOR INFORMATION

The most up-to-date information is provided by the **Greater Miami Convention and Visitor's Bureau,** 701 Brickell Ave., Suite 700, Miami, FL 33131 (*©* **800/933-8448** or 305/539-3000; fax 305/530-3113; www.tropicool miami.com).

If you arrive at the Miami International Airport, you can pick up visitor information at the airport's main visitor counter on the second floor of Concourse E: It's open 24 hours a day.

Always check local newspapers for special events during your visit. The city's only daily, the *Miami Herald,* is a good source for current-events listings, particularly the "Weekend" section in Friday's edition and the paper's entertainment weekly offshoot, *The Street,* available free every Friday in freestanding boxes anchored to city streets. Even better is the free weekly alternative paper, the *Miami New Times,* available in bright red boxes throughout the city.

Information on everything from dining to entertainment in Miami is available on the Internet at www.miami.citysearch.com, www.digitalcity.com/south florida, www.miaminewtimes.com, or at www.herald.com.

CITY LAYOUT

Miami may seem confusing at first, but it quickly becomes easy to navigate. The small cluster of buildings that makes up the downtown area is at the geographical heart of the city. In relation to downtown, the airport is northwest, the beaches are east, Coconut Grove is south, Coral Gables is west, and the rest of the city is north.

FINDING AN ADDRESS   Miami is divided into dozens of areas with official and unofficial boundaries. Street numbering in the city of Miami is fairly straightforward, but you must first be familiar with the numbering system. The mainland is divided into four sections (NE, NW, SE, and SW) by the intersection of Flagler Street and Miami Avenue. Flagler divides Miami from north to south and Miami Avenue divides the city from east to west. It's helpful to remember that avenues generally run north-south, while streets go east-west. Street numbers (1st St., 2nd St., and so forth) start from here and increase as you go farther out from this intersection, as do numbers of avenues, places, courts, terraces, and lanes. Streets in Hialeah are the exceptions to this pattern; they are listed separately in map indexes.

Getting around the barrier islands that make up Miami Beach is somewhat easier than moving around the mainland. Street numbering starts with 1st Street, near Miami Beach's southern tip, and increases to 192nd Street, in the northern part of Sunny Isles. Collins Avenue makes the entire journey, from head to toe of the island. As in the city of Miami, some streets in Miami Beach have numbers as well as names. When they are part of listings in this book, both name and number are given.

The numbered streets in Miami Beach are not the geographical equivalents of those on the mainland, but they are close. For example, the 79th Street Causeway runs into 71st Street on Miami Beach.

It's easy to get lost in sprawling Miami while you're first settling in, so a reliable map is essential. The **Trakker Map of Miami** is a four-color accordion map that encompasses all of Dade County. Some maps of Miami list streets according to area, so you'll have to know which part of the city you are looking for before the street can be found. All the listings in this book include area information for this reason.

THE NEIGHBORHOODS IN BRIEF

South Beach—The Art Deco District South Beach's 10 miles of beach are alive with a frenetic, circuslike atmosphere and are center stage for a motley crew of characters, from eccentric locals, seniors, snowbirds, and college students to gender benders, celebrities, club kids, and curiosity-seekers: Individuality is as widely accepted on South Beach as Visa and MasterCard.

Bolstered by a Caribbean-chic cafe society and a sexually charged, tragically hip nightlife, people-watching on South Beach (1st St.–23rd St.) is almost as good as a front-row seat at a Milan fashion show. And although the beautiful people do flock to South Beach, the models aren't the only sights worth drooling over: The thriving Art Deco District within South Beach contains the largest concentration of Art Deco architecture in the world (in 1979, much of South Beach was listed in the National Register of Historic Places). The pastel-hued structures are supermodels in their own right—only *these* models improve with age.

Miami Beach In the fabulous '50s, Miami Beach was America's true Riviera. The stamping ground of choice for the Rat Pack and notorious mobsters such as Al Capone, its huge self-contained resort hotels were vacations unto themselves, providing a full day's worth of meals, activities, and entertainment. Then, in the 1960s and 1970s, people who fell in love with Miami began to buy apartments rather than rent hotel rooms. Tourism declined, the Rat Pack fled to Vegas, Capone disappeared, and many area hotels fell into disrepair.

However, since the late 1980s and South Beach's renaissance, Miami Beach (24th St. and up) has experienced a tide of revitalization. Huge beach hotels are finding their niche with new international tourist markets and are attracting large convention crowds. New generations of Americans are quickly rediscovering the qualities that originally made Miami Beach so popular, and they are finding out that the sand and surf now come with a thriving international city.

Surfside, Bal Harbour, and **Sunny Isles** make up the north part of the beach (island). Hotels, motels, restaurants, and beaches line Collins Avenue and, with some outstanding exceptions, the farther north one goes, the cheaper lodging becomes. All told, excellent prices, location, and facilities make Surfside and Sunny Isles attractive places to stay, although, despite a slow-going renaissance, they are still a little rough around the edges. However, a revitalization is in the works for these areas, and, while it's highly unlikely they will ever become as chic as South Beach, there is potential for this, especially as South Beach falls prey to the inevitable spoiler: commercialism. Keep in mind that beachfront properties are at a premium, so many of the area's moderately priced hotels have been converted to condominiums, leaving fewer and fewer affordable places to stay.

In exclusive and ritzy Bal Harbour, where well-paid police officers are instructed to ticket drivers who go above the 30 mph speed limit, few hotels remain amid the many beachfront condominium towers. Instead, fancy homes, tucked away on the bay, hide behind gated communities, and the Rodeo Drive of Miami (known as the Bal Harbour Shops) attracts shoppers who don't flinch at four-, five-, and six-figure price tags.

Note that **North Miami Beach,** a residential area near the Dade-Broward County line (north of 163rd St.; part of N. Dade County), is a misnomer. It is actually northwest of Miami Beach, on the mainland, and has no beaches, though it does have some of Miami's better restaurants and shops. Located within North Miami Beach is the posh residential community of **Aventura,** best known for its high-priced condos, the Turnberry Isle Resort, and the Aventura Mall.

Note: South Beach, the historic Art Deco District, is treated as a separate neighborhood from Miami Beach.

Key Biscayne Miami's forested and secluded Key Biscayne is technically one of the first islands in the Florida Keys. However, this island is nothing like its southern neighbors. Located south of Miami Beach, off the shores of Coconut Grove, Key Biscayne is protected from the troubles of the mainland by the long Rickenbacker Causeway and its $1 toll.

Largely an exclusive residential community, with million-dollar homes and sweeping water views, Key Biscayne also offers visitors great public beaches, some top (read: pricey) resort hotels, and several good restaurants. Hobie Beach, adjacent to the causeway, is the city's premier spot for windsurfing, sailboarding, and jet-skiing. On the island's southern tip, Bill Baggs State Park has great beaches, bike paths, and dense forests for picnicking and partying.

Downtown Miami's downtown boasts one of the world's most beautiful cityscapes. Unfortunately, that's about all it offers—for now. During the day, a vibrant community of students, businesspeople, and merchants makes its way through the bustling streets where vendors sell fresh-cut pineapples and mangoes while young consumers on shopping sprees lug bags and boxes. However, at night, downtown is mostly desolate (except for NE 11th St., where there is a burgeoning nightlife scene) and not a place in which you'd want to get lost. The downtown area does have a mall (Bayside Marketplace, where many cruise passengers come to browse), some culture (Metro-Dade Cultural Center), and a few decent restaurants, as well as the sprawling American Airlines Arena (home to the Miami Heat). Additionally, a downtown revitalization project is in the works, in which a cultural arts center, urban chic dwellings and lofts, and an assortment of hip boutiques, eateries, and bars are starting to bring downtown back to a life it never really had.

Design District With restaurants springing up between galleries and furniture stores galore, the Design District is, as locals say, the new South Beach, adding a touch of New York's SoHo to an area formerly known as downtown Miami's "Don't Go." The district, which is a hotbed for furniture-import companies, interior designers, architects, and more, has also become a player in Miami's ever-changing nightlife, with bars, lounges, clubs, and restaurants ranging from über-chic and retro to progressive and indie that have helped the area become hipster central for South Beach expatriates and artsy bohemian types. In anticipation of its growing popularity, the district has also banded together to create an up-to-date website, www.design miami.com, which includes a calendar of events, such as the internationally lauded Art Basel, which attracts the who's who of the art world, and is chock-full of information. The district is loosely defined as the area bounded by NE 2nd Avenue, NE 5th Avenue East and West, and NW 36th Street to the south.

Biscayne Corridor From downtown, near Bayside, to the 70s (affectionately known as the Upper East Side), where trendy curio shops and upscale restaurants are slowly opening, Biscayne Boulevard is aspiring to reclaim itself as a safe thoroughfare where tourists can wine, dine, and shop. Previously known for sketchy, dilapidated 1950s- and 1960s-era hotels that had fallen on hard times, residents fleeing the high prices of the beaches in search of affordable housing are renovating Biscayne block by block, trying to make this once-again famous boulevard worthy of a Sunday drive. With the trendy Design District immediately west of 36th and Biscayne by 2 blocks, there is hope for the area.

Little Havana If you've never been to Cuba, just visit this small section of Miami and you'll come pretty close. The sounds, tastes, and rhythms are very reminiscent of Cuba's capital city, and some even jokingly say you don't have to speak a word of English to live an independent life here—even street signs are in Spanish and English.

Cuban coffee shops, tailor and furniture stores, and inexpensive restaurants line "Calle Ocho" (pronounced *Ka*-yey *O*-choh), SW 8th Street, the region's main thoroughfare. In Little Havana, salsa and merengue beats ring loudly from old record stores while old men in *guayaberas* (loose-fitting cotton or gauzy shirts, short sleeved, used to keep cool in Cuba and now a fashion statement in Miami) smoke cigars over their daily game of dominoes. The spotlight focused on

the neighborhood during the Elian Gonzalez situation in 2000, but the area was previously noted for the groups of artists and nocturnal types who have moved their galleries and performance spaces here, sparking a culturally charged neobohemian nightlife.

Coral Gables "The City Beautiful," created by George Merrick in the early 1920s, is one of Miami's first planned developments. This is not Levittown: The houses here were built in a Mediterranean style along lush, tree-lined streets that open onto beautifully carved plazas, many with centerpiece fountains. The best architectural examples of the era have Spanish-style tiled roofs and are built from Miami oolite, native limestone commonly called "coral rock." The Gables's European-flaired shopping and commerce center is home to many thriving corporations. Coral Gables also has landmark hotels, great golfing, upscale shopping to rival Bal Harbour, and some of the city's best restaurants, headed by world-renowned chefs.

Coconut Grove An arty, hippie hangout in the psychedelic '60s, Coconut Grove has given way from swirls of tie-dyes to the uniform color schemes of the Gap. Chain stores, theme restaurants, a megaplex, and bars galore make Coconut Grove a commercial success, but this gentrification has pushed most alternative types out. Ritzier types have now resurfaced here, thanks, in part, to the anti-boho Ritz-Carlton Coconut Grove. The intersection of Grand Avenue, Main Highway, and McFarlane Road pierces the area's heart. Right in the center of it all is CocoWalk and the Shops at Mayfair, filled with boutiques, eateries, and bars. Sidewalks here are often crowded, especially at night, when University of Miami students (who frequent this adopted college town) come out to play.

Southern Miami–Dade County
To locals, South Miami is both a specific area, southwest of Coral Gables, and a general region that encompasses all of southern Dade County, including Kendall, Perrine, Cutler Ridge, and Homestead. For the purposes of clarity, this book has grouped all these southern suburbs under the rubric "Southern Miami–Dade County." Similar attributes unite the communities: They are heavily residential and packed with strip malls amid a few remaining plots of farmland. Tourists don't usually stay in these parts, unless they are on their way to the Everglades or the Keys. However, Southern Miami–Dade County contains many of the city's top attractions (see later in this chapter), meaning that you're likely to spend at least some of your time in Miami here.

2 Getting Around

Officially, Dade County has opted for a "unified, multimodal transportation network," which basically means you can get around the city by train, bus, and taxi. However, in practice, the network doesn't work very well. Things may improve when the city hopefully completes its transportation center in 2005, but until then, unless you are going from downtown Miami to a not-too-distant spot, you are better off in a rental car or taxi.

With the exception of downtown Coconut Grove and South Beach, Miami is not a walker's city. Because it is so spread out, most attractions are too far apart to make walking between them feasible. In fact, most Miamians are so used to driving that they do so even when going just a few blocks.

BY PUBLIC TRANSPORTATION

BY RAIL Two rail lines, operated by the **Metro-Dade Transit Agency** (© **305/770-3131** for information; www.co.miami-dade.fl.us/mdta), run in concert with each other.

Metrorail, the city's modern high-speed commuter train, is a 21-mile elevated line that travels north-south, between downtown Miami and the southern suburbs. Locals like to refer to this semiuseless rail system as Metro*fail.* If you are staying in Coral Gables or Coconut Grove, you can park your car at a nearby station and ride the rails downtown. However, that's about it. There are plans to extend the system to service Miami International Airport, but until those tracks are built, these trains don't go most places tourists go, with the exception of Vizcaya (p. 132) in Coconut Grove. Metrorail operates daily from about 6am to midnight. The fare is $1.25.

Metromover, a 4½-mile elevated line, circles the downtown area and connects with Metrorail at the Government Center stop. This is a good way to get to Bayside (a waterfront marketplace) if you don't have a car. Riding on rubber tires, the single-car train winds past many of the area's most important attractions and its shopping and business districts. You may not go very far on the Metromover, but you will get a beautiful perspective from the towering height of the suspended rails. System hours are daily from about 6am to midnight, and the ride is free.

Additionally, the city of Coral Gables now offers the **Coral Gables Trolley** (www.coralgables.com/r1_trolley.htm), a free service running Monday through

Friday on three different shifts around the city's most popular shopping and sightseeing routes.

BY BUS   Miami's suburban layout is not conducive to getting around by bus. Lines operate and maps are available, but instead of getting to know the city, you'll find that relying on bus transportation will acquaint you only with how it feels to wait at bus stops. In short, a bus ride in Miami is grueling. You can get a bus map by mail, either from the Greater Miami Convention and Visitor's Bureau (see "Visitor Information," earlier in this chapter) or by writing the Metro-Dade Transit System, 3300 NW 32nd Ave., Miami, FL 33142. In Miami, call © **305/770-3131** for public-transit information. The fare is $1.25.

BY CAR

Tales circulate about vacationers who have visited Miami without a car, but they are very few indeed. If you are counting on exploring the city, even to a modest degree, a car is essential. Miami's restaurants, hotels, and attractions are far from one another, so any other form of transportation is relatively impractical. You won't need a car, however, if you are spending your entire vacation at a resort, are traveling directly to the Port of Miami for a cruise, or are here for a short stay centered in one area of the city, such as South Beach, where everything is within walking distance and parking is a costly nightmare.

When driving across a causeway or through downtown, allow extra time to reach your destination because of frequent drawbridge openings. Some bridges open about every half-hour for large sailing vessels to make their way through the wide bays and canals that crisscross the city, stalling traffic for several minutes.

RENTALS   It seems as though every car-rental company, big and small, has at least one office in Miami. Consequently, the city is one of the cheapest places in the world to rent a car. Many firms regularly advertise prices in the neighborhood of $140 per week for their economy cars. You should also check with the airline you have chosen to get to Miami: There are often special discounts when you book a flight and reserve your rental car simultaneously. A minimum age, generally 25, is usually required of renters, while some rental agencies have also set maximum ages!

National car-rental companies, with toll-free numbers, include **Alamo** (© 800/327-9633; www.goalamo.com), **Avis** (© 800/331-1212; www.avis.com), **Budget** (© 800/527-0700; www.budget.com), **Dollar** (© 800/800-4000 or 800/327-7607; www.dollar.com), **Hertz** (© 800/654-3131; www.hertz.com), **National** (© 800/328-4567; www.nationalcar.com), and **Thrifty** (© 800/367-2277; www.thrifty.com). One excellent company that has offices in every conceivable part of town and offers extremely competitive rates is **Enterprise** (© 800/325-8007; www.enterprise.com). Call around and comparison-shop before you make any decisions—car-rental prices can fluctuate more than airfares.

Many car-rental companies also offer cellular phones or electronic map rentals. It might be wise to opt for these additional safety features (the phone will definitely come in handy if you get lost), although the cost can be exorbitant.

Finally, think about splurging on a convertible (at most companies, the price for convertibles is approximately 20% more). Not only are convertibles one of the best ways to see the beautiful surroundings, but they're also an ideal way to perfect a tan!

PARKING   Always keep plenty of quarters on hand to feed hungry meters. Or, on Miami Beach, stop by the chamber of commerce at 1920 Meridian Ave. or any Publix grocery store to buy a magnetic **parking card** in denominations of $10, $20, or $25. Parking is usually plentiful (except on South Beach and Coconut Grove), but when it's not, be careful: Fines for illegal parking can be stiff, starting at $18 for an expired meter and going way up from there.

In addition to parking garages, valet services are commonplace and often used. Because parking is such a premium in bustling South Beach as well as in Coconut Grove, prices tend to be jacked up—especially at night and when there are special events (day or night). You can expect to pay an average of $5 to $15 for parking in these areas.

BY TAXI

If you're not planning on traveling much within the city (and especially if you plan on spending your vacation within the confines of South Beach's Art Deco District), an occasional taxi is a good alternative to renting a car and the parking hassles that come with renting your own car. Taxi meters start at $1.70 for the first quarter-mile and cost $2.20 for each additional mile. There are standard flat-rate charges for frequently traveled routes—for example, Miami Beach's Convention Center to Coconut Grove will cost about $16.

Major cab companies include **Yellow Cab** (© **305/444-4444**) and, on Miami Beach, **Central** (© **305/532-5555**).

BY BIKE

Miami is a biker's paradise, especially on Miami Beach, where the hard-packed sand and boardwalks make it an easy and scenic route. However, unless you are a former New York City bike messenger, you won't want to use a bicycle as your main means of transportation.

For more information on bicycles, including where to rent the best ones, see "Affordable Outdoor Pursuits," later in this chapter.

FAST FACTS: Miami

Business Hours   Banking hours vary, but most banks are open weekdays from 9am to 3pm. Several stay open until 5pm or so at least 1 day during the week, and most banks feature automated teller machines (ATMs) for 24-hour banking. Most stores are open daily from 10am to 6pm; however, there are many exceptions (noted in "Shopping A to Z," beginning on p. 148). As far as business offices are concerned, Miami is generally a nine-to-five town.

Dentists   **A&E Dental Associates,** 11400 N. Kendall Dr., Mega Bank Building (© 305/271-7777), offers round-the-clock care and accepts MasterCard and Visa.

Doctors   In an emergency, call an ambulance by dialing © **911** (a free call) from any phone. The Dade County Medical Association sponsors a **Physician Referral Service** (© 305/324-8717), weekdays from 9am to 5pm. **Health South Doctors' Hospital,** 5000 University Dr., Coral Gables (© 305/666-2111), is a 285-bed acute-care hospital with a 24-hour physician-staffed emergency department.

Drugstores See "Pharmacies," below.

Emergencies To reach the police, ambulance, or fire department, dial ℂ **911** from any phone. No coins are needed. Emergency hot lines include **Crisis Intervention** (ℂ **305/358-HELP** or 305/358-4357) and the **Poison Information Center** (ℂ **800/222-1222**).

Eyeglasses **Pearle Vision Center**, 7901 Biscayne Blvd. (ℂ **305/754-5144**), can usually fill prescriptions in about an hour.

Hospitals See "Doctors," above.

Internet Access Internet access is available at **Kafka's Cyber Cafe**, 1464 Washington Ave., South Beach (ℂ **305/673-9669**), the **South Beach Internet Cafe**, 1106 Collins Ave. (ℂ **305/532-4331**), and, no joke, the swanky all-in-one **Mobil Station**, at 2500 NW 87th Ave., Doral (ℂ **305/477-2501**).

Laundry/Dry Cleaning For dry cleaning, self-service machines, and a wash-and-fold service by the pound, call **All Laundry Service**, 5701 NW 7th St. (ℂ **305/261-8175**); it's open daily from 7am to 10pm. **Clean Machine Laundry**, 226 12th St., South Beach (ℂ **305/534-9429**), is convenient to South Beach's Art Deco hotels and is open 24 hours a day. **Coral Gables Laundry & Dry Cleaning**, 250 Minorca Ave., Coral Gables (ℂ **305/446-6458**), has been dry cleaning, altering, and laundering since 1930. It offers a lifesaving same-day service and is open weekdays from 7am to 7pm and Saturday from 8am to 3pm.

Lost Property If you lost something at the airport, call the **Airport Lost and Found** office (ℂ **305/876-7377**). If you lost something on the bus, Metrorail, or Metromover, call **Metro-Dade Transit Agency** (ℂ **305/770-3131**). If you lost something anywhere else, phone the **Dade County Police Lost and Found** (ℂ **305/375-3366**). You may also want to fill out a police report for insurance purposes.

Pharmacies **Walgreens Pharmacy** has dozens of locations all over town, including 8550 Coral Way (ℂ **305/221-9271**), in Coral Gables; 1845 Alton Rd. (ℂ **305/531-8868**), in South Beach; and 6700 Collins Ave. (ℂ **305/861-6742**), in Miami Beach. The branch at 5731 Bird Rd. at SW 40th Street (ℂ **305/666-0757**) is open 24 hours, as is **Eckerd Drugs**, 6460 S. Dixie Hwy., in South Miami (ℂ **305/661-0778**).

Police For emergencies, dial ℂ **911** from any phone. No coins are needed for this call. For other police matters, call ℂ **305/595-6263**.

Post Office The **Main Post Office**, 2200 Milam Dairy Rd., Miami, FL 33152 (ℂ **800/275-8777**), is located west of the Miami International Airport. Conveniently located post offices include 1300 Washington Ave. in South Beach and 3191 Grand Ave. in Coconut Grove. There is one central number for all post offices: ℂ **800/275-8777**.

Safety As always, use your common sense and be aware of your surroundings at all times. Don't walk alone at night, and be extra wary when walking or driving though downtown Miami and surrounding areas.

Reacting to several highly publicized crimes against tourists several years ago, both local and state governments have taken steps to help protect visitors. These measures include special highly visible police units patrolling the airport and surrounding neighborhoods and better signs on the state's most tourist-traveled routes.

Taxes A 6% state sales tax (plus 0.5% local tax, for a total of 6.5% in Miami–Dade County [from Homestead to North Miami Beach]) is added on at the register for all goods and services purchased in Florida. In addition, most municipalities levy special taxes on restaurants and hotels. In Surfside, hotel taxes total 10.5%; in Bal Harbour, 9.5%; in Miami Beach (including South Beach), 11.5%; and in the rest of Dade County, a whopping 12.5%. In Miami Beach, Surfside, and Bal Harbour, the resort (hotel) tax also applies to hotel restaurants and restaurants with liquor licenses.

Weather Hurricane season in Miami runs August through November. For an up-to-date recording of current weather conditions and forecast reports, call ✆ 305/229-4522. Also see the "When to Go" section in chapter 2 for more information on the weather.

3 Accommodations You Can Afford

While Miami is notorious for pricey hotels, with a little help you can still find a decent room at a fair cost. In the Art Deco District, for instance, many hotels are actually less Ritz-Carlton than they are Holiday Inn (unless, of course, they've been renovated). Many of these hotels were built in the 1930s for the middle class and are a wise choice for those who don't plan to spend much time in their room. Smart vacationers can almost name their price if they're willing to live without a few luxuries, such as an oceanfront view.

Below are our suggestions for some of the best values within Miami. If you happen to arrive without a reservation and run into trouble, check out South Beach's Collins Avenue, where there are also dozens of hotels and motels to choose from. If you do try the walk-in routine, don't forget to ask to see a room first. A few dollars extra could mean all the difference between flea and fabu.

Whenever booking your room, always ask how close your room will be to the center of the nightlife crowd; trying to sleep directly on Ocean Drive or Collins and Washington avenues, especially during the weekend, is next to impossible, unless your lullaby of choice happens to include throbbing salsa and bass beats.

While South Beach may be the nucleus of all things hyped and hip, it's not the only place with cool and swanky hotels. The advantage to staying on South Beach as opposed to, say, Coral Gables or Coconut Grove, is that the beaches are within walking distance, the nightlife and restaurant options are aplenty, and, basically, everything you would need is right there. However, staying there is definitely not for everyone. If you're wary, don't worry: South Beach is centrally located and only about a 15- to 30-minute drive from most other parts of Miami.

For a less expensive stay that's only a 10-minute cab ride from South Beach, Miami Beach proper (the area north of 23rd St. and Collins Ave. all the way up to 163rd St. and Collins Ave.) offers a slew of reasonable stays, right on the beach, that won't cost you your kids' college education fund.

SEASONS & RATES   South Florida's tourist season is well defined, beginning in mid-November and lasting until Easter. Hotel prices escalate until about March, after which they begin to decline. During the off season, hotel rates are typically 30% to 50% lower than their winter highs.

South Beach

WHERE TO STAY ■
Abbey Hotel **6**
Aqua **23**
Clay Hotel &
   International Hostel **25**
The Creek **2**
Crest Hotel Suites **14**
The Lily Leon Hotel **35**
The Loft Hotel **34**
Townhouse **10**
Villa Paradiso **26**
Whitelaw Hotel **36**

WHERE TO DINE ◆
A La Folie **24**
Big Pink **41**
Cafeteria **20**
Casa Tua **13**
David's Café **18**
El Rancho Grande **22**
Escopazzo **28**
Grillfish **26**
Jerry's Famous Deli **26**
Joe Allen **11**
Joe's Stone Crab
   Restaurant **43**
La Sandwicherie **27**
Lincoln Road Café **16**
Macaluso's **12**
Mama Vieja **1**
Mark's South Beach **30**
Metro Kitchen + Bar **32**
News Café **37**
Nobu **9**
Piola **21**
Prime 112 **42**
Puerto Sagua **38**
San Loco Tacos **27**
Sport Café **39**
Van Dyke Cafe **17**

ATTRACTIONS ●
Art Deco Welcome
   Center **33**
Bass Museum of Art **5**
Collins Park **4**
Colony Theater **15**
Fritz's Skate Shop **19**
Holocaust Memorial **7**
Miami Beach Bicycle
   Center **40**
Miami Beach
   Botanical Garden **8**
Miami Beach public courts
   at Flamingo Park **29**
Miami Beach Regional
   Library **3**
Wolfsonian-Florida
   International University **31**

To Central Miami Beach ↗

The Bass Museum of Art

COLLINS PARK

22nd St.

Park Ave.
20th St.
19th St.
18th St.

Dade Boulevard

Miami Beach Convention Center

Jackie Gleason Theater of Performing Arts

17th St.

James Ave.

Collins Ave.

Lincoln Road Mall
Lincoln Rd.

16th St.

Drexel Ave.

15th St.

Española Way

14th St.
Miami Beach Post Office
13th St.
12th St.
11th St.

Alton Rd.

Lenox Ave.
Michigan Ave.
Jefferson Ave.
Meridian Ave.
Euclid Ave.

FLAMINGO PARK

Pennsylvania Ave.

Washington Ave.

Ocean Dr.

Beach Patrol Station

Art Deco Welcome Center

10th St.
9th St.
8th St.
7th St.
6th St.
5th St.
4th St.
3rd St.
2nd St.
1st St.

LUMMUS PARK

Lummus Park Beach

ATLANTIC OCEAN

Commerce St.

Biscayne St.

Government Cut

SOUTH POINTE PARK

0   1/4 mi
0   0.25 km

N

But timing isn't everything. In many cases, rates also depend on your hotel's proximity to the beach and how much ocean you can see from your window. Small motels a block or two from the water can be up to 40% cheaper than similar properties right on the sand.

Rates below have been broken down into two broad categories: winter (generally, Thanksgiving–Easter) and off season (about mid-May to Aug). The months in between, the shoulder seasons, should fall somewhere in between the highs and lows, while rates always go up on holidays. Remember, too, that state and city taxes can add as much as 12.5% to your bill in some parts of Miami, and don't forget that parking is a pricey endeavor. Some hotels, especially those in South Beach, also tack on additional service charges.

LONG-TERM STAYS   If you plan to visit Miami for a month, a season, or more, think about renting a condominium apartment or a room in a long-term hotel. Long-term accommodations exist in every price category, from budget to deluxe, and in general are extremely reasonable, especially during the off season. Check with the reservation services below, or write a short note to the chamber of commerce in the area where you plan to stay. In addition, many local real estate agents also handle short-term rentals (meaning less than a year).

RESERVATION SERVICES   **Central Reservation Service** (© **800/950-0232** or 305/274-6832; www.reservation-services.com) works with many of Miami's hotels and can often secure discounts of up to 40%. It also gives advice on specific locales, especially in Miami Beach and downtown. During holiday time, there may be a minimum of a 3- to 5-day stay to use their services. Call for more information.

For bed-and-breakfast information throughout the state, contact **Florida Bed and Breakfast Inns** (© **800/524-1880;** www.florida-inns.com).

SOUTH BEACH

Choosing a hotel on South Beach is similar to deciding whether you'd rather pay $1.50 for french fries at Denny's or $8.50 for the same fries—but let's call them *pomme frites*—in a pricey haute cuisinerie. It's all about atmosphere. The rooms of some hotels may *look* ultrachic, but they can be as comfortable as sleeping on a concrete slab. Many Art Deco hotels, while pleasing to the eye, may be a bit run-down inside. Par for the course on South Beach, appearances are at times deceiving. Fortunately, for every chichi hotel in South Beach—and there are many—there are just as many moderately priced, more casual options.

Not so long ago, Courtyard by Marriott (© **800/321-2211** or 305/604-8887) debuted a 90-room, moderately priced hotel on a seedy stretch of Washington Avenue, smack in the middle of Clubland, a horror to many a South Beach trendoid.

For a map of the hotels in this section, see the "South Beach" map on p. 87.

Aqua ✯ *Value*   It's been described as the Jetsons meets Jaws, but the Aqua isn't all Hollywood. Animated, yes, but with little emphasis on special effects and more on a friendly staff, Aqua is a good catch for those looking to stay in style without compromising their budget. Rooms are ultramodern in an Ikea sort of way; in other words, cheap chic. There are apartment-like junior suites, suites, and a really fabulous penthouse, but the standard deluxe rooms aren't too shabby either, with decent-size bathrooms and high-tech amenities. It's a favorite amongst Europeans and young hipsters on a budget. This '50s-style motel has definitely been spruced up and its sun deck, courtyard garden, and small pool are popular hangouts for those who prefer to stay off the nearby sand. A small yet sleek lounge inside is a good place for a quick cocktail, breakfast, or a snack.

1530 Collins Ave., Miami Beach, FL 33139. ℂ **305/538-4361.** Fax 305/673-8109. www.aquamiami.com. 45 units. Winter $160 double, $200–$400 suite; off season $95 double, $125–$395 suite. Rates include European-style breakfast buffet. AE, DISC, MC, V. Valet parking $18. **Amenities:** Lounge; bar; small pool. *In room:* A/C, TV, minibar, CD player, Web TV.

The Loft Hotel   A boutique hotel along the lines of the Aqua hotel (above), though less whimsical, enticing, and airy-feeling, this renovated apartment building (which really gives you the feeling of staying in an apartment rather than a hotel) offers 20 suites, all surrounding a tidy, tropically landscaped garden. Rooms are especially spacious, with queen-size beds, breakfast room, conversation area, and hardwood or tile floors. Bathrooms are brand new and, for an old Art Deco building, pretty spacious. This hotel is popular with young, hip European types, just as the Aqua hotel is, but there isn't that much difference between the two hotels other than the fact that the Loft's rooms have fully equipped kitchens while Aqua's rooms don't, and Aqua has a bar/restaurant while the Loft does not. Prices at the Loft are very reasonable and the owners, who hail from Villa Paradiso, are extremely accommodating.

952 Collins Ave., Miami Beach, FL 33139. ℂ **305/534-2244.** Fax 305/538-1509. www.thelofthotel.com. 57 units. Winter $139–$179 double; off season $89–$129 double. AE, DC, MC, V. Valet parking $20. **Amenities:** On-site laundry; VIP passes to local nightclubs. *In room:* A/C, TV/VCR, kitchen, hair dryer.

Villa Paradiso ★★ *Finds*   This guesthouse, like Brigham Gardens, is more like a cozy apartment house than a hotel. There's no elegant lobby or restaurant, but the amicable hosts, Lisa and Pascal Nicolle, are happy to give you a room key and advice on what to do. The recently renovated spacious apartments are simple but elegant—hardwood floors, French doors, and stylish wrought-iron furniture—and are remarkably quiet considering their location, a few blocks from Lincoln Road and all of South Beach's best clubs. All have full kitchens, and guests have a choice of either a queen or two double beds or foldout couches for extra friends. Bathrooms have recently been renovated with marble tile. All rooms overlook the hotel's pretty courtyard garden.

1415 Collins Ave., Miami Beach, FL 33139. ℂ **305/532-0616.** Fax 305/673-5874. www.villaparadiso hotel.com. 17 units. Winter $100–$165 apartment; off season $75–$129 apartment. Weekly rates are 10% cheaper. Additional person $10. AE, DC, MC, V. Parking nearby $15. Pets (including small "nonbarking" dogs) accepted for $10 with a $100 deposit. **Amenities:** Coin-op washers and dryers. *In room:* A/C, TV, kitchen, fridge, coffeemaker.

SUPER-CHEAP SLEEPS

Clay Hotel & International Hostel ★ *Value*   A member of the International Youth Hostel Federation (IYHF), the Clay occupies a beautiful 1920s-style Spanish Mediterranean building at the corner of historic Española Way. Like other IYHF members, this hostel is open to all ages and is a great place to meet people. The usual smattering of Australians, Europeans, and other budget travelers makes it Miami's best clearinghouse of "insider" travel information. Even if you don't stay here, you might want to check out the ride board or mingle with fellow travelers over a beer at the sidewalk cafe.

Although a thorough renovation in 1996 made this hostel an incredible value and a step above any others in town, don't expect nightly turndown service or chocolates. But, for a hostel, it's full of extras. Ninety rooms have private baths and 12 VIP rooms have balconies overlooking quaint Española Way. There are also male and female dorm rooms with four to six beds and private bathrooms.

You will find occasional movie nights, an outdoor weekend market, and a tour desk with car rental available. Reservations for private rooms are essential in season and recommended year-round. Don't bother with a car in this congested area.

1438 Washington Ave. (at Española Way), South Beach, FL 33139. © 800/379-2529 or 305/534-2988. Fax 305/673-0346. www.clayhotel.com. 120 units. $42–$88 double; $16–$20 dorm beds. During the off season, pay for 6 nights in advance and get 7th night free. MC, V. Parking $10. **Amenities:** Cafe; access to nearby health club; bike rental; concierge; computer center; coin-op washers and dryers; lockers; kitchen. *In room:* A/C, TV, dataport, fridge, hair dryer.

The Creek   This funky and arty hostel-like hotel, formerly known as the Banana Bungalow, is cheap, campy, and quintessentially Miami Beach. Popular with the MTV set, The Creek is a redone (to the tune of $1 million that provoked the hotel to challenge other renovations, saying, "Bob Villa is a wuss.") 1950s two-story motel where it's always Spring Break. The hotel's clever website humanizes the hotel, saying it "thinks it's in an episode of Playboy's Penthouse," but also calls it a Jetsonian space-age hotel. The Creek is one of those that you have to see to fully appreciate, but in the wise words of the hotel itself, "Why does style and cool and fun have to cost you $400 a night? The Creek is a laid back, kick your feet up on the table, hunker down for a cold beverage, relax in the sun, chow down on a burger type place."

The lobby is a retro fabulous homage to the '50s. Contradictions at the Creek abound, which makes the place all the more amusing and ironic. The hotel surrounds an 8,000-square-foot pool deck complete with underwater music, top-of-the-line DJ equipment, and a fully stocked, 40-foot open air bar where everyone hangs out. Oh, and you'll also find a Ms. Pac Man video game, a theater with movies available for viewing at the front desk, a guest kitchen, and a dining room.

There are three types of rooms here: The Waterway Standard, no frills rooms that face a narrow canal where motorboats and kayaks are available for a small charge; the noisier Cabana Room, which opens to the pool deck (which boasts a serious sound system that the hotel turns off around midnight); and the Signature Rooms, 18 "altered living spaces" designed by artists and on the second floor facing the pool deck. I highly recommend the Signature Rooms in terms of decor and privacy, something you won't have if you face out onto the buzzing pool deck. There also happen to be 25 shared rooms with four to six bunk beds for backpackers on a serious budget.

2360 Collins Ave., Miami Beach, FL 33139. © 866/445-4800 or 305/538-1951. Fax 305/531-3217. www. thecreeksouthbeach.com. 85 units. Winter $20 per person in shared units, $79–$139 double; off season $18 per person in shared units, $50–$60 double. MC, V. Parking $5. **Amenities:** Cafe; bar; large pool; access to nearby health club; game room; coin-op laundry; Internet access; theater. *In room:* A/C, TV, fridge.

WORTH A SPLURGE

Abbey Hotel ⭐⭐ *Finds*   This charming, off-the-beaten-path '40s-revival boutique hotel is possibly the best deal on the entire beach. A haven for artists looking for quiet inspiration, the Abbey has recently undergone a $2.5 million renovation that restored its original Deco glory. Rooms are furnished with oversize earth-toned chairs and chrome beds that are surprisingly comfortable. Soft white-covered chairs and candles grace the lobby, which doubles as a chic Mediterranean-style restaurant (earning an "exceptional" from the *Miami Herald*), the Abbey Dining Room. It's extremely quiet at this hotel, as it is located in the midst of a sleepy residential neighborhood, but it's only 1 block from the beach and within walking distance of the Jackie Gleason Theater, the Convention Center, the Bass Museum of Art, and the Miami City Ballet.

300 21st St., Miami Beach, FL 33139. © **888/61-ABBEY** or 305/531-0031. Fax 305/672-1663. www.abbey hotel.com. 50 units. Winter $155–$225 double, $225 studio; off season $99–$130 double, $130 studio. AE, DC, DISC, MC, V. Off-site parking $17. Pets accepted for $25 for the 1st 3 days and $5 for each additional day. **Amenities:** Restaurant; bar; exercise room; concierge; business services; room service; laundry and dry cleaning service. *In room:* A/C, TV/VCR, dataport, hair dryer, iron; safe and stereo w/CD player in studios only.

Crest Hotel Suites ★ *Finds*   One of South Beach's best-kept secrets, the Crest Hotel is located next to the pricier, trendier Albion Hotel (and around the corner from Lincoln Road, in the heart of the Art Deco District) and features a quietly fashionable, contemporary, relaxed atmosphere with fantastic service. Built in 1939, the Crest was restored to preserve its Art Deco architecture, but the interior of the hotel is thoroughly modern, with rooms resembling cosmopolitan apartments. All suites have a living room/dining room area, kitchenette, and executive work space. An indoor/outdoor cafe with terrace and poolside dining isn't besieged with trendy locals, but does attract a younger crowd.

1670 James Ave., Miami Beach, FL 33139. © **800/531-3880** or 305/531-0321. Fax 305/531-8180. www. cresthotel.com. 64 units. Winter $155 double, $235 suite; off season $115 double, $175 suite. Packages available and 10% discount offered if booked on website. AE, MC, V. **Amenities:** Restaurant; cafe; pool; laundry and dry cleaning service. *In room:* A/C, TV, dataport, kitchenette, fridge, coffeemaker (select units).

The Lily Leon Hotel ★ *Finds*   A great hotel with little attitude, which recently merged with the neighboring Lily Guesthouse, the Lily Leon Hotel (formerly known as the Hotel Leon) is like a reasonably priced high-fashion garment found hidden on a rack full of overpriced threads. This charismatic sliver of a property has won the loyalty of fashion industrialists and romantics alike. Built in 1929 and restored in 1996, the hotel still retains many original details such as facades, woodwork, and even fireplaces (every room has one, not that you'll need to use it). The very central location (1 block from the ocean) is a plus, especially since the Leon lacks a pool. Most of the spacious and stylish rooms are immaculate and reminiscent of a loft apartment; spacious bathrooms with large, deep tubs are especially enticing.

Wood floors and simple, pale furnishings are appreciated in a neighborhood where many others overdo the Art Deco motif. However, some rooms are dark and have not seen such upgrades (we have gotten complaints) and are to be avoided; do not hesitate to ask to change rooms. Service is warm, friendly, and accommodating. We've also gotten complaints about the music coming from the hotel next door, but you have to realize that if you're staying on Collins or Washington avenues, you're going to hear noise: South Beach isn't known for its quiet, peaceful demeanor! The lobby has an informal bar and restaurant, not to mention a large communal table at which guests—production crews, fashion photographers, Europeans, and young hipsters—tend to mix and mingle. Because its entrance is not directly on pedestrian-heavy Collins Avenue, the Hotel Leon remains one of South Beach's most understated, yet coolest, stays.

841 Collins Ave., South Beach, FL 33139. © **305/673-3767.** Fax 305/673-5866. www.lilyguesthouse.com. 18 units. Winter $145–$245 suite, $395 penthouse; off season $100–$195 suite, $335 penthouse. Additional person $10. AE, DC, MC, V. Valet parking $18. "Well-behaved" pets accepted for $10 per night. **Amenities:** Restaurant and lobby bar; reduced rates at local gym; concierge; business services; room service (breakfast). *In room:* A/C, TV, minibar, hair dryer, safe, CD player.

Townhouse ★★   New York hipster Jonathan Morr felt that Miami Beach had lost touch with the bons vivants who gave the city its original cachet, so he decided to take matters into his own hands. His solution: this 72-room, five-story hotel in which standard rooms started at just $99 during its opening in the fall of 2000. The $99 rate proved too good to be true, but even the revised starting rates of $175 during season and $130 off season are still a great deal. The charm of this hotel is found in its clean and simple yet chic design with quirky details: exercise equipment that stands alone in the hallways, free laundry machines in the lobby, and a water bed–lined rooftop. Comfortable, shabby chic rooms boast L-shaped couches for extra guests (for whom you aren't charged). Though the rooms are all pretty much the same, consider the ones with the partial ocean view. The hotel's basement features the hot New York import, Bond St. Lounge.

150 20th St., South Beach, FL 33139. © **877/534-3800** or 305/534-3800. Fax 305/534-3811. www.town househotel.com. 72 units. Winter $175–$225 double, $450 penthouse; off season $130–$155 double, $395 penthouse. Rates include Parisian-style (coffee and pastry) breakfast. AE, MC, V. Valet parking $18. **Amenities:** Restaurant; bar; workout stations; bike rental; free laundry; rooftop terrace with water beds. *In room:* A/C, TV/VCR, dataport, fridge, hair dryer, safe, CD player.

Whitelaw Hotel 🌜 With a slogan that reads "clean sheets, hot water, and stiff drinks," the Whitelaw Hotel stands apart from the other boutique hotels with a fierce sense of humor, but never compromises on its fabulous amenities. Only half a block from Ocean Drive, this hotel, like its clientele, is full of distinct personalities, pairing such disparate elements as luxurious Belgian sheets with shag carpeting to create a completely innovative setting. All-white rooms manage to be homey and plush and not at all antiseptic. Bathrooms are large and well stocked with just about everything you may have forgotten at home. Complimentary cocktails in the lobby every night from 7 to 8pm contribute to a very social atmosphere.

808 Collins Ave., Miami Beach, FL 33139. © **305/398-7000.** Fax 305/398-7010. www.whitelawhotel.com. 49 units. Winter $165–$190 double, $210 minisuite; off season $125–$145 double, $145–$160 minisuite. Rates include complimentary continental breakfast and free cocktails in the lobby (7–8pm daily). AE, DC, MC, V. Parking $18. **Amenities:** Lounge; concierge; business services; laundry service; free airport pickup (to and from MIA); complimentary passes to area nightclubs. *In room:* A/C, TV, dataport, minibar, hair dryer, safe, CD player.

MIAMI BEACH: SURFSIDE, BAL HARBOUR & SUNNY ISLES

The area just north of South Beach, known as Miami Beach, encompasses Surfside, Bal Harbour, and Sunny Isles. Unrestricted by zoning codes throughout the 1950s, 1960s, and especially the 1970s, area developers went crazy, building ever-bigger and more brazen structures, especially north of 41st Street, which is now known as "Condo Canyon." Consequently, there's now a glut of medium-quality condos, with a few scattered holdouts of older hotels and motels casting shadows over the beach by afternoon. In April of 2003, Donald Trump unveiled his Trump International Sonesta Beach Resort (© **800/SONESTA**), a 390-room Sunny Isles monstrosity done up in the typically bombastic Trump style, setting a glitzier standard for its much less glamorous neighbors (though it's totally devoid of personality or style).

For a map of the hotels in this section, see the "Where to Stay & Dine in Miami Beach, Surfside, Bal Harbour, Sunny Isles & North Beach" map on p. 93.

Indian Creek Hotel ★★ *Finds* Located off the beaten path, the Indian Creek Hotel is a meticulously restored 1936 building featuring one of the beach's first operating elevators. It's also the most charming hotel in the area. Besides that, the service is impeccable. Because of its location facing the Indian Creek

Where to Stay & Dine in Miami Beach, Surfside, Bal Harbour, Sunny Isles & North Beach

ACCOMMODATIONS ■

Beach House Bal Harbour **3**

Circa39 Hotel **10**

Days Inn Oceanside **9**

Fontainebleau Hilton **7**

Indian Creek Hotel **11**

DINING ◆

Cafe Prima Pasta **4**

Crystal Cafe **8**

Lagoon **1**

Oggi Caffe **6**

Ouzo's Greek Taverna and Bar **5**

Sheldon's Drugs **2**

Timo **1**

Wolfie Cohen's Rascal House **1**

waterway and its lush landscaping, this place feels more like an old-fashioned Key West bed-and-breakfast than your typical Miami Beach Art Deco hotel. The rooms are outfitted in Art Deco furnishings, such as an antique writing desk, pretty tropical prints, and small but spotless bathrooms. All the rooms have been completely renovated. Just 1 short block from a good stretch of sand, the hotel is also within walking distance of shops and restaurants and has a landscaped pool area that is a great place to lounge in the sun. If you're looking for charm, friendly service, and peace and quiet, stay away from the South Beach hype and come here instead.

2727 Indian Creek Dr. (1 block west of Collins Ave. and the ocean), Miami Beach, FL 33140. *©* 800/491-2772 or 305/531-2727. Fax 305/531-5651. www.indiancreekhotel.com. 61 units. Winter $150–$240 double; off season $90–$150 double. Additional person $25. Group packages and summer specials available. AE, DC, DISC, MC, V. **Amenities:** Restaurant; bar; pool; concierge; car-rental desk; limited room service; laundry and dry cleaning service. *In room:* A/C, TV/VCR, dataport, fridge (in suites), hair dryer, CD player.

SUPER-CHEAP SLEEPS

Days Inn Oceanside *Value*   One of the most economical choices for travelers, this hotel has been refurbished in splashy pastels and bright lavenders. It's clean and cheap, and children under 17 stay free. A kosher Chinese restaurant is on the premises.

4299 Collins Ave., Miami Beach, FL 33140. *©* 800/356-3017 or 305/673-1513. Fax 305/538-0727. 143 units. Winter $99–$119 double; off season $79–$99 double. AE, MC, V. Valet parking $13. Pets accepted. **Amenities:** 2 restaurants; lounge; pool; access to nearby watersports; concierge; room service; laundry service; dry cleaning. *In room:* A/C, TV, dataport, fridge on request, coffeemakers in some rooms, iron, safe.

WORTH A SPLURGE

Beach House Bal Harbour ★★ *Finds*   The Beach House Bal Harbour is the closest thing the city has to a summer beach home—comfortable, unpretentious, and luxurious, yet decidedly low-key. In place of an elaborate hotel lobby, the public spaces of the Rubell-owned Beach House are divided into a series of intimate homey environments, from the wicker-furnished screened-in porch to the Asian-inspired Bamboo Room, with overstuffed Ralph Lauren leather couches and Japanese bric-a-brac. The 24-hour Pantry, inspired by Long Island's Sagaponack General Store, is packed with all the needs of the hotel's "unplugged" urban clientele. The ultraspacious rooms (those ending in 04 are the most spacious) are literally brimming with the comforts of home. The 200-foot private beach, hammock grove, and topiary garden are so lush, they're said to have caused several New York hipsters to renege on their summer shares in the Hamptons in favor of this Beach House.

9449 Collins Ave., Surfside, FL 33154. *©* 877/RUBELLS or 305/535-8606. Fax 305/535-8602. www.rubell hotels.com. 170 units. Winter $215–$315 double, $245–$305 junior suite; off season $180–$210 double, $230–$270 junior suite; year-round $350 1-bedroom suite. AE, DC, DISC, MC, V. Valet parking $15. **Amenities:** Restaurant; pantry; bar (until 11pm); heated pool; health club; spa; watersports equipment; children's playground; business center. *In room:* A/C, TV, dataport, fridge, hair dryer, iron, stereo/CD player, wireless TV Web access.

Circa39 Hotel ★   Some folks like to get away, take a holiday from the neighborhood, which is why Circa39 had the wisdom to open up where it did—close enough to the South Beach action for those who want to play, but far enough away to actually get some sleep when you want it. The 86-room boutique (what else?) hotel known as the Copley Plaza circa 1939, hence the name, has been redone and spruced up with modern amenities such as high-speed Internet access, the requisite bistro conducive to attracting hipsters, pool deck, tropical garden with massage cabanas, and fitness center. If you're looking to stay in a hip hotel but don't want to deal with the hubbub of being smack in the middle of things, this is a great option. Otherwise, consider staying in one of the countless boutiques on South Beach, where you'll get a lot more scene for your buck.

3900 Collins Ave., South Beach, FL 33139. ⓒ 877/824-7223 or 305/538-4900. Fax 305/538-4998. www. circa39.com. 86 units. Winter $169–$229 double; off season $109–$169 double. Additional person $15. AE, DISC, MC, V. Valet parking $18. **Amenities:** Bistro; bar; concierge; fitness center; laundry service; dry cleaning. In room: A/C, TV, minibar, fridge, coffeemaker, hair dryer, iron, safe, CD player, high-speed Internet access.

Fontainebleau Hilton ★★ *Overrated* *Kids*   In many ways, this is the quintessential Miami Beach hotel. Designed by the late and legendary Morris Lapidus, who oversaw an expansion in 2000, this grand monolith symbolizes Miami decadence. Since its opening in 1954, the Fontainebleau has hosted presidents, pageants, and movie productions, including the James Bond thriller *Goldfinger*. This is where all the greats, including Sinatra and his pals, performed in their prime, and to pay homage to the Rat Pack, the hotel has redone its lobby bar to reflect the era of swagger, attitude, raffish cool, and panache, featuring large, bordering on tacky but still swell silhouettes of Frank, Sammy, Dino, Joey, and Peter, and the live music of The Pack, a really good Rat Pack cover band. Club Tropigala is reminiscent of Ricky Ricardo's Tropicana and features a Las Vegas–style floor show with dozens of performers and two orchestras. Rooms are luxurious and decorated in various styles from 1950s to ultramodern; bathrooms are done up in Italian marble a la Caesar's Palace. In 2001, the hotel underwent a $10 million food and beverage renovation, introducing the massive, cruise-ship-esque 150-seat Bleu View Mediterranean restaurant and cocktail lounge. Adding to the Fontainebleau's opulence is the 7,000-square-foot Cookie's World water park; the water slide and river-raft ride bring a bit of Disney to Deco-land. The water park, along with supervised children's activities, is great for (though not reserved for) the little ones.

4441 Collins Ave., Miami Beach, FL 33140. ⓒ 800/HILTONS or 305/538-2000. Fax 305/674-4607. www. fontainebleau.hilton.com. 876 units. Winter $289–$459 double; off season $209–$329 double; year-round $525–$1,300 suite. Additional person $30. Packages available. AE, DC, DISC, MC, V. Overnight valet parking $17. Pets accepted at no extra cost. **Amenities:** 4 restaurants; 3 cocktail lounges; 2 large outdoor pools; 7 lighted tennis courts (after 2005's renovations); state-of-the-art health club; 3 whirlpool baths; watersports rentals; children's programs; game rooms; concierge; tour desk; car-rental desk; business center; shopping arcade; salon; room service; in-room massage; babysitting; laundry and dry cleaning service. In room: A/C, TV, fax, dataport, minibar, coffeemaker, hair dryer, iron, safe.

KEY BISCAYNE
WORTH A SPLURGE

Sonesta Beach Resort Key Biscayne ★★ *Kids*   The Sonesta is an idyllic, secluded resort on Key Biscayne—like a souped-up summer camp. Families and couples alike love this place for its oceanfront location and its many high-caliber amenities, which make it almost impossible to want to venture off the property.

Each of the plush recently upgraded 292 rooms has a private balcony or terrace. There are also 12 one- and two-bedroom suites. Room no. 828 is particularly appealing, with its sweeping views of the ocean, comfortable (to say the least) king bed, and top-floor location.

Known for having the best piña coladas in the entire city, the pool and beach bars are popular with locals and vacationers alike. The hotel's Two Dragons restaurant is good, featuring Chinese, Thai, and Japanese food. A fantastic, free, and fully supervised kids' program (ages 3–12) will actually allow parents to have a vacation of their own, perhaps at the resort's 10,000-square-foot spa or at the Water Tai Chi Program in the outdoor, heated Olympic pool. Although you may not want to leave the lush grounds, Bill Baggs Cape Florida State Park (p. 132) and the area's best beaches are nearby and worth the trip. Travelers here are only about 15 minutes from Miami Beach and even closer to the mainland and Coconut Grove. A fun new addition to the hotel is the Relay Segway Excursion Center, where you can rent high-tech Segway Human Transporters on which you can tool around the hotel on your own or take guided tours for $25 to $100.

350 Ocean Dr., Key Biscayne, FL 33149. © 800/SONESTA or 305/361-2021. Fax 305/361-3096. www. sonesta.com. 292 units. Winter $295–$445 double, $635–$1,070 suite; off season $179–$330 double, $435–$950 suite. 15% gratuity added to food and beverage bills. Special packages available. AE, DC, DISC, MC, V. Valet parking $15. **Amenities:** 4 restaurants; 2 bars; lounge; outdoor heated Olympic-size pool; access to nearby golf; 9 tennis courts; fitness center; full-service spa; 2 waterfront Jacuzzis; extensive watersports equipment rental; bike and moped rental; children's programs; shuttle service to shopping and entertainment; business center; salon; limited room service; laundry and dry cleaning service; sports court; sailing lessons. *In room:* A/C, TV, dataport, minibar, coffeemaker, hair dryer, iron, safe.

DOWNTOWN

If you've ever read Tom Wolfe's *Bonfire of the Vanities,* you may understand what downtown Miami is all about. If not, it's this simple: Take a wrong turn and you could find yourself in some serious trouble. Desolate and dangerous at night, downtown is trying to change its image, but it's a long, tedious process. Recently, however, part of the area has experienced a renaissance in terms of nightlife, with several popular dance clubs and bars opening up in the environs of NE 11th Street off Biscayne Boulevard. Most downtown hotels cater primarily to business travelers and pre- and post-cruise passengers. Although business hotels are expensive, quality and service are of a high standard. Look for discounts and packages for the weekend, when offices are closed and rooms often go empty. If you're the kind of person who digs an urban setting, you may enjoy downtown, but if you're looking for shiny, happy Miami, you're in the wrong place (for now). As posh, pricey lofts keep going up in the area faster than the nation's deficit, this area is about to experience the renaissance it has been waiting for. Keep your eyes peeled on this area. You read it here first: Like orange being the new black, Downtown Miami is the new South Beach.

Miami River Inn ★★★ *Finds* The Miami River Inn, listed on the National Register of Historic Places, is a quaint country-style hideaway (Miami's *only* bed-and-breakfast!) consisting of four cottages smack in the middle of downtown Miami. In fact, it's so hidden that most locals don't even know it exists, which only adds to its panache. Every room has hardwood floors and is uniquely furnished with antiques dating from 1908. In one room, you might find a hand-painted bathtub, a Singer sewing machine, and an armoire from the turn of the 20th century, restored to perfection. Thirty-eight rooms have private bathrooms—four have a shower only, six have a tub only, and 28 have a splendid shower and tub combo. One- and two-bedroom apartments are available as well. In the foyer, you can peruse a library filled with books about old Miami, with histories of this land's former owners: Julia Tuttle, William Brickell, and Henry Flagler. It's close to public transportation, restaurants, and museums, and only 5 minutes from the business district.

118 SW South River Dr., Miami, FL 33130. © 800/468-3589 or 305/325-0045. Fax 305/325-9227. www.miamiriverinn.com. 40 units. Winter $99–$229 double; off season $69–$109 double. Rates include continental breakfast. Additional person $15. AE, DC, DISC, MC, V. Free parking. Pets accepted for $25 per night. **Amenities:** Small, lushly landscaped swimming pool; access to nearby YMCA facilities; Jacuzzi; babysitting; coin-op washers and dryers; laundry and dry cleaning service. *In room:* A/C, TV, hair dryer (upon request), iron (upon request).

Where to Stay & Dine in Key Biscayne, Downtown Miami, North Dade, Little Havana, Coral Gables & Coconut Grove

Hy-Vong **14**
Jimbo's **29**
Jimmy's East Side Diner **4**
Joe's Seafood **6**
La Carreta **14**
Latin American Cafeteria **21**
Le Bouchon du Grove **24**
Miss Saigon Bistro **17**
190 **4**
Ortanique on the Mile **19**
Perricone's Marketplace **12**
Porcao **11**
Rusty Pelican **30**
Tobacco Road **9**
Versailles **14**

WHERE TO STAY ■
Best Western ChateauBleau **15**
Days Inn **3, 5**
Don Shula's Hotel and Golf Club **2**
Grove Isle Club and Resort **28**
Hampton Inn **26**
Holiday Inn **22**
Hotel Place St. Michel **16**
Mandarin Oriental, Miami **10**
Miami River Inn **8**
Sonesta Beach Resort Key Biscayne **32**
Terrace Inn **22**
Wyndham Miami Airport **1**

WHERE TO DINE ◆
Andiamo Brick Oven Pizza **4**
Anokha **24**
Azul **10**
Baleen **28**
Bayside Seafood Hut **31**
Big Fish **9**
Brasserie Les Halles **20**
Cafe Tu Tu Tango **25**
Caffe Abbracci **18**
Casa Juancho **13**
Chispa **23**
Daily Bread Marketplace **27**
Dogma Grill **4**
The Fish Joint **4**
continues opposite

97

WORTH A SPLURGE

Mandarin Oriental, Miami ★★★   Corporate big shots and celebrities not in the mood for the South Beach spotlight finally have a high-end luxury hotel to stay in while wheeling and dealing their way through Miami. Catering to business travelers, conventioneers, big-time celebrities (J-Lo, Jacko, and so on), and the occasional leisure traveler who doesn't mind spending in excess of $500 a night for a room, the swank Mandarin Oriental features a waterfront location, residential-style rooms with Asian touches (most with balconies), and several upscale dining and bar facilities. The waterfront view of the city is the hotel's best asset, both priceless and absolutely stunning. Much of the hotel's staff was flown in from Bangkok and Hong Kong to demonstrate the hotel's unique brand of superattentive Asian-inspired service. The hotel's two restaurants, the high-end Azul and the more casual Café Sambal, are up to Mandarin standards and are both wonderful, as is the 15,000-square-foot The Spa at Mandarin Oriental in which traditional Thai massages and Ayurvedic treatments are your tickets to nirvana. At press time, the Mandarin Oriental Miami had just opened its 20,000-foot white sand beach club, complete with beds with white cushions and canopies, beach butlers, and beachside cabana treatments, which is nice considering the hotel is 15 minutes from the beach. *Celeb tidbit:* Michael Jackson felt it necessary to autograph one of the paintings inside his suite even though he didn't paint it.

500 Brickell Key Dr., Miami, FL 33131. ℂ **305/913-8288.** Fax 305/913-8300. www.mandarinoriental.com. 329 units. Year-round $575 single; $600 double; $1,200–$5,000 suite. AE, DC, DISC, MC, V. Valet parking $24. **Amenities:** 2 restaurants; bar; outdoor pool; beach; beach club; state-of-the-art fitness center; full-service holistic spa; outdoor Jacuzzi; concierge; 24-hr. business center. *In room:* A/C, TV, dataport, minibar, hair dryer, iron, safe.

COCONUT GROVE

This waterfront village hugs the shores of Biscayne Bay, just south of U.S. 1 and about 10 minutes from the beaches. Once a haven for hippies, head shops, and arty bohemian characters, the Grove succumbed to the inevitable temptations of commercialism and has become a Gap nation, featuring a host of fun, themey restaurants, bars, a megaplex, and lots of stores. Outside of the main shopping area, however, you will find the beautiful remnants of old Miami in the form of flora, fauna, and, of course, water.

For a map of the hotels in this section, see the "Where to Stay & Dine in Key Biscayne, Downtown Miami, West Miami, Airport Area, North Dade, Little Havana, Coral Gables & Coconut Grove" map on p. 97.

Hampton Inn   This very standard chain hotel is a welcome reprieve in an area otherwise known for very pricey accommodations. The rooms are nothing exciting, but the freebies, like local phone calls, parking, in-room movies, breakfast buffet, and hot drinks around the clock, make this a real steal. Although there is no restaurant or bar, it is close to lots of both—only about half a mile to the heart of the Grove's shopping and retail area and about as far from Coral Gables. Rooms are brand new, sparkling clean, and larger than that of a typical motel. Located at the residential end of Brickell Avenue, it's a quiet, convenient location 15 minutes from South Beach and 5 minutes from Coconut Grove. If you'd rather save your money for dining and entertainment, this is a good bet.

2800 SW 28th Terrace (at U.S. 1 and SW 27th Ave.), Coconut Grove, FL 33133. ℂ **305/448-2800.** Fax 305/442-8655. www.Hampton-inn.com. 137 units. Winter $109–$154 double; off season $79–$124 double. Rates include continental breakfast buffet and local calls. AE, DC, DISC, MC, V. Free parking. **Amenities:** Large outdoor pool; exercise room; Jacuzzi. *In room:* A/C, TV, microwave and fridge on request.

WORTH A SPLURGE

Grove Isle Club and Resort ⭐   Hidden away in the bougainvillea and lushness of the Grove, the Grove Isle Resort is off the beaten path on its own lushly landscaped 20-acre island, just outside the heart of Coconut Grove. The isolated exclusivity of this resort contributes to a country club vibe, though, for the most part, the people here aren't snooty; they just value their privacy and precious relaxation time. Everyone dresses in white and pastels, and if they're not on their way to a set of tennis, they're not in a rush to get anywhere. You'll step into rooms that are elegantly furnished with mosquito-netted canopy beds and a patio overlooking the bay. You'll need to reserve early here—rooms go very fast. Baleen (p. 118), a fantastic yet pricey haute cuisinerie, serves fresh seafood and other regional specialties in a spectacular, elegant dining room, or, better yet, outside on the water.

4 Grove Isle Dr., Coconut Grove, FL 33133. ℭ **800/88-GROVE** or 305/858-8300. Fax 305/854-6702. www. groveisle.com. 49 units. Winter $409 suite; off season $199–$219 suite. Rates include breakfast with certain packages only. AE, DC, MC, V. Valet parking $17. **Amenities:** Large outdoor heated pool; 12 outdoor tennis courts; deluxe health club; concierge; secretarial services; salon; room service; in-room massage; babysitting; laundry and dry cleaning service. *In room:* A/C, TV/VCR, dataport, minibar, hair dryer, iron, safe.

CORAL GABLES

Translated appropriately as "City Beautiful," the Gables, as it's affectionately known, was one of Miami's original planned communities and is still among the city's prettiest, pedestrian-friendly, albeit preservation-obsessed, neighborhoods. Coral Gables has a number of wonderful luxury hotels, but fewer options for those on a smaller budget. Two popular and well-priced chain hotels in the area are a **Holiday Inn** (ℭ **800/HOLIDAY** or 305/667-5611) at 1350 S. Dixie Hwy., with rates between $89 and $189, and a **Terrace Inn** (ℭ **305/665-7501**) at 1430 S. Dixie Hwy., with rates ranging from $59 to $89. Both are located directly across the street from the University of Miami and are popular with families and friends of students.

SUPER-CHEAP SLEEPS

Best Western ChateauBleau ⭐   Finding a bargain hotel in the heart of Coral Gables is like finding a pot of gold at the end of a rainbow. At last, the Best Western ChateauBleau is that accommodating pot of gold, a no-frills, albeit very clean hotel with spacious, recently renovated rooms, most with balconies overlooking Coral Gables. A nice pool as well as a very good Greek restaurant, Mylos, make this hotel an attractive choice in an area where the concept of value is pretty much a foreign one. A complimentary shuttle to and from the Miami International Airport is a bonus, too.

1111 Ponce de León Blvd., Coral Gables, FL 33134. ℭ **305/448-2634.** Fax 305/448-2017. www.hotel chateaubleau.com. 120 units. Winter $79 double; off season $69 double. AE, DC, DISC, MC, V. Free parking. **Amenities:** Restaurant; bar; small pool; free airport shuttle; room service (8am–10pm); self-service laundry. *In room:* A/C, TV.

WORTH A SPLURGE

Hotel Place St. Michel ⭐⭐⭐   This European-style hotel, in the heart of Coral Gables, is one of the city's most romantic options. The accommodations and hospitality are straight out of old-world Europe, complete with dark wood–paneled walls, cozy beds, beautiful antiques, and a quiet elegance that seems startlingly out of place in trendy Miami. Everything here is charming— from the brass elevator and parquet floors to the paddle fans. One-of-a-kind furnishings make each room special. Bathrooms are on the smaller side but are hardly cramped. All have shower/tub combos except for two, which have either or. If you're picky, request your preference. Guests are treated to fresh fruit upon arrival and enjoy perfect service throughout their stay. The exceptional Restaurant St. Michel is a very romantic dining choice.

162 Alcazar Ave., Coral Gables, FL 33134. **©** **800/848-HOTEL** or 305/444-1666. Fax 305/529-0074. www. hotelplacestmichel.com. 27 units. Winter $165 double, $200 suite; off season $125 double, $160 suite. Additional person $10. Rates include continental breakfast and fruit basket upon arrival. AE, DC, MC, V. Self-parking $7. **Amenities:** Restaurant; lounge; access to nearby health club; concierge; room service; laundry and dry cleaning service. *In room:* A/C, TV, dataport, hair dryer, iron (available upon request).

NEAR THE AIRPORT/WEST MIAMI

As Miami continues to grow at a rapid pace, expansion has begun westward, where land is plentiful. Several resorts have taken advantage of the space to build world-class tennis and golf courses. While there's no sea to swim in, a plethora of facilities can definitely make up for the lack of an ocean view.

For a map of the hotels in this section, see the "Where to Stay & Dine in Key Biscayne, Downtown Miami, West Miami, Airport Area, North Dade, Little Havana, Coral Gables & Coconut Grove" map on p. 97.

Don Shula's Hotel and Golf Club   Guests come to Shula's mostly for the golf, but there's plenty here to keep nongolfers busy, too. Opened in 1992 to much fanfare from the sports and business community, Shula's resort is an all-encompassing oasis in the middle of the planned, quaint residential neighborhood of Miami Lakes, complete with a Main Street and nearby shopping facilities—a good thing, since the site is more than a 20-minute drive from anything. The guest rooms, located in the main building or surrounding the golf course, are plain but pretty in typical, uninspiring Florida decor—pastels, wicker, and light wood. As expected, the hotel's Athletic Club features state-of-the-art equipment and classes, but costs hotel guests $10 per day or $35 per week. The award-winning Shula's Steak House and the more casual Steak House Two get high rankings nationwide. They serve huge Angus beef steaks and seafood, which can be worked off with a round of golf the next day.

6842 Main St., Miami Lakes, FL 33014. **©** **800/24-SHULA** or 305/821-1150. Fax 305/820-8094. www. donshulahotel.com. 330 units. Winter $129–$289 suite; off season $99–$209 suite. Additional person $10. Business packages available. AE, DC, MC, V. **Amenities:** 2 restaurants; 1 bar; 2 pools; golf course and driving range; 9 tennis courts; sporting courts; health club; Jacuzzi; saunas; room service. *In room:* A/C, TV/VCR, dataport, coffeemaker, hair dryer, iron.

BARGAIN CHAINS

If you must stay near the airport, consider any of the dozens of moderately priced chain hotels. You'll find one of the cheapest and most recommendable options at either of the **Days Inn** locations at 7250 NW 11th St. or 4767 NW 36th St. (**©** **800/329-7466** for both or 305/888-3661 or 305/261-4230, respectively), each about 2 miles from the airport. The larger property on 36th Street offers slightly cheaper rates with singles starting as low as $49. The 11th Street locale may charge more for weekends, but prices usually start at $70. Prices include free transportation from the airport.

A more luxurious option is the **Wyndham Miami Airport,** at 3900 NW 21st St. (**©** **305/871-3800**), with rates from $100 to $225.

4 Great Deals on Dining

Don't be fooled by the plethora of superlean model types you're likely to see posing throughout Miami: Contrary to popular belief, dining in this city is as much a sport as the in-line skating on Ocean Drive. With over 6,000 restaurants to choose from, dining out in Miami has become a passionate pastime for locals and visitors alike. Our star chefs have fused Californian-Asian with Caribbean and Latin elements to create a world-class flavor all its own: *Floribbean*. Think mango chutney splashed over fresh swordfish or a spicy sushi sauce served alongside Peruvian ceviche.

Formerly synonymous with early-bird specials, Miami's new-wave cuisine, 10 years in the making, now rivals that of San Francisco—or even New York. Nouveau Cuban chef Douglas Rodriguez may have fled his Miami kitchen in favor of one in Manhattan, but he's coming back to a yet-to-open restaurant at 5061 Biscayne Blvd. In addition, other Food Network–caliber stellar chefs such as the Food Network's own Michelle Bernstein, Mark Militello, Allen Susser, Norman van Aken, and Jonathan Eismann remain firmly planted in the city's culinary scene, fusing local ingredients into edible masterpieces. Indulging in this New World cuisine is not only high in calories, it's high in price. But if you can manage to splurge at least once, it'll be worth it.

Thanks to a thriving cafe society in both South Beach and Coconut Grove, you can also enjoy a moderately priced meal and linger for hours without having a waiter hover over you. In Little Havana, you can chow down on a meal that serves about six for less than $10. And since seafood is plentiful, it doesn't have to cost you an arm and a leg to enjoy the appendages of a crab or lobster. Don't be put off by the looks of our recommended seafood shacks in places such as Key Biscayne—oftentimes these spots get the best and freshest catches.

Whatever you're craving, Miami's got it—with the exception of decent Chinese food and a New York–style slice of pizza. If you're craving a scene with your steak, then South Beach is the place to be. Like many cities in Europe and Latin America, it is fashionable to dine late in South Beach, preferably after 9pm, sometimes as late as midnight. Service on South Beach is notoriously slow and arrogant, but it comes with the turf. (Of course, it is possible to find restaurants that defy the notoriety and actually pride themselves on friendly service.) On the mainland—especially in Coral Gables, and, more recently, downtown and on Brickell Avenue—you can also experience fine, creative dining without the pretense.

The biggest complaint when it comes to Miami dining isn't the haughtiness, but rather the dearth of truly moderately priced restaurants, especially in South Beach and Coral Gables. It's either really cheap or really expensive; the in-between somehow gets lost in the culinary shuffle. Quick-service diners don't really exist here as they do in other cosmopolitan areas. I've tried to cover a range of cuisines in a range of prices. But with new restaurants opening on a weekly basis, you're bound to find a savory array of dining choices on every budget.

Many restaurants keep extended hours in season (roughly Dec–Apr) and may close for lunch and/or dinner on Mondays when the traffic is slower. Always call ahead, since schedules do change. Also, always look carefully at your bill—many Miami restaurants add a 15% gratuity to your total. *Feel free to adjust it* if you feel your server deserves more or less.

SOUTH BEACH

The renaissance of South Beach started in the early '90s and is still continuing as classic cuisine gives in to mod-temptation by inevitably fusing with more chic, nouveau developments created by faithful followers and devotees of the Food Network school of cooking. The ultimate result has spawned dozens of first-rate restaurants. In fact, big-name restaurants from across the country have capitalized on South Beach's international appeal and opened, and continue to open, branches here with great success. A few old standbys remain from the *Miami Vice* days, but the flock of newcomers dominates the scene, with places going in and out of style as quickly as the tides.

The Lincoln Road area is packed with places offering good food and a great atmosphere. Since it's impossible to list them all, I recommend strolling and browsing: Most restaurants post a copy of their menu outside.

With very few exceptions, the places on Ocean Drive are crowded with tourists and priced accordingly. You'll do better to venture a little farther into the pedestrian-friendly streets just west of Ocean Drive.

For a map of the restaurants in this section, see the "South Beach" map on p. 87.

Big Pink ★ *Kids* AMERICAN   Real Food for Real People is the motto to which this restaurant strictly adheres. Located on what used to be a gritty corner of Collins Avenue, Big Pink—owned by the folks at the higher-end Nemo— is quickly identified by a whimsical Pippi Longstocking–type mascot on a sign outside. Scooters and motorcycles line the streets surrounding the place, which is a favorite among beach bums, club kids, and those craving Big Pink's comforting and hugely portioned pizzas, sandwiches, salads, and hamburgers. The fare is above average at best, and the menu is massive, but it comes with a good dose of kitsch, such as their "gourmet" spin on the classic TV dinner, which is done perfectly, right down to the compartmentalized dessert. Televisions line the bar area, and the family-style table arrangement (there are several booths, too) promotes camaraderie among diners. Outdoor tables are available. Even picky kids will like the food here, and parents can enjoy the family-friendly atmosphere (not the norm for South Beach) without worrying if their kids are making too much noise.

157 Collins Ave. ✆ 305/532-4700. Main courses $13–$20. AE, DC, MC, V. Sun–Thurs 9am–1am; Fri–Sat 9am–2am.

Cafeteria ★ AMERICAN   Another New York City import has landed on South Beach, causing a fabulous frenzy amongst the hipster crowds who don't mind munching on $6 macaroni and cheese amidst a stark white backdrop filled with people who look as if they've been peeled off the latest Calvin Klein ads. Cafeteria is also the canteen of choice for those who wouldn't be caught dead in Denny's. Beautiful people and lackadaisical service aside, you can't beat a place that serves pizzas, meatloaf, and fabulous mac and cheese worthy of its price tag 24 hours a day, 7 days a week. As of press time, the former Cadillac dealership was working on its rooftop garden, which will surely be command central for the kinds of people for whom the name Paris conjures up a spoiled heiress and not the wonderful city of lights.

546 Lincoln Rd. ✆ 305/672-3448. Main courses $6–$16. AE, MC, V. Daily 24 hr.

David's Cafe ★ CUBAN   The farthest thing from a trendy spot, David's Cafe's Cuban food is so good, cheap, and available 24 hours a day, that Michael Jackson even sauntered up to the outdoor counter to order a cafe Cubano. Enjoy supercheap breakfasts (two eggs, home fries or grits, coffee, and toast is $4.75), Cuban sandwiches (ham, pork, Swiss, pickles, and mustard), midnight arroz con pollo, fantastic cheeseburgers, a wonderful $4 grilled cheese sandwich, *ropa vieja* Habanera (shredded sirloin and sauce), and pretty much anything you can think of—even, oddly enough, brown rice. Hey, this is South Beach, what can you expect?

1654 Meridian Ave. ℂ 305/672-8707. Main courses $4–$11. AE, MC, V. Daily 24 hr.

El Rancho Grande ★★ MEXICAN   Hidden on a side street off of Lincoln Road, El Rancho Grande is a favorite local cantina that has attracted the likes of Cher and Matt Damon thanks to its ultrafresh fare and unassuming ambience. With a Pottery Barn meets Acapulco decor, El Rancho Grande doesn't hold anything back when it comes to the cuisine. The Aztec Soup, a hot and spicy blend of chicken and tortilla strips, is some of the best I've had. The salsa here is not at all watery and is freshly made—a tongue tickling blend of spices, cilantro, tomatoes, onions, and peppers, and the Mexican favorites of burritos, enchiladas, and fajitas are all very well represented at this restaurant. All portions are huge and can be shared or taken home for extra meal mileage. There is a scene here, but it's very relaxed. Margaritas are a little weak when frozen and better ordered on the rocks. Expect a wait at the small bar for your table, especially on weekends. Limited outdoor seating is also available.

1626 Pennsylvania Ave. ℂ 305/673-0480. Main courses $10–$19. AE, DC, MC, V. Daily 11am–11pm.

Grillfish ★★ SEAFOOD   From the beautiful Byzantine-style mural and the gleaming oak bar, you'd think you were eating in a much more expensive restaurant, but Grillfish manages to pay the exorbitant South Beach rent with the help of a loyal local following who come for fresh, simple seafood in a relaxed but upscale atmosphere.

The servers are friendly and know the menu well. The barroom seafood chowder is full of chunks of shellfish, as well as some fresh whitefish filets in a tomato broth. The small ear of corn, included with each entree, is about as close as you'll get to any type of vegetable offering besides the pedestrian salad. Still, at these prices, it's worth a visit to try some local fare including mako shark, swordfish, tuna, marlin, and wahoo.

1444 Collins Ave. (corner of Española Way). ℂ 305/538-9908. www.grillfish.com. Reservations for 6 or more only. Main courses $9–$26. AE, DC, DISC, MC, V. Daily 11:30am–4pm and 5:30pm–midnight.

Jerry's Famous Deli ★ DELI   Answering the cries for a real, New York–style deli on South Beach is Jerry's Famous Deli, actually a Los Angeles import, which now occupies the cavernous space that used to house the very decadent gay disco, the Warsaw Ballroom. In a way, Jerry's still channels that same decadence, albeit with a menu that features over 700 monstrously-portioned items, from your typical corned beef on rye to your atypical brisket burrito. While the quality of the food is excellent, the service pales in comparison: This 24-hour deli is not a place to go if you're in a rush. The modern cafeteria, complete with full bar and a very Los Angeleno nonsmoking policy (which has expanded to all of Florida restaurants), is dimly lit with a disco soundtrack that is somewhat reminiscent of its predecessor. People come here to linger over sandwiches that can feed at least two people, if not more, and should you be craving a Reuben sandwich after a night of clubbing at 5am, Jerry's is command central for that set as well as the original early birders who are first waking at 5am and will have their dinner at 5pm. One thing, though: This is *not* your grandfather's deli, where sandwiches were only a few bucks. Prepare to shell out at least $10 and up for one of Jerry's. What do you expect? It's 21st-century South Beach!

1450 Collins Ave. ℂ 305/532-8030. Main courses $7–$15. AE, DC, DISC, MC, V. Daily 24 hr.

Lincoln Road Café ⭐ *Value* CUBAN   The Van Dyke Cafe (p. 105) is good for people-watching and reliable food, but if you're starving, not in the mood to wait for a table, and don't want to spend more than $10 for breakfast, head over to the Lincoln Road Café. Although it harkens back to the days of old South Beach, before the trendoids came and took over Lincoln Road with minimalistic, ultramodern decor and uncomfortable chairs, Lincoln Road Café remains a local hot spot for cheap breakfasts, lunches, and dinners. Breakfast is the real bargain, however, where for a mere $6, you can gorge yourself on eggs, bacon, ham, sausage, Cuban toast, and a mind-blowing, brain-buzzing *café con leche*. For lunch and dinner, there are hefty portions of Cuban faves from black beans and rice to arroz con pollo, all at low, low prices. Lincoln Road Café doesn't need Philippe Starck's designs to help bring in crowds: Thanks to cheap, good food, this unassuming eatery is a hot spot in its own right.

941 Lincoln Rd. ⓒ 305/538-8066. Items $7–$11. AE, DC, MC, V. Daily 8am–midnight.

Mama Vieja ⭐ COLOMBIAN   This funky Colombian hangout looks like a total dive from the outside, but once inside you will want to dive right in to the supremely fresh national specialties such as *pargo rojo estofado a la mama vieja* (red snapper stuffed with a supercreamy and delicate seafood sauce in a rice base). Brightly painted walls and elevated porches look out onto a large-screen TV showing music videos from the old country. The walls and ceilings are decorated with hundreds of hats that have been donated by customers and signed in exchange for a free meal. Bring in an interesting hat and mention it to the server before placing your order so that he or she can bring you to the attention of the owner. All the dishes here are worth trying and are so reasonably priced that it's easy to order a lot. Try to save room for the milky sweet desserts and a good strong coffee—you'll need it if you want to dance it off after at Lola, the very popular, unpretentious hotspot next door. If not, there's live music here, too.

235 23rd St. (just west of Collins Ave.). ⓒ 305/538-2400. Main courses $4.95–$15. AE, DC, DISC, MC, V. Mon and Wed noon–11pm; Thurs–Sun noon–midnight. Nightclub Thurs–Sun midnight–5am.

News Cafe ⭐ AMERICAN   This South Beach cafe cum landmark hasn't fallen off the radar as far as buzz and hype are concerned. The quintessential South Beach experience, News is still *au courant,* albeit swarming with mostly tourists. Unless it's appallingly hot or rainy out, you should wait for an outside table, which is where you need to be to fully appreciate the experience. Service is abysmal and often arrogant (perhaps because the tip is included), but the menu is reliable, running the gamut from sandwiches and salads to pasta dishes and omelets. My favorite here is the Middle Eastern platter, a dip lover's paradise, with hummus, tahini, tabbouleh, babaghanouj, and fresh pita bread. If it's not too busy, feel free to order just a cappuccino—your server may snarl, but that's what News is all about; creative types like to bring their laptops and sit here all day (or all night—this place is open 24 hr. a day). If you're by yourself and need something to read, there's an extensive collection of national and international newspapers and magazines at the in-house newsstand. News Cafe also opened another clone, Café Cardozo, at the Cardozo Hotel at 1300 Ocean Dr. on South Beach, in case 5 blocks is too much to walk to the original.

800 Ocean Dr. ⓒ 305/538-6397. Items $5–$20. AE, DC, MC, V. Open 24 hr.

Piola ⭐ PIZZA   This hip Italian import miraculously transforms pizza from an eat-out-of-the-box-stuff-a-slice-into-your-mouth experience into a fun, sit-down meal that's hard to beat for the price, quality, and quantity. An unabridged menu of nearly 80 different kinds of pizzas-for-one that are really enough to share between two people is mind-numbing and mouthwatering. I suggest that you order several pizzas, depending on how many people you are dining with (two is more than enough for two, for example). Start with the quattro formaggio pizza—brie, Gorgonzola, Parmesan, and mozzarella—and then consider a funkier version, say, smoked salmon and caviar. All pizzas are thin crusted and full of flavor. Waitstaff is extremely friendly, too, but be prepared for a lengthy wait, especially on weekend nights when the movie-going crowds next door spill over for a snack.

1625 Alton Rd. ☎ 305/674-1660. Reservations accepted. Main courses $7–$15. AE, DC, MC, V. Daily 6pm–1am.

Puerto Sagua ⭐ CUBAN/SPANISH   This brown-walled diner is one of the only old holdouts on South Beach. Its steady stream of regulars ranges from *abuelitos* (little old grandfathers) to hipsters who stop in after clubbing. It has endured because the food is good, if a little greasy. Some of the less heavy dishes are a superchunky fish soup with pieces of whole flaky grouper, chicken, and seafood paella, or marinated kingfish. Also good are most of the shrimp dishes, especially the shrimp in garlic sauce, which is served with white rice and salad.

This is one of the most reasonably priced places left on the beach for simple, hearty fare. Don't be intimidated by the hunched, older waiters in their white button-down shirts and black pants. Even if you don't speak Spanish, they're usually willing to do charades. Anyway, the extensive menu, which ranges from BLTs to grilled lobsters to yummy fried plantains, is translated into English. Hurry, before another boutique goes up in its place.

700 Collins Ave. ☎ 305/673-1115. Main courses $6–$24; sandwiches and salads $5–$10. AE, DC, MC, V. Daily 7:30am–2am.

Sport Café ⭐ ITALIAN   If you're in the mood for great Italian food—nothing fancy—but don't feel like dressing up and dealing with surly hosts and "reservations only" rudeness, look no further than Sport Café, known for its delicious, down-home, reasonably priced, and homemade Italian food. Seating is either inside the casual dining room or outside in the more romantic, less sporty private outdoor garden. The menu is pretty simple—penne al arrabiata, spaghetti, and so on—but always check the daily specials. The vibe here ranges from quiet and intimate to frenetic, especially when the soccer matches being broadcast on the restaurant's televisions kick the crowd into a European-style frenzy. Make sure to ask if the owners' mama is in the kitchen, where she cooks her not-always-offered secret lasagna and fabulous gnocchi.

560 Washington Ave. ☎ 305/674-9700. Reservations accepted for 4 or more. Main courses $7–$20; sandwiches and pizzas $6–$9. AE, MC, V. Daily noon–12:30am.

Van Dyke Cafe ⭐ AMERICAN   News Cafe's younger, less harried sibling, Van Dyke is a locals' favorite, at which people-watching is also premium, but attitude is practically nonexistent. Like News, the menu here is pretty cut and dry—sandwiches, salads, eggs, and so on, but the Van Dyke's warm, wood-floored interior, upstairs jazz bar, accessible parking, and intense chocolate soufflé make it a less taxing alternative. Also, unlike News, Van Dyke turns into a sizzling nightspot, featuring live jazz nearly every night of the week (a $5 cover charge is added to your bill if you sit at a table; the bar's free). Outside there's a vast tree-lined seating area that provides a front-row seat to the people-watching. Those allergic to or afraid of dogs may want to reconsider eating here, as Van Dyke is also a canine hotspot.

846 Lincoln Rd. ✆ 305/534-3600. Reservations recommended for dinner. Main courses $9–$17. AE, DC, MC, V. Daily 8am–2am.

SUPER-CHEAP EATS

A La Folie ★★ FRENCH   The Left Bank took a wrong turn and ended up on the quiet(er) end of Española Way in the form of A La Folie. Reflecting the *positive* things about our former allies, A La Folie is an authentic French cafe in which wooden booths and walls full of foreign newspapers and magazines make you have to take a second look at your plane ticket to make sure you're still in Miami. In addition to the affected, *très* French waitstaff (not snotty, but aloof), A La Folie features some of the best cafe fare in Miami including delicious, hugely portioned sandwiches such as the French fave croque-monsieur, salads, crepes, and, of course, cafe au lait and plenty of wine. Indoor and outdoor seating are equally conducive to whiling away many hours sipping coffee, reading a magazine, and reflecting on that whole Freedom Fry controversy back in the early 2000s.

516 Española Way. ✆ 305/538-4484. Main courses $5–$10. MC, V. Daily 9am–midnight.

La Sandwicherie SANDWICHES   You can get mustard, mayo, or oil and vinegar on sandwiches elsewhere in town, but you'd be missing out on all the local flavor. This gourmet sandwich bar, open until the crack of dawn, caters to ravenous club kids, biker types, and the body artists who work in the tattoo parlor next door. For many people, in fact, no night of clubbing is complete without capping it off with a turkey sub from La Sandwicherie.

229 14th St. (behind the Amoco station). ✆ 305/532-8934. Sandwiches and salads $6–$12. AE, MC, V. Daily 9am–5am. Delivery 9:30am–11pm.

San Loco Tacos ★ MEXICAN   There are no talking Chihuahuas to promote this excellent fast-food Mexican joint, but word of human mouth seems to do the trick. The food is served quickly, with no frills attached, but it's done very well and the place is open late—perfect for an after-clubbing bite. The guacamole is very fresh, and the tacos, burritos, enchiladas, and a host of other Mexican munchies are zesty, not skimpy, and really cheap. Salsa is not watered down or prepackaged and comes in mild, medium, or painfully hot. There are a few tables inside, but most people prefer to pick up their chow and take it out with them.

235 14th St. ✆ 305/538-3009. Items $2–$7. No credit cards. Sun–Thurs 11am–5am; Fri–Sat 11am–6am.

WORTH A SPLURGE

Casa Tua ★★★ *Finds* ITALIAN   The stunning Casa Tua is a sleek and chic country Italian-style establishment set in a refurbished 1925 Mediterranean-style house cum hotel. It has several dining areas, including a resplendent outdoor garden, comfy Ralph Lauren-esque living room, and a communal eat-in kitchen. The lamb chops are stratospheric in price ($42) but sublime in taste. Service is, as always with South Beach eateries, inconsistent, ranging from ultra-professional to absurdly lackadaisical. For these prices, they should be wiping our mouths for us. After or before dinner, head upstairs to the lounge area, where the beautiful people convene over $15 cocktails.

1700 James Ave. © 305/673-1010. Reservations required. Main courses $24–$42. AE, DC, MC, V. Mon–Sat 7pm–midnight.

Escopazzo ★★★ ITALIAN   Escopazzo means "I'm going crazy" in Italian, but the only sign of insanity in this primo Northern Italian eatery is the fact that it only seats 90. The wine bottles have it better—the restaurant's cellar holds 1,000 bottles of various vintages. Should you be so lucky to score a table at this romantic local favorite (choose one in the back dining room that's reminiscent of an Italian courtyard complete with water fountain and faux windows; it's not cheesy at all), you'll have trouble deciding between dishes that will have you swearing off the Olive Garden with your first bite. Among these, squid ink pasta with ragout of mussels, clams, and calamari in a crispy pasta basket, or Smithfield pork tenderloin filled with smoked mozzarella in a Madeira, sage, and amarena cherry sauce. The hand-rolled pastas and risotto are near perfection. Eating here is like dining with a big Italian family—it's never boring (the menu changes five or six times a year), the service is excellent, and nobody's happy until you are blissfully full.

1311 Washington Ave. © 305/674-9450. Reservations required. Main courses $18–$32. AE, MC, V. Mon–Fri 6pm–midnight; Sat 6pm–1am; Sun 6–11pm.

Joe Allen ★ *Finds* AMERICAN   It's hard to compete in a city with haute spots everywhere you look, but Joe Allen, a restaurant that has proven itself in both New York and London, has stood up to the challenge by establishing itself off the beaten path in possibly the only area of South Beach that has managed to remain impervious to trendiness and overdevelopment. Located on the bay side of the beach, Joe Allen is nestled in an unassuming building conspicuously devoid of neon lights, valet parkers, and fashionable pedestrians. Inside, however, one discovers a hidden jewel: a stark yet elegant interior and no-nonsense, fairly priced, ample-portioned dishes such as meatloaf, pizza, fresh fish, and salads. The scene has a homey feel favored by locals looking to escape the hype without compromising quality.

1787 Purdy Ave./Sunset Harbor Dr. (3 blocks west of Alton Rd.). © 305/531-7007. Reservations recommended, especially on weekends. Main courses $15–$25. MC, V. Daily 11:30am–11:30pm.

Joe's Stone Crab Restaurant ★★ SEAFOOD   Unless you grease the palms of one of the stone-faced maitre d's with some stone-cold cash, you'll be waiting for those famous claws for up to 2 hours—if not more. As much a Miami landmark as the beaches themselves, Joe's is a microcosm of the city, attracting everyone from T-shirted locals to a bejeweled Ivana Trump. Whatever you wear, however, will be eclipsed by a kitschy, unglamorous plastic bib that your waiter will tie on you unless you say otherwise. Open only during stone-crab season (Oct–May), Joe's reels in the crowds with the freshest, meatiest stone crabs and their essential accouterments: creamed spinach and excellent sweet-potato fries. The claws come in medium, large, or jumbo. Some say size doesn't matter; others swear by the jumbo (and more expensive) ones. Whatever you choose, pair them with a savory mustard sauce (a perfect mix of mayo and mustard) or hot butter. Not feeling crabby? The fried chicken and liver and onions on the regular menu are actually considered by many as far superior—they're definitely far cheaper—to the crabs. Oh yeah, and save room for dessert. The Key lime pie here is the best in town. If you don't feel like waiting, try Joe's Take Away, which is located next door to the restaurant—it's a lot quicker and just as tasty.

11 Washington Ave. (at Biscayne St., just south of 1st St.). (305/673-0365 or 305/673-4611 for takeout. www.joesstonecrab.com. Reservations not accepted. Market price varies but averages $63 for a serving of jumbo crab claws, $43 for large claws. AE, DC, DISC, MC, V. Daily 11:30am–2pm; Sun 4–10pm; Mon–Thurs 5–10pm; Fri–Sat 5–11pm. Open mid-Oct to mid-May.

Macaluso's ★★ ITALIAN   This restaurant epitomizes the Italians' love for—and mastery of—savory, plentiful, down-home Staten Island–style food. While the storefront restaurant is intimate and demure in nature, there's nothing delicate about the bold mix of flavors in every meat and pasta dish here. Catch the fantastic clam pie when in season—the portions are huge. Pricier items vary throughout the season, but will likely feature fresh fish handpicked by Chef (and owner) Michael, the Don of the kitchen, who is so accommodating he'll take special requests or even bring to your table a complimentary signature meatball. If he doesn't, don't hesitate to ask your waiter for one, he'll be glad to bring it to you. Everyone will recommend perennial favorites such as the rigatoni and broccoli rabe. There are also delicious desserts that range from homemade anisette cookies to Patricia Scott's pastries. The wine list is also good. The Georges Dubœuf Beaujolais, at $22 a bottle, is a steal, when you consider that it comes nicely chilled with slices of luscious Georgia peaches, which make a great and affordable dessert by themselves. *Celeb alert:* Macaluso's is where Demi Moore and tadpole Ashton Kutcher made their official debut as a couple while in Miami.

1747 Alton Rd. (305/604-1811. No reservations accepted. Main courses $14–$28; pizza $8–$13. MC, V. Tues–Sat 6pm–midnight; Sun 6–11pm. After 10:30pm, only pizza pies are served.

Mark's South Beach ★★ NEW WORLD/MEDITERRANEAN   Named after owner and chef Mark Militello, this is one of the best restaurants in all of Miami. But because celebrities don't go here, it's not on the A-list as far as scene is concerned, and for true foodies, this is a blissful thing. A cozy, contemporary restaurant nestled in the basement of the quietly chic Hotel Nash, Mark's New World and Mediterranean-influenced menu changes nightly. What doesn't change is the consistency and freshness of the restaurant's exquisite cuisine. The roasted rack of Colorado lamb with semolina gnocchi is exceptional and worth every bit of cholesterol it may have. Crispy-skinned yellowtail snapper with shrimp, tomato, black olives, oregano, and crumbled feta cheese is in a school of its own. Desserts, including an impressive cheese cart, are outrageous, especially the pistachio cake with chocolate sorbet. Unlike many South Beach eating establishments, the knowledgeable servers are here because of their experience in the restaurant—not modeling—business. If you're expecting to spot celebs and be part of the "scene," then Mark's is not the place for you. For a few bucks extra and a trip over the causeway, go to Azul at the Mandarin Oriental Miami instead.

In the Hotel Nash, 1120 Collins Ave. ⓒ **305/604-9050.** Reservations recommended. Main courses $26–$41. AE, DC, DISC, MC, V. Wed–Sun 7–11am and noon–3pm; Wed–Sat 7pm–midnight; Sun 7–11pm.

Metro Kitchen + Bar ✿ FUSION Diehard foodies find it hard to accept that anything has replaced the Astor Place Bar and Grill, but hipsters welcome the change thanks to the fact that Mynt co-owner and former Joia owner Nicola Siervo owns the Hotel Astor's new restaurant, and when he builds things, celebs come. Besides the fact that Cameron Diaz, Justin Timberlake, and even O.J. Simpson have been spotted dining here, it's not just about the scene. The decor is described as "tropical urban Art Deco," but I prefer to call it cosmopolitan chic, with its glass ceiling, plush banquettes, and rich wood accents. The outdoor garden, set up on what used to be the hotel's minipool, is gorgeous when it's not too hot out. Metro definitely looks as if it belongs in a metropolis. So does the smart looking crowd. The cuisine, created by Chef Rob Boone, formerly of Bambu, is a combination of modern American, Asian, French, and Italian cuisines. For dinner, do not miss the tomato tartlette appetizer with Majorero cheese and aged sherry vinegar. For a main course, choose from strip steak with truffle fries—the best fries you'll ever eat, pan-cooked snapper with udon noodles, or duck breast with grilled apples and fresh spinach. On Tuesday nights, Metro becomes a big scene as local luminaries convene here for cocktails, kibitzing, and star spotting.

In the Hotel Astor, 956 Washington Ave. ⓒ **305/672-7217.** Reservations recommended. Main courses $26–$29. AE, DC, DISC, MC, V. Daily 11:30am–2:30pm; Sun–Thurs 7pm–midnight; Fri–Sat 7pm–1am.

Nobu ✿✿✿ SUSHI When Madonna ate here, no one really noticed. Same thing happened when Justin Timberlake and Cameron Diaz canoodled here. Not because they were purposely trying not to notice, but because the real star at Nobu is the sushi. The raw facts: Nobu has been hailed as one of the best sushi restaurants in the world, with always-packed eateries in New York, London, and Los Angeles. The Omakase, or Chef's Choice—a multicourse menu entirely up to the chef for $70 per person and up—gets consistent raves. And although you won't wait long for your food to be cooked, you will wait forever to score a table here.

At the Shore Club Hotel, 1901 Collins Ave. ⓒ **305/695-3232.** Reservations for parties of 6 or more. Main courses $10–$30. AE, MC, V. Sun 7–11pm; Mon–Thurs 7pm–midnight; Fri–Sat 7pm–1am.

Prime 112 ✿✿✿ STEAKHOUSE Part of the ever expanding culinary empire of Nemo, Big Pink, and Shoji Sushi, Prime 112 is the latest darling to join the exclusive group of restaurants in the hot South of 5th Street area of South Beach. A sleek steakhouse ambience and bustling bar (complete with dried strips of bacon in lieu of nuts) plays second fiddle to the beef, which is arguably the best in the entire city. The 12-ounce filet mignon is seared to perfection and can be enhanced with optional dipping sauces (for a price)—truffle, garlic herb, foie gras, and chipotle. The 22-ounce bone-in rib-eye is fabulous, as is the gigantic 48-ounce porterhouse. Prime 112 also features a Kobe beef burger, a $30 version of sheer ecstasy, although fries are extra at $8, as are all the side dishes (the broccoli rabe sautéed in garlic is outstanding as are the scalloped potatoes)—typical in a steakhouse, but the prices here are hefty. A powerhouse crowd gathers here for lunch and dinner and reservations are more rare than the yellowfin tuna tartare appetizer, but should you be lucky enough to score such a, um, prime reservation, take it without hesitation.

112 Ocean Dr. (in The Browns Hotel). ℂ 305/532-8112. www.prime112.com. Reservations recommended. Main courses $28–$42. AE, DISC, MC, V. Daily 6:30pm–midnight; Mon–Fri 11:30am–3pm.

MIAMI BEACH: SURFSIDE, BAL HARBOUR & SUNNY ISLES

The area north of the Art Deco District—from about 21st Street to 163rd Street—had its heyday in the 1950s when huge hotels and gambling halls blocked the view of the ocean. Now, many of the old hotels have been converted into condos or budget lodgings, and the bayfront mansions have been renovated by and for wealthy entrepreneurs, families, and speculators. The area has many more residents, albeit seasonal, than visitors. On the culinary front, the result is a handful of superexpensive, traditional restaurants as well as a number of value-oriented spots.

For a map of the restaurants in this section, see the "Where to Stay & Dine in Miami Beach, Surfside, Bal Harbour, Sunny Isles & North Beach" map on p. 93.

Cafe Prima Pasta ★★ ITALIAN   Once a small unknown trattoria on a very trafficky, tacky street, Cafe Prima Pasta has expanded into a place to be for amazing Italian food and quite a bit of fanfare. Because there was always a massive wait that spilled out onto the street, the cafe has expanded to include ample outdoor seating that is set back from the street noise and traffic thanks to some creative landscaping. The pasta here is homemade and the kitchen's choice ingredients include prize-worthy ripe, juicy tomatoes; imported olive oil that would cost you a boatload if you bought a bottle in the store; fresh, drippy mozzarella; and fish that tastes as if it had just been caught right out back. The zesty, spicy garlic and oil that is brought out as dip for the bread is something you may want to keep with you during the course of your meal as it doubles as extra seasoning for your food, not that it's necessary. Though tables are packed in a bit, the atmosphere still manages to be romantic. Because of the chef's fancy for garlic, this is a three Altoid restaurant, so be prepared to pop a few or request that they go light on the stuff.

414 71st St. (half a block east of the Byron movie theater), Miami Beach. ℂ 305/867-0106. Reservations not accepted (except for parties of 6 or more). Main courses $9–$19; pastas $12–$19. V, MC. Mon–Thurs noon–midnight; Fri noon–1am; Sat 1pm–1am; Sun 5pm–midnight.

Oggi Caffe ★ ITALIAN   Tucked away in a tiny strip mall on the 79th Street Causeway, this neighborhood favorite makes fresh pastas daily. Each one, from the agnolotti stuffed with fresh spinach and ricotta to the wire-thin spaghettini, is tender and tasty. A hearty *pasta e fagiola* is filled with beans and vegetables and could almost be a meal. I also recommend the daily soups, especially the creamy spinach soup when it's on the menu. Though you could fill up on the starters, the entrees, especially the grilled dishes, are superb. The salmon is served on a bed of spinach with a light lemon-butter sauce. The place is small and a bit rushed, but it's worth the slight discomfort for this authentic, moderately priced food. Another Oggi Caffe opened at 7921 NW 2nd St. in downtown Miami and a sister restaurant, Caffe DaVinci, 1009 Kane Concourse in Bay Harbor Islands, just west of Bal Harbour, has been attracting a faithful following for several years.

1740 79th St. Causeway (in the White Star shopping center next to the Bagel Café), North Beach. ℭ **305/866-1238.** Reservations recommended. Main courses $14–$25; pastas $9–$13. AE, DC, MC, V. Mon–Fri 11:30am–2:30pm; daily 6–11pm.

Ouzo's Greek Taverna and Bar ★★★ GREEK   Opa! Here you can have a meal that's large enough to have fed the entire Olympic Village in Athens *and* a bottle of wine for about $25. You can't beat the taste, service, and ambience at this lovely neighborhood taverna, where spinach pie, grape leaves, souvlakia, moussaka, and, yes, the eponymous potent liqueur, all taste as if they've been shipped right from the Greek Islands. Occasionally belly dancers and live music make this indoor/outdoor cafe a lively weekend hotspot.

940 71st St., North Beach. ℭ **305/864-9848.** Main courses $7–$12; appetizers $3–$6. AE, DC, MC, V. Daily noon–late.

Wolfie Cohen's Rascal House ★ DELI   Although Jerry's Famous Deli on South Beach has taken away some of the Rascal House's younger patrons, the retro fabulous vibe at Wolfie's is inimitable. Open since 1954 and still going strong, this historic, nostalgic culinary extravaganza is one of Miami Beach's greatest traditions. Scooch into one of the vinyl booths, practically antique relics of the days when Frank Sinatra and his Rat Pack used to dine here after performances, and review the huge menu that's loaded with authentic Jewish staples. Consider the classic corned beef sandwich, stuffed cabbage, brisket, or potato pancakes. Make sure to warm up to the servers, many of whom have been here since day one, and they will provide you with a coveted wax paper bag (a culinary souvenir, if you will) so you can take home your uneaten Danish and rolls. There is another Wolfie's in Boca Raton, at 2006 NW Executive Center Circle (ℭ **561/982-8899**).

17190 Collins Ave. (at 163rd St.), Sunny Isles. ℭ **305/947-4581.** Main courses $8–$30. AE, MC, V. Sun–Thurs 6:30am–1am; Fri–Sat 6:30am–2am.

SUPER-CHEAP EATS

Sheldon's Drugs ★ *Value* AMERICAN   This typical old-fashioned drugstore counter was a favorite breakfast spot of Isaac Bashevis Singer. Consider stopping into this historic site for a good piece of pie and a side of history. According to legend, the author was sitting at Sheldon's eating a bagel and eggs when his wife got the call in 1978 that he had won the Nobel Prize for Literature. The menu hasn't changed much since then. You can get eggs and oatmeal and a good tuna melt. A blue-plate special might be generic spaghetti and meatballs or grilled frankfurters. The food is pretty basic, but you can't beat the prices.

9501 Harding Ave., Surfside. ℭ **305/866-6251.** Main courses $4–$8; soups and sandwiches $2–$7. AE, DISC, MC, V. Mon–Sat 7am–7pm; Sun 7am–4pm.

WORTH A SPLURGE

Crystal Café ★★★ CONTINENTAL/NEW WORLD   Although there is no shortage of trendy, swanky, sceney restaurants in the South Beach and Miami Beach areas, what *is* lacking is that charming, cozy, local gourmet restaurant where the chef/owner seems to know everybody's name. Enter Crystal Café, the missing link in the chain of food establishments that prides itself more on the celebrity clientele than the stellar cuisine. This place dares to be different—and not in a postmodern minimalistic decor-cuisine kind of way, either. Not only is the food spectacular, but the ambience is also extremely inviting and romantic and one that you will want to revisit. Chef/owner Klime is a mastermind of exquisite culinary preparation and attention to detail, from his drool-worthy goat cheese terrine appetizer to his masterful filet mignon. The shrimp cake appetizer is the size of a bread plate and rests on top of a small mound of lightly sautéed watercress and mushrooms. Surrounding the delicately breaded disk are concentric circles of beautiful sauces. The veal Marsala is served in a luscious brown sauce thickened not with heavy cream or flour, but with delicate vegetable broth and a hearty mix of mushrooms. The *osso buco* is a masterpiece. The wine list is award winning and recognized by experts from all over the world as one of the best. And it's constantly evolving. So is the menu. And I could go on. Words really can't do Crystal Café the justice it deserves. When you go, however, ask for Chef Klime. He will be more than happy to say hello and explain his philosophy that has made his restaurant one of Miami's tastiest standouts.

726 41st St., Miami Beach. © **305/673-8266.** Reservations recommended on weekends. Main courses $13–$28. AE, DC, DISC, MC, V. Sun and Tues–Thurs 5–10pm; Fri–Sat 5–11pm.

Timo ★★★ ITALIAN/MEDITERRANEAN   Finally! A hip, haute restaurant in Sunny Isles, where, until recently, Tony Roma's was the hottest eatery. Owned by Tim Andriola, former executive chef of Mark's South Beach, Timo is a stylish Italian Mediterranean restaurant catering to mostly North Miami Beach locals who have been yearning for something else besides the fabulous Chef Allen's. Among the specialties, try the handcrafted pastas, including semolina gnocchi with braised oxtail; a traditional Sicilian pasta pie consisting of thin slices of eggplant wrapped around macaroni with crushed red pepper and buffalo mozzarella; and a phenomenal veal scaloppini. Less pricey, less heavy items are also available such as a delicious ricotta and fontina wood-fired pizza with white truffle oil—perfect for lunch or a happy-hour snack. At Timo, a cool bistro meets lounge atmosphere gives way to a decidedly cool vibe, something which was always conspicuously lacking at Tony Roma's.

17624 Collins Ave., Sunny Isles. © **305/936-1008.** Reservations required. Main courses $11–$24. AE, DC, MC, V. Daily 11:30am–3pm; Sun–Thurs 6pm–10:30pm; Fri–Sat 6pm–11pm.

NORTH MIAMI BEACH
WORTH A SPLURGE

The Fish Joint ★★ SEAFOOD   People jonesing for an out-of-this-world high that won't get them arrested can usually be found lining up at this small neighborhood seafood spot where the frills are on the fish and not the decor. Industrial kitsch is the best description of The Fish Joint's interior, which tends to be on the loud side, but you don't go here for the decor: Simple, fresh fish is the draw, prepared in a multitude of ways, including the Chilean sea bass in sweet and sour glaze or the grouper oreganato. If you like shrimp, order the shrimp cocktail—the crustaceans are absolutely Jurassic-size! As an added touch, every meal comes with irresistible potato pancakes rather than your average boring baked potato. No matter what you order, however, you're guaranteed to experience a high of sorts thanks to the stellar quality of this one-of-a-kind fish joint.

2570 NE Miami Gardens Dr. © **305/936-8333.** Main courses $17–$24. AE, DC, MC, V. Sun–Thurs 5–10pm; Fri–Sat 5–11pm.

Lagoon ★ SEAFOOD/CONTINENTAL   This old bayfront fish house has been around since 1936. Major road construction nearby should have guaranteed its doom years ago, but the excellent view and incredible specials make it a worthwhile stop. If you can disregard the somewhat dirty bathrooms and nonchalant service, you'll find the best-priced juicy Maine lobsters around.

Yes, it's true! Lobster lovers can get two 1¼ pounders for $26. Try them broiled with a light buttery-seasoned coating. This dish is not only inexpensive but incredibly succulent, too. Side dishes include fresh vegetables, like broccoli or asparagus, as well as a huge baked potato, stuffed or plain.

488 Sunny Isles Blvd. (163rd St.). ℂ 305/947-6661. Reservations accepted. Main courses $20–$47; appetizers $10–$14. AE, MC, V. Daily 4:30–10pm. Happy hour daily 4:30–6pm.

DOWNTOWN

For a map of the restaurants in this section, see the "Where to Stay & Dine in Key Biscayne, Downtown Miami, West Miami, Airport Area, North Dade, Little Havana, Coral Gables & Coconut Grove" map on p. 97.

SUPER CHEAP EATS

Andiamo Brick Oven Pizza ⭐ PIZZA   Leave it to visionary Mark Soyka (News Cafe, Van Dyke Cafe, Soyka) to turn a retro-style 1960s car wash into one of the city's best pizza places. The brick-oven pizzas are to die for, whether you choose the simple Andiamo pie (tomato sauce, mozzarella, and basil) or the more designer combos of pancetta and caramelized onions; hot and sweet sausage with broccoli rabe; or portobello mushrooms with truffle oil and goat cheese. Pizzas come in three sizes—10-inch, 13-inch, and 16-inch. And while the pizza is undeniably delicious here, the most talked about aspect of Andiamo is the fact that while you're washing down slice after slice, for a fee, you can get your car washed and detailed at Leo's, the space's original and still-existing occupant, out back, killing two birds with one, uh, slice.

5600 Biscayne Blvd. ℂ 305/762-5751. Main courses $3–$15. MC, V. Sun–Thurs 11am–11pm; Fri–Sat 11am–midnight.

Dogma Grill ⭐⭐ HOT DOGS   A little bit of LA comes to a gritty stretch of Biscayne Boulevard in the form of this very tongue and cheeky hot dog stand whose motto is "A Frank Philosophy." Owned by a former MTV executive, Dogma will change the way you view hot dogs, offering a plethora of choices from your typical chili dog to Chicago style with celery salt, hot peppers, onions, and relish. The tropical version with pineapple is a bit funky but fitting for this stand, which attracts a very colorful, arty crowd from the nearby Design District. The buns here are softer than feather pillows and the hot dogs are grilled to perfection. Try the garlic fries and the lemonade, too.

7030 Biscayne Blvd. ℂ 305/759-3433. Main courses $3–$4. No credit cards. Daily 11am–9pm.

Jimmy's East Side Diner ⭐ DINER   The only thing wrong with this quintessential, consummate greasy spoon diner is that it's not open 24 hours. Other than that, for the cheapest breakfasts in town, not to mention lunches and early dinners, Jimmy's is a dream come true. Try the banana pancakes, corned beef hash, roasted chicken, or Philly cheese steak. Located on the newly hip Upper East Side of Biscayne Boulevard, Jimmy's is a very neighborhood-y place at which late Bee Gee Maurice Gibb used to dine every Sunday. Adding to the aging regulars is a new, eclectic contingency of hung-over hipsters for whom Jimmy's is a sweet—and cheap—morning-after salvation.

7201 Biscayne Blvd. ℂ 305/759-3433. Main courses $3–$11. No credit cards. Daily 7am–4pm.

Latin American Cafeteria ⭐⭐ CUBAN   The name may sound a bit generic, but this no-frills indoor-outdoor cafeteria has the best Cuban sandwiches in the entire city. They're big enough for lunch and a doggie-bagged dinner, too. Service is fast, prices are cheap, but be forewarned: English is truly a second language at this chain, so have patience—it's worth it.

9796 Coral Way. © **305/226-2393**. Main courses $5–$9. AE, MC, V. Daily 7:30am–11pm.

Perricone's Marketplace ✿ ITALIAN   A large selection of groceries and wine, plus an outdoor porch and patio for dining, makes this one of the most welcoming spots downtown. Its rustic setting in the midst of downtown is a fantastic respite from city life. Sundays offer buffet brunches and all-you-can-eat dinners, too. But it's most popular weekdays at noon, when the suits show up for delectable sandwiches, quick and delicious pastas, and hearty salads.

15 SE 10th St. (corner of S. Miami Ave.). © **305/374-9693**. Sandwiches $5.95 and up; pastas $13 and up. AE, MC, V. Sun–Mon 7am–10pm; Tues–Sat 7am–11pm.

Tobacco Road AMERICAN   Miami's oldest bar is a bluesy Route 66–inspired institution favored by barflies, professionals, and anyone else who wishes to indulge in good and greasy bar fare—chicken wings, nachos, and so on—for a reasonable price in a down-home, gritty-but-charming atmosphere. The burgers are also good—particularly the Death Burger, a deliciously unhealthy combo of choice sirloin topped with grilled onions, jalapeños, and pepper jack cheese—bring on the Tums! Also a live music venue, the Road, as it is known by locals, is well traveled, especially during Friday's happy hour and Tuesday's lobster night, when 100 1¼-pound lobsters go for only $11 apiece.

626 S. Miami Ave. © **305/374-1198**. www.tobacco-road.com. Main courses $7–$10 and $12–$15 for nightly specials. AE, DC, MC, V. Mon–Sat 11:30am–5am; Sun noon–5am. Cover charge $5 or $6 Fri–Sat night.

WORTH A SPLURGE

Azul ★★★ GLOBAL FUSION   If there were an epicurean version of the Academy Awards, this restaurant would win best director, hands down. Executive chef Michelle Bernstein, Miami's wunderkind in the kitchen, creates a tour de force of international cuisine, inspired by Caribbean, French, Argentine, Asian, and even American flavors. Like a stunning designer gown, the restaurant's decor, with its waterfront view, high ceilings, walls burnished in copper, and silk-covered chairs, is complemented by sparkling jewels—in this case, the food. The hamachi carpaccio appetizer is a sumptuous arrangement of yellowtail (imported from Japan), shaved fennel, mixed greens, and cucumber. Entrees, or "Plates of Resistance" as they're called here, include braised langoustine openfaced ravioli; ginger-lemon-grass–glazed Chilean sea bass served with black rice, kimchi, and Napa cabbage; and chicken with red Thai curry. Desserts range from fruity to chocolaty and shouldn't be skipped. If you can't afford dinner here, consider the chef's bargain lunch special. "Michelle's Way" is a $25, threecourse lunch that will undoubtedly give you incentive to save your pennies for a future dinner here.

At the Mandarin Oriental, 500 Brickell Key Dr. © **305/913-8254**. Reservations strongly recommended. Main courses $24–$38. AE, DC, DISC, MC, V. Mon–Fri noon–3pm; Mon–Sat 7–11pm.

Big Fish ★★ *Finds* SEAFOOD/ITALIAN   This scenic seafood shack on the Miami River is a real catch—if you can find it. Hard to locate, but well worth the search, Big Fish's remote location keeps many people biting. In fact, it added some Italian options to its all-seafood menu in the hopes of luring more people, and that worked, too. Big Fish has a sweeping view of the Miami skyline and some of the freshest catch around; the pasta served with it is only a starchy diversion. But the spectacular setting may be the real draw, right there on the Miami River where freighters, fishing boats, dinghies, and sometimes yachts slink by to the amusement of the faithful diners who no longer have to fish around for a charming, serene seafood restaurant. However, you should beware of Friday nights, when Big Fish turns into a big happy-hour scene.

55 SW Miami Ave. Rd. ℂ **305/373-1770.** Main courses $15–$28. AE, DC, MC, V. Mon–Thu noon–11pm; Fri–Sat noon–midnight. Cross the Brickell Ave. Bridge heading south and take the 1st right on SW 5th St. The road narrows under a bridge. The restaurant is just on the other side.

Joe's Seafood ⭐ *Finds* SEAFOOD   A good catch on the banks of the Miami River, Joe's Seafood (not to be confused with Joe's Stone Crab) has a great waterfront setting and a fairly simple, yet tasty menu of fresh fish cooked in a number of ways—grilled, broiled, fried, or, the best in my opinion, in garlic or green sauce. Meals are quite the deal here, all coming with green salad or grouper soup and yellow rice or french fries. The complimentary fish spread appetizer is also a nice touch. Because of this, not to mention the great, gritty ambience that takes you away from neon, neo-Miami in favor of the old seafaring days, there's usually a wait for a table.

400–404 NW N. River Dr. ℂ **305/381-9329.** Reservations recommended. Main courses $14–$23. AE, DC, DISC, MC, V. Sun–Thurs 11am–10pm; Fri–Sat 11am–11pm.

190 ⭐⭐⭐ *Finds* CONTINENTAL/FUSION   190 is *the* coolest restaurant in Miami. There's no water view and no gimmicks, just a fabulous Haight Ashbury/East Village meets Miami boho vibe in which a decidedly funky, arty—not trendy—crowd gathers for delicious food, sangria, live music, poetry readings, backgammon, pool, and, on Sundays, a stellar, all-you-can-eat $15 brunch that serves, among other things, fried green tomatoes and a makeshift buffet slash pool table full of delicious things. If you're not in the mood for a full dinner, grab a stool at the bar and enjoy a slew of $3 tapas including cheeses, olives, meats, and more. On the dinner menu, however, are some irresistible items including some of the best, least expensive foie gras in town, a quiche of the night for only $6 with stuffings such as brie and sautéed artichokes, a tangy shrimp ceviche, and an outstanding seared salmon with lemon and garlic. For dessert, do not miss the white chocolate–black pepper mousse. Like the restaurant itself, this one is wholly unique.

190 NE 46th St. ℂ **305/576-9779.** Main courses $6–$16. MC, V. Tues–Thurs 6–11pm; Fri–Sat 6pm–midnight; Sun 11am–5pm.

Porcao ⭐⭐ BRAZILIAN   The name sounds eerily like "pork out," which is what you'll be doing at this exceptional Brazilian *churrascaria* (a Brazilian-style restaurant devoted mostly to meat—it's the Portuguese translation of steakhouse). For about $37, you can feast on salads and meats *after* you sample the unlimited gourmet buffet, which includes such fillers as pickled quail eggs, marinated onions, and an entire pig. Do not stuff yourself here, as the next step is the meaty part: Choose as much lamb, filet mignon, chicken hearts, and steaks as you like, grilled, skewered, and sliced right at your table. Side dishes also come with the meal, including beans and rice and fried yucca.

801 Brickell Bay Dr. ℂ **305/373-2777.** Reservations accepted. Prix fixe $37 per person, all you can eat. AE, DC, MC, V. Daily noon–midnight.

LITTLE HAVANA

The main artery of Little Havana is a busy commercial strip called Southwest 8th Street, or Calle Ocho. Auto-body shops, cigar factories, and furniture stores line this street, and on every corner there seems to be a pass-through window serving superstrong Cuban coffee and snacks. In addition, many of the Cuban,

Dominican, Nicaraguan, Peruvian, and other Latin American immigrants have opened full-scale restaurants ranging from intimate candlelit establishments to bustling stand-up lunch counters.

For a map of the restaurants in this section, see the "Where to Stay & Dine in Key Biscayne, Downtown Miami, West Miami, Airport Area, North Dade, Little Havana, Coral Gables & Coconut Grove" map on p. 97.

Hy-Vong ★★ VIETNAMESE   A must in Little Havana, expect to wait hours for a table, and don't even think of mumbling a complaint. Vietnamese cuisine combines the best of Asian and French cooking with spectacular results. Food at Hy-Vong is elegantly simple and superspicy. Appetizers include small, tightly packed Vietnamese spring rolls and kimchi, a spicy, fermented cabbage (which they ran out of on my last visit here because I got there too late—get there early!). Star entrees include pastry-enclosed chicken with watercress cream-cheese sauce and fish in tangy mango sauce. Unfortunately, service here is not at all friendly or stellar—in fact it borders on abysmal, but once you finally do get your food, all will be forgotten.

Enjoy the wait with a traditional Vietnamese beer and lots of company. Outside this tiny storefront restaurant, you'll meet interesting students, musicians, and foodies who come for the large, delicious portions.

3458 SW 8th St. (between 34th and 35th aves.). ℭ **305/446-3674.** Reservations accepted for parties of 5 or more. Main courses $7–$19. AE, DISC, MC, V. Sun–Thurs 6–11pm; Fri–Sat 6–11:30pm. Closed 2 weeks in Aug.

La Carreta ★ CUBAN   This cavernous family-style restaurant is filled with relics of an old farm and college kids eating *medianoches* (midnight sandwiches with ham, cheese, and pickles) after partying all night. Waitresses are brusque but efficient and will help Anglos along who may not know the lingo. The menu is vast and very authentic, but is known for its sandwiches and smaller items. Try the *sopa de pollo,* a rich golden stock loaded with chunks of chicken and fresh vegetables, or the *ropa vieja,* a shredded beef stew in thick brown sauce. Because of its immense popularity and low prices, La Carreta has opened seven branches throughout Miami, including a counter in the Miami airport. Check the White Pages for other locations.

3632 SW 8th St. ℭ **305/444-7501.** Main courses $5–$22. AE, DC, DISC, MC, V. Daily 24 hr.

Versailles ★★ CUBAN   Versailles is the meeting place of Miami's Cuban power brokers, who meet daily over café con leche to discuss the future of the exiles' fate. A glorified diner, the place sparkles with glass, chandeliers, murals, and mirrors meant to evoke the French palace. There's nothing fancy here—nothing French, either—just straightforward food from the home country. The menu is a veritable survey of Cuban cooking and includes specialties such as *Moors and Christians* (flavorful black beans with white rice), *ropa vieja* (shredded beef stew), and fried whole fish. Versailles is the place to come for mucho helpings of Cuban kitsch. With its late hours, it's also the perfect place to come after spending your night in Little Havana.

3555 SW 8th St. ℭ **305/444-0240.** Soup and salad $2–$10; main courses $5–$20. DC, DISC, MC, V. Mon–Thurs 8am–2am; Fri 8am–3am; Sat 8am–4:30am; Sun 9am–1am.

WORTH A SPLURGE

Casa Juancho ★★ SPANISH   A generous taste of Spain comes to Miami in the form of the cavernous Casa Juancho, which looks like it escaped from a production of *Don Quixote.* The numerous dining rooms are decorated with traditional Spanish furnishings and enlivened nightly by strolling Spanish musicians who tend to be annoying and expect tips—do not encourage them to play at your table; you'll hear them loud and clear from other tables, trust me. Try not to be frustrated with the older staff that doesn't speak English or respond quickly to your subtle glance—the food's worth the frustration. Your best bet is to order lots of *tapas*, small dishes of Spanish finger food. Some of the best include mixed seafood vinaigrette, fresh shrimp in hot garlic sauce, and fried calamari rings. A few entrees stand out, like roast suckling pig, baby eels in garlic and olive oil, and Iberian-style snapper.

2436 SW 8th St. (just east of SW 27th Ave.). (✆ **305/642-2452.** Reservations recommended, but not accepted on Fri–Sat after 8pm. Main courses $15–$34; tapas $6–$10. AE, DC, DISC, MC, V. Sun–Thurs noon–midnight; Fri–Sat noon–1am.

KEY BISCAYNE

Key Biscayne has some of the world's nicest beaches, hotels, and parks, yet it is not known for great food. Locals, or "Key rats" as they're known, tend to go off-island for meals or takeout, but here are some of the best on-the-island choices.

For a map of the restaurants in this section, see the "Where to Stay & Dine in Key Biscayne, Downtown Miami, West Miami, Airport Area, North Dade, Little Havana, Coral Gables & Coconut Grove" map on p. 97.

SUPER-CHEAP EATS

Bayside Seafood Hut ⭐ *Finds* SEAFOOD   Known by locals as "the Hut," this ramshackle restaurant and bar is a laid-back outdoor Tiki hut and terrace that serves pretty good sandwiches and fish platters on paper plates. A blackboard lists the latest catches, which can be prepared blackened, fried, broiled, or in a garlic sauce. The fish dip is wonderfully smoky and moist, if a little heavy on mayonnaise. Local fishers and yachties share this rustic outpost with equal enthusiasm and loyalty. A completely new air-conditioned area for those who can't stand the heat is a welcome addition, as are the new deck and spruced-up decor. But behind it all, it's nothing fancier than a hut—if it was anything else, it wouldn't be nearly as appealing.

3501 Rickenbacker Causeway. (✆ **305/361-0808.** Reservations accepted for 15 or more. Appetizers, salads, and sandwiches $5–$15; platters $7–$13. AE, MC, V. Daily 10am until closing (which varies).

Jimbo's *Finds* SEAFOOD   Locals like to keep quiet about Jimbo's, a ramshackle seafood shack that started as a gathering spot for fishermen and has since become the quintessential South Florida watering hole, snack bar, and hangout for those in the know. If ever Miami had a backwoods, this was it, right down to the smoldering garbage can, stray dogs, and chickens. Do *not* get dressed up to come here—you will get dirty. Go to the bathroom before you get here, too, because the Porta-Potties are absolutely rancid. Grab yourself a dollar can of beer (there's only beer, water, and soda, but you are allowed to bring your own choice of drink if you want) from the cooler and take in the view of the tropical lagoon where they shot *Flipper.* You may even see a manatee or two. Vacant shacks that served as backdrops for films such as *True Lies* surround this hidden enclave, which attracts everyone from shrimpers and politicians to well-oiled beach bums. Oddly enough, there's even a bocce court here, and the owner, Jimbo, may challenge you to a game. Play if you must, but word has it he never loses. Jimbo's smoked fish—marlin or salmon—is the best in town, but be forewarned: There are no utensils or napkins. When I asked for some, the woman said, "Lady, this is a place where you eat with your hands." I couldn't have said it better.

Off the Rickenbacker Causeway at Sewerline Rd., Virginia Key. ✆ 305/361-7026. Smoked fish about $8 a pound. No credit cards. Mon–Fri 6am–6:30pm; Sat–Sun 6am–7:30pm. Head south on the main road toward Key Biscayne, make a left just after the MAST Academy (there will be a sign that says VIRGINIA KEY), tell the person in the toll booth you're going to Jimbo's, and he'll point you in the right direction.

WORTH A SPLURGE

Rusty Pelican ⭐ SEAFOOD   The Pelican's private tropical walkway leads over a lush waterfall into one of the most romantic dining rooms in the city, located right on beautiful blue-green Biscayne Bay. The restaurant's windows look out over the water onto the sparkling stalagmites of Miami's magnificent downtown. Inside, quiet wicker paddle fans whirl overhead and saltwater fish swim in pretty table-side aquariums. The restaurant's surf-and-turf menu features conservatively prepared prime steaks, veal, shrimp, and lobster. The food is good, but the atmosphere—the reason why you're here—is even better, especially at sunset, when the view over the city is magical.

3201 Rickenbacker Causeway. ✆ 305/361-3818. Reservations recommended. Main courses $16–$30. AE, DC, MC, V. Daily 11:30am–4pm; Sun–Thurs 5–11pm; Fri–Sat 5pm–midnight.

COCONUT GROVE

Coconut Grove was long known as the artists' haven of Miami, but the rush of developers trying to cash in on the laid-back charm of this old settlement has turned it into something of an overgrown mall. Still, there are several great dining spots both in and out of the confines of Mayfair or CocoWalk.

For a map of the restaurants in this section, see the "Where to Stay & Dine in Key Biscayne, Downtown Miami, West Miami, Airport Area, North Dade, Little Havana, Coral Gables & Coconut Grove" map on p. 97.

Cafe Tu Tu Tango ⭐ SPANISH/INTERNATIONAL   This restaurant in the bustling CocoWalk is designed to look like a disheveled artist's loft. Dozens of original paintings—some only half-finished—hang on the walls and on studio easels. Seating is either inside, among the clutter, or outdoors, overlooking the Grove's main drag. Flamenco and other Latin-inspired tunes complement a menu with a decidedly Spanish flair. Hummus spread on rosemary flat bread and baked goat cheese in marinara sauce are two good starters. Tapas items include roast duck with dried cranberries, toasted pine nuts, and goat cheese, plus Cajun chicken egg rolls filled with corn, cheddar cheese, and tomato salsa. Pastas, ribs, fish, and pizzas round out the eclectic offerings, and several visits have proved each consistently good. Try the sweet, potent sangria and enjoy the warm, lively atmosphere from a seat with a view.

3015 Grand Ave. (on the 2nd floor of CocoWalk). ✆ 305/529-2222. Reservations not accepted. Tapas $3–$9.50. AE, MC, V. Sun–Wed 11:30am–midnight; Thurs 11:30am–1am; Fri–Sat 11:30am–2am.

WORTH A SPLURGE

Anokha ⭐⭐⭐ INDIAN   This is the best Indian restaurant in Miami. Anokha's motto is "A guest is equal to God and should be treated as such," and they do stick to it. The food here is from the gods, with fantastic tandooris, curries, and stews. The restaurant's location at the end of a quiet stretch of Coconut Grove is especially enticing because it prevents the throngs of pedestrians from overtaking what some people consider a diamond in the rough.

3195 Commodore Plaza (between Main Hwy. and Grand Ave.). ✆ 786/552-1030. Main courses $12–$40. AE, DC, MC, V. Sun and Tues–Wed 6–10:30 pm; Thurs–Sat 6–11:30 pm.

Baleen ⭐⭐⭐ SEAFOOD/MEDITERRANEAN   While the prices aren't lean, the cuisine here is worth every pricey, precious penny. Oversize crab cakes, oak-smoked diver scallops, and steakhouse-quality meats are among Baleen's excellent offerings. The lobster bisque is the best on Biscayne Bay. Everything here is a la carte, so order wisely, as it tends to add up quicker than you can put your fork down. The restaurant's spectacular waterfront setting makes Baleen a true knockout. Request one of the few tables that are actually on the water's edge; lit with Tiki torches and an illuminated backdrop of Biscayne Bay, Baleen is the kind of restaurant that you'd expect a reality show like *The Bachelor* to use as the place where the happy couple expresses their love for each other.

4 Grove Isle Dr. (in the Grove Isle Hotel). ✆ 305/858-8300. Reservations recommended. Main courses $18–$46. AE, DC, MC, V. Sun–Wed 7am–10pm; Thurs–Sat 7am–11pm.

Le Bouchon du Grove ★★ FRENCH   This very authentic, exceptional bistro is French right down to the waitstaff, who may only speak French to you, forgetting that they are in the heart of Coconut Grove, USA. But it matters not. The food, prepared by an animated French (what else) chef, is superb. An excellent starter is the wonderful *gratinée Lyonnaise* (traditional French onion soup). Fish is brought in fresh daily; try the Chilean sea bass when in season *(filet de loup poele)*. Though it is slightly heavy on the oil, it is delivered with succulent artichokes, tomato confit, and seasoned roasted garlic that is a gastronomic triumph. The *carre d'agneau roti* (roasted rack of lamb with Provence herbs) is served warm and tender, with an excellent amount of seasoning. There is also an excellent selection of pricey but doable French and American red and white wines.

3430 Main Hwy. ✆ 305/448-6060. Reservations recommended. Main courses $18–$26. AE, MC, V. Mon–Fri 10am–3pm; Mon–Thurs 5–11pm; Fri 5pm–midnight; Sat 8am–3pm and 5pm–midnight; Sun 8am–3pm and 5–11pm.

CORAL GABLES

Coral Gables is a foodie's paradise—a city in which you certainly won't go hungry. What Starbucks is to most major cities, excellent gourmet and ethnic restaurants are to Coral Gables, where there's a restaurant on every corner, and everywhere in between.

For a map of the restaurants in this section, see the "Where to Stay & Dine in Key Biscayne, Downtown Miami, West Miami, Airport Area, North Dade, Little Havana, Coral Gables & Coconut Grove" map on p. 97.

Miss Saigon Bistro ★★ VIETNAMESE   Unlike Andrew Lloyd Webber's bombastic Broadway show, this Miss Saigon is small, quiet, and not at all flashy. Servers at this family-run restaurant—among them, Rick, the owners' son—will graciously offer to recommend dishes or even to custom-make something for you, and if you're lucky, he may even sing you an aria with a voice ironically tailored to Webber shows. The menu is varied and reasonably priced and the portions are huge—large enough to share. Noodle dishes and soup bowls are hearty and flavorful; caramelized prawns are fantastic, as is the whole snapper with lemon grass and ginger sauce. Despite the fact that there are few tables inside and a hungry crowd usually gathers outside in the street, they will not rush you through your meal, which is worth savoring. There is also a new, much larger location at 9503 S. Dixie Hwy., in South Miami's Pinecrest (✆ **305/661-2911**).

148 Giralda Ave. (at Ponce de Le_n and 37th Ave.). ✆ 305/446-8006. Main courses $9–$18. AE, DC, DISC, MC, V. Mon–Fri 11:30am–3pm; Mon, Wed, Thurs, Sun 5:30–10pm; Tues 6:30–10pm; Fri–Sat 5:30–11pm.

SUPER-CHEAP EATS

Daily Bread Marketplace GREEK   This place is great for takeout food and homemade breads. The falafel and gyro sandwiches are large, fresh, and filling.

The spinach pie for less than $1 is also recommended, though it's short on spinach and heavy on pastry. Salads and spreads, including luscious tabbouleh, hummus, and eggplant, are also worth a go. To eat in or take out, the Middle Eastern fare here is a real treat, especially in an area so filled with fancy French and Cuban fare. Plus, you can pick up groceries such as grape leaves, fresh olives, couscous, fresh nuts, and pita bread. Daily Bread has taken its success to another level, opening **Oasis Lounge,** a sit-down Middle Eastern restaurant with a lounge on South Beach at 840 1st St. at Alton Road (© **305/673-2252**).

2400 SW 27th St. (off U.S. 1 under the monorail). © **305/856-0363** or 305/856-0366. Sandwiches and salads $4–$7. MC, V. Mon–Sat 9am–8pm; Sun 11am–5pm.

WORTH A SPLURGE

Brasserie Les Halles ✩✩ FRENCH   Known especially for its fine steaks and delicious salads, this very welcome addition to the Coral Gables dining scene became popular as soon as it opened in 1997 and has since continued to do a brisk business. The modest and moderately priced menu is particularly welcome in an area of overpriced, stuffy restaurants. For starters, try the mussels in white-wine sauce and the escargot. For a main course, the duck confit is an unusual and rich choice. Pieces of duck meat wrapped in duck fat are slow-cooked and served on salad frissé with baby potatoes with garlic. Service by the young French staff is polite but a bit slow. The tables tend to be a little too close, although there is a lovely private balcony space overlooking the long, thin dining room where large groups can gather.

2415 Ponce de León Blvd. (at Miracle Mile). © **305/461-1099.** Reservations recommended on weekends. Main courses $13–$26. AE, DC, DISC, MC, V. Daily 11:30am–midnight.

Caffe Abbracci ✩✩ ITALIAN   You'll understand why this restaurant's name means "hugs" in Italian the moment you enter the dark, romantic enclave: Your appetite will be embraced by the savory scents of fantastic Italian cuisine wafting through the restaurant. The homemade black and red ravioli filled with lobster in pink sauce, risotto with porcini and portobello mushrooms, and the house specialty—grilled veal chop topped with tricolor salad—are irresistible and perhaps the culinary equivalent of a warm, embracing hug. A cozy bar and lounge was added recently to further encourage the warm and fuzzy feelings.

318 Aragon Ave. (1 block north of Miracle Mile, between Salzedo St. and Le Jeune Rd.). © **305/441-0700.** Reservations recommended for dinner. Main courses $15–$30; pastas $15–$20. AE, DC, MC, V. Mon–Fri 11:30am–3pm; Sun–Thurs 6–11:30pm; Fri–Sat 6pm–12:30am.

Chispa ✩✩✩ CONTEMPORARY LATIN   Simply put, Chispa rocks. The brainchild of star chef Robin Haas (formerly of Baleen), this cavernous, stylish nouveau Latin restaurant will blow you away. If you've ever tasted the delicious, greasy *croquettas* at any Cuban bodega, wait until you try Chispa's gourmet version—a magnificent shrimp and black-eyed pea *croquetta* that renders the greasy ones only good for hangovers. For a real Cuban experience, try Sergio's Spit Roasted Young Suckling Pig; I hear it's great, but just couldn't bring myself to dine on Porky. A slew of fantastic seafood ceviches, an unparalleled mahimahi with sour orange aioli, those addictive shrimp and black-eyed *croquettas,* and wood-roasted mushrooms atop a seared cornmeal stew prove that there is, indeed, a way to be creative with Cuban food. A 40-foot bar and massive booths seating 8 to 10 people make Chispa a great place for large groups. The acoustics, however, need to be improved as it's louder than a Celia Cruz tribute in here.

225 Altara Ave. © **305/648-2600.** Reservations strongly recommended. Main courses $17–$25. AE, DC, MC, V. Sun–Thurs 11:30am–2:30pm and 5:30–10:30pm; Fri–Sat 5:30–11:30pm.

Ortanique on the Mile ★★ NEW WORLD CARIBBEAN You'll be greeted as you walk in by soft spiderlike lights and canopied mosquito netting that will make you wonder whether you're on a secluded island or inside one of King Tut's temples. Chef Cindy Hutson has truly perfected her tantalizing New World Caribbean menu that also graces the tables of her two other Ortaniques in D.C. and Vegas. For starters, an absolute must is the pumpkin bisque with a hint of pepper sherry. For those who absolutely refuse to eat foie gras (goose liver), Chef Hutson makes it worth trying again thanks to the jerk spices in which she marinates the love-it-or-leave-it delicacy. Afterward, move on to the tropical mango salad with fresh marinated Sable hearts of palm, julienne mango, baby field greens, toasted Caribbean candied pecans, and passion-fruit vinaigrette. For an entree, I recommend the pan-sautéed Bahamian black grouper marinated in teriyaki and sesame oil. It's served with an ortanique (an orange-like fruit) orange liqueur sauce and topped with steamed seasoned chayote, zucchini, and carrots on a lemon-orange boniato–sweet plantain mash. For dessert, try the chocolate mango tower—layers of brownie, chocolate mango mousse, meringue, and sponge cake, accompanied by mango sorbet and tropical-fruit salsa. Entrees may not be cheap, but they're a lot less than airfare to the islands, from where most, if not all, the ingredients used here hail.

278 Miracle Mile (next to Actor's Playhouse). ✆ 305/446-7710. Reservations requested. Main courses $19–$36. AE, DC, MC, V. Mon–Tues 6–10pm; Wed–Sat 6–11pm; Sun 5:30–9:30pm.

SOUTH MIAMI & WEST MIAMI

Though mostly residential, these areas nonetheless have a couple eating establishments worth the drive.

El Toro Taco Family Restaurant ★★★ *(Finds)* MEXICAN Until I discovered this Mexican oasis in the midst of South Florida farmland, I'd never had good enough reason to leave my quasi-cosmopolitan confines in Miami for rural Homestead way down south. This 96-seat family-run restaurant has put major miles on my car since I first stumbled upon it a few years ago when I was lost and very hungry. Fabulous, and I mean fabulous, Mexican fare, including tacos, enchiladas, and burritos drenched with the freshest and zestiest salsa this side of Baja, is what you'll find here in abundance. It may sound odd to travel from a big city with tons of restaurants to farm country for Mexican food, but trust me, it's so cheap and delicious, it's worth the trip.

1 S. Krome Ave., Homestead. ✆ 305/245-8182. Main courses $1.75–$12. DISC, MC, V. Sun and Tues–Fri 10am–9pm; Fri–Sat 10am–10pm. Take 836 W (Dolphin Expwy.) toward Miami International Airport. Take Florida Tpk. S ramp toward Florida City/Key West. Take U.S. 41/SW 8th St. exit (#25) and turn left onto SW 8th St. Take SW 8th St. to Krome Ave. (½ mile) and turn left onto Krome Ave.

Shorty's ★ BARBECUE A Miami tradition since 1951, this honky-tonk of a log cabin is still serving some of the best ribs and chicken in South Florida. People line up for the smoke-flavored, slow-cooked meat that's so tender it seems to fall off the bone. The secret, however, is to ask for your order with sweet sauce. The regular stuff tastes bland and bottled. All the side dishes, including the coleslaw, corn on the cob, and baked beans, look commercial, but are necessary to complete the experience. This is a jeans and T-shirt kind of place, but you may want to wear an elastic waistband, as overeating is not uncommon.

9200 S. Dixie Hwy. (between U.S. 1 and Dadeland Blvd.), South Miami. ✆ 305/670-7732. Main courses $5–$9. DISC, MC, V. Sun–Thurs 11am–10pm; Fri–Sat 11am–11pm.

5 Hitting the Beach

Perhaps Miami's most popular attraction is its incredible 35-mile stretch of beachfront, which runs from the tip of South Beach north to Sunny Isles and circles Key Biscayne and the numerous other pristine islands dotting the Atlantic. The characteristics of Miami's many beaches are as varied as the city's population: There are beaches for swimming, socializing, or serenity; for family, seniors, or gay singles; some to make you forget you're in the city, others darkened by huge condominiums. Whatever type of beach vacation you're looking for, you'll find it in one of Miami's two distinct beach areas: Miami Beach and Key Biscayne.

MIAMI BEACH'S BEACHES Collins Avenue fronts more than a dozen miles of white-sand beach and blue-green waters from 1st to 192nd streets. Although most of this stretch is lined with a solid wall of hotels and condos, beach access is plentiful. There are lots of public beaches here, wide and well maintained, complete with lifeguards, bathroom facilities, concession stands, and metered parking (bring lots of quarters). Except for a thin strip close to the water, most of the sand is hard-packed—the result of a $10 million Army Corps of Engineers Beach Rebuilding Project meant to protect buildings from the effects of eroding sand.

In general, the beaches on this barrier island (all on the eastern, ocean side of the island) become less crowded the farther north you go. A wooden boardwalk runs along the hotel side of the beach from 21st to 46th streets—about 1½ miles—offering a terrific sun-and-surf experience without getting sand in your shoes. Aside from "Miami's Best Beaches," listed below, Miami's lifeguard-protected public beaches include 21st Street, at the beginning of the boardwalk; 35th Street, popular with an older crowd; 46th Street, next to the Fontainebleau Hilton; 53rd Street, a narrower, more sedate beach; 64th Street, one of the quietest strips around; and 72nd Street, a local old-timers' spot.

KEY BISCAYNE'S BEACHES If Miami Beach doesn't provide the privacy you're looking for, try Virginia Key and Key Biscayne. Crossing the Rickenbacker Causeway ($1 toll), however, can be a lengthy process, especially on weekends, when beach bums and tan-o-rexics flock to the Key. The 5 miles of public beach there, however, are blessed with softer sand and are less developed and more laid-back than the hotel-laden strips to the north.

MIAMI'S BEST BEACHES

Crandon Park Beach ⭐ On Crandon Boulevard in Key Biscayne, you'll find this beach, National Lampoon's *Vacation* on the sand. It's got a diverse crowd consisting of dedicated beach bums and lots of leisure-seeking families, set to a soundtrack of salsa, disco, and reggae music blaring from a number of competing stereos. With 3 miles of oceanfront beach, bathrooms, changing facilities, 493 acres of park, 75 grills, three parking lots, several soccer and softball fields, and a public 18-hole championship golf course, Crandon is like a theme park on the sand. Admission is $4 per vehicle. It's open daily from 8am to sunset.

Lummus Park Beach ⭐⭐ Also called Glitter Beach, Lummus Park beach runs along Ocean Drive from about 6th to 14th streets on South Beach. It's the best place to go if you're seeking entertainment as well as a great tan. On any day of the week, you might spy models primping for a photo shoot, nearly naked (topless is legal on this beach) sun-worshippers avoiding tan lines, and an assembly line of washboard abs off which you could (but shouldn't) bounce your

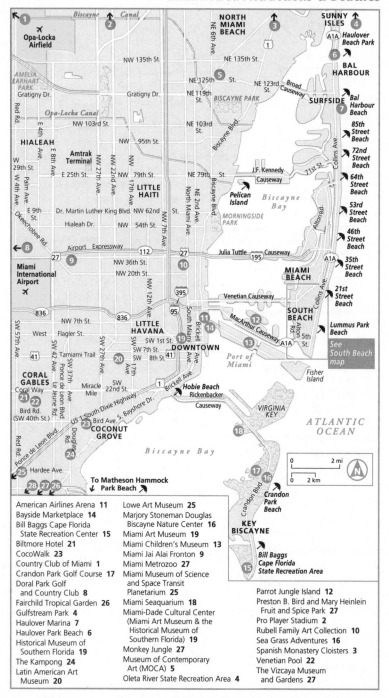

Miami Area Attractions & Beaches

American Airlines Arena **11**
Bayside Marketplace **14**
Bill Baggs Cape Florida
  State Recreation Center **15**
Biltmore Hotel **21**
CocoWalk **23**
Country Club of Miami **1**
Crandon Park Golf Course **17**
Doral Park Golf
  and Country Club **8**
Fairchild Tropical Garden **26**
Gulfstream Park **4**
Haulover Marina **7**
Haulover Park Beach **6**
Historical Museum of
  Southern Florida **19**
The Kampong **24**
Latin American Art
  Museum **20**

Lowe Art Museum **25**
Marjory Stoneman Douglas
  Biscayne Nature Center **16**
Miami Art Museum **19**
Miami Children's Museum **13**
Miami Jai Alai Fronton **9**
Miami Metrozoo **27**
Miami Museum of Science
  and Space Transit
  Planetarium **25**
Miami Seaquarium **18**
Miami-Dade Cultural Center
  (Miami Art Museum & the
  Historical Museum of
  Southern Florida) **19**
Monkey Jungle **27**
Museum of Contemporary
  Art (MOCA) **5**
Oleta River State Recreation Area **4**

Parrot Jungle Island **12**
Preston B. Bird and Mary Heinlein
  Fruit and Spice Park **27**
Pro Player Stadium **2**
Rubell Family Art Collection **10**
Sea Grass Adventures **16**
Spanish Monastery Cloisters **3**
Venetian Pool **22**
The Vizcaya Museum
  and Gardens **27**

Cheap Thrills: What to See & Do for Free (or Almost) in Miami

- **Watch the sun set over downtown.** Driving west over the Julia Tuttle Causeway (Fla. 112), you can catch the best views in the city. Aqua, pink, and orange lights explode behind a cluster of skyscrapers, and the surrounding water reflects it all. Head back in the other direction, and catch the glow of neon decorating a cluster of towering palms.
- **Indulge in Ocean Drive's eye candy.** All along South Beach's Ocean Drive, the Champs Elysees of Miami, well-toned and tanned bodies abound. Scantily clad boys and girls, gender benders, leggy models, in-line skaters, and gawking tourists alike parade along the wide promenade, with a backdrop of cotton candy–colored Art Deco buildings on one side and the glistening ocean on the other. If you're around in winter, you're almost guaranteed to find a preview fashion shoot in progress. Stake out a front row seat at any of the sidewalk cafes lining the strip where, for the price of a soda or a glass of wine, you'll be amused for hours.
- **Taste some Latin flavor in Little Havana.** To experience a little slice of Cuba on U.S. soil, stroll down Calle Ocho (8th St.) and stop into any of the shops catering to the huge exile population. Visit **Maximo Gomez Park,** 801 SW 15th Ave., where *viejitos* (old men) face off over chess boards from morning until sunset. Between 15th and 13th avenues is the street of *estrellas,* where stars like Celia Cruz have their names etched in the sidewalk, Hollywood-style. Visit a cigar factory, and then savor a *café con leche* at a local diner like Versailles (p. 116). There's no better way to get a feel for this city. (And if you don't *habla Español,* bring along a phrase book.)
- **Tour downtown from the Metrorail.** For 25¢, you can get a spectacular overview of Miami's bustling metropolis. The best part is, you can enjoy it all seated in the cool comfort of air-conditioned cars. It's like the monorail at Disney, but without the commentary.
- **Swim, stroll, and lounge on the beach.** Most of Miami's beaches are entirely free, though some in park areas do charge a fee for vehicles.

---

bottle of sunscreen. Restrooms and changing facilities are available on the beach, but don't expect to have a Cindy Crawford encounter in one of these. Most people tend to prefer using the somewhat drier, cleaner restrooms of the restaurants on Ocean Drive.

85th Street Beach ✮ Along Collins Avenue, this beach is located away from the maddening crowds and is a great place to head for a swim. It's one of Miami's only stretches of sand with no condos or hotels looming over sunbathers. Lifeguards patrol the area throughout the day and restrooms are available, though they are not exactly the benchmark of cleanliness.

Hobie Beach ✮✮ On the side of the causeway leading to Key Biscayne, Hobie Beach is not really so much a beach as an inlet with predictable winds. This spot is perfect for windsurfing, and numerous rental spots dot the area in response. Restrooms are available.

You can enjoy miles of wide sandy beaches all along Miami Beach, where the water is calm and warm. South Beach between 5th and 20th streets has the most characters, from topless European women to superbuff bodybuilders.

- **Walk through the lobby of The Delano Hotel.** The **Delano**, 1685 Collins Ave., South Beach (© 305/672-2000), is a tragically trendy outpost of seeing and being seen, with a gorgeous staff that competes for attention with the outlandish yet brilliantly minimalistic Philippe Starck decor. Check out the overflowing pool, out-of-proportion chess set, and funky (and pricey) gift shop. Splurge on a $10 drink poolside, and settle in for a few hours of celeb-spotting and people-watching. You won't be disappointed.

- **Sample the flavor of South Beach at its most venerated gourmet store.** A bunch of tomatoes might cost you $5 at **Epicure**, 1656 Alton Rd., Miami Beach (© 305/672-1861), but if you can resist the temptation of buying the high-ticket items, this is a great place to browse and snack (for free—if you don't ask, you don't get!). On most days, a busy booth offers samples of anything from salsa to olive oils. Stop by the cheese department and taste a wedge of something exotic or familiar. The deli folks will happily share a forkful of chicken salad or a generous slice of nova to anyone who asks for a nibble, and the tough cookies at the bakery counter will soften up if you ask to sample a pastry or two.

- **Rock out with headliners and legends at the Gulfstream Park Concert Series.** While some may consider acts like REO Speedwagon, Air Supply, and Cindy Lauper to be has-beens, devoted fans flock to see these groups and others live at this very popular concert series held at 21301 Biscayne Blvd., Hallandale. From January to April, the cost is free outside of the $5 charged for admission to the park. Call © 954/457-6940 for specific dates and times.

Bal Harbour Beach ✦   You'll find plenty of colorful shells at Bal Harbour Beach, Collins Avenue at 96th Street. There's also an exercise course and good shade—but no lifeguards, restrooms, or changing facilities.

Haulover Beach   For that all-over tan, head here, just north of the Bal Harbour border, and join nudists from around the world in a top-to-bottom tanning session. Should you choose to keep your swimsuit on, however, there are changing rooms and restrooms. This area also gets some of Miami's biggest swells and is very popular with surfers.

Matheson Hammock Park Beach ✦✦✦   Located at 9610 Old Cutler Rd. in South Miami (© 305/665-5475), this beach is the epitome of tranquillity, tucked away from the scene. It's a great beach for those seeking "alone time." It's also a great place to bring young children: Because of its man-made lagoon, which is fed naturally by the tidal movement of the adjacent Biscayne Bay, the waters are extremely calm, not to mention safe, and the area is secluded enough for families to keep an eye on the kids. Restrooms and changing facilities are available.

6 The Art Deco District

"You know what they used to say? 'Who's Art?'" recalls Art Deco revivalist Dona Zemo, "You'd say, 'This is an Art Deco building,' and they'd say, 'Really, who is Art?' These people thought 'Art Deco' was some guy's name."

How things have changed. This guy Art has become one of the most popular Florida attractions since, well, that mouse Mickey. The district is roughly bounded by the Atlantic Ocean on the east, Alton Road on the west, 6th Street to the south, and Dade Boulevard (along the Collins Canal) to the north.

Simply put, Art Deco is a style of architecture that, in its heyday of the 1920s and 1930s, used to be considered ultramodern. Today, fans of the style consider it retro-fabulous. And while some people may not consider the style fabulous, it's undoubtedly retro. According to the experts, Art Deco made its debut in 1925 in an exposition in Paris in which it set a stylistic tone, with buildings based on early neoclassical styles with the application of exotic motifs like flora, fauna, and fountains based on geometric patterns. In Miami, Art Deco is marked by the pastel-hued buildings that line South Beach and Miami Beach. But it's a lot more than just color. If you look carefully, you will see the intricacies and impressive craftsmanship that went into each building back in the day—which, in Miami's case, was the '20s, '30s, and '40s, and now, thanks to intensive restoration, today.

Most of the finest examples of the whimsical Art Deco style are concentrated along three parallel streets—Ocean Drive, Collins Avenue, and Washington Avenue—from about 6th to 23rd streets.

After years of neglect and calls for the wholesale demolition of its buildings, South Beach got a new lease on life in 1979. Under the leadership of Barbara Baer Capitman, a dedicated crusader for the Art Deco region, and the Miami Design Preservation League, founded by Baer Capitman and five friends, an area

---

Finds Walking by Design

The Miami Design Preservation League offers several tours of Miami Beach's historic architecture, which all leave from the Art Deco Welcome Center, located at 1001 Ocean Dr. in Miami Beach. A self-guided audio tour (available 7 days a week, from 10am–4pm) turns the streets into a virtual outdoor museum, taking you through Miami Beach's Art Deco district at your own leisure, with tours in several languages for just $10 per person. Guided tours conducted by local historians and architects offer an in-depth look at the structures and their history. The 90-minute Ocean Drive and Beyond tour (offered every Wed and Sat at 10:30am) takes you through the district, pointing out the differences between Mediterranean Revival and Art Deco for $15 per person. If you're not blinded by neon, the Thursday night Art Deco District Up-to-Date tour (leaving at 6:30pm) will whisk you around for 90 minutes, making note of how certain local hot spots were architecturally famous way before the likes of Madonna and Co. entered the scene. The cost is $15. For more information on tours or reservations, call © 305/672-2014.

made up of an estimated 800 buildings was granted a listing on the National Register of Historic Places. Designers then began highlighting long-lost architectural details with soft sherbet shades of peach, periwinkle, turquoise, and purple. Developers soon moved in, and the full-scale refurbishment of the area's hotels was under way.

Not everyone was pleased, though. Former Miami Beach commissioner Abe Resnick said, "I love old buildings. But these Art Deco buildings are 40, 50 years old. They aren't historic. They aren't special. We shouldn't be forced to keep them." But Miami Beach kept those buildings, and Resnick lost his seat on the commission.

Today, hundreds of new establishments—hotels, restaurants, and nightclubs—have renovated, or are in the process of renovating, these older, historical buildings and are moving in, making South Beach on the cutting edge of Miami's cultural and nightlife scene.

EXPLORING THE AREA

If you're touring this unique neighborhood on your own, start at the **Art Deco Welcome Center,** 1001 Ocean Dr. (© **305/531-3484**), which is run by the Miami Design Preservation League. The only beachside building across from the Clevelander Hotel and bar, the center gives away lots of informational material, including maps and pamphlets, and runs guided tours about the neighborhood. Art Deco books (including *The Art Deco Guide,* an informative compendium of all the buildings here), T-shirts, postcards, mugs, and other paraphernalia are for sale. It's open daily from 10am to 7:30pm.

7 Miami Art & Museums

Miami has never been known as a cultural mecca as far as museums are concerned. Though several exhibition spaces have made forays into collecting nationally acclaimed work, limited support and political infighting have made it a difficult proposition. Recently, however, things have changed as museums such as the Wolfsonian, the Museum of Contemporary Art, the Bass Museum of Art, and the Miami Art Museum have gotten on the bandwagon, boasting collections and exhibitions high on the list of art aficionados. It's now safe to say that world-class exhibitions start here. Listed below are the most lauded museums that have become a part of the city's cultural heritage, and as such, are as diverse as the city itself.

Work continues to proceed on the **Collins Park Cultural Center,** which comprises a trio of arts buildings on Collins Park and Park Avenue (off Collins Ave.), bounded by 21st to 23rd streets—the newly expanded Bass Museum of Art (see below), the new Arquitectonica-designed home of the Miami City Ballet, and the Miami Beach Regional Library, an ultramodern building designed by architect Robert A. M. Stern, scheduled to open at some point in 2006, which will have a special focus on the arts. The Library Café will be located on the library's first floor, serving coffee and pastries and exuding that cafe society ambience. Collins Park, the former site of the Miami Beach Library, will return to its original incarnation as an open space extending to the Atlantic, but it will also be the site of large sculpture installations and cultural activities planned jointly by the organizations that share the space.

Bass Museum of Art ★★★ The Bass Museum of Art has expanded and received a dramatically new look, rendering it Miami's most progressive art museum. World-renowned Japanese architect Arata Isozaki designed the magnificent new facility, which has triple the former exhibition space, and added an outdoor sculpture terrace, a museum cafe and courtyard, and a museum shop, among other improvements. In addition to providing space in which to show the permanent collection, exhibitions of a scale and quality not previously seen in Miami will now be featured at the Bass. The museum's permanent collection includes European paintings from the 15th through the early 20th centuries with special emphasis on Northern European art of the Renaissance and baroque periods, including Dutch and Flemish masters such as Bol, Flinck, Rubens, and Jordaens. Past exhibitions have included the works of Picasso, Frida Kahlo, and Francois-Marie Banier. The museum also has a lab, The New Information Workshop, making it possible for all aspiring artists to create their own masterpieces on computers for free or a nominal charge.

2121 Park Ave. (1 block west of Collins Ave.), South Beach. ✆ 305/673-7530. www.bassmuseum.org. Admission $6 adults, $4 students and seniors, free for children 6 and under. Free 2nd Thurs of the month 6–9pm. Tues–Wed and Fri–Sat 10am–5pm; Thurs 10am–9pm; Sun 11am–5pm.

Holocaust Memorial ★★★   This heart-wrenching memorial is hard to miss and would be a shame to overlook. The powerful centerpiece, Kenneth Triester's *Sculpture of Love & Anguish,* depicts victims of the concentration camps crawling up a giant, yearning hand, stretching up to the sky, marked with an Auschwitz number tattoo. Along the reflecting pool is the story of the Holocaust, told in cut marble slabs. Inside the center of the memorial is a tableau that is one of the most solemn and moving tributes to the millions of Jews who lost their lives in the Holocaust I've seen. You can walk through an open hallway lined with photographs and the names of concentration camps and their victims. From the street, you'll see the outstretched arm, but do stop and tour the sculpture at ground level.

1933 Meridian Ave. (at Dade Blvd.), South Beach. ✆ 305/538-1663. www.holocaustmmb.org. Free admission. Daily 9am–9pm.

Latin American Art Museum   In addition to the permanent collection of contemporary artists from Spain and Latin America, this 3,500-square-foot museum hosts monthly exhibitions of works from Latin America and the Caribbean Basin. Usually, the exhibitions focus on a theme, such as international women or surrealism. It's not a major attraction, but worth a stop if you're interested in Latin American art. On the same block, you'll find great design stores and a few other galleries.

2206 SW 8th St., Little Havana. ✆ 305/644-1127. Free admission (though donation suggested). Tues–Fri 11am–5pm; Sat 11am–4pm. 2nd Friday of every month 6:30–10pm. Closed major holidays.

Lowe Art Museum ★★   Located on the University of Miami campus, the Lowe Art Museum has a dazzling collection of 8,000 works that include American paintings, Latin American art, Navajo and Pueblo Indian textiles, and Renaissance and baroque art. Traveling exhibits such as *Rolling Stone* magazine's photo collection also stop here. For the most part, the Lowe is known for its collection of Greek and Roman antiquities, and, as compared to the more modern MOCA, Bass, and Miami Art Museum, features mostly European and international art hailing back to ancient times.

University of Miami, 1301 Stanford Dr. (at Ponce de León Blvd.), Coral Gables. ✆ 305/284-3603. www.lowemuseum.org. Admission $5 adults, $3 seniors and students with ID. Donation day is 1st Tues of the month. Tues, Wed, Fri, and Sat 10am–5pm; Thurs noon–7pm; Sun noon–5pm.

Miami Art Museum at the Miami–Dade Cultural Center ★★★   The Miami Art Museum (MAM) features an eclectic mix of modern and contemporary works by such artists as Eric Fischl, Max Beckmann, Jim Dine, and Stuart Davis. Rotating exhibitions span the ages and styles, and often focus on Latin American or Caribbean artists. There are also fantastic themed exhibits such as the Andy Warhol exhibit, which featured all-night films by the artist, make-your-own pop art, cocktail hours, and parties with local DJs. JAM at MAM is the museum's popular happy hour, which takes place the third Thursday of the month and is tied in to a particular exhibit. Almost as artistic as the works inside the museum is the composite sketch of the people—young and old—who attend these events.

The Miami–Dade Cultural Center, where the museum is housed, is a fortresslike complex designed by Phillip Johnson. In addition to the acclaimed Miami Art Museum, the center houses the main branch of the Miami–Dade Public Library, which sometimes features art and cultural exhibits, and the Historical Museum of Southern Florida, which highlights the fascinating history of the area. Unfortunately, the plaza onto which the complex opens is home to many of downtown Miami's homeless population, which makes it a bit off-putting but not dangerous.

101 W. Flagler St., Miami. ℂ 305/375-3000. www.miamiartmuseum.org. Admission $5 adults, $2.50 seniors and students, free for children under 12. Tues–Fri 10am–5pm; 3rd Thurs of each month 10am–9pm; Sat–Sun noon–5pm. From I-95 south, exit at Orange Bowl–NW 8th St. and continue south to NW 2nd St.; turn left at NW 2nd St. and go 1½ blocks to NW 2nd Ave.; turn right.

Miami Children's Museum ★★ *Kids*   This brand new museum, located across the MacArthur Causeway from Parrot Jungle Island, is a modern, albeit odd looking, 56,500-square-foot facility that includes 12 galleries, classrooms, a parent/teacher resource center, a Kid Smart educational gift shop, a 200-seat auditorium, and a Subway restaurant. The museum offers hundreds of bilingual, interactive exhibits as well as programs and classes and learning materials related to arts, culture, community, and communication. Even as an adult, I have to say I was tempted to participate in some kids-only activities and exhibitions, such as the miniature Bank of America and Publix Supermarket, and a re-creation of the NBC 6 television studio. There's also a re-creation of a Carnival Cruise ship and even a port stop in a re-created Brazil. Perhaps the coolest thing of all is the World Music Studio in which aspiring Britneys, Justins, and Lenny Kravitzes can lay down a few tracks and play instruments.

980 MacArthur Causeway, Miami Beach. ℂ 305/373-5437. www.miamichildrensmuseum.org. Admission $8 adults and children, $4 for city residents. Daily 10am–6pm.

Miami Museum of Science and Space Transit Planetarium ★★ *Kids*   The Museum of Science features more than 140 hands-on exhibits that explore the mysteries of the universe. Live demonstrations and collections of rare natural history specimens make a visit here fun and informative. Many of the demos involve audience participation, which can be lots of fun for willing and able kids and adults alike. There is also the Wildlife Center, with more than 175 live reptiles and birds of prey. The adjacent Space Transit Planetarium projects astronomy and laser shows as well as interactive demonstrations of upcoming computer technology and cyberspace features. Call or visit their website for a list of upcoming exhibits and laser shows.

3280 S. Miami Ave. (just south of the Rickenbacker Causeway), Coconut Grove. © **305/646-4200** for general information. www.miamisci.org. Admission $10 adults, $8 seniors and students, $6 children 3–12, free for children 2 and under; laser shows $7 adults, $4 seniors and children 3–12. $2 off admission after 4:30pm. Call for laser show times. Ticket prices include entrance to all museum galleries, planetarium shows, and the Wildlife Center. Museum of Science, daily 10am–6pm; call for planetarium show times. Closed on Thanksgiving and Christmas Day.

Museum of Contemporary Art (MOCA) ★★★

MOCA boasts an impressive collection of internationally acclaimed art with a local flavor. It is also known for its forward thinking and ability to discover and highlight new artists. A high-tech screening facility allows for film presentations to complement the exhibitions. You can see works by Jasper Johns, Roy Lichtenstein, Larry Rivers, Duane Michaels, and Claes Oldenburg, plus there are special exhibitions by such artists as Yoko Ono, Sigmar Polke, John Baldessari, and Goya. Guided tours are offered in English, Spanish, French, Creole, Portuguese, German, and Italian.

770 NE 125th St., North Miami. © **305/893-6211.** Fax 305/891-1472. www.mocanomi.org. Admission $5 adults, $3 seniors and students with ID, free for children 12 and under, Tues by donation. Tues–Sat 11am–5pm; Sun noon–5pm.

Rubell Family Art Collection ★★★ *Finds*

This impressive collection, owned by the Miami hotelier family, the Rubells, is housed in a two-story 40,000-square-foot former Drug Enforcement Agency warehouse in a sketchy area north of downtown Miami. The building looks like a fortress, which is fitting: Inside is a priceless collection of more than a thousand works of contemporary art, by the likes of Keith Haring, Damien Hirst, Julian Schnabel, Jean-Michel Basquiat, Paul McCarthy, Charles Ray, and Cindy Sherman. But be forewarned: Some of the art is extremely graphic and may be off-putting to some. The gallery changes exhibitions twice yearly and there is a seasonal program of lectures, artists' talks, and performances by prominent artists.

95 NW 29th St. (on the corner of NW 1st Ave. near the Design District), Miami. © **305/573-6090.** Admission $5 adults, $2 students and seniors. Wed–Sun 10am–6pm.

Spanish Monastery Cloisters ★★★ *Finds*

Did you know that the alleged oldest building in the Western Hemisphere dates from 1133 and is located in Miami? The Spanish Monastery Cloisters were first erected in Segovia, Spain for St. Bernard de Clairvaux, an influential church figure. Centuries later, newspaper magnate William Randolph Hearst purchased and brought them to America in pieces. The carefully numbered stones were quarantined for years until they were finally reassembled on the present site in 1954. It has often been used as a backdrop for weddings, movies, and commercials and is a very popular tourist attraction.

16711 W. Dixie Hwy. (at NE 167th St.), North Miami Beach. © **305/945-1461.** www.spanishmonastery.com. Admission $5 adults, $2.50 seniors and students with ID, $2 children 3–12. Mon–Sat 9am–5pm; Sun 1–5pm. Call ahead because the monastery closes for special events without it being announced.

Venetian Pool ★★★ *Kids*

Miami's most beautiful and unusual swimming pool, dating from 1924, is hidden behind pastel stucco walls and is honored with a listing in the National Register of Historic Places. Underground artesian wells feed the free-form lagoon, which is shaded by three-story Spanish porticos and features both fountains and waterfalls. It can be cold in the winter months. During summer, the pool's 800,000 gallons of water are drained and refilled nightly thanks to an underground aquifer, ensuring a cool, *clean* swim.

Drive-by Art

You can see the following pieces of public art and prized architecture from the comfort of your car, if you like. Each is a free roadside attraction and a great photo opportunity if you're in the area.

- **Versace Mansion (Amsterdam Palace):** Morbid curiosity has led hordes of people to the only private home on Ocean Drive, better known as the Versace mansion. If you can get past the fact that the late designer was murdered on the steps of this palatial estate, you should definitely observe the intricate Italian architecture that makes this house stand out from its streamlined Deco neighbors. It was built in the 1930s as a replica of Christopher Columbus's son's palace in Santo Domingo. Today the house is owned by a private citizen from Texas. It's located at the northwest corner of Ocean Drive and 11th Street, South Beach.

- **Estefan Enterprises:** Miami's royal family—Gloria and Emilio Estefan—may reside on private Star Island, but the headquarters of their musical empire is located in a whimsical building designed by the world-famous Arquitectonica architecture company. Its facade is carved with color-lined waves and fanciful shapes. The address is 420 Jefferson Ave. (at 5th St.), Miami Beach.

- **Miami Beach Post Office:** Post offices are rarely considered a must-see, but this one's an exception. Built in 1937, this unusual and modern-looking Depression-era building features a fabulous rotunda. Utterly Floridian are the coral steps that lead to the entrance. Inside this magnificent building, an intricate sun motif on the ceiling surrounds a lantern, which illuminates an epic mural depicting some of South Florida's history. Find the post office at 1300 Washington Ave., Miami Beach.

- **Mermaid Sculpture:** A pop art masterpiece designed by Roy Lichtenstein, this sculpture captures the buoyant spirit of Miami Beach and its environs. It's in front of the Jackie Gleason Theater of the Performing Arts, 1700 Washington Ave., Miami Beach.

- **Morris Lapidus on Lincoln Road:** Famed designer/architect, the late Morris Lapidus—the "high priest of high kitsch"—who is best known for the Fontainebleau Hotel, created a series of sculptures that are angular, whimsical, and quirky. In addition to the sculptures on Lincoln Road (at Washington Ave.), which you can't miss, Lapidus also created the Colony Theater, 1040 Lincoln Rd., which was built by Paramount in 1943; the 1928 Sterling Building, 927 Lincoln Rd., whose glass blocks and blue neon are required evening viewing; and the Lincoln Theater, 555 Lincoln Rd., which features a remarkable tropical bas-relief.

Visitors are free to swim and sunbathe here, just as Esther Williams and Johnny Weissmuller did decades ago. For a modest fee, you or your children can learn to swim during special summer programs.

2701 DeSoto Blvd. (at Toledo St.), Coral Gables. (℃) **305/460-5356.** www.venetianpool.com. Admission and hours vary seasonally. Nov–Mar $6 for those 13 and older, $3 children under 13; Apr–Oct $9 for those 13 and older, $5 children under 13. Children must be 3 years old and provide proof of age with birth certificate, or 38 in. tall, to enter. Hours are at least 11am–4:30pm but are often longer. Call for more information.

The Vizcaya Museum and Gardens ★★★   Sometimes referred to as the "Hearst Castle of the East," this magnificent villa is more Gatsby-esque than anything else you'll find in Miami. It was built in 1916 as a winter retreat for James Deering, co-founder and former vice president of International Harvester. The industrialist was fascinated by 16th-century art and architecture and his ornate mansion, which took 1,000 artisans 5 years to build, became a celebration of that period. If you love antiques, this place is a dream come true, packed with European relics and works of art from the 16th to the 19th centuries. Most of the original furnishings, including dishes and paintings, are still intact. You will see very early versions of a telephone switchboard, central vacuum cleaning system, elevators, and fire sprinklers. A free guided tour of the 34 furnished rooms on the first floor takes about 45 minutes. The second floor, which consists mostly of bedrooms, is open to tour on your own. The spectacularly opulent villa wraps itself around a central courtyard. Outside, lush formal gardens, accented with statuary, balustrades, and decorative urns, front an enormous swath of Biscayne Bay. Definitely take the tour of the rooms, but immediately thereafter, you will want to wander and get lost in the resplendent gardens.

3251 S. Miami Ave. (just south of Rickenbacker Causeway), North Coconut Grove. (℃) **305/250-9133.** www. vizcayamuseum.com. Admission $12 adults, $5 children 6–12, free for children 5 and under. Villa daily 9:30am–5pm (ticket booth closes at 4:30pm); gardens daily 9:30am–5:30pm.

Wolfsonian-Florida International University ★★★ *(Finds)*   Mitchell Wolfson Jr., heir to a family fortune built on movie theaters, was known as an eccentric, but I'd call him a pack rat. A premier collector of propaganda and advertising art, Wolfson was spending so much money storing his booty that he decided to buy the warehouse that was housing it. It ultimately held more than 70,000 of his items, from controversial Nazi propaganda to King Farouk of Egypt's match collection. Thrown in the eclectic mix are also zany works from great modernists such as Charles Eames and Marcel Duchamp. He then gave this incredibly diverse collection to Florida International University. The former 1927 storage facility has been transformed into a museum that is the envy of curators around the world. The museum is unquestionably fascinating and hosts lectures and rather swinging events surrounding particular exhibits.

1001 Washington Ave., South Beach. (℃) **305/531-1001.** www.wolfsonian.org. Admission $5 adults, $3.50 seniors, students with ID, and children 6–12. Mon, Tues, Fri, and Sat 11am–6pm; Thurs 11am–9pm; Sun noon–5pm.

8 Nature Preserves, Parks & Gardens

The Miami area is a great place for outdoors types, with beaches, parks, nature preserves, and gardens galore. For information on South Florida's two national parks, the Everglades and Biscayne National Park, see chapter 6.

At the historic **Bill Baggs Cape Florida State Park** ★, 1200 Crandon Blvd. ((℃) **305/361-5811**), at the southern tip of Key Biscayne about 20 minutes from downtown Miami, you can explore the unfettered wilds and enjoy some of the most secluded beaches in Miami. There's also a historic lighthouse that was built in 1825, which is the oldest lighthouse in South Florida. The lighthouse was damaged during the Second Seminole War (1836) and again in 1861 during the

Civil War. Out of commission for a while, in 1978 the U.S. Coast Guard restored it to working lighthouse condition. A rental shack leases bikes, hydro-bikes, kayaks, and many more water toys. It's a great place to picnic, and a newly constructed restaurant serves homemade Latin food, including great fish soups and sandwiches. Just be careful that the raccoons don't get your lunch—the furry black-eyed beasts are everywhere. Wildlife aside, however, Bill Baggs has been consistently rated as one of the top 10 beaches in the U.S. for its 1¼ miles of wide, sandy beaches and its secluded, serene atmosphere. Admission is $5 per car with up to eight people (or $3 for a car with only one person; $1 to enter by foot or bicycle). Open daily from 8am to sunset. Tours of the lighthouse are available every Thursday through Monday at 10am and 1pm. Arrive at least half an hour early to sign up—there is only room for 10 people on each tour. Take I-95 to the Rickenbacker Causeway and take that all the way to the end.

Fairchild Tropical Garden ✦✦✦, at 10901 Old Cutler Rd. in Coral Gables (© **305/667-1651;** www.ftg.org), is the largest of its kind in the continental United States. A veritable rainforest of both rare and exotic plants, as well as 11 lakes and countless meadows, are spread across 83 acres. Palmettos, vine pergola, palm glades, and other unique species create a scenic, lush environment. More than 100 species of birds have been spotted at the garden (ask for a checklist at the front gate), and it's home to a variety of animals. You should not miss the 30-minute narrated tram tour (tours leave on the hour 10am–3pm weekdays and 10am–4pm on weekends) to learn about the various flowers and trees on the grounds. There is also a museum, a cafe, a picnic area, and a gift shop with fantastic books on gardening, cooking, and edible gifts. The 2-acre rainforest exhibit, Windows to the Tropics, will save you a trip to the Amazon. Expect to spend a minimum of 2 hours here. Admission is $10 for adults, $9 for seniors, $5 for children 3 to 12, and is free for children under 3. Open daily, except December 25, from 9:30am to 4:30pm. Take I-95 south to U.S. 1, turn left onto Le Jeune Road, and follow it straight to the traffic circle; from there, take Old Cutler Road 2 miles to the park.

Located on Biscayne Bay in Coconut Grove (4013 Douglas Rd.; www.ntbg.org/kampong.html), the **Kampong** ✦✦ is a 7-acre botanical garden featuring a stunning array of flowering trees and tropical fruit trees including mango, avocado, and pomelos. In the early 1900s, noted plant explorer David Fairchild traveled the world seeking rare plants of economic and aesthetic value that might be cultivated in the United States. In 1928, he and his wife, Marian (daughter of Alexander Graham Bell), built a two-story residence here (listed on the National Register of Historic Places) amid some of his collections, borrow-ing the Malaysian word *kampong* for his home in a garden. In the 1960s, the Fairchilds sold the Kampong to Catherine Hauberg Sweeney, who donated the property to the National Tropical Botanical Garden to promote and preserve this South Florida treasure. It's a must-see for those interested in horticulture. Admission and tours are by appointment only, from Monday to Friday. For tour information, call © **305/442-7169** from 9am to 5pm Monday through Friday. Admission is $10 a person. Take U.S. 1 to Douglas Road (SW 37th Ave.). Go east on Douglas Road for about a mile. The Kampong will be on your left.

Named after the late champion of the Everglades, the **Marjory Stoneman Douglas Biscayne Nature Center** ✦, 6767 Crandon Blvd., Key Biscayne (© **305/361-6767;** www.biscaynenaturecenter.org), is housed in a brand-new $4 million facility and offers hands-on marine exploration, hikes through coastal hammocks, bike trips, and beach walks. Local environmentalists and historians lead intriguing trips through the local habitat. Call to reserve a spot on a regularly scheduled weekend tour or program. Be sure to wear comfortable closed-toe shoes for hikes through wet or rocky terrain. Open daily 10am to 4pm. Admission to the park is $4 per person; admission to the nature center is free. Call for weekend programs. To get there, take I-95 to the Rickenbacker Causeway Exit (#1) and take the causeway all the way until it becomes Crandon Boulevard. The center is on the east side of the street (the Atlantic Ocean side). Driving time is about 25 minutes from downtown Miami.

Because so many people are so focused on the beach itself, the **Miami Beach Botanical Garden,** 2000 Convention Center Dr., Miami Beach (℗ **305/673-7256**), remains, for the most part, a secret garden. The lush, tropical 4½-acre garden is a fabulous, all-natural retreat from the hustle and bustle of the silicone-enhanced city. Open Tuesday through Sunday from 9am to 5pm; admission is free.

The **Oleta River State Recreation Area** 🐾🐾, 3400 NE 163rd St., North Miami (℗ **305/919-1846**), consists of 993 acres—the largest urban park in the state—on Biscayne Bay. The beauty of the Oleta River combined with the fact that you're essentially in the middle of a city makes this park especially worth visiting. With miles of bicycle and canoe trails, a sandy swimming beach, shaded picnic pavilions, and a fishing pier, Oleta River State Recreation Area offers visitors an outstanding outdoor recreational experience cloistered from the confines of the big city. There are 14 cabins on the premises, sleeping four people and featuring air-conditioning. The cost is $51 per night and guests are required to bring their own linens. Bathrooms and showers are outside, and a fire circle with grill is available for cooking. For reservations, call ℗ **800/326-3521.** Open daily from 8am to sunset. Admission for pedestrians and cyclists is $1 per person. By car: driver plus car costs $3; driver plus one to seven passengers and car costs $5. Take 1-95 to exit 17 (S.R. 826 E.) and go all the way east until just before the causeway. The park entrance is on your right. Driving time from downtown Miami is about a half-hour.

A testament to Miami's unusual climate, the **Preston B. Bird and Mary Heinlein Fruit and Spice Park** 🐾, 24801 SW 187th Ave., Homestead (℗ **305/247-5727**), harbors rare fruit trees that cannot survive elsewhere in the country. If a volunteer is available, you'll learn some fascinating things about this 30-acre living plant museum, where the most exotic varieties of fruits and spices—ackee, mango, Ugli fruits, carambola, and breadfruit—grow on strange-looking trees with unpronounceable names. There are also original coral rock buildings dating back to 1912. The Strawberry Folk Festival in February and an art festival here in January are among the park's most popular—and populated—events.

The best part? You're free to take anything that *naturally* falls to the ground. You'll also find samples of interesting fruits and jellies made from the park's bounty as well as exotic ingredients and cookbooks in the gift store.

Admission to the spice park is $5 for adults and $1.50 for children under 12. It's open daily from 10am to 5pm; closed on Christmas. Tours are included in the price of admission and are offered at 11am, 1:30pm, and 3pm. Take U.S. 1 south, turn right on SW 248th Street, and go straight for 5 miles to SW 187th Avenue. The drive from Miami should take 45 minutes to an hour.

9 Animal Parks

For a tropical climate, Miami's got a lot of nontropical animals to see, and we're not talking about the motorists on I-95. Everything from dolphins and alligators to lions, tigers, and bears call Miami home (most in parks, some in nature).

Miami Metrozoo ★★ *Kids*   This 290-acre, sparsely landscaped complex (it was devastated by Hurricane Andrew) is quite a distance from Miami proper and the beaches—about 45 minutes—but worth the trip. Isolated and never really crowded, it's also completely cageless—animals are kept at bay by cleverly designed moats. This is a fantastic spot to take younger kids (the older ones seem bored and unstimulated here); there's a wonderful petting zoo and play area, and the zoo offers several daily programs designed to educate and entertain. Mufasa and Simba (of Disney fame) were modeled on a couple of Metrozoo's lions. Other residents include two rare white Bengal tigers, a Komodo dragon, rare koala bears, a number of kangaroos, and an African meerkat. The air-conditioned Zoofari Monorail tour offers visitors a nice overview of the park. An Andean Condor exhibit opened in 2000, and the zoo is always upgrading its facilities, including the impressive aviary. *Note:* The distance between animal habitats can be great, so you'll be doing *a lot* of walking here. Also, because the zoo can be miserably hot during summer months, plan these visits in the early morning or late afternoon. Expect to spend about 3 hours here.

12400 SW 152nd St., South Miami. © 305/251-0400. www.miamimetrozoo.com. Admission $12 adults, $7 children 3–12. Daily 9:30am–5:30pm (ticket booth closes at 4pm). Free parking. From U.S. 1 south, turn right on SW 152nd St. and follow signs about 3 miles to the entrance.

Miami Seaquarium ★ *Kids* *Overrated*   If you've been to Orlando's SeaWorld, you may be disappointed with Miami's version, which is considerably smaller and not as well maintained. It's hardly a sprawling seaquarium, but you will want to arrive early to enjoy the effects of its mild splash. You'll need at least 3 hours to tour the 35-acre oceanarium and see all four daily shows starring a number of showy ocean mammals. You can cut your visit to 2 hours if you limit your shows to the better, albeit corny, Flipper Show and Killer Whale Show. The highly regarded Water and Dolphin Exploration Program (WADE) allows visitors to touch and swim with dolphins in the Flipper Lagoon. The program costs $140 per person participating, $32 per observer, and is offered twice daily, at noon and 3:30pm, 7 days a week. Children must be at least 52 inches tall to participate. Reservations are necessary for this program. Call © **305/365-2501** in advance for reservations.

4400 Rickenbacker Causeway (south side), en route to Key Biscayne. © **305/361-5705.** www.miamise aquarium.com. Admission $25 adults, $20 children 3–9, free for children under 3. Daily 9:30am–6pm (ticket booth closes at 4pm).

Monkey Jungle ★ *Overrated*   Personally, I think this place is disgusting. It reeks, the monkeys are either sleeping or in heat, and it's really far from the city, even farther than the zoo. But if primates are your thing and you'd rather pass on the zoo, you'll be in paradise. You'll see rare Brazilian golden lion tamarins and Asian macaques. There are no cages to restrain the antics of the monkeys as they swing, chatter, and play their way into your heart. Screened-in trails wind through acres of "jungle," and daily shows feature the talents of the park's most progressive pupils. People who go here are not monkeying around—many of the park's frequent visitors are scientists and anthropologists, who speak to the seriousness of the park's mission. An interesting archaeological exhibition excavated from a Monkey Jungle sinkhole displays 10,000-year-old artifacts including human teeth and animal bones. A somewhat amusing attraction here, if you can call it that, is the Wild Monkey Swimming Pool, a show in which you get to watch Sea Monkeys diving for food. If you can stand the humidity, the smell, and the bugs (flies, mosquitoes, and so on), expect to spend about 2 hours here. The park's website sometimes offers downloadable discount coupons, so if you have Internet access, take a look before you visit.

14805 SW 216th St., South Miami. © 305/235-1611. www.monkeyjungle.com. Admission $16 adults, $13 seniors and active-duty military, $9.95 children 4–12. Daily 9:30am–5pm (tickets sold until 4pm). Take U.S. 1 south to SW 216th St., or from Florida Turnpike, take exit 11 and follow the signs.

Parrot Jungle Island *(Kids)* This Miami institution took flight from its lush, natural South Miami environment and headed north in the winter of 2003 to a new, overly fabricated, disappointing $46 million home on Watson Island, along the MacArthur Causeway near Miami Beach. While the island doubles as a protected bird sanctuary, the jungle's former digs in the heart of South Miami in a circa-1900 coral rock structure were a lot more charming and kitschier. The new, overpriced 18.6-acre park features an Everglades exhibit, a petting zoo, and several theaters, jungle trails, and aviaries. Watch your heads because flying above are hundreds of parrots, macaws, peacocks, cockatoos, and flamingos. But it's not all a loss. Be sure to check out the Crocosaurus, a 20-foot-long saltwater crocodile who hangs out in the park's Serpentarium, which also houses the park's reptile and amphibian collection. Also a pleasant surprise here is the Ichimura Japanese Garden. Continuous shows star roller-skating cockatoos, card-playing macaws, and numerous stunt-happy parrots. There are also tortoises, iguanas, and a rare albino alligator on exhibit. The park's website sometimes offers downloadable discount coupons, so if you have Internet access, take a look before you visit, because you definitely won't want to pay full price for this park. If you do get your money's worth and see all the shows and exhibits, expect to spend upwards of 4 hours here.

1111 Parrot Jungle Trail, Watson Island (on the north side of MacArthur Causeway/I-395). © 305/372-3822. www.parrotjungle.com. Admission $24 adults, $22 seniors and military, $19 children 3–10. Parking an additional $6 per vehicle. Daily 10am–6pm. From I-95, take I-395 East (MacArthur Causeway), make a right on Parrot Jungle Trail which is the first exit after the bridge. Follow the road around and under the causeway to the parking garage on the left-hand side.

Sea Grass Adventures ★ *(Value)* *(Kids)* Even better than the Seaquarium is Sea Grass Adventures, in which a naturalist from the Marjory Stoneman Douglas Biscayne Nature Center will introduce ($10 per person) kids and adults to an amazing variety of creatures that live in the sea grass beds of the Bear Cut Nature Preserve near Crandon Beach on Key Biscayne. Not just a walking tour, you will be able to wade in the water with your guide and catch an assortment of sea life in nets provided by the guides. At the end of the program, participants gather on the beach while the guide explains what everyone's just caught, passing the creatures around in miniature viewing tanks. Call for available dates, times, and reservations.

Marjory Stoneman Douglas Biscayne Nature Center, 6767 Crandon Blvd., Key Biscayne. © 305/361-6767. The center is free. Daily 10am–4pm.

10 Sightseeing Cruises & Organized Tours

BOAT & CRUISE-SHIP TOURS

You don't need a boating license or a zillion-dollar yacht to explore Miami by boat. Thanks to several enterprising companies, boat tours are easy to find, affordable, and are an excellent way to see the city from a more liquid perspective.

Fast Cats Ferry Service   Finally, a ferry that goes from Miami to Key West. It's about time. The PurrSeavearance may be a cheesy name for a luxury $7.5 million catamaran, but the trip is hardly so. The 102-foot boat can hold up to 149 passengers and will make the 4-hour cruise (driving only takes 3 hr., but with traffic it can take up to 5) four times a week starting at $69 each way. VIP tickets cost $98 and include preferential seating. Food and alcoholic beverages are available but not included in the price.

1635 N. Bayshore Dr., Sealine Marina, Downtown. ✆ 305/400-6446. www.fastcats.org. Round-trip $110–$212. Tours leave Miami Thurs–Sun at 7:30am and push off from Key West at 5:30pm.

Heritage Miami II Topsail Schooner   This relaxing ride aboard Miami's only tall ship is a fun way to see the city, since it's on a schooner (as opposed to the other tour company's cruising boats), which gives you more of a feel of the water. The 2-hour cruise passes by Villa Vizcaya, Coconut Grove, and Key Biscayne and puts you in sight of Miami's spectacular skyline and island homes. Call to make sure the ship is running on schedule. On Friday, Saturday, and Sunday evenings, there are 1-hour tours to see the lights of the city for $15 per person.

Bayside Marketplace Marina, 401 Biscayne Blvd., Downtown. ✆ 305/442-9697. Fax 305/442-0119. Tickets for day tours $20 adults, $15 children 12 and under. Sept–May only. Tours leave daily at 1:30, 4, and 6:30pm and Fri–Sun also at 9, 10, and 11pm.

Miami Duck Tours   Hands down, this is the corniest, kookiest tour in the entire city. In fact, the company prefers to call these tours the "quackiest" way to visit Miami and the beaches. Whatever you call it, it's weird. The *Watson Willy* is the first of several planned Miami Duck Tours "vesicles," not a body part, but a hybrid name that means part vessel, part vehicle (technical name: Hydra Terra Amphibious Vehicle). Each "vesicle" seats 49 guests, plus a captain and tour guide and leaves from Watson Island behind Parrot Jungle Island, traveling through downtown Miami and South Beach. If you're image conscious, you may want to reconsider traveling down Ocean Drive in a duck. That's right, a duck, which is what the "vesicle" looks like. After driving the streets in the duck, you'll end up cruising Biscayne Bay, past all the swanky houses. Embarrassing or downright hilarious, Miami Duck Tours is definitely something unique.

Bayside Marketplace (on land), 401 Biscayne Blvd., Downtown. ✆ 877/DUCK-TIX. www.ducktours miami.com. Tickets $24 adults, $21 seniors and military, $17 children 12 and under.

SIGHTSEEING TOURS

While there are several sightseeing tour operators in Miami, most, unfortunately, either don't speak English or are just plain shoddy. The following is the one we'd recommend:

Miami Nice Excursion Travel and Service ✪   Pick your destination, and the Miami Nice tours will take you to the Everglades, Fort Lauderdale, South Beach, the Seaquarium, Key West, Cape Canaveral, or wherever else you desire. The best trip for first-timers is the City Tour, a comprehensive tour of the entire city and its various neighborhoods. If you've got the time, you will definitely want to add on a side trip to the Everglades and/or Key West (though I suggest exploring the Everglades on your own). Included in most Miami trips is a fairly comprehensive city tour narrated by a knowledgeable guide. The company is one of the oldest in town.

18801 Collins Ave., Miami Beach. ℂ 305/949-9180. www.miaminicetours.com. Tours $32–$115 adults, $29–$100 children 3–9. Mon–Sat 7am–10pm; closed Sun. Call ahead for directions to various pickup areas.

SPECIALIZED TOURS

In addition to those listed below, a great option for seeing the city is to take a tour led by **Dr. Paul George.** Dr. George is a history teacher at Miami–Dade Community College and a historian at the Historical Museum of Southern Florida. He also happens to be "Mr. Miami." There's a set calendar of tours (including the Murder, Mystery, and Mayhem Bus Tour detailed below), and all of them are fascinating to South Florida buffs. Tours focus on neighborhoods, such as Little Havana, Brickell Avenue, or Key Biscayne, and on themes, such as Miami cemeteries and the Miami River. The often long-winded discussions can be a bit much for those who just want a quick look around, but Dr. George certainly knows his stuff. The cost is $17 to $37; reservations are required (ℂ **305/375-1621**). Tours leave from the Historical Museum at 101 W. Flagler St., Downtown. Call for a schedule.

Biltmore Hotel Tour ★★★ *Value*   Take advantage of these free Sunday walking tours to enjoy the hotel's beautiful grounds. The Biltmore is chock-full of history and mystery, including a few ghosts; go out there and see for yourself. In addition, there are also free weekly fireside sessions that are open to the public and presented by Miami Storytellers. Learn about the hotel's early days and rich stories of the city's past. These wonderful sessions are held in the main lobby by the fireplace and are accompanied by a glass of champagne. Call ahead to confirm.

1200 Anastasia Ave., Coral Gables. ℂ 305/445-1926. www.biltmorehotel.com. Free admission. Tours depart on Sun at 1:30, 2:30, and 3:30pm. Storytelling sessions are held every Thurs at 7:30pm.

Eco-Adventure Tours ★★★   For the eco-conscious traveler, the Miami–Dade Parks and Recreation Department offers guided nature, adventure, and historic tours involving biking, canoeing, snorkeling, hiking, and bird-watching all over the city. Contact them for more information.

ℂ 305/365-3018. www.miamidade.gov/parks.

Herencia Hispana Tour   For those looking to immerse themselves in Miami's rich Latin-American culture, the Herencia Hispana Tour is the ideal way to explore it all. Hop on a bus and zoom past such hotbeds of Latin activity as downtown's Flagler Street, the unavoidable Elian Gonzalez house, the Latin American Art Museum, and Little Havana's Domino Park and Tower Theater, among others. Not just a sightseeing tour, this one includes two very knowledgeable, albeit corny, guides who know just when to infuse a necessary dose of humor into a segment of history that some people may not consider so amusing.

Tours depart from the Steven P. Clark Government Center, 111 NW 1st St. ℂ 305/884-7567. Tours (which are in Spanish or English, but you must specify which one you require) are free, but advanced reservations are required. Tours depart at 9, 9:30, and 10am every Sat in Oct.

Miami Design Preservation League ★★   On Thursday evenings and Saturday mornings, the Design Preservation League sponsors walking tours that offer a fascinating inside look at the city's historic Art Deco District. Tour-goers meet for a 1½-hour walk through some of America's most exuberantly "architectured" buildings. The league led the fight to designate this area a National Historic District and is proud to share the splendid locale with visitors. Also, see p. 126 for more information.

Art Deco Welcome Center, 1001 Ocean Dr., South Beach. ℂ **305/672-2014**. www.mdpl.org. Walking tours $15 per person. Tours leave Wed and Sat at 10:30am and Thurs at 6:30pm. Self-guided audio tours also available daily for $10. No reservations necessary but arrive 15 min. early. Call ahead for updated schedules.

Murder, Mystery, and Mayhem Bus Tour ★★★ Visit the past by video and bus to Miami-Dade's most celebrated crimes and criminals from the 1800s to the present. From the murder spree of the Ashley Gang to the most notorious murders and crimes of our century, including the murder of designer Gianni Versace, historian Paul George conducts a most fascinating 3-hour tour of scandalous proportions.

Tours depart from the Dade Cultural Center, 101 W. Flagler St., Miami. ℂ **305/375-1621**. Tickets $37. Advance reservations required. Held twice a year, usually in Apr and Oct.

11 Affordable Outdoor Pursuits

In addition to the outdoor options below, see the "Hitting the Beach" and "Nature Preserves, Parks & Gardens" sections, both earlier in this chapter.

BIKING

The cement promenade on the southern tip of South Beach is a great place to ride. Biking up the beach (on either the beach or along the beach on a cement pathway—which is a lot easier!) is great for surf, sun, sand, exercise, and people-watching—just be sure to keep your eyes on the road, as the scenery can be most distracting. Most of the big beach hotels rent bicycles, as does the **Miami Beach Bicycle Center,** 601 5th St., South Beach (ℂ **305/674-0150**), which charges $8 per hour or $20 for up to 24 hours. It's open Monday through Saturday from 10am to 7pm, Sunday from 10am to 5pm.

Bikers can also enjoy more than 130 miles of paved paths throughout Miami. The beautiful and quiet streets of Coral Gables and Coconut Grove (several bike trails are spread throughout these neighborhoods) are great for bicyclists, where old trees form canopies over wide, flat roads lined with grand homes and quaint street markers.

The terrain in Key Biscayne is perfect for biking, especially along the park and beach roads. If you don't mind the sound of cars whooshing by your bike lane, **Rickenbacker Causeway** is also fantastic, since it is one of the only bikeable inclines in Miami from which you get fantastic elevated views of the city and waterways. However, be warned that this is a grueling ride, especially going up the causeway. **Key Cycling,** 61 Harbor Dr., Key Biscayne (ℂ **305/361-0061**), rents mountain bikes for $5 an hour or $15 a day, with a 2-hour minimum. It's open Tuesday through Friday from 10am to 7pm, Monday and Saturday from 10am to 6pm, and Sunday from 10am to 3pm.

If you want to avoid the traffic altogether, head out to **Shark Valley** in the Everglades National Park—one of South Florida's most scenic bicycle trails and a favorite haunt of city-weary locals. For more information on Shark Valley and the Everglades, see chapter 6.

For a decent list of trail suggestions throughout South Florida, visit www.geocities.com/floutdoorzone/bike.html. *Biking note:* Children under the age of 16 are required by Florida law to wear a helmet, which can be purchased at any bike store or retail outlet selling biking supplies.

BOATING

Private rental outfits include **Boat Rental Plus,** 2400 Collins Ave., Miami Beach (ℂ **305/534-4307**), where 50-horsepower, 18-foot powerboats rent for some of the best prices on the beach. There's a 2-hour minimum and rates go from $99 to $449, including taxes and gas. They also have great specials on Sundays. Cruising is permitted only in and around Biscayne Bay (ocean access is prohibited) and renters must be 21 to rent a boat. The rental office is at 23rd Street, on the inland waterway in Miami Beach. It's open daily from 10am to sunset. If you want a specific type of boat, call ahead to reserve. Otherwise, show up and take what's available.

Club Nautico of Coconut Grove, 2560 S. Bayshore Dr. (© **305/858-6258;** www.realpagessites.com/clubnauticomiami), rents high-quality powerboats for fishing, water-skiing, diving, and cruising in the bay or ocean. All boats are Coast Guard equipped, with VHF radios and safety gear. Rates start at $299 for 4 hours and $419 for 8 hours. Club Nautico is open daily from 8am to 6pm (weather permitting). Other locations include the Crandon Park Marina, 4000 Crandon Blvd., Key Biscayne (© **305/361-9217**), with the same rates and hours as the Coconut Grove location; and the Miami Beach Marina, Pier E, 300 Alton Rd., South Beach (© **305/673-2502**), where rates start at $299 for 4 hours and $399 for 8 hours. Nautico on Miami Beach is open daily from 9am to 5pm.

FISHING

Fishing licenses are required in Florida. If you go out with one of the fishing charter boats listed below, you are automatically accredited because the companies are. If you go out on your own, however, you must have a Florida fishing license, which costs $17 for Florida residents and $32 for nonresidents. Call © **888/FISH-FLO** or visit www.wildlifelicense.com for more information.

Some of the best surf-casting in the city can be had at **Haulover Beach Park** at Collins Avenue and 105th Street, where there's a bait-and-tackle shop right on the pier. **South Pointe Park,** at the southern tip of Miami Beach, is another popular fishing spot and features a long pier, comfortable benches, and a great view of the ships passing through Government Cut, the deep channel made when the port of Miami was dug.

You can also do some deep-sea fishing in the Miami area. One bargain outfitter, the **Kelley Fishing Fleet,** at the Haulover Marina, 10800 Collins Ave. (at 108th St.), Miami Beach (© **305/945-3801**), has half-day, full-day, and night fishing aboard diesel-powered "party boats." The fleet's emphasis on drifting is geared toward trolling and bottom fishing for snapper, sailfish, and mackerel. Half-day and night fishing trips are $31 for adults and $22 for children up to 10 years old; full-day trips are $49 for adults and $39 for children; prices are $5 cheaper if you have your own rod. Daily departures are scheduled at 9am, and 1:45 and 8pm; reservations are recommended.

Also at the Haulover Marina is the charter boat *Helen C* (10800 Collins Ave.; © **305/947-4081;** www.fishmiamibeach.com). Although there's no shortage of private charter boats here, Capt. Dawn Mergelsberg is a good pick, since she puts individuals together to get a full boat. Her *Helen* is a twin-engine 55-footer, equipped for big-game "monster" fish like marlin, tuna, dolphin fish, shark, and sailfish. The cost is $100 per person. Private, full-day trips are available for groups of six people per vessel and cost $900; half days are $500. Group rates and specials are also available. Sailings are scheduled for 8am to noon and 1 to 5pm daily; call for reservations. Children are welcome.

Key Biscayne offers deep-sea fishing to those willing to get their hands dirty and pay a bundle. The competition among the boats is fierce, but the prices are basically the same no matter which you choose. The going rate is about $400 to

$450 for a half day and $600 to $700 for a full day of fishing. These rates are usually for a party of up to six, and the boats supply you with rods and bait as well as instruction for first-timers. Some will also take you out to the Upper Keys if the fish aren't biting in Miami.

You might also consider the following boats, all of which sail out of the Key Biscayne marina and are in relatively good shape and nicer than most out there: **Sunny Boy** (© **305/361-2217**), **Top Hatt** (© **305/361-2528**), and **L & H** (© **305/361-9318**). Call for reservations.

Bridge fishing in Biscayne Bay is also popular in Miami; you'll see people with poles over almost every waterway. But look carefully for signs telling you whether it's legal to do so wherever you are: Some bridges forbid fishing.

GOLF

There are more than 50 private and public golf courses in the Miami area. Contact the **Greater Miami Convention and Visitor's Bureau** (© **800/933-8448**; www.miamiandbeaches.com) for a list of courses and costs.

The best hotel courses in Miami are found at the **Doral Golf Resort and Spa** (4400 NW 87th Ave., Miami; © **800/71-DORAL** or 305/592-2000), home of the legendary Blue Monster course as well as the Gold Course, designed by Raymond Floyd; the Great White Shark Course; and the Silver Course, refinished by Jerry Pate.

Other hotels with excellent golf courses include the **Fairmont Turnberry Isle Resort & Club** (19999 W. Country Club Dr., Aventura; © **800/327-7028** or 305/936-2929), with two Robert Trent Jones Sr.–designed courses for guests and members, and the **Biltmore Hotel** ★★ (1200 Anastasia Ave., Coral Gables; © **800/727-1926** or 305/445-1926), which is my pick for best public golf course because of its modest greens fees and an 18-hole par-71 course located on the hotel's spectacular grounds. It must be good: Despite his penchant for privacy, former President Bill Clinton prefers teeing off at this course over any other in Miami!

Otherwise, the following represent some of the area's best public courses. **Crandon Park Golf Course,** formerly known as the Links, 6700 Crandon Blvd., Key Biscayne (© **305/361-9129**), is the number-one-ranked municipal course in the state and one of the top five in the country. The park is situated on 200 bayfront acres and offers a pro shop, rentals, lessons, carts, and a lighted driving range. The course is open daily from dawn to dusk; greens fees (including cart) are $137 per person during the winter and $58 per person during the summer. Special twilight rates are also available.

One of the most popular courses among real enthusiasts is the **Doral Park Golf and Country Club,** 5001 NW 104th Ave., West Miami (© **305/591-8800**); it's not related to the Doral Hotel or spa. Call to book in advance since this challenging, semi-private 18-holer is extremely popular with locals. The course is open from 6:30am to 6pm during the winter and until 7pm during the summer. Cart and greens fees vary, so call © **305/592-2000** ext. 2104 for information.

Known as one of the best in the city, the **Country Club of Miami,** 6801 Miami Gardens Dr., at NW 68th Avenue, North Miami (© **305/829-8456**), has three 18-hole courses of varying degrees of difficulty. You'll encounter lush fairways, rolling greens, and some history to boot. The west course, designed in 1961 by Robert Trent Jones Sr. and updated in the 1990s by the PGA, was where Jack Nicklaus played his first professional tournament and Lee Trevino won his first professional championship. The course is open daily from 7am to sunset. Cart and greens fees are $38 to $71 per person during the winter, and $20 to $34 per person during the summer. Special twilight rates are available.

Golfers looking for some cheap practice time will appreciate **Haulover Beach Park,** 10800 Collins Ave., Miami Beach (© **305/940-6719**), in a pretty bayside location. The longest hole on this par-27 course is 125 yards. It's open daily from 7:30am to 6pm during the winter, and until 7:30pm during the summer. Greens fees are $6.40 per person during the winter and summer. Handcarts cost $1.90.

IN-LINE SKATING

Miami's consistently flat terrain makes in-line skating a breeze. Lincoln Road, for example, is a virtual skating rink as bladers compete with bikers and walkers for a slab of slate. But the city's heavy traffic and construction do make it tough to find long routes suitable for blading.

Because of the popularity of blading and skateboarding, the city has passed a law prohibiting skating on the west side (the cafe-lined strip) of Ocean Drive in the evenings as well as a law that all bladers must skate slowly and safely. Also, if you're going to partake in the sport, remember to keep a pair of sandals or sneakers with you, since many area shops won't allow you inside with skates on.

Despite all the rules, you can still have fun, and the following rental outfit can help chart an interesting course for you and supply you with all the necessary gear. In South Beach, **Fritz's Skate Shop,** 730 Lincoln Rd. Mall (© **305/532-1954**), rents top-quality skates, including safety pads, for $8 per hour, $24 per day, and $34 overnight. They provide free lessons at 10:30am on Sundays when you rent equipment, or they can hook you up with an instructor for private lessons. The shop also stocks lots of gear and clothing.

JET SKIS/WAVERUNNERS

Don't miss a chance to tour the islands on the back of your own powerful watercraft. Bravery is, however, a prerequisite, as Miami's waterways are full of speeding jet skiers and boaters who think they're in the Indy 500. Many beachfront concessionaires rent a variety of these popular (and loud) water scooters. The latest models are fast and smooth. Try **Tony's Jet Ski Rentals,** 3501 Rickenbacker Causeway, Key Biscayne (© **305/937-0302**), one of the city's largest rental shops, located on a private beach in the Miami Marine Stadium lagoon. There are three models available accommodating up to three people. Rates range from $45 for a half-hour to $80 for a full hour, depending on the number of riders. Tony's is open daily from 10:30am to 6:30pm.

KAYAKING

The laid-back **Urban Trails Kayak Company** rents boats at 3400 NE 163rd St. in Oleta River Park (© **305/947-1302;** www.urbantrails.com). The outfitters here give interested explorers a map to take with them and quick instructions on how to work the paddles and boats. They also operate very scenic 4-hour guided tours through rivers with mangroves and islands as your destination—less than 10 people on the tour costs $45 per person; more than 10 people costs $35 per person. These must be booked in advance. Rates are $8 an hour, $20 for up to 4 hours, and $25 for the whole day. Tandems (for two people) are $12 an hour, $30 for up to 4 hours, and $35 for the day. To keep the kayaks overnight is an extra $10. They also rent mountain bikes. Open daily from 9am to 5pm in the winter and 9am to 6pm in the summer.

SAILING

You can rent sailboats and catamarans through the beachfront concessions desk of several top resorts, such as the Doral Golf Resort and Spa (4400 NW 87th Ave., Miami; ℂ **800/71-DORAL** or 305/592-2000).

Sailboats of Key Biscayne Rentals and Sailing School, in the Crandon Marina (next to Sundays on the Bay), 4000 Crandon Blvd., Key Biscayne (ℂ **305/361-0328** days, 305/279-7424 evenings), can also get you out on the water. A 22-foot sailboat rents for $35 an hour or $110 for a half day and $175 for a full day. A Cat-25 or J24 is available for $35 an hour, $110 for a half day, and $175 for a full day. If you've always had a dream to win the America's Cup but can't sail, the able teachers at Sailboats will get you started. They offer a 10-hour course over 5 days for $300 for one person or $400 for you and a buddy.

SCUBA DIVING & SNORKELING

In 1981, the U.S. government began a wide-scale project designed to increase the number of habitats available to marine organisms. One of the program's major accomplishments has been the creation of nearby artificial reefs, which have attracted all kinds of tropical plants, fish, and animals. In addition, Biscayne National Park (see the park's section in chapter 6, beginning on p. 224) offers a protected marine environment just south of downtown.

Several dive shops around the city offer organized weekend outings, either to the reefs or to one of over a dozen old shipwrecks around Miami's shores. Check "Divers" in the Yellow Pages for rental equipment and for a full list of undersea tour operators.

Diver's Paradise of Key Biscayne, 4000 Crandon Blvd. (ℂ **305/361-3483**), offers one dive expedition per day during the week and two per day on the weekends to the more than 30 wrecks and artificial reefs off the coast of Miami Beach and Key Biscayne. You can take a 3-day certification course for $399, which includes all the dives and gear. If you already have your C-card, a dive trip costs about $90 if you need equipment and $45 if you bring your own gear. It's open Tuesday through Friday from 10am to 6pm and Saturday and Sunday from 8am to 6pm. Call ahead for times and locations of dives. For snorkeling, they will also set you up with equipment and maps on where to see the best underwater sights. Rental for mask, fins, and snorkel is $45.

South Beach Divers, 850 Washington Ave., Miami Beach (ℂ **305/531-6110;** www.southbeachdivers.com), will also be happy to tell you where to go under the sea and will provide you with scuba rental equipment as well for $40. You can rent snorkel gear for $15. They also do dive trips to Key Largo three times a week and do dives off Miami on Sundays at $100 for a two-tank dive.

SWIMMING

There is no shortage of water in the Miami area. See the Venetian Pool listing (p. 130) and the "Miami's Best Beaches" section earlier in this chapter for descriptions of good swimming options.

TENNIS

Hundreds of tennis courts in South Florida are open to the public for a minimal fee. Most courts operate on a first-come, first-served basis and are open from sunrise to sunset. For information and directions, call the **City of Miami Beach Recreation, Culture, and Parks Department** (ℂ 305/673-7730) or the **City of Miami Parks and Recreation Department** (ℂ 305/575-5256).

⌒
Tips **A Fisherman's Friend**

The Biscayne Bay area is prime tarpon fishing country and a pretty good spot for a lot of other trophy sportfish: snook, bonefish, dolphin fish, swordfish, and sailfish. For a fee, local guides are happy to show you the hot spots and make sure you reel one in. One such guide is **Capt. David Parsons** (✆ **305/968-9603**), who owns a great 28-foot boat, *Hakuna Matada*. He knows where the fish are biting and will take you from Biscayne Bay to the Atlantic Ocean in search of the best catch of the day for $550 for four people (swordfish can be caught at nighttime only; those trips run at $600), including rods, gear, and bait. All you bring is food/drink. Capt. Parsons also leads trips to Bimini for those who want to explore the fishing in the Bahamas.

Of the 590 public tennis courts throughout Miami, the three hard courts and seven clay courts at the **Key Biscayne Tennis Association,** 6702 Crandon Blvd. (✆ **305/361-5263**), are the best and most beautiful. Because of this, they often get crowded on weekends. You'll play on the same courts as Lendl, Graf, Evert, McEnroe, and other greats; this is also the venue for one of the world's biggest annual tennis events, the Nasdaq 100 Open. There's a pleasant, if limited, pro shop, plus many good pros. Only four courts are lit at night, but if you reserve at least 24 to 48 hours in advance, you can usually take your pick. They cost $6 per person per hour. The courts are open Monday through Friday from 8am to 9pm, Saturday and Sunday until 6pm.

Other courts are pretty run of the mill and can be found in most neighborhoods. I do, however, recommend the **Miami Beach public courts at Flamingo Park,** 1001 12th St. in South Beach (✆ **305/673-7761**), where there are 19 clay courts that cost $4 per person an hour for Miami Beach residents and $8 per person an hour for nonresidents. It's first-come, first-served. Open 8am to 9pm Monday through Friday, 8am to 8pm Saturday and Sunday.

Hotels with the best tennis facilities are the Biltmore, Fairmont Turnberry Isle Resort and Spa, the Doral Resort and Spa, and the Inn and Spa at Fisher Island. See the "Golf" section above for the contact information for these places.

WINDSURFING

Many hotels rent windsurfers to their guests, but if yours doesn't have a watersports concession stand, head for Key Biscayne. **Sailboards Miami,** Rickenbacker Causeway, Key Biscayne (✆ **305/361-SAIL;** www.sailboardsmiami.com), operates out of two big yellow trucks on Windsurfer Beach, the most popular (though our pick for best is Hobie Beach) windsurfing spot in the city. For those who've never ridden a board but want to try it, they offer a 2-hour lesson for $69 that's guaranteed to turn you into a wave warrior or you get your money back. After that, you can rent a board for $25 to $30 an hour. If you want to make a day of it, a 10-hour prepaid card costs $180. These cards require you to prepay, but they also reduce the price by about $70 for the day. You can use the card year-round, until the time on it runs out. Open Tuesday through Sunday from 10am to 5:30pm. Make your first right after the tollbooth (at the beginning of the causeway—you can't miss it) to find the outfitters. They also rent kayaks.

12 Spectator Sports

Check the *Miami Herald*'s sports section for a daily listing of local events and the paper's Friday "Weekend" section for comprehensive coverage and in-depth reports. For last-minute tickets, call the venue directly, since many season ticket holders sell singles and return unused tickets. Expensive tickets are available from brokers or individuals listed in the classified sections of the local papers. Some tickets are also available through **Ticketmaster** (© 305/358-5885).

BASEBALL

The 2003 World Champion **Florida Marlins** shocked the sports world in 1997 when they became the youngest expansion team to win a World Series, but then floundered as their star players were sold off by former owner Wayne Huizenga. They shocked the sports world again in 2003 by winning the World Series and turned many of Miami's apathetic sports fans into major league ball fans. If you're interested in catching a game, be warned: The summer heat in Miami can be unbearable, even in the evenings.

Home games are held at the **Pro Player Stadium,** NW 199th St., North Miami Beach (© 305/623-6200). Tickets cost from $4 to $50. Box office hours are Monday to Friday from 8:30am to 5:30pm and before games; tickets are also available through Ticketmaster. The team currently holds spring training in Melbourne, Florida.

BASKETBALL

The **Miami Heat** (© 786/777-1000), no longer led by celebrity coach Pat Riley, made their NBA debut in November 1988 and their games remain one of Miami's hottest tickets. Courtside seats are full of visiting celebrities from Puff Daddy to Madonna. The season lasts from October to April, with most games beginning at 7:30pm. They play in the brand-new waterfront **American Airlines Arena,** located downtown on Biscayne Boulevard. Tickets are $14 to $100 or much more. Box office hours are Monday through Friday from 10am to 5pm (until 8pm on game nights); tickets are also available through Ticketmaster (© 305/358-5885).

FOOTBALL

Miami's golden boys are the **Miami Dolphins,** the city's most recognizable team, followed by thousands of "dolfans." The team plays at least eight home games during the season, between September and December, at **Pro Player Stadium,** 2269 NW 199th St., North Miami Beach (© 305/620-2578). Tickets cost between $20 and much, much more. The box office is open Monday through Friday from 8:30am to 5:30pm; tickets are also available through Ticketmaster (© 305/358-5885).

HORSE RACING

Located on the Dade–Broward County border in Hallandale (just north of North Miami Beach/Aventura) is **Gulfstream Park,** at U.S. 1 and Hallandale Beach Boulevard (© 305/931-7223; www.gulfstreampark.com), South Florida's very own version of the Kentucky Derby, albeit not nearly as sceney. This horse track is a haven for serious gamblers and voyeurs alike. Large purses and important races are commonplace at this sprawling suburban course, and the track is typically crowded, especially during its amusing and entertaining concert series from January to April, which features has-beens and one-hit wonders such as Cindy Lauper, REO Speedwagon, and Bryan Adams on the front

Jai Alai Explained

Jai alai originated in the Basque country of northern Spain, where players used to use church walls as their courts. The game looks very much like lacrosse, actually, with rules very similar to handball or tennis and is played on a court with numbered lines. What makes the game totally unique, however, is the requirement that the ball must be returned in one continuous motion. The server must bounce the ball behind the serving line and with the basket, must hurl the ball to the front wall, with the aim being that, upon rebound, the ball will bounce between lines four and seven. If it doesn't, it is an under- or overserve and the other team receives a point.

lawn for just $5. Call for schedules. Admission is $3 to the grandstand weekdays and $5 weekends and $5 to the clubhouse; parking is free. Children under 17 are free. January through March, post times are 1:30pm on weekdays and 1pm on weekends. Closed Tuesdays.

ICE HOCKEY

The young **Florida Panthers** (© 954/835-7000) have amassed a legion of fans who love them. Much to the disappointment of Miamians, they moved to a new venue in Sunrise, the next county north of Miami-Dade, more than an hour from downtown Miami. Call for directions and ticket information.

JAI ALAI

Jai alai, sort of a Spanish-style indoor lacrosse, was introduced to Miami in 1924 and is regularly played in two Miami-area frontons (the buildings in which jai alai is played). Although the sport has roots stemming from ancient Egypt, the game, as it's now played, was invented by Basque peasants in the Pyrenees Mountains during the 17th century.

Players use woven baskets, called *cestas,* to hurl balls, called *pelotas,* at speeds that sometimes exceed 170 mph. Spectators, who are protected behind a wall of glass, place bets on the evening's players. The Florida Gaming Corporation owns the jai alai operations throughout the state, making betting on this sport as legal as buying a lottery ticket.

The **Miami Jai Alai Fronton,** 3500 NW 37th Ave., at NW 35th Street (© 305/633-6400), is America's oldest fronton, dating from 1926. It schedules 13 games per night, which typically last 10 to 20 minutes, but can occasionally go much longer. Admission is $1 to the grandstand, $5 to the clubhouse. There are year-round games. On Wednesdays, Thursdays, and Sundays, there are matinees only that run from noon to 5:30pm. Fridays, Saturdays, and Mondays, there are matinees in addition to evening games from 7pm to midnight. The fronton is closed on Tuesdays. See p. 235 for information on **Dania Jai Alai.**

13 A Bargain-Hunter's Shopping Guide

Miami is one of the world's premier shopping cities; more than 10 million visitors came here last year and they spent in excess of $13 billion. People come to Miami from all over—from Latin America to Hong Kong—in search of some products that are all-American (such as, Levi's, Nikes, and so on).

Miami offers many unique shopping spots, such as the up-and-coming area near downtown known as the Biscayne Corridor, where funky boutiques dare to defy the Gap, and Little Havana, where you can buy hand-rolled cigars and *guayabera* shirts.

You may want to order the Greater Miami Convention and Visitors Bureau's "Shop Miami: A Guide to a Tropical Shopping Adventure." Although it is limited to details on the bureau's paying members, it provides some good advice and otherwise unpublished discount offers. The glossy little pamphlet is printed in English, Spanish, and Portuguese and provides information about transportation from hotels, translation services, and shipping. Call © **800/283-2707** or 305/539-3000 for more information.

As a general rule, shop hours are Monday through Saturday from 10am to 6pm and Sunday from noon to 5pm. Many stores stay open late (until 9pm or so) one night of the week (usually Thurs). Shops in Coconut Grove are open until 9pm Sunday through Thursday and even later on Friday and Saturday nights. South Beach's stores also stay open later—as late as midnight. Department stores and shopping malls also keep longer hours, with most staying open from 10am to 9 or 10pm Monday through Saturday, and noon to 6pm on Sunday. With all these variations, call ahead to specific stores to find out what their hours are.

The 6.5% state and local sales tax is added to the price of all nonfood purchases. Food and beverage in hotels and restaurants are taxed via the resort tax, which is 3% in Miami/South Beach and Bal Harbour, 4% in Surfside, and 2% in the rest of Miami–Dade County.

SHOPPING AREAS

Most of Miami's shopping happens at the many megamalls scattered from one end of the county to the other; however, there is also some excellent boutique shopping and browsing to be done in the following areas:

AVENTURA On Biscayne Boulevard between Miami Gardens Drive and the county line at Hallandale Beach Boulevard is a 2-mile stretch of major retail stores including Best Buy, Borders, Circuit City, Linens N' Things, Marshall's, Sports Authority, and more. Also here is the mammoth Aventura Mall, housing a fabulous collection of shops and restaurants.

CALLE OCHO For a taste of Little Havana, take a walk down 8th Street between SW 27th Avenue and SW 12th Avenue, where you'll find some lively street life and many shops selling cigars, baked goods, shoes, furniture, and record stores specializing in Latin music. For help, take your Spanish dictionary.

COCONUT GROVE Downtown Coconut Grove, centered on Main Highway and Grand Avenue and branching onto the adjoining streets, is one of Miami's most pedestrian-friendly zones. The Grove's wide sidewalks, lined with cafes and boutiques, can provide hours of browsing pleasure. Coconut Grove is best known for its chain stores (Gap, Banana Republic, and so on) and some funky holdovers from the days when the Grove was a bit more bohemian, plus excellent sidewalk cafes centered on CocoWalk and the Streets of Mayfair.

MIRACLE MILE (CORAL GABLES) Actually only a half-mile long, this central shopping street was an integral part of George Merrick's original city plan. Today, the strip still enjoys popularity, especially for its bridal stores, ladies' shops, haberdashers, and gift shops. Recently, newer chain stores, like Barnes & Noble, Old Navy, and Starbucks, have been appearing on the Mile. The hyper upscale Village of **Merrick Park,** a mammoth, 850,000-square-foot upscale outdoor shopping complex between Ponce de León Boulevard and Le Jeune Road, just off the Mile, opened in the fall of 2002 with Nordstrom, Neiman Marcus, Armani, Gucci, Jimmy Choo, and Yves St. Laurent on board, to name a few.

DOWNTOWN MIAMI If you're looking for discounts on all types of goods—especially watches, fabric, buttons, lace, shoes, luggage, and leather—Flagler Street, just west of Biscayne Boulevard, is the best place to start. I wouldn't necessarily recommend buying expensive items here, as many stores seem to be on the shady side and do not understand the word *warranty*. However, you can still have fun here as long as you are a savvy shopper and don't mind haggling with people who may not have the firmest grasp on the English language. Most signs are printed in English, Spanish, and Portuguese; however, many shopkeepers may not be entirely fluent in English. Most recently, the developers responsible for Coconut Grove's CocoWalk shopping and entertainment complex broke ground on Mary Brickell Village, a 192,000-square-foot urban entertainment center west of Brickell Avenue and straddling South Miami Avenue between 9th and 10th streets downtown. The $80 million complex (slated to open in the beginning of 2005) will consist of a slew of trendy restaurants, boutiques, and, of course, the "required" Starbucks—a sure sign that a neighborhood has been revitalized.

BISCAYNE CORRIDOR ✦ Amidst the ramshackle old motels of yesteryear exist several funky, kitschy, and arty boutiques along the stretch of Biscayne Boulevard from 50th Street to about 79th Street known as the Biscayne Corridor. Everything from hand-painted tank tops to expensive Juicy Couture sweat suits can be found here, but it's not just about fashion. Several furniture stores selling antiques and modern pieces exist along here as well, so look carefully as you may find something here that would cause the appraisers on Antiques Road Show to lose their wigs.

SOUTH BEACH ✦ Slowly but surely South Beach has come into its own as far as shopping is concerned. While the requisite stores—Gap, Banana Republic, and others—have anchored here, several higher-end stores have also opened on the southern blocks of Collins Avenue, which has become the Madison Avenue of Miami. For the hippest clothing boutiques (including Armani Exchange, Ralph Lauren, Versace, Benetton, Levi's, Barneys Co-Op, Diesel, Guess?, Club Monaco, Kenneth Cole, and Nicole Miller, among others), stroll along this pretty strip of the Art Deco District.

For those who are interested in a little more fun with their shopping, consider South Beach's legendary Lincoln Road. This pedestrian mall, originally designed in 1957 by Morris Lapidus, recently underwent a multimillion-dollar renovation, restoring it to its former glory. Here, shoppers find an array of clothing, books, tchotchkes, and art as well as a menagerie of sidewalk cafes flanked on one end by a multiplex movie theater, and at the other, the Atlantic Ocean.

SHOPPING A TO Z
BOOKS
You can find local branches of **Barnes & Noble** at 152 Miracle Mile (© 305/446-4152), 5701 Sunset Dr. (© 305/662-4770), 18711 NE Biscayne Blvd. (© 305/935-9770), 7710 N. Kendall (© 305/598-7292), and 12405 N. Kendall Dr. (© 305/598-7727). **Borders** can be found at 9205 S. Dixie Hwy. (© 305/665-8800), 11401 NW 12th St. (© 305/597-8866), 3390 Mary St. (© 305/447-1655), 19925 Biscayne Blvd. (© 305/935-0027), and 8811 SW 107th Ave. (© 305/271-7457).

Books & Books   A dedicated following turns out to browse at this warm and wonderful little independent shop. Enjoy the upstairs antiquarian room, which specializes in art books and first editions. If that's not enough intellectual stimulation for you, the shop hosts free lectures from noted authors, experts, and personalities almost nightly, from Monica Lewinsky to Martin Amis. At another location (933 Lincoln Rd., South Beach; ✆ 305/532-3222), you'll rub elbows with tanned and buffed South Beach bookworms sipping cappuccinos at the Russian Bear Cafe inside the store. This branch stocks a large selection of gay literature and also features lectures. 265 Aragon Ave., Coral Gables. ✆ 305/442-4408. www.booksandbooks.com.

Kafka's Cyberkafe   Check your e-mail and surf the Web while you sip a latte or snack on a sandwich or pastry with friendly neighborhood regulars. This popular used bookstore also stocks a wide range of foreign and domestic magazines and caters to an international-youth-hostel-type crowd. 1464 Washington Ave., South Beach. ✆ 305/673-9669.

CIGARS

Although it is illegal to bring Cuban cigars into the United States, somehow, forbidden *Cohibas* show up at every dinner party and nightclub in town. Not that I condone it, but if you hang around the cigar smokers in town, no doubt one will be able to tell you where you can get some of the highly prized contraband. Be careful, however, of counterfeits, which are typically Dominican cigars posing as Cubans. Cuban cigars are illegal and unless you go down a sketchy alley to buy one from a dealer (think of it as shady as a drug deal), you are going to be smoking Dominican ones.

The stores listed below sell excellent hand-rolled cigars made with domestic- and foreign-grown tobacco. Many of the *viejos* (old men) got their training in Cuba working for the government-owned factories in the heyday of Cuban cigars.

La Gloria Cubana Cigar   This tiny storefront shop employs about 45 veteran Cuban rollers who sit all day rolling the very popular torpedoes and other critically acclaimed blends. They're usually back-ordered, but it's worth stopping in: They will sell you a box and show you around. 1106 SW 8th St., Little Havana. ✆ 305/858-4162.

Mike's Cigars Distributor's Inc. *Finds*   Mike's may have abandoned its old digs for a bigger, newer location, but it's one of the oldest and best smoke shops in town. Since 1950, Mike's has been selling the best from Honduras, the Dominican Republic, and Jamaica, as well as the very hot local brand, La Gloria Cubana. Many say it has the best prices, too. Mike's has the biggest selection of cigars in town and the employees speak English. 1030 Kane Concourse (at 96th St.), Bay Harbor Island. ✆ 305/866-2277. www.mikescigars.com.

COSMETICS, FRAGRANCES, BEAUTY PRODUCTS & A SALON

Brownes & Co. Apothecary *Finds*   Designed to look like an old-fashioned apothecary, this recently expanded beauty emporium combines the best selection of makeup and hair products—MAC, Shu Uemura, Kiehl's, Stila, Molton Brown, Francois Nars, and Dr. Hauschka, just to name a few—with lots of delicious-smelling bath and body stuff, plus a full-service beauty salon. Feel free to browse and sample here, as perfume-spritzing salespeople won't bother you. If you do need help, the staff is a collection of experts when it comes to beauty and hair products. Upstairs is the Browne's Beauty Lounge, in which you can get fabulously coiffed, colored, buffed, and waxed by the experts at the store's renowned salon, Some Like It Hot. For those of you looking for that J-Lo glow, she shops here, so ask one of the staff to point you in the right direction. 841 Lincoln Rd., South Beach. ℭ 305-532-8703. www.brownesbeauty.com.

FASHION: CLOTHING & ACCESSORIES
Miami didn't become a fashion capital until—believe it or not—the pastel-hued, Armani-clad cops on *Miami Vice* had their close-ups on the tube. Before that, Miami was all about old men in white patent leather shoes and well-tanned women in bikinis. How things have changed! Miami is now a fashion mecca in its own right, with some of the same high-end stores you'd find on Rue de Fauborg St. Honore in Paris or Bond Street in London. You'll find all the chichi labels, including Prada and Gucci, right here at the posh Bal Harbour Shops. For funkier frocks, South Beach is the place, where designers such as Cynthia Rowley, Betsey Johnson, and Giorgio Armani compete for window-shoppers with local up-and-coming designers, some of whom design for drag queens and club kids only. The strip on Collins Avenue between 7th and 10th streets has become quite upscale, including such shops as Armani Exchange and Nicole Miller, along with the inescapable Gap and Banana Republic. Of course, there's also more mainstream (and affordable) shopping in the plethora of malls and outdoor shopping and entertainment complexes that are sprinkled throughout the city.

Women's
Place Vendome For cheap and funky club clothes from zebra-print pants to bright, shiny tops. Two locations: 934 Lincoln Rd., South Beach ℭ 305/673-4005, and Aventura Mall, North Miami Beach ℭ 305/932-8931.

Men's
La Casa de las Guayaberas (*Finds*) Miami's premier purveyor of the traditional yet retro-hip Cuban shirt known as the *guayabera*—a loose-fitting, pleated, button-down shirt—was founded by Ramon Puig, who emigrated to Miami over 40 years ago. He still uses the same scissors he did back then, only now he's joined by a team of seamstresses who hand-sew 20 shirts a day in all colors and styles. Prices range from $15 to $375. 5840 SW 8th St., Little Havana. ℭ 305/266-9683.

Yo Yo Skateboarders, hip-hoppers, and graffiti artists love this funky shop for its cool vintage t-shirts and x-treme clothing and accessories. 742 NE 79th St., Miami. ℭ 305754-4279.

MUSIC STORES
Blue Note Records (*Finds*) Here for more than 18 years, Blue Note is music to the ears of music fanatics with a good selection of hard-to-find progressive and underground music. There are new, used, and discounted CDs and old vinyl, too. Call to find out about performances; some great names show up occasionally. A second location features jazz and LPs only. 16401 NE 15th Ave., North Miami Beach. ℭ 305/940-3394. For jazz/LPs: 2299 NE 164th St., North Miami Beach. ℭ 305/354-4563. www.bluenoterecords.com.

Casino Records Inc. The young, hip salespeople here speak English and tend to be music buffs. This store has the largest selection of Latin music in Miami, including pop icons such as Willy Chirino, Gloria Estefan, Albita, and local boy

Nil Lara. Their slogan translates to: "If we don't have it, forget it." Believe me, they've got it. 1208 SW 8th St., Little Havana. © 305/856-6888.

Yesterday and Today Records *(Finds)* This is Miami's most unique and well-stocked store for vinyl—you know, the audio dinosaur that went out with the Victrola? Y & T, as it's known, is a collector's heaven, featuring every genre of music imaginable on every format. Chances are, you could find some eight-track tapes, too. 7902 NW 36th St., Miami. © 305/468-0311.

THRIFT STORES/RESALE SHOPS

The Children's Exchange *(Kids)* Selling everything from layettes to overalls, this pleasant little shop is chock-full of good Florida-style stuff for kids to wear to the beach and in the heat. 1415 Sunset Dr., Coral Gables. © 305/666-6235.

Douglas Gardens Jewish Home and Hospital Thrift Shop Prices here are no longer the major bargain they once were, but for housewares and books, you can do all right. Call to see if they are offering any specials for seniors or students. 5713 NW 27th Ave., North Miami Beach. © 305/638-1900.

Rags to Riches This is an old-time consignment shop where you might find some decent rags, and maybe even some riches. Though not as upscale as it used to be, this place is still a good spot for costume jewelry and shoes. 12577 Biscayne Blvd., North Miami. © 305/891-8981.

Red White & Blue Thrift Store *(Finds)* Miami's best-kept secret is this mammoth thrift store that is meticulously organized and well stocked. You've got to search for great stuff, but it is there. There are especially good deals on children's clothes and housewares. 12640 NE 6th Ave., North Miami. © 305/893-1104.

14 Affordable Fun After Dark

With all the hype, you'd expect Miami to have long outlived its 15 minutes of fame by now. But you'd be wrong. Miami's nightlife, in South Beach *and,* slowly but surely, downtown, is hotter than ever before—and still getting hotter.

Practically every club in the area has installed closely guarded velvet ropes to create an air of exclusivity. Don't be fooled or intimidated by them—*anyone* can go clubbing in the magic city, and throughout this chapter, I've provided tips to ensure you gain entry to the venue you want to go to.

South Beach is certainly Miami's uncontested nocturnal nucleus, but more and more diverse areas, such as the Design District, South Miami, and even Little Havana, are increasingly providing fun alternatives without the ludicrous cover charges, "fashionably late" hours of operation (things don't typically get started on South Beach until after 11pm), the lack of sufficient self-parking, and outrageous drink prices that come standard in South Beach.

And while South Beach dances to a more electronic beat, other parts of Miami dance to a Latin beat—from salsa and merengue to tango and cha cha. However, if you're looking for a less frenetic good time, Miami's bar scene offers something for everyone, from haute hotel bars to sleek, loungey watering holes.

Parts of downtown Miami, such as the Biscayne Corridor, the Miami River, and the Design District, are in the throes of a trendy makeover a la New York City's Meatpacking District, in which, slowly but surely, cool lounges, bars, and clubs are popping up and providing the "in" and arty crowds with another, newer, more urban-chic nocturnal pasture.

But if the possibility of a celebrity sighting in one of the city's lounges, bars, or clubs doesn't fulfill your cultural needs, Miami also offers a variety of first-rate diversions in theater, music, and dance, including a world-class ballet (under the aegis of Edward Villella), a recognized symphony, and a talented opera company.

For up-to-date listing information, and to make sure the club of the moment hasn't expired, check the *Miami Herald*'s "Weekend" section, which runs on Friday, or the more comprehensive listings in *New Times*, Miami's free alternative weekly, available each Wednesday, or visit www.miami.citysearch.com online.

THE CLUB & MUSIC SCENE
DANCE CLUBS

Clubs are as much a cottage industry in Miami as is, say, cheese in Wisconsin. Clubland, as it is known, is not just a nocturnal theme park but a way of life for some. On any given night in Miami, there's something going on—no excuses are needed to throw a party here. Short of throwing a glammy event for the grand opening of a new gas station, Miami is very party hearty, celebrating everything from the fact that it's Tuesday night to the debut of a hot new DJ. Within this very bizarre after-dark community, a very colorful assortment of characters emerges, from your (a)typical nine-to-fivers to shady characters who have reinvented themselves as hot shots on the club circuit. While this scene of seeing and being seen may not be your cup of Absolut, it's certainly never boring.

The club music played on Miami's ever-evolving social circuit is good enough to get even the most rhythmically challenged wallflowers dancing. To keep things fresh in Clubland, local promoters throw one-nighters, which are essentially parties with various themes or motifs, from funk to fashion. Because these change so often, we can't possibly list them here. Word of mouth, local advertising, and listings in the free weekly *New Times*, www.miami.citysearch.com, or the "Weekend" section of the *Miami Herald* are the best ways to find out about these ever-changing events.

Before you get all decked out to hit the town as soon as the sun sets, consider the fact that Miami is a very late town. Things generally don't get started here before 11pm. The Catch-22 is that if you don't arrive on South Beach early enough, you may find yourself driving around aimlessly for parking, as it is very limited outside of absurd $20 valet charges. Municipal lots fill up quickly, so your best bet is to arrive on South Beach somewhat early and kill time by strolling around, having something to eat, or sipping a cocktail in a hotel bar. Another advantage of arriving a bit earlier than the crowds is that some clubs don't charge a cover before 11pm or midnight, which could save you a wad of cash over time. Most clubs are open every night of the week, though some are only open Thursday to Sunday and others are only open Monday though Saturday. Call ahead to get the most up-to-date information possible: Things change very quickly around here, and a call in advance can help you make sure that the dance club you're planning to go to hasn't become a video arcade. Cover charges are very haphazard, too. If you're not on the ubiquitous guest list (ask your concierge to put you on the list—he or she usually has the ability to do so, which won't help you with the wait to get in, but will eliminate the cover charge), you may have to fork over a ridiculous $20 to walk past the ropes. Don't fret, though. There are many clubs and bars that have no cover charge—they just make up for it by charging $13 for a martini!

Tips Ground Rules: Stepping Out in Miami

- Nightlife on South Beach doesn't really get going until after 11pm. As a result, you may want to consider taking what is known as a disco nap so that you'll be fully charged until the wee hours.
- If you're unsure of what to wear out on South Beach, your safest bet will be anything black.
- Do *not* try to tip the doormen manning the velvet ropes. That will only make you look desperate and you'll find yourself standing outside for what will seem like an ungodly amount of time. Instead, try to land your name on the ever-present guest lists by calling the club early in the day yourself, or, better yet, having the concierge at your hotel do it for you. Concierges have connections. If you don't have connections and you find yourself without a concierge, then act assertive, not surly, at the velvet rope, and your patience will usually be rewarded with admittance. If all else fails—for men, especially—surround yourself with a few leggy model types and you'll be noticed quicker.
- If you are a man going out with a group of men, unless you're going to a gay bar, you will most likely not get into any South Beach hot spot unless you are with women.
- Finally, have fun. It may look like serious business when you're on the outside, but once you're in, it's another story. Attacking Clubland with a sense of humor is the best approach to a successful, memorable evening out.

Club Space ✸ Clubland hits the mainland with this cavernous downtown warehouse of a club. With over 30,000 square feet of dance space, you can spin around a la Stevie Nicks (albeit to a techno beat) without having to worry about banging into someone. On Saturday and Sunday nights, the party usually extends to the next morning, sometimes as late 10am. It's quite a sight to see club kids rushing off to work straight from Space on a Monday morning. Known as the venue of choice for world-renowned DJs, Club Space sometimes charges ludicrous admission fees to cover their hefty price tags. *Note:* Club Space doesn't really get going until around 3 am. Call for more information, as it doesn't have a concrete schedule. 34 NE 11th St., Miami. ℂ **305/372-9378.** Cover $0–$20.

crobar ✸ Still haunted by the ghost of clubs past, the space formerly known as the Cameo Theatre is now possessed by the mod, millennial, industrial spirit that is crobar. With its intense, dance-heavy sound system, an industrially chic ambience, and crowds big enough to scare away any memories of a sadly abandoned Cameo, this Chicago import has raised the bar on South Beach nightlife with crazy theme nights (the monthly Sex Night is particularly, uh, stimulating), top-name DJs, and the occasional celebrity appearance. On Sunday, the club hosts an extremely popular gay night known as Anthem (p. 156). Open Thursday through Monday from 10pm to 5am. 1445 Washington Ave., South Beach. ℂ **305/531-8225.** www.crobarmiami.com. Cover Thurs, Sun, Mon $20; Fri–Sat $25.

I/O Although I'd like to call this new warehouse-y club "ghetto fabulous," I don't want to give out mixed messages. I/O is the club for that funky, arty/hipster set that listens to music by the likes of Belle and Sebastian and other groups that your Britney-loving sister probably never heard of. The club is composed of three areas—a bar area in which Japanese anime is played, a dance area where live music is performed and cool kids do their best break dancing (or whatever they're calling it these days), and an outdoor bar area, which is cool during winter months but brutally hot in the summer. The best nights here are Thursday night's Latin-flavored Fuacata! and Saturday night's Pop Life, an homage to the Depeche Mode era of New Wave. 30 NE 14th St., Downtown Miami. ✆ 305/358-8007. Cover $5–$10.

Nikki Beach Club *Finds* What the Playboy Mansion is to L.A., the Nikki Beach Club is to South Beach. This place is the product of local nightlife royalty Tommy Pooch and Eric Omores. Half-naked ladies and men actually venture into the daylight on Sundays (around 4pm, which is ungodly in this town) to see, be seen, and, at times, be obscene. At night, it's very Brady-Bunch-goes-to-Hawaii–seeming, with a sexy Tiki hut/Polynesian theme style, albeit rated R. The Sunday-afternoon beach party is almost legendary and worth a glimpse— that is, if you can get in. This is not your equal-opportunity beach club. Egos are easily shattered, as surly doormen are known to reject those who don't drive up in a Ferrari. Also located within this bastion of hedonism is the superhot **Pearl,** a mod-ish, 380-seat, orange-hued restaurant and lounge that features a Continental menu created by Nikki chef Brian Rutherford. But you'd do better to forget the food and go for the eye candy. 101 Ocean Dr., South Beach. ✆ 305/538-1111. Cover $10–$20.

Opium Garden Housed in the massive, open-air space, Opium Garden is a highly addictive nocturnal habit for those looking for a combination of sexy dance music, scantily clad dancers, celebrities such as J-Lo, Janet Jackson, Lenny Kravitz, and P. Diddy, and, for the masochists out there, an oppressive door policy in which two sets of velvet ropes are set up to keep those deemed unworthy out of this see-and-be-sceney den of inequity. Opium has a sushi restaurant (decent) and an ultra-VIP, celeb-saturated lounge, Prive, whose own separate door policy makes the aforementioned seem like a romp in the sand. 136 Collins Ave., South Beach. ✆ 305/531-5535. Cover $20.

Rumi Named after a 13th-century Sufi mystic, South Beach's first upscale supper club is command central for hipsters hailing from all coasts. Designed by hot NYC designers Nancy Mah and Scott Kester, Rumi is an urbane oasis of reds, tans, and chocolates, reminiscent of the golden age of supper clubs of the '30s and '40s. This bi-level space features intimate lounge areas as well as private and public dining rooms, in which haute Floribbean cuisine is served until around 11pm, when the tables conspicuously disappear and give way to a neo-Zen-like stamping ground for South Beach's chic elite. Make sure to check out the queen-size Murphy bed that snaps down from the wall to make room for late-night lounging. As long as you can get past the velvet ropes (by either looking pretty, being on the guest list, or just getting the doorman on a good day), there is no cover to bask in this bastion of South Beach scene-dom. 330 Lincoln Rd., South Beach. ✆ 305/672-4353. www.rumimiami.com.

SoHo Lounge *Finds* This multi-leveled, multi-faceted Design District club is tons of fun if you are into either '80s music or electroclash. Cheap drinks, a sprawling outdoor patio, and several different nooks, crannies, bars, and dance areas are available for perusal. The best area in the entire club is the two-story dance floor in which a big screen shows everything from Tronn to anime. Music ranges from the '80s greatest hits to more obscure music from Europe. One of the best venues in town for live music, SoHo Lounge has hosted the likes of Peaches and Electro-cute, and if those names don't ring a bell, consider going to SoHo to become acquainted with them. 175 NE 36th St., Design District. ℭ **305/576-1988.** Cover $0–$10.

LATIN CLUBS

Considering that Hispanics make up a large part of Miami's population and that there's a huge influx of Spanish-speaking visitors, it's no surprise that there are some great Latin nightclubs in the city.

Plus, with the meteoric rise of the international music scene based in Miami, many international stars come through the offices of MTV Latino, SONY International, and a multitude of Latin TV studios based in Miami—and they're all looking for a good club scene on weekends. Most of the Anglo clubs also reserve at least 1 night a week for Latin rhythms.

Casa Panza *Finds* This *casa* is one of Little Havana's liveliest and most popular nightspots. Every Tuesday, Thursday, and Saturday night, Casa Panza, in the heart of Little Havana, becomes the House of Flamenco, with shows at 8 and 11pm. You can either enjoy a flamenco show or strap on your own dancing shoes and participate in the celebration. Enjoy a fantastic Spanish meal before the show, or just a glass of sangria before you start stomping. Open until 4am, Casa Panza is a hot spot for young Latin club kids, and, occasionally, a few older folks who are so taken by the music and the scene that they've failed to realize that it's well past their bedtime. 1620 SW 8th St. (Calle Ocho), Little Havana. ℭ **305/643-5343.**

La Covacha *Finds* This hut, located virtually in the middle of nowhere (West Miami), is the hottest Latin joint in the entire city. Sunday features the best in Latin rock, with local and international acts. But the shack is really jumping on weekend nights when the place is open until 5am. Friday is *the* night here, so much so that the owners had to place a red velvet rope out front to maintain some semblance of order. It's an amusing sight—a velvet rope guarding a shack—but once you get in, you'll understand the need for it. Do not wear silk here, as you *will* sweat. 10730 NW 25th St. (at NW 107th Ave.), West Miami. ℭ **305/594-3717.** Cover $0–$10.

Mango's Tropical Café Claustrophobic types do not want to go near Mango's. Ever. One of the most popular spots on Ocean Drive, this outdoor enclave of Latin liveliness shakes with the intensity of a Richter-busting earthquake. Welcome and *bienvenido,* Mango's is *Cabaret,* Latin style. Nightly live Brazilian and other Latin music, not to mention scantily clad male and female dancers, draw huge gawking crowds in from the sidewalk. But pay attention to the music if you can: Incognito international musicians often lose their anonymity and jam with the house band on stage. Open daily from 11am to 5am. 900 Ocean Dr., South Beach. ℭ **305/673-4422.** Cover $5–$15.

THE GAY & LESBIAN SCENE

Miami and the beaches have long been host to what is called a "first-tier" gay community. Similar to the Big Apple, the Bay Area, or LaLa land, Miami has had a large alternative community since the days when Anita Bryant used her citrus power to boycott the rise in political activism in the early '70s. Well, things have changed and Miami–Dade now has a gay-rights ordinance.

Newcomers intending to party in any bar, whether downtown or certainly on the beach, will want to check ahead for the schedule, as all clubs must have a gay or lesbian night to pay their rent, since their gay nights bring in major crowds and profits. Miami Beach, in fact, is a capital of the gay circuit party scene, rivaling San Francisco, Palm Springs, and even the mighty Sydney, Australia, for tourist dollars. However, ever since South Beach got bit by the hip-hop bug, many of Miami's gays have been crossing county lines into Fort Lauderdale, where there are surprisingly many more gay establishments.

Anthem Sunday nights at crobar sing the gay anthem with this hyperpopular one-nighter featuring Miami's own superstar DJ Abel. 1445 Washington Ave., South Beach. ✆ 877/CRO-SOBE or 305/531-5027. Cover $20.

O-Zone This is the zone of choice for gay men with an aversion to South Beach's cruisy, scene-heavy vibes. It's known for a heavily Latin crowd (mixed with a few college boys from nearby University of Miami) and fantastic, outlandish drag shows on the weekends. 6620 SW 57th Ave. (Red Rd.), South Miami. ✆ 305/667-2888. No cover for men on Sat; other nights $5–$10.

Score There's a reason this Lincoln Road hotbed of gay social activity is called Score. In addition to the huge pick-up scene, Score offers a multitude of bars, dance floors, loungelike areas, and outdoor tables in case you need to come up for air. Sunday afternoon Tea Dances are legendary here. 727 Lincoln Rd., South Beach. ✆ 305/535-1111.

Twist One of the most popular bars (and hideaways) on South Beach, this recently expanded bar (which is literally right across the street from the police station) has a casual yet lively local atmosphere. 1057 Washington Ave., South Beach. ✆ 305/538-9478.

LIVE MUSIC
Unfortunately, Miami's live music scene is not thriving. Instead of local bands garnering devoted fans, local DJs are more admired, skyrocketing much more easily to fame—thanks to the city's lauded dance-club scene. However, there are still several places that strive to bring Miami up to speed as far as live music is concerned. You just have to look—and listen—for it a bit more carefully. The following is a list of places where you can, from time to time, catch some live acts, be it a DJ or an aspiring Nirvana.

Churchill's Hideaway *(Finds* British expatriate Dave Daniels couldn't live in Miami without a true English-style pub, so he opened Churchill's Hideaway, the city's premier space for live rock music. Filthy and located in a rather unsavory neighborhood, Churchill's is committed to promoting and extending the lifeline of the lagging local music scene. A fun no-frills crowd hangs out here. Bring earplugs with you, as it is deafening once the music starts. Monday is open mic night while Wednesday is reserved for ladies' wrestling. 5501 NE 2nd Ave., Little Haiti. ✆ 305/757-1807. www.churchillspub.com. Cover $0–$6.

Jazid *(Finds* Smoky, sultry, and illuminated by flickering candelabras, Jazid is the kind of place where you'd expect to hear Sade's "Smooth Operator" on constant rotation. Instead, however, you'll hear live jazz (sometimes on acid), soul, and funk. Past surprise performers at Jazid include former Smashing Pumpkin's front man Billy Corgan. An eclectic mix of mellow folk convenes here for a much necessary respite from the surrounding Washington Avenue mayhem. 1342 Washington Ave., South Beach. ✆ 305/673-9372. Cover $10.

Tobacco Road   Al Capone used to hang out here when it was a speakeasy. Now, locals flock here to see local bands perform, as well as national acts such as George Clinton and the P-Funk All-Stars, Koko Taylor, and the Radiators. Tobacco Road (the proud owner of Miami's very first liquor license) is small and gritty and meant to be that way. Escape the smoke and sweat in the backyard patio, where air is a welcome commodity. The downright cheap nightly specials, such as the $11 lobster on Tuesday, are quite good and are served until 2am; the bar is open until 5am. 626 S. Miami Ave. (over the Miami Ave. Bridge near Brickell Ave.), Downtown. (C) 305/374-1198. Cover $5–$10 Thurs–Sat.

Upstairs at the Van Dyke Cafe *Finds*   The cafe's jazz bar, located on the second floor, resembles a classy speakeasy in which local jazz performers play to an intimate, enthusiastic crowd of mostly adults and sophisticated young things, who often huddle at the small tables until the wee hours. 846 Lincoln Rd., Miami Beach. (C) 305/534-3600. Cover Sun–Thurs $5, Fri–Sat $10 for a seat; no cover at the bar.

BARS & LOUNGES

There are countless bars and lounges in and around Miami (most require proof that you are over 21 to enter), with the highest concentration on trendy South Beach. The selection listed here is a mere sample. Keep in mind that many of the popular bars—and the easiest to get into—are in hotels (with a few notable exceptions—see below). For a clubbier scene, if you don't mind making your way through hordes of inebriated club kids, a stroll on Washington Avenue will provide you with ample insight into what's hot and what's not. Just hold onto your bags. It's not dangerous, but, occasionally, a few shady types manage to slip into the crowd. Another very important tip when in a club: *Never put your drink down out of your sight*—there have been unfortunate incidents in which drinks have been spiked with illegal chemical substances. For a less hard-core, more collegiate nightlife, head to Coconut Grove. Oh, yes, and when going out in South Beach, make sure to take a so-called disco nap, as things don't get going until at least 11pm. If you go earlier, be prepared to face an empty bar or club. Off of South Beach and in hotel bars in general, the hours are fashionably earlier, with the action starting as early as, say, 7pm.

Automatic Slim's   This is *the* bar where Ozzie and Harriet types become more like Ozzy and Sharon. As South Beach's most popular, unpretentious bar, Automatic Slim's is indeed a slim space of bar, but it packs people in thanks to an exhaustive list of cheap(er) drinks, lack of attitude, great rock music, and a decor that can only be described as white trash chic. 1216 Washington Ave., South Beach. (C) 305/695-0795. No cover.

Blue   A very laid-back, very locals scene set to a sultry soundtrack of deep soul and house music has Miami's hipsters feeling the blues here on a nightly basis from 10pm to 5am. Before you whip out the St. John's Wort, dive into this so-not-trendy-it's-trendy lounge, in which the pervasive color blue will actually heighten your spirits as an eclectic haze of models, locals, and lounge lizards gather to commiserate in their dreaded trendy status. 222 Española Way (between Washington and Collins aves.), South Beach. (C) 305/534-1009. No cover.

Clevelander   If wet T-shirt contests and a fraternity party atmosphere are your thing, then this Ocean Drive mainstay is your kind of place. Popular with tourists and locals who like to pretend they're tourists, the Clevelander attracts a lively, sporty, adults-only crowd (the burly bouncers *will* confiscate fake IDs) who have no interest in being part of a scene, but, rather, taking in the very revealing scenery. A great time to check out the Clevelander is on a weekend afternoon, when beach Barbies and Kens line the bar for a post-tanning beer or frozen cocktail. 1020 Ocean Dr., South Beach. 🕻 305/531-3485. No cover.

Forge The Forge bar hosts an unusual mix of the uptight and those who wear their clothes too tight. (Door policy tends to be a bit exclusive; dress up and you should have no problem.) It's also where surgically altered ladies look for their cigar-chomping sugar daddies in a setting that somehow reminds me of *Dynasty*. Call well in advance if you want to watch the parade of characters from a dinner table. The Forge owners also own a ritzier nightclub (which is attached to the club), reminiscent of a cruise-ship lounge, called Jimmy'z (they say it's a private club, but if you dine at the restaurant or are acquainted with someone in the know, you can get in). 432 41st St., Miami Beach. 🕻 305/538-8533.

Grass Restaurant and Lounge Though Grass is truly a restaurant, it's also one of the city's biggest nocturnal hot spots and has one of the most oppressive door policies in town. Regardless, the place is übercool, with its *chickee hut* decor and its lounge-spinning DJs. The best way for you to get into Grass is by making a dinner reservation and dressing as if you were going up for inspection before Vogue Magazine's Cruella De Vil of Fashion, Anna Wintour. 28 NE 40th St., Design District. 🕻 305/573-3355.

Laundry Bar This is the only place in Miami where it's okay to let friends drink and dry. Laundry Bar features working washers, dryers, a fully stocked bar, and several other distractions to help make doing your laundry a fun rather than a dreaded chore. It's also one of the only bars on South Beach open from 7am to 5am daily. Thursdays are the hottest laundry nights on South Beach, when a DJ here spins the best in house music. On Wednesdays and Fridays, gospel diva Marvel Epps sings live to an always packed and lively house. And although it's most popular with the gay community, Laundry Bar draws a mixed crowd; on weekends, the place is packed like an overloaded washing machine. Daily happy hours (4 to 9pm) with two-for-one drinks allow you to save your change for the washing machines. 721 N. Lincoln Lane (behind Burdines off Lincoln Rd.), South Beach. 🕻 305/531-7700. www.laundrybar.com.

Mac's Club Deuce Standing on its own amidst an oasis of trendiness, Mac's Club Deuce is the quintessential dive bar, with cheap drinks and a cast of characters ranging from your typical barfly to your atypical drag queen. It's got a well-stocked jukebox, friendly bartenders, a pool table, and best of all, it's an insomniac's dream, open daily from 8am to 5am. 222 14th St., South Beach. 🕻 305/673-9537.

Mansion Housed in the space formerly known as Level, this latest nocturnal venture from the same team behind the utterly addictive Opium Garden (p. 154) is a massive, multi-leveled lounge that, according to the owners and promoters, is entirely "VIP," meaning you best know someone to get in or else you'll be amongst the masses outside and not even close to the manse. Live DJs, models, and celebrities galore—ubiquitous Paris Hilton, Tara Reid, Shannen

---

Impressions

There are two shifts in South Beach. There's nine to five. And then there's nine to five.

—South Beach artist Stewart Stewart

Moments Stargazing

The most popular places for celebrity sightings include Mynt, Opium Garden, Skybar, poolside at the Shore Club or the Delano, and, when it comes to J-Lo, somewhere on the beach around 20th street. Miami Heat basketball games are also star magnets.

Doherty, members of *NSync, and more, not to mention high ceilings, wood floors, brick walls, and a decidedly non-smoky interior make this Mansion, despite its cheesy name, a must of the list of see and be scenesters. Open Tuesday through Sunday from 11pm to 5am. 1235 Washington Ave., South Beach. ☎ 305/531-5535. Cover varies from $10–$40.

Mynt   This hyper-stylish, hip lounge is reminiscent of a space-age cafeteria. A massive 6,000-square-foot place, Mynt is nothing more than a huge living room in which models, celebrities, and assorted hangers-on bask in the green glow to the beats of very loud lounge and dance music. If you want to dance—or move, for that matter, this is not the place in which to do so. It's all about striking a pose in here. And unless you know the person at the door, be prepared to be ridiculed, emasculated, and socially shattered as you may be forced to wait outside upwards of an hour. If that's the case, forget it; it's not worth it. Wait next door at the Greek place if you want a celebrity sighting, since you'll have a better chance seeing people from there than actually waiting in the melee at the door or inside. 1921 Collins Ave., South Beach. ☎ 786/276-6132. Cover $10–20.

The Purdy Lounge   With the exception of a wall of lava lamps, Purdy is not unlike your best friend's basement, featuring a pool table and a slew of board games such as Operation to keep the attention-deficit disordered from getting bored. Because it's a no-nonsense bar with relatively cheap cocktails (by South Beach standards), Purdy gets away with not having to have a star DJ or fancy bass-heavy Bose sound system. A CD player somehow does the trick, although lately, in order to keep up with the Joneses, Purdy has been employing some disc-spinning DJs. With no cover and no attitude, a line is inevitable (it gets crowded inside), so be prepared to wait. Saturday night has become the preferred night for locals, while Friday night's happy hour draws a young professional crowd on the prowl. 1811 Purdy Ave./Sunset Harbor, South Beach. ☎ 305/531-4622.

Rok Bar   Larger than life rocker Tommy Lee has assembled a motley Miami crew at this paradox of a bar that combines down 'n' dirty rock and roll with the swank comforts of a chic lounge. The place is claustrophobic with limited seating (unless you're Pamela Anderson, forget about scoring a table), high priced drinks, and an oxymoronic soundtrack of Lynyrd Skynyrd, Michael Jackson, and Kid Rock, but it's fun nevertheless. 1905 Collins Ave., South Beach. ☎ 305/538-7171.

Rose Bar at the Delano   If every rose has its thorn, the thorn at this painfully chic hotel bar is the excruciatingly high-priced cocktails. Otherwise, the crowd here is full of the so-called glitterati, fabulatti, and other assorted poseurs who view life through (Italian-made) rose-colored glasses. 1685 Collins Ave., South Beach. ☎ 305/672-2000.

Segafredo Espresso   Although Segafredo is technically a cafe, it has become an integral part of Miami's nightlife in terms of its status as command central

Late-Night Bites

Although some dining spots in Miami stop serving at 10pm, many are open very late or even around the clock—especially on weekends. So, if it's 4am and you need a quick bite after clubbing, don't fret. There are a vast number of pizza places lining Washington Avenue in South Beach that are open past 6am. Especially good are **La Sandwicherie**, 229 14th St. (behind the Amoco station; ☎ **305/532-8934**), which serves up a great late-night sandwich until 5am; and its next-door neighbor **San Loco Tacos** (235 14th St.; ☎ **305/538-3009**), which slings tacos until 5am on week-nights and 6am on weekends. Another place of note for night owls is the **News Café**, 800 Ocean Dr. (☎ **305/538-6397**), a trendy and well-priced cafe that has an enormous menu offering great all-day breakfasts, Middle Eastern platters, fruit bowls, or steak and potatoes—and everything is served 24 hours a day. If you're craving a corned beef on rye at 5am, **Jerry's Famous Deli**, 1450 Collins Ave. (☎ **305/534-3244**), is open 24/7. If your night out was at one of the Latin clubs around town, stop in at **Versailles**, 3555 SW 8th St. (☎ **305/444-0240**), in Little Havana. What else but a Cuban *medianoche* (midnight sandwich) will do? It's not open all night, but its hours extend well past midnight—usually until 3 or 4am on weekends—to cater to gangs of revelers, young and old.

---

for Euros who miss that very special brand of European cafe society. Not in the mood for a club or bar but want to hear great music, sip a few cocktails, snack on some delicious sandwiches and pizza, and sit outside and people watch? This is the place. European lounge music, tons of outdoor tables around a fountain on a prime corner of Lincoln Road, and always a mob scene make 'Fredo one of my—and many other Miamians'—favorite nocturnal diversions. 1040 Lincoln Rd., South Beach. ☎ **305/673-0047**.

Skybar at the Shore Club Skybar lives up to its name in terms of loftiness; something this place has perfected better than anyone else, whether at its original L.A. location at the Mondrian, or at the sprawling South Beach location at the Shore Club. If you're not a hotel guest, not Beyonce, not on the "list," or you're a guy with several other guys and no girls, fugghedabout it. For those of you who can't get in, the Skybar is basically the entire backyard area of the Shore Club, consisting of several areas including the Moroccan-themed garden area, the hip-hop-themed indoor Red Room, the Sand Bar by the beach, and the Rum Bar by the pool. Popular on any given night, Sky Bar is yet another brilliant example of how hotelier Ian Schrager has managed to control the hipsters in a most Pavlovian way. At the Shore Club, 1901 Collins Ave., South Beach. ☎ **305/695-3100**.

Taverna Opa Although this Greek taverna (also located in Hollywood and Ft. Lauderdale) calls itself a restaurant, I consider it more of a raucous dance club that just happens to serve excellent Greek food. How many restaurants do you know of that allow patrons to dance suggestively with waiters on tables, throw napkins in the air as if they were confetti, and guzzle ouzo straight from the bottle, all to the tune of some very loud, jazzed up Greek dance music? Get here early, as the place is always packed—and I mean packed as in Standing Room Only. Although there is an outdoor bar, the real fun and scenery is indoors in the dining room where the tables double as dance floors and some very animated characters channel their best Zorbas. Be prepared for a big fat Greek hangover the next day. 36 Ocean Dr., South Beach. ☏ 305/673-6730.

Vino Nobody can figure out why this place opened in frat-ridden Coconut Grove, which is why Vino moved to South Beach after a year in the quasi college town, but nonetheless, Vino is the city's *only* bona fide wine bar with a collection of over 300 bottles and 60 wines by the glass. Decorated as if it came straight out of a West Elm catalogue, this chic, Manhattan-esque wine bar is known for many things, especially the fact that it's a chill lounge in which the 30 and over set can hang out, have audible conversations, sip wine, and even enjoy cheeses, fondues, and delicious desserts. Vino also has a monthly wine-tasting event with experts hailing from particular regions from around the world. 1601 Washington Ave. Ste. 110, Miami Beach, FL 33139; ☏ 305/532-8466.

Wet Willie's With such telling drinks as Call a Cab, this beachfront oasis is not the place to go if you have a long drive ahead of you. A well-liked pre- and postbeach hangout, Wet Willie's inspires serious drinking. Popular with the Harley Davidson set, tourists, and beachcombers, this bar is best known for its rooftop patio (get there early if you plan to get a seat) and its half-nude bikini beauties. 760 Ocean Dr., South Beach. ☏ 305/532-5650.

THE PERFORMING ARTS

Highbrows and culture vultures complain that there is a dearth of decent cultural offerings in Miami. What do locals tell them? Go back to New York! In all seriousness, however, in recent years Miami's performing arts scene has improved greatly. The city's Broadway Series features Tony Award–winning shows (the touring versions, of course), which aren't always Broadway caliber, but they are usually pretty good and not nearly as pricey. Local arts groups such as the Miami Light Project, a not-for-profit cultural organization that presents live performances by innovative dance, music, and theater artists, have had huge success in attracting big-name artists such as Nina Simone and Philip Glass to Miami. In addition, a burgeoning bohemian movement in Little Havana has given way to performance spaces that have become nightclubs in their own right.

THEATER

The **Actors' Playhouse** (Kids), a musical theater at the newly restored Miracle Theater at 280 Miracle Mile, Coral Gables (☏ 305/444-9293; www.actors playhouse.org), is a grand 1948 Art Deco movie palace with a 600-seat main theater and a smaller theater/rehearsal hall that hosts a number of excellent musicals for children throughout the year. In addition to these two rooms, the Playhouse recently added a 300-seat children's balcony theater. Tickets run from $27 to $40.

The **Coconut Grove Playhouse,** 3500 Main Hwy., Coconut Grove (☏ 305/442-4000; www.cgplayhouse.org), is also a former movie house, built in 1927 in an ornate Spanish rococo style. Today, this respected venue is known for its original and innovative staging of both international and local dramas and musicals. The house's second, more intimate Encore Room is well suited to alternative and experimental productions. Tickets run from $35 to $45.

The **Gables Stage** at the Biltmore Hotel, Anastasia Avenue, Coral Gables (☏ 305/445-1119), stages at least one Shakespearean play, one classic, and one contemporary piece a year. This well-regarded theater usually tries to secure the rights to a national or local premiere as well. Tickets cost $35; $15 and $32, respectively, for students and seniors.

The **Jerry Herman Ring Theatre** is on the main campus of the University of Miami in Coral Gables (℃ **305/284-3355**). The University's Department of Theater Arts uses this stage for advanced-student productions of comedies, dramas, and musicals. Faculty and guest actors are regularly featured, as are contemporary works by local playwrights. Performances are usually scheduled Tuesday through Saturday during the academic year. In the summer, don't miss "Summer Shorts," a selection of superb one-acts. Tickets sell for $14 to $16.

The **New Theater,** 4120 Laguna St., Coral Gables (℃ **305/443-5909**), prides itself on showing world-renowned works from America and Europe. As the name implies, you'll find mostly contemporary plays, with a few classics thrown in for variety. Performances are staged Thursday through Sunday year-round. Tickets are $35 on Thursdays, $40 on Fridays and Saturdays, and $35 to $40 on Sundays. If tickets are available on the day of the performance—and they usually are—students pay half price.

CLASSICAL MUSIC

In addition to a number of local orchestras and operas (see below), which regularly offer quality music and world-renowned guest artists, each year brings a slew of classical music special events and touring artists to Miami. The **Concert Association of Florida (CAF)** (℃ **877/433-3200**) produces one of the most important and longest-running series. Known for more than a quarter of a century for its high-caliber, star-packed schedules, CAF regularly arranges the best "serious" music concerts for the city. Season after season, the schedules are punctuated by world-renowned dance companies and seasoned virtuosos like Itzhak Perlman, Andre Watts, and Kathleen Battle. Since CAF does not have its own space, performances are usually scheduled in the Miami–Dade County Auditorium or the Jackie Gleason Theater of the Performing Arts (see the "Major Venues" section below). The season lasts October through April, and ticket prices range from $20 to $70.

Florida Philharmonic Orchestra South Florida's premier symphony orchestra, under the direction of James Judd, presents a full season of classical and pops programs interspersed with several children's and contemporary popular music performances. The Philharmonic performs downtown in the Gusman Center for the Performing Arts and at the Miami–Dade County Auditorium (see the "Major Venues" section below). 4120 Leguna St., Coral Gables. ℃ 800/226-1812. Tickets $15–$60. When extra tickets are available, students are admitted free on day of performance.

Miami Chamber Symphony This professional orchestra is a small, subscription-series orchestra that's not affiliated with any major arts organizations and is therefore an inexpensive alternative to the high-priced classical venues. Renowned international soloists perform regularly. The season runs October to May, and most concerts are held in the Gusman Concert Hall, on the University of Miami campus. 5690 N. Kendall Dr., Kendall. ℃ 305/284-6477. Tickets $12–$30.

New World Symphony This organization, led by artistic director Michael Tilson Thomas, is a stepping stone for gifted young musicians seeking professional careers. The orchestra specializes in ambitious, innovative, energetic performances and often features renowned guest soloists and conductors. The symphony's season lasts from October to May, during which time there are many free concerts. 541 Lincoln Rd., South Beach. (℃ 305/673-3331. www.nws.org. Tickets free–$58. Rush tickets (remaining tickets sold 1 hr. before performance) $20. Students $10 (1 hr. before concerts; limited seating).

OPERA

Florida Grand Opera   Around for over 60 years, this company regularly features singers from top houses in both America and Europe. All productions are sung in their original language and staged with projected English supertitles. Tickets become scarce when Placido Domingo or Luciano Pavarotti (who made his American debut here in 1965) comes to town. The opera's season runs roughly from November to April, with five performances each week. A new multimillion-dollar headquarters for the opera is scheduled to open in about May of 2006; until then, performances take place at the Miami–Dade County Auditorium and the Broward Center for the Performing Arts, about 40 minutes from downtown Miami. Box office: 1200 Coral Way, Southwest Miami. (℃ 800/741-1010. www.fgo.org. Tickets $19–$145. Student discounts available.

DANCE

Several local dance companies train and perform in the Greater Miami area. In addition, top traveling troupes regularly stop at the venues listed below. Keep your eyes open for special events and guest artists.

Ballet Flamenco La Rosa   For a taste of local Latin flavor, see this lively troupe perform impressive flamenco and other styles of Latin dance on Miami stages. (They also teach Latin dancing.) 13126 W. Dixie Hwy., North Miami. (℃ 305/899-7729. Tickets $25 at door, $20 in advance, $18 for students and seniors.

Miami City Ballet   This artistically acclaimed and innovative company, directed by Edward Villella, features a repertoire of more than 60 ballets, many by George Balanchine, and has had more than 20 world premieres. The company moved into a new $7.5 million headquarters in January 2000—the Ophelia and Juan Jr. Roca Center at the Collins Park Cultural Center in Miami Beach. This three-story center features eight rehearsal rooms, a ballet school, a boutique, and ticket offices. The City Ballet season runs from September to April. Ophelia and Juan Jr. Roca Center, Collins Ave. and 22nd St., South Beach. (℃ 305/929-7000 or 305/929-7010 for box office. Tickets $17–$50.

MAJOR VENUES

The **Colony Theater,** on Lincoln Road in South Beach ((℃ 305/674-1040), which has become an architectural showpiece of the Art Deco District, is presently closed for a $4.3 million renovation that will add wing and fly space, improve access for those with disabilities, and restore the lobby to its original Art Deco look.

At the **Miami–Dade County Auditorium,** West Flagler Street at 29th Avenue, Southwest Miami ((℃ 305/547-5414), performers gripe about the lack of space, but for patrons, this 2,430-seat auditorium is the only Miami space in which you can hear the opera—for now. A multimillion-dollar performing arts center downtown has been in the works for years (see below). For now, though, the Miami–Dade County Auditorium is home to the city's Florida Grand Opera, and it also stages productions by the Concert Association of Florida, many programs in Spanish, and a variety of other shows.

At the 1,700-seat **Gusman Center for the Performing Arts,** 174 E. Flagler St., downtown Miami ((℃ 305/372-0925), seating is tight, and so is funding, but the sound is superb. In addition to hosting the Florida Philharmonic

Orchestra and the Miami Film Festival, the elegant Gusman Center features pop concerts, plays, film screenings, and special events. The auditorium was built as the Olympia Theater in 1926, and its ornate palace interior is typical of that era, complete with fancy columns, a huge pipe organ, and twinkling "stars" on the ceiling.

Not to be confused with the Gusman Center (above), the **Gusman Concert Hall,** 1314 Miller Dr. at 14th Street, Coral Gables (© 305/284-6477), is a roomy 600-seat hall that gives a stage to the Miami Chamber Symphony and a varied program of university recitals.

The elegant **Jackie Gleason Theater of the Performing Arts,** located in South Beach at Washington Avenue and 17th Street (© 305/673-7300; www. gleasontheater.com), is the home of the Miami Beach Broadway Series, which has recently presented *Rent, Phantom of the Opera,* and *Les Misérables.* This 2,705-seat hall also hosts other big-budget Broadway shows, classical music concerts, and dance performances.

At press time, the city granted a budget in excess of $200 million for its official Performing Arts Center. Planned are a 2,400-seat ballet/opera house and a 2,000-seat concert hall for the Florida Philharmonic Orchestra, Florida Grand Opera, New World Symphony, Miami City Ballet, and a major concert series. Designed by world-renowned architect Cesar Pelli, it will be the focal point of a planned Arts, Media, and Entertainment District in mid-Miami. The complex will be wrapped in limestone, slate, decorative stone, stainless steel, glass curtain walls, and tropical landscaping, and is slated to be complete in mid-2006. For more information, check out their website at www.pacfmiami.org.

CINEMAS

In addition to the annual Miami Film Festival in February and other, smaller film events, Miami has nearly as many multiplex cinemas as it does palm trees. And for good reason. When it rains in Miami, what else is there to do besides go to the movies, a museum, or the mall? But if 40 screens of *Jurassic Park III* isn't your idea of a day at the movies, consider the following artsy theater, known for playing lots of subtitled, foreign films as well as those that get bumped off the big screen by the *Jurassic Parks* of the celluloid world.

The **Bill Cosford Cinema,** at the University of Miami, is located on the second floor of the memorial building off Campo Sano Avenue (© 305/284-4861). This well-endowed little theater was recently revamped and boasts high-tech projectors, new air-conditioning, and a new decor. It sponsors independent films as well as lectures by visiting filmmakers and movie stars. Andy Garcia and Antonio Banderas are a few of the big names this theater has attracted. It also hosts the African American Film Festival, a Student Film Festival, and collaborations with the Fort Lauderdale Festival (a very small film festival). Admission is $6, seniors $3.

5

The Keys

The drive from Miami to the Keys is a slow descent into an unusual but breathtaking American ecosystem: On either side of you, for miles ahead, lies nothing but emerald waters. (On weekends, however, you will also see plenty of traffic.) Strung out across the Atlantic Ocean like loose strands of cultured pearls, more than 400 islands make up this 150-mile-long chain of the Keys.

Despite the usually calm landscape, these rocky islands can be treacherous, as a series of tropical storms, hurricanes, and tornadoes reminded residents in the summer and fall of 1998, when millions of dollars of damage was inflicted. The exposed coast has always posed dangers to those on land as well as at sea.

When Spanish explorers Juan Ponce de León and Antonio de Herrera sailed amid these craggy, dangerous rocks in 1513, they and their men dubbed the string of islands "Los Martires" (The Martyrs), because they thought the rocks looked like men suffering in the surf. It wasn't until the early 1800s that rugged and ambitious pioneers, who amassed great wealth by salvaging cargo from ships sunk nearby, settled the larger islands (legend has it that these shipwrecks were sometimes caused by the "wreckers," who occasionally removed navigational markers from the shallows to lure unwitting captains aground). At the height of the salvaging mania (in the 1830s), Key West boasted the highest per capita income in the country.

However, wars, fires, hurricanes, mosquitoes, and the Depression took their toll on these resilient islands in the early part of the 20th century, causing wild swings between fortune and poverty. In 1938, the spectacular Overseas Highway (U.S. 1) was finally completed atop the ruins of Henry Flagler's railroad (which was destroyed by a hurricane in 1935, leaving only bits and pieces still found today), opening the region to tourists, who had never before been able to drive to this sea-bound destination.

These days, the highway connects more than 30 of the populated islands in the Keys. The hundreds of small, undeveloped islands that surround these "mainline" keys are known locally as the "backcountry" and are home to dozens of exotic animals and plants. Therein lie some of the most renowned outdoor sporting opportunities, from bonefishing to spear fishing and—at appropriate times of the year—diving for lobsters. To get to the backcountry, you must take to the water—a vital part of any trip to the Keys. Whether you fish, snorkel, dive, or just cruise, include some time on a boat in your itinerary; otherwise, you haven't truly seen the Keys.

Of course, people go to the Keys for the peaceful waters and the year-round warmth, but the sea and the teeming life beneath it are the main attractions here: Countless species of brilliantly colored fish can be found swimming above the ocean's floor, and you'll discover a stunning abundance of tropical and exotic plants, birds, and reptiles.

The warm, shallow waters (waters are deeper and rougher on the eastern/Atlantic side of the Keys) nurture living coral that supports a complex, delicate ecosystem of plants and animals—sponges, anemones, jellyfish, crabs, rays, sharks, turtles, snails, lobsters, and thousands of types of fish. This vibrant underwater habitat thrives on one of the only living tropical reefs in the entire North American continent. As a result, anglers, divers, snorkelers, and watersports enthusiasts of all kinds come to explore.

Heavy traffic has taken its toll on this fragile ecoscape, but conservation efforts are underway (traffic laws are strictly enforced on Deer Key, for example, due to deer crossings that have been contained thanks to newly installed fences). In fact, environmental efforts in the Keys exceed those in many other high-traffic visitor destinations.

Although the atmosphere throughout the Keys is that of a laid-back beach town, don't expect to find many impressive beaches here, especially after the damaging effects of the tropical storms and hurricanes in 1998. Beaches are mostly found in a few private resorts, though there are some small, sandy beaches in John Pennekamp Coral Reef State Park, Bahia Honda State Park, and in Key West. One great exception is Sombrero Beach in Marathon (p. 170), which is well maintained by Monroe County and is larger and considerably nicer than other beaches in the Keys. Sombrero Beach features a beachfront park, picnic facilities, a playground, and a protected cove for children at the west end of the beach.

The Keys are divided into three sections, both geographically and in this chapter. The Upper and Middle Keys are closest to the Florida mainland, so they are popular with weekend warriors who come by boat or car to fish or relax in towns like Key Largo, Islamorada, and Marathon. Further on, just beyond the impressive Seven-Mile Bridge (which actually measures only 6½ miles), are the Lower Keys, a small, unspoiled swath of islands teeming with wildlife. Here, in the protected regions of the Lower Keys, is where you're most likely to catch sight of the area's many endangered animals—with patience, you may spot the rare eagle, egret, or Key deer. You should also keep an eye out for alligators, turtles, rabbits, and a huge variety of birds.

Key West, the most renowned—and last—island in the Lower Keys, is literally at the end of the road. The southernmost point in the continental United States (made famous by the Nobel Prize–winning Ernest Hemingway), this tiny island is the most popular destination in the Florida Keys, overrun with cruise-ship passengers and day-trippers, as well as franchises and T-shirt shops. More than 1.6 million visitors pass through each year. Still, this "Conch Republic" has a tightly knit community of permanent residents who cling fiercely to their live-and-let-live attitude—an atmosphere that has made Key West famously popular with painters, writers, and free spirits.

EXPLORING THE KEYS BY CAR

After you have gotten off the Florida Turnpike and landed on U.S. 1, which is also known as the Overseas Highway (see "Getting There," under "Essentials," below), you'll have no trouble negotiating these narrow islands, since it is the only main road connecting the Keys. The scenic, lazy drive from Miami can be very enjoyable if you have the patience to linger and explore the diverse towns and islands along the way. If you have the time, I recommend allowing at least 2 days to work your way down to Key West and 3 or more days once there.

Most of U.S. 1 is a narrow, two-lane highway, with some wider passing zones along the way. The speed limit is usually 55 mph (35–45 mph on Big Pine Key and in some commercial areas). Despite the protestations of island residents,

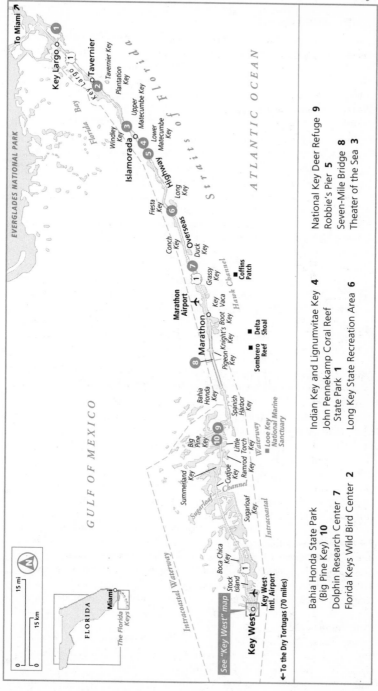

Bahia Honda State Park
(Big Pine Key) **10**

Dolphin Research Center **7**

Florida Keys Wild Bird Center **2**

Indian Key and Lignumvitae Key **4**

John Pennekamp Coral Reef
State Park **1**

Long Key State Recreation Area **6**

National Key Deer Refuge **9**

Robbie's Pier **5**

Seven-Mile Bridge **8**

Theater of the Sea **3**

Tips Don't Be Fooled

Avoid the many "Tourist Information Centers" that dot the main high-way. Most are private companies hired to lure visitors to specific lodgings or outfitters (anything that says FREE DISNEY TICKETS or something like that is probably a scam or timeshare racket). You're better off sticking with the official, not-for-profit centers (the legit ones usually don't advertise on the turnpike) that are extremely well located and staffed.

---

there has been talk of expanding the highway, but plans have not been finalized. Even on the narrow road, you can usually get from downtown Miami to Key Largo in just over an hour. If you're determined to drive straight through to Key West, allow at least 3½ hours. Weekend travel is another matter entirely: When the roads are jammed with travelers from the mainland, the trip could take upward of 5 to 6 hours (when there's an accident, traffic is at an absolute stand-still). If at all possible, I strongly urge you to avoid driving anywhere in the Keys on Friday afternoons or Sunday evenings.

To find an address in the Keys, don't bother looking for building numbers; most addresses (except in Key West and parts of Marathon) are delineated by mile markers (MM), small green signs on the roadside that announce the distance from Key West. The markers start at number 127, just south of the Florida mainland. The zero marker is in Key West, at the corner of Whitehead and Fleming Streets. Addresses in this chapter are accompanied by a mile marker (MM) designation when appropriate.

1 The Upper & Middle Keys: Key Largo ★★ to Marathon ★

58 miles SW of Miami

The Upper Keys are a popular, year-round refuge for South Floridians, who take advantage of the islands' proximity to the mainland. This is the fishing and diving capital of America, and the swarms of outfitters and billboards never let you forget it.

Key Largo, once called Rock Harbor but renamed to capitalize on the success of the 1948 Humphrey Bogart film (which wasn't actually filmed there), is the largest key and is more developed than its neighbors to the south. Dozens of chain hotels, restaurants, and tourist-information centers service the many water enthusiasts who come to explore the nation's first underwater state park, **John Pennekamp Coral Reef State Park,** and its adjacent marine sanctuary. **Isla-morada,** the unofficial capital of the Upper Keys, offers the area's best atmosphere, food, fishing, entertainment, and lodging. It's an unofficial "party capital" for mainlanders seeking a quick tropical excursion. Here (Islamorada is actually composed of four islands), nature lovers can enjoy walking trails, historic explorations, and big-purse fishing tournaments. For a more tranquil, quieter, less party-hearty Keys experience, all other Keys besides Key West and Islamorada are better choices. **Marathon,** smack in the middle of the Florida Keys, is one of the most populated keys and is known as the heart of the Keys. It is part fishing village, part tourist center, and part nature preserve. This area's highly developed infrastructure includes resort hotels, a commercial airport, and a highway that expands to four lanes.

Moments **No Place Like Homestead**

On its own, there's not much to the waterfront shack that is **Alabama Jack's.** The bar serves beer and wine only, and the restaurant specializes in delicious, albeit, greasy bar fare. But this quintessential Old Floridian dive, located between Homestead and Key Largo, is a colorful must on the drive south, especially on Sundays, when bikers mix with line dancers and Southern belles who look as if they just got off the *Hee Haw* set in all their fabulous frill. Hordes of Harley-Davidson bikers, local Miamians, barflies, and anglers flock here with much devotion, and the views of the mangroves are spectacular. Live country music resurrects the legendary sounds of Johnny Cash and Co. Pull up a bar stool, order a cold one, and take in the sights—in the bay and at the bar. To get there, pick up Card Sound Road (the old Rte. 1) a few miles after you pass Homestead, heading toward Key Largo. Alabama Jack's is on the right side and can't be missed (5800 Card Sound Rd., Homestead; © **305/248-8741**).

ESSENTIALS

GETTING THERE   From Miami International Airport (there is also an airport in Marathon), take Le Jeune Road (Northwest 42nd Ave.) to Route 836 west. Follow signs to the Florida Turnpike south (about 7 miles). The turnpike extension connects with U.S. 1 in Florida City. Continue south on U.S. 1. For a scenic option, weather permitting, take Card Sound Road south of Florida City, a backcountry drive that reconnects with U.S. 1 in upper Key Largo. The view from the Card Sound Bridge is spectacular and well worth the $1 toll.

If you're coming from Florida's west coast, take Alligator Alley to the Miami exit and then turn south onto the turnpike extension. The turnpike ends in Florida City, at which time you will be dumped directly onto the one-lane road, U.S. 1, that leads to the Keys. Have plenty of quarters (at least $10 worth, round-trip) for the tolls.

Greyhound (© **800/231-2222;** www.greyhound.com) has three buses leaving Miami for Key West every day, which also stop in Key Largo, Tavenier, Islamorada, Marathon, Big Pine Key, Cudjoe Key, Sugarloaf, and Big Coppit on their way south. Prices range up from about $13 to $32 one-way and take between an hour and 40 minutes to 4 hours and 40 minutes, depending on how far south you're going. Seats fill quickly in season, so come early. It's first-come, first-served.

VISITOR INFORMATION   Make sure you get your information from official, not-for-profit centers. The **Key Largo Chamber of Commerce,** U.S. 1 at MM 106, Key Largo, FL 33037 (© **800/822-1088** or 305/451-1414; fax 305/451-4726; www.keylargo.org), runs an excellent facility, with free direct-dial phones and plenty of brochures. Headquartered in a handsome clapboard house, the chamber operates as an information clearinghouse for all of the Keys and is open daily from 9am to 6pm.

The **Islamorada Chamber of Commerce,** housed in an actual little red caboose, U.S. 1 at MM 82.5, P.O. Box 915, Islamorada, FL 33036 (© **800/322-5397** or 305/664-4503; fax 305/664-4289; www.islamoradachamber.com), also offers maps and literature on the Upper Keys.

You can't miss the big blue visitor center at MM 53.5, the **Greater Marathon Chamber of Commerce,** 12222 Overseas Hwy., Marathon, FL 33050(© **800/262-7284** or 305/743-5417; fax 305/289-0183; www.floridakeysmarathon.com).

Cheap Thrills: What to See & Do for Free (or Almost) in the Keys

- **Take in the view from Seven-Mile Bridge.** Getting weary on that road trip south? Get out and stretch your legs at Seven-Mile Bridge, between MM 40 and 47 on U.S. 1. Its apex is the highest point in the pancake-flat Keys, which makes it an excellent place to admire the watery panorama.
- **Feed some giant fish at Robbie's Pier.** In the shallow waters off this Islamorada pier (at MM 77.5), scores of jumbo, valiant tarpon loiter, waiting for a snack or two from benevolent passersby. For $1 admission and a $2 bucket of fish, you can feed these oversize, prehistoric-looking fish, some of which can grow to up to 200 pounds. Also included in the $1 entry fee is an hour-long guided tour by park rangers, whose expertise can help make sense of your beautiful surroundings.
- **Soak up the sunset and the scene at Mallory Square.** In what has become an evening ritual, artists, acrobats, food hawkers, and animal acts gather for some end-of-the-day revelry at Mallory Square, ground zero for Key West's eccentric set. Nab a spot on the docks (at the westernmost end of Duval St.) to take it all in.
- **Explore one man's inventive whimsy: the Sugarloaf Bat Tower.** Developer Clyde Perkey hated mosquitoes—so much so that in 1929 he built a 45-foot-high, wooden, flat-topped pyramid to lure bug-eating bats to the region. Alas, despite a pervasive bat aphrodisiac, the critters never materialized. Now empty and deserted (and devoid of any explanatory signage), the Sugarloaf Bat Tower (at MM 17) is the only human-made attraction in the Lower Keys. Admission is free.
- **Go wild—with the birds, that is.** The **Florida Keys Wild Bird Rehabilitation Center** (at MM 94, in Tavernier) serves as a hospital for the

Here, you can receive free information on local events, festivals, shows, attractions, dining, and lodging.

OUTDOOR SIGHTS & ACTIVITIES

Anne's Beach (at MM 73.5, on Lower Matecumbe Key, at the southwest end of Islamorada) is really more of a picnic spot than a full-fledged beach, but die-hard suntanners still congregate on this lovely but tiny strip of coarse sand that was damaged beyond recognition during the series of storms in 1998. Plans are in place to reconstruct the boardwalk and huts, but at press time, work had not yet started.

A better choice for real beaching is **Sombrero Beach** ✦✦ in Marathon at the end of Sombrero Beach Road (near MM 50). This wide swath of uncluttered beachfront actually benefited from Hurricane George in September 1998, with generous deposits of extra sand and a face-lift courtesy of the Monroe County Tourist Development Council. More than 90 feet of sand is dotted with palms, Australian Pines, and Royal Poincianas as well as with barbecue grills, clean bathrooms, and some brand-new Tiki huts for relaxing in the shade.

If you are interested in seeing the Keys in their natural state, before modern development, you must venture off the highway and take to the water. Two backcountry islands that offer a glimpse of the "real" Keys are **Indian Key** and many native species of birds found here. Narrow wooden walkways, overhung by dense mangrove canopies, will take you past broad-winged hawks, great blue and white herons, roseate spoonbills, white ibises, cattle egrets, and a variety of pelicans. Come at feeding time (usually about 3:30pm) and see the dedicated staff feed the hundreds of those hungry beaks. This not-for-profit center doesn't charge admission but does request donations.

- **Reef madness—snorkel in an underwater state park. John Pennekamp Coral Reef State Park** contains part of the nation's first undersea preserve, and the only living coral reef in the continental United States. To experience this park, get in the water, which is shallow enough to make the 40 species of corals and more than 650 species of fish more than accessible to divers, snorkelers, and glass-bottom-boat passengers. Mention this guide at **Hall's Dive Center & Career Institute,** U.S. 1 at MM 48.5, Marathon (© **305/743-5929**), and you'll get special discounted rates for snorkeling and diving. Park admission is $2.50 per vehicle for one occupant; for two or more, it is $5 per vehicle, plus 50¢ per passenger; $1.50 per pedestrian or bicyclist.

- **Take the Key lime challenge.** The Key lime is to Key West what chocolate is to Belgium. Wherever you go, you are bound to be tempted by the most famous Key lime concoction of all—the Key lime pie. For free samples of pies, cookies, candies, and ice creams, the **Key Lime Pie Co.** (© **305/294-6567**) has two locations for taste testing, one at 701 Caroline St., and the other at 424 Greene St.

Lignumvitae Key ★★★. Visitors come to these to relax and enjoy the islands' colorful birds and lush hammocks (elevated pieces of land above a marsh).

Named for the lignum vitae ("wood of life") trees found there, **Lignumvitae Key** supports a virgin tropical forest, the kind that once thrived on most of the Upper Keys. Over the years, human settlers imported "exotic" plants and animals to the Keys, irrevocably changing the botanical makeup of many back-country islands and threatening much of the indigenous wildlife. Over the past 25 years, however, the Florida Department of Natural Resources has successfully removed most of the exotic vegetation from this key, leaving this 280-acre site much as it existed in the 18th century. The island also holds the Matheson House, a historic house built in 1919 that has survived numerous hurricanes. You can go inside the house, but this is interesting only if you have a hankering for coral rock, which the house is made out of. It's now a museum dedicated to the history, nature, and topography of the area. More interesting is actually seeing the area via the Botanical Gardens, which surround the house and are a state preserve. Lignumvitae Key has a visitor center at MM 88.5 (© **305/664-2540**).

Indian Key, a much smaller island on the Atlantic side of Islamorada, was occupied by Native Americans for thousands of years before European settlers arrived. The 10-acre historic site was also the original seat of Dade County before the Civil War. Interestingly, from an archaeological standpoint, you can see the ruins of the previous settlement and tour the lush grounds on well-marked trails (off Indian Key Fill, Overseas Highway, MM 79). To get information about Indian Key, call the Florida Park Service at © **305/664-4815** or check out www.abfla.com/parks/IndianKey/indiankey.html.

If you want to see both islands, plan to spend at least half a day. To get there, you can rent your own powerboat at **Robbie's Rent-A-Boat,** U.S. 1 at MM 77.5 on the bay side (p. 176), on Islamorada. It's then a $1 admission fee to each island, which includes an informative hour-long guided tour by park rangers. This is a good option if you are a confident boater.

However, I also recommend taking Robbie's **ferry service.** A visit to one island costs $15, $10 for kids 12 and under, which includes the $1 park admission; trips to both islands cost $25 per person. (If you have time for only one island, make it Lignumvitae.) Not only is the ferry more economical, but it's easier to enjoy the natural beauty of the islands when you aren't negotiating the shallow reefs along the way. The runabouts, which carry up to six people, depart from Robbie's Pier Thursday through Monday at 9am and 1pm for Indian Key, and at 10am and 2pm for Lignumvitae Key. In the busy season, you may need to book as early as 2 days before departure. Call © **305/664-4815** for information from the park service, or © **305/664-9814** for Robbie's.

Pigeon Key ★★   At the curve of the old bridge on Pigeon Key is an intriguing historical site that has been under renovation since late 1993. This 5-mile-long island was once the camp for the crew that built the old railway in the early part of the 20th century, and later served as housing for the bridge builders. From here, your vista includes both the vestiges of Henry Flagler's old Seven-Mile Bridge as well as the one on which traffic presently soars, many old wooden cottages, and a truly tranquil stretch of lush foliage and sea. If you miss the shuttle tour from the Pigeon Key Visitor Center or would rather walk or bike to the site, it's about 2½ miles. Either way, you may want to bring a picnic to enjoy after a brief self-guided walking tour of the Key and museum visit to what has become an homage to Flagler's railroad, featuring artifacts and photographs of the old bridge. There is also an informative 28-minute video of the island's history offered every hour starting at 10am. Parking is available at the Knight's Key end of the bridge, at MM 48, or at the visitor center at MM 47, on the ocean side.

East end of the Seven-Mile Bridge near MM 47, Marathon. © **305/743-5999**. www.pigeonkey.org. Admission $8.50 adults, $5 for children under 13. Price includes shuttle transportation from the visitor center. Daily 10am–3pm; shuttle tours run every hr. 10am–4pm.

Seven-Mile Bridge ★★★   A stop at the Seven-Mile Bridge is a rewarding and relaxing break from the drive south. Built alongside the ruins of oil magnate Henry Flagler's incredible Overseas Railroad, the "new" bridge (between MMs 40 and 47) is considered an architectural feat. The wide-arched span, completed in 1985 at a cost of more than $45 million, is impressive, and its apex is the highest point in the Keys. The new bridge and its now-defunct neighbor provide an excellent vantage point from which to view the stunning waters of the Keys. In the daytime, you may want to walk, jog, or bike along the scenic 4-mile stretch of old bridge, or join local anglers, who catch barracuda, yellowtail, and dolphin (the fish, not the mammal) on what is known as "the longest fishing pier in the world." Parking is available on both sides of the bridge.

Between MMs 40 and 47 on U.S. 1. © **305/289-0025**.

VISITING WITH THE ANIMALS

Dolphin Research Center ★★★ *Kids*   If you've always wanted to touch, swim, or play with dolphins, this is the place to do it. Of the three such centers in the continental United States (all located in the Keys), the Dolphin Research Center is the most organized and informative. Although some people argue that training dolphins is cruel and selfish, this is one of the most respected of the institutions that study and protect the mammals. Knowledgeable trainers at the Dolphin Research Center will also tell you that the dolphins need stimulation and enjoy human contact. They certainly seem to. They nuzzle and seem to smile and kiss the lucky few who get to swim with them in the daily program. The "family" of 15 dolphins swims in a 90,000-square-foot natural saltwater pool carved out of the shoreline.

If you can't get into the swim program, you can still watch the frequent shows, sign up for a class in hand signals, or feed the dolphins from docks. Because the Dolphin Encounter swimming program is the most popular, reservations must be made in advance (call more than a month in advance to make sure you get in). The cost is $155 per person. If you're not brave enough to swim with the dolphins or you have a child under 12 (not permitted to swim with dolphins), try the Dolphin Splash program, in which participants stand on an elevated platform from which they can "meet and greet" the dolphins. A height requirement of 44 inches is enforced, and an adult must hold up children under the required height. Cost for this program is $80 per person; free for children under 3.

U.S. 1 at MM 59 (on the bay side), Marathon. (© 305/289-1121. www.dolphins.org. Educational walking tours 5 times daily: 10 and 11am, and 12:30, 2, and 3:30pm. Admission $18 adults, $15 seniors, $12 children 4–12, free for children 3 and under. Daily 9am–4pm.

Florida Keys Wild Bird Center ★   Wander through lush canopies of mangroves on narrow wooden walkways to see some of the Keys' most famous residents—the large variety of native birds, including broad-wing hawks, great blue and white herons, roseate spoonbills, white ibis, cattle egrets, and a number of pelicans. This not-for-profit center operates as a hospital for the many birds that have been injured by accident or disease. In 2002, the World Parrot Mission was established here, focusing on caring for parrots and educating the public about the birds. Visit at feeding time, usually about 3:30pm, when you can watch the dedicated staff feed the hundreds of hungry birds.

U.S. 1 at MM 93.6, Bayside, Tavernier. (© 305/852-4486. www.fkwbc.org. Donations suggested. Daily 8:30am–6pm.

Robbie's Pier ★★★ *Value*   One of the best and definitely one of the cheapest attractions in the Upper Keys is the famed Robbie's Pier. Here, the fierce steely tarpons, a prized catch for backcountry anglers, have been gathering for the past 20 years. You may recognize these prehistoric-looking giants that grow to up to 200 pounds; many are displayed as trophies and mounted on local restaurant walls. To see them live, head to Robbie's Pier, where tens and sometimes hundreds of these behemoths circle the shallow waters waiting for you to feed them. Robbie's Pier also offers ranger-led boat tours and guided kayak tours to Indian Key, where you can go snorkeling or just bask in the glory of your surroundings.

U.S. 1 at MM 77.5, Islamorada. (© 305/664-9814. Admission $1. Bucket of fish $2. Daily 8am–5pm. Look for the Hungry Tarpon restaurant sign on the right after the Indian Key channel.

Theater of the Sea ★ *Kids*   Established in 1946, the Theater of the Sea is one of the world's oldest marine zoos. Recently refurbished, the park's dolphin and sea lion shows are entertaining and informative, especially for children, who can also see sharks, sea turtles, and tropical fish. If you want to swim with dolphins and you haven't booked well in advance, this is the place you may be able to get into with just a few hours', or days', notice as opposed to the more rigid Dolphin Research Center (see above) in Marathon. (While the Dolphin Research Center is a legitimate, scientific establishment, this is more of a theme-parky attraction. That's not to say the dolphins are mistreated, but it's just not as, say, educational and professional as it is at the Dolphin Research Center.) Theater of the Sea also permits you to swim with the sea lions and stingrays. Children under 5 are not permitted to participate. There are also twice daily 4-hour adventure and snorkel cruises, $65 for adults and $40 for children 3–12, in which you can learn about the history and ecology of the marine environment. The facility also serves as a haven for dozens of stray cats that have free run of the grounds and gift shop.

U.S. 1 at MM 84.5, Islamorada. ⓒ 305/664-2431. www.theaterofthesea.com. Admission $20 adults, $12 children 3–12. Dolphin swim $140; sea lion swim $95; stingray swim $45 per person. Reservations a must. Daily 10am–5pm (ticket office closes at 4pm).

TWO EXCEPTIONAL STATE PARKS

One of the best places to discover the diverse ecosystem of the Upper Keys is in its most famous park, **John Pennekamp Coral Reef State Park** ✸✸✸, located on U.S. 1 at MM 102.5, in Key Largo (ⓒ **305/451-1202;** www.pennekamp park.com). Named for a former *Miami Herald* editor and conservationist, the 188-square-mile park is the nation's first undersea preserve: It's a sanctuary for part of the only living coral reef in the continental United States. The original plans for Everglades National Park included this part of the reef within its boundaries, but opposition from local homeowners made its inclusion politically impossible.

Because the water is extremely shallow, the 40 species of coral and more than 650 species of fish here are particularly accessible to divers, snorkelers, and glass-bottom-boat passengers. To experience this park, visitors must get in the water—you can't see the reef from the shore. Your first stop should be the visitor center, which is full of educational fish tanks and a mammoth 30,000-gallon saltwater aquarium that re-creates a reef ecosystem. At the adjacent dive shop, you can rent snorkeling and diving equipment and join one of the boat trips that depart for the reef throughout the day. Visitors can also rent motorboats, sailboats, windsurfers, and canoes. The 2-hour glass-bottom-boat tour is the best way to see the coral reefs if you don't want to get wet. Watch for the lobsters and other sea life residing in the fairly shallow ridge walls beneath the coastal waters. *But remember:* These are protected waters, so you can't remove anything from the water.

Canoeing around the park's narrow mangrove channels and tidal creeks is also popular. You can go on your own in a rented canoe or, in winter, sign up for a tour led by a local naturalist. Hikers have two short trails from which to choose: a boardwalk through the mangroves and a dirt trail through a tropical hardwood hammock. Ranger-led walks are usually scheduled daily from the end of November to April. Phone ⓒ **305/451-1202** for schedule information and reservations.

Park admission is $2.50 per vehicle for one occupant; for two or more, it is $5 per vehicle, plus 50¢ per passenger; $1.50 per pedestrian or bicyclist. On busy weekend days, there's often a line of cars to get into the park. On your way into the park, ask the ranger for a map. Glass-bottom-boat tours cost $20 for adults and $12 for children 11 and under. Snorkeling tours are $27 for adults and $22 for children 17 and under, including equipment. Sailing and snorkeling tours are

$32 for adults, $27 for children 17 and under, including equipment. Canoes rent for $10 per hour. For experienced boaters only, four different-size reef boats (powerboats) rent for $38 to $50 per hour, with cheaper half-day and full-day rates available; call © **305/451-6325** for more information. A $400 deposit (and up depending on boat size, starting at a 22-ft. boat) is required. The park's boat rental is open daily from 8am to 5pm—the last boat rented is at 3pm; phone for tour and dive times. Reservations are recommended for all of the above. Also, see below for more options on diving, fishing, and snorkeling these reefs.

Long Key State Recreation Area ★★★, U.S. 1 at MM 68, Long Key (© **305/664-4815;** www.abfla.com/parks/LongKey/longkey.html), is one of the best places in the Middle Keys for hiking, camping, snorkeling, and canoeing. This 965-acre site is situated atop the remains of an ancient coral reef. At the entrance gate, ask for a free flyer describing the local trails and wildlife.

There are three nature trails that can be explored via foot or canoe: The Golden Orb Trail is a 40-minute walk through mostly just plants; the Layton Trail is a 15-minute walk along the bay; and the Long Key Canoe Trail glides along a shallow-water lagoon. Campsites are located along the Atlantic Ocean and the swimming, snorkeling, and saltwater fishing (license required) are top-notch here. Educational programs on the aforementioned are available, too, for novices. Snorkeling is shallow and on the shoreline of the Atlantic Ocean. The nearest place to rent snorkeling equipment is Holiday Isle, 84001 U.S. 1, Islam-orada (© **800/327-7070**).

The park's excellent 1½-mile canoe trail is also short and sweet, allowing visitors to loop around the mangroves in about an hour. You can rent canoes at the trail head for about $4 per hour. Long Key is also a great spot to stop for a picnic if you get hungry on your way to Key West.

Railroad builder Henry Flagler created the Long Key Fishing Club here in 1906, and the waters surrounding the park are still popular with game fishers. In summer, sea turtles lumber onto the protected coast to lay their eggs, all lined up on the coast. It's a big event, and educational programs are available to view this phenomenon.

Admission is $3.25 per car plus 50¢ per person (except for the Layton Trail, which is free). Open daily from 8am to sunset.

AFFORDABLE WATERSPORTS

There are literally hundreds of outfitters in the Keys who will arrange all kinds of water activities, from cave dives to parasailing. If those recommended below are booked up or unreachable, ask the local chamber of commerce for a list of qualified members.

BOATING   In addition to the rental shops in the state parks, you will find dozens of outfitters along U.S. 1 offering a range of runabouts and skiffs for boaters of any experience level. **Captain Pip's,** U.S. 1 at MM 47.5, Marathon (© **800/707-1692** or 305/743-4403), rents 18- to 24-foot motorboats with 90- to 225-horsepower engines for $130 to $250 per day. Overnight accommodations are available and include a free boat rental; 2-night minimum $220 to $255; weekly $1,190 to $1,890. Rooms are Key West comfortable and charming, with ceiling fans, tile floors, and pine paneling. But the best part about it is that every room comes with an 18- to 21-foot boat for your use during your stay.

CANOEING & KAYAKING   I can think of no better way to explore the uninhabited, shallow backcountry on the Gulf side of the Keys than by kayak or canoe, since you can reach places big boats just can't get to because of their large draft. Sometimes manatees will even cuddle up to the boats, thinking them another friendly species.

Many area hotels rent kayaks and canoes to guests, as do the outfitters listed here. **Florida Bay Outfitters,** U.S. 1 at MM 104, Key Largo (© **305/451-3018**), rents canoes and sea kayaks for use in and around John Pennekamp Coral Reef State Park for $25 to $45 for a half day and $40 to $60 for a whole day. At **Coral Reef Park Co.,** on U.S. 1 at MM 102.5, Key Largo (© **305/451-1621**), you can rent canoes and kayaks for $8 per hour, $28 for a half day; most canoes are sit-on-tops. **Florida Keys Kayak and Sail,** U.S. 1 at MM 75.5, Islamorada (© **305/664-4878**), at Robbie's Pier, offers backcountry tours, botanical preserve tours of Lignumvitae Key, historical site tours of Indian Key, and sunset tours through the mangrove tunnels and saltwater flats. Tour rates are from $39 to $49; rental rates range from $15 per hour to $45 per day for single kayak and $20 per hour to $60 per day for double kayak. **Reflections Nature Tours** (© **305/872-4668**) is a small mobile company that specializes in kayak, hiking, and bike tours through the lower Keys. Guided kayak tours cost $50 per person for a 3-hour tour; guided bike tours cost $35 per person for a 2-hour tour; and guided walking tours cost $13 per person for an hour tour. All tours are by appointment only.

DIVING & SNORKELING Located just 6 miles off Key Largo is a U.S. Navy Landing Ship Dock, the latest artificial wreck site to hit the Keys—or, rather, to be submerged 130 feet *below* the Keys.

The **Florida Keys Dive Center,** on U.S. 1 at MM 90.5, Tavernier (© **305/852-4599**), takes snorkelers and divers to the reefs of John Pennekamp Coral Reef State Park and environs every day. PADI (Professional Association of Diving Instructors) training courses are also available for the uninitiated. While some people have complained that employees are rude here, others disagree. We suggest you decide for yourselves. Tours leave at 8am and 12:30pm and cost $30 per person to snorkel (plus $9 rental fee for mask, snorkel, and fins) and $60 per person to dive (plus an extra $20 if you need to rent all the gear).

At **Hall's Dive Center & Career Institute,** U.S. 1 at MM 48.5, Marathon (© **305/743-5929**), snorkelers and divers can choose to dive at Looe Key, Sombrero Reef, Delta Shoal, Content Key, and Coffins Patch. Tours are scheduled daily at 9am and 1pm. You will spend 1 hour at each of two sites per tour. If you mention this book, you will get a special discounted rate ($5–$10 off) of $35 per person to snorkel (additional gear is $11) and $45 per person to dive (tanks are $8.50 each).

FISHING **Robbie's Partyboats & Charters,** on U.S. 1 at MM 84.5, Islamorada (© **305/664-8070** or 305/664-4196), located at the south end of the Holiday Isle Docks, offers day and night deep-sea and reef fishing trips aboard a 65-foot party boat. Big-game fishing charters are also available, and "splits" are arranged for solo fishers. Party-boat fishing costs $25 for a half-day morning tour (rod and reel rental is $3); it's $15 extra if you want to go back out on an afternoon tour. Charters run $400 for a half day, $600 for a full day; splits begin at $65 per person. Phone for information and reservations.

Bud n' Mary's Fishing Marina, on U.S. 1 at MM 79.8, Islamorada (© **800/742-7945** or 305/664-2461), one of the largest marinas between Miami and Key West, is packed with sailors offering guided backcountry fishing charters. This is the place to go if you want to stalk tarpon, bonefish, and snapper. If the seas are not too rough, deep-sea and coral fishing trips can also be arranged. Charters cost $500 to $550 for a half day, $750 to $800 for a full day, and splits begin at $125 per person.

Acquaint Yourself

Fans of stone crabs can get further acquainted with those seasonal crustaceans thanks to Keys Fisheries' 3-hour tours aboard 40- to 50-foot vessels, which leave from Marathon. The tour includes views of fishermen as they collect crabs from traps and process their claws. The $425 tour cost includes up to six passengers and up to 6 pounds of fresh claws iced for travel or prepared at a dockside restaurant. Stone crab season is from October 15 to May 15. Call © **305/743-4353** or check the Web at www. keysfisheries.com for more information.

SHOPPING

On your way to the Keys, you'll find an outlet center, the **Prime Outlets at Florida City** (© **305/248-4727**), at 250 E. Palm Dr. (where the Florida Turnpike meets U.S. Hwy. 1), in Florida City. The center holds more than 60 stores, including Nike Factory Store, Bass Co. Store, Levi's, OshKosh, and Izod. Travelers can pick up a free discount coupon booklet called the Come Back Pack from the Customer Service Center. The outlet is open Monday to Saturday from 10am to 9pm, Sunday from 11am to 6pm.

The Upper and Middle Keys have no shortage of tacky tourist shops selling shells and T-shirts (the ubiquitous "beads and trinkets") and other hokey souvenirs, but for real Keys-style shopping, check out the weekend flea markets. The best, **The Key Largo Storage/Flea Market,** is held every Saturday and Sunday bayside at MM 103.5 (© **305/451-0677**). Dozens of vendors open their stalls from 9am until 4 or 5pm, selling every imaginable sort of antiques, T-shirts, plants, shoes, books, toys, and games, as well as a hearty dose of good old-fashioned junk. Also decent is the **Grassy Key Flea Market,** at MM 60, on the ocean side. Other flea markets in the area are more unpredictable.

A mecca for fishing and sports enthusiasts, **The World Wide Sportsman** (© **305/664-4615**) at MM 81.5 is not only the largest fishing store in the Keys, but also a meeting place for anglers from all over the world. Every possible gizmo and gadget, plus hundreds of T-shirts, hats, books, and gift items are displayed in its more than 25,000 square feet. The salespeople are knowledgeable and eager to help. Travel specialists can even arrange for charter trips and backcountry tours. The store is open daily from 7am until 8:30pm.

ACCOMMODATIONS YOU CAN AFFORD

U.S. 1 is lined with chain hotels in all price ranges. In the Upper Keys, the best moderately priced option is the **Ramada Limited Resort & Casino** (© **800/ THE-KEYS** or 305/451-3939) at MM 100, off of U.S. 1 in Key Largo, which has three pools and a casino boat and is just 3 miles from John Pennekamp Coral Reef State Park. Another good option in the Upper Keys is **Islamorada Days Inn,** U.S. 1 at MM 82.5 (© **800/DAYS-INN** or 305/664-3681). In the Middle Keys, the **Wellesley Inn** at 13351 Overseas Hwy., MM 54 in Marathon (© **305/743-8550**), also offers reasonably priced ocean-side rooms.

For the best value in the Keys, plan your trip in the off season. That doesn't necessarily mean the scorching days of summer. Try September or May for great deals; midweek specials abound year-round as well. But be sure to check that your trip doesn't coincide with a major holiday, fishing tournament, or festival.

Since the real beauty of the Keys lies mostly beyond the highways, there is no better way to see this area than by boat. Why not stay in a floating hotel?

Especially if you're traveling with a group, houseboats can be economical. To rent a houseboat, call Ruth and Michael Sullivan at **Smilin' Island Houseboat Rentals** (MM 99.5), Key Largo (© **305/451-1930**). Rates are from $750 to $1,350 for 3 nights. Boats accommodate up to six people.

For land options, consider the recommendations below.

Banana Bay Resort & Marina 🐒🐒 *Finds* It doesn't look like much from the sign-cluttered Overseas Highway, but when you enter the lush grounds of Banana Bay, you will realize you're in one of the most bucolic and best-run properties in the Upper Keys. Built in the early 1950s as a place for fishermen to stay during extended fishing trips, the resort is a beachfront maze of two-story buildings hidden among banyans and palms. The rooms are moderately sized, and many have private balconies where you can enjoy your complimentary coffee and newspaper every morning. Recent additions to the hotel include a recreational activity area with horseshoe pits, a bocce court, picnic areas with barbecue grills, and a giant lawn chessboard.

U.S. 1 at MM 49.5, Marathon, FL 33050. © **800/BANANA-1** or 305/743-3500. Fax 305/743-2670. www. bananabay.com. 60 units. Winter $135–$225 double; off season $95–$175 double. Rates include continental breakfast. 3- and 7-night honeymoon and wedding packages available. AE, DC, DISC, MC, V. **Amenities:** Restaurant; 3 bars; pool; tennis courts; health club; Jacuzzi; watersports rental; self-service laundromat; small beach and snorkel area; charter fishing; sailing and diving. *In room:* A/C, TV, dataport, fridge, hair dryer, iron.

Conch Key Cottages 🐒 *Finds* Here's your chance to play castaway in the Keys. Occupying its own private microisland just off U.S. 1, Conch Key Cottages is a comfortable hideaway run by live-in owners Ron Wilson and Wayne Byrnes, who are constantly fixing and adding to their unique property. This is a place to get away from it all; the cottages aren't located close to much, except maybe one or two interesting eateries. The cabins, which were built at different times over the past 40 years, overlook their own stretch of natural, but very small, private beach and have a screened-in porch, cozy bedroom, bathroom, hammock, barbecue grill, and a two-person kayak. Request one of the two-bedroom cottages—especially if you are traveling with the family. They are the most spacious and are well designed, practically tailor-made for couples or families. On the other side of the pool are a handful of efficiency apartments (all with fully equipped kitchens) that are similarly outfitted but enjoy no beach frontage.

Near U.S. 1 at MM 62.3, Marathon, FL 33050. © **800/330-1577** or 305/289-1377. Fax 305/743-8207. www.conchkeycottages.com. 12 cottages. Dec 15–Sept 8 $110–$288; Sept 9–Dec 14 $74–$215. DISC, MC, V. **Amenities:** Pool; complimentary kayaks; laundry facilities. *In room:* A/C, TV, kitchen, coffeemaker, no phone.

Ragged Edge Resort 🐒🐒 This small oceanfront property's Tahitian-style 11 units are spread out along more than half a dozen gorgeous, grassy waterfront acres. All are immaculately clean and comfortable, and most are outfitted with full kitchens and tasteful furnishings. There's no bar, restaurant, or staff to speak of, but the retreat's affable owner, Jackie Barnes, is happy to lend you bicycles or offer good advice on the area's offerings. A large dock attracts boaters and a good variety of local and migratory birds. An outdoor, heated freshwater pool is a bonus for those months when the temperature gets a bit chilly—for Florida anyway.

243 Treasure Harbor Rd. (near MM 86.5), Islamorada, FL 33036. © **800/436-2023** or 305/852-5389. www. ragged-edge.com. 11 units. Winter $79–$199; off season $49–$142. AE, MC, V. **Amenities:** Outdoor pool; free use of bikes; laundromat. *In room:* A/C, kitchen (most units), fridge, coffeemaker.

SUPER-CHEAP SLEEPS

Bay Harbor Lodge 🐒 A small, simple retreat that's big on charm, the Bay Harbor Lodge is an extraordinarily welcoming place. The lodge is far from fancy, though it features new windows and paint, and the widely ranging accommodations are not created equal. The motel rooms are small and ordinary in decor, but even the least expensive is recommendable. The efficiencies are larger motel rooms with fully equipped kitchenettes. The oceanfront cottages are larger still, have full kitchens, and represent one of the best values in the Keys. The vinyl-covered furnishings and old-fashioned wallpapers won't win any design awards, but elegance isn't what the "real" Keys are about. The 1½ lush acres of grounds are planted with banana trees and have an outdoor heated pool and several small barbecue grills. A small beach is ideal for some quiet sunning and relaxation. Guests are free to use the rowboats, paddleboats, canoes, kayaks, and snorkeling equipment. Bring your own beach towels.

97702 Overseas Hwy., U.S. 1 at MM 97.7 (off the southbound lane of U.S. 1), Key Largo, FL 33037. ℭ **800/ 385-0986** or 305/852-5695. thefloridakeys.com/bayharborlodge. 16 units. Winter $55–$145 double, $85– $195 cottage; off season $75–$135 double, $105–$165 cottage. MC, V. **Amenities:** Freshwater pool. *In room:* A/C, TV, fridge, coffeemaker, hair dryer, microwave.

WORTH A SPLURGE

Kona Kai Resort & Gallery ★★   Unique to the Upper Keys, this little haven, with just 11 units, is both casual and elegant. Quaint rooms and complete suites dot the lushly landscaped 2-acre property, which boasts a large variety of native vegetation like palms, bougainvillea, and ferns, plus an impressive collection of fruit-bearing trees, such as carambola, passion fruit, banana, Key lime, guava, and coconut, which you can sample. An orchid house has over 250 beautiful flowers. Lounge chairs, hammocks, a Jacuzzi, and a compact beach are available for those who just want to relax (no phones in the rooms make relaxing imperative), while the owners will organize excursions to the Everglades, the backcountry, or wherever. All the rooms are very private and simply furnished; bathroom amenities are fabulous, with lotions, soaps, and shampoos made from tropical fruits. Smoking is not permitted in the rooms.

97802 Overseas Hwy. (U.S. 1 at MM 97.8), Key Largo, FL 33037. ℭ **800/365-7829** or 305/852-7200. Fax 305/852-4629. www.konakairesort.com. 11 units. Winter $149–$259 double, $177–$748 1- to 2-bedroom suite; off season $159–$192 double, $192–$561 1- to 2-bedroom suite. AE, DISC, MC, V. Closed Sept. Children under 16 not permitted. **Amenities:** Heated pool; tennis court; spa; Jacuzzi; watersports equipment rental; concierge; in-room massage and facials; boat ramp/dockage. *In room:* A/C, TV/VCR, kitchen, fridge, hair dryer, CD player (suites only).

CAMPING

John Pennekamp Coral Reef State Park ★★   One of Florida's best parks (p. 174), Pennekamp offers 47 well-separated campsites, half of which are available by advance reservation, the rest distributed on a first-come, first-served basis. The tent sites are small but well equipped with bathrooms, hot water, and showers. Note that the local environment provides fertile breeding grounds for insects, particularly in the late summer, so bring insect repellant or you will be sorry. Two man-made beaches and a small lagoon nearby attract many large wading birds. Reservations are held until 5pm, and the park must be notified of late arrival by phone on the check-in date. Pennekamp opens at 8am and closes around sundown.

U.S. 1 at MM 102.5 (P.O. Box 487), Key Largo, FL 33037. ℭ **305/451-1202.** www.pennekamppark.com. 47 campsites. Reservations can be made in advance by calling Reserve America (ℭ 800/326-3521). $24 (without electricity) to $26 (with electricity) per site. Park entry $4 per vehicle (50¢ for each additional person). Yearly permits and passes available. AE, DISC, MC, V. No pets.

Long Key State Park ★   The Upper Keys' other main state park is more secluded than its northern neighbor—and more popular. All sites are located ocean-side and are surrounded by narrow rows of trees and nearby toilet and bathroom facilities. Reserve well in advance, especially in winter.

U.S. 1 at MM 67.5 (P.O. Box 776), Long Key, FL 33001. ℂ **305/664-4815.** www.floridastateparks.org/longkey/default.asp. 60 oceanfront sites. $24–$26 per site for 1–4 people. $3.25 per vehicle. AE, DISC, MC, V. No pets.

GREAT DEALS ON DINING

Although not known as a culinary hot spot (though always improving), the Upper and Middle Keys do offer some excellent restaurants, most of which specialize in seafood. Often, visitors (especially those who fish) take advantage of accommodations that have kitchen facilities and cook their own meals. Some restaurants will even clean and cook your catch, for a fee.

Barracuda Grill ★★ SEAFOOD Owned by Lance Hill and his wife, Jan (a former sous chef at Little Palm Island, an exclusive island getaway on Little Torch Key), this small, casual spot serves excellent seafood, steaks, and chops, but unfortunately, it's open only for dinner. Some of the favorite dishes are the Caicos Gold Conch and Mangrove Snapper and Mango. Try the Tipsy Olives appetizer, marinated in gin or vodka, to kick-start your meal. For fans of spicy food, try the red-hot calamari. Decorated with barracuda-themed art, the restaurant also features a well-priced American wine list with lots of California vintages.

U.S. 1 at MM 49.5 (bay side), Marathon. ℂ **305/743-3314.** www.barracudagrill.com. Main courses $10–$26. AE, MC, V. Mon–Sat 6–10pm.

Calypso's Seafood Grill ★ SEAFOOD Here you'll find inventive seafood dishes in a casual and rustic waterside setting. If it's available, try the butter-pecan sauce over whatever fish is freshest. Don't miss the white-wine sangria, full of tangy oranges and limes and topped with a dash of cinnamon. The prices are surprisingly reasonable, but the service can be a little more laid-back than you're used to. The toughest part is finding the place. From the south, turn right at the blinking yellow lights near MM 99.5 to Ocean Bay Drive and then turn right. Look for the blue vinyl-sided building on the left.

1 Seagate Blvd. (near MM 99.5), Key Largo. ℂ **305/451-0600.** Main courses $9–$18. MC, V. Wed–Thurs and Sun–Mon 11:30am–10pm; Fri–Sat 11:30am–11pm.

Green Turtle Inn ★ SEAFOOD The Green Turtle Inn was established in 1947 as a place where anglers and travelers to and from Key West could stop for local delicacies made from sea turtles harvested in local waters. It has become the quintessential Keys eatery, with a friendly, local flavor and delicious and *different* fare, such as turtle steaks, soups, and chowders. Alligator steak is also popular and, yes, it does taste like chicken. The Turtle Chowder is what the Inn has become best known for.

U.S. 1 at MM 81.5, Islamorada. ℂ **305/664-9031.** Main courses $12–$22. AE, DISC, MC, V. Tues–Sun noon–10pm.

Islamorada Fish Company ★★ SEAFOOD Pick up a cooler of stone crab claws in season (mid-Oct to Apr), or try the great fried-fish sandwiches, served with melted American cheese, fried onions, and coleslaw. A few hundred yards up the road (at MM 81.6) is Islamorada Fish Company Restaurant & Bakery, the newer establishment, which looks like an average diner but has a selection of fantastic seafood and pastas. It's also the place for breakfast. Locals gather for politics and gossip as well as delicious grits, oatmeal, omelets, and homemade pastries. Keep your eyes open while dining outside—the last time I was here, there were baby manatees floating around, waiting for their close-ups.

U.S. 1 at MM 81.5 (up the street from Cheeca Lodge), Islamorada. ℂ **800/258-2559** or 305/664-9271. www.islamoradafishco.com. Reservations not accepted. Main courses $8–$27; appetizers $4–$7. DISC, MC, V. Sun–Thurs 11am–9pm; Fri–Sat 11am–10pm.

Lazy Days Oceanfront Bar and Seafood Grill ⭐ SEAFOOD/AMERICAN Opened in 1992, the Lazy Days quickly became one of the most popular restaurants around, mostly because of its large portions and lively atmosphere. Dining on the oceanfront outdoor veranda is highly recommended. Meals are pricier than the casual dining room would suggest, but the food is good enough and the menu varied. Steamed clams with garlic and bell peppers make a tempting appetizer. The menu focuses on—what else?—seafood, but you can also find good pasta dishes such as linguine with littleneck clams. Most main courses come with baked potato, vegetables, a tossed salad, and French bread, making appetizers redundant.

U.S. 1 at MM 79.9, Islamorada. ℂ **305/664-5256.** Main courses $11–$30. AE, DISC, MC, V. Wed–Sun 11:30am–10pm.

Time Out Barbecue ⭐⭐ BARBECUE This barbecue joint serves up hot and hearty old-fashioned barbecue that is among the best around. According to management, the secret is in the slow cooking—more than 10 hours for the melt-in-your-mouth soft pork sandwich. Topped off with delicious, not-too-creamy coleslaw and sweet baked beans, any of the many offerings are worth a stop. You can grab a seat at the one big picnic table on the grassy lawn next to the Trading Post.

U.S. 1 at MM 81.5 (ocean side). ℂ **305/664-8911.** Sandwiches $4.25–$6; rib and chicken platters to share $7–$15. MC, V. Daily 11am–10pm.

WORTH A SPLURGE

Atlantic's Edge ⭐⭐⭐ SEAFOOD/REGIONAL Ask for a table by the oceanfront window to feel really privileged at this restaurant, the most elegant in the Keys. Although the service and food are generally first-rate, don't get dressed up—a sports coat for men will be fine but isn't necessary. You can choose from an innovative, varied menu, which offers several choices of fresh fish, steak, chicken, and pastas. The crab cakes, made with stone crab when in season, are the very best in the Keys; served on a warm salad of baby greens with a mild sauce of red peppers, they're the stuff cravings are made of. Other excellent dishes include a Thai-spiced fresh baby snapper and the vegetarian angel-hair pasta with mushrooms, asparagus, and peppers in a rich broth. Service can sometimes be less than efficient but is always courteous and professional.

In the Cheeca Lodge, U.S. 1 at MM 82, Islamorada. ℂ **305/664-4651.** Reservations recommended. Main courses $20–$36. AE, DC, DISC, MC, V. Daily 6–10pm.

Kaiyo ⭐⭐⭐ JAPANESE/SUSHI This funky, colorful restaurant looks out of place in an area where most restaurants are housed in shanty shacks, and its exquisite, modern sushi and Japanese cuisine is a first for Islamorada; but the food is so good, people from all over South Florida plan trips around a meal at Kaiyo. The brainchild of Chef Dawn Sieber, former executive chef at Cheeca Lodge, Kaiyo isn't your typical sushi restaurant, but one that fuses Florida's fine ingredients with some of the freshest raw fish this side of Tokyo. Signature sushi rolls such as the Spicy Volcano Conch roll and the Key Lime Lobster roll are outstanding, as are the farm-raised raw oysters and farmed baby conch tempura. A hip, modern interior is an amusing contrast to the casually dressed, Key-ed up diners, and service here is of five-star caliber—something not typically found in the laid-back Keys. Before you say how you came to the Keys not for trendy sushi, but for fresh fish and conch fritters, do have a meal at Kaiyo. It *will* change the way you view Keys cuisine.

81701 Old Highway, U.S. 1 at MM 82, Islamorada. © 305/664-5556. Reservations recommended. Main courses $12–$15; sushi $4.50–$12. AE, DC, MC, V. Mon–Sat noon–10pm.

THE UPPER & MIDDLE KEYS AFTER DARK

Nightlife in the Upper Keys tends to start before the sun goes down, often at noon, since most people—visitors and locals alike—are on vacation. Also, many anglers and sports-minded folk go to bed early.

Hog Heaven opened in the early 1990s, the joint venture of some young locals tired of tourist traps. Located at MM 85.3, just off the main road on the ocean side in Islamorada (© 305/664-9669), it's a welcome respite from the neon-colored cocktail circuit. This whitewashed biker bar offers a waterside view and diversions that include big-screen TVs and video games. The food isn't bad, either. The atmosphere is cliquish since most patrons are regulars, so start up a game of pool to break the ice. Open from 11am to 4am daily.

No trip to the Keys is complete without a stop at the **Tiki Bar at the Holiday Isle Resort,** U.S. 1 at MM 84, Islamorada (© 800/327-7070 or 305/664-2321). Hundreds of revelers visit this ocean-side spot for drinks and dancing at any time of day, but the live rock music starts at 8:30pm. The thatched-roof Tiki Bar draws a high-energy but laid-back mix of thirsty people, all in pursuit of a good time. In the afternoon and early evening (when everyone is either sunburned, drunk, or just happy to be dancing to live reggae), head for **Kokomo's,** just next door. Kokomo's often closes at 7:30pm on weekends (5:30pm on weekdays), so get there early. For information, call the Holiday Isle Resort.

Woody's Saloon and Restaurant, on U.S. 1 at MM 82, Islamorada (© 305/664-4335), is a lively, wacky, loud, gritty, raunchy, local legend of a place serving up mediocre pizzas, buck naked strippers, and live bands almost every night. The house band, Big Dick and the Extenders, showcases a 300-pound Native American who does a lewd, rude, and crude routine of jokes and songs starting at 9pm, Tuesday through Sunday. He is a legend. By the way, don't think you're lucky if you are offered the front table: It's the target seat for Big Dick's haranguing. Avoid the lame karaoke performance on Sunday and Monday evenings. There's a small cover charge most nights. Drink specials, contests, and the legendary Big Dick keep this place packed until 4am almost every night. *Note:* This place is not for the faint of heart (or tact!), but more for those of the Howard Stern school of nightlife.

For a more subdued atmosphere, try the handsome stained-glass and mahogany-wood bar and club at **Zane Grey's** (on the second floor of World Wide Sportsman at MM 81.5). Outside, enjoy a view of the calm waters of the bay; inside, soak up the history of some real longtime anglers. It is open from 11am to 11pm, and later on weekends. Call to find out who is playing on weekends (© 305/664-4244), when there is live entertainment and no cover charge.

2 The Lower Keys: Big Pine Key to Coppitt Key

128 miles SW of Miami

Unlike their neighbors to the north and south, the Lower Keys (including Big Pine, Sugarloaf, and Summerland) are devoid of rowdy spring-break crowds, boast few T-shirt and trinket shops, and have almost no late-night bars. What they do offer are the very best opportunities to enjoy the vast natural resources on land and water that make the area so rich. Stay overnight in the Lower Keys, rent a boat, and explore the reefs—it might be the most memorable part of your trip.

ESSENTIALS

GETTING THERE   See "Essentials" for the Upper and Middle Keys (p. 169) and continue south on U.S. 1. The Lower Keys start at the end of the Seven-Mile Bridge. There are also airports in Marathon and Key West.

VISITOR INFORMATION   The **Big Pine and Lower Keys Chamber of Commerce,** ocean side of U.S. 1 at MM 31 (P.O. Box 430511), Big Pine Key, FL 33043 (© **800/872-3722** or 305/872-2411; fax 305/872-0752; www.lower keyschamber.com), is open Monday through Friday from 9am to 5pm and Saturday from 9am to 3pm. The pleasant staff will help with anything a traveler may need. Call, write, or stop in for a comprehensive, detailed information packet.

WHAT TO SEE & DO

Once the centerpiece (these days, it's Big Pine Key) of the Lower Keys and still a great asset is **Bahia Honda State Park** ⚐, U.S. 1 at MM 37.5, Big Pine Key (© **305/872-2353;** www.bahiahondapark.com), which, even after the violent storms of 1998, has one of the most beautiful coastlines in South Florida. Bahia Honda (pronounced *Bah*-ya) is a great place for hiking, bird-watching, swimming, snorkeling, and fishing. The 524-acre park encompasses a wide variety of ecosystems, including coastal mangroves, beach dunes, and tropical hammocks. There are miles of trails packed with unusual plants and animals and a small, white beach. Shaded seaside picnic areas are fitted with tables and grills. Although the beach is never wider than 5 feet even at low tide, this is the Lower Keys' best beach area.

True to its name (Spanish for "deep bay"), the park has relatively deep waters close to shore, and they are perfect for snorkeling and diving. Easy offshore snorkeling here gives even novices a chance to lie suspended in warm water and simply observe diverse marine life passing by. Or else head to the stunning reefs at Looe Key, where the coral and fish are more vibrant than anywhere else in the United States. Snorkeling trips go from the Bahia Honda concessions to Looe Key National Marine Sanctuary (4 miles offshore). They depart twice daily March through September and cost $28 for adults, $23 for youths 6 to 14, and are free for children 5 and under. Call © **305/872-3210** for a schedule.

Admission to the park is $5 per vehicle (plus 50¢ per person), $1.50 per pedestrian or bicyclist, free for children 5 and under. If you are alone in a car, you'll pay only $2.50. Open daily from 8am to sunset.

The most famous residents of the Lower Keys are the tiny Key deer. Of the estimated 300 existing in the world, two-thirds live on Big Pine Key's **National Key Deer Refuge** ⚐ which recently expanded with the acquisition of 20 acres of beach and waterfront property. To get your bearings, stop by the rangers' office at the Winn-Dixie Shopping Plaza near MM 30.5 off U.S. 1. They'll give you an informative brochure and map of the area. The refuge is open Monday through Friday from 8am to 5pm.

If the office is closed, head out to the Blue Hole, a former rock quarry now filled with the fresh water that's vital to the deer's survival. To get there, turn right at Big Pine Key's only traffic light onto Key Deer Boulevard (take the left fork immediately after the turn) and continue 1½ miles to the observation-site parking lot, on your left. The half-mile **Watson Hammock Trail,** about a third of a mile past the Blue Hole, is the refuge's only marked footpath. Try coming out to the footpath in the early morning or late evening to catch a glimpse of these gentle, dog-size deer. There is an observation deck there from which you can watch and photograph the protected species. They are more active in cool hours and in cooler times of the year. Refuge lands are open daily from half an hour before sunrise to half an hour after sunset. Don't be surprised to see a lazy alligator warming itself in the sun, particularly in outlying areas around the Blue Hole. If you do see a gator, do not go near it, do not touch it, and do not provoke it. Keep your distance; and if you must get a photo, use a zoom lens. Also, whatever you do, do not feed the deer—it will threaten their survival. Call the **park office** (© **305/872-2239**) to find out about the infrequent free tours of the refuge, scheduled throughout the year.

AFFORDABLE OUTDOOR ACTIVITIES

BICYCLING   If you have your own bike, or your lodging offers a rental (many do), the Lower Keys are a great place to get off busy U.S. 1 to explore the beautiful back roads. On Big Pine Key, cruise along Key Deer Boulevard (at MM 30). Those with fat tires can ride into the National Key Deer Refuge.

BIRD-WATCHING   Bring your birding books. A stopping point for migratory birds on the Eastern Flyway, the Lower Keys are populated with many West Indian bird species, especially during spring and fall. The small, vegetated islands of the Keys are the only nesting sites in the United States for the great white heron and the white-crowned pigeon. They're also some of the very few breeding places for the reddish egret, the roseate spoonbill, the mangrove cuckoo, and the black-whiskered vireo. Look for them on Bahia Honda Key and the many uninhabited islands nearby.

BOATING   Dozens of shops rent powerboats for fishing and reef exploring. Most also rent tackle, sell bait, and have charter captains available. For instance, **Jaybird's Powerboats,** U.S. 1 at MM 33, Big Pine Key (© **305/872-8500**), is an excellent option, but they rent for full days only. Prices start at $155 for a 19-footer.

CANOEING & KAYAKING   The Overseas Highway (U.S. 1) touches on only a few dozen of the many hundreds of islands that make up the Keys. To really see the Lower Keys, rent a kayak or canoe—perfect for these shallow waters. **Reflections Kayak Nature Tours,** operating out of Parmer's Resort, on U.S. 1 at MM 28.5, Little Torch Key (© **305/872-4668**), offers fully outfitted backcountry wildlife tours, either on your own or with an expert. The expert, Mike Wedeking, a former U.S. Forest Service guide, keeps up an engaging discussion describing the area's fish, sponges, coral, osprey, hawks, eagles, alligators, raccoons, and deer. The 3-hour tours cost $49 per person and include spring water, fresh fruit, granola bars, and use of binoculars. Bring a towel and sea sandals or sneakers.

FISHING   A day spent fishing, either in the shallow backcountry or in the deep sea, is a great way to ensure yourself a fresh fish dinner, or you can release your catch and just appreciate the challenge. Whichever you choose, **Larry Threlkeld's Strike Zone Charters,** U.S. 1 at MM 29.5, Big Pine Key (© **305/ 872-9863**), is the charter service to call. Prices for fishing boats start at $450 for a half day and $595 for a full day. If you have enough anglers to share the price, it isn't too steep. They may also be able to match you with other interested visitors.

HIKING   You can hike throughout the flat, marshy Keys, on both marked trails and meandering coastlines. The best places to trek through nature are **Bahia Honda State Park** at MM 29.5 and **National Key Deer Refuge** at MM 30 (for more information on both, see "What to See & Do," above). Bahia Honda Park has a free brochure describing an excellent self-guided tour along the Silver Palm Nature Trail. You'll traverse hammocks, mangroves, and sand dunes and cross a lagoon. The walk (which is less than a mile) explores a great cross-section of the natural habitat in the Lower Keys and can be done in under half an hour.

SNORKELING & DIVING   Snorkelers and divers should not miss the Keys' most dramatic reefs at the **Looe Key National Marine Sanctuary.** Here, you'll see more than 150 varieties of hard and soft coral—some, centuries old—as well as every type of tropical fish, including gold and blue parrotfish, moray eels, barracudas, French angels, and tarpon. **Looe Key Dive Center,** U.S. 1 at MM 27.5, Ramrod Key (© 305/872-2215), offers a mind-blowing 5-hour tour aboard a 45-foot catamaran with two shallow 1-hour dives for snorkelers and scuba divers. Snorkelers pay $25, and divers with their own equipment pay $40; on Wednesdays and Saturdays you can do a fascinating dive to the *Adolphus Busch Sr.,* a shipwreck sunk off Looe Key in 100 feet of water, for $45. Good-quality rentals are available. (See "What to See & Do," above, for other diving options.)

ACCOMMODATIONS YOU CAN AFFORD

There are a number of cheap, fairly unappealing fish shacks along the highway for those who want bare-bones accommodations. So far, there are no national hotel chains in the Lower Keys. For information on lodging in cabins or trailers at local campgrounds, see "Camping," below.

Big Pine Key Fishing Lodge *Value*   Sitting on 6 acres of lush ocean-side land, this superaffordable and well-maintained property is a favorite of campers and boaters. Most of the lodges contain full kitchenettes, and nearly all offer microwaves and refrigerators. Though you won't find a phone in your room, there are plenty of conveniently located pay phones. A large heated pool with a sun deck and lounge chairs is a plus, especially since there isn't any real beach here (a tiny swath of artificial beach suffices for determined sand lovers). The lodge also boasts an on-site marina.

In addition to the lodges, this spot also maintains 102 campsites right off the ocean, equipped with water, electricity, sewer, and satellite TV. Hurricanes George and Irene destroyed most of the trees in the camping area, so it's a good idea to bring along something that will provide you with some shade.

P.O. Box 513, MM 33, Big Pine Key, FL 33043. © 305/872-2351. 16 units (showers only), 102 campsites. Year-round $95–$115 single or double; $89–$130 loft room for 1–4 people; $30–$37 campsites for tent or with full hookup. Discounts for stays longer than a week. Extra person $10. DISC, MC, V. **Amenities:** Heated pool; game room; laundry. *In room:* A/C, TV (kitchenette, fridge, and microwave in some), no phone.

Deer Run Bed and Breakfast ★★ *Finds*   Located directly on the beach, Sue Abbott's small, homey, smoke-free Caribbean-style B&B is a real find. One upstairs and two downstairs guest rooms are comfortably furnished with queen-size beds, good closets, and touch-sensitive lamps. Rattan and 1970s-style chairs and couches furnish the living room, along with 13 birds and 3 cats. Breakfast, which is served on a pretty, fenced-in porch, is cooked to order by Sue herself. The wooded area around the property is full of Key deer, which are often spotted on the beach as well. A hot tub overlooking the ocean is especially nice. Ask to use one of the bikes to explore nearby nature trails.

Long Beach Dr. (P.O. Box 431), Big Pine Key, FL 33043. © 305/872-2015. Fax 305/872-2842. deerrunbb@ aol.com. 3 units. Winter from $110 double; off season from $95 double. Rates include full American breakfast. No credit cards. From U.S. 1 S., turn left at the Big Pine Fishing Lodge (MM 33); continue for about 2 miles. No children under 16. **Amenities:** Jacuzzi; free use of bikes. *In room:* A/C, TV.

Parmer's Resort ⊛   Parmer's, a fixture here for more than 20 years, is well known for its charming hospitality and helpful staff. This downscale resort offers modest but comfortable cottages, each of them unique. Some are waterfront, many have kitchenettes, and others are just a bedroom. Room no. 26, aka Wahoo, a one-bedroom efficiency, is especially nice, with a small sitting area that faces the water. Room no. 6, a small efficiency, has a kitchenette and an especially large bathroom. The rooms have been recently updated—and are consistently very clean. Many can be combined to accommodate large families. The hotel's waterfront location, not to mention that it's only a half-hour from lively Key West, almost makes up for the fact that you must pay extra for maid service.

565 Barry Ave. (P.O. Box 430665), near MM 28.5, Little Torch Key, FL 33043. © 305/872-2157. Fax 305/ 872-2014. www.parmersresort.com. 45 units. Winter $85–$150 double, from $105 efficiency; off season $65–$105 double, from $85 efficiency. Rates include continental breakfast. AE, DISC, MC, V. From U.S. 1, turn right onto Barry Ave. Resort is ½ mile down on the right. **Amenities:** Heated pool; bike rental; kayak rentals; coin-op washers and dryers; boat ramp. *In room:* A/C, TV.

CAMPING

Bahia Honda State Park ⊛⊛⊛ (© 800/326-3521; www.abfla.com/parks/ BahiaHonda/bahiahonda.html) offers some of the best camping in the Keys. It is as loaded with facilities and activities as it is with campers. However, don't be discouraged by its popularity—this park encompasses more than 500 acres of land, 80 campsites spread throughout three areas, and six spacious and comfortable cabin units (fitting six people each) that were reconstructed between 2000 and 2001. Cabins hold up to eight guests and come complete with linens, kitchenettes, and utensils as well as a wraparound terrace, barbecue pit, and rocking chairs.

For one to four people, camping here costs about $25 per site without electricity and $26 with electricity. Depending on the season, cabin prices change: Prices range from $50 to $110. Additional people (over four) cost $6 each. MasterCard and Visa are accepted.

Another excellent value can be found at the **KOA Sugarloaf Key Resort** ⊛⊛, near MM 20. This ocean-side facility has 200 fully equipped sites, with water, electricity, and sewer, which rent for about $85 a night (no-hookup sites cost about $45). Or pitch a tent on the 5 acres of lush waterfront property. This site is especially nice because of its private beaches and access to diving, snorkeling, and boating; and its grounds are nice and well maintained. The resort also rents travel trailers. The 25-foot Dutchman sleeps six and is equipped with eating and cooking utensils. It costs about $120 a day. More luxurious trailers go for $180 a day. All major credit cards are accepted. For details, write them at P.O. Box 420469, Summerland Key, FL 33042 (© 800/562-7731 or 305/745-3549; fax 305/745-9889; www.koa.com).

GREAT DEALS ON DINING

Coco's Kitchen ✮ CUBAN/AMERICAN   This tiny storefront has been dishing out black beans, rice, and shredded beef to fans of Cuban cuisine for more than 10 years. The owners, who are actually from Nicaragua, cook not only superior Cuban food but also some local specialties, Italian food, and Caribbean food. Specialties include fried shrimp, whole fried yellowtail, and Cuban-style roast pork (available only on Sat). The best bet is the daily special, which may be roasted pork or fresh grouper, served with rice and beans or salad and crispy fries. Top off the huge, cheap meal with a rich caramel-soaked flan.

283 Key Deer Blvd. (in the Winn-Dixie Shopping Center), Big Pine Key. © 305/872-4495. Main courses $6–$15; breakfast $2–$5. MC, V. Mon–Sat 7am–7:30pm. Turn right at the traffic light near MM 30.5. Stay in the left lane.

Mangrove Mama's Restaurant SEAFOOD/CARIBBEAN   As the dedicated locals who come daily for happy hour will tell you, this is a true Lower Keys institution and a dive (the restaurant is a shack that used to have a gas pump as well as a grill) in the best sense of the word. Guests share the property with some miniature horses (out back) and stray cats. A handful of simple tables, inside and out, are shaded by banana trees and palm fronds. Fish is the menu's mainstay, although soups, salads, sandwiches, and omelets are also good. Grilled teriyaki chicken and club sandwiches are tasty alternatives to fish, as are meatless chef's salads and spicy barbecued baby back ribs.

U.S. 1 at MM 20, Sugarloaf Key. © 305/745-3030. Main courses $10–$20; lunch $6–$9; brunch $5–$7. MC, V. Daily 11am–3pm and 5:30-10pm.

Monte's SEAFOOD   Certainly nobody goes to this restaurant/fish market for its atmosphere: Plastic place settings rest on plastic-covered picnic-style tables in a screen-enclosed dining patio. But Monte's doesn't need great atmosphere, since it has survived for more than 20 years on its very good and incredibly fresh food. The day's catch may include shark, tuna, lobsters, stone crabs, or shrimp.

U.S. 1 at MM 25, Summerland Key. © 305/745-3731. Main courses $13–$17; lunch $6–$10. No credit cards. Mon–Sat 9am–10pm; Sun 10am–9pm.

THE LOWER KEYS AFTER DARK

Although the mellow islands of the Lower Keys aren't exactly known for wild nightlife, there are some friendly bars and restaurants where locals and tourists gather to hang out and drink.

One of the most scenic is **Sandbar** (© **305/872-9989**), a wide-open breezy wooden house built on slender stilts and overlooking a wide channel on Barry Avenue (near MM 28.5). It attracts an odd mix of bikers and blue-hairs daily from 11am to 10pm and is a great place to overhear local gossip and colorful metaphors. Pool tables are the main attraction, but there's also live music some nights. The drinks are reasonably priced and the food isn't too bad, either. For another fun bar scene, see **No Name Pub,** listed above in "Great Deals on Dining."

3 Key West ✮✮✮

159 miles SW of Miami

There are two schools of thought on Key West—one is that it has become way too commercial, and the other is that it's still a place where one can go and not worry about being prim, proper, or even well groomed. I think it's a bizarre fusion of both—a fascinating look at small-town America in which people truly live by the (off)beat of their own drum, albeit one with a Gap and Banana Republic—but not yet a Starbuck's—thrown in to bring you back to some reality. The locals, or "conchs" (pronounced *conks*), and the developers here have been at odds for years. This once low-key island has been thoroughly commercialized—there's a Hard Rock Cafe smack in the middle of Duval Street and thousands of cruise-ship passengers descend on Mallory Square each day. It's definitely not the seedy town Hemingway and his cronies once called their own. Or is it?

Laid-back Key West still exists, but it's now found in different places: the backyard of a popular guesthouse, for example, or an art gallery, a secret garden, a clothing-optional bar, or the hip hangouts of Bahama Village. Fortunately there are plenty of these, and Key West's greatest historic charm is found just off the beaten path. Don't be afraid to explore these residential areas, as conchs are notoriously friendly. In fact, exploring the side streets always seems to yield a new discovery of some sort. Of course, there are always the calm waters of the Atlantic and the Gulf of Mexico all around.

The heart of town offers party people a good time—that is, if your idea of a good time is the smell of stale beer, loud music, and hardly shy revelers. Here, you'll find good restaurants, fun bars, live music, rickshaw rides, and lots of shopping. Key West is still very gay-centric, except during the time of spring break. Same-sex couples walking hand in hand are the norm here, and if you're not open-minded and would prefer to avoid this scene, just look for the ubiquitous rainbow flag hanging outside of gay establishments and you'll know what to expect. For the most part, however, the scene is extremely mixed and colorful. If partying isn't your thing, then avoid Duval Street (the Bourbon St. of South Florida) at all costs. Instead, take in the scenery at a dockside bar or ocean-side Jacuzzi. Whatever you do, don't bother with a watch or tie—this is the home of the perennial vacation.

ESSENTIALS

GETTING THERE For directions by car, see "Essentials" for the Upper and Middle Keys (p. 169) and continue south on U.S. 1. When entering Key West, stay in the far-right lane onto North Roosevelt Boulevard, which becomes Truman Avenue in Old Town. Continue for a few blocks and you will find yourself on **Duval Street** ⋆, in the heart of the city. If you stay to the left, you'll also reach the city center after passing the airport and the remnants of historic houseboat row, where a motley collection of boats once made up one of Key West's most interesting neighborhoods.

Several regional airlines fly nonstop (about 55 min.) from Miami to Key West; fares are about $120 to $300 round-trip. **American Eagle, Continental, Delta,** and **US Airways Express** land at **Key West International Airport,** South Roosevelt Boulevard (© **305/296-5439**), on the southeastern corner of the island.

Greyhound (© **800/231-2222;** www.greyhound.com) has buses leaving Miami for Key West every day for about $30 to $32 one-way and $57 to $60 round-trip. Seats fill up in season, so come early. The ride takes about 4½ hours.

There's also, finally, a ferry that goes from Miami (from downtown's Sealine Marina) to Key West. It's about time. **Fast Cats'** PurrSeavearance (© **786/205-8683;** www.fastcats.org) may be a cheesy name for a luxury $7.5 million catamaran, but the trip is hardly so. The 102-foot boat can hold up to 149

passengers and will make the 4½-hour cruise (driving only takes 3 hr., but with traffic, it can take up to 5) four times a week starting at $65 each way. VIP tickets cost $98 and include preferential seating. Food and alcoholic beverages are available but not included in the price. Tours leave Miami Thursday through Sunday at 7:30am and push off from Key West on Sundays at 5:30pm.

GETTING AROUND   With limited parking, narrow streets, and congested traffic, driving in Old Town Key West is more of a pain than a convenience. Unless you're staying in one of the more remote accommodations, consider trading in the car for a bicycle. The island is small and as flat as a board, which makes it easy to negotiate, especially away from the crowded downtown area. Many tourists also choose to cruise by moped, an option that can make navigating the streets risky, especially since there are no helmet laws in Key West. So be careful and spend the extra few bucks to rent a helmet; hundreds of visitors are seriously injured each year.

Rates for simple one-speed cruisers start at about $8 per day (from $40 per week). Mopeds start at about $12 for 2 hours, $25 per day, and $100 per week. The best shops include **The Bicycle Center** at 523 Truman Ave. (© **305/294-4556**); the **Moped Hospital,** 601 Truman Ave. (© **305/296-3344**); and **Tropical Bicycles & Scooter Rentals** at 1300 Duval St. (© **305/294-8136**). **The Bike Shop,** 1110 Truman Ave. (© **305/294-1073**), rents cruisers for $8 per day and $40 per week. A $150 deposit is required.

PARKING   Parking in Key West's Old Town is particularly limited, but there is a well-placed **municipal parking lot** at Simonton and Angela streets, just behind the firehouse and police station. If you have brought a car, you may want to stash it here while you enjoy the very walkable downtown part of Key West.

VISITOR INFORMATION   The **Key West Chamber of Commerce,** 402 Wall St., Key West, FL 33040 (© **800/527-8539** or 305/294-2587; www. keywestchamber.com), offers both general and specialized information. The lobby is open daily from 8:30am to 6pm; phones are answered from 8am to 8pm. The **Key West Visitor Center** is the area's best for information on accommodations, goings-on, and restaurants; the number is © **800/LAST-KEY.** It's open weekdays from 8am to 5:30pm and weekends from 8:30am to 5pm. Gay travelers will want to call the **Key West Business Guild** (© **305/294-4603**), which represents more than 50 guesthouses and B&Bs in town, as well as many other gay-owned businesses (ask for its color brochure) or **Good Times Travel** (© **305/294-0980**), which will set up lodging and package tours on the island.

While you're in one of the above offices, be sure to pick up a free copy of Sharon Wells' Walking & Biking Guide to Historic Key West. Though I still couldn't find all the spots I wanted to in the Key West Cemetery (p. 193) while using her guide, it was helpful for historical descriptions throughout town (and it's free). She also leads guided walking tours around the island. Contact her (© **305/294-8380;** www.seekeywest.com) for more information.

ORIENTATION   A mere 2-by-4-mile island, Key West is simple to navigate, even though there is no real order to the arrangement of streets and avenues. As you enter town on U.S. 1 (also called Roosevelt Blvd.), you will see most of the moderately priced chain hotels and fast-food restaurants. The better restaurants, shops, and outfitters are crammed onto Duval Street, the main thoroughfare of Key West's Old Town. Surrounding streets contain many inns and lodges in picturesque Victorian/Bahamian homes. On the southern side of the island is the coral beach area and some of the larger resort hotels.

The area called Bahama Village has only recently become known to tourists. With several newly opened, trendy restaurants and guesthouses, this hippie-ish neighborhood, complete with street-roaming chickens and cats, is the most urban and rough you'll find in the Keys. You might see a few seedy drug dealings on street corners, but it's nothing to be overly concerned with: It looks worse than it is and resident business owners tend to keep a vigilant eye on the neighborhood. The area is actually quite funky and should be a welcome diversion from the Duvalian mainstream.

SEEING THE SIGHTS

Before shelling out big bucks for any of the dozens of worthwhile attractions in Key West, I recommend getting an overview on either of the two comprehensive island tours, **The Conch Tour Train** or the **Old Town Trolley** (see "Organized Tours," below). There are simply too many attractions and historic houses to list. I've highlighted my favorites below but encourage you to seek out others.

Audubon House & Tropical Gardens ★★   This well-preserved home, dating from the early 19th century, stands as a prime example of early Key West architecture. Named after renowned painter and bird expert John James Audubon, who was said to have visited the house in 1832, the graceful two-story home is a peaceful retreat from the bustle of Old Town. Included in the price of admission is a self-guided audio tour that lasts about half an hour and spotlights rare Audubon prints, gorgeous antiques, historical photos, and lush tropical gardens. With voices of several characters from the house's past, the tour never gets boring—although it is at times a bit hokey. Even if you don't want to spend the time and money to explore the grounds and home, check out the impressive gift shop, which sells a variety of fine mementos at reasonable prices.

205 Whitehead St. (between Greene and Caroline sts.). © 305/294-2116. www.audubonhouse.com. Admission $9 adults, $5 children 6–12. Daily 9:30am–5pm (last admission at 4:30pm). Discounts for students and AAA and AARP members.

Ernest Hemingway Home and Museum ★   Hemingway's particularly handsome stone Spanish Colonial house, built in 1851, was one of the first on the island to be fitted with indoor plumbing and a built-in fireplace, and it contains the first swimming pool built on Key West (look for the penny he pressed into the cement near the pool). The author owned the home from 1931 until his death in 1961, and he lived there with about 50 cats, whose descendants, including the famed six-toed cats, still roam the premises. It was during those years that the Nobel Prize winner wrote some of his most famous works, including *For Whom the Bell Tolls, A Farewell to Arms,* and *The Snows of Kilimanjaro.* Fans may want to take the optional half-hour tour, where you'll see rooms of his house with glass cabinets that store certain artifacts, books, and pieces of mail addressed to him as well as his study. It's interesting (to an extent) and included in the price of admission. If you don't take the tour or have no literary interest in Hemingway, the admission price is really a waste of money, except for the house's lovely architecture and garden. If you're feline phobic, beware: There are cats everywhere.

907 Whitehead St. (between Truman Ave. and Olivia St.). © **305/294-1136.** Fax 305/294-2755. www.hemingwayhome.com. Admission $10 adults, $6 children. Daily 9am–5pm. Limited parking.

Harry S Truman Little White House Museum ★★   President Harry Truman used to refer to the White House as the "Great White Jail." On temporary leave from the big house, Truman discovered the serenity of Key West and made

Going, Going, Gone: Where to Catch the Famous Key West Sunset

A tradition in Key West, the Sunset Celebration can be relaxing or overwhelming, depending on your vantage point. If you're in town, you must check out this ritual at least once. Every evening, locals and visitors gather at the docks behind Mallory Square (at the westernmost end of Whitehead St.) to celebrate the day gone by. Secure a spot on the docks early to experience the carnival of portrait artists, acrobats, food vendors, animal acts, and other performers trading on the island's bohemian image. But the carnival atmosphere isn't for everyone: In season, the crowd can be overwhelming, especially when the cruise ships are in port. Also, hold onto your bags and wallets as the tight crowds make Mallory Square at sunset prime pickpocketing territory.

A more refined choice is the Hilton's **Sunset Deck** (© **305/294-4000**), a luxurious second-floor bar on Front Street, right next door to Mallory Square. From the civilized calm of a casual bar, you can look down on the mayhem with a drink in hand.

Also near the Mallory madness is the **Ocean Key Resort's** bar. This long open-air pier serves up drinks and decent bar food against a dramatic pink- and yellow-streaked sky. It's located at the very tip of Duval Street (© **800/328-9815** or 305/296-7701).

For the very best potent cocktails and great bar food on an outside patio or enclosed lounge, try **Pier House Resort and Caribbean Spa's Havana Docks** at 1 Duval St. (© **305/296-4600**). There's usually live music and a lively gathering of visitors enjoying this island's bounty. The bar is right on the water and is a prime sunset-viewing spot.

his escape to what became known as the Little White House, which is open to the public for touring. The house is fully restored, and the exhibits document Truman's time in the Keys. Tours are every 15 minutes and last between 45 and 50 minutes. For fans of all things Oval Office–related, there's a presidential gift shop on the premises.

111 Front St. © **305/294-9911**. www.trumanlittlewhitehouse.com. Admission $10 adults, $5 children under 12. Daily 9am–4:30pm.

Heritage House Museum ★ *Finds*   For a glimpse into one of the oldest houses in Key West, check out the Heritage House Museum, the former 1834 home of Jesse Porter, a Key West preservationist who hosted the likes of Robert Frost, Tennessee Williams, Gloria Swanson, and Tallulah Bankhead in his home cum salon. Furnished with 19th-century antiques, the house is a fascinating look at 19th- and early-20th-century Key West. Guided tours are informative and entertaining, sort of like an antique version of an *E! True Hollywood Story.*

410 Caroline St. © **305/296-3573** for tour reservations. www.heritagehousemuseum.org. Free admission. Mon–Sat 10am–4pm.

Key West Aquarium ★★ *Kids*   The oldest attraction on the island, the Key West Aquarium is a modest but fascinating exhibit. A long hallway of eye-level displays showcases dozens of varieties of fish and crustaceans. You'll see delicate sea horses swaying in the backlit tanks. Kids can touch sea cucumbers and sea anemones in a shallow tank in the entryway. If you can, catch one of the free guided tours, where you can witness the dramatic feeding frenzy of the sharks, tarpon, barracudas, stingrays, and turtles. Expect to spend about 1 to 1½ hours here.

1 Whitehead St. (at Mallory Sq.). (✆) 305/296-2051. www.keywestaquarium.com. Admission $9 adults, $4.50 children 4–12, free for children under 4. Tickets are good for 2 consecutive days. Look for discount coupons at local hotels, at Duval St. kiosks, and from trolley and train tours. Daily 10am–6pm; tours at 11am and 1, 3, and 4pm.

Key West Cemetery ✖✖✖ *Finds* This funky, picturesque cemetery is the epitome of the quirky Key West image, as irreverent as it is humorous. Many tombs are stacked several high, condominium style—the rocky soil made digging 6 feet under nearly impossible for early settlers. Headstones reflect residents' lighthearted attitudes toward life and death. I TOLD YOU I WAS SICK is one of the more famous epitaphs, as is the tongue-in-cheek widow's inscription AT LEAST I KNOW WHERE HE'S SLEEPING TONIGHT. Pick up a copy of Sharon Wells' Walking & Biking Guide to Historic Key West (p. 190). Though some of the inscriptions are hard to find, even with the free walking tour guide, it's fun to walk through.

Entrance at the corner of Margaret and Angela sts. Free admission. Daily dawn–dusk.

Key West Lighthouse Museum ✖ When the Key West Lighthouse opened in 1848, it signaled the end of a profitable era for the pirate salvagers who looted reef-stricken ships. The story of this and other Keys lighthouses is illustrated in a small museum that was formerly the keeper's quarters. It's worth mustering the energy to climb the 88 claustrophobic steps to the top, where you'll be rewarded with magnificent panoramic views of Key West and the ocean.

938 Whitehead St. (✆) 305/294-0012. Admission $8 adults, $6 seniors and locals, $4 children 7–12, free for children 6 and under. Daily 9:30am–4:30pm.

Mel Fisher Maritime Heritage Museum ✖✖ This museum honors local hero Mel Fisher, whose death in 1998 was mourned throughout South Florida, and who, along with a crew of other salvagers, found a multimillion-dollar treasure trove in 1985 aboard the wreck of the Spanish galleon *Nuestra Señora de*

⸙ *Moments* A Great Escape

Many people complain that Key West's quirky, quaint panache has been lost to the vulture of capitalism, evidenced by the glut of T-shirt shops and tacky bars. But that's not entirely so. For a quiet respite, visit the Key West Botanical Gardens, a little-known slice of serenity tucked between the Aqueduct Authority plant and the Key West Golf Course. The 11-acre gardens—maintained by volunteers and funded by donations—contain the last hardwood hammock in Key West, plus a colorful representation of wildflowers, butterflies, and birds. A genetically cloned tree is the latest addition to the gardens. Although the gardens received a terrible blow from the storms of 1998, the calm remains within them. Located at Botanical Garden Way and College Road, Stock Island. Free admission. Open daily from 8am to sunset. Follow College Road; then turn right just past Bayshore Manor.

Atocha. If you're into diving, pirates, and sunken treasures, check out this small, informative museum, full of doubloons, pieces of eight, emeralds, and solid-gold bars (one of them you can lift!). A 1700 English merchant slave ship, the only tangible evidence of the transatlantic slave trade, is on view on the museum's second floor. A dated but informative film provides a good background for Fisher's incredible story. An exhibition telling the story of over 1,400 African slaves captured in Cuban waters and brought to Key West for sanctuary is the museum's latest, most fascinating one to date.

200 Greene St. ℭ **305/294-2633.** www.melfisher.org. Admission $7.50 adults, $3.75 children 6–12, free for children 5 and under. Daily 9:30am–5pm. Take U.S. 1 to Whitehead St. and turn left on Greene.

Oldest House/Wrecker's Museum ⭐ Dating from 1829, this old New England Bahama House has survived pirates, hurricanes, fires, warfare, and economic ups and downs. The 1½-story home was designed by a ship's carpenter and incorporates many features from maritime architecture, including portholes and a ship's hatch designed for ventilation before the advent of air-conditioning. Especially interesting is the detached kitchen building outfitted with a brick "beehive" oven and vintage cooking utensils. Although not a must-see on the Key West tour, history and architecture buffs will appreciate the finely preserved details and the glimpse of a slower, easier time in the island's life.

322 Duval St. ℭ **305/294-9502.** Admission $5 adults, $1 children 6–12, free for children 5 and under. Daily 10am–4pm.

ORGANIZED TOURS

BY TROLLEY-BUS & TRAM Yes, it's more than a bit hokey to sit on this 60-foot tram of yellow cars, but it's worth it—at least once. The city's whole story is packed into a neat, 90-minute package on the **Conch Tour Train,** which covers the island and all its rich, raunchy history. Operating since 1958, the trains are open-air, which can make the ride uncomfortable in bad weather. The "train's" engine is a propane-powered Jeep disguised as a locomotive. Tours depart from both Mallory Square and the Welcome Center, near where U.S. 1 becomes North Roosevelt Boulevard, on the less-developed side of the island. For more information, contact the **Conch** at ℭ **305/294-5161** or www.conchtour train.com. The cost is $20 for adults, $10 for children 4 to 12, and free for children 3 and under. Daily departures are every half-hour from 9am to 4:30pm.

The **Old Town Trolley** is the choice in bad weather or if you are staying at one of the many hotels on its route. Humorous drivers maintain a running commentary as the enclosed tram loops around the island's streets past all the major sights. Trolleys depart from Mallory Square and other points around the island, including many area hotels. For details, call ℭ **305/296-6688** or visit www.trolleytours.com. Tours are $20 for adults, $10 for children 4 to 12, and free for children 3 and under. Departures are daily every half-hour (though not always on the half-hour) from 9am to 4:30pm. Whichever you choose, these historic trivia-packed tours are well worth the price of admission.

BY AIR Proclaimed by the mayor as "the official air force of the Conch Republic," **Island Airplane Tours,** at Key West Airport, 3469 S. Roosevelt Blvd. (ℭ **305/294-8687**), offers windy rides in its open-cockpit 1940 Waco biplanes that take you over the reefs and around the islands. Thrill seekers—and only they—will also enjoy a spin in the company's S2-B aerobatics airplane, which does loops, rolls, and sideways figure-eights. Company owner Fred Cabanas was "decorated" in 1991, after he spotted a Cuban airman defecting to the United States in a Russian-built MIG fighter. Sightseeing flights cost $50 to $200, depending on the duration.

BY BOAT   The catamaran *The Pride of Key West* and *Fireball,* a glass-bottom boat, both at Zero Duval St. (© **305/296-6293;** fax 305/294-8704), depart on both day (noon and 2pm) coral-reef tours and evening sunset cruises (call for times). Reef trips cost $25 per person; sunset cruises are $30 per person. Kids 5 through 12 sail all cruises for $13.

Schooner *Western Union* (© **305/292-9830**) was built in 1939 and served as a cable-repair vessel until it was designated the flagship of the city of Key West and began day, sunset, and charter sailings. Sunset sailings are especially memorable and include entertainment, cocktails, and a cannon fire. Prices vary.

M/V *Heritage* (© **305/295-8687**) is Key West's newest water attraction, a 45-foot custom-designed schooner that offers 1-hour tours of Key West's historic harbor. Sites of interest on this tour include Fort Zachary Taylor, a Civil War–era fortification; the Truman Naval Station; the Key West National Wildlife Preserve; and Mallory Square. Tours are fully narrated to highlight the island's connection to pirates, wreckers, spongers, fishermen, and the U.S. Navy and Coast Guard. Tours depart daily at 9 and 11am and 1, 3, and 5pm from the Hilton Marina, 245 Front St. The cost is $12 per person.

OTHER TOURS   Sharon Wells (© **305/294-8380;** www.seekeywest.com) leads a slew of great tours throughout the island, focusing on things as diverse as literature, architecture, and places that have a connection to the island's gay and lesbian culture.

For a lively look at Key West, try a tour of the island's five **most famous pubs.** It starts daily at 2:30pm, lasts 1½ hours, costs $21, and includes four drinks. Another fun tour is the 1-mile, 90-minute **nightly ghost tour,** leaving at 8pm from the Holiday Inn La Concha, 430 Duval St. Cost is $18 for adults and $10 for children under 12. This spooky and interesting tour gives participants insight into many old island legends. The Key West Tour Association offers both tours.

Since the early 1940s, Key West has been a haven for gay luminaries such as Tennessee Williams and Broadway legend Jerry Herman. A new **tour of Gay Key West,** created by the Key West Business Guild, showcases the history, contributions, and landmarks associated with the island's flourishing gay and lesbian culture. Highlights of the tour include Williams's house, the art gallery owned by Key West's first gay mayor, and a variety of guesthouses whose gay owners fueled the island's architectural restoration movement. The 70-minute tours take place every Saturday at 11am, starting and ending at 511 South St. The cost is $20. Call © **305/294-4603** for more information.

For Jimmy Buffett fans, or Parrotheads as they're also known, there's **Trails of Margaritaville** (© **305/292-2040**), an amusing 90-minute walking tour providing fans with an officially sanctioned peek at the stamping grounds of Buffett's carefree days in Key West back in the 1970s. Decked out in full Parrothead regalia—Hawaiian shirts and parrot hats—the informative and often hilarious guides lead you past the hangouts and other high points of Buffett's Key West, spinning yarns about the musician and Key West in general. *Note:* If you're not a huge fan of Jimmy Buffett's, you might want to skip this tour as the price is relatively steep and you probably won't be as interested in these things as die-hard fans are or have as much fun as them, either. The tour departs daily at 4pm from **Captain Tony's Saloon** (428 Greene St.), where Buffett used to hang out and perform, and ends at, you guessed it, Margaritaville Cafe on Duval Street. Tour tickets are $18 for adults, $15 for locals with ID, and $10 for children ages 6 through 10. Bring cash or traveler's checks; no credit cards accepted. Reservations are required at least 2 days in advance.

AFFORDABLE OUTDOOR ACTIVITIES

BEACHES   Unlike the rest of the Keys, you'll actually find a few small beaches here, although they don't compare with the state's wide natural wonders up the coast: A narrow, rocky beach is typical of the Key's beaches. Here are your options: **Smathers Beach,** off South Roosevelt Boulevard west of the airport; **Higgs Beach,** along Atlantic Boulevard between White Street and Reynolds Road; and **Fort Zachary Beach,** located off the western end of Southard Boulevard.

A magnet for partying teenagers, **Smathers Beach** is Key West's largest and most overpopulated beach. Despite the number of rowdy teens, the beach is actually quite clean and it looks lovely since its renovation in the spring of 2000. If you go early enough in the morning, you may notice some people sleeping on the beach from the night before.

Higgs Beach is a favorite among Key West's gay crowds, but what many people don't know is that beneath the sand is an unmarked cemetery of African slaves who died while waiting for freedom. Higgs has a playground and tennis courts and is near the minute Rest Beach, which is actually hidden by the White Street Pier.

Although there is an entrance fee ($3.75 per car, plus more for each passenger), I recommend the beach at **Fort Zachary,** since it also includes a great historical fort, a Civil War museum, and a large picnic area with tables, barbecue grills, bathrooms, and showers. Plus, large trees scattered across 87 acres provide shade for those who are reluctant to bake in the sun. Hurricane George damaged the vulnerable point in 1998, but replanting of native vegetation has made it even better than before.

BICYCLING & MOPEDING   A popular mode of transportation for locals and visitors, bikes and mopeds are available at many rental outlets in the city (p. 190). Escape the hectic downtown scene and explore the island's scenic side streets by heading away from Duval Street toward South Roosevelt Boulevard and the beachside enclaves along the way.

DIVING   One of the area's largest scuba schools, **Dive Key West Inc.,** 3128 N. Roosevelt Blvd. (© **800/426-0707** or 305/296-3823; fax 305/296-0609; www.divekeywest.com), offers instruction on all levels and its dive boats take participants to scuba and snorkel sites on nearby reefs.

Key West Marine Park (© **305/294-3100**), the newest dive park along the island's Atlantic shore, incorporates no-motor "swim only" lanes marked by buoys, providing swimmers and snorkelers a safe way to explore the waters around Key West. The park's boundaries stretch from the foot of Duval Street to Higgs Beach.

Wreck dives and night dives are two of the special offerings of **Lost Reef Adventures,** 261 Margaret St. (© **800/952-2749** or 305/296-9737). Regularly scheduled runs and private charters can be arranged. Phone for departure information.

Also see **Mosquito Coast Outfitters,** under "Kayaking," below.

FISHING   As any angler will tell you, there's no fishing like Keys fishing. Key West has it all: bonefish, tarpon, dolphin, tuna, grouper, cobia, and more. Sharks, too.

> ⌒ *Tips* **Reel Deals**
>
> When looking for the best deals on fishing excursions, know that the bookers from the kiosks in town generally take 20% of a captain's fee in addition to an extra monthly fee. You can usually save yourself money by booking directly with a captain or going straight to one of the docks.

Step aboard a small exposed skiff for an incredibly diverse day of fishing. In the morning, you can head offshore for sailfish or dolphin (the fish, not the mammal), and then by afternoon, get closer to land for a shot at tarpon, permit, grouper, or snapper. Here in Key West, you can probably pick up more cobia—one of the best fighting and eating fish around—than anywhere else in the world. For a real fight, ask your skipper to go for the tarpon—the greatest fighting fish there is, famous for its dramatic "tail walk" on the water after it's hooked. Shark fishing is also popular.

You'll find plenty of competition among the charter-fishing boats in and around Mallory Square. You can negotiate a good deal at **Charter Boat Row,** 1801 N. Roosevelt Ave. (across from the Shell station), home to more than 30 charter-fishing and party boats. Just show up to arrange your outing, or call **Garrison Bite Marina** (© **305/292-8167**) for details.

The advantage of the smaller, more expensive charter boats is that you can call the shots. They'll take you where you want to go, to fish for what you want to catch. These "light tackles" are also easier to maneuver, which means you can go to backcountry spots for tarpon and bonefish, as well as out to the open ocean for tuna and dolphin. You'll really be able to feel the fish, and you'll get some good fights. Larger boats, for up to six or seven people, are cheaper and are best for kingfish, billfish, and sailfish. Consider Capt. Vinnie Argiro's **Heavy Hitters Charters** (© **305/745-6665**) if you want a light-tackle experience. For a larger boat, try Capt. Henry Otto's 44-foot *Sunday,* docked at the Hyatt in Key West (© **305/294-7052**).

The huge commercial party boats are more for sightseeing than serious angling, though you can get lucky and get a few bites at one of the fishing holes. One especially good deal is the *Gulfstream III* (© **305/296-8494**), an all-day charter that goes out daily from 9:30am to 4:30pm. You'll pay $35, plus $3 for a rod and reel. It's $25 for kids under 12. This 65-foot party boat usually has at least 30 other anglers. Bring your own cooler or buy snacks on the boat. Beer and wine are allowed.

Serious anglers should consider the light-tackle boats that leave from **Oceanside Marina** (© **305/294-4676**) on Stock Island, at 5950 Peninsula Ave., 1½ miles off U.S. 1. It's a 20-minute drive from Old Town on the Atlantic side. There are more than 30 light-tackle guides, which range from flatbed, backcountry skiffs to 28-foot open boats. There are also a few larger charters and a party boat that goes to the Dry Tortugas. Call for details.

For a light-tackle outing with a very colorful Key West flair, call **Capt. Bruce Cronin** at © **305/294-4929** or **Capt. Kenny Harris** at © **305/294-8843,** two of the more famous (and pricey) captains working these docks for over 20 years. You'll pay from $650 for a full day, usually about 8am to 4pm, and from $450 for half a day.

GOLF A relative newcomer in terms of local recreation, golf is gaining in popularity here as it is in many visitor destinations. The area's only public golf club is **Key West Golf Club** (© 305/294-5232), an 18-hole course located at the entrance to the island of Key West at MM 4.5 (turn onto College Rd. to the course entrance). Designed by Rees Jones, the course has plenty of mangroves and water hazards on its 6,526 yards. It's open to the public and has a new pro shop. Call ahead for tee-time reservations. Rates are $140 per player, including cart.

KAYAKING **Mosquito Coast Outfitters,** housed in a woodsy wine bar at 1017 Duval St. (© **305/294-7178**), operates a first-rate kayaking and snorkeling tour every day as long as the weather is mild. The tours depart at 9am sharp (and return around 3pm) and cost $55 per person. Included in the price are snacks, soft drinks, and a guided tour of the mangrove-studded islands of Sugar Key or Geiger Key just north of Key West. The tour is primarily for kayaking, but you will have the opportunity to get in the water for snorkeling if you're interested.

SHOPPING

You'll find all kinds of unique gifts and souvenirs in Key West, from coconut postcards to Key lime pies. On Duval Street, T-shirt shops outnumber almost any other business. If you must get a wearable memento, be careful of unscrupulous salespeople. Despite efforts to curtail the practice, many shops have been known to rip off unwitting shoppers. It pays to check the prices and the exchange rate before signing any sales slips. You are entitled to a written estimate of any T-shirt work before you pay for it.

At Mallory Square is the **Clinton Street Market,** an overly air-conditioned mall of kiosks and stalls designed for the many cruise-ship passengers who never venture beyond this supercommercial zone. Amid the dreck are some delicious coffee and candy shops and some high-priced hats and shoes. There's also a free and clean restroom.

Once the main industry of Key West, cigar making is enjoying renewed success at the handful of factories that survived the slow years. Stroll through **"Cigar Alley"** (while on Green St., go 2 blocks west and you'll hit Cigar Alley, also known as Pirate's Alley), where you will find *viejitos* (little old men) rolling fat stogies just as they used to do in their homeland across the Florida Straits. Stop at the **Conch Republic Cigar Factory,** at 512 Greene St. (© **305/295-9036**), for an excellent selection of imported and locally rolled smokes, including the famous El Hemingway. Remember, buying or selling Cuban-made cigars is illegal. Shops advertising "Cuban Cigars" are usually referring to domestic cigars made from tobacco grown from seeds that were brought from Cuba decades ago. To be fair, though, many premium cigars today are grown from Cuban seed tobacco—only it is grown in Latin America and the Caribbean, not Cuba.

If you are looking for local or Caribbean art, you will find nearly a dozen galleries and shops clustered on Duval Street between Catherine and Fleming streets. You'll also find some excellent shops scattered on the side streets. One worth seeking out is the **Haitian Art Co.,** 600 Frances St. (© **305/296-8932**), where you can browse through room upon room of original paintings from well-known and obscure Haitian artists in a range of prices from a few dollars to a few thousand. Also, check out **Cuba, Cuba!** at 814 Duval St. (© **305/295-9442**), where you'll find paintings, sculpture, and photos by Cuban artists as well as books and art from the island.

A favorite stop in the Keys is the deliciously fragrant **Key West Aloe** at 524 Front St., between Simonton and Duval streets (© **305/294-5592**). Since 1971, this shop has been selling a simple line of bath products, including lotions, shampoos, and soothing balms for those who want a reminder of the tropical breezes once they're back home. At the main shop (open until 8pm), you can find great gift baskets, tropical perfumes, and candies and cookies, too. In addition to frangipani, vanilla, and hibiscus scents, sample Key West for Men, a unique and alluringly musky bestseller.

For foodies, the **Key Lime Pie Co.** (© **305/294-6567**) is so popular for its pies, cookies, and pretty much anything you can think of made with Key lime (candles, soaps, lotions) that there are two on the tiny island. One is at 701 Caroline St. and the other is at 424 Greene St. From sweet to spicy, **Peppers of Key West** (© **305/295-9333**) at 602 Greene St. is a hot-sauce-lover's heaven, with hundreds of variations of sauce, from brutally spicy to mild. Grab a seat at the tasting bar and be prepared to let your taste buds sizzle.

Literature and music buffs will appreciate the many bookshops and record stores on the island. **Key West Island Bookstore** (© **305/294-2904**) at 513 Fleming St. carries new, used, and rare books and specializes in fiction by residents of the Keys, including Hemingway, Tennessee Williams, Shel Silverstein, Ann Beattie, Richard Wilbur, and John Hersey. It's open daily from 10am to 9pm. **Flaming Maggie's** (© **305/294-3931**) at 830 Fleming St. carries a wide selection of gay books. It's open Monday through Saturday from 10am to 6pm.

For anything else, from bed linens to candlesticks to clothing, go to downtown's oldest and most renowned department store, **Fast Buck Freddie's,** at 500 Duval St. (© **305/294-2007**). For the same merchandise at reduced prices, try **Half Buck Freddie's** ⋇, 726 Caroline St. (© **305/294-2007**), where you can shop for out-of-season bargains and "rejects" from the main store.

Also check out **KW Light Gallery,** 534 Fleming St. (© **305/294-0566**), for high-quality contemporary photography as well as historic images and other artworks that relate to the Keys or exemplify the concept of light and its varied interpretations. Open Thursday through Tuesday 10am to 6pm (summer hours are 10am–4pm).

ACCOMMODATIONS YOU CAN AFFORD

You'll find a wide variety of places to stay in Key West, from resorts with all the amenities to seaside motels, quaint bed-and-breakfasts, and clothing-optional guesthouses. Unless you're in town during Key West's most popular holidays—Fantasy Fest (around Halloween), where Mardi Gras meets South Florida for the NC-17 set, Hemingway Days (in July), where Papa is seemingly and eerily alive and well, and Christmas and New Year's—or for a big fishing tournament (many are held from Oct–Dec) or boat-racing tourney, you can almost always find a place to stay at the last minute. However, you may want to book early, especially in winter, when prime properties fill up and many require 2- or 3-night minimum stays. Prices at these times are also extremely high. Finding a decent room for under $100 a night is a real trick.

Another suggestion, and my recommendation, is to call **Vacation Key West** (© **800/595-5397** or 305/295-9500; www.vacationkw.com), which is a wholesaler that offers discounts of 20% to 30% and is skilled at finding last-minute deals. They represent mostly larger hotels and motels but can also place visitors in guesthouses. The phones are answered weekdays from 9am to 6pm and Saturday from 11am to 2pm. The **Key West Innkeepers Association,** P.O. Box

6172, Key West, FL 33041 (© **800/492-1911** or 305/292-3600), can also help find lodging in any price range from its dozens of members and affiliates.

Gay travelers will want to call the **Key West Business Guild** (© **305/294-4603**), which represents more than 50 guesthouses and B&Bs in town, as well as many other gay-owned businesses. Be advised that most gay guesthouses have a clothing-optional policy. One of the most elegant and popular ones is **Big Ruby's** (© **800/477-7829** or 305/296-2323; rates start at $145 for a double during peak season and $85 during the off season) at 409 Applerouth Lane (a little alley just off Duval St.). A low cluster of buildings surrounds a lushly landscaped courtyard where a hearty breakfast is served each morning and wine is poured at dusk. The mostly male guests hang out by a good-size pool, tanning in the buff. Also popular is **Oasis** at 823 Fleming St. (© **305/296-2131;** rates are $169–$229 in winter and $109–$169 in summer), which is superclean and friendly, with a central location and a 14-seat hot tub.

Another luxurious property is **The Florida Key Guesthouse** at 412 Frances St. (© **305/296-4719;** rates are $225 in season and $125 during the off season), which is more romantic and traditionally decorated and welcomes many lesbian travelers as well. *Out and About* gave it a five-star rating. For women only, **Pearl's Rainbow,** 525 United St. (© **800/74-WOMYN** or 305/292-1450), is a large, fairly well-maintained guesthouse with lots of privacy and amenities, including two pools and two hot tubs. Rates in season range from $109 to $229.

Ambrosia Key West ★★ *Finds* Although Key West is a tiny island, it's amazing to discover that even after visiting here countless times a year, every time I go back, I discover yet another hidden treasure. Ambrosia is one of them, a private compound situated on 2 acres of lush landscaping just a block away from Duval Street. Three tropical lagoon-style pools, suites, town houses, and a stand-alone cottage are all spread out on the grounds. Town houses have full living rooms, complete kitchens, and spiral staircases leading to master suites with vaulted ceilings and private decks. The cottage, overlooking a dip pool, is a perfect family retreat, featuring two bedrooms, two bathrooms, a living room, and a full kitchen. All rooms and suites feature private entrances, most with French doors opening up onto a variety of intimate outdoor spaces, including private verandas, patios, and gardens with sculptures, fountains, and pools. Fantastic service bolstered by the philosophy that it's better to have high occupancy than high rates explains why Ambrosia has a 90% year-round occupancy—a record in seasonal Key West.

622 Fleming St., Key West, FL 33040. © **800/535-9838** or 305/296-9838. Fax 305/296-2425. www.ambrosia keywest.com. 19 units. Winter $169–$499; off season $120–$289. Rates include breakfast. AE, DISC, MC, V. Off- and on-street parking. Pets accepted. **Amenities:** 3 outdoor heated pools; hot tub. *In room:* A/C, TV, kitchens (in some), fridge, coffeemaker, hair dryer, iron, CD player.

Angelina Guest House ★★ This former bordello and gambling hall turned youth hostel–type guesthouse is about the cheapest in town and conveniently located near a hot, hippie restaurant called Blue Heaven (see "Great Deals on Dining," below), one of the best restaurants in town. Though the neighborhood is definitely urban, it is generally safe and is full of character. The rooms are all furnished differently in a modest style, recently upgraded with new decor. Only three rooms do not have private bathrooms. Two rooms have full kitchens, and one has a microwave and small refrigerator; there are no televisions or telephones. A gorgeous lagoon-style heated pool with waterfall and tropical landscaping was an excellent addition. Even better are the poolside hammocks—get out there early, they go quickly! Even though the Angelina is sparse (perfect for the bohemian types who don't mind a little grit), it's a great place to crash if you are on the cheap.

302 Angela St. (at the corner of Thomas St.), Key West, FL 33040. © **888/303-4480** or 305/294-4480. Fax 305/272-0681. www.angelinaguesthouse.com. 14 units. Winter $79–$149 double; off season $59–$99 double. Rates include continental breakfast. DISC, MC, V. **Amenities:** Outdoor heated pool; concierge. *In room:* A/C, hair dryer, iron, no phone.

Casa Alante Guest Cottages ★★ *(Finds* This place is a hidden treasure situated on an acre of property amidst gardens, an orchid terrace, and mahogany trees. A bed-and-breakfast owned by a former Austrian baroness, Casa Alante features 10 charming units with names like Manatee, Dolphin, and Hemingway Cat, each with its own mailbox shaped in the form of whatever the room is named after. All units have full kitchens and private terraces, and, best of all, all rooms have fill-in-the-blank menus on which guests fill out their choices for breakfast, which is decorated on trays with tropical flowers and delivered to your porch front. Each unit is unique, ranging from large efficiencies and one-bedroom suites to a fabulous loft apartment. In addition to the lush gardens and small pool, there are five chickens that call Casa Alante home, so prepare to hear the clucking at an early-ish hour.

1435 S. Roosevelt Blvd., Key West, FL 33040. © **800/688-3942** or 305/293-0702. Fax 305/292-8699. www. casaalante.com. 10 units. Winter $125–$260; off season $80–$195. Rates include breakfast. AE, DC, DISC, MC, V. Private parking. Pets accepted. **Amenities:** Outdoor heated pool; free bikes; laundry facilities. *In room:* A/C, TV, kitchen, fridge, coffeemaker, hair dryer, CD player.

Chelsea House ★ Chelsea House caters to a mixed gay/straight clientele and displays its liberal philosophy most prominently on the clothing-optional sun deck. One of only a few guesthouses in Key West that offer TVs, VCRs, private bathrooms, and kitchenettes in each guest room, Chelsea House has a large number of repeat visitors. The apartments come with full kitchens and separate living areas, as well as palm-shaded balconies in back. The bathrooms and closets could be bigger, but both are adequate and serviceable. Breakfast is served outside by the pretty pool.

709 Truman Ave., Key West, FL 33040. © **800/845-8859** or 305/296-2211. Fax 305/296-4822. www.chelsea housekw.com. 20 units. Winter $135–$260 double; off season $79–$135 double. Rates include breakfast. AE, DC, DISC, MC, V. Private parking. Pets accepted, $15 per night. Children 17 and under not accepted. **Amenities:** Outdoor pool; access to nearby health club; bike rental; concierge. *In room:* A/C, TV/VCR, fax, kitchenette, fridge, hair dryer, iron, safe.

The Grand ★★ *(Finds* Don't expect cabbies or locals to know about this well-kept secret, located in a modest residential section of Old Town, about 5 blocks from Duval Street. It's got almost everything you could want, including a very moderate price tag. Proprietor Elizabeth Rose goes out of her way to provide any and all services for her appreciative guests. All rooms have private bathrooms, air-conditioning, and private entrances. Room no. 2 on the backside of the house is the best deal; it's small and there is no closet or dresser, just hooks on the walls, but it has a porch and the most privacy. Suites are a real steal, too. The large two-room units come with a complete kitchen. This place is undoubtedly the best bargain in town.

1116 Grinnell St. (between Virginia and Catherine sts.), Key West, FL 33040. © **888/947-2630** or 305/ 294-0590. Fax 305/294-0477. www.thegrandguesthouse.com. 11 units. Winter $98–$138 double, $148–$188 suite; off season $78–$98 double, $108–$118 suite. Rates include continental breakfast. AE, DISC, MC, V. **Amenities:** Bike/scooter rental; concierge. *In room:* A/C, TV, fridge.

Key West International Hostel & Seashell Motel This well-run, affordable hostel is a 3-minute walk to the beach and to Old Town. Very busy with European backpackers, it's a great place to meet people. The dorm rooms are dark, grimy, and sparse, but livable if you're desperate for a cheap room. The higher-priced motel rooms are a good deal, especially those equipped with full kitchens. Amenities include a pool table under a Tiki roof, and bicycle rentals for $8 per day. There's also cheap food available for breakfast, lunch, and dinner, as well as discounted prices for snorkeling, diving, and sunset cruises.

718 South St., Key West, FL 33040. ✆ **800/51-HOSTEL** or 305/296-5719. Fax 305/296-0672. www.keywest hostel.com. 96 units, 10 private rooms, 1 2-bedroom suite with Jacuzzi. Year-round members $20, nonmembers $23. Motel units $75–$105 in season; $55–$85 off-season. MC, V. Free parking. **Amenities:** Bike rental; kitchen. *In room:* A/C, TV, fridge, coffeemaker, hair dryer. Dorm rooms have only A/C.

Southernmost Point Guest House ★★ *Finds* *Kids* One of the few inns that actually welcome children and pets, this romantic and historic guesthouse is a real find. The antiseptically clean rooms are not as fancy as the house's ornate 1885 exterior, but each is unique and includes some combination of basic beds and couches and a hodgepodge of furnishings, including futon couches and high-back wicker chairs. Room no. 5 is best; situated upstairs, it has a private porch, an ocean view, and windows that let in lots of light. Every room has fresh flowers, a refrigerator, wine, and a full decanter of sherry. Mona Santiago, the hotel's kind, laid-back owner, provides chairs and towels that can be brought to the beach, which is just a block away. Guests can help themselves to free wine as they soak in the 14-seat hot tub. Kids will enjoy the backyard swings and the pet rabbits.

1327 Duval St., Key West, FL 33040. ✆ **305/294-0715.** Fax 305/296-0641. www.southernmostpoint.com. 6 units. Winter $115–$175 double, $235–$265 suite; off season $79–$110 double, $155–$165 suite. Rates include breakfast. AE, MC, V. Pets accepted, $5 in summer, $10 in winter. **Amenities:** Garden pool; hot tub; laundry facilities; barbecue grills. *In room:* A/C, TV/VCR, fridge, coffeemaker, hair dryer, iron.

Westwinds Inn ★ A close second to staying in your own private, 19th-century clapboard, tin-roofed house is this tranquil inn located just 4 blocks from Duval Street in the historic Seaport district. Lush landscaping—banana stalks, mango, and Spanish Lime trees—keeps the inn extremely private and secluded, and at times, you do feel as if you're alone. And that's not a scary thing; it's absolutely fabulous. Two pools, one heated in the winter, are offset by alcoves, fountains, and the extremely well-maintained whitewashed inn, which is actually composed of five separate houses. Rooms are comfortable, with wicker furnishings and fans, and with private bathrooms. All rooms are nonsmoking.

914 Eaton St., Key West, FL 33040. ✆ **800/788-4150** or 305/296-4440. Fax 305/293-0931. www.westwinds keywest.com. 19 units. Winter $135–$175 double, $195 suite; off season $80–$145 double, $130–$165 suite. Rates include continental breakfast. DISC, MC, V. **Amenities:** 2 pools (1 heated); bike rental; self-service laundry. *In room:* A/C (some rooms have TVs and kitchenettes).

WORTH A SPLURGE

The Gardens Hotel ★★★ *Finds* At last, the true garden of Eden has been located and it's on Angela Street in Key West. Once a private residence, The Gardens Hotel (whose main house is listed in the National Register of Historic Places) is hidden amidst the exotic Peggy Mills tropical botanical gardens. What lies behind the gardens is a luxurious, Bahamian-style hideaway featuring 17 luxuriously appointed accommodations including two suites; two historic rooms in the main house; 12 garden and courtyard rooms in the backyard, as carriage house-type rooms, not attached to the house; and one übersecluded cottage. I stayed in one of the courtyard rooms and didn't want to leave, even though the hotel is within walking distance of frenetic Duval Street. A gorgeous free-form swimming pool is right in the middle of the courtyard, and a Tiki bar is right there to serve up whatever libation you desire. The Jacuzzi is hidden behind beautiful landscaping. The rooms are resplendent, with Aveda products, Jacuzzi bathtubs, hardwood floors, brass and iron beds, marble bathrooms, and a sense of serenity that words can't describe. Winding brick pathways leading to secluded seating areas in the private gardens make for an idyllic romantic get-away that's the quintessence of paradise.

526 Angela St., Key West, FL 33040. (℃ **800/526-2664** or 305/294-2661. Fax 305/292-1007. 17 units. Winter $685 master suite, $265 historic rooms, $575 carriage house suite, $315 garden rooms, $355 courtyard rooms, $465 cottage; off season $485–$595 master suite, $155–$215 historic rooms, $385–$495 carriage house suite, $175–$245 garden rooms, $215–$285 courtyard rooms, $295–$395 cottage. Rates include continental breakfast. AE, DC, MC, V. **Amenities:** Bar, pool. *In room:* A/C, TV, hair dryer, safe.

GREAT DEALS ON DINING

With its share of the usual drive-through fast-food franchises (mostly up on Roosevelt Blvd.) and Duval Street succumbing to the lure of a Hard Rock Cafe, you might be surprised to learn that, over the years, an upscale and high-quality dining scene has begun to thrive in Key West. Wander Old Town or the newly spruced-up Bahama Village and browse menus after you have exhausted my list of picks below.

If you don't feel like venturing out, call **We Deliver** (℃ **305/293-0078**), a service that will bring you anything you want from any of the area's restaurants or stores for a small fee ($3–$6). We Deliver operates between 3 and 11pm. If you are staying in a condominium or efficiency, you may want to stock your refrigerator with groceries, beer, wine, and snacks from the area's oldest grocer, **Fausto's Food Palace.** Open since 1926, there are now two locations: 1105 White St. and 522 Fleming St. The Fleming Street location will deliver (℃ **305/ 294-5221** or 305/296-5663). Fausto's has a $25 delivery minimum.

Bahama Mama's Kitchen ✿ BAHAMIAN   Sit outside under an umbrella and enjoy the authentic Bahamian dishes made from recipes that have been handed down through owner Corey's family for the past 150 years. Prepared fresh daily, all dishes are created with their special "Bahamian" seasonings. Try the coconut shrimp butterflied, soaked in coconut oil, battered with egg, and then rolled in fresh shredded coconut and deep-fried. The fresh catch of the day comes blackened, broiled, or fried and is served with island plantains, shrimp hash cakes, and crab rice. The service is good and the staff is friendly.

In the Bahama Village Market, 324 Petronia St. (℃ 305/294-3355. Appetizers $4–$7; main courses $9–$13. MC, V. Daily 11am–10pm.

Banana Café ✿✿✿ *Finds* FRENCH   This is an upscale local eatery that's been discovered by savvy visitors on the less-congested end of Duval Street and kept its loyal clientele with affordable prices and delightful, light preparations. Banana Café's crepes are legendary on the island for breakfast or lunch, and fresh quality ingredients and a French-themed menu bring daytime diners back for the casual, classy, tropical-influenced dinner menu. Every Thursday night, there's live jazz.

1211 Duval St. (℃ **305/294-7227.** Main courses $4.80–$23; breakfast and lunch $2–$8.50. AE, DC, MC, V. Daily 8am–11pm.

Blue Heaven ★★ (Finds) SEAFOOD/AMERICAN/NATURAL   This little hippie-run gallery and restaurant has become the place to be in Key West—and with good reason. Be prepared to wait in line. The food here is some of the best in town, especially for breakfast. You can enjoy homemade granola, huge tropical-fruit pancakes, and seafood Benedict. Dinners are just as good and run the gamut from fresh-caught fish dishes to Jamaican-style jerk chicken, curried soups, and vegetarian stews. But if you're a neat freak, don't bother. Some people are put off by the dirt floors and roaming cats and birds, but frankly, it adds to the charm.

305 Petronia St. (✆) 305/296-8666. Main courses $10–$30; lunch $6–$14; breakfast $5–$11. DISC, MC, V. Daily 8–11:30am, noon–3pm, and 6–10:30pm; Sun brunch 8am–1pm. Closed mid-Sept to early Oct.

Mangia, Mangia ★ (Value) ITALIAN/AMERICAN[Locals appreciate that they can get good, inexpensive food here in a town filled with tourist traps. Off the beaten track, in a little corner storefront, this great Chicago-style pasta place serves some of the best Italian food in the Keys. The family-run restaurant offers superb homemade pastas of every description, including one of the tastiest marinaras around. The simple grilled chicken breast brushed with olive oil and sprinkled with pepper is another good choice, as is the Picadillo Pasta—black-bean pasta shells smothered in a Cuban-inspired sauce with meat, tomatoes, olives, capers, and spices.

900 Southard St. (at Margaret St.). (✆) 305/294-2469. Reservations not accepted. Main courses $9–$15. AE, MC, V. Daily 5:30–10pm.

PT's Late Night ★ (Finds) AMERICAN   This place is worth knowing about not only because it's one of the only places in town serving food past 10pm, but also because it happens to serve good food at extremely reasonable prices. PT's is more like a sports bar than a restaurant, and service can be a bit slow and brusque, but you'll enjoy their heaping plates of nachos, sizzling fajitas served with all the trimmings, and superfresh salads—so big they can be a meal in themselves.

920 Caroline St. (at the corner of Margaret St.). (✆) 305/296-4245. Main courses $6.95–$15. DISC, MC, V. Daily 11am–4am.

WORTH A SPLURGE

Cafe des Artistes ★★★ FRENCH   Open for nearly 2 decades, the Cafe des Artistes' impressive longevity is the result of its winning combination of food and atmosphere. The fact that it was once part of a hotel built in 1935 by Al Capone's bookkeeper adds to its allure, but it's really the food that people come for. Traditional French meals benefit from a subtle tropical twist. Start with the duck-liver pâté, made with fresh truffles and old cognac, or Maryland crab meat served with an artichoke heart and herbed-tomato confit. Ask about the escargot du jour. Nouvelle and traditional French entrees include lobster flambé with mango and basil, and wine-basted lamb chops rubbed with rosemary and ginger.

1007 Simonton St. (near Truman Ave.). (✆) 305/294-7100. Reservations recommended. Main courses $25–$38. AE, MC, V. Daily 6–11pm.

Café Marquesa ★★★ CONTEMPORARY AMERICAN   If you're looking for fabulous dining (and service) in Key West, and want to splurge, financially and gastronomically, this is the place. The intimate, 50-seat restaurant is something to look at, but it's really the food that you'll want to admire. Specialties include peppercorn-dusted, seared yellowfin tuna with saffron risotto; grilled Florida lobster tail and diver sea scallops with Thai basil sauce, black Thai rice, and Asian vegetables; and an almost perfect feta and pine nut–crusted rack of lamb with rosemary demi-glace, creamy polenta, and eggplant caponata.

In the Marquesa Hotel, 600 Fleming St. ℂ 305/292-1919. Reservations highly recommended. Main courses $20–$36. AE, DC, MC, V. Daily 7–11pm summer; 6–11pm winter. No smoking.

Louie's Backyard ★★ CARIBBEAN   Nestled amid blooming bougainvillea on a lush slice of the Gulf, Louie's remains one of the most romantic restaurants on earth. Famed chef Norman Van Aiken of Norman's in Miami brought his talents farther south and started what has become one of the finest dining spots in the Keys. As a result, this is one of the hardest places to score a reservation: Either call way in advance or hope that your hotel concierge has some pull. After dinner, sit at the dockside bar and watch the waves crash, almost touching your feet, while enjoying a cocktail at sunset. You can't go wrong with the fresh catch of the day, or any seafood dish, for that matter. The weekend brunches are also great. Even if you can't stay for dinner, go for lunch; this is one dining experience you won't want to miss.

700 Waddell Ave. ℂ 305/294-1061. Reservations highly recommended. Main courses $25–$30; lunch $8–$15. AE, DC, MC, V. Daily 11:30am–3pm and 6–10:30pm.

KEY WEST AFTER DARK

Duval Street is the Bourbon Street of Florida. Amid the T-shirt shops and clothing boutiques, you'll find bar after bar serving neon-colored frozen drinks to revelers who bounce from one to the next from noon till dawn. Bands and crowds vary from night to night and season to season. Your best bet is to start at Truman Avenue and head up Duval to check them out for yourself. Cover charges are rare, except in gay clubs (see "The Gay Scene," below), so stop into a dozen and see which you like. For the most part, Key West is a late-night town, and bars and clubs don't close until around 3 or 4am.

Captain Tony's Saloon   Just around the corner from Duval's beaten path, this smoky old wooden bar is about as authentic as you'll find. It comes complete with old-time regulars who remember the island before cruise ships docked here; they say Hemingway drank, caroused, and even wrote here. The owner, Capt. Tony Tarracino, a former controversial Key West mayor—"immortalized" in Jimmy Buffett's "Last Mango in Paradise"—has recently capitalized on the success of this once-quaint tavern by franchising the place. 428 Greene St. ℂ 305/294-1838.

Sloppy Joe's   You'll have to stop in here just to say you did. Scholars and drunks debate whether this is the same Sloppy Joe's that Hemingway wrote about, but there's no argument that this classic bar's early-20th-century wooden ceiling and cracked-tile floors are Key West originals. There's live music nightly as well as a cigar room and martini bar. 201 Duval St. ℂ 305/294-5717, ext. 10. www.sloppyjoes.com.

THE GAY SCENE

Key West's bohemian live-and-let-live atmosphere extends to its thriving and quirky gay community. Since Tennessee Williams and before, Key West has provided the perfect backdrop to a gay scene unlike that of many large urban areas. Seamlessly blended with the prevailing culture, there is no "gay ghetto" in Key West, where alternative lifestyles are embraced and even celebrated.

Although restaurants and businesses welcome visitors without discrimination, nightlife *is* inevitably nightlife. In Key West, the best music and dancing can be found at the predominantly gay clubs. While many of the area's other hot spots are geared toward tourists who like to imbibe, the gay clubs are for those who want to rave, gay or not. Covers vary, but are rarely more than $10.

Two adjacent popular late-night spots are the **801 Bourbon Bar/One Saloon** (801 Duval St. and 514 Petronia St.; *C* **305/294-9349** for both), featuring great drag and lots more disco. A mostly male clientele frequents this hot spot from 9pm until 4am. Another Duval Street favorite is **Aqua,** at 711 Duval St. (*C* **305/292-8500**), where you might catch drag queens belting out torch songs or judges voting on the best package in the wet jockey shorts contest.

Sunday nights are fun at two local spots. **Tea by the Sea,** on the pier at the Atlantic Shores Motel (510 South St.; *C* **800/520-3559**), attracts a faithful following of regulars and visitors alike. The clothing-optional pool is always an attraction. Show up after 7:30pm. Better known around town as La-Te-Da, **La Terraza de Martí,** the former Key West home of Cuban exile José Martí, at 1125 Duval St. (*C* **305/296-6706**), is a great spot to gather poolside for the best martini in town—but don't bother with the food. Just upstairs from there is **The Crystal Room** (*C* **305/296-6706**), with a high-caliber cabaret performance featuring the popular Randy Roberts in the winter.

6

The Everglades & Biscayne National Park

President Harry S Truman once declared the Everglades "an irreplaceable primitive area." And while those words don't exactly do the Everglades and its surrounding Biscayne National Park justice, he clarified, saying, "Here are no lofty peaks seeking the sky, no mighty glaciers or rushing streams wearing away the uplifted land. Here is land, tranquil in its quiet beauty, serving not as the source of water, but as the last receiver of it. To its natural abundance we owe the spectacular plant and animal life that distinguishes this place from all others in our country."

There's no better reality show than the one that exists in the Everglades, really. Up close and personal views of alligators, crocodiles, and bona fide wildlife—not the kind you'd find on, say, South Beach, after midnight—make for a very interesting, photo opportunistic experience even the Crocodile Hunter would find hard to mimic on his show.

Tourists who come to South Florida really shouldn't leave the area without taking time to see some of the wild plant and animal life in the swampy Everglades and the underwater treasures of Biscayne National Park.

1 A Glimpse of Everglades National Park ★★

35 miles SW of Miami

Before going, my conception of the Everglades was that it was one big swamp swarming with ominous creatures. For someone who'd rather endure an endless series of root canals than audition for a role on *Survivor* (the closest I'd ever been to nature was sleep-away camp), the Everglades may as well have been the *Never*glades. That is, until I finally decided to venture there. To my surprise, and contrary to popular belief, the Everglades isn't really a swamp at all, but one of the country's most fascinating natural resources.

For first-timers or those with dubious athletic skills, the best way to see the 'glades is probably via airboats, which actually aren't allowed in the park proper, but cut through the saw grass on the park's outskirts, taking you past countless birds, alligators, crocodiles, deer, and raccoons. A walk on one of the park's many trails will provide you with a different vantage point: up-close interaction with an assortment of tame wildlife. But the absolute best way to see the 'glades is via canoe, where you can get incredibly close to nature. Whichever method you choose, I guarantee you will marvel at the sheer beauty of the Everglades. Despite the multitude of mosquito bites (the bugs seem to be immune to repellent—wear long pants and cover your arms, if possible), an Everglades experience will definitely contribute to a newfound appreciation for Florida's natural (and beautiful) wonderland.

Everglades National Park

Tiger Key
Picnic Key

TEN THOUSAND
ISLANDS

Rabbit Key

Pavilion Key

Mormon Key

New Turkey Key &
Turkey Key

Ochopee
Everglades City
Gulf Coast Visitor Center
Chokoloskee

Sunday Bay Chickee

Lopez
River

The Watson
Place

Darwins Place

Plate Creek
Bay Chickee

Lostmans Five Bay

29
41 Tamiami Trail

Monroe
Station

Big Cypress
National Preserve
Visitor Center

BIG CYPRESS
NATIONAL
PRESERVE

Sweetwater Bay Chickee

94

Willy Willy

EVERGLADES

South Lostmans

Rogers River
Bay Chickee

Highland
Beach

Wilderness Waterway

Camp
Lonesome

Harney River Chickee

Graveyard Creek

Shark River
Chickee

Canepatch

Watson
River
Chickee

North
River
Chickee

Oyster Bay
Chickee

Joe River
Chickee

Roberts River
Chickee

Lane Bay
Chickee

Wilderness Waterway

CAPE SABLE

South Joe River Chickee

Gulf of
Mexico

Mrazek Pond

Middle Cape

East Cape

Clubhouse
Beach

Eco Pond
Flamingo

Flamingo
Visitor Center

FLORIDA

Map Area

Miami

0   10 mi
0   10 km

N

🏕 Campground

208

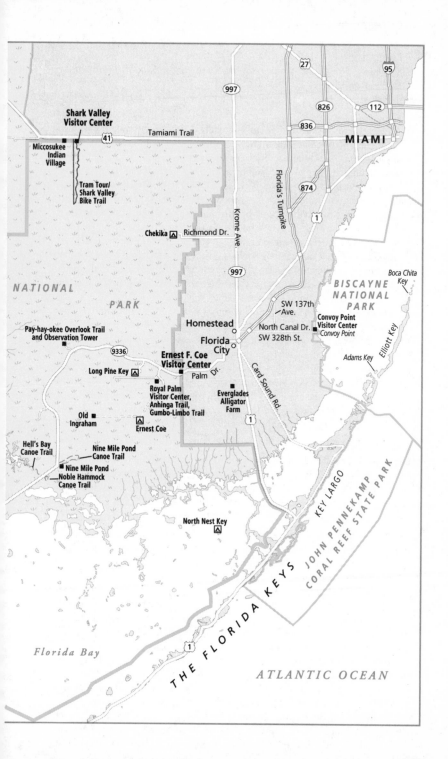

Shark Valley
Visitor Center

Miccosukee
Indian
Village

41 Tamiami Trail

997

27

826 112

836

MIAMI

Tram Tour/
Shark Valley
Bike Trail

Florida's Turnpike

874

1

Chekika Richmond Dr.

Krome Ave.

997

BISCAYNE
NATIONAL
PARK

Boca Chita
Key

NATIONAL

PARK

Pay-hay-okee Overlook Trail
and Observation Tower

9336

Long Pine Key

Ernest F. Coe
Visitor Center

Palm Dr.

SW 137th
Ave.

North Canal Dr.
SW 328th St.

Homestead

Florida
City

Convoy Point
Visitor Center
Convoy Point

Elliott Key

Adams Key

Royal Palm
Visitor Center,
Anhinga Trail,
Gumbo-Limbo Trail

Everglades
Alligator
Farm

Card Sound Rd.

Old
Ingraham

Ernest Coe

1

Hell's Bay
Canoe Trail

Nine Mile Pond
Canoe Trail

Nine Mile Pond
Noble Hammock
Canoe Trail

North Nest Key

KEY LARGO

JOHN PENNEKAMP
CORAL REEF STATE PARK

THE FLORIDA KEYS

Florida Bay

1

ATLANTIC OCEAN

Lazy River

It takes a month for 1 gallon of water to move through Everglades National Park.

This vast and unusual ecosystem is actually a shallow, 40-mile-wide, slow-moving river. Rarely more than knee-deep, the water is the lifeblood of this wilderness, and the subtle shifts in water level dictate the life cycle of the native plants and animals. In 1947, 1.5 million acres—less than 20% of the Everglades' wilderness—were established as Everglades National Park. At that time, few lawmakers understood how neighboring ecosystems relate to each other. Consequently, the park is heavily affected by surrounding territories and is at the butt end of every environmental insult that occurs upstream in Miami.

While there has been a marked decrease in the indigenous wildlife here, Everglades National Park nevertheless remains one of the few places where you can see dozens of endangered species in their natural habitat, including the swallowtail butterfly, American crocodile, leatherback turtle, southern bald eagle, West Indian manatee, and Florida panther.

Take your time on the trails, and a hypnotic beauty begins to unfold. Follow the rustling of a bush, and you might see a small green tree frog or tiny brown anole lizard, with its bright-red-spotted throat. Crane your neck to see around a bend and discover a delicate, brightly painted mule-ear orchid.

The slow and subtle splendor of this exotic land may not be immediately appealing to kids raised on video games and rapid-fire commercials, but they'll certainly remember the experience and thank you for it later. Meanwhile, you'll find plenty of dramatic fun around the park, such as airboat rides, alligator wrestling, and biking, to keep the kids satisfied for at least a day.

JUST THE FACTS

GETTING THERE & ACCESS POINTS   Although the Everglades may seem overwhelmingly large and unapproachable, it's easy to get to the park's two main areas—the northern section, which is accessible via Shark Valley and Everglades City, or the southern section, accessible through the Ernest F. Coe Visitor Center, near Homestead and Florida City.

Northern Entrances   A popular day trip for Miamians, **Shark Valley,** a 15-mile paved loop road, with an observation tower in the middle of the loop, overlooking the pulsating heart of the Everglades, is the fastest way to explore the Everglades. Just 25 miles west of the Florida Turnpike, Shark Valley is best reached via the Tamiami Trail, South Florida's pre-turnpike, two-lane road, which cuts across the southern part of the state along the park's northern border. Roadside attractions (boat rides and alligator farms, for example) along the Trail are operated by the Miccosukee Indian Village and are fun and worth a quick stop. An excellent tram tour (leaving from the Shark Valley Visitor Center) goes deep into the park along a trail that's also terrific for biking. This is also the best way to reach the park's only accommodation (and full-service outfitters), the Flamingo Lodge. Shark Valley is about an hour's drive from Miami.

A little less than 10 miles west along the Tamiami Trail from Shark Valley, you'll discover the **Big Cypress National Preserve,** in which stretches of vibrant green cypress and pine trees make for a fabulous Kodak moment. If you pick up State Road 29 and head south from the Tamiami Trail, you'll hit a modified version of civilization in the form of Everglades City (where the Everglades meet the Gulf of Mexico) and see another entrance to the park and the **Gulf Coast Visitor Center.** From Miami to Shark Valley: Go west on I-395 to State Road 821 south (the Florida Tpk.). Take the U.S. 41/SW 8th Street (Tamiami Trail) exit. The Shark Valley entrance is just 25 miles west. To get to Everglades City, continue west on the Tamiami Trail and head south on State Road 29.

Cheap Thrills: What to See & Do for Free (or Almost) in the Everglades & Biscayne National Park

If you're not in the mood to drop cash on tours and boat rides, the best thing to do when it comes to the Everglades is to get in your car and drive. You will likely see wildlife crossing and numerous Kodak moments without enduring the banter of frustrated comedians-slash-tourguides.

- **Tour Shark Valley.** Shark Valley Visitors Center, Everglades National Park, 40001 S.R. 9336 (© **305/221-8776**). Shark Valley is considered to be one of the last places that mimic the natural system of the Everglades. Take a tour of the park (anytime during the hours of 8:30am to 6pm) by walking, biking, or taking a tram through the swamp to see alligators, wading birds, and lots of other animals. Admission is $10 per car.

- **Take Offs and Landings.** If you've got a good eye, birdwatching is an excellent and free diversion in the 'Glades, since more than 350 species of birds make their homes here. Tropical birds from the Caribbean and temperate species from North America can be found, along with exotics that have blown in from more distant regions. Eco and Mrazek ponds, located near Flamingo, are two of the best places for birding, especially in early morning or late afternoon in the dry winter months. Pick up a free birding checklist from a visitor center so you can keep track of your fair feathered friends.

- **Gator Wrestling.** You get a lot of bang for your buck at **Gator Park,** 24050 SW 8th St. (© **305/559-2255**; www.gatorpark.com), which, despite its touristy name, happens to be one of the most informative and entertaining attractions around, not to mention one of the only airboat tour operators that give out free earplugs. After the boat ride, there's a free interactive wildlife show that features alligator wrestling and several other frightening acts involving scorpions. Take note of the gorgeous peacocks that live in the trees here. Admission for the boat ride and show is $19.25, $10.70 for children 6 through 11—prices are cheaper if you purchase tickets online. Kids under 6 ride free. Airboats depart every 20 minutes, so there's no worrying about missing the boat. Open daily from 9am to 7pm.

- **Get Acquainted. Ernest F. Coe Visitor Center,** located at the Park Headquarters' entrance, west of Homestead and Florida City, features state-of-the-art educational displays, films, and interactive exhibits, all free once you pay the park's entrance fee of $10 per vehicle.

Everglades City is approximately a 2½-hour drive from Miami, but because it is scenic, it may take longer if you stop or slow down to view your surroundings.

Southern Entrance—via Homestead & Florida City   If you're in a rush to hit the 'glades and don't care about the scenic route, this is your best bet. Just southeast of Homestead and Florida City, off of State Road 9336, the southern access (and main entrance) to the park will bring you directly to the Ernest F. Coe Visitor Center. Right inside the park, 4 miles beyond the Ernest F. Coe Visitor Center, is the Royal Palm Visitor Center, which is the starting point for the two most popular walking trails—Gumbo Limbo and Anhinga, on which you will witness a plethora of birds and wildlife roaming freely, unperturbed by their human voyeurs. If you go 13 miles west of the Ernest F. Coe Visitor Center, you will hit the Pa-hay-okee Overlook Trail, which is worth a trek across the boardwalk to reach the observation tower, over which vultures and hawks hover protectively amidst a resplendent, picturesque, bird's-eye view of the Everglades. From Miami to the southern entrance: Go west on I-395 to State Road 821 south (Florida Tpk.). The Turnpike will end in Florida City. Take your first right turn through the center of town (you can't miss it) and follow the signs to the park entrance on State Road 9336. The Ernest F. Coe Visitor Center is about 1½ hours from Miami.

VISITOR CENTERS & INFORMATION   General inquiries and specific questions should be directed to **Everglades National Park Headquarters,** 40001 S.R. 9336, Homestead, FL 33034 (© **305/242-7700**). Ask for a copy of *Parks and Preserves,* a free newspaper that's filled with up-to-date information about goings-on in the Everglades. Headquarters is staffed by helpful phone operators daily from 8:30am to 4:30pm. You can also try www.nps.gov/ever/visit/index.htm.

Note that all hours listed are for the high season, generally November through May. During the slow summer months, many offices and outfitters keep abbreviated hours. Always call ahead to confirm hours of operation.

Thirty-eight miles from the main entrance, at the park's southern access, is the **Flamingo Visitor Center,** which offers natural-history exhibits and information on Flamingo's visitor services.

Especially since its recent expansion, the **Ernest F. Coe Visitor Center,** located at the Park Headquarters' entrance, west of Homestead and Florida City, is the best place for gathering information for your trip. In addition to information on tours and boat rentals, and free brochures outlining trails, wildlife, and activities, you will also find state-of-the-art educational displays, films, and interactive exhibits. A gift shop sells postcards, film, unusual gift items, an impressive selection of books about the Everglades, and a supply of your most important gear: insect repellent. The shop is open from 8am to 5pm daily.

The **Royal Palm Visitor Center,** a small nature museum located 3 miles past the park's main entrance, is a smaller information center. The museum is not great (there are displays with recorded messages interpreting the park's ecosystem), but the center is the departure point for the popular Anhinga and Gumbo Limbo Trails. Open daily from 8am to 4pm.

Knowledgeable rangers, who provide brochures and personal insight into the park's activities, also staff the **Shark Valley Visitor Center,** at the park's northern entrance, and the **Flamingo Visitor Center.** Both are open daily from 8:30am to 5pm.

ENTRANCE FEES, PERMITS & REGULATIONS   Permits and passes can be purchased only at the main park, Chekika, or Shark Valley entrance station.

Even if you are just visiting the park for an afternoon, you'll need to buy a 7-day permit, which costs $10 per vehicle. Pedestrians and cyclists are charged $5 each.

An Everglades Park Pass, valid for a year's worth of unlimited admissions, is available for $25. You may also purchase a 12-month National Parks Pass for $50, which is valid for entrance into any U.S. national park. U.S. citizens aged 62 and older pay only $10 for a Golden Age Passport—that's valid for life. A Golden Access Passport is available free to U.S. citizens with disabilities.

Permits are required for campers to stay overnight either in the backcountry or in the primitive campsites. See "Camping in the Everglades," on p. 218.

Those who want to fish without a charter captain must obtain a standard State of Florida saltwater fishing license. These are available in the park at Flamingo Lodge or at any tackle shop or sporting goods store nearby. Nonresidents will pay $17 for a 7-day license or $7 for 3 days. Florida residents can get a fishing license good for the whole year for $14. Snook and crawfish licenses must be purchased separately at a cost of $2.

Charter captains carry vessel licenses that cover all paying passengers, but ask to be sure. Freshwater fishing licenses are available at various bait-and-tackle shops outside the park at the same rates as those offered inside the park. A good one nearby is **Don's Bait & Tackle,** located at 30710 S. Federal Hwy., in Homestead right on U.S. 1 (© **305/247-6616**). *Note:* Most of the area's freshwater fishing, limited to murky canals and artificial lakes near housing developments, is hardly worth the trouble when so much good saltwater fishing is available.

SEASONS   There are two distinct seasons in the Everglades: high season and mosquito season. High season is also dry season and lasts from late November to May. Despite the bizarre cold and wet weather patterns that El Niño brought in 1998, most winters here are warm, sunny, and breezy—a good combination for keeping the bugs away. This is the best time to visit because low water levels attract the largest variety of wading birds and their predators. As the dry season wanes, wildlife follows the receding water; and by the end of May, the only living things you are sure to spot will cause you to itch. The worst, called "no-see-ums," are not even swattable. If you choose to visit during the buggy season, be vigilant in applying bug spray.

Also, realize that many establishments and operators either close or curtail offerings in the summer, so always call ahead to check schedules.

RANGER PROGRAMS   More than 50 ranger programs, free with admission, are offered each month during high season and give visitors an opportunity to gain an expert's perspective. Ranger-led walks and talks are offered year-round from the Royal Palm Visitor Center, west of the main entrance, and at the Flamingo and Gulf Coast Visitor Centers, as well as the Shark Valley Visitor Center during the winter months. Park rangers tend to be helpful, well informed, and good-humored. Some programs occur regularly, such as Royal Palm Visitor Center's Glade Glimpses, a walking tour during which rangers point out flora and fauna and discuss issues affecting the Everglades' survival. These tours are scheduled at 12:30pm daily. The Anhinga Ambles, a similar program that takes place on the Anhinga Trail, starts at 10:30am or 3:30pm daily. Since times, programs, and locations vary from month to month, check a schedule, available at any of the visitor centers (see above).

SAFETY   There are many dangers inherent in this vast wilderness area. *Always* let someone know your itinerary before you set out on an extended hike. It's mandatory that you file an itinerary when camping overnight in the backcountry (which you can do when you apply for your overnight permit at either the Flamingo Visitor Center or the Gulf Coast Visitor Center). When you're on the water, watch for weather changes; severe thunderstorms and high winds often develop rapidly. Swimming is not recommended because of the presence of alligators, sharks, and barracudas. Watch out for the region's four indigenous poisonous snakes: diamondback and pygmy rattlesnakes, coral snakes (identifiable by their colorful rings), and water moccasins (which swim on the surface of the water). Again, bring insect repellent to ward off mosquitoes and biting flies. First aid is available from park rangers. The nearest hospital is in Homestead, 10 miles from the park's main entrance.

SEEING THE HIGHLIGHTS

Shark Valley, a 15-mile paved road (ideal for biking) through the Everglades, provides a fine introduction to the wonder of the Everglades, but don't plan on spending more than a few hours there. Bicycling or taking a guided tram tour (p. 218) are fantastic ways to see the park's highlights.

If you want to see a greater array of plant and animal life, make sure that you venture into the park through the main entrance, pick up a trail map, and dedicate at least a day to exploring from there.

Stop first along the Anhinga and Gumbo Limbo trails, which start right next to one another, 3 miles from the park's main entrance. These trails provide a thorough introduction to Everglades flora and fauna and are highly recommended to first-time visitors. Each of them is .5 mile round-trip. **Gumbo Limbo Trail** (my pick for best walking trail in the Everglades) meanders through a gorgeous shaded, junglelike hammock of gumbo limbo trees, royal palms, ferns, orchids, air plants, and a general blanket of vegetation, though it doesn't put you in close contact with much wildlife. **Anhinga Trail** is one of the most popular trails in the park because of its abundance of wildlife: There's more water and wildlife in this area of the park than in most parts of the Everglades, especially during dry season. Alligators, lizards, turtles, river otters, herons, egrets, and other animals abound, making this one of the best trails for seeing wildlife. Arrive early to spot the widest selection of exotic birds, like the Anhinga bird, the Trail's namesake, a large black fishing bird so accustomed to humans that many of them build their nests in plain view. Take your time—at least an hour is recommended for each trail. Both are wheelchair accessible. If you treat the trails and modern boardwalk as pathways to get through quickly, rather than destinations to experience and savor slowly, you'll miss out on the still beauty and hidden treasures that await.

If you want to get closer to nature, a few hours in a canoe along any of the trails allows paddlers the chance to sense the park's fluid motion and to become a part of the ecosphere. Visitors who choose this option end up feeling more like explorers than merely observers. (See "Sports & Affordable Outdoor Activities," below.)

No matter which option you choose (and there are many), I strongly recommend staying for the 7pm program, available during high season at the Long Pine Key Amphitheater. This talk and slide show, given by one of the park's rangers, will give you a detailed overview of the park's history, natural resources, wildlife, and threats to its survival.

SPORTS & AFFORDABLE OUTDOOR ACTIVITIES

BIKING The relatively flat 38-mile-long paved Main Park Road is great for biking because of the multitude of hardwood hammocks (treelike islands or dense stands of hardwood trees that grow only a few inches above land) and a dwarf cypress forest (stunted and thinly distributed cypress trees, which grow in poor soil on drier land), but Shark Valley is the best biking trail by far. Expect to spend 2 to 3 hours along either.

If the park isn't flooded from excess rain (which it often is, especially in spring), Shark Valley in Everglades National Park is South Florida's most scenic bicycle trail. Many locals haul their bikes out to the 'glades for a relaxing day of wilderness-trail riding. You'll share the flat, paved road only with other bikers and a menagerie of wildlife. (Don't be surprised to see a gator lounging in the sun or a deer munching on some grass. Otters, turtles, alligators, and snakes are common companions in the Shark Valley area.) There are no shortcuts, so if you become tired or are unable to complete the entire 15-mile trip, turn around and return on the same road. Allow 2 to 3 hours to bike the entire loop.

Those who love to mountain bike, and who prefer solitude, might check out the **Southern Glades Trail,** a 14-mile-long unpaved trail opened in late 1998 that is lined with native trees and teeming with wildlife such as deer, alligators, and the occasional snake. The remote trail runs along the C-111 canal, off State Road 9336 and Southwest 217th Street.

You can rent bikes at the Flamingo Lodge, Marina, and Outpost Resort (see "Accommodations You Can Afford," below) for $17 per 24 hours, $14 per full day, $8.50 per half day (any 4-hr. period), and $3 per hour. A $50 deposit is required for each rental. Rentals can be picked up from 7am and the bikes have to be returned by 5pm. Bicycles are also available from Shark Valley Tram Tours, at the park's Shark Valley entrance (© **305/221-8455**), for $5.25 per hour; rentals can be picked up anytime between 8:30am and 3pm and must be returned by 4pm.

BIRD-WATCHING   More than 350 species of birds make their homes in the Everglades. Tropical birds from the Caribbean and temperate species from North America can be found here, along with exotics that have blown in from more distant regions. Eco and Mrazek ponds, located near Flamingo, are two of the best places for birding, especially in early morning or late afternoon in the dry winter months. Pick up a free birding checklist from a visitor center (see "Just the Facts," on p. 210), and ask there what's been spotted in recent days.

CANOEING   Canoeing through the Everglades may be one of the most serene, surprisingly diverse adventures you'll ever have. From a canoe (where you're incredibly close to the water level), your vantage point is priceless. Canoers in the 'glades can coexist with the gators and birds there in a way no one else can; they behave as if you are part of the ecosystem—something that can't happen on an airboat. A ranger-guided boat tour is your best bet and costs $20, plus a required deposit. As always, a ranger will help you understand the surroundings and give you an education on what you're seeing.

Everglades National Park's longest "trails" are designed for boat and canoe travel, and many are marked as clearly as walking trails. The **Noble Hammock Canoe Trail,** a 2-mile loop, takes 1 to 2 hours and is recommended for beginning canoers. The **Hell's Bay Canoe Trail,** a 3- to 6-mile course for hardier paddlers, takes 2 to 6 hours, depending on how far you choose to go. Park rangers can recommend other trails that best suit your abilities, time limitations, and interests.

You can rent a canoe at the Flamingo Lodge, Marina, and Outpost Resort (p. 218) for $50 for 24 hours, $40 per full day (any 8-hr. period), $30 per half day (any 4-hr. period), and $12 per hour. Skiffs, kayaks, and tandem kayaks are also available. The concessionaire will shuttle your party to the trail head of your choice and pick you up afterward. Rental facilities are open daily from 6am to 8pm.

Overnight canoe rentals are available for $50 to $60. During ideal weather conditions (stay away during bug season!), you can paddle right out to the Gulf and camp on the beach. However, Gulf waters at beach sites can be extremely rough, and people in small watercraft such as a canoe should exercise caution.

You can also take a canoe tour from the Parks Docks on Chokoloskee Causeway on State Road 29, ½ mile south of the traffic circle at the ranger station in Everglades City. Call Everglades National Park Boat Tours at © **800/445-7724.**

FISHING About one-third of Everglades National Park is open water. Freshwater fishing is popular in brackish **Nine-Mile Pond** (25 miles from the main entrance) and other spots along the Main Park Road, but because of the high mercury levels found in the Everglades, freshwater fishers are warned not to eat their catch. Before casting, check in at a visitor center, as many of the park's lakes are preserved for observation only. Fishing licenses are required (see "Just the Facts" on p. 210 for more information).

Saltwater anglers will find snapper and sea trout plentiful. Charter boats and guides are available at Flamingo Lodge, Marina, and Outpost Resort (p. 218). Phone for information and reservations.

MOTORBOATING Motorboating around the Everglades seems like a great way to see plants and animals in remote habitats, and, indeed, is an interesting and fulfilling experience as you throttle into nature. However, environmentalists are taking stock of the damage motorboats (especially airboats) inflict on the delicate ecosystem. If you choose to motor, remember that most of the areas near land are "no wake" zones and that, for the protection of nesting birds, landing is prohibited on most of the little mangrove islands. Motorboating is allowed in certain areas such as Florida Bay, the backcountry toward Everglades City, and the Ten Thousand Islands area. In all the freshwater lakes, however, motorboats are prohibited if they're above 5 horsepower. There's a long list of restrictions and restricted areas, so get a copy of the park's boating rules from National Park Headquarters before setting out (see "Just the Facts," earlier).

The Everglades' only marina—accommodating about 50 boats with electric and water hookups—is the Flamingo Lodge, Marina, and Outpost Resort, in Flamingo. The well-marked channel to the Flamingo is accessible to boats with a maximum 4-foot draft and is open year-round. Reservations can be made through the marina store (© **239/695-3101,** ext. 304). Skiffs with 15-horsepower motors are available for rent. These low-power boats cost $90 per day, $65 per half day (any 5-hr. period), and $22 per hour. A $125 deposit is required.

ORGANIZED TOURS

AIRBOAT TOURS Shallow-draft, fan-powered airboats were invented in the Everglades by frog hunters who were tired of poling through the brushes. Airboats cut through the saw grass and are sort of like hydraulic boats in which at high enough speeds, the boat actually lifts above the saw grass and into the air. And even though airboats are the most efficient (not to mention fast and fun!) way to get around, they are not permitted in the park (these shallow-bottom runabouts tend to inflict severe damage on animals and plants). Just outside the boundaries of the Everglades, however, you'll find a number of outfitters offering rides (consider bringing earplugs; these high-speed boats are loud).

One of the best airboat outfitters is **Gator Park,** 12 miles west of the Florida Turnpike at 24050 SW 8th St. (© **305/559-2255**), which, despite its touristy name, happens to be one of the most informative and entertaining around, not to mention one of the only airboat tour operators that gives out free earplugs. Request, if you can, Rick, the best tour guide there, who deserves a medal for getting out into the water and poking around a massive alligator even though he's not really supposed to. After the boat ride, there's a free interactive wildlife show that features alligator wrestling and several other frightening acts involving scorpions. Take note of the gorgeous peacocks that live in the trees here. Admission for the boat ride and show is $15. Kids under 6 ride free. Airboats depart every 20 minutes, so there's no worrying about missing the boat. Open daily 9am to 7pm.

Another one we recommend is **Coopertown Airboat Tours** (© **305/226-6048**), located about 11 miles west of Florida's Turnpike on the Tamiami Trail (US41). Here, the superfriendly staff has helped the company garner the title of "Florida's Best" by the *Miami Herald* for 40 years in a row. You never know what you're going to see, but with great guides, you're sure to see *something* of interest on the 9-mile round-trip, 40-minute tours. There's also a restaurant and a small gator farm on the premises. Airboat rides cost $14 for anyone over 12, $8 for children 7 to 11, and are free for those 6 and under. Open daily from 8am to 6pm (tours leave frequently).

Airboat rides are also offered at the **Miccosukee Indian Village,** just west of the Shark Valley entrance on U.S. 41/the Tamiami Trail and MM 70 (© **305/223-8380**). The price is $10. However, *be warned and advised:* We are not recommending this particular outfit over others—they are merely the ones closest to the Shark Valley entrance. As always, the quality of your tour is only going to be as good as the quality of your tour guide, and, unfortunately, we have gotten some complaints about the Miccosukee tours.

The **Everglades Alligator Farm,** 4 miles south of Palm Drive on Southwest 192nd Avenue (© **305/247-2628**), offers half-hour guided airboat tours from 9am until 6pm daily. The price, which includes admission to the park, is $17 for adults, $10 for children 4 to 11, and free for children 3 and under. Prices are less for admission without the airboat ride. Another reputable company is **Captain Doug's,** located 35 miles south of Naples and 1 mile past the bridge in Everglades City (© **800/282-9194**).

CANOE TOURS   A fabulous way to explore the Everglades backcountry is via canoe. Slink through the mangroves, across saw grass prairies, or even walk the sands of the unfettered 10,000 Islands. Expert guides will lead you in the right direction. Contact **North American Canoe Tours** (© **239/695-3299**) at the Ivey House B&B (p. 220).

ECO TOURS   Although it's fascinating to explore on your own, it would be a shame for you to tour the Everglades without a clue as to what you're seeing. It's a lot more than saw grass and alligators in the 'glades backcountry, which is why **Everglades Rentals and Eco Adventures** (© **239/695-3299**), located within the Ivey House B&B (p. 220), is there to help guide, explain, entertain, and clear up key issues like the differences between alligators and crocodiles or swamps and the Florida Everglades.

MOTORBOAT TOURS   Both Florida Bay and backcountry tours are offered at the Flamingo Lodge, Marina, and Outpost Resort (p. 218). Florida Bay tours cruise nearby estuaries and sandbars, while six-passenger backcountry boats visit smaller sloughs. Passengers can expect to see birds and a variety of other animals

(I once saw a raccoon and some wild pigs). Both are available in 1½- and 2-hour versions that cost $12 or $18 for adults, $7 or $12 for children ages 6 through 13, free for those under 6. Tours depart throughout the day, and reservations are recommended. There are also charter-fishing and sightseeing boats that can be booked through the resort's main reservation number (© **239/695-3101**).

TRAM TOURS   At the park's Shark Valley entrance, open-air tram buses take visitors on 2-hour naturalist-led tours that delve 7½ miles into the wilderness and make up the best quick introduction you can get to the Everglades. At the trail's midsection, passengers can disembark and climb a 65-foot observation tower that offers good views of the 'glades, though the tower on the Pa-hay-okee trail is better. Visitors will see plenty of wildlife and endless acres of saw grass. Tours run December through April daily on the hour between 9am and 4pm and May through November at 9:30 and 11am and 1 and 3pm, and are sometimes stalled by flooding or particularly heavy mosquito infestation. Reservations are recommended from December to March. The cost is $12 for adults, $7.25 for children 12 and under, and $11 for seniors. For further information, contact **Shark Valley Tram Tours** at © **305/221-8455.**

ACCOMMODATIONS YOU CAN AFFORD

The only lodging in the park proper is the Flamingo Lodge, a fairly priced and very recommendable option. However, there are a few hotels just outside the park that are even cheaper. A $45 million casino hotel, the **Miccosukee Indian Village** (© **877/242-6464;** www.miccosukee.com), is located adjacent to the Miccosukee bingo and gaming hall on the northern edge of the park. And although bugs can be a major nuisance, especially in the warm months, camping is really the way to go in this very primitive environment.

LODGING IN EVERGLADES NATIONAL PARK

Flamingo Lodge, Marina, and Outpost Resort ★★   The Flamingo Lodge is the only lodging actually located within the boundaries of Everglades National Park. This woodsy, sprawling complex offers rooms (overlooking the Florida Bay) in either a two-story simple motel or the lodge. Either option feels very much like being at summer camp, with a few more amenities. Rooms are your standard, cookie-cutter, motel-style rooms, with functional bathrooms. No luxury here, but it's nonetheless a comfort for those who'd rather not experience the great outdoors while they sleep. More interesting than the actual motel, however, are the visitors who crop up on the lawn—alligators, raccoons, and other nomadic creatures. The hotel is open year-round, although the restaurant (p. 222) closes in the summer.

1 Flamingo Lodge Hwy., Flamingo, FL 33034. © **800/600-3813** or 239/695-3101. Fax 239/695-3921. www. flamingolodge.com. 97 units. Winter $79–$95 double, $89–$105 triple, $99–$115 quad, $110–$145 suite, $99–$135 cottage; off season $68 double, $78 triple, $88 quad, $102 suite, $92 cottage. Rates for cottages or suites are for 1–4 people. Children under 17 stay free. AE, DC, DISC, MC. Take Florida Tpk. south to Florida City; exit on U.S. 1. At 4-way intersection, turn right onto Palm Dr.; continue for 3 miles and turn left at Robert Is Here fruit stand. Turn right at the 3-way intersection. The park entrance is 3 miles ahead. Continue for about 38 miles more to reach lodge. **Amenities:** Waterside bar and restaurant; freshwater swimming pool; bike, canoe, and kayak rentals; marina with boat tours; boat rentals; houseboat and fishing charters; coin-op washers and dryers; convenience store. *In room:* A/C, TV in standard rooms and suites but not in cottages, kitchen in cottages and suites only.

CAMPING IN THE EVERGLADES

Campgrounds are available year-round in Flamingo and Long Pine Key. Both have drinking water, picnic tables, charcoal grills, bathrooms, and tent and trailer pads, and welcome RVs (Flamingo allows up to 40-ft. vehicles while Long Pine Key accepts up to 60 footers), though there are no electrical hookups. Flamingo has cold-water showers; Long Pine Key does not have showers or hookups for showers. Private ground fires are not permitted, but supervised campfire programs are conducted during winter months. Long Pine Key and Flamingo are popular and require reservations in advance. Reservations for Flamingo and Long Pine may be made through the National Park Reservations Service at *C* **800/365-CAMP** or online (from 10am–10pm) at www.nps.gov/ever/visit/camping.htm. Campsites are $14 per night with a 14-day consecutive stay limit, 30 days a year maximum.

Camping is also available in the **backcountry** (those remote areas accessible only by boat, foot, or canoe—basically most of the park) year-round on a first-come, first-served basis. Campers must register with park rangers/get a free permit (see the section on "Safety," on p. 213) in person or by telephone no less than 24 hours before the start of their trip. For more information, contact the Gulf Coast Visitor Center (*C* **239/695-3311**) or the Flamingo Visitor Center (*C* **239/695-2945**), which are the only two places that give out these permits. Once you have one, camping sites cost $14 (with a maximum of 8 people per site) or $28 for a group site (maximum of 15 people). Campers can use only designated campsites, which are plentiful and well marked on visitor maps.

Many backcountry sites are *chickee huts*—covered wooden platforms (with toilets) on stilts. They're accessible only by canoe and can accommodate free-standing tents (without stakes). Ground sites are located along interior bays and rivers, and beach camping is also popular. In summer especially, mosquito repellent is necessary gear.

LODGING IN EVERGLADES CITY

Since Everglades City is 35 miles southeast of Naples and 83 miles west of Miami, many people choose to explore this western entrance to Everglades National Park, located off the Tamiami Trail, on State Road 29. An annual seafood festival held the first weekend in February is a major event that draws hordes of people. Everglades City (the gateway to the Ten Thousand Islands), where the 'glades meet the Gulf of Mexico, is the closest thing you'll get to civilization in South Florida's swampy frontier, with a few tourist traps—er, shops, a restaurant, and two bed-and-breakfasts (see below).

Everglades Vacation Rentals and Day Spa ★★★ *Finds*   This very cute bed-and-breakfast is right on the money, as far as kitsch is concerned—it's a fabulous retreat from the lush greenery of the swampy Everglades to the even more lush greenery of money. Located in a building that was formerly the first bank established, in 1923, in Collier County, money is this place's premise, but it won't cost you too much to stay here. Rooms such as the Trust Room, the Checking Department, and the Stocks and Bond Rooms, all with bathrooms, are clean and comfortable and are located on the floor where banking used to be done until 1962. Perhaps the best things about the place, besides the congenial service, are that breakfast is served in the bank's fully restored vault and that original artifacts from the bank are still visible, such as the 3,000-pound cannonball safe. Unlike a real bank, however, the knowledgeable staff at the inn is happy to give free advice on what to do in the area. A new day spa on the premises provides all the necessary pampering after a long day exploring the swamps.

201 W. Broadway, Everglades City, FL 34139. *C* **239/695-3151.** Spa 239/695-1006. Fax 239/695-3335. www.banksoftheeverglades.com. 7 units. $100–$125. Rates include continental breakfast delivered to your door. AE, DISC, MC, V. **Amenities:** Free use of bikes; Everglades excursions available. *In room:* A/C, TV.

Ivey House B&B ★(★ *Finds*   Housed in what used to be a recreational center for the men who built the Tamiami Trail, the Ivey House offers three types of accommodations. In the original house, there are 10 small rooms that share communal bathrooms (one each for women and men). There are no televisions or phones in the rooms. One private cottage consists of two bedrooms, a full kitchen, a private bathroom, and a screened-in porch. The Ivey's newer inn (opened in 2001) adds 18 rooms (with private bathrooms, TVs, and phones) that face a courtyard with a screened-in shallow "conversation" pool. During the summer, however, the mosquitoes are out in full force and a trip to the pool could leave you with multiple bites as it did me (screens or not). Bring bug spray!

Owners Sandee and David Harraden are extremely knowledgeable about the Everglades, and usually the guests are as well. A living-room area offers guests the opportunity to mingle. A full hot breakfast is included in the price from 6:30 to 11am. Boxed lunches, stored in a cooler so you can bring them along for your Everglades excursions, are offered for $9.50 each. The Ivey House is closed in September and there's a 2-night minimum in February when the Everglades Seafood Festival is going on. *Note:* There is no smoking in any of the buildings.

107 Camellia St., Everglades City, FL 34139. ✆ 239/695-3299. Fax 239/695-4155. www.iveyhouse.com. 28 units. Winter $70–$175 main houses, $125–$175 cottage (2-night minimum); off season $50–$125 main house, cottages closed in the off season. MC, V. **Amenities:** Restaurant; small pool; free use of bikes; Everglades excursions available. *In room:* A/C, TV, fridge, kitchen (cottage only).

Rod & Gun Lodge ★   This rustic, old white clapboard house has plenty of history and all kinds of activities for sports enthusiasts, including a swimming pool, bicycle rentals, tennis center, and nearby boat rentals and private fishing guides. Sitting on the banks of the sleepy Barron River, the Rod & Gun Lodge was originally built as a private residence nearly 170 years ago, but Barron Collier turned it into a cozy hunting lodge in the 1920s. President Herbert Hoover vacationed here after his 1928 election victory, and President Harry S Truman flew in to sign Everglades National Park into existence in 1947 and stayed over as well. Other guests have included President Richard Nixon, Burt Reynolds, and Mick Jagger. The public rooms are beautifully paneled and hung with tarpon, wild boar, deer antlers, and other trophies. Guest rooms in this single-story building are unfussy but perfectly comfortable. Out by the swimming pool and riverbank, a screened veranda with ceiling fans offers a pleasant place for a libation. The excellent seafood restaurant serves breakfast, lunch, and dinner. The entire property is nonsmoking. *Note:* No credit cards are accepted.

Riverside Dr. and Broadway (P.O. Box 190), Everglades City, FL 34139. ✆ 239/695-2101. 17 units, all with bathroom and porches looking out on the river. Winter $110 double. No credit cards. Closed after July 4 for the summer. **Amenities:** Restaurant; pool; tennis courts; bicycle rentals. *In room:* A/C, TV.

NEARBY IN HOMESTEAD & FLORIDA CITY

Homestead and Florida City, two adjacent towns that were almost blown off the map by Hurricane Andrew in 1992, have come back better than before. Located about 10 miles from the park's main entrance, along U.S. 1, 35 miles south of Miami, these somewhat rural towns offer several budget lodging options, including a handful of chain hotels. There is a **Days Inn** (✆ 305/245-1260) in Homestead and a **Hampton Inn** (✆ 800/426-7866 or 305/247-8833) right off the turnpike in Florida City. However, the best option is listed below.

Best Western Gateway to the Keys   This two-story standard motel offers contemporary style and comfort about 10 miles from the park's main entrance.

A decent-size pool and a small spa make it an attractive option to some. Each identical standard room has bright, tropical bedspreads and oversize picture windows. The suites offer convenient extras like a microwave, a coffeemaker, an extra sink, and a small fridge. Clean and conveniently located, the only drawback is that in season, there is often a 3-day minimum stay requirement. You'd do best to call the local reservation line (© **305/246-5100**) instead of the toll-free number—on several occasions, the hotel made an exception to the rule while the central reservation line was not able to do the same.

411 S. Krome Ave. (U.S. 1), Florida City, FL 33034. © **800/528-1234** or 305/246-5100. Fax 305/242-0056. www.bestwestern.com. 114 units. Winter $135–$150 double; off season $109–$124 double. Rates include continental breakfast. During races and the very high season, there may be a 3-night minimum stay. AE, DC, DISC, MC, V. **Amenities:** Pool; spa; laundry service; dry cleaning. *In room:* A/C, TV, dataport, fridge, coffeemaker, hair dryer.

Super-Cheap Sleeps

Evergaldes International Hostel ★   This is what a hostel *should* be. Sure, I've seen cleaner, more modern ones, but the feeling of camaraderie here is what hostels are all about. Located in an old 1930s boarding house, this hostel has dorm rooms as well as doubles (all with shared baths) and a great kitchen plus a washer/dryer, high-speed Internet connection, bike rentals, and a garden (with tents, forts, and an outdoor chess board) to explore. The staff here is amazingly accommodating and friendly, and they run sightseeing/canoe trips to the Everglades as well as offering tons of helpful information.

20 SW 2nd Ave., Florida City, FL 33034. © **800/372-3874** or 305/248-1122. www.evergladeshostel.com. Dorm beds $14; private doubles $35; nonmember fee $3. **Amenities:** Bike rentals; laundry facilities; kitchen; Internet access; tours. *In room:* A/C (in some).

GREAT DEALS ON DINING IN & AROUND THE PARK

You won't find fancy nouvelle cuisine in this suburbanized farm country, but there are plenty of fast-food chains along U.S. 1 and a few old favorites worth a taste, listed below.

Here for nearly a quarter of a century, **El Toro Taco Family Restaurant** (p. 121) at 1 S. Krome Ave. (near Mowry Dr. and Campbell Dr.; © **305/245-8182**) opens daily at 9:30am and stays crowded until at least 9pm most days. The fresh grilled meats, tacos, burritos, salsas, guacamole, and stews are all mild and delicious. No matter how big your appetite, it's hard to spend more than $12 per person at this Mexican outpost. Bring your own beer or wine.

Housed in a squat, one-story, windowless stone building that looks something like a medieval fort, the **Capri Restaurant,** 935 N. Krome Ave., Florida City (© **305/247-1542**), has been serving hearty Italian-American fare since 1958. Great pastas and salads complement a full menu (portions are big) of meat and fish dishes. They serve lunch and dinner every day (except Sun) until 9:30pm weekdays and 10:30pm weekends.

The **Miccosukee Restaurant** (© **305/223-8380**), just west of the Shark Valley entrance on the Tamiami Trail (U.S. 41), serves authentic pumpkin bread, fry bread, fish, and not-so-authentic Native American interpretations of tacos and fried chicken. It's worth a stop for brunch, lunch, or dinner.

Near the Miccosukee reservation on 16400 SW 8th St. is **The Pit Bar-B-Q** (© **305/226-2272**), a total pit of a place known for some of the best smoked ribs, barbecue chicken, and cornbread this side of the deep south. Open daily from 11am–8pm.

In Everglades City, **The Oyster House** (© **239/695-2073**) on Chokoloskee Causeway, State Road (the locals call it Highway) 29 South, is a large but homey seafood restaurant with modest prices, excellent service, and a fantastic view of the 10,000 islands. Try their hush puppies.

Once inside the Everglades, you'll want to eat at the only restaurant within the boundaries of this huge park, **The Flamingo Restaurant** (© **239/695-3101**). Located in the Flamingo Lodge (p. 218), this is a very civilized and affordable restaurant. Besides the spectacular view of Florida Bay and numerous Keys from the large, airy dining room, you'll also find fresh fish that is grilled, blackened, or deep-fried. Dinner entrees come with salad or conch chowder, steamed vegetables, black beans, and rice or baked potato. The large menu has something for everyone, including basic and very tasty sandwiches, pastas, burgers, salads, and a kids' menu offering standard choices for less than $6. Prices are surprisingly moderate, with full meals starting at about $11 and going no higher than $22. You may need reservations for dinner, however, especially in season.

2 Biscayne National Park ⓐ★

35 miles S of Miami, 21 miles E of Everglades National Park

With only about 500,000 visitors each year (mostly boaters and divers), the unusual Biscayne National Park is one of the least-crowded parks in the country. Perhaps that's because the park is a little more difficult than most to access—more than 95% of its 181,500 acres are underwater.

The park's significance was first formally acknowledged in 1968 when, in an unprecedented move (and against intense pressure from developers), President Lyndon B. Johnson signed a bill to conserve the barrier islands off South Florida's east coast as a national monument—a protected status that's just a rung below national park. After being twice enlarged, once in 1974 and again in 1980, the waters and land surrounding the northernmost coral reef in North America became a full-fledged national park—the largest of its kind in the country.

To be fully appreciated, Biscayne National Park should be thought of more as a preserve than as a destination. I suggest using your time here to explore underwater life, of course, but also to relax.

The park consists of 44 islands, but only a few of them are open to visitors. The most popular one is **Elliott Key,** which has campsites and a visitor center plus freshwater showers (cold water only), restrooms, trails, and a buoyed swim area. It's located about 9 miles from **Convoy Point,** the park's official headquarters on land. During Columbus Day weekend, there is a very popular regatta in which a lively crowd of party people gathers—sometimes in the nude—to celebrate the long weekend. If you'd prefer to rough it a little more, the 29-acre island known as **Boca Chita Key,** once an exclusive haven for yachters, has now become a popular spot for all manner of boaters. Visitors can enjoy camping and tour the island's restored historic buildings, including the county's second-largest lighthouse and a tiny chapel.

The park's small mainland mangrove shoreline and keys are best explored by boat. Its extensive reef system is renowned by divers and snorkelers worldwide.

JUST THE FACTS

GETTING THERE & ACCESS POINTS   Convoy Point, the park's mainland entrance, is located 9 miles east of Homestead. To reach the park from Miami, take the Florida Turnpike to the Tallahassee Road (SW 137th Ave.) exit. Turn left, then left again at North Canal Drive (SW 328th St.) and follow signs to the park. Another option is to rent a speedboat in Miami and cruise south for about an hour and a half. If you're coming from U.S. 1, whether you're heading north or south, turn east at North Canal Drive (SW 328th St.). The entrance is approximately 9 miles away. The rest of the park is accessible only by boat.

Because most of Biscayne National Park is accessible only to boaters, mooring buoys abound, since it is illegal to anchor on coral. When no buoys are available, boaters must anchor on sand or on the new docks surrounding the small harbor off of Boca Chita. Boats can also dock there overnight for $15. Even the most experienced boaters should carry updated nautical charts of the area, which are available at Convoy Point's Dante Fascell Visitor Center. The waters are often murky, making the abundant reefs and sandbars difficult to detect—and there are more interesting ways to spend a day than waiting for the tide to rise. There's a boat launch at adjacent Homestead Bayfront Park and 66 slips on Elliott Key, available free on a first-come, first-served basis.

Transportation to and from the visitor center to Elliot Key costs $26 (plus tax) round-trip per person and takes about an hour. This is a convenient option, ensuring that you don't get lost on some deserted island by boating there yourself. Call (C) **305/230-1100** for a seasonal schedule.

VISITOR CENTERS & INFORMATION   The **Dante Fascell Visitor Center,** often still referred to by its older name, the **Convoy Point Visitor Center,** 9700 SW 328th St., Homestead, FL 33033-5634, at the park's main entrance ((C) **305/230-7275;** fax 305/230-1190; www.nps.gov/bisc), is the natural starting point for any venture into the park without a boat. In addition to providing comprehensive information about the park, on request, rangers will show you a short video on the park, its natural surroundings, and what you may see. The center is open daily from 9am to 5pm.

For information on transportation, glass-bottom boat tours, and snorkeling and scuba-diving expeditions, contact the park concessionaire, **Biscayne National Underwater Park, Inc.,** P.O. Box 1270, Homestead, FL 33030 ((C) **305/230-1100;** fax 305/230-1120; www.nps.gov/bisc). The company is open daily from 8:30am to 5pm.

ENTRANCE FEES & PERMITS   Entering Biscayne National Park is free. There is a $15 per night overnight docking fee at both Boca Chita Key Harbor and Elliott Key Harbor ($7.50 per night for holders of Golden Age or Golden Access Passports), which includes a campsite. Campsites are $10 for those staying without a boat. See p. 212 for information on fishing permits. Backcountry camping permits are free and can be picked up from the Dante Fascell Visitor Center. For information on fees and permits, call the park ranger at (C) **305/230-1144.**

SEEING THE HIGHLIGHTS

Since the park is primarily underwater, the only way to truly experience it is with snorkel or scuba gear. Beneath the surface of Biscayne National Park, the aquatic universe pulses with multicolored life: Bright parrotfish and angelfish, gently rocking sea fans, and coral labyrinths abound. See the "Snorkeling & Scuba Diving" section below for more information.

Afterward, take a picnic out to Elliott Key and taste the crisp salt air blowing off the Atlantic. Or head to Boca Chita, an intriguing island that was once the private playground of wealthy yachters.

SPORTS & AFFORDABLE OUTDOOR ACTIVITIES

CANOEING & KAYAKING   Biscayne National Park offers excellent canoeing, both along the coast and across the open water to nearby mangroves and artificial islands that dot the longest uninterrupted shoreline in the state of Florida. Since tides can be strong, only experienced canoeists should attempt to paddle far from shore. If you do plan to go far, first obtain a tide table from the visitor center (see "Just the Facts," above) and paddle with the current. Free ranger-led canoe tours are scheduled the second and fourth Saturdays from January 10 to April 24 from 9am to noon; phone for information. You can rent a canoe at the park's concession stand; rates are $9 an hour. Two person kayaks can be rented for $16 an hour. Call (C) **305/230-1100** for reservations, information, ranger tours, and boat rentals.

FISHING Ocean fishing is excellent year-round at Biscayne National Park; many people cast their lines right from the breakwater jetty at Convoy Point. A fishing license is required (see p. 212 for complete information). Bait is not available in Biscayne National Park but is sold in adjacent Homestead Bayfront Park. Stone crabs and Florida lobsters can be found here, but you're allowed to catch these only on the ocean side when they're in season. There are strict limitations on size, season, number, and method of take (including spear fishing) for both fresh- and saltwater fishing. The latest regulations are available at most marinas, bait-and-tackle shops, and the park's visitor centers. Or you can contact the **Florida Fish and Wildlife Conservation Commission,** Bryant Building, 620 S. Meridian St., Tallahassee, FL 32399-1600 ((C) **850/488-0331**).

HIKING & EXPLORING Since the majority of this park is underwater, hiking is not the main attraction here, but, nonetheless, there are some interesting sights and trails. At Convoy Point, you can walk along the 370-foot boardwalk and along the ½-mile jetty that serves as a breakwater for the park's harbor. From there, you can usually see brown pelicans, little blue herons, snowy egrets, and a few exotic fish.

Elliott Key is accessible only by boat, but once you're there, you have two good trail options. True to its name, the Loop Trail makes a 1.5-mile circle from the bay-side visitor center, through a hardwood hammock and mangroves, to an elevated ocean-side boardwalk. It's likely that you'll see purple and orange land crabs scurrying around the mangrove roots.

Reopened in 1998, Boca Chita Key was once the playground for wealthy tycoons, and it still offers the peaceful beauty that attracted elite anglers from cold climates. Many of the historical buildings are still intact, including an ornamental lighthouse, which was never put into use.

Take advantage of the tours, usually led by a park ranger and available every Sunday in the winter only at 1:30pm. The tour, including the boat trip, takes about 3 hours. The price is $24 for adults, $19 for seniors, and $16 for children under 12. However, call in advance to see if the sea is calm enough for the boat trip—the boats won't run in rough seas. See "Glass-Bottom Boat Tours," below, for information about the daily 10am tours.

SNORKELING & SCUBA DIVING The clear, warm waters of Biscayne National Park are packed with colorful tropical fish that swim in the offshore reefs. If you don't have your own gear, or don't want to lug it to the park, you can rent or buy snorkeling and scuba gear at the full-service dive shop at Convoy Point. Rates are in line with dive shops on the mainland.

The best way to see the park from underwater is to take a snorkeling or scuba diving tour operated by **Biscayne National Underwater Park, Inc.** ((C) **305/ 230-1100;** www.nps.gov/bisc). Snorkeling tours depart at 1:30pm daily, last about 3 hours, and cost $35 per person, including equipment. They also run weekend two-tank dives for certified divers. The price is $54, including two tanks and weights. Make your reservations in advance. The shop is open daily from 9am to 5pm.

Before entering the water, be sure to apply waterproof sunblock—once you begin to explore, it's easy to lose track of time, and the Florida sun is brutal, even during winter.

SWIMMING You can swim at the protected beaches of Elliott Key, Boca Chita Key, and adjacent Homestead Bayfront Park, but none of these match the width or softness of other South Florida beaches. Check the water conditions before heading into the sea: The strong currents that make this a popular destination for windsurfers and sailors can be dangerous, even for strong swimmers. Homestead Bayfront Park is really just a marina located next to Biscayne National Park, but it does have a beach and picnic facilities as well as fishing areas and a playground. It's located at Convoy Point, 9698 SW 328th St., Homestead (© **305/230-3034**).

GLASS-BOTTOM BOAT TOURS

If you prefer not to dive, the best way to see the sights is on a glass-bottom boat tour. **Biscayne National Underwater Park, Inc.** (© **305/230-1100;** www.nps.gov/bisc) offers daily trips to view some of the country's most beautiful coral reefs and tropical fish. Boats depart year-round from Convoy Point at 10am and stay out for about 3 hours. At $24 for adults, $19 for seniors, and $16 for children 12 and under, the scenic and informative tours are well worth the price. Boats carry fewer than 50 passengers; reservations are almost always necessary.

ACCOMMODATIONS YOU CAN AFFORD

Besides campsites, there are no facilities available for overnight guests to this watery park. Most noncamping visitors come for an afternoon, on their way to the Keys, and stay overnight in nearby Homestead, where there are many national chain hotels and other affordable lodgings (see p. 220 for more information).

CAMPING

Although you won't find hotels or lodges in Biscayne National Park, it does have some of the state's most pristine campsites. Since they are inaccessible by motor vehicle, you'll be sure to avoid the mass of RVs so prevalent in many of the state's other campgrounds. Sites are on Elliott Key and Boca Chita (p. 222) and can be reached only by boat. If you don't have your own, call © **305/230-1100** to arrange a drop-off. Transportation to and from the visitor center costs $26 (plus tax) per person. Boca Chita has only saltwater toilets (no showers or sinks); Elliot Key has freshwater, cold-water showers (and toilets) but is otherwise no less primitive. If you didn't pay for the overnight docking fee, campsites are $10.

With a backcountry permit, available free from the Visitor Center, you can pitch your tent somewhere even more private. Ask for a map at the Visitor Center, and be sure to bring plenty of bug spray. Sites cost $10 a night for up to six persons staying in one or two tents. Backcountry camping is allowed only on Elliot Key, which is a very popular spot (accessible only by boat) for boaters and campers. It is approximately 9 miles from Dante Fascell Visitor Center and offers hiking trails, fresh water, boat slips, showers, and restrooms. While there, don't miss the Old Road, a 7-mile tropical hammock trail that runs the length of Elliott Key. This trail is one of the few places left in the world to see the highly endangered Schaus' swallowtail butterfly, recognizable by its black wings with diagonal yellow bands. They're usually out from late April to July.

The Gold Coast: Hallandale to the Palm Beaches

Named not for the sun-kissed skin of the area's residents but for the gold salvaged from shipwrecks off its coastline, the Gold Coast embraces more than 60 miles of beautiful Atlantic shoreline—from the pristine sands of Jupiter in northern Palm Beach County to the legendary strip of beaches in Fort Lauderdale.

If you haven't visited the cities along Florida's southeastern coast in the last few years, you'll be amazed at how much has changed. Miles of sprawling grassland and empty lots have been replaced with luxurious resorts and high-rise condominiums. Taking advantage of their proximity to Miami, the cities that make up the Gold Coast have attracted millions looking to escape crowded sidewalks, traffic jams, and the everyday routines of life.

Fortunately, amid all the building, much of the natural treasure of the Gold Coast remains. There are 300 miles of Intracoastal Waterway, not to mention Fort Lauderdale's Venetian-inspired canals. And the unspoiled splendor of the Everglades is just a few miles inland.

The most popular areas in the Gold Coast are Fort Lauderdale, Boca Raton, and Palm Beach. While Fort Lauderdale is a favored beachfront destination, Boca Raton and Palm Beach are better known for their country-club lifestyles and excellent shopping. Farther north is the quietly popular Jupiter, best known for spring training at the Roger Dean Stadium and for its former resident, Burt Reynolds. In between these better-traveled destinations are a few things worth stopping for, but not much. Driving north along the coastline is one of the best ways to fully appreciate what the Gold Coast is all about—it's a perspective you certainly won't find in a shopping mall.

Tourists come here by the droves, but they aren't the only people coming; thousands of transplants, fleeing the increasing population influx in Miami and the frigid winters up North, have made this area their home. As a result, there has been a construction boom in the existing cities and even westward, into the swampy areas of the Everglades. More than 20 homes per day are being built in Broward County alone. There has also been a great revitalization of several downtown areas, including Hollywood, Fort Lauderdale, and West Palm Beach. These once-desolate urban centers have been spruced up and now attract more young travelers and families than ever before.

Unfortunately, like its neighbors to the south, the Gold Coast can be prohibitively hot and buggy in the summer. The good news is that bargains are plentiful in the summer months (May–Oct), when many locals take advantage of package deals and uncrowded resorts.

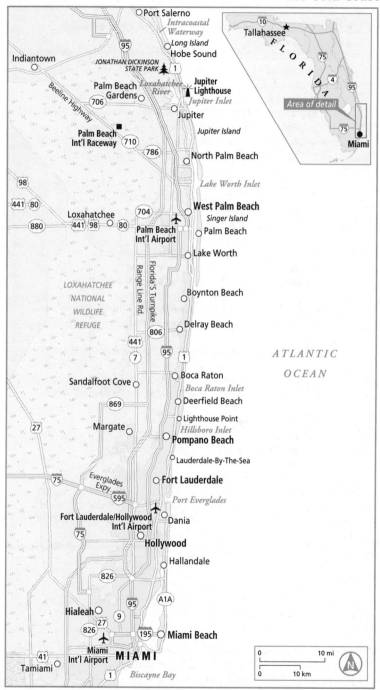

The Gold Coast

Port Salerno

Intracoastal Waterway

Long Island

Hobe Sound

Indiantown

95

JONATHAN DICKINSON STATE PARK

1

Loxahatchee River

Jupiter Lighthouse

Jupiter Inlet

Palm Beach Gardens

706

Jupiter

Jupiter Island

Beeline Highway

Palm Beach Int'l Raceway

710

786

North Palm Beach

98

Lake Worth Inlet

441 80

Loxahatchee

704

West Palm Beach

880

441 98 80

Palm Beach Int'l Airport

Singer Island

Palm Beach

Lake Worth

Boynton Beach

Range Line Rd.

Florida's Turnpike

LOXAHATCHEE NATIONAL WILDLIFE REFUGE

806

Delray Beach

441

7

95 1

ATLANTIC OCEAN

Sandalfoot Cove

Boca Raton

Boca Raton Inlet

869

Deerfield Beach

Lighthouse Point

Margate

Hillsboro Inlet

Pompano Beach

Lauderdale-By-The-Sea

27

75

Everglades Expy.

Fort Lauderdale

595

Port Everglades

Fort Lauderdale/Hollywood Int'l Airport

Dania

75

Hollywood

Hallandale

826

95

A1A

Hialeah

9

826 27

195

Miami Beach

Miami Int'l Airport

M I A M I

41

Tamiami

1

Biscayne Bay

FLORIDA

10

Tallahassee

75

4

95

Area of detail

75

Miami

0   10 mi
0   10 km

N

Cheap Thrills: What to See & Do for Free (or Almost) on the Gold Coast

- **Take a Broadwalk.** The 3-mile-long Hollywood Beach **Broadwalk,** modeled after Atlantic City's legendary boardwalk, is Hollywood's most popular beachfront pedestrian thoroughfare, a cement promenade that's 30 feet wide and stretches along the shoreline. Popular with runners, skaters, and cruisers, the Broadwalk is also renowned as a hangout for thousands of retirement-age snowbirds who get together for frequent dances and shows at a faded outdoor amphitheater
- **Drive the Strip.** The Fort Lauderdale "Strip," aka A1A, is perhaps one of the most scenic stretches of pavement you'll ever find. Drive along the Atlantic on A1A from Fort Lauderdale all the way up to Palm Beach and marvel at the mansions, blue water, and stunning scenery.
- **Trail Turtles.** In June and July, **John U. Lloyd Beach State Park,** 6503 N. Ocean Dr., Dania (© **954/923-2833**), is a haven for nesting turtles. The Sea Turtle Awareness Program is a fascinating program hosted by knowledgeable park rangers. The program begins at dusk with a lecture and slide show while scouts search the beach for nesting loggerhead sea turtles. Reservations are required and it only costs $3 to $5 per carload.
- **Hail a Water Taxi.** The **Water Bus of Fort Lauderdale** (© **954/467-6677;** www.watertaxi.com) cruise through the Intracoastal Waterways and make over 20 stops at local attractions, hotels, and restaurants in Fort Lauderdale. You'll never be able to ride in a regular taxi again. All-day tickets cost $5.
- **Forget Ringling Bros.** Move over Barnum and Bailey! **The Fort Lauderdale Swap Shop,** 3291 W. Sunrise Blvd. (© **954/791-SWAP**), features a *free* circus every day complete with elephants, lions, tigers, bears, and bargains.
- **Tell The Donald *He's* Fired:** Membership to Donald Trump's tonier-than-thou Mar-A-Lago country club may cost an arm and a leg, but it's still free to do a drive by and scream out your window, "You're fired," as you continue along past all the Palm Beach compounds and estates and wonder how the residents there got so rich.

For the purposes of this chapter, the Gold Coast will consist of the towns of Hallandale, Hollywood, Pompano Beach, Fort Lauderdale, Dania, Deerfield, Boca Raton, Delray Beach, Boynton Beach, Jupiter, and the Palm Beaches.

EXPLORING THE GOLD COAST BY CAR

Like most of South Florida, the Gold Coast consists of a mainland and an adjacent strip of barrier islands. You'll have to check the maps to keep track of the many bridges that allow access to the islands where most of the tourist activity is centered. Interstate 95, which runs north-south, is the area's main highway. Farther west is the Florida Turnpike, a toll road that can be worth the expense since the speed limit is higher and it is often less congested than I-95. Also on the mainland is U.S. 1, which generally runs parallel to I-95 (to the east) and is a narrower thoroughfare mostly crowded with strip malls and seedy hotels.

I recommend taking Fla. A1A, a slow oceanside road that connects the long, thin islands of Florida's whole east coast. Although the road is narrow, it is the most scenic and forces you into the relaxed atmosphere of these resort towns.

1 Broward County: Hallandale & Hollywood ⟨★⟩ to Fort Lauderdale ⟨★⟩⟨★⟩

23 miles N of Miami

Until the 2000 presidential election fiasco, most people had never heard of Broward County. Less exposed than the highly hyped Miami, Broward County is a lot calmer and, according to some, a lot friendlier than the magic city. In fact, a friendly rivalry exists between residents of Miami–Dade County and those of Broward County. Miamians consider themselves more sophisticated and cosmopolitan than their northern neighbors who, in turn, dismiss the alleged sophistication as snobbery and actually prefer their own county's gentler pace.

With more than 23 miles of beachfront and 300 miles of navigable waterways, Broward County is also a great outdoor destination. Scattered amid the shopping malls, condominiums, and tourist traps is a beautiful landscape lined with hundreds of parks, golf courses, tennis courts, and, of course, beaches.

The City of Hallandale Beach is a small, peaceful oceanfront town located just north of Dade County's Aventura. Condos are the predominant landmarks in Hallandale, which is still pretty much a retirement community, although the revamped multimillion-dollar Westin Diplomat Resort is trying to revitalize and liven up the area. Just north of Hallandale is the more energetic, burgeoning, Hollywood.

Like many other small American towns, South Florida's city of Hollywood has been working on redeveloping its downtown area for years. Once a sleepy community wedged between Fort Lauderdale and Miami, Hollywood is now a bustling area of 1.5 million people belonging to an array of ethnic and racial identities: from white and African American, to people of Jamaican, Chinese, and Dominican descent. (*Money* magazine trumpeted the self-described "City of the Future" as having an ethnic makeup that mirrors what America will look like by the year 2022.) In May of 2004, Hard Rock Cafe International debuted its $300 million **Seminole Hard Rock Hotel & Casino** (© **954/327-7625**) at the Seminole Indian Nation reservation land in Hollywood, with a 500-room hotel, a spa, and 130,000-square-foot casino. This could be exactly what the city needs to kick its slow renaissance up a notch.

Additionally, a spate of redevelopment has made the pedestrian-friendly center along Hollywood Boulevard and Harrison Street, east of Dixie Highway, a popular destination for travelers and locals alike. Some predict Hollywood will be South Florida's next big destination—South Beach without the attitude, traffic jams, and parking nightmares. While the prediction is a dubious one, Hollywood is definitely awakening from its long slumber. Prices are a fraction of those at other tourist areas, and a quasi-bohemian vibe is apparent in the galleries, clubs, and restaurants that dot the new "strip." Its gritty undercurrent, however, prevents it from becoming too trendy.

Fort Lauderdale, and its well-known strip of beaches, restaurants, bars, and souvenir shops, has also undergone a major transformation. Once famous (or infamous) for the annual mayhem it hosted during spring break, this area is now attracting a more affluent, better-behaved yachting crowd. Starwood Hotels has announced plans for a W Fort Lauderdale Hotel, a 346-room boutique hotel originally slated to open in South Beach but instead opening in Fort Lauderdale in December of 2006.

In addition to beautiful wide beaches, Fort Lauderdale, known as the Venice of America, has more than 300 miles of navigable waterways and innumerable canals, which permit thousands of residents to anchor boats in their backyards. Boating is not just a hobby here; it's a lifestyle. Visitors can easily get on the water, too, by renting a boat or simply hailing a moderately priced water taxi.

Huge cruise ships also take advantage of Florida's deepest harbor, Port Everglades, whose name is somewhat misleading because it is not part of the Florida Everglades. The seaport is actually located on the southeastern coast of the Florida peninsula, near the Fort Lauderdale–Hollywood International Airport on the outskirts of Hollywood and Dania Beach. Port Everglades is the second-busiest cruise-ship base in Florida after Miami and one of the top five in the world. For further information on cruises, see chapter 4, "Miami," and consult *Frommer's Caribbean Cruises & Ports of Call* (Wiley Publishing, Inc.).

ESSENTIALS

GETTING THERE If you're driving from Miami, it's a straight shot north to Hollywood or Fort Lauderdale. Visitors on their way to or from Orlando should take the Florida Turnpike to exit 53, 54, 58, or 62, depending on the location of your accommodations.

The **Fort Lauderdale–Hollywood International Airport** is small, easy to negotiate, and located just 15 minutes from both of the downtown areas it services. But the user-friendliness of this airport may not last much longer: Because of its popularity, the airport is undergoing a $650 million expansion and renovation that may render it just as maddening as any other major metropolitan airport.

Amtrak (© **800/USA-RAIL**) stations are at 200 SW 21st Terrace (Broward Blvd. and I-95), Fort Lauderdale (© **954/587-6692**), and 3001 Hollywood Blvd. (northwest corner of Hollywood Blvd. and I-95), Hollywood (© **954/921-4517**).

VISITOR INFORMATION The **Greater Fort Lauderdale Convention & Visitors Bureau,** 1850 Eller Dr., Suite 303 (off I-95 and I-595 east), Fort Lauderdale, FL 33316 (© **954/765-4466;** fax 954/765-4467; www.sunny.org), is an excellent resource for area information in English, Spanish, and French. I highly recommend calling them in advance to request a free comprehensive guide covering events, accommodations, and sightseeing in Broward County. In addition, once you are in town, you can contact an **information line** (© **954/527-5600;** www.activityline.net) to get easy-to-follow directions, travel advice, and assistance from multilingual operators who staff a round-the-clock help line. Also available for brochures, information, and vacation packages in Fort Lauderdale are operators at Greater Than Ever Fort Lauderdale (© **800/22-SUNNY**).

The **Greater Hollywood Chamber of Commerce,** 330 N. Federal Hwy. (on the corner of U.S. 1 and Taylor St.), Hollywood, FL 33020 (© **954/923-4000;** fax 954/923-8737; www.hollywoodchamber.org), is open Monday through Friday from 9am to 5pm. Here you'll find the lowdown on all of Hollywood's events, attractions, restaurants, hotels, and tours.

Fort Lauderdale, Hollywood & Pompano Beach Area

Banyan Marina
  Resort **19**
Bass Pro Shops
  Outdoor World **29**
Beach Place **21**
Bonnet House **20**
Broward Mall **14**
Carlos & Pepe **26**
Dania Jai Alai **29**
Design Center of
  the Americas **27**

The Diplomat
  Country Club
  and Spa **38**
Eduardo De San
  Angel **7**
Emerald Hills **31**
The Floridian
  Restaurant **18**
Fort Lauderdale
  Beach Hostel **9**

Fort Lauderdale Beach
  Promenade **13**
Fort Lauderdale
  Stadium **5**
The Fort Lauderdale
  Swap Shop **10**
Galleria **21**
Gulfstream Park **40**
Hamburger Mary's **8**
Hollywood Beach
  Broadwalk **32**
Jimmy Evert
  Tennis Center **17**
John U. Lloyd Beach
  State Park **28**
Lago Mar Resort
  and Club **24**

Le Tub **34**
A Little Inn
  By the Sea **6**
Mark's Las Olas **18**
Marriott's Harbor
  Beach **25**
Museum of Art
  Fort Lauderdale **16**
Museum of Discovery
  & Science **15**

Office Depot Center **2**
Orangebrook
  Golf Course **37**
Pillars Hotel **21**
Pompano Park Racing **4**
Sawgrass Mills **1**
Sea Downs (and
  the Bougainvillea) **33**
Seminole Hard Rock
  Hotel & Casino **11**

Stranahan House **19**
Sugar Reef **39**
Sunfish Grill **3**
Tarpon Bend **18**
Taverna Opa **35**
Tuscan Today
  Trattoria **12**
The Westin Diplomat
  Resort & Spa **39**

BEACHES

The southern part of the Gold Coast, Broward County, has the region's most popular and amenities-laden beaches, which stretch for more than 23 miles. Most do not charge for access, though all are well maintained. Here's a selection of some of the county's best from south to north.

Hollywood Beach, stretching from Sheridan Street to Georgia Street, is a major attraction in the city of Hollywood, a virtual carnival with a motley assortment of young hipsters, big families, and sunburned French Canadians who dodge bicyclers and skaters along the rows of tacky souvenir shops, T-shirt shops, game rooms, snack bars, beer stands, hotels, and even miniature-golf courses. The 3-mile-long Hollywood Beach **Broadwalk,** modeled after Atlantic City's legendary boardwalk, is Hollywood's most popular beachfront pedestrian thoroughfare, a cement promenade that's 30 feet wide and stretches along the shoreline. Popular with runners, skaters, and cruisers, the Broadwalk is also renowned as a hangout for thousands of retirement-age snowbirds who get together for frequent dances and shows at a faded outdoor amphitheater. Despite efforts to clear out a seedy element, the area remains a haven for drunks and scammers, so keep alert.

If you tire of the hectic diversity that defines Hollywood's Broadwalk, enjoy the natural beauty of the beach itself, which is wide and clean. There are lifeguards, showers, bathroom facilities, and public areas for picnics and parties.

The **Fort Lauderdale Beach Promenade,** along the beach, underwent a $26 million renovation, and it looks fantastic. It's especially peaceful in the mornings when there's just a smattering of joggers and walkers; but even at its most crowded on the weekend, the expansive promenade provides room for everyone. Note, however, that the beach is hardly pristine; it is across the street from an uninterrupted stretch of hotels, bars, and retail outlets. Also nearby is a megaretail and dining complex, Beach Place (p. 238), on Fla. A1A, midway between Las Olas Boulevard and Sunrise Boulevard.

Just across the road, on the sand, most days you will find hard-core volleyballers, who always welcome anyone with a good spike, and an inviting ocean welcoming swimmers of any level. The unusually clear waters are under the careful watch of some of Florida's best-looking lifeguards. Freshen up afterward in any of the clean showers and restrooms conveniently located along the strip. Pets have been banned from most of the beach in order to maintain the impressive cleanliness not commonly associated with such highly trafficked public beaches; a designated area for pets exists away from the main sunbathing areas.

Turtle Trail

In June and July, the John U. Lloyd beach is crawling with nature lovers who come for the spectacular Sea Turtle Awareness Program. Park rangers begin the evening with a lecture and slide show while scouts search the beach for nesting loggerhead sea turtles. If a turtle is located—plenty of them usually are—a beach walk is conducted, where participants can see the turtles nesting and, sometimes, their eggs hatching. The program begins at 9pm on Wednesdays and Fridays from mid-May through mid-July. Call ℂ **954/923-2833** for reservations. Comfortable walking shoes and insect repellent are recommended. The park entrance fee of $3 to $5 per carload applies.

Especially on weekends, parking along the ocean-side meters is nearly impossible to find. Try biking, skating, or hitching a ride on the water taxi instead. The strip is located on Fla. A1A, between SE 17th Street and Sunrise Boulevard.

Dania Beach's **John U. Lloyd Beach State Park,** 6503 N. Ocean Dr., Dania (© **954/923-2833**), is 251 acres of barrier island between the Atlantic Ocean and the Intracoastal Waterway, from Port Everglades on the north to Dania on the south. Its natural setting contrasts sharply with the urban development of Fort Lauderdale. Lloyd Beach, one of Broward County's most important nesting beaches for sea turtles, produces some 10,000 hatchlings a year. The park's broad, flat beach is popular for swimming and sunning. Self-guided nature trails are great for those who are too restless to sunbathe.

AFFORDABLE OUTDOOR ACTIVITIES & SPECTATOR SPORTS

BOATING   Often called the "yachting capital of the world," Fort Lauderdale provides ample opportunity for visitors to get out on the water, either along the Intracoastal Waterway or on the open ocean. If your hotel doesn't rent boats, try **Aloha Watersports,** Marriott's Harbor Beach Resort, 3030 Holiday Dr., Fort Lauderdale (© **954/462-7245**). They will outfit you with a variety of craft, including jet skis, WaveRunners, and catamarans. Rates start at $65 per half-hour for WaveRunners ($15 each additional rider; doubles and triples available), $70 to $125 for sailboats, $60 to $70 for catamarans, $20 per person per hour for ocean kayaks, and $60 per person for a 10- to 12-minute parasailing ride. Aloha also offers Coast Guard classes at 9am daily where adults can obtain their Florida Boaters License for $3.

CRUISES   The **Jungle Queen,** 801 Sea Breeze Blvd. (3 blocks south of Las Olas Blvd. on Fla. A1A), in the Bahia Mar Yacht Center, Fort Lauderdale (© **954/462-5596**), a Mississippi River–style steamer, is one of Fort Lauderdale's best-known attractions, cruising up and down the New River. All-you-can-eat 4-hour dinner cruises (departing nightly at 7pm and costing $31 for adults and $17 for children 2–10) and 3-hour sightseeing tours (scheduled daily at 10am and 2pm and costing $14 for adults and $9.25 for children 2–10) take visitors past Millionaires' Row, Old Fort Lauderdale, and the new downtown. They also have a seasonal 8-hour cruise that goes down to Miami (Bayside) leaving Wednesdays and Saturdays at 9:15am and costing $17 for adults and $12 for children.

If you're interested in gambling, several casino-boat companies operate day cruises out of Port Everglades and offer blackjack, slots, and poker. **Discovery Cruise Lines** (© **800/937-4477**) has daily cruises to the Bahamas, leaving at 7:45am, where you can gamble, eat, and party for 10 to 12 hours (you have about 3 hr. in the Bahamas to go to the Straw Market or to do even more gambling) for $113 Monday through Thursday, and $143 Friday through Sunday. The price includes breakfast, lunch, and dinner, but drinks cost extra.

Sea Escape (© **800/327-2005** or 954/453-3333) also launches daily casino cruises 15 times a week. But theirs don't travel more than a few miles offshore. These trips "to nowhere" are Monday through Sunday from 11am to 4:30pm; Monday through Friday from 7:30pm to 12:30am; and Saturday from 7:30pm to 1:30am. The daytime cruises are free on Mondays but cost $25 in advance for adults ($35 if you pay at the dock) and $13 for kids 2 through 12 (children not allowed on the evening cruises). Evening cruises have the same prices, except on Friday and Saturday, when adults pay $30 in advance, $40 at the dock. The party cruises offer buffet meals and full casinos for $30 to $40 per person. I'd

---

Great Adventures

While the Westin Diplomat Resort & Spa in Hollywood caters to the likes of Demi Moore and Ashton Kutcher, who stayed here along with Madonna during a kabbalah conference, it's not completely prohibitive to enjoy the hotel's offerings, even if you can't afford to stay there. Instead, try their **Adventure World** (© 954/457-9575; www.abcadventure world.com), a one-stop shop for adventure seekers looking for air cat excursions; kayak, canoe, and jet ski trips; fishing expeditions; tours on Segway human transporters; and more. Discount packages are available.

---

recommend spending an additional $20 for a cabin ($25 per cabin on the evening cruises—though do not expect *Love Boat* luxe here), so you can stretch out and relax between hands. Even though the cruises don't go far from the coast, 5 or 6 hours is a long time to spend at sea, especially if the weather is rough.

FISHING   Completed in 1999 at a cost of more than $32 million, the **IGFA (International Game Fish Association) World Fishing Center** at 300 Gulf Stream Way (© **954/922-4212;** www.igfa.org) in Dania Beach is an angler's paradise. One of the highlights of this museum, library, and park is the virtual-reality fishing simulator, which allows visitors to actually reel in their own computer-generated catch. Also included in the 3-acre park are displays of antique fishing gear, record catches, famous anglers, various vessels, and a wetlands lab. To get a list of local captains and guides, call **IGFA headquarters** (© **954/927-2628**) and ask for the librarian. Admission is $6 for adults, $5 for seniors and children between 3 and 16, and free for children under 3. The museum and library are open daily from 10am to 6pm. On the grounds is also **Bass Pro Shops Outdoor World,** a huge multifloor retail complex situated on a 3-acre lake.

GOLF   More than 50 golf courses in all price ranges compete for players. Some of the best include **Emerald Hills** at 4100 N. Hills Dr., Hollywood, just west of I-95 between Sterling Road and Sheridan Street. This beauty consistently lands on the "best of" lists of golf writers throughout the country. The 18th hole, on a two-tier green, is the challenging course's signature; it's surrounded by water and is more than a bit rough. The course is pricey—greens fees start at $125 for tee times after 1pm and $150 for tee times before noon Friday through Sunday, and $125 before noon and $100 after 1pm Monday through Thursday. Call © **954/961-4000** for tee times. **The Diplomat Country Club and Spa,** 501 Diplomat Pkwy., Hallandale Beach (© **954/602-6000;** www.diplomatcountryclub.com), is located across the Intracoastal from the Westin Diplomat Resort and has fabulous golf facilities with 8 acres of lakes and rolling fairways and a fantastic delivery service that brings lunch and drinks straight to your cart. You will pay for the services, however, with greens fees of $189 weekdays, $195 weekends, and 2pm twilights at $95 all week. For one of Broward's best municipal challenges, try the 18-holer at the **Orangebrook Golf Course** at 400 Entrada Dr. in Hollywood (© **954/967-GOLF**). Built in 1937, this is one of the state's oldest courses and one of the area's best bargains. Morning and noon rates range from $29 to $34. After 2pm, you can play for less than $20, including a cart. Men must wear collared shirts to play here, and no spikes are allowed.

SCUBA DIVING   In Broward County, the best wreck dive is the *Mercedes I*, a 197-foot freighter that washed up in the backyard of a Palm Beach socialite in 1984 and was sunk for divers the following year off Pompano Beach. The artificial reef, filled with colorful sponges, spiny lobsters, and barracudas, is located 97 feet below the surface, a mile offshore between Oakland Park Boulevard and Sunrise Boulevard. Dozens of reputable dive shops line the beach. Ask at your hotel for a nearby recommendation or contact **Neil Watson's Undersea Adventures,** 1525 S. Andrews Ave., Fort Lauderdale (© **954/462-3400;** www.neil watson.com).

SPECTATOR SPORTS   Baseball fans can get their fix at the **Fort Lauderdale Stadium,** 5301 NW 12th Ave. (© **954/828-4980**), where the Baltimore Orioles play Spring Training exhibition games starting in early March; call © **954/776-1921** for tickets. General admission is $6, a spot in the grandstand $9, $3 for kids 14 and under, and box seats $12. During the season, the Florida Marlins play just south of Hallandale at the **Pro Player Stadium** near the Dade–Broward County line. Call Ticketmaster for tickets (© **305/358-5885**), which range from $4 to $50. Tickets go on sale in January.

Pompano Park Racing, 1800 SW 3rd St., Pompano Beach (© **954/972-2000**), features parimutuel harness racing from October to early August. Both grandstand and clubhouse admission is free.

Jai alai, a sort of Spanish-style indoor lacrosse, was introduced to Florida in 1924 and still draws big crowds, who bet on the fast-paced action. Broward's only fronton, **Dania Jai Alai,** 301 E. Dania Beach Blvd. at the intersection of Fla. A1A and U.S. 1 (© **954/920-1511**), is a great place to spend an afternoon or evening.

Wrapped around an artificial lake, **Gulfstream Park,** at U.S. 1 and Hallandale Beach Boulevard, Hallandale (© **954/454-7000**), is pretty and popular. Large purses and important horse races are commonplace at this recently refurbished suburban course, and the track is often crowded. It hosts the Florida Derby each March. Call for schedules. Admission is $3 weekdays, $5 weekends to the grandstand, and always $5 to the clubhouse. Parking is free. From January 3 to April 25, post times are 1:30pm weekdays and 1pm weekends, and the doors open at 11:30am. Many weekends feature live concerts by well-known musicians.

In the sport of ice hockey, the young Florida Panthers (© **954/835-7000**) are loved by their fans. They play in Sunrise at the **Office Depot Center** at 2555 NW 137th Way (© **954/835-8000**). Tickets range from $14 to $100. Call for directions and ticket information.

TENNIS   There are hundreds of courts in Broward County, and plenty are accessible to the public. Many are at resorts and hotels. If one's not at yours, try one of these.

Famous as the spot where Chris Evert got in her early serves, the **Jimmy Evert Tennis Center,** 701 NE 12th Ave. (off Sunrise Blvd.), Fort Lauderdale (© **954/828-5378**), has 18 lighted clay and 3 hard courts. Her coach and father, James Evert, still teaches young players here, though he is very picky about whom he'll accept. Nonresidents of Fort Lauderdale pay $5 per hour before 4pm and $6 after. Reservations are accepted after 2pm for the following day but cost an extra $3.

SEEING THE SIGHTS

Billie Swamp Safari ⚑   Billie Swamp Safari is an up-close-and-personal view of the Seminole Indians' 2,200-acre Big Cypress Reservation. There are daily tours into reservation wetlands, hardwood hammocks, and areas where wildlife (seemingly strategically placed deer, water buffalo, bison, wild hogs, ornery ostriches, rare birds, and alligators) reside. Tours are provided aboard swamp buggies, customized motorized vehicles specially designed to provide visitors with an elevated view of the frontier while comfortably riding through the wetlands and cypress heads. For the more adventurous, you may want to take a fast-moving airboat ride or trek a nature trail. Airboat rides run about 20 minutes while the swamp buggy tours are about 1 hour long. A stop at an alligator farm reeks of Disney, but the kids won't care. You can also stay overnight in a native Tiki hut if you're really looking to immerse yourself in the culture.

Big Cypress Reservation, 1½-hr. drive west of Fort Lauderdale. © **800/949-6101**. Free admission. Swamp buggy tours $20 adults, $18 seniors 62 and up, $10 children 4–12; airboat tours $12 for all ages. Daily 8:30am–6pm. Airboats depart every 30 min. beginning at 9:30am; last ride at 4:30pm. Swamp buggy tours leave on the hour (except for 4pm) between 11am and 5pm.

Bonnet House ★★★   This historic 35-acre plantation home and estate, accessible by guided tour only, will provide you with a fantastic glimpse of old South Florida. Built in 1921, the sprawling two-story waterfront home (surrounded with formal tropical gardens) is really the backdrop of a love story, which the very chatty volunteer guides will share with you if you ask. Some have actually lunched with the former resident of the house, the late Evelyn Bartlett, the wife of world-acclaimed artist Frederic Clay Bartlett. The worthwhile 1¼-hour tour brings you quirky people, whimsical artwork, lush grounds, and interesting design. Inquire about the literary walks and science workshops, which are offered regularly on the grounds.

One If by Land, Taxi If by Sea

Plan to spend at least an afternoon or evening cruising Fort Lauderdale's 300 miles of waterways in the only way you can: by boat. The **Water Bus of Fort Lauderdale** (© **954/467-6677**; www.watertaxi.com) is one of the greatest innovations for water lovers since those cool Velcro sandals. A trusty fleet of older port boats serves the dual purpose of transporting and entertaining visitors as they cruise through "The Venice of America." Because of its popularity, the water taxis have welcomed several sleek, 70-passenger "water buses" (featuring indoor and outdoor seating with an atrium-like roof) to the fleet.

Taxis operate on demand and also along a fairly regular route, carrying up to 48 passengers to 20 stops. If you stay at a hotel on the route, you can be picked up at your hotel, usually within 15 minutes of calling, and then be shuttled to any of the dozens of restaurants, bars, and attractions on or near the waterfront. If you aren't sure where you want to go, ask one of the personable captains, who can point out historic and fun spots along the way.

Starting daily at 8am, boats run until midnight 7 days a week, depending on the weather. Check their website for exact times of pickup. The cost is $5 for a day pass; $4 for a one-way trip; $10 for a 3-day pass; and $25 for a weeklong pass. Tickets are available on board; no credit cards are accepted.

900 N. Birch Rd. (1 block west of the ocean, south of Sunrise Blvd.), Fort Lauderdale. ☎ **954/563-5393**. www.bonnethouse.org. Admission $10 adults, $9 seniors, $8 students under 18, free for children 6 and under. Call for hours and tour times.

Museum of Art Fort Lauderdale ★ *Kids* A fantastic modern art facility, the Museum of Art Fort Lauderdale features permanent collections including those from William Glackens; the CoBrA Movement in Copenhagen, Brussels, and Amsterdam featuring over 200 paintings; 50 sculptures; 1,200 works on paper from 1948–1951, including the largest repository of Asger Jorn graphics outside the Silkeborg Kunstmuseum in Denmark; a stunning collection of Picasso ceramics; and a contemporary collection of works from over 90 Cuban artists in exile around the world. Traveling exhibits such as Ansel Adams and constant art classes make the Museum a great place to spend a rainy day.

1 E. Las Olas Blvd., Fort Lauderdale. ☎ **954/525-5500**. www.moafl.org. Adults $6, students $3, children under 6 free. Wed and Fri–Mon 11am–7pm; Thurs 11am–9pm.

Museum of Discovery & Science ★★ *Kids* This museum's high-tech, interactive approach to education proves that science can equal fun. Adults won't feel as if they're in a kiddie museum, either. During the week, school groups meander through the cavernous two-story modern building. Kids 7 and under enjoy navigating their way through the excellent explorations in the "Discovery Center." Florida Ecoscapes is particularly interesting, with a living coral reef, bees, bats, frogs, turtles, and alligators. Most weekend nights, you'll find a diverse crowd ranging from hip high-school kids to 30-somethings enjoying a rock film in the IMAX 3-D theater, which also shows short, science-related, supersize films daily. Out front, see the 52-foot-tall "Great Gravity Clock," located in the museum's atrium, the largest kinetic-energy sculpture in the state. Call for changing exhibits.

401 SW 2nd St., Fort Lauderdale. ☎ **954/467-6637**. www.mods.org. Museum admission (includes admission to 1 IMAX film) $14 adults, $13 seniors, $12 children 3–12. Mon–Sat 10am–5pm; Sun noon–6pm. Movie theaters stay open later. From I-95, exit on Broward Blvd. E. Continue to SW 5th Ave.; turn right, garage on right.

Stranahan House ★★★ In a town whose history is younger than many of its residents, visitors may want to take a minute to see Fort Lauderdale's very oldest standing structure and a prime example of classic "Florida Frontier" architecture. Built in 1901 by the "father of Fort Lauderdale," Frank Stranahan, this house once served as a trading post for Seminole trappers, who came here to sell pelts. It's been a post office, town hall, and general store and now is a worthwhile little museum of South Florida pioneer life, containing turn-of-the-last-century furnishings and historical photos of the area. It is also the site of occasional concerts and social functions. Call for details.

335 SE 6th Ave. (Las Olas Blvd. at the New River Tunnel), Fort Lauderdale. ☎ **954/524-4736**. www.stranahanhouse.com. Admission $6 adults, $5 seniors, $3 students and children. Wed–Sat 10am–3pm; Sun 1–3pm. Tours are on the hour; last tour at 3pm. Accessible by water taxi.

SHOPPING & BROWSING

It's all about malls in Broward County. And while most of the best shopping is located within Fort Lauderdale proper, there are other areas in the county also worth browsing.

Dania is known as the Antique Capital of the South because within 1 square mile of Federal Highway, the city has more than 100 dealers selling everything from small collectibles to fine antiques. (If you want to peruse, it's best to park along Federal Highway, on the "row," which is where Federal Highway meets

U.S. 1.) For more information on "Antique Row," call ℭ **954/924-3627.** Also in Dania is the **Design Center of the Americas (DCOTA),** at the intersection of I-95 and Griffin Road (ℭ **954/920-7997;** www.designcenteroftheamericas. com), a 775,000-square-foot full-service interior design center with tons of furniture showrooms featuring everything from ultramod to classic, designer studios, and, from time to time, fabulous sample sales.

For bargain mavens, there's a strip of "fashion" stores on Hallandale Beach Boulevard's "Schmatta Row," east of Dixie Highway and the railroad tracks, where off-brand shoes, bags, and jewelry are sold at deep discounts. Hollywood Boulevard also offers some interesting shops, with everything from Indonesian artifacts to used and rare books, leather bustiers, and handmade hats. Dozens of shops line the pedestrian-friendly strip just west of Young Circle. The art galleries are clustered along Harrison Street, just east of Dixie Highway.

The area's only beachfront mall, **Beach Place,** is in Fort Lauderdale on Fla. A1A just north of Las Olas Boulevard. The recipient of a $1.6 million face-lift in 2001, this 100,000-square-foot giant sports the usual chains like Sunglass Hut, Limited Express, Banana Republic, and Gap, as well as lots of popular bars and restaurants. While it used to be all the rage with the spring-break set, Beach Place is now aiming for a much more upscale clientele, adding many new higher-end stores and restaurants.

Other more traditional malls include the upscale **Galleria,** at Sunrise Boulevard near the Fort Lauderdale Beach, and **Broward Mall,** west of I-95 on Broward Boulevard, in Plantation.

If you are looking for unusual boutiques, especially art galleries, head to quaint **Las Olas Boulevard** ✿ (located west of A1A and a block east of Federal Hwy./U.S. 1, off of SE 8th St.), where there are hundreds of shops with alluring window decorations (like kitchen utensils posing as modern art sculptures) and intriguing merchandise such as mural-size oil paintings.

On the edge of the Arts and Science District is **Las Olas Riverfront,** a retail complex with 260,000 square feet of restaurants, clothing stores, arcades, and a multiplex movie theater.

The Fort Lauderdale Swap Shop, 3291 W. Sunrise Blvd. (ℭ **954/791-SWAP**), is one of the world's largest flea markets. I think it's rather schlocky, actually. In addition to endless acres of vendors hawking everything from electronics to underwear, there's a miniature amusement park, a 13-screen drive-in movie theater, weekend concerts, and even a free daily circus complete with elephants, horse shows, high-wire acts, and clowns.

The monster of all outlet malls is **Sawgrass Mills,** 12801 W. Sunrise Blvd., Sunrise (ℭ **800-FL-MILLS** or 954/846-2350; fax 954/846-2312). Since the most recent expansion, completed in mid-1999, which added more than 30 new designer outlet stores, this behemoth (shaped like a Florida alligator) now holds more than 300 shops, kiosks, a 24-screen movie theater, and many restaurants and bars, including a Hard Rock Cafe. The enclosed area covers nearly 2.5 million square feet over 50 acres—there's no way to see it all in a day. New-ish at Sawgrass is **Wanadoo City,** a $50 million education and amusement center for kids featuring 140,000 square feet of "city" where they can role play being firefighters, TV anchors, actors, chefs, judges, doctors, pilots, archaeologists, and more. To get there, take I-95 to I-595 west to the Flamingo Road exit, turn right, and drive 2 miles to Sunrise Boulevard; you will see the large complex on the left. From the Florida Turnpike, exit Sunrise Boulevard west.

Fishing enthusiasts won't want to miss **Bass Pro Shops Outdoor World** (200 Gulfstream Way, Dania Beach; ℭ **954/929-7710**), a sprawling retail complex just west of I-95, where you can buy anything from yachts to lures.

ACCOMMODATIONS YOU CAN AFFORD

The Fort Lauderdale beach has a hotel or motel on nearly every block, and they range from the run-down to the luxurious. Both the **Howard Johnson** (ℭ **800/ 327-8578** or 954/563-2451), at 700 N. Atlantic Blvd. (on Fla. A1A, south of Sunrise Blvd.), and the **Days Inn** (ℭ **800/329-7466** or 954/563-2521), at 4221 N. Ocean Blvd., offer clean ocean-side rooms starting at about $150. For a more luxurious stay, the **St. Regis Resort, Spa and Residences** (ℭ **954/568- 4623**), featuring 197 suites, a gourmet restaurant, and a spa, at press time was slated to open in August of 2005. And, opened in May 2004, the **Seminole Hard Rock Hotel & Casino,** 1 Seminole Rd. (ℭ **954/327-7625**), a $300 million resort with 500 rooms, a health spa, beach club, and gaming facilities, undoubtedly brought new life to the Hollywood area.

In Hollywood, where prices are generally cheaper, the **Holiday Inn** at 101 N. Ocean Blvd. (ℭ **954/923-8700**) operates a full-service hotel right on the ocean. With prices starting at around $110 in season and discounts for AAA members, it's a great deal. **Howard Johnson** (ℭ **800/423-9867** or 954/925-1411) has a good location right on the beach at 2501 N. Ocean Dr. (I-95 to Sheridan St. east to Fla. A1A south).

Extended Stay America/Crossland Economy Studios (ℭ **800/398-7829**) has four superclean properties in Fort Lauderdale and offers year-round rates as low as $49 a night and $159 per week. The studios are designed with business travelers in mind. Each includes free local calls, a dataport, a kitchenette, a recliner, and a well-lit desk.

Especially for rentals for a few weeks or months, call **Florida Sunbreak** (ℭ **800-SUNBREAK**). Also, check out the annual list of small lodgings compiled by the **Greater Fort Lauderdale Convention & Visitors Bureau** (ℭ **954/ 765-4466**). It is especially helpful for those looking for privately owned, charming, and affordable lodgings.

Banyan Marina Resort ★★   These fabulous waterfront apartments, located on a beautifully landscaped residential island, may have you vowing never to stay in a hotel again. They're intimate, charming, *and* reasonably priced. Built around a stunning 75-year-old banyan tree, the Banyan Marina Resort is located directly on the active canals halfway between Fort Lauderdale's downtown and the beach. When available, you'll choose between one- and two-bedroom apartments, which have been recently renovated. All are comfortable and spacious, with French doors, full kitchens, and living rooms. There is a small outdoor heated pool and a marina for those with boats in tow.

111 Isle of Venice, Fort Lauderdale, FL 33301. ℭ **954/524-4430.** Fax 954/764-4870. www.banyanmarina. com. 10 units. Winter $95–$250 apt; off season $60–$170 apt. Weekly and monthly rates available. MC, V. Free parking. From I-95, exit Broward Blvd. E.; cross U.S. 1 and turn right on SE 15th Ave. At the first traffic light (Las Olas Blvd.), turn left. Turn left at the 3rd island (Isle of Venice). **Amenities:** Restaurant; pool; dock. *In room:* A/C, TV, dataport, kitchen, coffeemaker, hair dryer.

A Little Inn by the Sea ★   It's not fancy, but A Little Inn by the Sea sits on a primo piece of oceanfront, and most rooms have private balconies overlooking the ocean. There's also 300 feet of private, palm tree–lined beach, which isn't too shabby either. Rooms are hardly worthy of a spread in an interior design magazine, but the views make up for the lackluster decor. A free breakfast buffet, a rooftop terrace, and a heated freshwater pool are lovely perks.

4546 El Mar Dr., Lauderdale-by-the-Sea, FL 33308. © **800/492-0311** or 954/772-2450. Fax 954/938-9354. www.alittleinn.com. 29 units. Winter $119–$149 double, $160–$199 suite, $318 2-bedroom apartment; off season $79–$109 double, $129–$159 suite, $228–$248 2-bedroom apartment. MC, V. Free parking. **Amenities:** Heated pool; access to nearby tennis court; nearby children's playground; coin laundry. *In room:* A/C, TV.

Sea Downs (and the Bougainvillea) ★★

This bargain accommodation is often booked months in advance by returning guests who want to be directly on the beach without paying a fortune. The hosts of this superclean 1950s motel, Claudia and Karl Herzog, live on the premises and keep things running smoothly. Renovations completed in 1997 have replaced bathroom fixtures, and many rooms have been redecorated here and at the Herzogs' other even less expensive property next door, the 11-unit Bougainvillea. Guests at both hotels share the Sea Downs' pool.

2900 N. Surf Rd., Hollywood, FL 33019. © **954/923-4968.** Fax 954/923-8747. www.seadowns.com or www.bougainvilleahollywood.com. 12 units. Winter $63–$95 studio, $88–$140 1-bedroom apt; off season $60–$70 studio, $88–$108 1-bedroom apt. No credit cards. From I-95, exit Sheridan St. E. to Fla. A1A and go south; drive ½ mile to Coolidge St.; turn left. **Amenities:** Freshwater outdoor pool; concierge; laundry facilities. *In room:* A/C, TV, dataport, kitchen, fridge, coffeemaker.

SUPER-CHEAP SLEEPS

Fort Lauderdale Beach Hostel

For the young, or budget/backpack travelers, this hostel is a great option, offering both dorm beds and private rooms at bargain basement prices. Clean and conveniently located, the hostel is just 654 feet from the ocean, features free parking, free telephones, free self-cook food, a free breakfast buffet, and, if you're lucky, free surfboards or in-line skates lying around for your use.

2115 N. Ocean Blvd., Fort Lauderdale, FL 33305. © **954/567-7275.** www.fortlauderdalehostel.com. 12 units. Dorm beds $18 per night, $115 per week; private rooms $59 season, $42 off season. MC, V. **Amenities:** Free breakfast; Ping-Pong; free Internet access; sun deck; garden. *In room:* A/C, TV, iron.

Ronny Dee Resort Motel ★

The good news is that this family-owned motel is just 100 yards from the beach and is extremely affordable. The bad news is that it's located on busy Fla. A1A. Popular with European guests, the two-story yellow motel is wrapped around a central swimming pool; its guest rooms are wood-paneled (suburban style) and filled with an eclectic mix of furniture. A new coat of paint and new flooring helped to spruce up the place recently. It's clean but not overflowing with all the creature comforts of nearby chain motels.

717 S. Ocean Blvd., Pompano Beach, FL 33062. © **954/943-3020.** www.ronnydeeresort.com. Fax 954/783-5112. 35 units. Winter $69–$88 double; off season $39–$49 double. $5 per extra person. AE, MC, V. From I-95, exit Atlantic Blvd. E. to Fla. A1A N. **Amenities:** Outdoor heated pool; game room. *In room:* A/C, TV, dataport, fridge.

WORTH A SPLURGE

Lago Mar Resort and Club ★★ *Kids*

A charming lobby with a rock fireplace and saltwater aquarium sets the tone of this utterly inviting resort, a casually elegant piece of Old Florida that occupies its own little island between Lake Mayan and the Atlantic. Lago Mar guests have access to the broadest and best strip of beach in the entire city, not to mention the wonderful bougainvillea-lined, 9,000-square-foot swimming lagoon. Lago Mar is very family oriented, with lots of facilities and supervised activities for children. Service is spectacular. The rooms and suites have Mediterranean or Key West influences and are well appointed—but it's likely you won't be spending much time inside.

1700 S. Ocean Lane, Fort Lauderdale, FL 33316. © **800/524-6627** or 954/523-6511. Fax 954/524-6627. www.lagomar.com. 212 units. Winter $265 double, from $355 suite; off season $140–$165 double, from $165 suite. AE, DC, MC, V. Free valet parking. From Federal Hwy. (U.S. 1), turn east onto SE 17th St. Causeway; turn right onto Mayan Dr.; turn right again onto S. Ocean Dr.; turn left onto Grace Dr.; then left again onto S. Ocean Lane to the hotel. **Amenities:** 4 restaurants; cocktail lounge; wine room; outdoor pool and lagoon; 2 tennis courts; exercise room; watersports equipment rental; children's programs during holiday periods; game room; concierge; tour desk; business center; 24-hr. room service; laundry services; dry cleaning. *In room:* A/C, TV, dataport, kitchenette, coffeemaker (in some units), hair dryer.

Pillars Hotel ★★★ *Finds*   It took me a while to discover this hotel and, apparently, that's exactly the point. One of Fort Lauderdale's best-kept secrets, if not the best, Pillars Hotel transports you from the neon-hued flash and splash of Fort Lauderdale's strip and takes you to a two-story British Colonial, Caribbean-style retreat tucked away on the bustling Intracoastal Waterway. Since it has just 23 rooms, you feel as if you have the grand house all to yourself, albeit with white-tablecloth room service, an Eden-istic courtyard with free-form pool, lush landscaping, access to a water taxi, and signing privileges at nearby restaurants and spa. Rooms are luxurious and loaded with amenities such as private-label bath products, ultraplush bedding, and, if you're so inclined, a private masseuse to iron out your personal kinks. Upon arrival, you will be greeted with a welcome cocktail, and there's always free iced tea at the pool in case you're thirsty. A library area, with a grand piano and over 500 books and videos, is at your disposal as is pretty much anything you request here. The quintessential Fort Lauderdale retreat, the Pillars is the zenith of Fort Lauderdale accommodations. There are four suites and all rooms are nonsmoking.

111 N. Birch Rd., Fort Lauderdale, FL 33304. © **954/467-9639.** Fax 954/763-2845. www.pillarshotel.com. 23 units. Winter $199–$265 double, $299–$499 suite; off season $129–$209 double, $199–$409 suite. AE, DC, DISC, MC, V. Complimentary off-street parking. **Amenities:** Waterfront pool; 24-hr. concierge; business services; 24-hr. room service; same-day laundry service; signing privileges at Max's Beach Place restaurant; water-taxi service; preferred rates at beachfront and downtown health clubs. *In room:* AC, TV/VCR, dataport, minibar, hair dryer, iron, safe.

GREAT DEALS ON DINING

It took awhile for a more sophisticated, varied Epicurean scene to reach these shores, but Fort Lauderdale, and to some extent Hollywood, finally has several fine restaurants. Increasingly, ethnic options are joining the legions of surf-and-turferies that have dominated the area for so long. **Las Olas Boulevard** has so many eateries that the city has put a moratorium on the opening of new restaurants on the 2-mile-long street.

Carlos & Pepe ☆ MEXICAN   Tucked away in yet another strip mall, Carlos & Pepe is a restaurant that doesn't need fancy digs to convince you that its authentic homemade Mexican cuisine is worth eating. The salsa, in particular, is excellent, not the watery bottled version you find in many Mexican establishments. The food is extremely fresh and flavorful and typical of what you'd find on a Mexican menu: fajitas, burritos, quesadillas, and enchiladas. The margaritas are also quite good, but beware—they do not skimp on the tequila. A low-key local crowd tends to frequent this very casual restaurant.

1302 SE 17th St. (south of Broward Blvd.), Fort Lauderdale. © **954/467-7192.** Main courses $8–$16. AE, DC, DISC, MC, V. Mon–Thurs 11:30am–11pm; Fri–Sat 11:30am–midnight; Sun noon–10pm.

The Floridian Restaurant ☆ *Value* AMERICAN/DINER   The Floridian has been filling South Florida's diner void for over 63 years, serving breakfast, lunch, and dinner, 24/7. It's especially busy on weekend mornings when locals and tourists come in for huge omelets, fresh oatmeal, sausage, and biscuits.

1410 E. Las Olas Blvd., Fort Lauderdale. © **954/463-4041.** Fax 954/761-3930. Sandwiches $3–$7; breakfast combos $3.50–$8; hot platters $7–$14. No credit cards. Daily 24 hr.

Hamburger Mary's ★★ AMERICAN   For fans of kitsch, Hamburger Mary's is a place to fawn over and tell your friends about. For one, the check is presented to you in a stiletto heel from Frederick's of Hollywood. Secondly, the hamburgers are fabulous and full of tongue in cheeky names such as Buffy the Hamburger Slayer—a garlic and Swiss burger—Mary's Breast, and Mary Tyler S'mores. Located in the gay-friendly hamlet of Wilton Manors, Mary's is the neon spot on an already colorful neighborhood with its shabby chic decor that consists of lamps made from galvanized steel buckets, beads and feather boas, speakers covered by wigs, and shoes on the ceiling. An outdoor lanai area provides a fabulous setting for events such as Monday night's Martini and a Movie night in which campy classics are shown on a big screen, and Tuesday night's Mary's House of Blues, featuring live jazz and blues and $3 Tarantula Margaritas. On Sundays, live reggae music and $3 Absolut Peppar Bloody Marys bring in the crowds, which are as colorful as the restaurant itself.

2449 Wilton Dr., Wilton Manors. ① 954/567-1320. Main courses $6–$10. AE, DC, MC, V. Sun–Thurs 11:30am–11pm; Fri–Sat 11:30am–midnight. Bar stays open 2 hr. later.

Le Tub ★★ *Finds* AMERICAN   Hands down, this is one of the coolest, most unpretentious, quintessential, pre-swanky South Florida restaurants if not one of the coolest restaurants period. Established in 1959 as a Sunoco gas station, Le Tub was eventually closed by the energy crisis of the early '70s. In 1974, the place was purchased by a man who dedicated an entire year to personally transforming the place into this waterfront restaurant, made out of flotsam, jetsam, and ocean bone treasures gathered over 4 years of jogging on Hollywood Beach. But the waterfront location and unique building aren't the only things to marvel at. As you walk in, take note of the hand-painted bathtubs and toilet bowls (it's not at all gross; they're used as planters) lining the walkway. Inside the restaurant is a divey bar complete with pool table and jukebox, but outside seating on the deck is the real gem. Le Tub is famous for its burgers, chili, and seafood, but more than the food is the peaceful, easy feeling that exudes from the place.

1100 N. Ocean Dr., Hollywood. ① 954/931-9425. Main courses $6–$17. No credit cards. Daily 10:30am–4am.

Sugar Reef ★★ FRENCH VIETNAMESE/CARIBBEAN   I could go on about the restaurant's priceless, unobstructed ocean view, but the menu of Mediterranean, Caribbean, and French-Vietnamese dishes is just as outstanding. A pleasant tropical decor is bolstered by the fresh air wafting in from the Atlantic through the open windows. Seafood bouillabaisse in green curry and coconut broth and pork loin Benedict—layers of jerk-spiced pork and hollandaise sauce—are among the restaurant's most popular dishes. The restaurant puts a savory spin on duck, roasted and topped with sweet-chile-and-papaya salsa. This is not a restaurant you'd expect to find on a beach boardwalk, which makes it all the more delightful.

600 N. Surf Rd. (on the Broadwalk just north of Hollywood Blvd.), Hollywood. ① 954/922-1119. Reservations accepted for groups of 6 or more. Main courses $10–$24; sandwiches and salads $4–$9. AE, DISC, MC, V. Mon 4–10:30pm; Tues–Thurs 11am–10:30pm; Fri–Sun 11am–11pm (sometimes later in winter).

Tarpon Bend ★★ SEAFOOD/AMERICAN   This restaurant is one of the few places where the fishermen still bring the fish to the back door. The oysters from the raw bar are shucked to order and are incredible. Try the house specialty "smoked fish dip"—a kingfish smoked on premises. The steamed clambake, with half a Maine lobster, clams, potatoes, mussels, and corn on the cob, is scrumptious and served in its own pot. Also try some of the homemade side dishes. For chocolate lovers, the chocolate brownie sundae is a must. There's live entertainment Wednesday through Saturday and a full bar.

200 SW 2nd St., Fort Lauderdale. ✆ 954/523-3233. Reservations accepted for groups of 6 or more. Main courses $12–$15. AE, MC, V. Mon–Thurs 11:30am–1am; Fri–Sat 11:30am–3am.

Taverna Opa ★★ *Value* GREEK   Don't get nervous if you hear plates breaking when you enter this raucous, authentic Greek taverna—it's just the restaurant's lively staff making sure your experience here is 100% Greek. Entrees and delicious *meze* (appetizers), including a large Greek salad with hunks of fresh feta cheese, moist and savory stuffed grape leaves, and grilled calamari, are offered at ridiculously cheap prices. Order a variety of dishes to get the full experience of the restaurant. When you've had enough ouzo, you may want to consider hopping up on one of the tables and dancing to the jacked-up Greek music. If not, don't worry; the waiters usually wind up on the tabletop, encouraging diners to shout the restaurant's name, "Opa!," making sure you don't forget it. You won't. In addition to the two branches in Hollywood and Fort Lauderdale, there's also a branch in Miami's South Beach.

410 N. Ocean Dr., Hollywood. ✆ 954/929-4010. And 3051 NE 32nd Ave., Fort Lauderdale. ✆ 954/567-1630. www.tavernaoparestaurant.com. Reservations accepted weekdays only. Appetizers $2–$9.50; main courses $2.50–$28. AE, DC, DISC, MC, V. Daily from 4pm "until the ouzo runs out."

Tuscan Today Trattoria ★★ *Finds* ITALIAN   For classic Tuscan food in a charming atmosphere, Tuscan Today is something you should not put off until tomorrow. Inspired by the peasant origins of the original trattoria, the restaurant consistently turns out outstanding pizzas and flavorful meat and fish from a customized wood-burning brick oven imported from Tuscany. A reasonable and excellent wine list provides you with a difficult choice in two affordable price ranges: $19 and $23. Artichokes steamed in white-wine broth provide a flavorful balance between garlic and sun-dried tomatoes. Tagliatelle Arometto St. David is an elaborate name for an elaborate dish of fresh herbs marinated in extra-virgin olive oil and lightly tossed with flat semolina pasta, Parmigiano Reggiano cheese, then garnished with diced sweet peppers, olives, and tomatoes. It's outstanding. Grilled thin-crusted pizzas are prepared as the Italians prefer them—light on sauce and cheese but heavy on flavor. For pasta lovers, the powerful but surprisingly light gnocchi with spinach is a good way to go. And if you order a meat or fish entree, be sure to try the rosemary roasted potatoes.

1161 N. Federal Hwy., Fort Lauderdale. ✆ 954/566-1716. Reservations accepted for groups of 6 or more. Main courses $8.95–$15. AE, DC, DISC, MC, V. Sun–Thurs 11am–10pm; Fri–Sat 11am–11pm.

WORTH A SPLURGE

Eduardo De San Angel ★★★ MEXICAN   Gourmet Mexican is *not* an oxymoron, and for those who don't believe that, take one meal at the sublime Eduardo De San Angel and you'll see how true it is. Chef Eduardo Pria has a masterful way with food as seen in dishes such as Jaibas Rellenas, fresh Florida blue crab, plum tomatoes, onions, jalapeño peppers, and Spanish green olives baked in a shell with melted jack cheese au gratin; and mole poblano, herb-oil-brushed grilled breast of chicken topped with the traditional mole from Puebla, toasted sesame seeds, and sliced avocado. And then there's the roasted poblano pepper filled with fresh Florida blue crab, pickled jalapeño peppers, green olives, and tomatoes over stewed sweet onions baked in a parchment paper pocket.

Fresh flowers and candlelight, not to mention the fact that the restaurant resembles an intimate hacienda, also drive home the fact that this isn't your mom's Old El Paso taco dinner.

2822 E Commercial Blvd., Fort Lauderdale. (℡ 954/772-4731. Reservations essential. Main courses $18–$29. AE, DC, DISC, MC, V. Mon–Thurs 11:30am–10:30pm; Fri–Sat 5:30–10:30pm.

Mark's Las Olas ★★★ NEW WORLD CUISINE   Before star chef Mark Militello hit Las Olas Boulevard, there was really no reason to dine here. However, once he opened the doors to his sleek, modern restaurant, he opened the eyes and mouths of discriminating Fort Lauderdale gourmands to his excellent New World cuisine. Roasted garlic-stuffed grilled tenderloin of beef with caramelized sweet onion, Swiss chard, marrow toast, and red wine short-rib sauce is possibly the best item on the menu. If the kitchen is out of it—they tend to run out quickly—everything else on the menu, from the hot pepper pizza with chorizo to the crab-crusted black grouper with wild mushroom-salsify ragout, roasted potatoes, and horseradish butter, is delicious. Save room for a chocolate dessert—any one will do.

1032 E. Las Olas Blvd., Fort Lauderdale. (℡ 954/463-1000. Reservations suggested. Main courses $14–$30. AE, DC, MC, V. Mon–Fri 11:30am–2:30pm; Mon–Thurs 6–10:30pm; Fri–Sat 6–11pm; Sun 6–10pm.

Sunfish Grill ★★★ SEAFOOD   Unlike its fellow contemporary seafood restaurants, the Sunfish Grill chooses to focus on fish, not fusion. Chef Anthony Sindaco doesn't want to be a star, either. He'd prefer to leave the spotlight on his fantastic fish dishes, which are possibly the freshest in town thanks to the fact that he buys his fish at local markets and often from well-known local fishermen who appear at his back door with their catches of the day. The shrimp bisque cappuccino is a deliciously rich soup served in a demitasse cup—because it's that rich. Conch fritters are purely spectacular, not full of filler. Chilean sea bass, expertly cooked with roasted fennel, saffron potatoes, and a caramelized-onion broth, is wonderful, but the best thing in my opinion is the seared tuna resting on a bed of mushroom and oxtail ragout with garlic mashed potatoes. It's not your typical Japanese-style seared tuna. It's better. In fact, almost everything at the Sunfish Grill is better than at most seafood restaurants.

2771 E. Atlantic Blvd., Pompano Beach. (℡ 954/788-2434. Reservations accepted. Main courses $17–$28. AE, MC, V. Mon–Thurs 6–9:30pm; Fri–Sat 6–10:30pm.

THE HOLLYWOOD & FORT LAUDERDALE AREA AFTER DARK

Fort Lauderdale no longer mimics the raucous antics of *Animal House* as far as nightlife and partying are concerned. It has gotten hip to the fact that an active nightlife is vital to the city's desires to distract sophisticated, savvy visitors from the magnetic lure of South Beach. And while Fort Lauderdale is no South Beach, it has vastly improved the quality of nightlife throughout the city by welcoming places that wouldn't dare host wet-T-shirt and beer-chugging contests. It also lacks the South Beach attitude, which is part of the attraction.

Hollywood's nightlife seems to be in the throes of an identity crisis, touting itself as the next South Beach, while at the same time hyping its image as an attitude-free nocturnal playground. Here's the real deal: At press time, Hollywood nightlife was barely awake, with the exception of a few bars and one struggling dance club. If you're looking for a quiet night out, it's probably your best bet. But don't come too late—after midnight, the city is absolutely deserted.

For information on clubs and events, pick up a free copy of Fort Lauderdale's weekly newspaper, *City Link,* or the Fort Lauderdale edition of the *New Times.*

Where the Boys Are: Gay Fort Lauderdale

While South Beach is a magnet for the so-called circuit boys—gay men who party on a continual, ritualistic basis—Fort Lauderdale has more of a low-key, small-town scene similar to, say, Provincetown. Here, local gay-owned and -operated bars, clubs, and restaurants are the places of choice for those who find South Beach's scene too pretentious, superficial, and drug infested. The Fort Lauderdale neighborhood of Wilton Manors is the hub of gay life, but there is a smattering of gay establishments throughout the city.

The Copa, located at 2800 S. Federal Hwy. (east on I-595, near the airport; 𝄡 954/463-1507), is the hottest gay spot north of South Beach—the granddaddy of Fort Lauderdale's gay club scene. Patrons of **Cathode Ray** call this bar their "Cheers." It's located at 1105 E. Las Olas Blvd. (𝄡 954/462-8611). **Georgie's Alibi** is Wilton Manors' most popular gay bar. Find it at 2266 Wilton Dr., Wilton Manors (𝄡 954/ 565-2526). Two great dance clubs are the **Coliseum** (2520 S. Miami Rd.; 𝄡 954/832-0100) and **Club 84** (1000 W. S.R. 84; 𝄡 954/525-7883).

The Culture Room   If you consider rock and heavy metal to be culture, visit the Culture Room and bang your head to local bands. Open daily from 8pm to 3am. 3045 N. Federal Hwy. (at the corner of Oakland Park Blvd.), Fort Lauderdale. 𝄡 954/564-1074. Cover varies.

Elbo Room   Formerly spring break central, the Elbo Room has actually managed to maintain its rowdy and divey reputation by serving up frequent drink specials and live bands. Open daily from 10am to 2am. 241 S. Atlantic Blvd. on the corner of Las Olas Blvd. and Fla. A1A., Fort Lauderdale. 𝄡 954/463-4615.

Mai Kai *(Moments)*   Immerse yourself in this fabulous vestige of Polynesian kitsch: hula dancers, fire-eaters, and potent (and sickly sweet) drinks served in coconuts. The food, which draws an ambiguous line between Chinese, Polynesian, and other forms of Asian cuisine, is tasty enough but definitely overpriced. No matter; it's bound to get cold as you watch the hilarious show, which includes everything from Tahitian classics to Polynesian versions of American hits. Trippy and undeniably fun, a trip to Mai Kai is a must. *Note:* The cocktails cost almost as much as a meal. Open daily from 5pm until midnight. 3599 N. Federal Hwy. (between Commercial and Oakland Park blvds.), Fort Lauderdale. 𝄡 954/563-3272. Reservations required. Shows (2 nightly) are $9.95 for adults; free for children 12 and under.

O'Hara's   What used to be a mediocre jazz club has turned into a premier venue for excellent, live R&B, pop, and funk music. Two locations: 1905 Hollywood Blvd., Hollywood (𝄡 954/925-2555; 24-hr. Jazz & Blues Hot Line 𝄡 954/524-2801); and 722 E. Las Olas Blvd., Fort Lauderdale (𝄡 954/524-1764).

The Parrot   Fort Lauderdale's most famous—and fun—dive bar, The Parrot is a local's and out-of-towner's choice for an evening of beer (16 kinds on tap), bonding, and browsing of the bar's virtual gallery of photos of almost everyone who's ever imbibed here since its opening in 1970. Open Sunday through Thursday from 11am to 2am and Friday and Saturday from 11am to 3am. 911 Sunrise Lane, Fort Lauderdale. 𝄡 954/563-1493.

The Poor House   There's nothing poor about this microbrew hangout where excellent live music from local bands starts at midnight and goes on well into the wee hours. A friendly, lively, mixed crowd composes a generational cross-section where the gap is bridged by a common love of live music, cold beer, and good times. Open daily from 5pm to 2am. 110 SW 3rd Ave., Fort Lauderdale. © 954/522-5145.

Shooters   This waterfront bar is quintessential Fort Lauderdale. Inside, you'll find nautical types, families, and young professionals mixed in with a good dose of sunburned tourists enjoying the live reggae, jazz, or Jimmy Buffett–style tunes with the gorgeous backdrop of the bay and marinas all around. Open Monday through Friday from 11:30am to 2am; Saturday from 11:30am to 3am; and Sunday from 10am to 2am. 3033 NE 32nd Ave., Fort Lauderdale. © 954/566-2855.

2 Boca Raton ⋆⋆ & Delray Beach ⋆

26 miles S of Palm Beach, 40 miles N of Miami, 21 miles N of Fort Lauderdale

Boca Raton is one of South Florida's most expensive, well-maintained cities—home to ladies who lunch and SUV-driving yuppies. The city's name literally translates as "rat's mouth," but you'd be hard-pressed to find rodents in this area's fancy digs.

If you're looking for funky, wacky, and eclectic, look elsewhere. Boca is a luxurious resort community and, for some, the only place worth staying in South Florida. Although Jerry Seinfeld's TV parents retired to the fictional Del Boca Vista, Boca's just too pricey to be a retirement community. With minimal nightlife, entertainment in Boca is restricted to leisure sports, excellent dining, and upscale shopping. The city's residents and vacationers happily comply.

Delray Beach, named after a suburb of Detroit, grew up completely separate from its southern neighbor. This sleepy yet starting-to-awaken beachfront community was founded in 1894 by a Midwestern postmaster who sold off 5-acre lots through Michigan newspaper ads. Because of their proximity to each other, Boca and Delray can easily be explored together. Budget-conscious travelers would do well to eat and sleep in Delray and dip into Boca for sightseeing and beaching only. The 2-mile stretch of beach here is well maintained and crowded, but not mobbed. Delray's "downtown" area is confined to Atlantic Avenue, which is known for casual to chic restaurants, quaint shops, and art galleries. During the day, Delray is definitely asleep, but recently, thanks to the addition of trendy restaurants and bars, nighttime is much more animated, a burgeoning hotbed of hipster activity, young and old. Still, compared to Boca, Delray is much more laid-back, hardly as chichi, and more like a cute little beach town than the sprawling, swanky, suburban feel emitted by Boca.

ESSENTIALS

GETTING THERE   Like the rest of the cities on the Gold Coast, Boca Raton and Delray are easily reached from I-95 or the Florida Turnpike. Both the Fort Lauderdale–Hollywood International Airport and the Palm Beach International Airport are about 20 minutes away. Amtrak (© **800/USA-RAIL;** www.amtrak.com) trains make stops in Delray Beach at an unattended station at 345 S. Congress Ave.

VISITOR INFORMATION   Contact or stop by the **Palm Beach County Convention and Visitors Bureau,** 1555 Palm Beach Lakes Blvd., Suite 800, West Palm Beach, FL 33401 (© **800/554-PALM** or 561/233-3000; fax 561/471-3990; www.palmbeachfl.com). They're open Monday through Friday from

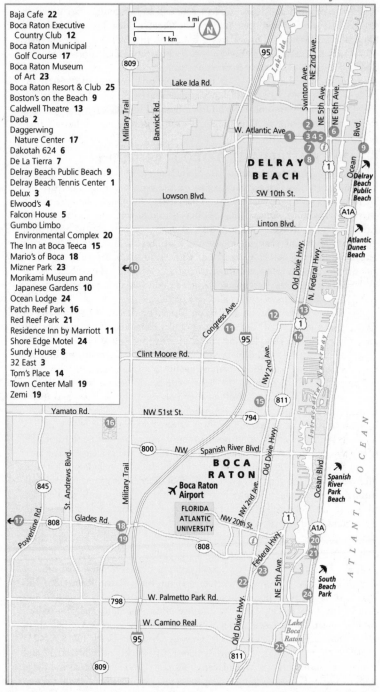

8:30am to 5:30pm and have excellent coupons and discounts. On weekdays from 8:30am until at least 4pm, stop by **The Greater Boca Raton Chamber of Commerce** at 1800 N. Dixie Hwy., 4 blocks north of Glades Road (© **561/ 395-4433;** fax 561/392-3780; www.bocaratonchamber.com), Boca Raton, FL 33432, for information on attractions, accommodations, and events in the area. Also, try the **Greater Delray Beach Chamber of Commerce** (© **561/278- 0424;** fax 561/278-0555; www.delraybeach.com) at 64 SE 5th Ave., half a block south of Atlantic Avenue on U.S. 1, Delray Beach, FL 33483; but I recommend the Palm Beach County Convention and Visitors Bureau since it has information on the entire county.

BEACHES & AFFORDABLE OUTDOOR ACTIVITIES

BEACHES   Thankfully, Florida had the foresight to set aside some of its most beautiful coastal areas for the public's enjoyment. Many of the area's best beaches are located in state parks and are free to pedestrians and bikers, though most do charge for parking. Among the beaches I recommend are Delray Beach's **Atlantic Dunes Beach,** 1600 S. Ocean Blvd., a 7-acre developed beach with lifeguards, restrooms, changing rooms, and a family park area; and Boca Raton's **South Beach Park,** 400 N. Ocean Blvd., with 1,670 feet of beach, 25 acres, lifeguards, picnic areas, restrooms, showers, and 955 feet of developed beach south of the Boca Inlet. South Beach Park charges $15 on weekdays and $17 on weekends. The two beaches below are also very popular.

The **Delray Beach Public Beach,** on Ocean Boulevard at the east end of Atlantic Avenue, is one of the area's most popular hangouts. Weekends especially attract a young and good-looking crowd of active locals and tourists. Regular volleyball, Frisbee, and paddleball games make for good entertainment. Refreshments, snack shops, bars, and restaurants are just across the street. Families enjoy the protection of lifeguards on the clean, wide beach. Gentle waters make it a good swimming beach, too. Restrooms and showers are available, and there's limited parking at meters along Ocean Boulevard.

Spanish River Park Beach, on North Ocean Boulevard (Fla. A1A), 2 miles north of Palmetto Park Road in Boca Raton, is a huge 95-acre oceanfront park with a ½-mile-long beach complete with lifeguards as well as a large grassy area, making it one of the best choices for picnicking. Facilities include picnic tables, grills, restrooms, showers, and a bi-level 40-foot observation tower. You can walk through tunnels under the highway to access nature trails that wind through fertile grasslands. Volleyball nets are ocean-side and always have at least one serious game going on. The park is open from 8am to 8pm. Admission is $16 for vehicles on weekdays and $18 on weekends and major holidays. Also, read about Red Reef Park under "Scuba Diving & Snorkeling," below.

GOLF   This area has plenty of good courses. The best ones, that are not located in a gated community, are found at the **Boca Raton Resort & Club** (501 E. Camino Real, Boca Raton; © **800/327-0101** or 561/395-3000) and **The Inn at Boca Teeca** (5800 NW 2nd Ave., Boca Raton; © **561/994-0400**). Another great place to swing your clubs is at the **Deer Creek Golf Club** in Deerfield Beach, 2801 Country Club Blvd., Deerfield Beach (© **954/421- 5550**), a 300-plus-yard driving range where a large bucket of balls costs $7 and a small one costs $4. Rates at the Deer Creek Golf Club are seasonal and range from $45 to $125. However, from May to October or November, about a dozen private courses open their greens to visitors staying in Palm Beach County hotels. This "Golf-A-Round" program is free or severely discounted (carts are additional), and reservations can be made through most major hotels. Ask at your hotel, or contact the **Palm Beach County Convention and Visitors Bureau** (© **561/471-3995**) for information on which clubs are available for play.

The semiprivate, 18-hole, par-61 course at the **Boca Raton Executive Country Club**, 7601 E. Country Club Blvd. (© **561/997-9410**), is usually open to the public and is an excellent choice for those looking to improve their game in a professional setting. A driving range is on the property as well as a restaurant and a pro shop, where you can rent clubs. If you like, take lessons from a PGA pro. Greens fees are $20 per person.

The **Boca Raton Municipal Golf Course,** 8111 Golf Course Rd. (© **561/ 483-6100**), is the area's best public golf course. There's an 18-hole, par-72 course covering approximately 6,200 yards as well as a 9-hole, par-30 course. There's a snack bar and a pro shop where clubs can be rented. Greens fees are $11 to $14 for 9 holes and $19 to $25 for 18 holes. Ask for special summer discount fees.

SCUBA DIVING & SNORKELING   **Moray Bend,** a 58-foot dive spot located about ¾ mile off Boca Inlet, is the area's most popular. It's home to three moray eels that are used to being fed by scuba divers. The reef is accessible by boat from **Force E Dive Center,** 877 E. Palmetto Park Rd., Boca Raton (© **561/368-0555**). Phone for dive times. Dives cost $40 to $45 per person.

Red Reef Park, 1400 N. Ocean Park Blvd. (© **561/393-7974**), a fully developed 67-acre oceanfront park in Boca Raton, has good swimming and year-round lifeguard protection. There's snorkeling for beginners around the rocks and reefs that lie just off the beach in 2 to 6 feet of water. The park also has restrooms and a small picnic area with grills and tables. Located ½ mile north of Palmetto Park Road, it is open daily from 8am to 10pm. You pay only if you drive in. It's $10 per car during the week or $12 on weekends.

TENNIS   The snazzy **Delray Beach Tennis Center,** 201 W. Atlantic Ave. (© **561/243-7360;** www.delraytennis.com), has 14 lighted clay courts and 5 hard courts available by the hour. Phone for rates and reservations.

The 17 public lighted hard courts at **Patch Reef Park,** 2000 NW 51st St. (© **561/997-0881;** www.ci.boca-raton.fl.us/parks/Patchreef.cfm), are available by reservation. The fee for nonresidents is $5.75 per person per hour. Courts are available Monday through Saturday from 7:30am to 10pm and Sunday from 7:30am to dusk; you can phone ahead to see if a court is available. To reach the park from I-95, exit at Yamato Road West and continue past Military Trail to the park.

SEEING THE SIGHTS

Boca Raton Museum of Art ★★   In addition to a relatively small but well-chosen permanent collection that's strongest in 19th-century European oils (Degas, Klee, Matisse, Picasso, Seurat), the museum stages a wide variety of excellent temporary exhibitions by local and international artists. Lectures and films are offered on a fairly regular basis, so call ahead for details.

Mizner Park, 501 Plaza Real, Boca Raton. © 561/392-2500. www.bocamuseum.org. Admission $8 adults, $6 seniors, $4 students, free for children under 12. Additional fees may apply for special exhibits and performances. Free on Wed except during special exhibitions. Tues, Thurs, and Sat 10am–5pm; Wed and Fri 10am–9pm; Sun noon–5pm.

Daggerwing Nature Center ★   Seen enough snowbirds? Head over to this 39-acre swampy splendor where birds of another feather reside, including herons, egrets, woodpeckers, and warblers. The park's trails come complete with a soundtrack provided by songbirds hovering above (watch your head). The park's Night Hikes will take you on a nocturnal wake-up call for owls at 6pm. Bring a flashlight.

S. County Regional Park, 11200 Park Access Rd., Boca Raton. ℭ 561/488-9953. Free admission. Tues–Fri 1–4:30pm; Sat 9am–4:30pm. Call for tour and activity schedule.

Gumbo Limbo Environmental Complex ★★★ If manicured lawns and golf courses aren't your idea of communing with nature, then head to Gumbo Limbo. Named for an indigenous hardwood tree with continuously shedding bronze bark, the 20-acre complex protects one of the few surviving coastal hammocks, or forest islands, in South Florida. Visitors can walk through the hammock on a ½-mile-long elevated boardwalk that ends at a 40-foot observation tower, from which you can see the Atlantic Ocean, the Intracoastal Waterway, and much of Boca Raton. From mid-April to September, sea turtles come ashore here to lay their eggs.

1801 N. Ocean Blvd. (on Fla. A1A between Spanish River Blvd. and Palmetto Park Rd.), Boca Raton. ℭ 561/338-1473. Fax 561/338-1483. Free admission. Mon–Sat 9am–4pm; Sun noon–4pm.

Morikami Museum and Japanese Gardens ★★★ Slip off your shoes and enter into a serene Japanese garden that dates from 1905, when an entrepreneurial farmer, Jo Sakai, came to Boca Raton to build a tropical agricultural community. The Yamato Colony, as it was known, was short-lived; by the 1920s only one tenacious colonist remained: George Sukeji Morikami. But Morikami was quite successful, eventually running one of the largest pineapple plantations in the area. The 200-acre Morikami Museum and Japanese Gardens (a stroll through the garden is actually ¾ mile), which opened to the public in 1977, was Morikami's gift to Palm Beach County and the State of Florida. The park section, dedicated to the preservation of Japanese culture, is constructed to appeal to all the senses. An artificial waterfall that cascades into a koi- and carp-filled moat; a small rock garden for meditation; and a large bonsai collection that includes miniature maple, buttonwood, juniper, and Australian pine trees are all worth contemplation. There's also a cafe with a Japanese- and Asian-inspired menu if you want to stay for lunch.

4000 Morikami Park Rd., Delray Beach. ℭ 561/495-0233. www.morikami.org. Museum $9 adults, $8 seniors, $6 children 6–18, free for members and children 5 and under. Museum Tues–Sun 10am–5pm; gardens Tues–Sat 10am–5pm. Closed major holidays.

SHOPPING & BROWSING

Even if you don't plan to buy anything, a trip to Boca Raton's **Mizner Park** is essential for capturing the essence of the city. Like Main Street in a small town, Mizner is the place to see and be seen, where Rolls-Royces and Ferraris are parked curbside, freshly coifed women sit amidst shopping bags at outdoor cafes, and young movers and shakers make evening plans on their constantly buzzing cellphones. Beyond the human scenery, however, Mizner Park is scenic in its own right with beautiful landscaping. It's really an outdoor mall, with 45 specialty shops, seven good restaurants, and a multiplex. Each shop front faces a grassy island with blue and green gazebos, potted plants, and garden benches. Mizner Park is located on Federal Highway (between Palmetto Park Rd. and Glades Rd.; ℭ 561/362-0606).

Boca's **Town Center Mall,** located on the south side of Glades Road, just west of I-95, has seven huge department stores, including Nordstrom, Bloomingdale's, Burdines, Lord & Taylor, and Saks Fifth Avenue. Add to that the hundreds of specialty shops, an extensive food court, and a range of other restaurants, and you have the area's most comprehensive shopping center.

A lifeless, overrated area, but good enough for a quick stroll, is the more artsy community of Delray Beach, known by many as Pineapple Grove. Here, along Atlantic Avenue, especially east of Swinton Avenue, you'll find a few antiques shops, clothing stores, and art galleries shaded by palm trees and colorful awnings. Pick up the "Downtown Delray Beach" map and guide at almost any of the stores on this strip, or call © **561/278-0424** for more information.

ACCOMMODATIONS YOU CAN AFFORD

A number of national chain hotels worth considering include a moderately priced **Holiday Inn Highland Beach Oceanside** at 2809 S. Ocean Blvd., on Fla. A1A, southeast of Linton Boulevard (© **800/234-6835** or 561/278-6241). Although you won't find rows of cheap hotels as in Fort Lauderdale and Hollywood, a handful of mom-and-pop motels have survived along Fla. A1A between the towering condominiums of Delray Beach. Look along the beach just south of Atlantic Boulevard. Especially noteworthy is the pleasant little two-story, shingle-roofed **Bermuda Inn** at 64 S. Ocean Blvd. (© **561/276-5288**).

Even more economical options can be found in Deerfield Beach, Boca's neighbor, south of the county line. A number of beachfront efficiencies offer great deals, even in the winter months. Try the **Panther Motel and Apartments** at 715 S. A1A (© **954/427-0700**). This clean and convenient motel has rates starting as low as $40, although in season you may have to book for a week at a time. Weekly rates in season start at $457.

Ocean Lodge ✪   Situated around a small heated pool and sun deck, this two-story motel is a particularly well-kept accommodation in an area of run-down or overpriced options. The large rooms offer furnishings and decor that are clean but a bit impersonal. A recent renovation that added modern Formica and floral wallpaper lifts this a notch above a basic motel. Ask for a room in the back, since the street noise can be a bit loud, especially in season. The bonus is that you are across the street from the ocean and in one of Florida's most upscale resort towns.

531 N. Ocean Blvd. (just north of Palmetto Park Rd. on Fla. A1A), Boca Raton, FL 33432. © 800/STAY-BOCA or 561/395-7772. Fax 561/395-0554. 18 units. Winter $99–$125 double; off season $75–$99 double. AE, MC, V. **Amenities:** Pool. *In room:* A/C, TV.

Residence Inn by Marriott ✪   You certainly get a lot of bang for your buck here, where studios are large open rooms with a living room area complete with fireplace (not that you'll need it) and sofa bed. There are also one-bedroom suites and penthouse suites, which come with cool retro-fab Murphy beds. Best of all, all rooms have full kitchens complete with dishwasher and fridge. There's also an outdoor pool and sports court set up for basketball, paddle tennis and volleyball and guests of the hotel receive free passes to the nearby Bally's Gym and discounted rates for golf and tennis at the nearby Palm Aire Country Club.

525 NW 77th St., Boca Raton, FL 33487. © 800/228-9290 or 561/994-3222. Fax 561994-3339. 120 units. Winter $129–$149; off season $99–$119. Rates include complimentary buffet breakfast. AE, DC, DISC, MC, V. **Amenities:** Outdoor pool; access to nearby health and country club. *In room:* A/C, TV, dataport, kitchen, hair dryer, iron, safe.

Shore Edge Motel   Another relic of the 1950s, this motel has been recently spiffed up with new landscaping and some redecorating and is a good choice, especially because of its location—across the street from a public beach, just north of downtown Boca Raton. It's the quintessential South Florida motel: a small, pink, single-story structure surrounding a modest swimming pool and courtyard. Although the rooms are on the small side, they're very neat and clean. The higher-priced accommodations are larger and come with full kitchens.

425 N. Ocean Blvd. (on Fla. A1A, north of Palmetto Park Rd.), Boca Raton, FL 33432. ℂ **561/395-4491.** Fax 561/347-8759. 16 units. Winter $85–$99 double; off season $55–$65 double. AE, MC, V. **Amenities:** Pool. *In room:* A/C, TV.

WORTH A SPLURGE

Sundy House ★★★   Sundy House is a bona fide 1902 Queen Anne house that has been restored to its full Victorian glory—on the outside, at least. Inside, however, the apartments are in a style that is best described as Caribbean funky, adorned in brilliant colors and with state-of-the-art audiovisual equipment, full modern kitchens, and laundry facilities. Six new guest rooms known as The Stables are equestrian chic, with more rustic appointments, including dark woods and wooden floors. And while the rooms here are comfortable and gorgeous in their own rights, it's the surrounding property of the Sundy House that garners the most oohs and aahs. Set on an acre of lush gardens, the Sundy House is surrounded by over 5,000 species of exotic plants, gently flowing streams, and colorful parrots. And going along with the whole nature theme is the hotel's swimming pond, literally that, in which guests can swim with the fish (in a good way!). One of South Florida's best kept secrets (though not for much longer), Sundy House is paradise rediscovered.

106 S. Swinton Ave., Delray Beach, FL 33444. ℂ **877/439-9601** or 561/272-5678. Fax 561/272-1115. www.sundyhouse.com. 11 units. Winter $250–$500 1- or 2-bedroom or cottage; off season $175–$500 1- or 2-bedroom or cottage. AE, DC, DISC, MC, V. **Amenities:** Restaurant; bar; swimming pond; limited room service. *In room:* A/C, TV/DVD, kitchen, minibar, coffeemaker, hair dryer, safe, CD player, washer/dryer.

GREAT DEALS ON DINING

Boca Raton, and its surrounding area, is the kind of place where you discuss dinner plans at the breakfast table. Nightlife in Boca means going out to a restaurant. But who cares? These are some of the best restaurants in South Florida.

Baja Cafe ★ MEXICAN   A jeans and T-shirt kind of place with wooden tables, Baja Cafe serves fantastic Mexican food at even better prices. It's located right by the Florida East Coast Railway tracks, so don't be surprised if you feel a little rattling. Live music and entertainment in the evening make this place a hot spot for an unpretentious crowd.

201 NW 1st Ave., Boca Raton. ℂ **561/394-5449.** No reservations. Main courses $6–$10. No credit cards. Mon–Thurs 11:30am–10pm; Fri–Sat 11:30am–11pm; Sun 5–10pm.

Mario's of Boca ★ ITALIAN   This extremely popular, bustling Italian bistro (which moved into new digs in the spring of 2003) keeps Boca's biggest mouths busy with massive portions of great homemade Italian food. The garlic rolls and the pizza are especially worth piping down for. If you're really hungry, there's an all-you-can-eat buffet 7 days a week.

1901 N. Military Trail (at the Holiday Inn, opposite from Kings Market), Boca Raton. ℂ **561/392-5595.** Reservations not accepted. Main courses under $15. AE, MC, V. Daily breakfast 7–10:30am; Mon–Thurs 11:30am–10pm; Fri–Sat 11:30am–11pm; Sun noon–9:30pm.

32 East ★★ NEW AMERICAN   The menu changes every day at this very popular people-watching outpost of tasty, contemporary American food that has finally added a little hip to the Delray Beach dining scene. Among the standouts are crispy Key West shrimp in lemon mint butter with endives and spicy melon coulis; Oregon porcini, corn, and lobster risotto with herb salad in a Vidalia vinaigrette; and mesquite-grilled skirt steak and treviso on fontina polenta with horseradish gremolata. A hip ambience abuzz with activity makes 32 East a popular hangout spot for the cocktail set.

32 E. Atlantic Ave., Delray Beach. © 561/276-7868. Reservations recommended. Main courses $10–$16. AE, DC, MC, V. Sun–Thurs 5:30–10pm; Fri–Sat 5:30–11pm; bar until 2am.

Tom's Place ★★ *Finds* BARBECUE   There are two important factors in a successful barbecue: the cooking and the sauce. Tom and Helen Wright's no-nonsense shack wins on both counts, offering flawlessly grilled meats paired with well-spiced sauces. Beef, chicken, pork, and fish are served soul-food style, with your choice of two sides such as rice with gravy, collard greens, black-eyed peas, coleslaw, or mashed potatoes.

7251 N. Federal Hwy., Boca Raton. © 561/997-0920. Reservations not accepted. Main courses $8–$15; sandwiches $5–$6; early-bird special $7.95. AE, MC, V. Tues–Thurs 11:30am–10:30pm; Fri 11:30am–10pm; Sat noon–10pm.

WORTH A SPLURGE

De La Tierra ★★★ FLORIBBEAN   Although chef Johnny Vinczenz left, this restaurant remains a stunning experience that combines elegant indoor dining and lush tropical outdoor settings with gastronomic wizardry that's a product of the fresh fruits, vegetables, and spices grown on the hotel's 5-acre farm. Each dish is prepared with a palpable, edible precision. Consider the following: smoked tomato soup is served with tiny grilled brie sandwiches and cilantro sour cream; leg of duck confit cakes are served with mango coleslaw; calamari is breaded with blue cornmeal, fried crispy, and plated with chipotle lime vinaigrette, red chili aioli, and tropical fruit salsa; diver scallops are caramelized and served with truffle braised oyster mushrooms, corn broth, caviar, and microgreens; slightly smoked salmon is served with chive potato latkes, papaya/apple chutney, and dill shallot sour cream; and chicken is marinated in pesto and served with mushroom risotto, truffled roasted chicken broth, baby carrots, and broccoli rapini. Save room for dessert, which includes a phenomenal American blueberry cobbler and mango and jackfruit shortcake.

106 South Swinton Ave., Delray Beach. © 561/272-5678. Reservations essential. Main courses $14–$26. AE, DC, DISC, MC, V. Daily 11:30am–2:30pm and 6–10pm; Sunday brunch 10:30am–2:30pm.

Zemi ★★★ NEW AMERICAN   Zemi is a sleek and chic neo-American restaurant. Chef Michael Schwartz, formerly of South Beach's Nemo, is responsible for the fabulous fare, not to mention a loyal clientele that will schlep to wherever Schwartz goes. Chile-crusted shrimp with manchego cheese, roasted garlic, sun-dried tomatoes, lemon oil, and cilantro; grilled pork T-bone in a pear-ginger compote; and the marinated, grilled skirt steak with vegetable hash and crispy onions are all superb.

5050 Town Center Circle, in the Boca Center, Boca Raton. © 561/391-7177. Reservations strongly recommended. Main courses $18–$28. AE, DC, DISC, MC, V. Mon–Fri 11:30am–2:30pm; Mon–Thurs and Sun 6–10pm; Fri–Sat 6–11pm.

BOCA RATON & DELRAY BEACH AFTER DARK
THE BAR, CLUB & MUSIC SCENE

Atlantic Avenue in Delray Beach has finally gotten quite hip to nightlife and is now lined with sleek and chic restaurants, lounges, and bars that attract the Palm Beach County "in crowd," along with a few randoms such as the Elvis of New Age, aka Yanni, who has a house nearby. Although it's hardly South Beach or Fort Lauderdale's Las Olas and Riverfront, Atlantic Avenue holds its own as far as a vibrant nightlife is concerned. In Boca Raton, Mizner Park is the nucleus of a makeshift nightlife, with restaurants masking themselves as nightclubs or, at the very least, very sceney bars, such as Gigi's Tavern, 346 Plaza Real, in Mizner Park (ⓒ **561/368-4488**), and Mark's Mizner Park, 334 Plaza Real (ⓒ **561/395-0770**).

Boston's on the Beach This is a family restaurant with a somewhat lively bar scene. It's a good choice for postsunbathing, supercasual happy hours Monday through Friday from 4 to 8pm, or live reggae on Monday. With two decks overlooking the ocean, Boston's is an ideal place to mellow out and take in the scenery. Open daily from 7am to 2am. 40 S. Ocean Blvd., Delray Beach. ⓒ **561/278-3364.**

Dada Located in a two-story, 1924 house, Dada is a nocturnal outpost of food, drink, music, art, culture, and history. In other words, this is the place you can expect to find neo bohemian, arty types lingering in their black glasses and berets on one of the living room's cozy couches listening to music, poetry, or dissertations on the latest in life. Live music, great food, a bar, an outdoor patio area, and a very eclectic crowd makes Dada the coolest hangout in Delray. Open daily from 5:30pm to 2am. 52 N. Swinton Ave., Delray Beach. ⓒ **561/330-DADA.**

Dakotah 624 Creative cocktails such as the Kissing Cousin (Southern Comfort, Fris vodka, lime juice, and triple sec) and its own line of cigars attract a hip, young clientele to this vaguely Southwestern-style bar on the beach. Open Monday through Wednesday from 4pm to midnight, Thursday 4pm to 1am, Friday and Saturday from 4pm to 2am, and Sunday from 4 to 11pm. 270 E. Atlantic Ave., Delray Beach. ⓒ **561/274-6244.**

Delux No Doubt's Gwen Stefani partied at Delux, requesting the DJ to play reggae. Believe it or not, this red-hued dance club on Atlantic Avenue is cooler than some of South Beach's big-shot dance clubs thanks to a soundtrack of sexy house music, bedlike seating, and a beautiful crowd in which someone as striking as Stefani can actually blend in without being noticed—at least for a second anyway. Open Wednesday through Sunday from 7pm to 2am. 16 E. Atlantic Ave., Delray Beach. ⓒ **561/279-4792.**

Elwood's Over the train tracks just a few feet from the sleek and chic bars and restaurants on Atlantic Avenue is this fabulous blues-themed biker bar housed in a former gas station and garage. No fancy martinis here, just cold beer and good tunes. Open Monday through Friday from 5pm to 2am, Saturday from 11am to 2am, and Sunday from 11am to midnight. 301 E. Atlantic Ave., Delray Beach. ⓒ **561/272-7427.**

Falcon House A cozy wine and tapas bar located on a side street off the Atlantic Avenue bustle, Falcon House is reminiscent of a bar you'd expect to find in Napa Valley, with an impressive selection of wines and a well-heeled, hip crowd. Falcon House is a haven for those who are over the whole hip-hop loungey scene that's found on Atlantic. Open Monday through Saturday from 5pm to 2am. 116 NE 6th Ave., Delray Beach. ⓒ **561/243-9499.**

THE PERFORMING ARTS

For details on upcoming events, check the *Boca News* or the *Sun-Sentinel,* or call the **Palm Beach County Cultural Council** information line at ⓒ **800/882-ARTS.** During business hours, a staffer can give details on current performances. After hours, a recorded message describes the week's events.

The **Florida Symphonic Pops,** a 70-piece professional orchestra, performs jazz, swing, rock, big band, and classical music throughout Boca Raton. For nearly 50 years, this ever-growing musical force has entertained audiences of every age. Call ℭ **561/393-7677** for a schedule of concerts.

Boca's best theater company is the **Caldwell Theatre,** and it's worth checking out. Located in a strip shopping center at 7873 N. Federal Hwy., this equity showcase does well-known dramas, comedies, classics, off-Broadway hits, and new works throughout the year. Prices are reasonable (usually $29–$38). Full-time students with ID will be especially interested in the little-advertised "Student Rush." When available, tickets are sold for $5 to those who arrive at least an hour in advance. Call ℭ **561/241-7432** for details.

3 Palm Beach ⟨★⟩⟨★⟩ & West Palm Beach ⟨★⟩

65 miles N of Miami, 193 miles E of Tampa, 45 miles N of Fort Lauderdale

Palm Beach County encompasses cities from Boca Raton in the south to Jupiter and Tequesta in the north. But it is Palm Beach, the small island town across the Intracoastal Waterway, which has been the traditional winter home of America's aristocracy—the Kennedys, the Rockefellers, the Pulitzers, the Trumps, titled socialites, and plenty of CEOs. For a real-time perspective on what it means to put on the ritz, there is no better place than Palm Beach, where teenagers cruise around in their parents' Rolls-Royces and socialites, seen only in society publications, seem to jump out of the glossy pages and into an even glossier, glitzier real life. It's really something to be seen, despite the fact that some may consider it all over the top and, frankly, obscene. But it is not only a city of upscale resorts and chic boutiques. In fact, Palm Beach holds some surprises, from a world-class art museum to one of the top bird-watching areas in the state.

Across the water from Palm Beach proper, or the "island" as locals call it, is downtown West Palm Beach, which is where everybody else lives. Clematis Street is the area's nightlife hub, with a great selection of bars, clubs, and restaurants. City Place is West Palm's version of Mizner Park; shops, restaurants, and other entertainment options liven up this once-dead area of West Palm. In addition to good beaching, boating, and diving, you'll find great golf and tennis throughout the county.

Note: Palm Beach's population swells from 20,000 in the summer to 40,000 in the winter. Book early if you plan to visit during the winter months.

ESSENTIALS

GETTING THERE   If you're driving up or down the Florida coast, you'll probably reach the Palm Beach area by way of I-95. Exit at Belvedere Road or Okeechobee Boulevard and head east to reach the most central part of Palm Beach.

Visitors on their way to or from Orlando or Miami should take the Florida Turnpike, a toll road with a speed limit of 65 mph. Tolls are pricey, though; you may pay upward of $9 from Orlando and $4 from Miami. If you're coming from Florida's west coast, you can take either State Route 70, which runs north of Lake Okeechobee to Fort Pierce, or State Route 80, which runs south of the lake to Palm Beach.

All major **airlines** fly to the Palm Beach International Airport, at Congress Avenue and Belvedere Road (ℭ **561/471-7400**). **Amtrak** (ℭ **800/USA-RAIL;** www.amtrak.com) has a terminal in West Palm Beach, at 201 S. Tamarind Ave. (ℭ **561/832-6169**).

GETTING AROUND Although a car is almost a necessity in this area, a recently revamped public transportation system is extremely convenient for getting to some attractions in both West Palm and Palm Beach. **Palm Tran** underwent a major expansion in late 1996, increasing service to 32 routes and more than 140 buses. The fare is $1 for adults and 50¢ for children ages 3 to 18, seniors, and riders with disabilities. Free route maps are available by calling ℂ **561/ 233-4-BUS.** Information operators are available from 6am to 7pm, except Sunday.

In downtown West Palm, free shuttles from City Place to Clematis Street operate Monday through Friday from 9am until 4pm, with plans to expand operations to evenings and weekends, too. Allegedly, the shuttles come every 5 minutes, but I'd count on them taking longer. Look for the bubble gum–pink minibuses throughout downtown. Call ℂ **561/833-8873** for more details.

For a more nostalgic route, consider the stately wicker chariots that run in the downtown area, especially on weekends and during special events. Rates vary according to the time of day but average $1 to $2 per block, plus a per-person charge of $1. Call ℂ **561/835-8922** for pickup or information.

VISITOR INFORMATION The **Palm Beach County Convention and Visitors Bureau,** 1555 Palm Beach Lakes Blvd., Suite 204, West Palm Beach, FL 33401 (ℂ **800/554-PALM** or 561/471-3995; www.palmbeachfl.com), distributes an informative brochure and will answer questions about visiting the Palm Beaches. Ask for a map as well as a copy of its "Arts and Attractions Calendar," a day-to-day guide to art, music, stage, and other events in the county.

BEACHES & AFFORDABLE OUTDOOR ACTIVITIES

BEACHES Public beaches are a rare commodity here in Palm Beach. Most of the island's best beaches are fronted by private estates and are inaccessible to the general public. However, there are a few notable exceptions, including **Midtown Beach,** east of Worth Avenue, on Ocean Boulevard, between Royal Palm Way and Gulfstream Road, which boasts more than 100 feet of undeveloped beach. This newly widened sandy coast is now a centerpiece and a natural oasis in a town dominated by commercial glitz. There are no restrooms or concessions here, although a lifeguard is on duty until sundown. About 1½ miles north of there, near Dunbar Street, is a popular hangout for locals, who prefer it to Midtown Beach because of the relaxed and serene atmosphere. Parking is available at meters along Fla. A1A. At the south end of Palm Beach, there's a less-popular but better-equipped beach at **Phipps Ocean Park.** On Ocean Boulevard, between the Southern Boulevard and Lake Avenue Causeways, is a large and lively public beach encompassing more than 1,300 feet of groomed and guarded oceanfront. With picnic and recreation areas, as well as plenty of parking, the area is especially good for families.

BIKING Rent anything from an English single-speed to a full-tilt mountain bike at the **Palm Beach Bicycle Trail Shop,** 223 Sunrise Ave. (ℂ **561/659- 4583**). The rates are $8 an hour, $20 a half day (9am–5pm), or $26 for 24 hours and include a basket and lock (not that a lock is necessary in this fortress of a town). The most scenic route is called the Lake Trail, running the length of the island along the Intracoastal Waterway. On it, you'll see some of the most magnificent mansions and grounds and will enjoy the views of downtown West Palm Beach as well as some great wildlife.

GOLF There's good golfing in the Palm Beaches, but many of the private-club courses are maintained exclusively for the use of their members. Ask at your

Palm Beach & West Palm Beach

The Sport of Kings

The posh Palm Beach Polo and Country Club is one of the world's premier polo grounds and hosts some of the sport's top-rated players. Even if you're not a sports fan, you must attend a match at this field, which is actually on the mainland in an area called Wellington. Rest assured, however, that the spectators, and many of the players, are pure Palm Beach. After all, a day at the pony grounds is one of the only good reasons to leave Palm Beach proper. Don't worry, you need not be a Vanderbilt or a Kennedy to attend—matches are open to the public and are surprisingly affordable.

Even if you haven't a clue as to how the game is played, you can spend your time people-watching. Stargazers have spotted Prince Charles, Sylvester Stallone, Tommy Lee Jones, Bo Derek, and Ivana Trump, among others, in recent years. Dozens of lesser-known royalty, and just plain old characters, keep box seats or chalets right on the grounds.

Dress is casual; a navy or tweed blazer over jeans or khakis is a standard for men, while neat-looking jeans or a pantsuit is the norm for women. On warmer days, shorts and, of course, a polo shirt are fine, too.

General admission is $6 to $10; box seats cost $10 to $36. Matches are held throughout the week. Schedules vary, but the big names usually compete on Sunday at 3:30pm from January to April.

The fields are located at 11809 Polo Club Rd., Wellington, 10 miles west of the Forest Hill Boulevard exit of I-95. Call ℂ **561/793-1440** for tickets and a detailed schedule of events.

hotel, or contact the **Palm Beach County Convention and Visitors Bureau** (ℂ **561/471-3995**) for information on which clubs are currently available for play. In the off season, some private courses open their greens to visitors staying in a Palm Beach County hotel. This "Golf-A-Round" program offers free greens fees (carts are additional); reservations can be made through most major hotels.

The best hotel for golf in the area is the **PGA National Resort & Spa** (400 Ave. of the Champions, Palm Beach Gardens; ℂ **800/633-9150**), which features a whopping 90 holes of golf.

One of the state's best courses open to the public is **Emerald Dunes Golf Course** ⊛, 2100 Emerald Dunes Dr. in West Palm Beach (ℂ **561/687-1700**). Designed by Tom Fazio, this dramatic 7,006-yard, par-72 course was voted "One of the Best 10 You Can Play" by *Golf* magazine. It is located just off the Florida Turnpike at Okeechobee Boulevard. Bookings are taken up to 30 days ahead. Fees start at $130, including carts.

The **Palm Beach Public Golf Course,** 2345 S. Ocean Blvd. (ℂ **561/547-0598**), a popular public 18-hole course, is a par-54. The course opens at 8am and runs on a first-come, first-served basis. Club rentals are available. Greens fees start at $22 per person.

SCUBA DIVING   Year-round warm waters, barrier reefs, and plenty of wrecks make South Florida one of the world's most popular places for diving. One of the best-known artificial reefs in this area is a vintage Rolls-Royce Silver Shadow, which was sunk offshore in 1985. Nature has taken its toll, however, and divers can no longer sit in the car, which has been ravaged by time and saltwater.

Call either of the following outfitters for gear and excursions: **Ocean Sports Scuba Center,** 1736 S. Congress Ave., West Palm Beach (© **561/641-1144**) or **Jim Abernaethy's Scuba Adventures,** at 2116 Avenue B. in Riviera Beach (© **561/691-5808**).

TENNIS   There are hundreds of tennis courts in Palm Beach County. Wherever you are staying, you are bound to be within walking distance of one. In addition to the many hotel tennis courts, you can play at **Currie Park,** 2400 N. Flagler Dr., West Palm Beach (© **561/835-7025**), a public park with three lighted hard courts. They are free and available on a first-come, first-served basis.

WATERSPORTS   Call the **Seaside Activities Station** (© **561/835-8922**) to arrange sailboat, jet ski, bicycle, kayak, water-ski, and parasail rentals.

SEEING THE SIGHTS

Flagler Museum ★★★   The Gilded Age is preserved in this luxurious mansion commissioned by Standard Oil tycoon Henry Flagler as a wedding present to his third wife. *Whitehall,* also known as the "Taj Mahal of North America," is a classically columned Edwardian-style mansion containing 55 rooms, including a Louis XIV music room and art gallery, a Louis XV ballroom, and 14 guest suites outfitted with original antique European furnishings. Out back, climb aboard "The Rambler," Mr. Flagler's private restored railroad car. Allow at least 1½ hours to tour the stunning grounds and interior. School and group tours are available, but, for the most part, this is a self-guided museum.

One Whitehall Way (at Cocoanut Row and Whitehall Way), Palm Beach. © 561/655-2833. www.flagler.org. Admission $10 adults, $3 children 6–12. Tues–Sat 10am–5pm; Sun noon–5pm.

Norton Museum of Art ★★★   Since a 1997 expansion doubled the Norton's space, the museum has gained even more prominence in the art world. It is world famous for its prestigious permanent collection and top temporary exhibitions. The museum's major collections are divided geographically. The American galleries contain major works by Edward Hopper, Georgia O'Keeffe,

Unreal Estate

No trip to Palm Beach is complete without at least a glimpse of Mar-A-Lago, the stately residence of Donald Trump, the 21st century's answer to Jay Gatsby. In 1985, Trump purchased Mar-A-Lago, the former estate of cereal heiress Marjorie Merriweather Post, for what was considered a meager $8 million (for a fully furnished beachfront property of this stature, it was a relative bargain, actually), to the great consternation of locals, who feared that he would turn the place into a casino. Instead, Trump, who sometimes resides in a portion of the palace, opened the house to the public—for a price, of course—as a tony country club (membership fee: $100,000).

While there are currently no tours open to the public, you can glimpse the gorgeous manse as you cross the bridge from West Palm Beach into Palm Beach. 1100 S. Ocean Blvd., Palm Beach.

and Jackson Pollock. The French collection contains Impressionist and post-Impressionist paintings by Cézanne, Degas, Gauguin, Matisse, Monet, Picasso, Pissarro, and Renoir. And the Chinese collection contains more then 200 bronzes, jades, and ceramics, as well as a collection of monumental Buddhist sculptures. Allow about 2 hours to see this museum, depending on your level of interest. Recent exhibitions in 2004 include JFK and Art, featuring the various and sometimes complicated responses of American and European artists to John Fitzgerald Kennedy, and The Beatles, an exhibition of photographer Harry Benson's shots of the fab four from 1964 to 1970.

1451 S. Olive Ave., West Palm Beach. © 561/832-5196. Fax 561/659-4689. www.norton.org. Admission $8 adults, $3 13–21, free for children 12 and under. Mon–Sat 10am–5pm; Sun 1–5pm. Closed Mon (May–Oct) and all major holidays. Take I-95 to exit 52 (Okeechobee Blvd. E.). Travel east on Okeechobee to Dixie Hwy.; then south ½ mile to the Norton. Parking may be accessed through entrances on Dixie Hwy. and S. Olive Ave.

Playmobil Fun Park ★★ Kids In a child's mind, it doesn't get any better than this. The 17,000-square-foot Playmobil Fun Park is housed in a replica castle and loaded with themed areas for imaginative play: a medieval village, a Western town, a fantasy dollhouse, and more. Plus, there are two water-filled tables on which kids can play with the Playmobil boats. Tech-minded kids could get bored, but toddlers (and up to age 5 or so) will love this place. You *could* spend hours here and not spend a penny, but parents beware: Everything is available for purchase.

8031 N. Military Trail, Palm Beach Gardens. © **800/351-8697** or 561/691-9880. Fax 561/691-9517. www. playmobil.com. Admission $1. Mon–Sat 10am–6pm; Sun noon–5pm. From I-95, go north to Palm Beach Lakes Blvd.; then west to Military Trail. Turn left, and the park is about a mile down on the right.

NATURE PRESERVES & ATTRACTIONS

Lion Country Safari ★★ Kids More than 1,300 animals on this 500-acre preserve (the nation's first cageless drive-through safari) are divided into their indigenous regions, from the East African preserve of the Serengeti to the American West. Elephants, lions, wildebeest, ostriches, American bison, buffalo, watusi, pink flamingos, and many other more unusual species roam the preserve. When I visited, most of the lions were asleep; when they are awake, they travel freely throughout the cageless grassy landscape (this can be very scary). In fact, you're the one who's confined in your own car without an escort (no convertibles allowed). You're given a detailed informational pamphlet with photos and descriptions and are instructed to obey the 15 mph speed limit—unless you see the rhinos charge (a rare occasion), in which case you're encouraged to floor it. To drive the loop takes just over an hour, though you could make a day of just watching the chimpanzees play on their secluded islands or the calming and graceful giraffes. Included in the admission price is Safari World, an amusement park with paddleboats, a carousel, miniature golf, and a nursery for baby animals born in the preserve. Picnics are encouraged, and camping is available (call for reservations). The best time to go is late afternoon right before the park closes, when they herd up all the animals; plus, it's much cooler then, so the lions are more active. Though some may consider this a tourist trap, I had a great time. Plus, it's way cheaper than flying to Africa for a real safari.

Southern Blvd. W. at S.R. 80, West Palm Beach. © **561/793-1084**, or 561/793-9797 for camping reservations. www.lioncountrysafari.com. Admission $18 adults, $16 seniors, $14 children 3–9, free for children under 3. Van rental $8 per hr. Daily 9:30am–5:30pm (last vehicle admitted at 4:30pm). From I-95, exit on Southern Blvd. Go west for about 18 miles.

Palm Beach Zoo at Dreher Park ★ If you want animals, go to Lion Country Safari. Unlike big-city zoos, this intimate 23-acre park is more like a stroll in the park than an all-day excursion. It features about 500 animals representing more than 100 different species. A special monkey exhibit and petting zoo are favorites with kids. Stroller and wagon rental are available. Allow at least 2 hours to see all of the sights here. The Zoo's newest attraction is the Tropics of the Americas, a 3-acre jungle path and complex that will immerse zoo guests into the animals, plants, and culture of a New World Rainforest. Visitors will encounter many rare animals such as jaguars, monkeys, giant anteaters, tapirs, bats, birds, snakes, and more.

1301 Summit Blvd. (east of I-95 between Southern Blvd. and Forest Hill Blvd.). 𝒞 561/547-WILD. Fax 561/585-6085. www.palmbeachzoo.org. Admission $7.50 adults, $6 seniors, $5 children 3–12, free for children under 3. Daily 9am–5pm. Closed Thanksgiving.

SHOPPING & BROWSING

No matter what your budget is, be sure to take a stroll down Worth Avenue, "the Rodeo Drive of the South," and a window-shopper's dream. Between South Ocean Boulevard and Cocoanut Row, there are more than 200 boutiques, posh shops, art galleries, and upscale restaurants. If you want to fit in, dress as if you were going to an elegant luncheon and not to the mall down the street.

Despite the presence of the usual suspects (**Gucci, Chanel, Armani, Hermès, Louis Vuitton,** among others), Worth Avenue is not impervious to the mainstream. **Victoria's Secret, Limited Express,** and several other chains have sneaked in here, too, but so have a good number of unique boutiques. **History Buff,** 32 Via Mizner (𝒞 **561/366-8255**), is a virtual museum, selling every genre of original historical autographs, some dating back to the 1600s, as well as vintage signed photos, first-edition books, and memorabilia. A similar store is **Treasures Gallery,** at 217 Worth Ave. (𝒞 **561/835-1891**), an autograph gallery with a priceless collection of John Hancocks, including those of Joe DiMaggio, Mickey Mantle, Andrew Jackson, Abraham Lincoln, Howard Hughes, and hundreds more, all displayed in beautiful frames. For privileged feet, **Stubbs & Wooton,** 4 Via Parigi (𝒞 **561/655-4105**), sells velvet slippers that are a favorite of the loofahed locals. **The Purple Turtle,** 150 Worth Ave. (𝒞 **561/655-1625**), in the Esplanade shopping promenade, sells designer clothes for infants, including Baby Dior and Baby Armani. For rare and estate jewelry, **Richter's of Palm Beach,** 224 Worth Ave. (𝒞 **561/655-0774**), has been specializing in priceless gems since 1893. Just off Worth Avenue, at 374 S. County Rd., is the **Church Mouse** (𝒞 **561/659-2154**), a great consignment/thrift shop with antique furnishings and tableware as well as lots of good castaway clothing and shoes, all reasonably priced. This shop usually closes for 2 months during the summer. Call to be sure.

City Place, Okeechobee Road (at I-95), West Palm Beach (𝒞 **561/820-9716**), is a $550 million, Mediterranean-style shopping, dining, and entertainment complex that's responsible for revitalizing what was once a lifeless downtown West Palm Beach. Among the 78 mostly chain stores are **Macy's, FAO Schwarz, Benetton,** which has an in-line skating track inside, **Armani Exchange, Pottery Barn,** and **SEE** eyewear. Restaurants include a Ghirardelli ice-cream shop, Legal Seafoods, City Cellar Wine Bar and Grill, Cheeburger Cheeburger, and Cheesecake Factory. Best of all is the Muvico Parisian, a 20-screen movie theater where you can wine and dine while watching a feature.

Elsewhere, Downtown West Palm Beach has a scant number of interesting boutiques along Clematis Street. In addition to a large and well-organized bookstore, **Clematis Street Books,** at 206 Clematis (𝒞 **561/832-2302**), there are a few used-record stores, clothing shops, and several art galleries.

The **Palm Beach Outlet Center,** at 5700 Okeechobee Blvd. (3 miles west of I-95), West Palm Beach, is the most elegant outlet mall I have ever seen. Upscale clothing, luggage, and shoes are offered at bargain prices in lushly decorated surroundings. The fully enclosed mall also sports a food court.

As if there weren't enough shopping malls in South Florida, enter the newest one, **The Mall at Wellington Green** (10300 W. Forest Hill Blvd., Wellington; ℂ 561/227-6900), featuring 140 specialty stores and department stores such as Nordstrom, Lord & Taylor, and Dillard's.

ACCOMMODATIONS YOU CAN AFFORD

The island of Palm Beach is the epitome of *Lifestyles of the Rich and Famous,* oozing with glitz, glamour, and the occasional scandal. Royalty and celebrities come to winter here, and there are plenty of lavishly priced options to accommodate them. Happily, there are also a few special inns that offer reasonably priced rooms in elegant settings. But the more modest places to lay your straw hat are mostly surrounding the island.

A few of the larger hotel chains operating in Palm Beach include the **Palm Beach Marriott/Fairfield Inn and Suites,** at 2870 S. Ocean Blvd. (ℂ 800/228-2800 or 561/582-2581), which is across the street from the beach. Also beachside is the pricey **Palm Beach Hilton,** at 2842 S. Ocean Blvd. (ℂ 800/433-1718 or 561/586-6542). An excellent and affordable alternative right in the middle of Palm Beach's commercial section is a condominium that operates as a hotel, too: the **Palm Beach Hotel,** at 235 Sunrise Ave. (between County Rd. and Bradley Place, across the street from the Publix supermarket; ℂ 561/659-7794). With winter prices starting at about $105, this clean and comfortable accommodation is a great option for those looking for the rare bargain in Palm Beach.

In West Palm Beach, the chain hotels are mostly located on the main arteries close to the highways and a short drive from the activities in downtown. They include a **Best Western,** 1800 Palm Beach Lakes Blvd. (ℂ 800/331-9569 or 561/683-8810), and, just down the road, a **Comfort Inn,** 1901 Palm Lakes Blvd. (ℂ 800/221-2222 or 561/689-6100). Farther south is the **Parkview Motor Lodge,** 4710 S. Dixie Hwy., just south of Southern Boulevard (ℂ 561/833-4644). This 28-room, single-story motel is the best of the many motels along Dixie Highway (U.S. 1). With rates starting at $50 for a room with television, air-conditioning, and telephone, you can't ask for more.

For other options, contact **Palm Beach Accommodations** at ℂ 800/543-**SWIM.**

Hibiscus House ⭐⭐ *Finds*   Inexpensive bed-and-breakfasts are rare in Southeast Florida, making the Hibiscus House, one of the area's firsts, a true find. Located a few miles from the coast in a quiet residential neighborhood, this 1920s-era B&B is filled with handsome antiques and tapestries in luxurious fabrics. Every room has its own private terrace or balcony. The Red Room has a fabulous new bathroom with Jacuzzi. The backyard, a peaceful retreat, has been transformed into a tropical garden, complete with heated swimming pool and lounge chairs. Also, there are plenty of pretty areas for guests to enjoy inside; one little sitting room is wrapped in glass and is stocked with playing cards and board games. *Beware:* Breakfast portions are enormous. The gourmet creations are as filling as they are beautiful. Ask for any special requests in advance; owners Raleigh Hill and Colin Rayer will be happy to oblige.

501 30th St., West Palm Beach, FL 33407. (℃ **800/203-4927** or 561/863-5633. Fax 561/863-5633. www.hibiscushouse.com. 8 units. Winter $100–$175 double; off season $85–$150 double. Rates include breakfast. AE, DC, DISC, MC, V. From I-95, exit onto Palm Beach Lakes Blvd. E. and continue 4 miles. Turn left onto Flagler Dr. and continue for about 20 blocks. Then turn left onto 30th St. Pets accepted. **Amenities:** Heated pool; concierge. *In room:* A/C, TV, hair dryer.

Hotel Biba ★★ *Finds*   As West Palm Beach came into its own as far as nightlife is concerned, it was only a matter of time before a hip boutique hotel made its appearance in the historic El Cid neighborhood, located 1 mile from City Place and nightlife-heavy Clematis Street. The very cool Hotel Biba answers the call for an inexpensive, chic hotel that young hipsters can call their own. A word of advice, however: The hotel is not exactly soundproof. Rooms may be cloistered by fence and gardens, but they are still extremely close to a major thoroughfare. Try to ask for one that's on the quieter Belvedere Road as opposed to those facing South Olive Avenue. Housed in a renovated Colonial-style 1940s motor lodge, Biba has been remarkably updated on the inside by de rigueur designer Barbara Hulanicki and features a sleek and chic lobby with the requisite hip hotel bar, the Biba Bar; a gorgeously landscaped outdoor pool area with Asian gardens; and a reflection pond. Rooms are equally fabulous, with private patios, mosaic-tile floors, custom-made mahogany furniture, Egyptian cotton linens, down pillows, exquisite bathroom products, and high-tech amenities. The bold color schemes mix nicely with the high-fashion crowd that convenes here.

320 Belvedere Rd., West Palm Beach, FL 33405. (℃ **561/832-0094**. Fax 561/833-7848. www.hotelbiba.com. 43 units. Year-round $99–$135 double, $140–$179 suite. **Amenities:** Restaurant; lounge; outdoor pool; concierge. *In room:* A/C, TV, dataport, hair dryer, CD player.

ParkView Motor Lodge ★   The best of the many hotels along shabby U.S. 1, this single-story, clean, family-run spot is a real find in the Palm Beaches. There's no pool, but there are charming touches, like the colored sheets and towels in the rooms, and the bougainvillea that grows in pretty terra-cotta pots along the hallways. The nondescript rooms all have refrigerators, and the location is ideal, only 3 miles from downtown.

4710 S. Dixie Hwy., West Palm Beach, FL 33405. (℃ **561/833-4644**. Fax 561/833-4644. 28 units, some with shower only, some with tub only. Winter $82–$98 single or double; off season $56–$70 single or double. Rates include continental breakfast. AE, DC, DISC, MC, V. Extra person $8 in winter, $5 off season. *In room:* A/C, TV, fridge.

WORTH A SPLURGE
Palm Beach Historic Inn ★★   Built in 1923, the Palm Beach Historic Inn is an area landmark located within a block's walking distance of the beach (on which chairs and towels are provided for guests of the hotel), Worth Avenue, and several good restaurants. The small lobby is filled with antiques, books, magazines, and an old-fashioned umbrella stand, all of which add to the homey feel of this intimate bed-and-breakfast. In your room, wine, fruit, snacks, tea, and cookies ensure that you won't go hungry—never mind the excellent continental breakfast that is brought to you daily. All the rooms are on the second floor, are uniquely decorated, and feature hardwood floors, down comforters, Egyptian cotton linens, fluffy bathrobes, and plenty of good-smelling toiletries. Gone are the frills, floral prints, sheer curtains, and plethora of lace that once made this inn feel like staying at your grandmother's house. What you'll find here, thanks to new innkeepers who took over in July 2001, is a casual elegance that's comfortable for everyone. In addition, a baby grand piano and guitars for the musically inclined, as well as videotapes to keep the kids entertained, have been added to the hotel's amenities.

365 S. County Rd., Palm Beach, FL 33480. © 561/832-4009. Fax 561/832-6255. www.palmbeach
historicinn.com. 13 units. Winter $150–$185 double, $250–$375 suite; off season $85–$105 double,
$150–$175 suite. Rates include continental breakfast. Children stay free in parent's room. AE, MC, V. Small
pets accepted. No smoking. *In room:* A/C, TV/VCR, fridge, hair dryer, iron.

GREAT DEALS ON DINING

Palm Beach has some of the area's swankiest restaurants. Thanks to the development of downtown West Palm Beach, however, there is also a great selection of
trendier, less expensive spots. Dress here is slightly more formal than in most
other areas of Florida: Men wear blazers, and women generally put on modest
dresses or chic suits when they dine out, even in the oppressively hot days of
summer. You should also check out the dining options at City Place (see it's
description under "Shopping & Browsing" above for more information).

Big City Tavern ★★ AMERICAN   If the Palm Beach–proper dining scene is
too stuffy for you, head over the bridge to Clematis Street, downtown West
Palm's hub of urban chic, where you will find this yuppie enclave of brick and
pressed tin in which people-watching is at a premium. Despite its all-American
appearance, Big City Tavern offers a varied menu, including coconut shrimp
tempura with a salmon inside-out sushi roll and a delicious bowl of littleneck clams in wine broth with roasted garlic and escarole. On weekends, the
Tavern is mobbed, so be prepared for a long wait that's best spent at the action-
packed bar.

224 Clematis St., West Palm Beach. © 561/659-1853. Reservations suggested. Main courses $7.95–$28.
AE, MC, V. Daily 10:30am–2pm; Sun–Tues 5:30–10:30pm; Wed–Sat 5:30pm–midnight.

Green's Pharmacy ★ *Value* AMERICAN   This neighborhood corner pharmacy offers one of the best meal deals in Palm Beach. Both breakfast and lunch
are served coffee-shop style either at a Formica bar or at plain tables placed on a
black-and-white checkerboard floor. Breakfast specials include eggs and omelets
served with home fries and bacon, sausage, or corned-beef hash. At lunch, the
grill serves burgers and sandwiches, as well as ice-cream sodas and milkshakes to
a loyal crowd of pastel-clad Palm Beachers.

151 N. County Rd., Palm Beach. © 561/832-0304. Fax 561/832-6502. Breakfast $2–$5; burgers and sandwiches $3–$6; soups and salads $2–$7. AE, DISC, MC, V. Mon–Sat 7am–5pm; Sun 7am–3pm.

John G's ★ AMERICAN   This coffee shop is the most popular in the county.
For decades, John G's has been attracting huge breakfast crowds; lines run out
the door (on weekends, all the way down the block). Stop in for some good,
greasy spoon–style food served in heaping portions right on the beachfront. This
place is known for fresh and tasty fish and chips and its selection of creative
omelets and grill specials.

10 S. Ocean Blvd., Lake Worth. © 561/585-9860. www.johngs.com. Reservations not accepted. Breakfast
$3–$8.50; lunch $5–$14. No credit cards. Daily 7am–3pm. From the Florida Tpk., take the Lake Worth exit and
head toward the ocean.

Montezuma ★★ MEXICAN   The 50 seats here manage to accommodate
patient patrons who wait for some of the freshest burritos, tacos, mariscos, and
tortillas in Palm Beach County. Try any of the huge egg platters for breakfast.
For lunch or dinner, try the huge enchiladas, salads, tacos, and enormous platters of steak, chicken, or pork dishes. Also offered is authentic tongue in green
sauce.

5607 S. Dixie Hwy. (between Forest Hill and Southern blvds.), West Palm Beach. © 561/586-7974. Main
courses $6–$14. AE, DC, DISC, MC, V. Sun–Thurs 8am–10pm; Sat–Sun 8am–11pm.

Sandwiches by the Sea SANDWICHES   Large classic subs that put Subway to great shame, healthful salads, and pita pockets for the price of a meal at McDonald's make this little narrow take-out shop a real find in pricey Palm Beach. Breakfast choices are limited to fruit salads, muffins, breads, and croissants, but lunch choices include hearty homemade soups and overstuffed sandwiches. Choose the daily special sandwich and a large drink for about $5. Fresh white meat chicken salad and tuna are favorites. Also tempting are frozen yogurt treats, brownies, and cookies. This is the place to come for picnic supplies or a superbargain lunch to enjoy at a tiny counter.

363 S. County Rd., Palm Beach. (© 561/655-7911. Salads and hoagies $4–$6. No credit cards. Mon–Sat 9am–4pm.

WORTH A SPLURGE

Rhythm Café ★ Finds ECLECTIC AMERICAN   This funky hole-in-the-wall is where those in the know come to eat some of West Palm Beach's most laidback gourmet food. On the handwritten, photocopied menu (which changes daily), you'll always find a fish specialty accompanied by a hefty dose of greens and garnishes. Also reliably outstanding is the sautéed medallion of beef tenderloin, served on a bed of arugula with a tangy rosemary vinaigrette. Salads and soups are a great bargain, since portions are relatively large and the display usually spectacular. The kitschy decor of this tiny cafe comes complete with vinyl tablecloths and a changing display of paintings by local amateurs. Young, handsome waiters are attentive but not solicitous. The old drugstore where the restaurant recently relocated features an original 1950s lunch counter and stools.

3800 S. Dixie Hwy., West Palm Beach. (© 561/833-3406. Reservations recommended on weekends. Main courses $12–$31. AE, DISC, MC, V. Tues–Sat 6–10pm; Sun (Dec–Mar) 5:30–9pm; closed in early Sept. From I-95, exit east on Southern Blvd. Go 1 block north of Southern Blvd.; restaurant on the right.

THE PALM BEACHES AFTER DARK
THE BAR, CAFE & MUSIC SCENE

A decade-old project to revitalize downtown West Palm Beach has finally become a reality, with **Clematis Street** at its heart. Artist lofts, sidewalk cafes, bars, restaurants, consignment shops, and galleries dot the street from Flagler Drive to Rosemary Avenue, creating a hot spot for a night out, especially on weekends, when yuppies mingle with stylish Euros and disheveled artists. Every Thursday night is a mob scene of 20- and 30-somethings who come out for "Clematis by Night." Each week features a different rock, blues, or reggae band plus an art show. Vendors sell food and drinks, and the street's bars and restaurants are packed. It is a bit raucous at times, but fun. Minors unaccompanied by their guardians are not permitted in the downtown area around Clematis Street after 10pm on weeknights and after 11pm on weekend nights. Otherwise, most of the nightspots listed below are open until about 3 or 4am.

Over the bridge, it's a completely different world. Palm Beach is much quieter and better known for its rather private society balls and estate parties. With the exception of some restaurants that are more of a scene (such as **Ta-boo;** see below), Palm Beach nightlife is more likely to entail sipping port at one of the finer hotels like The Breakers, The Colony, the Ritz-Carlton, the Four Seasons, or the Chesterfield.

West Palm Beach

E. R. Bradley's   What used to be a swank saloon on the island of Palm Beach is now a very casual, friendly indoor/outdoor bar in downtown West Palm, attracting a mixed crowd. The later-night bar scene is a real draw. If you are hungry, try the "crab bomb," Maryland lump crabmeat baked in a light cream sauce with steamed vegetables. Open Sunday through Wednesday from 8am to 3am and Thursday through Saturday from 8am to 4am. 104 Clematis St. ℂ 561/ 833-3520.

Respectable Street Café   This is one of the premier live music venues in South Florida. In addition to the requisite DJs, this grungy bar features an impressive lineup of alternative music acts. The cafe's plain store-front exterior belies its funky, high-ceilinged interior decorated with large black booths, psychedelic wall murals, and a large checkerboard-tile dance floor. Open Wednesday and Thursday 9pm to 3am; Friday and Saturday from 9pm to 4am. 518 Clematis St. ℂ 561/832-9999. Cover varies $5–$20.

Palm Beach

The Leopard Lounge *Finds*   *The Flintstones* meets *Dynasty* at this spotty lounge in the Chesterfield Hotel, in which the carpeting, tablecloths, and waitstaff's waistcoats are all in leopard print. There's live music every night from Cole Porter to swing. The crowd's a bit older here, but younger couples and a celebrity or two often find their way here, which makes for an amusing scene. Open daily from 6pm to 1:30am. 363 Cocoanut Row. ℂ 561/659-5800.

Ta-boo   Ta-boo is reminiscent of an upscale TGI Fridays (with food that's about on the same level)—one that caters to a well-heeled crowd—with lots of greenery, a fireplace, and a somewhat cheesy Southwestern decor. But make no mistake, Ta-boo is not about the food: This stellar after-dinner spot is where bejeweled socialites spill out of fancy cars to show off their best Swarovski and salsa. Just find somewhere else to eat first. Open for lunch daily 11:30am to 5pm, Sunday through Thursday from 5 to 10pm and Friday and Saturday from 5 until 11pm. 221 Worth Ave., Palm Beach. ℂ 561/835-3500.

GAMBLING

The *Palm Beach Princess* (ℂ 800/841-7447 or 561/845-7447) is a small cruise ship (421 ft.) offering reasonably priced casino gambling cruises out of the Port of Palm Beach (U.S. 1 between 45th St. and Blue Heron Blvd.) every day and evening. Choose from craps, roulette, poker, blackjack, and slots. Cruises include a large buffet with average food like spaghetti and meatballs, chicken, Greek salad, and vegetables; best is the prime rib at the carving board. Cruises sail daily between 11am and 4:30pm and 6:30 and 11:45pm. Friday and Saturday evening cruises go from 6:30pm to 12:30am. Sunday cruises sail from 11am to 5pm and 6:30 to 11:30pm. Prices during the week are $30 per person; on weekends, it's $40 per person. If your birthday is in the month you plan to sail, you'll pay $25 weekdays, $35 weekends. Florida residents, AARP, and AAA discounts are available.

THE PERFORMING ARTS

With a number of dedicated patrons and enthusiastic supporters of the arts, this area happily boasts many good venues for those craving culture. Check the *Palm Beach Post* or the *Palm Beach Daily News* for up-to-date listings and reviews.

The **Raymond F. Kravis Center for the Performing Arts,** 701 Okeechobee Blvd., West Palm Beach (ℂ 561/832-7469; www.kravis.org), is the area's largest and most active performance space. With a huge curved-glass facade and more than 2,500 seats in two lushly decorated indoor spaces, plus a new outdoor amphitheater, The Kravis, as it is known, stages more than 300 performances each year. Phone or check their website for a current schedule of Palm Beach's best music, dance, and theater.

4 Jupiter ⟨★ & Northern Palm Beach County ⟨★

20 miles N of Palm Beach, 81 miles N of Miami, 60 miles N of Fort Lauderdale

While Burt Reynolds is Jupiter's hometown hero (and Celine Dion just built a sprawling manse there, too), the true stars of quaint Jupiter are the beautiful beaches. In the springtime, you can also catch a glimpse of the St. Louis Cardinals and the Montreal Expos during their spring-training seasons. North Palm Beach County's other towns—Tequesta, Juno Beach, North Palm Beach, Palm Beach Gardens, and Singer Island—are inviting for tourists who want to enjoy the many outdoor activities that make this area so popular with retirees, seasonal residents, and families.

ESSENTIALS

GETTING THERE   The quickest route from West Palm Beach to Jupiter is on the Florida Turnpike or the sometimes-congested I-95. You can also take a slower but more scenic coastal route, U.S. 1 or Fla. A1A. Since Jupiter is so close to Palm Beach, it's easy to fly into the **Palm Beach International Airport** (© **561/471-7420**) and rent a car there. The drive should take less than half an hour.

VISITOR INFORMATION   A **Visitor Information Center** is located between I-95 and the Florida Turnpike at 8020 Indiantown Rd. in Jupiter (© **561/575-4636;** www.jupiterfloridausa.com) and is open from 8:30am to 5:30pm Monday through Friday.

BEACHES, AFFORDABLE OUTDOOR ACTIVITIES & SPECTATOR SPORTS

BASEBALL   The **Roger Dean Stadium,** 4751 Main St. (© **561/775-1818**), hosts spring training for both the St. Louis Cardinals and the Montreal Expos, along with minor-league action from Florida's state league, the Hammerheads. Tickets range in price from $6 to $18. Call for schedules and specific ticket information.

BEACHES   The farther north you head from populated Palm Beach, the more peaceful and pristine the coast becomes. Just a few miles north of the bustle, castles and condominiums give way to wide open space and public parkland. There are dozens of recommendable spots. Following are a few of the best.

John D. MacArthur Beach is a spectacular beach that preserves the natural heritage of the subtropical coastal habitat that once covered Southeast Florida. This state park has a remarkable 4,000-square-foot Nature Center with exhibits, displays, and a video interpreting the barrier island's plant and animal communities. Dominating a large portion of Singer Island, the barrier island just north of Palm Beach, this beach has lengthy frontage on both the Atlantic Ocean and Lake Worth Cove. The beach is great for hiking, swimming, and sunning. Bathrooms and showers are available. To reach the park from the mainland, cross the Intracoastal Waterway on Blue Heron Boulevard and turn north on Ocean Boulevard.

Jupiter Inlet meets the ocean at **Dubois Park,** a 29-acre beach that is popular with families. The shallow waters and sandy shore are perfect for kids, while adults can play in the rougher swells of the lifeguarded inlet. A footbridge leads to **Ocean Beach,** an area popular with windsurfers and surfers. There's a short fishing pier and plenty of trees shading barbecue grills and picnic tables. Visitors can also explore the Dubois Pioneer Home, a small house situated atop a shell mound built by the Jaega Indians. Made from cypress, the home was built in

1898 by Harry Dubois, a citrus worker, as a wedding gift to his wife Susan, whose pictures are still in the house. You will see an original butter churn and pump sewing machine in the living room, and the dining room and bedroom are almost straight out of *Little House on the Prairie.* The park entrance is on Dubois Road, about a mile south of the junction of U.S. 1 and Fla. A1A.

BIKING   Rent a bike from **Raleigh Bicycles of Jupiter,** at 103 U.S. 1, Unit F1 (℃ **561/746-0585**). Prices for cruisers are $17 per day and $50 per week. For all-terrain bikes, prices are $19 per day and $70 per week. Bike enthusiasts will enjoy exploring this flat and uncluttered area. North Palm Beach has hundreds of miles of smooth, paved roads. Loggerhead Park in Juno Beach or Fla. A1A along the ocean also has great trails for starters. You'll find many more scenic routes over the bridges and west of the highway.

CANOEING   You can rent a boat at several outlets throughout northern Palm Beach County, including **Canoe Outfitters,** 9060 W. Indiantown Rd. (west of I-95), North Jupiter (℃ **561/746-7053**), which provides access to one of the area's most beautiful natural waterways. Canoers start at Riverbend Park along an 8-mile stretch of Intracoastal Waterway, where the lush foliage supports dozens of exotic birds and reptiles. Keep your eyes open for the gators, who love to sunbathe on the shallow shores of the river. You'll end up, exhausted, at Jonathan Dickinson Park about 5 or 6 hours later. A pamphlet describing local flora and fauna is available for $1. Trips run Thursday through Monday and cost $40 for two people in a double canoe. Guided trips are also available for $35 per person.

CRUISES   Several sightseeing cruises offer tours of the magnificent waterways that make up northern Palm Beach County. Water taxis conduct daily narrated tours through the scenic waters. One interesting excursion that will take you past the mansions of the rich and famous, and possibly past the manatees swimming off the port of Palm Beach, departs from **Panama Hatties** at PGA Boulevard and the Intracoastal Waterway. Prices are $17 for adults, $15 for seniors, and $9 for children under 12 for the 1½-hour ride. Call ℃ **561/775-2628.** The *Manatee Queen,* 1065 N. Ocean Blvd. (at the Crab House), Jupiter (℃ **561/744-2191**), is a 40-foot catamaran with bench seating for up to 49 people. Two-hour tours of Jupiter Island depart daily at 2:30pm, passing Burt Reynolds's and Perry Como's former mansions, among other spots of historical and natural interest. They also have a daily sunset cruise from 5 to 6:30pm. Reservations are highly recommended, especially in season; call for the current schedule of offerings. Prices are $20 for adults and $13 for children ages 6 through 12. Bring your own lunch or purchase chips and sodas at the mini–snack bar.

FISHING   Before you leave, send for an information-packed fishing kit with details on fish camps, charters, and tournament and tide schedules distributed by the **West Palm Beach Fishing Club** (℃ **561/832-6780**). The cost is $10 and well worth it. Allow at least 4 weeks for delivery.

Once in town, several outfitters along U.S. 1 and Fla. A1A have vessels and equipment for rent if your hotel doesn't. One of the most complete facilities is the **Sailfish Marina & Resort,** 98 Lake Dr. (off Blue Heron Blvd.), Palm Beach Shores (℃ **561/844-1724**). Call for equipment, bait, guided trips, or boat rentals.

GOLF   Even if you're not lucky enough to be staying at the **PGA National Resort & Spa,** you may still be able to play on their award-winning courses. If

Discovering a Remarkable Natural World

North Palm Beach is well known for the giant sea turtles that lay their eggs on the county's beaches from May to August. These endangered marine animals return here annually, from as far away as South America, to lay their clutches of about 115 eggs each. Nurtured by the warm sand, but targeted by birds and other predators, only about one or two babies from each nest survive to maturity.

Many environmentalists recommend that visitors take part in an organized turtle-watching program (rather than going on their own) to minimize disturbance to the turtles. The Jupiter Beach Resort (5 N. A1A, Jupiter; © 800/228-8810 or 561/746-2511) and the Marinelife Center of Juno Beach (see below) both sponsor free guided expeditions to the egg-laying sites from May to August. Phone for times and reservations.

Just south of Jupiter, in Juno Beach, is the **Marinelife Center of Juno Beach,** in Loggerhead Park, 14200 U.S. 1, Juno Beach (© 561/627-8280). Combining a science museum and nature trail, the small Marinelife Center is dedicated to the coastal ecology of northern Palm Beach County. Hands-on exhibits teach visitors about wetlands and beach areas, as well as offshore coral reefs and the local sea life. Visitors are encouraged to walk the center's sand-dune nature trails, all of which are marked with interpretive signs. This is one place in which you're guaranteed to see live sea turtles year-round. During high breeding season (June–July), the center conducts narrative walks along a nearby beach. Reservations are a must. The booking list opens on May 1 and is usually full by midmonth. Admission to the center is free, though donations are accepted. Open Monday through Saturday from 10am to 4pm and Sunday from noon to 3pm.

you or someone in your group is a member of another golf or country club, have the head pro write a note on club letterhead to Jackie Rogers at PGA (400 Ave. of the Champions, Palm Beach Gardens, FL 33418; © **561/627-2000**) to request a play date. Be sure the pro includes his PGA number and contact information. Allow at least 2 weeks for a response. Also, ask about the "Golf-A-Round" program, where selected private clubs open to nonmembers for free or discounted rates. Contact the **Palm Beach County Convention and Visitors Bureau** (© **561/471-3995**) for details.

Plenty of other great courses dot the area, including the **Golf Club of Jupiter,** 1800 Central Blvd., Jupiter (© **561/747-6262**), where a well-respected 18-hole, par-70 course is situated on more than 6,200 yards featuring narrow fairways and fast greens. Fees are $56 until noon, $45 after noon, and $25 after 2pm, and include a mandatory cart. The course borders I-95.

HIKING   In an area that's not particularly known for extraordinary natural diversity, **Blowing Rocks Preserve** has a terrific hiking trail along a dramatic limestone outcropping. You won't find hills or scenic vistas, but you will see Florida's unique and varied tropical ecosystem. The well-marked mile-long trail passes oceanfront dunes, coastal strands, mangrove wetlands, and a coastal hammock. The preserve, owned and managed by The Nature Conservancy, also protects an important habitat for West Indian manatees and loggerhead turtles. Located along South Beach Drive (Fla. A1A), north of the Jupiter inlet, the preserve is about a 10-minute drive northeast of Jupiter. Free guided tours are available Fridays at 1pm and Sundays at 11am, and no reservations are necessary. From U.S. 1, head east on S.R. 707 and cross the Intracoastal Waterway to the park. Admission is $3 for adults; kids 12 and under are free. For more information, contact The Nature Conservancy, 574 South Beach Rd., Hobe Sound, FL 33455 (© **561/744-6668**).

SCUBA DIVING & SNORKELING   Year-round warm, clear waters make northern Palm Beach County great for both diving and snorkeling. The closest coral reef is located ¼ mile from shore and can easily be reached by boat. Three popular wrecks are clustered near each other, less than a mile offshore of the Lake Worth Inlet at about 90 feet. The best wreck, however, is the 16th- or 17th-century Spanish galleon discovered by lifeguard Peter Leo just off Jupiter Beach. If your hotel doesn't offer dive trips, call the **South Florida Dive Headquarters,** 101 N. Riverside Dr., Pampono Beach (© **800/771-DIVE** or 954/ 783-2299); or **Seafari Dive and Surf,** 75 E. Indiantown Rd., Suite 603, Jupiter (© **561/747-6115**).

TENNIS   In addition to the many hotel tennis, you can swing a racquet at a number of local clubs. The **Jupiter Bay Tennis Club,** 353 U.S. 1, Jupiter (© **561/744-9424**), has seven clay courts (three lighted) and charges $12 per person per day. Reservations are highly recommended.

More economical options are available at relatively well-maintained municipal courts. Call for locations and hours (© **561/966-6600**). Many are available free on a first-come, first-served basis.

A HISTORIC LIGHTHOUSE

Jupiter Inlet Lighthouse ☆   Completed in 1860, this redbrick structure is the oldest extant building in Palm Beach County. Still owned and maintained by the U.S. Coast Guard, the lighthouse is now home to a small historical museum, located at its base. The Florida History Museum sponsors tours of the lighthouse, enabling visitors to explore the cramped interior, which is filled with artifacts and photographs illustrating the rich history of the area. A 15-minute video explains the various shipwrecks, Indian wars, and other events that helped shape this region. Helpful volunteers are eager to tell colorful stories to highlight the 1-hour tour.

500 S.R. 707, Jupiter. © 561/747-8380. Admission $6. Sat–Wed 10am–4pm (last tour departs at 3:15pm). Children must be 4 ft. or taller to climb. No open-backed shoes.

SHOPPING

Northern Palm Beach County may not have the glitzy boutiques of Worth Avenue, but it does have an impressive indoor mall, the **Gardens of the Palm Beaches,** at 3101 PGA Blvd., where you can find large department stores including **Bloomingdale's, Burdines, Macy's,** and **Saks Fifth Avenue,** as well as more than 100 specialty shops. A large, diverse food court and fine sit-down restaurants in this 1.3-million-square-foot facility make this shopping excursion an all-day affair. Call © **561/775-7750** for store information.

ACCOMMODATIONS YOU CAN AFFORD

The northern part of Palm Beach County is much more laid-back and less touristy than the rest of the Gold Coast. Here, there are relatively few fancy hotels or attractions. In addition to several **Holiday Inns** (℃ **800/325-8193**), there is a reasonably priced and recently renovated **Wellesley Inn,** 34 Fisherman's Wharf (I-95, exit east on Indiantown Rd.; turn left before the bridge), in Jupiter (℃ **800/444-8888**). Suites include sofa beds, refrigerators, and microwaves and cost $55 year-round. Although not within walking distance of the beach, the inn is located near shops and restaurants and Fla. A1A.

Baron's Landing Motel & Apartments ★ *Value* This charming family-run inn is a perfect little beach getaway. It's not elegant, but it is cozy. The single-story motel fronting the Intracoastal Waterway is often full in winter with snowbirds who dock their boats at the hotel's marina for weeks or months at a time. Nearly all rooms, which are situated around a small pool, have small kitchenettes. Each unit has a funky mix of used furniture, and some have pullout sofas. Bathrooms have been remodeled. Considering that you're a few blocks from some of the most expensive real estate in the country, this is a good deal.

18125 Ocean Blvd. (Fla. A1A at the corner of Clemens St.), Jupiter, FL 33477. ℃ 561/746-8757. 8 units. Winter $75–$125 double, $1,350–$1,700 monthly; off season $45–$75 double, $700–$900 monthly. No credit cards. **Amenities:** Small pool. *In room:* A/C, TV, fax, dataport, kitchen, fridge, coffeemaker, iron.

Cannonsport Marina & Resort A great find at the southern tip of Singer Island, this small and exclusive apartment house was recently renovated and is located just on the lake's edge where guests enjoy a marina, barbecue grill, hammocks, and comfy lounge furniture. There is also a good-size pool and hot tub. Plus, it's just 2 blocks from the ocean. Still, the best part is that all apartments have fully stocked kitchens with stoves and ranges. The best are the two-bedroom apartments, which have private sun decks. A renovation in 2001 included new furniture and remodeled kitchens.

178 Lake Dr., Palm Beach Shores, FL 33404. ℃ **800/627-8328** or 561/844-5588. Fax 561/844-9007. www.cannonsport.com. 14 units. Winter $110–$200; off season $90–$180. AE, DC, DISC, MC, V. **Amenities:** Pool; Jacuzzi; watersports equipment; fishing equipment; free shuttle to town; laundry facilities. *In room:* A/C, TV/VCR, kitchen, fridge, coffeemaker, iron.

Cologne Motel A modest roadside motel, the Cologne is a well-maintained one-story building with very little in the way of amenities. The bathrooms are small but clean. The area is safe if not scenic and only about a 5-minute drive to the beach. A more direct route by foot gets you there in about 15 minutes.

220 U.S. 1, Tequesta/Jupiter, FL 33469. ℃ **561/746-0616.** 10 units. Winter $78 double; off season $46 double. Weekly rates available. AE, MC, V. *In room:* A/C, TV, fridge.

GREAT DEALS ON DINING

In addition to all the national fast-food joints that line Indiantown Road and U.S. 1, you'll find a number of touristy fish restaurants serving battered and fried everything. There are only a few really exceptional eateries in North Palm Beach and Jupiter. Try those listed below for guaranteed good food at reasonable prices.

Capt. Charlie's Reef Grill ★★ SEAFOOD/CARIBBEAN The trick here is to arrive early, ahead of the crowd of local foodies who come for the more than a dozen daily local-catch specials prepared in dozens of styles. Imaginative appetizers include Caribbean chili, a rich chunky stew filled with fresh seafood; and a tuna spring roll big enough for two. The enormous Cuban crab cake is moist and perfectly browned without tasting fried and is served with homemade mango chutney and black beans and rice. Sit at the bar to watch the hectic kitchen turn out perfect dishes on the 14-burner stove. Somehow, the pleasant waitresses keep their cool even when the place is packed.

12846 U.S. 1 (behind O'Brian's and French Connection), Juno Beach. © **561/624-9924**. Reservations not accepted. Main courses $9.95–$22. MC, V. Sun–Fri 11:30am–3pm and 5–9:30pm.

Nick's Tomato Pie ⭐ ITALIAN   A fun, family restaurant, Nick's is a popular attraction that's known to bring folks even from Miami for a piece of this pie. With a huge menu of pastas, pizzas, fish, chicken, and beef, this cheery (and noisy) spot has something for everyone. On Saturday night, you'll see lots of couples on dates and some families leaving with takeout bags left over from the impossibly generous portions. The homemade sausage is a delicious treat, served with sautéed onions and peppers. The *pollo Marsala,* too, is good and authentic.

1697 W. Indiantown Rd. (1 mile east of I-95, exit 59A), Jupiter. © **561/744-8935**. Reservations accepted for groups of 6 or more. Main courses $12–$20; pastas $10–$15. AE, DC, DISC, MC, V. Mon–Thurs and Sun 5–9:30pm; Fri–Sat 5–10:30pm.

SUPER-CHEAP EATS

Athenian Cafe ⭐ *Finds* GREEK   Peter Papadelis and his family have been running this pleasant storefront cafe for more than a decade. Tucked in the corner of a strip mall, this place is a favorite with businesspeople, who stop in for a heaping portion of rich and meaty moussaka or a flaky spinach pie made fresh by Peter himself. You could make a meal of the thick and lemony Greek soup and the large, fresh antipasto. In a town replete with tourist-priced fish joints, this is a welcome alternative. Early-bird specials, served until 7pm, include many Greek favorites and broiled local fish with soup or salad, rice, vegetables, pita, dessert, and coffee or tea.

In the Chasewood Shopping Center, 6350 Indiantown Rd., Suite 7, Jupiter. © **561/744-8327**. Main courses $5–$16. AE, MC, V. Daily 11am–9pm.

Lanna Thai THAI   There are dozens of great choices at Lanna Thai, including all the old reliables like pad Thai, panang curry, pad king, and pad puck to pair with meat, chicken, or fish. This inauspicious storefront has a quaint, whitewashed dining room where only a dozen tables sit beneath latticework bedecked with fake plants. Come for the lunch specials that include spring rolls, soup, and fried rice for less than $6.

4300 S. U.S. 1 (in the Bluff's Square Shopping Center, between Indian Town and Donald Ross rds.), Jupiter. © **561/694-1443**. Reservations not accepted. Main courses $10; chef's specials $10–$18. MC, V. Mon–Fri 11am–3pm; daily 5–10pm.

JUPITER & NORTHERN PALM BEACH COUNTY AFTER DARK

With one notable exception, there just isn't much going on here after dark. However, **Club Safari,** 4000 PGA Blvd. (just east of I-95), in Palm Beach Garden's Marriott Hotel (© **561/622-8888**), has a hilarious Vegas-style safari-themed decor. There is DJ music, a large video screen, and a modest cover charge on the weekends. It's open nights, Wednesday through Sunday. For more options, check your hotel or do what most people do—go to West Palm Beach.

8

The Treasure Coast:
Stuart to Sebastian

The area north of Palm Beach is known as the Treasure Coast for the same reason that the area from Fort Lauderdale to Palm Beach is known as the Gold Coast—it was the site of a number of shipwrecks that date back over 300 years, which led to the discovery of priceless treasures in the water (some historians believe that treasures from these sunken vessels *still* lie buried deep beneath the ocean floor).

The difference, however, is that while the Gold Coast is a bit, well, tarnished as far as development is concerned, the Treasure Coast remains, for the most part, an unspoiled, quiet natural jewel. Miles of uninterrupted beaches and aquamarine waters attract swimmers, boaters, divers, anglers, and sun worshippers who love to dip, dive, and surf. If you love the great outdoors and prefer a more understated environment than hyperdeveloped Miami and Fort Lauderdale, the Treasure Coast is a real find.

For hundreds of years, Florida's east coast was a popular stopover for European explorers, many of whom arrived from Spain to fill coffers with gold and silver. Rough weather and poor navigation often took a toll on their ships, but in 1715, a violent hurricane stunned the northeast coast and sank an entire fleet of Spanish ships laden with gold. Although Spanish salvagers worked for years to collect the lost treasure, much of it remained buried beneath the shifting sand. Workers hired to excavate the area in the 1950s

and 1960s discovered centuries-old coins under their tractors.

Today, you can still see shipwrecks and incredible barrier reefs in St. Lucie County, which can be reached from the beaches of Fort Pierce and Hutchinson Island. On these same beaches, you'll also find an occasional treasure hunter trolling the sand with a metal detector, alongside swimmers and sunbathers who come to enjoy the stretches of beach that extend into the horizon. The sea, especially around Sebastian Inlet, is a mecca for surfers, who find some of the largest swells in the state.

Along with the pleasures of the talcum-powder sands, the Treasure Coast also offers good shopping, sporting, and numerous other opportunities to take a reprieve from the hubbub of the rat race. Visitors to this part of South Florida should not miss the extensive array of wildlife, which includes the endangered West Indian manatee, loggerhead and leatherback turtles, tropical fish, alligators, deer, and exotic birds. For sports enthusiasts, there are boundless sporting opportunities here—from golf and tennis to polo, motorcar racing, the New York Mets during their spring training, and the best freshwater fishing around.

The downtown areas of the Treasure Coast have been experiencing a rebirth in the past few years, along with the influx of unprecedented numbers of new residents. Fortunately, the area's growth has occurred at a reasonable pace so that the neighborhoods have

Cheap Thrills: What to See & Do for Free (or Almost) on the Treasure Coast

- **Take in the scenery.** One of the most scenic areas on this stretch of the coast is **Jonathan Dickinson State Park** ⭐, 12 miles south of Stuart at 16450 S. Federal Hwy. (U.S. 1), Hobe Sound (© **772/546-2771**). The park intentionally receives less maintenance than other, more meticulously maintained parks so that it will resemble the rough-around-the-edges, wilderness-like environment of hundreds of years ago, before Europeans started chopping, dredging, and "improving" the area. Dozens of species of Florida's unique wildlife, including alligators and manatees, live on the park's more than 11,300 acres. Bird-watchers will also be delighted by glimpses of rare and endangered species such as the bald eagle, the Florida scrub-jay, and the Florida sandhill crane, which still call this park home. You can rent canoes from the concession stand to explore the Loxahatchee River on your own. Admission is $4 per car of up to eight adults. Day hikers, bikers, and walkers pay $1 each. The park is open from 8am until sundown. See "Accommodations You Can Afford," below, for details on camping.
- **Glimpse a wildlife refuge.** Close to Jonathan Dickinson State Park is **Hobe Sound Wildlife Refuge,** on North Beach Road off S.R. 708, at the north end of Jupiter Island (© **772/546-6141**). This is one of the best places to see sea turtles that nest on the shore in the summer months, especially in June and July. Because it's home to a large variety of other plant and animal species, the park is worth visiting at other times of year as well. Admission is $4 per car, and the preserve is open daily from sunrise to sunset. Exact times are posted at each entrance and change seasonally.
- **Walk among the turtles.** For turtle walks on Hutchinson Island, call © **877/375-4386.** These walks take place from May 22 to July 22 at 9pm, Friday and Saturday. Reservations are necessary and should be made well in advance, as walks are limited to 50 people. Reservations are accepted as of May 1.

been able to retain their small-town feel. The result is a batch of freshly spruced-up accommodations, shops, and restaurants from Stuart to Sebastian.

Southern Martin County's well-to-do Hobe Sound, in particular, is a Treasure Coast hot spot with its pristine beaches, Banyan tree–canopied streetscapes, one-of-a-kind antiques shops, and art galleries. Hobe Sound rests at the front door of the Gold Coast and the back door of the Treasure Coast, and it has immediate access to the Atlantic Ocean and the Intracoastal Waterway. Real estate here is at a premium, with million-dollar waterfront mansions lining the shores.

For the purposes of this chapter, the Treasure Coast runs roughly from Hobe Sound in the south to the Sebastian Inlet in the north, encompassing some of Martin, St. Lucie, and Indian River Counties and all of Hutchinson Island.

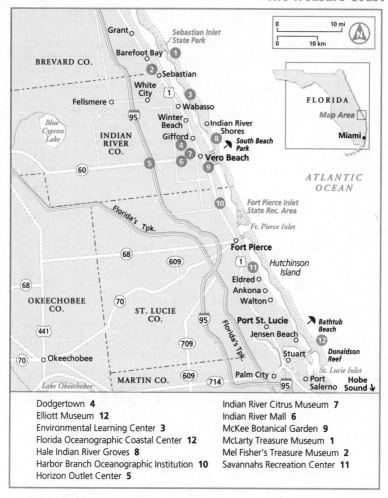

The Treasure Coast

Dodgertown **4**	Indian River Citrus Museum **7**
Elliott Museum **12**	Indian River Mall **6**
Environmental Learning Center **3**	McKee Botanical Garden **9**
Florida Oceanographic Coastal Center **12**	McLarty Treasure Museum **1**
Hale Indian River Groves **8**	Mel Fisher's Treasure Museum **2**
Harbor Branch Oceanographic Institution **10**	Savannahs Recreation Center **11**
Horizon Outlet Center **5**	

TREASURE COAST ESSENTIALS
GETTING THERE

Since virtually every town described in this chapter runs along a straight route along the Atlantic Ocean, I've given all directions below.

BY PLANE   The **Palm Beach International Airport** (© 561/471-7420), located about 35 miles south of Stuart, is the closest gateway to this region if you're flying. See the "Getting There" section on Palm Beach, on p. 255, in chapter 7 for complete information. If you are traveling to the northern part of the Treasure Coast, **Melbourne International Airport,** off U.S. 1 in Melbourne (© 321/723-6227), is less than 25 miles north of Sebastian and about 35 miles north of Vero Beach.

BY CAR   If you're driving up or down the Florida coast, you'll probably reach the Treasure Coast via I-95. If you are heading to Stuart or Jensen Beach, take exit 61 (Rte. 76/Tanner Hwy.) or 62 (Rte. 714); to Port St. Lucie or Fort Pierce, take exit 63 or 64 (Okeechobee Rd.); to Vero Beach, take exit 68 (S.R. 60); to Sebastian, take exit 69 (County Rd.).

You can also take the Florida Turnpike; this toll road is the fastest (but not the most scenic) route, especially if you're coming from Orlando. If you are heading to Stuart or Jensen Beach, take exit 133; to Fort Pierce, take exit 152 (Okeechobee Rd.); to Port St. Lucie, take exit 142 or 152; to Vero Beach, take exit 193 (S.R. 60); to Sebastian, take exit 193 to S.R. 60 east and connect to I-95 north.

If you are staying in Hutchinson Island, which runs almost the entire length of the Treasure Coast, you should check with your hotel or see the listings below to find the best route to take.

Finally, if you're coming directly from the west coast, you'll probably take S.R. 70, which runs north of Lake Okeechobee to Fort Pierce, located just up the road from Stuart.

BY RAIL **Amtrak** (© **800/USA-RAIL;** www.amtrak.com) stops in West Palm Beach at 201 S. Tamarind Ave., and in Okeechobee at 801 N. Parrot Ave., off U.S. 441 north.

BY BUS **Greyhound** buses (© **800/231-2222;** www.greyhound.com) service the area with terminals in Stuart, at 1308 S. Federal Hwy.; in Fort Pierce, at 7005 Okeechobee Rd. (© **772/461-3299**); and in Vero Beach, at U.S. 1 and S.R. 60 (© **772/562-6588**).

GETTING AROUND
A car is a necessity in this large and rural region. Although heavy traffic is not usually a problem here, on the smaller coastal roads, like A1A, expect to travel at a slow pace, usually between 25 and 40 mph.

1 Hobe Sound ⭐⭐⭐, Stuart (North Hutchinson Island ⭐⭐) & Jensen Beach

Once just a stretch of pineapple plantations, the towns of Martin County, which include Hobe Sound, Stuart, and Jensen Beach, still retain much of their rural character. Dotted between citrus groves and mangroves are modest homes and an occasional high-rise condominium. Although the area is definitely still seasonal (with a distinct rise in street and pedestrian traffic beginning after the Christmas holidays), the atmosphere is pure small town. Even in historic downtown Stuart, the result of a successful, ongoing restoration, expect the storefronts to be dark and the streets abandoned after 10pm.

ESSENTIALS
The **Stuart/Martin County Chamber of Commerce,** 1650 S. Kanner Hwy., Stuart, FL 34994 (© **800/524-9704** or 772/287-1088; fax 772/220-3437; www.goodnature.org), is the region's main source for information. The **Jensen Beach Chamber of Commerce,** 1901 NE Jensen Beach Blvd., Jensen Beach, FL 34957 (© **772/334-3444;** fax 772/334-0817; www.jensenchamber.com), also offers visitors information about its simple beachfront town.

AFFORDABLE OUTDOOR ACTIVITIES
BEACHES Hutchinson Island, located in Stuart, is one of the most popular beach destinations of the Treasure Coast, located just north of Palm Beach on the Atlantic Ocean. Some 70 miles of excellent beaches and laid-back, Old Florida ambience make for an idyllic frozen-cocktail-on-the-beach resort vacation.

The best of them is **Bathtub Beach,** on North Hutchinson Island. Here, the calm waters are protected by coral reefs, and visitors can explore the region on dune and river trails. Pick a secluded spot on the wide stretch of beach, or enjoy marked nature trails across the street. Facilities include showers and toilets open during the day. To reach Bathtub Beach from the northern tip of Hutchinson Island, head east on Ocean Boulevard (Stuart Causeway) and turn right onto MacArthur Boulevard. The beach is about a mile ahead on your left, just north of the Hutchinson Island Marriott Beach Resort and Marina. Parking is plentiful.

CANOEING   Jonathan Dickinson State Park (see "Cheap Thrills: What to See & Do for Free (or Almost) on the Treasure Coast," above) is the most popular area for canoeing. The route winds through a variety of botanical habitats. You'll see lots of birds and the occasional manatee. Canoes cost $6 per hour and can be rented through the concession located in the back of the park. The concession (© 561/746-1466) is open Monday through Friday from 9am to 5pm and Saturday and Sunday from 8am to 5pm.

FISHING   Several independent charter captains operate on Hutchinson Island and Jensen Beach. One of the largest operators is the **Sailfish Marina,** 3565 SE St. Lucie Blvd., in Stuart (© 772/221-9456), which maintains half a dozen charter boats for fishing excursions year-round. Also on-site are a bait-and-tackle shop and a knowledgeable, helpful staff. Other reputable charter operators include **Hungry Bear Adventures, Inc.,** docked at Indian River Plantation Marriott Resort, 4730-1 SE Teri Place in Stuart (© 772/285-7552; www. hungrybear.net); and **Bone Shaker Sportfishing,** 3585 SE St. Lucie Blvd., in Stuart (© 772/286-5504; veejay4842@aol.com).

GOLF   Try the Champions Club at Summerfield, on U.S. 1, south of Cove Road in Stuart (© 772/283-1500), a somewhat challenging championship course designed by Tom Fazio. This rural course, the best in the area, offers great glimpses of wildlife amid the wetlands. Winter greens fees are around $65, and carts are mandatory. Reservations are a must and are taken 4 days in advance.

SCUBA DIVING & SNORKELING   Three popular artificial reefs off Hutchinson Island provide excellent scenery for both novice and experienced divers. The **USS *Rankin*** lies 7 miles east-northeast of the St. Lucie Inlet. The Rankin is a 459-foot ship that lays on its port side in 80 feet of water. This ship was used in World War II for troop transportation and was sunk in 1988. Deck hatches on the wreck are open and allow exploration. Inside, there are thousands of Atlantic Spiny oysters, and a cannon is attached to the bow. The 58-foot-deep **Donaldson Reef** consists of a cluster of steel tanks and barrels sunk in 58 feet of water to create the artificial reef. It's located due east of the Gilbert's House of Refuge Museum (see below). The **Ernst Reef,** made from old tires, is a 60-foot dive located 4½ miles east-southeast of the St. Lucie inlet. Local dive shops have "tips" on the best spots and rules and regulations for safe diving.

SEEING THE SIGHTS

Balloons Over Florida ★★★ *Finds*   For a lofty view of Martin County's wildlife, take a hot-air balloon ride above the animals' natural habitat. Two fully licensed and insured balloons and pilots will take a maximum of four people up, up, and away for about an hour, depending on wind and weather conditions. After you've landed, drink in the sights over a glass of complimentary champagne and a continental breakfast.

Tours begin at approximately 6:30am from a takeoff point to be determined. 🕐 **772/334-9393.** $175 per person, including continental breakfast and champagne.

Elliott Museum ★★ A treasure trove of wacky artifacts that really personify Americana, the Elliott Museum is a rich tribute to inventors, sports heroes, and collectors. The museum was created by the son of turn-of-the-20th-century inventor Sterling Elliott to display the genius of the American spirit. Among the bizarre things you'll see here are displays of an apothecary, ice-cream parlor, barbershop, other old-fashioned commercial enterprises, and an authentic handcarved miniature circus. Sports fans will appreciate the baseball memorabilia—a half-million dollars' worth—including an autographed item from every player in the Baseball Hall of Fame.

A gallery of patents and models of machines, invented by the museum's founder, Harmon Parker Elliott, and his son, provides an intriguing glimpse into the business of tinkering. Their collection of restored antique cars is also impressive. Expect to spend at least an hour seeing the highlights.

825 NE Ocean Blvd. (north of Indian River Plantation Resort), Hutchinson Island, Stuart. 🕐 **772/225-1961.** Admission $6 adults, $2 children 6–13, free for children 5 and under. Mon–Sat 10am–4pm.

Florida Oceanographic Coastal Center ★★ This is a nature lover's Disney World. Opened by the South Florida Oceanographic Society in late 1994, this 44-acre site (surrounded by coastal hammock and mangroves) is its own little ecosystem and serves as an outdoor classroom, teaching visitors about the region's flora and fauna. The modest main building houses saltwater tanks and wet and dry "discovery tables" with small indigenous animals. The incredibly eager staff of volunteers encourages visitors to wander the lush, well-marked nature trails.

890 NE Ocean Blvd. (across the street from the Elliott Museum), Hutchinson Island, Stuart. 🕐 **772/225-0505.** www.fosusa.org. Admission $6 adults, $3 children 3–12, free for children under 3. Mon–Sat 10am–5pm; Sun noon–4pm.

A BOAT TOUR

The _Loxahatchee Queen_ ★★★, a 35-foot, 44-passenger pontoon boat (🕐 **772/746-1466**) in Jonathan Dickinson State Park in Hobe Sound, makes daily tours of the area's otherwise inaccessible backwater, where curious alligators, manatees, eagles, and tortoises often peek out to see who's in their yard. Try to catch the 2-hour tour, given Wednesday through Sunday as the tide permits, when it includes a stop at Trapper Nelson's home. Known as the "Wildman of Loxahatchee," Nelson lived in primitive conditions on a remote stretch of the water in a log cabin he built himself, which is preserved for visitors to see. Tours leave four times daily at 9 and 11am and 1 and 3pm and cost $12 for adults, $7 for children 6 to 12, and free for children 5 and under. See the "Cheap Thrills: What to See & Do for Free (or Almost) on the Treasure Coast" box on p. 274 for more information on the park.

SHOPPING

Downtown Stuart's historic district, along Flagler Avenue between Confusion Corner and St. Lucie Avenue, offers shoppers diversity and quality in a small old-town setting. Shops offer a range of goods: antique bric-a-brac, old lamps and fixtures, books, gourmet foods, furnishings, and souvenirs. For bargains, check out the **B & A Flea Market** (🕐 **772/288-4915**), the Treasure Coast's oldest and largest flea market.

ACCOMMODATIONS YOU CAN AFFORD

Although the area boasts some beautiful beaches, the bulk of the hotel scene is downtown, where the nicer (and more reasonably priced) accommodations can be found among the shops and restaurants. There are, however, a few excellent beachfront hotels and inns. One of the bigger hotel chains in the area is the **Holiday Inn.** Its recently renovated, stunning beachfront property is at 3793 NE Ocean Blvd., on Hutchinson Island in Jensen Beach (© **800/992-4747** or 772/225-3000). Rates in season range from $150 to $209. Holiday Inn also has a downtown location at 1209 S. Federal Hwy. (© **772/287-6200**). This simple two-story building on a busy main road is kept in very good shape and is convenient to Stuart's downtown historic district. Rates range from $129 to $149. *Note:* In 2002, a 2% tax was added on accommodations in the Stuart-Hutchinson Island area.

Harborfront Inn Bed & Breakfast ★★ *Finds*   A bona fide return to Old Florida, the Harborfront Inn has the advantage of being right on the river, where you can sail, kayak, and water-ski. It consists of a series of little blue-trimmed shingled cottages within walking distance of the restaurants of downtown Stuart. Each room (all with a sitting area and a private bathroom) has its own private entrance. The two best rooms are the bright Garden Suite, which has a queen-size bed, rattan furnishings, and a deck with river and garden views; and the Guest House, which has an extra-large bathroom with two sinks and can be rented with an adjoining full kitchen. An enclosed porch surrounds the inn's cozy public areas where breakfast (usually including fresh fruit from the trees that grow on the property) is served. A must-do is the in-room candlelight dinner. Smoking is not permitted here.

310 Atlanta Ave., Stuart, FL 34994. © 800/294-1703 or 561/288-7289. Fax 561/221-0474. 6 units. Winter $90–$183 double. Off-season discounts available. Rates include breakfast. DISC, MC, V. Free dockage. From I-95 take Exit 61 heading east to U.S. 1 N. Turn left on W. Ocean Blvd. and make the first right (Atlanta Ave.). Children not allowed. **Amenities:** Jacuzzi; watersports equipment/rentals. *In room:* A/C, TV/VCR, hair dryer.

WORTH A SPLURGE

Hutchinson Island Marriott Beach Resort and Marina ★★★ *Kids*   This sprawling 200-acre compound offers many diversions for active (or not-so-active) vacationers, and families in particular. This is definitely Hutchinson Island's best resort, occupying the lush grounds of a former pineapple plantation. Activities include tennis, golfing, boating, sport fishing (especially for sailfish), scuba diving, and other watersports.

Some rooms overlook the Intracoastal and the resort's marina, while others face the ocean or the gardens. All are generously sized and have fully equipped kitchens. In the summer months, be sure to sign up for a "turtle watch," so you can observe turtles crawling onto the sand to lay their eggs. Another great activity, offered at an extra cost, is a sightseeing cruise along the St. Lucie and Indian rivers.

555 NE Ocean Blvd., Hutchinson Island, Stuart, FL 34996. © 800/775-5936 or 772/225-3700. Fax 772/225-0003. www.marriott.com. 298 units. Winter $179–$259 double, $265–$399 suite; off season $99–$109 double, $129–$299 suite. AE, MC, V. From downtown Stuart, take E. Ocean Blvd. over 2 bridges to NE Ocean Blvd.; turn right. Pets accepted with a $50 deposit. **Amenities:** Restaurant; coffee shop; lounge; 4 large pools; 18-hole golf course; 13 tennis courts; fitness center and spa; extensive watersports; bike rental; children's programs; game room; concierge; on-property transportation; limited room service; babysitting; laundry services; dry cleaning. *In room:* A/C, TV, dataport, kitchenette, minibar, coffeemaker, hair dryer, iron.

CAMPING

There are comfortable campsites (rustic cabins or sites for your tent or camper) in **Jonathan Dickinson State Park** in Hobe Sound (see the "Cheap Thrills:

What to See & Do for Free (or Almost) on the Treasure Coast" box on p. 274). The River Camp area of the park offers the benefit of the nearby Loxahatchee River, while the Pine Grove site has beautiful shade trees. There are concession areas for daytime snacks and 135 campsites with showers, clean restrooms, water, optional electricity, and an open-fire pit for cooking. Overnight rates in the winter are $18 without electricity, $20 with electricity. In the summer, rates are about $14 for four people.

For a more cushy camping experience, reserve a wood-sided cabin with a furnished kitchen, a bathroom with shower, heat and air-conditioning, and an outdoor grill. Bring your own linens. Cabins rent for $85 (one bed and a pullout couch), $95 (two beds and a pullout couch), and up a night and sleep four people comfortably, six if your group is really into togetherness. Call ℂ 772/546-2771 Monday through Friday from 9am to 5pm, well in advance, to reserve a spot. A $50 key deposit is required.

GREAT DEALS ON DINING

Black Marlin ℱ FLORIDA REGIONAL   Although it sports the look and feel of a dank English pub, the Black Marlin offers full Floridian flavor. The salmon BLT is typical of the dishes here—grilled salmon on a toasted bun topped with bacon, lettuce, tomato, and coleslaw. Designer pizzas are topped with shrimp, roasted red peppers, and the like; and main dishes, all of which are served with vegetables and potatoes, include a lobster tail with honey-mustard sauce, and a charcoal-grilled chicken breast served on radicchio with caramelized onions.

53 W. Osceola St., downtown Stuart. ℂ 772/286-3126. Reservations not accepted. Salads and sandwiches $4–$8; full meals $9–$24. AE, MC, V. Mon–Thurs 5–10pm; Fri–Sat 5–11pm (the bar is open later).

Conchy Joe's Seafood ★★ *Finds* SEAFOOD   Known for fresh seafood and Old Florida hospitality, Conchy Joe's enjoys an excellent reputation that's far bigger than the restaurant itself. Shorts and flip-flops are the attire of choice here, and dining is either indoors, at red-and-white cloth-covered tables, or on a covered patio overlooking the St. Lucie River. The restaurant features a wide variety of freshly shucked shellfish and daily-catch selections that are baked, broiled, or fried, and the conch chowder is sublime. The large bar here is especially popular at night and during weekday happy hours.

3945 NE Indian River Dr. (½ mile from the Jensen Beach Causeway), Jensen Beach. ℂ 772/334-1130. Reservations not accepted. Main courses $12–$20. AE, DISC, MC, V. Daily 11:30am–2:30pm and 5–10pm.

Harry and the Natives ★★ AMERICAN   When you dine at this wild and wacky, kitschy old Florida institution (to which both Harleys and Bentleys flock), you'll get decent bar fare—try the venison burger—with a fabulous dish of local color and humor (sometimes very un-PC humor) on the side. The menu itself is hilarious, especially "Acceptibles: Visa, Mastercard, our gift certificates, cash, oceanfront homes, table dancing, honeydripping and dishwashing." No offense to our Canadian friends, but the menu also kiddingly has a "Canadian Breakfast—(no tip) $20." Hilarious. The food ranges from eggs, omelets, and banana pancakes to the "President Bush Omelet—$1,000,000,000 Profits go to the Palm Beach County Election Supervisor to buy more butterfly ballots, voting machines and incompetent help." I don't want to spoil it all for you, so just make sure to read the entire menu. There's live music Wednesday, Friday, and Saturday. Make sure you request that the band play the Harry and the Natives theme song.

11910 S. Federal Hwy., Hobe Sound. ℂ 772/546-3061. Main courses $5–$10. MC, V. Daily 6:30am–2:30am.

WORTH A SPLURGE

11 Maple Street ★★★ AMERICAN The most highly rated restaurant in Jensen Beach, 11 Maple Street occupies a cozy, converted, old house. Dining is both indoors and out, in any one of a series of cozy dining rooms or on a covered patio surrounded by gardens. Interesting dishes not typically found in these parts of Florida include the wood-grilled venison with French green lentils, broccoli rabe, caramelized turnip, hazelnut, and white bean purée with grilled tomato sauce; and the braised Moulard duck leg with wood-grilled Oregon quail, Tuscan cabbage, butternut squash, and chestnut tart with a balsamic pear reduction. The restaurant also uses organically grown produce from its own garden (when available) and poultry and meats that are farm raised and free of chemical additives.

11 Maple St., Jensen Beach. © 772/334-7714. Reservations recommended. Main courses $18–$30. MC, V. Wed–Sun 6–10pm. Head east on Jensen Beach Blvd. and turn right after the railroad tracks.

STUART & JENSEN BEACH AFTER DARK

No list of Jensen nightlife would be complete without mention of Conchy Joe's Seafood (see "Great Deals on Dining," above), one of the region's most active spots. Inside, locals chug beer and watch a large-screen TV, while outside on the waterfront patio, live bands perform a few nights a week for a raucous crowd of dancers. Happy hours, weekdays from 3 to 6pm, draw large crowds with low-priced drinks and snacks. There is no cover.

The centerpiece of Stuart's slowly expanding cultural offerings is the newly restored **Lyric Theater** at 59 SW Flagler Ave. (© **772/286-7827**). This beautiful 1920s-era, 600-seat theater hosts a variety of shows, readings, concerts, and films throughout the year.

2 Port St. Lucie & Fort Pierce

Port St. Lucie and Fort Pierce (two Old Florida towns, reminiscent of pre-Neon, pre-condo-maniacal Florida, which are sleepy, different worlds when compared to the Gold Coast and Miami) thrive on sport fishing. A seemingly endless row of piers juts out along the Intracoastal Waterway and the Fort Pierce Inlet for both river and ocean runs. Here visitors can also dive, snorkel, beachcomb, and sunbathe in an area that has been left untouched by the overdevelopment that has altered its neighbors to the south and north.

Most sightseeing takes place along the main beach road (the strip across from the Ocean/A1A). Driving along Fla. A1A on Hutchinson Island, you'll discover several secluded beach clubs interspersed with 1950s-style homes, a few small inns, grungy raw bars, and a few high-rise condominiums. Much of this island is government owned and kept undeveloped for the public's enjoyment.

ESSENTIALS

The **St. Lucie County Chamber of Commerce,** 2200 Virginia Ave., Fort Pierce, FL 34982 (© **772/595-9999;** www.stluciechamber.org), is the region's main source of information. There's another branch at 1626 SE Port St. Lucie Blvd., in Port St. Lucie. Both spots are open Monday through Friday from 9am to 5pm.

BEACHES & NATURE PRESERVES

North Hutchinson Island's beaches are the most pristine in this area. You won't find restaurants, hotels, or shopping; instead, spend your time swimming, surfing, fishing, and diving. Most of the beaches along this stretch of the Atlantic Ocean are private, but thankfully, the state has set aside some of the best areas for the public.

Fort Pierce Inlet State Recreation Area (© 772/468-3985) is a stunning 340-acre park with almost 4,000 feet of sandy shores that were once the training ground for the original navy frogmen. A short nature trail leads through a canopy of live oaks, cabbage palms, sea grapes, and strangler figs. The western side of the area has swamps of red mangroves that are home to fiddler crabs, osprey, and a multitude of wading birds. Jack Island State Preserve, in the State Recreation Area, is popular with bird-watchers and offers hiking and nature trails. Jutting out into the Indian River, the mangrove-covered peninsula contains several marked trails, varying in distance from .5 mile to over 4 miles. The trails go through mangrove forests and lead to a short observation tower.

The best beach in the recreation area, called Jetty Park, lies in the northern part of the state recreation area. Families enjoy the picnic areas and barbecue grills. There are restrooms and outdoor showers, and lifeguards look after swimmers.

The park is located at 905 Shorewinds Dr., north of Fort Pierce Inlet. To get there from I-95, take exit 66 east (Rte. 68) and turn left onto U.S. 1 north; in about 2 miles, you will see signs to Fla. A1A and the North Bridge Causeway. Turn right on A1A and cross over to North Hutchinson Island. Admission is $3.25 per vehicle, and the park is open daily from 8am to sunset.

BASEBALL & AFFORDABLE OUTDOOR ACTIVITIES

BASEBALL The **New York Mets** hold spring training in Port St. Lucie from late February to the end of March at the **Thomas J. White Stadium,** 525 NW Peacock Blvd. (© 772/871-2115). Tickets for spring training exhibition games and practices cost $3 to $15. From April to August, their farm team, the Port St. Lucie Mets, plays home games in the stadium.

FISHING The **Fort Pierce City Marina,** 1 Ave. A, Fort Pierce (© 772/464-1245), has more than a dozen charter captains who keep their motors running for anglers anxious to catch a few. Brochures available at the marina list all the privately owned charter operators, who organize trips on an as-desired basis. The price usually starts at $150 per person for half-day tours, depending on the season.

GOLF The most notable courses in Port St. Lucie are at the **PGA Golf Club at the Reserve** (© 772/467-1300), at 1916 Perfect Dr. The club's first of three 18-hole public golf courses opened in January 1996 and was designed by Tom Fazio; another course was designed by Pete Dye. The South Course, a classic Old Florida–style course, is set on wetlands, offers views of native wildlife, and is the most popular. The center also offers lessons for amateurs. The club is open from 7am to 6pm daily. Greens fees are usually $89, but after 2pm they go down to $35. Reserve at least 9 days in advance.

SEEING THE SIGHTS

Harbor Branch Oceanographic Institution ★★ Harbor Branch is a working nonprofit scientific institute that studies oceanic resources and welcomes visitors on regularly scheduled tours. The first stop is the J. Seward Johnson Marine Education Center, which houses institute-built submersibles that are used to conduct marine research at depths of up to 3,000 feet. A video details current research projects, and several large aquariums simulate the environments of the

Indian River Lagoon and a saltwater reef. Tourists are then shuttled by minibus to the Aqua-Culture Farming Center, a research facility that contains shallow tanks growing seaweed and other oceanic plants. The 90-minute Lagoon Wildlife Tour, on a pontoon boat, examines the Indian River Lagoon and is a fascinating tour. The bus tour of the 600-acre campus is $10 and leaves Monday through Saturday at 10am, noon, and 2pm.

5600 U.S. 1 N., Fort Pierce. © 772/465-2400. www.hboi.edu. Admission $10 adults, $6 children 6–12, free for children 5 and under. Boat tours are Mon–Sat at 10am and 1 and 3pm and cost $17 for adults, $12 for children 6–12. Mon–Fri 8am–5pm; visitor center gift shop Mon–Sat 9am–5pm. Arrive at least 20 min. before tour.

Savannahs Recreation Area ★★★ *Finds* A 550-acre former reservoir, Savannahs is one of the most interesting places in these parts—it's a veritable wilderness, with botanical gardens, nature trails, campsites, a petting zoo, and scenery reminiscent of the Florida Everglades, but in a much more contained environment.

1400 E. Midway Rd., Fort Pierce. © 772/464-7855. Admission $1 per car. Daily 8am–6pm.

ACCOMMODATIONS YOU CAN AFFORD

The Port St. Lucie mainland is pretty run-down, but there are a number of inexpensive hotel options on scenic Hutchinson Island that are both charming and well priced. Probably the best option is the **Hampton Inn** (© 800/426-7866 or 772/460-9855), 2831 Reynolds Dr., which is relatively new and beautifully maintained. However, if you want to be closer to the water, try the **Days Inn Hutchinson Island,** 1920 Seaway Dr. (© 800/325-2525 or 772/461-8737), a small motel that sits along the Intracoastal inlet and is simple but very well kept.

Budget travelers will be glad to know about the **Edgewater Motel and Apartments,** 1160 Seaway Dr. (next door to and under the same ownership as the Dockside–Harborlight Inn and Resort), Fort Pierce (© 800/286-1745 or 772/468-3555). Motel rooms start at less than $70 in high season, and efficiencies are also available from $80. Guests can enjoy a private pool, shuffleboard courts, and a nearby fishing pier.

Dockside–Harborlight Inn and Resort ★ Fronting the Intracoastal Waterway, the Harborlight is a great choice for boating and fishing enthusiasts, offering 15 boat slips and two private fishing piers. The hotel itself carries on the nautical theme with pierlike wooden stairs and rope railings. While not exactly captain's quarters, the rooms (straight out of Rooms to Go, albeit with a bit of a nautical flair, with wood headboards and wicker) are attractive enough. Higher-priced rooms have either waterfront balconies or small kitchenettes.

1160 Seaway Dr., South Hutchinson Island, FL 34949. © 800/286-1745 or 772/468-3555. Fax 772/489-9848. www.docksideinn.com. 64 units. Winter $65 standard rooms, $79–$130 efficiencies; off season $49–$89 standard rooms and efficiencies. AE, DC, DISC, MC, V. From I-95, exit at 66A east to U.S. 1 north to Seaway Dr. **Amenities:** 2 outdoor heated pools; self-service laundry; 5 lighted fishing docks; boat dockage; grilling areas. *In room:* A/C, TV, dataport, kitchenette (in higher-priced rooms), minibar, coffeemaker.

WORTH A SPLURGE

Villa Nina Island Inn ★★ *Finds* This is a very private inn in a simple but new home on 8 acres of the river's edge. Although privacy is paramount at Villa Nina, silence isn't necessarily deafening here, as it's more serene than quiet. In fact, the atmosphere is rather cheery and extremely romantic. Innkeepers Nina and Glenn Rappaport live in the main house and have built riverfront rooms along the back, each with a private entrance and either a fully equipped kitchen or a kitchenette. Riverfront rooms are very homey, with comfortable beds and private bathrooms. Enjoy breakfast poolside or delivered to your room (you may also opt out of breakfast for a $10 nightly savings). Possibly the best deal—and best room—in the Inn is the Grand View Suite, with high ceilings, a massive sitting area, sweeping views of the river and pool, floor-to-ceiling windows, breakfast nook, and marble shower, all for $165 off season and $195 during high season. Smoking is not permitted anywhere in the inn. On this stunning 8-acre property, you can use canoes and rowboats for river rides.

3851 N. S.R. A1A, North Hutchinson Island, FL 34949. ℂ/fax 772/467-8673. www.villanina.com. 5 units. Year-round $113–$240. DISC, MC, V. **Amenities:** Outdoor heated pool; canoe, diving gear, and snorkel rental; bike rental; free laundry facilities; private beach access. *In room:* A/C, TV, kitchen or kitchenette, minibar (in most rooms), fridge, coffeemaker.

GREAT DEALS ON DINING

There are a number of good seafood restaurants in the Fort Pierce and St. Lucie area, but it's also easy to drive to Stuart for more diverse dining options. See section 1 of this chapter for my recommendation in Stuart.

Le Brittany's ⭐⭐ FRENCH   Strip mall dining never tasted as good as this French Continental find in which seafood is paramount and prix fixe bargains make haute cuisine an accessible reality. Try the smoked salmon, duck pâté, Dover sole, and Grand Marnier. Chef Denis Floch and his wife Francoise definitely know their French food.

899 Prima Vista Blvd., Port St. Lucie. ℂ 772/871-2231. Reservations accepted. Main courses $12–$20. MC, V. Wed–Sun 4:30–9pm.

Mangrove Mattie's ⭐⭐ SEAFOOD   A rustic restaurant on the Fort Pierce Inlet, Mangrove Mattie's is the best place for outdoor dining, with its priceless location—right on the inlet, affording panoramic views of the Atlantic—and excellent fresh seafood. Weekday happy hours (4–7pm) are especially popular, thanks to the view and the free buffet.

1640 Seaway Dr., Fort Pierce. ℂ 772/466-1044. Reservations accepted. Main courses $11–$18. AE, DISC, MC, V. Daily 11:30am–10pm.

Theo Thudpucker's Raw Bar and Seafood Restaurant ⭐ SEAFOOD Located in a little building by the beach and wallpapered with maps and newspapers, Thudpucker's is a straightforward chowder bar. There's not much more to the dining room than one long bar and a few simple tables. Chowder and stews, often made with sherry and half-and-half, make excellent starters or light meals. The most recommendable (and filling) dinner dishes are sautéed scallops, deviled crabs, and deep-fried Okeechobee catfish.

2025 Seaway Dr., Fort Pierce. ℂ 772/465-1078. Reservations not accepted. Main courses $12–$29. MC, V. Mon–Thurs 11:30am–9:30pm; Fri–Sat 11:30am–11pm; Sun 1–9:30pm.

PORT ST. LUCIE/FORT PIERCE AFTER DARK

ArtWalk, a monthly event to showcase the downtown galleries, restaurants, and shops of Fort Pierce, takes place the second Wednesday of every month from 5 to 8pm and costs $5 per person, beginning in front of downtown's Sunrise Theater (ℂ 772/466-3880). All galleries are usually open to the public for this event, and they supply free beverages and cheese. The **Friday Fest Street Festival** occurs on the first Friday of every month at the Historic Downtown Riverfront in Fort Pierce and is free of charge, featuring live music and refreshments for sale. The **St. Lucie Blues Club,** 338 Port St. Lucie Blvd. (ℂ 772/873-1111), features live jazz, blues, and rock music Tuesday through Sunday nights. Reservations are recommended.

3 Vero Beach ⭐ & Sebastian ⭐⭐

Old Florida is thriving in these remote and tranquil villages. Vero Beach, known for its exclusive and affluent winter population, and Sebastian, known as one of the last remaining fishing villages, are located at the northern tip of the Treasure Coast region in Indian River County. These two beach towns are populated with folks who knew Miami and Fort Lauderdale in the days before massive high-rises and overcrowding. They appreciate the area's small-town feel, and that's exactly the area's appeal for visitors: a laid-back, relaxed atmosphere, friendly people, and friendlier prices.

A crowd of well-tanned surfers from all over the state descends on the region, especially the Sebastian Inlet, to catch some of the state's biggest waves. Other watersports enthusiasts enjoy the area's fine diving and windsurfing. Anglers are also in heaven here, and in spring, baseball buffs can catch some action from the L.A. Dodgers as they train in exhibition games.

ESSENTIALS

The **Indian River County Tourist Council,** 1216 21st St., Vero Beach, FL 32961 (✆ **772/567-3491;** fax 772/778-3181; www.vero-beach.fl.us/chamber), will send visitors an incredibly detailed information packet on the entire county (which includes Vero Beach and Sebastian), with a full-color map of the area, a comprehensive listing of upcoming events, a hotel guide, and more.

BEACHES & OTHER AFFORDABLE OUTDOOR ACTIVITIES

BEACHES   You'll find plenty of free and open beachfront along the coast—most are uncrowded and are open from 7am until 10pm.

South Beach Park, on South Ocean Drive, at the end of Marigold Lane, is a busy, developed, lifeguarded beach with picnic tables, restrooms, and showers. It's known as one of the best swimming beaches in Vero Beach and attracts a young crowd that plays volleyball and Frisbee in a tranquil setting. A nicely laid-out nature walk takes you into beautiful secluded trails.

At the very north tip of the island, **Sebastian Inlet State Park** ⭐ has flat, sandy beaches with lots of facilities, including kayak, paddleboat, and canoe rentals; a well-stocked surf shop (there's supposedly some of the hottest surfing on the East Coast on the north jetty in this park); picnic tables; and a snack shop. The winds seem to stir up the surf with no jetty to stop their swells, to the delight of surfers and boarders, who get here early to catch the big waves. At press time, the park was readying itself for the arrival of cozy cabins ranging from 1,150 to 1,600 square feet and featuring high-tech amenities such as Internet access as well as woodsy ones such as rocking chairs, porches, and fireplaces. Call ✆ **321/984-4852** for rental fees and more information. Campers enjoy fully equipped sites in a woody area. Admission to the Sebastian Inlet State Park, 9700 S. Fla. A1A, Melbourne, is $5 per car and $1 for those who walk or bike in.

FISHING   Capt. Jack Jackson works 7 days a week out of **Vero's Tackle and Sport-Shop,** 57–59 Royal Palm Point (✆ **772/567-6550**), taking anglers on his 25-foot boat for private river excursions (all equipment is provided). Half-day jaunts on the Indian River cost $250 for one or two people (the minimum required for a charter), tackle, rigs, and everything included; $50 extra for a third person. You can either bring your own food and drinks or purchase food from the shop.

Many other charters, guides, party boats, and tackle shops operate in this area. Consult your hotel for suggestions, or call the **Vero Beach Chamber of Commerce** (© 772/567-3491) for a list of local operators. You can also contact **Captain Hiram's** (© 772/589-4345; www.hirams.com), a restaurant/bar/hotel/marina that houses many charter fishing boats.

GOLF   Hard-core golfers insist that of the dozens of courses in the area, only a handful are worth their plot of grass.

Set on rolling hills with uncluttered views of sand dunes and sky, the **Sandridge Golf Club** (© 772/770-5000), at 5300 73rd St., Vero Beach, offers two par-72 18-holers. The Dunes is a long course with rolling fairways, and the newer Lakes course has lots of water. Both charge $38, including a cart. Weekends the cost is $32 after noon. A small snack bar sells drinks and sandwiches. Reservations are recommended and are taken 2 days in advance.

Although less challenging, the **Sebastian Municipal Golf Course** (© 772/589-6800), at 1010 E. Airport Dr., is a good 18-hole par-72. It's scenic, well maintained, and a relative bargain. Greens fees are $35 per player with a cart, and about half that if you want to play 9 holes after 1:30pm.

Also, see "Dodgertown," below.

SEEING THE SIGHTS

Environmental Learning Center ★★ (Kids)   The Indian River is not really a river at all, but a large brackish lagoon that's home to a greater variety of species than any other estuary in North America—it has thousands of species of plants, animals, fish, and birds, including 36 species on the endangered list. The privately funded Environmental Learning Center was created to protect the local habitat and educate visitors about the Indian River area's environment. Situated on 51 island acres, the center features a 600-foot boardwalk through the mangroves and dozens of hands-on exhibits that are geared to both children and adults. There are live touch-tanks, exhibits, and microscopes for viewing the smallest sea life up close. The best thing to do here is join one of the center's interpretive canoe trips, offered by reservation only.

255 Live Oak Dr. (just off the 510 Causeway), Wabasso Island (a 51-acre island sitting in the middle of the Indian River Lagoon). © 772/589-5050. www.elcweb.org. Free admission. Canoe trips $10 for adults, $5 for children ages 6–12. Tues–Fri 10am–4pm; Sat 9am–noon; Sun 1–4pm. From Vero Beach via U.S. 1, turn right at the intersection of U.S. 1 and CR 510 in Wabasso. Go over the Wabasso causeway but before going over the tall Wabasso bridge, turn right onto Wabasso Island Lane. The Environmental Learning Center sign is on the south (right) side of CR 510 at this intersection. Take an immediate right turn onto Live Oak Drive. The ELC is less than ¼-mile down on the right side.

McKee Botanical Garden ★★   This impressive 18-acre attraction was originally opened in 1932 and featured a virtual jungle of orchids, exotic and native trees, monkeys, and birds. After years of neglect, it was placed on the National Register of Historic Places in 1998. It underwent a top-to-bottom overhaul that was completed in February 2000, and you can now again experience the full charms of this little Eden.

350 U.S. 1, Vero Beach. © 772/794-0601. Fax 772/794-0602. www.mckeegarden.org. Admission $6 adults, $5 seniors, $3.50 children 5–12. Tues–Sat 10am–5pm; Sun noon–5pm.

McLarty Treasure Museum ★   If you're unconvinced about why this area is called the Treasure Coast, then this is a must-see. Erected on the actual site of a salvaging camp from a 1715 shipwreck, this quaint little museum is full of interesting history. It may not have the vast treasures of the nearby Mel Fisher museum (see below), but it does offer a very engaging 45-minute video describing the many aspects of treasure hunting. You'll also see household items salvaged from the Spanish fleet and dioramas of life in the 18th century.

13180 N. Fla. A1A, Sebastian Inlet State Recreation Area, Vero Beach. (℃ 772/589-2147. Admission $1, free for children under 6. Daily 10am–4:30pm.

Mel Fisher's Treasure Museum ★★   This museum (where you can see millions of dollars of treasures from the doomed Spanish fleet that went down in 1715) is truly priceless. Although not as extensive as the museum in Key West (p. 193), this exhibit includes gold coins, bars, and Spanish artifacts that are worth a look. Also, the preservation lab shows how the goods are extricated, cleaned, and preserved.

1322 U.S. 1, Sebastian. (℃ 772/589-9874. www.melfisher.com. Admission $6.50 adults, $5 seniors over 55, $2 children 6–12, free for children 5 and under. Mon–Sat 10am–5pm; Sun noon–5pm.

DODGERTOWN

Vero is the winter home of the **Los Angeles Dodgers** (at least for the time being; there's been talk of a move), and the town hosts the team in grand style. The 450-acre compound, Dodgertown, at 3901 26th St. (℃ **772/569-4900**), encompasses Spring Training Camp, two golf courses, a conference center, a country club, a movie theater, a recreation room, citrus groves, and a residential community. It is a city unto its own for baseball fanatics and retirees. You can watch afternoon exhibition games during the winter (usually between mid-Feb and the end of Mar) in the comfortable 6,500-seat outdoor stadium. Even if the game sells out, you can sprawl on the lawn for just $8 (the stadium has never turned away an eager fan). Even when spring training is over, you can still catch a game; the Dodgers' farm team, the Vero Beach Dodgers, has a full season of minor-league baseball in summer.

Admission to the complex is free; tickets to games are $15 for a reserved seat, and the complex is open daily from 9am to 5pm; game time is usually 1pm. From I-95, take the exit for S.R. 60 east to 43rd Avenue and turn left; continue to 26th Street and turn right.

SHOPPING

Ocean Boulevard and Cardinal Drive are Vero's two main shopping streets. Both are near the beach and are lined with specialty boutiques, including antiques and home-decorating shops.

If you want to send fruit back home, the local source is **Hale Indian River Groves,** 615 Beachland Blvd. (℃ **800/562-4502;** www.halegroves.com), a shipper of local citrus and jams since 1947, with four locations in Vero Beach. The grove is closed 2 to 3 months a year, usually from summer through early fall, depending on the crops; the season generally runs from November to Easter.

The **Horizon Outlet Center,** at S.R. 60 and I-95, Vero Beach (℃ **877/GO-OUTLET** or 772/770-6171), contains more than 80 discount stores selling name-brand shoes, kitchenware, clothing, and more. The center is open Monday through Saturday from 9am to 8pm and Sunday from 11am to 6pm.

Indian River Mall (℃ **772/770-6255**), 6200 20th St. (S.R. 60, about 5 miles east of I-95), is a monster mall with all the big national chains (Gap, Structure, and Victoria's Secret) as well as several department stores. It's open Monday through Saturday from 10am to 9pm and Sunday from noon to 6pm.

ACCOMMODATIONS YOU CAN AFFORD

You can choose from accommodations on the mainland or on the beach. As you might expect, the beachfront accommodations are a bit more expensive—but, I think, worth it. There are deals to be had in the chain hotels and some lovely privately-owned properties, especially on weekdays and during the off season. A great spot to know, especially if you are planning to fish, is the **Key West Inn at Captain Hiram's** (1580 U.S. 1, Sebastian; ℭ **772/388-8588;** www.hirams. com; see "Fishing," above, and also "Vero Beach & Sebastian After Dark," below), where there are 70 rooms available adjacent to the restaurant and over-looking the water.

Comfortable and inexpensive chain options near the Vero Beach Outlet Center off S.R. 60 include a **Holiday Inn Express** (ℭ **800/465-4329** or 772/567-2500) and a **Hampton Inn** (ℭ **800/426-7866** or 772/770-4299). Rates for both run between $70 and $80 and include breakfast and free local calls.

Davis House Inn ★★   Each of the dozen rooms in this contemporary three-story B&B has a private entrance. The rooms are large and clean, although somewhat plain, and each has a king-size bed, a pullout sofa, and a small kitch-enette, making the rooms popular with long-term guests. The bathrooms are equally ample and have plenty of counter space. Guests will find a large wooden deck for sunbathing and a sunny second-floor breakfast room. The inn is a bit out of the way but is within walking distance of some nearby restaurants; the beach is a 10-minute drive away.

607 Davis St., Sebastian, FL 32958. ℭ **772/589-4114.** Fax 772/589-1722. 12 units. Winter $69–$79 double; off season $50–$69 double. 7-night min. in Feb. Weekly and monthly rates available. AE, DISC, MC, V. From I-95, take exit 69, heading east to Indian River Dr. and turn left. Go 1¼ miles to Davis St.; turn left. **Amenities:** Coin-op washers and dryers. In room: A/C, TV.

Driftwood Resort ★★ *Finds*   Originally planned in the 1930s as a private estate by eccentric entrepreneur Waldo Sexton, the Driftwood was opened to the public in the late '30s after several travelers stopped by to inquire about renting a room here, since it was the largest property in Vero Beach and people assumed it was an attraction or, at least, a hotel. All of the guest rooms were renovated in 2000, and each is unique. Some feature terra cotta–tiled floors and lighter fur-niture, while others have a more rustic feel with hardwoods and antiques. Some of the rooms contain Jacuzzis, and all are equipped with full kitchens. Two of the best rooms at the Driftwood are the Captain's Quarters, which overlooks the ocean with a private staircase to the pool, and the town house located in the breezeway building, featuring a spiral staircase as well as living room and bed-room views of the ocean. The resort is listed on the National Register of Historic Places and, to say the least, has lots of quirky charm.

3150 Ocean Dr., Vero Beach, FL 32963. ℭ **772/231-0550.** Fax 772/234-1981. www.thedriftwood.com. 100 units. Winter $130–$160 double; off season $79–$120 double. AE, DISC, MC, V. **Amenities:** 2 outdoor heated pools; dry cleaning service. In room: A/C, TV, kitchen (in most 1-bedroom and all 2-bedroom units), cof-feemaker, Jacuzzi (in some rooms).

Islander Inn ★   This is one of the most comfortable and welcoming inns in the area. Well located in downtown Vero Beach, this small, quaint Key-West-meets-Old-Florida–style motel is just a short walk to the beach, restaurants, and shops. Every breezy guest room has a small refrigerator, either a king-size bed or two double beds, paddle fans, wicker furniture, and vaulted ceilings, and opens onto a pretty courtyard and sparkling pool. Efficiencies have full kitchens.

3101 Ocean Dr., Vero Beach, FL 32963. ℂ **800/952-5886** or 772/231-4431. 16 units. Winter $105–$120 double; off season $72–$99 double. Efficiencies cost $10 extra. AE, MC, V. **Amenities:** Cafe; pool. *In room:* A/C, TV, fridge.

Sea Turtle Inn & Azalea Lane Apartments ✸   This two-part nonsmoking property offers the best value on the beach (just 2 blocks from the ocean). The 1950s motel and an adjacent apartment building have been fully renovated and outfitted with understated but efficient furnishings. You won't find any fancy amenities (or even a phone, for that matter, unless you request one), but its price and location make up for what it lacks in frills. The properties share a small pool and sun deck. Book early, especially in season, since it fills up quickly with long-term visitors.

835 Azalea Lane, Vero Beach, FL 32963. ℂ **772/234-0788.** Fax 772/234-0717. www.vero-beach.fl.us/ seaturtle. 20 units. Winter $69–$109 double; off season $59–$89 double. Weekly and monthly rates available. MC, V. From I-95, go east on S.R. 60 (about 10 miles to Cardinal Dr.; turn right onto Azalea Lane). **Amenities:** Small pool; bike rental; laundry facilities. *In room:* A/C, TV, small fridge, coffeemaker, no phone.

CAMPING

The Vero Beach and Sebastian area of the Treasure Coast area is popular with campers, who can choose from nearly a dozen camping locations throughout. If you aren't camping at the scenic and very popular **Sebastian Inlet** (see "Beaches," on p. 285), then try the **Vero Beach KOA RV Park,** 8850 U.S. 1, Wabasso (ℂ **772/589-5665**). This 120-site campground is 2 miles from the ocean and the Intracoastal Waterway and ¼ mile from the Indian River, a big draw for fishing fanatics. There's access to running water and electricity, as well as showers, a shop, and hookups for RVs. Rates are $30 per site and $25 for tents. To get there, take I-95 to exit 69 east; at U.S. 1, turn left.

GREAT DEALS ON DINING

Black Pearl Brasserie and Grill ✸✸ CONTINENTAL   This sophisticated brasserie may seem out of place in this beachy town, but it happens to be one of Vero Beach's trendiest spots. The restaurant's small list of appetizers includes salads, chilled sweet-potato vichyssoise, crispy fried-chicken fingers with mango dipping sauce, and grilled oysters with tangy barbecue sauce. Equally creative main courses are uniformly good. Don't miss their signature dish, an onion-crusted mahimahi with caramel-citrus glaze; the herb-crusted tilapia with roasted tomato beurre blanc is also fab. All fruits and vegetables used here come from local markets, farms, and groves. Both this original, unassuming restaurant and its newer counterpart, The **Black Pearl Riverfront,** at 4445 N. Fla. A1A (ℂ **772/234-4426**), serve fantastically fresh and inventive food. The riverfront location is more formal and serves only dinner, starting at 5pm.

2855 Ocean Dr., Vero Beach. ℂ **772/234-7426.** Fax 772/234-9074. Reservations recommended. Main courses $12–$21. AE, DC, DISC, MC, V. Mon–Sun 11:30am–10pm; Sun brunch 10:30am–2pm.

Nino's Cafe ✸ ITALIAN   This little beachside cafe looks like a stereotypical pizza joint, complete with fake brick walls, murals of the Italian countryside, and red-and-white checked tablecloths. The atmosphere is pure cheese and so is much of the food—pizza and parmigiana dishes are smothered in the stuff. Still, the thin crust and fresh toppings make the pizza here a cut above the rest. Entrees and pastas are also tasty.

1006 Easter Lily Lane (off Ocean Dr., next to Humiston Park), Vero Beach. ℂ **772/231-9311.** Main courses $9–$13. No credit cards. Mon–Thurs 11am–9pm; Fri–Sat 11am–10pm; Sun 4–9pm.

SUPER-CHEAP EATS

Beachside Restaurant at the Palm Court Resort $\bigstar$ *Value* AMERICAN/ DINER   For a great big, cheap American breakfast with an ocean view, this is the place to go. You can get omelets, home fries, cream chipped beef, corned-beef hash, pancakes, Belgian waffles, and even grits. Friendly waitresses also serve lunch and dinner in the comfy wooden booths. The best dishes, like chili, fried chicken, and steaks, are hearty and delicious. No smoking.

3244 Ocean Dr., Vero Beach. ℂ 772/234-4477. Breakfast $2–$5; full dinners $8.95 and up. AE, DC, DISC, MC, V. Mon–Sat 6am–9pm; Sun 6am–1:30pm.

A PRIX-FIXE STEAL

Chez Yannick $\bigstar\bigstar\bigstar$ FRENCH/CONTINENTAL   Excellent cooking, a comprehensive wine list, and white-glove service complement the crystal and gilded decor at this French standout, complete with fireplaces and a piano player, and steeped in old-world charm. Excellent starters include a succulent sliced duckling breast, cream of lobster soup, and hearts-of-palm salad with a slightly spicy vinaigrette. Some items, like lobster and shrimp in a cognac-dill sauce, are available as either an appetizer or an entree. Other main courses include beef tenderloin stuffed with Gorgonzola cheese and sautéed soft-shell crabs. Desserts might include profiteroles with ice cream and chocolate or rasp-berry sauce, crème caramel, chocolate-mousse pie, or raspberry sorbet.

1605 S. Ocean Dr., Vero Beach. ℂ **772/234-4115.** Reservations recommended. Main courses $15–$30; fixed-price dinner $19–$21 available in the off season. AE, MC, V. Mon–Sat open at 6pm; closing time varies based on last reservation.

VERO BEACH & SEBASTIAN AFTER DARK

More than half the residents in this area are retirees, so it shouldn't be a surprise that even on weekends, this town retires relatively early. Hotel lounges often have live music and a good bar scene, however, especially in high season, and sometimes stay open as late as 1am, if you're lucky. For beachside drinks, go to the Driftwood Resort (p. 288).

A mostly 30-something and younger crowd goes to **Bombay Louie's** in Vero Beach, at 398 21st St. (ℂ 772/978-0209), where a DJ spins dance music after 9pm Wednesday through Saturday. Vero Beach is also known as an artsy enclave, hosting galleries such as **The Art Works,** 2855 Ocean Dr., Vero Beach (ℂ 772/ 231-4688), and the **Bottalico Gallery,** 3121 Ocean Dr., Vero Beach (ℂ 772/231-0414). **The Civic Arts Center** at Riverside Park is a hub of culture, including the **Riverside Theatre** (ℂ 772/231-6990), the **Agnes Wahlstrom Youth Play-house** (ℂ 772/234-8052), and the **Center for the Arts** (ℂ 772/231-0707), known for films and an excellent lecture series.

In Sebastian, you'll find live music every weekend (and daily in season) at **Captain Hiram's,** 1606 N. Indian River Dr. (ℂ **772/589-4345**), a salty out-door restaurant and bar on the Intracoastal Waterway that locals and tourists love at all hours of the day and night (well, until it closes at 11pm, that is). The feel is tacky Key West, complete with a sand floor and thatched-roof bar.

North of the inlet, head for the tried-and-true **Sebastian Beach Inn** (SBI to locals), 7035 S. Fla. A1A (ℂ **321/728-4311**), for live music on the weekends. Jazz, blues, or sometimes rock 'n' roll starts at 9pm on Friday and Saturday. On Sunday, it's old-style reggae after 2pm. The inn is open daily for drinks from 11am until anywhere from midnight to 2am.

4 A Side Trip Inland: Fishing at Lake Okeechobee ✮✮✮

60 miles SW of West Palm Beach

Many visitors to the Treasure Coast come to fish, and they certainly get their fill of it off the miles of Atlantic shore and on the inland rivers. But if you want to fish freshwater and nothing else, head for "The Lake"—**Lake Okeechobee,** that is. The state's largest, it's chock-full of good eating fish. Only about a 1½-hour drive from the coast, it makes a great day or weekend excursion.

ESSENTIALS

GETTING THERE From Palm Beach, take I-95 south to Southern Boulevard (U.S. 98 west) in West Palm Beach, which merges with S.R. 80 and S.R. 441. Follow signs for S.R. 80 west through Belle Glade to South Bay. In South Bay, turn right onto U.S. 27 north, which leads directly to Clewiston.

VISITOR INFORMATION Contact the **Clewiston Chamber of Commerce,** 544 W. Sugarland Hwy., Clewiston, FL 33440 (© **863/983-7979;** www.clewiston.org), for maps, business directories, and the names of numerous fishing guides throughout the area. In addition, you might contact the **Pahokee Chamber of Commerce,** 115 E. Main St., Pahokee, FL 33476 (© **772/924-5579;** fax 772/924-8116; www.pahokee.com); they'll send a complete package of magazines, guides, and accommodations listings.

ACCOMMODATIONS YOU CAN AFFORD

If you aren't camping (see below), book a room at the **Clewiston Inn** ✮✮, 108 Royal Palm Ave., Clewiston (© **800/749-4466** or 863/983-8151). Built in 1938, this Southern plantation–inspired hotel is the oldest in the Lake Okeechobee region. Its 52 rooms are simply decorated and nondescript. The lounge area sports a 1945 mural depicting the animals of the region. Double rooms start at $99 a night; suites begin at $129. All have air-conditioning and TVs.

Another choice, especially if you're here to fish, is **Roland Martin,** 920 E. Del Monte (© **800/473-6766** or 863/983-3151), the "Disney of fishing." This RV park (no tent sites) also offers modest motel rooms, efficiencies, condominiums, apartments, or sites for your RV, with two heated pools, gift and marina shops, and a restaurant. The modern complex, dotted with prefab buildings painted in white and gray, is clean and well manicured. Rooms rent for $68 and efficiencies cost $88. Condominiums are about $150 a night with a 3-night minimum. RV sites are about $25 with TV and cable hookup.

CAMPING

During the winter, campers own the Clewiston area. Campsites are jammed with regulars, who come year after year for the simple pleasures of the lake and, of course, the warm weather. Every manner of RV, from simple pop-top Volkswagens to Winnebagos to fully decked-out mobile homes, finds its way to the many campsites along the lake. (Also see Roland Martin, above.)

Okeechobee Landings, U.S. 27 east (© **863/983-4144**), is one of the best; it has every conceivable amenity included in the price of a site. More than 250 sites are situated around a small lake, clubhouse, snack bar, pool, Jacuzzi, horseshoe pit, shuffleboard court, and tennis court. Full hookup includes a sewage connection, which is not the case throughout the county. RV spots are sold to regulars, but there are usually some spots available for rental to one-time visitors. Rates start at $25 a day or $150 weekly plus tax, including hookup. Year-round

Going After the Big One

Fishing on Lake Okeechobee is a year-round affair, though the fish tend to bite a little better in the winter, perhaps for the benefit of the many snowbirds who flock here (especially in Feb–Mar). RV camps are mobbed almost year-round with fish-frenzied anglers who come down for weeks at a time for a decent catch.

You'll need a fishing license to go out with a rod and reel. It's a simple matter to apply. The chamber of commerce and most fishing shops can sign you up on the spot. The cost for non-Florida residents for 7 days is $17 or $32 for the year.

You can rent, charter, or bring your own boat to Clewiston; just be sure to schedule your trip in advance. You don't want to show up during one of the frequent fishing tournaments only to find you can't get a room, campsite, or fishing boat. All tournaments are held at Roland Martin's marina (see below). For more information on tournaments, log on to their website at www.rolandmartinmarina.com.

There are several marinas where you can rent or charter boats. If it's your first time on the lake, I suggest chartering a boat with a guide who can show you the lake's most fertile spots and help you handle your tackle. **Roland Martin,** 920 E. Del Monte (✆ **863/983-3151**), is the one-stop spot where you can find a guide, tackle, rods, bait, coolers, picnic supplies, and a choice of boats. Rates for a guided fishing tour are $200 for a half day and $300 for a full day for one to two people. You need a fishing license, which is available there for $17. They also have boat rentals: A 16-foot johnboat is $40 for half a day and $60 for a full day with a $40 deposit.

Another reputable boat-rental spot is **Angler's Marina,** 910 Okeechobee Blvd. (✆ **800/741-3141** or 863/983-BASS). Rentals for a 14-footer start at $40 for a half day, for a maximum of four people. A full day is $60. If you want a guide, rates start at $150 (for two people) for a half day, though in the summer (June–Oct), when it's slow, you can usually get a cheaper deal.

rates for trailer rentals, which sleep two people, start at $32 Sunday through Thursday and from $37 on Friday and Saturday.

GREAT DEALS ON DINING

If you aren't frying up your own catch for dinner, you can find a number of good eating spots in town. At the **Clewiston Inn** (see "Accommodations You Can Afford," above), you can get catfish, beef stroganoff, ham hocks, fried chicken, and liver and onions in a setting as Southern as the food. The dining room is open daily from 6am to 2pm and 5 to 9pm, and entrees cost $9 to $18. **L&L Restaurant,** 265 N. Devils Garden Rd. (✆ **863/983-6666**), is a good Spanish restaurant, with entrees ranging from $8 to $12. **Pinky's On the Green Pub,** Highway 80 (✆ **863/983-8464**), is a no-frills diner, with entrees under $8.

9

Southwest Florida

Although there are no adobe houses, cacti, deserts, and, as far as we know, no John Edwards's *Crossing Over*-esque mystics hawking crystals here, Southwest Florida is definitely the Southwest in terms of serenity, golf, retirees, and expensive homes. While the area, itself, may be staid, and the ride there, through the Everglades, may be the closest thing to adventure you're going to get in terms of this neck of the So Flo woods, it's definitely an area worth exploring.

As primitive as it gets, Alligator Alley (I-75) is the closest thing to a dirt road that South Florida's got. Once a desolate two-lane road connecting Southeast Florida with the Gulf Coast, Alligator Alley is still pretty quiet, but hardly lifeless thanks to the presence of the egrets, wood storks, owls, herons, osprey, red-shouldered hawks, belted kingfishers, and, of course, alligators that call the area behind the fenced in, protected shoulders home. As you go through Alligator Alley, en route to or from Southwest Florida, your cellphone will not work and the only option for refueling will be at the Miccosukee Indian Reservation. Driving through Alligator Alley is like entering a time warp. When you reach the end, you will enter another world, where million-dollar mansions, posh resorts, golf courses, and all signs of the good life juxtapose with nature.

Bordered on the east by the Everglades and on the west by an intriguing island-studded coast, Southwest Florida traces its nature-loving roots to inventor and amateur botanist Thomas A. Edison, who was so enamored of it that he spent his last 46 winters in Fort Myers. His friend Henry Ford liked it, too, and built his own winter home next door. The world's best tarpon fishing lured President Theodore Roosevelt and his buddies to the 10,000 or so islands dotting this coast. Some of the planet's best shelling helped entice the du Ponts of Delaware to Gasparilla Island, where they founded the Nantucket-like village of Boca Grande. The unspoiled beauty of Sanibel and Captiva islands so entranced Pulitzer Prize–winning political cartoonist J. N. "Ding" Darling that he campaigned to preserve many of those islands in their natural states. And the millionaires who built Naples enacted tough zoning laws that to this day make their town one of the most alluring—and expensive—in Florida.

Southwest Florida International Airport, on the eastern outskirts of Fort Myers, is this region's major airport (see "Essentials," in section 1, below). From here it's only 20 miles to Sanibel Island, 35 miles to Naples, or 46 miles to Marco Island. If you have a car, you can see the area's sights and participate in most of its activities easily from one base of operations.

EXCURSIONS TO THE EVERGLADES & KEY WEST You won't be in Southwest Florida for long before you see advertisements for excursions to the Everglades. Naples is only 36 miles from Everglades City, the "back door" to wild and wonderful Everglades National Park, so it's easy to combine a visit to the national park with your stay in Southwest Florida. See chapter 6 for full details about the Everglades.

You also can easily make a day trip to Key West from here by air or sea. **Cape Air** (© **800/352-0714;** www.flycapeair.com) shuttles its small planes several times a day between Key West and both Southwest Florida International Airport and the Naples Municipal Airport. The same-day round-trip fare is about $180.

The **Key West Shuttle** (© **888/ 539-2628** or 239/732-7744; www.keywestshuttle.com) runs to Key West from both Fort Myers Beach and Marco Island November through May, departing in the morning, arriving in Key West about midday, and beginning the return voyage about 5pm. That will give you about 5 hours in Key West, so you may want to stay there overnight in order to more thoroughly explore the town. Round-trip fare is about $120 for adults, $90 for children 6 to 12. Contact the shuttle for schedules and reservations.

See chapter 5 for full details about Key West and the rest of the Keys.

1 Fort Myers

148 miles NW of Miami, 142 miles S of Tampa, 42 miles N of Naples

You know how there are two schools of martini drinkers—one whose students consider themselves shaken not stirred purists and the other whose students believe in candy-flavored and -colored cocktails, the brighter and sweeter, the better? The purists usually shudder at the candy cocktailers and vice versa. Now replace those opposing martini camps with fans of technological progress and those who thought things were just fine the way they were, and you're on your way to understanding the dual mindset of historical Fort Meyers. You see, inventor Thomas Alva Edison came here in 1885 to regain his health after years of incessant toil and the death of his first wife. But unlike most new arrivals, he didn't just merge quietly into the population. Rather, his presence turned the city into one big lightbulb: The cows didn't know what hit 'em. Some regret the lightbulb ever making its way into Fort Myers. Others could care less.

Today, however, the debate is moot, and, in fact, the city's prime attractions are the homes Edison and Henry Ford built on the banks of the Caloosahatchee. Edison planted lush tropical gardens around the two homes and royal palms in front of the properties along McGregor Boulevard, once a cow trail leading from town to the docks at Punta Rassa. Had those two never showed up, Fort Myers would probably have been yet another Denny's-lined truck stop. Now lining McGregor Boulevard for miles, the trees give Fort Myers its nickname: The City of Palms.

After you've seen the Edison and Ford homes, you'll want to high-tail it to the sands at nearby Fort Myers Beach or on Sanibel or Captiva islands (see sections 2 and 3, later in this chapter). You also can venture inland and observe incredible numbers of wildlife in their river and swamp habitats, including those at the Babcock Ranch, largest of the surviving cattle producers and now a major game preserve. *Note:* If you're looking for action of the *Girls Gone Wild, MTV Spring Break* kind, this area is *not even close* to where you want to be.

ESSENTIALS

GETTING THERE This entire region is served by **Southwest Florida International Airport** (© 239/768-1000; www.swfia.com), on Daniels Parkway east of I-75. You can get here on **Air Canada** (© 888/247-2262), **AirTran** (© 800/ 247-8726), **America West** (© 800/235-9292), **American** (© 800/433-7300),

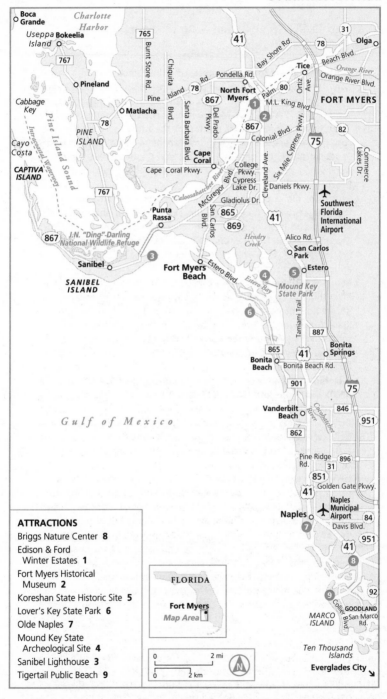

Southwest Florida

ATTRACTIONS

Briggs Nature Center **8**

Edison & Ford
Winter Estates **1**

Fort Myers Historical
Museum **2**

Koreshan State Historic Site **5**

Lover's Key State Park **6**

Olde Naples **7**

Mound Key State
Archeological Site **4**

Sanibel Lighthouse **3**

Tigertail Public Beach **9**

FLORIDA

Fort Myers
Map Area

0   2 mi

0   2 km

Cheap Thrills: What to See & Do for Free (or Almost) in Southwest Florida

- **Catch the "green flash" at sunset.** Like the Tampa Bay Area to the north (see chapter 10, "The Tampa Bay Area"), Southwest Florida has mile after mile of beaches facing due west, thus providing glorious sunsets over the Gulf of Mexico and a chance to see the elusive "green flash," the moment the top of the sun dips below the horizon. The best places to watch for free are anywhere along Fort Myers Beach, at Blind Pass between Sanibel and Captiva islands, from the Naples Pier, and at the public access area on Marco Island's Crescent Beach.

- **Search for oldies but goodies at Fleamasters.** Florida has numerous flea markets where bargain hunters can browse for antiques, crafts, fashions, and fresh produce. With more than 800 busy booths, Fort Myers's weekend **Fleamasters,** 4135 Dr. Martin Luther King, Jr. Blvd. (*C* **239/334-7001**), is one of the biggest and best. It has snack bars and entertainment, too.

- **Canoe down a lazy river.** An official Florida canoe trail, the Estero River south of Fort Myers, winds its way into Estero Bay, which is itself a state aquatic preserve. Near the mouth of the river lies Mound Key State Archeological Site, a Calusa Indian shell midden dating back some 2,000 years. **Koreshan State Historic Site,** on the river at U.S. 41 and Corkscrew Road (*C* **239/992-0311**), rents canoes for just $5.30 an hour, $27 per day.

- **Worship at a diamond.** With both the **Boston Red Sox** (*C* **239/334-4700**) and **Minnesota Twins** (*C* **800/338-9467** or 239/768-4270) holding their spring training here from mid-February through March, Fort Myers is a great place to see some of your favorite big league baseball stars get ready for the regular grind. Great seats close to the action cost $10 to $15, a bargain compared to what you'll pay when the boys of spring get back north.

- **Love nature on Lover's Key.** Possessed of one of Florida's best undeveloped beaches, the **Lover's Key State Park** south of Fort Myers Beach (*C* **239/463-4288**) is a great place to spend a day swimming, sunning, and shelling—a place where you'll find birds instead of condos as your neighbors. Admission is $2 for single-occupant vehicles, $4 for vehicles with two to eight occupants, and $1 for pedestrians and bicyclists. After that, the restrooms, showers, and tram ride through the mangroves to the deserted beach are free.

- **Walk or ride along Wildlife Drive.** The mangrove swamps, winding waterways, and uplands of Sanibel Island's **J. N. "Ding" Darling**

American Trans Air (*C* 800/225-2995), **Continental** (*C* 800/525-0280), **Delta** (*C* 800/221-1212), **JetBlue** (*C* 800/538-2583), **LTU International** (*C* 800/888-0200), **Midwest Express** (*C* 800/452-2022), **Northwest/KLM** (*C* 800/225-2525), **Royal** (*C* 800/667-7692), **Spirit** (*C* 800/772-7117), **Sun Country** (*C* 800/359-5786), **United** (*C* 800/241-6522), and **US Airways** (*C* 800/428-4322).

National Wildlife Refuge (© **239/472-1100**) are great places to see alligators, raccoons, otters, and hundreds of species of birds. You can see many of the creatures from the 5-mile, one-way Wildlife Drive, which costs $5 per vehicle or $1 per pedestrian or biker. A naturalist will explain what you're seeing on a 2-hour narrated tram tour—a very good value at $10 for adults and $5 for children 12 and under.

- **Stoop for shells.** Okay, you'll have to pay a $3 toll to get here and a small fee to park your car (or lock your bike to a tree for nothing), but you can stroll Sanibel Island's world-famous shelling beaches as long as you want for free. After a few hours hunched over in the "Sanibel stoop," you're sure to go home with a prize find or two.
- **Bike on Sanibel Island.** Affluent but nature-loving Sanibel Island has one of the best networks of paved biking/blading/hiking trails in Florida. The trails end at Blind Pass, between Sanibel and Captiva, but catching a sunset here will make every pump of the pedal worth the effort. Ride your own across the 3-mile causeway from Fort Myers to the island, or rent a basic model from several Sanibel firms for $5 per hour or $15 to $25 a day.
- **Watch the millionaires from Naples Pier.** Olde Naples residents love to stroll out on their ancient pier to fish, catch a sunset, or look at Millionaires' Row, a string of magnificent mansions along the town's lovely beach. Now a state historic site, the pier is open 24 hours a day and is free, although it will cost you a few quarters to park in the nearby municipal lots.
- **Swank around on 3rd Street.** It costs not a penny to window-shop the ritzy 3rd Street district in Olde Naples. This town has industrial-strength money, but it's so Midwestern-friendly that nobody will care if you maxed out your credit cards just to get here.
- **Hunker down at happy hour.** Right on the beach and facing the glorious Gulf sunsets, the *chickee hut* (a traditional Native American hut with open sides and a thatched roof) bar at **Vanderbilt Inn Naples,** a motel about 4 miles north of Olde Naples (© **800/643-8654** or 239/597-3151), cuts the price of libation during happy hour Monday to Friday from 4:30 to 8:30pm and on Saturday and Sunday from 3:30 to 7:30pm. The place really fills up on Sunday, when bands play. You can almost crawl here after a day on the undeveloped beach at Delnor-Wiggins State Park, next door.

The two baggage-claim areas have information booths (with maps) and free phones to various hotels in the region.

Alamo (© 800/327-9633), **Avis** (© 800/331-1212), **Budget** (© 800/527-0700), **Dollar** (© 800/800-4000), **Enterprise** (© 800/325-8007), **Hertz** (© 800/654-3131), **National** (© 800/CAR-RENT), and **Thrifty** (© 800/367-2277) have rental cars here.

Vans and taxis are available at a booth across the street from the baggage claim. The maximum fares for one to three passengers are $26 to downtown Fort Myers, $38 to Fort Myers Beach, $40 to $47 to Sanibel Island, $60 to Captiva Island, $60 to Naples, and $75 to Marco Island. Each additional passenger pays $8.

Amtrak provides bus connections between Fort Myers and its nearest station, in Tampa (© **800/USA-RAIL;** www.amtrak.com). The Amtrak buses arrive and depart the **Greyhound/Trailways** bus station, 2275 Cleveland Ave. (© **800/ 231-2222;** www.greyhound.com).

VISITOR INFORMATION   For advance information about Fort Myers, Fort Myers Beach, and Sanibel and Captiva islands, contact the **Lee Island Coast Visitor and Convention Bureau,** 2180 W. 1st St., Suite 100, Fort Myers, FL 33901 (© **800/237-6444** or 239/338-3500; fax 239/334-1106; www.lee islandcoast.com).

Volunteers staff information booths in the baggage-claim areas at Southwest Florida International Airport.

Once you're here, the **Greater Fort Myers Chamber of Commerce** (© **800/ 366-3622** from outside Florida, or 239/332-3624; fax 239/332-7276; www. fortmyers.org) has a walk-in visitor center at the corner of Edwards Drive and Lee Street on the downtown waterfront. Open Monday through Friday from 9am to 4:30pm.

There's also an information booth at the Edison and Ford Winter Estates (see "Exploring the Area," below).

GETTING AROUND   LeeTran (© **239/275-8726;** www.rideleetran.com) operates public buses. System maps are available from the Greater Fort Myers Chamber of Commerce (see "Visitor Information," above). There's no public bus service to Sanibel and Captiva islands, but you can connect to the Fort Myers Beach trolleys (see "Getting Around," in section 2, later in this chapter).

For a taxi, call **Yellow Cab** (© **239/332-1055**), **Bluebird Taxi** (© **239/275-8294**), or **Admiralty Taxi** (© **239/275-7000**).

EXPLORING THE AREA
TOURING THE ESTATES

Edison and Ford Winter Estates ★★   Thomas Edison and his second wife, Mina, brought their family to this Victorian retreat—they called it Seminole Lodge—in 1886 and wintered here until the inventor's death in 1931. Mrs. Edison gave the 14-acre estate to the city of Fort Myers in 1947, and today it's Southwest Florida's top historic attraction. It looks exactly as it did during Edison's lifetime. Costumed actors portraying the Edisons, the Fords, and their friends such as Harvey Firestone give "living history" accounts of how the wealthy lived in those days.

An avid amateur botanist, Edison experimented with the exotic foliage he planted in the lush tropical gardens surrounding the mansion (he turned goldenrod into rubber and used bamboo for light-bulb filaments). Some of his light bulbs dating from the 1920s still burn in the laboratory where he and his staff worked on some of his 1,093 inventions. The monstrous banyan tree that shades the laboratory was 4 feet tall when Harvey S. Firestone presented it to Edison in 1925; today it's the largest banyan in Florida. A museum displays some of Edison's inventions, as well as his unique Model-T Ford, a gift from friend Henry Ford. In 1916, Ford and his wife, Clara, built **Mangoes,** their bungalow-style house, next door, so they could winter with the Edisons. Like Seminole Lodge,

ACCOMMODATIONS ■

Courtyard
by Marriott **13**
Fairfield Inn
by Marriott **15**
The Hibiscus House
Bed and Breakfast **4**
Holiday Inn Riverwalk
& Marina **5**
Quality Inn
Historic District **9**
Sanibel Harbour
Resort & Spa **14**
Super 8 **12**

ATTRACTIONS ●

Burroughs Home **1**
City of Palms Park **8**
Edison and Ford
Winter Estates **7**
Fort Myers Historical
Museum **2**
Imaginarium **3**
Koreshan State
Historic Site **17**

DINING ◆

Farmers Market
Restaurant **10**
Mel's Diner **16**
Oasis Restaurant **6**
Sasse il Pizzaiuolo **11**
Toucan Charlie's
Bar and Grill **5**

Mangoes is furnished as it appeared in the 1920s. The Fords' home is not as interesting as the Edisons', but when you go to the Edison House, you have no choice but to go through the Ford House, too, since the only way to see either one is on a guided tour, which includes both.

Allow an extra hour here to take a scenic ride on the river in a replica of Edison's electric boat *Reliance*.

2350 McGregor Blvd. ℂ **239/334-3614** for a recording, or 239/334-7419. www.edison-ford-estate.com. Admission $15 adults, $8.50 children 6–12, free for children 5 and under. Boat rides $4 per person. Homes open Mon–Sat 9am–5:30pm; Sun noon–5:30pm (1½-hr. tours of both homes depart continuously; last tour daily departs at 4pm). Boat rides Mon–Fri 9am–3pm (weather permitting). Closed Thanksgiving, Christmas Eve, and Christmas Day.

OTHER DOWNTOWN ATTRACTIONS

A good way to explore downtown Fort Myers during the winter season is on a leisurely, 2-hour guided walking tour hosted by the **Fort Myers Historical Museum,** 2300 Peck St., at Jackson Street (ℂ **239/332-5955;** www.cityftmyers.com/attractions/historical.htm). The tours are held on Wednesdays from 10am to noon and cost $5 a head. Reservations are required.

The historical museum itself is housed in the restored Spanish-style depot served by the Atlantic Coast Line from 1924 to 1971. Inside you'll see exhibits depicting the city's history from the ancient Calusa peoples and the Spanish conquistadors to the first settlers, including the remains of a P-39 Aircobra, which helps explain the town's role in training fighter pilots in World War II. Outside stands a replica of an 1800s "cracker" home and the *Esperanza,* the longest and one of the last of the plush Pullman private cars. Admission is $9.50 for adults,

$8.50 for seniors, $4 for children 3 to 12, free for kids under 3. Open Tuesday through Saturday from 10am to 5pm and Sunday from noon to 4pm.

The Georgian Revival **Burroughs Home,** 2505 1st St., at Fowler Street (© **239/332-6125;** http://downtownfortmyers.com/burroughshome), was built on the banks of the Caloosahatchee River in 1901 by cattleman John Murphy and later sold to the Burroughs family. You must take a 30-minute tour; they usually are given from mid-October to mid-May, Tuesday through Friday, on the hour from 11am to 3pm and by appointment off season, but call ahead any time of year. Admission is $6 for adults, $3 for children 3 to 12, free for children under 3. At press time, the home was under renovation and closed until approximately October 2005, so call before you go to make sure it's open.

Rather than have the kids go batty on a rainy day, head for the **Imaginarium,** 2000 Cranford Ave., at Martin Luther King Jr. Boulevard (© **239/337-3332;** www.cityftmyers.com/Attractions/imaginarium.htm), a hands-on museum in the old city water plant. A host of toylike exhibits explains basic scientific principles such as gravity and the weather. Admission is $7 for adults, $6.50 for seniors, and $4 for children 3 to 12. Open Monday through Saturday from 10am to 5pm, Sunday noon to 5pm. Closed Thanksgiving and Christmas.

A NEARBY HISTORICAL ATTRACTION

Koreshan State Historic Site   Worth a 15-mile drive south of downtown Fort Myers if you're into canoeing or quirky gurus, these 300 acres on the narrow Estero River were home to the Koreshan Unity Movement (pronounced Ko-*resh*-en), a sect led by Chicagoan Cyrus Reed Teed. The Koreshans—who should not be confused with the late, disturbing Branch Davidian leader David Koresh—who believed that humans lived *inside* the earth and—ahead of their time—that women should have equal rights, established a self-sufficient settlement here in 1894. You can visit their garden and several of their buildings, plus view photos from their archives. Canoeists will find marked trails winding down the slow-flowing river to **Mound Key,** an islet made of the shells discarded by the Calusa Indians (see "Canoeing & Kayaking" under "Affordable Outdoor Activities & Spectator Sports," below). There's also a picnic and camping area with 60 wooded sites for tents or RVs. For information, contact the park superintendent at P.O. Box 7, Estero, FL 33928.

U.S. 41 at Corkscrew Rd., Estero (15 miles south of downtown Fort Myers). © **239/992-0311.** www.florida stateparks.org/koreshan/default.asp. Admission $4 per vehicle for up to 8 people, $3 for a single occupant vehicle, $1 pedestrians or bikers; tours $2 adults, $1 children 6–12. Canoes $3 an hr., $15 per day. Camping winter $16; off season $10. Park daily 8am–sunset; settlement buildings daily 8am–5pm; 1-hr. tours Sat–Sun 1pm. From I-75, take Corkscrew Rd. (exit 19), go 2 miles west, and cross U.S. 41 into the site.

SHOPPING

Outlet shoppers will find a large Levi's store among other major-brand shops at the **Sanibel Tanger Factory Stores,** on the way to the beaches at the junction of Summerlin Road and McGregor Boulevard (© **888/SHOP-333** or 239/454-1616; www.tangeroutlet.com). Another Levi's store, plus Brooks Brothers, Donna Karan, Dockers, Fila, Nike, Reebok, Maidenform, Nautica, OshKosh B'Gosh, and many more stores are at the much larger **Miromar Outlets,** on Corkscrew Road at I-75 in Estero (© **239/948-3766;** www.miromar.com), about halfway between Fort Myers and Naples. Both outlet malls are open Monday through Saturday from 10am to 9pm, Sunday from 11am to 6pm.

AFFORDABLE OUTDOOR ACTIVITIES & SPECTATOR SPORTS

CANOEING & KAYAKING   The area's slow-moving rivers and quiet, island-speckled inland waters offer fine canoe and kayak ventures; you'll visit with birds and manatees along the way. Two popular local venues are the winding water-ways around Pine Island west of town and the Estero River south of Fort Myers. The Estero River route is an official Florida canoe trail and leads 3½ miles from U.S. 41 to Estero Bay, which is itself a state aquatic preserve. Near the mouth of the river lies **Mound Key State Archaeological Park,** one of the largest Calusa shell middens. Scholars believe that this mostly artificial island dates back some 2,000 years and was the capital of the Calusa chief who ruled all of South Florida when the Spanish arrived. There's no park ranger on the key, but signs explain its history. Also see the "Go the Blueway" box on p. 318.

Koreshan State Historic Site, ½ mile south of the bridge at the intersection of U.S. 41 and Corkscrew Road (✆ 239/992-0311), rents canoes (see "A Nearby Historical Attraction," above). Less than a mile from the site, **Estero River Tackle & Canoe Outfitters,** 20991 S. Tamiami Trail (U.S. 41), Estero, at the Estero River bridge (✆ 239/992-4050; www.all-florida.com/swestero.htm), has guided historic and nature tours (call for schedule and prices) and rents canoes and kayaks from 8am to 4pm at prices ranging from $18 to $30 a day. Open daily from 8am to sunset.

In addition to its cruises mentioned below, **Tropic Star Cruises,** based at Knight's Landing marina, 16499 Porto Bello in Bokeelia on Pine Island (✆ 239/283-0015; www.tropicstarcruises.com), rents kayaks and has guided tours over 18 miles of paddling trails. Rentals cost $35 a day for single-seaters, $45 for doubles. Call for schedule and prices of guided tours. The company also has a ferry service to Cayo Costa State Park, where it rents kayaks (p. 328).

CRUISES   J. C. Boat Cruises (✆ 239/334-7474; www.floridatravel.com/jccruises) presents a variety of year-round cruises on the Caloosahatchee River and its tributaries, including lunch and dinner voyages on the stern-wheeler *Captain J. P.* The 3-hour Everglades Jungle Cruise is a good way to observe the area's wildlife, with lots of manatees to be seen from November to April. Once a week, a full-day cruise goes all the way up the Caloosahatchee to Lake Okeechobee and back. The ticket office is at the downtown Fort Myers City Yacht Basin, Edwards Drive at Lee Street, opposite the chamber of commerce. Prices range from $14 to $75 for adults. Schedules change and advance reservations are required, so call ahead.

If you're headed out to Cabbage Key, Cayo Costa State Park, or Boca Grande (see "Nearby Island Hopping," in section 3, later in this chapter, beginning on p. 326), **Tropic Star Cruises** (✆ 239/283-0015; www.tropicstarcruises.com) are a faster way to get there from Fort Myers than driving to Captiva Island and taking a boat from there. Tropic Star's all-day nature cruises on Pine Island Sound depart from Knight's Landing marina, 16499 Porto Bello in Bokeelia on Pine Island, daily at 9:30am. They include a stop at Cayo Costa and Cabbage Key and cost $25 for adults, $15 for kids under 12. The company also runs daily ferries to Cayo Costa State Park ($20 for adults, $15 for those under 12) and to Boca Grande ($30 adults, $15 for those under 12). The ferries take less than 30 minutes to cross the sound. Call for departure times.

Much more luxurious, the sleek, 100-foot-long yacht *Sanibel Harbour Princess* (✆ 239/466-2128) goes on sunset dinner cruises from its base at Sanibel Harbour Resort & Spa (p. 304). Evening cruises start at $53 for adults,

$33 for children 6 though 12, including tax and gratuity. A 2-hour Sunday-brunch cruise costs $33 for adults, $23 for children 6 though 12, including tax and gratuity. Call ahead for departure times and reservations.

GOLF   For an excellent rundown of Southwest Florida golf courses, pick up a free copy of *Golfer's Guide,* available at the visitor information centers and many hotel lobbies, or on the Internet at www.golfersguide.com. See "Special-Interest Trips," in chapter 2, for information about subscribing or ordering the current edition. And don't forget that you can call **Tee Times USA** (*©* **800/374-8633** or 888/465-3356; www.teetimesusa.com) to book starting times at Florida courses.

Although it looks like an exclusive private enclave, the **Fort Myers Country Club,** McGregor Boulevard at Hill Avenue (*©* **239/936-2457**), actually is a municipal course. Designed in 1917 by Donald Ross, it's flat and uninteresting by today's standards, but it's right in town. A steak-and-seafood restaurant now occupies the fine old clubhouse. The city's other municipal course is the more challenging **Eastwood Golf Club,** on Ortiz Avenue between Colonial Boulevard and Dr. Martin Luther King Jr. Boulevard in the eastern suburbs (*©* **239/275-4848**). Greens fees at both range from about $25 in summer to $60 during winter. Nonresidents must book tee times at least 24 hours in advance.

Other area courses open to the public include the Tom Fazio–designed **Gateway Golf & Country Club,** on Daniels Parkway east of the airport (*©* **239/561-1010**), and the two nationally acclaimed **Pelican's Nest** courses in Bonita Springs (*©* **239/947-4600**).

SPECTATOR SPORTS   While many Major League **baseball** teams have jumped around Florida for their **spring training,** the Boston Red Sox and the Minnesota Twins have worked out in Fort Myers for years. The **Boston Red Sox** play at the 6,500-seat City of Palms Park, at Edison Avenue and Broadway (*©* **877/733-7699** or 239/334-4799; www.redsox.mlb.com). Tickets range from $6 to $21. The **Minnesota Twins** work out at the 7,500-seat William Hammond Stadium in the Lee County Sports Complex on Six Mile Cypress Parkway between Daniels Parkway and Metro Parkway (*©* **800/338-9467** or 239/768-4200; www.twins.mlb.com). The Twins' minor-league affiliate, the **Fort Myers Miracle** (*©* **239/768-4210;** www.miraclebaseball.com), play in the stadium April through August.

The **Texas Rangers** hold their spring training at **Charlotte County Stadium** (*©* **817/273-5222;** www.rangers.mlb.com), about an hour's drive north of Ft. Myers. To get there from Ft. Myers, take I-75 north to exit 31 and go south on Kings Highway (Fla. 769); then take an immediate right on Veterans Boulevard (Fla. 776) to the stadium on the left.

The **Florida Everblades** (*©* **239/948-7825;** www.floridaeverblades.com) play minor-league professional hockey October through March at TECO Arena, at exit 19 off I-75 in Estero. Tickets range from $8 to $29.

ACCOMMODATIONS YOU CAN AFFORD

If you're looking for a stay with personality in Fort Myers proper, you're not going to find it. For that, you'll have to head to Fort Myers Beach (see the next section of this chapter). But if you're looking for bargains and don't mind driving to the beach, Fort Myers has just about every chain hotel imaginable. Most are quite clean and reliable.

As in the rest of southern Florida, room rates here are highest, and reservations essential, during winter, from mid-December to April. Even the chain hotels and motels along U.S. 41 in Fort Myers—most brands are represented along this busy thoroughfare—charge premium rates then. During the off season, however, they drop by as much as 50% or more.

If you can't get a room at the properties mentioned below, the **Lee Island Coast Visitor and Convention Bureau** operates a free reservation service (ⓒ **800/733-7935**) covering many more accommodations in Fort Myers, Fort Myers Beach, and Sanibel and Captiva islands.

A few blocks from the Edison and Ford homes, the recently renovated and under-new-management inn formerly known as Li-Inn Sleeps is now known as **The Hibiscus House Bed and Breakfast,** 2135 McGregor Blvd., at Clifford Street (ⓒ **239/332-2651;** fax 239/332-8922; www.cyberstreet.com/users/ li-inn/li-inn.html), and is a must-stay for B&B fans, with five comfortable rooms, each with private bathroom, in a charming wooden house built a century ago in North Fort Myers. The building, full of antiques and collectibles, was later split in two, floated across the river, and nailed back together. The inn's new owner brings 20-plus years of culinary experience (as the former owner of haute caterer A Moveable Feast in New York's tony Hamptons). Renovations here include new linens, new paint, the addition of a television, and a dining area reminiscent of a Tuscan trattoria. Rates range from $100 to $130 in winter, $85 to $115 off season, including full breakfast.

Chain hotels in the area include **Courtyard by Marriott** (4455 Metro Pkwy., at the corner of Colonial Blvd.; ⓒ **800/321-2211** or 239/275-8600; www. Marriott.com), **Fairfield Inn by Marriott** (7090 Cypress Terrace, off U.S. 41 a block south of Daniels Pkwy.; ⓒ **800/228-2800** or 239/437-5600; www. Marriott.com), and **Super 8** (2717 Colonial Blvd.; ⓒ **800/800-8000** or 239/ 275-3500; www.super8.com).

Many business travelers opt for the Art Deco **Quality Inn Historic District,** 2431 Cleveland Ave. (U.S. 41), at Edison Avenue (ⓒ **800/998-0466** or 239/332-3232). Its location, a 2-block walk to the Boston Red Sox training facility and a short drive to the Edison and Ford homes, is a plus for vacationers, too. Minor-league hopefuls stay here during baseball spring training, so you could meet a future major-leaguer.

All hotel bills in Southwest Florida are subject to a 9% tax.

The only campground with tent sites near here is at **Koreshan State Historic Site** (p. 301).

Holiday Inn Riverwalk & Marina   This islandlike riverside hotel is a convenient base from which to explore the nearby Edison and Ford Winter Estates and other downtown attractions. The L-shaped building wraps around an attractively landscaped pool area. A riverfront building known as La Marina holds Toucan Charlie's Bar and Grill (see "Great Deals on Dining," below), which has live music Friday and Saturday nights. The bands stop playing by 11pm, but you should ask for a room at the front of the property, which will be far enough removed from the action to escape most of the noise. Some of these have Jacuzzi tubs and small patios. Other units here lack both patios and balconies.

2220 W. 1st St. (at Euclid Ave.), Fort Myers, FL 33901. ⓒ 800/HOLIDAY or 239/334-3434. Fax 239/334-3844. 146 units. Year round $66–$110 double. Weekend rates available. AE, DC, DISC, MC, V. **Amenities:** Restaurant; bar; outdoor adult and children's pools; activities desk; salon with massage; limited room service; coin-op washers and dryers. *In room:* A/C, TV, fridge, coffeemaker, hair dryer, iron.

WORTH A SPLURGE

Sanibel Harbour Resort & Spa ★★★ *Kids* This secluded, sports-oriented resort overlooks San Carlos Bay and Sanibel Island (a complimentary shuttle takes guests to the island's beaches and to a bike-rental shop three times a day). The main hotel and the boutique-style **Inn at Sanibel Harbour** are both modern and luxurious throughout. All of the hotel rooms (refurbished in 2003) and most of the condominium apartments have wonderful water and island views from their balconies, including spectacular sunsets over Sanibel. A large, attractive pool and sunning complex sit by the water, but don't be disappointed by the quality of the beach here—this is the bay and not the Gulf, after all, so stay over on the islands if a great beach is among your top priorities. The spa here has just been enhanced and features over 60 sublime treatments. If tennis is your game, the resort has 8 clay courts and a 5,000-seat stadium that has hosted Davis Cup matches. *Note:* The resort was heavily damaged by Hurricane Charley, but it is set to be fully repaired and reopened by February of 2005.

17260 Harbour Pointe Rd., Fort Myers, FL 33908. © 800/767-7777 or 239/466-4000. Fax 239/466-2150. www.sanibel-resort.com. 401 units, including 54 condo apts. Winter $329–$459 double, $389–$519 suite, $469–$689 condo apt; off season $169–$310 double, $219–$379 suite, $299–$449 condo apt. $12 per unit per day resort benefits fee. Packages available. AE, DC, DISC, MC, V. Free self-parking; valet parking $10. Take the last exit off Summerlin Rd. before the Sanibel Causeway toll plaza. **Amenities:** 3 restaurants; 2 bars; 6 heated outdoor pools; 8 clay tennis courts; health club and spa; watersports equipment/rentals; children's programs; concierge; activities desk; business center; 24-hr. room service; laundry service; dry cleaning. *In room:* A/C, TV, kitchen (condos only), minibar (main building only), fridge, coffeemaker, hair dryer, iron, safe, high-speed Internet access.

GREAT DEALS ON DINING

Some Southwest Florida restaurants adjust their hours from season to season and even from year to year, so you may want to call ahead to make sure of an establishment's business hours.

Fort Myers's main commercial strip, Cleveland Avenue (U.S. 41), has most national fast-food and family chain restaurants, especially near College Parkway. There's a branch of **Mel's Diner,** the excellent regional chain, at 4820 S. Cleveland Ave., opposite Page Field (© **239/275-7850**), offering inexpensive diner-style fare including breakfast served anytime.

Sasse il Pizzaiuolo ★★ *Finds* CONTINENTAL/ITALIAN In a small shopping strip north of the Edison Mall, this informal, often-noisy spot offers one of the area's most unusual and reasonably priced dining experiences. Aromas waft from the wood-fired oven in the open kitchen, from which come enormous slabs of pizzalike bread (served with seasoned olive oil for dipping). The selections change daily, although you can usually count on braised lamb shank served over polenta, and veal scallopini stuffed with prosciutto, roasted peppers, and mozzarella. It's all of a quality rarely found at these prices, and the portions are so huge that most patrons carry home doggie bags. Note that reservations are not accepted (and preference is sometimes given to regulars), so be prepared to wait for a table, especially on weekends. We have gotten complaints about the service here, though we've never had a bad experience.

3651 Evans Ave., in Carrell Corner shopping center (between Carrell Rd. and Winkler Ave.). © 239/278-5544. Reservations not accepted. Main courses $8–$18. No credit cards. Tues–Fri 11:30am–1:15pm; Wed–Sat 5:30–8:15pm.

Toucan Charlie's Bar and Grill ⊛ INTERNATIONAL In the La Marina part of the Holiday Inn Riverwalk & Marina, this restaurant's sliding-glass walls opening to a riverside deck make it the most attractive place in town for taking a relaxing, alfresco lunch break while seeing the sights, or for watching the sun set over the Caloosahatchee. The Caribbean slash seafood cuisine is fine, but the restaurant is best known for its spectacular views and its rockin' Tiki Bar, which features live music on weekends.

At Holiday Inn Riverwalk & Marina, 2220 W. 1st St. (at Euclid Ave.). ℂ **239/334-2727**. Main courses $7–$20; salads and sandwiches $2.95–$7.95. AE, DC, DISC, MC, V. Daily 7am–10pm (bar open later).

SUPER-CHEAP EATS

Farmers Market Restaurant ⭐⭐ *Finds* SOUTHERN Cabbage, okra, green beans, and tomatoes at the retail Farmers Market next door provide the fodder for some of the best country-style cooking in Florida at this plain and simple restaurant frequented by everyone from business executives to truck drivers. Specialties are beef and pork barbecue from the tin smokehouse out by Edison Avenue, plus other Southern favorites like country-fried steak, fried chicken livers and gizzards, and smoked ham hocks with a bowl of lima beans. Yankees can order fried chicken, roast beef, or pork chops, and they can have hash browns instead of grits with their big breakfast. But forget about Southern Comfort: No alcohol is served, nor is smoking permitted.

2736 Edison Ave. (at Cranford Ave.). ℂ **239/334-1687**. Breakfast $3–$7.50; sandwiches $3–$6; meals $7.50. No credit cards. Mon–Sat 6am–8pm; Sun 6am–7pm.

Oasis Restaurant AMERICAN A fine place for breakfast before touring the nearby Edison and Ford homes, Bonnie Grunberg and Tammie Shockey's narrow storefront spot also appeals to local professionals who don't mind sitting elbow to elbow recovering from a night at Shooters Waterfront Cafe USA (just behind this shopping center) with a "hangover" omelet chock-full of bacon, cheese, peppers, tomatoes, and onions.

In Edison-Ford Sq., 2222 McGregor Blvd. (at Euclid Ave.). ℂ **239/334-1566**. Breakfast $3–$6; sandwiches, burgers, and salads $4–$6. No credit cards. Mon–Fri 8am–3pm; Sat–Sun 7am–2pm.

FORT MYERS AFTER DARK

For the most part, Fort Myers shuts down after dark and the pay-per-view on your hotel room's television may just be your best bet for entertainment. But there are some activities that happen when the sun goes down around here. For entertainment ideas and schedules, consult the daily *News-Press* (www.news-press.com), especially Friday's "Gulf Coasting" section. Also be on the lookout for *Happenings,* a tabloid-size entertainment guide distributed free at the visitor information offices and in some hotel lobbies. Tickets for most events are available from **Ticketmaster** (ℂ **239/334-3309**).

The city's showcase performing-arts venue is the **Barbara B. Mann Performing Arts Hall** ⭐, 8099 College Pkwy., at Summerlin Road (ℂ **800/440-7469** or 239/481-4849 for tickets; www.bbmannpah.com), on the campus of Edison Community College. It features world-famous performers and Broadway plays.

Originally a downtown vaudeville playhouse, the 1908-vintage **Arcade Theater,** 2267 1st St., between Bay and Hendry streets (ℂ **239/332-4488**), presents a variety of performances.

2 Fort Myers Beach ⭐⭐

13 miles S of Fort Myers, 28 miles N of Naples, 12 miles E of Sanibel Island

Often overshadowed by trendy Sanibel and Captiva islands to the north and ritzy Naples to the south, down-to-earth Fort Myers Beach, which occupies all of skinny Estero Island, offers just as much sun and sand as its affluent neighbors, both a half-hour drive away, but at more moderate prices. In fact, if you're looking for that Jimmy Buffet style of slacking, Fort Myers Beach is where it's at.

Droves of families and young singles flock to the busy intersection of San Carlos Boulevard and Estero Boulevard, an area so packed with bars, beach-apparel shops, restaurants, and motels that the locals call it "Times Square." That Coney Island image certainly doesn't apply to the rest of Estero Island, where old-fashioned beach cottages, manicured condominiums, and quiet motels beckon couples and families in search of more sedate vacations. In fact, promoters of the southern end of the island say that they're not in Fort Myers Beach; they're on Estero Island. It's their way of distinguishing their part of town from congested Times Square.

Narrow Matanzas Pass leads into broad Estero Bay, which separates the island from the mainland. While the pass is the area's largest commercial fishing port (when they say "fresh off the boat" here, they aren't kidding), the bay is an official state aquatic preserve inhabited by a host of birds as well as manatees, dolphins, and other sea life. Nature cruises go forth onto this lovely protected bay, which is dotted with islands.

A few miles south of Fort Myers Beach, a chain of pristine barrier islands includes unspoiled **Lover's Key,** a state park where a tractor-pulled tram runs through a mangrove forest to one of Florida's best beaches. Many people seem to feel the need to prove that they belong on Lover's Key, so beware of where you walk or park your car, and don't be surprised if you see steamy windows.

ESSENTIALS

GETTING THERE   See section 1 on Fort Myers, beginning on p. 294, for information about Southwest Florida International Airport, car-rental firms, Amtrak's trains, and Greyhound/Trailways bus service to the area.

VISITOR INFORMATION   You can get advance information from the Lee Island Coast Visitor and Convention Bureau (p. 298) and from the **Fort Myers Beach Chamber of Commerce,** 17200 San Carlos Blvd., Fort Myers Beach, FL 33931 (© **800/782-9283** or 239/454-7500; fax 239/454-7910; www.fmb chamber.com), which provides free information, sells a detailed street map for $2, and operates a visitor welcome center on the mainland portion of San Carlos Boulevard just south of Summerlin Road. The chamber is open Monday through Friday from 8am to 5pm, Saturday from 10am to 5pm, and Sunday from 11am to 5pm.

GETTING AROUND   Estero Island is absolutely inundated with traffic during the peak winter months, but you can get around on the **Beach Trolley,** which operates every 15 minutes daily from 7am to 9:30pm along the full length of Estero Boulevard from Bowditch Regional Park at the north end south to Lover's Key. It operates year-round. During the winter, the **Beach Park & Ride Trolley** runs daily from 6:30am to 9:30pm between Summerlin Square Shopping Center, on the mainland at Summerlin Road and San Carlos Boulevard, to Bowditch Regional Park. Rides on both trolleys cost 25¢ per person. Ask your hotel staff or call **LeeTran** (© 239/275-8726; www.rideleetran.com) for more information.

For a cab, call **Local Motion Taxi** (© **239/463-4111**).

There are no bike paths per se here, although many folks ride along the paved shoulders of Estero Boulevard. A variety of rental bikes, scooters, and in-line

ACCOMMODATIONS ■

Best Western Pink Shell
  Beach Resort **2**
Diamond Head All Suite
  Beach Resort **6**
Edison Beach House
  All Suite Hotel **3**
Island House Motel **3**
Outrigger Beach Resort **7**

DINING ◆

Beach Pierside Grill **4**
Channel Mark **1**
The Dragonfly Bistro **1**
The Fish House **8**
Gulf Shore Grill **4**
Loggerheads **8**
Pappa Mondo Ristorante
  Italiano **5**

skates are available at **Fun Rentals,** 1901 Estero Blvd. at Ohio Avenue (✆ **239/ 463-8844**). Charges start at $40 a day for one-passenger scooters, $14 a day for bikes.

HITTING THE BEACH

A prime attraction for both beachgoers and nature lovers is the gorgeous **Lover's Key State Park** ★★★, 8700 Estero Blvd. (✆ **239/463-4588;** www.floridastate parks.org/loverskey/default.asp), on the totally preserved Lover's Key, south of Estero Island. Although the highway runs down the center of the island, access to this unspoiled beach from the parking lot is restricted to footpaths or a tractor-pulled tram through a bird-filled forest of mangroves. The beach itself is known for its multitude of shells. There are bathhouses with outdoor showers, and a snack shop here. The park is open daily from 8am to sunset. Admission is $4 per vehicle with two to eight occupants, $2 for vehicles with a single occupant, and $1 for pedestrians and bicyclists. No alcohol is allowed, nor are pets permitted on the beach or in the water (you must keep them on a leash elsewhere in the park).

On Estero Island, **Lynn Hall Memorial Park** features a fishing pier and beach in the middle of Times Square. It has changing rooms, restrooms, and one of the few public parking lots in the area; the meter costs 75¢ per hour, but keep it fed—there's a $32 fine if your time runs out. At the island's north end, **Bowditch Regional Park** has picnic tables, cold-water showers, and changing rooms. It has parking only for drivers with disabilities permits, but it's the turnaround point for the Beach Connection Trolley.

Several beach locations are hotbeds of parasailing, jet skis, sailboats, and other beach activities. **Times Square,** at the intersection of San Carlos Boulevard and

Estero Boulevard, and the **Best Western Beach Resort,** about ¼ mile north, are popular spots on Estero's busy north end. Other hotbeds are **Diamond Head All Suite Beach Resort,** just south of Times Square, and the **Junkanoo Beach Bar** in the middle beach area (see "Fort Myers Beach After Dark," later in this chapter). Down south, activities are centered at the **Outrigger Beach Resort** (see "Accommodations You Can Afford," below).

AFFORDABLE OUTDOOR ACTIVITIES

BOATING & BOAT RENTALS Powerboats are available from the **Mid Island Marina** (© 239/765-4371), the **Fort Myers Beach Marina** (© 239/463-9552), the **Fish Tale Marina** (© 239/463-3600), and **Salty Sam's Marina** (© 239/463-7333). **Dockside Boat Rentals** (© 239/765-4433) rents them at the Best Western Pink Shell Beach Resort on Estero Island's northern end. Boats cost about $125 for half a day, $200 for a full day.

CRUISES A good way to get out on the water and see some of this area's wildlife is on a nature cruise aboard the *Island Princess* (© **239/765-4433**), an open-air pontoon boat based at the Best Western Pink Shell Beach Resort marina on the north end of the island (see "Accommodations You Can Afford," below). The boat usually goes on 1½-hour nature cruises Monday through Saturday afternoons. Prices are $13 for adults, $7 for children 6 though 12. The *Island Princess* also has bay fishing trips departing at 9am on Monday, Wednesday, Friday, and Saturday ($25 adults, $23 children 6–12) and shelling trips at 9am on Tuesday and Thursday ($25 adults, $12 children 6–12). Call ahead for reservations, which are required, and to learn what time the afternoon nature cruises depart.

FISHING You can surf-cast, throw your line off the pier at Times Square, or venture offshore on a number of charter-fishing boats here. The staff at **Getaway Marina,** 18400 San Carlos Blvd., about ½ mile north of the Sky Bridge (© **239/466-3600**), is very adept at matching clients with skilled charter-boat skippers. Expect to spend about $60 a day for a full day's fishing for up to six persons and $37 for a half day.

No reservations are required on "party boats" that take groups out. Operating year-round, the *Great Getaway* and *Great Getaway II* (© 239/466-3600) sail from the Getaway Marina, about ½ mile north of the bridge. The *Island Lady* (© **239/482-2005**) is docked at Fisherman's Wharf, virtually under the San Carlos Island end of the Skyway Bridge. They all depart between 8 and 9:30am; charge between $30 and $50 per person, depending on the length of the voyage; and have air-conditioned lounges with bars. Call for details and reservations.

SCUBA DIVING & SNORKELING Scuba diving is available at **Seahorse Scuba,** 15600 San Carlos Blvd. (© **239/454-3111**). Two-tank dives start at $69. In business since 1989, the company also teaches diver-certification courses.

The live-aboard dive boat *Ultimate Getaway,* based at Getaway Marina, 18400 San Carlos Blvd. (© **239/466-3600;** fax 239/644-7529; www.ultimate getaway.net), makes 4-day voyages to the Dry Tortugas (70 miles west of Key West). This 100-foot vessel carries a maximum of 20 divers and is equipped with a dive platform, chase boat, and TV/VCR. Trips cost about $500 per person, including meals, beer, air, and weights, but bring your own regulator, mask, and fins. Reservations are essential.

ACCOMMODATIONS YOU CAN AFFORD

The hostelries recommended below are removed from the crowds of Times Square, but three chain motels offer comfortable accommodations right in the center of the action: **Ramada Inn** (© 800/544-4592 or 239/463-6158), **Days Inn** (© 800/544-4592 or 239/463-9759), and **Howard Johnson Inn** (© 800/544-4592 or 239/463-9231). The mid-rise **Best Western Beach Resort** (© 800/336-4045 or 239/463-6000) is ¼ mile north, just far enough to escape the noise but still have a lively beach.

Sunstream Resorts, 6640 Estero Blvd., Fort Myers Beach, FL 33931 (© 800/625-4111; fax 239/463-3060; www.sunstream.com), manages three "condominium hotels" here, including the plush **Casa Playa,** 510 Estero Blvd. (© 800/569-4876 or 239/765-0510; www.casaplayaresort.com), and the **Lover's Key Beach Club & Resort,** 8771 Estero Blvd. (© 877/798-4879 or 239/765-1040; www.loverskey.com), both of which opened in 2000. The latter is on the north end of Lover's Key. The 60 spacious apartments in the older, 16-story **Pointe Estero Island Resort,** 6640 Estero Blvd. (© 239/765-1155), all have whirlpool bathtubs and screened balconies with gorgeous Gulf or bay views. The less expensive **Santa Maria,** 7317 Estero Blvd. (© 239/765-6700), is on the bay side of the island.

For information about rate seasons, see the "Accommodations You Can Afford" portion of the "Fort Myers" section, beginning on p. 302.

For campers, the somewhat-cramped **Red Coconut RV Resort,** 3001 Estero Blvd. (© 239/463-7200; fax 239/463-2609; www.redcoconut.com), has sites for RVs and tents both on the Gulf side of the road and right on the beach. They start at $40 a night during winter and are $25 off season.

Island House Motel ★ *Value*   Sitting on stilts in the Old Florida fashion, but with modern furnishings, Ken and Sylvia Lachapelle's clapboard-sided Island House Motel enjoys a quiet location along a bayside channel, directly across the boulevard from the Best Western Beach Resort and within walking distance of busy Times Square. Four of their units have screened porches; all have kitchens and ceiling fans. Ken and Sylvia maintain an open-air lounge with a small library beneath one of the units. They also provide free beach chairs and bikes. Book as early as possible for February and March. The Lachapelles also operate the three-story **Edgewater Inn,** less than a block away at 781 Estero Blvd. (same phone, fax, and website). The two one-bedroom and four two-bedroom apartments there all have screened lanais. They are available on a weekly basis during winter and for 3-day minimum stays off season.

701 Estero Blvd., Fort Myers Beach, FL 33931. © 800/951-9975 or 239/463-9282. Fax 239/463-2080. www.edgewaterfmb.com. 5 units. Winter $119–$139 double; off season $59–$79 double. Rates include local phone calls. Weekly rates available. MC, V. **Amenities:** Heated outdoor pool; access to nearby health club; bicycles lent for free; coin-op washers and dryers. *In room:* A/C, TV, kitchen, coffeemaker, hair dryer, iron.

Outrigger Beach Resort   Well known for its beachside Tiki bar, this clean, pleasant motel has been owned and operated by the same family since 1965. Their "garden efficiencies" in the original building have the feel of small cottages, with excellent ventilation through both front and rear windows and doors opening to backyard decks. Other buildings here are two-story blocks containing motel-style rooms and efficiencies, which have views of the large parking lot. The beachside bar is one of the best places in Fort Myers Beach to watch the sun set.

6200 Estero Blvd., Fort Myers Beach, FL 33931. © **800/749-3131** or 239/463-3131. Fax 239/463-6577. www.outriggerfmb.com. 144 units. Winter $120–$215 double; off season $85–$185 double. AE, MC, V. **Amenities:** Restaurant; bar; heated outdoor pool; small exercise room; game room; coin-op washers and dryers. *In room:* A/C, TV, dataport, kitchen (in efficiencies only), fridge, coffeemaker (in efficiencies only), hair dryer, safe.

WORTH A SPLURGE

Best Western Pink Shell Beach Resort ⭐ Not to be confused with the nearby Best Western Beach Resort, this popular, family-oriented establishment fronts 12 acres of the Gulf and the Matanzas Pass from its perch on Estero's quiet northern end. It has efficiencies, suites, and one- and two-bedroom fully-equipped apartments in three mid-rise, Gulf-front buildings with lovely views of Sanibel Island from screened balconies. The standard efficiencies are the least-expensive units here. Old Florida–style cottages on stilts are pure kitsch. Rooms underwent a thorough renovation in 2001 and are still in pretty good shape. For a more luxurious stay, choose one of the beachfront White Sand Villas. More oceanfront villas—Captiva Villas—should be completed in 2005. Sailboats and nature and sightseeing cruises pick up guests at the bayside marina, which rents boats and bikes. The scenic Hungry Pelican Cafe, on a covered deck overlooking the channel, is a great spot for breakfast or lunch.

275 Estero Blvd., Fort Myers Beach, FL 33931. © **800/554-5454** or 239/463-6181. Fax 239/463-1229. www.pinkshell.com. 234 units. Winter $205–$515 condo or cottage; off season $145–$500 condo or cottage. Packages and weekly rates available. AE, DC, DISC, MC, V. **Amenities:** Restaurant; bar; 4 heated outdoor pools; lighted tennis courts; watersports equipment rental; bike rental; babysitting; laundry service; coin-op washers and dryers. *In room:* A/C, TV, dataport, kitchen, fridge, coffeemaker, hair dryer, iron, safe, microwave.

Edison Beach House All Suite Hotel ⭐⭐ No standardized list of amenities does justice to this hyper, almost obsessive compulsively clean, intimate, five-story, nonsmoking beachside inn, for when owner Larry Yax built it in 1999, he equipped every unit as if he were going to live in it. Each of the light and airy units has a balcony, a ceiling fan, a fully equipped kitchen (look for your complimentary bag of popcorn in the microwave oven), a writing desk stocked with office supplies, and a linen closet packed with extra towels. Most of the bathrooms also have a combo washer-dryer. The freshly-laundered bedspreads provided each new guest are but one example of the premium Larry puts on cleanliness. The beachfront units have the best view, but much more romantic are the "A" suites, whose queen-size beds are almost surrounded by windows formed by a turret on one corner of the building—as in, you fall asleep and wake up to a panoramic view spanning from Gulf to bay.

830 Estero Blvd., Fort Myers Beach, FL 33931. © **800/399-2511** or 239/463-1530. Fax 239/765-9430. www.edisonbeachhouse.com. 24 units. Winter $145–$325 double; off season $95–$175 double. AE, DISC, MC, V. **Amenities:** Heated outdoor pool; laundry service. *In room:* A/C, TV, dataport, kitchen, coffeemaker, hair dryer, iron.

GREAT DEALS ON DINING

The busy area around Times Square has fast-food joints to augment several local restaurants catering to the beach crowds. The pick is the moderately priced **Beach Pierside Grill,** directly on the beach at the foot of Lynn Hall Memorial Pier (© **239/765-7800**), a lively pub with bright-blond wood trim and vivid fabric colors reminiscent of establishments in Miami's South Beach. It all opens onto a large beachside patio with dining at umbrella tables, outstanding sunsets, and live bands playing at night. The reasonably priced fare is a catch-all of conch fritters, shrimp and fish baskets, burgers, and seafood main courses. They take reservations—a plus in this busy area. Food is served daily from 11am to 11pm.

Channel Mark ★★ SEAFOOD Maryland-style crab cakes, delicately seasoned with Old Bay spice in true Maryland fashion, are enough to make this the beach's best place for seafood. Nestled by the "Little Bridge" leading onto San Carlos Island's northern end, every table here looks out on a maze of channel markers on Hurricane Bay. A dock with palms growing through it makes this a tranquil place for a waterside lunch. At night, a relaxed tropical ambience is ideal for kindling romance. The adjacent lounge offers the same menu and has live entertainment on weekends.

19001 San Carlos Blvd. (at the north end of San Carlos Island). ℂ 239/463-9127. Reservations recommended on major holidays; not accepted other times. Main courses $10–$21. AE, DISC, MC, V. Sun–Thurs 11am–10pm; Fri–Sat 11am–11pm.

Gulf Shore Grill SEAFOOD/AMERICAN On the southern fringes of Times Square, this old clapboard building offers splendid views of the Gulf and the beach. It began life in the 1920s as the Crescent Beach Casino and has seen various incarnations as a bathhouse, gambling casino, dance hall, and rooming house. These days, an extensive salad bar accompanies traditional Florida-style main courses such as baked grouper imperial, grilled mahimahi, and shrimp wrapped in bacon and coated with honey. This is one of the best breakfast spots on the beach, with choices ranging from biscuits under sausage gravy to eggs served on a muffin under Alaskan crab meat and a charon sauce. The kitchen also provides the pub fare for **The Cottage Bar,** an open-air drinking establishment next door (open daily 11am–2am).

1270 Estero Blvd. (on the beach at Ave. A). ℂ 239/765-5440. Reservations recommended for dinner. Main courses $13–$25; breakfast $4–$11; sandwiches and burgers $6–$13. AE, DISC, MC, V. Daily 8am–3pm and 5–10pm.

Loggerheads SEAFOOD/AMERICAN The motto "The Local's Nest" accurately describes this friendly storefront restaurant, the best bet on the island's south end. Charter-boat captains and other locals congregate around a big square bar on one side of the knotty pine–accented dining room. The menu offers a wide range of appetizers, big salads, sandwiches, burgers, and main course options from both land and sea. Grouper prepared in a number of satisfying if not spectacular ways leads the main courses, but you can also order traditionally fried, grilled, broiled, or blackened seafood plus pastas, steaks, ribs, and jerk chicken.

In Santini Marina Plaza, 7205 Estero Blvd. (at Lennel Rd.). ℂ 239/463-4644. Reservations recommended on weekends. Main courses $12–$18; sandwiches and burgers $7–$8. AE, DISC, MC, V. Sun–Thurs 11am–11pm; Fri–Sat 11am–midnight.

Pappa Mondo Ristorante Italiano ★★ (Value) NORTHERN ITALIAN Pasquale Riso (he's the chef) and Andrea Mazzonetto hail from Italy, and the fare they present in their attractive dining room—or out on their roadside patio—is authentic old-country cooking. They make everything from scratch—you can watch them producing pasta at a big machine behind a large picture window. Especially tasty is the ravioli, either ricotta cheese topped with butter and sage sauce, or stuffed with veal and served with a light cream sauce tinged with balsamic vinegar.

1821 Estero Blvd. (at Ohio Ave.). ℂ 239/765-9660. Reservations recommended. Main courses $11–$16. AE, MC, V. Daily 3:30–10pm. Closed Christmas.

SUPER-CHEAP EATS

The Fish House SEAFOOD   You'll find the beach's least-expensive outdoor dining at the dockside tables of this no-frills friendly pub. You'll also see charter-boat skippers slaking their thirst at a large wooden bar occupying about half the open-air but screened dining room. Go for the fried or grilled grouper and other fish the captains have just landed. Sandwiches are available all day, including a tasty grouper version.

7225 Estero Blvd. (at Fish Tale Marina, behind Santini Marina Plaza). ✆ 239/765-6766. Main courses $7–$20; sandwiches $6.50–$9. AE, DISC, MC, V. Winter daily 11am–11pm; off season daily 11am–10pm. Closed Thanksgiving and Christmas.

WORTH A SPLURGE

The Dragonfly Bistro ★★ AMERICAN   Chef Preston Dishman (what better name for a chef?), graduate of New York City's French Culinary Institute, set his sights on this sleek restaurant after working at New York's famed Le Bernadin restaurant, and Fort Myers couldn't be luckier. Rich red banquettes contribute to the coolness of the restaurant, but the menu, which changes with the seasons, even though Florida doesn't really experience seasons, is cooler and richer. Everything but the sorbet is made from scratch here. Salivate over local handpicked jumbo lump crab salad with aged cheddar and corn blini with tomato vinaigrette, and crisp bacon; seared fresh Maine sea scallops with roasted cauliflower, Yukon gold potatoes, sweet garlic greens, and mustard butter; and chargrilled prime steak with Yukon gold fries and caramelized onion aioli.

19051 San Carlos Blvd. ✆ 239/765-8200. Reservations recommended. Main courses $21–$27. AE, DC, MC, V. Mon–Sat 7:30–9am; Sun 7:30–10am; Mon–Fri 11:15am–3pm; Sat 11:15am–4pm; Mon–Sat 5pm until "the customers stop coming in the door."

FORT MYERS BEACH AFTER DARK

To find out what's going on while you're here, pick up copies of the daily *News-Press* (www.news-press.com) and of the *Beach Bulletin* and the *Fort Myers Beach Observer*, two local tabloid newspapers. They're available at the chamber of commerce (p. 306).

The area around Times Square is always active, every day during winter and on weekends off season. In the very heart of Times Square, at the foot of Lynn Hall Memorial Pier, the **Beach Pierside Grill,** 1000 Estero Blvd. (✆ 239/765-7800), has live entertainment on its beachside patio. Facing due west, **Jimmy's Beach Bar,** in the Days Inn at 1130 Estero Blvd. (✆ 239/463-9759), has live music nightly for the "best sunsets on the island" (actually, you can say that of all the beachside establishments here). It's not directly on the beach, but locals in the know head for the rooftop bar at **The Beached Whale,** 1249 Estero Blvd. (✆ 239/463-5505), which supplies free chicken wings during their nightly happy hour. Rock and reggae music is played downstairs for nighttime dancing.

Away from the crowds in the "middle beach" area, the **Junkanoo Beach Bar,** under Anthony's on the Gulf, 3040 Estero Blvd. (✆ 239/463-2600), attracts a more affluent crowd for its bohemian-style parties that run from 11:30am to 1:30am daily. Live bands here specialize in reggae and other island music. The menu offers inexpensive subs, sandwiches, burgers, and pizzas, and a concessionaire rents beach cabanas and watersports toys, making it a good place for a lively day at the beach.

On Sunday afternoons, revelers jam the docks for the famous outdoor reggae parties at **The Bridge Waterfront Restaurant,** 708 Fisherman's Wharf (✆ 239/765-0050), which is under the Sky Bridge on San Carlos Island.

3 Sanibel & Captiva Islands ★★★

14 miles W of Fort Myers, 40 miles N of Naples

Sanibel and Captiva are Florida's unfussy cousins. Au natural is how they prefer to be so that you can appreciate their natural beauty. They don't need lip gloss and eye shadow to make them pretty. Leave the Tammy Faye makeup for Miami and Orlando. Here you will find none of the neon signs, amusement parks, and high-rise condominiums that clutter most beach resorts in the state. Indeed, Sanibel's main drag, Periwinkle Way, runs under a canopy of whispery pines and gnarled oaks so thick they almost obscure the small signs for chic shops and restaurants. This wooded ambience is the work of local voters, who have saved their trees and tropical foliage, limited the size and appearance of signs, and permitted no building higher than the tallest palm and no WaveRunner or other noisy beach toy within 300 yards of their gorgeous, shell-strewn beaches. And although they haven't yet banned cacophonous cellphones, don't be surprised if they eventually do. It's *that* peaceful.

Nevertheless, the islands still have wildlife: More than half of the two islands is preserved in its natural state as wildlife refuges. Here you can ride, walk, bike, canoe, or kayak through the J. N. ("Ding") Darling National Wildlife Refuge, one of Florida's best.

Legend says that Ponce de León named the larger of these two barrier islands "San Ybel," after Queen Isabella of Spain. Another legend claims that Captiva's name comes from the captured women kept here by the infamous pirate Jose Gaspar. The modern era of the islands dates from 1892, when a few farmers settled on the islands. One of them, Clarence Chadwick, started an unsuccessful Key lime and copra plantation on Captiva; many of his towering coconut palms still stand, adding to that skinny island's tropical luster.

ESSENTIALS

GETTING THERE See "Getting There," in section 1 of this chapter, for information about air, train, bus, and rental-car services. The Amoco station at 1015 Periwinkle Way, at Causeway Road, is the Sanibel agent for **Enterprise Rent-a-Car** (© **800/325-8007** or 239/395-2880).

VISITOR INFORMATION The **Sanibel & Captiva Islands Chamber of Commerce,** 1159 Causeway Rd., Sanibel Island, FL 33957 (© **239/472-1080;** fax 239/472-1070; www.sanibel-captiva.org), maintains a visitor center on Causeway Road as you drive onto Sanibel from Fort Myers. The chamber gives away an island guide and sells a detailed street map for $3. Other books are for sale, including comprehensive shelling guides and a helpful collection of menus from the islands' restaurants. There are phones for making hotel and condominium reservations (check the brochure racks for discounts during summer and Dec). Open Monday through Saturday from 9am to 7pm, Sunday from 10am to 5pm.

GETTING AROUND Neither Sanibel nor Captiva has public transportation. **No parking** is permitted on any street or road on Sanibel. Free beach parking is available on the Sanibel Causeway. Other municipal lots either are reserved for local residents or have a 75¢ hourly fee. Accordingly, many residents and visitors get around by bicycle (see "More Ways to Enjoy the Outdoors," below).

If you need a cab, call **Sanibel Taxi** (© **239/472-4160**).

PARKS & NATURE PRESERVES

Named for the *Des Moines Register* cartoonist who was a frequent visitor here and who started the federal Duck Stamp program, the outstanding **J. N. ("Ding") Darling National Wildlife Refuge** ★★★, on Sanibel-Captiva Road, is home to alligators, raccoons, otters, and hundreds of species of birds. Occupying more than half of Sanibel Island, this 6,000-plus-acre area of mangrove swamps, winding waterways, and uplands has a 2-mile boardwalk nature trail and a 5-mile, one-way **Wildlife Drive.** The visitor center shows brief videos about the refuge's inhabitants every half-hour and sells a map keyed to numbered stops along the Wildlife Drive. The best times for viewing the wildlife are early morning, late afternoon, and at low tide (tables are posted at the visitor center and are available at the chamber of commerce). Mosquitoes and "no-see-ums" (tiny, biting sand flies) are especially prevalent at dawn and dusk, so bring repellent.

Admission to the visitor center is free. The Wildlife Drive costs $5 per vehicle, $1 for hikers and bicyclists (free to holders of current federal Duck Stamps and National Park Service access passports). The visitor center is open from November to April, daily from 9am to 5pm; off season, daily from 9am to 4pm. The center is open on federal holidays January through May, closed on holidays the rest of the year. The Wildlife Drive is open year-round, Saturday through Thursday from 1 hour after sunrise to 1 hour before sunset.

For more information, contact the refuge at 1 Wildlife Dr., Sanibel Island, FL 33957 (© **239/472-1100**).

You'll get a lot more from your visit by taking a naturalist-narrated tram tour given by **Tarpon Bay Recreation,** at the north end of Tarpon Bay Road (© **239/472-8900;** www.dingdarlingsociety.org). The tours last 2 hours and cost $10 for adults, $5 for children 12 and under. Schedules are seasonal, so call ahead.

Tarpon Bay Recreation also offers a variety of guided **canoe and kayak tours,** with an emphasis on the historical, cultural, and environmental aspects of the refuge (call for the schedule and reservations, which are required). It also rents canoes, kayaks, and small boats with electric trolling motors (see "More Ways to Enjoy the Outdoors," below).

A short drive from the visitor center, the nonprofit **Sanibel/Captiva Conservation Foundation,** 3333 Sanibel-Captiva Rd. (© **239/472-2329;** www.sccf. org), maintains a nature center, a native plant nursery, and 4½ miles of nature trails on 1,100 acres of wetlands along the Sanibel River. You can learn more about the islands' unusual ecosystems through environmental workshops, guided 1½-hour trail walks, beach walks, and a 2-hour natural-history boat cruise (call for seasonal schedules and reservations). Various items are for sale, including native plants and publications about the islands' birds and other wildlife. Admission is $3 for adults, free for children 16 and under. The nature center is open from November 15 to April 14, Monday through Friday from 8:30am to 4pm, Saturday from 10am to 3pm; off season, Monday through Friday from 8:30am to 3pm.

Also nearby, the **Clinic for the Rehabilitation of Wildlife (C.R.O.W.),** 3883 Sanibel-Captiva Rd. (© **239/472-3644;** www.crowclinic.org), is dedicated to the care of sick, injured, or orphaned wildlife. Tours of the facility usually take place year-round Monday through Friday at 11am, but call to make sure. Tours cost $3 per person.

ACCOMMODATIONS ■

Buttonwood Cottages **22**
Captiva Island Inn
  Bed & Breakfast **5**
Gulf Breeze Cottages **26**
Palm View Motel **25**
South Seas Resort **1**
Sundial Beach Resort **12**
Tarpon Tale Inn **24**
'Tween Waters Inn **6**

ATTRACTIONS ●

Bailey-Matthews
  Shell Museum **11**
Clinic for the
  Rehabilitation of
  Wildlife (C.R.O.W.) **8**
J.N. (Ding) Darling
  National Wildlife
  Refuge **9**
Sanibel Lighthouse **23**
Sanibel/Captiva
  Conservation
  Foundation **10**
Tarpon Bay
  Recreation **13**

DINING ◆

The Bubble Room **2**
The Cabbage Key
  Restaurant **27**
Grandma Dot's
  Seaside Saloon **20**
The Green Flash **4**
Hungry Heron **15**
Jerry's Family
  Restaurant **17**
The Lazy Flamingo II **19**
Lighthouse Cafe **21**
Mad Hatter **7**
McT's Shrimp House
  & Tavern **18**
Mucky Duck **3**
R.C. Otter's
  Island Eats **2**
Sanibel Cafe **16**
Sanibel Grill **14**
The Timbers Restaurant
  & Fish Market **14**

HITTING THE BEACH: SHELLING & SEA LIFE

BEACHES   Sanibel has four public beach–access areas with metered parking:
the eastern point around **Sanibel Lighthouse,** which has a fishing pier; **Gulf-side City Park,** at the end of Algiers Lane, off Casa Ybel Road; **Tarpon Bay Road Beach,** at the south end of Tarpon Bay Road; and **Bowman's Beach,** off
Sanibel-Captiva Road. **Turner Beach,** at Blind Pass between Sanibel and
Captiva, is highly popular at sunset since it faces due west; there's a small free
parking lot on the Captiva side, but parking on the Sanibel side is limited
to holders of local permits. All except Tarpon Bay Road Beach have restrooms.
Be forewarned: Although nude bathing is illegal, the end of Bowman's Beach
near Blind Pass often sees more than its share of bare straight and gay bodies.

Another popular beach on Captiva is at the end of Andy Rosse Lane in front
of the Mucky Duck Restaurant. It's the one place here where you can rent
motorized watersports equipment (see "More Ways to Enjoy the Outdoors,"
below), but you'll have to use the Mucky Duck's restrooms if you need to go.
There's limited free parking just north of here, at the end of Captiva Drive
(go past the entrance to South Seas Resort to the end of the road).

SHELLING   Sanibel and Captiva are famous for their seashells, and local res-idents and visitors alike can be seen in the "Sanibel stoop" or the "Captiva
crouch" while searching for some 200 species.

Only if you're a hard-core shell fanatic should you check out the **Bailey-Matthews Shell Museum** ★★, 3075 Sanibel-Captiva Rd. ((© **888/679-6450**

> **_Tips_ Don't Take Live Shells**
>
> Florida law prohibits taking live shells (those with living creatures inside them) from the beaches, and federal regulations prevent them from being removed from the J. N. ("Ding") Darling National Wildlife Refuge.

or 239/395-2233; www.shellmuseum.org), the only museum in the United States devoted solely to saltwater, freshwater, and land shells (yes, snails are included). If you don't get shell-shocked over the stuff, then stick to the beaches. This, however, is a far cry from the ubiquitous, tourist trappy shell factories you will see throughout the state. Shells from as far away as South Africa surround a 6-foot globe in the middle of the main exhibit hall, thus showing their geographic origins. A spinning wheel–shaped case identifies shells likely to wash up on Sanibel. Other exhibits are devoted to shells in tribal art, fossil shells found in Florida, medicinal qualities of various mollusks, the endangered Florida tree snail, and "sailor's Valentines"—shell craft made by natives of Barbados for sailors to bring home to their loved ones. The upstairs library attracts serious malacologists—for the uninitiated, those who study mollusks—and a shop purveys clever shell-themed gifts. The museum is open Tuesday through Sunday from 10am to 4pm; admission is $6 adults, $3 children 8 to 16, free for children under 8.

The months from February to April, or after any storm, are the prime times of the year to look for whelks, olives, scallops, sand dollars, conch, and many other varieties of shells. Low tide is the best time of day. The shells can be sharp, so wear Aqua Socks or old running shoes whenever you go walking on the beach.

With so many residents and visitors scouring Sanibel, you may have better luck finding that rare shell on the adjacent shoals and nearby islands, such as Upper Captiva and Cayo Costa (see "Nearby Island Hopping," later in this chapter). **Captiva Cruises** ★★ (© **239/472-5300;** www.captivacruises.com) has shelling trips from the South Seas Resort on Captiva daily at 9am and noon. They cost $35 for adults, $18 for children. Reservations are required. Captiva Cruises also has popular dolphin-watching and wildlife cruises, with narration by a naturalist from the Sanibel-Captiva Conservation Foundation, daily from 4 to 5:30pm. These cost $20 for adults, $10 for kids. All of Captiva Cruises' boats are air-conditioned and have restrooms and snack bars.

At least 15 charter-boat skippers also offer to take guests on shelling expeditions to these less-explored areas. Their half-day rates are about $200 for up to four people, so get up a group to go. Several operate from the **'Tween Waters Inn Marina** (© **239/472-5161**) on Captiva, including **Capt. Mike Fuery** (© **239/466-3649**). Others are based at **Jensen's Twin Palms Marina,** on Captiva (© **239/472-5800**), and at the **Sanibel Marina,** on North Yachtsman Drive, off Periwinkle Way east of Causeway Boulevard (© **239/472-2723**). They all distribute brochures at the chamber of commerce visitor center (p. 313) and are listed in the free tourist publications found there.

MORE WAYS TO ENJOY THE OUTDOORS

BICYCLING, WALKING, JOGGING & IN-LINE SKATING   Paved bicycle paths follow alongside most major roads, including the entire length of Periwinkle Way and along Sanibel-Captiva Road to Blind Pass, making Sanibel a paradise for cyclists, walkers, joggers, and in-line skaters. And you can walk or bike the 5-mile, one-way nature trail through the J. N. ("Ding") Darling National Wildlife Refuge.

The chamber of commerce visitor center has bike maps, as do Sanibel's rental firms: **Finnimore's Cycle Shop,** 2353 Periwinkle Way (© 239/472-5577); **The Bike Rental,** 2330 Palm Ridge Rd. (© 239/472-2241); **Billy's Rentals,** 1470 Periwinkle Way (© 239/472-5248); **Boats, Bikes & Beach Stuff,** 2427 Periwinkle Way (© 239/472-8717); and **Tarpon Bay Recreation,** at the north end of Tarpon Bay Road (© 239/472-8900). On Captiva, **Jim's Bike & Skate Rentals** on Andy Rosse Lane (© 239/472-1296) rents bikes and beach equipment. Bike rates range from $7 for up to 4 hours to $15 a day for basic models. Both Finnimore's and Jim's also rent in-line skates.

There are no bike paths on Captiva, where trees alongside the narrow roads can make for dangerous riding.

BOATING & FISHING   On Sanibel, rental boats and charter-fishing excursions are available from **The Boat House** at the Sanibel Marina, on North Yachtsman Drive (© **239/472-2531**), off Periwinkle Way east of Causeway Road. **Tarpon Bay Recreation,** at the north end of Tarpon Bay Road (© **239/472-8900**), rents boats with electric trolling motors and tackle for fishing.

On Captiva, check with **Sweet Water Rentals** at the 'Tween Waters Inn Marina (© **239/472-6376**), **Jensen's Twin Palms Marina** (© **239/472-5800**), and **McCarthy's Marina** (© **239/472-5200**), all on Captiva Road. Rental boats cost about $125 for half a day, $200 for a full day.

Many **charter-fishing captains** are docked at these marinas. Half-day rates are about $300 for up to four people. The skippers leave free brochures at the chamber of commerce visitor center (p. 313), and they're also listed in the free tourist publications found there.

CANOEING & KAYAKING   As noted under "Parks & Nature Preserves," above, **Tarpon Bay Recreation** (© **239/472-8900**; www.tarponbay.com) has guided canoe and kayak trips in the J. N. ("Ding") Darling National Wildlife Refuge. Do-it-yourselfers can rent canoes and kayaks here. They cost $20 for the first 2 hours, $5 for each additional hour. **Captiva Kayak Co./WildSide Adventures,** based at McCarthy's Marina (© **877/395-2925** or 239/395-2925), rents canoes and kayaks on Captiva, as does **'Tween Waters Inn Marina** (© **239/472-5161**).

Naturalist, avid environmentalist, and former Sanibel mayor Mark "Bird" Westall of **Canoe Adventures** ★★ (© 239/472-5218; fax 239/472-6833) takes visitors on guided canoe trips through the wildlife refuge and on the Sanibel River. His excursions are timed for low tide and cost $45 for adults, $25 for children under 18. He will tailor shorter trips to accommodate children or anyone else not up to 2½ to 3 hours in a canoe. Naturalist **Brian Houston** leads kayaking trips from 'Tween Waters Inn Marina on Captiva, but make your reservations at Tarpon Bay Recreation on Sanibel (© **239/472-8900**). Brian also charges $45 per person. **Captiva Kayak Co./WildSide Adventures,** based at McCarthy's Marina on Captiva (© **877/395-2925** or 239/395-2925), has both day and night back-bay ecology trips for $35 for adults, $25 for teenagers, $20 for children (add $10 to each price for night trips). They will customize tours, including camping on Cayo Costa (see "Nearby Island Hopping," later in this chapter) for advanced kayakers. Reservations are essential with all these operators. Also see the "Go the Blueway" box.

Go the Blueway

Inspired by the Calusa Native Americans, the first residents of the area, The Great Calusa Blueway encompasses two distinct regions of the Gulf of Mexico coast in over 40 miles of a new paddling trail for kayakers and canoers covering the waters of Lovers Key State Recreation Area, Mound Key State Archaeological Site, Koreshan State Historic Site, Fort Myers Beach, Sanibel, Captiva, and Pine islands, ending at Cayo Costa. Even cooler, the Blueway utilizes Global Positioning System (GPS) technology, marking key points along the trail to aid in navigation. The first portion of the trail meanders through Estero Bay, while the second segment, which opened in late 2004, centers on Pine Island Sound. Outfitters offer guided trips to view sunrises and sunsets, bird rookeries, manatees and dolphins, shelling, archaeology, and history. Starlight and full-moon excursions are special treats not to be missed. For those of you who want to go it alone, there are numerous rentals, launch areas, and trail maps also available. For more information on the Blueway, contact Lee County Parks & Recreation at ☎ 239/461-7400 or www.greatcalusablueway.com.

GOLF & TENNIS   Golfers may view a gallery of wild animals while playing the 5,600-yard, par-70, 18-hole course at the **Dunes Golf and Tennis Club,** 949 Sandcastle Rd., Sanibel (☎ 239/472-2535; www.dunesgolfsanibel.com), whose back 9 runs across a wildlife preserve. Call a day in advance for seasonal greens fees and a tee time. The Dunes also has seven tennis courts.

You can also play 9 water-bordered holes at **Beachview Golf Club,** 1100 Par View Dr. (☎ 239/472-2626). The **South Seas Resort** does have tennis courts and a 9-hole golf course, but they're for guests only.

SAILING   If you want to learn how to sail, noted yachties Steve and Doris Colgate have a branch of their **Offshore Sailing School** at the South Seas Resort (☎ 888/454-9002 or 239/472-5111, ext. 7141; www.offshore-sailing.com). You can either learn to sail or polish your skills here. Clinics ranging from half a day to a full week are available. Also ask about their popular women-only, father/son, and mother/daughter programs.

Also based on Captiva, two sailboats take guests out on the waters of Pine Island Sound: the *Adventure* (☎ 239/472-5300) and the *New Moon* (☎ 239/395-1782). They cost $95 per hour with a 2-hour minimum. Reservations are required.

Do-it-yourselfers can rent small sailboats from **Captiva Kayak Co./WildSide Adventures,** based at McCarthy's Marina (☎ 877/395-2925 or 239/395-2925). Prices range from $25 to $55 an hour, depending on the size of the craft.

WATERSPORTS   Sanibel may prohibit motorized watersports equipment on its beaches, but Captiva doesn't. **Yolo Watersports** (☎ 239/472-9656) offers parasailing and WaveRunner rentals on the beach in front of the Mucky Duck Restaurant, at the Gulf end of Andy Rosse Lane on Captiva.

MORE TO SEE & DO

At the east end of Periwinkle Way, the **Sanibel Lighthouse** has marked the entrance to San Carlos Bay since 1884. The lightkeepers used to live in the cottages at the base of the 94-foot tower. The now-automatic lighthouse makes for a lovely Kodak moment a la the Leaning Tower of Pisa, but it isn't open to visitors, though the grounds and beach are.

The best way to get the lay of the land and learn all about the islands' history is on a 2-hour **Sanibel Island Eco-History Trolley Tour,** staged by Adventures in Paradise (℅ **239/472-8443;** www.adventureinparadiseinc.com). Tours depart the chamber of commerce (p. 313) Monday through Saturday at 10:30am and 1pm and cost $30 for adults, $15 for children, and are free for kids 3 and under. Call for reservations.

In addition to its other trips, **Captiva Cruises** (℅ **239/472-5300;** www. captivacruises.com) goes out daily on sunset cruises from the South Seas Resort on Captiva. These cost $18 for adults, $10 for children ages 6 through 12. Call for daily departure times and reservations.

SHOPPING

For excellent window-shopping, you can burn up a rainy day at Sanibel's numerous upscale boutiques carrying expensive jewelry, apparel, and gifts. Many are in **Periwinkle Place** and **Tahitian Gardens,** the main shopping centers along Periwinkle Way. The larger Periwinkle Place sports mostly high-end men's and women's clothiers, while Tahitian Gardens has some excellent gift shops, including **The Cheshire Cat** (℅ **239/482-8697**), offering nature toys and other unique items for kids.

More than a dozen Sanibel galleries feature original works of art; pick up a gallery guide at the chamber of commerce visitor center (p. 313). On Captiva, the treehouselike **Jungle Drums,** on Andy Rosse Lane (℅ **239/395-2266**), has the area's most unique collection of wildlife art.

Founded in 1899, **Bailey's General Store** is still going strong at the corner of Periwinkle Way and Tarpon Bay Road (℅ **239/472-1516**), with a supermarket, deli, salad bar, hardware store, beach shop, shoe repair, and Western Union all under one roof.

Bailey's General Store is open daily from 7am to 9pm. Most other shops are open Monday through Saturday from 9am to 6pm, Sunday from noon to 5pm.

ACCOMMODATIONS YOU CAN AFFORD

Sanibel & Captiva Central Reservations, Inc. (℅ **800/325-1352** or 239/472-0457; fax 239/472-2178; www.sanibel-captivarent.com), and **1-800-SANIBEL** (℅ **800/726-4235** or 239/472-1800; fax 239/395-9690; www.1-800-sanibel. com) are reservations services that will book you into most condominiums and cottages here.

In general, Sanibel and Captiva room and condominium rates are highest during the shelling season, February through April. January is usually somewhat less expensive. But note that most rates fall drastically during the off season. Don't hesitate to ask for a discount or special deal then. Since most properties on the islands are geared to 1-week vacations, you can also save by purchasing a package deal if you're staying for 7 nights or longer.

The islands' sole campground, the **Periwinkle Trailer Park,** 1119 Periwinkle Way, Sanibel Island (℅ **239/472-1433**), is so popular it doesn't even advertise. No other camping is permitted on either Sanibel or Captiva.

SANIBEL ISLAND

Palm View Motel In a quiet residential area less than a block from the Holiday Inn Beach Resort and Morgan's Forest restaurant, this little property is one of Sanibel's few inexpensive motels. The best choices here are the spacious, well-ventilated one- and two-bedroom apartments, but even the smaller efficiencies have kitchens and separate living and sleeping areas. There's a hot tub in the backyard plus fire pits and barbecues, and pets are allowed. A 2001 renovation included a remodeling of the suites, new brick walkways, major plantings, outdoor retreats, gardens, and water effects.

706 Donax St., Sanibel Island, FL 33957. © 239/472-1606. Fax 239/472-6733. www.palmviewsanibel.com. 5 units. Winter $145–$185 efficiency and apts; off season $85–$135 efficiency and apts. Weekly rates available. MC, V. Pets accepted ($10 per day). **Amenities:** Jacuzzi; free guest laundry; free bike, beach chair, and umbrella lending. *In room:* A/C, TV/VCR, kitchen, coffeemaker, hair dryer, iron, microwave.

Tarpon Tale Inn ✰ *Finds* Owners Dawn and Joe Ramsey preside over this low-slung gray building in Sanibel's Old Town, the island's first settlement where the ferries from Fort Myers used to dock near the lighthouse. White walls and tile floors make their comfortable units bright; French doors lead to gardens dense with sea grape, palm, and ficus trees, which provide privacy for a large outdoor hot tub. Three of their five units (which are attached yet completely private bungalows hidden amidst palms, bougainvillea, hibiscus, ferns, sea grapes, gumbo limbos, and Key limes) have separate bedrooms, while two other "deluxe studios" actually are two-bedroom suites. All units have shower-only bathrooms. Continental breakfast makings are delivered the night before. Smoking is not permitted inside the inn's rooms. There is no daily maid service, though towels and linens are exchanged every 3 days or as needed.

367 Periwinkle Way, Sanibel Island, FL 33957. © 888/345-0939 or 239/472-0939. Fax 239/472-6202. www.tarpontale.com. 5 units. $99–$159 double (depending on which room and length of stay). Rates include continental breakfast. AE, DC, DISC, MC, V. Some pets accepted for a fee; call first. **Amenities:** Jacuzzi; free use of bikes; free use of beach chairs and umbrellas; coin-op washers and dryers; free local calls. *In room:* A/C, TV/VCR, kitchen w/stove and microwave, coffeemaker, hair dryer and iron on request, CD player, no phone (though guest phones are in common room and laundry room).

Worth an Off-Season Splurge

Sundial Beach Resort ✰✰ *Kids* The largest resort on Sanibel, this condominium complex lacks intimacy but has lots to keep families occupied (they even provide jogging strollers so you don't have to schlep your own), from a palm-studded, beachside pool area to a complimentary marine biology program and a small ecology center with a touch tank. The one-, two-, and three-bedroom condominiums are housed in two- and three-story buildings (as high as they get on Sanibel) and have screened balconies overlooking the beach or tropically landscaped gardens. Rooms are pleasantly decorated in a Golden Girls kind of way.

1451 Middle Gulf Dr., Sanibel Island, FL 33957. © 800/237-4184 or 239/481-3636. Fax 239/481-4947. www.sundialresort.com. 270 units. Winter $349–$519 condo apt; off season $179–$429 condo apt. Packages available. AE, DC, DISC, MC, V. **Amenities:** 4 restaurants; 2 bars; 5 heated outdoor pools; 12 tennis courts; exercise room; Jacuzzi; watersports equipment rental; bike rental; children's programs; game room; concierge; activities desk; business center; limited room service; massage; babysitting; laundry service; coin-op washers and dryers. *In room:* A/C, TV/VCR, kitchen, coffeemaker, hair dryer, iron.

CAPTIVA ISLAND
An Off-Season Deal

Captiva Island Inn Bed & Breakfast ✰ This B&B complex sits virtually surrounded by restaurants, art galleries, and boutiques along Captiva's block-long commercial street. That can make it a bit too busy for some eyes and ears, but it has its charms. Two suites in the Key West–style main building open to porches overlooking the lane, while four Dutch clapboard cottages sit out back on the fringes of a gravel parking lot (you get just enough yard here for hammocks and a gas grill). The ceiling in one Martha's Vineyard-esque cottage that once housed aviator Charles Lindbergh has clouds painted against a blue sky. It and the rest of the units have ceiling fans, kitchens, large bathrooms, queen-size sofa beds in their living rooms, cool tile floors, and designer bed linens (including down comforters for the occasional chilly night). Some rooms have only showers in their bathrooms. Guests also get free use of bicycles and towels and chairs for the beach (a block away) and get a complimentary full breakfast at the **Keylime Bistro,** which has good American-style food and superb Key lime cheesecake and is open from 8am to 10pm daily.

11509 Andy Rosse Lane (P.O. Box 848), Captiva Island, FL 33924. © **800/454-9898** or 239/395-0882. Fax 239/395-0862. www.captivaislandinn.com. 12 units, 1 5-bedroom, 5-bathroom house. Winter $190–$300 double; off season $99–$150 double. Rates include full breakfast. AE, DISC, MC, V. **Amenities:** Access to nearby spa; free use of bikes. *In room:* A/C, TV, fridge, coffeemaker.

Worth an Off-Season Splurge

'Tween Waters Inn ★★   Wedged between the Gulf beach and the bay on the narrowest part of Captiva, this venerable establishment was the regular haunt of cartoonist J. N. ("Ding") Darling. Anne Morrow Lindbergh also dined here often while writing *A Gift from the Sea.* Just as Darling preserved the islands' wildlife, the 'Tween Waters has saved the cottages he stayed in. Situated in a sandy palm grove, these pink shiplap buildings have been upgraded but still capture Old Florida. Some face the Gulf, others, the bay. Themed to honor their famous guests, they range in size from the bayside honeymoon cottage with barely enough room for its king-size bed and a tiny kitchen to a three-bedroom, two-bathroom house. The spacious hotel rooms and apartments are in three modern buildings on stilts; they all have screened balconies facing the Gulf or the bay.

15951 Captiva Rd., Captiva Island, FL 33924. © **800/223-5865** or 239/472-5161. Fax 239/472-0249. www.tween-waters.com. 138 units. Winter $245–$285 double, $250–$585 suite; $290–$650 cottage; off season $155–$230 double, $210–$440 suite, $210–$460 cottage. Rates include continental breakfast. Packages available. AE, DC, MC, V. Pets accepted in some units ($15 per day). **Amenities:** 2 restaurants; 2 bars; outdoor pool; 3 tennis courts; exercise room; massage room; Jacuzzi; watersports equipment rentals; bike rentals; coin-op washers and dryers. *In room:* A/C, TV, dataport, kitchen (suites and cottages), fridge, coffeemaker, hair dryer, iron (suites only), safe.

COTTAGES

The islands have several Old Florida–style cottages that offer charming and often less-expensive alternatives to hotels and condominiums. Some of the best are members of the **Sanibel-Captiva Small Inns & Cottages Association.** You can contact the association (via its website only) at www.sanibelsmallinns.com for a complete listing of properties.

Sitting between two condominium complexes off Middle Gulf Drive, **Gulf Breeze Cottages** ★★, 1081 Shell Basket Lane, Sanibel Island, FL 33957 (© **800/388-2842** or 239/472-1626; www.gbreeze.com), is a collection of clapboard cottages separated from the beach by a lawn with covered picnic area and outdoor shower. One two-story building is divided into four efficiencies (the pick is no. 7, with a two-way view of the Gulf from its big picture windows). Rates are $215 to $350 a day in winter, $115 to $230 a day off season.

With only one monstrous mansion standing between them and a narrow bay beach near Sanibel Lighthouse, **Buttonwood Cottages** ★, 1234 Buttonwood

Lane, Sanibel Island, FL 33957 (℃ **887/395-COTTAGE** or 239/395-9061; fax 239/395-2620; www.buttonwoodcottages.com), are less expensive options at $125 to $220 a day in winter, $75 to $160 off season. Remodeled and equipped with many modern amenities, the five units occupy two long cottages built on stilts. Four of them have screened porches, with two overlooking a lushly tropical backyard sporting two hammocks and two hot tubs. The Lighthouse Cafe (see "Great Deals on Dining," below) is around the corner.

GREAT DEALS ON DINING

No restaurant can survive on these affluent islands without serving good food, so you're assured of getting a fine meal wherever you go. Oddly, only a handful of restaurants offer dining with water views.

SANIBEL ISLAND

Much of the "help" on this affluent island dines at **Jerry's Family Restaurant,** 1700 Periwinkle Way at Casa Ybel Road (℃ **239/472-9300**), which offers wholesome and inexpensive diner fare (ingredients come fresh from the adjacent Jerry's Supermarket). Both the restaurant and the supermarket are open daily from 6am to 11pm. Breakfast is served from 6am to 4pm, and you can usually get a table quickly here (which can't be said of Sanibel's other popular breakfast spots).

You'll find very reasonably priced pub fare at Sanibel's sports bars, such as **The Lazy Flamingo II** (see below) and **Sanibel Grill,** 703 Tarpon Bay Rd., near Palm Ridge Road (℃ **239/472-3128**), which actually serves as the bar for Timbers, the fine seafood restaurant next door (see below).

For picnics at Sanibel's beaches or on a canoe, the deli and bakery in **Bailey's General Store,** at Periwinkle Way and Tarpon Bay Road (℃ **239/472-1516**), carries a gourmet selection of breads, cheeses, and meats. **Huxter's Deli and Market,** 1203 Periwinkle Way, east of Donax Street (℃ **239/472-6988**), has sandwich fixings and "beach box" lunches to go.

Hungry Heron ✦✦ *Kids* AMERICAN   This tropically decorated eatery is Sanibel's most popular family restaurant. There's something for everyone on the huge, tabloid-size menu—from hot and cold appetizers and overstuffed "seawiches" to pasta and steamed shellfish. And if the 280 regular items aren't enough, there's a list of nightly specials. Seafood, steaks, and stir-fries from a sizzling skillet are popular with local residents, who bring the kids here for fun and a children's menu. An all-you-can-eat breakfast buffet on Saturday and Sunday mornings is an excellent value.

In Palm Ridge Place, 2330 Palm Ridge Rd. (at Periwinkle Way). ℃ 239/395-2300. Reservations not accepted, but call for preferred seating. Main courses $9–$18; sandwiches, burgers, and snacks $6–$11; weekend breakfast buffet $9 adults, $5 children under 10. AE, DISC, MC, V. Mon–Fri 11am–9pm; Sat–Sun 7:30am–9pm (breakfast buffet 11am Sat, to noon Sun).

McT's Shrimp House & Tavern SEAFOOD   Shrimp reigns at this casual Old Florida–style establishment, where you'll see a line outside at 4pm waiting

---

(*Tips* **Deals on Meals**

Local restaurants often run advertisements containing discount coupons in the "Sanibel-Captiva Shopper's Guide," a free publication available at the chamber of commerce visitor center.

for the early-bird specials served to the first 100 persons in the door. Everyone else gets to view the daily catch displayed in a chiller case, including the night's shrimp ready for the chef to prepare in one of at least a dozen ways, from steamed to fried in a coconut-and-almond batter. There are also grouper and swordfish, plus steaks and chicken for the land-minded, but stick to the shrimp here (see below for The Timbers Restaurant & Fish Market, which does a much better job of cooking fish). McT's Tavern offers an extensive choice of appetizers and light dinners. All you can eat peel-and-eat shrimp and stone crabs are available nightly, though if it's not stone crab season (Oct–May) the crab will likely be frozen.

1523 Periwinkle Way (at Fitzhugh St.). (C) 239/472-3161. Main courses $13–$22; early-bird specials $10. AE, DC, DISC, MC, V. Shrimp House daily 4:45–10pm. McT's Tavern daily 4pm–midnight. Closed Thanksgiving and Christmas.

Sanibel Cafe ★ *Value* AMERICAN   Seashells are the not-so-original theme at Lynda and Ken Boyce's pleasant cafe, whose tables are museum-like glass cases containing delicate fossilized specimens from the Miocene and Pliocene epochs. Fresh-squeezed orange and grapefruit juice, Danish Havarti omelets, and homemade muffins and biscuits highlight the breakfast menu (eggs Benedict and fruit-filled waffles are served until closing). Lunch features specialty sandwiches; shrimp, Greek, and chicken-and-grape salads made with a very light, fat-free dressing; and a limited list of main courses such as grilled or blackened chicken breast. At dinner, they add homemade meatloaf, crunchy grouper, and certified Angus steaks. Fatten up on Lynda's homemade red-raspberry jam, apple or cherry crisps, and terrific Key lime pie.

In the Tahitian Gardens Shops, 2007 Periwinkle Way. (C) 239/472-5323. Call ahead for preferred seating. Main courses $7.50–$17; breakfast $3.50–$9; salads, sandwiches, and burgers $4.50–$13. MC, V. Daily 7am–9pm.

Super-Cheap Eats

Grandma Dot's Seaside Saloon SEAFOOD   One of Sanibel's most popular lunch spots, this open-air but screened cafe on the docks of Sanibel Marina offers excellent salads (try the seafood Caesar) and fine sandwiches plus a few main courses led by broiled grouper in a sauce of lemon, dill, butter, and white wine.

At Sanibel Marina, 634 N. Yachtsman Dr. (C) 239/472-8138. Reservations not accepted. Main courses $6–$23; salads and sandwiches $6–$12. MC, V. Daily 11:30am–7:30pm.

The Lazy Flamingo II *Value* SEAFOOD/PUB FARE   The Lazy Flamingo is a down-homey type place where the food is consistently good. Locals and visitors become repeat customers who flock here for reasonably priced food, a wide choice of beers iced down in a huge box behind the bar, and sports TVs. Some of that beer is used to steam shrimp and a finger-stinging collection of oysters, clams, and spices known as "The Pot." Best pick, however, is grouper from the charcoals, as either a main course or a sandwich. The flamingo-pink menu also has an array of sandwiches, burgers, fish platters, and very spicy "Dead Parrot Wings." Fillet your own catch, and the chef will cook it to order for you. Happy-hour prices prevail whenever football games are on the TVs. A sister institution, the **Lazy Flamingo I,** 6520-C Pine Ave., at Sanibel-Captiva Road, ¼ mile south of Blind Pass ((C) **239/472-5353**), has the same menu and hours.

1036 Periwinkle Way, west of Causeway Blvd. (C) 239/472-6939. Reservations not accepted. Main courses $11–$15; sandwiches and snacks $5–$9. Cook your catch $8. AE, DISC, MC, V. Daily 11:30am–1am.

Lighthouse Cafe ⭐ *Value* AMERICAN   This casual storefront establishment dishes up breakfast omelets that are meals in themselves, especially the ocean frittata containing delicately seasoned scallops, crab meat, shrimp, broccoli, and fresh mushrooms, and crowned with an artichoke heart and creamy Alfredo sauce. Seafood Benedict is one of the more decadent offerings. For the light(er) eater, a slew of creative sandwiches are served after 11am. Reasonably priced cafe-style dinners are served during winter only. For the best pancakes ever, the Lighthouse Cafe has cornered the market, using a special recipe that draws up to 700 people a day in season. For just $3.95, you can go nuts on malted blueberry or banana pancakes, or pretend to be healthy with granola nut wholewheat hot cakes with sliced bananas.

In Seahorse Shops, 362 Periwinkle Way (at Buttonwood Lane, east of Causeway Rd.). ℂ 239/472-0303. Call ahead to get on waiting list. Main courses $10–$15; breakfast $3.50–$7.50; sandwiches and salads $4.50–$8.50. MC, V. Mid-Dec to Easter daily 7am–3pm and 5–9pm; Easter to mid-Dec daily 7am–3pm.

Worth a Splurge

Mad Hatter ⭐⭐ ECLECTIC   One of Sanibel's best choices for a romantic special dinner, this New American Gulf-front restaurant has only 12 tables, but each has a view that's perfect at sunset. The ever-changing eclectic menu features flavors from around the world, such as Thai-style peanut sauce over a seared, sesame-encrusted yellowfin tuna steak. The jumbo shrimp Wellington is a fascinating twist on the classic beef dish, and the stuffed crab served with a lobster velouté is another winner.

6467 Sanibel-Captiva Rd., at Blind Pass. ℂ 239/472-0033. Reservations highly recommended. Main courses $26–$34. AE, MC, V. Dec 15–Jan 31 daily 5–9pm; Feb 1–Easter Sun–Mon 5–9:30pm, Tues–Sat 11:30am–2pm and 5–9:30pm; Easter–May 31 daily 5–9:30pm; June 1–Dec 14 Mon–Sat 5–9:30pm. Closed Sept after Labor Day.

The Timbers Restaurant & Fish Market ⭐⭐ SEAFOOD/STEAK   This casual upstairs restaurant, with bamboo railings, oversize canvas umbrellas, and paintings of tropical scenes through faux windows, consistently is Sanibel's best place for fresh fish and aged beef hot off the charcoal grill. It's true what they say—"We serve it fresh or we don't serve it at all." In the fish market out front, you can view the catch and have the chef charcoal-grill or blacken it to order. The steaks, cut on the premises, are the island's best.

703 Tarpon Bay Rd. (between Periwinkle Way and Palm Ridge Rd.). ℂ 239/472-3128. Main courses $15–$23; early birds get $2.50 off regular price. AE, MC, V. Winter daily 4:30–9:30pm; off season daily 5–9:30pm.

CAPTIVA ISLAND

Big deli sandwiches and picnic fare are available at the **Captiva Island Store,** Captiva Road at Andy Rosse Lane (ℂ **239/472-2374**), and the gourmet-oriented **C. W.'s Market and Deli,** at the entrance to the South Seas Resort (ℂ **239/472-5111**). The beach is a block from these stores.

Also, see the review for the Captiva Island Inn Bed & Breakfast on p. 320 for information on the **Keylime Bistro.**

The Bubble Room ⭐⭐⭐ *Kids* STEAK/SEAFOOD   Imagine Walt Disney on acid and you'll understand where the Bubble Room is coming from. The kitschiest restaurant you'll probably ever find, the Bubble Room's tongue-in-cheeky American cuisine is complemented by a decor that's filled with Christmas and Hollywood memorabilia from the '30s, '40s, and '50s. Distracting, to say the least—but in a very good way—The Bubble Room makes it hard to decide which is cooler, the Henny Young-One boneless breast of young chicken, the prime ribs Weissmuller, or the thousands of movie stills, puppets, antique juke-boxes, or toy trains. *Note:* We've gotten complaints about the "awful" food here (others recommend the diagonally opposite **Keylime Bistro**—see p. 321—instead), but we still think The Bubble Room is fun, with good (though admit-tedly not fabulous) food and a great atmosphere.

15001 Captiva Rd. (at Andy Rosse Lane). © 239/472-5558. www.bubbleroomrestaurant.com. Reservations not accepted, but call for preferred seating. Main courses $17–$30. AE, DC, DISC, MC, V. Daily 11:30am–2:30pm and 5–10pm. Closed Christmas.

The Cabbage Key Restaurant ★★★ AMERICAN   You can only get here by boat, but there are constant shuttles from Captiva, so get on one and experi-ence the true meaning of cheeseburgers in paradise. Jimmy Buffet allegedly wrote his famous song here, and when you get here, you'll understand why. The cheeseburgers rock, the setting is sublime, and there are no fried foods or microwave in sight. It's a place rich in history—and in money: there are thou-sands of dollar bills here, signed and stuck to the walls and ceiling with masking tape.

Intracoastal Water Marker 60, North Fort Myers. © 239/283-22781. Main courses $5–$15. Mon–Sat 7:30–9am; Sun 7:30–10am; Mon–Fri 11:15am–3pm; Sat 11:15am–4pm; Mon–Sat 6–8:30pm; Sun 6–7pm.

The Green Flash ★ SEAFOOD   You can't miss this restaurant, which sits at the infamous "curve" where Captiva Road takes a sharp turn to the north. You won't see the real "green flash" as the sun sets here, because this modern build-ing looks eastward across Pine Island Sound, but it does make for a nice view at lunch. And seeing the full moon turn the sound into glistening silver is worth having at least an evening drink here. The overall quality of the cuisine here is very good, and the prices are very reasonable for Captiva. Start with oysters Rockefeller or shrimp bisque. Both are house specialties, as is the garlicky grouper "café de Paris" and salmon with a dill-accented béarnaise sauce.

15183 Captiva Rd. © 239/472-3337. Reservations recommended. Main courses $13–$22. AE, DC, DISC, MC, V. Daily 11:30am–3:30pm and 5:30–9:30pm (bar open 11:30am–9:30pm).

Mucky Duck ★ SEAFOOD/PUB FARE   A Captiva institution since 1976, this lively, British-style pub, named after a pub of the same name in Shake-speare's Stratford-Upon-Avon in the U.K., is the only place on either island where you can dine right by the beach. If you don't get a real seat with this great view, the humorous staff will gladly roll a fake window over to appease you. The menu offers a selection of fresh seafood items, plus English fish and chips, steak-and-sausage pie, and a ploughman's lunch. There's also a vegetarian platter. No smoking is allowed inside. You can't make a reservation, but you can order drinks, listen to live music (Mon–Sat), and bide your wait at beachside picnic tables out front (come early for sunset).

Andy Rosse Lane (on the Gulf). © 239/472-3434. Reservations not accepted. Lunch $5.50–$11; dinner main courses $13–$19. AE, DC, DISC, MC, V. Mon–Sat 11am–2:30pm and 5–9:30pm.

R. C. Otter's Island Eats ★★ *Value* AMERICAN   Occupying an old clap-board-sided island cottage, this Key West–style cafe brings informality and good, inexpensive food to Captiva. In contrast to the island's 15 or so formal haute-cuisine restaurants, you can dine here in your bare feet and not spend a fortune for an excellent breakfast, snack, lunch, or full meal. The tables are cov-ered with wrapping paper, and rolls of paper towels substitute for napkins. The choice seats are under ceiling fans on the front porch or beneath umbrellas on the brick patio. In hot weather, you can opt for the air-conditioned dining room, whose walls are adorned with the works of local artists. The wide-ranging menu includes salads, hot dogs, burgers, sandwiches, stir-fries, meatloaf, country-fried steak, broiled fish, and soft-shell crabs, plus delicious nightly specials. The island's best breakfasts are equally varied, from bacon and eggs to a seafood quesadilla. Musicians perform out in the yard every day.

11506 Andy Rosse Lane. © 239/395-1142. Reservations not accepted, but call for preferred seating. Main courses $10–$20; breakfast $6–$12; salads, sandwiches, and burgers $6–$12. AE, DISC, MC, V. Daily 7:30am–10pm (breakfast to 11:30am).

SANIBEL & CAPTIVA ISLANDS AFTER DARK

You won't find glitzy nightclubs on these family-oriented islands, but night owls do have some fun places to roost at the resorts and restaurants mentioned above. Here's a brief recap:

ON SANIBEL   The Sundial Beach Resort's **Beaches Bar & Grill,** 1451 Middle Gulf Dr. (© **239/472-4151**), features entertainers during dinner, then live bands for dancing from 9pm on. The **Patio Lounge,** in the Jacaranda, 1223 Periwinkle Way (© **239/472-1771**), attracts an affluent crowd of middle-agers and seniors to its live music every evening. **McT's Tavern,** 1523 Periwinkle Way (© **239/472-3161**), has darts, video games, and a large-screen TV for sports fans. The **Sanibel Grill,** 703 Tarpon Bay Rd. (© **239/472-4453**), and the two **Lazy Flamingo** branches (see "Great Deals on Dining," above) are other popular sports bars.

The Pirate Players, a group of professional actors, perform Broadway dramas and comedies from November to April in Sanibel's state-of-the-art, 150-seat **J. Howard Wood Theatre,** 2200 Periwinkle Way (© **239/472-4109**). The **Old Schoolhouse Theater,** 1905 Periwinkle Way (© **239/472-6862;** www.old schoolhousetheater.com), complements its neighbor by offering Broadway musicals and revues from December to April. Call for the current schedule and prices.

ON CAPTIVA   Local songwriters perform their works nightly at **R. C. Otter's Island Eats,** 11500 Andy Rosse Lane (© **239/395-1142**). The **Crow's Nest Lounge,** in the 'Tween Waters Inn, on Captiva Road (© **239/472-5161**), is Captiva's top nightspot for dancing. **Chadwick's Lounge,** at the entrance to the South Seas Resort (© **239/472-5111**), has a large dance floor and music from 9pm on.

NEARBY ISLAND HOPPING

Sanibel and Captiva are jumping-off points for island-hopping boat trips to barrier islands and keys teeming with ancient legends and Robinson Crusoe–style beaches. You don't have to get completely lost out there, however, because several islets have comfortable inns and restaurants. The trip across shallow Pine Island Sound is itself a sightseeing adventure, with playful dolphins surfing on the boats' wakes and a variety of cormorants, egrets, frigate birds, and (in winter) rare white pelicans flying above or lounging on sandbars between meals.

Captiva Cruises (© **239/472-5300;** www.captivacruises.com) has daily trips from the South Seas Resort on Captiva. One vessel goes daily to Cabbage Key, departing at 10:30am and returning at 3:30pm. It stops at Useppa Island going and coming Tuesday through Sunday. During the winter months, another goes to Boca Grande by way of Cayo Costa State Park, departing Tuesday through Saturday at 10:30am and returning at 4pm. These day trips cost $28 for adults, $15 for children ages 6 through 12 to Cabbage Key or Useppa; $35 for adults,

$18 for children ages 6 through 12 to Boca Grande or Cayo Costa. Reservations are required.

From Pine Island off Fort Myers, you can take **Tropic Star Cruises'** daily ferry service (① **239/283-0015;** www.tropicstarcruises.com) to Cayo Costa (see below).

CABBAGE KEY ★★

You never know who's going to get off a boat at 100-acre Cabbage Key and walk unannounced into the funky **Cabbage Key Inn** ★★, a rustic house built in 1938 by the son and daughter-in-law of mystery novelist Mary Roberts Rinehart. Ernest Hemingway liked to hang out here in the early days, and novelist John D. MacDonald was a frequent guest 30 years later. Today, you could find yourself rubbing elbows at the bar with the likes of Walter Cronkite, Ted Koppel, Sean Connery, or Julia Roberts. Singer and avid yachtie Jimmy Buffett likes Cabbage Key so much that it inspired his hit song "Cheeseburger in Paradise."

A path leads from the tiny marina across a lawn dotted with coconut palms to this white clapboard house that sits atop an ancient Calusa shell mound. Guests dine in the comfort of two screened porches and seek libations in the Rineharts' library-turned-bar, its pine-paneled walls now plastered with dollar bills left by visitors. The straight-back chairs and painted wooden tables show their age, but that's part of Cabbage Key's laid-back, don't-give-a-you-know-what charm.

In addition to the famous thick, juicy cheeseburgers so loved by Jimmy Buffett (and erroneously thought by the misinformed to have hailed from Key West), the house specialties are fresh broiled fish and shrimp steamed in beer. Lunches range from $5 to $10; main courses at dinner, $15 to $25.

Most visitors come out here for the day, but if you want to stay overnight, the Cabbage Key Inn has six rooms and six cottages. The more expensive cottages, four of which have kitchens, are preferable to the rooms. Although the units have private bathrooms and air conditioners, they are very basic by today's standards, and some of their original 1920s furnishings have seen better days. Service for overnight guests can leave a lot to be desired, and there's no place on the islet to buy snacks or sundries. If you do decide to rough it, rates are $89 single or double for rooms, $145 to $239 for cottages. For information or reservations, contact Cabbage Key Inn, P.O. Box 200, Pineland, FL 33945 (① **239/283-2278;** fax 239/283-1384; www.cabbage-key.com).

Captiva Cruises (① **239/472-5300;** www.captivacruises.com) goes to Cabbage Key daily from Captiva Island, charging $28 for adults, $15 for children ages 6 through 12 (reservations are required). You can also get here from Pine Island via **Tropic Star Cruises** (① **239/283-0015;** www.tropicstarcruises.com), which depart from Knight's Landing marina daily (p. 301). Fares are $25 for adults, $15 for children under 7. Call for departure times. You can also get here from Pine Island with **Island Charters** (① **800/340-3321** or 239/283-1113).

CAYO COSTA ★★★

Short of Tom Hanks in *Castaway,* you can't get any more deserted than at **Cayo Costa State Park** ★★★ (pronounced *Kay*-oh *Cos*-tah), which occupies a 2,132-acre, completely unspoiled barrier island with miles of white-sand beaches, pine forests, mangrove swamps, oak-palm hammocks, and grasslands. Other than natural wildlife, the only permanent residents here are park rangers.

Day-trippers can bring their own supplies and use a picnic area with pavilions. A free tram carries visitors from the sound-side dock to the Gulf beach.

Fishing with the Bushes

Former President George Bush, present President George W. Bush, Florida Governor Jeb Bush—indeed, the entire Bush clan—like to retreat to **Boca Grande** ★★ for a little rest and relaxation every now and then. And well they should, for this charming village on Gasparilla Island is a head-of-state's kind of place. The du Ponts, the Astors, the Morgans, the Vanderbilts, and other moneyed folk started coming here in the 1920s and still turn the island into a Florida version of Nantucket during their winter "social season." In addition to the warm weather, the lure was then, and still is, some of the world's best tarpon fishing. Descendants of the watermen who were here first still guide the rich and famous. They live in modest homes on streets named Dam-If-I-Know, Dam-If-I-Care, and Dam-If-I-Will. You can see their backyards full of boats and fishnets, but high hedges hide the manicured "beachfronter" mansions over by the Gulf.

You can explore the little village in a few hours on foot or on a bike rented from **Island Bike 'n' Beach,** 333 Park Ave. (© **941/964-0711**). The pink-brick **Railroad Depot,** at the corner of Park Avenue and 4th Street, has been restored to the turn-of-the-20th-century grandeur it enjoyed when the rich arrived by train. It now houses a cluster of upscale boutiques and the **Loose Caboose** restaurant and ice-cream parlor (© **941/964-0440**), where movie stars have been seen satiating their sweet

The state maintains 12 very basic cabins and a primitive campground on the northern end of the island near Johnson Shoals, where the shelling is spectacular. Cabins cost $20 a day, and campsites are $13 a day year-round. For camping or cabin reservations, call © **800/326-3521** or go to www.reserveamerica. com. There's running water on the island but no electricity.

The park is open daily from 8am to sundown. There's a $1-per-person honor-system admission fee for day visitors. You can rent single-seat kayaks for $35 a day, $45 a day for two-seaters; for reservations, call the *Tropic Star* on Pine Island (© **239/283-0015;** www.tropicstarcruises.com).

For more information contact **Cayo Costa State Park,** P.O. Box 1150, Boca Grande, FL 33921 (© **941/964-0375;** www.floridastateparks.org/cayocosta). Office hours are Monday through Friday from 8am to 5pm.

UPPER (NORTH) CAPTIVA

Cut off by a pass from Captiva, its northern barrier-island sibling is occupied by the upscale resort of **North Captiva Island Club,** P.O. Box 1000, Pineland, FL 33945 (© **800/576-7343** or 239/395-1001; fax 239/472-5836; www.north captiva.com). Despite the development, however, about 750 of the island's 1,000 acres are included in a state preserve. The club rents accommodations ranging from efficiencies to luxury homes. There's scheduled water-taxi service from **Jensen's Twin Palms Marina** on Captiva (© **239/472-5800**), or you can get here from Matson Marine on Pine Island with **Island Charters** (© **800/340-3321** or 239/283-1113). Both charge $25 per person round-trip.

teeth. **Banyan Street** (actually 2nd St.) is canopied with tangled banyan trees and is one of the prettiest places for a stroll. The **Johann Fust Community Library,** at Gasparilla Road and 10th Street (© **941/964-2488**), contains the extraordinary **Du Pont Shell Collection,** gathered by Henry Francis du Pont during nearly 50 years of combing the island's beaches. At the island's south end, **Boca Grande Lighthouse Museum and Visitor's Center** (© **941/964-0060**) occupies the wood-frame lighthouse that began marking the pass into Charlotte Harbor in 1890. Exhibits explain the island's history, its tarpon fishing, and its wildlife and seashells. The white-sand beaches of **Gasparilla Island State Recreation Area** (© **941/ 964-0375;** www.floridastateparks.org/gasparillaisland) trim the lighthouse.

Captiva Cruises (© **239/472-5300**) has daily trips here during the winter season (see "Nearby Island Hopping," above). The fare is $35 for adults, $18 for children under 7, and reservations are required. *Tropic Star* cruises (© **239/283-0015;** www.tropicstarcruises.com) come here daily from Pine Island off Fort Myers (p. 301). Fares are $25 for adults and $15 for children ages 6 through 12. Call for departure times.

For more information, contact the **Boca Grande Area Chamber of Commerce,** 5800 Gasparilla Rd. (P.O. Box 704), Boca Grande, FL 33921 (© **941/964-0568;** fax 941/964-0620; www.bocagrandechamber.com).

USEPPA ISLAND

Useppa was a refuge of President Theodore Roosevelt and his tarpon-loving industrialist friends at the turn of the 20th century. New York advertising magnate Barron G. Collier bought the island in 1906 and built a lovely wooden home overlooking Pine Island Sound. His mansion is now the **Collier Inn,** where day-trippers and overnight guests can partake of lunches and seafood dinners in a country-club ambience. They can also visit the **Useppa Museum,** which explains the island's history and displays 4,000-year-old Calusa artifacts. Admission is by $2 donation.

The Collier Inn is the centerpiece of the **Useppa Island Club,** an exclusive development with more than 100 luxury homes, all in the clapboard-sided, tin-roofed style of Old Florida. For information, rates, and reservations, contact **Collier Inn & Cottages,** P.O. Box 640, Bokeelia, FL 33922 (© **888/735-6335** or 239/283-1061; fax 239/283-0290; www.useppa.com).

4 Naples ★★★

42 miles S of Fort Myers, 106 miles W of Miami, 185 miles S of Tampa

Ah, sleepy, swanky Naples. A place that may have defined the meaning of R&R, considering the fact that there's not much to do here besides linger on the beach, play golf, and dream that this isn't just a vacation but a way of life, Naples is easily Southwest Florida's most sophisticated city. And while Naples has its requisite waterfront mansions, sprawling country club fairways, and a thoroughfare of pricey boutiques and restaurants, it's not nearly as upper crusty as, say, Palm Beach or Beverly Hills. Although the people are indeed very Ralph Lauren upper crusty types, heavy on the starch, the snobbery factor and upper tax bracket lockjaw is conspicuously absent here, unlike how people usually characterize the east coast of Florida, which is just as monied, but nowhere near as friendly or laid-back.

Don't even think of thumbing your nose at the long-bearded man dressed in ratty shorts and a Hawaiian T-shirt until you make sure he doesn't hop into a Bentley or zillion-dollar yacht. Therein lies the beauty of Naples. People are wealthy here, but have no need to flaunt it. What they do flaunt are St. Tropez tans and a general *joie de vivre.* And leave the kids at home. Even though there's a zoo and a teddy bear museum here, it's not a place where the little ones will have fun. Your relaxation *will* be disturbed when little Johnny and Jane start tugging at your shirt whining of boredom. Naples is a romantic spot for couples; it's not a swinging singles scene whatsoever. In fact, this is the kind of city where the young singles need to try out for reality shows in order to find a mate. But you never know if the Mr. or Ms. Howell sitting at the bar is recently divorced and looking for a companion to share their wealth. The median age in Naples can't be much lower than 45, but Naples itself isn't a spring chicken, either.

Naples was born in 1886, when a group of 12 Kentuckians and Ohioans bought 8,700 acres fronted by a gorgeous beach, laid out a town, and started selling lots. They built a pier and the 16-room Naples Hotel, whose first guest was President Grover Cleveland's sister Rose. She and other notables soon built a line of beach homes known as "Millionaires' Row." Today that area is known as Olde Naples and is carefully protected by its modern residents. Despite a recent building boom that has expanded the city to the north and east, the original settlement still retains the air of that time a century ago.

Although high-rise buildings now line the beaches north of the old town, the newer sections of Naples still have their charm, thanks to Ohio manufacturer Henry B. Watkins Sr. In 1946, Watkins and his partners bought the old hotel and all the town's undeveloped land and laid out the Naples Plan, which created the very wealthy but environmentally conscious city you see today.

About 4 miles north of Olde Naples, Vanderbilt Beach has a more traditional beach-resort character than the historic district. Lined with a mix of two-story, 1960s-style motels and high-rise hotels and condominiums, the main beach here sits like an island of development between two preserved areas: Delnor-Wiggins Pass State Park to the north, and a county reserve fronting the expensive Pelican Bay golf-course community to the south.

ESSENTIALS

GETTING THERE   Most visitors arrive at the **Southwest Florida International Airport,** 35 miles north of Naples in Fort Myers (p. 294). **Naples Municipal Airport,** on North Road off Airport-Pulling Road (© 239/643-6875; www.flynaples.com), is served by the commuter arms of **American** (© 800/433-7300) and **United/US Airways** (© 800/428-4322), which means you'll have to change planes in Miami, Tampa, or Orlando. Taxis await all flights outside the small terminal building. **Avis** (© 800/331-1212), **Budget** (© 800/527-0700), **Hertz** (© 800/654-3131), and **National** (© 800/CAR-RENT) have booths at the airport. **Enterprise** (© 800/325-8007) is in town.

VISITOR INFORMATION   The most comprehensive source of information is the **Naples Area Chamber of Commerce,** which maintains a visitor center at 895 5th Ave. S. (at U.S. 41), Naples, FL 34102 (© **239/262-6141;** fax 239/435-9910; www.napleschamber.org). The center has a host of free information and phones for making hotel reservations, and it sells a detailed street map for

Naples

ACCOMMODATIONS ■
Hotel Escalante **14**
Inn by the Sea **19**
Lighthouse Inn Motel **2**
Naples Beach Hotel
  & Golf Club **10**
Park Shore Resort **4**
The Registry Resort **3**
The Ritz-Carlton Golf
  Resort, Naples **2**
Vanderbilt Inn Naples **2**

ATTRACTIONS ●
Caribbean Gardens **6**
Clam Pass County Park **1**
The Conservancy's
  Naples Nature Center **7**
Delnor-Wiggins Pass
  State Park **2**
Lowdermilk Park **9**
Naples Museum of Art **2**
Naples Trolley
  General Store and
  Marketplace **17**
Old Marine Marketplace
  at Tin City **12**
Palm Cottage (Naples
  Historical Society) **19**
Vanderbilt Beach **2**

DINING ◆
Cheeburger
  Cheeburger **15**
Chop's City Grill **11**
The Dock at
  Crayton Cove **21**
First Watch **8**
Mel's Diner **5**
Old Naples Pub **19**
Riverwalk Fish &
  Ale House **12**
Tony's Off Third **20**
Wynn's on Fifth **16**
Yabba Island Grill **11**
Zoë's **11**

Clam
Bay

Seagate Dr.

Pine Ridge Rd.

West Blvd.

Blvd. N.
Gulf
Shore

Neapolitan Way

Granada Blvd.

Crayton Rd.

Venetian
Bay
Park

9th St. N.

Solano Rd.

Goodlette

Ohio
Dr.

Anchor Rode Dr.

Frank

Outer
Doctors
Bay

Crayton

Rd.

Harbour Dr.

Rd.

Wedge Dr.

41

Mooring Line Dr.

Gulf Shore

SpringLine Dr.

Tamiami Trail N.

Golden Gate

Pkwy

886

Banyan Blvd.

Lowdermilk Park
& Public Beach

Blvd. N.

Goodlette Frank Rd. N.

7th Ave. N.

**OLDE
NAPLES**

9th St. S.

Central Ave.

3rd St.

41 851

5th Ave. S.

Gulf Shore Blvd. S.

8th Ave. S.

9th St. S.

18th 19th 19th

Broad Ave. S.

Naples

Naples Pier

13th Ave. S.

15th Ave. S.

18th Ave. S.

Bay

County Rd.

Gordon River

Naples
Municipal
Airport

■ Terminal
✈
North   Rd.

Airport Rd.

41 84   Davis Blvd.

31

G u l f   o f   M e x i c o

⚑ Golf Course
ⓘ Information
Ⓟ Police Station
✉ Post Office

FLORIDA

Naples ●
  ● Miami

$2. By mail, it will send you a free list of accommodations and other basic information, or you can order a complete Naples vacation packet for $8 ($12 to Canada and other countries) and the street map for $5. The visitor center is open Monday through Saturday from 9am to 5pm.

GETTING AROUND   The **Naples Trolley** (© 239/262-7300; www.naples trolleytours.com) clangs around 25 stops between the Naples Trolley General Store and Welcome Center, 1010 6th Ave. S. at 10th Street South (2 blocks west of Tin City in Olde Naples), and Vanderbilt Beach Monday through Saturday from 8:30am to 5:15pm and Sunday from 10:15am to 5:15pm. Daily fares are $17 for adults, $7 for children 4 to 12, free for children under 4, with free reboarding. Schedules are available in brochure racks in the lobbies of most hotels and motels. The drivers provide narration, so the entire loop makes a good 2-hour sightseeing tour.

For taxis, call **Yellow Cab** (© 239/262-1312), **Checker Cab** (© 239/455-5555), **Maxi Taxi** (© 239/262-8977), or **Naples Taxi** (© 239/775-0505).

HITTING THE BEACH

Unlike many Florida cities where you have to drive over to a barrier island to reach the beach, this city's beach is right in Olde Naples. And rather than being fronted by tall condominium buildings, here, the mansions along Millionaires' Row form the backdrop. Access to the gorgeous white sand is at the Gulf end of each avenue, although parking in the neighborhood can be brutal. Try the metered lots on 12th Avenue South near the **Naples Pier,** the town's most popular beaching spot (see "Exploring the Town," below), where there are also restrooms and a food concession. Families gather on the beach north of the pier, while local, bored teens aimlessly congregate on the south side.

Also popular, the very Norman Rockwellian **Lowdermilk Park,** on Millionaires' Row at Gulf Shore Boulevard and North Banyan Boulevard, has a pavilion, restrooms, showers, a refreshment counter, professional-quality volleyball courts (the area's best players practice here), a duck pond, and picnic tables. There's also metered parking, so bring quarters. A few blocks farther north is another metered parking lot with beach access beside the Naples Beach Hotel & Golf Resort, 851 Gulf Shore Blvd. N., at Golf Drive.

Nature lovers head to the Pelican Bay development north of the historic district and the popular **Clam Pass County Park** ★★ (© 239/353-0404). A free tram takes you along a 3,000-foot boardwalk winding through mangrove swamps and across a back bay to a beach of fine white sand. It's a strange sight, what with high-rise condominiums standing beyond the mangrove-bordered backwaters, but this actually is a miniature wilderness. Some 6 miles of canoe and kayak trails—with multitudes of birds and an occasional alligator—run from Clam Pass into the winding streams. The beach pavilion here has a bar—drinking is a sport in Naples—restrooms with foot showers only, picnic tables, and beach equipment rentals, including one- and two-person kayaks and 12-foot canoes. Entry is from a metered parking lot beside The Registry Resort at the end of Seagate Drive. There's a $4-per-vehicle parking fee. You can push, but not ride, bicycles on the boardwalk.

At Vanderbilt Beach, about 4 miles north of Olde Naples, the **Delnor-Wiggins Pass State Park** ★★★, at the west end of Bluebill Avenue–111th Avenue North (© 239/597-6196; www.floridastateparks.org/delnor-wiggins), has been listed among America's top 10 stretches of sand. It has bathhouses, a boat ramp, and the area's best picnic facilities. A concessionaire sells hot dogs, sandwiches, and ice cream and rents beach chairs, umbrellas, kayaks, canoes, and snorkeling gear. Fish viewing is great over a small reef under 12 feet of water about 150 feet offshore. Fishing from the beach is excellent here, too. Rangers provide nature tours throughout the year, with the most interesting during the Loggerhead turtle nesting season from June to October (call or check the website for the schedule). People nesting season is in the winter, when most Naples residents are at their winter homes. Naples is *very* seasonal.

The area is open daily from 8am to sunset. Admission is $2 per vehicle with one occupant, $5 for vehicles with two to eight occupants, and $1 for pedestrians and bikers. To get here from Olde Naples, go north on U.S. 41 about 4 miles and take a left on 111th Avenue, which turns into Bluebill Avenue before reaching the beach. Note that 111th Avenue is known as Immokalee Road east of U.S. 41.

OTHER AFFORDABLE OUTDOOR ACTIVITIES

BOATING   Powerboat and WaveRunner rentals are available from **Club Nautico,** at the Boat Haven Marina, 1484 E. Tamiami Trail (© 239/417-3474), on the east bank of the Gordon River behind Kelly's Fish House; and from **Port-O-Call Marina,** also behind Kelly's Fish House (© 239/774-0479).

CRUISES   The Gordon River and Naples Bay from the U.S. 41 bridge on 5th Avenue South to the Gulf are prime territory for sightseeing, dolphin-watching, and sunset cruises. Day Star Charters is a great outfit featuring the double-decked *Double Sunshine* (© 239/263-4949), which sallies forth onto the river and bay daily from Tin City, where it has a ticket office. The 1½-hour cruises usually leave at 10am, noon, 2pm, and an hour before sunset. They cost $23 for adults and $12 for children under 12.

The *Sweet Liberty* (© 239/793-3525; www.sweetliberty.com), a 53-foot sailing catamaran, makes 3-hour morning shelling cruises to Keewaydin Island. The vessel then spends the afternoon on 2-hour sightseeing cruises (you'll usually see dolphins playing in the river on this one) and 2-hour sunset cruises on Naples Bay before docking at Boat Haven Marina on the east side of the Gordon River Bridge. Shelling cruises cost $35 for adults, $15 for children 12 and under; sightseeing and sunset cruises cost $25 for adults, $15 for children 12 and under.

For a good deal more luxury, the 83-foot *Naples Princess* (© 800/728-2970 or 239/649-2275; www.naplesprincesscruises.com) has narrated breakfast, lunch, and sunset dinner cruises from Port-O-Call Marina, on the eastern shore of the Gordon River. With extensive buffets, the sightseeing, lunch, sunset, and dinner cruises are good values at $24, $30, $31, and $44 to $50 per person, respectively. Call for schedules and reservations.

FISHING   The locals like to fish from the **Naples Pier** (see "Exploring the Town," below). The pier has tables on which to clean your catch, but watch out for the ever-present pelicans, which are master thieves. You can buy tackle and bait from the local marinas (see "Boating," above). The pier is open around the clock, and admission is free. No fishing license is required.

The least expensive way for singles, couples, and small families to fish without paying for an entire boat is on the 45-foot *Lady Brett* (© 239/263-4949), which makes two daily half-day trips from Tin City for $50 for adults, $45 for kids under 12. Rod, reel, bait, and fishing license are included, but bring your own drinks and lunch. Its sister boat, the *Captain Paul,* goes on half-day backcountry fishing trips, departing daily at 9am. These cost $45 for adults, $40 for children 12 and under.

A number of charter boats are based at the marinas mentioned under "Boating," above; call or visit them for booking information and prices.

GOLF   Naples has an extraordinary number of fine golf courses for a city its size. Most are out in the suburbs, but not the flat but challenging 18 holes at the **Naples Beach Hotel & Golf Club** ⭐⭐, 851 Gulf Shore Blvd. N. (✆ **239/261-2222**), which are right in the middle of town. Nonguests can play here, but call ahead for a tee time.

Two of the best-known courses are **Lely Flamingo Island Club** ⭐⭐ and the **Lely Mustang Golf Club,** both on U.S. 41 between Naples and Marco Island (✆ **800/388-GOLF** or 239/793-2223). Robert Trent Jones Sr. designed the Lely Flamingo course, and its hourglass fairways and fingerlike bunkers present many challenges. Designed by Lee Trevino, the Lely Mustang course is more forgiving but still fun. Former PGA Tour player Paul Trittler has his golf school at these courses. You'll pay a price here in winter, when 18-hole fees are about $135 at Lely Flamingo and $150 at Lely Mustang, including cart and range balls, but they drop progressively after Easter to about $40 and $50, respectively, in the muggy summer months.

Boyne South, on U.S. 41 between Fla. 931 and Fla. 92 (✆ **239/732-5108**), is another winner, with lots of wildlife inhabiting its many lakes (a 16-ft. alligator reportedly resides near the 17th hole). There are a driving range, practice facility, and restaurant; instruction is available. Wintertime fees are about $70, but in the off season they drop to $45 or less. Tee times are taken up to 4 days in advance.

Another local favorite is the player-friendly **Hibiscus Golf Club,** ½ mile east of U.S. 41 off Rattlesnake Hammock Road in East Naples (✆ **239/774-0088**). A pro shop and teaching professional are available. Fees are about $70 in winter, cart included, dropping to about $30 in summer.

At the intersection of Vanderbilt Beach and Airport-Pulling Roads, the Greg Norman–designed 27 championship holes at the **Tiburón Golf Club** ⭐⭐, 2620 Tiburón Dr. (✆ **877/WCI-PLAY** or 239/594-2040), play like a British Open course—but without the thick-thatch rough. Fees reach $200 in winter but drop as low as $70 in summer. The course is home to the **Rick Smith Golf Academy** (✆ **877/464-6531** or 239/593-1111) and The Ritz-Carlton Golf Resort, Naples.

The area also has several other courses worth playing, most described in the Naples–Fort Myers edition of the *Golfer's Guide* available at the chamber of commerce visitor center (or check the magazine's website at www.golfersguide.com). On the Web, www.naplesgolf.com is also a good source of information about area courses.

SCUBA DIVING   Kevin Sweeney's **SCUBAdventures,** 971 Creech Rd., at Tamiami Trail (✆ **239/434-7477;** www.scubadventureslc.com), which also has a base on Marco Island (see section 5, later in this chapter), takes divers into the Gulf, teaches diver-certification courses, and rents watersports equipment.

TENNIS   In Olde Naples, the city's **Cambier Park Tennis Center** ⭐⭐, 755 8th Ave. S., at 9th Street South (✆ **239/213-3060;** www.cambiertennis.com), is one of the country's finest municipal facilities. In fact, it matches those found at many luxury resorts. Play on its 12 lighted clay courts costs $25 an hour. Book at the pro shop upstairs in the modern building, which has restrooms but no showers. The shop is open Monday through Friday from 8am to 9pm, Saturday and Sunday from 8am to 5pm.

WATERSPORTS **Naples Watersports,** 550 Port A Call Way (✆ **239/774-0479**), will hook you up with WaveRunners, jet skis, and all requisite water toys. Hobie Cats and windsurfers can also be rented on the beach at the **Naples Beach Hotel & Golf Club,** 851 Gulf Shore Blvd. N. (✆ **239/261-2222**), and at **Clam Pass County Park,** at the end of Seagate Drive (✆ **239/353-0404**). See p. 332 for more about Clam Pass.

EXPLORING THE TOWN
OLDE NAPLES ★★★

Its history may go back only to 1886, but the beach skirting **Olde Naples** still has the charm of that Victorian era. The heart of the district lies south of 5th Avenue South (that's where U.S. 41 takes a 45-degree turn). The town docks are on the bay side, the stunning **Naples Beach** along the Gulf. Laid out on a grid, the tree-lined streets run between many houses, some dating from the town's beginning, and along Millionaires' Row between Gulf Shore Boulevard and the beach. With these gorgeous homes virtually hidden in the palms and casuarinas, Naples Beach seems a century removed from the high-rise condominiums found farther north.

The **Naples Pier,** at the Gulf end of 12th Avenue South, is a focal point of the neighborhood. Built in 1888 to let steamers land potential real-estate customers, the original 600-foot-long, T-shaped structure was destroyed by hurricanes and damaged by fire. Local residents have rebuilt it because they like strolling its length to catch fantastic Gulf sunsets—and to get a glimpse of Millionaires' Row from the Gulf side. The pier is now a state historic site. It's open 24 hours a day, but parking in the nearby lots is restricted between 11pm and 7am.

Nearby, **Palm Cottage,** 137 12th Ave. S., between 1st Street and Gordon Drive (✆ **239/261-8164**), was built in 1885 by one of Naples's founders, *Louisville Courier-Journal* publisher Walter Haldeman, as a winter retreat for his chief editorial writer. After World War II, its socialite owners hosted many galas attended by Hollywood stars such as Hedy Lamarr, Gary Cooper, and Robert Montgomery. One of the few remaining Southwest Florida houses built of tabby mortar (made by burning shells), Palm Cottage today is the home of the Naples Historical Society, which maintains it as a museum filled with authentic furniture, paintings, photographs, and other memorabilia. Tours are given during winter, Monday through Friday from 1 to 3:30pm. Adult admission is $5, free for children 12 and under.

Near the Gordon River Bridge on 5th Avenue South, the old corrugated waterfront warehouses are now a cheesy shopping-and-dining complex known as the **Old Marine Marketplace at Tin City,** which tourists throng to and local residents assiduously avoid during the winter months. It does, however, look cool from the outside.

MUSEUMS & ZOOS

Caribbean Gardens ★ *Kids*   The only zoo in Florida to have rare, Indochinese tigers and a supporting cast of lions, leopards, spotted hyenas, and African wild dogs, Caribbean Gardens is an oasis of animal activity. In addition to the standard caged animals, the zoo also has boat rides, primate islands, a large display of flora, and close encounters with kangaroos, alligators, and pythons. You can see them on a boat safari that slinks through spectacular lush tropical gardens and the islands of the park's Lake Victoria, where monkeys, lemurs, and apes live. Everyone gets to handle some of the animals and reptiles at the "Scales &

Tails" area. The Safari Canyon presentation is a cool multimedia presentation that combines video, music, and live animals that swim, leap, stalk, and slither around the natural rock-work theater that's only a splash away from the audience. You will easily fill 3 to 4 hours here. If you have kids with you, perhaps you may want to break the zoo up into several days of sightseeing so that you have something to do with them when they get antsy from swimming at the beach or pool. Should all this animal activity make you hungry, a Subway branch sells sandwiches, and there are picnic facilities on the premises.

1590 Goodlette-Frank Rd. (at Fleischmann Blvd.). ⓒ 239/262-5409. www.caribbeangardens.com. Admission $16 adults, $10 children 4–15, free for children 3 and under. Daily 9:30am–5:30pm. Closed Easter, Thanksgiving, and Christmas.

Naples Museum of Art ★★   If anything's a sign of the emerging sophistication of a sleepy seaside town, it's the appearance of this three-story, 30,000-square-foot art museum, attached to the Naples Philharmonic Center for the Arts. The first full-scale art museum in Southwest Florida, the Naples Museum of Art features an impressive 15 different galleries, highlighting paintings, sculptures, and drawings, with major permanent collections concentrating on both the American Modern and Ancient Chinese genres. Touring shows and exhibitions bring a welcome element of eclecticism to the museum, whose very structure, including a 90-foot by 45-foot glass dome and 14-foot entrance gates, is a dramatic work of art on its own. Tuesdays through Saturdays October through May, there are free guided tours at 11am and 2pm.

5833 Pelican Bay Blvd. (at West Blvd.). ⓒ 239/597-1900. www.thephil.org. Admission $8 adults, $4 students; more for special exhibitions. May 2–July 31 and Sept 8–Oct 31 Tues–Sat 10am–4pm and Sun noon–4pm; Nov 2–May 1 Tues–Sat 10am–5pm and Sun noon–5pm. Closed Mondays, month of Aug–Labor Day, Easter, Memorial Day, Fourth of July, Labor Day, Thanksgiving Day, Christmas Eve Day, Christmas Day, New Year's Eve Day, and New Year's Day.

A NATURE PRESERVE

You can experience Southwest Florida's abundant natural life—and we don't mean those without silicone—without leaving town at **The Conservancy's Naples Nature Center** ★, 14th Avenue North, east of Goodlette-Frank Road (ⓒ 239/262-0304; www.conservancy.org), one of two preserves operated by The Conservancy of Southwest Florida (see the Briggs Nature Center on p. 343). There are nature trails and an aviary with bald eagles and other birds. You can take 45-minute guided boat rides on the hour, between 10am and 3pm, weather permitting. The naturalist guides will explain the vegetation along the upper reaches of the Gordon River, which isn't all that interesting unless you're a vegetation fanatic, but what is interesting is the wildlife—including an occasional monkey escapee from Caribbean Gardens next door (see "Museums & Zoos," above). You can also rent canoes and kayaks and see the area by yourself. An excellent nature store carries gift items. Admission fees of $7.50 for adults and $2 for children 3 to 12 (free for children under 3) include the boat rides. Canoes and kayaks cost $15 for 2 hours, $7.50 for each additional hour. The center is open year-round Monday through Saturday from 9am to 4:30pm, and from February through April, it's also open from 1 to 5pm on Sundays. Closed July 4, Labor Day, Thanksgiving, Christmas Eve, and Christmas Day.

GREAT WINDOW-SHOPPING

A 2-block stretch of **3rd Street South** ★★, at Broad Avenue, aspires to be the Rodeo Drive of Naples, but with the conspicuous absence of Gucci, Prada, and Tiffany and Co., remains just an ordinary, albeit lovely, pricey place for window-shopping. This glitzy collection of jewelers, clothiers, and art galleries may be too rich for many wallets, but the window-shopping here is unmatched. Be sure to pick up a free brochure from the chamber of commerce visitor center (p. 336); it lists the merchants and has a map of the area.

Nearby, the **5th Avenue South** ✪ shopping area, between 3rd and 9th streets south, has seen a renaissance in recent years and is now Naples's hottest wining and dining spot, complete with requisite Starbucks, though the avenue is longer and a bit less chic than 3rd Street South, with stockbrokerages and real-estate offices thrown into the mix of boutiques and antiques dealers.

Even the malls in Naples have their charms. And if it rains, you will definitely want to go to the mall since there's not much to do otherwise. The **Village at Venetian Bay,** 4200 Gulf Shore Blvd., at Park Shore Drive (© **239/643-0835**), evokes images of its Italian namesake, with 50 canal-side shops featuring high-fashion men's and women's clothiers and fine-art galleries. Ornate Mediterranean architecture and a tropical waterfall highlight the open-air **Waterside Shops at Pelican Bay,** Seagate Drive at North Tamiami Trail (U.S. 41; © **239/598-1605**), where the anchor stores are Saks Fifth Avenue and Jacobson's. There's also a huge Barnes & Noble bookstore across Seagate Drive.

Discount shoppers can head to **Prime Outlets Naples,** on Fla. 951, about a mile south of U.S. 41 on the way to Marco Island (© **888/545-7196** or 239/775-8083; www.primeoutlets.com). The 43 shops are open from 10am to 8pm Monday through Saturday and 11am to 6pm on Sunday.

ACCOMMODATIONS YOU CAN AFFORD

Branches of most chain hotels sit along U.S. 41, but these tend to be of higher quality and better value than their counterparts elsewhere in Southwest Florida.

One of the most reasonably priced of the town's many condominium complexes, **Park Shore Resort,** 600 Neapolitan Way, Naples, FL 34103 (© **800/548-2077** or 239/263-2222; fax 239/263-0946; www.parkshorefl.com), has 156 attractive one- and two-bedroom condominiums surrounding an artificial lagoon with waterfalls cascading on its own island. Guests can walk across a bridge to the artificial island, where they can swim in the heated pool, barbecue on gas grills, or order a meal from the restaurant or a drink from the bar. There's also once-a-day (11am) complimentary transport to the beach (to return from the beach, make a reservation at the front desk to catch a ride back at 2pm). The condominiums range from $145 to $260 in winter but drop to $99 to $119 off season.

One of the biggest condominium-rental agents here is **Bluebill Properties,** 26201 Hickory Blvd., Bonita Springs, FL 33923 (© **800/237-2010** or 239/992-6620; www.naplesvacation.com).

Inn by the Sea ✪   Listed in the National Register of Historic Places, this übercharming bed-and-breakfast, 2 blocks from the beach in the heart of Olde Naples, was built in 1937 as a boardinghouse. The Federal-style house still has much of its original pine floors and pine or cypress ceilings and woodwork. With windows on three sides, the Sanibel on the ground floor is the lightest and airiest unit here, while the Bokeelia suite is the most romantic, with its bed set at an angle in one corner. For those looking for an even more natural setting, the one-bedroom cottage in the garden is a splendid choice. Bikes, beach chairs, and towels are provided; in season, guests are served oranges from the backyard tree. You'll have to do without a phone or TV in your room here; however, there is a TV in the common living space area.

287 11th Ave. S., Naples, FL 34102. ℂ 800/584-1268 or 239/649-4124. Fax 239/434-2842. www.innbythe sea-bb.com. 5 units, 1 1-bedroom cottage. Winter $149–$189 double; off season $94–$114 double. Rates include extended continental breakfast. AE, DISC, MC, V. Children 10 and under not accepted. **Amenities:** Access to nearby health club; free use of bikes. *In room:* A/C, hair dryer, no phone.

Lighthouse Inn Motel A relic from decades gone by, Judy and Buzz Dugan's no-frills but spotlessly clean motel sits across the street from other more expensive Gulf-side properties on Vanderbilt Beach. The efficiencies and apartments are simple, with cinder-block walls and small kitchens. The one kitchenless room has a small fridge and coffeemaker, but note: No unit has a telephone, and four of them have shower-only bathrooms. Most guests take advantage of weekly and monthly rates in winter, when it's heavily booked.

9140 Gulf Shore Dr. N., Naples, FL 34108. ℂ 239/597-3345. Fax 239/597-5541. 15 units. Winter $105 double, $110 efficiency, $120 apt; off season $49 double, $59 efficiency, $69 apt. MC, V. From Olde Naples, go 3½ miles north on U.S. 41; take a left on Vanderbilt Beach Rd. (C.R. 862). Turn right on Gulf Shore Dr. to hotel on right. **Amenities:** Restaurant; bar; heated outdoor pool. *In room:* A/C, TV, kitchen, fridge, coffeemaker, no phone.

An Off-Season Deal

Vanderbilt Inn Naples ✪ Beach casual decor in the accommodations and public areas sets the tempo for a casual, fun vacation at this two-story motel right on Vanderbilt Beach, where you can go parasailing and rent boats and watersports equipment. Nature lovers can walk along the beach and into Delnor-Wiggins Pass State Park next door (p. 332). The 16 efficiencies (with kitchens) on the ends of the building open to the beach. About half of the standard motel-style rooms face a magnificently landscaped courtyard with a kidney-shaped swimming pool surrounded by a brick terrace, while the other, less-expensive units open to parking lots. Although the rooms are entered from exterior walkways, their big windows are darkly tinted to provide privacy. A thatch-roof bar and full-service outdoor restaurant serve lunches and dinners by the beach and draw a crowd for sunset happy hour. The indoor dining room, Splash, serves breakfast and dinner. Another restaurant turns lively when bands play on Friday and Saturday nights. Kids 12 and under dine free when accompanied by adults here.

11000 Gulf Shore Dr., Naples, FL 34108. ℂ 800/643-8654 or 239/597-3151. Fax 239/597-3099. www.vanderbiltinn.com. 147 units. Winter $145–$350 double; off season $110–$220 double. Weekly rates available. AE, DC, DISC, MC, V. From Olde Naples, go 4 miles north on U.S. 41; take a left on 111th Ave. (which becomes Bluebill Ave.) to hotel on left. **Amenities:** 2 restaurants; 2 bars; heated outdoor pool; Jacuzzi; watersports equipment rental; business center. *In room:* A/C, TV, dataport, fridge, coffeemaker (efficiencies only), safe, microwave (efficiencies only).

Worth a Splurge

Hotel Escalante ✪✪ On the western end of the 5th Avenue shopping district and 2 blocks from the beach, this romantic boutique hotel is perfect for couples who want convenience, no crowds, and a bit of pampering. The closest thing to Italy that you'll find in Naples, *Florida,* this 71-room Mediterranean villa–style hotel is only blocks away from the beach and worlds away from the hustle and bustle of the real world, ensconced in 4 acres of lush, private gardens with over 300 species of plants, walkways of old brick, and fountains. The large rooms and spacious one-bedroom suites are in eight one- and two-story buildings spread out over most of a city block. The cottagelike suites have private patios opening to the lush courtyards. All units are luxuriously appointed.

290 5th Ave. S., Naples, FL 34102. ℂ 877/GULF-INN or 239/659-3466. Fax 239/262-8748. www.hotel escalante.com. 71 units. Winter $195–$655; off season $165–$400. Rates include continental breakfast. AE,

DC, DISC, MC, V. **Amenities:** Bar; heated outdoor pool; exercise room; day spa; Jacuzzi; sauna; 24-hr. room service; massage; laundry service. *In room:* A/C, TV, dataport, minibar, fridge, coffeemaker, hair dryer, iron.

GREAT DEALS ON DINING

Naples's beaches are ideal for picnics. In Olde Naples, you can get freshly baked breads and pastries, prepackaged gourmet sandwiches, and fruit plates at **Tony's Off Third,** 1300 3rd St. S. (© **239/262-7999**). **Wynn's on Fifth,** 745 5th Ave. S. (© **239/261-0901**), between 8th Street and Park Street South, has high-quality deli items, prepackaged sandwiches, salads, takeout meals, and gourmet pastries at very reasonable prices. Both have a few sidewalk tables and are fine places for coffee or a snack while window-shopping on 3rd and 5th avenues South.

You'll find budget-priced fast-food and family-style restaurants along U.S. 41, including a branch of the inexpensive **Mel's Diner,** 3650 Tamiami Trail N. (© **239/643-9898**).

The Dock at Crayton Cove ★ *Value* SEAFOOD   Located right on the City Dock, this locals hangout is the best place in town for a supercasual open-air meal or a cool drink while watching the boats go back and forth across Naples Bay. Servers are friendly and conversational, which, depending on how you look at it, can be a good or not so good thing. The chow ranges from hearty chowders by the mug to seafood with a Floribbean fare, with Jamaican-style jerk shrimp thrown in for spice; main courses are moderately priced. Grilled seafood Caesar salad and a good selection of sandwiches, hot dogs, and other pub-style fare also appear on the menu. "Margarita madness" happy hour and a half-price raw bar (don't miss the steamed mussels with French bread for dipping the garlic sauce) run daily from 9:30 to 11:30pm.

12th Ave. S. (at the City Dock in Olde Naples). © 239/263-9940. Reservations not accepted. Main courses $11–$26; sandwiches $9–$13. AE, DISC, MC, V. Daily 11am–midnight.

Old Naples Pub ★★ *Value* AMERICAN/PUB FARE   You would never guess that the person sitting next to you at the bar here is a mogul of some sort, so relaxed is this small, somewhat-cramped pub in the middle of the fabulous 3rd Street South shops. Diners fortunately find more room at tables on the shopping center's patio. The menu features very good pub fare (and at extraordinarily inexpensive prices for Olde Naples), including homemade soups, nachos, burgers, and sandwiches ranging from charcoal-grilled bratwurst to fried grouper. Only six main courses are offered: platters with New York strip steak, grilled tuna, the catch of the day, fried grouper or clam strips, and baby back ribs. Best bets are the chicken salad with grapes and walnuts, and the burgers, steaks, and fish from the charcoal grill. You can catch live entertainment here nightly during winter, Wednesday through Saturday off season.

255 13th Ave. S. (between 3rd and 4th sts. S.). © 239/649-8200. Main courses $11–$15; salads, sandwiches, and burgers $5–$9. AE, DISC, MC, V. Mon–Sat 11am–10pm; Sun noon–9pm.

Yabba Island Grill ★ *Value* CARIBBEAN   Perhaps the noisiest, most crowded spot on Fifth Avenue, Yabba Island Grill attempts to channel the Caribbean with loud music, a massive bar, and a tropical decor and does a very decent job doing it. The food here makes as loud a statement as Yabba's pastel color scheme, with most items providing a riot of flavors from across the Caribbean. And if the party hearty crowd that convenes here isn't enough to entice you, consider the St. Croix Sizzler, a terrific combination of small lobster tail, a chunk of mahimahi, and mussels over a bed of peppers, onions, and a sweet mango-curry sauce. Also worthy of a repeat: the Monsoon salad consisting of grilled chicken breast, hearts of palm, candied pecans, and mushrooms under a warm bacon-and-berry vinaigrette and topped with crispy onion rings. If you're looking for a peaceful and quiet meal, get here super early—in fact, at 4:30pm, right when they open, before all the antsy vacationers start piling in.

711 5th Ave. S. (between 8th St. S. and Park Ave. S.). ℂ 239/262-5787. Reservations recommended. Main courses $10–$24; sandwiches $8–$10. AE, DISC, MC, V. Daily 4:30–11pm (bar to 2am Fri–Sat).

SUPER-CHEAP EATS

Cheeburger Cheeburger ★★ Though this is a chain restaurant, with no decor to speak of, if you're hankering after a good, no, make that great, burger with a side of fries or onion rings and a milkshake, this is definitely the place to go. Choose the size burger you want and any of more than a dozen toppings, and enjoy (there are also salads for those who want to be healthy).

505 5th Ave. S. (between 5th and 6th sts.). ℂ 239/435-9796. Burgers $4.25–$10. Daily 11am–9pm.

First Watch *Value* AMERICAN Just like its siblings elsewhere in Florida, this diner is a favorite local haunt for breakfast, late brunch, or a mid-day meal. You may have to wait for a table, but once seated, a young staff will provide quick and friendly service. The menu leans heavily on healthy selections, but you can get your cholesterol from a sizzling skillet of fried eggs served over layers of potatoes, vegetables, and melted cheese. Lunch features large salads, sandwiches, and quesadillas. In addition to the dining room, there's more seating at umbrella tables in the shopping center's courtyard.

In Gulf Shore Sq., 1400 Gulf Shore Blvd. (at Banyan Rd.). ℂ 239/434-0005. Most items $3.50–$8. AE, DISC, MC, V. Daily 7am–2:30pm. Closed Christmas.

WORTH A SPLURGE

Chop's City Grill ★★ STEAKS/SEAFOOD The smell of steak and money waft through this urbane bistro that's more Miami hip than Naples nautical. Aged, top-quality steaks and lamb chops are the house specialties, either chargrilled to perfection and served with thick onion rings and mashed potatoes, or peppered and served with a blackberry and cabernet-wine sauce. Fresh fish from the grill is another good choice. Asian influences appear here, too, such as deelish Mongolian beef, sea scallops "shocked" in a wok with Thai curry sauce and served over noodles with wild mushrooms and stir-fried vegetables.

837 5th Ave. S. (between 8th and 9th sts. S.). ℂ 239/262-4677. Reservations recommended. Main courses $15–$30. AE, DC, DISC, MC, V. Sun–Thurs 5–10pm; Fri–Sat 5–11pm.

NAPLES AFTER DARK

For entertainment ideas, check the *Naples Daily News* (www.naplesnews.com), especially the "Neapolitan" section in Friday's edition.

PERFORMING ARTS Known locally as "The Phil," the impressive **Philharmonic Center for the Arts** ★★, 5833 Pelican Bay Blvd., at West Boulevard (ℂ **800/597-1900** or 239/597-1900; www.thephil.org), is the home of the Naples Philharmonic, but its year-round schedule is filled with cultural events, concerts by celebrated artists and internationally known orchestras, and Broadway plays and shows aimed at children and families. Call or check the website for its seasonal calendar.

A fine local theater group, the **Naples Players,** holds their winter-season performances in the new Sugden Community Theatre, 701 5th Ave. S. (ℂ **239/263-7990;** www.naples.net/presents/theatre). Tickets can be hard to come by, so call well in advance.

THE CLUB & BAR SCENE Remember: Naples is not South Beach nor does it portend to be. It does, however, realize that some people like to party well past the early-bird hours and, as a result, there are a few good spots here to get your groove on. The restaurants and bistros along 5th Avenue South are popular watering holes, especially for young professional singles who make this their "meat market" on Friday nights. **Zoë's,** 720 5th Ave. S. (© **239/261-1221**), turns into a high-energy nightclub Friday and Saturday from 10:30pm to 2am. Nearby, **McCabe's Irish Pub,** 699 5th Ave. S. (© **239/403-7170**), features traditional Irish music nightly. For a lot of camp with your cabaret, the **Ridgway Bar and Grill,** 3rd Street South and 13th Avenue (© **239/262-5500**), is a hot spot thanks to pianist Jim Badger, whose bawdy shows bring in crowds of all ages (under 18 not recommended).

In the 3rd Street South shopping area, **Old Naples Pub,** 255 13th Ave. S. (© **239/649-8200**), has live music nightly during winter, Wednesday through Saturday nights off season. See "Great Deals on Dining," above.

The touristy **Old Marine Marketplace at Tin City,** comprised of the restored waterfront warehouses on 5th Avenue South on the west side of the Gordon River, comes alive during the winter when visitors flock to its shops and the **Riverwalk Fish & Ale House** (© 239/262-2734), which has live entertainment during the season.

Some of the hotels mentioned earlier in this section have entertainment throughout the year. The beachside *chickee hut* bar at the **Naples Beach Hotel & Golf Club,** 851 Gulf Shore Blvd. N. (© 239/261-2222), is always popular, has live entertainment many nights, and is *the* place to go on Sunday afternoon and early evening. So is the beachside bar at the **Vanderbilt Inn Naples** (© 239/597-3151).

5 Marco Island

15 miles SE of Naples, 53 miles S of Fort Myers, 100 miles W of Miami

Marco Island is reminiscent of a sleepy, albeit swanky, beachfront retirement community. When the sun goes down, you can hear a pin drop, though. There is absolutely no life after dark here, but still Captain William Collier would hardly recognize Marco Island if he were to come back from the grave today. No relation to Collier County founder Barron Collier, the captain settled his family on the north end of this island, the largest of Florida's Ten Thousand Islands, back in 1871. He traded pelts with the Native Americans, caught and smoked fish to sell to Key West and Cuba, and charged fishermen and other guests $2 a day for a room in his home. A few turn-of-the-20th-century buildings still stand here, but Captain Collier would be shocked to come across the high-rise bridge to the island and see it now sliced by man-made canals and virtually covered by resorts, condominiums, shops, restaurants, and winter homes. These are the products of an extensive real-estate development begun in 1965, which means that Marco lacks any of the charm found in Naples and on Sanibel and Captiva islands. Much of the sales effort here was aimed at the northeastern states, so the island smacks more of New York and Massachusetts than of the laid-back Midwestern style of its neighbors.

Marco's only real attractions are its crescent-shaped beach and access to the nearby waterways running through a maze of small islands, its excellent boating and fishing, and the island's proximity to thousands of acres of wildlife preserves.

ESSENTIALS

GETTING THERE   See p. 294 and 330 for information about the **Southwest Florida International Airport** and the **Naples Municipal Airport,** respectively, and about Amtrak's train service and Greyhound/Trailways buses to those cities.

VISITOR INFORMATION   The **Marco Island Area Chamber of Commerce,** 1102 N. Collier Blvd., Marco Island, FL 34145 (© **800/788-6272** or 239/394-7549; fax 239/394-3061; www.marcoislandchamber.org), provides free information about the island. A message board and a phone are located outside for making hotel reservations even when the office is closed. The chamber is open Monday through Friday from 9am to 5pm and Saturday from 10am to 3pm during winter.

GETTING AROUND   **Marco Island Trolley Tours** (© **239/394-1600**) makes four complete loops around the island and into the wacky, shacky fishing village of Goodland from 10am to 3:15pm Monday through Saturday. The conductors sell tickets and render an informative narration about the island's history. Daily fare is $17 for adults, $7 for children 11 and under, with free reboarding. The entire loop takes about 1 hour and 45 minutes.

   Enterprise Rent-a-Car (© **800/325-8007** or 239/642-4488) has an office here. For a cab, call **A-Action Taxi** (© **239/394-4400**), **Classic Taxi** (© **239/394-1888**), or **A-Okay Taxi** (© **239/394-1113**).

   Depending on the type, rental bicycles cost $5 an hour to $65 a week at **Scootertown,** 845 Bald Eagle Dr. (© **239/394-8400**), north of North Collier Boulevard near Olde Marco. Scooters cost about $50 for 24 hours.

HITTING THE BEACH & OTHER AFFORDABLE OUTDOOR ACTIVITIES

BEACHES   The sugar-white Crescent Beach curves for 3½ miles down the entire western shore of Marco Island. Its southern 2 miles are fronted by an unending row of high-rise condominiums and hotels, but the northern 1½ miles are preserved in **Tigertail Public Beach** (© **239/642-8414**). There are restrooms, cold-water outdoor showers, a children's playground, a watersports rental concessionaire, and a snack bar. The park is at the end of Hernando Drive. It's open daily from dawn to dusk. There's no admission charge to the beach, but parking in the lot costs $3 per vehicle.

   The beaches in front of the Marriott, Hilton, and Radisson resorts have parasailing, windsurfing, and other watersports activities, all for a fee.

   If you're not staying at the big resorts, Collier County maintains a $3-per-vehicle parking lot and access to the developed beach on the southern end of the island, on Swallow Avenue at South Collier Boulevard.

OUTDOOR ACTIVITIES   **Marco River Marina,** 951 Bald Eagle Dr. (© **239/394-2502;** www.marcoriver.com), is the center for boat rentals, fishing, and cruises. Operating from a booth on the marina's dock, **Sunshine Tours** (© **239/642-5415;** www.sunshinetoursmarcoisland.com) will book offshore fishing charters and arrange back-bay fishing ($47 adults, $37 kids under 10), shelling excursions to the small islands ($37 adults, $27 children under 10), sunset cruises ($30 adults, $15 children under 10), and dinner cruises ($49 per person). The back-bay fishing trips go at high tide, the shelling trips at low tide, so call for the schedule and reservations.

SCUBAdventures has a base at 845 Bald Eagle Dr. (© **239/389-7889**) in Olde Marco. Two-tank dives range from $65 to $85 depending on distance offshore.

Naples's Lely and Boyne South golf courses are a short drive away (see "Other Affordable Outdoor Activities," in section 4, earlier in this chapter). The closest public courses are the **Marco Shores Golf Club,** 1450 Mainsail Dr. (© **239/ 394-2581**), and **The Rookery at Marco** (© **239/793-6060**), both in the marshlands off Fla. 951 north of the island. Fees range from about $120 in winter down to $75 in summer.

A NATURE PRESERVE

Operated by The Conservancy and part of the Rookery Bay National Estuarine Research Reserve, the **Briggs Nature Center** 🐾, on Shell Island Road, off Fla. 951 between U.S. 41 and Marco Island (© **239/775-8569;** www.conservancy. org), has a ½-mile boardwalk through a pristine example of Florida's disappearing scrublands, home to the threatened scrub jays and gopher tortoises. Rangers lead a variety of nature excursions (call for the seasonal schedule), and there is a self-guided canoe trail, with canoes for rent Tuesday through Saturday mornings (you must return them by 1pm) at $13 for the first 2 hours, $5 for each additional hour. The center is open Monday through Saturday from 9am to 4:30pm. Admission to the boardwalk is $4 for adults, $2 for children 3 to 12, free for children under 3. For more information, contact **The Conservancy of Southwest Florida,** 1450 Merrihue Dr., Naples, FL 34102 (© **239/262-0304;** fax 239/262-0672; www.conservancy.org).

ACCOMMODATIONS YOU CAN AFFORD

The only chain hotels on Marco Island (none inexpensive) are the large Marriott, Hilton, and Radisson properties that stand in a row along Crescent Beach on the island's southwestern corner. **Century 21 First Southern Trust** (© **800/ 523-0069** or 239/394-7653; fax 239/394-8048; www.c21marco.com) is one of the largest agents representing rental property owners.

As elsewhere in South Florida, the high season here is from mid-December to mid-April. Rates drop precipitously in the off season.

Boat House Motel *Value*   One of the best bargains in these parts, this pleasant little motel is a throwback to the '50s and sits beside the Marco River in Olde Marco, on the island's northern end. The rooms are in an old school two-story, lime-green-and-white building that ends at a wooden dock with a small heated swimming pool, lounge furniture, picnic tables, and barbecue grills. Two rooms on the end have their own decks, and all open to tiny courtyards. Bright paint, ceiling fans, and louvered shutters add a tropical ambience throughout. The one-bedroom condominiums next door open to a riverside dock, upon which is built a two-bedroom cottage named "The Gazebo," whose peaked roof is supported by umbrella-like spokes from a central pole. There's a heated waterfront pool, too.

1180 Edington Place, Marco Island, FL 34148. © **800/528-6345** or 239/642-2400. Fax 239/642-2435. www.theboathousemotel.com. 25 units. Winter $99–$155 double, $170–$260 apt or cottage; off season $63–$130 double, $125–$220 apt or cottage. MC, V. Pets accepted ($15 fee plus $5 per day). **Amenities:** Heated outdoor pool; coin-op washers and dryers. *In room:* A/C, TV, fridge, iron.

OFF-SEASON DEALS

Marco Island Hilton Beach Resort ★★   About half the size of the nearby Marco Island Marriott Resort, Golf Club & Spa but nevertheless a group-oriented hotel, this 11-story beachside tower overlooks the Gulf and a courtyard with a multiangled swimming pool wrapped around four coconut palms. The spacious units have curved balconies angled to give water views. One-bedroom units have cooking facilities.

560 S. Collier Blvd., Marco Island, FL 34145. (C) 800/HILTONS or 239/394-5000. Fax 239/394-8410. www. marcoisland.hilton.com. 298 units. Winter $199–$359 double; off season $89–$189 double. $9 per unit per day resort amenities fee (includes local calls). Packages available. AE, DC, DISC, MC, V. Free parking. **Amenities:** 2 restaurants; 2 bars; heated outdoor pool; 3 tennis courts; exercise room; Jacuzzi; sauna; watersports equipment rental; children's programs; game room; concierge; activities desk; business center; salon; limited room service; massage; babysitting; laundry service; concierge-level rooms. *In room:* A/C, TV, dataport, kitchen (suites only), minibar, fridge, coffeemaker, hair dryer, iron, safe.

GREAT DEALS ON DINING

For inexpensive fare, head for the Town Center Mall, at the corner of North Collier Boulevard and Bald Eagle Drive, where you'll find two good choices. **Susie's Diner** (C) **239/642-6633**) is popular with the locals for breakfasts and especially for Susie's inexpensive full-meal lunch specials. She's open Monday to Saturday from 6:30am to 2:30pm and Sunday from 6:30am to 1pm (for breakfast only). **Breakfast Plus** (C) **239/642-6900**) has eye-openers ranging from bacon and eggs to kippers to latkes. It's open daily from 7am to 2:30pm.

The island's popular sports bars also offer inexpensive pub fare to go with their multitudinous TVs. Most popular are **Rookie's Bar & Grill,** in Mission de San Marco Plaza at the corner of South Collier Boulevard and Winterberry Drive (C) **239/394-6400**), and the **Crazy Flamingo,** in the Town Center Mall, North Collier Boulevard at Bald Eagle Drive (C) **239/642-9600**).

Cafe de Marco ★★ SEAFOOD   Purveyor of some of the island's finest cuisine, this homelike establishment at the Marco Village shops was originally constructed as housing for maids at Captain William Collier's Olde Marco Inn. The chef specializes in excellent treatments of fresh seafood, from your choice of shrimp or fresh baked fish with mushrooms, seasoned shallots, and garlic butter to his own luscious creation of seafood and vegetables combined in a lobster sauce and served over linguine. If your waistline can stand it, finish with a Cafe Puff, an almond praline ice-cream ball rolled in chocolate cookie crumbs, placed in a puff pastry shell, and served with whipped cream. Early-bird specials here are a very good value. You can dine inside or on a screened patio.

244 Palm St., Olde Marco. (C) **239/394-6262**. Reservations recommended. Main courses $16–$30; early-bird specials $13. Minimum charge $13 per adult, $4.50 per child. AE, MC, V. Winter daily 5–10pm; off season Mon–Sat 5–10pm. Early-bird specials 5–6pm.

Kretch's ★★ *Value* SEAFOOD/CONTINENTAL   Noted pastry chef Bruce Kretschmer rules this shopping-center roost, Marco's best all-around restaurant. Bruce has created a sinfully rich seafood strudel by combining shrimp, crab, scallops, cheeses, cream, and broccoli in a flaky Bavarian pastry and serving it all under a lobster sauce. It's available in appetizer or main course–size portions. Cholesterol counters can choose from broiled or charcoal-grilled fish, shrimp, Florida lobster tail, steaks, or lamb chops. Bruce's popular "Mexican Friday" lunches feature delicious tacos and other inexpensive south-of-the-border selections. Sunday is home-cooking night during winter, with chicken and dumplings, Yankee pot roast, and braised lamb shanks.

527 Bald Eagle Dr. (south of N. Collier Blvd.). (C) **239/394-3433**. Reservations recommended in winter. Main courses $14–$25. DISC, MC, V. Mon–Fri 11am–3pm and 5–9pm; Sat–Sun 5–9pm. Closed Sun off season and Easter, July 4, Thanksgiving, Christmas Eve, and Christmas Day.

Snook Inn SEAFOOD   The choice dinner seats at this Old Florida establishment are in an enclosed dock right beside the scenic Marco River, but for lunch or libation (they make fabulous Bloody Marys with pickled okra), head to the dockside Chickee Bar, a fun place anytime but especially at sunset. A new garden courtyard isn't a bad place to be, either, as long as it's not mosquito season, in which case, avoid all outdoor areas unless you've bathed in Off. Live entertainment is featured out there both day and night during the winter season, nightly the rest of the year. Although seafood is the specialty, tasty steaks, chicken, burgers, and sandwiches are among the choices. Even the sandwiches come with a trip to the salad bar at dinner, making them a fine bargain. Bring a filet of that fish you caught today and the chef will cook it for you. Call A-Okay Taxi (see "Essentials," above) for a free ride from anywhere on Marco Island to Snook Inn.

1215 Bald Eagle Dr. (at Palm St.), Olde Marco. (© **239/394-3313**. Reservations not accepted. Main courses $12–$21; sandwiches $8–$10; cook-your-catch $11. AE, DC, DISC, MC, V. Daily 11am–4pm and 4:30–10pm. Closed Thanksgiving and Christmas.

MARCO ISLAND AFTER DARK

Marco Island nightlife is an oxymoron. When the sun sets, so does everything else here, for the most part. With the exception of the island's movie theater and a few hotel bars, there's not much doing here after dark. A drive to Naples is necessary for those looking to burn the midnight oil.

To find out what's going on, check the *Naples Daily News* (www.naplesnews. com), especially the "Neapolitan" section in Friday's edition and its weekly "The Marco Islander" section, available at the chamber of commerce (p. 342).

It's not after dark, but one of the biggest parties in Florida takes place every Sunday afternoon at **Stan's Idle Hour Seafood Restaurant,** on County Road 892 in Goodland (© **239/394-3041**), where owner Stan Gober—an Ernest Hemingway look-alike—plays host and fires up the barbecue grills; bands crank up country music for dancing the "Buzzard Lope"; and men compete to see who has the best legs. Stan's Goodland Mullet Festival, always the weekend before the Super Bowl, is the mother of all parties.

Marco Island's much tamer but nevertheless entertaining version is the **Snook Inn** (see the "Great Deals on Dining" section, above), where bands play out in the dockside Chickee Bar.

Much more sedate are the lounges in the **Marriott** and **Hilton** resorts, which provide pianists every evening.

It seems like everyone turns out for free outdoor entertainment at the **Mission San Marco Plaza** shopping center, South Collier Boulevard at Winterberry Drive, every Tuesday night year-round, and at the **Town Center Mall,** at North Collier Boulevard and Bald Eagle Drive, every Thursday night.

10

The Tampa Bay Area

San Francisco isn't the country's only Bay Area. In fact, when some people hear the word "Tampa," they typically think of Busch Gardens and never even mention the Bay Area. They'd be missing out: Tampa Bay is a stunning, picturesque city, and while it may not have a red bridge, it does have an array of colors reflecting off of the sparkling waters. If you haven't had a chance to explore Florida's Bay Area, do so now. There's so much more to the Tampa Bay area than beer and amusement parks. Sure, you can chug as much Busch Beer here as you want, but you can also do (and see, and eat, and experience) much more here.

Florida's very own city by the bay, Tampa is a scenic spot. It's also got its own vibrant culture with roots firmly implanted in Cuban and American history. Many families visiting Orlando's theme parks eventually drive an hour west on I-4 to another major theme park, Busch Gardens in Tampa. But this area shouldn't be a mere side trip from Disney World, for Florida's west-central coast is an exciting destination unto itself.

The city of Tampa is the commercial center of Florida's west coast—a growing seaport and center of banking and high-tech manufacturing. You can come downtown during the day to see the sea life at the Florida Aquarium and stroll through the Henry B. Plant Museum, housed in an ornate, Moorish-style hotel built more than a century ago to lure tourists to the city. A short trolley ride will take you from downtown Tampa to Ybor City, the historic Cuban enclave, which is now a bustling, often rowdy, nightlife and dining hot spot.

Two bridges and a causeway will whisk you west across Old Tampa Bay to St. Petersburg, Pinellas Park, Clearwater, Dunedin, Tarpon Springs, and other cities on the Pinellas Peninsula, one of Florida's most densely packed urban areas. Over here on the bayfront, photo-ready downtown St. Petersburg is famous for wintering seniors, a shopping and dining complex built on a pizer, and, surprisingly, the world's largest collection of Salvador Dalí's surrealist paintings.

Keep driving west and you'll come to a line of barrier islands where St. Pete Beach, Clearwater Beach, and other Gulf-side communities boast 28 miles of sunshine, surf, and white sand.

Heading south, I-275 will take you across the mouth of Tampa Bay to Sarasota and another chain of barrier islands that stretches 42 miles along the coast south of Tampa Bay. One of Florida's cultural centers, affluent Sarasota is the gateway to St. Armands and Longboat keys, two playgrounds of the rich and famous, and to Lido and Siesta keys, both attractive to families of more modest means.

1 Tampa

200 miles SW of Jacksonville, 85 miles SW of Orlando, 254 miles NW of Miami

Even if you stay on the beaches 20 miles to the west, you should consider driving into Tampa for a mild taste of metropolis. If you have children in tow, they may *demand* that you go into the city so they can ride the rides and see the animals at Busch Gardens. Once there, you can also educate them (and yourself) at the Florida Aquarium and the city's other fine museums. Additionally, historic Ybor City has the bay area's liveliest and hottest nightlife.

Tampa was once a sleepy little port when Cuban immigrants founded Ybor City's cigar industry in the 1880s. A few years later, Henry B. Plant put Tampa on the tourist map by building a railroad that ran into town and constructing the bulbous minarets over his garish Tampa Bay Hotel, now a museum named in his honor. During the Spanish-American War, Teddy Roosevelt trained his Rough Riders here and walked the Ybor City streets with Cuban revolutionary José Martí. A land boom in the 1920s gave the city its charming, Victorian-style Hyde Park suburb, now a gentrified redoubt for the baby boomers just across the Hillsborough River from downtown.

Today's downtown skyline is the product of the 1980s and 1990s booms, when banks built skyscrapers and the city put up an expansive convention center, a performing-arts center, and the St. Pete Times Forum (formerly the Ice Palace), a 20,000-seat bayfront arena that is home to professional hockey's Tampa Bay Lightning. The renaissance hasn't been as rapid as planned, given the recent economic recession, but it is continuing into the 21st century with redevelopment of the seaport area east of downtown. There the existing Florida Aquarium and the Garrison Seaport Center (a major home port for cruise ships bound for Mexico and the Caribbean) are being joined by office buildings, apartment complexes, and a major shopping-and-dining center known as Channelside (in the Channel District) at Garrison Seaport.

You won't want to spend your entire Florida vacation in Tampa, but everything it offers adds up to a fast-paced, modern city on the go.

ESSENTIALS

GETTING THERE Tampa International Airport (© 813/870-8770; www.tampaairport.com), 5 miles northwest of downtown Tampa, is the major air gateway to this area (**St. Petersburg–Clearwater International Airport** has limited service; see section 2, "St. Petersburg," later in this chapter). Most major and many no-frills airlines serve Tampa International, including **Air Canada** (© 800/268-7240 in Canada, or 800/776-3000 in the U.S.), **AirTran** (© 800/247-8726), **America West** (© 800/235-9292), **American** (© 800/433-7300), **British Airways** (© 800/247-9297), **Continental** (© 800/525-0280), **Delta** (© 800/221-1212), **JetBlue** (© 800/538-2583), **Lufthansa** (© 800/824-6200), **MetroJet** (© 800/428-4322), **Midway** (© 800/446-4392), **Midwest Express** (© 800/452-2022), **Northwest** (© 800/225-2525), **Southwest** (© 800/435-9792), **Spirit** (© 800/722-7117), **United** (© 800/241-6522), and **US Airways** (© 800/428-4322).

Alamo (© 800/327-9633), **Avis** (© 800/331-1212), **Budget** (© 800/527-0700), **Dollar** (© 800/800-4000), **Enterprise** (© 800/325-8007), **Hertz** (© 800/654-3131), **National** (© 800/227-7368), and **Thrifty** (© 800/367-2277) all have rental-car operations here.

The Limo/SuperShuttle (© 800/282-6817 or 727/527-1111; www.super shuttle.com) operates van services between the airport and hotels throughout the Tampa Bay area. Fares for one person range from $13 to $33 round-trip, depending on your destination. Taxis are plentiful at the airport; the ride to downtown Tampa takes about 15 minutes and costs $11 to $19.

Amtrak trains arrive downtown at the Tampa Amtrak Station, 601 Nebraska Ave. N. (© 800/872-7245; www.amtrak.com).

VISITOR INFORMATION   Contact the Tampa Bay Convention & Visitors Bureau, 400 N. Tampa St., Tampa, FL 33602-4706 (© 800/448-2672, 800/368-2672, or 813/223-2752; www.visittampabay.com), for advance information. If you're downtown, you can head to the bureau's visitor information center at 400 N. Tampa St. (Channelside), Suite 2800 (© 813/223-1111). It's open Monday through Saturday from 9:30am to 5:30pm.

Operated by the Ybor City Chamber of Commerce, the Centro Ybor Museum and Visitor Information Center, in Centro Ybor, 1514½ E. 8th Ave. (between 15th and 16th sts. E.), Tampa, FL 33605 (© 813/248-3712; www.ybor.org), distributes information and has exhibits about the area's history. A 7-minute video will help get you oriented with this area—an 8-block stretch of Seventh Avenue. The center is open Monday through Saturday from 10am to 6pm, Sunday from noon to 6pm.

GETTING AROUND   Like most other Florida destinations, it's virtually impossible to see Tampa's major sights and enjoy its best restaurants without a car. You can get around downtown via the free Uptown-Downtown Connector Trolley, which runs north-south between Harbor Island and the city's North Terminal bus station on Marion Street at I-275. The trolleys run every 10 minutes from 6am to 6pm Monday through Friday. Southbound they follow Tampa Street between Tyler and Whiting streets, and Franklin Street between Whiting Street and Harbor Island. Northbound trolleys follow Florida Avenue from the St. Pete Times Forum to Cass Street. It's operated by the Hillsborough Area Regional Transit/HARTline (© 813/254-4278; www.hartline.org), the area's transportation authority, which also provides scheduled bus service ($1.25–$3) between downtown Tampa and the suburbs. Pick up a route map at the visitor information center (see above).

The transportation situation has gotten somewhat better, not to mention nostalgic, with the TECO Line Street Car System, a new 2⅓-mile but old-fashioned streetcar system, complete with overhead power lines, that hauls passengers between downtown and Ybor City via the St. Pete Times Forum, Channelside, Garrison Seaport, and the Florida Aquarium. The cars run every 30 minutes, and one-way fares are $1.25. Check with the visitor center or call HARTline for schedules.

Taxis in Tampa don't normally cruise the streets for fares, but they do line up at public places, such as hotels, the performing-arts center, and bus and train depots. If you need a taxi, call Tampa Bay Cab (© 813/251-5555), Yellow Cab (© 813/253-0121), or United Cab (© 813/253-2424). Fares are $1 at flag fall, plus $1.50 for each mile.

EXPLORING THE THEME & ANIMAL PARKS

Adventure Island (Kids)   If the summer heat gets to you before one of Tampa's famous thunderstorms brings late-afternoon relief, you can take a waterlogged break at this 25-acre outdoor water theme park near Busch Gardens Tampa Bay (see below). You can also frolic here during the cooler days of spring and fall,

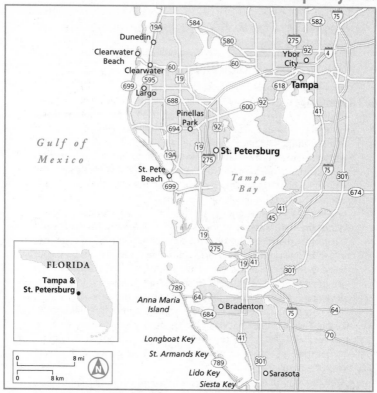

when the water is heated. The Key West Rapids, Tampa Typhoon, Gulf Scream, and other exciting water rides will drench the teens, while other, calmer rides are geared toward younger kids. Wahoo Run plunges up to five riders more than 15 feet per second as the half-enclosed tunnel corkscrews more than 600 feet to a waiting splash pool. There are also places to picnic and sunbathe, a games arcade, a volleyball complex, and an outdoor cafe. Although some people tend to go barefoot here, I suggest you make sure you bring and wear your shoes at all times as it gets kind of nasty out there after a while.

10001 Malcolm McKinley Dr. (between Busch Blvd. and Bougainvillea Ave.). © **813/987-5600.** www. 4adventure.com. Admission at least $30 adults, $28 children 3–9, plus tax; free for children 2 and under. Combination tickets with Busch Gardens Tampa Bay (1 day each) $65 adults, $55 children 3–9, free for children under 3. Website sometimes offers discounts. Parking $5. Mid-Mar to Labor Day daily 10am–5pm; Sept–Oct Fri–Sun 10am–5pm (extended hours in summer and on holidays). Closed Nov to early March. Take exit 50 off I-275 and go east on Busch Blvd. for 2 miles. Turn left onto McKinley Dr. (N. 40th St.) and entry is on right.

Busch Gardens Tampa Bay ★★ *Kids*   Although its heart-stopping thrill rides get much of the ink, this venerable theme park (it predates Disney World) ranks among the largest zoos in the country. It's a don't-miss attraction for children and adults, who can see, in person, all those wild beasts they've watched on the *Animal Planet*—and they'll get better views of them here than at Disney's Animal Kingdom in Orlando (p. 449). Busch Gardens has several thousand animals living in naturalistic environments that help carry out the park's overall African theme. Most authentic is the 80-acre plain, strongly reminiscent of the real

Cheap Thrills: What to See & Do for Free (or Almost) in the Tampa Bay Area

- **Hike, bike, or blade along Bayshore Boulevard.** The best view of downtown Tampa's skyline is from Bayshore Boulevard, a broad promenade facing the city from the western side of Hillsborough Bay. Its sidewalk is the city's favorite place to stroll, bike, or in-line skate, especially at sunset when lights in the high-rise buildings begin to twinkle on the water.
- **Party for Free in Ybor City.** Weekend afternoons turn into parties with live music in the patio of **Centro Ybor** (© 813/241-4545), the new dining-entertainment complex in the midst of Tampa's historic Ybor City district. You may find yourself paying for a pitcher of sangria in one of the center's lively pubs, but the music outside is free.
- **Watch the setting sun paint the sky.** Facing due west, the St. Pete and Clearwater beaches offer glorious sunsets over the Gulf. If you can afford to stay right on the beach, watch the colorful show from your balcony or patio. For the rest of us, the area's many public beaches are good vantage points, and most are free. The two with the least development to spoil the moment are Fort Desoto Park, south of St. Pete Beach, and Sand Key Park, just across the inlet from Clearwater Beach. They both close at dark, but by then, you may have seen the "green flash" just as the top of the sun hits the horizon. And don't forget the area's many beachside bars, where you can watch for the cost of a drink.
- **Take the ferry to a great beach.** You'll have to pay admission to Honeymoon Island State Recreation Area and another $8 for adults or $4.50 per kid to ride the ferry, but that's a small price to pay to reach **Caladesi Island State Park,** north of Clearwater (© 727/469-5942), and one of Florida's best beaches—a lovely, relatively secluded stretch of fine soft sand edged in sea grass and palmettos. You might even see dolphins cavorting offshore, or perhaps rattlesnakes, black racers, raccoons, armadillos, or rabbits from the park's nature trail.
- **Help birds to mend.** You can visit more than 500 sea and land birds recuperating at the **Suncoast Seabird Sanctuary** in Indian Shores (© 727/391-6211), the nation's largest wild-bird hospital. Cormorants, great white herons, birds of prey, ubiquitous brown pelicans: They're all here. Down Sarasota way, the **Pelican Man's Bird**

Serengeti of Tanzania and Kenya, upon which zebras, giraffes, and other animals graze. Unlike the animals on the real Serengeti, however, the grazing animals have nothing to fear from lions, hyenas, crocodiles, and other predators, which are confined to enclosures—as are hippos and elephants.

The park has eight areas, each of which has its own theme, animals, live entertainment, thrill rides, kiddie attractions, dining, and shopping. A Skyride cable car soars over the park, offering a bird's-eye view of it all. Turn left after the main gate and head to **Morocco,** a walled city with exotic architecture, craft demonstrations, a sultan's tent with snake charmers, and an exhibit featuring alligators

Sanctuary (© 941/388-4444) treats more than 5,000 injured birds and other wildlife each year. Admission is free to both, but you'll want to make a donation.

- **Poke through a rustic museum dedicated to sponges.** The highlight of any stroll along the carnival-like Sponge Docks in Tarpon Springs is the rickety **Spongeorama** (© 727/943-9509), a warehouse-turned-museum dedicated to sponges and sponge divers. You can buy a wide variety of fresh-from-the-Gulf sponges here and watch a 30-minute video about sponge-diving. Admission is free. The docks also have a host of inexpensive restaurants featuring authentic Greek cuisine brought here by the town's sponge-diving settlers.

- **Play great golf on the cheap.** A round of golf in southern Florida can cost $70 and up in winter, but Sarasota's municipal **Bobby Jones Golf Complex** (© 941/365-GOLF) has two 18-hole championship layouts and a 9-hole executive course. But get this: Greens fees range from just $5 to $25, some even including cart rental.

- **Find out what the Big Top bought.** Adults pay $12 to $15 to get in, but you'll have three "rings" to visit at the **FSU Ringling Center for the Cultural Arts** in Sarasota (© 941/359-5700, or 941/351-1660 for recorded information), which houses the phenomenal collections of circus master John Ringling. A pink Italian-Renaissance villa is filled with more than 500 years of European and American art, including one of the world's most important collections of grand 17th-century baroque paintings. The Ringlings' 30-room winter residence displays their personal mementos. And the Circus Galleries are devoted to memorabilia from "The Greatest Show on Earth."

- **Hide your plastic at St. Armand's Circle.** Don't bring your credit cards, but by all means do some window-shopping on Sarasota's St. Armand's Circle, the lushly landscaped home to more than 150 international boutiques, gift shops, and galleries rivaling those in Palm Beach and on Naples's Third Avenue South. Plan to take a break at lunch, when the otherwise expensive restaurants here offer some good deals.

and turtles. The Moorish-style Moroccan Palace Theater features an ice show, which many families consider to be the park's best entertainment for both adults and children. Here you can also attend a song-and-dance show in the Marrakech Theater. Overlooking it all is the Crown Colony Restaurant, the park's largest.

After watching the snake charmers, walk eastward past Anheuser-Busch's fabled Clydesdale horses to **Egypt,** where you can visit King Tut's tomb with its replicas of the real treasures and listen to comedian Martin Short narrate "Akbar's Adventure Tours," a wacky simulator that "transports" one and all across Egypt via camel, biplane, and mine car. The whole room moves on this

Tampa & St. Petersburg

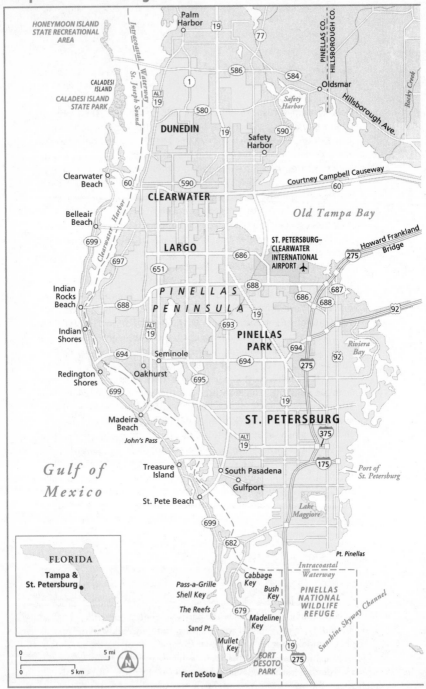

HONEYMOON ISLAND
STATE RECREATIONAL
AREA

Palm
Harbor

19

77

Intracoastal Waterway

St. Joseph Sound

586

584

PINELLAS CO.
HILLSBOROUGH CO.

CALADESI
ISLAND

CALADESI ISLAND
STATE PARK

1

ALT
19

580

Oldsmar

Safety
Harbor

Hillsborough Ave.

Rocky Creek

DUNEDIN

19

590

Safety
Harbor

Clearwater
Beach

60

590

Courtney Campbell Causeway

60

CLEARWATER

Old Tampa Bay

Belleair
Beach

699

Clearwater Harbor

LARGO

686

ST. PETERSBURG–
CLEARWATER
INTERNATIONAL
AIRPORT ✈

Howard Frankland
Bridge

275

697

651

PINELLAS

688

686

687

688

92

Indian
Rocks
Beach

688

PENINSULA

19

693

Riviera
Bay

Indian
Shores

ALT
19

PINELLAS
PARK

694

694

Seminole

695

275

92

Oakhurst

Redington
Shores

699

Madeira
Beach

John's Pass

ST. PETERSBURG

19

ALT
19

375

Gulf of
Mexico

Treasure
Island

South Pasadena

Gulfport

175

Port of
St. Petersburg

St. Pete Beach

Lake
Maggiore

699

682

Pt. Pinellas

FLORIDA

Tampa &
St. Petersburg

Pass-a-Grille
Shell Key

The Reefs

Sand Pt.

Cabbage
Key

Bush
Key

679

Madeline
Key

Intracoastal
Waterway

PINELLAS
NATIONAL
WILDLIFE
REFUGE

Sunshine Skyway Channel

Mullet
Key

FORT
DESOTO
PARK

19

275

Fort DeSoto

0   5 mi

0   5 km

N

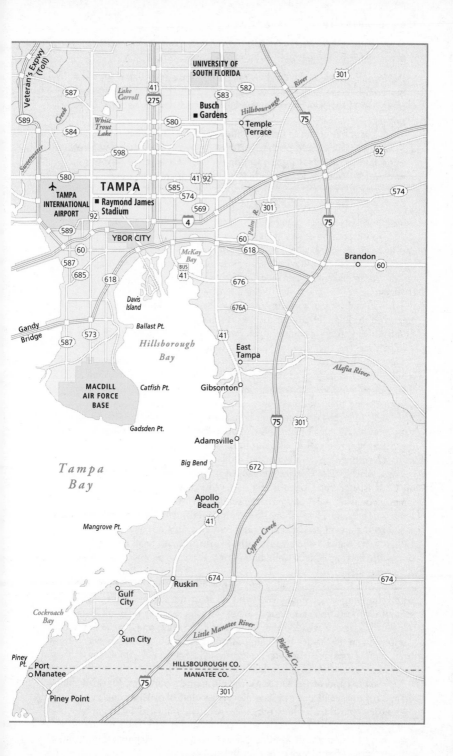

> ## Tips If You Need Another Day
>
> Once you're inside Busch Gardens Tampa Bay and decide you really need more time to see it all, check to see if the park has (frequently offered) **Next-Day Tickets,** which let you back in the next day for about $16 per person.
>
> Also, if you're going to Orlando, Busch Gardens Tampa Bay is included in the five-park version of the **FlexTicket,** a 14-day pass that also gives admission to Universal Studios Florida, SeaWorld, Islands of Adventure, and Wet 'n' Wild for $210 for adults and $176 for children 3 to 9.

ride, which lasts only 5 minutes—much less time than the usual wait to get inside. Youngsters can dig for their own ancient treasures in a sand area. Adults and kids 54 inches or taller can ride Montu, the tallest and longest inverted roller coaster in the world with seven upside-down loops. Your feet dangle loose on Montu, so make sure your shoes are tied tightly and your lunch has had time to digest.

From Egypt, walk to the **Edge of Africa,** the most unique of the park's eight areas, and the home of most of the large animals. Go immediately to the Expedition Africa Gift Shop and see if you can get on one of the park's zoologist-led wildlife tours (see the "How to See Busch Gardens" box, below).

Next stop is **Nairobi,** the most beautiful part of the park, where you can see gorillas and chimpanzees in the Myombe Reserve in a lush area that replicates their natural rainforest habitat. Nairobi also has a baby animal nursery, a petting zoo, turtle and reptile displays, an elephant exhibit (alas, the magnificent creatures seem to be bored to the point of madness), and Curiosity Caverns, where bats, reptiles, and small mammals that are active in the dark are kept in cages (it's the most traditional zoolike area here). The entry to Rhino Rally, the park's safari adventure, is at the western end of Nairobi.

Next, head to **The Congo,** highlighted by rare white Bengal tigers that live on Claw Island. The Congo is also home to two roller coasters: Kumba, the largest and fastest roller coaster in the southeastern United States (54-in. minimum height); and The Python (48-in. minimum), which twists and turns for 1,200 feet. You will get drenched—and refreshed on a hot day—by riding the Congo River Rapids, where you're turned loose in round boats that float down the swiftly flowing "river" (42-in. minimum). There are bumper cars and kiddie rides here, too.

From The Congo, walk south into **Stanleyville,** a prototype African village, with a shopping bazaar, orangutans living on an island, and the Stanleyville Theater, usually featuring shows for children. Two more water rides are here: the Tanganyika Tidal Wave (48-in. minimum height), where you'll come to a very damp end and the Stanley Falls Flume (an aqua version of a roller coaster). Also here, serving ribs and chicken, the picnic-style Stanleyville Smokehouse has some of the best chow in the park.

Up next is **Land of the Dragons,** the most entertaining area for small children. They can spend an entire day enjoying a variety of play elements in a fairy-tale setting, plus just-for-kids rides. The area is dominated by Dumphrey, a whimsical dragon who interacts with visitors and guides children around a three-story treehouse with winding stairways, tall towers, stepping stones, illuminated water geysers, and an echo chamber.

The next stop is **Bird Gardens,** the park's original core, offering rich foliage, lagoons, and a free-flight aviary for hundreds of exotic birds, including golden and American bald eagles. Be sure to see the Florida flamingos and Australian koalas while you're here.

Then you're off to take a break at the **Hospitality House,** which offers piano entertainment and free samples of Anheuser-Busch's famous beers. You must be

---

⌒Tips   How to See Busch Gardens

You can save a few dollars and avoid waiting in long lines by buying your tickets to Busch Gardens Tampa Bay at the privately owned **Tampa Bay Visitor Information Center,** opposite the park at 3601 E. Busch Blvd., at North Ednam Place (℃ **813/985-3601;** www.hometown. aol.com\tpabayinfoctr). Owner Jim Boggs worked for the park for 13 years and gives expert advice on how to get the most out of your visit. He sells slightly-discounted tickets (buying here will also save you from standing in line to buy tickets at the parks) to Busch Gardens, Adventure Island, and other attractions, and he will book hotel rooms and car rentals for you, often at a discount. The center is open Monday through Saturday from 10am to 5:30pm, Sunday from 10am to 2pm, except Christmas.

Arrive early and allow at least a day to see the park. Try not to come when it's raining, since some rides may not be operating. Bring comfortable shoes; and, remember, you will get wet on some of the rides, so wear or bring appropriate clothing (shops near the rides sell plastic ponchos for $5 or $6, but they're cheaper in the outside world). There are lockers throughout the park where you can stash your gear.

As soon as you're through the turnstiles, pick up a copy of a park map and the day's activity schedule, which tells what's showing and when at the 14 entertainment venues in the park. Then take a few minutes to carefully plan your time—it's a big park with lots to see and do.

Although you'll get close to Busch Garden's predators, hippos, and elephants in their glass-walled enclosures, the only way to mingle with the grazers is on a tour. The best is a **VIP Animal Adventure Tour,** on which you'll roam the plains in the company of a zoologist. These 2-hour excursions cost a pricey $100 per person (in addition to the park's entry fee) and usually leave about 1:30pm daily. The tours can fill up fast, and you can't call ahead for reservations, so as soon as you enter the park, go to the Expedition Africa Gift Shop, opposite the Crown Colony Restaurant in the Edge of Africa, to reserve a spot. Another (though less attractive) alternative is the 30-minute, zoologist-led **Serengeti Safari Special Tours,** in which you ride out among the grazers on the back of a flatbed truck. These are worth an extra $30 per person regardless of age. You can make reservations for the morning tour at the Expedition Africa Gift Shop, but the midday and afternoon tours are first-come, first-served. Note that children under 5 are not allowed on either tour.

Tampa

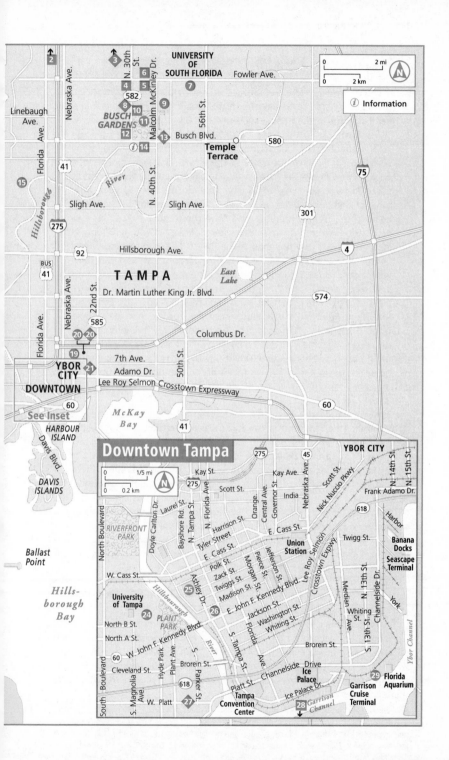

Fun Fact **Step Right Up . . . Lobster Boy Slept Here**

If you're looking for a true attraction, not of the animatronic, electronic, or supersonic ilk, deviate off the beaten path from Tampa and head straight to the little seaside town of Gibsonton. Best known as "Freaktown, USA," this town of 7,000 residents boasts the country's largest concentration of carnies (people who make their livings by working in traveling circuses and sideshows). Today, these people, once proudly known as "professional freaks," primarily work as ticket takers, clowns, acrobats, and animal trainers, but over 50 years ago, some of them were better known as "The Bearded Lady," "The Blockhead," "The Hermaphrodite," and "The Three-Legged Man." At one point in this colorful town's history, the police chief was an 8-foot, 4-inch giant while the fire chief was a dwarf. Gibsonton is also where Lobster Boy (the frequent Jerry Springer Show guest who was born with a genetic condition that caused his fingers and toes to fuse into two digit claws) called home. Surprisingly, the town wasn't very pleased with his penchant for self-exploitation and appearing on trash television. Although the sideshow stars are, for the most part, gone from Gibsonton (thanks to advanced depilatory techniques, the Bearded Lady is now clean shaven), if you're lucky you may stumble upon a bona fide barker who'll invite you to step right up to his mobile home so he can regale you with tales of the sideshow days of yore.

---

21 to imbibe (there's a limit of two free mugs per seating), but soft drinks are also available.

If your stomach can take another hair-raising ride, try **Gwazi** (48-in. minimum), an adrenaline-pumping attraction where a pair of old-fashioned wooden roller coasters (named the Lion and the Tiger) start simultaneously and whiz within a few feet of each other six times as they roar along at 50 mph and rise to 90 feet. In Gwazi's "Water Wars," participants shoot water-filled balloons at each other with big slingshots. It's a soaking way to end your visit.

If you want to experience the park's fifth and final roller coaster, head to **Timbuktu** and climb aboard the **Scorpion,** a high-speed number with a 60-foot drop and 360-degree loop (42-in. height minimum).

Added attractions include a $325, 6-hour zookeeper-for-a-day program, the devotion of 26 acres of its 65-acre Serengeti Plain to free-roaming white rhinos, and a 4-D multisensory R.L. Stine film in a new theater.

You can exchange foreign currency in the park, and interpreters are available.

Note: You can get to Busch Gardens from Orlando via shuttle buses, which pick up at area hotels between 8:00 and 10:15am for the 1½- to 2-hour ride, with return trips starting at 5pm and continuing until the park closes. Round-trip fares are $5 per person. Call ✆ **800/511-2450** for schedules, pickup locations, and reservations.

3000 E. Busch Blvd. (at McKinley Dr./N. 40th St.). ✆ **888/800-5447** or 813/987-5283. www.buschgardens. com. *Note:* Admission and hours vary so call ahead, check website, or get brochure at visitor centers. Admission single-day ticket $54 adults, $45 children 3–9, plus tax; free for children 2 and under. Daily 10am–6pm (extended hours to 7 and 8pm in summer and on holidays). Parking $8. Take I-275 north of downtown to Busch Blvd. (exit 50) and go east 2 miles. From I-75, take Fowler Ave. (exit 54) and follow the signs west.

Florida Aquarium ★★ (Kids)   See more than 5,000 aquatic animals and plants that call Florida home at this entertaining and informative attraction. The exhibits follow a drop of water from the pristine springs of the Florida Wetlands Gallery, through a mangrove forest in the Bays and Beaches Gallery, and out onto the Coral Reefs, where an impressive 43-foot-wide, 14-foot-tall panoramic window lets you look out to schools of fish and lots of sharks and stingrays. Also worth visiting are the "Explore a Shore" playground to educate the kids, a deep-water exhibit, and a tank housing moray eels. You can also go out on the bay to look for birds and sea life on 90-minute Eco-Tour cruises in the *Bay Spirit*, a 64-foot diesel-powered catamaran. The aquarium also offers a **Dive with the Sharks** program (© 813/367-4005) that gives certified scuba divers the chance to swim with blacktip reef, sand tiger, and nurse sharks for 30 minutes. The $150 price tag includes a souvenir photo and T-shirt.

701 Channelside Dr. © 813/273-4000. www.flaquarium.net. Admission $18 adults, $15 seniors, $12 children 3–11, free for children under 3. Eco-Tour $19 adults, $18 seniors, $14 children 3–11, free for children under 3. Combination aquarium admission and Eco-Tour $30 adults, $27 seniors, $20 children 3–11, free for children under 3. Website sometimes offers discounts. Parking $5. Daily 9:30am–5pm. Dolphin Quest Mon–Fri 2pm; Sat–Sun 1 and 3pm. Closed Thanksgiving and Christmas.

Lowry Park Zoo ★ (Kids)   The opportunity to watch 3,000-pound manatees, Komodo dragons, Persian leopards, and rare red pandas makes this a worth-while, albeit not entirely necessary, excursion after the kids have seen the plains of Africa at Busch Gardens. With lots of greenery, bubbling brooks, and cas-cading waterfalls, this 24-acre zoo displays animals in settings similar to their natural habitats. Other major exhibits include a Florida wildlife display, an Asian Domain, a Primate World, an Aquatic Center, a free-flight aviary with a birds-of-prey show, a hands-on Discovery Center, and an endangered-species carousel ride. The new Wallaroo Station has kids' rides, a small water park, a kangaroo walk-about, and a petting zoo. Lowry Park has one of Florida's three manatee hospital and rehabilitation centers. It's also a sanctuary for Florida pan-thers and red wolves.

1101 W. Sligh Ave. © 813/935-8552, or 813/932-0245 for recorded information. www.lowryparkzoo.com. Admission $12 adults, $11 seniors, $8 children 3–11, free for children 2 and under. Daily 9:30am–5pm. Closed Thanksgiving and Christmas. Take I-275 to Sligh Ave. (exit 48) and follow the signs.

VISITING THE MUSEUMS

Henry B. Plant Museum   Originally built in 1891 by railroad tycoon Henry B. Plant as the super-chichi 511-room Tampa Bay Hotel, this ornate building alone is worth a short trip across the river from downtown to the University of Tampa campus. Its 13 silver minarets and distinctive Moorish architecture, modeled after the Alhambra in Spain, make this National Historic Landmark a focal point of the Tampa skyline. Although the building is the highlight of a

---

A Free Attraction

The Tampa Electric Company is a hot spot, not just because it provides the juice that makes the city tick, but because the waters surrounding the plant are a haven for manatees who revel in the fact that the water here is warm—manatees need to be in water at least 68°F (20°C), and the Electric Company's water is at least that warm. The **Manatee Viewing Center** (© 813/228-4289; www.tampaelectric.com) is open from November 1 to April 15 from 10am to 5pm for viewing the manatees.

visit, don't skip its contents: art and furnishings from Europe and the Orient, and exhibits that explain the history of the original railroad resort, Florida's early tourist industry, and the hotel's role as a staging point for Theodore Roosevelt's Rough Riders during the Spanish-American War.

401 W. Kennedy Blvd. (between Hyde Park and Magnolia aves.). © 813/254-1891. www.plantmuseum. com. Free admission; suggested donation $5 adults, $2 children 12 and under. Tues–Sat 10am–4pm; Sun noon–4pm. Closed Thanksgiving, Christmas Eve, and Christmas Day. Take Kennedy Blvd. (Fla. 60) across the Hillsborough River.

MOSI (Museum of Science and Industry) ★★ *Kids*   A great place to take the kids, MOSI is the largest science center in the Southeast and has more than 450 interactive exhibits. You can step into the Gulf Hurricane and experience 74 mph winds or explore the human body in The Amazing You. If your heart is up to it, you can ride a bicycle across a 98-foot-long cable suspended 30 feet above the lobby (don't worry: you'll be harnessed to the bike). You can also watch stunning movies in Florida's first IMAX dome theater or take a 5-minute ride in a flight simulator ($3.50 additional charge). Outside, trails wind through a 47-acre nature preserve with a butterfly garden.

4801 E. Fowler Ave. (at N. 50th St.). © 813/987-6100. www.mosi.org. Admission $15 adults, $13 seniors, $12 children 2–12, free for children under 2. Admission includes IMAX movies. Daily 9am–5pm or later. From downtown, take I-275 north to the Fowler Ave. E. exit (#51). Take this 2 miles east to museum on right.

Tampa Museum of Art   Located on the east bank of the Hillsborough River, next to the round NationsBank building (locals facetiously call it the "Beer Can"), this fine-arts complex offers eight galleries with changing exhibits ranging from classical antiquities to contemporary Florida art. There's also a 7-acre riverfront park and sculpture garden. Call or check the website for the schedule of temporary exhibits. If you only have time allotted for one art museum on this trip, skip this one and head to St. Petersburg for the more innovative Salvador Dalí Museum.

600 N. Ashley Dr. (at Twiggs St.), downtown. © 813/274-8130. www.tampamuseum.com. Admission $7 adults, $6 seniors, $3 children 6–18 and students with ID cards, free for children under 6, by donation Thurs 5–8pm and Sat 10am–noon. Tues–Wed and Fri–Sat 10am–5pm; Thurs 10am–8pm; Sun 11am–5pm. Parking 90¢ per hour. Take I-275 to exit 44 (Ashley Dr.).

YBOR CITY

Northeast of downtown, the city's historic Latin district takes its name from Don Vicente Martinez Ybor (*Ee*-bore), a Spanish cigar maker who arrived here in 1886 via Cuba and Key West. Soon his and other Tampa factories were producing more than 300,000 hand-rolled stogies a day.

It may not be the cigar capital of the world anymore, but Ybor is still smokin' as the happening part of Tampa and it's one of the best places in Florida to buy hand-rolled cigars. It's not on a par with New Orleans's Bourbon Street, Washington's Georgetown, or Miami's South Beach, but good food and great music dominate the scene, especially on weekends when the streets bustle until 4am (note to claustrophobes: avoid it at all costs on weekends). Live-music offerings run the gamut from jazz and blues to rock.

At the heart of it all is **Centro Ybor,** a dining-shopping-entertainment complex sprawling between 7th and 8th avenues and 16th and 17th streets (© 813/ 242-4660; www.centroybor.com). Here you'll find a multiscreen cinema, a comedy club, several restaurants, and a large open-air bar. The Ybor City Chamber of Commerce has its visitor center here (see "Essentials," earlier in this chapter), and the Ybor City State Museum's gift shop is here as well (see below).

Check with the visitor center about **walking tours** of the historic district. **Ybor City Ghost Walks** (© 813/242-4660) will take you to the spookier parts of the area beginning at 4pm Thursday and Saturday. They cost $10 per person, last 75 minutes, and are by reservation only.

Even if you're not a cigar smoker, you'll enjoy a stroll through the **Ybor City State Museum** ✦, 1818 9th Ave., between 18th and 19th streets (© 813/247-6323; www.ybormuseum.org), housed in the former Ferlita Bakery (1896–1973). You can take a self-guided tour around the museum to see a collection of cigar labels, cigar memorabilia, and works by local artisans. Admission is $2 per person. Depending on the availability of volunteer docents, admission includes a 15-minute guided tour of **La Casita,** a renovated cigar worker's cottage adjacent to the museum; it's furnished as it was at the turn of the last century. The museum is open daily from 9am to 5pm, but the best time to visit is between 11am and 3pm, when you have the best chance for the guided tour of La Casita. Better yet, plan to catch the cigar-rolling demonstrations (ongoing; no specific schedule) Friday through Sunday from 10am to 3pm.

Housed in a 100-year-old, three-story former cigar factory, **Ybor City Brewing Company,** 2205 N. 20th St., facing Palm Avenue, produces Ybor Gold and other brews, none with preservatives.

Like any area with trendy bars and restaurants, things are always changing, going out of business, and opening, so you may want to check with www.ybortimes.com for the latest in what's hot in Ybor City.

ORGANIZED TOURS

Swiss Chalet Tours, 3601 E. Busch Blvd. (© 813/985-3601; www.hometown.aol.com\tpabayinfoctr), opposite Busch Gardens in the privately run Tampa Bay Visitor Information Center (see the "How to See Busch Gardens" box, above), operates guided bus tours of Tampa, Ybor City, and environs. The 4-hour tours of Tampa are given from 10am to 3pm daily, with a stop for lunch at the Columbia Restaurant in Ybor City. They cost $45 for adults and $40 for children 12 and under. The full-day tours (10am–5pm) of both Tampa and St. Petersburg give a good overview of the two cities and the beaches; these cost $70 for adults and $65 for children 12 and under. Reservations are required at least 24 hours in advance; passengers are picked up at major hotels and various other points in the Tampa/St. Petersburg area. The company can also book bus tours to Orlando, Sarasota, Bradenton, and other regional destinations (call for schedules, prices, and reservations).

AFFORDABLE OUTDOOR ACTIVITIES & SPECTATOR SPORTS

BIKING, IN-LINE SKATING & JOGGING   Bayshore Boulevard, a 7-mile-long promenade, is famous for its sidewalk right on the shores of Hillsborough Bay and is a favorite for runners, joggers, walkers, and in-line skaters. The route goes from the western edge of downtown in a southward direction, passing stately old homes in Hyde Park, a few high-rise condominiums, retirement communities, and houses of worship, ending at Ballast Point Park. The view from the promenade across the bay to the downtown skyline is unmatched here (Bayshore Blvd. is also great for a drive).

FISHING   For charters, try **Captain Jim's Inshore Sportfishing Charters,** 512 Palm Ave., Palm Harbor (© 727/439-9017; www.captainhud.com), which offers private sport-fishing trips for tarpon, redfish, trout, and snook. Rates are $300 to $450 for two anglers. Call for schedule and required reservations.

GOLF Tampa has three municipal golf courses where you can play for about $30 to $35, a relative pittance when compared with fees at the privately owned courses here and elsewhere in Florida. The **Babe Zaharias Municipal Golf Course,** 11412 Forest Hills Dr., north of Lowry Park (© 813/631-4374), is an 18-hole, par-70 course with a pro shop, putting greens, and a driving range. It is the shortest of the municipal courses, but its small greens and narrow fairways present ample challenges. Water provides obstacles on 12 of the 18 holes at **Rocky Point Golf Course,** 4151 Dana Shores Dr. (© 813/673-4316), located between the airport and the bay. It's a par-71 course with a pro shop, a practice range, and putting greens. On the Hillsborough River in north Tampa, the **Rogers Park Golf Course,** 7910 N. 30th St. (© 813/673-4396), is an 18-hole, par-72 championship course with a lighted driving and practice range. All the courses are open daily from 7am to dusk, and lessons and club rentals are available.

You can book starting times and get information about these and the area's other courses by calling **Tee Times USA** (© 800/374-8633; www.teetimes usa.com).

If you want to do some serious work on your game, the **Arnold Palmer Golf Academy World Headquarters** is at Saddlebrook Resort, 5700 Saddlebrook Way, Wesley Chapel, 12 miles north of Tampa (© 800/729-8383 or 813/973-1111; www.saddlebrookresort.com). Half-day and hourly instruction is available as well as 2-, 3-, and 5-day programs for adults and juniors. You have to stay at the resort or enroll in the golf program to play at Saddlebrook.

For course information online, go to **www.golf.com** and **www.florida golfing.com,** or call the **Florida Sports Foundation** (© 850/488-8347) or **Florida Golfing** (© 866/833-2663).

SPECTATOR SPORTS National Football League fans can catch the Super Bowl champ **Tampa Bay Buccaneers** at the modern, 66,000-seat Raymond James Stadium, 4201 N. Dale Mabry Hwy., at Dr. Martin Luther King Jr. Boulevard (© 813/879-2827; www.buccaneers.com) August through December. Single-game tickets (starting at $30) are very hard to come by.

The National Hockey League's **Tampa Bay Lightning,** winners of the 2004 Stanley Cup, play in the St. Pete Times Forum, beginning in October (© 813/301-6500; www.tampabaylightning.com). You can usually get single-game tickets ($8–$155) on game day.

New York Yankees fans can watch the Bronx Bombers during baseball spring training from mid-February to the end of March at Legends Field (© 813/879-2244 or 813/875-7753; www.yankees.mlb.com), opposite Raymond James Stadium. This scaled-down replica of Yankee Stadium is the largest spring-training facility in Florida, with a 10,000-seat capacity. Tickets are $10 to $16. The club's minor-league team, the **Tampa Yankees** (same phone and website), plays at Legends Field April through August.

The only thoroughbred racecourse on Florida's west coast, **Tampa Bay Downs,** 11225 Racetrack Rd., Oldsmar (© 800/200-4434 in Florida, or 813/855-4401; www.tampadowns.com), is the home of the Tampa Bay Derby. Races are held from December to May ($2 general admission, $3 clubhouse), and the track presents simulcasts year-round. Call for post times.

TENNIS Players at all levels can sharpen their games at the **Hopman Tennis Program,** at the Saddlebrook Resort. You must be a member or a guest to play here.

SHOPPING

Hyde Park and Ybor City are two areas of Tampa worth some window-shopping, perhaps sandwiched around lunch at one of their fine restaurants (see "Great Deals on Dining," later in this chapter).

On the mall front, the newest player in town is the upscale **International Plaza** (© 813/342-3790; www.shopinternationalplaza.com) near Tampa International Airport, where the headliners include Neiman Marcus, Nordstrom, and Lord & Taylor.

CIGARS Ybor City is no longer a major producer of hand-rolled cigars, but you can still watch artisans making stogies at the **Gonzalez y Martinez Cigar Factory,** 2025 7th Ave., in the Columbia Restaurant building (© 813/247-2469). Gonzalez and Martinez are recent arrivals from Cuba and don't speak English, but the staff does at the adjoining **Columbia Cigar Store** (it's best to enter here). Rollers are on duty Monday through Saturday from 10am to 6pm.

You can stock up on fine domestic and imported cigars at **El Sol,** 1728 E. 7th Ave. (© 813/247-5554), the city's oldest cigar store; **King Corona Cigar Factory,** 1523 E. 7th Ave. (© 813/241-9109); and **Metropolitan Cigars & Wine,** 2014 E. 7th Ave. (© 813/248-3304).

SHOPPING CENTERS **Old Hyde Park Village,** 1507 W. Swann Ave., at South Dakota Avenue (© 813/251-3500; www.oldhydeparkvillage.com), is a terrific alternative to cookie-cutter suburban malls. Walk around little shops in the sunshine and check out Hyde Park, one of the city's oldest and most historic neighborhoods at the same time. The cluster of 50 upscale shops and boutiques is set in a village layout. The selection includes Williams-Sonoma, Pottery Barn, Restoration Hardware, Brooks Brothers, Crabtree & Evelyn, and Godiva, to name a few. There's a free parking garage on South Oregon Avenue behind Jacobson's department store. Most shops are open Monday through Saturday from 10am to 7pm and Sundays from noon to 5pm. There's a farmers' market (at Swan and Dakota avenues) every Saturday from 9am to 2pm offering local produce, seafood, and assorted tchotchkes.

The centerpiece of the downtown seaport renovation, the massive mall known as **Channelside at Garrison Seaport,** on Channelside Drive between the Garrison Seaport and the Florida Aquarium (© 813/223-4250; www.channelside.com), has stores, restaurants, a dance club, a games arcade, and a multiscreen cinema with an IMAX screen.

In Ybor City, the new **Centro Ybor,** on 7th Avenue East at 16th Street (© 813/242-4660; www.centroybor.com), is primarily a dining and entertainment complex, but you'll find a few national stores here such as American Eagle, Birkenstock, Urban Outfitters, and Victoria's Secret.

ACCOMMODATIONS YOU CAN AFFORD

Hillsborough County adds 12% tax to your hotel room bill.

The nearest chain motel to the park is **Howard Johnson Hotel Near Busch Gardens Maingate,** 4139 E. Busch Blvd. (© 800/4061411 or 813/988-9191), an older property that was extensively renovated in 1999. It's 1½ blocks east of the main entrance. A bit farther away, the 500-room **Embassy Suites Hotel and Conference Center,** 3705 Spectrum Blvd., facing Fowler Avenue (© 800/362-2779 or 813/977-7066; fax 813/977-7933), is the plushest and most expensive establishment near the park. Almost across the avenue stands **LaQuinta Inn & Suites,** 3701 E. Fowler Ave. (© 800/687-6667 or 813/910-7500; fax 813/910-7600). Side-by-side, just south of Fowler Avenue, are editions of **AmeriSuites,**

Tips **Discount Packages**

Many Tampa hotels combine tickets to major attractions such as Busch Gardens in their packages, so always ask about special deals.

11408 N. 30th St. (© **800/833-1516** or 813/979-1922; fax 813/979-1926), and **DoubleTree Guest Suites,** 11310 N. 30th St. (© **800/222-8733** or 813/971-7690; fax 813/972-5525).

Baymont Inn & Suites *Value*   Fake banana trees and a parrot cage welcome guests to the terra cotta–floored lobby of this comfortable and convenient member of the small chain of cost-conscious but amenity-rich motels. All rooms are spacious and have ceiling fans and desks. Rooms with king beds also have recliners; business rooms sport dataport phones and extra large desks; and the suites have refrigerators and microwave ovens. Outside, a courtyard with an unheated swimming pool has plenty of space for sunning. There's no restaurant on the premises, but plenty are within walking distance.

9202 N. 30th St. (at Busch Blvd.), Tampa, FL 33612. © **800/428-3438** or 813/930-6900. Fax 813/930-0563. www.baymontinns.com. 146 units. Winter $89–$119 double; off season $79–$99 double. Rates include continental breakfast and local phone calls. AE, DC, DISC, MC, V. **Amenities:** Outdoor pool; game room; coin-op washers and dryers. *In room:* A/C, TV, dataport, fridge, coffeemaker, hair dryer, iron.

Best Western All Suites Hotel *Value*   This three-story all-suites hotel is the most beachlike vacation venue you'll find close to the park. Whimsical signs lead you around a lush tropical courtyard with heated pool, hot tub, and a lively, sports-oriented Tiki bar. They pride themselves on being "so close" to Busch Gardens that "the parrots escape to our trees," hence the hotel's nickname "that parrot place." The bar can get noisy before closing at 9pm, and ground-level units are musty, so ask for an upstairs suite away from the action. Suite living rooms are well equipped and separate bedrooms have narrow screened patios or balconies. Great for kids, 11 "family suites" have bunk beds in addition to a queen-size bed for parents.

Behind Busch Gardens, 3001 University Center Dr. (faces N. 30th St. between Busch Blvd. and Fowler Ave.), Tampa, FL 33612. © **800/786-7446** or 813/971-8930. Fax 813/971-8935. www.thatparrotplace.com. 150 units. Winter $99–$159 suite for 2; off season $79–$99 suite for 2. Rates include hot and cold breakfast buffet. AE, DC, DISC, MC, V. **Amenities:** Restaurant (breakfast and dinner only); bar; heated outdoor pool; access to nearby health club; Jacuzzi; game room; limited room service; laundry service; coin-op washers and dryers. *In room:* A/C, TV, dataport, fridge, coffeemaker, hair dryer, iron.

GREAT DEALS ON DINING

We have organized the restaurants that follow by geographic area: near Busch Gardens, in or near Hyde Park (across the Hillsborough River from downtown), and in Ybor City. Although Ybor City is better known, Tampa's trendiest dining scene is along South Howard Avenue—"SoHo" to the locals—between West Kennedy Boulevard and the bay in affluent Hyde Park.

NEAR BUSCH GARDENS

You'll find the national fast food and family restaurants east of I-275 on Busch Boulevard and Fowler Avenue.

Ristorante Francesco ✦ NORTHERN ITALIAN   Gregarious owner Francesco "Frankie" Murchesini patrols the tables in the hottest dining spot in

North Tampa (as witnessed by the photos of famous patrons adorning the walls). When not playing his harmonica to celebrate someone's birthday, Frankie's making sure everyone is enjoying his delicious *cernia portofino* (scrumptious grouper in a brandy sauce with shrimp) and other Northern-Italian dishes. His sister makes the pasta, which shows up in more traditional fare such as seafood over linguini with a choice of marinara or white-wine sauce. Be sure to start with half a Caesar salad.

In La Place Village Shopping Center, 1441 E. Fletcher Ave. (between 14th and 15th sts.). 𝒞 **813/971-3649.** Reservations recommended. Main courses $10–$27. AE, DC, DISC, MC. V. Mon–Fri 11:30am–2:30pm and 5:30–10pm; Sat 5:30–10pm; Sun 5–9pm.

Shells 𝄐 *Value* SEAFOOD You'll see Shells restaurants in many parts of Florida, and with good reason, for this casual, award-winning chain consistently provides excellent value. They all have virtually identical menus, prices, and hours. Particularly good are the spicy Jack Daniel's buffalo shrimp and scallop appetizers. Main courses range from the usual fried seafood platters to pastas and charcoal-grilled shrimp, fish, steaks, and chicken.

11010 N. 30th St. (between Busch Blvd. and Fowler Ave.). 𝒞 **813/977-8456.** Main courses $9–$20 (most $10–$12). AE, DISC, MC, V. Sun–Thurs 11:30am–10pm; Fri–Sat 11:30am–11pm.

Super-Cheap Eats

Mel's Hot Dogs *Kids* AMERICAN Catering to everyone from businesspeople on a lunch break to hungry families craving inexpensive all-beef hot dogs, Mel Lohn's red-and-white cottage offers everything from "bagel-dogs" to bacon/cheddar Reuben-style hot dogs. All choices are served on a poppy-seed bun and can be ordered with french fries and a choice of coleslaw or baked beans. Even the decor is dedicated to wieners: The walls and windows are lined with hot-dog memorabilia, and there's usually a wiener-mobile parked out front. And just in case hot-dog mania hasn't won you over, there are a few alternative choices (chicken, beef and veggie burgers, and terrific onion rings).

Amish Country South?

Twelve miles east of Tampa, you'll find **Behind the Fence,** 1400 Viola Dr. at Country Side Street (𝒞 **813/685-8201**), a fabulous and secluded country-style B&B in Brandon, Florida. Innkeeper Larry Yoss, raised in an Amish area in Ohio, brought his heritage to Florida by encouraging traveling artisans to hang out in the inn's backyard where they'd demonstrate their skills in soap-making, candle dipping, basket weaving, blacksmithing, looming, and open-hearth cooking. This became a yearly August to September weekend trip into the past, which is often carried over to Christmas, during which time Behind the Fence re-creates itself as an homage to Christmas in the 1800s (though it's a great place to stay at any time of the year). The inn itself is as charming as it sounds, with a porch overlooking a pool, breakfasts including Amish sweet rolls, and three guest rooms in the main house usually rented by friends and families because they share a single bathroom. The two cottage rooms by the pool are authentically furnished and have their own facilities including claw-foot tubs. Rates are Amishly reasonable, from $69 to $89.

4136 E. Busch Blvd., at 42nd St. ⓒ 813/985-8000. Most items $4–$9. No credit cards (but they have an ATM machine on premises). Sun–Thurs 11am–8pm; Fri–Sat 11am–9pm.

HYDE PARK

Bella's Italian Cafe ⋆ Ⓥⁿˡᵘᵉ ITALIAN   Creative dishes and very reasonable prices make this sophisticated yet informal cafe one of SoHo's most popular neighborhood hangouts. Although you can order the wood-fired pizzas and homemade pasta under traditional Bolognese or Alfredo sauces, the stars here feature the tasty likes of blackened chicken in a creamy tomato sauce over fettuccine, or shrimp and scallops in a roasted tomato sauce over bow-tie pasta. Finish with the house version of tiramisu. Local professionals flock to the friendly bar during two-for-one happy hours nightly from 4 to 7pm and from 11pm until closing. The open kitchen provides only appetizers, salads, pizzas, and desserts after 11pm.

1413 S. Howard Ave. (at Mississippi Ave.). 813/254-3355. Reservations not accepted. Main courses $7–$15; pizza $7.50–$9.50. AE, DC, DISC, MC, V. Mon–Tues 11:30am–11:30pm; Wed–Thurs 11:30am–12:30am; Fri 11am–1:30am; Sat 4pm–1:30am; Sun 4–11:30pm.

Four Green Fields IRISH/AMERICAN   Just across the bridge from the downtown convention center, this thatched-roof Irish pub may be surrounded by palm trees instead of potato fields, but it still offers the ambience and tastes of Ireland. Staffed by Irish immigrants, the large room with a square bar in the center smells of Bass and Harp ales. The Gaelic stew is predictably bland, but the salads and sandwiches are passable. The live Irish music Thursday through Saturday nights and on Sunday afternoon draws a fun crowd ranging from post-college to early retirees.

205 W. Platt St. (between Parker St. and Plant Ave.). ⓒ 813/254-4444. www.fourgreenfields.com. Reservations accepted. Main courses $9.50–$15; sandwiches $6–$7. AE, MC, V. Daily 11am–3am.

Wine Exchange ⋆⋆ MEDITERRANEAN   This Tampa hot spot is an oenophile's dream come true, in which each dish is paired with a particular wine available by the bottle or glass. While the menu is rather simple, featuring pizzas, pastas, salads, and sandwiches, the daily specials are more elaborate, including grilled Delmonico steak, blackened pork tenderloin, or dijon-crusted salmon. The outdoor patio is a great place to sit, that is, if there's room. There's almost always a wait at this buzzworthy eatery.

1611 W. Swan Ave. ⓒ 813/254-9463. Reservations not accepted. Main courses $10–$22. AE, DC, DISC, MC, V. Mon–Fri 11:30am–10pm; Sat 11am–11 pm, Sun 11am–9 pm; brunch on Sat and Sun 11am–3pm.

Worth a Splurge

Bern's Steak House ⋆⋆ STEAKHOUSE   The exterior of this famous steakhouse looks like a factory. Inside, however, some say it looks like a brothel with eight ornate dining rooms with themes such as Rhône, Burgundy, and Irish Rebellion. However you perceive the decor, this is a carnivore's paradise, one to which I actually drove from Miami and back just for dinner. At Bern's you order and pay for expertly charcoal-grilled steaks of perfectly aged beef according to the thickness and weight (the 60-oz., 3-in.-thick Porterhouse can feed four adults). The phone book–size wine list—one of the restaurant's most famous attributes—offers more than 7,000 selections, with many available by the glass. Ask your server for a sampling before you purchase a bottle.

Upstairs, the restaurant's other most famous attribute—the dessert quarters—have 50 romantic booths paneled in aged California redwood, which can privately seat from 2 to 12 guests each. All of these little chambers are equipped with phones for placing your order and closed-circuit TVs for watching and listening to a resident pianist. The dessert menu offers almost 100 selections, plus some 1,400 after-dinner drinks. It's possible to reserve a booth for dessert only, but preference is given to those who dine.

The big secret here is that steak sandwiches are available at the bar but are not mentioned on the menu. Smaller versions of the chargrilled steaks served in the dining rooms, they come with a choice of french fries or crispy onion rings. Add a salad and you have a terrific meal for about half the price of the least-expensive main course. **Sidebern's,** 2208 W. Morrison Ave. (at S. Howard Ave.) (*②* 813/258-2233), is the restaurant's New American offshoot, which is also quite good, but if you had to choose between the two, choose the original, because missing Bern's would be like seeing the remake of *Psycho* without ever seeing the original.

1208 S. Howard Ave. (at Marjory Ave.). *②* 813/251-2421. www.bernssteakhouse.com. Reservations recommended. Main courses $17–$59; sandwiches $9–$12. AE, DC, DISC, MC, V. Daily 5–11pm. Closed Christmas. Valet parking $5.

YBOR CITY

Big City Tavern 🐾 NEW AMERICAN   Although this restaurant is a chain, located in West Palm Beach and Fort Lauderdale, Ybor City's Big City Tavern take the prize for best decor, housed in a converted ballroom and featuring columns, floor to ceiling windows, and wrought-iron balconies. The food's pretty good, too, especially the roasted duck with mango and basil risotto, and the bar scene is a people-watching paradise as a youngish, well heeled, hip clientele gathers to trade tales of life in the big city.

1600 E. 8th Ave. *②* 813/247-3000. Reservations recommended. Main courses $11–$20. AE, MC, V. Sun–Thurs 11:30am–1am; Fri–Sat 11:30am–2am.

Carmine's Restaurant & Bar 🐾 CUBAN/ITALIAN/AMERICAN   Bright blue poles hold up an ancient pressed-tin ceiling above this noisy corner cafe. It's not the cleanest joint in town, but a great variety of loyal local patrons gather here for genuine Cuban sandwiches—smoked ham, roast pork, Genoa salami, Swiss cheese, pickles, salad dressing, mustard, lettuce, and tomato on crispy Cuban bread. There's a vegetarian version, too, and the combination half-sandwich and choice of black beans and rice or a bowl of Spanish soup made with sausages, potatoes, and garbanzo beans all make a hearty meal for just $7 at lunch, $8 at dinner. Main courses are led by Cuban-style roast pork, thin-cut pork chops with mushroom sauce, spaghetti with a blue-crab tomato sauce, and a few seafood and chicken platters.

1802 E. 7th Ave. (at 18th St.). *②* 813/248-3834. Reservations not accepted. Main courses $7–$17; sandwiches $4–$8. No credit cards. Mon–Tues 11am–11pm; Wed–Thurs 11am–1am; Fri–Sat 11am–3am; Sun 11am–6pm.

Worth a Splurge

Columbia 🐾🐾🐾 SPANISH   Dating from 1905, this hand painted tile building occupies an entire city block in the heart of Ybor City. Tourists flock here to soak up the ambience, and so do the locals because it's so much fun to clap along during fire-belching Spanish flamenco floor shows Monday through Saturday evenings ($6 per person additional charge). You can't help coming back time after time for the famous Spanish bean soup and original "1905" salad. The *paella a la valenciana* is outstanding, with more than a dozen ingredients from Gulf grouper and Gulf pink shrimp to calamari, mussels, clams, chicken, and pork. One of our favorites is *boliche* (eye of round stuffed with chorizo), accompanied by plantains and black beans and rice. All entrees come with a crispy hunk of Cuban bread with butter. Lighter appetites can choose from a limited menu of tapas, including "Cuban caviar" (actually a spicy black-bean dip). The decor throughout is graced with hand painted tiles, wrought-iron chandeliers, dark woods, rich red fabrics, and stained-glass windows. You can breathe your own fumes in the Cigar Bar.

2117 E. 7th Ave. (between 21st and 22nd sts.). ℂ 813/248-4961. www.columbiarestaurant.com. Reservations recommended. Main courses $14–$28. AE, DC, DISC, MC, V. Mon–Thurs 11am–10pm; Fri–Sat 11am–11pm; Sun noon–9pm.

TAMPA AFTER DARK

The Tampa/Hillsborough Arts Council maintains an **Artsline** (ℂ **813/229-2787**), a 24-hour information service providing the latest on current and upcoming cultural events. Racks in many restaurants and bars have copies of *Weekly Planet* (**www.weeklyplanet.com**), *Focus,* and *Accent on Tampa Bay,* three free publications detailing what's going on in the entire bay area. And you can also check the "BayLife" and "Friday Extra" sections of *The Tampa Tribune* (**www.tampatrib.com**) and the Thursday "Weekend" section of the *St. Petersburg Times* (**www.sptimes.com**). The visitor center usually has copies of the week's newspaper sections (see "Essentials," earlier in this chapter).

THE CLUB & MUSIC SCENE Ybor City is Tampa's favorite nighttime venue by far. All you have to do is stroll along 7th Avenue East between 15th and 20th streets, and you'll hear music blaring out of the clubs. The avenue is packed with people, a majority of them high schoolers and early 20-somethings, on Friday and Saturday from 9pm to 3am, but you'll also find something going on Tuesday through Thursday, and even on Sundays. The clubs change names and character frequently, so you don't need names, addresses, or phone numbers; your ears will guide you along 7th Avenue East. With all of the sidewalk seating, it is easy to judge what the clientele is like in any given place and make your choice from there.

Ybor City and Bern's Steak House are command central for the boozy sophisticates of Tampa, but if you go downtown, you'll find the true hub of Tampa's bar scene in the form of, well, The Hub, 719 N. Franklin St. (ℂ **813/229-1553**), a classic dive bar in which judges, lawyers, and the over-21 set shake and stir over stiff libations and a fabulous jukebox.

The center of the action these days is **Centro Ybor,** on 7th Avenue East at 16th Street (ℂ **813/242-4660;** www.thecentroybor.com), the district's large dining-and-entertainment complex. The restaurants and pubs in this family-oriented center tend to be considerably tamer than many of those along 7th Avenue, at least on nonweekend nights. You don't have to pay to listen to live music in the center's patio on weekend afternoons.

THE PERFORMING ARTS With a prime downtown location on 9 acres along the east bank of the Hillsborough River, the huge **Tampa Bay Performing Arts Center** ✸, 1010 N. MacInnes Place next to the Tampa Museum of Art

---

⌒ Tips Careful Where You Park

Parking can be scarce during nighttime in Ybor City, and the area has seen an occasional robbery late at night. Play it safe and use the municipal parking lots behind the shops on 8th Avenue East or the new parking garages near Centro Ybor, on 7th Avenue East at 16th Street.

(© **800/955-1045** or 813/229-7827; www.tampacenter.com), is the largest performing-arts venue south of the Kennedy Center in Washington, D.C. Accordingly, this four-theater complex is the focal point of Tampa's performing-arts scene, presenting a wide range of Broadway plays, classical and pop concerts, operas, cabarets, improv, and special events.

A sightseeing attraction in its own right, the restored **Tampa Theatre,** 711 Franklin St. (© **813/274-8286;** www.tampatheatre.org), between Zack and Polk streets, dates from 1926 and is on the National Register of Historic Places. It presents a varied program of classic, foreign, and alternative films, as well as concerts and special events. (And it's said to be haunted!)

The 66,321-seat **Raymond James Stadium,** 4201 N. Dale Mabry Hwy. (© **813/673-4300;** www.raymondjames.com/stadium), is sometimes the site of headliner concerts. The **USF Sun Dome,** 4202 E. Fowler Ave. (© **813/974-3111;** www.sundome.org), on the University of South Florida campus, hosts major concerts by touring pop stars, rock bands, jazz groups, and other contemporary artists.

Bars featuring live music include **Whiskey Joe's,** 2500 N. Rocky Point Dr. (© **813/281-0557**), a bayfront shack with plenty of visual and audible color; Ybor City's **Twilight,** 1507 E. 7th Ave. (© **813/247-4225**), an industrial-chic soundstage for the likes of local bands and national bands such as Seven Mary Three; and **Skipper's Smokehouse,** 910 Skipper Rd. (© **813/971-0666**), a Key West–style former smokehouse turned blues, jazz, zydeco, ska, and reggae hot spot.

Ticketmaster (© **813/287-8844**) sells tickets to most events and shows.

2 St. Petersburg ⊛

20 miles SW of Tampa, 289 miles NW of Miami, 84 miles SW of Orlando

On the western shore of the bay, St. Petersburg stands in contrast to Tampa, much like San Francisco compares to Oakland in California. Whereas Tampa is the area's business, industrial, and shipping center, St. Petersburg was conceived and built a century ago primarily for tourists and wintering snowbirds. Here you'll find one of the most picturesque and pleasant downtowns of any city in Florida, with a waterfront promenade and the famous, inverted pyramid-shaped Pier offering great views across the bay, plus quality museums, interesting shops, and a few good restaurants. Thanks to an urban redevelopment program, St. Pete has awoken from its slumber and is starting to actually resemble a city that could be considered "hip," with renewed, restored streetscapes full of punk'd out skateboarders, clubs, bars, and a vibrancy that goes well beyond the excitement surrounding Bingo night at the "adult" communities in town.

Away from downtown, the city pretty much consists of strip malls dividing residential neighborhoods, but plan at least to have a look around the charming bayfront area. If you don't do anything else, go out on The Pier and take a pleasant stroll along Bayshore Drive.

ESSENTIALS

GETTING THERE   **Tampa International Airport,** approximately 16 miles northeast of St. Petersburg, is the prime gateway for the area (see "Essentials," in section 1, earlier in this chapter). The primary carrier at **St. Petersburg–Clearwater International Airport,** on Roosevelt Boulevard (Fla. 686) about 10 miles north of downtown St. Petersburg (© **727/453-7800;** www.fly2pie.com), is **American Trans Air (ATA)** (© **800/435-9282;** www.ata.com). The Canadian

---

Fun Fact Sunny Days

St. Petersburg is listed in the Guinness Book of World Records as the city with the longest number of days of consecutive sunshine—768 to be exact. From February 9, 1967 to March 17, 1969, the city experienced not a drop of rain, no clouds, just pure, unadulterated, tanning-friendly sunshine!

---

carrier **Air Transat** (© 877/872-6728; www.airtransat.com) flies here during the winter months. **Amtrak** (© 800/USA-RAIL; www.amtrak.com) has bus connections from its Tampa station to downtown St. Petersburg (see "Getting There," in section 1, above).

VISITOR INFORMATION   For advance information about St. Petersburg and the beaches (see section 3, later in this chapter), contact the **St. Petersburg/Clearwater Area Convention & Visitors Bureau,** 14450 46th St. N., Clearwater, FL 34622 (© **800/345-6710,** or 727/464-7200 for hotel reservations; fax 727/464-7222; www.floridasbeach.com for information specific to the beaches).

When you arrive, you can head to the **St. Petersburg Area Chamber of Commerce,** 100 2nd Ave. N. (at 1st St.), St. Petersburg, FL 33701 (© **727/821-4069;** fax 727/895-6326; www.stpete.com). Across the street from the BayWalk shopping-and-dining complex, this downtown main office and visitor center is open Monday through Friday from 8am to 5pm, Saturday from 10am to 4pm, and Sunday from noon to 4pm. Ask for a copy of the chamber's visitor guide, which lists hotels, motels, condominiums, and other accommodations.

Also downtown, there are **walk-in information centers** on the first level of The Pier and in the lobby of the Florida International Museum (see "Seeing the Top Attractions," below).

The chamber also operates the **Suncoast Welcome Center** (© **727/573-1449**), on Ulmerton Road at exit 31B southbound off I-275 (there's no exit here for northbound traffic). The center is open daily from 9am to 5pm except New Year's Day, Easter, Thanksgiving, and Christmas.

GETTING AROUND   The **Pinellas Suncoast Transit Authority/PSTA** (© 727/530-9911; www.psta.net) operates regular bus service throughout St. Petersburg and the rest of the Pinellas Peninsula. Rides cost $1.25 for adults, 60¢ for seniors, and 75¢ for students.

If you need a cab, call **Yellow Cab** (© 727/821-7777) or **Independent Cab** (© 727/327-3444). Fares are $2 at flag fall, plus $1.60 for each additional mile.

SEEING THE TOP ATTRACTIONS

Florida Holocaust Museum 🔾   This thought-provoking museum (the fourth-largest Holocaust museum in the U.S.) has exhibits about the Holocaust (Jewish life before the Holocaust, the rise of the Nazi party, the world's response, and so on), including a boxcar used to transport human cargo to the Auschwitz death camp in Poland and a second-floor gallery of art relating to the Holocaust. Its main focus, however, is to promote tolerance and understanding in the present. It was founded by Walter P. Loebenberg, a local businessman who escaped Nazi Germany in 1939 and fought with the U.S. Army in World War II.

Downtown St. Petersburg

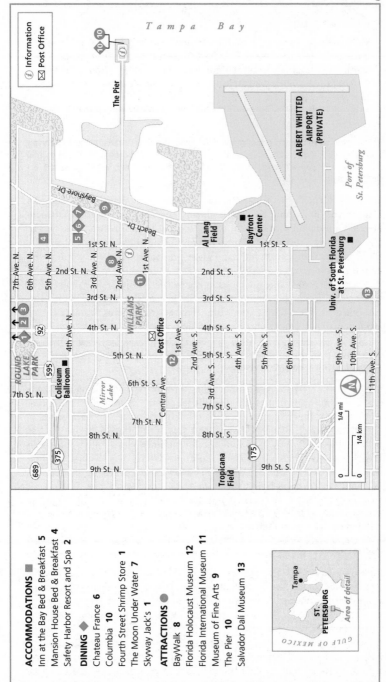

ACCOMMODATIONS ■
Inn at the Bay Bed & Breakfast **5**
Mansion House Bed & Breakfast **4**
Safety Harbor Resort and Spa **2**

DINING ◆
Chateau France **6**
Columbia **10**
Fourth Street Shrimp Store **1**
The Moon Under Water **7**
Skyway Jack's **1**

ATTRACTIONS ●
BayWalk **8**
Florida Holocaust Museum **12**
Florida International Museum **11**
Museum of Fine Arts **9**
The Pier **10**
Salvador Dali Museum **13**

Fun Fact Open-Air Mail

St. Petersburg residents don't have to go inside to get mail out of their boxes at St. Petersburg's open-air **Post Office,** at the corner of 1st Avenue North and 4th Street North. Built in 1917, this granite, arcaded Spanish Colonial structure is a popular local landmark and is often photographed by those enchanted by its charm.

---

55 5th St. S. (between Central Ave. and 1st Ave. S.). © **800/960-7448** or 727/820-0100. www.flholocaust museum.org. Admission $8 adults, $7 seniors and college students, $3 children 6–18, free for kids under 6. Mon–Fri 10am–5pm; Sat–Sun noon–5pm (last admission at 4pm). Closed Easter, Rosh Hashanah, Yom Kippur, Thanksgiving, and Christmas.

Florida International Museum ★★   Housed in the former Maas Brothers Department Store, long an area landmark, this excellent museum attracted 600,000 visitors from around the world when it opened its first exhibition in 1995, and the success has continued. Its outstanding exhibit on the Cuban Missile Crisis was such a smash hit that it's now permanent—and well worth seeing even if the two temporary exhibits don't catch your fancy. On the other hand, they very well could, since the museum is associated with—and gets some of its staff on loan from—the Smithsonian Institution in Washington, D.C. Call to see what's scheduled during your visit. Allow at least 3 hours to tour all three exhibitions. There's an excellent museum store here as well.

100 2nd St. N. (between 1st and 2nd aves. N.). © **800/777-9882** or 727/822-3693. www.floridamuseum. org. Admission to all exhibits $10 adults, $8 seniors, $5 children 6–18, free for children under 6. Mon–Sat 10am–5pm; Sun noon–5pm (last entry 4pm daily).

Museum of Fine Arts ★★   Resembling a Mediterranean villa on the waterfront, this museum houses an excellent permanent collection of European, American, pre-Colombian, and Far Eastern art, with works by such artists as Fragonard, Monet, Renoir, Cézanne, and Gauguin. Other highlights include period rooms with antiques and historical furnishings, plus a gallery of Steuben crystal, a new decorative-arts gallery, and world-class rotating exhibits. The best way to see it all is on a guided tour, which takes about 1 hour. Ask about classical-music performances from October to April.

255 Beach Dr. NE (at 3rd Ave. N.). © **727/896-2667.** www.fine-arts.org. Admission $8 adults, $7 seniors 65 and older, $4 students older than 6 with ID, free for children under 6 (special exhibits cost more). Admission includes guided tour. Tues–Sat 10am–5pm; Sun 1–5pm. Guided tours Tues–Sat 11am, 1, 2, and 3pm; Sun 1 and 2pm (no additional charge). Closed New Year's Day, Martin Luther King Jr. Day, Thanksgiving, and Christmas.

Salvador Dalí Museum ★★★   This starkly modern museum houses the world's most comprehensive (and most valuable, at $125 million) collection of works by the renowned Spanish surrealist—and for art lovers is reason enough to visit downtown St. Petersburg. Housing six of the artist's Masterworks, the museum was given three stars by the Michelin Guide—the highest-ranked museum in the entire South. It includes oil paintings, watercolors, drawings, and more than 1,000 graphics, plus posters, photos, sculptures, objets d'art, and a 5,000-volume library on Dalí and surrealism. Reynolds Morse, an Ohio plastics engineer, and his wife, Eleanore, discovered the Catalonian artist and began collecting his works in 1943. They moved the collection here in 1980 and are credited with introducing the seemingly normal city to the kind of skewed perception usually reserved for much larger metropolises. Make sure to take one of the free docent-led tours to get the most out of the museum and its artwork.

1000 3rd St. S. (near 11th Ave. S.). (© 727/823-3767. www.salvadordalimuseum.org. Admission $13 adults, $11 seniors, $7 students 10 and older and children 5–9, free for children 4 and under, Thurs between 5–8pm $5 for all. Mon–Wed and Fri–Sat 9:30am–5:30pm; Thurs 9:30am–8pm; Sun noon–5:30pm. Closed Thanksgiving and Christmas.

AFFORDABLE OUTDOOR ACTIVITIES & SPECTATOR SPORTS

You can get information about the city's parks and leisure activities on the Internet at **www.stpete.com/leisure.htm**.

BIKING, IN-LINE SKATING & HIKING   With miles of flat terrain, the St. Petersburg area is ideal for bikers, in-line skaters, and hikers. The **Pinellas Trail** is especially good, since it follows an abandoned railroad bed 47 miles from St. Petersburg north to Tarpon Springs (© **727/464-8201;** www.pinellascounty. org/trailgd/default.htm). The **St. Pete trail head** is on 34th Street South (U.S. 19) between 8th and Fairfield avenues south. It's packed on the weekends. Free strip maps of the trail are available at the St. Petersburg Area Chamber of Commerce (see "Visitor Information," above). The 2½-mile-long **Friendship TrailBridge** (www.friendshiptrail.org/index.html), linking Tampa and St. Petersburg, is another popular venue for hikers, bikers, bicyclists, anglers, and in-line skaters, but be careful going up and down the steep center span, especially if you're on skates.

GOLF   One of the nation's top 50 municipal courses, the **Mangrove Bay Golf Course** ★★, 875 62nd Ave. NE (© **727/893-7800**), hugs the inlets of Old Tampa Bay and offers 18-hole, par-72 play. Facilities include a driving range; lessons and golf-club rental are also available. Fees are about $30 in winter, slightly lower off season.

In Largo, the **Bardmoor Golf & Tennis Club,** 8001 Cumberland Rd. (© **727/392-1234**), is often the venue for major tournaments. Lakes punctuate 17 of the 18 holes on this par-72 championship course. Lessons and rental clubs are available, as is a Tom Fazio–designed practice range. Call the clubhouse for seasonal greens fees. The course is open daily from 7am to dusk. The par-3 Twin **Brooks Golf Course,** 3800 22nd Ave. S. (© **727/893-7445**), is a challenging course operated by the city of St. Petersburg. Fees range from about $20 to $30.

Call **Tee Times USA** (© **800/374-8633;** www.teetimesusa.com) to reserve times at these and other area courses.

For course information online, go to www.golf.com and www.floridagolfing. com, or call the **Florida Sports Foundation** (© **850/488-8347**) or **Florida Golfing** (© **866/833-2663**).

SAILING   Both Steve and Doris Colgate's **Offshore Sailing School** (© **888/ 454-8002** or 239/454-1700; www.offshore-sailing.com) and the **Annapolis Sailing School** (© **800/638-9192** or 727/867-8102; www.annapolissailing. com) have operations here. Various courses lasting from 2 days to a week are offered. Contact the schools for prices and schedules.

Tips Car Smarts

You can spend a small fortune in a parking garage or in feeding the meters in St. Petersburg, but you can cut costs substantially by parking at The Pier ($3 all day) and taking The Looper, the city's trolley service, which operates between The Pier and all major downtown attractions.

Mermaids & Manatees

Drive north of St. Petersburg for an hour on congested U.S. 19, and you'll come to one of Florida's original tourist attractions, the famous Weeki Wachee Springs (© **877/469-3354** or 352/596-2062; www.weeki wachee.com). "Mermaids" have been putting on acrobatic swimming shows here every day since 1947. It's a sight to see them doing their dances in waters that come from one of America's most prolific fresh-water springs, pouring some 170 million gallons of 72°F (22°C) water a day into the river. There's more than mermaids here; you can take a Wilderness River Cruise across the Weeki Wachee River and send the kids on the flume ride at Buccaneer Bay, the water-park part of the attraction. Admission is $20 for adults, $16 for children 3 to 10. Kids under 3 get in free (reduced prices are available when Buccaneer Bay is closed). Weeki Wachee Springs is open Monday through Thursday from 10am to 3pm and Friday through Sunday from 10am to 4pm. Buccaneer Bay water park is only open Fridays from 10am to 4pm and Saturday and Sunday from 10am to 5pm.

You can also rent canoes on the Weeki Wachee River for $33 a day (© **352/597-0360**).

From Weeki Wachee, travel 21 miles north to the **Homosassa Springs Wildlife State Park,** 4150 S. Suncoast Blvd. (U.S. 19) in Homosassa Springs (© **352/628-5343**; www.floridastateparks.org/homosassasprings). The highlight here is a floating observatory where visitors can "walk" underwater and watch manatees in a rehabilitation facility, as well as thousands of fresh- and saltwater fish. You'll also see deer, a bear, bob-cats, otters, egrets, and flamingos along unspoiled nature trails. The

SPECTATOR SPORTS   St. Petersburg has always been a baseball town, and **Tropicana Field,** a 45,000-seat domed stadium alongside I-175 between 9th and 16th streets (© **727/825-3100**), is the home of the American League **Tampa Bay Devil Rays** (© **888/326-7297** or 727/825-3137; www.devilrays. mlb.com). The baseball season runs April through October. Single-game tickets are $3 to $75 and usually are available on game days. Call or check the website for the schedule. The Devil Rays move outdoors to **Florida Power Park at Al Lang Field,** on 2nd Avenue South at 1st Street South, for their spring-training workouts and games from mid-February to the end of March.

The **Philadelphia Phillies** now play their spring-training season in new digs in Clearwater (**Bright House Networks Field;** 601 Old Coachman Rd.; © **727/442-8496**). Their minor-league affiliate, the **Clearwater Phillies** (© **727/441-8638;** www.clearwaterphillies.com; $7–$13), plays in the stadium April through August. The **Toronto Blue Jays** do their spring thing at Grant Field, 373 Douglas Ave. in Dunedin (© **800/707-8269** or 813/733-9302; www.bluejays.mlb.com; $13–$15), which also is home to their minor-league affiliate, the **Dunedin Blue Jays** (© **727/733-9302;** www.dunedinbluejays. com), April through August.

TENNIS   You can learn to play or hone your game at the **Phil Green Tennis Academy** at Safety Harbor Resort and Spa (p. 376).

park is open daily from 9am to 5:30pm (last ticket sold at 4pm). Admission is $9 for adults and $5 for children 3 to 12 and includes a 20-minute narrated boat ride. Kids under 3 get in free.

About 7 miles north of Homosassa Springs, more than 300 **manatees** spend the winter in Crystal River, and you can **swim or snorkel** with them ★★ in the warm-water natural spring of Kings Bay. **American Pro Diving Center,** 821 SE Hwy. 19, Crystal River, FL 34429 (② **800/291-3483** or 352/563-0041; fax 352/563-5230; www.americanprodive.com), offers daily swimming and snorkel tours. Early mornings are the best time to see the manatees, so try to take the 6:30am departure. The trips range from about $30 to $50 per person. Call for the schedule and reservations. American Pro Diving also rents cottages on the Homosassa River.

Baseball fans won't want to miss the **Ted Williams Museum & Hitters Hall of Fame,** 2455 N. Citrus Hills Blvd., off C.R. 486 west of Hernando (② **352/527-6566;** www.twmuseum.com). Built in the shape of a baseball diamond, the museum holds the great hitter's personal memorabilia, including his two Triple Crown batting titles. It's open Tuesday through Sunday from 10am to 4pm. Admission is $5 for adults, $1 for children.

For more information about the area, contact the **Citrus County Chamber of Commerce,** 28 NW Hwy. 19, Crystal River, FL 34428 (② **352/795-3149;** fax 352/795-4260; www.citruscountychamber.com). The chamber's visitor center is open Monday through Friday from 8:30am to 4:30pm, Saturday from 9am to 1pm.

SHOPPING

The Pier, at the end of 2nd Avenue Northeast houses more than a dozen boutiques and crafts shops; but nearby Beach Drive, running along the waterfront, is one of the most fashionable downtown strolling and shopping venues.

Downtown's new commercial showplace is **BayWalk** (② **727/895-9277;** www.stpete.org/baywalk.htm), an open-air shopping, dining, and entertainment complex bordered by 1st and 2nd streets and 2nd and 3rd avenues North. It has a branch of Ann Taylor and some small boutiques.

Haslam's Book Store, 2025 Central Ave. (② **727/822-8616;** www.haslams. com), is one of our favorite places to browse. Dating from 1933, its collection has grown to more than 350,000 volumes, making it Florida's largest bookstore. (As an added perk, it, too, is said to be haunted.)

Central Avenue is another shopping area, featuring the **Gas Plant Antique Arcade,** between 12th and 13th streets (② **727/895-0368**), the largest antiques mall on Florida's west coast, with more than 100 dealers displaying their wares. (Downtown has several antiques-and-collectibles dealers; get a list and map from the chamber of commerce.) The **Florida Craftsmen Gallery,** at 5th Street (② **727/821-7391;** www.floridacraftsmen.net), is a showcase for the works of more than 150 Florida artisans and craftspeople specializing in jewelry, ceramics, woodwork, fiber works, glassware, paper creations, and metalwork.

ACCOMMODATIONS YOU CAN AFFORD

The **St. Petersburg/Clearwater Area Convention & Visitors Bureau** (see "Essentials," earlier in this chapter) operates a free **reservations service** (✆ 800/ 345-6710), through which you can book rooms at most hotels and motels in St. Petersburg and at the beaches. The bureau also publishes a brochure that lists members of its Superior Small Lodgings program; all establishments have fewer than 50 rooms and have been inspected and certified for cleanliness and value.

Note: Sales and hotel taxes will add 11% to your bill.

Inn at the Bay Bed & Breakfast   You can walk to The Pier from this charming B&B with wraparound porches on all three of its stories. Built in 1901, the Key West–style house overlooks a flower-filled garden with a gazebo. The guest quarters have been furnished with ceiling fans and Victorian pieces, including a canopy bed in one room and feather beds in all rooms. The honeymoon suite is equipped with a large double shower, Jacuzzi, and bidet; the rest have both claw-foot tubs and modern showers in their bathrooms. Half of the rooms open onto the porches, while the rest have a separate sitting room and kitchenette.

126 4th Ave. NE (between Beach Dr. and 1st St. N.), St. Petersburg, FL 33701. ✆ 888/873-2122 or 727/ 822-1700. Fax 727/896-7412. www.innatthebay.com. 12 units. $119–$270 singles–suites. $20 additional person. Rates include continental breakfast. AE, DISC, MC, V. *In room:* A/C, TV/VCR, kitchenette (in some), coffeemaker, hair dryer, iron, stereo with CD player, high-speed Internet access.

Mansion House Bed & Breakfast ★★   Mirror images of each other, these two houses separated by a landscaped courtyard were built between 1901 and 1912. The comfortable living room in the main house, which has 6 of the 10 units here, opens to a sunroom, off which a small screened porch provides mosquito-free lounging and the only place where guests can smoke. Both houses have upstairs front parlors with TVs, VCRs, and libraries. Tall, old-fashioned windows let lots of light into the attractive guest rooms. The pick of the litter is the "Pembroke" room, upstairs over the carriage house. It has a four-poster bed with mosquito netting, and its residents have their own whirlpool in an outdoor, screened hut. The brick courtyard garden between the two houses (there's a heated swimming pool and Jacuzzi out there) is a popular spot for weddings, receptions, and other functions.

105 5th Ave. NE (at 1st St. NE.), St. Petersburg, FL 33701. ✆ 800/274-7520 or 727/821-9391. Fax 727/821-6909. www.mansionbandb.com. 10 units, all with bathroom. $99–$220 double. Rates include full breakfast. AE, DC, DISC, MC, V. **Amenities:** Heated outdoor pool; access to nearby health club; Jacuzzi; bicycle rentals; laundry service. *In room:* A/C, TV, dataport, hair dryer.

A NEARBY SPA WITH GOOD PACKAGE DEALS

Safety Harbor Resort and Spa ★★ *Value*   Hernando de Soto thought he had found Ponce de León's fabled Fountain of Youth when, in 1539, he happened upon five mineral springs in what is now Safety Harbor on the western shore of Old Tampa Bay (see the "Tampa & St. Petersburg" map on p. 352). You may not recover your youth at this venerable spa, which has been in operation since 1926 and got a face-lift in 1998, but you will be rejuvenated with such services as massage and hydrotherapy and a full menu of fitness classes from boxing to yoga. The mineral springs enable it to offer acclaimed water-fitness programs, and this is a good place to work on your games at the Quinzi Golf Academy and the Phil Green Tennis Academy. This sprawling complex of beige stucco buildings with Spanish-tile roofs and lame, old fogy–style rooms, sits on 22 waterfront acres in the sleepy town of Safety Harbor, north of St. Petersburg. The grounds of the place make up for what the rooms lack. Moss-draped Safety Harbor has a charming small-town ambience, with a number of shops and restaurants just outside the spa's entrance. Given the reasonable off-season room rates and special packages available, this is one of Florida's better spa values.

105 N. Bayshore Dr., Safety Harbor, FL 34695. ℂ **888/237-8772** or 727/726-1161. Fax 727/724-7749. www.safetyharborspa.com. 193 units. Winter $205–$235 double; off season $175–$205 double. Packages available. AE, DC, DISC, MC, V. Valet parking $10; free self-parking. Pets accepted ($35-per-night charge). **Amenities:** 2 restaurants; bar; heated indoor and outdoor pools; golf course; 9 tennis courts; full-service spa; bicycle rentals; concierge; activities desk; car-rental desk; business center; limited room service; laundry service; coin-op washers and dryers. *In room:* A/C, TV, dataport, coffeemaker, hair dryer, iron, high-speed Internet access.

GREAT DEALS ON DINING

Don't overlook the food court at **The Pier,** where the inexpensive chow is accompanied by a very rich, but quite free, view of the bay. Among The Pier's restaurants is a branch of Tampa's famous **Columbia** (ℂ **727/822-8000;** p. 367).

The Moon Under Water ⓖ ASIAN/MIDDLE EASTERN/AMERICAN Tables on the veranda or sidewalk in front of this pub are a great place to take a break during your downtown stroll. The British Raj rules supreme inside the darkly paneled dining room with its slowly twirling ceiling fans and plethora of colonial artifacts, including obligatory pith helmets. Your taste buds are in for a treat here, because the bill of fare covers a number of former British outposts, including America (burgers and Philly cheese steaks), but the emphasis here is on mild, medium, or blazing-hot Indian curries—with a recommended Irish, British, or Australian beer to slake the resulting thirst. For lighter fare, consider Mideastern tabbouleh. There's also live music on weekend evenings.

332 Beach Dr. NE (between 3rd and 4th aves.). ℂ 727/896-6160. Main courses $7.50–$17; sandwiches and salads $6–$8. AE, DC, DISC, MC, V. Sun–Thurs 11:30am–11pm; Fri–Sat 11:30am–midnight. Closed New Year's Day, Thanksgiving, and Christmas.

SUPER-CHEAP EATS

Fourth Street Shrimp Store ⓖⓖ *Value* SEAFOOD You'll pass a seafood market counter when you enter, from which comes the fresh namesake shrimp, the star here. You can also pick from grouper, clam strips, catfish, or oysters fried, broiled, or steamed, all served in heaping portions. This is the best and certainly the most interesting bargain in town. There's also limited outdoor seating.

1006 4th St. N. (at 10th Ave. N.). ℂ 727/822-0325. Main courses $5–$14; sandwiches $2.50–$7. MC, V. Daily 11am–9pm.

Skyway Jack's ⓖ BREAKFAST This is the restaurant that Cracker Barrel aspires to be, a down home, country kitchen with kitsch *and* outstanding breakfast fare. Start the day off with eggs Florentine, stuffed French toast, even sweetbreads and eggs, or go old school with eggs, grits, hash browns, and biscuits 'n' gravy. For early risers or late night partyers, Skyway Jack's greases its griddle starting at 5am.

2795 34th St. S. ℂ 727/867-1907. Main courses $2.75–$6.50. No credit cards. Daily 5am–3pm.

WORTH A SPLURGE

Chateau France ⓖⓖ CLASSICAL FRENCH Chef Antoine Louro provides St. Petersburg's most romantic setting in this charming pink Victorian house built in 1910. He specializes in French classics such as homemade pâté, Dover sole meunière, filet mignon au poivre, coq au vin, orange duck, and a rich seafood bouillabaisse. Fresh baby vegetables, Gruyère-cheese potatoes, and

Antoine's special Eiffel Tower salad accompany all main courses. The wine list is excellent, as are the bananas flambé and crêpes suzette.

136 4th Ave. N. (between Bayshore Dr. and 1st St. N.). (℃ 727/894-7163. Reservations recommended. Main courses $20–$38. AE, DC, DISC, MC, V. Daily 5–11pm.

ST. PETERSBURG AFTER DARK

Good sources of nightlife information are the Thursday "Weekend" section of the *St. Petersburg Times* (www.sptimes.com), the "BayLife" and "Friday Extra" sections of the *Tampa Tribune* (www.tampatrib.com), and the *Weekly Planet* (www.weeklyplanet.com), a tabloid available at the visitor information offices and in many hotel and restaurant lobbies.

The heart of downtown's nighttime scene is **BayWalk** (℃ 727/895-9277; www.stpete.org/baywalk.htm), downtown's new shopping-dining-entertainment complex bordered by 1st and 2nd streets and 2nd and 3rd avenues North. There, a 20-screen cinema and several restaurants and bars will keep you busy.

THE BAR, CLUB & MUSIC SCENE Ever since St. Pete started coming into its own as far as the hipster quotient is concerned, cool bars started appearing as quickly as Madonna changes her accent. Among them, **A Taste for Wine,** 241 Central Ave., (℃ 727/895-1623), is an upscale spot with polished woods and a granite bar offering terrific by-the-glass vintages, appetizers, and a gorgeous outdoor balcony; the **Haymarket Pub,** 8308 4th St. N., (℃ 727/577-9621), is the gay-friendly Cheers of St. Pete where audible conversation and reasonably priced drinks aren't implausible demands; **Janus Landing,** 200 1st Ave. N. (℃ 727/896-1244), is a fantastic outdoor concert venue and bar where mostly alternative and rock bands perform; **Ringside Cafe,** 2742 4th St. N. (℃ 727/894-8465), is a laid-back jazz and blues bar; and **Martini Bar,** 131 2nd Ave. N., (℃ 727/895-8558), where a crowd that looks as if it stepped off the set of *Sex and the City* or *Friends* convenes for some serious seeing and being seen.

A historic attraction as well as an entertainment venue, the Moorish-style **Coliseum Ballroom,** 535 4th Ave. N. (℃ 727/892-5202; www.stpete.org/coliseum.htm), has been hosting dancing, big bands, boxing, and other events since 1924 (it even made an appearance in the 1985 movie *Cocoon*). Come out and watch the town's many seniors doing the jitterbug just like it was 1945 again! Call for the schedule and prices.

PERFORMING ARTS VENUES The **Bayfront Center,** 400 1st St. S. (℃ 727/892-5767, or 727/892-5700 for recorded information), houses the 8,100-seat Bayfront Arena (www.stpete.org/bayfront.htm) and the 2,000-seat Mahaffey Theater (www.stpete.org/mahaffey.htm). The schedule includes a variety of concerts, Broadway shows, big bands, ice shows, and circus performances. **Ticketmaster** (℃ 813/287-8844) sells tickets to most events and shows.

Tropicana Field, 1 Stadium Dr. (℃ 727/825-3100), has a capacity of 50,000 for major concerts, but it also hosts a variety of smaller events when the Devil Rays aren't playing baseball.

3 St. Pete & Clearwater Beaches ★ ★

If you're looking for sun and sand, you'll find plenty of both on the 28 miles of slim barrier islands that skirt the Gulf shore of the Pinellas Peninsula. With some one million visitors coming here every year, don't be surprised if you have lots of company. But you'll also discover quieter neighborhoods geared to families, and some of the nation's finest beaches, some of which are protected from development by parks and nature preserves.

St. Pete & Clearwater Beaches

ACCOMMODATIONS ■

Beach Haven **8**

Best Western
Sea Stone Resort **19**

Clearwater Beach Hotel **13**

Clearwater Beach
International Hostel **11**

Great Heron Inn **3**

Island's End Resort **10**

Sun West Beach Motel **18**

The Westin Innisbrook
Resort **1**

DINING ◆

Bob Heilman's
Beachcomber **15**

Bobby's Bistro
& Wine Bar **16**

Frenchy's Original Cafe **14**

Frenchy's Rockaway Grill **12**

Guppy's Seafood
Grill & Bar **2**

Hurricane **9**

Lobster Pot **5**

Ted Peters' Famous
Smoked Fish **7**

ATTRACTIONS ●

Clearwater Marine
Aquarium **17**

John's Pass Village
and Boardwalk **6**

Suncoast Seabird
Sanctuary **4**

Clearwater Beach

At the southern end of the strip, St. Pete Beach is the granddaddy of the area's resorts: Visitors started coming here a century ago, and they haven't quit. Today, St. Pete Beach is heavily developed and often overcrowded during the winter season. If you like high-rises and mile-a-minute action, St. Pete Beach is for you. But even here, Pass-a-Grille, on the island's southern end, is a quiet residential enclave with eclectic shops and a fine, though crowded, public beach.

A more gentle lifestyle begins just to the north on the 3½-mile-long Treasure Island. From there, you cross famous John's Pass to Sand Key, a 12-mile-long island occupied by primarily residential Madeira Beach, Redington Shores, Indian Shores, Indian Rocks Beach, and Belleair Beach. Finally the road crosses a soaring bridge to Clearwater Beach, whose silky sands attract active families and couples.

If you like your great outdoors unfettered by development, the jewels here are Fort Desoto Park, south of St. Pete Beach at the mouth of Tampa Bay, and Caladesi Island State Park, north of Clearwater Beach. They are consistently rated among America's top beaches. Sand Key Park, looking at Clearwater Beach from the southern shores of Little Pass, which separates Clearwater Beach from Belleair Beach, is one of Florida's finest local beach parks.

ESSENTIALS

GETTING THERE   See "Getting There," in section 1, on p. 347, for information about getting to the beaches.

VISITOR INFORMATION   See "Visitor Information," in section 2 (p. 370), for the St. Petersburg/Clearwater Area Convention & Visitors Bureau and the St. Petersburg Area Chamber of Commerce. The bureau's website at www.floridasbeach.com has information specific to the beaches.

Once you're here, you can get beach information at the **Gulf Beaches of Tampa Bay Chamber of Commerce,** 6990 Gulf Blvd. (at 70th Ave.), St. Pete Beach, FL 33706 (© **800/944-1847** or 727/360-6957; fax 727/360-2233; www.gulfbeaches-tampabay.com). The chamber is open Monday through Friday from 9am to 5pm.

For advance information about Clearwater Beach, contact the **Clearwater Regional Chamber of Commerce,** 1130 Cleveland St., Clearwater, FL 33755 (© **727/461-0011;** fax 727/449-2889; www.clearwaterflorida.org). You can also walk into the **Clearwater Visitor Information Center,** on Causeway Boulevard in the lobby of the Clearwater Beach Marina Building (© **727/462-6531**). It's open Monday through Saturday from 9am to 5pm, Sunday from 1 to 5pm.

GETTING AROUND   The **Pinellas Suncoast Transit Authority/PSTA** (© **727/530-9911**) operates motorized trolley service along Gulf Boulevard (Fla. 699) between the Hurricane restaurant (p. 387) in St. Pete Beach and the Sheraton Sand Key Resort (this entire trip, one way, takes about an hour), where it connects with the **Jolly Trolley** (© **727/445-1200**), which continues on Gulf Boulevard through Clearwater Beach. The PSTA trolley runs daily, every 20 minutes between 5am and 10pm, to midnight on Friday and Saturday. Rides cost $1.25, or you can buy a daily pass for $3. One-ride fares on the Jolly Trolley are 50¢ per person, 25¢ for seniors. Call the trolleys for schedules, or pick up printed copies at the Gulf Beaches of Tampa Bay Chamber of Commerce (see above).

Along the beach, the major cab company is **BATS Taxi** (© **727/367-3702**). Fares are $2 at flag fall, plus 20¢ for each ½ mile.

HITTING THE BEACH

This entire stretch of coast is one long beach, but since hotels, condominiums, and private homes occupy much of it, you may want to sun and swim at one of the area's public parks. The very best are described below, but there's also the fine **Pass-a-Grille Public Beach,** on the southern end of St. Pete Beach, where you can watch the boats going in and out of Pass-a-Grille Channel and quench your thirst at the Hurricane restaurant (p. 387). This and all other Pinellas County public beaches have metered parking lots, so bring a supply of quarters. There are public restrooms along the beach.

Sand Key Park ⟨⟩, on the northern tip of Sand Key facing Clearwater Beach, sports a wide beach and gentle surf and is relatively off the beaten path in this commercial area. It's great to go out for a morning walk or jog here. The park is open from 8am to dark and has restrooms. Admission is free, but the parking lot has meters. For more information, call ⟨⟩ **727/464-3347.**

Clearwater Public Beach (also known as Pier 60) has beach volleyball, watersports rentals, lifeguards, restrooms, showers, and concessions. The swimming is excellent, and there is a fishing pier with a bait-and-tackle shop, plus a children's playground. Gated municipal parking lots here cost $1 per hour or $7 a day. The lots are right across the street from the Clearwater Beach Marina, a prime base for boating, cruises, and other waterborne activities (see "Affordable Outdoor Activities," below). A somewhat-less-crowded spot in Clearwater Beach is at the Gulf end of Bay Esplanade.

CALADESI ISLAND STATE PARK ★★★

Occupying a 3½-mile-long island north of Clearwater Beach, **Caladesi Island State Park** boasts one of Florida's top beaches—a lovely, relatively secluded stretch with fine, soft sand edged in sea grass and palmettos. Dolphins often cavort in the waters offshore. In the park itself is a nature trail, where you might see one of the rattlesnakes, raccoons, armadillos, or rabbits that live here. A concession stand, a ranger station, and bathhouses (with restrooms and showers) are available. Caladesi Island is accessible only by ferry from **Honeymoon Island State Recreation Area,** which is connected by Causeway Boulevard (Fla. 586) to Dunedin, north of Clearwater.

You'll first have to pay the admission to Honeymoon Island: $5 per vehicle with two to eight occupants, $2 per single-occupant vehicle, $1 for pedestrians and bicyclists. Beginning daily at 10am, the ferry (⟨⟩ **727/734-5263**) departs Honeymoon Island every hour. Round-trip rides cost $8 for adults, $4.50 for kids.

Neither Caladesi nor Honeymoon allows camping, but pets are permitted in the inland parts of the island and on South Beach (bring a leash and use it at all times).

The two parks are open daily from 8am to sunset and are administered by Gulf Islands Geopark, 1 Causeway Blvd., Dunedin, FL 34698 (⟨⟩ **727/469-5918;** www.floridastateparks.org/caladesiisland and www.floridastateparks.org/honeymoonisland).

To really get to know the islands, go with Linda Taylor of **It's Our Nature, Inc.** (⟨⟩ **888/535-7448** or 727/441-2599; www.itsournature.com), on one of her guided walks of Honeymoon and Caladesi . They last about 2 hours and cost $15 for adults, $8 for children, plus park admission and ferry fare. Call for reservations, which are required, and for information about other guided walks and nature experiences.

FORT DESOTO PARK ★★

South of St. Pete Beach at the very mouth of Tampa Bay, **Fort Desoto Park** encompasses all of Mullet Key, set aside by Pinellas County as a 900-acre bird, animal, and plant sanctuary. Besides the stunning white-sugar sand, it is best known for a Spanish-American War–era fort, which has a museum (open daily 9am–4pm). Other diversions include great fishing from piers, large playgrounds for kids, and 4 miles of trails winding through the park for in-line skaters, bicyclists, and joggers. Park rangers conduct nature and history tours, and you can rent canoes and kayaks to explore the winding mangrove channels along the island's bay side. The park has changing rooms and restrooms.

Sitting by itself on a heavily forested island, the park's **campground** ★★ is one of Florida's most picturesque (many sites are beside the bay). It's such great camping that the 233 tent and RV sites usually are sold out, especially on weekends, so it's best to reserve well in advance. But, there are a few catches: You must appear in person no more than 30 days in advance at the campground office, at 631 Chestnut St. in Clearwater, or at 150 5th St. N. in downtown St. Petersburg. You must pay when you make your reservation in cash or by traveler's check (no credit cards or personal checks). And, you must reserve for at least 2 nights, but you can stay no more than 14 nights in any 30-day period. Sites cost $33 a night January through July, $28 a night the rest of the year. All sites have water and electricity hookups.

Admission to the park is free. It's open daily from 8am to dusk, although campers and persons fishing from the piers can stay later. To get here, take the Pinellas Byway (50¢ toll) east from St. Pete Beach and follow Fla. 679 (35¢ toll) and the signs south to the park. For more information, contact the park at 3500 Pinellas Byway, Tierra Verde, FL 33715 (© **727/582-2267;** www.fortdesoto. com).

AFFORDABLE OUTDOOR ACTIVITIES

BOATING, FISHING & OTHER WATERSPORTS   You can indulge in parasailing, boating, deep-sea fishing, wave running, sightseeing, dolphin watching, water-skiing, and just about any other waterborne diversion your heart could desire in the St. Pete and Clearwater Beaches area. All you have to do is head to one of two beach locations: **Hubbard's Marina,** at John's Pass Village and Boardwalk (© **800/755-0677** or 727/393-1947; www.hubbards marina.com), in Madeira Beach on the southern tip of Sand Key; or **Clearwater Beach Marina,** at Coronado Drive and Causeway Boulevard (© **800/772-4479** or 727/461-3133), which is at the beach end of the causeway leading to downtown Clearwater. Agents in booths there will give you the schedules and prices (expect to pay $35–$45 for a half day of fishing on a large party boat, $65–$70 for a full day), answer any questions you have, and make reservations if necessary. Go in the early morning to set up the day's activities, or in the afternoon to book the next day's.

CRUISES   The top nature cruise here is the **Sea Life Safari** ★★ (© **888/239-9414** or 727/441-1790; www.cmaquarium.org), operated by the Clearwater Marine Aquarium. These 2½-hour safaris are available at 11am, 1:30, and 4pm, and are more like field trips than pleasure cruises. Aquarium biologists go along to explain what they pull up in trawl nets (don't worry: They throw it all back). You'll also see birds and other wildlife on a visit to a bird sanctuary islet. Dolphin sightings are likely, too. The cruises are well worth $19 for adults, $12 for kids 3 to 12. You can combine the cruise with aquarium admission and save $3.

Call for the schedule and to reserve. Also ask about sunset nature cruises from mid-April to mid-October.

Hubbard's Sea Adventures, based at John's Pass Village and Boardwalk in Madeira Beach (*©* **800/755-0677** or 727/393-1947; www.hubbardsmarina. com), offers a 2-hour dolphin watch and sightseeing cruise. It costs $12 for adults, $6 for kids 11 and under. There's also a 3-hour shelling tour ($20 for adults, $10 for kids), but the best outings are cruises to fascinating **Egmont Key State Park** *⭑* on historic Egmont Key at the mouth of Tampa Bay (www.florida stateparks.org/egmontkey). This uninhabited island is the site of a lighthouse, of now-crumbling Fort Dade (built in 1900 during the Spanish-American War but abandoned long ago), and of threatened gopher tortoises. Sea turtles also come ashore here to nest. You can go snorkeling and shelling here, so bring your swimsuit (snorkeling gear is available). The half-day cruises leave from St. Pete Beach Tuesday through Sunday and cost $35 for adults, $25 for children.

Another popular cruise target is lovely **Shell Key,** one of Florida's last completely undeveloped barrier islands. Shell Key is great for bird-watchers, who could spot a remarkable 88 different species, including some of North America's rarest shorebirds. Hubbard's Shell Key beachcombing trips usually depart at 9am Monday through Saturday, for $20 adults, $10 kids 12 and under. You can rent beach chairs, umbrellas, snorkeling gear, and other equipment once you get there. Call to confirm the schedule and make reservations, which are recommended.

You can also get there on the **Shell Key Shuttle,** Merry Pier, on Pass-a-Grille Way at the eastern end of 8th Avenue in southern St. Pete Beach (*©* **727/360-1348;** www.shellkeyshuttle.com). Boats leave daily at 10am, noon, and 2pm. Prices are $14 for adults, $7 for children 12 and under. The ride takes 15 minutes, and you can return on any shuttle you wish.

The most unusual outings here are with **Captain Memo's Pirate Cruise,** at Clearwater Beach Marina (*©* **727/446-2587;** www.captmemo.com), which sails the *Pirate's Ransom,* a reproduction of a pirate ship with a pirate crew, on 2-hour daytime cruises, as well as sunset and evening champagne cruises ($30–$32 adults, $25 seniors and children 13–17, $20 kids under 13).

Two paddle-wheel riverboats operate here: The *Show Queen* has lunch, sunset dinner, and Sunday-brunch cruises from Clearwater Beach Marina (*©* **800/772-4479** or 727/461-3113; www.showqueen.com). The *Starlite Princess* does likewise from 3400 Pasadena Ave. S. (*©* **800/444-4814** or 727/462-2628; www.starlitecruises.com), at the eastern side of the Corey Causeway linking St. Pete Beach to the mainland. Call for prices, schedules, and reservations.

SCUBA DIVING   You can dive on reefs and wrecks with **Diving Clearwater** (*©* **877/GO DIVIN;** www.divingclearwater.com) or Sea Fox Dive Charters (*©* **727/469-8979;** www.seafoxdivecharters.com).

SHOPPING

John's Pass Village and Boardwalk, on John's Pass in Madeira Beach has an unremarkable collection of beach souvenir shops, but the atmosphere makes it worth a stroll. The pick of the lot is the **Bronze Lady** (*©* **727/398-5994;** www.bronzelady2000.com), featuring a collection of works by the late comedian-artist Red Skelton, best known for his numerous clown paintings. The shops are open daily from 9am to 6pm or later.

If you're in the market for one-of-a-kind hand-hammered jewelry, try **Evander Preston Contemporary Jewelry,** 106 8th Ave., Pass-a-Grille

(© 727/367-7894), a unique gallery/workshop housed in a 75-year-old building in Pass-a-Grille's 1-block-long 8th Avenue business district. Check out the golden miniature train with diamond headlight (it's not for sale). Open Monday through Saturday from 10am to 5:30pm.

ACCOMMODATIONS YOU CAN AFFORD

St. Pete Beach and Clearwater Beach have national chain hotels and motels of every name and description. You can also use the St. Petersburg/Clearwater Convention & Visitors Bureau's free **reservations service** (© 800/345-6710) to book rooms at most of them. The **St. Petersburg Area Chamber of Commerce** lists a wide range of hotels, motels, condominiums, and other accommodations in its annual visitor guide (see p. 376 for more information on them), and it publishes a brochure listing all members of its Superior Small Lodgings program.

As is the case throughout Florida, there are more short- and long-term rental condominiums here than there are hotel rooms. Many of them are in high-rise buildings right on the beach. Among local rental agents, **JC Resort Management,** 17200 Gulf Blvd., North Redington Beach, FL 33708 (© 800/535-7776 or 727/397-0441; fax 727/397-8894; www.jcresort.com), has many from which to choose.

Rates are highest from January to April. Ask about special discounted packages in the summer. Any time of year, though, it's wise to make reservations early. The hotel tax in Pinellas County is 11%.

ST. PETE BEACH

Beach Haven ⚓ *Value*   Nestled on the beach between two high-rise condominiums, these low-slung, pink-with-white-trim structures look from the outside like the early 1950s motel they once were. But Jone and Millard Gamble, who used to own this motel and still have the charming Island's End Resort (see below), replaced the innards and installed bright tile floors, vertical blinds, pastel tropical furniture, and many modern amenities, including VCRs and refrigerators. Five of the original quarters remain as motel rooms (with shower-only bathrooms), but the others are linked to make 12 one-bedroom units and one two-bedroom unit, all with kitchens. The top choice is the one-bedroom suite with sliding-glass doors opening to a tiled patio beside an outdoor heated pool. There's also a sunning deck with lounge furniture by the beach. You don't get maid service on Sunday or holidays, and the rooms and bathrooms are 1950s smallish; but every unit here is bright, airy, and comfortable.

4980 Gulf Blvd. (at 50th Ave.), St. Pete Beach, FL 33706. © 727/367-8642. Fax 727/360-8202. www.beach havenvillas.com. 18 units. Winter $90–$150 double; off season $68–$122 double. AE, DISC, MC, V. **Amenities:** Heated outdoor pool; coin-op washers and dryers; concierge-level rooms. *In room:* A/C, TV, dataport, kitchen, coffeemaker, hair dryer, iron.

Island's End Resort ★★★ *Value*   A wonderful respite from the maddening crowd, and a great bargain to boot, this little all-cottage hideaway sits right on the southern tip of St. Pete Beach, smack-dab on Pass-a-Grille, where the Gulf of Mexico meets Tampa Bay. You can step from the six contemporary cottages right onto the beach. And since the island curves sharply here, nothing blocks your view of the emerald bay. Strong currents run through the pass, but you can safely swim in the Gulf or grab a brilliant sunset at the Pass-a-Grille public beach, just one door removed. Linked to each other by boardwalks, the comfortable one- or three-bedroom cottages have dining areas, living rooms, VCRs, and fully equipped kitchens. You will love the one monstrous unit with two living rooms (one can be converted to sleeping quarters), two bathrooms (one with a whirlpool tub and separate shower), and its own private bayside swimming pool. Maid service is available on request.

1 Pass-a-Grille Way (at 1st Ave.), St. Pete Beach, FL 33706. © 727/360-5023. Fax 727/367-7890. www. islandsend.com. 6 units. Winter $115–$235 cottage; off season $100–$235 cottage. Weekly rates available. Complimentary breakfast served Tues, Thurs, and Sat. MC, V. **Amenities:** Coin-op washers and dryers. *In room:* A/C, TV, kitchen, coffeemaker, hair dryer, iron.

INDIAN ROCKS BEACH AREA

Great Heron Inn *Value*   A real heron named Harry patrols the beach at this family-oriented motel owned and operated by transplanted Michiganders Ralph and Teena Hickerson. It sits at the narrowest section of Indian Rocks Beach, facing the Gulf on one side and its own Intracoastal Waterway dock on the other. The buildings flank a central courtyard, with a heated pool, which opens to the beach. The airy one-bedroom apartments offer modern furnishings and Berber carpets, and each has a full kitchen and dining area. There are no king- or queen-size beds here, only doubles (plus pullout sleeper sofas in the living rooms).

68 Gulf Blvd. (south of First Ave.), Indian Rocks Beach, FL 33785. © 727/595-2589. Fax 727/517-2705. www.heroninn.com. 16 units. Winter $110–$125 double; off season $85–$100 double. Weekly and monthly rates available. AE, DISC, MC, V. Hotel is 4 blocks south of Fla. 688. **Amenities:** Coin-op washers and dryers. *In room:* A/C, TV, fax, kitchen, coffeemaker.

CLEARWATER BEACH

Best Western Sea Stone Resort   Located just across the street from the Gulf in Clearwater Beach's busy south end, the Sea Stone is a six-story building of classic Key West–style architecture, containing 43 one-bedroom suites, each with a kitchenette and a living room. The living-room windows of the suites look across external walkways to the harbor. A few steps away, the older five-story Gulfview Wing offers 65 standard motel rooms, the least-expensive choices here.

445 Hamden Dr. (at Coronado Dr.), Clearwater Beach, FL 33767. © 800/444-1919 or 727/441-1722. Fax 727/441-1680. www.seastoneresort.com. 106 units. Winter $89–$179 double; off season $69–$129 double. AE, DC, DISC, MC, V. **Amenities:** Restaurant; bar; heated outdoor pool; Jacuzzi; coin-op washers and dryers. *In room:* A/C, TV, kitchen, fridge, coffeemaker, hair dryer, iron.

Sun West Beach Motel *Value*   Sitting among several small motels, a 2-block walk from the beach, Scott and Judy Barrows's simple one-story establishment dates from 1954, but it's well maintained, overlooks the bay, and has a fishing/boating dock and a heated bayside pool and sun deck. All units, which face the

---

Tips Cheap Bunks for the Young at Heart

The young and young at heart can find an inexpensive bed at **Clearwater Beach International Hostel**, 606 Bay Esplanade (©/fax 727/443-1211; www.clearwaterbeachhostel.com), in a predominately residential neighborhood a short walk north of the busy beach area. There's a swimming pool, communal kitchen, TV lounge with hundreds of videos to watch, canoes and other toys to borrow, and bicycles to rent. The hostel's 33 dorm beds rent for $13 a night, while four private rooms range from $34 to $57. MasterCard and Visa credit cards are accepted. Reservations are strongly advised during the winter and summer months. The hostel is affiliated with both Hostelling International and American Youth Hostels.

bay, the pool, or the sun deck, have tropical-style furnishings, which make the place seem more modern than it is. The four motel rooms have small refrigerators, the 10 efficiencies have kitchens, and a few suites have separate bedrooms. The biggest and best unit is the Bayside Suite, which has vaulted ceilings, a steam room in its bathroom, and a fully equipped kitchen.

409 Hamden Dr. (at Bayside Dr.), Clearwater Beach, FL 33767. © **727/442-5008.** Fax 727/461-1395. 15 units. Winter $63–$99 double; off season $42–$70 double. MC, V. **Amenities:** Heated outdoor pool; access to nearby health club; coin-op washers and dryers. In room: A/C, TV, kitchen (some units), fridge, coffeemaker.

Worth a Splurge

Clearwater Beach Hotel ★ Besides the idyllic beach location, you'll enjoy easy access to many nearby shops and restaurants from this Old Florida–style structure, built in 1986 to replace an old wooden hotel. The resort has been owned and operated by the same family since the 1950s and attracts a mixed clientele. Directly on the Gulf, the complex consists of the six-story main building and two contemporary motel-style wings. Some rooms have balconies, and the efficiencies in the wings have kitchenettes. Offering French cuisine, the formal dining room is romantic at sunset and offers great views of the Gulf, while the nautically themed lounge has entertainment nightly. A bar provides snacks and libations beside an outdoor heated swimming pool.

500 Mandalay Ave. (at Baymont St.), Clearwater Beach, FL 33767. © **800/292-2295** or 727/441-2425. Fax 727/449-2083. www.clearwaterbeachhotel.com. 157 units. Winter $145–$169 double; off season $125–$169 double. AE, DC, MC, V. Free valet parking. **Amenities:** Restaurant; bar; heated outdoor pool; access to nearby health club; concierge; limited room service; laundry service. In room: A/C, TV, kitchen (efficiencies only), fridge, coffeemaker.

A NEARBY GOLF RESORT

The Westin Innisbrook Resort ★★ *Golf Digest, Golf,* and other magazines pick this as one of the country's best places to play (provided you stay here, of course). Situated off U.S. 19 between Palm Harbor and Tarpon Springs, this 1,000-acre, all-condominium resort has 90 holes on championship courses that are more like the rolling links of the Carolinas than the usually flat courses found in Florida. Some golf magazines think the **Copperhead course** ★★, former home of the annual JCPenney Classic, is number one in Florida. If you want to learn, Innisbrook has the largest resort-owned and -operated golf school in North America, and it boasts a tennis center with instruction, too. It's similar to the sports-oriented Saddlebrook Resort near Tampa, except that the courses are more challenging here and you're much closer to the beach. A free shuttle runs around the property, and another goes to the beach three times a day. Ranging in size from suites to two-bedroom models, the quarters are privately owned condos spread all over the premises. The focal points are the golf and tennis clubhouses, all of which have restaurants and bars: This place is not for serious beachgoers.

36750 U.S. 19 N., Palm Harbor, FL 34684. © **877/752-1480** or 727/942-2000. Fax 727/942-5576. www.westin-innisbrook.com. 700 units. Winter $229–$485 suite; off season $145–$289 suite. Golf packages available. AE, DC, DISC, MC, V. **Amenities:** 7 restaurants; 7 bars; heated outdoor pools; 4 golf courses; 15 tennis courts; health club; Jacuzzis; sauna; children's programs; concierge; activities desk; car-rental desk; limited room service; massage; babysitting; laundry service; coin-op washers and dryers. In room: A/C, TV, dataport, kitchen, minibar, coffeemaker, hair dryer, iron.

GREAT DEALS ON DINING

We have grouped the restaurants by their geographic location: St. Pete Beach, including Pass-a-Grille; Indian Rocks Beach, including Madeira Beach, Redington

Beach, North Redington Beach, Redington Shores, and Indian Shores; and, finally, Clearwater Beach.

ST. PETE BEACH

Hurricane SEAFOOD   A longtime institution, across the street from Pass-a-Grille Public Beach, this three-level gray Victorian building with white ginger-bread trim is a great place to toast the sunset, especially at the rooftop bar. It's more beach pub than restaurant; but the grouper sandwiches are excellent, and there's always fresh fish to be fried, broiled, or blackened, and shrimp and crab to be steamed. Downstairs you can dine inside the knotty pine–paneled dining room or on the sidewalk terrace, where bathers from across Gulf Way are welcome (there's a walk-up bar for beach libation). The second-floor dining area also has seating on a wraparound veranda. You must be at least 21 years old to go up to the Hurricane Watch rooftop bar or to join the revelry when the second level turns into Stormy's Nightclub at 10pm Wednesday through Saturday.

807 Gulf Way (at 9th Ave.), Pass-a-Grille. (℃ 727/360-9558. www.thehurricane.com. Main courses $9–$18; sandwiches $5–$9. AE, MC, V. Daily 8am–1am.

Ted Peters' Famous Smoked Fish ⭐ *Value* SEAFOOD   This open-air eatery is an institution in these parts: Ted's has been around since the '50s. Some folks bring the fish they caught for the staff to smoke ($1.50 a pound), others figure fishing is a waste of time and come right to Ted's table for mullet, mackerel, salmon, and other fish slowly cooked over red oak. Enjoy the smell and sip a cold one while you wait for your order.

1530 Pasadena Ave. (just across St. Pete Beach Causeway), Pasadena. (℃ 727/381-7931. Main courses $8–$18. No credit cards. Wed–Mon 11am–7:30pm.

INDIAN ROCKS BEACH AREA

Guppy's Seafood Grill & Bar ⭐⭐ SEAFOOD   Locals also love this small bar and grill across from Indian Rocks Public Beach because they know they'll always get terrific chow (it's associated with the excellent Lobster Pot; see below). You won't soon forget the salmon coated with potatoes and lightly fried, then baked with a creamy leek and garlic sauce; it's fattening, yes, but also a bargain at $10. Another good choice is lightly cooked tuna finished with a peppercorn sauce. The atmosphere is casual beach friendly, with a fun bar in the middle of it all. Try the delicious upside-down apple-walnut pie topped with ice cream. You can dine outside on a patio beside the main road.

1701 Gulf Blvd. (at 17th Ave.), Indian Rocks Beach. (℃ 727/593-2032. Main courses $10–$18; sandwiches $6–$7. AE, DC, DISC, MC, V. Sun–Thurs 11:30am–10:30pm; Fri–Sat 11:30am–11pm.

Worth a Splurge

Lobster Pot ⭐⭐⭐ SEAFOOD/STEAKS   Step into this weathered-looking restaurant near the beach and experience some of the finest seafood in the area. The prices are high, but the variety of Maine lobster dishes is amazing. The lobster cardinal is a blend of meat, cream, and cognac baked to succulent perfection, and the bouillabaisse is as authentic as any you'd find in the south of France. In addition to lobster, there's a wide selection of grouper, snapper, salmon, swordfish, shrimp, scallops, crab, Dover sole, and steaks, most prepared with elaborate sauces. The children's menu here is definitely out of the ordinary: It features half a Maine lobster and a petite filet mignon.

17814 Gulf Blvd. (at 178th Ave.), Redington Shores. (℃ 727/391-8592. www.lobsterpotrestaurant.com. Reservations recommended. Main courses $16–$40. AE, DC, MC, V. Daily 4:30–10pm.

The Sponge Capital of the World ☆

One of Florida's most fascinating small towns and a fine day trip from Tampa, St. Petersburg, or the beaches (it's 30 miles north of St. Petersburg, 23 miles west of Tampa, and 13 miles north of Clearwater), **Tarpon Springs** calls itself "the Sponge Capital of the World." Greek immigrants from the Dodecanese Islands settled here in the late 19th century to harvest sponges, which grew in abundance offshore. By the 1930s, Tarpon Springs was producing more sponges than any other place in the world. A blight ruined the business in the 1940s, but the descendants of those early immigrants stayed on. Today they compose about a third of the population, making Tarpon Springs a center of transplanted Greek culture.

Sponges still arrive at the historic **Sponge Docks,** on Dodecanese Boulevard. With a lively, carnival-like atmosphere, the docks are a great place to spend an afternoon or early evening, poking your head into shops selling sponges and other souvenirs while Greek music comes from the dozen or so family restaurants purveying authentic Aegean cuisine. You can also venture offshore from here, because booths on the docks hawk sightseeing and fishing cruises. Make your reservations as soon as you get here; then go sightseeing ashore or grab a meal at one of the multitudinous Greek restaurants and bakeries facing the dock while waiting for the next boat to shove off.

You also can visit the tin-roofed **Spongeorama** (510 Dodecanese Blvd.; no phone; open daily 10am–5pm), a museum dedicated to sponges and sponge divers that sells a wide variety of sponges (they'll

CLEARWATER BEACH

Bobby's Bistro & Wine Bar ☆ AMERICAN   Son of Bob Heilman's Beachcomber, this chic bistro draws a more urbane crowd than its parent. A wine-cellar theme is amply justified by the real thing: a walk-in closet with several thousand bottles kept at a constant 55°F (12°C). Walk through and pick your vintage, then listen to jazz while you dine inside at tall, bar-height tables or outside on a covered patio. The chef specializes in gourmet pizzas on homemade focaccia crust (as a tasty appetizer), plus charcoal-grilled lamb chops, filet mignon, fresh fish, and monstrous pork chops with caramelized Granny Smith apples and a Mount Vernon mustard sauce. Everything's served a la carte here, so watch your credit card. On the other hand, there's a less expensive sandwich menu featuring the likes of bronzed grouper and chicken with a spicy Jack cheese.

447 Mandalay Ave. (at Papaya St., behind Bob Heilman's Beachcomber). ✆ 727/446-9463. Reservations recommended. Main courses $8–$22; sandwiches and pizzas $6–$10. AE, DC, DISC, MC, V. Sun–Thurs 5–11pm; Fri–Sat 5pm–midnight; bar later.

Super-Cheap Eats

Frenchy's Original Cafe SEAFOOD   Popular with locals and visitors in the know since 1981, this casual pub makes the best grouper sandwiches in the area and has all the awards to prove it. The sandwiches are fresh, thick, juicy, and delicious. The atmosphere is pure Florida casual style. There can be a wait ship your purchase home) and shows a 30-minute video several times a day about sponge diving. Admission is free. A scuba diver feeds sharks three times a day in the **Konger Tarpon Springs Aquarium** (850 Dodecanese Blvd.; ℂ **727/938-5378**; open Mon–Sat 10am–5pm, Sun noon–5pm), at the western end of the boulevard. Admission is $4.75 adults, $4 seniors, $2.75 for children 3 to 11, free for kids under 3.

South of the docks, the **Downtown Historic District** sports turn-of-the-last-century commercial buildings along Tarpon Avenue and Pinellas Avenue (Alt. U.S. 19). On Tarpon Avenue west of Pinellas Avenue, you'll come to the Victorian homes overlooking **Spring Bayou**. This creek-side area makes for a delightfully picturesque stroll.

The **Tarpon Springs Chamber of Commerce**, 11 E. Orange St., Tarpon Springs, FL 34689 (ℂ **727/937-6109**; fax 727/937-2879; www.tarpon springs.com), has an information office on Dodecanese Boulevard at the Sponge Docks, which is open Tuesday through Sunday from 10:30am to 4:30pm.

To get to Tarpon Springs from Tampa or St. Petersburg, take U.S. 19 north and turn left on Tarpon Avenue (C.R. 582). From Clearwater Beach, take Alt. U.S. 19 north through Dunedin. The center of the historic downtown district is at the intersection of Pinellas Avenue (Alt. U.S. 19) and Tarpon Avenue. To reach the Sponge Docks, go 10 blocks north on Pinellas Avenue and turn left at Pappas' Restaurant onto Dodecanese Boulevard.

during winter and on weekends year-round. For a similarly relaxed setting, directly on the beach, **Frenchy's Rockaway Grill,** at 7 Rockaway St. (ℂ **727/446-4844;** www.frenchysonline.com), has a wonderful outdoor setting, and it keeps a charcoal grill going to cook fresh fish.

41 Baymont St. ℂ 727/446-3607. www.frenchysonline.com. Sandwiches and burgers $5–$7.50. AE, MC, V. Mon–Thurs 11:30am–11pm; Fri–Sat 11:30am–midnight; Sun noon–11pm.

For a Few Bucks More

Bob Heilman's Beachcomber ⍟ AMERICAN   In a row of restaurants, bars, and T-shirt shops, this establishment has been popular with the locals since 1948. Each dining room here is unique: Large models of sailing crafts create a nautical theme in one, a pianist makes music in a second, works of art create a gallery in the third, and booths and a fireplace make for a cozy fourth. The menu presents a variety of well-prepared fresh seafood and beef, veal, and lamb selections. If you tire of fruits-of-the-sea, the "back to the farm" fried chicken—from an original 1910 Heilman family recipe—is incredible.

447 Mandalay Ave. (at Papaya St.). ℂ 727/442-4144. Reservations recommended. Main courses $13–$29. AE, DC, DISC, MC, V. Mon–Sat 11:30am–11pm; Sun noon–10pm.

THE BEACHES AFTER DARK

If you haven't already found it during your sightseeing and shopping excursions, the restored fishing community of **John's Pass Village and Boardwalk,** on Gulf Boulevard at John's Pass in Madeira Beach, has plenty of restaurants, bars, and shops to keep you occupied after the sun sets. Elsewhere, the nightlife scene at the beach revolves around rocking bars that pump out music until 2am. All of the places listed in this section are bars that have live music.

Pass-a-Grille has the popular, always-lively lounge at **Hurricane,** on Gulf Way at 9th Avenue, opposite the public beach (p. 387).

Up on the northern tip of Treasure Island, **Gators on the Pass** (© 727/ **367-8951**) claims to have the world's longest waterfront bar, with a huge deck overlooking the waters of John's Pass. The complex also includes a nonsmoking sports bar and a three-story tower with a top-level observation deck for panoramic views of the Gulf of Mexico. There's live music, from acoustic and blues to rock, most nights.

In Clearwater Beach, the **Palm Pavilion Grill & Bar,** on the beach at 18 Bay Esplanade (© 727/446-2742), has live music Tuesday through Sunday nights during winter and on weekends in the off season. Nearby, **Frenchy's Rockaway Grill,** at 7 Rockaway St. (© 727/446-4844; www.frenchysonline.com), is another popular hangout.

If you're into laughs, **Coconuts Comedy Club,** at the Howard Johnson motel, Gulf Boulevard at 61st Avenue in St. Pete Beach (© 727/360-5653), has an ever-changing program of live stand-up funny men and women. Call for the schedule, performers, and prices.

For a more highbrow evening, go to the Clearwater mainland and the 2,200-seat **Ruth Eckerd Hall,** 1111 McMullen-Booth Rd. (© 727/791-7400; www. rutheckerdhall.com), which hosts a varied program of Broadway shows, ballet, drama, symphonic works, popular music, jazz, and country music.

4 Sarasota ✮✮✮

52 miles S of Tampa, 150 miles SW of Orlando, 225 miles NW of Miami

Far enough away from Tampa Bay to have an identity very much its own, Sarasota is, surprisingly, one of Florida's cultural centers. In fact, many retirees spend their winters here because there's so much to keep them entertained and stimulated, including the Van Wezel Performing Arts Hall and the FSU Center for the Performing Arts, home of the annual Asolo Theatre Festival. Sarasota also has an extensive array of first-class resorts, restaurants, and upscale boutiques.

Offshore, more than 40 miles of gloriously white beaches fringe a chain of long, narrow barrier islands stretching from Tampa Bay to Sarasota. To the south, **Siesta Key** is a residential enclave popular with artisans and writers and is home to Siesta Village, this area's funky, laid-back, and often-noisy beach hangout. Shielded from the Gulf by **Lido Key,** which has a string of affordable hotels attractive to family vacationers, **St. Armands Key** sports one of Florida's ritziest shopping and dining districts, while adjacent **Longboat Key** is one of the country's swankiest islands.

ESSENTIALS

GETTING THERE You probably will get a less-expensive airfare by flying into **Tampa International Airport,** an hour's drive north of Sarasota (p. 347), and you could save even more since Tampa's rental-car agencies usually offer some of the best deals in Florida. If you don't rent a car, **Sarasota-Tampa Express** (© 800/326-2800 or 941/727-1344) provides bus connections for $22 for adults, $11 for children 3 to 12. Call in advance for schedule and pickup locations.

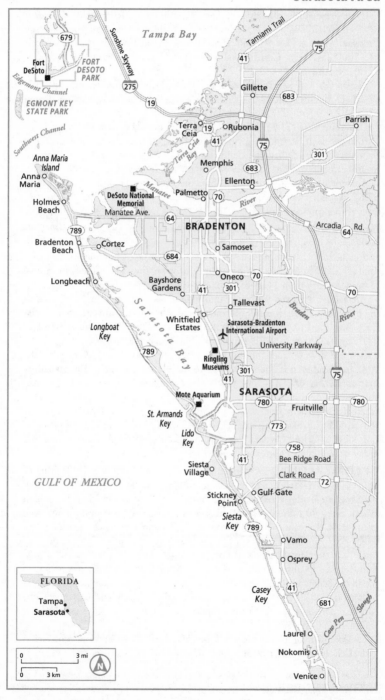

Sarasota Area

Tampa Bay

679

Fort
DeSoto

FORT
DESOTO
PARK

Edgemont Channel

EGMONT KEY
STATE PARK

Southwest Channel

Sunshine Skyway

275

19

Tamiami Trail

41

75

Gillette

683

Parrish

Terra
Ceia

19   Rubonia

41

Terra Ceia Bay

75

301

Memphis

683

Ellenton

Anna Maria
Island

Anna
Maria

Holmes
Beach

DeSoto National
Memorial
Manatee Ave.

Manatee

Palmetto

70

River

Arcadia   Rd.

64

789

64

BRADENTON

Bradenton
Beach   Cortez

684

Samoset

70

Longbeach

Bayshore
Gardens

41

Oneco

301

70

Tallevast

Sarasota Bay

Whitfield
Estates

Braden   *River*

Sarasota-Bradenton
International Airport

*Longboat
Key*

789

University Parkway

75

Ringling
Museums

301

41

SARASOTA

Mote Aquarium

780

Fruitville

780

*St. Armands
Key*

773

*Lido
Key*

758

41

Bee Ridge Road

GULF OF MEXICO

Siesta
Village

Clark Road

72

Stickney
Point   Gulf Gate

*Siesta
Key*   789

Vamo

Osprey

FLORIDA

Tampa
Sarasota

*Casey
Key*

41

681

Cau Pen   *Slough*

Laurel

0   3 mi

Nokomis

0   3 km

Venice

391

If you decide to fly directly here, **Sarasota-Bradenton International Airport** (© **941/359-2770**; www.srq-airport.com), north of downtown, off University Parkway between U.S. 41 and U.S. 301, is served by **American Trans Air** (© 800/225-2995), **Continental** (© 800/525-0280), **Delta** (© 800/221-1212), **Northwest** (© 800/225-2525), and **US Airways** (© 800/428-4322).

Alamo (© 800/327-9633), **Avis** (© 800/331-1212), **Budget** (© 800/527-0700), **Dollar** (© 800/800-4000), **Hertz** (© 800/654-3131), and **National** (© 800/227-7368) all have car-rental offices here.

Diplomat Taxi (© **941/355-5155**) has a monopoly on service from the airport to hotels in Sarasota and Bradenton. Look for the cabs at the west end of the terminal outside baggage claim. Fares range from about $10 to downtown Sarasota to $35 to Longboat Key or Anna Maria Island.

Amtrak has bus connections to Sarasota from its Tampa station (© **800/ 872-7245;** www.amtrak.com).

VISITOR INFORMATION   Contact the **Sarasota Convention and Visitors Bureau,** 655 N. Tamiami Trail (U.S. 41), Sarasota, FL 34236 (© **800/522-9799** or 941/957-1877; fax 941/951-2956; www.sarasotafl.org). The bureau and its helpful visitor center are in a blue pagoda-shaped building on Tamiami Trail (U.S. 41) at 6th Street. They're open Monday through Saturday from 9am to 5pm, Sunday from 11am to 3pm, closed holidays.

You can get a packet of advance information about Bradenton and surrounding Manatee County from the **Greater Bradenton Area Convention and Visitors Bureau,** P.O. Box 1000, Bradenton, FL 34206 (© **800/462-6283** or 941/729-9177; fax 941/729-1820; www.floridaislandbeaches.org).

If you're driving from the north via I-75, you can get off at U.S. 301 (exit 224) and head west if you want to go to the **Manatee County Tourist Information Center** (© **941/729-7040**), where volunteers are on hand to answer your questions and sell you excellent road maps for less than you'll pay elsewhere. It's open daily from 8:30am to 5pm except Easter Sunday, Thanksgiving, the day after Thanksgiving, and Christmas Day. The office also has an information kiosk at **Prime Outlets,** across I-75, which is open Monday through Saturday from 10am to 6pm and Sundays from 11am to 6pm.

GETTING AROUND   Operated by the Sarasota County Area Transit, or SCAT (© **941/861-1234;** www.co.sarasota.fl.us/public_works_scat/scat.asp), the **Sarasota Trolley** runs every 20 minutes from 9am to 5pm Monday through Friday, every 40 minutes on Saturday. The Scenic Loop Trolley operates from Island Park, Bayfront at Ringling Boulevard, through downtown Sarasota, north to the FSU Ringling Center for the Cultural Arts, and out to St. Armands and Lido Keys (but not to Siesta or Longboat keys). The Main Street Trolley goes from Island Park through downtown and eastward along Main Street. Fares are $1 on the Scenic Loop, 25¢ on the Main Street line, or you can buy a daily pass to both lines for $2. SCAT also operates regularly scheduled bus service. The Sarasota Convention and Visitors Bureau distributes route maps (see "Visitor Information," above).

Sarasota taxi companies include **Diplomat Taxi** (© **941/355-5155**), **Green Cab Taxi** (© **941/922-6666**), and **Yellow Cab of Sarasota** (© **941/955-3341**).

HITTING THE BEACH

Many of the area's 40-plus miles of beaches are occupied by hotels and condominium complexes, but there are excellent public beaches as well. The area's most popular is **Siesta Key Public Beach,** with a picnic area, a 700-car parking lot, crowds of families, and quartz sand reminiscent of the blazingly white beaches in Northwest Florida. There's also beach access at **Siesta Village,** which has a plethora of casual restaurants and pubs with outdoor seating (see "Great Deals on Dining," later in this chapter). The more secluded and quiet **Turtle Beach** is at Siesta Key's south end. It has shelters, boat ramps, picnic tables, and volleyball nets. Both beaches have bathroom facilities.

Unless you're staying on Longboat Key, you won't be able to hit the beach there, since luxury homes and condos block access to the Gulf. However, do drive the length of Longboat Key and admire the luxurious residences. Then, take a right off St. Armands Circle onto Lido Key and **North Lido Beach.** The south end of the island is occupied by **South Lido Beach Park,** with plenty of shade, making it a good spot for picnics and walks.

AFFORDABLE OUTDOOR ACTIVITIES & SPECTATOR SPORTS

BICYCLING & IN-LINE SKATING The flat terrain in this area makes for good in-line skating and for fine, though not challenging, bike riding. You can bike and skate from downtown Sarasota to Lido and Longboat keys, since paved walkways/bike paths run alongside the John Ringling Causeway and then up Longboat Key. **Siesta Sports Rentals,** 6551 Midnight Pass Rd., in the Southbridge Mall just south of Stickney Point Bridge on Siesta Key (© **941/346-1797;** www.siestasportsrentals.com), rents bikes of various sizes (including stroller attachments for kids), plus motor scooters, in-line skates, kayaks, and beach chairs and umbrellas. Bike rentals range from about $14 a day to $50 a week, while scooters go for $15 an hour, $50 a day, or $175 a week. The shop is open daily from 9am to 5pm.

BOAT RENTALS **All Watersports,** in the Boatyard Shopping Village, on the mainland end of Stickney Point Bridge (© **941/921-2754**), rents personal watercraft such as jet skis, speedboats, runabouts, and bow riders. At the island end of the bridge, **C. B.'s Saltwater Outfitters,** 1249 Stickney Point Rd. (© **941/349-4400**), and **Dockside Marine,** 1265 Old Stickney Point Rd. (© **941/349-8880**), both rent runabouts, pontoon boats, and other craft. Bait and tackle are available at the marinas.

CRUISES The area's best nature cruises go forth from Mote Aquarium (see the "Exploring the Area" section, below).

That paddle-wheeler you see going up and down the bay is the *Seafood Shack Showboat,* operated by the Seafood Shack restaurant, 4110 127th St. W., in Cortez (© **800/299-5048** or 941/794-5048). It has afternoon cruises to Sarasota Bay, Tampa Bay, and as far away as the Sunshine Skyway. Prices are $16 for adults, $15 for seniors, and $8 for children 4 to 10. The *Showboat* goes to a different destination each day, and its schedule is seasonal, so call a day ahead for the schedule. Reservations are not accepted.

FISHING Charter fishing boats dock at most marinas here. Check out www.sarasotaboating.com for a list. In downtown Sarasota, the **Flying Fish Fleet,** at Marina Jack's Marina, U.S. 41 at Island Park Circle (© **941/366-3373;** www.flyingfishfleet.com), offers party-boat charter-fishing excursions, with bait and tackle furnished. Prices for half-day trips are $35 adults, $30 seniors, and $25 kids 4 to 12. All-day voyages cost $55, $50, and $45, respectively. Call for the schedule. Charter boats also line up along the dock here.

GOLF The **Bobby Jones Golf Complex** ⚑, 1000 Circus Blvd. (© **941/365-4653**), is Sarasota's only municipal facility, but it has two 18-hole championship layouts—the American (par-71) and British (par-72) courses—and the 9-hole Gillespie executive course (par-30). Tee times are assigned 3 days in advance. Greens fees range from $25 to $35, including cart rental.

The semiprivate **Rolling Green Golf Club,** 4501 Tuttle Ave. (© **941/355-6620**), is an 18-hole, par-72 course. Facilities include a driving range, rental clubs, and lessons. Tee times are assigned 2 days in advance. Prices, including cart, are about $50 in winter and $30 off season. Also semiprivate, the **Sarasota Golf Club,** 7820 N. Leewynn Dr. (© **941/371-2431**), is an 18-hole, par-72 course. Facilities include a driving range, lessons, club rentals, a restaurant, a lounge, and a golf shop. Fees, including cart, are about $65 in winter, $45 off season.

If you have reciprocal privileges, **University Park Country Club,** west of I-75 on University Parkway (© **941/359-9999**), is Sarasota's only nationally ranked course. Fees, including cart, are about $55 year-round. The **Buffalo Creek Golf Course,** 8100 Erie Road (© **941/776-2611**), is a beautiful 18-hole, par-72 municipal course on the north side of the Bradenton River. Fees, with cart, are about $50 ($40 without) in winter; less than half that in the summertime.

Bradenton is home to the well-known **David Leadbetter Golf Academy,** 1414 69th Ave., at U.S. 41 (© **800/872-6425** or 941/755-1000; www.leadbetter.com), a part of the Nick Bollettieri Sports Academy (see "Tennis," below). Presided over by one of golf's leading instructors, this facility offers practice tee instruction, video analysis, scoring strategy, and more.

For course information online, go to www.golf.com or www.floridagolfing.com, or call the **Florida Sports Foundation** (© **850/488-8347**) or **Florida Golfing** (© **866/833-2663**).

KAYAKING   Based at Mote Aquarium (see "Exploring the Area," below), **Sarasota Bay Explorers** 🎣🎣 (© **941/388-4200;** www.sarasotabayexplorers.com) uses a 38-foot pontoon boat to ferry novice and experienced kayakers and their craft to a marine sanctuary, where everyone paddles through tunnels formed by mangroves. The paddling is easy and the waters are shallow. Experienced naturalists serve as guides. Wear swimsuits and tennis shoes or rubber-soled booties, and bring a towel and lunch. The 3-hour trips cost $50 for adults, $40 for children 5 to 17, and are free for kids under 5 (seats are provided for the youngsters). Reservations are required.

SAILING   Take a leisurely cruise on the waters of Sarasota Bay and the Gulf of Mexico aboard the 41-foot, 12-passenger sailboat *Enterprise,* docked at Marina Jack's Marina, U.S. 41 at Island Park Circle (© **888/232-7768** or 941/951-1833; www.sarasotaboating.com/sailingcharters.html). Cruises range from 3 hours for $45 per person to 4 hours for $55 a head, while 2-hour sunset cruises cost $35 per person. Departure times vary, and reservations are required. **Siesta Key Sailing,** 1219 Southport Dr. (© **941/346-7245;** www.siestakeysailing.com), charges the same for similar cruises in a 42-foot Morgan Outlander sloop. Reservations are essential. Call for rates.

You can also get to historic Egmont Key, 3 miles off the northern end of Anna Maria Island at the mouth of Tampa Bay (p. 383), on a 30-foot sloop-rigged sailboat with **Spice Sailing Charters** (© **941/778-3240**), based at the Galati Yacht Basin on Bay Boulevard on northern Anna Maria Island. The company also has sunset cruises. Rates start at $30 per person. Call for schedule and reservations, which are required.

SPECTATOR SPORTS   **Ed Smith Stadium,** 2700 12th St., at Tuttle Avenue, east of downtown Sarasota (© **941/954-4464**), is the winter home of the **Cincinnati Reds** (© 941/955-6501; www.cincinnatireds.com), who hold spring training here in February and March. Game tickets are $5 to $12. From April to August, the stadium is home to the **Sarasota Red Sox** (© 941/365-4460, ext. 2300; www.sarasox.com), a Class A minor-league affiliate of the Boston Red Sox. Tickets are $4 and $5.

The **Pittsburgh Pirates** (© 941/748-4610; www.pirateball.com) do their February-through-March spring training at 6,562-seat McKechnie Field, 9th Street West and 17th Avenue West, south of downtown Bradenton. Tickets are $6 to $9.

The **Sarasota Polo Club,** 8201 Polo Club Lane, Sarasota (© **941/907-0000**), at Lakewood Ranch, a planned community midway between Sarasota and Bradenton, is the site of weekly polo matches from mid-December to early April, on Sunday afternoons. General admission is $6, free for children under 13. Call for the schedule of matches.

TENNIS   The **Nick Bollettieri Sports Academy,** 5500 34th St. W. in Bradenton (© **800/872-6425** or 941/755-1000; www.bollettieri.com), is one of the world's largest tennis training facilities, with more than 70 championship grass, clay, and hard courts and a pro shop. It's open year-round, and reservations are required for all activities.

WATERSPORTS   You'll find watersports activities in front of the major hotels out on the keys (see "Accommodations You Can Afford," beginning on p. 399). **Siesta Sports Rentals,** 6551 Midnight Pass Rd. on Siesta Key (© **813/346-1797**; www.siestasportsrentals.com), rents kayaks and sailboats, plus beach chairs and umbrellas.

EXPLORING THE AREA
IN SARASOTA

Florida Ever-Glides, Inc. ★★   Ride the future (and get some history at the same time) when you take a tour with this great company, the first in the U.S. to offer historic and scenic guided tours using Segway Human Transporters, you know, those cool electric scooter-type things you've seen on TV (and saw George Bush, Jr. fall off of). The friendly staffers here will have you up, riding, and comfortable (I swear) in a matter of minutes, with orientation, training, and as many practice runs as you need before you start off on your 2-hour 9am or 2pm tour of Downtown Sarasota and the Bayfront, including the vintage 1920s Towles Court Artist Colony.

200 S. Washington Blvd., #11 (on the corner of Adams Lane). © 941/363-9556. Fax 941/363-9557. www.floridaever-glides.com. $59 per person. AE, DISC, MC, V. Daily 8am–5pm.

FSU Ringling Center for the Cultural Arts ★★★   By far the top attraction here, this 66-acre site is where showman and circus legend John Ringling and his wife, Mable, collected art and built houses on a grand scale. Now under the aegis of Florida State University, **The John and Mable Ringling Museum of Art** is the state's official art museum. It's filled with more than 500 years of European and American art, including one of the world's most important collections of grand 17th-century baroque paintings as well as collections of decorative arts and traveling exhibits. The old-master collection also includes five world-renowned tapestry cartoons by Peter Paul Rubens and his studio.

Built in 1924 and 1925 at a cost of $1.5 million and modeled after a Venetian palace, the Ringlings' spectacular 32-room palatial, bayfront, four-story

---

Tips   How to See the Ringling Museums

It's best to visit the FSU Ringling Center for the Cultural Arts on a week-day when the center offers adult guided tours and school tours of the art museum, house, and circus museum, which are included in the price of admission. Call ahead or check at the information desk as soon as you arrive for tour times. In between, explore the gardens and have lunch at The Banyan Cafe.

---

winter residence **Ca'd'Zan** ("House of John" in the Venetian dialect) has been recently restored. An 8,000-square-foot terrace leads down to the dock at which Mable Ringling moored her Venetian gondola. Don't miss a tour of this house to see the period furniture and stunning architecture and artwork; in fact, I'd make it the first stop on your Ringling itinerary.

The **Ringling Museum of the Circus** is devoted to circus memorabilia (which is, in a way, more fascinating than the circus itself) including parade wagons, calliopes, costumes, and colorful posters. The grounds also include a classical courtyard, a rose garden, a museum shop, and the historic **Asolo Theater,** a 19th-century Italian court playhouse, which the Ringlings moved here in the 1950s. It's now the centerpiece of the Florida State University Center for the Performing Arts. You'll need most of a day to see everything here.

5401 Bay Shore Rd. at N. Tamiami Trail (U.S. 41). ℂ **941/359-5700,** or 941/351-1660 for recorded information. www.ringling.org. Admission $15 adults, $12 seniors, $5 out-of-state students, free for Florida students and all children 12 and under. Daily 10am–5:30pm. Closed New Year's Day, Thanksgiving, and Christmas. From downtown, take U.S. 41 north to University Pkwy. and follow signs to museum.

G. Wiz (Gulfcoast Wonder & Imagination Zone)   This hands-on, state-of-the-art science center has two floors of fun exhibits that cover the physical, earth, and health sciences. In June 2002, G. Wiz opened its 3-year ExploraZone exhibit, which features annually rotating interactive exhibits from San Francisco's renowned Exploratorium. The 35 exhibits have themes ranging from sound and music to mathematics and motion, color and optics, sight and illusion, and others.

1001 Blvd. of the Arts (in the Blivas Science and Technology Center, 1 block west of U.S. 41). ℂ **941/9061851.** www.gwiz.org. Admission $7 adults, $6 seniors, $5 kids 2 and over, free 5–8pm the 1st Wed of the month. Tues–Sat 10am–5pm; Sun noon–5pm.

Marie Selby Botanical Gardens ★★   A must-see for serious plant lovers and a should-see for those looking for good photo ops, this peaceful retreat on the bay, just south of downtown, is said to be the only botanical garden in the world specializing in the preservation, study, and research of epiphytes, that is, "air plants" such as orchids. It's home to more than 20,000 exotic plants, including more than 6,000 orchids, as well as a bamboo pavilion, a butterfly and hummingbird garden, a medicinal plant garden, a waterfall garden, a cactus and succulent garden, a fernery, a hibiscus garden, a palm grove, two tropical food gardens, and a native shore-plant community. Selby's home and the Payne Mansion (both on the National Registry) are also located here.

811 S. Palm Ave. (south of U.S. 41). ℂ **941/366-5731.** www.selby.org. Admission $12 adults, $6 children 6–11, free for children 5 and under. Daily 10am–5pm. Closed Christmas.

Sarasota Classic Car Museum   There's more to this museum than its 90-plus classic and "muscle" autos, from Rolls-Royces and Pierce Arrows to the four cars used personally by circus czar John Ringling. Also here are more than 1,200 antique music boxes and several of Thomas Edison's early phonographs, including a 1909 diamond-tipped-needle model. Check out the Penny Arcade with antique games (with original prices), and grab a cone at the ice-cream and sandwich shop. In operation since 1953, this is now a nonprofit museum dedicated to preserving antique automobiles.

5500 N. Tamiami Trail (at University Pkwy.). ✆ 941/355-6228. www.sarasotacarmuseum.org. Admission $8.50 adults, $7.65 seniors, $5.75 children 13–17, $4 children 6–12, free for children under 6. Daily 9am–6pm. Take U.S. 41 north of downtown; museum is 2 blocks west of the airport.

ON ST. ARMANDS KEY

Mote Aquarium ★★ *Kids* Kids get to touch cool stuff like a stingray (minus the stinger, of course) and watch sharks in the shark tank at this excellent aquarium. Part of the noted Mote Marine Laboratory complex, it is more broad-based than Tampa's Florida Aquarium, which concentrates primarily on local sea life. The kids won't believe all the sea-horse babies that come from the dad's pouch (one of Mother Nature's strange-but-true surprises), and they surely will gawk at a 35-foot-long deceased giant squid (it was 45 ft. long when alive). They can see manatees in the Marine Mammal Center, a block's walk from the aquarium. There are also many research-in-progress exhibits. Start by watching the aquarium's 12-minute film on the feeding habits of sharks; then allow at least 90 minutes to take in everything on land. Add another 2 hours to take a narrated sea-life encounter cruise with **The Sarasota Bay Explorers** (✆ **727/388-4200;** www.sarasotabayexplorers.com). These fun and informative cruises visit a deserted island, and the guides throw out nets and bring up sea life for inspection. It's a good idea to make reservations for the cruise a day in advance. This company has unusual kayaking adventures, too (p. 394).

1600 Ken Thompson Pkwy. (on City Island). ✆ **800/691-6683** or 941/388-2541. www.mote.org. Admission $12 adults, $8 children 4–12, free for children under 4. Nature cruises $24 adults, $20 children 4–12, free for children under 4. Combination aquarium-cruise tickets $30 adults, $25 children. Daily 10am–5pm. Nature cruises daily 11am, and 1:30 and 4pm. From St. Armands Circle, go north toward Longboat Key; turn right just before the Lido-Longboat bridge.

IN & NEAR BRADENTON

DeSoto National Memorial Nestled on the Manatee River, west of downtown, this park attracts history buffs by re-creating the look and atmosphere of the period when Spanish explorer Hernando de Soto landed here in 1539. It includes a restoration of de Soto's original campsite and a scenic half-mile nature trail that circles a mangrove jungle and leads to the ruins of one of the first settlements in the area. Start by watching a 21-minute film about de Soto in America. From December to March, park employees dress in 16th-century costumes and portray the way the early settlers lived, including demonstrations of cooking and the firing of an arquebus, one of the world's earliest firearms.

DeSoto Memorial Hwy. (north end of 75th St. W.). ✆ 941/792-0458. www.nps.gov/deso. Free admission. Daily 9am–5pm. Take Manatee Ave. (Fla. 64) west to 75th St. W. and turn right; follow the road to its end and the entrance to the park.

Gamble Plantation ★ Situated northeast of downtown Bradenton, this is the oldest structure on the southwestern coast of Florida, and a fine example of an antebellum plantation home—something that's quite rare in Florida—over a 6-year period in the late 1840s by Major Robert Gamble, it was constructed primarily of "tabby mortar" (a mixture of oyster shells, sand, molasses, and water), with 10 rooms, verandas on three sides, 18 exterior columns, and eight fireplaces. Maintained as a state historic site, it includes a fine collection of 19th-century furnishings. Entrance to the house is by tour only, although you can explore the grounds on your own. The Prime Outlets Ellenton is a 5-minute drive from here via U.S. 301, so you can combine a plantation visit with some bargain hunting (see p. 399 for more information).

3708 Patten Ave. (U.S. 301), Ellenton. © 941/723-4536. www.floridastateparks.org/gambleplantation. Free admission to the grounds. Tours $4 adults, $2 children 6–12, free for children under 6. Thurs–Mon 9am–4:30pm; 30-min. guided house tour 9:30 and 10:30am, and 1, 2, 3, and 4pm. Take U.S. 301 north of downtown to Ellenton; the site is on the left, just east of Ellenton-Gillette Rd. (Fla. 683).

Solomon's Castle ★★ This attraction gets the vote and the award for the Weirdest and Wackiest (and boy, are there many) of Florida category. Howard Solomon, in 1974, began building what has become a 60-foot-tall, 12,000-square-foot castle in a Manatee County swamp. Solomon, a metal and wood sculptor by trade, built the huge structure (where he now lives) out of 22-by-34-inch offset aluminum printing plates discarded by a local newspaper. He and other tour guides (though try to get a tour led by him, or at least meet him and talk to him about his work) lead guests on a pun-filled tour of the castle, which is decked out with some of his smaller artistic creations, mostly made of other people's "trash," including a chair made out of 86 beer cans, an elephant pieced together with seven oil drums, a unicorn fashioned out of coat hangers, and about 80 stained-glass windows. Howard is continually building new things—you never know what you'll find. If that's not enough to tempt you, you can have lunch in the restaurant, which is in a Spanish galleon that Howard built in his spare time. You *have* to experience this to believe it. Seriously.

4533 Solomon Road, Ona. © 863/494-6007. www.solomonscastle.com. Admission $10 adults, $4 kids under 12. Tours Tues–Sun 11am–4pm, Oct–June. Closed July–Sept. Take Hwy. 64 east of I-75 29 miles to Hwy. 665, go south 9 miles and turn left at the sign to the castle.

South Florida Museum and Parker Manatee Aquarium *Kids* The star at this downtown complex is "Snooty," the oldest manatee born in captivity (1948) and Manatee County's official mascot. Snooty and his pal "Mo" live in the Parker Manatee Aquarium. The South Florida Museum tells the story of Florida's history, from prehistoric times to the present, including a Native American collection with life-size dioramas and a Spanish courtyard containing replicas of 16th-century buildings. (Fire recently damaged the museum's Bishop Planetarium, which is now closed.)

201 10th St. W. (on the riverfront, at Barcarrota Blvd.). © 941/746-4131. www.southfloridamuseum.org. Admission $9.50 adults, $7.50 seniors, $6 students with ID, $5 children 5–12, free for children 4 and under. Jan–Apr and July Mon–Sat 10am–5pm, Sun noon–5pm; rest of year Tues–Sat 10am–5pm, Sun noon–5pm. Closed New Year's Day, Thanksgiving, and Christmas. From U.S. 41, take Manatee Ave. west to 10th St. W. and turn right.

SHOPPING

Visitors come from all over the world to shop at **St. Armands Circle** ★★, on St. Armands Key. Wander around this outdoor circle of more than 150 international boutiques, gift shops, galleries, restaurants, and nightspots, all surrounded by lush landscaping, patios, and antiques. Pick up a map at the Sarasota Convention and Visitors Bureau (p. 392). Many shops here are comparable to those in Palm Beach and on Naples's Third Avenue South, so check your credit-card limits—or resort to some great window-shopping. We love to browse through **Global Navigator** (© 813/388-4514), a travel-equipment and apparel shop that reminds us of Banana Republic when it carried really cool stuff (open daily 10am–10pm).

> ⌒ *Tips* **Finding the Elusive Parking Space**
>
> Parking on or near St. Armands Circle can be scarce, and if you *can* find a spot, on-street parking is limited to 3 hours. Your best bets are the free, unrestricted lots on Adams Drive at Monroe and Madison drives.

For discount shopping, the focal point of this area is the **Prime Outlets Ellenton,** on U.S. 301 at exit 43 off I-75 in Ellenton (© **941/723-1150;** www.primeoutlets.com), about a 15-minute drive northeast of downtown Bradenton (turn left at the 1st stoplight east of I-75). This Spanish-style outdoor center has more than 100 factory and outlet stores. Shops are open Monday through Saturday from 10am to 9pm and Sunday from 11am to 6pm.

A NEARBY STATE PARK WITH A WILD & SCENIC RIVER

About 20 miles southeast of Sarasota, the **Myakka River State Park** ⋇, on Fla. 72 about 9 miles east of I-75, is Florida's largest, covering more than 35,000 acres flanking 14 miles of the Myakka River, one of two official Wild and Scenic Rivers in the state. It's an outstanding wildlife sanctuary and breeding ground, home to hundreds of species of plants and animals, including alligators. There are 39 miles of backcountry trails and boardwalks, including one snaking high up in the treetops, giving great views over the surrounding wetlands, prairies, and dense woodlands. The park is open daily from 8am to sunset. Admission is $5 per car with two to eight occupants, or $1 per pedestrian or bicyclist. You can stay out here in a campground or in five log cabins built by the Civilian Conservation Corps during the Great Depression (they now have air-conditioners, electric stoves, refrigerators, and hot-water showers). Campsites cost $22 a night year round. Cabins rent for $60 a night year-round. For camping reservations call © **800/326-3521** or go to the website www.reserveamerica.com. For more information about the park, contact the headquarters at 13207 S.R. 72, Sarasota, FL 34241 (© **941/361-6511;** www.myakkariver.org).

The best and certainly easiest ways to see the park are on 1-hour-long nature "safaris" by boat or tram with **Myakka Wildlife & Nature Tours** (© **941/365-0100**). The boat tours onto Myakka Lake are in the world's largest airboat, while on land, the tram tours take you into the wilderness where other vehicles aren't allowed. Either excursion costs $8 for adults, $4 for children 6 to 12, and is free for kids 5 and under. Call for the schedules, which change seasonally. Reservations are not accepted, so buy your tickets at the camp store as soon as you arrive.

ACCOMMODATIONS YOU CAN AFFORD

The beaches here are virtually lined with condominiums, many of which are actually all-condominium projects operated as hotels. Among the rental agencies requiring stays of less than a month are **Argus Property Management,** 2477 Stickney Point Rd., Sarasota, FL 34231 (© **941/927-6464;** fax 941/927-6767; www.argusmgmt.com), and **Florida Vacation Accommodations,** 4030 Gulf of Mexico Dr., Longboat Key, FL 34228 (© **800/237-9505** or 941/364-9505; fax 941/364-1830; www.vacationinfl.com).

Most visitors stay out at the beaches, but cost-conscious travelers will find some good deals on the mainland, such as the **Best Western Midtown,** 1425 S. Tamiami Trail (U.S. 41), at Prospect Street (© **800/722-8227** or 941/955-9841; fax 941/954-8948; www.bwmidtown.com). This older but well-maintained motel is 2 miles in either direction from the main causeways leading to the keys. Winter rates are $119 for a double room, dropping to $79 off season.

Most other national chain motels are near the airport, including a **Comfort Inn** (✆ **800/228-5150** or 941/355-7091), a **Days Inn** (✆ **800/329-7466** or 941/355-9271), and a **Hampton Inn** (✆ **800/336-9335** or 941/351-7734). All of recent vintage and thoroughly modern, they stand side-by-side on Tamiami Trail (U.S. 41) near the FSU Ringling Center for the Cultural Arts and the Asolo Center for the Performing Arts.

The high season is from January to April. The hotel tax here is 10%.

ON LIDO KEY
Worth a Splurge
The Helmsley Sandcastle ✿   Set on 600 feet of a private, white-sand beach on the Gulf of Mexico and only minutes from the upscale St. Armands Circle, the rooms here are nothing special, though they are large and most have great views of the water. With an incredibly friendly staff and a nice resorty feel, stay here if you want to relax in a perfectly fine location without dealing with the stuffiness of a fancier hotel.

1540 Ben Franklin Dr., Sarasota, FL 34236. ✆ **800/225-2181** or 941/388-2181. Fax 941/388-2655. www.helmsleyhotels.com. 179 units. Winter $169–$279 double; off season $109–$189 double. AE, DC, DISC, MC, V. **Amenities:** 3 restaurants; poolside bar; 2 outdoor heated pools; nearby golf and tennis; business center. *In room:* A/C, TV, fridge, coffeemaker, hair dryer, iron.

ON SIESTA KEY
Captiva Beach Resort ✿ *Value*   Owners Robert and Jane Ispaso have substantially upgraded and improved this older property in the Stickney Point business district, about half a block from the beach on a narrow, closely packed circle populated by other small motels. They pride themselves on being throwbacks to the 1950s, and it's said that if someone says good morning to you at this place, even if you are in the worst mood, hung-over, or antisocial, if you don't respond, it's considered rude. So if you're looking for a place where people keep to themselves, this isn't it. Every one of the comfortable, sparkling-clean units here has some form of cooking facility, and some have separate living rooms with sleeper sofas. These are older buildings, so you'll find window air conditioners mounted through the walls, and shower-only bathrooms in some units. It's very popular with longer-term guests during winter. You'll get fresh towels daily but maid service only once a week. This and the circle's other motels share a common pool area, and guests get complimentary use of beach towels, chairs, and umbrellas. Several restaurants are a short walk away.

6772 Sara Sea Circle, Siesta Key, FL 34242. ✆ **800/349-4131** or 941/349-4131. Fax 941/349-8141. www.captivabeachresort.com. 20 units. Winter $135–$215 double, $225–$305 bungalows and suites; off season $90–$170 double, $160–$180 bungalows and suites. Weekly and monthly rates available. AE, DISC, MC, V. **Amenities:** Heated outdoor pool; coin-op washers and dryers. *In room:* A/C, TV, kitchen, coffeemaker, hair dryer.

ON ANNA MARIA ISLAND
Bungalow Beach Resort ✿✿   If you want an Old Florida–style bungalow by the beach, owners Bert and Gayle Luper have them at this romantic little complex. In fact, white-sand walkways join the beach to these bright and airy clapboard cottages, built in the 1930s and 1940s but considerably spiffed up in recent years with hardwood floors, bright tropical furniture, and ceiling fans. Ranging in size from efficiencies to three bedrooms, they all have cooking

facilities and a deck or porch. A few have single-person whirlpool bathtubs. The five choice cottages open directly to the beach; the largest has a whirlpool bathtub with a steam maker, a full gourmet kitchen, and a deck. Three others are grouped around an outdoor swimming pool. There is no restaurant on the grounds, but several are within walking distance. No smoking is allowed in the units here.

2000 Gulf Dr. N. (between 17th and 22nd aves.), Bradenton Beach, FL 34217. (℃ 800/779-3601 or 941/778-3600. Fax 941/778-1764. www.bungalowbeach.com. 15 units, some with shower only. Winter $159–$369 double; off season $109–$269 double. AE, MC, V. **Amenities:** Heated outdoor pool; Jacuzzi; coin-op washers and dryers; concierge-level rooms. *In room:* A/C, TV, kitchen, coffeemaker, hair dryer.

Worth a Splurge

Harrington House Bed and Breakfast ★★   Flowers will be awaiting when you arrive at Jo and Frank Davis's exceptional bed-and-breakfast. In a tree-shaded setting on the beach overlooking the Gulf, this three-story coquina-and-rock house was built in 1925 and exudes an Old Florida ambience. The eight bedrooms are individually decorated with antique, wicker, or rattan furnishings. Some units have four-poster or brass beds, Jacuzzis, fireplaces, and French doors leading to balconies overlooking the Gulf. In addition to the bedrooms in the main house, four rooms are available in the adjacent Spangler Beach House, a remodeled 1940s captain's home, and four more are in the nearby Huth House, a beachside residence. Three units in the latter open to an expansive covered lanai facing the beach through a row of Australian pines. All guests enjoy use of the main house's high-ceilinged living room with fireplace, beachside pool, patio, and complimentary use of bicycles, kayaks, and other sports equipment. No smoking is allowed inside here.

5626 Gulf Dr. (at 58th St.), Holmes Beach, FL 34217. (℃ 888/828-5566 or 941/778-5444. Fax 941/778-0527. www.harringtonhouse.com. 14 units. Winter $189–$249 double; off season $139–$179. Rates include full breakfast. MC, V. No children under 12 allowed. **Amenities:** Heated outdoor pool; complimentary use of sports equipment. *In room:* A/C, TV, hair dryer.

GREAT DEALS ON DINING
IN DOWNTOWN SARASOTA

Downtown's best breakfast spot is the local branch of **First Watch,** 1395 Main St., at Central and Pineapple avenues (℃ **941/954-1395**). Like its siblings in Naples (see "Great Deals on Dining," in section 4 of chapter 9) and elsewhere, First Watch offers a wide variety of inexpensive breakfast and lunch fare. It's open daily from 7:30am to 2:30pm. If the wait's too long, walk south along Central Avenue; this block has several coffeehouses and cafes with sidewalk seating.

You'll find most of the national chain fast-food and family restaurants along U.S. 41.

Marina Jack   SEAFOOD/CONTINENTAL   Overlooking the waterfront with a wraparound 270-degree view of Sarasota Bay and Siesta and Lido keys, this establishment has spectacular water vistas and a carefree "on vacation" attitude, especially on the open-air raw-bar deck, which often is packed all afternoon on weekends and at sunset every day. The food is good but not the best in town, so come here for a relaxing, fun time. You may have to wait for a table or bar stool down on the deck, but be sure to make reservations if you want to have a meal in the upstairs dining room. Fresh local seafood is the star both upstairs and down—grilled grouper is your best bet. The downstairs lounge and raw bar also serves sandwiches and burgers.

In Island Park, Bayfront at Central Ave. ℂ **941/365-4232**. Reservations recommended in dining room. Dining room main courses $16–$35. Deck main courses $14–$17; sandwiches and salads $8–$11; Sun brunch $12–$24. AE, DISC, MC, V. Daily 11:30am–2am. Closed Christmas.

Yoder's ⭐ *Value* AMISH/AMERICAN   Just 3 miles east of downtown is an award-winning, value eatery operated by an Amish family (Sarasota and Bradenton have sizable Amish communities and several other Amish restaurants). Evoking the Pennsylvania Dutch country, the simple dining room displays handcrafts, photos, and paintings celebrating the Amish way. The menu emphasizes plain, made-from-scratch cooking such as home-style meatloaf, Southern fried chicken, country-smoked ham, and fried filet of flounder. Burgers, salads, soups, and sandwiches are also available. Leave room for Mrs. Yoder's traditional shoofly and other homemade pies, one of the restaurant's biggest draws. *Note:* Alcohol is neither served nor allowed here, so don't even think about sneaking in a flask.

3434 Bahia Vista St. (west of Beneva Rd.). ℂ **941/955-7771**. Main courses $6.25–$9.50; breakfast $2.50–$7; sandwiches, burgers, and salads $3.25–$8. No credit cards (ATM on premises). Mon–Sat 6am–8pm.

Worth a Splurge

Bijou Cafe ⭐⭐ INTERNATIONAL   Chef Jean-Pierre Knaggs prepares award-winning cuisines from around the world in his cafe, a former gas station, in the heart of the theater district. Although the more casual Michael's on East (see below) bistro draws a hefty after-theater crowd, this is the best place to dine within walking distance of the downtown entertainment venues. Jean-Pierre artfully presents the likes of prime veal Louisville (with crushed pecans and bourbon-pear sauce), pan-seared crab cakes served under a rémoulade and over a bed of fresh greens, and gently simmered lamb shanks with rosemary and garlic.

1287 1st St. (at Pineapple Ave.). ℂ **941/366-8111**. Reservations recommended. Main courses $17–$30. AE, DC, MC, V. Mon–Sat 11:30am–2pm; daily 5–9:30pm. Closed Sun June–Dec. Free valet parking nightly in winter, on weekends off season.

Michael's on East ⭐⭐ CREATIVE INTERNATIONAL   At the rear of the Midtown Plaza shopping center on U.S. 41 south of downtown, Michael Klauber's chic bistro is one of the top places here for fine dining and is the locals' favorite after-theater haunt. Huge cut-glass walls create three intimate dining areas, one a piano bar for pre- or after-dinner drinks. Prepared with fresh ingredients and a creative flair, the offerings here will tempt your taste buds. House specialties are the Dungeness crab cakes, pan-seared Chilean sea bass with couscous and artichoke hearts in a thyme-accented tomato coulis, and grilled duck breast with Bermuda onion, shiitake fondue, and pecan risotto.

1212 East Ave. S. (between Bahia and Prospect sts.). ℂ **941/366-0007**. Reservations recommended. Main courses $18–$36. AE, DC, DISC, MC, V. Winter Mon–Fri 11:30am–2pm, Sat 5:30–10pm, Sun 6–10pm; off season Mon–Fri 11:30am–2pm, Mon–Sat 6–10pm. Complimentary valet parking.

IN SOUTHSIDE VILLAGE

Sarasota's hottest dining area is **Southside Village,** centered on South Osprey Avenue between Hyde Park and Hillview streets, about 15 blocks south of downtown. Here you'll find several hip restaurants, including Fred's and Pacific Rim (see below). The village landmark is **Morton's Gourmet Market** ⭐, 1924 S. Osprey Ave. (ℂ **941/955-9856**), which offers a multitude of deli items, specialty sandwiches, a ton of fresh salads, freshly baked pastries and desserts, and cooked meals dispensed from a cafeteria-style steam table, which you can dine on picnic-fashion on sidewalk tables outside. Most ready-to-go items cost less than $7. Open Monday through Saturday from 8am to 8pm, Sunday from 10am to 5pm.

Fred's ⭐ CONTINENTAL   A popular hangout for the 20- and 30-something sets, especially on Friday nights, Fred's is the quintessential neighborhood brasserie serving an eclectic mix of American, European, Asian, and Latin influences in a stunning setting reminiscent of a sleek New York City bistro with copper ceilings and black-and-white checked floor. The food is essentially comfort food—rib-eye with mashed potatoes and penne pasta with chicken—and is pretty inconsistent, but what is consistent is the scene here, especially in the restaurant's cigar-friendly Tasting Room, which is abuzz with activity late into the night.

1923 S. Osprey Ave. 🕐 **941/364-5811.** Reservations recommended. Main courses $15–$30. AE, DC, MC, V. Mon–Thurs 11am–10pm; Fri–Sat 11am–1am; Sun 9am–10pm.

Pacific Rim ⭐ *Value* JAPANESE/THAI   Sarasotans love this chic and very casual restaurant for exceptional cuisine at economical prices. Japanese influence is felt at the authentic sushi bar along one side of the dining room, while Thai spices make a strong impact on the regular menu. The chargrilled shrimp with Thai curry and coconut-milk sauce is especially tasty, as is the combination of chicken and vegetables stir-fried in the wok. Here you can select your meat and vegetables separately from the sauce and the chefs will combine them on the grill, on the wok, or in the bowl (as in rice dishes).

In Hillview Centre, 1859 Hillview St. (between Osprey Ave. and Laurent Place). 🕐 **941/330-8071.** Main courses $7.50–$15. AE, DISC, MC, V. Mon–Thurs 11:30am–2pm and 5–9pm; Fri 11:30am–2pm and 5–10pm; Sat 5–10pm.

ON ST. ARMANDS KEY

While the locals are hanging out in Southside Village, part-year residents and visitors flock to St. Armands Circle. Plan to spend at least one evening here, since the nighttime scene is like a fair, with everyone strolling around the circle, poking heads into a few stores that stay open after dark, and window-shopping the others. It's fun and safe, so come early and plan to stay late. See "Shopping," earlier in this chapter, for parking tips.

The circle has a branch of Tampa's famous **Columbia** (p. 367) between John Ringling Boulevard and John Ringling Parkway (🕐 **941/388-3987**). The Spanish food is excellent, there's outdoor seating, and the Patio Lounge is one of the liveliest spots here for evening entertainment Thursday through Sunday. Like its sibling in Naples, the local edition of **Tommy Bahama's Tropical Cafe,** 300 John Ringling Blvd. (🕐 **941/388-2446**), draws a lively crowd of young professionals to its moderately priced seafood. It's upstairs over Tommy Bahama's clothing store.

At night, you may wish to forgo an expensive dessert and wander over to the local branch of **Kilwin's,** 312 John Ringling Blvd. (🕐 **941/388-3200**), for some gourmet chocolate, Mackinac Island fudge, or ice cream or yogurt in a homemade waffle cone. Enjoy your sweets on one of the sidewalk park benches—everyone else does.

Super-Cheap Eats

Blue Dolphin Cafe *Value* AMERICAN/DINER   On the John Ringling Boulevard spoke of St. Armands Circle, this informal diner is the affluent area's best inexpensive place to have breakfast, and the owners, Jill and Rob Ball, are a font of free information, too. They serve standard breakfast fare as well as fresh crab or lobster benedict, raspberry pancakes, and pecan-peach waffles.

Lunchtime highlights are homemade soups and grouper sandwiches. You can order breakfast anytime. The Blue Dolphin is open for dinner on Friday nights during the winter season, offering the likes of flaky-crust chicken potpie, slow-roasted prime rib, and spicy crab cakes.

470 John Ringling Blvd. (1 block off St. Armands Circle). ℂ **941/388-3566**. Breakfast $4.50–$10; sandwiches, burgers, and salads $5–$10. AE, DC, DISC, MC, V. Daily 7am–3pm.

Hungry Fox AMERICAN   This upstairs restaurant is the only place on St. Armands Circle offering three inexpensive meals a day year-round. It's not much to look at inside, with marble-look tables and plastic lawn chairs, so wait for a table out on the veranda, especially next to the railing where you can oversee all the action down below. Breakfast, which is served until noon, offers everything from lox and bagels to Virginia ham and eggs. Sandwiches and salads appear at lunch, followed by steaks, chicken, pastas, and spicy jambalaya for dinner. Most items are a good value for the price, but stay away from anything cooked in the deep fryer if you're concerned about your cholesterol.

419 St. Armands Circle (above Cha Cha Coconuts). ℂ **941/388-2222**. Main courses $11–$17; sandwiches, burgers, and salads $4.50–$9; breakfast $4.50–$10. AE, DISC, MC, V. Mon–Sat 8am–9pm; Sun 8am–2:30pm.

Worth a Splurge

Café L'Europe ★★★ CONTINENTAL   One of Sarasota's most lauded restaurants, Café L'Europe has been the recipient of countless awards and praises for its continental cuisine that fuses French, Caribbean, and Spanish influences into what the chef prefers to call New European Cuisine. An elegant ambience renders the restaurant a place to celebrate special occasions, whether over the classic Dover sole or an updated version of sweetbreads—crispy sweetbreads, this time, with mixed lettuces, poached pear, and mustard sauce. Sea bass, steamed in papillote, with spinach, zucchini, roasted garlic, fingerling potatoes, dill, and tomatoes matched with one of the restaurant's many vintages is a sublime choice as well. Service, as to be expected in a restaurant of this caliber, is outstanding.

431 St. Armands Circle (at John Ringling Blvd.). ℂ **941/388-4415**. Reservations recommended. Main courses $10–$30. AE, DC, MC, V. Daily 11am–10:30pm.

ON SIESTA KEY

Ocean Boulevard, which runs through **Siesta Village,** the area's funky, laid-back beach hangout, is virtually lined with restaurants and pubs. Most have outdoor seating and bars, which attract the beach crowd during the day. At night, rock-'n'-roll bands draw teenagers and college students to this lively scene.

Blasé Café ★★ *Finds* INTERNATIONAL   Tongue in cheeky, to say the least, this restaurant doesn't take itself seriously. One of Florida's most unusual restaurants, Ralph and Cindy Cole's supercasual establishment has tables indoors and a few under the cover of the Village Corner shopping center's walkway, but most are alfresco, on a wooden deck built around a palm tree in the center's asphalt parking lot. Never mind the cars pulling in and out virtually next to your chair: Ralph's food is so good that it draws droves of locals, who don't mind waiting for an umbrella table. This is Siesta Key's best breakfast spot, offering Italian- and Louisiana-flavored frittatas as well as plain old bacon and eggs. Lunch sees burgers, big salads, and platters such as chicken Alfredo and Florentine crepes with shrimp. At night, Ralph puts forth the likes of pan-seared sushi-quality yellowfin tuna with tangy wasabi and pickled ginger. You can while away the rest of the evening in the wine bar, where the Coles have installed the original bar from the Don CeSar Beach Resort & Spa in St. Pete Beach. There's also live music in there on weekends.

In Village Corner, 5263 Ocean Blvd. (at Calle Miramar), Siesta Village. © 941/349-9822. Reservations recommended. Main courses $10–$23; breakfast and lunch $5–$9. MC, V. Mon–Thurs 8:30am–9:30pm; Fri–Sat 8:30am–10pm. Closed Mon June–Nov.

Turtles AMERICAN   With tropical overtones and breathtaking water vistas across from Turtle Beach, this informal restaurant on Little Sarasota Bay has tables indoors and on an outside deck. Unique seafood offerings include snapper New Orleans and potato-encrusted mahimahi. You can't go wrong ordering grouper grilled, broiled, blackened, or fried. There's also a selection of pastas on the menu. The economical early-bird specials offer several choices ranging from a medium-size portion of mahimahi to spicy Szechuan shrimp.

8875 Midnight Pass Rd. (at Turtle Beach Rd.). © 941/346-2207. Main courses $11–$20; salads and sandwiches $7–$15; early-bird specials $9–$11. AE, DISC, MC, V. Mon–Sat 11:30am–9:30pm; Sun 10am–9pm. Early-bird specials daily 4–6pm.

ON LONGBOAT KEY

Euphemia Haye/The Haye Loft ★★★ INTERNATIONAL   This area's most extraordinary restaurant, the romantically lighted Euphemia Haye is best known for Chef Raymond Arpke's crispy roast duck filled with bread stuffing and accompanied by a tangy fruit sauce. His prime strip steak rolled in cracked peppercorns and served with an orange, brandy, and butter sauce is another winner, as are his shrimp in a delightful curry and coconut cream sauce. If all this sounds sweet, wait until you go upstairs to The Haye Loft, his casual dessert bar. Up here you can take your pick from fabulous pies topped with thick whipped cream or Ben & Jerry's ice cream. You can also sample the kitchen's offerings, for the loft has its own light-fare menu, including soups, appetizers, small pizzas, and sandwiches. If you're lucky, the night's special sandwich will be steak topped with Raymond's peppercorn sauce. Served open-face and garnished with a field-greens salad, it's a meal for about $10. Add a glass of superb wine and a slice of pie a la mode, and you've had a wonderful dinner for under $20.

5540 Gulf of Mexico Dr. (at Gulfbay Rd.). © 941/383-3633. www.euphemiahaye.com. Reservations recommended downstairs, not accepted in The Haye Loft. Main courses $18–$39; sandwiches, pizzas, and salads $7–$12. DC, DISC, MC, V. Restaurant Sun–Thurs 5–10pm; Fri–Sat 5–10:30pm. The Haye Loft daily 6pm–midnight.

Moore's Stone Crab SEAFOOD   Located in Longbeach, the old fishing village on the north end of Longboat Key, this popular bayfront restaurant began in 1967 as an offshoot of a family seafood business established 40 years earlier. From the outside, in fact, it still looks a little like a packing house, but the view of the bay dotted with mangrove islands makes a fine complement to stone crabs fresh from the family's own traps from October 15 to May 15. Otherwise, the menu offers an incredibly large variety of seafood, most of it fried or broiled. Sandwiches and salads are served all day.

800 Broadway (at Bayside Dr.). © 941/383-1748. Main courses $15–$23; stone crab market price (as much as $40–$45 in season, from mid-Oct to mid-May); sandwiches and salads $7–$13. AE, DISC, MC, V. Winter daily 11:30am–9:30pm; off season Mon–Fri 4:30–9:30pm; Sat–Sun 11:30am–9:30pm.

ON ANNA MARIA ISLAND

The Beachhouse ★ AMERICAN   This large, lively place sits right on Bradenton Beach with a huge open deck and a covered pavilion facing out to the Gulf. Even inside, wide windows let in the view. Owned by Ed Chiles, son of the late U.S. senator and Florida governor Lawton Chiles, the Beachhouse offers daily fresh fish, including the signature beechnut grouper (with nutty crust in citrus-butter sauce). There's also a good variety of fare, including seafood salads and pastas, crab cakes, fish and chips, and broiled steaks. Local musicians play on the patio most evenings.

200 Gulf Dr. N. (at Cortez Rd.), Bradenton Beach. (C) 941/779-2222. Reservations not accepted, but call for preferred seating. Main courses $12–$20; sandwiches $6–$10. AE, DC, DISC, MC, V. Daily 11:30am–10pm.

Sandbar ★ SEAFOOD Sitting on the site of the former Pavilion, built in 1913 when people from Tampa and St. Pete took the ferry here, this popular restaurant is perched right on the beach overlooking the Gulf. The air-conditioned, knotty-pine dining room offers several traditional as well as innovative preparations of seafood (crab cakes with a Creole mustard sauce, for example). The real action here is under the umbrellas on the lively beachside deck, where appetizers, sandwiches, salads, and platters are served all day and night. Live music makes a party on the deck Monday to Friday nights and on Saturday and Sunday beginning at 1pm. The inside bar is one of the few we've seen in Florida with no sports TVs.

100 Spring Ave. (east of Gulf Dr.), Anna Maria. (C) 941/778-0444. Reservations not accepted; call ahead to get on waiting list. Main courses $15–$20; salads and sandwiches $5–$12. AE, DC, DISC, MC, V. Daily 11:30am–10pm.

Super-Cheap Eats

Gulf Drive Café ★★ *Value* AMERICAN Locals flock to this bright Gulf-side cafe for one of the best bargains on any beach in Florida. With big windows, bentwood cafe chairs with colorful cushions, and lots of hanging plants and ceiling fans, the coral and green dining room opens to a beachside patio with tables shaded by a trellis (the wait is worth it). The breakfast fare is led by sweet Belgian waffles, which are available all day. You can also order salads, sandwiches, and burgers anytime here, with quiche du jour, Mediterranean seafood pasta, and regular seafood platters joining the show at 4pm.

900 Gulf Dr. N. (at 9th St.), Bradenton Beach. (C) 941/778-1919. Reservations not accepted. Main courses $7–$14; breakfast $3–$6; sandwiches and burgers $4.50–$6. DISC, MC, V. Daily 7am–9:30pm.

SARASOTA AFTER DARK

The cultural capital of Florida's west coast, Sarasota is home to a host of performing arts, especially during the winter season. To get the latest update on what's happening any time of year, call the city's 24-hour **Artsline** ((C) **941/365-2787**). Also check the "Ticket" section in Friday's *Herald-Tribune* (www.news coast.com), the local daily newspaper; the Sarasota Convention and Visitors Bureau usually has copies (p. 392).

THE PERFORMING ARTS Located at the FSU Ringling Center for the Cultural Arts (p. 395), the Florida State University Center for the Performing Arts, 5555 N. Tamiami Trail (U.S. 41; (C) **800/361-8388** or 941/351-8000; www. asolo.org), presents the winter-through-spring **Asolo Theatre Festival** ★★★. This annual program of ballet and Broadway-style musicals and drama is one of the state's finest. In addition to the Asolo Theatre, a 19th-century Italian court playhouse moved here from Asolo, Italy, in the 1950s by the Ringlings, the center uses the 487-seat Harold E. and Ethel M. Mertz Theatre, originally constructed in Scotland in 1900 and transferred piece by piece to Sarasota in 1987. The 161-seat Asolo Conservatory Theatre was later added as a smaller venue for experimental and alternative offerings. The complex is under the direction of Florida State University (FSU).

The city's other prime venue is the lavender, seashell-shaped **Van Wezel Performing Arts Hall** ★★★, 777 N. Tamiami Trail (U.S. 41), at 9th Street (© **800/826-9303** or 941/953-3368; www.vanwezel.org). Recently renovated, it offers excellent visual and acoustic conditions and a wide range of year-round programming, including touring Broadway shows and visiting orchestras and dance troupes. It and the FSU Center host performances by the **Florida West Coast Symphony** (© **941/953-4252;** www.fwcs.org), the **Jazz Club of Sarasota** (© **941/366-1552** or 941/316-9207; www.jazzclubsarasota.com), the **Sarasota Pops** (© **941/795-7677**), and the **Sarasota Ballet** (© **800/361-8388** or 941/351-8000; www.sarasotaballet.org).

Downtown Sarasota's theater district is home to the **Florida Studio Theatre,** 1241 N. Palm Ave., at Cocoanut Avenue (© **941/366-9000;** www.fst2000.org), which has contemporary performances from December to August, including a New Play Festival in May. Built in 1926 as the Edwards Theater, **The Opera House,** 61 N. Pineapple Ave., between Main and 1st streets (© **941/366-8450;** www.sarasotaopera.org), presents classical operas (in their original languages) as well as highbrow concerts. Next door to The Opera House, the **Golden Apple Dinner Theatre,** 25 N. Pineapple Ave. (© **941/366-5454**), presents cocktails, dinner, and a professional Broadway-style show year-round. The professional, nonequity **Theatre Works,** 1247 1st St., at Cocoanut Avenue (© **941/952-9170**), presents musical revues and other works year-round.

THE CLUB & MUSIC SCENE   You can find plenty of music to dance to on the mainland at **Sarasota Quay,** the downtown waterfront dining-shopping-entertainment complex on Tamiami Trail (U.S. 41), a block north of John Ringling Causeway. Just walk around this brick building and your ears will take you to the action. The laser sound-and-light crowd gathers at **In Extremis** (© **941/954-2008**), where a high-energy DJ spins Top 40 tunes for 20-somethings. Michael's Mediterranean Grill turns into **Anthony's After Dark** rocking disco at 10:30pm. An older but still energetic crowd dances to contemporary jazz at the **Downunder Jazz Bar** (© **941/951-2467**). In Siesta Key Village, **The Old Salty Dog,** 5023 Ocean Blvd. (© **941/349-0158**), offers a fabulous selection of British ales and a lovely outdoor patio.

Over on St. Armands Circle, the Patio Lounge in the **Columbia** restaurant (© **941/388-3987**) is one of the liveliest spots along the beach strip, featuring live, high-energy dance music Tuesday through Sunday evenings. And on Siesta Key, the pubs and restaurants along Ocean Boulevard in Siesta Village have noisy rock-'n'-roll bands entertaining a mostly young crowd, but you can retire to the pleasant confines of the wine bar at **Blasé Café** (© **941/349-9822**) for live jazz. See "Great Deals on Dining," above, for more about these two restaurants.

11

Walt Disney World & Orlando

by Laura Lea Miller

Welcome to Walt Disney World (WDW) and Orlando, a happy place presided over by an ageless rodent, where cash registers almost always sing happy songs (and they're not harmonizing over nickel-and-dime sales).

Before Disney's 1971 arrival, Gatorland was the biggest tourist show in town, and its tickets cost a seemingly meager $5. Even in the early 1980s, a family of four could get into the Magic Kingdom for under $100, eat at one of Orlando's finer restaurants for $30, and spend the night at Disney's Contemporary or Polynesian resorts for $90.

Today, the same 24-hour visit costs more than double what it did 2 decades ago. Yes, WDW is a world of dreams, but dreams aren't cheap anymore. The same resort rooms begin at $234 and $299, respectively; it's just over $200 to get two adults and two kids into a theme park; and you need a search and rescue team to find a spot where dinner for four is $50.

It seems impossible, but in Mickeyland, anything is possible—Mousketeer's honor.

Here, you'll find a better deal than other tourists but have as much fun or more. You'll discover where to discover bargains and discounts but still be chin deep in the action. And trust me: There's enough action to make your head spin.

Uncle Walt's world now encompasses four major theme parks and a dozen smaller attractions, two entertainment districts, tens of thousands of hotel rooms, scores of restaurants, and a pair of cruise ships. Universal Orlando and SeaWorld add four theme parks. Universal also has its own nightclub district, CityWalk. And Orlando and Lake Buena Vista have 80 or more smaller attractions, a landslide of eateries, and enough rooms to boost the city's total to 115,000 in 2005.

Disney has built such a lead over the wannabes that, despite growth, Universal and SeaWorld have joined Wet 'n Wild and Busch Gardens in Tampa to offer special packages and discounts. Their **FlexTickets** let you visit up to five parks for a flat price. (See "Passes & Coupons That Save Your Orlan-Dough," below.)

And you really must *plan ahead!* The number of attractions begging for your time and the hyper-commercial atmosphere can put a serious dent in your wallet and stamina. Once here, it's easy to get overwhelmed by the urge to do everything in the World and then some. Even if you have 2 weeks, it won't be long enough to hit everything.

1 Orientation

WHEN SHOULD I GO?

Orlando's busiest seasons are whenever kids are out of school: weekends, early June to Labor Day, mid-December to early January, and spring break. The experience is more enjoyable when crowds are thin and the weather is moderate, so the best times to go are the week after Labor Day until the day before Thanksgiving, the week after Thanksgiving until mid-December, and the 6 weeks before and after spring vacation. The worst time is summer: Crowds are huge and the days are hot and humid.

GETTING THERE
BY PLANE
THE MAJOR AIRLINES   Over 37 scheduled airlines and several more charter companies serve the more than 26 million Orlando passengers who arrive at **Orlando International Airport** (℃ **407/825-2001;** www.orlandoairports.net) each year. The best fares to Orlando are for travel during the months of November, December, and January, excluding holidays.

   Delta (℃ 800/221-1212; www.delta.com) provides nearly 20% of the flights to and from Orlando International Airport, offering service from roughly 150 cities. Other carriers include **Air Canada** (℃ 888/247-2262; www.aircanada. ca), **America West** (℃ 800/235-9292; www.americawest.com), **American** (℃ 800/433-7300; www.americanair.com), **British Airways** (℃ 800/247-9297; www.british-airways.com), **Continental** (℃ 800/525-0280; www. continental.com), **Delta Song** (℃800/FLY-SONG; www.flysong.com), **JetBlue Airways** (℃ 800/538-2583; www.jetblue.com), **Northwest** (℃ 800/225-2525; www.nwa.com), **Southwest Airlines** (℃ 800/435-9792; www.southwest.com), **United Airlines** (℃ 800/241-6522; www.united.com), **United's Ted** (℃ **800/ CALL-TED;** www.flyted.com), and **US Airways** (℃ 800/428-4322; www. usairways.com).

   Located only 25 miles from Walt Disney World, Orlando International is extremely easy to navigate and conveniently located to the city's tourist areas. For those of you who don't wish to rent a car **Mears Transportation** (℃ **407/ 423-5566;** www.mearstransportation.com) provides shuttle service to and from the airport with vans running 24 hours a day and departing every 15 to 25 minutes. Round-trip fares are $25 to $29 adults and $18 to $21 children ages 4 to 11 (actual price depends on the location you're going to); children 3 and under ride free.

BY CAR   From Atlanta, take **I-75** south to the Florida Turnpike to **I-4** west. From the Northeast, take **I-95** south to I-4 west. From Chicago, take **I-65** south to Nashville, **I-24** south to I-75, and then south to the Florida Turnpike to I-4 west. From Dallas, take **I-20** east to **I-49,** then south to **I-10,** east to I-75, and south to the Florida Turnpike to I-4 west.

BY TRAIN   **Amtrak** trains (℃ **800/872-7245;** www.amtrak.com) pull into stations both in downtown Orlando (23 miles from Walt Disney World) and Kissimmee (15 miles from Disney). There are also stops in Winter Park (10 miles north of downtown) and Sanford (23 miles northeast of downtown Orlando). The Sanford stop is the terminal for Amtrak's Auto Train as well.

   You can get train discounts if you book far in advance. There may be travel restrictions, mostly around holidays. Traveling into Orlando instead of Winter Park, about 10 miles away, will save you some money. Amtrak also offers money-saving packages—including hotel accommodations (some at WDW resorts), car rentals, tours, and more—with your train fare. For information, call ℃ **800/ 321-8684.**

BY BUS   **Greyhound** buses (℃ **800/231-2222;** www.greyhound.com) stop in terminals at 555 N. Magruder Blvd. (John Young Pkwy.), a few miles west of

Orlando/Walt Disney World Area

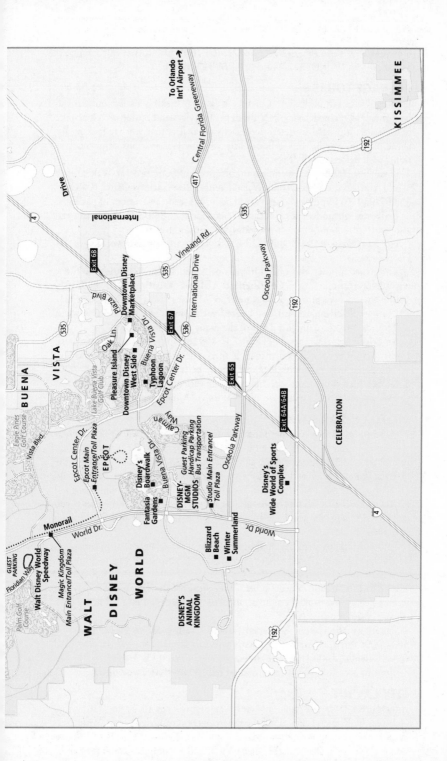

To Orlando Int'l Airport →

Central Florida Greeneway

KISSIMMEE

192

417

535

Drive

International

4

Vineland Rd.

Exit 68

535

Downtown Disney Marketplace

International Drive

Plaza Blvd.

Osceola Parkway

192

Oak Ln.

Exit 67

536

Pleasure Island

555

Buena Vista Dr.

Downtown Disney West Side

Typhoon Lagoon

VISTA

Lake Buena Vista Golf Club

Epcot Center Dr.

Exit 65

BUENA

Eagle Pines Golf Course

Cayman Way

Exit 64A/64B

Epcot Center Dr.

Epcot Main Entrance/Toll Plaza

CELEBRATION

EPCOT

Disney's Boardwalk

Guest Parking

Vista Blvd.

Buena Vista Dr.

Handicap Parking

Bus Transportation

Osceola Parkway

Disney's Wide World of Sports Complex

DISNEY-MGM STUDIOS

Studio Main Entrance/Toll Plaza

4

Monorail

Fantasia Gardens

World Dr.

GUEST PARKING

World Dr.

Blizzard Beach

Walt Disney World Speedway

Floridian Way

Winter Summerland

192

Magic Kingdom Main Entrance/Toll Plaza

WALT

Palm Golf Course

DISNEY

WORLD

DISNEY'S ANIMAL KINGDOM

411

downtown Orlando (© **407/292-3422**), and 16 E. Dakin Ave. in Kissimmee, 14 miles from Walt Disney World (© **407/847-3911**).

PACKAGE TOURS

Finding a vacation package to Orlando is easy; it's making a selection that can be difficult as each package offers a variety of services and options. To make the best choice, you need to determine exactly what it is that you are looking for ahead of time, whether it is airline tickets, car-rental reservations, resort reservations, park tickets, or all of the above.

If you're planning on spending the majority of your time at Walt Disney World, contact the **Walt Disney World Central Reservations Office (CRO)** at © 407/934-7639 or www.disneyworld.com for a wide assortment of packages.

Universal Orlando packages can be booked at © **888/322-5537.** You can also get information online at **www.universalorlando.com**.

For **SeaWorld,** call © **800/423-8368** or go to **www.seaworld.com** for information.

The major airlines also offer Orlando packages. **Delta** (© **800/872-7786;** www.deltavacations.com), **Continental Airlines Vacations** (© **800/301-3800;** www.coolvacations.com), **American Airlines Vacations** (© **800/321-2121;** www.americanair.com), and **United Vacations** (© **888/854-3899;** www. unitedvacations.com) are just a few of the many available options.

American Express Travel (© **800/732-1991;** http://travel.americanexpress. com/travel) offers packages that include special deals for their cardholders.

The **American Automobile Association,** better known as **AAA** (© **800/ 836-2582;** www.aaa.com), also offers a wide variety of vacation packages, and special amenities and savings are available for AAA members.

VISITOR INFORMATION

The **Orlando/Orange County Convention & Visitors Bureau,** 8723 International Dr., Suite 101, Orlando, FL 32819 (© **407/363-5872;** www.orlando info.com), can answer questions and send maps and brochures, such as the *Official Visitors Guide* and *Official Accommodations Guide.* The packet should reach you in a couple of weeks and also include the "Magicard," which is good for up to $500 in discounts on rooms, car rentals, attractions, and more. If you don't mind using an automated recording system, you can order by calling © **800/643-9492.**

For information about **Walt Disney World**—including vacation brochures and videos—contact Walt Disney World, Box 10000, Lake Buena Vista, FL 32830-1000 (© **407/934-7639** or 407/824-2222; www.disneyworld.com). The website is an especially good bet; Disney just revamped it and it is now easier to navigate and provides more detailed information than ever before on both the parks and the resorts.

For information about **Universal Orlando,** call © **800/837-2273** or 407/ 363-8000; surf the Internet to **www.universalorlando.com**, or write to Universal Orlando, 1000 Universal Studios Plaza, Orlando, FL 32819.

You can obtain SeaWorld information online at **www.seaworld.com**.

CITY LAYOUT

Interstate 4 (I-4) will take you everywhere you want to go in and around Orlando, with several exits along the way to get you to Walt Disney World, SeaWorld, and Universal Studios Orlando, not to mention the areas of International Drive (or I-Drive), Lake Buena Vista, and Kissimmee. *Note:* I-4 can be woefully congested. It's best to use it during non-peak hours, when the tourists

---

Fun Fact **Name Game**

Universal may be suffering an identity crisis. It changed the name of its umbrella company to Universal Studios Escape when local operations expanded beyond a single theme park. But critics thought that was confusing, so now it's Universal Orlando and that name seems to fit.

---

and locals aren't rushing to and from Orlando and the parks. There are many alternate routes that will allow you to avoid the highway completely, and I recommend you get a detailed road map of the area to check out what routes will work best with your touring plans.

The Florida Turnpike crosses I-4 and links to I-75 to the north. U.S. 192, a major east-west highway, runs along Kissimmee's major motel area to U.S. 27, where it crosses I-4 near the Disney World entrance. The Beeline Expressway goes east from I-4 past Orlando International Airport to Cape Canaveral.

NEIGHBORHOODS IN BRIEF

Walt Disney World Located southwest of the city of Orlando, WDW encompasses over 47 square miles and includes four major theme parks, two smaller water parks, several resorts, and a plethora of restaurants and shops including the Downtown Disney Marketplace, the entertainment district of Pleasure Island and Disney Westside, not to mention the Wide World of Sports Complex, and Disney Quest.

Lake Buena Vista Lake Buena Vista actually encompasses all of WDW, but also includes much of the area bordering the resort. Here you can find the "official" (but not Disney-owned) hotels located on Hotel Plaza Boulevard. The area along 535, or Apopka-Vineland as it is also known, is home to many a resort and restaurant. Though the region is bustling, many of the resorts, restaurants, and shops are set far off the main thoroughfare to maintain a quieter atmosphere.

Celebration What else would you expect from Disney, the original creators of this 4,900-acre community, but a picture-perfect town. This area, which some not so kiddingly refer to as Stepford or Pleasantville, offers not only beautiful homes, but also a charming collection of shops, restaurants, and even its own hotel.

Downtown Disney This is really not a neighborhood (nor is it downtown) as much as it is the area encompassing Disney's two nighttime entertainment districts, Pleasure Island and West Side, as well as its shopping complex, the Downtown Disney Marketplace. Full of clubs, entertainment venues, unique restaurants, and shopping experiences, you can celebrate New Year's Eve here every night, shop till you drop, or tempt your taste buds.

Kissimmee Thanks to a million dollar "Rebeautivacation" project, the neighborhood that was the region's tourist hot spot B.D. (Before Disney) has come back to life with the addition of extra wide sidewalks, colorful (and plentiful) streetlamps, landscaping, and location markers. Even U.S. 192 itself has been improved to handle traffic more easily and safely. Kissimmee is home to a variety of budget and moderate resorts and hotels, a plentitude of restaurants, and a handful of minor attractions.

International Drive Area (Hwy. 536) Known as **I-Drive,** this busy tourist zone is home to more than 100 resorts and hotels, countless restaurants, tacky attractions both big and small, shopping, entertainment, and even it's own transportation system—the I Ride Trolley. There is literally something here for everybody. The areas north of Sand Lake Road are the most congested with T-shirt shops and tourist traps,

and until you get south of the intersection at S.R. 528 (aka the Beeline Expwy.), the driving is slow going at best.

Downtown Orlando The actual downtown area is actually northeast of Walt Disney World on I-4. It offers restaurants, hotels, theaters, museums, the Orlando Science Center, nightclubs, and more. It's where you go to escape the Mouse.

GETTING AROUND

In a city that thrives on tourists, you won't find it difficult to get from point A to point B—especially if you have a car—but the going can be slow at times. If you're traveling outside or between the tourist areas, try to avoid the 7-day-a-week rush hour (7–9am and 4–6pm). Rush hours are bad anywhere, but commuter traffic here only compounds the tourist traffic.

ON INTERNATIONAL DRIVE Traffic on I-Drive can be absolutely infuriating, compounded exponentially if you are visiting at one of the busier times of year (the two weeks surrounding the Easter holiday being among the busiest). Its extremely high concentration of hotels, restaurants, shops, and attractions, not to mention the numerous traffic lights and alcoves located along the way make driving very slow going. The two ways to conquer the traffic of I-Drive are to travel by foot (while points of interest can be reasonably close together, keep in mind that safety can be a factor when walking here) and the **I-Ride Trolley** (© **407/248-9590;** www.iridetrolley.com), which stops about every 2 blocks from one end of I-Drive to the other. The trolley runs from 8am to 10:30pm (75¢ adults, 25¢ seniors, and children under 12 ride for free; *exact change is required*). Unlimited passes for between one and fourteen days are available as well and the cost averages out to about a dollar a day. It really is a fun way to get around the area.

BY THE DISNEY TRANSPORTATION SYSTEM If you plan to stay at and spend most of your time in Disney, there's an extensive, free transportation network that runs throughout the WDW property.

Disney resorts and official hotels offer unlimited free transportation via bus, monorail, ferry, or water taxi to all WDW properties throughout the day and, at times, well into the evening.

The system is free, saving you money on a rental car, insurance, and gas, as well as theme-park parking fees. The drawback, however, is that you're at the

---

Tips **Look Both Ways**

We don't recommend foot travel anywhere in Orlando, but occasionally you'll have to walk across a parking lot or street. *Be careful.* Orlando is among the most dangerous cities in the country for pedestrians, according to a Washington, D.C.–based research group. Wide roads designed to move traffic quickly and a shortage of sidewalks, streetlights, and crosswalks are to blame.

mercy of the Disney departure schedules and routes, which can often be slow and sometimes *very* indirect. A copy of the "WDW Transportation Guide Map" is available inside Disney's new shopping and dining guide. Ask for the guide at Guest Services desks inside any of the Disney resorts and theme parks.

BY SHUTTLE   Mears Transportation operates vans and buses that go to all of the theme parks, as well as the Kennedy Space Center and Busch Gardens (yes, in Tampa), among others. Rates vary according to destination. Call ℭ **407/ 423-5566** for rates.

BY TAXI   Taxis gather at the major resorts, and smaller properties will be happy to call a cab for you. **Yellow Cab** (ℭ **407/699-9999**) and **Ace Metro** (ℭ **407/855-0564**) are both good choices, though you should keep in mind that taxis are expensive and charges may run as much as $3.25 for the first mile and $1.75 per mile thereafter.

FAST FACTS: Walt Disney World & Orlando

Babysitters Many Orlando hotels, including all of Disney's resorts, offer babysitting services, usually from an outside service such as **Kids Night Out** (ℭ **800/696/8105** or 407/828-0920; www.kidsniteout.com), or **All About Kids** (ℭ **800/728-6506** or 407/812-9300; www.all-about-kids.com). Child-care rates usually run somewhere between $10 and $15 per hour for the first child and $1 per additional child, per hour. Several Orlando resorts have good child-care facilities with counselor-supervised activity programs right on the premises (the Disney resorts' programs are only for kids age 4–12 and cost $10 per hour). Reservations are a good idea (ℭ **407/939-3463**).

Business Hours Theme park operating hours vary depending on the time of year, even on the day of the week. While most open at 8 or 9am and close at 6 or 7pm, you should call or check a park's website for its most current schedule before arriving. Other businesses are generally open from 9am to 5pm, Monday through Friday.

Doctors & Dentists There are basic first-aid centers in all of the theme parks. There's also a 24-hour, toll-free number for the **Poison Control Center** (ℭ **800/282-3171**). To find a dentist, call **Dental Referral Service** at ℭ **800/235-4111** or go online to **www.dentalreferral.com**.

Disney offers in-room medical service 24 hours a day (ℭ **407/238-2000**). **Doctors on Call Service** (ℭ **407/399-3627**) makes house and room calls in most of the Orlando area. **Centra-Care** lists several walk-in clinics in the Yellow Pages, including ones on International Drive (ℭ **407/370-4881**), and at Lake Buena Vista near Disney (ℭ **407/934-2273**).

Emergencies Dial ℭ **911** for police, fire departments, and ambulance.

Hospitals **Sand Lake Hospital,** 9400 Turkey Lake Rd. (ℭ **407/351-8550**), is about 2 miles south of Sand Lake Road. From the WDW area, take I-4 east to the Sand Lake Road exit and make a left on Turkey Lake Road. The hospital is 2 miles up on your right. To avoid the highway, take Palm Parkway (off of Apopka-Vineland near Hotel Plaza Blvd.), it turns into Turkey Lake Road. The hospital is 2 miles up on your left. **Celebration Health** (ℭ **407/ 303-4000**), located in the near-Disney town of Celebration, is at 400

Celebration Place. From I-4, take the U.S. 192 exit. At the first traffic light, turn right onto Celebration Avenue. At the first stop sign, take another right.

Kennels The theme parks board pets for $6 per day. WDW also offers overnight boarding ($11 for the general public or $9 for Disney resort guests) at the Transportation and Ticket Center's kennel near the Polynesian Resort. Universal Orlando's resorts all welcome pets, which can stay with you right in your room.

Lost Children Every theme park has a designated spot for parents to reunite with lost children. Ask a park employee or check at guest services for details.

Pharmacies **Walgreens,** 7650 W. Sand Lake Rd. (© **407/345-9497**), operates a 24-hour pharmacy. Other locations can be found near Universal Orlando and Kissimmee by logging on to **www.walgreens.com**. There are scores of others located throughout the area as well, all listed in the Yellow Pages.

Post Office The post office most convenient to Disney and Universal is at 10450 Turkey Lake Rd. (© **800/275-8777**). It's open Monday through Friday from 9am to 4:30pm and Saturdays from 9am to noon.

Taxes A 6.5% to 7% sales tax (depending on which local county you happen to be in) is charged on all goods with the exception of most edible grocery-store items and medicines. Hotels add another 2% to 5% in resort taxes to your bill, so the total tax on accommodations can run you up to 12%.

Telephone If you're making a local call in Orlando, even to someone just across the street, *you must dial the 407 area code followed by the number you wish to call,* for a total of 10 digits.

Weather Call © **321/255-0212** for the local weather forecast or check out the Weather Channel at **www.weather.com** for the most up-to-date information.

2 Accommodations You Can Afford, In & Around the Parks

Psst! Beat the crowds. Reserve your room as early as you can—the minute you pick dates for your trip if possible. The average hotel rack rate for the metro area is $110 and increasing 5% to 10% a year. In some cases (but not at Disney properties), rates are lower in July, August, and September, though many places only have a few discounted rooms, and they go fast. The rates are higher in January, February, and March. And Orlando is a year-round destination thanks to tourists and the convention trade, so many hotels and motels don't offer much of a discount season. Also, make sure to factor the **11% or 12% hotel tax** into your budget.

HOW TO SAVE MONEY BY STAYING WITH MICKEY Many people assume that motels outside the Disney parks will cost less than stays on WDW premises, where the lowest rack rates are $77 to $126 at the All-Star resorts. Unless you are going in low season and the motel you choose charges for shuttle transportation to the parks—many charge $10 to $15 per person per day—that assumption is valid. Disney resort rates are usually 20% to 30% higher than the rates for comparable hotels and resorts outside of Mickeyville. That said, you can save money on transportation, parking, and tickets if you stay on the property, and you will gain the convenience of being in the center of the action.

Disney-owned hostelries and "official" hotels offer complimentary transportation to and from WDW parks and other areas. In general, however, the lower the room rate, the farther you are from the theme parks and the longer it takes to travel. You'll have to weigh time against cost to determine whether to rent a car. If you do rent a car, keep in mind that resort guests get free parking at the theme parks, so you'll save yourself $8 per day.

In or out of this World, if you book your hotel as part of a package (details below), you'll likely enjoy savings. Ask about discounts for students, government employees, seniors, military, firefighters, police, AFL-CIO, corporate clients, and, again, AARP, or AAA. Special Internet-only discounts and packages may also be featured on hotel websites, especially those of the larger chains. No matter what your landing zone, ask again when you arrive if there are any additional discounts or promotions available.

There are 31 hotels, resorts, villas, timeshares, and campsites that are owned by Disney or are "official" hotels—those that are privately owned but have earned Disney's seal of approval. The best of these within (and a few out of) our price range are described in the following pages. In addition to their proximity to the parks, there are a number of advantages to staying at a Disney property or "official" hotel. Even the budget choices offer extensive resort facilities. The following amenities are included at all Disney resorts; **some** are offered by the "official" hotels, but be sure to ask when booking:

- **Unlimited complimentary transportation** via bus, monorail, ferry, and/or water taxi to/from all four parks from 2 hours before opening until 2 hours after closing. Unlimited free rides are also provided to and from Downtown Disney, Typhoon Lagoon, Pleasure Island, Fort Wilderness, and other Disney resorts. This helps save money and also guarantees admission to all the parks, even during peak times when the parking lots sometimes fill. Note, however, that the Disney transportation system can be *excruciatingly slow.* Sometimes you have to take a ferry to catch a bus to get on the monorail to reach your hotel. The system makes a circuit, but may not necessarily take the most direct path for you. It can take an hour or more to get to a place that's right across the lagoon from you.
- The **Extra Magic Hour** (see the box "The Early Bird . . . ," below).
- Kids under 17 stay free in their parent's room, and **reduced-price children's menus** are available in most restaurants.
- A **guest-services desk** where you can purchase tickets to all WDW theme parks and attractions and obtain general information.

⌒Tips The Early Bird . . .

In October 2002, WDW launched its **Extra Magic Hour,** which lets resort guests into the parks an hour before other guests. The schedule can vary weekly so it is best to check at the desk when you arrive for an updated schedule.

Tips   Special Treatment

AAA (℃ **800/732-1991**; www.aaa.com) members can take advantage of special lodging programs at select WDW resorts and preferred parking at the theme parks if they purchase a AAA Disney vacation package or pre-purchase their park tickets at participating AAA locations. A member's Hospitality Desk located right inside the Magic Kingdom's Town Square provides basic member services.

- The ability to purchase reduced-price **Ultimate Park Hopper Passes** for the length of your stay. (Available at all "official" hotels as well.) The passes can offer some significant savings.
- Disney's **refillable mug program** lets you buy—for around $12—a bottomless mug for soda, coffee, tea, and/or cocoa at its resorts. The offer is for the length of your stay, but it isn't transferable to the theme parks. You can use it only at the property at which it is bought, with two exceptions: Mugs are transferable between the Beach Club and Yacht Club resorts or among the three All-Star resorts.
- Playing privileges, **preferred tee times,** and, in some cases, free transportation to one of the Disney golf courses.
- Resort guests can **charge** most purchases (including meals) made anywhere inside WDW to their room. In most cases, purchases made inside the theme parks can be delivered to your room at no extra charge.

WALT DISNEY WORLD CENTRAL RESERVATIONS OFFICE (CRO) & WALT DISNEY TRAVEL COMPANY

To book a room or package at Disney's resorts, campgrounds, and "official" hotels, through the **Walt Disney World Travel Company,** contact the **Central Reservations Office (CRO),** P.O. Box 10000, Lake Buena Vista, FL 32830-1000 (℃ **407/934-7639;** www.disneyworld.com).

CRO can recommend accommodations suited to your price range and specific needs, such as being near a particular park, facilities that offer supervised child-care centers, or a pool large enough to swim laps. But the staffers who answer the phones won't volunteer information about a better deal or a special *unless you ask.*

Be sure to inquire about Disney's numerous package plans, which can include meals, tickets, recreation, and other features. The right package can save you money and time; but having a comprehensive game plan first is helpful in computing the cost of your vacation in advance.

CRO can also give you information about various theme-park ticket options, the airlines, and car rentals. It can also make dinner-show reservations for you at the resort of your choice.

THE DISNEY RESORTS

Disney's Caribbean Beach Resort ⭐   The Caribbean Beach is a great value for families who don't require over the top frills and amenities. The rooms are grouped into five island "villages" surrounding a large duck-filled lake. The recently refurbished rooms are best, however the bathrooms are still fairly tight. Parrot Cay Island, where the main pool (of seven) is located, replicates a Spanish-style fort complete with a water slide, waterfalls, and cannons. The closest park is Disney–MGM Studios, but it can take up to 45 minutes to get there using the Disney Transportation system.

900 Cayman Way (off Buena Vista Dr.; P.O. Box 10000), Lake Buena Vista, FL 32830-1000. © **407/934-7639** or 407/934-3400. Fax 407/934-3288. www.disneyworld.com. 2,112 units. $133–$209 double. Extra person $15. Children 17 and under stay free in parent's room. AE, DC, DISC, MC, V. Free parking. Take I-4 to the Hwy. 536/Epcot Center Dr. exit and follow signs. Pets $9 a night. **Amenities:** Restaurant; grill; lounge; large heated outdoor pool and 6 smaller ones in the villages; kids' pool; Jacuzzi; watersports equipment; arcade; WDW Transportation System; transportation to non-Disney parks for a fee; limited room service; babysitting; guest laundry; nonsmoking rooms. *In room:* A/C, TV, fridge ($10 a night), hair dryer, iron, safe.

Disney's Fort Wilderness Resort & Campground ⟨⟩   Pines, cypress trees, and fish-filled lakes and streams surround this woodsy 780-acre camping resort. The biggest knock is that it's quite far from Epcot, Disney–MGM Studios, and Animal Kingdom. But it's close to the Magic Kingdom, and if you're a true outdoors type, you'll enjoy the break from some of the Mickey madness. There are 784 campsites for RVs, pull-behind campers, and tents (110/220-volt outlets, grills, and comfort stations with showers and restrooms). Guests can ride horses and attend nightly campfire programs.

Some sites are open to pets—at a cost of $3 per site, not per pet—which is cheaper than using the WDW overnight kennel, where you pay $9 per pet. The 408 wilderness cabins (actually trailers) are large enough for six people once you pull down the Murphy beds, and they also have kitchens.

3520 N. Fort Wilderness Trail (P.O. Box 10000), Lake Buena Vista, FL 32830-1000. © **407/934-7639** or 407/824-2900. Fax 407/824-3508. www.disneyworld.com. 784 campsites, 408 wilderness cabins. Campsite $35–$82 double; wilderness cabin $229–$329 double. Extra person $2 for campsite, $5 for cabin. Children 17 and under stay free in parent's room. AE, DC, DISC, MC, V. Free parking. Take I-4 to the Hwy. 536/Epcot Center Dr. exit and follow the signs. **Amenities:** 2 restaurants; grill; lounge; 2 heated outdoor pools; kids' pool; 2 lighted tennis courts; watersports equipment; outdoor activities (fishing, horseback and hay rides, campfires); 2 game rooms; WDW Transportation System; transportation to non-Disney parks for a fee; babysitting; guest laundry; nonsmoking homes; outdoor grill. *In room:* Cabins only: A/C, TV/VCR, kitchen, fridge, coffeemaker, hair dryer.

Disney's Port Orleans Resort ⟨⟩ *Value*   This resort, resembling turn-of-the-20th-century New Orleans, includes the old Dixie Landings property that was merged into it in 2000. It has the best location, landscaping, and the coziest atmosphere of all resorts in this class. Its Doubloon Lagoon pool is a hit with the kids as it has a water slide curving from out of a dragon's mouth. The rooms are big enough for four, but it makes for a tight fit. Make sure to ask for a recently refurbished room. All 1,080 rooms in the French Quarter side reopened in March 2004 after a large-scale refurbishment. The 2,048 rooms in Riverside will

---

Tips **Tight Squeeze**

An average hotel or motel room in Orlando has 350 to 400 square feet and beds for four, hardly a castle, but most travelers find that adequate for a short stay. We've made a special note in the listings of properties where the rooms are substantially larger or smaller than that average.

Although Disney's resort rooms have notoriously cramped bathrooms, all sport double sinks (the "value" resorts have only a single sink), usually set in a small dressing area outside the bathroom. So while you may bang your shin on the shower, at least you won't have to wait in line to brush your teeth.

Tips **Value in the Eyes of the Beholder**

Disney's All-Star resorts charge a "preferred room" rate, but don't expect much for the top rate of $126. Guests who book it are paying for location: Preferred rooms are closer to the pools, food court, and/or transportation. If you've got a rental car or don't mind walking, don't bother paying extra; some of the quietest rooms at the All-Stars are the standard ones.

---

be renovated in phases starting in the summer of 2004. Port Orleans is east of Epcot and Disney–MGM Studios.

2201 Orleans Dr. (off Bonnet Creek Pkwy.; P.O. Box 10000), Lake Buena Vista, FL 32830-1000. (C) 407/934-7639 or 407/934-5000. Fax 407/934-5353. www.disneyworld.com. 3,056 units. $133–$209 double. Extra person $15. Children 17 and under stay free in parent's room. AE, DC, DISC, MC, V. Free parking. Take I-4 to the Hwy. 536/Epcot Center Dr. exit and follow the signs. Pets $9 a night. **Amenities:** 2 restaurants; grill/food court; 2 lounges; 6 heated outdoor pools; 2 kids' pools; Jacuzzi; watersports equipment; 2 arcades; WDW Transportation System; transportation to non-Disney parks for a fee; limited room service; babysitting; guest laundry; nonsmoking rooms. *In room:* A/C, TV, fridge ($10 a night), hair dryer, iron, safe.

SUPER-CHEAP SLEEPS

Disney's All-Star Movie Resort Kids love the larger-than-life themes at the All-Star resorts, but adults usually cringe at the visual overload. Suck it up, because you're getting a deal (for Disney, anyway) here. Giant cartoon characters such as Buzz Lightyear adorn this one and help hide a 21st-century rendition of a 1950s Holiday Inn. The rooms are spartan and very small—the bathrooms are even worse. Like its two siblings, the All-Star Movie Resort is buried in WDW's southwest corner to avoid frightening the higher-paying guests.

Note: Disney has two additional All-Star resorts—the All-Star Music Resort and the All-Star Sports resort—both identical to the Disney's All Star Movie resort where it counts (like room size and layout). The only major difference is the change in theme: One offers musical themes ranging from jazz to Calypso, and the other sports surfing, basketball, football, and tennis themes. All three of the All Star resorts are located out in the Disney boonies, and the closest park is Animal Kingdom.

1991 W. Buena Vista Dr., Lake Buena Vista, FL 32830-1000. (C) 407/934-7639 or 407/939-7000. Fax 407/939-7111. www.disneyworld.com. 1,900 units. $77–$126 double. Extra person $10. Children 17 and under stay free in parent's room. AE, DC, DISC, MC, V. Free self-parking. Take I-4 east to Exit 67, Hwy. 536/Epcot Center Dr. Follow signs to WDW, then to the resort. Pets $9 a night. **Amenities:** Food court; lounge; 2 outdoor heated pools; kids' pool; arcade; WDW Transportation System; transportation to non-Disney parks for a fee; limited room service; babysitting; guest laundry; nonsmoking rooms. *In room:* A/C, TV, dataport, fridge ($10 a night), safe.

Disney's Pop Century Resort *Value* While kids may not appreciate the kitsch factor at this whimsical resort, you probably will. Gigantic memorabilia from decades past—remember the 8-track and the Rubik's Cube?—mark the exteriors at Disney's newest value resort. While there might not be a lot of frills, the price is right for families on a budget who want to bunk with Mickey. The rooms and bathrooms—just like Disney's All-Star properties—are tiny, but will work for a family of four with a concerted bit of effort. The resort opened its first phase, covering the 1950s to the 1990s, in December 2003; additional "decades" are scheduled to open in the near future. The resort is closest to the Wide World of Sports Complex.

1050 Century Dr. (off the Oceola Pkwy; P.O. Box 10000), Lake Buena Vista, FL 32830-1000. © **407/938-4000** or 407/939-6000. Fax 407/938-4040. www.disneyworld.com. 2880 units. $77–$126 double. Extra person $10. Children 17 and under stay free in parent's room. AE, DC, DISC, MC, V. Free parking. Take I-4 east to Exit 67, Hwy. 536/Epcot Center Dr. Follow signs to WDW, then to the resort. Pets $9 a night. **Amenities:** Food court; lounge; 2 heated outdoor pools; kids' pool; arcade; WDW Transportation System; transportation to non-Disney parks for a fee; limited room service; babysitting; guest laundry; nonsmoking rooms. *In room:* A/C, TV, dataport, fridge ($10 a night), safe.

AN "OFFICIAL" HOTEL AT LAKE BUENA VISTA

The "official" Disney hotels are located on or around Hotel Plaza Boulevard, on the northeast side of Disney property and adjacent to Downtown Disney. Guests can enjoy some of the perks of staying in a WDW resort (free transportation to the Disney parks being one of them) while staying in a location somewhat more central to the rest of Orlando's offerings. You can reserve a room through Central Reservations Operations (© **407/934-7639**), but it's best to call the individual hotel or parent chain to check on the availability of special deals or packages.

Tips Enjoying the Parks Without Getting Fleeced

It's easy to get seduced by the smiley-faced goodwill of the theme-park fantasylands—and soon you believe that 10 bucks for a hamburger *(without trimmings)* is a fair price. But a level head, advance planning, and open ear (heed our advice) will help you maximize park experiences without the usual wallet drain.

1. **Bring bottled water and snacks** with you to the parks, more so if you're traveling with small fry. You can't bring coolers inside (who wants to lug one around, anyway?), but you can carry a light lunch in a backpack and save a bundle, considering that bottled water runs $2.50, a smoked turkey drumstick is nearly $5, and a counter-service lunch costs $6 to $9 per person. You'll get away with a fraction of that by picking up a carry-in lunch and water at a grocery.

2. Continuing that thought, **eat bigger and better early in the day.** As frequent and thrifty park visitors, we've learned to make it through the day on a slim budget when finances insist. If you have wheels, look for steakhouses and other places pitching buffet breakfasts ($3–$7) on billboards and in hotel handouts. Then, go light at noon in the parks and let your budget determine your evening meal.

3. Before coming here, **buy cheap rain ponchos** for everyone. All major parks include water rides and, trust us, it's miserable to walk around wet all day, even in summer. They'll also come in handy during summer storms, which arrive quickly and violently. Something you can buy at home for $2 costs $6 in the parks. You can find the same kind of savings on **camera gear and film.**

4. **Drink up.** Most Disney resorts offer "bottomless" refills that allow you unlimited drinks at the hotel food courts. It's worth the cost, especially if you consume a lot of coffee or soda. (See "How to Save Money by Staying with Mickey," on p. 416 for more information.)

Best Western Lake Buena Vista Hotel *(Value)* This 12-acre lakefront hotel has nicer rooms and public areas than you might find in others within the chain. Rooms are in an 18-story tower, and all of them come with balconies. The views improve from the eighth floor up, and guests on the west side have a better chance of seeing something Disney. The hotel's 18th-floor lounge offers an excellent view of the Magic Kingdom's fireworks. You can reserve an oversize room (20% larger) or one with a view of WDW fireworks for $15 more a night.

2000 Hotel Plaza Blvd. (between Buena Vista Dr. and Apopka-Vineland Rd./Hwy. 535), Lake Buena Vista, FL 32830. © **800/348-3765** or 407/828-2424. Fax 407/828-8933. www.downtowndisneyhotels.com or www.orlandoresorthotel.com. 325 units. $99–$159 for 4 persons; $199–$339 suite. $5 daily resort fee. 5th person $15. AE, DC, DISC, MC, V. Free parking. From I-4, take the Hwy. 535/Apopka-Vineland Rd. exit north to Hotel Plaza Blvd. and go left. It's the 1st hotel on the right. **Amenities:** Restaurant; grill; heated outdoor pool; kids' pool; guest-services desks; complimentary bus service to WDW parks; transportation to non-Disney parks for a fee; limited room service; guest laundry; nonsmoking rooms. *In room:* A/C, TV w/pay movies, coffeemaker, hair dryer, iron, safe, Nintendo.

Holiday Inn in The Walt Disney Resort *(Value)* This former Courtyard by Marriott recently changed hands and is very popular with families. The inner and outer glass elevators in the center of the hotel offer a fun ride for everyone. The rooms are what you'd expect of a Holiday Inn and can comfortably fit four. For a great view of the Magic Kingdom's fireworks display, a room on the west side is best, and the higher up the better.

1805 Hotel Plaza Blvd. (between Lake Buena Vista Dr. and Apopka-Vineland Rd./Hwy. 535), Lake Buena Vista, FL 32830. © **888/782-9722** or 407/828-8888. Fax 407/827-4623. www.downtowndisneyhotels.com or www.holiday-inn.com. 323 units. $86–$199 double. AE, DC, DISC, MC, V. Free parking. From I-4, take the Hwy. 535/Apopka-Vineland Rd. exit north to Hotel Plaza Blvd. and go left. It's the 3rd hotel on left. **Amenities:** Restaurant; 2 lounges; 2 heated outdoor pools; kids' pool; Jacuzzi; arcade; guest-services desk; complimentary bus service to WDW parks; transportation to non-Disney parks for a fee; car-rental desks; limited room service; guest laundry; nonsmoking rooms. *In room:* A/C, TV w/pay movies, coffeemaker, hair dryer, iron, safe, Nintendo.

LAKE BUENA VISTA AREA HOTELS

The hotels in this section are within a few minutes' drive of WDW parks. They offer the location but not the privileges of staying at an "official" hotel.

WORTH A SPLURGE

Marriott's Orlando World Center ★★ *(Finds)* Golf, tennis, and spa lovers will find plenty to do at this 230-acre resort, which caters to couples and business travelers but is also very suitable for families. The sports facilities are first-class and the largest of its five pools has water slides and waterfalls. The location, only 2 miles from the Disney parks, is a fabulous plus. The large, comfortable and beautifully decorated rooms sleep four, and the higher poolside floors offer views of Disney.

8701 World Center Dr. (on Hwy. 536 between I-4 and Hwy. 535), Orlando, FL 32821. © **800/621-0638** or 407/239-4200. Fax 407/238-8777. www.marriottHotels.com/MCOWC. 2,111 units. $189–$410 for up to 5; $425–$2,400 suite. $5 daily resort fee. Children 17 and under stay free in parent's room. AE, DC, DISC, MC, V. Free self-parking; valet $12. Take I-4 to the Hwy. 535/Apopka-Vineland Rd. exit, go south 1½ miles, then right/west on Hwy. 536, and go ⅓ mile. **Amenities:** 4 restaurants; 2 lounges; 3 heated outdoor pools; heated indoor pool; kids' pool; 18-hole golf course; 8 lighted tennis courts; health club; spa; whirlpool; sauna; concierge; car-rental desk; transportation to all theme parks for a fee; business center; salon; 24-hr. room service; massage; babysitting; guest laundry; nonsmoking rooms. *In room:* A/C, TV w/pay movies, dataport, minibar, coffeemaker, hair dryer, iron, safe.

Nickelodeon Family Suites Resort ★★ *(Finds)* *(Kids)* This all-suite property, a former award-winning Holiday Inn, is one of the absolute best resorts in the

Orlando area for families. Its two-bedroom Kid Suites feature a second bedroom for the kids with either bunk or twin beds and full kitchens. The resort has themed activity nights (movies, magic, variety shows) and a wide variety of recreational activities including a small minigolf area, playground, and children's activity center. In 2004, the property teamed up with Nickelodeon to make many "Nickprovements," adding Nick character breakfasts, wake-up calls from a favorite Nick star, and many other amenities. The introduction of the three-bedroom Kid Suite in 2005, offering three bedrooms (room for nine), two bathrooms, and a full kitchen, will only add to the appeal of this resort.

14500 Continental Gateway (off Hwy. 536), Lake Buena Vista, FL 32821. ℂ 877/387-5437 or 407/387-5437 or 866/GO2-NICK. Fax 407/387-1489. www.nickhotel.com. 800 units. $146–$199 suite. AE, DC, DISC, MC, V. Free self-parking. From I-4, take the Hwy. 536/International Dr. exit east 1 mile to the resort. **Amenities:** Restaurant; several fast-food counters; lounge; large lap pool; family swimming pool; minigolf course; fitness center; 2 Jacuzzis; game room; complimentary recreation center for ages 4–12; tour desk; free shuttle to Disney parks; transportation to non-Disney parks for a fee; coin-op washers and dryers; 3 outdoor Ping-Pong tables; 2 shuffleboard courts. *In room:* A/C, TV w/pay movies and VCR (some with Nintendo), dataport, fridge, coffeemaker, hair dryer, iron, safe, microwave.

Staybridge Suites Lake Buena Vista ★★   A Summerfield Suites in a previous life, this recent edition to the Staybridge Suites chain is located just off Apopka-Vineland, close to the action of Downtown Disney and the theme parks, as well as many restaurants. Featured are one- and two-bedroom suites, all with full kitchens (the two-bedroom suites have two bathrooms). The suites' separate living areas are larger and more comfortable than similar ones at other all-suite hotels. A unique plus here for those who'd rather not spend time in a supermarket on their vacation is the complimentary grocery shopping service, which allows you to select items for delivery to your room (you don't have to be there, and only the service is free—you still have to pay for the groceries).

8751 Suiteside Dr., Orlando, FL 32836. ℂ 800/866-4549 or 407/238-0777. Fax 407/238-2640. www.ichotelsgroup.com. 150 units. $119–$289. Rates include continental breakfast. Rollaway beds and cribs available at no charge. AE, DC, DISC, MC, V. Free self-parking. From I-4, take the exit for 535 (exit #68), turn right; follow to Vinings Way Rd., turn right; the hotel is located on the left. **Amenities:** Deli; outdoor heated pool; children's pool; 24-hr. exercise room; Jacuzzi; 24-hr. game room; free shuttle to Disney parks; guest services desk; convenience store; 24-hr. guest laundry; nonsmoking rooms; accessible suites; complimentary grocery delivery service; high-speed Internet access. *In room:* A/C, TV/VCR, dataport, kitchen, hair dryer, iron, ironing board, safe.

ON U.S. 192/KISSIMMEE AREA

This very eclectic stretch of highway is dotted with fast-food eateries and tourist traps. It's hardly what you'd call scenic, but it has a lot of inexpensive accommodations that are within 1 to 8 miles of the Disney parks. All the hostelries listed below are clean and well run. There are also two branches of the budget **Motel 6** (ℂ **800/466-8356;** www.motel6.com) in Kissimmee on U.S. 192. One branch is at 5731 W. Irlo Bronson Memorial Hwy. (ℂ **407/396-6333**); the other, at 7455 W. Irlo Bronson Memorial Hwy. (ℂ **407/396-6422**), is a tad nicer. They have pools, cable TV, a tolerance for small pets, and blue-light special rates ($40–$56).

A system of highway markers has been erected along Irlo Bronson Highway to help motorists better find their way. These towers by the side of the road are aptly dubbed "Marker" along with a number. For example, a property may be located between Marker 5 and Marker 6. We've included those designations where appropriate.

SUPER-CHEAP SLEEPS

Days Inn Eastgate This two-story, pink stucco Days Inn forms an attractively landscaped courtyard around a large swimming pool. Families will appreciate the picnic tables and a play area on the lawn. The rooms are nicely decorated. Some have fridges and microwaves. There's a restaurant where kids eat free.

5245 W. Irlo Bronson Memorial Hwy. (U.S. 192, between Poinciana and Polynesian Isle boulevards, near Marker 12), Kissimmee, FL 34746. ✆ **800/423-3864** or 407/396-7700. Fax 407/396-0293. www.daysinn eastgate.com. 200 units. $30–$89 for up to 4. Rates may be higher during major events. AE, DC, DISC, MC, V. Free parking. From I-4, take the U.S. 192/Irlo Bronson Memorial Hwy. exit; it's about 3½ miles on 192. **Amenities:** Restaurant (American); lounge; heated outdoor pool; video arcade; guest services desk; free transportation to Disney parks; transportation for a fee to others; guest laundry. *In room:* A/C, TV.

Hampton Inn Maingate West Just 1½ miles west of WDW, this welcoming motel is a good choice for the budget-conscious vacationer. The rooms are nicely decorated, but are a bit on the small side, making them a snug fit for four. While there are not a lot of frills, the property is well maintained and provides the basics with good taste. There's no restaurant, but a free breakfast is served in the lobby and there are more than enough dining choices just a minute or two away to keep you from going hungry.

3000 Maingate Lane, Kissimmee, FL 34747. ✆ **800/936-9417** or 407/396-5457. Fax 407/396-8989. www. hamptoninnmaingatewest.com. 118 units. $69–$119 double. Extra person $10. Rates include continental breakfast. Children 17 and under stay free in parent's room. AE, DC, DISC, MC, V. Free self-parking. From I-4, take the U.S. 192 exit west; go 3 miles, then right on Maingate Lane (across the street from Celebration). **Amenities:** Outdoor heated pool; guest services desk; free shuttle to Disney parks; transportation to non-Disney parks for a fee; nonsmoking rooms. *In room:* A/C, TV, dataport, coffeemaker, iron.

La Quinta Inn Lakeside ★★ (Kids) (Value) The hand painted exteriors, lobby, and common areas of this recently renovated hotel give it a unique charm not found in its hotel brethren. Just up the road from the Disney entrance, this 24-acre resort looks deceptively small when you first pull up (most of the accommodations are hidden behind the lobby area), but amenities include numerous recreational options (pools, playgrounds, and so on), a food court, convenience store, and a bountiful free breakfast. Rooms are standard in size and offerings, but are nicely decorated and will comfortably sleep four. Other pluses include a childcare facility and free transport to *all* the major theme parks.

7769 Irlo Bronson Memorial Hwy. (U.S. 192), Kissimmee, FL 34747. ✆ **800/531-5900** or 407/396-2222. Fax 407/396-7087. www.LaquintainnLakeside.com. 651 units. $59–$109 double. Extra person $10. Rates include continental breakfast. Children 17 and under stay free in parent's room. Discount packages available. Small pets accepted ($25 fee). AE, DC, DISC, MC, V. Free self-parking. From I-4, take Exit 64B/U.S. 192, 3 miles up on your right. Small pets accepted ($25 fee). **Amenities:** 2 restaurants; food court; 3 outdoor heated pools; 2 kids' pools; Jacuzzi; small minigolf; 2 tennis courts; playgrounds; exercise room; guest services desk; free bus to Disney, Universal, and SeaWorld parks; guest laundry; nonsmoking rooms. *In room:* A/C, TV w/pay movies and PlayStation, dataport, fridge, coffeemaker, hair dryer, iron, safe.

WORTH A SPLURGE

Comfort Suites Maingate East ★ (Value) Set back from the main drag, this fairly new and welcoming hotel is one of the nicest in the area. The lobby and accommodations—consisting of studio and one-bedroom suites—are bright and inviting. The main pool and the children's pool, with an umbrella fountain to keep everyone cool, are open around the clock. For entertainment, Old Town (a small-scale shopping, dining, and entertainment complex) is next door, and a great miniature golf course is located just in front of the property.

2775 Florida Plaza Blvd., Kissimmee, FL 34746. ℂ **888/782-9772** or 407/397-7848. Fax 407/396-7045. www.comfortsuitesfl.com. 198 units. $65–$150 double. Extra person $10. Rates include continental breakfast. Children 17 and under stay free in parent's room. AE, DC, DISC, MC, V. Free self-parking. From I-4 take the U.S. 192 exit east; go 1¾ miles, then right on Florida Plaza Blvd. **Amenities:** Outdoor heated pool; kids' pool; fitness center; game room; concierge; free shuttle to Disney, Universal, and SeaWorld parks; business center; guest laundry; nonsmoking suites available. *In room:* A/C, TV, dataport, fridge, coffeemaker, hair dryer, iron, safe, microwave.

So You Didn't Book a Room . . .

If you're looking for a basic room, you can try these chain hotels and motels. They're all moderate or inexpensive in price and located in the budget motel corridors of Kissimmee/U.S. 192 or International Drive. While I can't vouch for them personally, their brand names generally mean reliability.

In Kissimmee:

- **Comfort Suites Maingate Hotel,** 7888 W. Irlo Bronson Memorial Hwy., Kissimmee (ℂ **407/390-9888**).
- **Comfort Suites Resort Maingate East,** 2775 Florida Plaza Blvd., Kissimmee (ℂ **407/397-7848**).
- **Days Inn East of the Magic Kingdom,** 5840 W. Irlo Bronson Memorial Hwy., Kissimmee (ℂ **407/396-7969**).
- **Days Inn Maingate–West,** 7980 W. Irlo Bronson Memorial Hwy., Kissimmee (ℂ **407/997-1000**).
- **DoubleTree Maingate,** 4787 W. Irlo Bronson Memorial Hwy., Kissimmee (ℂ **407/397-0555**).
- **Howard Johnson Maingate West,** 8660 W. Irlo Bronson Memorial Hwy., Kissimmee (ℂ **407/396-4500**).
- **Quality Suites Maingate East,** 5876 W. Irlo Bronson Memorial Hwy., Kissimmee (ℂ **407/396-8040**).
- **Travelodge Kissimmee,** 2261 E. Irlo Bronson Memorial Hwy., Kissimmee (ℂ **407/846-2221**).

In the International Drive Area:

- **Days Inn Convention Center/SeaWorld,** 9990 International Dr., Orlando (ℂ **407/352-8700**).
- **Days Inn East of Universal Studios,** 5827 Caravan Court, Orlando (ℂ **407/351-3800**).
- **Days Inn International Drive,** 7200 International Dr., Orlando (ℂ **407/351-1200**).
- **Holiday Inn Express International Drive,** 6323 International Dr., Orlando (ℂ **407/351-4430**).
- **Sheraton Studio City Hotel,** 5905 International Dr., Orlando (ℂ **407/351-2100**).
- **Travelodge International Drive,** 5859 American Way, Orlando (ℂ **407/345-8880**).

You also can try **Central Reservation Service** (ℂ **407/740-6442;** www.reservation-services.com) and **Hotel Kingdom** (ℂ **407/294-9600;** www.discounthotelsamerica.com).

Holiday Inn Nikki Bird Resort ⋆ Here's another family-friendly inn with a roaming mascot (Nikki Bird) and a dedication to kids. This 26-acre resort features standard rooms as well as Kid Suites (themes vary) that have a separate sleeping area for youngsters. Their recreational facilities are extensive, including three pools and two toddler pools with squirting fountains, tennis courts, and more. Kids 12 and under eat free (two kids per paying adult); they also get entertainment, including puppet shows, songs, and games.

7300 W. Irlo Bronson Memorial Hwy. (U.S. 192), Kissimmee, FL 34747. ✆ **800/206-2747** or 407/396-7300. Fax 407/396-7555. www.hicentralflorida.com. 530 units. $89–$139 for up to 4. Extra person $10. AE, DC, DISC, MC, V. Free self-parking. Take I-4 Exit 64B/U.S. 192 west. It's 1½ miles past the Disney entrance on the left. **Amenities:** Restaurant; grill; lounge; 3 outdoor heated pools; 2 kids' pools; 3 lighted tennis courts; exercise room; Jacuzzi; kids' club; game room; concierge; car-rental desk; free shuttle to Disney parks; transportation to non-Disney parks for a fee; room service 6:30am–10:00pm; guest laundry; nonsmoking and accessible rooms available; volleyball; basketball; playground. *In room:* A/C, TV w/pay movies, dataport, fridge, coffeemaker, hair dryer, iron, microwave, newspaper, CD players (in some).

INTERNATIONAL DRIVE AREA
SUPER-CHEAP SLEEPS

Fairfield Inn International Drive ⋆ *Value* If you're looking for I-Drive's best value, it's hard to beat the Fairfield. This one combines a quiet location off the main drag, down-to-earth rates, and a clean, modern motel in one package. The rooms are very comfortable and there are a number of restaurants within walking distance of the hotel. A new transportation service to and from Disney costs $8 roundtrip.

8342 Jamaican Court (off International Dr. between the Beeline Expressway and Sand Lake Rd.), Orlando, FL 32819. ✆ **800/228-2800** or 407/363-1944. Fax 407/363-1944. www.fairfieldinn.com. 135 units. $69–$99 for up to 4. Rates include continental breakfast. AE, DC, DISC, MC, V. Free self-parking. From I-4, take Exit 74A, Sand Lake Rd./Hwy. 482, go east 1 block, turn right on I-Drive, then right on Jamaican Court. Hotel is on the right. **Amenities:** Outdoor heated pool; guest services desk; transportation for a fee to the parks; guest laundry; valet; nonsmoking rooms. *In room:* A/C, TV w/pay movies, dataport, safe.

WORTH A SPLURGE

La Quinta Inn & Suites Convention Center ⋆ Opened in 1998, this is one of a handful of upscale, moderately priced motels on Universal Boulevard, which runs parallel to (but isn't as congested as) International Drive. The hotel is aimed at business travelers, but this is Orlando, so families traveling with kids are welcomed with open arms. King rooms come with a fridge and microwave. There are a limited number of two-room suites offering separate living and sleeping areas.

8504 Universal Blvd., Orlando, FL 32819. ✆ **800/531-5900** or 407/345-1365. Fax 407/345-5586. www. laquinta.com. 185 units. $90–$150 double. Extra person $10. Rates include continental breakfast. Children 18 and under stay free in parent's room. AE, DC, DISC, MC, V. Free self-parking. Take I-4 to the Sand Lake Rd./Hwy. 482 exit, go east toward Universal, then right. **Amenities:** Outdoor heated pool; exercise room; Jacuzzi; transportation to all theme parks for a fee; guest laundry; nonsmoking rooms. *In room:* A/C, TV w/pay movies, dataport, coffeemaker, hair dryer, iron, Nintendo.

3 Great Deals on Dining, In & Around the Parks

Because many Orlando visitors spend most of their time in the Walt Disney World area, we've focused on the best and most reasonably priced choices throughout that vast empire. Also listed are some worthwhile places beyond the realm, including some at CityWalk, the dining and entertainment district at Universal Orlando.

There are plenty of other places to eat in Orlando. International Drive and U.S. 192 (Irlo Bronson Memorial Hwy.) are packed with a variety of budget restaurants. Parents find that just about every restaurant in town offers a low-priced children's menu and usually provides some kind of kid's activity as well. The downside of restaurants that cater to kids is that they're noisy; if you're looking for a quiet meal, head for restaurants listed as "Worth a Splurge."

HOW TO ARRANGE PRIORITY SEATING AT WALT DISNEY WORLD RESTAURANTS

Priority Seating *isn't* a reservation. It's exactly what its name implies: You will get priority over any others waiting for a table at the time you schedule. There may still be a wait, but it will generally be significantly shorter than it would be if you didn't have one. And if you don't use Priority Seating, especially for the most popular restaurants such as Cinderella's Table or Victoria & Albert's, you may miss out all together as these popular restaurants are usually booked well in advance, leaving little or no room at all for the guests who decide to just show up for a table. To arrange for Priority Seating at any WDW restaurant (in the parks or at the resorts), call © **407/939-3463.** You can book as far as 90 days (180 in some cases) in advance of your arrival for most restaurants (which may be necessary during the busier times of year and is essential at some restaurants).

If you're staying on Disney property, you can arrange Priority Seating right at your resort; otherwise head to the Guest Relations desks inside each of the theme parks or make arrangements at your chosen restaurant.

TIPS ON WALT DISNEY WORLD RESTAURANTS

All park restaurants (as well as all restaurants in Florida) are **nonsmoking.**

Magic Kingdom restaurants don't serve alcohol, but those at Animal Kingdom, Epcot, and Disney–MGM Studios do.

Sit-down restaurants in WDW take American Express, Diners Club, Discover, MasterCard, Visa, and the Disney Card.

Unless otherwise noted, *restaurants in the parks require park admission.* Also, unless you're using WDW transportation or are a Disney resort guest, there is an additional $8 parking fee.

Nearly all WDW restaurants with sit-down or counter service offer children's menus with items ranging anywhere from around $4 to $6.

Keep in mind that theme-park eateries as a general rule are about 25% more expensive than comparable places in the "outside" world. The prices that follow are for entrees only; other courses, drinks, and tax are extra.

Also see the listings for dinner shows in "Walt Disney World & Orlando After Dark," later in this chapter. For online information, go to **www.disneyworld. com**.

Value Bargain Buffets

We won't list them all, but International Drive and U.S. 192/Irlo Bronson Memorial Highway have billboards peddling all-you-can-eat breakfast buffets for $4 to $6. This is a good way to fill up early and go easy on lunch, especially on days spent in the parks, where food is overpriced. Buffets are served by **Golden Corral,** 8033 International Dr. (© **407/352-6606**); **Ponderosa Steak House,** 6362 International Dr. (© **407/352-9343**), and 7598 U.S. 192 W. (© **407/396-7721**); and **Sizzler Restaurant,** 9142 International Dr. (© **407/351-5369**), and 7602 U.S. 192 W. (© **407/397-0997**).

INSIDE THE WDW THEME PARKS

With few exceptions, you won't find Disney's park restaurants winning accolades from *Food & Wine* or *Bon Appétit.* The food at most of them is on par with the food at Universal Orlando—filling and palatable, but overpriced for the quality. The following list includes the Magic Kingdom, Epcot, Disney–MGM Studios, and Animal Kingdom. Get information on all Disney restaurants by calling © 407/939-3463 or visiting **www.disneyworld.com**.

EPCOT

The World Showcase has some of the best dining options inside the WDW theme parks, thanks to the cultural cuisine of its 11 nation pavilions. Although many consider a meal here an essential part of the experience, I must point out that the food (as in all the parks) is priced higher than comparable fare in the free world.

The restaurants below are arranged geographically, beginning at the Canada pavilion and proceeding counterclockwise around the World Showcase Lagoon. *Prices are for entrees only* and don't include tax, tip, and beverages.

CANADA   Le Cellier Steakhouse has a castlelike ambience accentuated by vaulted stone arches. Red-meat main events (all Midwest, corn-fed) include the usual range of cuts—filet, porterhouse, prime rib, veal chop, and so on. They do, however, offer some choices in the way of pasta and seafood as well. Lunch runs $10 to $21; dinner is $16 to $27.

UNITED KINGDOM   The Tudor-beamed **Rose & Crown** is a cozy pub suggestive of Victorian England. Visitors from the U.K. flock to this spot, where folk music and saucy servers entertain you as you feast on a short but joyfully traditional menu including prime rib with Yorkshire pudding or fish and chips. The outdoor dining area overlooks the lagoon and is a good place to see the IllumiNations fireworks display. Lunch is $11 to $14; dinner is $14 to $20.

FRANCE   Chefs de France has an Art Nouveau interior agleam with mirrors and brass chandeliers. Three French chefs designed the menu, which is respectable by park standards. The dinner entrees include Mediterranean seafood casserole (grouper, scallops, and shrimp dusted with saffron, then swum in a mild garlic sauce) and a garlicky braised lamb shank. Lunch is $11 to $18; dinner is $15 to $30.

MOROCCO   Of all the Epcot restaurants, **Marrakesh** ⊛ best exemplifies the spirit of the park, yet a lot of guests don't know it's there or ignore it because they're worried that the menu is too exotic. Expect belly dancers to entertain while you feast on options like marinated beef shish kabob, braised chicken with green olives, and a medley of seafood, chicken, and lamb. Most entrees come with couscous. Lunch costs $12 to $18; dinner is $17 to $26.

JAPAN   If you've been to any of the Japanese steakhouse chains, you know what to expect at **Teppanyaki:** Guests sit around large grill tables while white-hatted chefs rapidly dice, slice, stir-fry, and launch the occasional shrimp tail onto your plate with amazing skill. The culinary acrobatics here are a sight to see, the cuisine however, is average. Lunch is $12 to $22; dinner is $13 to $32. The adjoining **Yakitori House** is a bamboo-roofed cafeteria that serves casual fare including noodle dishes and chicken, beef, or shrimp brochettes. Meals here are generally under $10.

Tips **Best Protein Snack in the Parks**

For our money, you can't beat the smoked turkey drumsticks sold in WDW parks for under $5. How popular are they? Last year, Disney guests gobble-gobbled 1.6 million of them.

ITALY **L'Originale Alfredo di Roma,** set inside one of the most beautiful of the world pavilions, is Epcot's most popular restaurant. Singing waiters top off the dining experience here. The menu includes the celebrated namesake fettuccine. For something on the meatier side of the menu, try the veal chops served with chianti-and-truffle sauce, mushrooms, asparagus, and roasted potatoes. If you want a quieter setting, ask for a seat on the veranda. Lunch costs $10 to $25; dinner runs $17 to $38.

GERMANY ✦ The **Biergarten** simulates a Bavarian village at Oktoberfest, and has a very festive atmosphere. The all-you-can-eat buffet is filled with traditional Bavarian fare (assorted sausages, pork schnitzel, sauerbraten, spaetzle with gravy, sauerkraut, and a large assortment of trimmings). The lunch buffet is $15 for adults, $7 for kids 3 to 11; dinner is $20 for adults, $8 for children. At **Sommerfest,** a cafeteria, you can purchase bratwurst sandwiches with sauerkraut. All items there are under $7.

CHINA When it comes to decor, the **Nine Dragons** shines with carved rosewood furnishings and a dragon-motif ceiling. Some windows overlook the lagoon outside. Portions here are small when compared with those at most Chinese restaurants. Lunch runs $9.50 to $19; dinners go for $13 to $30. If you want something lighter, the open-air **Lotus Blossom Café** sells egg rolls, pork fried rice, and stir-fried chicken and vegetables served over noodles ($4–$6.50).

NORWAY **Akershus** is a re-created 14th-century castle where you can sample a 40-item smorgasbord of *smavarmt* (hot) and *koldtbord* (cold) dishes. The reasonably good entrees usually include such dishes as venison stew, roast pork, gravlax, smoked mackerel, and mustard herring. The lunch buffet costs $14 for adults, $7 for children 4 to 9; the dinner buffet is $20 for adults, $9 for kids. The **Kringla Bakeri og Kafe** sells open-face sandwiches, sugar-sprinkled waffles, and fresh-baked Norwegian pastries. All items there cost under $6.

MEXICO ✦ It's always night at the **San Angel Inn** ✦, where candlelit tables set a romantic mood, and the menu delivers reasonably authentic food. A popular choice is the *mole poblano* (chicken brought to life with more than 20 spices, carrots, and a hint of chocolate). Another favorite: *filete motuleno* (grilled beef tenderloin served over black beans, melted cheese, pepper strips, and fried plantains). Lunch runs $9.25 to $18 and dinners around $18 to $24. The **Cantina de San Angel,** a cafeteria with outdoor seating at umbrella tables overlooking the lagoon, offers tacos, burritos, and other items under $8.

Future World

At the Living Seas pavilion, the mood is half the fun at the **Coral Reef,** where the tables circle a 5.6-million-gallon aquarium that has 4,000 denizens of the deep. Tiered seating ensures everyone a good view. Highlights include panseared salmon with garlic-pesto mashed potatoes and candied carrots, and Caribbean lobster with summer squash and potatoes. Lunch is $14 to $21; dinner is $16 to $32.

IN THE MAGIC KINGDOM

In addition to the restaurant listed below, there are plenty of fast-food outlets located throughout the park of which Pecos Bill Cafe, Cosmic Ray's Starlight Cafe, and the Columbia Harbour House are your best choices. That said, you may find that a quiet, sit-down meal is an essential, if brief, getaway from the day's activities.

Fantasyland   Romantics may find it hard to beat the ambience of eating at **Cinderella's Royal Table** ⭐ in Cinderella Castle, the Magic Kingdom's icon. Servers treat you like a lord or lady while fetching you headliners such as spice-crusted salmon, a New York strip, or roasted chicken. Lunch costs $9 to $26; dinner sells for $21 to $26. Don't forget to make Priority Seating arrangements if you want to eat here.

The **Crystal Palace,** named for its glass exterior, is a favorite with the young set because of its all-you-can eat character buffets (where kids and adults can pick and choose from a decent variety of meats, veggies, and desserts). Lunch costs $18 for adults and $10 for children (3–11). Dinner runs $22 for adults and $10 for children (3–11). Priority Seating is a must.

DISNEY–MGM STUDIOS

There are more than a dozen places to refuel in this Hollywood-style theme park. The ones listed below are the best of the bunch. Again, Priority Seating is a must.

Modeled after the Los Angeles celebrity haunt where Louella Parsons and Hedda Hopper held court, the **Hollywood Brown Derby** offers a good time and a pricey meal. The Derby's signature dessert, grapefruit cake with cream-cheese icing, is a perfect meal-capper. Entrees go for $14 to $19 at lunch; $19 to $27 at dinner.

The **50's Prime Time Café** is like going home to mom's kitchen for dinner— back in the 1950s. The atmosphere delivers with black-and-white TV sets showing *My Little Margie* and servers threatening to withhold dessert if you don't eat all your food. Although the desserts are good, the meatloaf and pot roast aren't quite as good as mom used to make. Meals cost $14 to $19 at lunch and dinner.

The best bets at **Mama Melrose's Ristorante Italiano** are the wood-fired and brick-baked specialties including the flat breads (grilled pepperoni, portobello mushroom, and four cheese). Lunch is $12 to $21; dinner is $12 to $22.

Take the above review for the 50's Prime Time Café, give it a science-fiction spin, and welcome to the **Sci-Fi Dine-In Theater Restaurant.** Diners sit in chrome-plated convertibles with the Hollywood hills as a backdrop and are treated to newsreels, cartoons, and "B" horror flicks. The meals here are served with less culinary flair than in other Disney restaurants. Lunches run $11 to $17; dinners are $14 to $19.

If you must eat at Disney–MGM, we recommend you stick to one of the following counter-service options, all of which sell items for under $8 or $10:

- **Toy Story Pizza Planet,** located in the Muppets Courtyard, offers what the name implies along with salads, espresso, and cappuccino.
- **Rosie's All-American Café,** located on Sunset Boulevard near the Rock 'n' Roller Coaster, sells burgers including veggie burgers, cold sandwiches, soups, and salads.
- The **ABC Commissary,** on Commissary Lane, has burgers, chicken, and wraps.
- **Catalina Eddie's,** next to Rosie's, serves pizza and salads.

ANIMAL KINGDOM

You'll find only a few options in Animal Kingdom, and most of those are of the grab-and-go style. There is a branch of the Rainforest Café outside the park's entrance, but it's overpriced for the value received. The **Tusker House** inside the park offers some tasty options, including grilled chicken salad in focaccia bread; rotisserie or fried chicken; and wraps with turkey, chicken, and ham. Prices run $7 to $8.

AT DISNEY RESORTS

Maya Grill AMERICAN/CAJUN   Some call it "Nuevo Latino." But it's nothing fancier than steaks, chicken, shellfish, and other seafood items raised an octave by Southwestern-style spices. The atmosphere, though, is more than a notch higher than that of the food courts, and in the morning, breakfast arrives with the same kind of warm-you-up flavor. A breakfast buffet menu is available daily from 7am to 11am at $13 for adults and $7.95 for kids.

1000 Buena Vista Dr. (in Disney's Coronado Springs Resorts). ✆ 407/934-7639 for Priority Seating. Main courses and breakfast items under $9; dinner $9–$18. AE, DC, DISC, MC, V. Daily 7–11:30am and 5–10pm.

SUPER-CHEAP EATS

Intermission Food Court INTERNATIONAL   This cheerful food court, adorned with music paraphernalia and memorabilia, has stations ranging from baked goods and pizza to subs. You can get a barbecued beef, chicken, or pork dinner for under $13. Wine and beer are available, and kids can head to a video arcade while Mom and Dad linger over coffee. All-you-can-eat buffet breakfasts cost under $10 for those 9 and older and under $7 for those under 9.

The **End Zone Food Court** at the adjoining All-Star Sports Resort (✆ **407/ 939-5000**) and the **World Premiere Food Court** at the All-Star Movie Resort (✆ **407/939-7000**) have similar menus and prices.

1801 W. Buena Vista Dr. (at Disney's All-Star Music Resort, at World Dr. and Osceola Pkwy.). ✆ **407/ 939-6000**. Reservations not accepted. Most items under $10. AE, DC, DISC, MC, V. Daily 7am–11pm (bakery opens at 6am; pizza served to midnight).

Market Street Old Port Royale Food Court AMERICAN   This place has all of the usual food-court offerings (rotisserie chicken, sandwiches, pizza, salads, cookies, cakes, pies, ice cream cones, and sundaes). Kids will enjoy the large video-game arcade on the premises and a room where Disney movies and cartoons are aired.

⸜Tips⸝ Special Tastes

Looking for kosher food? Worried WDW can't entertain your vegetarian taste buds? Disney usually can handle those diets and other special ones (people who need fat-free or sugar-free meals, folks who have allergies or a lactose intolerance, for instance) as long as guests give Disney advance notice—usually no more than 24 hours. You can do that when you make Priority Seating arrangements (✆ **407/939-3463** or, if you're staying at a Disney resort, at its guest services desk). If you're not staying at WDW, call ✆ **407/824-2222**. Some options are available without prior notice at counter-service spots throughout the parks—ask a park employee if you're looking for something specific. That said, the price will be high for less than haute cuisine.

900 Cayman Way (at Disney's Caribbean Beach Resort, off Buena Vista Dr.). ℭ 407/934-3400. Reservations not accepted. Most items under $10. AE, DC, DISC, MC, V. Daily 7am–11pm (bakery opens at 6am; pizza served to midnight).

WORTH A SPLURGE

Artist Point ✶ *Finds* SEAFOOD/STEAKS   Enjoy a grand view of Disney's Wilderness Lodge in this rustically elegant establishment. Select from a season-ally-changing menu that might include grilled buffalo sirloin with a sweet potato and hazelnut gratin; or a cedar-plank roasted Silver Bay salmon with maple-whiskey glaze. *Note:* Artist Point has a more relaxed atmosphere than some of the busier WDW resort restaurants.

901 W. Timberline Dr., in Disney's Wilderness Lodge. ℭ 407/939-3463 or 407/824-1081. www.disney world.com. Priority Seating recommended. Main courses $23–$34. AE, DC, DISC, MC, V. Daily 5:30–10pm. Free self- and valet parking.

'Ohana ✶ PACIFIC RIM   Its star is earned on the fun front, but the decibel level will turn some off. As your luau is being prepared over an 18-foot-wide fire pit, the staff keeps you busy with coconut races, hula lessons, and other shenani-gans. The feed bag includes salad, fruit, fresh-baked focaccia bread, turkey, shrimp, pork loin, and steak, plus dessert. A full bar offers tropical drinks, including non-alcoholic ones for kids, and there's a limited selection of wines.

1600 Seven Seas Dr., at Disney's Polynesian Resort. ℭ 407/939-3463 or 407/824-2000. www.disney world.com. Priority Seating strongly encouraged. $24 adults, $10 children 3–11. AE, DC, DISC, MC, V. Daily 7:30–11am and 5–10pm. Valet or free self-parking.

MEALS WITH DISNEY CHARACTERS

Dining with the Disney characters is a treat for almost any Disney fan, but it's a special one for those under the age of 10. The characters will greet, sign auto-graphs, pose for photos, and interact with the entire family. These dining expe-riences are extremely popular, so make Priority Seating arrangements (ℭ **407/ 939-3463**) as early as possible, and call for schedules. Prices vary, but generally expect breakfast (most serve it) to be $17 to $20 for adults, $9 to $10 for kids 3 to 11; those that serve dinner charge $21 to $24 for adults and $10 to $11 for kids.

Character meals are offered at **Cape May Café** (in Disney's Beach Club Resort), **Chef Mickey's** (at Disney's Contemporary Resort), **Cinderella's Royal Table** (in Cinderella Castle, Magic Kingdom), **Crystal Palace Buffet** (at Crystal Palace, Magic Kingdom), **Donald's Prehistoric Breakfastosaurus** (in

---

⟨*Value* **Bring on the Barbecue**

It's always an adventure traveling off the beaten path, especially when you hit a place like **Bubbalou's Bodacious BBQ** ✶, 1471 Lee Rd., Winter Park (ℭ 407/628-1212; www.bubbalous.com), which serves some of the best barbecue in Florida and is well worth the drive (about 5 min. from Downtown Orlando). Go for the full pork platter that comes with a heap-ing helping of pork and all the fixin's. The uninitiated should stay away from the "Killer" sauce if they value their taste buds; you might even taste-test the mild sauce before moving up to the hot. Main courses run $4 to $13. It's open Monday through Saturday from 10am to 9pm. To get here, take the I-4 Lee Rd. exit and follow your nose; Bubbalou's is on the left next to a dry cleaner.

Dinoland U.S.A., Animal Kingdom), **Garden Grill** (in The Land Pavilion at Epcot), **Liberty Tree Tavern** (in Liberty Square, in the Magic Kingdom), **'Ohana** (at Disney's Polynesian Resort), **Princess Storybook Breakfast** (at Akershus Castle in Epcot's Norway Pavilion), and **1900 Park Fare** (at Disney's Grand Floridian Resort & Spa).

Note: We strongly recommend against promising children they will meet a specific character at a meal. If you have your heart set on meeting a certain character, call to confirm his or her appearance when making your Priority Seating arrangement.

UNIVERSAL ORLANDO

Universal stormed onto the restaurant scene with the mid-1999 opening of its dining and club venue, CityWalk, located between and in front of its two parks, Universal Studios Florida and Islands of Adventure (© **407/363-8000;** www. citywalk.com).

Note: Parking will cost you $8 before 6pm at the following restaurants.

SUPER-CHEAP EATS

Bob Marley—A Tribute to Freedom CARIBBEAN   Part club and part restaurant, Marley's is a replica of the late reggae singer's home in Kingston, complete with tile roof and green-shuttered windows. There's live reggae nightly. The menu has nothing but modestly priced Jamaican fare, including a jerk snapper sandwich on coca bread with yucca fries, a tomato-based fish chowder, and grouper fingers lightly breaded, fried, and topped with red and green peppers. Of course, most folks don't leave without sipping at least one Red Stripe—Jamaica's national beer.

1000 Universal Studios Plaza, in CityWalk. © **407/224-3663.** www.universalorlando.com. Reservations not accepted. Main courses $6–$9. AE, DISC, MC, V. Daily 4pm–2am. Parking $8 (free after 6pm). From I-4, take Exit 75B, Kirkman Rd./Hwy. 435, and follow the signs to Universal.

Pastamore Ristorante SOUTHERN ITALIAN   The antipasto primo here is a meal unto itself, and includes bruschetta, eggplant Caponata, melon with prosciutto, grilled portobello mushrooms, Italian cold cuts, olives, plum tomatoes, mozzarella, and more. The menu also has traditional options such as veal Marsala, chicken piccata, shrimp scampi, fettuccine Alfredo, lasagna, and pizza. An open kitchen allows diners a view of the chefs at work. You can also eat in a cafe where lighter fare—breakfast and sandwiches—is served from 8am to 2am.

1000 Universal Studios Plaza, in CityWalk. © **407/363-8000.** www.universalorlando.com. Reservations accepted. Main courses $7–$18. AE, DISC, MC, V. Daily 5pm–midnight. Parking $8 (free after 6pm). From I-4, take the Kirkman Rd./Hwy. 435 exit and follow the signs to Universal.

WORTH A SPLURGE

Tchoup Chop ★★ PACIFIC RIM   Pronounced "chop chop," Emeril Lagasse's second restaurant in Orlando is named for the location of his original restaurant, Tchoupitoulous Street in New Orleans. The exhibition kitchen offers a look at chefs making Polynesian- and Asian-influenced entrees such as Kona coffee–glazed duck breast with duck and vegetable chow mein; and grilled rib-eye steak with garlic mashed potatoes, fried Maui onions, teriyaki sauce, and stir-fried vegetables.

6300 Hollywood Way, in Universal's Royal Pacific Hotel. © **407/503-2467.** www.emerils.com. Reservations strongly recommended. Main courses $15–$24. AE, DISC, MC, V. Daily 11:30am–2pm; Sun–Thurs 5:30–10pm; Fri-Sat 5:30–11pm. Valet parking $4. From I-4, take the Kirkman Rd./Hwy. 435 exit, and follow the signs to Universal.

Tips Saving with Take-Out

Even if you don't rent an efficiency or kitchenette, you can save some on your meal budget by getting take-out. In addition to places like delis, pizza joints, and fast-food restaurants, a number of Orlando-area supermarkets sell ready-to-eat meals. Some of the more notable ones are Publix, Winn-Dixie, Albertson's, and Gooding's. You can find them in the Yellow Pages under "Grocers."

IN THE LAKE BUENA VISTA AREA

There are a number of good choices in this area, which is outside Disney but adjacent to its theme parks.

SUPER-CHEAP EATS

Pebbles ★★ *Finds* FLORIDIAN   If you want to dine like a gourmet without the hefty price, this is the restaurant for you. This local chain has a reputation for great food and creative appetizers. Its pleasant Key West style is casual and comfortable, and portions are generous and presented with an artistic flair. The delicious Ybor Gold twin filets are seared, and then bathed in the namesake lager and delivered with caramelized onions and three-cheese potatoes.

12551 Apopka-Vineland Rd., in the Crossroads Shopping Center. ℂ 407/827-1111. www.pebblesworld wide.com. Reservations not accepted. Main courses $10–$18. AE, DC, DISC, MC, V. Sun–Thurs noon–11pm; Fri–Sat 11am–11pm. Free self-parking. Take the I-4 Hwy. 535/Apopka-Vineland Rd. exit north to the Crossroads Shopping Center on the right.

Romano's Macaroni Grill ★ *Value* NORTHERN ITALIAN   Though it's part of a multi-state chain, Romano's has the down-to-earth cheerfulness of a mom-and-pop joint. The laid-back atmosphere makes it a good place for families or those looking for a casual dinner at a good price. The menu offers thin-crust pizzas made in a wood-burning oven and topped with such items as barbecued chicken. The grilled chicken Portobello (simmering between smoked mozzarella and spinach orzo pasta) is worth the visit. Premium wines are served by the glass.

12148 Apopka–Vineland Rd. (just north of County Rd. 535/Palm Pkwy.). ℂ 407/239-6676. www.macaroni grill.com. Main courses $6–$15 at lunch, $8–$17 at dinner (most under $12). AE, DC, DISC, MC, V. Sun–Thurs 11am–10pm; Fri–Sat 11am–11pm. Free self-parking. Take I-4 Exit 68, Hwy. 535/Apopka–Vineland Rd. north and continue straight when Hwy. 535 goes to the right. Romano's is about 2 blocks on the left.

INTERNATIONAL DRIVE & VICINITY

International Drive has one of the area's larger collections of fast-food joints, but the midsection and southern third also have some of this region's better restaurants. I-Drive is 10 minutes by auto from the Walt Disney World parks.

Bahama Breeze ★ *Value* CARIBBEAN   This chain restaurant sports a creative menu that offers a variety of delicious sandwiches and chicken, fish, and pasta entrees with Caribbean twists. The Cuban sandwich is the most authentic around. If that is not to your liking, try the pan-seared pork, or Bahamian chicken kabobs. The atmosphere is island casual, with rich wood and wicker throughout. On a warm evening ask to eat outside. Once famous for its long waits, the restaurant now accepts call-ahead reservations—be sure and do so.

8849 International Drive, Orlando. ℂ 407/248-2499. www.bahamabreeze.com. Call ahead is available. Lunch and dinner $9–$25. AE, DISC, MC, V. Mon–Fri 4pm–1:30am; Sat noon–1:30am; Sun noon–1am. Free self-parking. From I-4, take exit 74A, follow I-Drive 1 mile south.

B-Line Diner AMERICAN   You can sink into upholstered booths or belly up to the counter on a stool in this '50s-style diner. The round-the-clock menu features comfort foods such as a chicken potpie that's up to what mom made; a ham and cheese sandwich on a baguette; and roast pork with grilled apples, sundried cherry stuffing, and brandy-honey sauce. The portions are hearty, but so are the prices. And though it is a diner-style restaurant, it is not particularly kid friendly, unless your children are particularly well behaved.

9801 International Dr., in the Peabody Orlando. © **407/345-4460.** www.peabodyorlando.com. Reservations not accepted. Main courses $4–$14 at breakfast, $7–$17 at lunch, $9–$26 (most under $17) at dinner. AE, DC, DISC, MC, V. Daily 24 hr. Free self- and validated valet parking. From I-4, take Exit 74A, Sand Lake Rd./Hwy. 528, east to International Dr., then south. Hotel is on the left across from the Convention Center.

Siam Orchid ★ *Finds* THAI   Tim and Krissnee Martsching grow the mint, chiles, cilantro, lemon grass, and wild lime that go into their entrees. The star attractions include Pad Thai (rice noodles tossed with ground pork, garlic, shrimp, crab claws, crab meat, and crushed peanuts in a tongue-twanging sweet sauce) and Royal Thai (a curry with chicken chunks, potato, and onion in yellow curry sauce). The split-level dining room seats diners in cushioned booths and banquettes and bamboo chairs; some tables overlook a lake. Siam Orchid serves sake, plum wine, and Thai beers from a full bar.

7575 Universal Dr. (between Sand Lake Rd. and Carrier Dr.). © **407/351-0821.** Reservations recommended. Main courses $12–$24. AE, DC, DISC, MC, V. Mon–Fri 11am–2pm; daily 5–11pm. Free self-parking. From I-4, take the Sand Lake Rd./Hwy. 528 exit east to Universal, then go north to the restaurant (on the left).

SUPER-Cheap Eats

Café Tu Tu Tango ★★ *Finds* INTERNATIONAL/TAPAS   Authentic cuisine and the eclectic atmosphere of a Mediterranean artists' loft—complete with working artist—are the main draws at this interesting tapas bar. The portions are small, but the tastes are big. The roasted pears on pecan crisps—topped with Spanish bleu cheese and a balsamic reduction—are a must. The staff is fabulous and your server will be happy to educate you about the menu or make suggestions. Wine is available by the glass or bottle.

8625 International Dr. © **407/248-2222.** www.cafetututango.com. Reservations accepted but not required. Tapas (small plates) $4–$11. AE, DC, DISC, MC, V. Sun–Thurs 11:30am–11pm; Fri-Sat 11:30am–midnight. Free self-parking. From I-4, take exit 74A, Sand Lake Rd./Hwy 528, east to International Dr., then south. It is on the left.

Max's Café AMERICAN   Located in the town of Celebration, its Art-Deco decor is a re-creation of yesterday's "blue-plate special" joints that served stick-to-your-ribs, comfort favorites, such as roast turkey with cornbread stuffing and mashed 'taters. You get your money's worth in sandwiches (try the Havana or portobello melt) and meals such as honey-glazed ribs, roast pork, and Dijon-crusted chicken, all of which come in hearty helpings. The meatloaf may be better than Mom's (with all due respect).

701 Front St., Celebration. © **407/566-1144.** www.maxsrestaurants.com. Main courses $7–$12. AE, DC, DISC, MC, V. Sun–Thurs 11am–9pm; Fri-Sat 9am–10pm. Free self-parking.

WORTH A SPLURGE

Dux ★★ *Finds* INTERNATIONAL   Named for the Peabody's famous mallards, Dux offers a marvelous and oft-changing menu, as well as impeccable service. If it's there, try the succulent oven-roasted grouper with bok choy, mushrooms, and ginger sauce; or sample the tender veal chop marinated in apple cider and honey and served medium rare. The candle-lit dining room provides a wonderful atmosphere, and Dux is best reserved for a very special night out or a meal on an expense account.

9801 International Dr., in the Peabody Orlando. ✆ 407/345-4550. www.peabodyorlando.com. Reservations recommended. Main courses $26–$45. AE, DC, DISC, MC, V. Mon–Sat 6–10pm. Free self- and validated valet parking. From I-4, take the Sand Lake Rd./Hwy. 528 exit east to International Dr., then south. Hotel is on the left across from the Convention Center.

ELSEWHERE IN ORLANDO

Rolando's ✩ *Finds* CUBAN Big portions and authentic cuisine are the main draws at this mom-and-pop eatery. My favorites include *arroz con pollo* (chicken with yellow rice), *ropa vieja* (shredded beef), and, if you call a day in advance, *paella* (fish and shellfish served on a bed of rice). Entrees come with yucca or plantains. Soft lighting adds a smidgen of ambience, and there's a very limited beer and wine list.

870 E. Hwy. 436/Semoran Blvd., Casselberry. ✆ 407/767-9677. Reservations accepted. Main courses $4–$6 lunch, $8–$18 dinner. AE, DC, DISC, MC, V. Mon–Fri 11am–9:30pm; Sat noon–10pm; Sun noon–8:30pm. Free self-parking. From I-4, take Exit 82A, Hwy. 408/East–West Expwy., head east, and make a left on Hwy. 436.

SUPER-CHEAP EATS

Little Saigon ✩ *Finds* VIETNAMESE Asian immigrants created the demand for this great little eatery that's yet to be discovered by tourists. Try the summer rolls—a soft wrap filled with rice, shrimp, and pork served with a delicious peanut sauce. Head next for the grilled pork and egg over rice and noodles or barbecued beef with fried egg and rice. The numbered menu isn't translated well, but your server or the manager can help.

1106 E. Colonial Dr./Hwy. 50 (near downtown Orlando). ✆ 407/423-8539. Reservations not accepted. Main courses under $5 lunch, $5–$10 dinner. AE, DISC, MC, V. Daily 10am–9pm. Free self-parking. Take Exit 83B, Colonial Dr./Hwy. 50, off I-4 and head east. Turn right on Thorton Ave. The parking lot is immediately to the left.

WORTH A SPLURGE

Le Provence ✩ NEW FRENCH This upscale local favorite serves dishes that feature duck, veal, lobster, scallops, and tuna. If you're in the mood for creative seafood, try the snapper stuffed with shrimp mousse, then wrapped in phyllo with smoked tomato compote and braised cabbage. Wow! Duck lovers can drool over a combo plate: breast meat grilled in a subtle citrus marinade and a leg with natural juices and pineapple salsa. Few restaurants in town offer rabbit, and none do it better than Le Provence, where the loin is stuffed with pâté and vegetables and served in cognac sauce. There are eight fixed-price menus that range from three to six courses. You can enjoy a martini or an after-dinner drink and a cigar next door at Monaco's, which also serves lunch.

Note: In addition to the valet parking noted below, early birds have a shot at a small amount of metered street parking.

50 E. Pine St., in downtown Orlando. ✆ 407/843-1320. www.cenfla.com/res/leprovence. Reservations recommended. Main courses $5–$10 at lunch; $16–$34 at dinner (most under $25); $30–$58 prix fixe. AE, DC, MC, V. Mon–Fri 11:30am–2pm and 5:30–9:30pm; Sat 5:30–10:30pm. Valet parking $6. From I-4 take the Anderson St. exit east to Church St., then left/north on Court Ave. It's near the corner of Court and Pine.

4 Tips for Visiting Walt Disney World Attractions

No wonder they call it a world. Walt Disney World encompasses the Magic Kingdom; Epcot; Disney–MGM Studios; Animal Kingdom; Downtown Disney (including Cirque du Soleil, DisneyQuest, and Pleasure Island, among others); two water parks (Typhoon Lagoon and Blizzard Beach); scores of restaurants; and 19 Disney-owned resorts.

PLANNING YOUR TRIP

Planning is essential. Unless you're staying for considerably more than a week, you won't have time to experience all of the rides, shows, attractions, and recreational options. You'll only wear yourself to a frazzle trying—it's better to follow a relaxed itinerary, including leisurely meals, than to make a marathon.

INFORMATION   Call or write **Walt Disney World,** P.O. Box 10000, Lake Buena Vista, FL 32830-1000 (✆ **407/934-7639**), for a copy of the very informative *Walt Disney World Vacations,* an invaluable planning aid. Once you've arrived in town, guest-services, concierge, or front desks in area hotels—especially Disney properties and "official" hotels—have **up-to-the-minute information** about what's going on in the parks. If your hotel doesn't have this information, call ✆ **407/824-4321.**

Once you get inside the parks, go to the **Guest Relations** desks marked on the guide map you get immediately upon entry.

There's plenty of park info on the Web at **www.disneyworld.com, www. orlandosentinel.com**, and **www.orlandoinfo.com**. A great unofficial site that offers cool tips and loads of information is **Deb's Unofficial Walt Disney World Information Guide (http://allearsnet.com)**.

ESSENTIALS

Arrive Early   Get to the parks 30 to 45 minutes before the opening bell, thus avoiding a traffic jam entering them and a long line at the gate. Early arrival also lets you experience one or two major attractions before long lines form at them. In high season, the parking lots sometimes fill and you may have to wait to get in. The longest lines in all parks are between 11am and 4pm.

Parking   Cars, light trucks, and vans pay $8. Visitors with disabilities can park in special areas near the entrances; ask the parking-lot attendants or call ✆ **407/ 824-4321.** *Don't forget* to write down where you parked (area and row number), because after a long day at the parks, they all start to look and sound alike.

When You Arrive   Grab a park map. It not only tells you where the fun is but where to eat and where to shop as well. Pick up a copy of the daily entertainment schedule too. If you want to see certain shows or parades, you will need to know when to go. Don't forget to arrive early so you get a good seat.

Best Times to Visit   There isn't really an off season in Orlando, but crowds are usually thinner from mid-January to March and from mid-September until the week before Thanksgiving. The busiest days at all theme parks are generally Saturdays and Sundays, when the locals visit. Beyond that, Monday, Thursday, and Saturday are pretty frantic in the Magic Kingdom; Tuesday and Friday are hectic at Epcot; Sunday and Wednesday are crazy at Disney–MGM Studios; and Monday, Tuesday, and Wednesday are a zoo at Animal Kingdom. Major

---

Tips   **Advanced Pass Purchase Saves Money**

If you plan on purchasing a Premium Pass, doing so ahead of time can result in savings. You can save up to $11 per person by purchasing passes (only those 5 to 7 days in length) for guests ages 10 and over in advance. A 7-Day Premium Pass purchased at the gate would cost $279, but if you buy it before you arrive (through Disney online, a participating Disney Store, or travel agent), it's only $268.

holidays attract scores of visitors: from Christmas to New Year's is a frenzied time and the week preceding and following Easter are out of control busy.

Note: Summer is the worst time to visit, because of the crowds, the heat, and the humidity.

Operating Hours   Park hours vary and are influenced by special events as well as the economy. Call ahead or go to **www.disneyworld.com** to check for operating times otherwise you could find yourself expecting to stay all night when in reality the park closes at 6:00pm. Not only will hours vary from park to park, but from week to week, and even day to day. This can greatly affect your plans in regards to what park you visit, and when so don't just assume, check the schedule ahead of time or once you arrive.

Tickets   In 2005, Disney revamped its entire ticketing structure, giving visitors who stay at WDW for a few days far better deals than those who come for just a day (and making the whole process a touch confusing). The following *don't include 6.5% sales tax* unless noted. *Note:* Price hikes and changes are frequent occurrences, so call (© **407/824-4321**) or visit WDW's website (**www.disney world.com**) for up-to-the-minute fees. Also, be advised that Disney has changed its ticket expiration policy, so unless you buy an expensive add-on that we cannot recommend, your multiday pass will expire 14 days from the first day it is used.

⟨Value **Passes & Coupons That Save Your Orlan-Dough**

- **It's Not Just Disney Anymore.** Universal Orlando, SeaWorld, and Wet 'n Wild have joined to fight Disney's multipark pass system. The **FlexTicket** lets you see the "other-than-Disney" parks with these passes, which counter Disney's Park Hopper tickets. With the **FlexTicket,** you pay one price to visit any of the participating parks during a 14-day period. A four-park pass to Universal Studios Florida, Islands of Adventure, Wet 'n Wild, and SeaWorld is $179.95 for adults and $145.95 for children 3 to 9. A five-park pass, which adds Busch Gardens in Tampa, is $214.95 for adults and $179.95 for kids. The **FlexTicket** can be ordered through Universal (© **407/363-8000;** www. universalorlando.com); SeaWorld (© **407/351-3600;** www.seaworld. com); or Wet 'n Wild (© **800/992-9453** or 407/351-9453; www.wetn wild.com).
- **Extra! Extra! Local Newspaper Saves You Money.** There's no shortage of golf courses in the Orlando area; the best way to find a good deal is to look in the sports section of the *Orlando Sentinel* for discount coupons and otherwise unadvertised specials. The **Friday** "Calendar" section of the *Sentinel* often includes two-for-one dinner special coupons or other entertainment discounts. It also lists cultural events and concerts around Central Florida, some of which are free or have a nominal admission charge.
- **More Coupons.** Hotel lobbies, restaurants, newspaper racks, and some of the attractions have other free newspapers and brochures that are filled with discounts or two-for-one specials on meals, tickets, rooms, and souvenirs.

Tips **Smoking Alert**

Disney long has prohibited smoking in shops, attractions, restaurants, ride lines, and other areas. All WDW parks stopped selling cigarettes in 1999, and in 2000 smokers were allowed to light up only in designated areas.

1-day/1-park tickets, for admission to the Magic Kingdom, Epcot, Animal Kingdom, or Disney–MGM, cost $59.75 for adults, $48 for children 3 to 9. (Ouch!) **Multiday tickets** allow you to visit *one park per day*. A 7-day ticket costs $199 for adults, $160 for kids.

A **Park Hopper** add-on ($35 *per ticket*, per person*)* allows visitors unlimited admission to the Magic Kingdom, Epcot, Animal Kingdom, and Disney–MGM Studios for the length of their ticket. A 1-day adult Park Hopper ticket costs $94.75, while the 7-day version costs $234 — making the latter a far better deal.

Premium Passes are Park Hopper tickets that also allow visitors their choice of two to five admissions to Typhoon Lagoon, Blizzard Beach, Pleasure Island, DisneyQuest, or Disney's Wide World of Sports (the number of admissions you get depends on the number of days on your pass). Prices range from an obscene $139.95 for a 1-day adult pass to $268 for a 7-day pass (a very good deal).

One-day ticket to Typhoon Lagoon or Blizzard Beach is $32 for adults, $26 for children.

One-day ticket to Pleasure Island is $21. Because this is primarily an 18-and-over entertainment complex, there's no bargain price for children.

5 The Magic Kingdom

The Magic Kingdom offers 40 attractions plus shops and restaurants in a 107-acre package. Its centerpiece and symbol, Cinderella Castle, forms the hub of a wheel whose spokes reach to **seven themed "lands."**

From the parking lot, you have to walk or take a tram, then a ferry or monorail to the entrance. While rides are short, the wait isn't during peak periods. In this park's case, arrive an hour early because it takes 35 to 45 minutes to reach the action.

Upon entering the park, get a Magic Kingdom guide map. It shows every shop, restaurant, and attraction. Consult its entertainment schedule to see what's cooking today. There are parades, musical extravaganzas, fireworks, band concerts, barbershop quartets, character appearances, and more.

If you have questions, **City Hall,** on your left as you enter, is an information center and, like Toontown Fair, a great place to meet costumed characters.

MAIN STREET, USA

The gateway to the Kingdom, Main Street resembles a turn-of-the-20th-century American street (okay, so it leads to a 13th-century European castle). Main Street is best left for the end of the day when you're heading back to your hotel.

Right as you enter Main Street, you can board the **Walt Disney World Railroad,** an authentic 1928 steam-powered train for a 15-minute trip clockwise around the perimeter of the park. It's a good way to travel if you're headed to one of its three stations—the park entrance, Frontierland, and Mickey's Toontown Fair—or if you just want to go for a relaxing ride with shorter lines.

ADVENTURELAND

Cross a bridge and stroll through an exotic jungle of foliage, thatched roofs, and totems. Amid dense vines and stands of bamboo, drums are beating and swashbuckling adventures are beginning.

On the 10-minute **Jungle Cruise,** you sail through an African veldt in the Congo, an Amazon rainforest, and the Nile river in Egypt among others. Dozens of animatronic creatures inhabit the hanging vines, cascading waterfalls, and tropical foliage.

The first major ride added to Adventureland since 1971, the **Magic Carpets of Aladdin** delights wee ones and some older kids. Its 16 four-passenger carpets circle a giant genie's bottle while the camels spit water at the passengers. The flying carpets spin and move up, down, forward, and back.

In the classic **Pirates of the Caribbean**, the pirates chase "wenches" as your boat passes audio-animatronic figures that include "yo-ho-hoing" pirates raiding a Caribbean town. After a lot of looting and boozing, the pirates pass out. This ride might be a bit scary for kids under 5 due to the unexpected yet small waterfalls and bits of darkness.

The Enchanted Tiki Room Under New Management is a very upbeat and enchanting show featuring a slew of tropical birds singing and telling jokes. It is a bit loud on the decibel front, but is otherwise cute and entertaining.

FRONTIERLAND

From Adventureland, step into the wild and woolly past of the American frontier. The landscape is straight out of the Wild West, complete with log cabins and rustic saloons.

The low-key **Big Thunder Mountain Railroad** roller coaster has tight turns and dark descents rather than sudden, steep drops. It's situated in a 200-foot-high, red-stone mountain with 2,780 feet of track through caves and

---

Tips FASTPASS

Don't want to stand in long lines? Disney parks use a reservation system whereby you go to the most popular rides, feed your theme-park ticket into a small ticket-taker machine, and get an assigned time to return. When you reappear at the appointed time, you get into a reasonably short line and then hop aboard. Here's the drill:

Hang onto your ticket stub when you enter, and head to the hottest ride of your choosing. If it's a FASTPASS attraction (they're noted in the guide map you get when you enter) and there's a line, feed your ticket stub into the waist-level ticket taker. Retrieve both your ticket stub and the FASTPASS stub that comes with it. Look at the two times stamped on the FASTPASS. Come back during that 1-hour window and you can enter the ride with almost no wait. In the interim, venture on out and experience another attraction or show.

Note: Early in the day, your window may begin as close as only 40 minutes after you feed the FASTPASS machine, but later in the day it could be hours. Initially, Disney allowed you to do this on only one ride at a time, however now you can get a pass for a second attraction 2 hours after your first assigned time.

canyons. Your train careens through the ribs of a dinosaur, under a thundering waterfall, past geysers and bubbling mud pots, and over a bottomless volcanic pool. It's tailor-made for kids and grown-ups who want a thrill but aren't quite up to tackling the big coasters. *Note:* You must be 40 inches or taller to ride.

The **Country Bear Jamboree** ⚜⚜ is a hoot. It's a 15-minute show featuring audio-animatronic bears belting out rollicking country tunes and crooning plaintive love songs.

Based on Disney's 1946 film *Song of the South,* **Splash Mountain** ⚜⚜⚜ takes you flume-style past 26 colorful scenes that include swamps, bayous, caves, and waterfalls. Riders are caught in the schemes of Brer Fox and Brer Bear as they chase the ever-wily Brer Rabbit. Your hollow-log vehicle twists, turns, and splashes, sometimes plummeting in darkness as the ride leads to a 45-degree, 52-foot-long, 40 mph splashdown in a briar-filled pond. *Note:* You must be at least 40 inches tall to ride.

LIBERTY SQUARE

This zone depicts 18th-century America. Thirteen lanterns, symbolizing the colonies, hang from the Liberty Tree, an immense live oak. And you might encounter a fife-and-drum corps on the cobblestone streets.

Every American president is represented by a lifelike audio-animatronic figure in the **Hall of Presidents** ⚜. Look closely, and you'll see them fidget and whisper. The show begins with a film, and then the curtain rises on America's leaders. Each president's costume reflects his period's fashion, fabrics, and tailoring techniques.

Once inside the **Haunted Mansion** ⚜⚜, darkness, spooky music, howling, and screams enhance the ambience. The slow-motion ride has bizarre scenes: a ghostly banquet and ball, a graveyard band, a suit of armor that comes alive, a talking head in a crystal ball, and weird flying objects. At the end, a ghost joins your car. It's a classic that's more amusing than terrifying.

FANTASYLAND

The attractions in this happy land are themed after classics such as *Snow White, Peter Pan,* and *Dumbo.* If your kids are 8 and under, you may want to make this and Mickey's Toontown your primary stops in the Magic Kingdom.

There's not a lot to do at **Cinderella Castle** ⚜, but its status as the Magic Kingdom's icon makes it a must (not that you can really miss it, as it stands at 185 ft. tall). The namesake character appears on occasion, and Cinderella's Royal Table restaurant is located inside.

The elaborate and beautiful **Cinderella's Golden Carousel** ⚜⚜ was constructed by Italian carvers in 1917 and refurbished by Disney artists, who added 18 hand painted scenes from Cinderella on a wooden canopy above the horses. Kids of all ages will enjoy this ride.

Dumbo the Flying Elephant ⚜ is a very tame kids' ride, in which the Dumbos go around in a circle, gently rising and dipping. If you can stand the lines, and they are usually quite long here, it's very exciting for wee ones.

Built for the 1964 New York World's Fair, **It's a Small World** ⚜ takes you to countries inhabited by appropriately costumed audio-animatronic dolls singing "It's a small world after all," in tiny doll-like voices. Every adult who has ever ridden this in the past will remember the tune as it can be difficult to get it out of your mind. *Note:* This ride is closed for refurbishment until mid-2005.

Mad Tea Party is a traditional amusement park ride with an *Alice in Wonderland* theme that's always a hit with the younger set. Riders sit in big pastel-hued teacups on saucers that careen around a circular platform while tilting and spinning. Adults may want to ground themselves when they get off as the kids tend to spin as fast as physically possible.

Debuting in 2003, **Mickey's PhilharMagic** ★★★ is by far the most amazing 3-D film I've ever seen. Covering one of the largest screens ever made for a 3-D movie, the production's special effects (similar in style to those in **Jim Henson's Muppet*Vision 3D,** p. 447) are incredible. Many of Disney's most beloved characters make an appearance to help (or in some cases hinder) the attempts of Donald Duck to retrieve Mickey's magical sorcerer's hat. This is a must see for everyone.

On **Peter Pan's Flight** ★ you'll ride in airborne versions of Captain Hook's ship, and take a calm flight over nighttime London to Never-Never Land. You will fly overhead the mermaids, the ticking crocodile, the Lost Boys, Princess Tiger Lilly, Tinker Bell, Hook, and Smee. It's a fun ride for younger kids and Peter Pan fans of all ages.

Though it may still scare kids under 5, contrary to its name, in **Snow White's Scary Adventures** the storyline is bright, and the title heroine appears in pleasant scenes, such as one at a wishing well, and rides off to live happily ever after.

MICKEY'S TOONTOWN FAIR

Where's Mickey? This 2-acre site is a great place for small children to find him and his pals. Toontown offers a chance to meet Disney characters, including Mickey, Minnie, Donald, and Goofy and even have your photo taken with them (if you can make it through the sometimes seemingly endless lines).

The Barnstormer at Goofy's Wiseacre Farm ★★ is a mini–roller coaster likely inspired by Woody Woodpecker's Nuthouse Coaster at Universal Orlando (p. 454). It looks and feels like a crop duster that flies off-course and through Goofy's barn. The ride has very little in the dip-and-drop department, but a bit of zip on the spin-and-spiral front. (It even gets squeals from adults.) The 60-second corkscrew ride has a 35-inch height minimum.

Donald's Boat (S.S. Miss Daisy) ★ offers a lot of interactive fun, and the "waters" around it feature fountains of water snakes and other wet fun things that earn squeals of joy (and relief on hot days).

Mickey's & Minnie's Country Houses ★ are separate cottages that offer a lot of visual fun and some marginal interactive areas for youngsters. Mickey's place features garden and garage playgrounds. Minnie's lets kids play in her kitchen, where popcorn goes wild in a microwave and a cake comes to life in the oven as the utensils play melodies.

TOMORROWLAND

In 1994, WDW folks decided Tomorrowland (originally designed in the 1970s) was beginning to look like "Yesteryear," so it was revamped to add a more futuristic feel. The newly-opened (late 2004), family-friendly **Stitch's Great Escape** recruits riders to help capture the infamous "experiment 626," who is wreaking havoc while loose in the galaxy. Disney animatronics bring this adventure to life.

On **Buzz Lightyear's Space Ranger Spin** ★★, join Buzz and try to save the universe while flying your cruiser through a world you'll recognize from the original *Toy Story* movie. Kids enjoy using the dashboard-mounted laser cannons as they spin through the sky (filled with gigantic toys instead of stars). If they're good shots, they can set off sight and sound gags with their lasers. You may be riding this more than once if you have kids.

The cosmic coaster, **Space Mountain** ✪ usually has *long* lines (if you don't use FASTPASS), even though it's years past its prime. Once aboard a "rocket," you'll climb and dive through the inky, starlit blackness of outer space. The hairpin turns and plunges make it seem as if you're going at breakneck speed, but your car doesn't go any faster than 28 mph. *Note:* Riders must be at least 44 inches tall.

The Timekeeper is hosted by a robot/mad scientist (Robin Williams) and his assistant, 9-EYE, a flying, camera-headed droid that moonlights as a time-machine test pilot. In this jet-speed escapade, the audience hears Mozart as a young prodigy playing for French royalty, watches da Vinci work, and floats in a hot-air balloon over Red Square. It's more for adults than kids.

Younger kids love **Tomorrowland Indy Speedway,** especially if their adult companion lets them drive (without a big person, there's a 52-in. height minimum for driving a lap). Teens and other fast starters find it just too slow—the cars go only 7 mph and are loosely locked into lanes.

PARADES, FIREWORKS & MORE

For up-to-the-moment information, see the entertainment schedule given in the park guide map that you get when entering the park.

Magic Kingdom's first new fireworks display in just over 30 years, **Wishes** ✪✪✪ debuted in October of 2003 to lots of acclaim. It's precise mix of choreographed bursts, music and story is just amazing and has to be experienced to be appreciated. This is absolutely the best way to end your day in the Magic Kingdom. The fireworks go off nightly during peak periods, but only on selected nights the rest of the year.

A 20-minute after-dark display, **SpectroMagic** ✪✪ combines fiber optics, holographic images, old-fashioned twinkling lights, and a soundtrack featuring classic Disney tunes. The parade runs on a *very limited basis.*

6 Epcot

Epcot is an acronym for Experimental Prototype Community of Tomorrow, and it was Walt Disney's dream for a planned residential community. But, long after his death, it opened in 1982 as Central Florida's second Disney theme park.

The 260-acre park has two sections, **Future World** and **World Showcase.** It's so large that hiking World Showcase from tip to tip (1½ miles) can be exhausting. That's why some folks say Epcot really stands for "Every Person Comes Out Tired." Depending on how long you intend to linger at each of the 11 countries in World Showcase, this park can be seen in 1 day, but it's better to do it over 2 to take it all in properly.

Conserve your energy by taking launches across the lagoon from the edge of Future World to Germany or Morocco. Double-deckers circle World Showcase, making stops at Norway, Italy, France, and Canada.

FUTURE WORLD

Future World is centered on Epcot's icon, a giant geosphere known as Spaceship Earth (or "that big golf ball"). Major corporations sponsor most of its themed areas, and the focus is on discovery, scientific achievements, and tomorrow's technologies in areas running from energy to undersea exploration. Here are the headliners:

The fountains at the **Imagination** ★★ pavilion are magical—they fire "water snakes" that arch in the air and dare kids to avoid their "bite." The 3-D *Honey I Shrunk the Audience* ★★ show shrinks you, then terrorizes you with giant mice, a cat, and a 5-year-old who gives you a sound shaking. **Journey into Your Imagination** ★ features a park favorite, Figment the dragon.

Innoventions ★ is divided into two sections. House of Innoventions in **Innoventions East** heralds a smart house equipped with a refrigerator that can make your grocery list and a picture frame that can send photos to other smart frames. The exhibits in **Innoventions West** are led by Sega's Video Games of Tomorrow.

The largest of Future World's pavilions, **The Land** ★ looks at our relationships to food and nature. **Living with the Land** ★ is a 13-minute boat ride through a rainforest, an African desert, and the windswept American plains. **Circle of Life** ★ blends spectacular live-action footage with animation in a 15-minute, 70mm motion picture based on *The Lion King* that delivers a cautionary environmental message.

The Living Seas ★ pavilion's 5.7-million-gallon aquarium has a reef and 4,000 sea creatures, such as sharks, barracudas, parrotfish, rays, and dolphins. A 2½-minute multimedia preshow about today's ocean technology is followed by a 7-minute film on the formation of the earth and seas as a means to support life. After the films, you enter "hydrolators" for a hokey "descent" to the simulated ocean floor, where you get close-up views through acrylic windows of the denizens in a natural coral-reef habitat.

Get set to blast off to Mars on **Mission: Space** ★★★, Epcot's newest attraction. Sophisticated simulator technology developed in partnership with NASA and Hewlett Packard launch you on an amazing ride through space that feels a lot like the real deal (so some NASA astronauts have claimed, anyway). This one is definitely not for the faint at heart, and has a 44-inch height limit.

Spaceship Earth is the large, silvery geosphere that is Epcot's icon, but all that awaits inside is a bland 15-minute show/ride that takes you through the history of communications. *Tip:* Skip it.

Test Track ★★ is a marvel that combines GM engineering and Disney Imagineering. The line for this one can be more than an hour long, so consider FASTPASS. Once you're in your six-passenger convertible, the 5-minute ride follows what looks like a real highway and includes a brake test, climb, and tight S-curves. There's also a 12-second burst of speed that reaches 65 mph on the straightaway. *Note:* Riders must be at least 40 inches tall.

Sponsored by Exxon, the **Universe of Energy** ★ pavilion is home to a 32-minute ride, **Ellen's Energy Adventure**, which features comedian Ellen DeGeneres being tutored by Bill Nye the Science Guy to be a *Jeopardy!* contestant. In the process, you learn about energy resources from fossil fuels and take a ride through the dinosaur age.

Housed in a vast geodesic dome fronted by a 75-foot-tall replica of a DNA strand, **Wonders of Life** ★★ offers some of Future World's most engaging shows and attractions. The *Making of Me* is a captivating 15-minute motion picture combining live action (starring Martin Short) with animation and spectacular in-utero photography to create the sweetest introduction imaginable to the facts of life. (Be aware; if your kids are under 8, this show may prompt certain questions about reproduction that you may or may not be ready for.) In **Body Wars,** you're "reduced" to the size of a cell in order to join a medical rescue inside the immune system of a human body. The motion simulator takes you on a wild ride through gale-force winds in the lungs and pounding heart chambers. This one isn't a smart choice for those prone to motion sickness or who generally prefer to be stirred rather than shaken. *Note:* Riders must be at least 40 inches tall. In the hilarious, multimedia **Cranium Command** ✮✮, you tag along with Buzzy, an audio-animatronic brain-pilot-in-training charged with a seemingly impossible task—controlling the brain of a typical 12-year-old boy. Celebrities play the boy's body parts as he encounters preadolescent traumas such as meeting a girl and having a run-in with the principal. *Note:* This pavilion is only open during busy periods and high season.

WORLD SHOWCASE

This community of 11 miniaturized nations surrounds a 40-acre lagoon at the park's south end. All of these "countries" have indigenous architecture, landscaping, restaurants, and shops. The nations' cultural facets are explored in art exhibits, dance or other live performances, and innovative films. The employees in each pavilion are natives of that country. The World Showcase opens at 11am or noon, so there's time for Future World if you arrive earlier.

The architecture in **Canada** ✮✮ ranges from a mansard-roofed replica of Ottawa's 19th-century, French-style Château Laurier (here called Hôtel du Canada) to a British-influenced stone building modeled after a landmark near Niagara Falls. But the highlight is *O Canada!* ✮✮, a dazzling, 18-minute, 360-degree CircleVision film that shows Canada's scenic splendor, from a dog-sled race to the thundering flight of thousands of snow geese.

Bounded by a serpentine wall that wanders its perimeter, the **China** ✮ pavilion is entered via a triple-arched ceremonial gate inspired by the Temple of Heaven in Beijing, a summer retreat for Chinese emperors. Passing through the gate, you'll see a half-size replica of this ornately embellished red-and-gold circular temple, built in 1420 during the Ming dynasty. Gardens simulate those in Suzhou, with miniature waterfalls, fragrant lotus ponds, bamboo groves, corkscrew willows, and weeping mulberry trees. **Wonders of China** ✮✮ is a 20-minute, 360-degree CircleVision film that explores 6,000 years of dynastic and communist rule and the breathtaking diversity of the Chinese landscape. Outside, the amazing **Dragon Legend Acrobats** provide live thrills.

The **France** pavilion focuses on La Belle Epoque, a period from 1870 to 1910 in which French art, literature, and architecture flourished. It's entered via a replica of the Pont des Arts footbridge over the Seine and leads to a ⅒-scale model of the Eiffel Tower constructed from Gustave Eiffel's original blueprints. The pièce de résistance here is *Impressions de France* ✮✮. Shown in a palatial sit-down theater á la Fontainebleau, this 18-minute film is a scenic journey through diverse French landscapes that's enhanced by the music of French composers and shown on a vast, 200-degree wraparound screen.

Enclosed by castle walls and towers, the festive **Germany** pavilion is centered on a cobblestone square with pots of colorful flowers girding a fountain statue of St. George and the Dragon. The adjacent clock tower has glockenspiel figures that herald each hour with quaint melodies. Sixteenth-century facades replicate a merchant's hall in the Black Forest and the town hall in Römerberg Square.

Note: Model-train enthusiasts and kids enjoy the exquisitely detailed miniature version of a small **Bavarian town** ⍟, complete with working train station.

One of the prettiest World Showcase pavilions, **Italy,** lures visitors over an arched footbridge to a replica of Venice's pink-and-white Doge's Palace. Other highlights include an 83-foot-tall bell tower, Venetian bridges, and a central piazza enclosing a version of Bernini's Neptune Fountain. You can shop for Italian specialties such as Murano glass.

At **Japan** ⍟⍟, a flaming red *torii* (gate of honor) leads the way to the Goju No To pagoda, inspired by a shrine built at Nara in A.D. 700. In a traditional Japanese garden, cedars, yews, bamboos, willows, and flowering shrubs frame pebbled footpaths, rustic bridges, waterfalls, rock landscaping, and a pond of koi. The Yakitori House is based on the 16th-century Katsura Imperial Villa in Kyoto, considered the crowning achievement of Japanese architecture. Another highlight is the moated **White Heron Castle,** a replica of the Shirasagi-Jo, a 17th-century fortress overlooking the city of Himeji. The drums of **Matsuriza** ⍟⍟—one of the best performances in the World Showcase—entertain guests daily.

You'll hear marimbas and mariachi bands (including **Mariachi Cobre**) as you approach the festive **Mexico** ⍟ showcase, fronted by a towering Mayan pyramid modeled on the Aztec temple of Quetzalcoatl (God of Life) and surrounded by dense Yucatán jungle landscaping. Upon entering the pavilion, you'll find yourself in a museum of pre-Colombian art and artifacts. Down a ramp, after you have passed through the local shops, **El Rio del Tiempo (River of Time)** ⍟ offers an 8-minute cruise through Mexico's past and present.

When you enter **Morocco** ⍟⍟, note the imperfections in the mosaic tile in the Koutoubia Minaret, the prayer tower of a 12th-century mosque in Marrakech. They were put there intentionally in accordance with the belief that only Allah is perfect. The **Medina** (old city), entered via a replica of an arched gateway in Fez, leads to Fez House (a traditional Moroccan home) and the narrow, winding streets of the *souk,* a bustling marketplace where all manner of authentic handcrafted merchandise is on display. **Treasures of Morocco** is a daily, 35-minute guided tour (1–5pm) that highlights this country's culture, architecture, and history.

Inside **Norway** ⍟, a *stavekirke* (stave church), styled after the 13th-century Gol Church of Hallingdal, features changing exhibits. A replica of Oslo's 14th-century **Akershus Castle,** next to a cascading woodland waterfall, is the setting for the pavilion's restaurant (p. 429). **Maelstrom** ⍟, a ride in a dragon-headed Viking vessel, traverses fjords before you crash through a gorge into the North Sea, where you're hit by a storm (albeit a relatively calm one). Passengers disembark at a 10th-century Viking village to view the 70mm film *Norway,* which documents Norwegian history.

⌒ **Moments**   **A Grand Nightcap**

IllumiNations ⍟⍟ is a blend of fireworks, lasers, and fountains in a display that's signature Disney. The show is worth the crowds that flock to the parking lot when it's over—don't miss it! **Tip:** Stake your claim to the best viewing areas a half-hour before show time (listed in your entertainment schedule). The ones near Showcase Plaza have a head start for the exits. The Rose & Crown Pub in the U.K. pavilion (see earlier), offers a great view of the proceedings.

The **United Kingdom** pavilion beckons you with **Britannia Square,** a formal London-style park complete with copper-roofed gazebo bandstand, a stereotypical red phone booth, and a statue of the Bard. Four centuries of architecture are represented along quaint cobblestone streets. A formal garden with low box hedges in geometric patterns, flagstone paths, and a stone fountain replicates the landscaping of 16th- and 17th-century palaces. *Tip:* Don't miss **The British Invasion** ⭐, a group that impersonates the Beatles daily except Sundays, and pub pianist Pam Brody (Tues, Thurs, Fri, and Sun).

Housed in a Georgian-style structure, the 29-minute **U.S.A.—The American Adventure** ⭐ is a dramatization of U.S. history using video, rousing music, and a cast of audio-animatronic figures, including narrators Mark Twain and Ben Franklin. You'll see Jefferson writing the Declaration of Independence, Matthew Brady photographing a family being divided by the Civil War, the stock market crash of 1929, the attack on Pearl Harbor, and the *Eagle* heading for the moon. Entertainment includes the **Spirit of America Fife & Drum Corps** and **Voices of Liberty,** an a cappella group that sings patriotic songs.

7 Disney–MGM Studios

Disney bills this park as "the Hollywood that never was and always will be." Once inside, you'll find pulse-quickening rides and movie- and TV-themed shows. Movie sets remember the golden age of Hollywood and street performers dressed as starlets, gossip columnists, and studio execs wander around, interacting with the crowds (you might even get a chance to yell "cut!").

MAJOR ATTRACTIONS & SHOWS

The 35-minute **Disney–MGM Studios Backlot Tour** ⭐ takes you behind the scenes via tram for a look at the vehicles, props, costumes, sets, and special effects used in movies and TV shows. But the real fun begins once you reach **Catastrophe Canyon,** where an earthquake causes canyon walls to rumble. A raging oil fire, massive explosions, torrents of rain, and flash floods threaten you and other riders before you're taken behind the scenes to see how filmmakers use special effects to make such disasters.

Producers adapted the 30-minute **Beauty and the Beast Live on Stage** ⭐ show from the same-name movie. The sets and costumes are lavish, and the production numbers are pretty spectacular. Arrive early to get a good seat.

On **The Great Movie Ride,** film footage and 50 audio-animatronic replicas of movie stars re-create some of the most famous scenes in film. It's 22 minutes of sheer bliss for the cinema buff.

Peek into the world of movie stunts at the 30-minute **Indiana Jones Epic Stunt Spectacular** ⭐⭐⭐, which re-creates major scenes from the Indiana Jones films. Arrive early and sit near the stage for your shot at being an audience participant. Alas, this is a job for adults only.

Kermit and Miss Piggy star in **Jim Henson's Muppet*Vision 3D** ⭐⭐, a must-see film that marries Jim Henson's puppets with Disney audio-animatronics, special-effects, 70mm film, and 3-D technology. The coming-at-you action includes flying Muppets, cream pies, and cannonballs, as well as high winds, fiber-optic fireworks, bubble showers, even an actual spray of water. The 25-minute show runs continuously.

At press time, **Disney** was revamping the **Magic of Disney Animation,** ditching the old but beloved tour hosted by Walter Cronkite and Robin Williams in favor of more interactive options. The new attraction is set to feature characters

---

(*Moments* **A Nighttime Spectacle**

The fireworks, laser lights, and choreography of **Fantasmic!** ★★★ make it a spectacular, 25-minute, end-of-day experience. The extravaganza features shooting stars, fireballs, animated fountains, a cast of 50, a giant dragon, a king cobra, and one million gallons of water. And everything is orchestrated by a sorcerer mouse who looks more than remotely familiar. Throughout, musical scores and characters from Disney classics entertain you.

Tip: Make a Priority Seating reservation for the Hollywood Brown Derby, Mama Melrose's Ristorante Italiano, or Hollywood & Vine and, when you do, ask for the Fantasmic! package (pricing depends on restaurant selected; ☎ 407/939-3463). After dinner you'll get preferred seating at the show.

---

from Disney's *Mulan* interacting with a live actor and a video on the making of that film. Visitors will also get a chance to watch real animators at work and ask questions about the animation process before attempting their own Disney character drawings while under the supervision of a working animator.

Younger audiences (2–5) love the 20-minute **Playhouse Disney—Live on Stage!,** where they meet characters from *Bear in the Big Blue House, The Book of Pooh,* and others. It encourages preschoolers to dance, sing, and play along with the cast. It happens several times a day. Check your schedule.

Want the best thrill ride WDW has to offer? Then tackle the fast-and-furious **Rock 'n' Roller Coaster** ★★★. You sit in a 24-passenger "stretch limo" with 120 speakers that blare Aerosmith at 32,000 watts as you blast from 0 to 60 mph in 2.8 seconds, then fly into the first gut-tightening inversion at 5Gs. Then you're off on a wild ride through a make-believe California freeway system in the semidarkness. *Note:* Riders must be at least 48 inches tall.

Cutting-edge when it opened, **Star Tours,** based on the original *Star Wars* trilogy, is now a couple of rungs below the latest technology but is still fun. You board a 40-seat "spacecraft" for an otherworldly journey that greets you with sudden drops, crashes, and oncoming laser blasts as it careens out of control. *Note:* Riders must be at least 40 inches tall.

Disney continues to fine-tune **The Twilight Zone Tower of Terror** ★★★ into a true stomach-lifter. As legend has it, during a violent storm on Halloween night 1939, lightning struck the Hollywood Tower Hotel, causing an entire wing and an elevator full of people to disappear. And you're about to meet them as you star in a special episode of *The Twilight Zone.* The ride now features random drop sequences, allowing for a real sense of unknown, and new visual, audio, and olfactory effects have also been added to make the experience even more frightening. It's definitely a couple of grades above Doctor Doom's Fearfall at Islands of Adventure (p. 455). *Note:* You must be at least 40 inches tall to ride.

Hazy lighting creates an underwater effect in a reef-walled theater and helps set the mood for the charming musical show, **Voyage of the Little Mermaid** ★, which combines live performers with puppets, film clips, and more. All the movie's major songs, including the theme, "Under the Sea," are featured. The 17-minute show is a great place to rest and sing along.

Contestants can't win $1 million on **Who Wants to Be a Millionaire—Play It!** ★, but they can win points used to buy prizes ranging from collectible pins to a leather jacket or a trip to New York to meet Regis Philbin. Based on Disney-owned ABC TV's game show, the theme-park version features lifelines (such as asking the audience or calling a stranger on two phones set up in the park). Games run continuously in the 600-seat studio. Audience members play along on keypads. The fastest to answer qualifying questions become contestants.

8 Animal Kingdom

Disney's fourth major park combines exotic animals, elaborate landscapes, and a handful of rides to create yet another reason that many guests don't venture outside this World of Disney very often.

Animal Kingdom is a 500-acre park for animals, a conservation venue as much as an attraction, so it's easy for most of the animals to escape your eyes here. Busch Gardens (p. 349) at 335 acres has fewer places for critters to play hide-and-seek, so it's easier to see them there if you're up for the 3-hour round-trip to Tampa. Animal Kingdom wins the battle of the shows with **Tarzan Rocks!** and **Festival of the Lion King,** but Busch wins hands-down the battle of thrill rides with its five roller coasters.

DISCOVERY ISLAND

Like Cinderella Castle in the Magic Kingdom, the 14-story **Tree of Life** ✮✮ is the park's central landmark. WDW artisans built the tree, which has 8,000 limbs, 103,000 leaves, and 325 mammals, reptiles, amphibians, bugs, birds, Mickeys, and dinosaurs carved into its trunk, limbs, and roots. Teams of artisans worked for a year creating its sculptures, and it's worth a walk around its roots, especially on the way to see *It's Tough to Be a Bug!* ✮✮, a 3-D movie with pretty impressive special effects. Grab your glasses and settle into a creepy-crawly seat. It's not a good one for very young kids (it's dark and loud) or bug haters, but for others it's a fun, sometimes poignant look at life from a smaller perspective. Near the conclusion, a stinkbug truly awakens your senses.

DINOLAND U.S.A.

Enter by passing under "Olden Gate Bridge," a 40-foot Brachiosaurus reassembled from fossils. You'll also find a replica of "Sue," a 67-million-year-old Tyrannosaurus Rex skeleton that was worked on by paleontologist here before being shipped to her new home at Chicago's Field Museum.

Kids love the chance to slip, slither, slide, and slink through **The Boneyard** ✮, a giant playground, where they can discover the real-looking remains of Triceratops, T-Rex, and other vanished giants. It's also a great place for parents to take a break from the pavement pounding of a day in the park.

Dinosaur hurls you through darkness in CTX Rover "time machines" that pass an array of snarling (though somewhat hokey) dinosaurs. Young children may find the dinos and darkness a bit frightening. *Note:* You must be 40 inches or taller to climb aboard.

Disney introduced **Primeval Whirl,** a spinning, free-style twin roller coaster in 2002. You control the action through its wacky maze of curves, peaks, and dippity-do-dahs. This is a modern version of those old carnival roller coasters of the '50s and '60s. *Note:* It carries a 48-inch height minimum.

Phil Collins's soundtrack and a cast of 27 very live performers (tumblers, dancers, and in-line skating daredevils) put on quite a show during the 28-minute **Tarzan Rocks!** ✮. The costumes and music are spectacular, second in Animal Kingdom only to "Festival of the Lion King" (see below).

TriceraTop Spin is a minithrill for youngsters. Dinosaurs attached to arms circle a hub while moving up and down and all around much like Dumbo (p. 441) at the Magic Kingdom.

CAMP MINNIE-MICKEY

Characters and one of the best theme-park shows in town are the main attractions in this small area of Animal Kingdom.

The **Character Greeting Trails** ⭐ are a must-do for people traveling with children. A variety of Disney characters, from Winnie the Pooh and Pocahontas to Timon and Baloo, have separate trails where you can meet and mingle. Mickey, Minnie, Goofy, and Pluto also make periodic appearances.

Everyone in the audience comes alive when the music starts at the rousing, 28-minute **Festival of the Lion King** ⭐⭐⭐ in the Lion King Theater. The festival celebrates nature's diversity, with a very talented troupe of singers, dancers, and life-size critters that lead the way to an inspiring sing-along that gets the crowd caught up in the fun. The action is onstage as well as moving around the audience. It is a sight and sound spectacular that shouldn't be missed. Make sure to arrive at least 20 minutes early.

AFRICA

Enter through the town of Harambe, a representation of an African coastal village on the edge of the 21st century. A central marketplace is surrounded by structures built of coral stone and thatched with reed by craftspeople from Africa.

Animal Kingdom doesn't have many rides, so calling **Kilimanjaro Safaris** ⭐⭐⭐ the best may sound like a qualified endorsement. But the animals make it a winner as long as your timing is right. They're scarce at midday most times of year (in cooler months you may get lucky), so *ride this one as close to the park's opening or closing as you can.* Your vehicle is a very large truck that takes you through a simulated African landscape. You might see black rhinos, hippos, crocodiles, antelopes, wildebeests, zebras, or a lion.

Hippos, tapirs, ever-active mole rats, and some other critters are often on the **Pangani Forest Exploration Trail** ⭐⭐ for your viewing, but the real prize is getting a look at the gorillas. They're not always cooperative, especially in hot weather when they tend to spend most of the day in shady areas out of view. Those who come early, stay late, are patient, or make return visits can be rewarded with a close look at some special creatures.

ASIA

Disney's Imagineers did a good job of creating the mythical kingdom of **Anandapur.** The intricately painted artwork is just another example of the lengths that Disney has gone to transport you from the everyday real world to the places of your imagination.

Kali River Rapids ⭐ is a good raft ride—slightly better than Congo River Rapids at Busch Gardens in Tampa, but not quite as good as Popeye & Bluto's Bilge-Rat Barges at Islands of Adventure (p. 454). Its churning water mimics real rapids, and some optical illusions will have you wondering if you're about to drop over the falls. You *will* get wet. *Note:* There's a 38-inch height minimum.

With **Maharajah Jungle Trek** ⭐, Disney keeps its promise to provide up-close views of animals. If you don't show up in the midday heat, you may see Bengal tigers through the thick glass, while nothing but air divides you from dozens of giant fruit bats (wing spans up to 6 ft.) in another habitat.

9 Other Walt Disney World Attractions

TYPHOON LAGOON ★★★

A storm-stranded fishing boat—the *Miss Tilly*—sits atop 95-foot-high Mount Mayday and overlooks this Disney water park. Every few minutes the boat blows its stack, shooting a 50-foot geyser into the air. It has several other attractions.

Castaway Creek's rafts and inner tubes glide along a 2,100-foot-long river that circles most of the park and includes a rainforest, caves, and grottoes. At **Water Works,** jets of water spew from shipwrecked boats.

Ketchakiddie Creek is for 2- to 5-year-old guests. An innovative water playground, it has bubbling fountains to frolic in, mini–water slides, a pint-size "white-water" tubing run, spouting whales and squirting seals, rubbery crocodiles to climb on, grottoes to explore, and waterfalls to loll under.

At **Shark Reef,** guests get free equipment and instructions for a 15-minute swim through this very small snorkeling area that includes a simulated reef populated by parrotfish, rays, and small sharks.

Typhoon Lagoon ★★, the park's 2.75-million-gallon wave pool, launches **big breakers** every 90 seconds. A foghorn warns you when, in case you want to head for cover. Young children can wade in the lagoon's more peaceful tidal pools—**Blustery Bay** or **Whitecap Cove.**

Humunga Kowabunga consists of three 214-foot Mount Mayday slides that propel you down the mountain on a serpentine route through waterfalls and bat caves and past nautical wreckage before depositing you into a bubbling catch pool. *Note:* You must be 48 inches or taller to ride this. **White-Water Rides** at Mount Mayday is the setting for three white-water rafting adventures—**Keelhaul Falls, Mayday Falls,** and **Gangplank Falls**—all offering steep drops coursing through caves and passing lush scenery.

Typhoon Lagoon is open from 10am to 5pm, with extended hours during holiday periods and summer (✆ **407/560-4141;** www.disneyworld.com). A 1-day ticket is $32 for adults, $26 for children 3 to 9.

BLIZZARD BEACH ★★★

This 66-acre "ski resort" in the midst of a tropical lagoon is centered on the 90-foot Mount Gushmore.

Its 2,900-foot-long **Cross Country Creek** is a lazy tube run, but watch out for the cave, where you'll get splashed with melting ice. **Runoff Rapids** offers another tube job. This one lets you careen down one of three twisting, turning runs through semidarkness.

Ski-Patrol Training Camp, designed for preteens, features a rope swing, a T-bar hanging over the water, the wet and slippery **Mogul Mania** slide, and an ice-floe walk along slippery floating icebergs.

Snow Stormers has three flumes descending from the top of Mount Gushmore, following a switchback course through slalom-type gates.

Summit Plummet ★★★ is one of the most breath-defying adventures in any water park. Read every speed, motion, vertical-dip, wedgie, and hold-onto-your-breast-plate warning before hopping on. This starts slow, with a lift ride to the 120-foot summit. But it finishes as the world's fastest body slide—a test of your courage and swimsuit—that virtually goes straight down and has you moving sans vehicle at 60 mph into the catch pool. *Note:* It has a 48-inch height minimum.

Teamboat Springs is this World's longest white-water raft ride, twisting down a 1,200-foot series of rushing waterfalls.

Tike's Peak is a kiddie version of Mount Gushmore. It has short water slides, animals to climb aboard, a snow castle, a squirting ice pond, and a fountain play area for young guests.

Blizzard Beach is open from 10am to 5pm, with extended hours during some holiday periods and summer (© **407/560-3400;** www.disneyworld.com). A 1-day ticket is $32 for adults, $26 for children 3 to 9.

MINIATURE GOLF ⊛

Hippos, ostriches, and alligators decorate the **Fantasia Gardens** course. This course is a good bet for beginners and kids. Seasoned minigolfers probably will prefer the second 18-hole course, **Fantasia Fairways,** which is a scaled-down golf course complete with sand traps, water hazards, tricky putting greens, and holes ranging from 40 to 75 feet—this one can be tricky.

Santa Claus and his elves provide the theme for **Winter Summerland,** which offers two more 18-hole courses. The summer course is pure Florida, from sand castles to surfboards to a visit with Santa on the "Winternet."

Tickets are about $10 for adults and $8 for kids 3 to 9. The courses are open from 10am to 10 or 11pm daily. For information about Fantasia Gardens, call © **407/560-4582.** For information on Winter Summerland, call © **407/560-3000.** Find both on the Internet at **www.disneyworld.com.**

---

10 Touring the Non-Disney Parks: Universal Orlando & SeaWorld

---

There are so many attractions in Orlando (over 95) that it's impossible to see half of them unless you're here for a month. The following should help you finish picking your must-see list.

UNIVERSAL STUDIOS FLORIDA

Even with fast-paced, grown-up rides such as Twister, Terminator, and Men in Black Alien Attack, Universal Studios Florida is fun for kids. And as a plus, it's a working motion-picture and TV studio, so occasionally there's filming being done at Nickelodeon's sound stages or elsewhere in the park. **Hanna-Barbera characters** usually are on hand to greet visitors, as is a talented group of actors portraying a wide range of characters.

TICKET PRICES   A **1-day ticket** costs $59 for adults, $48 for children 3 to 9. A 2-day, two-park unlimited-access pass is $100 for adults, $89 for children 3 to 9; a two-park preferred annual pass will run $169. This includes free parking and has no blackout dates. The two-park annual power pass is less expensive at $99; however, most holidays and a lot of weekends are blacked out and parking is not included.

As with Disney, Universal offers savings on ticket purchases if you purchase them before you leave home. If you buy your tickets online, you can get a 5-day ticket (good for both Universal parks and select CityWalk clubs) for the price of a 2-day ticket ($100 adult, $89 kids ages 3–9). You can pick your tickets up at the front gate of either park or have them sent (for a delivery charge) to your home.

THE FLEXTICKET   The least expensive way to see Universal, SeaWorld, *and* Wet 'n Wild is with a FlexTicket. This pass lets you pay one price for unlimited admission to participating parks during a 14-day period. A four-park pass

---

(*Tips* **Goodbye Kong, Hello Mummy**

Kongfrontation was part of Universal Studios Florida when it opened in 1990, but the ride closed in September 2002 and was replaced as this book went to press with **Revenge of the Mummy.** The new $40-million indoor roller coaster relies on speed, pyrotechnics, and robotics to induce screams as riders hurtle through Egyptian sets, passageways, and tombs in cars that move forward and in reverse. Even the preshow for the waiting victims—riders, I mean riders—lends to the ominous atmosphere and includes several surprise interactive areas and a storyline that plays out as you get closer to boarding the ride.

---

to Universal Studios Florida, Islands of Adventure, Wet 'n Wild, and SeaWorld is $180 for adults and $146 for children 3 to 9. A five-park pass, which adds Busch Gardens in Tampa, is $215 for adults and $180 for kids. The **FlexTicket** can be ordered through Universal (© **800/711-0080** or 407/363-8000; www. universalorlando.com) or the other participating parks.

PARKING   Parking is $8 for cars, light trucks, and vans. Valet is $14.

MAJOR ATTRACTIONS

On **Back to the Future: The Ride** 🌟🌟🌟, you blast through the space-time continuum in a flight simulator built to look like the movie's famous DeLorean car. You twist, turn, dip, and dive—all the while feeling like you're really flying. *Note:* It's bumpy and might not be a good idea if you're prone to dizziness or motion sickness. Riders must be at least 40 inches tall.

Set in a parklike theater-in-the-round, the 25-minute musical, **A Day in the Park with Barney,** stars the Purple One, Baby Bop, and BJ. It uses song, dance, and interactive play to deliver an environmental message. This could be the highlight of the day for preschoolers, though for many adults, it can have serious, brain-eating effects.

Not long after you climb on a San Francisco BART train at **Earthquake— The Big One** 🌟🌟, there's an earthquake that's 8.3 on the Richter scale! As you sit helplessly trapped, concrete slabs collapse around you, a propane truck bursts into flames, a runaway train hurtles your way, and the station floods.

Soar with E.T. on a mission to save his ailing planet at **E.T. Adventure** 🌟, and you'll pass through the forest and into space aboard a bicycle.

The $45-million *Jaws* 🌟 features a boat ride into a 7-acre, 5-million-gallon lagoon, where a 3-ton, 32-foot-long, mechanical great white shark will attack you. You'll truly feel the heat when a wall of flame surrounds your boat as you char-grill the fish.

Buckle up for **Jimmy Neutron's Nicktoon Blast** 🌟🌟, one of Universal's new rides. Jimmy's Rocket Pod hurtles you through hyperspace thanks to sophisticated computer graphics, state-of-the-art ride technology, animation, and programmable motion-based seats. The attraction also features other popular characters, including SpongeBob SquarePants and Rugrats.

In **Men in Black Alien Attack** 🌟🌟🌟, you board a six-passenger cruiser, buzz the streets of New York, and use your "zapper" to splatter up to 120 bug-eyed targets. You have to contend with return fire and light, noise, and clouds of liquid nitrogen (aka fog) that can spin you out of control. Your laser tag–style gun fires infrared bullets. The 4-minute, $70-million ride relies on 360-degree spins rather than speed for its thrill factor. *Note:* Guests must be at least 42 inches tall for this $70 million ride.

At the **Nickelodeon Studios** (★), you'll tour the sound stages where Nick shows are produced. You'll also view concept pilots, visit the kitchen where Gak and green slime are made, and try new Sega video games. This 45-minute behind-the-scenes walking tour is a fun escape from the hustle of the midway. A child volunteer gets slimed, but don't worry—it's only green applesauce or a reasonable facsimile.

Another new ride, **Shrek 4-D** (★) is a 20-minute show that can be seen, heard, felt and smelled thanks to motion simulator technology, OgreVision glasses, and special effects, such as water spritzers. The theater's seats are pneumatic air propulsion nodules that can turn and tilt. I expected more from Universal in the seating effects department, but the movie is definitely worthwhile.

James Cameron, who directed T2, supervised the $60 million **Terminator 2: 3-D Battle Across Time** (★★), which features Arnie and other original cast members (on film). It combines three huge screens with technical effects and live action on stage, including a custom-built Harley and six 8-foot-tall cyberbots. The crisp 3-D effects are among the best in any Orlando park. *Note:* Universal has given this show a PG-13 rating.

Two million cubic feet of air per minute (enough to fill four full-size blimps) create a funnel cloud, five stories tall at **Twister . . . Ride It Out** (★★). The roar of a freight train, at rock-concert decibel level, fills the theater as cars, trucks, and a cow fly by while the audience watches just 20 feet away. Crowds sometimes applaud when it's all over. *Note:* This show also has a PG-13 rating.

Woody Woodpecker's Nuthouse Coaster (★★) is a kiddie coaster that will thrill some moms and dads, too. Although only 30 feet at its peak, it offers quick, banked turns. The ride lasts only about 60 seconds and waits can be 30 minutes or more, but few kids will want to miss the experience. *Note:* The coaster has a 36-inch height minimum.

ISLANDS OF ADVENTURE

At 110 acres, Universal's second theme park (opened in 1999) is the same size as its big brother, Universal Studios Florida, but it seems larger. Roller coasters roar above pedestrian walkways and water rides slice through the park. It is, bar none, *the* Orlando theme park for thrill-ride junkies.

A few words of caution: *Nine of the park's 14 major rides have height restrictions.* Many of the same rides may not be suitable for those who are tall enough but are pregnant or have health problems, physical restrictions, heart, neck, or back problems, or a tendency toward motion sickness.

TICKET PRICES See the "Ticket Prices" information for Universal Studios Florida on p. 452.

THE FLEXITICKET See "The FlexTicket" information for Universal Studios Florida on p. 452.

PARKING Parking is $8 for cars, light trucks, and vans. Valet is $14.

MAJOR ATTRACTIONS
Port of Entry

This park gateway has five shops, four restaurants, and the **Island Skipper Tours,** which ferry passengers to **Jurassic Park.**

Seuss Landing

You will feel as if you have jumped right into the pages of a Dr. Seuss classic as you enter Seuss Landing. The main attractions here are aimed at youngsters, however anyone who loved the good Doctor as a child will enjoy the nostalgic fun.

Seuss fans recognize the giant candy-striped hat looming over the entrance to **The Cat in the Hat** 𝕩𝕩, and probably the chaotic journey. Comparable to, but a lot spunkier than It's a Small World at WDW, The Cat in the Hat puts you in a spinning couch that travels through 18 scenes from the famous book, retelling the tale of a day gone very much awry.

One Fish, Two Fish, Red Fish, Blue Fish 𝕩 is a kiddie charmer similar to the Dumbo ride at WDW (including the ridiculously long line). Here, your controls let you move your funky fish up or down 15 feet as you spin around on an arm attached to a hub. Watch out for "squirt posts," which spray unsuspecting riders who don't follow the rhyme (and some who do).

Forget tradition and hop on **Caro-Seuss-El** 𝕩𝕩𝕩. The not-so-normal carousel gives you a chance to ride whimsical characters from Dr. Seuss, including Cowfish, elephant birds, and Mulligatawnies.

The 19-station **If I Ran the Zoo** 𝕩𝕩 interactive play land features flying water snakes and a chance to tickle the toes of a Seussian animal. Kids can also spin wheels, explore caves, fire water cannons, climb, slide, and otherwise burn off excited energy that most adults can't remember ever having.

Marvel Super Hero Island

Thrill junkies love the twisting, turning, stomach-churning rides on this island filled with building-tall murals of Marvel superheroes.

The original web master is the star of the exceptional, special effects–laden **The Amazing Adventures of Spider-Man** 𝕩𝕩𝕩, which is arguably the best in town. Passengers wearing 3-D glasses squeal as their 12-passenger cars twist and spin, plunge, and soar through a comic-book universe. There's a simulated 400-foot drop that feels an awful lot like the real thing.

Look! Up in the sky! It's a bird, it's a plane . . . uh, it's you falling 150 feet, if you're courageous enough to climb aboard **Doctor Doom's Fearfall** 𝕩. The screams that can be heard far from the ride's entrance add to the anticipation. You're fired to the top, with feet dangling, and dropped in intervals, leaving your stomach at several levels. The fall isn't quite up to Disney's Tower of Terror (p. 448), but it's still frightful. *Note:* Minimum height is 52 inches.

On the **Incredible Hulk Coaster** 𝕩𝕩𝕩, you're launched from a dark tunnel and hurtled into the lower ozone while accelerating from 0 to 40 mph in 2 seconds. You will spin upside down 128 feet from the ground, feel weightless, and careen through the center of the park. Coaster-lovers will be pleased to know this ride, which lasts 2 minutes and 15 seconds, includes seven inversions and two deep drops. *Note:* Riders must be at least 54 inches tall.

Toon Lagoon

More than 150 lifesize cartoon images let you know you've entered an island dedicated to your favorites from the Sunday funnies.

Dudley Do-Right's Ripsaw Falls 𝕩𝕩, which lies under Dudley's staid red hat, has a lot more speed and drop than onlookers think. Six-passenger logs launch you into a 75-foot dip at 50 mph. You *will* get wet on this ride. *Note:* Riders must be 44 inches or taller.

The three-story boat, **Me Ship, The Olive** 𝕩 is family-friendly from bow to stern. Kids can toot whistles, clang bells, or play the organ. Sweet Pea's Playpen is fun for young guests. Adults and kids 6 and up love Cargo Crane, which lets you drench riders on Popeye & Bluto's Bilge-Rat Barges (see below).

Popeye & Bluto's Bilge-Rat Barges ★★ are similar to the rafts at WDW's Kali River Rapids (p. 450), but they're faster and bouncier. Adding to the fun, you'll be squirted by water cannons fired from Me Ship, The Olive (above). The rafts bump and dip 14 feet at one point, as you travel a *c-c-cold* white-water course. You will get *soaked!* Riders must be at least 42 inches tall.

Jurassic Park

All of the basics and some of the high-tech wizardry from Stephen Spielberg's wildly successful films are incorporated in this lushly landscaped tropical locale that includes a replica of the visitor center from the *Jurassic Park* movie.

The **Camp Jurassic** ★★ play area has everything from lava pits with dino bones to a rainforest. Watch out for the spitters that lurk in dark caves. The multilevel play area has plenty of places for kids to crawl, explore, and spend energy. But keep an eye on young ones: It's easy to get confused in the caverns.

Jurassic Park Discovery Center is an amusing, educational pit stop that offers life-size dinosaur replicas and interactive games. The sequencer lets you combine your DNA with a dinosaur's. "Beasaur" allows you to see and hear as "they" did. The highlight is watching a velociraptor "hatch" in the lab.

On the **Jurassic Park River Adventure** ★★, after you enjoy a leisurely raft tour along a faux river, things get dicey. A T-Rex thinks you look like a tasty morsel, and spitters launch "venom" your way. The only way out: an 85-foot plunge in your log-style life raft. It's steep and quick enough to lift your fanny out of the seat. Expect to get wet. *Note:* Guests must be at least 42 inches tall.

The Lost Continent

Universal has created a foreboding mood in this section of the park, whose entrance is marked by menacing stone griffins.

Coaster crazies love **Dueling Dragons** ★★★, an intertwined set of two leg-dangling racers that climb to 125 feet, invert five times, and three times come within 12 inches of each other as the dragons test your bravery and bowels. There's a special (longer!) line for the front seat. *Note:* Riders must be at least 54 inches tall.

The Flying Unicorn ★★ is a small roller coaster that travels through a mythical forest with a fast, corkscrew run sure to earn squeals, but probably not at the risk of losing one's lunch. Riders must be at least 36 inches tall.

Those who notice it have fun at **The Mystic Fountain** ★, a "smart" fountain that especially delights kids. It can "see," "hear," and talk, leading to a lot of kibitzing with those who stand before it and take the time to kibitz back. But be careful: It can squirt you.

The park's best show (given the lack of competition, that's something of a backhanded compliment), **Poseidon's Fury** ★ has changed a couple of times, but still revolves around a battle between the evil Poseidon, god of the sea, and Zeus, king of the gods. Speaking of revolving, you'll pass through a small room that has a 42-foot vortex where 17,500 gallons of water swirl around you, barrel-roll style, and see the gods hurl fireballs at each other.

SEAWORLD

This 200-acre marine-life park explores the mysteries of the deep by combining conservation awareness with entertainment. Over the years it has expanded by adding more rides, additional entertainment venues, and of course more wildlife. While not as large as its neighbors (Universal and Disney), and won't leave you as thoroughly exhausted as its neighbors can, SeaWorld (© **800/327-2424** or 407/351-3600; www.seaworld.com) is a must see for anyone visiting the Orlando area.

TICKET PRICES   A **1-day ticket** costs $53.95 for ages 10 and over, $44.95 for children 3 to 9, plus 6% sales tax. If you purchase tickets online (at home only) at least 7 days in advance from the time of your visit, you can save an additional 10%, making the tickets $49 for an adult and $40.45 for kids 3 to 9.

MULTI-PARK PASSES   For information on the **FlexTicket,** see p. 452. The **Value Ticket** is a 2-day pass good for 1 day at SeaWorld and 1 day at Bush Gardens Tampa Bay. Prices are $89.95 adult and $80.95 kids ages 3 to 9. (This is a savings of up to $18 if tickets are purchased separately).

Multi-day and multi-park **Passports** are also available. These are essentially annual passes, good for either 1 or 2 years, and cover one, two, or three parks, depending on which level you choose—gold, silver, or platinum. The passes start at $90 and run up to $295. For more information, check **www.seaworld.com**.

PARKING   Parking is $8 for cars, light trucks, and vans. For a few dollars more, you can park close to the entrance in a special designated section.

MAJOR ATTRACTIONS

A lovable sea lion and otter, with a supporting cast of walruses and harbor seals, appear in **Clyde & Seamore Take Pirate Island** 🐟, fish-breath comedy with a swashbuckling conservation theme. It's corny, but allot of fun. Just watch out if you enter to close to showtime; the mime entertaining the crowds ahead of time may target you for the audiences amusement.

Taking a cue from Disney Imagineers, SeaWorld created a story to go with its $30 million water coaster, **Journey to Atlantis** 🐟🐟. But what really matters is the drop—a wild plunge from 60 feet with lugelike curves. *Note:* Riders must be at least 42 inches tall, and pregnant women as well as those with heart, neck, or back problems should not ride.

Atlantic bottlenose dolphins perform flips and high jumps, twirl, swim on their backs, and give rides to trainers at **Key West Dolphin Fest.** The tricks are impressive, but it's like any other dolphin show. If you go, see this before Shamu. He puts these little mammals to shame.

Kraken 🐟🐟🐟, SeaWorld's deepest venture into thrill rides, starts slow but ends with speed. Its floor-less, open-sided 32-passenger trains plant you on a pedestal high above the track. You climb 151 feet, fall 144 feet, hit 65 mph, go underground three times (spraying bystanders with water), and make seven loops during a 4,177-foot-long course. It may be the longest 3 minutes and 39 seconds of your life. *Note:* Kraken has a 54-inch height minimum.

Tips Shuttle Service

SeaWorld and **Busch Gardens** (p. 349), both owned by Anheuser-Busch, offer round-trip shuttle service ($10 per person) to get you from Orlando to Tampa and back. The 1½- to 2-hour one-way shuttle runs daily and has five pickup locations in Orlando, including at Universal and on International Drive. The schedule allows for about 7 hours at Busch Gardens. The service is free if you have a FlexTicket. Call © **800/221-1339** for details.

In **Manatees: The Last Generation?** ⭐, underwater viewing stations, innovative cinema techniques, and interactive displays combine for a tribute to these gentle marine mammals. While this isn't as good as seeing them in the wild, it's as close as most folks get, and it's a much roomier habitat than the tight quarters their kin have at Epcot's The Living Seas (p. 444).

You are transported by moving sidewalk through Arctic and Antarctic displays at **Penguin Encounter.** You'll get a glimpse of penguins as they preen, socialize, and swim at bullet speed in their 22°F (−5°C) habitat. You'll also see puffins and murres in a similar, separate area. While it gives you a nice view of the penguins (and they are always a hit with the kids) the surroundings about the viewing area leave a bit to be desired.

The 3-acre **Shamu's Happy Harbor** ⭐ play area has a four-story net tower with a 35-foot-high crow's nest, water cannons, remote-controlled vehicles, nine slides, a submarine, and a water maze. Most kids relish the freedom of running, jumping, and climbing (and, of course, getting wet) after hearing "don't wander too far away from us" all day long.

Everyone comes to SeaWorld to see Shamu and his friends—the stars of the well-choreographed show, **The Shamu Adventure** ⭐⭐⭐. When you hear the warning that Hurricane Shamu is approaching, it's time for those sitting in the first 14 rows to hightail it. Those who don't are drenched with *icy water* as the orcas race around the pool, creating a huge wave that rolls over the edge and into the audience.

More than 220 species of aquatic predators reside in the park's **Shark Encounter** ⭐⭐ attraction. The pools out front have small sharks and rays (feeding isn't allowed). The interior aquariums have big eels, poisonous lionfish, menacing barracudas, and bug-eyed pufferfish.

Enveloping guests in the beauty, exhilaration, and danger of a polar expedition, **Wild Arctic** ⭐ combines a high-definition adventure film with flight-simulator technology to display breathtaking Arctic panoramas. After a hazardous flight over the frozen north, visitors emerge into an exhibit where you can see a playful polar bear, beluga whales, and walruses. Kids and those prone to motion sickness may find the ride bumpy. There's a separate line if you want to skip the flight.

A prime example of SeaWorld's ongoing expansion is **The Waterfront,** a 5-acre themed seaport village offering a variety of desperately needed restaurants, shops, and shows for all to enjoy.

DINING AT SEAWORLD

The park offers a trio of entertaining dining experiences. **Dine with Shamu** ($32 adults, $18 kids ages 3–9) offers visitors the experience of seeing Shamu up close (inside an area usually restricted to trainers during normal hours) while enjoying a buffet style meal. **Makahiki Luau** offers both island-style entertainment as well as a luau-style meal. The cost is $43 adults, $28 kids 3 to 9 (theme park admission is *not* required). The new **Sharks Underwater Grill** is an upscale restaurant geared mostly to adults that allows up-close viewing of sharks through a wall of glass. Entrees ($16–$27) are on the pricey side for park dining, but the food is very good and not the usual park blah. The interesting menu features such dishes as coconut-crusted chicken spears, Caribbean seafood ragout, herb crusted tuna, and scallops and shrimp with mango-papaya salsa.

DISCOVERY COVE: A DOLPHIN ENCOUNTER

Anheuser-Busch spent $100 million building SeaWorld's sister park, which debuted in 2000. Prices vary seasonally, but range from $229 to $249 per person (plus 6% sales tax) for ages 6 and up if you want to swim with the dolphins; and $129 to $149 if you will forego the dolphin swim. Double-check prices when you make your reservations (required to enter the park).

The **dolphin encounter** ★★★ stars an amazing group of 28 of these mammals. They do tricks and take guests on brief but thrilling rides. The experience lasts 90 minutes, 35 to 40 minutes of which is spent in the lagoon with a dolphin. The rest is a classroom experience on these remarkable mammals.

Here's what you get for your money, with or without the dolphin encounter:

- A limit of *no more than 1,000 other guests a day.* (The average daily attendance at Disney's Magic Kingdom is 41,000.) This ensures your experience will be more relaxing and private—which is really part of what you are paying for in the first place anyway.
- Lunch, a towel, locker, sunscreen, snorkeling gear including a flotation vest, a souvenir photo, and free parking are also part of the deal.
- Other 9am-to-5:30pm activities include a chance to swim near (but on the other side of Plexiglas from) **barracudas and black-tip sharks.** There are no barriers, however, between you and the gentle rays and brightly colored tropical fish in the 1.3 million-gallon coral reef. The 3,300-foot-long Tropical River is a great place to swim or float in a mild current—it goes through a cave, two waterfalls, and a 100-foot-long, 30-foot-high aviary where you can take a stroll, becoming a human perch. There also are beaches for tanning.
- Seven consecutive days of **unlimited admission** to either SeaWorld *or* Busch Gardens. For an additional $30 per person, you can upgrade this option to 14 days of unlimited admission to both SeaWorld *and* Busch Gardens.

Get more information on Discovery Cove by calling © **877/434-7268** or go to **www.discoverycove.com**. If you want to try it, make a reservation as far in advance as possible. Despite the price, it reaches its capacity almost every day.

11 Other Area Attractions

We've covered the monster parks. Now, we're going to explore some of the best smaller attractions. Many of these require less than a day (or a fortune) to see, so we'll note how much time and money to budget. **Add 6.5% sales tax** to the prices below unless otherwise noted.

IN KISSIMMEE

Kissimmee's tourist strip is 10 to 15 minutes west of Disney.

Gatorland ★   Founded in 1949 with only a handful of alligators living in huts and pens, Gatorland now houses thousands of alligators and crocodiles on its 70-acre spread. The four shows here are *Gator Wrestlin'*, which is more of an environmental awareness program; the *Gator Jumparoo,* in which one of the big reptiles lunges 4 or 5 feet out of the water to snatch a long-dead chicken from a trainer's hand; *Up Close Encounters,* which features a variety of wildlife, including some venomous snakes; and *Jungle Crocs of the World,* which showcases the toothy reptiles. The park has an open-air restaurant where you can try smoked gator ribs and nuggets and a shop where you can buy gator leather products. (Gatorland operates a breeding farm for meat and hides.) Younger guests enjoy the park's water play area and petting zoo.

14501 S. Orange Blossom Trail (U.S. 441; between Osceola Pkwy. and Hunter's Creek Blvd.). © 800/393-5297 or 407/855-5496. www.gatorland.com. Admission $20 adults, $9.95 children 3–12 (plus tax). Open daily at 9am; closing times vary. Free parking. From I-4, take the Osceola Pkwy. exit east to U.S. 17/92/441 and go left/north. Gatorland is 1½ miles on the right.

ON INTERNATIONAL DRIVE

Like Kissimmee attractions, these are a 10- to 15-minute drive from the Disney area and 5 to 10 minutes from Universal Orlando.

Wet 'n Wild ★★ Orlando's favorite non-Disney water park offers 25 acres of fun including: **Fuji Flyer,** a six-story, four-passenger toboggan run through 450 feet of banked curves; **The Surge,** one of the longest (580 ft. of curves) and fastest multipassenger tube rides in the Southeast; and **Black Hole,** a two-person, spaceship-style raft that makes a 500-foot, twisting, turning voyage through darkness (all three require that kids 36–48 in. tall be accompanied by an adult). You also can ride **Raging Rapids,** a simulated white-water run with a waterfall plunge; **Blue Niagara,** a 300-foot-long, six-story loop-and-dipster that also has a plunge (48-in. height minimum); **Knee Ski,** a cable-operated knee-boarding course that's open in warm-weather months only (56-in. height minimum); and **Mach 5,** a trio of twisting, turning flumes. The park also has a large kids' area with miniversions of the big rides. Plan on a full day here.

In addition to the admission prices below, Wet 'n Wild is part of the multi-day **FlexTicket package** that includes admission to Universal Orlando (which owns this attraction), SeaWorld, and Busch Gardens in Tampa. See "The FlexTicket" on p. 452 for details and prices.

6200 International Dr. (at Universal Blvd.). ℂ 800/992-9453 or 407/351-1800. www.wetnwild.com. Admission $35.25 adults, $26.95 children 3–9. Hours vary seasonally, weather permitting. You can rent tubes ($4), towels ($2), and lockers ($5); all require an additional $2 deposit refundable upon return. Parking is $6 for cars, light trucks, and vans. From I-4, take the Universal Orlando exit and follow the signs.

ELSEWHERE IN ORLANDO

These attractions are about a 30-minute drive from the Disney area.

Orlando Museum of Art ★ This local heavyweight handles some of the most prestigious traveling exhibits in the nation. It hosts special exhibits throughout the year, but even if you miss one it's worth a stop to see the rotating permanent collection of 19th- and 20th-century American art, pre-Columbian art dating from 1200 B.C. to A.D. 1500, and African art. Allow 2 to 3 hours.

2416 N. Mills Ave. (in Loch Haven Park). ℂ 407/896-4231. www.omart.org. Admission $12 adults, $11 seniors and students, $5 children 7–18. Tues–Fri 10am–4pm; Sat–Sun noon–4pm. Free parking. Take the I-4 Princeton St. exit east and follow signs to Loch Haven Park.

Orlando Science Center ★★ *Finds* The four-story center has 10 exhibit halls that explore everything from swamps to the plains of Mars. One of the big attractions is the **Dr. Phillips CineDome,** a 310-seat theater that presents films, planetarium shows, and laser-light displays. **KidsTown** has a pint-size park and construction site. **Science City** includes a power plant, and **123 Math Avenue** uses puzzles and other things to make learning fun. Allow 3 to 4 hours.

777 E. Princeton St. (between Orange and Mills aves., in Loch Haven Park). ℂ 888/672-4386 or 407/514-2000. www.osc.org. Admission (includes exhibits, Cinedome film, and planetarium show) $15 adults, $14 seniors 55 and older, $10 children 3–11. Tues–Thurs 9am–5pm; Fri–Sat 9am–9pm; Sun noon–5pm. Parking available in a garage across the street for $3.50. Take the I-4 Princeton St. exit east and cross Orange Ave.

12 Affordable Sports & Recreational Activities

If you want some exercise other than walking the parks, Walt Disney World and the surrounding areas have plenty of recreational options. Most of the following are open to everyone, no matter where you're staying (we note the exceptions below).

BICYCLING Bike rentals (single and multispeed bikes for adults, tandems, baby seats, and children's bikes including those equipped with training wheels) are available from the **Bike Barn** (✆ 407/824-2742) at Fort Wilderness Resort and Campground. Rates are $8 per hour, $22 per day (including tax). Fort Wilderness offers good bike trails.

BOATING   With a ton of man-made lakes and lagoons, WDW owns a navy of pleasure boats. **Capt. Jack's** at Downtown Disney rents Water Sprites and canopy boats ($23–$37 per half-hour). For information call ✆ **407/828-2204.**

The **Bike Barn** at Fort Wilderness (✆ **407/824-2742**) rents canoes and paddleboats ($6.50 per half-hour, $12 per hour).

GOLF   Disney operates five 18-hole, par-72 golf courses and one 9-hole, par-36 walking course. The rates are $130 to $175 per 18-hole round for resort guests ($10 more if you're not staying at a WDW property). For tee times and information, call ✆ **407/824-2270** up to 7 days in advance (up to 30 days for guests of the Disney resort and official properties). Call ✆ **407/934-7639** about golf packages.

The **Grand Cypress Golf Club** (✆ **800/233-1234;** www.grandcypress.com) at the **Hyatt Regency Grand Cypress Resort** is one of the best in the country. Its four Jack Nicklaus–designed courses offer 45 challenging holes. The best of the lot is the New Course, an 18-hole tribute to the venerable Old Course at St. Andrews. The courses are open to guests only and greens fees run $115 to $175, depending on the season. Golf packages are available.

Beyond Mickey's shadow, **Golfpac** (✆ **888/848-8941** or 407/260-2288; www.golfpacinc.com) is an organization that packages golf with accommodations and arranges tee times at more than 40 Orlando-area courses. **Tee Times USA** (✆ **888/465-3356;** www.teetimesusa.com) and **Florida Golfing** (✆ **866/833-2663;** www.floridagolfing.com) are reservation services that offer packages and course information.

HORSEBACK RIDING   **Disney's Fort Wilderness** offers 45-minute guided trail rides daily. The cost is $32 per person. Children must be at least 9. Maximum weight limit is 250 pounds. For information, call ✆ **407/824-2832.**

The **Villas of Grand Cypresses' Equestrian Center** (✆ **800/835-7377** or 407/239-1938; www.grandcypress.com) offers 45-minute walk-trot trail rides for $45. A 30-minute private lesson is $55; an hour lesson is $100.

SWIMMING   The **YMCA Aquatic Center** has a full fitness center, racquetball courts, and an indoor Olympic-size pool. Admission is $10 per person, $25 for families. It's at 8422 International Dr. (✆ **407/363-1911**).

TENNIS   There are 26 tennis courts (most of them lighted) scattered throughout the Disney properties. Most are free and open to resort guests only on a first-come, first-served basis. Call ✆ **407/939-7529** to make reservations or for more information. The Racquet Club at the Contemporary Resort ($15 an hour per court) has six clay courts, all lighted for evening play, and offers lessons ($40–$70, depending on duration of lesson).

SPECTATOR SPORTS
BASEBALL   The **Atlanta Braves** play 18 spring-training games at Disney's Wide World of Sports beginning in early March. Tickets are $12 to $20. Call ✆ **407/839-3900** or see **www.atlantabraves.com** for more information. From April to September, the **Orlando Rays,** the Tampa Bay Devil Rays' Class AA Southern League affiliate, play their 70 home games at the same complex. Tickets through **Ticketmaster** (✆ **407/839-3900**) sell for $5 to $8.

BASKETBALL   The **TD Waterhouse Centre,** 600 W. Amelia St., between I-4 and Parramore Avenue, is the home of the **Orlando Magic,** which plays 41 of its regular season games here from October to April. Call ℂ **407/896-2442** or check out **www.nba.com/magic.** Single-game tickets are $25 to $175.

13 Shopping

I've driven all the way up from Miami on a Saturday just to go shopping in Orlando. The outlets here rock (see below) and offer discounts unlike anything down south.

On International Drive, look for **Pointe Orlando,** 9101 International Dr. (ℂ **407/248-2838;** www.pointeorlandofl.com), an open-air complex with three dozen stores including Tommy Hilfiger and Abecrombie and Fitch.

There are several factory outlets, but their publicized discounts of 25% to 75% are often a mirage. You can avoid being taken by knowing suggested retail prices, so you can decide whether you're making a killing. **Belz Factory Outlet World,** 5401 W. Oak Ridge Rd. (at the north end of International Dr.; ℂ **407/354-0126;** www.belz.com), and **Orlando Premium Outlets,** 8200 Vineland Ave. (ℂ **407/ 238-7787;** www.PremiumOutlets.com), and **Lake Buena Vista Factory Stores,** 155591 Apopka-Vineland Rd. (ℂ **407/238-9301;** www.lbvfs.com), are the better ones, with the Premium Outlets having the best variety and nicest atmosphere to shop in.

Mall at Millenia, 4200 Conroy Rd. (ℂ **407/363-3555;** www.mallatmillenia. com), is the new upscale kid on the block (Bloomingdale's, Neiman Marcus, Tiffany), while **Florida Mall,** 8001 S. Orange Blossom Trail (ℂ **407/851-6255;** www.shopsimon.com), has Saks, Dillards, and more.

Old-stuff buffs love **Antique Row** on Orange Avenue in downtown Orlando. This collection of two-dozen shops is about as far away as you can get from the manufactured fun of Disney. Headliners include **Flo's Attic** (ℂ **407/895-1800;** www.flosattic.net), which sells traditional antiques.

14 Walt Disney World & Orlando After Dark

Central Florida has plenty for night owls to do. Parties last into the wee hours at **Pleasure Island, Downtown Disney, CityWalk,** and other hot spots.

DISNEY DINNER SHOWS

Hoop-Dee-Doo Musical Revue ⍟ *(Moments*   As WDW's most popular show, Hoop-Dee-Doo requires Priority Seating reservations, which should be made as early as possible. The reward: You can feast on an all-you-can-eat barbecue. While you stuff yourself silly, performers in 1890s garb lead you in a footstomping, hand-clapping high-energy show that includes jokes you haven't heard since second grade.

3520 N. Fort Wilderness Trail (at WDW's Fort Wilderness Resort and Campground). ℂ 407/939-3463. www.disneyworld.com. Reservations required. Adults $49, kids 3–11 $25, including tax and gratuity. Free parking. Show times 5, 7:15, and 9:30pm daily.

Spirit of Aloha Dinner Show *(Moments*   While not quite as much in demand as the Hoop-Dee-Doo, the Polynesian Resort presents a delightful (and new) 2-hour show that's like a big neighborhood party. This Polynesian luau features Tahitian, Samoan, and Hawaiian singers, drummers, and dancers who entertain you while you feast on a menu that includes tropical appetizers, Lanai roasted chicken, Polynesian wild rice, South Seas vegetables, dessert, wine, beer and other beverages. It all takes place 5 nights a week in an open-air theater (dress for nighttime weather).

1600 Seven Seas Dr. (at Disney's Polynesian Resort). © 407/939-3463. www.disneyworld.com. Reservations required. Adults $49, kids 3–11 $25, including tax and gratuity. Free parking. Show times 5:15 and 8pm Tues–Sat.

ENTERTAINMENT MECCAS
AT DISNEY

PLEASURE ISLAND   This 6-acre complex has clubs, restaurants, shops, and movie theaters where during the day you can enjoy for free whatever's open (only the restaurants). At night, for one admission price ($21 plus tax; © **407/939-2648**), you can go club-hopping and rock into the wee hours every night of the week. The mood is festive, especially at midnight, when the New Year's Eve party gets started. *Note:* At night, this is primarily an adult venue. Here's the lineup:

Adventurers Club 🎭🎭   The most unique of Pleasure Island's clubs, Adventurers occupies a multistory building chock-full of artifacts like 1940s aviation photos, hunting trophies, shrunken heads, Buddhas, and a mounted "yakoose"—a half yak, half moose that occasionally speaks, whether you've been drinking or not. In the Mask Room, the 100 or so masks move their eyes, jeer, and make bizarre pronouncements. Improv comedy takes place throughout the evening in the salon.

BET Soundstage 🎭   This club grooves with traditional R&B and the rhyme of hip-hop. If you like the BET Cable Network, you'll love it. Boogie on an expansive dance floor or kick back on the terrace. The club sometimes has concerts for a separate charge. Call © **407/934-7666.**

Mannequins Dance Palace 🎭🎭   Housed in a vast dance hall with a small-town movie-house facade, Mannequins is supposed to be a converted mannequin warehouse (remember, you're still in Disney World). This high-energy club has a big, rotating dance floor, and its popularity makes it one of the toughest nightspots to get into. It offers three levels of bars and hangout space that are festooned with elaborately costumed mannequins and moving scenery suspended from the overhead rigging. A deejay plays contemporary tunes filtered through speakers that could wake the dead, and there are high-tech lighting effects. You must be 21 to get in, and they're *very* serious about it.

The Pleasure Island Jazz Company   This big, barnlike club features contemporary and traditional live jazz. Most performers are locals, but about once a month there's a big name, such as Kenny Rankin or Maynard Ferguson.

⌒Moments   Not Your Ordinary Circus

Cirque du Soleil, the famous no-animals circus in Downtown Disney West Side, seems to put all 64 performers onstage at once in the trampoline routine. Trapeze artists, high-wire walkers, an aerial gymnast, a strongman, and two zany clowns cement a show called *La Nouba* 🎭🎭🎭 (it means "live it up") into a five-star, multiact performance.

But, in a world of pricey attractions, this is one of the priciest. There are two ticket categories: $87 for adults and $52 for kids 3 to 9 (including tax) for center of the theater seats; $77 and $47, respectively, to the right and left of the stage. The 90-minute shows are at 6 and 9pm; days rotate. Call © **407/939-7600** or check out **www.cirquedusoleil.com** for details.

Rock 'n' Roll Beach Club Live bands play classic rock from the 1960s through the 1990s. There are bars on all three floors. The first level has a dance floor; the others offer arcade-style games, pizza, and more.

Motion Pleasure Island's newest dance club is a hyperactive joint that features Top-40 tunes and alternative rock, and uses moody blue lighting to halfway convey the sensation that you're dancing the night away in space.

DOWNTOWN DISNEY WEST SIDE

House of Blues This three-tier, barnlike building may be a little difficult for those with disabilities to maneuver in, but there really isn't a bad seat in the house. The atmosphere is dark, perfect for the oft-featured bluesy sounds that raise the rafters. The dance floor is big enough to boogie without doing the bump with a stranger, and food is served. ℂ 407/934-2583. www.hob.com. Cover charges vary.

CITYWALK

Located between Islands of Adventure and Universal Studios Florida, this 30-acre club-and-restaurant district (ℂ **407/363-8000;** www.citywalk.com) is five times larger than Pleasure Island. Alcohol is prominently featured, so an adult should accompany all children and free-flowing peers.

You can walk the district for free or visit individual clubs for the cover charges in the following listings. CityWalk also offers two **party passes.** A pass to all clubs costs $8.95 plus tax. For $12 plus tax, you get a club pass and a movie at Universal Cineplex (ℂ **407/354-5998**). *Note:* Daytime parking in the Universal Orlando garages costs $8, but parking is free after 6pm.

Bob Marley—A Tribute to Freedom This hybrid bar/restaurant has a party atmosphere that makes the food more appealing as the night wears on. Jamaican food is served amid portraits of the original Rastamon. Reggae bands, local and national, perform on a microdot-size stage. The hours are daily from 4pm to 2am. ℂ 407/224-2262. Cover $5 after 8pm, more on special nights. Must be 21 to enter after 10pm.

CityJazz The cover includes the **Downbeat Jazz Hall of Fame** (which has memorabilia from Louie Armstrong and other greats) as well as the **Thelonious Monk Institute of Jazz,** a performance venue that's also the site of jazz workshops. The two-story, 10,500-square-foot building has more than 500 pieces of memorabilia representing Dixieland, swing, bebop, and jazz and is open Sunday through Thursday from 8pm to 1am and Friday and Saturday from 7pm to 2am. ℂ 407/224-2189. Cover $5 (more for special events). Must be 18 to enter.

the groove This club is Universal's answer to Mannequins at Pleasure Island, though it's not quite as popular and, therefore, has less of a waiting list. There's a high-tech sound system that will blow your hair back and a spacious dance floor in a room gleaming with chrome. A deejay plays tunes most nights, featuring the latest in hip-hop, jazz-fusion, techno, and alternative music. Bands occasionally play the house, too. The hours are Sunday through Wednesday from 9pm to 2am and Thursday through Saturday from 9pm to 3am. ℂ 407/363-8000. Cover $5. Must be 21 to get in.

Jimmy Buffett's Margaritaville Music from the maestro drifts through the building, and live tunes are performed on a small stage inside later in the evening. A Buffett sound-alike also strums on the back porch. Inside, there are three themed bars. If you opt for dinner among the palm trees, go for the true Key West experience. Early in the day that means a cheeseburger; later, it's one of several kinds of fish. Open daily from 11am to 2am. $\textit{C}$ 407/224-2155. Cover $5 after 10pm.

Latin Quarter   This two-level restaurant/nightclub offers you a chance to absorb the salsa-and-samba culture and cuisine of 21 Latin nations. If you don't know how to move your hips, there's a dance instructor to lend a hand. The music ranges from merengue to Latin rock. The sound system is loud enough to blow you into the next county, but before that happens you can leave on your own to peruse a Latin American art gallery. Open Saturday and Sunday from noon to 2am and Monday through Friday from 5pm to 2am. The restaurant closes at 10pm and the nightclub hours are 10pm to 2am. $\textit{C}$ 407/363-5922. Cover $5–$10 Thurs–Sat after 10pm.

Pat O'Brien's *Overrated*   Just like the French Quarter, which is home to the original Patty O's, drinking, drinking, and more drinking are the highlights here. Enjoy dueling Baby Grands and a flame-throwing fountain while you suck down the drink of the Big Easy, a Hurricane. Open daily from 4pm to 2am. $\textit{C}$ 407/363-8000. Cover $5 after 9pm. Must be 21 to enter.

12

Northeast Florida

When driving through the elongated state of Florida, many people make the grave mistake of gunning their engines and jetting through the Northeast part of the state without as much as a single stop beyond the Cracker Barrels, Denny's, and gas stations lining the highways. Thankfully, Juan Ponce de León actually made the *fortunate* mistake of playing accidental tourist and discovering just how magnificent the Northeast part of the state truly is. You would do well to explore in his footsteps.

Northeast Florida traces its roots back to 1513, when the wanderlusty Spaniard Juan Ponce de León, who later undertook a misguided quest for the Fountain of Youth, sighted this coast and landed somewhere between present-day Jacksonville and Cape Canaveral. (He was a bit off course—he meant to land in what is now Bimini—but who can blame a guy who didn't have GPS?) Observing the land's lush foliage, he named it *La Florida,* or "the flowery land." In 1565, the Spanish established a colony at St. Augustine, a city that remains the country's oldest continuous settlement.

Not much, if anything at all, has changed in St. Augustine (in a wonderful way). The streets of the restored Old City look much as they did in Spanish times. But not everything in Northeast Florida is antiquated.

To the south there's the Jetsonian "Space Coast," where rockets blast off from the Kennedy Space Center at Cape Canaveral. In nearby Cocoa Beach you can witness the retro-fabulous phenomenon of surfers riding the rather sizeable waves. And in Daytona Beach, brace yourself for the deafening roar of the stock cars and motorbikes that make this beach town the "World Center of Racing." And don't blink, because you wouldn't want to miss Daytona's other pop cultural phenom, known as the MTV Spring Break bikini crowd.

A far cry from spring breakers on a budget, if you go north along the coast, you'll come to the monied haven of Ponte Vedra Beach, where golf definitely takes precedence over manual labor. Over in Jacksonville, Florida's largest metropolis and a thriving port city and naval base, experience a little taste of so-called city life before retreating back to the beach.

Up near the Georgia border, cross a bridge to Amelia Island, where you'll discover exclusive resorts taking full advantage of 13 miles of beautiful beaches. Amelia's Victorian-era town, Fernandina Beach, is yet another throwback to the past, helping to further render the Northeast region of Florida a fascinating juxtaposition of old, new, and somewhere delightfully in between. However you perceive it, just make sure not to make the mistake of missing it. After all, Ponce de León didn't blow off Bimini for nothing, you know.

1 Cocoa Beach, Cape Canaveral, the Kennedy Space Center & Melbourne ⊀

46 miles SE of Orlando, 186 miles N of Miami, 65 miles S of Daytona

The "Space Coast," the area around Cape Canaveral, was once a sleepy place where city dwellers escaped the crowds from the exploding urban centers of Miami and Jacksonville. But then came the NASA space program. Today, the region produces and accommodates its own crowds, especially hordes of tourists who come to visit the Kennedy Space Center and enjoy the area's 72 miles of beaches (this is, after all, the closest beach to Orlando's mega-attractions) and excellent fishing, surfing, and golfing.

Thanks to NASA, this is also a prime destination for nature lovers. The space agency originally took over much more land than it needed to launch rockets. Rather than sell off the unused portions, it turned them over to the Canaveral National Seashore and the Merritt Island National Wildlife Refuge (www.nbbd.com/godo/minwr), which have preserved these areas in their pristine natural states.

A handful of Caribbean-bound cruise ships also depart from the man-made Port Canaveral, and the number has grown slowly over the years. The south side of the port is lined with seafood restaurants and marinas, which serve as home base for gambling ships and the area's deep-sea charter and group fishing boats.

ESSENTIALS

GETTING THERE The nearest airport is **Melbourne International Airport** (© **321/723-6227;** www.mlbair.com), 22 miles south of Cocoa Beach, which is served by **Continental** (© **800/525-0280;** www.continental.com) and **Delta** (© **800/221-1212;** www.delta.com). **Orlando International Airport,** about 35 miles to the west, is a much larger hub with many more flight options and generally less expensive fares (p. 409). It's an easy 45-minute drive from the Orlando airport to the beaches via the Beeline Expressway (Fla. 528, a toll road)—it can take almost that long from the Melbourne airport, where **Avis, Budget, Hertz,** and **National** have car-rental desks. **The Melbourne Airport Shuttle** (© **321/724-1600**) will take you from the Melbourne airport to most local destinations for about $10 to $20 per person.

VISITOR INFORMATION For information about the area, contact the **Florida Space Coast Office of Tourism/Brevard County Tourist Development Council,** 8810 Astronaut Blvd., Suite 102, Cape Canaveral, FL 32920 (© **800/872-1969** or 321/868-1126; www.space-coast.com). The office is in the Sheldon Cove building, on Fla. A1A a block north of Central Boulevard, and is open Monday through Friday from 8am to 5pm.

The office also operates an information booth at the Kennedy Space Center Visitor Complex (see below).

GETTING AROUND A car is essential in this area. If you're not coming by car, you can rent one at the airport. **Space Coast Area Transit** (© **321/633-1878;** www.ridescat.com) operates buses ($1 adults, 50¢ seniors and students), but routes tend to be circuitous and therefore extremely time-consuming.

ATTRACTIONS

In addition to the attraction below, Brevard College's **Astronaut Memorial Planetarium and Observatory,** 1519 Clearlake Rd., Cocoa Beach (© **321/634-3732;** www.brevardcc.edu/planet), south of Fla. 528, has its own International Hall of

468 CHAPTER 12 · NORTHEAST FLORIDA

Cheap Thrills: What to See & Do for Free (or Almost) in Northeast Florida

- **Watch a space shuttle blast off from Cape Canaveral.** Although you'll have to pay to get in, the best place to watch the space shuttles blasting off from Cape Canaveral is at the Kennedy Space Center itself (© **321/449-4444**). On the other hand, it costs not a cent to watch from the causeways leading to the islands, and on U.S. 1 as it skirts the waterfront in Titusville. Call © **321/867-4636** or check NASA's official website (www.ksc.nasa.gov) for a schedule of upcoming take-offs. You can buy launch tickets at the Kennedy Space Center Visitor Complex or online at www.ksctickets.com.

- **Contemplate skinny dipping at Playalinda Beach.** It isn't legal any-more, but you'll feel like stripping it all off on beautiful and deserted **Playalinda Beach,** in the Canaveral National Seashore (© **321/267-1110**), a protected 13-mile stretch of barrier-island beach backed by cabbage palms, sea grapes, palmettos, marshes, and Mosquito Lagoon. The $5 per vehicle, $1 per pedestrian or cyclist admission is a small price to pay to visit this wild beach. The seashore and the adjacent **Merritt Island National Wildlife Refuge** (© **321/861-0667**) also are great places to see herons, egrets, ibises, and other birds, plus giant sea turtles nesting from May to August.

- **Vroom around Daytona International Speedway.** You can't really drive your own race car around Daytona Beach's world center of racing, but the next best thing is the action-packed IMAX film *Daytona USA* (© **386/947-6800**). You'll think you're in the winner's seat of the Day-tona 500. You also can participate in a pit stop on a NASCAR Winston Cup stock car, see the actual winning car still covered in track dust, talk via video with favorite competitors, and play radio or television announcer by calling the finish of a race. Compared to admissions to other Florida theme parks, Daytona USA charges a reasonable $16 for adults, $13 for seniors, and $8 for children 6 to 12. Kids 5 and under get in free.

Space Explorers, but its big attractions are sound and light shows in the planetar-ium. Call or check the website for schedules and prices.

John F. Kennedy Space Center ★★★ Whether you're a space buff or not, you'll appreciate the sheer grandeur of the facilities and technological achieve-ments displayed at NASA's primary space-launch facility. Astronauts departed Earth at this site in 1969 en route to the most famous "small step" in history—humankind's first walk on the moon—and today's space shuttles still regularly lift off from here on their latest missions.

Since all roads other than Fla. 405 and Fla. 3 are closed to the public in the space center, you must begin your visit at the **Kennedy Space Center Visitor Complex.** A bit like a themed amusement park, this privately operated complex has been undergoing an ambitious $130 million renovation and expansion, so check to see that they have not changed their tours and exhibits before going. Call beforehand to see what's happening on the day you intend to be here, and

- **Relive the past in America's oldest city.** Older than either Jamestown or Plymouth Rock, St. Augustine's restored Spanish Quarter offers a look back to America's very beginnings. You'll have to pay a few dollars to enter sites such as the nation's oldest store and oldest jail, but you can freely stroll these narrow streets for hours, poking your head into antiques shops, peering into lush yards surrounding ancient buildings, and watching the boats out on the Matanzas River. Or for $16 adults, $5 children, you can ride around town on a trolley, train, or horse-drawn carriage.

- **Stroll along a lazy river.** City leaders have developed appealing, park-like commercial complexes on the banks of the broad, slow-moving St. Johns River. On the north stands **Jacksonville Landing** (© 904/353-1188), a 6-acre dining/shopping/entertainment center with a small maritime museum, more than 65 shops, about half a dozen full-service restaurants, and an inexpensive food court with indoor and outdoor seating overlooking the river. The Landing is the scene of special events such as arts festivals and free outdoor rock, blues, country, and jazz concerts. On the opposite shore, you can stroll along the 1¼-mile wooden zigzag boardwalk of the Southbank Riverwalk.

- **Visit a new breed of national park.** Jacksonville's Timucuan Ecological and Historic Preserve is not your usual national park. For one thing, it's a vast, intriguing system of sites on both sides of the St. Johns River. And for another, admission is free. The prime attraction is the **Fort Carolina National Memorial** (© 904/641-7155), the site of a 16th-century French Huguenot settlement wiped out by the Spanish who landed at St. Augustine. On the north side of the river, the **Zephaniah Kingsley Plantation** (© 904/251-3537) was an early 19th-century manse owned by Zephaniah Kingsley, a white man who married a Senegalese woman he once owned and then moved his family to Haiti to escape racism at home. You can make a donation, but admission to the park is free.

arrive early to plan your visit. You'll need at least 2 hours to see the highlights on the bus tour through the space center, up to 5 hours if you linger at the stops along the way, and a full day to see and do everything here. Buy a copy of the *Official Tour Book;* it's easier to use than the rental cassette tapes, and you can take it home as a colorful souvenir (though some of our readers think you don't need any extra information because the bus tours are narrated and the exhibits have good descriptions).

The visitor complex has real NASA rockets and the actual Mercury Mission Control Room from the 1960s. Exhibits look at early space exploration and where it's going in the new millennium. There are space-related hands-on activities aimed at kids, a daily "Encounter" with a real astronaut, several dining venues, and a shop selling a variety of space memorabilia and souvenirs. IMAX movies shown on five-and-a-half-story-high screens are informative and entertaining.

While you could spend your entire day at the visitor complex, you must take a **KSC Tour** to see the actual space center where rockets and shuttles are prepared and launched. Plan to take the bus tour early in your visit (the lines for these are brutal) and be sure to hit the restrooms before boarding the bus—there's only one out on the tour. The buses depart every 10 minutes or so, and you can reboard as you wish. They stop at the LC-39 Observation Gantry, with a dramatic 360-degree view over launch pads where space shuttles blast off; the International Space Station Center, where scientists and engineers prepare additions to the space station now in orbit; and the Apollo/Saturn V Center, which includes artifacts, photos, films, interactive exhibits, and the 363-foot-tall Saturn V, the most powerful rocket ever launched by the United States. The bus tour was the low point of our recent visit. Though the commentary on the bus itself was interesting, the stops themselves were relatively dull and waiting to board and reboard buses was more than frustrating (though touching a moon rock at the Apollo/Saturn V Center was pretty cool): Stick around the visitor's center if you're short on time.

Don't miss the Astronaut Memorial, a moving black-granite monument that has the names of the U.S. astronauts (the names of those who perished in the recent *Columbia* tragedy should be up there by the time this book hits the shelves) who have died on missions or while in training. The 60-ton structure rotates on a track that follows the movement of the sun (on clear days, of course), causing the names to stand out above a brilliant reflection of the sky.

On launch days, the center is closed at least part of the day. These aren't good days to see the center, but they're great days to observe history in the making. For $38 adults and $28 for kids 3 through 11, you get a **combined ticket** that entitles you to admission to the center for the shortened operating hours, plus at least a two-hour excursion to *NASA Parkway* to see the liftoff. You must pick up tickets, available 5 days before the launch, on site.

An out of this world experience is to do lunch with an astronaut, a once in a lifetime opportunity that is available every day during lunch hours ($20 adults, $10 kids 3–11). Some of the greatest astronauts have participated, including

---

Tips Out to Launch

If you'd like to see a shuttle launch at the **Kennedy Space Center,** first call ☎ **321/867-5000** or check NASA's official website (www.ksc.nasa.gov) for a schedule of upcoming takeoffs. (However, you should note that since the *Columbia* accident, possible takeoffs could be a long way off or policies for viewing could have changed.) You can buy launch tickets at the Kennedy Space Center Visitor Complex (☎ **321/449-4444**) or online at www.ksctickets. com. (*A word of caution:* Shuttle launches are frequently delayed due to weather, equipment malfunctions, or other factors, so you might have to make multiple visits to see one. If you don't have that flexibility, the launch window may be delayed beyond your going-home date.)

If you can't get into the space center, other good viewing spots are on the causeways leading to the islands and on U.S. 1 as it skirts the waterfront in Titusville. The **Holiday Inn Riverside–Kennedy Space Center,** on Washington Avenue (U.S. 1) in Titusville (☎ **800/465-4329** or 321/269-2121; www.holiday innksc.com), also has a clear view of the launch pads across the Indian River, but area motels raise their rates and often book up during launch periods.

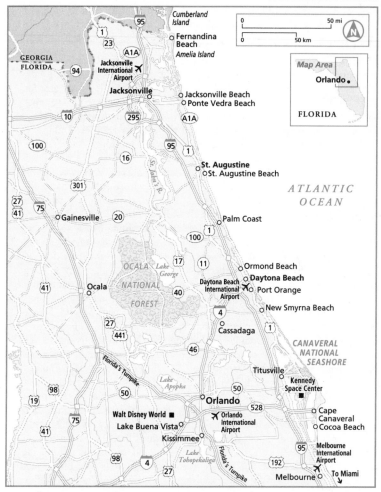

GEORGIA
FLORIDA

Cumberland
Island

Fernandina
Beach
Amelia Island

Jacksonville
International
Airport

Jacksonville

Jacksonville Beach
Ponte Vedra Beach

St. Augustine
St. Augustine Beach

ATLANTIC
OCEAN

Palm Coast

Ormond Beach
Daytona Beach
Daytona Beach
International
Airport
Port Orange

New Smyrna Beach

OCALA Lake
George

NATIONAL

FOREST

Cassadaga

CANAVERAL
NATIONAL
SEASHORE

Florida's Turnpike

Gainesville

Ocala

Lake
Apopka

Titusville
Kennedy
Space Center

Orlando

Walt Disney World
Lake Buena Vista
Kissimmee

Orlando
International
Airport

Cape
Canaveral
Cocoa Beach

Lake
Tohopekaliga

Melbourne
International
Airport

Melbourne

To Miami

Map Area
Orlando

FLORIDA

0   50 mi
0   50 km

John Glenn, Jim Lovell, Walt Cunningham, Story Musgrave, and Jon McBride. Call ℂ **321/449-4400** to make a reservation. Seating is limited.

Note: The financially troubled **Astronaut Hall of Fame** in Titusville closed its doors in fall 2002. Kennedy Space Center acquired many of its exhibits and added them as a separate attraction at the KSC visitor center ($14 adults and $9.95 kids 3–11, or $31 adults and $21 kids for a 2-day Maximum Access Admission to the Center and the Hall of Fame). The new attraction includes displays, exhibits, and tributes to the heroes of the Mercury, Gemini, and Apollo space programs. There's also a collection of spacecraft, including a Mercury 7 capsule, a Gemini training capsule, and an Apollo 14 command module. And in "Simulator Station," guests can experience the pressure of four times the force of gravity, ride a rover across Mars, and land a Space Shuttle.

NASA Pkwy. (Fla. 405), 6 miles east of Titusville, ½ mile west of Fla. 3. ℂ **321/449-4444** for general information, or 321/449-4444 for guided bus tours and launch reservations. www.kennedyspacecenter.com. Admission $35 adults, $25 children 3–11. Annual passes $44 adults, $28 children 3–11. Audio tours $5 per person. All tours and movies free for children under 3. Daily 9am–5:30pm. Shuttle-bus tours daily 9:45am–2:15pm. Closed Christmas and some launch days.

BEACHES & WILDLIFE REFUGES

To the north of the Kennedy Space Center, **Canaveral National Seashore** ✸✸✸ is a protected 13-mile stretch of barrier-island beach backed by cabbage palms, sea grapes, palmettos, marshes, and Mosquito Lagoon. This is a great area for watching herons, egrets, ibises, willets, sanderlings, turnstones, terns, and other birds. You might also glimpse dolphins and manatees in Mosquito Lagoon. Canoeists can paddle along a marked trail through the marshes of Shipyard Island, and you can go backcountry camping November through April (permits required—see below).

The main **visitor center** is at 7611 S. Atlantic Ave., New Smyrna Beach, FL 32169 (✆ **321/867-4077,** or 321/867-0677 for recorded information; www. nps.gov/cana), on Apollo Beach, at the north end of the island. The southern access gate to the island is 8 miles east of Titusville on Fla. 402, just east of Fla. 3. A paved road leads from the gate to undeveloped **Playalinda Beach** ✸✸✸, one of Florida's most beautiful. While it's illegal, nude sunbathing has long been a tra-dition here (at least for those willing to walk a few miles to the more deserted areas). The beach has toilets but no running water or other amenities, so bring everything you will need. The seashore is open daily from 6am to 8pm during day-light saving time, daily from 6am to 6pm during standard time. Admission fees are $5 per motor vehicle, $3 for pedestrians or bicyclists. National Park Service passports are accepted. Backcountry camping permits cost $10 for up to six peo-ple and must be obtained from the New Smyrna Beach visitor center (see above). For advance information, contact the seashore headquarters at 308 Julia St., Titusville, FL 32796 (✆ **321/867-4077** or 321/267-1110; www.nps.gov/cana).

Its neighbor to the south and west is the 140,000-acre **Merritt Island National Wildlife Refuge** ✸✸, home to hundreds of species of shorebirds, waterfowl, reptiles, alligators, and mammals, many of them endangered. Stop and pick up a map and other information at the visitor center, on Fla. 402 about 4 miles east of Titusville (it's on the way to Playalinda Beach). The center has a ¼-mile-long boardwalk along the edge of the marsh and has displays showing the animals you may see here. You can see them from the 6-mile-long Black Point Wildlife Drive or one of the nature trails through the hammocks and marshes. The visitor center is open Monday through Friday from 8am to 4:30pm, Satur-day from 9am to 5pm, Sun 9am to 5pm November to March (closed Sun Apr–Oct). Admission is free. For more information and a schedule of interpre-tive programs, contact the refuge at P.O. Box 6504, Titusville, FL 32782 (✆ **321/ 861-0667;** www.nbbd.com/godo/minwr).

Note: Those parts of the national seashore near the Kennedy Space Center and all of the refuge close 4 days before a shuttle launch and usually reopen the day after a launch.

Another good beach area is **Lori Wilson Park,** on Atlantic Avenue at Antigua Drive in Cocoa Beach (✆ **321/868-1123**), which preserves a stretch of beach backed by a forest of live oaks. It's home to a small but interesting nature cen-ter, and it has restrooms by the beach. The park is open daily from sunrise to sunset, the nature center, Monday through Friday from 1 to 4pm.

The beach at **Cocoa Beach Pier,** on Meade Avenue east of Fla. A1A (✆ **321/ 783-7549**), is a popular spot, especially with surfers, who consider it the East Coast's surfing capital. The rustic pier was built in 1962 and has 842 feet of fish-ing, shopping, and food and drinks overlooking a wide, sandy beach (see "Great

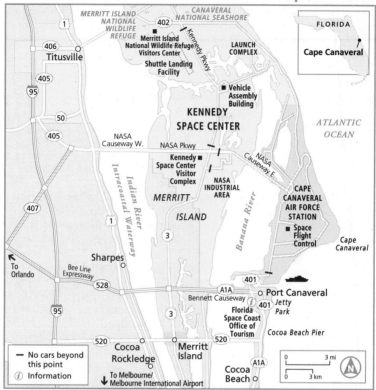

Deals on Dining," below). Because this is not a public park, there are no restrooms other than the ones in the restaurants on the pier.

Jetty Park, 400 E. Jetty Rd. (© **321/783-7111;** www.portcanaveral.org/funport/parks.htm), at the south entry to Port Canaveral, has lifeguards, a fishing pier with bait shop, a children's playground, a volleyball court, a horseshoe pit, picnic tables, a snack bar, a grocery store, restrooms and changing facilities, and the area's only campground. From here you can watch the big cruise ships as they enter and leave the port's narrow passage. The park is open daily from 7am to 10pm, and the pier is open 24 hours for fishing. Admission is $3 per car, $7 for RVs. The 150 tent and RV campsites (some of them shady, most with hookups) cost $17 to $26 a night, depending on location and time of year. No pets are allowed.

AFFORDABLE OUTDOOR ACTIVITIES

ECOTOURS Funday Discovery Tours (© **321/725-0796;** www.fundaytours.com) offers a variety of day trips, including dinner and sunset cruises, airboat and swamp-buggy rides, dolphin-watching cruises, bird-watching expeditions, and personalized tours of the Kennedy Space Center and Merritt Island National Wildlife Refuge. Reservations are required, so call, check the website, or pick up a copy of their list of trips from the visitor center (see "Essentials," above).

FISHING Head to Port Canaveral for catches such as snapper and grouper. **Jetty Park** (© **321/783-7111**), at the south entry to the port, has a fishing pier equipped with a bait shop (see "Beaches & Wildlife Refuges," above). The south bank of the port is lined with charter boats, and you can go deep-sea fishing on the *Miss Cape Canaveral* (© **321/783-5274** or 321/648-2211 in Orlando; www. misscape.com), one of the party boats based here. All-day voyages departing daily at 8am cost $45 to $60 for adults, $40 to $55 for seniors, $35 to $50 for students 11 to 17, and $25 to $40 for kids 6 to 10.

GOLF   You can read about Northeast Florida's best courses in the free *Golfer's Guide,* available at the tourist information offices and in many hotel lobbies. See p. 58 for information about ordering copies.

In Cocoa Beach, the municipal **Cocoa Beach Country Club,** 500 Tom Warringer Blvd. (© **321/868-3351**), has 27 holes of golf and 10 lighted tennis courts set on acres of natural woodland, rivers, and lakes. Greens fees are about $40 in winter, dropping to about $35 in summer, including cart.

On Merritt Island south of the Kennedy Space Center, **The Savannahs at Sykes Creek,** 3915 Savannahs Trail (© **321/455-1377**), has 18 holes over 6,636 yards bordered by hardwood forests, lakes, and savannahs inhabited by a host of wildlife. You'll have to hit over a lake to reach the 7th hole. Fees with cart are about $40 in winter, less in summer.

The best nearby course is the Gary Player–designed **Baytree National Golf Club,** 8010 N. Wickham Rd., ½ mile east of I-95 in Melbourne (© **321/259-9060**), where challenging marshy holes are flanked by towering palms. This par-72 course has 7,043 yards with a unique red-shale waste area. Fees are about $90 in winter, dropping to about $50 in summer, including cart.

For course information online, go to **www.golf.com** and **www.floridagolfing.com**, or call the **Florida Sports Foundation** (© **850/488-8347**) or **Florida Golfing** (© **866/833-2663**).

SURFING   Rip through some occasionally awesome waves (by Florida's standards, not California's or Hawaii's) at the **Cocoa Beach Pier** area or down south at **Sebastian Inlet.** Get outfitted at Ron Jon Surf Shop (4151 N. Atlantic Ave.; © **321/799-8888;** www.ronjons.com) or learn how to hang five or 10 with **Cocoa Beach Surfing School** ♠, 150 E. Columbia Lane (© **321/868-1980;** www.cocoabeachsurfingschool.com). They offer equipment and lessons for beginners or pros at area beaches. Be sure to bring along a towel, flip-flops, sunscreen, and a lot of nerve.

ACCOMMODATIONS YOU CAN AFFORD

The hotels listed below are all in Cocoa Beach, the closest resort area to the Kennedy Space Center, about a 30-minute drive to the north. For TV and pop culture junkies, Cocoa Beach was where the show *I Dream of Jeannie* took place. Closest to the space center and Port Canaveral is the **Radisson Resort at the Port,** 8701 Astronaut Blvd. (Fla. A1A) in Cape Canaveral (© **800/333-3333** or 321/784-0000; www.Radisson.com). It isn't on the beach, but you can relax in a landscaped courtyard with a waterfall cascading over fake rocks into an outdoor heated pool. This comfortable, well-equipped hotel caters to business travelers and passengers waiting to board cruise ships (free transportation to the port and free parking while you cruise) departing from nearby Port Canaveral and has a great complimentary breakfast.

The newest chain motels in this area are the **Hampton Inn Cocoa Beach,** 3425 Atlantic Blvd. (© **877/492-3224** or 321/799-4099; www.hamptoninncocoabeach.com), and **Courtyard by Marriott,** 3435 Atlantic Blvd. (© **800/321-2211** or 321/784-4800; www.marriott.com). Opened in 2000 and 2001, respectively, they stand side-by-side and have access to the beach via a pathway through a condominium complex.

The **Florida Space Coast Office of Tourism** (8810 Astronaut Blvd. #102; Cape Canaveral, FL 32920; ℂ **800/93-OCEAN** or 321/868-1126; www.spacecoast.com) publishes a booklet of the area's Superior Small Lodgings.

The area has a plethora of rental condominiums and cottages. **King Rentals Inc.,** 102 W. Central Blvd., Cape Canaveral, FL 32920 (ℂ **888/295-0934** or 321/784-5046; www.kingrentals.com), has a wide selection in its inventory.

Given the proximity of Orlando, the generally warm weather year-round, and business travelers visiting the space complex, there is little if any seasonal fluctuation in room rates here. They are highest weekends, holidays, and during special events, such as space shuttle launches.

Tent and RV camping are available at **Jetty Park** in Port Canaveral (see "Beaches & Wildlife Refuges," above).

You'll pay a 4% hotel tax on top of the Florida 6% sales tax here.

DoubleTree Hotel Cocoa Beach Oceanfront ⭐ This six-story hotel was extensively remodeled and upgraded in 1998, and although not particularly upscale, it's the pick of the full-service beachside hotels here. All rooms have balconies with ocean views and easy chairs, and 10 suites have living rooms with sleeper sofas and separate bedrooms. A charming dining room facing the beach serves decent Mediterranean fare and opens to a bi-level brick patio with water cascading between two heated swimming pools. Conference facilities draw groups.

2080 N. Atlantic Ave., Cocoa Beach, FL 32931. ℂ 800/552-3224 or 321/783-9222. Fax 321/799-3234. www.cocoabeachdoubletree.com. 148 units. $125–$179 double; $185–$275 suite. AE, DC, DISC, MC, V. **Amenities:** Restaurant; bar; 2 heated outdoor pools; exercise room; game room; limited room service; laundry service; coin-op washers and dryers; concierge-level rooms. *In room:* A/C, TV, dataport, coffeemaker, hair dryer, iron.

Riverview Hotel ⭐⭐⭐ Located right on the Intracoastal Waterway in New Smyrna Beach, the Riverview Hotel, a former fishing and hunting shack for sportsmen scoping the Indian River Lagoon, is a spectacularly restored, 18-room hotel featuring a 5,000-foot spa complete with a mineral pool. Every night, there's jazz on the deck and, to boot, a fabulous restaurant, Riverview Charlie's, which some consider to be one of the state's best seafood spots, is on the premises. The owners, Christa and Jim Kelsey used to work at the Faro Blanco Marina Resort in the Florida Keys, so they are well versed in the art of hospitality. Some rooms have private patios or porches and all rooms are immaculate, charming in a Little House on the Prairie Way, and come complete with modern amenities such as cable television. If I had a choice, however, I'd choose the two-bedroom cottage or house with private pool, which are bargains at $175 to $210!

103 Flagler Ave., New Smyrna Beach, FL 32169. ℂ 800/945-7416 or 386/428-5858. Fax 321/423-8927. www.riverviewhotel.com. 18 units. $100–$120 double. Rates include expanded continental breakfast. AE, DISC, MC, V. **Amenities:** Restaurant; heated pool; spa; sauna; massage. *In room:* A/C, TV.

WORTH A SPLURGE

The Inn at Cocoa Beach ⭐⭐⭐ Despite having 50 units, an intimate bed-and-breakfast ambience prevails at this seaside inn, far and away the most romantic place to stay in the area (which is why it draws so many couples). The inn began as a beachfront motel but underwent a transformation under current owner Karen Simpler, a skilled interior decorator. She has furnished each unit with an elegant mix of pine, tropical, and French country pieces. Rooms in the three- and four-story buildings are much more spacious and have better sea views from their balconies than the "standard" units in the original two-story motel wing (all but six units here have balconies or patios). The older units open to a courtyard with a swimming pool tucked behind the dunes. Highest on the romance scale are two rooms with Jacuzzi tubs, large showers, and easy chairs facing gas fireplaces. In addition to the complimentary breakfast, guests are treated to evening wine-and-cheese socials and afternoon tea. There's also an honor bar where you can pour your own drinks and a library from which to feed your head.

4300 Ocean Blvd., Cocoa Beach, FL 32932. © **800/343-5307** or 321/799-3460. Fax 321/784-8632. www. theinnatcocoabeach.com. 50 units. $135–$295 double. Rates include continental breakfast and afternoon tea. AE, DISC, MC, V. No children under 12 accepted. **Amenities:** Bar (guests only); heated outdoor pool; sauna; massage; laundry service. *In room:* A/C, TV, dataport.

GREAT DEALS ON DINING

On the **Cocoa Beach Pier,** at the beach end of Meade Avenue, you'll get a fine view down the coast to accompany the seafood offerings at **Atlantic Ocean Grill** (© **321/783-7549**) and the mediocre pub fare at adjacent **Marlins Good Times Bar & Grill** (same phone). The restaurants may not justify spending an entire evening on the pier, but the outdoor, tin-roofed **Boardwalk Tiki Bar** ✦, where live music plays most nights, is a prime spot to have a cold one while watching the surfers or a sunset.

Bernard's Surf/Fischer's Seafood Bar & Grill ✦ SEAFOOD/STEAKS Photos on the walls testify that many astronauts—and Russian cosmonauts, too—come to these adjoining establishments to celebrate their landings. It all started as Bernard's Surf, which has been serving standard steak-and-seafood fare in a nautically dressed setting since 1948. Bernard's offers house specials such as stone crab claws, Florida lobster tails stuffed with crab, char-grilled red snapper, and a belly-busting platter of shrimp, scallops, grouper, crab cakes, lobster, and oysters. You can even get some Russian Beluga or Sevruga caviar if you so desire. The fresh seafood also finds its way into Fischer's Seafood Bar & Grill, a friendly, *Cheers*-like lounge popular with the locals. Fischer's menu features fried combo platters, shrimp and crab-claw meat sautéed in herb butter, and mussels with a wine sauce over pasta, to mention a few worthy selections. Fischer's also provides sandwiches, burgers, and other pub fare, and it has the same 25¢ happy-hour oysters and spicy wings as a branch of **Rusty's Seafood & Oyster Bar** (see below), also part of this complex.

2 S. Atlantic Ave. (at Minuteman Causeway Rd.), Cocoa Beach. © **321/783-2401.** Reservations recommended in Bernard's, not accepted in Fischer's. Bernard's main courses $14–$55. Fischer's main courses $9–$16; sandwiches and salads $4–$9. AE, DC, DISC, MC, V. Bernard's Mon–Fri 4–10pm; Sat 4–11pm. Fischer's Mon–Fri 11am–10pm; Sat 11am–11pm. Closed Christmas.

Rusty's Seafood & Oyster Bar *Value* SEAFOOD This lively sports bar beside Port Canaveral's man-made harbor offers inexpensive chow ranging from very spicy seafood gumbo to a pot of seafood that will give two people their fill of steamed oysters, clams, shrimp, crab legs, potatoes, and corn on the cob. Raw or steamed fresh oysters and clams from the raw bar are first rate and a very good value, as is a lunch buffet on weekdays. Seating is available indoors or out, but the inside tables have the best view of fishing boats and cruise liners going in and out of the port. Daily happy hours from 3 to 6pm see beers drafted at 60¢ a mug, and tons of raw or steamed oysters and spicy Buffalo wings go for 25¢ each. It's a busy and sometimes noisy joint, especially on weekend afternoons, but the clientele tends to be somewhat older and better behaved than at some other pubs along the banks of Port Canaveral. There's another **Rusty's** in the

Bernard's Surf/Fischer's Seafood Bar & Grill restaurant complex in Cocoa Beach (see above). It has the same menu.

628 Glen Cheek Dr. (south side of the harbor), Port Canaveral. ℂ 321/783-2033. Main courses $7–$25; sandwiches and salads $4–$7; lunch buffet $6. AE, DC, DISC, MC, V. Sun–Thurs 11am–11:30pm; Fri–Sat 11am–12:30am (lunch buffet Mon–Fri 11am–2pm).

WORTH A SPLURGE

The Mango Tree ★★ CONTINENTAL Gourmet seafood, pastas, and chicken are served in a plantation-home atmosphere with elegant furnishings in this stucco house, the finest dining venue here. Although the ambience borders on Tavern on the Green touristy tacky, the restaurant is, much like Tavern, rather picturesque. Goldfish ponds inside and a waterfall splashing into a Japanese koi pond out in the lush tropical gardens provide pleasing backdrops. Start with finely seasoned Indian River crab cakes, then go on to the chef's expert spin on fresh tuna filets, roast Long Island duckling, beef tips with peppercorn-mushroom sauce, and other excellent dishes drawing their inspiration from the continent.

118 N. Atlantic Ave. (Fla. A1A, between N. 1st and N. 2nd sts.), Cocoa Beach. ℂ 321/799-0513. Reservations recommended. Main courses $15–$39. AE, MC, V. Tues–Sun 6–10pm.

THE SPACE COAST AFTER DARK

For a rundown of current performances and exhibits, call the **Brevard Cultural Alliance's Arts Line** (ℂ 321/690-6819). For live music, walk out on the **Cocoa Beach Pier,** on Meade Avenue at the beach, where **Oh Shuck's Seafood Bar & Grill** (ℂ 321/783-7549), **Marlins Good Times Bar & Grill** (ℂ 321/783-7549), and the alfresco **Boardwalk Tiki Bar** ★ (same phone as Marlins) have bands on weekends, more often during the summer season. The Tiki bar is a great place to hang out over a cold beer all afternoon and evening.

2 Daytona Beach ★/★

54 miles NE of Orlando, 251 miles N of Miami, 78 miles S of Jacksonville

Daytona Beach is a town with many personalities. It is at once the self-proclaimed "World's Most Famous Beach" and "World Center of Racing," a mecca for tattooed motorcyclists and pierced spring-breakers, *and* the home of a surprisingly good art museum. The city and developers are also spending millions of dollars to turn the somewhat seedy beachfront area (complete with the requisite T-shirt and souvenir shops), around the famous Main Street Pier, into Ocean Walk Village, a redevelopment area of shops, entertainment, and resort facilities.

Daytona Beach has been a destination for racing enthusiasts since the early 1900s when "horseless carriages" raced on the hard-packed sand beach. One thing is for sure: Daytonans still love their cars. Recent debate over the environmental impact of unrestricted driving on the beach caused an uproar from citizens who couldn't imagine it any other way. As it worked out, they can still drive on the sand, but not everywhere, and especially not in areas where sea turtles are nesting.

Today, hundreds of thousands of race enthusiasts come to the home of the National Association for Stock Car Auto Racing (NASCAR) for the Daytona 500, the Pepsi 400, and other races throughout the year. The Speedway is also home to DAYTONA USA, a state-of-the-art motor-sports entertainment attraction worth a visit even by nonracing fans.

Be sure to check the "Florida Calendar of Events," in chapter 2, to know when the town belongs to college students during spring break, hundreds of thousands of leather-clad motorcycle buffs during Bike Week (March) and Bike-toberfest (Oct), or racing enthusiasts for big competitions. You can't find a hotel room, drive the highways, or enjoy a peaceful vacation when they're in town.

ESSENTIALS

GETTING THERE   **Continental** (© 800/525-0280) and **Delta** (© 800/221-1212) fly into the small, pleasant, and calm **Daytona Beach International Airport** (© 386/248-8030; http://flydaytonafirst.com), 4 miles inland from the beach on International Speedway Boulevard (U.S. 92), but you usually can find less expensive fares to **Orlando International Airport** (p. 409), about an hour's drive away. **Daytona-Orlando Transit Service (DOTS)** (© 800/231-1965 or 386/257-5411; www.dots-daytonabeach.com) provides van transportation to and from Orlando International Airport. Fares are about $27 for adults one-way, $49 round-trip; fares for children 11 and under are $14 one-way and $28 round-trip. The service brings passengers to the company's terminal at 1034 N. Nova Rd., between 3rd and 4th streets, or to beach hotels for an additional fee.

If you fly into the Daytona airport, rates for the **Daytona Shuttle** (© 386/255-2294) range up to $12 per person, $14 per couple, or $6 per person for parties of three or more. The ride from the airport to most beach hotels via **Yellow Cab Co.** (© 386/255-5555) is between $7 and $18.

Alamo (© 800/327-9622), **Avis** (© 800/831-2847), **Budget** (© 800/527-0700), **Dollar** (© 800/800-4000), **Enterprise** (© 800/325-8007), **Hertz** (© 800/654-3131), and **National** (© 800/227-7368) have booths at the airport. If it suits you, why not rent a Harley? This is Daytona, after all. Contact **Daytona Harley-Davidson** (© 800/307-4464 or 386/258-0638; www.daytonahd.com). Rates are $125 to $135 daily, $600 to $640 weekly.

Amtrak (© 800/872-7245; www.amtrak.com) trains stop at Deland, about 15 miles southwest of Daytona Beach, with connecting bus service from Deland to the beach.

VISITOR INFORMATION   The **Daytona Beach Area Convention & Visitors Bureau,** 126 E. Orange Ave. (P.O. Box 910), Daytona Beach, FL 32115 (© 800/544-0415 or 386/255-0415; www.daytonabeach.com), can help you with information on attractions, accommodations, dining, and events. The office is on the mainland just west of the Memorial Bridge. The information area of the lobby is open daily from 9am to 5pm. The bureau also maintains a branch at DAYTONA USA, 1801 W. International Speedway Blvd. (open daily 9am–7pm), and a kiosk at the airport.

GETTING AROUND   Although Daytona is primarily a driver's town, VOTRAN, Volusia County's public transit system (© 386/761-7700; http://votran.org), runs a **free shuttle** around the Main Street Pier/Ocean Walk Village area and a pay **trolley** along Atlantic Avenue on the beach, Monday through Saturday from noon to midnight. Trolley fares are $1 for adults, 50¢ for seniors and children 6 to 17, and free for kids under 6 riding with an adult. VOTRAN also runs **buses** throughout downtown and the beaches.

For a taxi, call **Yellow Cab** (© 386/255-5555) or **Southern Komfort Cab** (© 386/252-2222).

Daytona Beach

ACCOMMODATIONS ■

Adam's Mark Daytona Beach Resort **4**

Old Salty's Inn **11**

The Plaza Resort & Spa **3**

The Villa Bed & Breakfast **2**

DINING ◆

The Cellar **7**

Down the Hatch **12**

Frappes North **1**

McK's Dublin Station **6**

Ocean Deck Restaurant & Beach Club **5**

ATTRACTIONS ●

Daytona International Speedway/ DAYTONA USA **9**

Daytona Flea and Farmer's Market **10**

Museum of Arts and Sciences **8**

Ponce de León Inlet Lighthouse & Museum **12**

Crossing Over Into Cassadaga

If you're in the Daytona Beach/Orlando area, suspend your disbelief for a few hours and make a pit stop in Cassadaga, the tiny century-old community composed completely of psychics and mediums who will be happy to tell you your future, your fortune, or put you in touch with the deceased—for a price, of course.

Should you find the whole concept of psychics and talking to the dead completely kooky and out of whack, consider the history of Cassadaga, which is fascinating in its own right.

Without sounding too much like the intro to the SciFi Channel show *Crossing Over with John Edward,* as a young man from New York, George Colby was told during a séance that he would someday establish a spiritualist community in the South. In 1875, the prophecy came true when Colby was led through the wilderness of Central Florida by his spiritual guide to a 35-acre area that was to become the Cassadaga Spiritualist Camp.

Although it sounds like a bizarre cult, it's not. Consisting of about 57 acres and 55 no-nonsense clapboard houses, Cassadaga caters to those who have chosen to share in a community of like-minded people who happen to believe in the otherworldly. Yes, the people are eccentric, to say the least, but they are all very friendly. Designated a Historic District on the National Register of Historic Places, Cassadaga is the Spiritualist version of Lourdes, to which skeptics and believers alike flock for answers, or at least kicks.

When you get to town, head straight for the **Information Center** (for directions, see below), where you can find out which psychics and mediums are working that day, and make an appointment for a session, which ranges from $25 and up for a palm reading to $50 and up for a session with a medium. A general store, restaurant, hotel, and a few curious shops selling crystals and potions of sorts are there to keep you occupied while you wait for your appointment. Whether you're a believer or not, an hour or two in Cassadaga will make for interesting cocktail conversation.

From Daytona, take I-4 to exit 114. Turn right onto Highway 472 at the end of the exit ramp toward Orange City/Deland. At the traffic light, turn right onto Dr. Martin Luther King Parkway. Turn right at the first light, which is Cassadaga Road. Continue 1½ miles to the intersection with Stevens Street. The Information Center is on the right. For more information, call © **386/228-3171** or log on to www.cassadaga.org.

A VISIT TO THE WORLD CENTER OF RACING

Daytona International Speedway/DAYTONA USA ★★   You don't have to be a racing fan to enjoy a visit to the **Daytona International Speedway,** 4 miles west of the beach. Opened in 1959 with the first Daytona 500, this 480-acre complex is one of the keynotes of the city's fame. The track presents about nine weekends of major racing events annually, featuring stock cars, sports cars, motorcycles, and go-karts, and is used for automobile and motorbike testing and other events many other days of the year. Its grandstands can accommodate more than 150,000 fans. Big events sell out months in advance (tickets to the Daytona 500 in Feb can be gone a year ahead of time), so get your tickets and hotel reservations as early as possible.

Start your visit at the **World Center of Racing Visitors Center,** in the NASCAR office complex at the east end of the speedway. Admission to the center is free, and you can walk out and see the track during nonrace days (there's a small admission to the track during qualifying races leading up to the main events). Entertaining 30-minute guided tram tours of the facility (garage area, pit road, and so on) depart from the visitor center and are well worth taking.

The visitor center houses a large souvenir shop, a snack bar, and the phenomenally popular **DAYTONA USA,** a 60,000-square-foot, state-of-the-art interactive motor-sports entertainment attraction. Here you can learn about the history, color, and excitement of stock car, go-kart, and motorcycle racing in Daytona. In Daytona Dream Laps, one of its newest "rides," you get the feel of what it's like to zoom around the track in a Daytona 500 race from a 32-seat motion simulator. If that doesn't get your stomach churning, hop inside your own 80% scale NASCAR car in Acceleration Alley, buckle up, and roar up to 200 mph in a spectacular simulator that combines motion, video, projection, and sound for the ultimate virtual reality–like racing experience ($5 per ride above the admission price, below). On the milder side, you can participate in a pit stop on a NASCAR Winston Cup stock car, see an actual winning Daytona 500 car still covered in track dust, talk via video with favorite competitors, and play radio or television announcer by calling the finish of a race. An action-packed IMAX film will put you in the winner's seat of a Daytona 500 race.

To really experience what it's like, you can actually make (for $106) three laps around the track in a stock car from May to October with the **Richard Petty Driving Experience Ride-Along Program** (© 800/237-3889; www.1800 bepetty.com). Professional drivers (sorry, none are named Petty) are at the wheel as you see and feel what it's like to travel an average 115 mph.

Allow at least 4 hours to see everything, and bring your video camera.

1801 W. International Speedway Blvd. (U.S. 92, at Bill France Blvd.). © 386/253-7223 for race tickets, 386/253-7223 for information, or 386/947-6404 or 386/947-6800 for DAYTONA USA. www.daytonaintlspeedway.com and www.daytonausa.com. Speedway free admission except on race days; tram rides $7. DAYTONA USA admission $16 adults, $13 seniors, $8 children 6–12. Combination DAYTONA USA–tram tour $20 adults, $17 seniors, $14 children 6–12. Tram rides and DAYTONA USA free admission for children under 6. Speedway daily 9am–7pm; trams depart every 30 min. 9:30am–5pm except during races and special events. DAYTONA USA daily 9am–7pm (later during race events). Closed Christmas.

HITTING THE WORLD'S MOST FAMOUS BEACH

The beautiful and hard-packed beach here runs for 24 miles along a skinny peninsula separated from the mainland by the Halifax River. The bustling hub of activity is at the end of Main Street, near the Adam's Mark Daytona Beach Resort, where you'll find the **Main Street Pier,** which was the longest wooden pier on the East Coast until Hurricane Floyd washed away about a third of its 1,006 feet in 1999. Out here you'll find a restaurant, bar, bait shop, beach-toy concessions, a chairlift running its length, and views from the 180-foot-tall Space Needle. Admission as far out as the restaurant and bar is free (at about a third of the way, this is far enough for a good view down the beach), but you'll have to pay $1 to walk beyond that point, and more than that if you fish (see "Affordable Outdoor Activities," below). Beginning at the pier, the city's famous ocean-side **Boardwalk** is lined with restaurants, bars, and T-shirt shops, as are the 4 blocks of Main Street nearest the beach. The city's Ocean Walk Village redevelopment project begins here and runs several blocks north.

There's another busy beach area at the end of **Seabreeze Boulevard,** which has a multitude of restaurants, bars, and shops.

Couples seeking greater privacy usually prefer the northern or southern extremities of the beach. **Ponce Inlet,** at the very southern tip of the peninsula, is especially peaceful, since there is little commerce or traffic there to disturb the silence.

AFFORDABLE OUTDOOR ACTIVITIES

CRUISES Take a leisurely cruise on the Halifax River aboard the 14-passenger, 25-foot *Fancy,* a replica of an 1890s-style fantail launch. It's operated by **A tiny Cruise Line River Excursions,** 425 S. Beach St., at Halifax Harbor Marina (② **386/226-2343**). Captain Jim regales passengers with river lore and points out dolphins (which are more commonly spotted in the mornings), manatees, herons, diving cormorants, pelicans, egrets, osprey, oyster beds, and other natural phenomena during his 2-hour midday cruise. In the afternoon, you can see the man-made estates along the river. Cruises range from $9.50 to $15 for adults, $6 to $8 for children 4 to 12, and free for children 3 and under. Weather permitting, the midday cruises depart year-round (with a brief hiatus during the holidays), Monday through Saturday at 11:30am. The 1-hour tour of riverfront homes is at 2pm and of historic downtown at 3:30pm; there are no Monday cruises in winter months. Call for reservations. Romantic sunset cruises are also available.

FISHING The easiest and least-expensive way to fish offshore for marlin, sailfish, king mackerel, grouper, red snapper, and more is with the **Critter Fleet,** 4950 S. Peninsula Dr., just past the lighthouse in Ponce Inlet (② **800/338-0850** or 386/767-7676; www.critterfleet.com), which operates two party boats. One goes on all-day trips (about $60 adults, $35 kids under 12), while the other makes morning and afternoon voyages (about $40 adults, $25 kids under 12). The fares include rod, reel, and bait. Call for schedules, prices, and reservations.

Save the cost of a boat and fish with the locals from the **Main Street Pier,** at the ocean end of Main Street near the Adam's Mark Daytona Beach Resort (② **386/253-1212**). Admission for anglers is $3.50 for adults, $2 for kids under 12. Bait and fishing gear are available, and no license is required.

GOLF There are more than 25 courses within 30 minutes of the beach, and most hotels can arrange starting times for you. **Golf Daytona Beach,** 126 E. Orange Ave., Daytona Beach, FL 32114 (② **800/881-7065** or 386/239-7065; fax 386/239-0064), publishes an annual brochure describing the major courses. It's available at the tourist information offices (see "Essentials," above).

For course information online, go to www.golf.com and www.floridagolfing. com, or call the **Florida Sports Foundation** (② **850/488-8347**) or **Florida Golfing** (② **866/833-2663**).

Two of the nation's top-rated links for women golfers are at the **LPGA International** 🌟🌟, 1000 Championship Dr. (② **386/274-5742;** www.lpga international.com): Those are the Champions course designed by Rees Jones and the Legends course designed by Arthur Hills. Both boast 18 outstanding holes. LPGA International is a center for professional and amateur women golfers (workshops and teaching programs), and the pro shop carries a great selection of ladies' equipment and clothing. Greens fees with a cart are usually about $75, less in summer. *Pssst*—They let guys play here, too!

A Lloyd Clifton–designed course, the centrally located 18-hole, par-72 **Indigo Lakes Golf Course,** 2620 W. International Speedway Blvd. (© **386/ 254-3607;** www.indigolakesgolf.com), has flat fairways and large bunkered Bermuda greens. Fees here are about $65 in winter, including a cart, less in summer.

The semiprivate South Course at **Pelican Bay Country Club,** 550 Sea Duck Dr. (© **386/756-0034;** www.pelicanbaygolfclub.com), is one of the area's favorites, with fast greens to test your putting skills. Fees are about $45 with cart in winter, less in summer (no walking allowed). The North Course is for members only.

The city's prime municipal course is the **Daytona Beach Country Club,** 600 Wilder Blvd. (© **386/258-3119**), which has 36 holes. Winter fees are about $20 to walk, $30 to share a cart. They drop $3 in summer.

HELICOPTER RIDES   Take a helicopter ride around the Daytona area to see the city from a different point of view. **Air Florida** (© **386/257-6993;** www. airfloridahelicopters.com) offers rides starting at $20 (two person minimum), leaving from the Daytona Flea and Farmer's Market (see below).

HORSEBACK RIDING   **Shenandoah Stables,** 1759 Tomoka Farms Rd., off U.S. 92 (© **386/257-1444**), offers daily trail rides and lessons. Call for prices and schedules.

SPECTATOR SPORTS   The **Daytona Cubs** (© **386/872-2827;** www.daytona cubs.com), a Class A minor-league affiliate of the Chicago Cubs, play baseball April through August at Jackie Robinson Ballpark, on City Island downtown. A game here is a treat, since the park has been restored to its classic 1914 style by the designers of Baltimore's Camden Yards and Cleveland's Jacobs Field. Tickets are $4 to $7.

WATERSPORTS   Watersports equipment, bicycles, beach buggies, and mopeds, can be rented along the Boardwalk, at the ocean end of Main Street (see "Hitting the World's Most Famous Beach," above), and in front of major beachfront hotels.

MUSEUMS & ATTRACTIONS

Museum of Arts and Sciences ★★   An exceptional institution for a town of Daytona's size and reputation (as a culturally devoid, trashy, spring break mecca), this museum is best known for its Cuba: A History of Art exhibit, with paintings acquired in 1956, when Cuban dictator Fulgencio Batista donated his private collection to the city. Among them is a portrait of Eva ("Evita") Perón, said to be the only existing painting completed while she was alive (it hangs near the lobby, not within the Cuban exhibit). The Dow Gallery displays Smithsonian-quality examples of American decorative arts, and the Bouchelle Study Center for the Decorative Arts contains American and European jewelry, furniture, mirrors, and more. Other rooms worth visiting include the Schulte Gallery of Chinese Art; Africa: Life and Ritual, with the largest collection of Ashante gold ornaments (these are stunning) in the United States; and the Center for Florida history, with the skeleton of a 13-foot-tall, 130,000-year-old giant ground sloth. A recent addition is the unique collection of the late Chapman S. Root, a Daytona philanthropist and a founder of the Coca-Cola empire; among the Root memorabilia is the mold for the original Coke bottle as well as many other changing exhibitions (the collection is very large). The Root family's two private railroad cars are also on display. The planetarium presents 30-minute shows of what the night sky will look like on the date of your visit. Even though this is a first-class art museum, except for the skeleton and the model railroads, children are apt to be bored here.

1040 Museum Blvd. (off Nova Rd./Fla. 5A between International Speedway Blvd. and Bellevue Ave.). © 386/ 255-0285. www.moas.org. Museum $8 adults, $4 children and students with ID, free for children 5 and under. Planetarium shows $3 adults, $2 children and students. Tues–Fri 9am–4pm; Sat–Sun noon–5pm. Planetarium shows Tues–Fri 2pm; Sat–Sun 1 and 3pm. Closed Thanksgiving, Christmas Eve, and Christmas Day. Take International Speedway Blvd. west, make a left on Nova Rd. (Fla. 5A), and look for a sign on your right.

Ponce de León Inlet Lighthouse & Museum ★★ This National Historic Landmark is well worth a stop even if you're not a lighthouse enthusiast. The 175-foot brick-and-granite structure is the second-tallest lighthouse in the United States. (Only the beacon at Cape Hatteras, North Carolina, is taller.) Built in the 1880s, the lighthouse and the graceful Victorian brick buildings surrounding it have been restored (it's one of the only light stations in the United States to have all its original buildings still standing). There are no guided tours, but you can walk through the 12 areas, which feature different exhibits (lighthouse lenses, historical artifacts, and a film of early car racing on the nearby beach), and around the tugboat *F. D. Russell,* now sitting high-and-dry in the sand. Use common sense if you climb the 203 steps to the top of the lighthouse; it's a grinding ascent, but the view from up there is spectacular.

4931 S. Peninsula Dr., Ponce Inlet. © 386/761-1821. www.ponceinlet.org. Admission $5 adults, $1.50 children under 12. Memorial Day to Labor Day daily 10am–9pm; rest of year daily 10am–5pm. Follow Atlantic Ave. south, make a right on Beach St., and follow the signs.

SHOPPING

On the mainland, Daytona Beach's main riverside drag, **Beach Street,** is one of the few areas in town where people actually stroll. The street is wide and inviting, with palms down its median and decorative wrought-iron archways and fancy brickwork overlooking a branch of the Halifax River that separates downtown from City Island, home of municipal offices and the lovingly restored Jackie Robinson Ballpark (see "Spectator Sports," above). Today, Beach Street, between Bay Street and Orange Avenue, offers antiques and collectibles shops, art galleries, clothiers, a magic shop, the local historical museum, and several good cafes. At 154 S. Beach St., you'll find the home of the **Angell & Phelps Chocolate Factory** (© **386/252-6531;** www.angellandphelps.com), which has been making candy for more than 75 years. Come here to watch the goodies being made (and get a free sample!) or just to buy some of the handmade treats.

"Hog" riders will find several shops to their liking along Beach Street, north of International Speedway Boulevard, including the **Harley-Davidson Store,** 290 N. Beach St., at Dr. Mary McLeod Bethune Boulevard (© **386/253-2453**), a 20,000-square-foot retail outlet and diner serving breakfast and lunch. It's one of the nation's largest dealerships. In addition to hundreds of gleaming new and used Hogs, you'll find as much fringed leather as you've ever seen in one place.

The **Daytona Flea and Farmer's Market,** on Tomoka Farms Road at the junction of I-95 and U.S. 92, a mile west of the Speedway (© **386/253-3330;** www.daytonafleamarket.com), is huge, with 1,000 covered outdoor booths plus 100 antiques and collectibles vendors in an air-conditioned building. Most of the booths feature new (though not necessarily first-rate) wares along the lines of socks, sunglasses, luggage, handbags, jewelry, tools, and the like. It's open year-round Friday through Sunday from 8am to 5pm. Admission and parking are free.

ACCOMMODATIONS YOU CAN AFFORD

Room rates here are among the most affordable in Florida. Some properties have as many as 20 rate periods during the year, but generally they are somewhat higher from the beginning of the races in February all the way to Labor Day. They skyrocket during major events at the Speedway, during bikers' gatherings, and during college spring break (see "Florida Calendar of Events," in chapter 2, beginning on p. 41), when local hotels fill to the bursting point. Even if you can find a room then, there's often a minimum-stay requirement.

Hundreds of hotels and motels line Atlantic Avenue along the beach, many of them family owned and operated. The Daytona Beach Area Convention & Visitors Bureau (see "Essentials," earlier in this chapter) distributes a brochure that lists **Superior Small Lodgings** for Daytona Beach, Deland, and New Smyrna Beach. All of the small motels listed below are members.

If you're going to the races and don't care about staying on the beach, some upper-floor rooms at the new **Hilton Garden Inn Daytona Beach Airport,** 189 Midway Ave. (© 877/944-4001 or 386/944-4000), overlook the international speedway track. Unlike most members of Hilton's Garden Inn chain, this one has a restaurant.

Thousands of rental condominiums line the beaches here. Among the most luxurious is the new, 150-unit condominium hotel **Ocean Walk Resort,** 300 N. Atlantic Ave., Daytona Beach, FL 32118 (© 800/649-3566 or 386/323-4800; www.oceanwalkresort.com), which is part of the Ocean Walk Village redevelopment. Near the Main Street Pier, it's in the center of the action and has one- and two-bedroom apartments with fully equipped kitchens, washers and dryers, and all of the usual hotel amenities, plus a wondrous computer golf simulator, a "lazy river" in the outdoor pool, an island putting green, and much more—including the gaudiest lobby we've ever seen. One of the largest rental agents is **Peck Realty,** 2340 S. Atlantic Ave., Daytona Beach Shores, FL 32118 (© 800/447-3255 or 386/257-5000; www.peckrealty.com).

In addition to the 6% state sales tax, Volusia County levies a 4% tax on hotel bills.

Old Salty's Inn *(Value)* The most unusual of the many mom-and-pop beachside motels here, Old Salty's is a lush tropical enclave carrying out a *Gilligan's Island* theme, with old motors, rotting boats, life preservers, and a Jeep lying about. The TV series' main characters are depicted in big murals painted on the buildings. The two-story wings flank a courtyard festooned with palms and banana trees (you can pick one for breakfast). Facing this vista, the bright rooms have microwaves, refrigerators, and front and back windows to let in good ventilation. The choice units have picture windows overlooking the beach. There are gas grills and rocking chairs under a gazebo by a heated beachside swimming pool.

1921 S. Atlantic Ave. (Fla. A1A, at Flamingo Ave.), Daytona Beach Shores, FL 32118. © 800/417-1466 or 386/252-8090. Fax 386/947-9980. www.oldsaltys.com. 19 units. $53–$71 doubles; $63–$93 efficiencies; $75–$121 suites. AE, DISC, MC, V. **Amenities:** Heated outdoor pool; free use of bikes; coin-op washers and dryers. *In room:* A/C, TV, kitchen, fridge, coffeemaker, hair dryer, iron.

The Plaza Resort & Spa *(★★)* Remodeled in 2000 to the tune of $26 million (the original seven-story hotel was built in the early 20th century), these elegant adjoining 7- and 13-story buildings now hold some of Daytona Beach's best rooms (in a much more tasteful atmosphere than many of the neighboring hotels)—provided you don't need a large bathroom. The choice units are the corner suites, which have sitting areas and two balconies overlooking the

Atlantic; some even have a Jacuzzi. All units have balconies and microwaves (an on-premises convenience store sells frozen dinners).

600 N. Atlantic Ave. (at Seabreeze Ave.), Daytona Beach, FL 32118. © 800/874-7420 or 386/255-4471. Fax 386/238-7984. www.plazaresortandspa.com. 323 units. $69–$215 doubles; $189–$449 suites. AE, DC, DISC, MC, V. **Amenities:** Restaurant; bar; heated outdoor pool; exercise room; spa; Jacuzzi; watersports equipment rentals; game room; business center; limited room service; massage; babysitting; laundry service; coin-op washers and dryers; concierge-level rooms. *In room:* A/C, TV, dataport, fridge, coffeemaker, hair dryer, iron, microwave.

The Villa Bed & Breakfast ★★★   You'll think you're in Iberia upon entering this 70+-year-old Spanish mansion's great room with its fireplace, baby grand piano, terra-cotta floors, and walls hung with Mediterranean paintings. A sunroom equipped with a TV and VCR, a formal dining room, and a breakfast nook are also located downstairs. The lush backyard surrounds a swimming pool and a covered, four-person Jacuzzi. Upstairs, the nautically themed Christopher Columbus room has a vaulted ceiling and a small balcony overlooking the pool. The largest quarter here is the King Carlos suite, the original master bedroom with a four-poster bed, entertainment system, refrigerator, rooftop deck, dressing area, and bathroom equipped with a four-head shower. The Queen Isabella room has a portrait of the queen over a queen-size bed, and the Marco Polo room has Chinese black-lacquer furniture and Oriental rugs evoking the great explorer's adventures.

801 N. Peninsula Dr. (at Riverview Blvd.), Daytona Beach, FL 32118. ©/fax 386/248-2020. www.thevillabb. com. 4 units, all with bathroom. $100–$250 double. Rates include continental breakfast. AE, MC, V. No children or pets accepted. **Amenities:** Heated outdoor pool; Jacuzzi. *In room:* A/C, TV, hair dryer, no phone.

GREAT DEALS ON DINING

Daytona Beach has a few interesting dining venues, but not many are likely to leave an indelible memory. A profusion of fast-food joints line the major thoroughfares, especially along Atlantic Avenue on the beach and International Speedway Boulevard (U.S. 92) near the racetrack. Restaurants come and go in the Beach Street district on the mainland, and along Main Street and Seabreeze Boulevard on the beach. A casual restaurant serves burgers and chicken wings and lots of suds out on the Main Street Pier.

The local **Shells** seafood restaurant is on the beach at 200 S. Atlantic Ave. (© **386/258-0007;** www.shellsseafood.com), a block north of International Raceway Boulevard. See p. 365 for details about this inexpensive chain. **Buca di Beppo** (a boisterous, fun, and loud restaurant serving "immigrant southern Italian specialties" family style) is open for dinners only, until 10pm (11pm Fri–Sat). Expect to take home leftovers, as the portions are huge—but don't worry, you'd want to anyway: The food is surprisingly good, especially for a "theme" restaurant (2514 W. International Speedway Blvd.; © **386/253-6523;** www.bucadibeppo.com).

AT THE BEACHES

Down the Hatch ★ (Value SEAFOOD   Occupying a 1940s fish camp on the Halifax River, Down the Hatch serves big portions of fresh fish and seafood (note its shrimp boat docked outside). Inexpensive burgers and sandwiches are available, too. The scenic views include boats and shorebirds visible through the big picture windows—you might even see dolphins frolicking. At night, arrive early to catch the sunset over the river, and also to beat the crowd at this very popular place. In summer, light fare is served outside on an awning-covered deck.

4894 Front St., Ponce Inlet. Ⓒ **386/761-4831**. Call ahead for Priority Seating. Main courses $9–$25 (most $10–$16); breakfast $2–$5; burgers and sandwiches $3–$6.50; early-bird menu (served 11am–5pm) $6–$8. AE, MC, V. Daily 8am–10pm. Closed 1st week in Dec. Take Atlantic Ave. south, make a right on Beach St., and follow the signs.

Ocean Deck Restaurant & Beach Club *(Value)* SEAFOOD/PUB FARE Known by spring-breakers, bikers, and other beachgoers as Daytona's best "beach pub" since 1940, the Ocean Deck is also the best restaurant in the busy area around the Main Street Pier. Opening to the sand and surf, the downstairs reggae bar is as sweaty, noisy, and packed as ever (a band plays down there nightly from 9pm–2:30am). The upstairs dining room can be noisy, too, but you can come here for some good food, reasonable prices, and great ocean views. You can choose from a wide range of seafood, chicken, sandwiches, and the best burgers on the beach, but don't pass up the mahimahi (look for "trophy" on the menu), first broiled with peppery Jamaican spices and then finished off on a grill, a bargain at $9. There's valet parking after dark, or you can park free at the lot behind the Ocean Deck's Reggae Republic surf shop, a block away on Atlantic Avenue.

127 S. Ocean Ave. (at Kemp St.). Ⓒ **386/253-5224**. www.oceandeck.com. Main courses $9–$18; salads and sandwiches $5–$8. AE, DISC, MC, V. Daily 11am–2am (bar to 3am).

ON THE MAINLAND
Super-Cheap Eats

The Cellar ⚐ AMERICAN   An excellent place for ladies who lunch, this tea-room occupies the basement of a Victorian home built in 1907 as President Warren G. Harding's winter home (he spent election eve here in 1920) and now is listed in the National Register of Historic Places. It couldn't be more charm-ing, with low ceilings, backlit reproduction Tiffany windows, fresh flowers everywhere, linen tablecloths and napkins, and china teacups. If you can play the piano, help yourself to the baby grand. A wide-ranging lunch menu offers the likes of the house signature chicken salad as a platter or croissant sandwich, a quiche du jour, crab-cake sandwich, vegetarian lasagna, or chicken potpie. In the warm months, there's outdoor seating at umbrella tables on a covered gar-den patio.

220 Magnolia Ave. (between Palmetto and Ridgewood aves.). Ⓒ **386/258-0011**. Soups, salads, and sand-wiches $6–$9. AE, DISC, MC, V. Mon–Fri 11am–3pm.

McK's Dublin Station AMERICAN/IRISH   Worth knowing about because it serves food after midnight, this upscale Irish pub has an eclectic menu. The fare includes club sandwiches, burgers, a mahimahi wrap, and a few main courses of steaks, fish, and chicken. The food isn't exceptional, but it's perfectly acceptable after a few Bass ales. The service is sometimes rushed, but usually pleasant.

218 S. Beach St. (between Magnolia St. and Ivy Lane). Ⓒ **386/238-3321**. Reservations not accepted. Main courses $6–$15; salads and sandwiches $5–$8. AE, MC, V. Mon–Wed 11am–9pm; Thurs–Sat 11am–10pm__ (bar open later).

Worth a Splurge

Frappes North ⚐⚐ CREATIVE AMERICAN/FUSION   It's worth the 6-mile drive north to Bobby and Meryl Frappier's sophisticated, hip establishment, at which they provide this area's most entertaining cuisine. Several chic dining rooms—one has beams extending like spokes from a central pole—set the stage for an inventive, ever-changing "Menu of the Moment" fusing a multitude of styles. Ingredients are always fresh, and the herbs come from the restaurant's garden. You may run into treats such as organically groovy chicken with goat cheese, prosciutto, shiitake mushrooms, and Madeira wine sauce or maple-glazed crispy duck. Bobby and Meryl always have at least one vegetarian (though not necessarily nondairy) main course. Lunch is a steal here, with dinner-size main courses at a fraction of dinnertime prices. The restaurant is in a storefront on the mainland stretch of Granada Boulevard, Ormand Beach's main drag.

123 W. Granada Blvd. (Fla. 40; between Ridgewood Ave. and Washington St.), Ormand Beach. 🕿 **386/615-4888.** www.frappesnorth.com. Reservations recommended. Main courses $15–$25; lunch $7–$11. AE, MC, V. Mon–Fri 11:30am–2:30pm; Mon–Sat 5–10pm. From the beaches, drive 4 miles north on Fla. A1A to left on Granada Blvd. (Fla. 40); cross Halifax River to restaurant on right.

DAYTONA BEACH AFTER DARK

Check the Friday edition of the Daytona Beach *News-Journal* (www.n-jcenter. com) for its weekly "Go-Do" and the Sunday edition for the "Master Calendar" section, which list upcoming events. Other good sources are *Happenings Magazine* and *Backstage Pass Magazine,* two tabloids available at the visitor center (see "Essentials," earlier in this chapter) and in many hotel lobbies.

There are also ghost tours led by certified ghost hunters. Merging legends with science, you're guaranteed to have a spooky time (at least it's more interesting than most touristy ghost tours). A portion of all proceeds goes to cemetery preservation and restoration, so at least you can feel good about the fee. Tickets are $8 per person, children under 6 are free. Contact **Haunts of Daytona** (🕿 **386/253-6034;** www.hauntsofdaytona.com) for tours and start times.

THE PERFORMING ARTS The city-operated **Peabody Auditorium,** 600 Auditorium Blvd., between Noble Street and Wild Olive Avenue (box office 🕿 **386/254-4545** or 386/671-3460), is Daytona's major venue for serious performance, including concerts by the local Symphony Society (🕿 **386/253-2901**). Professional actors perform Broadway musicals during winter and summer at the **Seaside Music Theater,** 176 N. Beach St., downtown (🕿 **800/854-5592** or 386/252-6200; www.seasidemusictheater.org).

Under the city auspices, the **Oceanfront Bandshell** (🕿 **386/671-3400**), on the boardwalk next to the Adam's Mark Hotel, hosts a series of free big-name concerts every Sunday night from early June to Labor Day. It's also the scene of raucous spring-break concerts.

THE CLUB & BAR SCENE In addition to the following, the sophisticated **Clocktower Lounge** at the Adam's Mark Daytona Beach Resort is worth a visit.

600 North, 600 North Atlantic (🕿 **904/255-4471**), *is* Baywatch revisited, with buxom bikini babe staffers who have actually been extras on the show, and a year-round spring-break vibe with assorted drinking and thong sporting contests.

The **Boot Hill Saloon,** 310 Main St. (🕿 **904/258-9506**), is a bluesy, brewsy honky tonk especially popular during race and bike weeks. If line dancing is your thang, then scoot your boots over to the **Rockin' Ranch,** 801 S. Nova Rd. (🕿 **904/947-0785**), an überfun country-western bar with live music and even line-dancing lessons.

Main Street and **Seabreeze Boulevard** on the beach are happening areas where dozens of bars (and a few topless shows) cater to leather-clad bikers.

A popular beachfront bar for more than 40 years, the **Ocean Deck Restaurant & Beach Club,** 127 S. Ocean Ave. (🕿 **386/253-5224;** see "Great Deals on Dining," above), is packed with a mix of locals and tourists, young and old, who come for live music and cheap drinks. Reggae or ska bands play after

9:30pm. There's valet parking after dark, or leave your vehicle at Ocean Deck's Reggae Republic surf shop on Atlantic Avenue.

3 St. Augustine: America's First City ⋆⋆

105 miles NE of Orlando, 302 miles N of Miami, 39 miles S of Jacksonville

With its 17th-century fort, old city gates, horse-drawn carriages clip-clopping along narrow streets, historic buildings, and reconstructed 18th-century Spanish Quarter, St. Augustine seems more like a picturesque European village than a modern Floridian city. This is, after all, the oldest continuous European settlement in the United States (no, it wasn't Jamestown in 1607 or the Pilgrims at Plymouth Rock in 1620). A group of French Huguenots settled in 1562 near the mouth of the St. Johns River, in present-day Jacksonville. Three years later, a Spanish force under Pedro Menéndez de Avilés arrived on the scene, wiped out the Huguenot men (de Avilés spared their women and children), and established a settlement on the harbor he named "St. Augustín."

The colony survived a succession of attacks by pirates, Indians, and the British over the next 2 centuries. The Treaty of Paris, ending the French and Indian War, ceded the town to Britain in 1763, but the British gave it back 20 years later. The United States took control when it acquired Florida from Spain in 1821.

Tourism is St. Augustine's main industry these days; but despite the daily invasion (with good reason—there are a plethora of interesting attractions), it's an exceptionally charming town, with good restaurants, a small-town nightlife, and shopping bargains. Give yourself 2 days here just to see the highlights, longer to savor this historic gem: St. Augustine is one of those places that actually lives up to most of the sickly sweet and sentimental promotional literature written about it.

ESSENTIALS

GETTING THERE   The Daytona Beach airport (p. 478) is about an hour's drive south of St. Augustine, but services are more frequent—and fares usually lower—at Jacksonville's international airport, about the same distance north (p. 503). Amtrak's nearest train station is in Jacksonville. See "Essentials," in sections 2 and 4 of this chapter, for details.

VISITOR INFORMATION   Before you go, contact the **St. Augustine, Ponte Vedra & The Beaches Visitors and Convention Bureau,** 88 Riberia St., Suite 400, St. Augustine, FL 32084 (② **800/653-2489** or 904/829-1711; www. visitoldcity.com), and request the *Visitor's Guide,* detailing attractions, events, restaurants, accommodations, shopping, and more.

The **St. Augustine Visitor Information Center** is at 10 Castillo Dr., at San Marco Avenue, opposite the Castillo de San Marcos National Monument (② **904/825-1000**). There are numerous ways to see the city, depending on your interest and time, and this is a good place to make your plans. For $1, you can watch "Struggle to Survive," a 42-minute video about the town's difficult first 14 years (history buffs will enjoy it; otherwise, it's a good way to kill an hour on a rainy day). However, the free 22-minute orientation video is more helpful in planning your visit. Once you've looked through their extensive information and made a plan, you can buy tickets for sightseeing trains and trolleys, which include discount admissions to the attractions (see "Getting Around," below). The center is open daily, from 8:30am to 5:30pm.

GETTING AROUND   Once you've parked at the visitor center, you can walk or take one of the sightseeing trolleys, trains, or horse-drawn carriages around the historic district. The trolleys and trains follow 7-mile routes, stopping at the visitor center and at or near most attractions between 8:30am and 5pm daily. You can get off at any stop, visit the attraction, and step aboard the next vehicle that comes along. Several vehicles make continuous circuits along the route throughout the day; you won't have to wait more than 20 minutes. If you don't get off at any attractions, it takes about 1 hour and 10 minutes to complete the tour. They don't all go to the same sights, so speak with their agents at the visitor center to pick the right one for you. You can buy tickets there or from the drivers. The companies also sell **discounted tickets** to some attractions.

St. Augustine Historical Sightseeing (© **904/826-4218** or 904/829-3800) operates the green-and-white, open-air buses (and enclosed buses when it rains, a definite advantage). You can park your car at the headquarters (the Authentic Old Jail and the Florida Heritage Museum at the Authentic Old Jail, which are also stops on the tour). The bus tours cost $15 for adults, $5 for kids 6 to 12, free for kids under 6.

St. Augustine Sightseeing Trains (© **800/226-6545** or 904/829-6545; www.redtrains.com) cover all the main sites except the Authentic Old Jail and the Florida Heritage Museum at the Authentic Old Jail, but its red open-air trains are small enough to go down more of the narrow historic-district streets. Tickets are $14 for adults, $5 for kids 6 to 12, free for kids under 6, and are good for 3 consecutive days. The company also sells package tickets for your convenience.

You may also want to see the sights from the back of a horse-drawn carriage. **St. Augustine Transfer Company** (© **904/829-2391;** www.staugustinetransfer. com) has been showing people around town since 1877. The carriages line up on Avenida Menendez, south of Castillo de San Marcos National Monument. Slow-paced, entertainingly driver-narrated 45-minute to 1-hour rides past major landmarks and attractions are offered from 8am to midnight. Private tours and hotel and restaurant pickups are available. Carriage tours cost $20 for adults, $10 for kids 5 to 11, free for kids under 6. Add $3 if you want to take a ride after dark.

For more personalized tours, call **Tour Saint Augustine** (© **800/797-3778** or 904/825-0087), which offers guided walking tours around the historical area. Tours range from $10 per person for 1 hour.

You can also search for old spirits with the nightly **Ghost Tours of St. Augustine** ★★ (© **888/461-1009** or 904/461-1009; www.ghosttoursofstaugustine. com), in which guides in period dress lead you through the historic district or to the St. Augustine Lighthouse; tickets are $10 to $20 per person, depending on the tour you choose, children under 6 free. They also have 1-hour ghost

---

(**Tips**   **Where to Park in "St. Aug"**

On-street parking is nonexistent in St. Augustine's historic district, and metered parking lots are difficult to find and are often full. Your best bet is to park in the large lots behind the visitor center on Castillo Drive. The $3 fee is good for 2 consecutive days, so you may leave and return at will. Plus, most of the top historic attractions are within walking distance of the center, as it is virtually across the street from the Old City Gates.

cruises on the river in a 72-foot-tall-mast schooner. They cost $28 per person including soft drinks and snacks. Call for schedule and reservations.

The Sunshine Bus Company (© **904/823-4816**) runs public bus routes Monday through Saturday from 6am to 7pm. The north-south line runs between the St. Augustine Airport on U.S. 1 and the historic district via San Marco Avenue and the Greyhound bus terminal on Malaga Street. Rides cost $1 per person. Call for the schedule.

For a taxi, call **Yellow Cab** (© **904/824-6888**).

Solano Cycle, 61 San Marco Ave., at Locust Avenue (© **904/825-6766;** www.solanocycle.com), 2 blocks north of the visitor center, rents bicycles, mopeds, and scooters. Bikes cost $14 a day; scooters are $56, and mopeds are $38. Open daily from 10am to 6pm.

SEEING THE TOP HISTORIC ATTRACTIONS

St. George Street from King Street north to the Old City Gate (at Orange St.) is the heart of the historic district. Lined with a plethora of restaurants and boutiques selling everything from T-shirts to antiques, these 4 blocks get the lion's share of the town's tourists. You'll have much less company if you poke around the narrow streets of the primarily residential neighborhood south of King Street.

Most of the town's attractions do not have guided tours, but most do have docents on hand to answer questions.

Be sure to drive through the parking lot of the Howard Johnson Express Inn, at 137 San Marco Ave., to see a gorgeous and stately **live oak tree** ★★ that is at least 600 years old and then continue east to **Magnolia Avenue** ★★, which is a spectacularly beautiful street with a lovely canopy of old magnolia trees.

Castillo de San Marcos National Monument ★   As far as fortresses are concerned, this one's pretty cool. America's oldest and best-preserved masonry fortification took 23 years (1672–95) to build. It is stellar in design, with a double drawbridge (the only way in or out) over a 40-foot dry moat. Diamond-shaped bastions in each corner, which enabled cannons to set up a deadly crossfire, contained domed sentry towers. The seemingly indestructible Castillo was never captured in battle, and its coquina (limestone made from broken sea shells and corals) walls did not crumble when pounded by enemy artillery or violent storms throughout more than 300 years. Today, the old bombproof storerooms surrounding the central plaza house exhibits documenting the history of the fort, a national monument since 1924. You can also tour the vaulted powder magazine, a dank prison cell (supposedly haunted), the chapel, and guard rooms. Then, climb the stairs to get a great view of the Matanzas Bay. A self-guided tour map and brochure are provided at the ticket booth. If available, the 20- to 30-minute ranger talks are well worth attending. There are popular torchlight tours of the fort in winter (call for schedule).

If you like forts, you should also check out **Fort Matanzas,** built on an island in the 1740s to warn St. Augustine of enemy attacks from the south (which were out of reach of the Castillo de San Marcos). For more information, call © **904/ 471-0116** or visit www.nps.gov/foma. The monument is open daily from 8:30am to 5:30pm, and both admission to the fort and the ferry ride to the island are free, though donations are accepted.

1 E. Castillo Dr. (at San Marco Ave.). © **904/829-6506**. www.nps.gov/casa. Admission $5 adults for 7-day pass, $2 children 6–16, free for children under 6 with an adult. Fort daily 8:45am–4:45pm; grounds daily 5:30am–midnight.

Colonial Spanish Quarter and Spanish Quarter Museum ★★   If H.G. Wells were alive, he'd think he was witnessing living proof of a bona fide time-travel machine when he got a load of this recreated colonial Spanish village, complete with costumed folk doing things they used to do back in the 1700s. Watch as the blacksmiths, carpenters, leatherworkers, and home makers demonstrate their skills and show you what life was like before the Internet. All architecture and landscape have been recreated within this 2-square-block park, which, in my opinion, is infinitely more fun than the museum itself. Do take a 20-minute guided tour of the **DeMesa-Sanchez House** (ca. 1740–60), the only authentic colonial-era structure in the compound (the others are reproductions). If you're into all this recreated history, then do not miss the Old St. Augustine Village Museum (see below), which covers even more history.

33 St. George St. (between Cuna and Orange sts.). ℭ **904/825-6830**. www.historicstaugustine.com. Admission $7 adults, $6 seniors, $4 students 6–18, free for children 5 and under; or $13 per family. Daily 9am–5:30pm (last entry at 4:30pm).

Lightner Museum ★★★   Now *this* is a museum. Henry Flagler's opulent Spanish Renaissance–style Alcazar Hotel, built in 1889, closed during the Depression and stayed vacant until Chicago publishing magnate Otto C. Lightner bought the building in 1948 to house his vast collection of Victoriana. The building is an attraction in itself and makes a gorgeous museum, centering on an open palm courtyard with an arched stone bridge spanning a fishpond. The first floor houses a Victorian village, with shop fronts representing emporia selling period wares. A Victorian Science and Industry Room displays shells, rocks, minerals, and Native American artifacts in beautiful turn-of-the-20th-century cases. Other exhibits include stuffed birds, an Egyptian mummy, steam-engine models, and amazing examples of Victorian glassblowing (yes, it's a strange amalgamation for a museum, but there's sure to be *something* you're interested in). Plan to spend about 90 minutes exploring it all, and be sure to be here at 11am or 2pm, when a room of automated musical instruments erupts in concerts of period music. Check out where the cafe is, too, which is housed in what used to be a stunning indoor pool. The imposing building across King Street was Henry Flagler's rival resort, the Ponce de León Hotel. It now houses **Flagler College,** which runs don't-miss-it 45-minute tours daily (at 10am and 2pm) of its magnificent Tiffany stained-glass windows, ornate Spanish-Renaissance architecture, and gold-leafed Maynard murals ($5 adults, $1 kids under 12; call ℭ **904/823-3378** or visit www.flagler.edu/news_events/tours.html for more information). Across Cordova Street stands another competitor of the day, the 1888-vintage Casa Monica Hotel (p. 500).

75 King St. (at Granada St.). ℭ **904/824-2874**. www.lightnermuseum.org. Admission $8 adults, $2 college students with ID and children 12–18, free for children 11 and under. Daily 9am–5pm (last tour 4pm).

The Oldest Store Museum ★★   The C&F Hamblen General Store, think a prehistoric WalMart, was St. Augustine's one-stop shopping center from 1835 to 1960, and the museum on its premises today replicates the emporium at the turn of the 20th century. On display are more than 100,000 items sold here in that era, many of them gleaned from the store's attic. They include high-button shoes, butter churns, spinning wheels, 1890s bathing suits, barrels of dill pickles (you can purchase one), and medicines that were 90% alcohol. Some 19th-century brand-name products shown here are still available today, among them Hershey's chocolate, Coca-Cola, Ivory soap, and Campbell's soups. It all makes for about 30 minutes of fascinating browsing.

4 Artillery Lane (between St. George and Aviles sts. behind Trinity Episcopal Church). © 904/829-9729. www.oldcity.com/oldstore. Admission $5 adults, $4.50 seniors over 60, $1.50 children 6–12, free for children 5 and under. Mon–Sat 10am–4pm; Sun noon–4pm.

Old St. Augustine Village Museum ★★   More time travel in St. Augustine is available at this awesome museum recreating life back in the old days. Operated by Daytona Beach's excellent Museum of Arts and Sciences (p. 483), this museum brings to life each period of the city's history, from Spanish colonial times to the early 20th century. The 10 restored homes here—built between 1790 and 1910—are original and on their original building sites. The oldest was owned for a year in the early 19th century by Achille Murat, Napoleon's exiled nephew (original letters from the French emperor are among the many fascinating exhibits). Many of the houses have varying exhibits inside, though since this museum is a work in progress, some are also closed, temporarily, until refurbishments are complete. The reconstructed Star General Store sells preserves and other Victorian-era goods. You'll need 2 hours to see it all, including the 30-minute guided tour. Admission is good all day, so if you miss the start of a tour, you can leave and come back.

250 St. George St. (entry on Bridge St. between St. George and Cordova sts.). © 904/823-9722. www.old-staug-village.com. Admission $7 adults, $6 seniors, $5 children under 12. Daily 9am–5pm. Guided tours on the hour 10am–3pm except 1pm.

MORE HISTORIC ATTRACTIONS

Authentic Old Jail   It's no Alcatraz, but in a sinister way, this old jail is kind of quaint. This compact prison, a mile north of the visitor center, may be authentic, but it is not particularly historic. It was built in 1890 and served as the county jail until 1953. The sheriff and his wife raised their children upstairs and used the same kitchen facilities to prepare the inmates' meals and their own. Among the "regular" cells, you can also see a maximum-security cell where murderers and horse thieves were confined, a cell housing prisoners condemned to hang (they could see the gallows being constructed from their window), and a grim solitary-confinement cell—with no windows or mattress. A restaurant here serves inexpensive lunch fare.

167 San Marco Ave. (at Williams St.). © 904/829-3800. Admission $5 adults, $4 children 6–12, free for children 5 and under. Daily 8:30am–5pm.

Fountain of Youth Archaeological Park *Overrated*   Considering that Botox and plastic surgery are the real fountains of youth, why bother? Never mind that Juan Ponce de León never found the Fountain of Youth, this 25-acre archaeological park bills itself as North America's first historic site. Smithsonian Institution archaeological digs have established that a Timucuan Indian village existed on this site some 1,000 years ago, but there's no evidence that Ponce de León visited here during his 1513 voyage of discovery. You can wander around the not-so-interesting grounds yourself, but you'll learn more on a 45-minute guided tour or a planetarium show about 16th-century celestial navigation. **Be warned:** This place could be a secondary dictionary definition for the phrase *tourist trap* (not to mention the water from the fountain smells and tastes *awful*). Nevertheless, the grounds are lovely and the nonfountain exhibits are okay, which is good, because people feel the need to come here, even though it's basically a waste of time.

11 Magnolia Ave. (at Williams St.). © 800/356-8222 or 904/829-3168. Admission $6 adults, $5 seniors, $3 children 6–12, free for children 5 and under. Daily 9am–5pm.

Mission of Nombre de Dios   This serene setting overlooking the Intracoastal Waterway is believed to be the site of the first permanent mission in the United States, founded in 1565. The mission is a popular destination of religious pilgrimages. Whatever your beliefs, it's a beautiful tree-shaded spot, ideal for quiet meditation.

27 Ocean Ave. (east of San Marco Ave.). © **904/824-2809.** Free admission; donations appreciated. Daily 8am–5:30pm.

St. Augustine Lighthouse & Museum   Photo-op alert! This 165-foot-tall structure, Florida's first official lighthouse, was built in 1875 (with a signature black-and-white spiral stripe and red lantern) to replace the old Spanish lighthouse that had stood at the inlet since 1565. Sitting in a shady grove of live oaks, the lightkeeper's Victorian cottage was destroyed by fire in 1970 but was meticulously restored to its Victorian splendor. Also new is a Victorian-style visitor center that houses a museum explaining the history of the lighthouse and the area. You should be in good physical condition (children must be at least 7 years old *and* 4 ft. tall) to climb the 219 steps to the top of the lighthouse, where you can see as far as 19 nautical miles on a clear day.

81 Lighthouse Ave. (off Fla. A1A east of the Bridge of Lions). © **904/829-0745.** www.staugustinelighthouse. com. Admission to museum and tower $6.95 adults, $5.95 seniors, $4.50 children 7–11, free for kids under 7 and all active-duty and retired military personnel. Daily 9am–6pm. Follow Fla. A1A south across Bridge of Lions; take last left before turnoff to Anastasia State Park.

OTHER ENTERTAINING ATTRACTIONS

St. Augustine Alligator Farm and Zoological Park ★★ *Kids*   If you have gotten over the shock of Steve Irwin aka The Crocodile Hunter's Jacko-esque foible in which he dangled his three month old infant in front of a massive crocodile, then head over to the St. Augustine Alligator Farm and Zoological Park, where gators and crocs are a dime a dozen. In fact, there are more than 2,700 gators and crocodiles—including some rare white ones—on display at this more-than-century-old attraction. In fact, it houses the world's only complete collection of all 22 species of crocodilians, a category that includes alligators, crocodiles, caimans, and gavials. Other creatures living here include geckos, prehensile-tailed skinks, lizards, snakes, tortoises, monkeys, and exotic birds. There are ponds and marshes filled with a variety of ducks, geese, swans, herons, egrets, ibises, wood storks, and other native wading birds as well as a petting zoo with pygmy goats, potbellied pigs, miniature horses, mouflon sheep, and deer. Entertaining (and educational) 20-minute alligator and reptile shows take place hourly throughout the day, and spring through fall you can often see narrated feedings. There's also a stuffed (and famous) giant crocodile from New Guinea named Gomek on display.

999 Anastasia Blvd. (Fla. A1A), east of Bridge of Lions at Old Quarry Rd. © **904/824-3337.** www.alligator farm.com (check for discounts). Admission $16 adults, $9 children 3–10, free for children under 3. Daily 9am–5pm; summer hours 9am–6pm.

HITTING THE BEACH

There are several places to find sand and sea: in **Vilano Beach,** on the north side of St. Augustine Inlet; and in **St. Augustine Beach,** on the south side (the inlet dumps the Matanzas and North rivers into the Atlantic). Be aware, however, that erosion has almost swallowed the beach from the inlet as far south as Old Beach Road in St. Augustine Beach. The U.S. Army Corps of Engineers is reclaiming the sand, but in the meantime, hotels and homes here have rock seawalls instead of sand bordering the sea.

Where Golf Is King

Passionate golf fans can easily spend a day at the **World Golf Hall of Fame** ⭐ (© **904/940-4123**), a state-of-the-art museum honoring professional golf, its great players, and the sport's famous supporters (including comedian Bob Hope and singer Dinah Shore). It's the centerpiece of **World Golf Village,** which is a complex of hotels, shops, offices, and 18-hole golf courses (see "Affordable Outdoor Activities" below). There's an IMAX screen next door.

Museum admission is $12 adults, $11 seniors and students, $7 children 5 to 12. IMAX movie tickets range from $9 to $14 adults, $6 to $12 seniors and students, $5 to $9 children 5 to 12. Combination tickets to the museum and one IMAX movie cost $17 for adults, $15 seniors and students, $11 children 5 to 12. A round on the putting green costs $7 for adults, $6 seniors and students, and $5 for children 5 to 12. Admission and movies are free for children under 5. The museum is open daily from 10am to 6pm (IMAX movies run until 8pm Fri–Sat).

You don't have to play the real courses, because the village is built around a lake with a "challenge hole" sitting out in the middle, 132 feet from the shoreline. You can hit balls at it or play a round on the nearby putting course. The Walkway of Champions (whose signatures appear in pavement stones) circles the lake and passes a shopping complex whose main tenant is the two-story **Tour Stop** (© **904/940-0422**), a purveyor of pricey apparel and equipment.

The village is at exit 95A off I-95. For more information, contact World Golf Village, 21 World Golf Place, St. Augustine, FL 32092 (© **904/ 940-4000**; www.wgv.com).

Erosion has made a less noticeable impact on the beautiful **Anastasia State Park** ⭐⭐, on Anastasia Boulevard (Fla. A1A) across the Bridge of Lions and just past the Alligator Farm, where the 4 miles of beach (on which you can drive and park) are still backed by picturesque dunes. On its riverside, the area faces a lagoon flanked by tidal marshes. Amenities and activities include shaded picnic areas with grills, restrooms, windsurfing, sailing and canoeing (on a saltwater lagoon), a nature trail, and saltwater fishing (for bluefish, pompano, sea trout, redfish, and flounder—a license is required for out-of-state residents). In summer, you can rent chairs, beach umbrellas, and surfboards. There's good birdwatching here, too, especially in spring and fall; pick up a brochure at the entrance. The 139 wooded campsites are in high demand year-round. They have picnic tables, grills, and electricity. Admission to the park is $5 per vehicle and $1 for bicyclists and pedestrians. Campsites cost $23. For camping reservations, call © **800/326-3521** or go to the website at www.reserveamerica.com. The day-use area is open daily from 8am to sunset. You can bring your pets. For more information, contact Anastasia State Park, 1340A Fla. A1A S., St. Augustine, FL 32084 (© **904/461-2033;** www.floridastateparks.org/anastasia).

All St. Augustine beaches charge a fee of $3 per car at official access points from Memorial Day to Labor Day; the rest of the year you can park free, but there are no lifeguards on duty or toilet facilities on the beach.

ST. AUGUSTINE: AMERICA'S FIRST CITY

AFFORDABLE OUTDOOR ACTIVITIES

For additional outdoor options, contact the St. Augustine, Ponte Vedra & The Beaches Visitors and Convention Bureau (p. 489) and ask them to send you a copy of their *Outdoor Recreation Guide.*

CRUISES   The Usina family has been running **St. Augustine Scenic Cruises** (© **904/824-1806;** www.scenic-cruise.com) on Matanzas Bay since the turn of the 20th century. They offer 75-minute narrated tours aboard the double-decker *Victory III,* departing from the Municipal Marina just south of the Bridge of Lions. You can sometimes spot dolphins, brown pelicans, cormorants, and king-fishers. Snacks, soft drinks, beer, and wine are sold on board. Departures are normally at 11am and 1, 2:45, and 4:30pm daily except Christmas, with an additional tour at 6:15pm from April 1 to May 21 and Labor Day to October 15; from May 22 to Labor Day there are two additional tours, at 6:45 and 8:30pm. Call ahead—schedules can change during inclement weather. Fares are $12 adults, $8.50 seniors, $7.50 juniors 13 to 18, $5.75 children 4 to 12, free for children under 4. If you're driving, allow time to find parking on the street.

You can also take the free ferry to Fort Matanzas on Rattlesnake Island. There are often dolphins in the water as you make the trip, and the fort is interesting if you have the time. Ferries take off from 8635 Highway A1A (follow A1A south out of St. Augustine for about 15 miles). Call © **904/471-0116** or visit www.nps.gov/foma for more information.

FISHING   You can fish to your heart's content at **Anastasia State Park** (see "Hitting the Beach," above). You can also cast your line off **St. Johns County Fishing Pier,** on the north end of St. Augustine Beach (© **904/461-0119**). The pier is open 24 hours daily and has a bait shop with rental equipment that is open from 6am to 10pm. Admission is $2 ($1 children under 12) for fishing, 50¢ per person for sightseeing.

For full-day, half-day, and overnight **deep-sea fishing** excursions (for snapper, grouper, porgy, amberjack, sea bass, and other species), contact the **Sea Love Marina,** 250 Vilano Rd. (Fla. A1A north), at the eastern end of the Vilano Beach Bridge (© **904/824-3328;** www.sealovefishing.com). Full-day trips on the party boat *Sea Love II* cost about $50, half-day trips, $35. No license is required, and rod, reel, bait, and tackle are supplied. Bring your own food and drink.

GOLF   The area's best golf resorts are in Ponte Vedra Beach—about a half-hour's drive north on Fla. A1A, closer to Jacksonville than St. Augustine (see "Accommodations You Can Afford," in section 4, later in this chapter, for details).

At World Golf Village, 12 miles north of St. Augustine at exit 95A off I-95 (see the box, "Where Golf Is King," above), **The Slammer & The Squire** and **The King & The Bear** (© **904/940-6088;** www.wgv.com) together offer 36 holes amid a wildlife preserve. Locals say they're not as challenging as their greens fees, about $100 in summer, $165 in winter, including cart. For those not schooled in golf history, the "Slammer" is in honor of Sam Sneed, the "Squire" is for Gene Sarazen, the "King" is Arnold Palmer, and the "Bear" is Jack Nicklaus. Palmer and Nicklaus actually collaborated in designing their course.

Nicklaus also had a hand in the stunning course at the **Ocean Hammock Golf Club** ★★ (© **386/477-4600;** www.oceanhammock.com), on Fla. A1A in Palm Coast, about halfway between St. Augustine and Daytona Beach. Opened in late 2000 with 6 of its holes skirting the beach, it is the first truly oceanside course built in Florida since the 1920s.

There are only a few courses in St. Augustine, including a rather flat 18 at the **Ponce de León Hotel, Golf & Conference Resort** and the **St. Augustine Shores Golf Club,** 707 Shores Blvd., off U.S. 1 (© **904/794-4653**). The latter is a par-70 course featuring 18 holes, lots of water, a lighted driving range and putting green, and a restaurant and lounge. Greens fees usually are under $30, including cart.

For more course information online, go to www.golf.com and www.florida golfing.com, or call the **Florida Sports Foundation** (© **850/488-8347**) or **Florida Golfing** (© **866/833-2663**).

SAILING   You can spend 4 hours under sail with Captain Paul Kulik on board his *Voyager* (© **904/347-7183;** www.villavoyager.com), a 22-foot-wide tri-maran, which departs the Municipal Marina next to the Bridge of Lions. The cruises cost $38 per person, including sandwiches, soft drinks, and beer. The boat can carry a maximum of six guests, so call for reservations and schedule.

WATERSPORTS   Jet skis and surfing and windsurfing equipment can be rented at **Surf Station,** 1020 Anastasia Blvd. (Fla. A1A), a block south of the Alligator Farm (© **904/471-9463**); and at **Raging Water Sports,** at the Conch House Marina Resort, 57 Comares Ave. (© **904/829-5001**), which is off Anastasia Avenue (Fla. A1A) halfway between the Bridge of Lions and the Alligator Farm.

SHOPPING

The winding streets of the historic district are home to dozens of **antiques stores** and **art galleries** stocked full of original paintings, sculptures, bric-a-brac, fine furnishings, china, and other treasures. Brick-lined **Aviles Street,** 1 block from the river, has an especially good mix of shops for browsing, as does **St. George Street** south of the visitor center and the Uptown area on **San Marco Avenue** a few blocks north of the center. The **Alcazar Courtyard Shops** at the Lightner Museum (© **904/824-2874**) have a good selection of antiques shops (p. 492). The visitor center has lists of art galleries and antiques shops, or you can contact the **Antique Dealers Association of St. Augustine,** 60 Cuna St., St. Augustine, FL 32084 (no phone).

Experience chocolate heaven at **Whetstone Chocolates,** 2 Coke Rd. (Fla. 312), between U.S. 1 and the Mickler O'Connell Bridge (© **904/825-1700**). Free self-guided tours of the store and factory usually take place Monday through Saturday from 10am to 5pm, but call to make sure of the factory's schedule. Whetstone has a retail outlet at 42 St. George St. in the historic district.

Outlet shoppers will find plenty of good hunting 7 miles northwest of down-town on Fla. 16 at I-95 in the **St. Augustine Outlet Mall** (© **904/825-1555;** www.staugustineoutlets.com), on the west side of I-95; and the enclosed, air-conditioned **Belz Factory Outlet World** (© **904/826-1311;** www.belz.com), on the east side of the Interstate. Stores in both malls are open Monday through Saturday from 9am to 9pm, Sunday from 10am to 6pm.

ACCOMMODATIONS YOU CAN AFFORD

There are plenty of moderate and inexpensive motels and hotels in St. Augustine. Most convenient to the historic district is the 40-room **Best Western Spanish Quarter Inn,** 6 Castillo Dr. (© **800/528-1234** or 904/824-4457; www.staugustinebestwestern.com), directly across the street from the visitor center. It's completely surrounded by an asphalt parking lot but does have a swimming pool and hot tub.

St. Augustine has more than two dozen bed-and-breakfasts in restored historic homes. They all provide free parking, complimentary breakfast, 24-hour refreshments, and plenty of atmosphere (the St. Francis Inn has a spectacular walled courtyard), but most accept neither young children nor guests who smoke (check before booking). Those listed below are in the historic district. For more choices, contact **St. Augustine Historic Inns,** P.O. Box 5268, St. Augustine, FL 33085-5268 (no phone; www.staugustineinns.com), for descriptions of its member properties.

Almost all accommodations increase their prices on weekends, when the town is most crowded with visitors, so if you're coming on a weekend expect the higher end of the listed rates. St. Johns County charges a 9% tax on hotel bills.

Bayfront Westcott House Bed & Breakfast Inn ★ Overlooking Matanzas Bay, this romantic, two-story, Key West–style wood-frame house offers rare opportunities for an uncluttered view from the porch, the second-story veranda, and a shady courtyard. The rooms—some with bay windows, two-person whirlpool tubs, and working fireplaces—are exquisitely furnished and immaculate. Yours might have authentic Victorian furnishings and a brass bed made up with a white quilt and lace dust ruffle.

146 Avenida Menendez (between Bridge and Francis sts.), St. Augustine, FL 32084. ✆ **800/513-9814** or 904/824-4301. Fax 904/824-4301. www.westcotthouse.com. 9 units, all with bathroom. $129–$229 double. Rates include full breakfast. AE, DISC, MC, V. **Amenities:** Access to nearby health club; Jacuzzi; free bicycles; massage. *In room:* A/C, TV, hair dryer.

Carriage Way Bed and Breakfast ★ *Value* Primarily occupying an 1883 Victorian wood-frame house fronted by roses and hibiscus, this bed-and-breakfast isn't fancy or formal, but it is comfortable, relaxed, and a good value. Rooms in the main house are furnished with simple antique reproductions, including many four-poster beds. One room even retains its original fireplace. A console TV, books, magazines, and games are provided in a homey parlor. For more privacy, two more rooms are down the street in "The Cottage," a one-story clapboard house built in 1885. It has its own living room and kitchen, and both the Miranda and the Ashton rooms have claw-foot bathtubs. Miranda also sports a two-person Jacuzzi, and Ashton has its own small back porch. Special packages can provide you with nice little touches as a gourmet picnic lunch, a horse drawn carriage around the city, and breakfast in bed.

⟨ *Tips* **A Swashbuckling Hostel**
────────────────────────────────

International travelers on the cheap congregate at the **Pirate Haus Inn & Hostel**, 32 Treasury St., at Charlotte Street (✆ **904/808-1999;** www.pirate haus.com), smack in the middle of the historic district. Done up in a pirate theme, this Spanish-style building has a communal kitchen, living room, and rooftop terrace. Affiliated with both Hostelling International and American Youth Hostels, the inn has five private rooms (three with their own bathrooms) equipped with either a queen or double bed plus one or two bunk beds. Two other rooms have dormitory-style bunk beds. Rooms cost $42 to $56 a night (higher on some weekends), while dorm beds go for $17 a night. MasterCard and Visa credit cards are accepted. Reservations are advised, especially on weekends. Rates include the hostel's famous all-you-can-eat pancake breakfast.

70 Cuna St. (between Cordova and Spanish sts.), St. Augustine, FL 32084. © 800/908-9832 or 904/829-2467. Fax 904/826-1461. www.carriageway.com. 11 units, all with bathroom. $89–$159 double. Rates include full breakfast. AE, DISC, MC, V. **Amenities:** Free use of bikes. *In room:* A/C, dataport.

Kenwood Inn   There's lots of pink here, but what makes this inn so unusual is its relatively large outdoor space, which includes a swimming pool, a lushly landscaped sun deck, and a secluded garden courtyard (complete with a koi pond and neat flower bed under a sprawling pecan tree). The Victorian wood-frame house with graceful verandas has served as a boardinghouse or inn since the late 19th century. Everything from the carpeting to the linens to the china is first class. Rooms are larger and more private than most other accommodations in converted single-family homes. Some rooms have neither televisions nor telephones.

38 Marine St. (at Bridge St.), St. Augustine, FL 32084. © 800/824-8151 or 904/824-2116. Fax 904/824-1689. www.oldcity.com/kenwood. 14 units, all with bathroom. $95–$175 double; bridal suite $225. Rates include continental breakfast. DISC, MC, V. **Amenities:** Outdoor pool; free use of bikes. *In room:* A/C, TV (in some), fax, dataport, kitchen, minibar, fridge, coffeemaker, hair dryer, iron, no phone (in some).

Monterey Inn *(Value)*   For the price, you can't find a better choice than this modest, wrought iron–trimmed motel overlooking the Matanzas Bay and close to the attractions and nightlife of the Old City. Three generations of the Six family have run this simple two-story motel, and they keep the 1960s building and grounds clean and functional. Rooms are not especially spacious but they are good enough to sleep in after a day on the beach.

16 Avenida Menendez (between Cuna and Hypolita sts.), St. Augustine, FL 32084. © 904/824-4482. Fax 904/829-8854. www.themontereyinn.com. 59 units. $59–$159 double. AE, DC, DISC, MC, V. **Amenities:** Heated outdoor pool. *In room:* A/C, TV, dataport, hair dryer.

Victorian House *(Kids)*   This 1897-vintage Victorian bed-and-breakfast features a wraparound porch and an adjoining old store, now dubbed the "Carriage House." The latter is divided into four units, one of which has a kitchenette. What's unusual is that children are welcome to stay in the Carriage House units, all of which have TVs and private entrances. Kids are not welcome to stay in the main house, however, whose rooms lack TVs. Country Victorian antiques adorn all units here, but none of the units have telephones.

11 Cadiz St. (between Aviles and Charlotte sts.), St. Augustine, FL 32084. © 877/703-0432 or 904/824-5214. Fax 904/824-7990. www.victorianhouse-inn.com. 8 units, all with bathroom. $95–$175 double. Rates include full breakfast. AE, DISC, MC, V. **Amenities:** Free bikes. *In room:* A/C, TV (4 units), kitchen (1 unit), no phone.

WORTH A SPLURGE

Casa Monica Hotel ★★★   This Moorish revival hotel was built in 1888 as a luxury hotel by Bostonian and YMCA founder Franklin W. Smith. Unfortunately, Smith never really opened it, since the furniture he'd purchased for the hotel never made it to St. Augustine, thanks to Henry Flagler, who owned the railroad the furniture was to be shipped on as well as the neighboring—and thus competing—hotel. In a bind and losing too much money, Smith finally sold the hotel to Flagler, for 25¢ on the dollar of what he originally spent, and the furniture mysteriously appeared almost immediately! (This Spanish-Moorish–style building—look for the atmospheric, arched, old-time carriage entrance near the present garage—was also used as the St. Johns County Courthouse from the 1960s until 1997.)

Now totally restored, it's easily the best hotel in town, with top-notch rooms and services. Most of the lovely guest quarters are spacious and fully modern hotel rooms, with Iberian-style armoires, wrought-iron headboards, and tapestry drapes. "Premium" rooms have sitting areas with sofas and easy chairs. All units have big bathrooms equipped with high-end toiletries and either a large walk-in shower or a combination tub-shower. Much more interesting are the "signature suites" installed in the building's two tile-topped towers and fortresslike central turret. Each of these one- to four-bedroom units is unique. One in the turret has a half-round living room with gun-port windows overlooking the historic district, while a three-story town house model in one of the towers has a huge whirlpool bathroom on its top floor.

95 Cordova St. (at King St.), St. Augustine, FL 32084. © 800/648-1888 or 904/827-1888. Fax 904/819-6065. www.casamonica.com. 138 units. $149–$239 double. Packages available. AE, DC, DISC, MC, V. Valet parking $13; limited free self-parking 2 blocks from hotel. **Amenities:** Restaurant; marketplace; bar; heated (and cooled) outdoor pool; access to nearby health club; exercise room; Jacuzzi; bike rental; children's programs; concierge; business center; limited room service; babysitting; coin-op washers and dryers. *In room:* A/C, TV, dataport, fridge, coffeemaker, hair dryer, iron, safe, high-speed Internet access.

GREAT DEALS ON DINING

In a town with as much tourist traffic as St. Augustine, there are, of course, a fair number of "tourist trap" restaurants. But on the whole, the food in St. Augustine, even at the popular eateries, is fairly priced and of good quality.

The historic district has a branch of Tampa's famous **Columbia** restaurant, at 98 St. George St., at Hypolita Street (© **904/824-3341**). Like the original in Ybor City (p. 367), this one sports Spanish architecture, including intricate tile work and courtyards with fountains.

A1A Ale Works ⭐ SEAFOOD Anyone who has ever chugged from a beer bong, entered a beer drinking contest, or simply just loves beer must visit the A1A Ale Works, the quintessential brew pub. You can't miss this two-story Victorian-style building on the waterfront opposite the Bridge of Lions. One of the city's most popular and fun watering holes, the noisy downstairs bar offers nightly entertainment, which sometimes filters upstairs into the restaurant. Despite the noise potential, the kitchen turns out a surprisingly good blend of new-world Floribbean, Cuban, Caribbean, and Latino styles, in a nice setting with big windows and outside balcony seating overlooking the river and Bridge of Lions. Most of the seafood is very fresh, and the sauces are made to order. The spicy ahi stick appetizer (sushi-grade tuna, pickled ginger, and sesame seeds wrapped in a wonton skin, cooked rare, served over Caribbean slaw and topped with a wasabi and siracha aioli) is as good as it gets, and you shouldn't leave without trying it. Don't overlook the nightly specials, either, especially the fresh fish. The house brew ranges from a very light lager to a nonalcoholic root beer.

1 King St. (at Avenida Menendez). © 904/829-2977. Call for preferred seating. Main courses $12–$28; sandwiches $7–$9. AE, DC, DISC, MC, V. Sun–Thurs 11am–10:30pm; Fri–Sat 11am–11pm. Late-night menu served downstairs.

Gypsy Cab Co. ⭐⭐ *Value* NEW AMERICAN Billing itself as a temple of "urban cuisine," owner-chef Ned Pollack's high-energy establishment, with gaudy purple neon stripes outside and bright, art-filled dining rooms inside, offers the town's most interesting culinary experience. Ned's creative menu changes daily, although a hearty black-bean soup is a constant winner. If it's available, try the veal with bacon-horseradish cream or the grouper in a tomato-basil sauce. As a capper, we recommend Amaretto cheesecake or Key lime pie. Also worthy of note, the house salad dressing is so good they sell it by the bottle. Lunch is served (Mon–Fri 11am–4pm) in the Gypsy Bar & Grill next door, which has live music Wednesday, Friday, and Saturday evenings (© **904/808-1305**). Taking the concept a little too far, there's also a Gypsy Comedy Club right next door.

828 Anastasia Blvd. (Fla. A1A, at Ingram St., east of the Bridge of Lions). ✆ **904/824-8244**. www.gypsycab. com. Reservations not accepted. Main courses $12–$25. AE, DC, DISC, MC, V. Mon–Thurs 4:30–10pm; Fri 4:30–11pm; Sat 11am–11pm; Sun 10:30am–10pm.

SUPER-CHEAP EATS

The Bunnery Bakery & Café ⚘ *Value* BAKERY/DELI   If you suffer from attacks of the raging sweet tooth, get thee to the Bunnery. Alluring aromas waft from this bakery and cafe in the heart of the historic district. It's lovely to come here for breakfast or for a fresh pastry and hot cup of latte, cappuccino, or espresso anytime you need a break from sightseeing. At lunch, plop yourself into one of the colorful booths and indulge in soup, salads, burgers, panini, or a croissant stuffed with walnut-and-pineapple chicken salad. Order at the counter; the staff will call your number when it's ready.

121 St. George St. (between Treasury and Hypolita sts.). ✆ **904/829-6166**. Breakfast $3–$7; sandwiches and salads $3.50–$8. No credit cards. Daily 8am–6pm. Closed New Year's Day, Easter, Thanksgiving, Christmas Eve, and Christmas.

The Spanish Bakery COLONIAL   Occupying a reconstructed 17th-century kitchen building, this little family-operated establishment bakes almond, lemon, and cinnamon cookies, using recipes from the Spanish colonial period, when a lack of refrigeration limited the use of milk and eggs. A couple of these crunchy morsels, eaten at the picnic tables outside, make a fine snack while you're touring the historic district. Or you can have lunch here, choosing from daily specials such as spicy Spanish-style chili over rice.

Rear of 42½ St. George St. (between Cuna and Orange sts.). ✆ **904/471-3046**. Reservations not accepted. Lunch specials $5; cookies and rolls 40¢–50¢ each. No credit cards. Daily 9:30am–3pm. Closed Thanksgiving and Christmas.

WORTH A SPLURGE

La Parisienne ⚘⚘ CONTEMPORARY FRENCH   Somewhat of an accidental tourist in these parts, La Parisienne is a welcome respite from all the nearby Americana. Despite its name, this lovely dining room evokes the French countryside, with a rough-hewn beamed-pine ceiling, lace-curtained windows, and ladder-back chairs. Changing seasonally, the menu always features fresh seafood, and in fall you'll see venison and quail. If they're offered, begin with pan-seared sea scallops in a citrus sauce; then go on to steak au poivre with a Cognac-cream sauce, roast rack of lamb Provençal, or the day's treatment of fresh local fish. A fixed-price, five-course menu offers a choice of meat or seafood appetizers and main courses plus cheeses and dessert. The weekend brunch menu offers beignets, eggs Benedict, and scrambled eggs with smoked salmon.

60 Hypolita St. (between Spanish and Cordova sts.). ✆ **904/829-0055**. www.laparisienne.net. Reservations recommended. Main courses $19–$28; 5-course prix fixe menu $60. AE, DISC, MC, V. Tues–Fri 5–9pm; Sat–Sun 11am–3pm and 5–9pm.

ST. AUGUSTINE AFTER DARK

Especially on weekends, the Old Town is full of strollers and partyers making the rounds to the dozens of active bars, clubs, and restaurants. For up-to-date details on what's happening in town, check the local daily, the *St. Augustine Record* (www.staugustine.com), or the irreverent *Folio Weekly* (www.folioweekly.com).

The best-looking and rowdiest crowd in town can be found at the **A1A Ale Works** (see "Great Deals on Dining," above). Twenty-something hipsters and middle-aged partyers mingle at this handsome New Orleans–style microbrewery and restaurant. Thursday through Saturday nights, downstairs at the bar, on a crowded window-front stage, you'll find live music, usually light rock and R&B tunes.

Ann O'Malley's, 23 Orange St., near the Old City Gate (© **904/825-4040**), is an Irish pub, open until 1am. Besides the selection of ales, stouts, and drafts, this is one of the only spots in town where you can grab a late-night bite.

Also popular with locals, **Mill Top Tavern,** 19½ St. George St., at the Fort (© **904/829-2329**), is a warm and rustic tavern housed in a 19th-century mill building (the waterwheel is still outside). Weather permitting, it's an open-air space. There's music here every day from 1pm until 1am.

At **Scarlett O'Hara's,** 70 Hypolita St., at Cordova Street (© **904/824-6535;** www.scarlettoharas.net), a catacomb of cozy rooms with working fireplaces in a rambling, 19th-century wood-frame house is the setting for everything from DJs and karaoke to live music. Sporting events are also aired on a large-screen TV.

Across the river, the **Gypsy Bar & Grill,** part of the Gypsy Cab Co. restaurant (see "Great Deals on Dining," above), 828 Anastasia Blvd. (© **904/824-8244**), often has live music as well as a next-door comedy club.

You can also take one of the many ghost tours that are offered nightly.

4 Jacksonville

36 miles S of the Georgia border, 134 miles NE of Orlando, 340 miles N of Miami

Once infamous for its smelly paper mills, the sprawling metropolis of Jacksonville—residents call it "Jax," from its airport abbreviation—is now one of the South's insurance and banking capitals. Development was rampant throughout Duval County during the 1990s, with hotels, restaurants, attractions, and clubs springing up, especially in suburban areas near the interstate highways. Nevertheless, there are 20 miles of Atlantic Ocean beaches upon which to sun and swim, many championship golf courses to play, and an abundance of beautiful and historic national and state parks to roam.

Spanning the broad, curving St. Johns River, downtown Jacksonville is a vibrant center of activity during weekdays and on weekend afternoons and evenings, when many locals return to the restaurants and bars of Jacksonville Landing and Southbank Riverwalk, two dining-and-entertainment complexes facing each other across the river that have helped to revitalize downtown.

ESSENTIALS

GETTING THERE   Jacksonville International Airport, on the city's north side about 12 miles from downtown (© 904/741-2000; www.jaxairports.org), is served by **Air Canada** (© 888/247-2262), **AirTran** (© 800/247-8726), **American** (© 800/433-7300), **Continental** (© 800/525-0280), **Delta** (© 800/221-1212), **Midway** (© 800/446-4392), **Northwest** (© 800/225-2525), **Southwest** (© 800/435-9792), **United** (© 800/241-6522), and **Metro Jet** and **US Airways** (© 800/428-4322).

Alamo (© 800/327-9633), **Avis** (© 800/331-1212), **Budget** (© 800/527-0700), **Dollar** (© 800/800-4000), **Enterprise** (© 800/325-8007), **Hertz** (© 800/654-3131), and **National** (© 800/227-7368) have rental-car booths at the airport.

Gator City Taxi (© **904/741-0008** at the airport, or 904/355-8294 elsewhere) provides cab service. Fares for up to four persons are about $20 to downtown, $38 to $45 to beach hotels, $55 to $65 to St. Augustine, and $40 to Amelia Island. **Express Shuttle** (© **904/353-8880**) provides van service to and from hotels and resorts throughout the area. Per-person fares are about $17 to downtown Jacksonville, $22 to $28 to the beaches, $57 to $67 to St. Augustine, and $35 to Amelia Island.

There's an **Amtrak** station in Jacksonville at 3570 Clifford Lane, off U.S. 1, just north of 45th Street (© **800/USA-RAIL**; www.amtrak.com).

VISITOR INFORMATION Contact the **Jacksonville and the Beaches Convention & Visitors Bureau,** 201 E. Adams St., Jacksonville, FL 32202 (© **800/733-2668** or 904/798-9111; fax 904/789-9103; www.jaxcvb.com), for maps, brochures, calendars, and advice. The bureau is open Monday through Friday from 8am to 5pm. It operates information booths in the upstairs food court of **Jacksonville Landing.** The latter is open Monday through Saturday from 10am to 7pm, Sunday from 12:30 to 5:30pm. The bureau also has a walk-in information office in **Jacksonville Beach** at 403 Beach Blvd., between 3rd and 4th streets (© **904/242-0024**), which is open Monday through Saturday from 10am to 6pm.

GETTING AROUND You can get around downtown Jacksonville via the **Skyway,** an elevated and completely automated train that runs down Hogan Street from the Florida Community College Jacksonville campus through downtown and across the river via the Acosta/Fla. 13 bridge to the Southbank Riverwalk. The Skyway operates Monday through Friday from 6am to 11pm, Saturday from 10am to 11pm, and Sunday only for special events. Skyway rides cost 35¢. **The Trolley** connects with the Skyway and runs east-west through downtown, primarily along Bay Street. It's free and operates Monday through Friday from 6:30am to 7pm and Saturday 8am to 6pm. Get maps and sched-ules from the convention and visitors bureau or at the visitor information booth at Jacksonville Landing (see above). Both are operated by the **Jacksonville Transportation Authority** (© **904/630-3181**; www.jtaonthemove.com), which also provides local bus service.

Otherwise, you're better off having a car if you want to explore this vast area. You can hail a **taxi** downtown if you spot one, although it is usually best to call **Gator City Taxi** (© **904/355-8294**) or **Yellow Cab** (© **904/260-1111**) for a pickup. Fares are $1.50 when the flag drops, and 25¢ for each ⅙ mile thereafter.

Out at the beaches, the **St. Johns River Ferry** (© **904/241-9969**; www.stjohnsferry.com) shuttles vehicles across the river between Mayport, an Old Florida fishing village on the south side, and Fort George on the north shore. The boats run daily. (Times vary, so call for the current schedule.) One-way fare is $2.75 per two-axle private vehicle, 50¢ for pedestrians and bicyclists. Even if you have to wait 30 minutes for the next ferry, the 5-minute ride greatly short-ens the trip between the Jacksonville beaches and Amelia Island.

EXPLORING THE AREA

Cummer Museum of Art & Gardens ★★ Built on the grounds of a private Tudor mansion, this modestly sized but impressive museum is worth a visit for anyone who appreciates the visual arts. The permanent collection encompasses works from 2000 B.C. to the present. It's especially rich in American Impression-ist paintings and includes an impressive collection of 18th-century porcelain and 18th-century Japanese woodblock prints. Personally, I find the art here a bit bor-ing and too focused on landscapes, but that's my taste. Frankly, and art snobs may gasp at this statement, the actual landscaping of the museum is infinitely more spectacular. Don't miss the stunning Italian and English gardens set on the scenic

Jacksonville

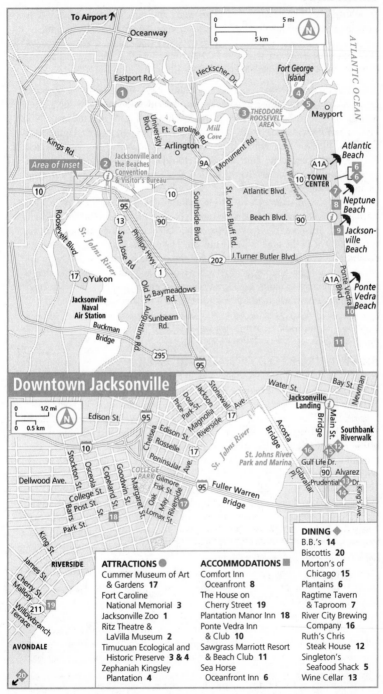

St. Johns River. The museum hosts temporary and traveling exhibits and sponsors a multitude of activities during the year, so call to see what's happening.

829 Riverside Ave. (between Post and Fisk sts.). ℂ **904/356-6857.** www.cummer.org. Admission $6 adults, $4 seniors over 65 and military, $3 students, $1 children under 5; free Tues after 4pm. Tues and Thurs 10am–9pm; Wed and Fri–Sat 10am–5pm; Sun noon–5pm.

Jacksonville Zoo ⭐ *Kids*   Another city, another zoo. But this isn't just any zoo. Located between downtown and the airport, this environmentally sensitive zoo is well on its way to becoming one of the Southeast's best. While the zoo's Wild Florida area presents local fauna, including black bears, red wolves, Florida panthers, and alligators, the main exhibits feature an extensive and growing collection of lions, rhinos, elephants, antelopes, Nile crocodiles, cheetahs, monkeys, western lowland gorillas, and other African wildlife. You'll enter the 73-acre park through an authentic thatched roof built in 1995 by 24 Zulu craftsmen. Whether you go on foot or by tram, allow at least 3 hours to tour this vast and lush zoo. When you arrive, ask about current animal shows and special events. Strollers and wheelchairs are available for rent. The newest attraction, Range of the Jaguar opened in the spring of 2004 to the tune of $15.4 million. The exhibit focuses on a neotropical rainforest setting that can be found in Central or South America. Although this attraction spotlights the jaguar, you will see other animals here as well, such as golden lion tamarins, tapirs, capybaras, giant river otters, anteaters and a variety of bird, reptile, amphibian, and fish species including the anaconda.

8605 Zoo Pkwy. ℂ **904/757-4462** or 904/757-4463. www.jaxzoo.org. Admission $9.50 adults, $8 seniors, $5 children 3–12, free for children under 3. Daily 9am–5pm. Closed Thanksgiving and Christmas. Take I-95 north to Hecksher Dr. (exit 124A) and follow the signs.

AN UNUSUAL BREED OF NATIONAL PARK

Named after the American Indians who inhabited Central and North Florida some 1,000 years before European settlers arrived, the **Timucuan Ecological and Historic Preserve** offers visitors an opportunity to explore untouched wilderness, historical buildings, and informative exhibits on the area's natural history. Unusual for a national park, this 46,000-acre preserve hasn't been hacked off from the rest of the community and drawn within arbitrary boundaries. The result is a vast, intriguing system of sites joined by rural roads alongside tumbledown fish camps, trailer parks, strip malls, condominiums, and stately old homes.

Admission to all park facilities is free (though donations are accepted). The visitor centers at Fort Caroline National Memorial and Zephaniah Kingsley Plantation (see below) are open daily from 9am to 5pm except New Year's Day, Thanksgiving, and Christmas. The Theodore Roosevelt Area is open daily from 7am to 5pm during Eastern Standard Time, daily from 7am to 8pm during daylight savings time. Closed Christmas.

The preserve's prime attractions are 14 miles northeast of downtown on the south bank of the St. Johns River. Your starting point is the **Fort Caroline National Memorial** ⭐, 12713 Ft. Caroline Rd. (ℂ **904/641-7155;** www.nps. gov/timu), which serves as the preserve's visitor center. This was the site of the 16th-century French Huguenot settlement that was wiped out by the Spanish who landed at St. Augustine. This two-thirds–size replica shows you what the original was like. You can see archaeological artifacts and two well-produced half-hour videos highlighting the area as well.

The fort sits at the northwestern edge of the 600-acre **Theodore Roosevelt Area,** a beautiful woodland and marshland rich in history that has been undisturbed since the Civil War. On a 2-mile hike along a centuries-old park trail, you'll see a wide variety of birds, wildflowers, and maritime hammock forest. Bring binoculars if you have them, since such birds as endangered wood storks, great and snowy egrets, ospreys, hawks, and painted buntings make their home here in spring and summer. On the ground, you might catch sight of a gray fox or raccoon. You may also want to bring a blanket and picnic basket to spread out under the ancient oak trees that shade the banks of the wide and winding St. Johns River. After the trail crosses Hammock Creek, you're in ancient Timucuan country, where their ancestors lived as far back as 500 B.C. Farther along is the site of a cabin in the wilderness that belonged to the reclusive brothers Willie and Saxon Browne, who lived without the modern conveniences of indoor plumbing or electricity until the last brother's death in 1960.

If you're here on a weekend, take the fascinating 1½-hour guided tour of the fort and Theodore Roosevelt Area, offered every Saturday and Sunday (when weather and staffing permit). Call the fort for details and schedules.

The **Ribault Monument,** on St. Johns Bluff about ½ mile east of the fort, was erected in 1924 to commemorate the arrival in 1562 of French Huguenot Jean Ribault, who died defending Fort Caroline from the Spanish. It's worth a stop for the dramatic view of the area.

To get here from downtown Jacksonville, take Atlantic Boulevard (Fla. 10) east, make a left on Monument Road, and turn right on Fort Caroline Road; the Theodore Roosevelt Area is entered from Mt. Pleasant Road, about 1 mile southeast of the fort; look for the trail head parking sign and follow the narrow dirt road to the parking lot.

HITTING THE BEACH

You can fish, swim, snorkel, sail, sunbathe, or stroll on the sand dunes (at least Mar–Nov, since winter can get downright chilly here). All of these activities are just a 20- to 30-minute drive east of downtown at Jacksonville's four beach communities.

Atlantic Boulevard (Fla. 10) will take you to **Atlantic Beach** and **Neptune Beach.** The boulevard divides the two towns, and where it meets the ocean, you'll come to **Town Center,** a quaint community with a number of shops, restaurants, pubs, and a few inns.

Beach Boulevard (U.S. 90) dead-ends at **Jacksonville Beach,** where you'll find beach concessions, rental shops, and a fishing pier. This is also the most popular local surfing beach.

To the south, J. Turner Butler Boulevard (Fla. 202) leads from I-95 to the boundary between Jacksonville Beach and Ponte Vedra Beach. A right turn there will take you to **Ponte Vedra Beach** (pronounced here as Ponti *Vee*-dra). This ritzy, golf-oriented enclave actually is in St. Johns County (St. Augustine), but it's so much closer to Jacksonville that we've included it in this chapter.

AFFORDABLE OUTDOOR ACTIVITIES & SPECTATOR SPORTS

CRUISES **Jacksonville River Cruises** (© **904/396-2333;** www.rivercruise. com) operates sightseeing, dinner, and dancing cruises on the stern-wheel paddleboats the *Lady St. Johns* and the *Annabelle Lee.* They usually dock at the Radisson Riverwalk Hotel on the Southbank Riverwalk. Prices are $30 to $45; schedules vary greatly by season, so call ahead or check the website.

FISHING The least-expensive way to fish for red snapper, grouper, sea bass, small sharks, amberjack, and more, 15 to 30 miles offshore in the Atlantic Ocean, is aboard the *King Neptune,* a 65-foot air-conditioned deep-sea party boat. The full-day trips depart at 7:30am daily from Monty's Marina, 4378 Ocean St. (Fla. A1A), ½ mile south of the Mayport Ferry landing (© **904/ 246-7575**), and return at 4:30pm. Price is $50 per person, including bait and tackle. You don't need a license, but reservations are required.

GOLF   The Jacksonville area offers a great variety of golf courses, some of which are ranked among the top in the country. In Ponte Vedra Beach, the Sawgrass Marriott Resort (see "Accommodations You Can Afford," below, for information about the resort) sits on the most famous course, the **TPC at Sawgrass** ★★★, home of the Players Championship in March. Ranked among the nation's top courses, its island hole is one of the most photographed in the world. Nearby are the Ocean and Lagoon courses at the Ponte Vedra Inn & Club.

Top courses open to the public include the **Golf Club of Jacksonville,** at 10440 Tournament Lane (© **904/779-0800**), which is managed by the PGA Tour. It's a great bargain, with greens fees ranging from $30 to $45. The semiprivate **Cimarrone,** at 2690 Cimarrone Blvd. (© **904/287-2000**), is a fast and watery course with greens fees ranging from $30 to $65.

Be on the lookout for the free *Golfer's Guide* in visitor centers and hotel lobbies (see "Special-Interest Trips," on p. 58, for information about ordering copies).

For course information online, go to www.golf.com and www.floridagolfing. com, or call the **Florida Sports Foundation** (© **850/488-8347**) or **Florida Golfing** (© **866/833-2663**).

HORSEBACK RIDING   For a scenic ride along the sand and dunes (or lessons), try **Sawgrass Stables,** 23900 Marsh Landing Pkwy., off Fla. A1A in Ponte Vedra Beach (© **904/285-3791**). Call for rates and reservations.

SPECTATOR SPORTS   The 73,000-seat **Alltel Stadium,** 1 Stadium Place, at East Duval and Haines streets (© **904/353-3309** to charge tickets), hosts the annual Florida-Georgia football game every October, and other college football games September through December. It also is the home field of the National Football League's **Jacksonville Jaguars** (© **877/452-4784** or 904/633-2000 for ticket information; www.jaguars.com). One of the stadium's biggest draws is the **Toyota Gator Bowl,** usually on New Year's Day.

Adjacent to the stadium, the 10,600-seat **Jacksonville Veterans Memorial Coliseum,** 1145 E. Adams St. (© **904/630-3900** for information, or 904/353-3309 to charge tickets), hosts National Hockey League exhibition games, college basketball games, ice-skating exhibitions, wrestling matches, and various family shows.

SHOPPING & BROWSING

Jacksonville has plenty of shopping opportunities, including an upscale mall, **The Avenues Mall,** south of town at 10300 Southside Blvd., as well as a number of flea markets, including the **Beach Boulevard Flea and Farmer's Market** on Beach Boulevard (Fla. 90; © **904/645-5961**). More than 600 vendors show up Saturday and Sunday from 9am to 5pm to sell their wares in a partially covered facility. Some booths are open other days of the week as well.

San Marco Square, at San Marco and Atlantic boulevards, south of the river, is a quaint shopping district in the middle of a stunning residential area. Shops in meticulously refashioned Mediterranean-revival buildings sell antiques and home furnishings, in addition to wares such as clothing, books, and records.

Another worthwhile neighborhood to explore is the **Avondale/Riverside** historic district southwest of downtown on St. Johns Avenue between Talbot Avenue and Boone Park, on the north bank of the river. More than 60 boutiques, antiques stores, art galleries, and cafes line the wide, tree-lined avenue.

Nearby, the younger set hangs out at **Five Points,** on Park Street at Avondale Avenue, where used-record stores, vintage clothiers, coffee shops, and funky art galleries stay open late.

Like St. Augustine, Jacksonville is a mecca for chocoholics, particularly **Peterbrooke Chocolatier Production Center,** 1470 San Marco Blvd., on San Marco Square (© **904/398-2489;** www.peterbrooke.com). If you've never tried chocolate-covered popcorn or pretzels, well, this is the place if you're up to the experience. Open Monday through Friday from 10am to 5pm. Peterbrooke also has a retail shop on St. Johns Avenue in Avondale.

ACCOMMODATIONS YOU CAN AFFORD

Because Jacksonville hasn't yet made it onto the hip list, there are no boutique hotels in the city—yet. Instead, you have a choice of either a large chain hotel a la Hilton or Omni, or, preferably, much cozier, more charming bed and breakfasts.

We've arranged the accommodations listed below geographically, in and around downtown first, followed by the beach scene. The suburbs have dozens more options to choose from, especially along I-95. Many are clustered south of downtown in the **Southpoint** (exit 101, Turner Butler Blvd./Fla. 202) and **Baymeadows** (exit 101, Baymeadows Rd./Fla. 152) areas. These locales have a multitude of chain restaurants, and you can hop on the highways and zoom to the beach or downtown—although you aren't really at either one if you stay out there.

Rates in the downtown hotels are higher midweek when rooms are in demand by business travelers. Beach accommodations are somewhat less expensive in the cold months from December through March.

Note: Hotel taxes in the area tack on an additional 12% to 14%!

IN JACKSONVILLE

Prudential Drive in the Southbank Riverwalk area is home to the **Radisson Riverwalk Hotel** (© **800/333-3333** or 904/396-5100), the **Hampton Inn Central** (© **800/426-7866** or 904/396-7770), and the all-suites **Extended Stay American Downtown** (© **800/398-7829** or 904/396-1777; www.extendedstay.com).

The House on Cherry Street 🐦🐦   This colonial-style, wood-frame house, on the St. Johns River in the Riverside neighborhood, is ideal for a romantic B&B vacation. French doors open to a delightful screened-in back porch furnished with rocking chairs; it overlooks an expanse of tree-shaded lawn (where guests play croquet) leading to the river (where they play with kayaks and canoes). You might select the Rose or the Duck room, both with canopied four-poster beds and river views. Ducks are rather a theme here, with hundreds of antique decoys on display. All accommodations offer adjacent sitting rooms and ceiling fans and have fresh flowers, books, and magazines. This place gets booked up fast, so make reservations as early as possible.

1844 Cherry St. (on the St. Johns River), Jacksonville, FL 32205. © 904/384-1999. Fax 904/384-5013. www. 1bbweb.com/cherry. 4 units, all with bathroom. $75–$105 double. Rates include full breakfast. AE, MC, V. No small children accepted. **Amenities:** Free use of bikes; canoes; kayaks. *In room:* A/C, TV, hair dryer, no phone.

Worth a Splurge

Plantation Manor Inn 🐦🐦   The setting for many weddings and special events, this three-story plantation-style bed-and-breakfast in the historic Riverside district is blocks from the river, 10 minutes from downtown, and a short drive to Avondale's shopping and dining. Its homey interior, outfitted with a mix of thrift-store antiques, features glossy pine floors and gorgeous cypress paneling, wainscoting, and carved moldings. Breakfast, including freshly baked muffins and breads, is served in a lovely dining room with a working fireplace. When the sun is shining, take the morning meal on a brick patio, a delightful setting with ivy-covered walls, flower beds, and garden furnishings under the shade of a massive oak tree. The patio also contains a lap pool and whirlpool spa. On the second floor, you can enjoy a big wraparound porch with seating amid potted geraniums, hibiscus, and bougainvillea. All but one of the rooms here have shower-only bathrooms.

1630 Copeland St. (between Oak and Park sts.), Jacksonville, FL 32204. ✆ **904/384-4630.** Fax 904/387-0960. www.plantationmanorinn.com. 9 units, all with bathroom. $150–$180 double. Rates include full breakfast. AE, DC, MC, V. **Amenities:** Outdoor pool; Jacuzzi. *In room:* A/C, TV, hair dryer, iron.

AT THE BEACHES

A dozen modest hotels line Jacksonville Beach's 1st Street, along the Atlantic Ocean. Completely renovated in 1998, the **Comfort Inn Oceanfront,** 1515 N. 1st St., 2 blocks east of Fla. A1A (✆ **800/654-8776** or 904/241-2311; fax 904/ 249-3830; www.comfortinnjaxbeach.com), is one of the better values. Its rooms have balconies or screened patios, and guests can enjoy a large pool with four rock waterfalls and a palm-fringed sun deck, a secluded grotto whirlpool, an exercise room, a gift/sundries shop, and a multicourt sand-volleyball park.

Sawgrass Marriott Resort & Beach Club ★★ Swingers love this hotel. No, not *that* kind of swinger, but, rather the kind that emulates Tiger Woods. One of the nation's largest golf resorts, this duffer's paradise is virtually surrounded by 99 holes, including the Pete Dye–designed **TPC at Sawgrass** ★★★, home of the annual Players Championship in March. In fact, this course has appeared on every golf critic's "best of" list since it opened in 1980. Overlooking the TPC's picturesque 13th hole, the seven-story hotel sits beside one of the lakes that make the course so challenging. The view augments the gourmet fusion cuisine served in the Augustine Grille, the hotel's signature restaurant. The guest rooms in the hotel are comfortable but of modest size. Best for families are the fully equipped one- and two-bedroom "villa suites" (condominium apartments) on or near a golf course, which offer large furnished patios or balconies. Especially luxurious are the one- to three-bedroom beachfront units, which sport huge kitchens, living rooms with working fireplaces, full dining rooms, and large screened wooden decks. A complimentary shuttle takes guests to the oceanside Cabana Beach Club for snacks and meals.

1000 PGA Tour Blvd. (off Fla. A1A between U.S. 210 and J. Turner Butler Blvd.), Ponte Vedra Beach, FL 32082. ✆ **800/228-9290** or 904/285-7777. Fax 904/285-0906. www.sawgrassmarriott.com. 508 units. $109–$135 double, $175–$205 suite. Golf packages available. AE, DC, DISC, MC, V. Free self-parking; valet parking $12. **Amenities:** 6 restaurants; 4 bars; 3 outdoor pools (2 heated); 5 golf courses; 17 tennis courts; 2 health clubs; Jacuzzi; watersports equipment rentals; bike rental; children's programs; game room; concierge; activities desk; business center; limited room service; babysitting; laundry service; coin-op washers and dryers; concierge-level rooms. *In room:* A/C, TV, dataport, kitchen (condos only), minibar, coffeemaker, hair dryer, iron.

Sea Horse Oceanfront Inn *Value* This old-school beachfront motel offers clean, spacious rooms with ocean views from balconies or patios. Families will appreciate the six units here with kitchenettes, not to mention a big beachfront lawn with pool, shuffleboard, picnic tables, and a barbecue grill. And others will enjoy proximity to some of Jacksonville's top nightspots. The pool itself boasts a happening watering hole, The Lemon Bar. If you have a large family or group, consider the vast and lovely third-floor penthouse—it has a big living room and dining area, full kitchen, separate bedroom as well as sofa beds, and a huge balcony furnished with a dining table and chaise longues. A coffee shop adjoins the motel, and Town Center's restaurants and bars are across the street.

120 Atlantic Blvd. (at beach end of Atlantic Blvd.), Neptune Beach, FL 32266. ℭ **800/881-2330** or 904/
246-2175. Fax 904/246-4256. www.seahorseresort.com. 38 units. $109–$119 double; $200–$225 penthouse
suite for up to 6. AE, DC, DISC, MC, V. **Amenities:** Bar; heated outdoor pool. *In room:* A/C, TV, dataport,
kitchen (6 units).

GREAT DEALS ON DINING

The convention and visitors bureau's annual guide contains a complete list of
restaurants. For more choices, check listings in the "Shorelines" and "Go" sections
of Friday's *Florida Times-Union* (**www.jacksonville.com**) and in *Folio Weekly* (**www.
folioweekly.com**), the free local alternative paper available at restaurants, hotels,
and nightspots all over town. We have concentrated here on restaurants in downtown Jacksonville and at the beaches.

IN DOWNTOWN JACKSONVILLE

Southbank Riverwalk is the city's up-and-coming mecca for eating out. In addition to B.B.'s and the River City Brewing Company, both reviewed below, the
area has riverfront branches of **Ruth's Chris Steak House,** in the Hilton Jacksonville Riverfront, 1201 Riverplace Blvd. (ℭ **904/396-6200**); **Morton's of
Chicago,** 1510 Riverplace Blvd. (ℭ **904/399-3933**); and the **Wine Cellar,**
1314 Prudential Dr. (ℭ **904/398-8989**), offers very good Continental fare and
has a wine list to justify its name.

You will also find a plethora of good cafes and restaurants in the San Marco
Square and Avondale neighborhoods, to break up your shopping excursions.

Don't forget that on the north side of the river, **Jacksonville Landing** has several full-service restaurants and an inexpensive food court with outdoor seating
(p. 469).

B.B.'s ★★ ECLECTIC South of the Southbank Riverwalk, this bistro son of
Biscottis (see below) is one of the city's hottest restaurants. You'll find local yuppies congregating at the big marble-top bar on one side of the sometimes noisy
Art Deco dining room, especially during weekday "wine-downs" featuring beer
and wine specials and discounted appetizers (the mozzarella bruschetta is a big
hit here and at Biscottis), from 4 to 7pm. There's a small but inventive selection
of sandwiches, salads, and individual-size pizzas available all day. Featuring local
seafood, the nightly main-course specials run the gamut from roasted sea bass
with citrus couscous to seared scallops with lemon grass–scented rice, sun-dried
tomatoes, and lobster-flavored butter. Save room for the famous desserts, available for inspection in the chiller case near the open kitchen. Saturday brunch
sees the likes of yummy Benedict-style crab cakes and flaming bananas Foster.

1019 Hendricks Ave. (between Prudential Dr. and Home St.). ℭ **904/306-0100.** Call for Priority Seating.
Main courses $12–$23; sandwiches and salads $5–$8.50; pizzas $6–$8. AE, DC, DISC, MC, V. Mon–Thurs
11am–10:30pm; Fri 11am–midnight; Sat 10am–midnight (Sat brunch 10am–2pm).

Biscottis ★★ *Value* ECLECTIC This brick-walled little gem in the trendy
Avondale neighborhood might easily have come out of New York's East Village.
Start your day here (except on Mon) with a pastry and cup of joe. For lunch and
dinner, daily specials such as pan-seared tuna or pork loin are always fresh and
beautifully presented. The huge and inventive salads are especially good: Try the
Oriental version with chicken breast, orange slices, roasted peppers, and creamy
sesame dressing. Pizzas, too, are served with wonderfully exotic and delicious
toppings—ever try guacamole and black beans on your slice? And by all means,
don't leave without sampling the wonderful desserts. On warm days, choose a
tiny sidewalk table for great people-watching. *Note:* If the wait's too long here,

several other choices ranging from a neighborhood diner to expensive haute cuisine line these 2 blocks of St. Johns Avenue in Avondale.

3556 St. Johns Ave. (between Talbot and Ingleside aves. in Avondale). ✆ 904/387-2060. Main courses $9–$19; sandwiches and salads $5–$8.50; pizzas $7–$8.50. AE, DC, DISC, MC, V. Mon 11am–10pm; Tues–Thurs 7am–10pm; Fri 7am–midnight; Sat 8am–midnight; Sun 8am–3pm.

River City Brewing Company ★★ NEW AMERICAN/LOUISIANA   Occupying a prime location on the Southbank Riverwalk, this gorgeous restaurant and microbrewery has dramatic waterfront and skyline views. For an even better vantage point, sit outside on the enormous covered deck. The quality of the cuisine very nearly lives up to the vista, especially the coconut shrimp served with a sweet Mandarin-orange sauce. For a main course, try the Cajun chicken linguine with mushrooms and ham in a spicy cream sauce, or pretzel-encrusted mahimahi with a mustard-cream sauce. While you can easily drop a bundle in the main dining room, you can devise an inexpensive, simpler meal (burgers and such) in the Brew Haus, a large sports bar that opens to the big covered deck and the riverbank. Bands play on the deck weekend evenings. Sunday brunch brings incredible buffets with decadent desserts.

835 Museum Circle (on Southbank Riverwalk). ✆ 904/398-2299. Main courses $15–$18; sandwiches and salads $5–$11; Sun brunch buffet $22 adults, $16 seniors, $12 children 3–12. AE, DC, DISC, MC, V. Dining room Sun–Thurs 11am–3pm and 5–10pm; Fri–Sat 11am–3pm and 5–11pm; Sun 10:30am–2:30pm and 5–10pm. Pub and deck (light fare) Sun–Thurs 3–10pm (bar to midnight); Fri–Sat 3–11pm (bar to 2am). Closed Christmas. Valet parking available on weekends.

AT THE BEACHES

In addition to the Ragtime Tavern & Taproom (see below), you'll have several dining (and drinking) choices in the brick storefronts of Town Center, the old-time beach village at the end of Atlantic Boulevard. Among the best is the ocean-front **Plantains,** in the Sea Turtle Inn.

Ragtime Tavern & Taproom ★★ SEAFOOD/CAJUN   In the heart of Town Center, this lively sister of St. Augustine's A1A Ale Works (p. 501) offers six handcrafted brews, including a refreshing pilsner known as Dolphin's Breath. You can imbibe at one of two bars on either end of the building. In between, a rabbit warren of dining rooms provides fine enough fare to keep it filled with local professionals right through the cool winter months. Try the conch fritters or the coconut shrimp as an appetizer. For a main course, you can select from seared sesame-coated yellowfin tuna (the best dish here if you like rare fish) or several other treatments of fish, shrimp, chicken, and pastas. Save room for some New Orleans–style beignets for dessert. Also from the Big Easy, po' boy sandwiches are served at all hours. Good local bands play here Thursday through Sunday evenings.

207 Atlantic Blvd. (at 1st Ave.), Atlantic Beach. ✆ 904/241-7877. Call to get on waiting list. Main courses $12–$22; sandwiches and salads $6–$8. AE, DC, DISC, MC, V. Sun–Thurs 11am–10:30pm; Fri–Sat 11am–11pm (bar open later).

Singleton's Seafood Shack ★★ (Value) SEAFOOD   This rustic fish camp has been serving every imaginable kind of fresh-off-the-boat seafood since 1969. And rustic it is, constructed primarily of unpainted, well-weathered plywood nailed to two-by-fours. Unlike most other fish camps that tend to overwork the deep fryer, the fried standbys such as conch fritters, shrimp, clam strips, oysters, and squid actually retain their seafood taste! (Usually, that means they change the oil before it gets the too-fishy or burnt taste of the last entree.) Singleton's also offers other preparations such as blackened mahimahi and Cajun shrimp.

Best bets at lunch are the fried shrimp or oyster po'boy sandwiches covered in crispy onion rings. At dinner your Styrofoam plate will come stacked with a choice of side items such as black beans and rice, marvelous horseradishy coleslaw, fries, and hush puppies. They have a selection of chicken dishes, but stick to seafood.

4728 Ocean St. (Fla. A1A, at St. Johns River Ferry landing), Mayport. © 904/246-4442. Main courses $10–$18; sandwiches $2–$7. AE, DISC, MC, V. Sun–Thurs 10am–9pm; Fri–Sat 10am–10pm.

JACKSONVILLE AFTER DARK

In addition to the spots recommended below, check the listings in the "Shorelines" and "Go" sections of Friday's *Florida Times-Union* (**www.jacksonville.com**) and *FolioWeekly* (**www.folioweekly.com**), the free local alternative paper, available at restaurants, at hotels, and all over town. Another source is **www.jaxevents.com**.

THE PERFORMING ARTS   Jacksonville has plenty of seats for concerts, touring Broadway shows, dance companies, and big-name performers with the 73,000-seat **Alltel Stadium,** at East Duval and Haines streets (© **904/630-3900**); the 10,600-seat **Jacksonville Veterans Memorial Coliseum,** 1145 E. Adams St. (© **904/630-3900** for information or 904/353-3309 to charge tickets); the 3,200-seat **Florida Times-Union Center for the Performing Arts,** 300 Water St., between Hogan and Pearl streets (© **904/630-3900**); and the revitalized **Ritz Theatre** (© **904/632-5555**). Call or check the sources above for what's playing.

THE BAR SCENE   You will find several libation options downtown at **Jacksonville Landing** (p. 469), including, if you must, a lively waterfront **Hooters** (© **904/356-5400**), plus free outdoor rock, blues, country, and jazz concerts every Friday and Saturday night except during winter. There's also live music on weekends across the river at the **River City Brewing Company** (see "Great Deals on Dining," above).

Out at Town Center, at the ocean end of Atlantic Boulevard, one of several popular spots is **Ragtime Tavern & Taproom** (see "Great Deals on Dining," above), where local groups play live jazz and blues Wednesday through Sunday nights. Weekends, especially, the place is really jumping and the crowd is young, but it's lively rather than rowdy. Across the street is the **Sun Dog Diner,** at 207 Atlantic Blvd. (© **904/241-8221**), with nightly acoustic music and decent diner food. If these don't fit your mood, walk around Town Center until you find something you like. The **Freebird Café,** 200 N. 1st St. (© **904/246-2473**), is a two-story homage to native Jacksonville band Lynyrd Skynyrd, run by late lead singer Ronnie Van Zant's widow and daughter and featuring live music 6 nights a week as well as pretty good nouveau Southern cuisine. Music fans of a different genre shouldn't miss **Stella's Piano Café,** 1521 Margaret St. (© **904/353-2900**), a restaurant housed in an old Victorian home with a second floor piano bar.

5 Amelia Island ★★

32 miles NE of Jacksonville, 192 miles NE of Orlando, 372 miles N of Miami

Alas, paradise is found on the northernmost barrier island of Florida. With 13 beautiful miles of beach and a quaint Victorian town, Amelia Island is a charming getaway about a 45-minute drive northeast of downtown Jacksonville. Overall, this skinny barrier island, 18 miles long by 3 miles wide, has more in common with the Low Country of Georgia (across Cumberland Sound from here) and South Carolina. In fact, it's more like St. Simons Island in Georgia or Hilton Head Island in South Carolina than other beach resorts in Florida.

Amelia has five distinct personalities. First is its southern end, an exclusive real-estate development built in a forest of twisted, moss-laden live oaks. Here you will find world-class tennis and golfing at two of Florida's most luxurious resorts. Second is modest **American Beach,** founded in the 1930s so that African Americans would have access to the ocean in this then-segregated part of the country. Today it's a modest, predominately black community tucked away among all that south-end wealth. Third is the island's middle, a traditional beach community with a mix of affordable motels, cottages, condominiums, and a seaside inn. Fourth is the historic bayside town of **Fernandina Beach** ★★★, which boasts a 50-square-block area of gorgeous Victorian, Queen Anne, and Italianate homes listed in the National Register of Historic Places. And fifth is lovely **Fort Clinch State Park,** which keeps developers from turning the island's northern end into more ritzy resorts.

The town of Fernandina Beach dates from the post–Civil War period, when Union soldiers who had occupied Fort Clinch began returning to the island. In the late 19th century, Amelia's timber, phosphate, and naval-stores industries boomed. Back then, the town was an active seaport, with 14 foreign consuls in residence. You'll see (and occasionally smell) the paper mills that still stand near the small seaport here. The island experienced another economic explosion in the 1970s and 1980s, when real-estate developers built condominiums, cottages, and two big resorts on the island's southern end. In recent years, Fernandina Beach has seen another big boom, this time in bed-and-breakfast establishments.

ESSENTIALS

GETTING THERE   The island is served by **Jacksonville International Airport** (p. 503), which is 12 miles north of Jacksonville's downtown and 43 miles from the island. Skirting the Atlantic in places, the scenic drive here from downtown Jacksonville is via Fla. A1A and the St. Johns River Ferry. The fast, four-lane way is via I-95 north and the Buccaneer Trail (Fla. A1A) east.

VISITOR INFORMATION   For advance information, contact the **Amelia Island–Fernandina Beach–Yulee Chamber of Commerce,** 102 Centre St. (P.O. Box 472), Fernandina Beach, FL 32035 (© **800/226-3542** or 904/277-0717; fax 904/261-6997; www.ameliaisland.org). The chamber's visitor information center, in the rustic train station at the bay end of Centre Street, is open Monday through Friday from 9am to 5pm, Saturday from 10am to 2pm.

GETTING AROUND   There's no public transportation on this 13-mile-long island, so you'll need a vehicle. An informative and entertaining way to tour the historic district is on a 30-minute ride with **Old Towne Carriage Company** (© **904/277-1555**), whose horse-drawn carriages leave from the waterfront on Centre Street between 6:30 and 9pm. Advance reservations are essential. Rides cost $15 for adults, $7.50 for kids under 13, with a minimum of $55 per ride. The carriage company closes from November to April when the horses get a much-deserved rest.

Another excellent way to see the town is on a walking tour sponsored by the Amelia Island Museum of History (see the "An Old Jail Turned Historic Museum," section below).

HITTING THE BEACH

Thanks to a reclamation project, the widest beaches here are at the exclusive enclave on the island's southern third. Even if you aren't staying at one of the swanky resorts there, you can enjoy this section of beach at **Peters Point Beach**

Amelia Island

See inset

ACCOMMODATIONS ■
Fairbanks House **9**
Florida House Inn **7**
Hampton Inn & Suites **5**

ATTRACTIONS ●
Amelia Island Museum
 of History **10**
Fort Clinch State Park **1**

DINING ◆
Beech Street Grill **8**
Florida House Inn **7**
Joe's 2nd Street Bistro **6**
Marina Restaurant **4**

NIGHTLIFE ★
O'Kanes Irish Pub & Eatery **3**
Palace Saloon **2**

Amelia Island

FLORIDA

Fernandina Beach

Franklin St.
Escambia St.
Dade St.
Alachua St.
Centre St.
Ash St.
Beech St.
Cedar St.
Elm St.
Gum St.

Amelia River

N. Front St.
N. 2nd St.
N. 3rd St.
N. 4th St.
N. 5th St.
N. 6th St.
N. 7th St.
N. 8th St.
N. 9th St.
N. 10th St.
N. 11th St.

S. Front St.
S. 3rd St.
S. 6th St.
S. 7th St.
S. 8th St.

200

0   1 mi
0   1 km

Cumberland
Sound
St. Marys Entrance
Fort Clinch
South Jetty
FORT CLINCH STATE PARK
Little Tiger Island
N. 14th St.
N. Fletcher Av.
Franklin St.
Front St.
Centre St.
Atlantic Av.
Little Amelia Island
Fir St.
Jasmine St.
Citrona Dr.
Main Beach
A1A 105
■ **Public Access**
Clinch Dr.
S. 8th St.
S. 14th St.
Will Hardee Rd.
Citrona St.
Fletcher Av.
A1A
108
Sadler Rd.
■ **Public Access**
Royal Amelia Golf Links
Citrona Ext.
S. 14th St.
S. 1st Av.
To I-95
↖
Amelia Island Pkwy
Simmons Rd.
■ **Public Access**
↖ **Beach**
Minnlota Rd.
Crane Island
Fernandina Beach Municipal Golf Course
Kingsley Creek
The Buccaneer Trail
Scott Rd.
■ **Peters Point Beach Front Park**
Kingsley Creek
Amelia Island Pkwy
Amelia River
Golf Club of Amelia Island
↖ **American Beach**
Harrison Creek
Amelia Rd.
Walker Creek
AMELIA ISLAND STATE PARK
A1A 105
Nassau River
Nassau Sound
↘ **To Mayport**

A T L A N T I C   O C E A N

Front Park, on Fla. A1A, north of the Ritz-Carlton. The park has picnic shelters and restrooms. North of the resort, the beach has public-access points with free parking every ¼ mile or so. The center of activity is **Main Beach,** at the ocean end of Atlantic Avenue (Fla. A1A), with good swimming, restrooms, picnic shelters, showers, a food concession, and a playground. There's also lots of free parking, and this area is popular with families.

The beach at **Fort Clinch State Park** 🏝🏝, which wraps around the island's heavily forested northern end, is backed by rolling dunes and is filled with shells and driftwood. A jetty and pier jutting into Cumberland Sound are popular with anglers. There are showers and changing rooms at the pier. Elsewhere in the park, you might see an alligator—and certainly some of the 170 species of birds that live here—by hiking the Willow Pond nature trail. Rangers lead nature tours on the trail, usually beginning at 10:30am on Saturday. There are also 6 miles of off-road bike trails here. Construction on the remarkably well-preserved **Fort Clinch** began in 1847 on the northern tip of the island and was still underway when Union troops occupied it in 1862. The fort was abandoned shortly after the Civil War, except for a brief reactivation in 1898 during the Spanish-American War. Reenactors gather the first full weekend of each month to re-create how the Union soldiers lived (including wearing their wool underwear, even in summer!) in the fort in 1864. Rangers are on duty at the fort year-round, and they lead candlelight tours on Friday and Saturday evenings during summer, beginning about an hour after sunset. The candlelight tours cost $3 per person. You can arrange guided tours at other times for an extra fee. The park entrance is on Atlantic Avenue near the beach. Entrance fees are $5 per vehicle with up to eight occupants, $1 for pedestrians and bicyclists. Admission to the fort costs $2, free for children under 5. The park is open daily from 8am to sunset, the fort, daily from 9am to 5pm. For a current schedule of tours and events, contact the park at 2601 Atlantic Ave., Fernandina Beach, FL 32034 (© **904/277-7274;** www.floridastateparks.org/fortclinch).

The park also has 62 **campsites,** some behind the dunes at the beach (no shade out there), most in a forest along the sound side. They cost $21 per night with electricity, $19 without, including tax. Pets cost an extra $2 a night. You can reserve a site up to 11 months in advance (a very good idea in summer) by calling © **800/326-3521** or surfing the Web to www.reserveamerica.com.

Pets on leashes are allowed on all the island's public beaches and in Fort Clinch State Park.

AFFORDABLE OUTDOOR ACTIVITIES

BOATING, FISHING, SAILING & KAYAKING   The **Amelia Island Charter Boat Association,** at Tiger Point Marina on 14th Street north of the historic district (though the boats dock at Centre St.) (© **800/229-1682** or 904/261-2870), can help arrange deep-sea fishing charters, party-boat excursions, and dolphin-watching and sightseeing cruises. Other charter boats also dock at Fernandina Harbor Marina, downtown at the foot of Centre Street.

Windward Sailing School, based at Fernandina Harbor Marina, 3977 1st Ave. (© **904/261-9125;** www.windwardsailing.com), will teach you to skipper your boat and also has charters and boat rentals. Call for details and reservations.

You have to be careful in the currents, but the backwaters here are great for kayaking, whether you're a beginner or a pro. However, you'll have to travel just off the island to do it. Ray and Jody Hetchka's **Kayak Amelia** 🏝🏝 (© **888/ 305-2925** or 904/251-0016; www.kayakamelia.com) is based near Talbot Island State Park (technically in Jacksonville) and offers beginner- and advanced-level trips on back bays, creeks, and marshes. Half-day trips go for about $55 per person, all-day costs about $95. Reservations are required.

GOLF   If you're not staying in a resort with a golf course, try the new 18-hole **Royal Amelia Golf Links** (© 904/491-8500; www.royalamelia.com), for $95 a person, or the older and less expensive 27-hole **Fernandina Municipal Golf Course** (© 904/277-7370), where prices start at $37 weekdays, $41 weekends (note that these courses can be extremely expensive).

For course information online, go to www.golf.com and www.floridagolfing. com, or call the **Florida Sports Foundation** (© 850/488-8347) or **Florida Golfing** (© 866/833-2663).

HORSEBACK RIDING   You can go horseback riding on the beach with the **Kelly Seahorse Ranch** (© 904/491-5166; www.kellyranchinc.com), located on the southernmost tip of Amelia Island within the Amelia Island State Park. Cost is $45 per person for a one-hour ride; the ranch is open daily from 8am to 6pm and reservations are required. *Note:* Riders must be age 13 or older and weigh less than 230 pounds. No experience is necessary.

AN OLD JAIL TURNED HISTORIC MUSEUM

Amelia Island Museum of History ⭐   Housed in the old Nassau County jail, built of brick in 1878, this award-winning local museum explains Amelia Island's fascinating history, from Timucuan Indian times through its possession by France, Spain, Great Britain, the United States, and the Confederacy (the island changed flags eight times). Only an upstairs photo gallery is open for casual inspection, so plan to take the 1-hour, 15-minute docent-led tour of the newly remodeled ground floor if you want to get the most out of this museum.

The museum also offers excellent **walking tours** of historic Centre Street on Thursday and Friday September through June. These depart at 3pm from the chamber of commerce (see "Essentials," above) and cost $8 for adults, $3 for students. You can't make a reservation; just show up. Longer tours of the entire 50-square-block historic district can be arranged with 24-hour notice; these cost $10 per person, with a minimum of four persons required.

233 S. 3rd St. (between Beech and Cedar sts.). © 904/261-7378. www.ameliaislandmuseumofhistory.org. Admission by donation. Tours $5 adults, $3 students. Mon–Sat 10am–4pm. Tours Mon–Sat 11am and 2pm.

SHOPPING

Stroll down **Centre Street** in downtown Fernandina Beach, with its vintage storefronts and charming boutiques. Quality antiques shops, consignment shops, and bookstores line the wide boulevard ending at the marina. Be sure to go around the corner and poke your head into the **Island Art Association Gallery,** 18 N. 2nd St. (© 904/261-7020), a co-op exhibiting works by local artists.

On the south end of the island on Fla. A1A, **Palmetto Walk,** under a canopy of live oaks, and the **Village Shops,** at the entrance to the Amelia Island Plantation (© 877/624-1854), are other good shopping bets.

ACCOMMODATIONS YOU CAN AFFORD

More than two-dozen of the town's charming Victorian and Queen Anne houses have been restored and turned into B&Bs. For a complete list, contact the chamber of commerce (p. 514) or the **Amelia Island Bed & Breakfast Association** (© 888/277-0218; www.ameliaislandinns.com). You can tour all the B&Bs during an island-wide open house the first weekend in December.

A number of agencies will book vacation properties ranging from affordable cottages to magnificent mansions. Contact **Amelia Island Lodging Systems,**

584 S. Fletcher Ave., Fernandina Beach, FL 32034 (© **800/872-8531** or 904/ 261-4148; www.amelialodgings.com), which even has two lighthouse replicas for rent. *Warning:* Some properties on the website aren't as nice as they seem. Be sure to check very carefully before booking a specific property.

Your best **camping** option here is **Fort Clinch State Park** (see "Hitting the Beach," above).

Note: Rates are subject to a 9% hotel tax.

Florida House Inn ✸ (Value) Built near a railroad in 1857, this clapboard Victorian building is Florida's oldest operating hotel. Ulysses S. Grant stayed here, as did Cuban revolutionary José Martí; and the Rockefellers and Carnegies broke bread at the boardinghouse-style dining room that still provides family-style, all-you-can-eat traditional Southern fare. You can rock away on the two gingerbread-trimmed front verandas (Grant made a speech from the upstairs porch) or on a back porch overlooking a brick courtyard shaded by a huge oak tree. The 11 rooms in the original building, all mostly up to modern standards, are loaded with antiques. Most have working fireplaces, and some have claw-foot tubs. Four rooms are in a wing added in 1998; one of these has log-cabin walls, and the others are done country-style. All have fireplaces and whirlpool tubs.

20 S. 3rd St. (between Centre and Ash sts.), Fernandina Beach, FL 32034. © **800/258-3301** or 904/261-3300. Fax 904/277-3831. www.floridahouse.com. 15 units. $99–$219 double. Rates include full breakfast. AE, DISC, MC, V. Dogs accepted ($10 nightly fee). **Amenities:** Restaurant; bar; coin-op washers and dryers. *In room:* A/C, TV, coffeemaker, hair dryer, iron.

Hampton Inn & Suites ✸✸ A Hampton Inn that garners two stars, you ask? Believe it or not, it's true. When plans were announced a few years ago to build this four-story hotel in the center of the historic district, they created quite a stir among preservationists. But the all-woman hotel firm of Miriam Taylor & Co. put those fears to rest by designing one of the most unusual Hampton Inns we've ever seen. Although there's only one building, the exterior looks like a row of different structures, all in the styles and sherbet hues of the Victorian storefronts lining Centre Street. Above a curving staircase rising in the two-story Victorian-style lobby, quadrants of an unusual ceiling clock have been painted to represent the 4 centuries of Fernandina Beach's history. Wooden floors taken from an old Jacksonville church, slatted door panels evocative of 19th-century sailing schooners, and many other touches add to the Victorian ambience. About half of the guest rooms are near the top of the romance scale: king beds, gas-burning fireplaces, and two-person whirlpool tubs. The standard suites are large enough for families, and the other standard rooms are adequately equipped for business travelers, making this a good choice for everyone. About a third of the units have balconies. Those higher up on the west side have fine views over the river and marshes. The only drawback: Trains slowly rumble by on the west side a few times a day.

19 S. 2nd St. (between Centre and Ash sts.), Fernandina Beach, FL 32034. © **800/426-7866** or 904/491-4911. Fax 904/491-4910. www.hamptoninn.com. 122 units. $109–$189 double. Rates include extensive breakfast buffet. AE, DC, DISC, MC, V. **Amenities:** Outdoor pool; exercise room; Jacuzzi; business center; babysitting; laundry service; coin-op washers and dryers. *In room:* A/C, TV, dataport, fridge, coffeemaker, hair dryer, iron.

WORTH A SPLURGE

Fairbanks House ✸✸ Having all the amenities and almost as much privacy as a first-class hotel in a superbly refurbished 1885 Italianate home, the Fairbanks House is a top B&B choice in the historic district. As gorgeous as it is, it used to be known as "Fairbanks' Folly," because of its pronounced decor. Many rooms and all of the cottages offer private entrances for guests who prefer not to walk through the main house. Room no. 3, in the back of the house on the main floor, is one of the finest rooms, with a private entrance, large sitting room, plush king-size bed, period antiques, porcelain, oil paintings, and fresh flowers. Occupying the entire top floor, the two-bedroom Tower Suite has plenty of room to spread out, plus 360-degree views and its own whirlpool tub. Five other units here have whirlpool tubs. Note that Fairbanks is the only B&B on the island with a swimming pool. No smoking indoors or out. Kids over 12 are welcome.

227 S. 7th St. (between Beech and Cedar sts.), Fernandina Beach, Amelia Island, FL 32034. (℃) 888/891-9882 or 904/277-0500. Fax 904/277-3103. www.fairbankshouse.com. 9 units, 3 detached cottages, all with bathroom. $170–$295 double; $220–$295 cottage. Rates include full breakfast and evening social hour (beverages and hors d'oeuvres). Packages available. AE, DISC, MC, V. **Amenities:** Heated outdoor pool. *In room:* A/C, TV, dataport, kitchen (cottage only), minibar, fridge, coffeemaker, hair dryer, iron.

GREAT DEALS ON DINING

You'll find several restaurants, pubs, and snack shops along Centre Street, between the bay and 8th Street (Fla. A1A), in Fernandina Beach's old town. Additionally, the **Florida House Inn** (see "Accommodations You Can Afford," above) serves boardinghouse-style, all-you-can-eat lunches and dinners Tuesday through Saturday from 11:30am to 2:30pm ($7 per person) and from 5:30 to 9pm ($13 per person).

Marina Restaurant *Value* AMERICAN   Occupying a brick store built in the 1880s, this quintessential small-town restaurant has been feeding Low Country fare to the locals since 1965. A lot of the seafood here is fried and broiled, but you can order crab-stuffed shrimp or flounder as well as grouper topped with scallops and a garlicky wine sauce. Budgeteers love the $10-and-under list of Southern favorites such as country-fried steak, breaded veal cutlet, grilled pork chops, and fried chicken. Meatloaf with tomato-and-basil gravy, stuffed bell peppers with a Greek-style tomato sauce, and other lunchtime specials come with three fresh country-style vegetables, which are themselves worth the price of the meal. Hearty breakfasts feature eggs, omelets, French toast, and hotcakes.

101 Centre St. (at Front St.), Fernandina Beach. (℃) **904/261-5310.** Main courses $8–$19; breakfast $3–$6; sandwiches $5–$9. DC, MC, V. Daily 7–10am and 11:30am–9pm.

WORTH A SPLURGE

Beech Street Grill ★★ REGIONAL NEW AMERICAN   The cosmopolitan chic Beech Street Grill pleases all palates with a rich menu of fish, chicken, and meat choices, including seasonal game dishes such as roasted venison loin in a black-currant sauce with sweet-potato-and-onion hash. Nightly fish specialties are always exceptional (some can be pricier than printed menu options). A Parmesan-encrusted red snapper with a mustard-basil sauce is superb. Seared tuna is always perfect, too. The dense and tasty crab cakes and the chewy steamed dumplings are great choices for starters, as is the huge mixed-green salad with mustard-basil vinaigrette, toasted pecans, and blue cheese. Housed in a century-old landmark home and in a newer wing to one side, five dining rooms offer a lively atmosphere. The upstairs features a pianist.

801 Beech St. (at 8th St./Fla. A1A), Fernandina Beach. (℃) **904/277-3662.** Reservations strongly recommended. Main courses $22–$35. AE, DC, DISC, MC, V. Daily 6–10pm.

Joe's 2nd Street Bistro ★★★ NEW AMERICAN   In the heart of the Fernandina Beach historic district, you'll find this diminutive restored 1900s home that is full of massive flavor. The island-inspired dining room features a brick fireplace, and upstairs is a private dining room, but I suggest grabbing a table—weather permitting—outside on the covered front porch. Eating here is almost like eating in a chef's home, a quaint and delectable experience to say the least. Try the pecan-breaded breast of duck with wild rice pancakes and red currant sauce, or loin lamb chops with a southwestern-style rub served over a three bean ragout with roasted tomatoes and tobacco fried onions. Yowza! For dessert, the apple bread pudding kicks that part of your body where perhaps the calories will end up. It rocks. Joe's rocks. Don't miss it. Eat at Joe's.

101 Centre St. (at Front St.), Fernandina Beach. ℂ **904/261-5310.** Reservations recommended. Main courses $14–$26. AE, DC, MC, V. Daily 6–9:30pm.

AMELIA ISLAND AFTER DARK

This romantic island goes to bed early. If you tire of the lounges in the island's resorts, check out the **Palace Saloon,** 117 Centre St., at 2nd Street (ℂ **904/261-6320**). It claims to be Florida's oldest watering hole (open since 1878). Complete with a pressed-tin ceiling and a 40-foot-long mahogany bar, it once hosted the Carnegies and the du Ponts. Some nights you'll even find live local blues or rock. It's open daily from 11am until 2am.

Another popular local watering hole, **O'Kane's Irish Pub & Eatery,** 318 Centre St., at 4th Street (ℂ **904/261-1000**), has live music until midnight Monday through Thursday; until 1:30am on weekends.

13

Northwest Florida: The Panhandle

The Florida Panhandle is kind of like the Jan Brady of the state. Consider that Cindy, the cute sister, could represent Orlando and Tampa, with their amusements and attractions, while South and Southwest Florida could be Marcia, the gorgeous sister whom everyone fawns over and talks about. And then there's the misrepresented, misunderstood, underestimated Jan, in this case Northwest Florida, aka the Panhandle, always getting the shaft, even though she's got some great qualities all her own, if only people took the time to discover them. For the Panhandle, this is a particular shame, since it is, undeniably, a dynamic, uncommonly beautiful part of the state.

If you like beaches, you'll love the Panhandle, the land of the two-way sun, which runs east to west along the Gulf of Mexico and, therefore, offers sunrises *and* sunsets. Once and sometimes erroneously still known as the Redneck Riviera (thanks to fans in Georgia, Alabama, and Louisiana)—a refreshing change from the glitz and glamour oozing from Florida's south, the Panhandle, while still rugged in a sexy, Marlboro Man kind of way, has slowly shed that rep with the emergence of upscale residential developments and boutique hotels.

Three other reasons to love this zone: water as turquoise as colored contact lenses, smaller crowds than other Florida beaches, and ghost-white sand that's so talcumlike it squeaks when you walk on it. (The sand in these parts is so brilliantly white,

because over thousands of years, quartz particles were washed downstream from the eroding Appalachian Mountains and pummeled into grains as fine and soft as baby powder before finally landing at its final resting place under towels of the three million sunbathers who flock here every year.) Speaking of walking, you can, for some 100 miles of these incomparable sands are protected in state parks and the gorgeous Gulf Islands National Seashore.

Pensacola, Destin, Fort Walton Beach, and Panama City Beach are summertime meccas for families, couples, and singles from the aforementioned adjoining states—a geographic proximity that lends this area the languid charm of the Deep South. Indeed, Southern specialties such as collard greens and cheese grits (in the South it's a two-syllable word, pronounced *gree*-its) appear frequently on menus here.

But there's more to the northwestern Panhandle than beaches and Southern charm. Record catches of grouper, amberjack, snapper, mackerel, cobia, sailfish, wahoo, tuna, and blue marlin have made Destin one of the world's fishing capitals. In the interior near Pensacola, the Blackwater, Shoal, and Yellow rivers teem with bass, bream, catfish, and largemouth bass, and also feature some of Florida's best canoeing and kayaking adventures.

The area is also steeped in history. Rivaling St. Augustine as Florida's oldest town, picturesque Pensacola preserves a heritage derived from Spanish, French,

Cheap Thrills: What to See & Do for Free (or Almost) in Northwest Florida

- **Hit a powdery beach.** Admission is free to most of 100-plus miles of powdery, snow-white beaches that make this area special. A few bucks will let you into the **Gulf Islands National Seashore** at Pensacola, the **Henderson Beach** and **Grayton Beach** parks at Destin, the **St. Andrews State Park** at Panama City Beach, and the **St. George Island State Park** near Apalachicola. You won't soon forget the time you spend on these protected sands and dunes, all consistently ranked among the nation's finest beaches.

- **Stroll through Florida's second oldest town.** You'll have to pay to go into its homes and museums, but you can walk the streets of **Historic Pensacola Village** (✆ 850/444-8905) for free. Built in 1823, the village boasts some of Florida's oldest homes, along with charming boutiques and interesting restaurants. During summer, costumed characters go about their daily chores and demonstrate old crafts, and archaeologists unearth the old Spanish commanding officer's compound.

- **Visit the Blue Angels and Top Guns.** Next to the Smithsonian Institution's National Air and Space Museum in Washington, D.C., the best places to see our nation's war planes on display are at the **National Museum of Naval Aviation** in Pensacola (✆ 850/452-3604) and at the **U.S. Air Force Armament Museum** in Fort Walton Beach (✆ 850/882-4062). Admission to both is free. The IMAX films shown at the naval museum will make you believe you're flying in a Blue Angel's cockpit (there's a charge for the films). Near the Pensacola museum and also free, historic **Fort Barrancas** (✆ 850/934-2600) dates from 1797, when the Spanish built its water battery. The incredibly intricate brickwork of the upper section was laid by American troops between 1839 and 1844.

- **Get away from it all on Shell Island.** The round-trip boat fare costs $9.50 for adults, $5.50 for kids 11 and under, but the ride over to Shell Island, off Panama City Beach (✆ 850/233-5140; www.shellisland shuttle.com), will take to you to an uninhabited natural preserve that's great for shelling, swimming, suntanning, or just relaxing. Bring chairs, beach gear, coolers, food, and beverages. The boat shuttles daily, every half hour between 9am and 5pm, between the island and St. Andrews State Recreation Area.

- **Celebrate the air conditioner.** Without air-conditioning, Florida would be an uncomfortable place to live or visit during its hot, humid summers. In the late 1800s, Doctor John Gorrie of Apalachicola invented a cooling machine to keep his malaria patients comfortable. It was a moment of great note in Florida's history, duly celebrated by his hometown's **John Gorrie State Museum** (✆ 850/653-9347). For $1

English, and American conquests. Famous for its oysters, Apalachicola saw the invention of the air conditioner, a moment of great historical note for Florida. And Tallahassee, seat of state government since 1824, has a host of 19th-century buildings, including the majestic Old State Capitol, not to (children under 6 are free), you can see a working replica of his device, the prototype of the air-conditioning units that make Florida summers bearable today.

- **Look down on the capital and out to the Gulf.** State legislators meet in Tallahassee's $43-million skyscraper **New Capitol Building** (© 850/487-1902) from March to May, but you can take the elevators to the 22nd-floor observatory any day and look down over all of the capital—and on a clear day, all the way to the Gulf of Mexico, some 20 miles away. Also free are guided tours of the building and the Old Capitol, directly in front of the skyscraper. With its majestic dome, the old building has been restored to its original 19th-century beauty and has an eight-room exhibit portraying Florida's political history.

- **Learn about black history and art.** Florida A&M University in Tallahassee is one of the country's leading all-black colleges, and it's a wonderful place to learn about African-American history and see some of that community's major works of art. Housed in a columned library built by Andrew Carnegie in 1908, the **Black Archives Research Center and Museum** (© 850/561-2603) displays one of the nation's most extensive collections of African-American artifacts and historical materials, while **The Florida A&M University Art Gallery** (© 850/599-3161) focuses on works by African-American artists, with a wide variety of paintings, sculptures, and more. Admission is free to both.

- **Take in the camellias and azaleas at Maclay State Gardens.** It'll cost a few bucks to get through the gate, but you won't find many places as naturally magnificent in springtime as Maclay State Gardens, on the northeastern outskirts of Tallahassee (© 850/487-4556). The more than 300 acres here feature more than 200 varieties of flowers, with 28 acres devoted exclusively to azaleas and camellias. This floral wonderland surrounds the beautifully restored 1923 home of New York financier Alfred B. Maclay and his wife, Louise. The blooming season is January to April, with the peak about mid-March. The park also offers nature trails, canoe rentals, boating, picnicking, swimming, and fishing.

- **See where Johnny Weissmuller played Tarzan.** Wakulla Springs, 15 miles south of Tallahassee, is so jungly that some of the 1930s Tarzan movies starring Johnny Weissmuller were filmed here. Today they are within the 2,860 acres of **Edward W. Ball Wakulla Springs State Park** (© 850/922-3632), which means you'll have to pay a few dollars to get in. You can also pay $6 for adults, $4 for children, to take glass-bottom-boat sightseeing and wildlife-observation tours. You can swim in the lake formed by the springs, but watch for alligators!

mention a cool little town named, yes, Havana, which is one of the Southeast's largest antiques centers.

One note to those traveling the entire state: While "season" in South Florida tends to fall in the winter months, because of the Panhandle's geographic location and tendency to get chilly to downright cold during winter months, their "season" is during the summer, so hotel rates will be higher during that time while it's the opposite down south.

EXPLORING NORTHWEST FLORIDA BY CAR

Both I-10 and U.S. 98 link Tallahassee and Pensacola, some 200 miles apart. The fastest route is I-10, but all you'll see is a huge pine forest divided by two strips of concrete. Plan to take U.S. 98 instead, a scenic excursion in itself. Although it can be traffic-clogged in the beach towns during summer, U.S. 98 has some beautiful stretches out in the country, particularly as it literally skirts the bay east of Apalachicola and the Gulf west of Port St. Joe. It's also lovely along skinny Okaloosa Island and across the high-rise bridge between Fort Walton Beach and Destin. From the bridge you'll see the brilliant hue of the Gulf and immediately understand why they call this the Emerald Coast. If you turn off U.S. 98 onto 30A, a 20-mile drive along the coastline, you will immediately be transported back in time, to the pre-Golden Arch–lined highways of Florida. Along this scenic stretch, you'll not only see sand and surf, but, believe it or not, pine forests, saw palmettos, the Choctawhatchee Bay, and Hogtown Bayou, a magnet for fiery sunsets.

1 Pensacola ★ ★

191 miles W of Tallahassee, 354 miles W of Jacksonville

A charming blend of Old Spanish brickwork, colonial French balconies reminiscent of New Orleans, and magnificent Victorian mansions built by British and American lumber barons, Pensacola is definitely worthy of its motto, "City of Five Flags," but, today, it's much more than just pretty buildings and a nice vibe. Thanks to the Pensacola Downtown Improvement Board, work has continued to progress on the revitalization of downtown, promoting the full occupancy of once abandoned, 125-year-old buildings and the emergence of downtown businesses, stores, historic theaters, restaurants, bars, and events such as the Florida Springfest, a 3-day music festival that lures big names like Bonnie Raitt, Trace Adkins, The Allman Brothers, and Jethro Tull, with coverage by VH-1.

West of town, the excellent National Museum of Naval Aviation at the U.S. Naval Air Station celebrates the storied past of U.S. Navy and Marine Corps pilots who trained at Pensacola. The Blue Angels, who are based here, demonstrate the high-tech present with thrilling exhibitions of precision flying in the navy's fastest fighters.

A Friendly Feud

Native Americans left pottery shards and artifacts in the coastal dunes in Pensacola centuries before Tristan de Luna arrived with a band of Spanish colonists in 1559. Although his settlement lasted only 2 years, modern Pensacolans claim de Luna made their town the oldest in North America. Pensacola actually dates its permanence from a Spanish colony established here in 1698, however, so St. Augustine wins this friendly feud, having been continuously settled since 1565. France, Great Britain, the United States, and the Confederacy subsequently captured (and in one case recaptured) this strategically important deep-water port.

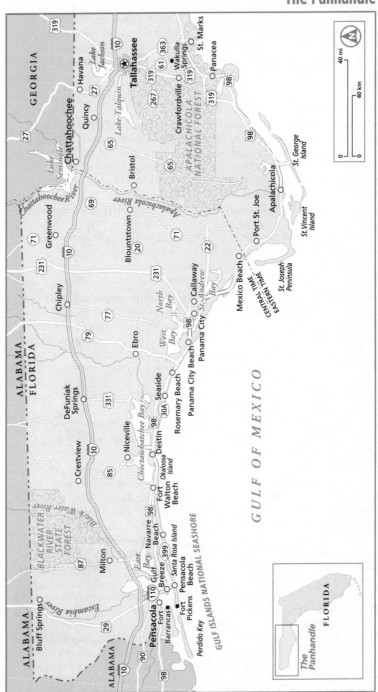

GULF OF MEXICO

FLORIDA

The Panhandle

Also on the Naval Station, historic Fort Barrancas looks across the bay to Perdido Key and Santa Rosa Island, which reach out like narrow pinchers to form the harbor. Out there, powdery white-sand beaches beckon sun-and-surf lovers to their spectacular Gulf shores, which include Pensacola Beach, a small family-oriented resort, and most of Florida's share of Gulf Islands National Seashore, home of historic Fort Pickens.

ESSENTIALS

GETTING THERE   **Pensacola Regional Airport** (© 850/436-5005; www.flypensacola.com), on 12th Avenue at Airport Road, is served by **AirTran** (© 800/247-8726), **Continental** (© 800/525-0280), **Delta** (© 800/221-1212), **Northwest** (© 800/225-2525), and **US Airways** (© 800/428-4322).

Alamo (© 800/327-9633), **Avis** (© 800/331-1212), **Budget** (© 800/527-0700), **Dollar** (© 800/800-4000), **Enterprise** (© 800/325-8007), **Hertz** (© 800/654-3131), and **National** (© 800/227-7368) have rental-car operations here.

Taxis wait outside the modern terminal. Fares are approximately $11 to downtown, $17 to Gulf Breeze, and $22 to Pensacola Beach.

The **Amtrak** transcontinental Sunset Limited stops in Pensacola at 980 E. Heinberg St. (© 800/872-7245; www.amtrak.com).

VISITOR INFORMATION   The **Pensacola Visitor Information Center,** 1401 E. Gregory St., Pensacola, FL 32501 (© **800/874-1234** or 850/434-1234; fax 850/432-8211; www.visitpensacola.com), gives away helpful information about the Greater Pensacola area, including maps of self-guided tours of the historic districts, and sells a detailed street map of the area. The office is at the mainland end of the Pensacola Bay Bridge and is open daily from 8am to 5pm (until 4pm Sat–Sun Oct–Mar).

For information specific to the beach, contact the **Pensacola Beach Chamber of Commerce,** 735 Pensacola Beach Blvd. (P.O. Box 1174), Pensacola Beach, FL 32561 (© **800/635-4803** or 850/932-1500; fax 850/932-1551; www.visit pensacolabeach.com). The chamber's offices and visitor center are on the right as you drive onto Santa Rosa Island across the Bob Sikes Bridge. They're open daily from 9am to 5pm.

GETTING AROUND   To see the historic sights in town, park at the Pensacola visitor center (see above) and take the **Five Flags Trolley** (© **850/436-9383**). The one-way East Bay (Blue) Line runs Monday through Friday from 9am to 4pm between the visitor center and downtown. The Palafox (Red) Line runs Monday through Friday from 7am to 6pm north-south along Palafox Street between the waterfront and North Hill Preservation District. Both pass through Historic Pensacola Village. The 25¢ fare includes a transfer between the two lines. The visitor center has free route maps.

A free Tiki Trolley operates along the full length of Pensacola Beach Memorial Day weekend through Labor Day weekend, Friday and Saturday from 10am to 3am, Sunday from 10am to 10pm.

Both trolleys are operated by **Escambia County Area Transit System (ECAT)** (© **850/595-3228;** www.ecat.pensacola.com), which also runs public buses around town Monday through Saturday ($1; 50¢ seniors)—but not to the beach. Call for schedules.

If you need a cab, call **Airport Express Taxi/City Cab** (© **850/478-4477**), Orange Cab (© **850/478-0222**), or Yellow Cab (© **850/433-3333**). Fares are $1.50 at flag fall, plus $1.60 a mile.

Downtown Pensacola

ACCOMMODATIONS ■
New World Inn **12**
Springhill Guesthouse **1**

DINING ◆
Hopkins' Boarding House **1**
Jamie's **6**
Marina Oyster Barn **2**
McGuire's Irish Pub **3**
Skopelos on the Bay **2**

ATTRACTIONS ●
Civil War Soldiers Museum **8**
Historic Pensacola Village **7**
Pensacola Civic Center **4**
Pensacola Historical Museum **10**
Pensacola Museum of Art **11**
Saenger Theatre **8**
Vietnam Memorial **5**

NIGHTLIFE ★
McGuire's Irish Pub **3**
Seville Quarter **9**

North Hill Preservation District
Palafox Historic District
Seville Historic District

You can rent bicycles from **Key Sailing**, 500 Quietwater Beach Rd. (© **877/ 932-7272** or 850/932-5520; www.keysailing.com), in Pensacola Beach. Rentals are $10 for 4 hours and $15 for a full day.

TIME   Pensacola is in the Central Time zone, 1 hour behind Miami, Orlando, and Tallahassee.

HITTING THE BEACH: GULF ISLANDS NATIONAL SEASHORE & MORE

Stretching eastward 47 miles, from the entrance to Pensacola Bay to Fort Walton Beach, skinny Santa Rosa Island is home to the resorts, condominiums, cottages, restaurants, and shops of Pensacola Beach, the area's prime vacation spot. This relatively small and low-key resort began life a century ago as the site of a beach pavilion, or "casino" as such facilities were called back then; and the heart of town—at the intersection of Pensacola Beach Boulevard, Via de Luna, and Fort Pickens Road—is still known as Casino Beach. This lively area at the base of the town's water tank sports restaurants, snack bars, a games arcade for kids, a minigolf course, public restrooms, walk-up beach bars with live bands blaring away, an indoor sports bar, and an outdoor concert pavilion with summertime entertainment. And the shops, restaurants, and bars of Quietwater Boardwalk are just across the road on the bay side of the island. If you want an active beach vacation, it's all here in one compact zone.

One reason Pensacola Beach is so small is that most of Santa Rosa Island is included in the **Gulf Islands National Seashore** ★★★. Jumping from island to island from Mississippi to Florida, this magnificent preserve, possibly the best beach in the entire state, includes 150 miles of undeveloped and federally protected white-sand beach and rolling dunes covered with sea grass and sea oats. Established in 1971, the national seashore is a protected environment for more than 280 species of birds.

The most interesting part of the seashore is **Fort Pickens** (© 850/934-2635), on the western end of Santa Rosa Island, about 7 miles west of Pensacola Beach. Built in the 1830s to team with Fort Barrancas in guarding Pensacola's harbor entrance, this huge brick structure saw combat during the Civil War, but it's best known as the prison home of Apache medicine man Geronimo from 1886 to 1888. The visitor center has a small museum featuring displays about Geronimo, coastal defenses, and the seashore's ecology. Plan to be here at 2pm, when rangers lead 45-minute tours of the fort (the schedule can change, so call the fort to make sure). Seven-day admission permits (that's the minimum you can get) to the Fort Pickens area are $7 per vehicle, $3 per pedestrian or bicyclist, free for holders of National Park Service passports. The fort and museum are open March through October daily from 9:30am to 5pm, November through February daily from 8:30am to 4pm. Both are closed on Christmas.

The Fort Pickens area has 200 campsites (135 with electricity) in a pine forest on the bay side of Santa Rosa Island. Nature trails lead from the camp through Blackbird Marsh and to the beach. A small store sells provisions. Sites cost $15 a night without power, $20 a night with it, and you have to pay the admission fee to the Fort Pickens area. Golden Age and Golden Access cardholders get a 50% discount. Call © 800/365-2267 for reservations (enter code GUL) or 850/934-2621 for recorded information. You can make reservations up to 5 months in advance.

The national seashore's headquarters are in the 1,378-acre Naval Live Oaks Area, on U.S. 98, a mile east of Gulf Breeze (© 850/934-2600). This former federal tree plantation is a place of primitive beauty, with nature trails leading through the oaks and pines to picnic areas and a beach. Pick up a map at the headquarters building, which has a small museum and a gorgeous view through the pines to Santa Rosa Sound. Picnic areas and trails are open from 8am to sunset year-round except Christmas. Admission is free. The visitor center is open daily from 8am to 5:30pm.

The national seashore also maintains historic Fort Barrancas on the U.S. Naval Air Station west of town. See the "Pensacola's Other Fort" box on p. 532 for details.

For more information, contact the Gulf Islands National Seashore, 1801 Gulf Breeze Pkwy., Gulf Breeze, FL 32561 (© 850/934-2600; www.nps.gov/guis).

AFFORDABLE OUTDOOR ACTIVITIES

FISHING Red snapper, grouper, mackerel, tuna, and billfish are abundant off the Panhandle. The easiest way to drop a line into the Gulf is off the new **Pensacola Beach Gulf Fishing Pier,** on Fort Pickens Road in Pensacola Beach

Florida's Canoe Capital

The little town of Milton, the official "Canoe Capital of Florida" (by an act of the state legislature, no less), is about 20 miles northeast of Pensacola via U.S. 90. It's a well-earned title, because the nearby Blackwater River, Coldwater River, Sweetwater Creek, and Juniper Creek are perfect for canoeing, kayaking, tubing, rafting, and paddleboating.

The Blackwater is considered one of the world's purest sand-bottom rivers. It has remained a primordial, backwoods beauty, thanks chiefly to Florida's largest state forest (183,000 acres of oak, pine, and juniper) and **Blackwater River State Park** ★★, 7720 Deaton Bridge Rd., Holt, FL 32564 (© 850/983-5363; www.floridastateparks.org/blackwaterriver) where you can closely observe plant life and wildlife along nature trails. The park has facilities for fishing, picnicking, and camping. Admission is $3 per day per vehicle, $1 more for extra passengers, pedestrians, or bicyclists. Campsites cost $12 plus $2 per pet with tags and vaccination papers. For camping reservations call © 800/326-3521 or go to the website (www.reserveamerica.com).

Adventures Unlimited, Route 6, Box 283, Milton, FL 32570 (© 800/239-6864 or 850/623-6197; fax 850/626-3124; www.adventuresunlimited.com), is a year-round resort with day and overnight canoeing, kayaking, and rafting expeditions. Special arrangements are made for novices. Canoe trips start at $17 per person (4 miles), kayaking adventures from $22. Inner tubes start at $6. Campsites cost $15 a night, $20 with electricity. The resort also has 14 cottages on the Coldwater River ($49–$129 a night), and bed-and-breakfast accommodations at the Wolfe Creek Old School House Inn (eight rooms, all with bathrooms, $89–$109 double). Two-night minimum stays are required, 3 nights on holidays. Call for schedules and reservations for trips, accommodations, and camping.

Blackwater Canoe Rental, 10274 Pond Rd., Milton, FL 32570 (© 800/967-6789 or 850/623-0235; www.blackwatercanoe.com), also rents canoes, kayaks, floats, tubes, and camping equipment. It has day and overnight camping trips by canoe or kayak, or inner tubes ranging from $11 to $19 per person and overnight excursions ranging from $22 to $33 per person. Tents, sleeping bags, and coolers are available for rent.

(© 850/934-7200; www.fishpensacolabeachpier.com). At 1,471 feet, it's the longest fishing pier on the Gulf coast. The pier is open 24 hours a day year-round. Fees to fish are $6.50 per day for adults, $5.50 for seniors, and $3.50 for children 6 to 12. Bait and equipment cost extra. Observers can watch for $1 per person.

Fishing-charter services are offered at Pensacola by the **Beach Marina Fishing Fleet** (© 877/650-3474 or 850/932-0304) and at Pensacola Beach by **Reel Eazy Charters** (© 877/733-5329 or 850/932-8824). Expect to pay between $400 and $900 for one to four passengers, depending on the length of your trip. You may be able to save by driving to Destin, where party boats charge less per person (p. 542). Sightseeing and evening cruises here go for $50 to $200 per person.

GOLF The Pensacola area has its share of Northwest Florida's numerous championship golf courses. Look for free copies of *South Coast Golf Guide,* an annual directory describing all of them, at the visitor information offices and in many hotel lobbies (see "Special-Interest Trips," in chapter 2, for information about ordering copies). Reasonably priced golf packages can be arranged through many local hotels and motels.

For course information online, go to www.golf.com and www.floridagolfing. com or call the **Florida Sports Foundation** (✆ 850/488-8347) or **Florida Golfing** (✆ 866/833-2663).

Among this region's best courses is **Marcus Pointe,** on Marcus Pointe Boulevard off North W Street (✆ 800/362-7287 or 850/484-9770), which has hosted the Nike Tour, the American Amateur Classic, and the Pensacola Open. *Golf Digest* magazine described this 18-hole course as a "great value," and that's not far off: Greens fees with cart are about $40 to $65, depending on the season.

The Moors, on Avalon Boulevard north of I-10 (✆ 800/727-1010 or 850/ 995-4653), also has greeted the Nike Tour and is home to the Emerald Coast Classic, a PGA Seniors event. Pot bunkers here make you think you're playing in Scotland. Greens fees are similarly priced. The Moors also has a lodge with eight luxury rooms.

Others worth considering are the **Lost Key Golf Club** on Perdido Key (✆ 888/256-7853 or 850/492-1300), one of the area's more difficult courses; **Scenic Hills,** on U.S. 90 northwest of town (✆ 850/476-9611), whose rolling fairways are unique for this mostly flat area; the 36-hole **Tiger Point,** 1255 Country Club Rd. east of Gulf Breeze by Santa Rosa Sound (✆ 850/932-1330), overlooking the water (the 5th-hole green of the East Course actually sits on an island); **Hidden Creek,** 3070 PGA Blvd., in Navarre between Gulf Breeze and Fort Walton Beach (✆ 850/939-4604); **Creekside Golf Course,** 2355 W. Michigan Ave. (✆ 850/944-7969); and **Osceola Municipal Golf Course,** 300 Tonawanda, off Mobile Highway (✆ 850/456-2761).

In addition, **The Sportsman Golf Resort,** 1 Doug Ford Dr. (✆ 866/319-2471 or 850/492-1223; www.sportsmanresort.com), on the mainland north of Perdido Key, has accommodations available for visiting golfers. It was the home of the PGA Pensacola Open from 1978 to 1987, when it was known as the Perdido Bay Golf Resort. Greens fees here range from $55 to $65.

WATERSPORTS Visibility in the waters around Pensacola can range from 30 to 50 feet deep inshore to 100 feet deep 25 miles offshore. Although the bottom is sandy and it's too far north for coral, the battleship USS *Massachusetts,* submerged in 30 feet of water 3 miles offshore, is one of some 35 artificial reefs where you can spot loggerhead turtles and other creatures. There are also good snorkeling sites just off the beach; get a map from the Gulf Islands National Seashore (see "Hitting the Beach: Gulf Islands National Seashore & More," above).

Scuba Shack, 711 S. Palafox St. (✆ 850/433-4319), offers sales, rentals, classes, and diving and fishing charters on the *Wet Dream,* moored behind the office. **Divers Den,** 512 N. 9th Ave. (✆ 850/438-0650; www.diversden.com), also provides trips, equipment rental, and PADI instruction. **MBT Divers** (✆ 850/455-7702; www.mbtdivers.com) has rentals, instruction, and trips to several sites, including the habitats of sea turtles, manta rays, and nurse sharks. **Gulf Breeze Dive Pros,** 297B Gulf Breeze Pkwy. (U.S. 98), in Gulf Breeze (✆ 850/934-8845), has a menu that includes rentals, all levels of instruction, and diving excursions on the 30-foot *Easy Dive.*

Key Sailing Center, 500 Quietwater Beach Rd., on the Quietwater Beach Boardwalk (© 877/932-7272 or 850/932-5520; www.keysailing.com), and Radical Rides, 444 Pensacola Beach Blvd., near the Bob Sikes Bridge (© 850/ 934-9743), rent Hobie Cats, pontoon boats, WaveRunners, jet skis, and wind-surfing boards.

EXPLORING HISTORIC PENSACOLA

Adjacent to the Historic Pensacola Village, the city's Vietnam Memorial, on Bayfront Parkway at 9th Avenue, is known as the "Wall South," since it is a three-quarter–size replica of the national Vietnam Veterans Memorial in Washington, D.C. Look for the "Huey" helicopter atop the wall.

Civil War Soldiers Museum ✪   Founded by Dr. Norman Haines Jr., a local physician who started collecting Civil War relics in Sharpsburg, Maryland, when he was growing up, this 4,200-square-foot storefront museum in the heart of the Palafox Street business district emphasizes how ordinary soldiers lived during that bloody conflict. The doctor's collection of military medical equipment and treatment methods is especially informative. A 23-minute video tells of Pensacola's role during the Civil War. The museum's bookstore carries more than 600 titles about the war.

108 S. Palafox St. (south of Romana St.). © 850/469-1900. www.cwmuseum.org. Admission $5 adults, $2.50 children 6–12, free for children 5 and under. Tues–Sat 10am–4:30pm. Closed New Year's Day, Thanksgiving, Christmas Eve, and Christmas Day.

Historic Pensacola Village ✪✪✪   History buffs as well as those who appreciate delightful architecture will *love* this retro-fabulous old-school village that's comparable to Long Island's Old Bethpage Village Restoration or Virginia's Colonial Williamsburg. Bounded by Government, Taragona, Adams, and Alcanz streets, this original part of Pensacola resembles a shady English colonial town—albeit with Spanish street names—complete with town green and Christ Church, built in 1832 and resembling Bruton Parish in Williamsburg, Virginia. Some of Florida's oldest homes, now owned and preserved by the state, are here, and the village has charming boutiques and interesting restaurants. All twenty of the Village's properties are on the National Register as a historic district. During summer, costumed characters go about their daily chores and demonstrate old crafts, and University of Florida archaeologists unearth the old Spanish commanding officer's compound at Zaragosa and Tarragona streets. Among the landmarks you can visit are the Museum of Industry, the Museum of Commerce, the French Creole–style Charles Lavalle House, the elegant Victorian Dorr House, the French Colonial–Creole Quina House, and St. Michael's Cemetery (land was deeded by the king of Spain). The Julee Cottage Black History Museum, 204 E. Zaragosa St., is another fascinating site. Built around 1790, this small house was owned by Julee Panton, a freed slave who ran her business, invested in real estate, and loaned money to slaves so they could buy their freedom. Today the museum recalls her life and deeds. Start your tour by buying tickets at Tivoli House, 205 E. Zaragosa St., just east of Tarragona Street, where you can get free maps and brochures. Try to take one of the 90-minute guided walking tours of the village, which will take you through Christ Church and other buildings not otherwise open to the public.

Admission to the village includes the T. T. Wentworth Jr. Florida State Museum, 330 S. Jefferson St. (© 850/595-5985), at Church Street downtown, a classic yellow-brick building housing exhibits of Western Florida's history and a special hands-on Discovery Museum for children. The museum's newest exhibition is "La Frontera de Pensacola," a hands-on exhibit highlighting local heritage.

205 E. Zaragosa St. (east of Tarragona St.). ℂ 850/595-5985. www.historicpensacola.org. Admission $6 adults, $5 seniors, $2.50 children 4–16, free for children 3 and under. Mon–Fri 10am–4pm; 90-min. guided tours 11am and 1pm. Closed New Year's Day, Thanksgiving, Christmas Eve, Christmas Day, and all other state holidays.

National Museum of Naval Aviation ✮✮ Given the present world circumstances, this museum should be required attendance for everyone. Yes, it's fascinating, but it also gives you a look into just how much blood, sweat, and tears go into defending this country. The U.S. Navy and Marine Corps have trained at the sprawling U.S. Naval Air Station since they began flying airplanes early in the last century. Celebrating their heroics, this remarkable museum has more than 100 aircraft dating from the 1920s to the space age plus interesting exhibits on subjects such as POWs. There's even a torpedo bomber flown by former President George (the first) Bush during World War II. Both children and adults can sit at the controls of a jet trainer, and the mock-ups of aircraft carrier conning towers and hanger decks are realistic. You can almost feel the tug of gravity while watching the Blue Angels and other naval aviators soaring about the skies in the stunning *Magic of Flight,* one of two IMAX films shown at the museum. If the movie doesn't get your stomach churning, then a 15-minute ride in the museum's flight-motion simulator will. Using high-tech video and real

---

Pensacola's Other Fort

Standing on Taylor Road near the National Museum of Naval Aviation, **Fort Barrancas** ✮✮ (ℂ 850/455-5167) is definitely worth a visit while you're at the naval station. This imposing brick structure sits on a bluff overlooking the deep-water pass into Pensacola Bay. The Spanish built the water battery in 1797. Linked to it by a tunnel, the incredibly intricate brickwork of the fort's upper section was constructed by American troops between 1839 and 1844. Entry is by means of a drawbridge across a dry moat, and an interior scarp gallery goes all the way around the inside of the fort. Meticulously restored and operated by the National Park Service as part of Gulf Islands National Seashore, the fort is open March through October, daily from 9:30am to 4:45pm; November through February, daily from 8:30am to 3:45pm. Ranger-led, 1-hour guided tours are well worth taking. The schedule changes seasonally, so call for the latest information. Admission and the tours are free.

The **Pensacola Lighthouse,** opposite the museum entrance on Radford Boulevard, has guided ships to the harbor entrance since 1825. Except for occasional guided tours (call the Pensacola visitor centers, listed earlier in this chapter, for a schedule), the lighthouse is not open to the public, but you can drive right up to it. The nearby **Lighthouse Point Restaurant** (ℂ 850/452-3251) offers bountiful, all-you-can-eat luncheon buffets and magnificent bay views for about $5.50 per person Monday through Thursday and $6.25 per person on Fridays; it's open Monday through Friday from 10:30am to 2pm (closed Sat–Sun), and reservations are not required.

motion, it simulates a high-speed, low-level mission in the navy's F-18 Hornet jet fighter. All guides are retired naval and Marine Corps aviators, which adds a personal touch to the hour-long museum tours. Allow at least half a day here, and save 20 minutes for a Flight Line bus tour of more than 40 aircraft parked outside the museum's restoration hangar.

Radford Blvd., U.S. Naval Air Station. © 850/452-3604. www.naval-air.org. Free admission. IMAX movies $6.50 adults; $6.00 seniors, military, and children 5–13; free for children under 5. Add $3 for second movie. Flight-motion simulator rides $3.50 per person. Daily 9am–5pm. Guided tours daily at 9:30 and 11am, and 1 and 2:30pm. Flight Line bus tours daily every 30 min. 10am–noon and 1–4pm. IMAX movies on the hour daily 10am–4pm. Flight-motion simulator every 15 min. 9am–4:45pm. Closed New Year's Day, Thanksgiving, and Christmas. Enter naval station either at the Main Gate at the south end of Navy Blvd. (Fla. 295) or at the Back Gate on Blue Angel Pkwy. (Fla. 173) and follow the signs. No passes are required.

Pensacola Museum of Art ★   Housed in what was the city jail from 1906 to 1954, this museum showcases an impressive collection of European and American decorative glass, some African tribal art, and sometimes minor works by Salvador Dalí, John Marin, Ansel Adams, Thomas Hart Benton, Lynda Benglis, Milton Avery, George Rodrigue, Alexander Calder, Pablo Cano, and Rembrandt among others, all displayed in the former cell blocks. They also sponsor cool events such as Art After Dark, in which you are invited to use the walls of the museum as your personal canvas in your best display of personal, artistic expression. Call before going to see what's on.

407 S. Jefferson St. (at Main St.). © 850/432-6247. www.pensacolamuseumofart.org. Free admission on Tues; other days $5 adults, $2 students and active-duty military, free for children under 6. Tues–Fri 10am–5pm; Sat–Sun noon–5pm.

HISTORIC DISTRICTS

In addition to Historic Pensacola Village (see above) in the Seville Historic District (see references below), the city has two other preservation areas worth a stroll. The Pensacola Visitor Information Center provides free walking-tour maps (see "Essentials," earlier in this chapter) if you're interested.

PALAFOX HISTORIC DISTRICT ★★   Running up Palafox Street from the water to Wright Street, the Palafox Historic District is also the downtown business district. Beautiful Spanish Renaissance and Mediterranean-style buildings stand from the early days, including the ornate Saenger Theatre. In 1821, General Andrew Jackson formally accepted Florida into the United States during a ceremony in Plaza Ferdinand VII, now a National Historic Landmark. His statue commemorates the event.

For architecture buffs, this district is a theme park, with the 1902 Theisen Building and its vivid displays of Beaux Arts details, and the 1925 Seanger Theatre, with its terra-cotta ornamentation and grille work on the front facade showcasing it as an elegant gem of the Spanish Baroque style.

The Palafox district is home to the **Pensacola Historical Museum;** the **Pensacola Museum of Art,** in the old city jail; and the **T. T. Wentworth Jr. Florida State Museum** (see "Exploring Historic Pensacola," above).

And, no visit to the Palafox District is complete without visits to the **Hopkins' Boarding House** restaurant, 900 N. Spring St. (© 850/438-3979), for family-style grub in a turn-of-the-century house (p. 536), and, for boozehounds, **The Palace Oyster Bar,** 130 E. Government St. (© 850/434-6211), which includes a bar from the old Palace Hotel, where Florida's first liquor license was issued.

NORTH HILL PRESERVATION DISTRICT ★   Another entry in the National Register of Historic Places, the North Hill Preservation District covers the 50 square blocks north of the Palafox Historic District bounded by Wright, Blount, Palafox, and Reus streets. Descendants of Spanish nobility, timber barons, British merchants, French Creoles, buccaneers, and Civil War soldiers still live in some of the more than 500 homes. They are not open to the public but are a bonanza for anyone interested in architecture. In 1863, Union troops erected a fort in Lee Square, at Palafox and Gadsden streets. It later was dedicated to the Confederacy, complete with a 50-foot-high obelisk and sculpture based on John Elder's painting *After Appomattox.*

SHOPPING

Sightseeing and shopping can be combined in Pensacola's Palafox and Seville Historic Districts, where many shops are housed in renovated centuries-old buildings. The **Quayside Art Gallery,** on Plaza Ferdinand at the corner of Zaragosa and Jefferson streets (℗ 850/438-2363; www.quaysidegallery.com), is the largest cooperative gallery in the Southeast. More than 100 artists display their works here, and the friendly staff will direct you to other nearby galleries.

North T Street between West Cervantes Street and West Fairfield Drive has so many antiques dealers and small flea markets that it's known as Antique Alley. Other dealers have booths in the **Ninth Avenue Antique Mall,** 380 N. 9th Ave. between Gregory and Strong streets (℗ 850/438-3961). Get a complete list of local antiques dealers from the Pensacola Visitor Information Center (p. 526).

Browsers will enjoy poking through the 400 dealer spaces at the **Flea Market,** on U.S. 98, opposite The Zoo, 15 miles east of Pensacola (℗ 850/934-1971). It's open on Saturday and Sunday from 9am to 5pm. Admission is free.

ACCOMMODATIONS YOU CAN AFFORD

The Pensacola Visitor Information Center (p. 526) publishes a complete list of rental condominiums and cottages. Among the leading rental agents are **JME Management,** 22-A Via de Luna, Pensacola Beach, FL 32561 (℗ 800/554-3695; www.jmevacations.com), and **Tristan Realty,** 1020 Fort Pickens Rd., Pensacola Beach, FL 32561 (℗ 800/445-9931 or 850/932-7363; fax 850/932-8361; www. tristanrealty.com).

The **Fort Pickens Area** of Gulf Islands National Seashore is your best bet here for camping (p. 528).

Escambia County adds 11.5% tax to all hotel and campground bills.

The accommodations listed below are arranged by geographic area: downtown Pensacola and Pensacola Beach. Bear in mind that Pensacola Beach is at least a 15-minute drive from downtown.

DOWNTOWN PENSACOLA

The University Mall complex at I-10 and Davis Highway, about 5 miles north of downtown, has a host of chain motels, and there's an ample supply of inexpensive restaurants on Plantation Road and in the adjacent mall. Another good bet is the 1998-vintage **Hampton Inn Airport,** 2187 Airport Blvd. (℗ 800/426-7866 or 850/478-1123; fax 850/478-8519). This area is not as congested as that around University Mall. The inn runs a free shuttle to nearby Cordova Mall and its adjacent chain restaurants.

Several of the town's Victorian homes have been turned into luxurious bed-and-breakfasts. Among the best is **Springhill Guesthouse,** 903 N. Spring St. (℗ 800/475-1956 or 850/438-6887; www.bbonline.com/fl/springhill), whose wraparound porch faces the extraordinary Hopkins' Boarding House across the street (see "Great Deals on Dining," below).

> **Tips When Room Rates Are Lowest**
>
> Room rates at all Panhandle beaches are highest from mid-May to mid-August, and premiums are charged at Easter, Memorial Day, July 4, and Labor Day. Hotel or motel reservations are essential during these periods. There's another high-priced peak in March, when thousands of raucous college students invade during spring break. Economical times to visit are April (except Easter) and September—the weather is warm, most establishments are open, and room rates are significantly lower than during summer. The least-expensive rates are available during winter, but many attractions and some restaurants may be closed then.

New World Inn   Near the scenic bay and in the historic district, this urban version of a comfortable country inn (it looks more like a concrete fortress) is part of a meeting facility known as New World Landing. Inside, however, is an entirely different—much more pleasing to the eye—story. From the colonial-style lobby, a grand staircase leads to high-ceilinged and spacious rooms and suites artistically decorated with antiques.

600 S. Palafox St. (at Pine St.), Pensacola, FL 32501. ✆ 850/432-4111. Fax 850/432-6836. www.newworld landing.com. 15 units. $75–$95 double; $125–$145 suite. Rates include continental breakfast. AE, MC, V. **Amenities:** Access to nearby health club; laundry service. *In room:* A/C, TV, dataport.

Seville Inn   Best thing about this dated two-story motel is its location at the edge of the Seville Historic District, across the street from the Civic Center and about 4 blocks from Palafox Street and the Saenger Theatre. It has two outdoor swimming pools open during the warm months; one is covered so you can swim even on rainy days. Local phone calls are free, and guests get passes to the nearby Seville Quarter entertainment complex (see "Pensacola After Dark," below). You can save a few dollars off the room rate by picking up a discount coupon at the Pensacola visitor center (see "Essentials," earlier in this section).

223 E. Garden St. (between Alcaniz and Manresa sts.), Pensacola, FL 32501. ✆ 800/277-7275 or 850/433-8331. Fax 850/432-6849. 120 units. Summer $69–$84 single or double; off season $39–$69 single or double. Rates include continental breakfast. AE, DC, DISC, MC, V. **Amenities:** Restaurant (regional); bar; 2 outdoor pools; exercise room; Jacuzzi; sauna; bike rentals; business center; coin-op washers and dryers. *In room:* A/C, TV, fridge, iron.

PENSACOLA BEACH

Best Western Pensacola Beach Resort   It's a Best Western, yes, but this hotel has a better view than some fancier hotels could ever dream of, right on the Gulf, and it's notable for bright, clean, and extra-spacious accommodations, complete with refrigerators, coffeemakers, microwaves, and wet bars. Outside corridors lead to all rooms. Although none has its own balcony or patio, units facing the beach have great views but higher prices. Two pools and a kids' playground are on the beach, and restaurants are within walking distance.

16 Via de Luna Dr., Pensacola Beach, FL 32561. ✆ 800/934-3301 or 850/934-3300. Fax 850/934-4366. www.bestwestern.com. 123 units. Summer $149–$189 double; off season $79–$149 double. Rates include continental breakfast. Golf packages available. AE, DC, DISC, MC, V. **Amenities:** 2 outdoor pools; watersports equipment rentals; game room. *In room:* A/C, TV, dataport, fridge, coffeemaker, hair dryer, iron, microwave.

Clarion Suites Resort & Convention Center ★★   This most unusual of Pensacola Beach's resorts resembles a village of tin-roofed, pastel-sided cottages located on the sand dunes and reminiscent of a tony rental community in New York's Hamptons. Pretty swank for Clarion Suites, I'd say. The attractively decorated accommodations are one-bedroom suites with kitchens and two televisions that can accommodate four people. The best units are those directly facing the beach. They have balconies or patios, while the others do not. There are no restaurants in the resort, and if you don't feel like cooking in your suite's kitchen, area eateries are within walking distance. The outdoor pool is lovely, but why use the pool when you're right on this stunning beach?

20 Via de Luna Dr., Pensacola Beach, FL 32561. (C) **800/874-5303** or 850/932-4300. Fax 850/934-9112. www.clarionsuitesresort.com. 86 units. Summer $119–$199 up to 4 persons; off season $84–$119 up to 4 persons. Rates include continental breakfast. AE, DC, DISC, MC, V. **Amenities:** Heated outdoor pool; watersports equipment rentals; coin-op washers and dryers. *In room:* A/C, TV, dataport, kitchen, coffeemaker, hair dryer, iron.

Five Flags Inn *(Value)* Sitting between the Holiday Inn Express and The Dunes, this basic but friendly motel looks like a jail from the road and the rooms have cinder block walls, but if it's location and view you're looking for at a bargain basement rate, flag this hotel. Big picture windows in the rooms overlook the swimming pool (heated Mar–Oct) and the gorgeous white-sand beach, which comes right up to the property. Although the accommodations are small, trust us on this: The rates are a bargain for clean, Gulf-front rooms.

299 Fort Pickens Rd., Pensacola Beach, FL 32561. (C) **850/932-3586.** Fax 850/934-0257. www.fiveflagsinn. com. 49 units. Summer $99 double; off season $49–$85 double; $20 more for holidays. AE, DC, DISC, MC, V. **Amenities:** Heated outdoor pool. *In room:* A/C, TV, hair dryer, iron.

GREAT DEALS ON DINING
PENSACOLA

Hopkins' Boarding House ★★★ *(Value)* SOUTHERN You haven't had true comfort food until you dine at this extraordinary Victorian boardinghouse founded by Arkie Dell Hopkins in 1949 and now run by her son Ed in the heart of the North Hill Preservation District, where it feels as if you are dining at your own grandma's house. Outside, ancient trees shade a wraparound porch with old-fashioned rocking chairs in which you'll wait the next available place at the large dining tables inside. It's all-you-can-eat family-style, so you could be seated next to a football star, the mayor, or a mechanic, since everyone in town dines here. Platters are piled high with staples of down-home Southern cooking: black-eyed peas, collard greens, and other seasonal vegetables from nearby farms. Tuesday is famous as Fried Chicken Day, and you're likely to be served fried fish on Friday. Yankees should sample the piping-hot grits accompanying each bountiful breakfast (slop on some butter or salt and pepper to give them taste but never use sugar on this staple that some Yankees confuse with Cream of Wheat). In true boardinghouse fashion, you'll bus your own dishes and pay on the way out. No alcoholic beverages are served, but the "don't-call-it-sweet-if-you-want-to-be-considered-a-local" iced tea is a sweet treat.

900 N. Spring St. (at Strong St.). (C) **850/438-3979.** Breakfast $3.50–$8; lunch and dinner full meals $8. No credit cards. Tues–Sun 7–9:30am and 11:15am–2pm; Tues and Fri 5–7:30pm.

Marina Oyster Barn ★ *(Value)* SEAFOOD Exuding the ambience of the quickly vanishing Old Florida fish camps, this plain but clean restaurant at the Johnson-Rooks Marina is to seafood what the Hopkins' Boarding House is to grits. It's been a local favorite since 1969, for its view and its down-home–style seafood. Freshly shucked oysters, served raw, steamed, fried, or Rockefeller-style, are the main feature; but the seafood salad here is also first-rate, and the fish, shrimp, and oysters are breaded with cornmeal in true Southern fashion. The daily luncheon specials give you a light meal at a bargain price.

505 Bayou Blvd. (on Bayou Texar). © **850/433-0511.** Main courses $5–$15; sandwiches $2.50–$5.50; lunch specials $3.75–$6.50. AE, DISC, MC, V. Tues–Sat 11am–9pm (lunch specials 11am–2pm). Go east on Cervantes St. (U.S. 90) across the Bayou Texar Bridge, then take 1st left on Stanley Ave., and left again to the end of Strong St.

McGuire's Irish Pub ✿ STEAKS/SEAFOOD   Every day and night is St. Patrick's Day at this lively and popular pub. The menu is delectably Irish, complete with corned beef and cabbage, Irish stew, and other such Dublin delicacies. Supersize steaks are the best offerings, however, as are hickory-smoked ribs and chicken. You can also order seafood, including a hearty bouillabaisse with shrimp, red snapper, clams, mussels, and oysters. The big burgers come with a choice of more than 20 toppings, from smoked Gouda cheese to sautéed Vidalia onions. You can watch your ale being brewed in copper kettles and dine in a cellarlike room with 8,000 bottles of wine on display. More than 125,000 dollar bills line the bar's walls and ceilings. Live music is offered most nights.

600 E. Gregory St. (between 11th and 12th aves.). © **850/433-6789.** www.mcguiresirishpub.com. Main courses $16–$25; snacks, burgers, and sandwiches $8–$12. AE, DC, DISC, MC, V. Daily 11am–midnight; later on weekend.

Worth a Splurge

Jamie's ✿✿✿ TRADITIONAL FRENCH   Occupying a restored Victorian home in Historic Pensacola Village, the town's classiest and most romantic restaurant enhances the dining experience with a stellar ambience augmented by working fireplaces, fabulous antiques, candlelight, and subdued background music. The excellent French Provincial fare includes roast leg of lamb, tournedos of beef, and seafood specials. The wine list is also exquisite. This is as fine as Pensacola's cuisine gets.

424 E. Zaragoza St. (between Alcanz and Florida Blanca). © **850/434-2911.** Reservations recommended at both lunch and dinner. Main courses $17–$30. AE, DISC, MC, V. Mon–Sat 11:30am–2pm and 5:30–9pm (sometimes later).

Skopelos on the Bay ✿ SEAFOOD/STEAKS/GREEK   If you didn't know any better—or drank too much ouzo, you'd think you were in Santorini. Perched on a bluff overlooking the bay, this family-owned restaurant has been famous hereabouts since 1959 for its great views and creative seafood dishes, such as the scamp Cervantes (scamp is a deepwater fish with white, flaky meat). Other seafood selections range from broiled scallops to Mediterranean-style grouper prepared with a sauce of tomato and roasted eggplant. The menu also features charcoal-grilled steaks and chicken and roast leg of lamb. Befitting the owner's Greek heritage, roast lamb is served with moussaka, dolmades, titopita, and spanakopita. In warm weather, opt for an outside table with a bay view.

670 Scenic Hwy. (U.S. 90 east, at E. Cervantes St.). © **850/432-6565.** Reservations recommended. Main courses $15–$35. AE, DISC, MC, V. Tues–Thurs and Sat 5–10:30pm; Fri 11:30am–2:30pm and 5–10:30pm.

PENSACOLA BEACH

Bobaloo's on the Beach ✿ SEAFOOD   Waterfront views aside, Bobaloo's is proudest of serving the "largest seafood platter on the beach," in addition to delicious southern cooking such as fried dill pickles, fried crawfish tails, and collard greens. The fishing motif is most apropos, but the best part about the place is that they will cook, fry, boil, or do whatever to any fish caught right there by one of the many charter boats scouting the waters. Live music and a lively crowd make Bobaloo's a great choice for lunch, dinner, or just kicking back with a beer, some fried food, and a phenomenal sunset.

699 Pensacola Beach Blvd. © **850/934-3434.** Main courses $3.25–$13. MC, V. Daily 11:30am–1am.

Flounder's Chowder & Ale House ★★ SEAFOOD Floundering around for a place where you can get fresh fish cooked any way, and live reggae almost nightly? Then Flounder's Chowder & Ale House is where you need to be, on the boardwalk, overlooking the Santa Rosa Sound, and serving great food for breakfast, brunch, lunch, dinner, or late night snacks. The best of the offerings include the Maine lobster and chargrilled tuna, grouper, and mahimahi. If you're lucky, a big smoker grill outside will be producing more fish and some exceptional ribs. Burgers, salads, and sandwiches are offered all day. The dining room is cool and not at all what you'd expect from a fish house, with stained glass windows imported from a convent, of all places, confessional booth walls straight from a church, and bookshelves contributing to a cozy, Nantucket in the winter kind of feel. But when the weather's warm, you'll definitely want to be outdoors.

800 Quietwater Beach Rd. (at Via de Luna and Fort Pickens Rd.). ℂ 850/932-2003. Reservations not accepted. Main courses $15–$21; burgers and sandwiches $8–$10. AE, DC, DISC, MC, V. Sun–Thurs 11am–midnight (to 11pm in winter); Fri–Sat 11am–2am (to 11pm in winter).

PENSACOLA AFTER DARK

For what's hip and happening when the sun goes down, pick up the daily *Pensacola News Journal* (www.pensacolanewsjournal.com), especially its Friday entertainment section. Another good source is the *Pensacola Downtown Crowd* (www.burchell publishing.com/downtown.asp), a free publication available at the Pensacola Visitor Information Center (p. 526) covering the nightly events going on in downtown Pensacola.

THE PERFORMING ARTS Pensacola has a surprisingly sophisticated array of entertainment choices for such a relatively small city. For a schedule of upcoming events, get a copy of *Vision*, a bimonthly newsletter published by the Arts Council of Northwest Florida (ℂ 850/432-9906; www.artsnwfl.org). Also pick up **Sneak Preview**, a calendar of events at the Pensacola Civic Center and the Saenger Theater. Both publications are available at the Pensacola Visitor Information Center (p. 526). Tickets for all major performances can be purchased from **Ticketmaster** (ℂ 800/488-5252 or 850/433-6311; www.ticketmaster.com).

The highlight venue here is the ornate **Saenger Theatre** ★, 118 S. Palafox St., near Romana Street (ℂ 850/444-7686; www.pensacolasaenger.com), a painstakingly restored masterpiece of Spanish baroque architecture that locals call the Grande Dame of Palafox. Presentations include the local opera company and symphony orchestra, Broadway musicals, and touring performers. The 10,000-seat **Pensacola Civic Center,** 201 E. Gregory St., at Alcaniz Street (ℂ 850/432-0800; www.pensacolaciviccenter.com), hosts a variety of concerts, exhibitions, sports events, and conventions. Call ahead for the current schedule.

THE CLUB & BAR SCENE Pensacola's downtown nighttime entertainment center is **Seville Quarter,** 130 E. Government St., at Jefferson Street (ℂ 850/434-6211; www.rosies.com), in the Seville Historic District. This restored antique-brick complex with New Orleans–style wrought-iron balconies is actually a collection of pubs and restaurants whose names capture the ambience: Rosie O'Grady's Goodtime Emporium, Lili Marlene's Aviator's Pub, Apple Annie's Courtyard, End o' the Alley Bar, Phineas Phogg's Balloon Works (a dance hall, not a balloon shop), and Fast Eddie's Billiard Parlor (which has electronic games, too). The pubs serve libations, food, and live entertainment from Dixieland jazz to country and western. Get a monthly calendar at the information booth next to Rosie O'Grady's. Open daily from 11am to 2am.

Fun Fact The Last Great Road House ★★★

Sitting precisely on the Florida-Alabama state line on Perdido Key, about 15 miles west of downtown Pensacola, the **Flora-Bama Lounge,** 17401 Perdido Key Dr. (© 850/492-0611; www.florabama.com), is almost a shrine to country music. Billing itself as the "Last Great American Road House," this slapped-together Gulf-side pub is famous for its special jam sessions from noon until way past midnight on Saturday and Sunday. Flora-Bama is the prime sponsor and a key venue for the Frank Brown International Songwriters' Festival during the first week of November. But the wackiest shindig held here has to be the Interstate Mullet Toss and Beach Party (the last weekend in Apr), which defies more in-depth description. The raw oyster bar is popular all the time. Granted, the joint can get a bit rough from time to time, but you won't soon forget the great Gulf views while sipping a cold one at the Deck Bar. The Flora-Bama is open daily from 8:30am to 2:30am.

Every night is party time at **McGuire's Irish Pub,** the city's popular Irish pub, brewery, and eatery (p. 537). Irish bands appear nightly during summer, on Saturday and Sunday the rest of the year.

Beach nightlife centers around **Quietwater Boardwalk,** Via de Luna at Fort Pickens Road (no phone), a shopping/dining complex on Santa Rosa Sound. With the lively beach and reggae bar at **Flounder's Chowder House** (p. 538) just a few steps away, it's easy to barhop until you find a band to your liking. Across Via de Luna at Casino Beach is **The Dock** (© 850/934-3314), which has live bands nightly in summer, on weekends in off season. And **Sidelines Sports Bar & Restaurant** (© 850/934-3660) has a great game lineup.

2 Destin, Fort Walton Beach ★★ & Seaside

40 miles E of Pensacola, 160 miles W of Tallahassee

Sitting on a round harbor off East Pass, which lets broad and beautiful Choctawhatchee Bay flow into the Gulf of Mexico, Destin, along with Fort Walton Beach and Okaloosa Island, comprise the Emerald Coast, is justly famous for its fishing fleet, the largest in the state. It's also Northwest Florida's fastest-growing and most upscale vacation destination, with a multitude of high-rise condominiums, the huge Sandestin resort, several golf courses, and some of the Panhandle's best restaurants and lively nightspots. By and large, Destin attracts a more affluent crowd than Fort Walton Beach, its more down-to-earth neighbor.

Although Fort Walton Beach has its own strip of white sand on Okaloosa Island, it is a city whose economy is supported less by tourism than by the sprawling Eglin Air Force Base. Covering more than 700 square miles, Eglin is the world's largest air base and is home to the U.S. Air Force's Armament Museum and the 33rd Tactical Fighter Wing, the "Top Guns" of Operation Desert Storm in 1991.

To the east of Destin, development is picking up steam along the beaches of southern Walton County. Still, this picturesque area has mostly cottages nestled among rolling sand dunes covered with sea oats. Here you'll find Grayton Beach State Park, which sports one of America's finest beaches, and the quaint, albeit Stepford-esque planned village of **Seaside** ★★, which served as the set for Jim Carrey's movie *The Truman Show.* Seaside was built on a lovely stretch of beach in the 1980s—but with Victorian architecture that makes it look a century older. The village's Gulf-side honeymoon cottages make for one of Florida's most romantic retreats; and the village has interesting shops and art galleries, a stamp-size, Greek Revival–style post office, and a resident population of artists, writers, and other creative folks, who permit only their own cars in their relatively expensive little enclave. Don't worry; there are parking spaces for tourists on the one main road through Seaside, but you can't drive into the village itself unless you live there. Although I appreciate Seaside for what it is, the last time I was there I couldn't help feeling like the secret had gotten too far out and that Seaside was slowly falling under the weight of commercialism and too much tourism.

ESSENTIALS

GETTING THERE   Flights arriving at and departing from **Okaloosa Regional Airport** (© **850/651-7160;** www.co.okaloosa.fl.us/airport.html) actually use the enormous strips at Eglin Air Force Base. The terminal is on Fla. 85 north of Fort Walton Beach and is served by **Delta** (© 800/221-1212), **Northwest** (© 800/225-2525), and **US Airways** (© 800/428-4322).

   Avis (© 800/331-1212), **Budget** (© 800/527-0700), **Hertz** (© 800/654-3131), and **National** (© 800/CAR-RENT) have rental cars at the airport, and **Enterprise** (© 800/325-8007) is in town.

   AAA Annie's Shuttle (© **850/978-2450**) provides 24-hour van transportation to and from the airport. Fares for up to three people are based on a zone system: $15 to $18 to Fort Walton Beach, $27 to Destin, and $40 to Sandestin and southern Walton County.

   The Sunset Limited transcontinental service on **Amtrak** (© **800/872-7245;** www.amtrak.com) stops at Crestview, 26 miles north of Fort Walton Beach.

VISITOR INFORMATION   For advance information about both Fort Walton Beach and Destin, contact the **Emerald Coast Convention and Visitors Bureau,** P.O. Box 609, Fort Walton Beach, FL 32549 (© **800/322-3319** or 850/651-7122; fax 850/651-7149; www.destin-fwb.com). The bureau shares quarters with the **Okaloosa County Visitors Welcome Center** in a tin-roofed, beachside building on Miracle Strip Parkway (U.S. 98) on Okaloosa Island at the eastern edge of Fort Walton Beach. Stop there for brochures, maps, and other information. The welcome center is open Monday through Friday from 8am to 5pm, Saturday and Sunday from 10am to 4pm.

   The **Destin Area Chamber of Commerce,** 4484 Legendary Dr., Destin, FL 32541 (© **850/837-6241;** fax 850/654-5612; www.destinchamber.com), gives away brochures and sells maps of the area. The chamber is in an office complex at the entry to Regatta Bay Golf & Country Club, on U.S. 98, ½ mile east of the Mid-Bay Bridge. It's open Monday through Friday from 9am to 5pm, closed holidays.

   For information about the beaches of South Walton, contact the **South Walton Tourist Development Council,** P.O. Box 1248, Santa Rosa Beach, FL 32459 (© **800/822-6877** or 850/267-1216; fax 850/267-3943; www.beachesofsouth walton.com). Its **visitor center** is at the intersection of U.S. 98 and U.S. 331 in Santa Rosa Beach (© **850/267-3511**). Open daily from 8:30am to 5:30pm.

GETTING AROUND   The Okaloosa County Tourist Development Authority (© **850/651-7131**) operates a free **Island Shuttle** trolley during the summer months along the entire length of Santa Rosa Boulevard on Okaloosa Island. The two trolleys run every 30 minutes Sunday through Thursday from 7am to 10pm, Friday and Saturday from 7am to 1am. They also connect the island to the Uptown Bus station, on Eglin Parkway NE on the Fort Walton Beach mainland.

Tips   How to Find a Street Address

Don't worry about getting lost, since most of what you'll want to see and do in Destin and Fort Walton Beach is either on, or no more than a few blocks from, U.S. 98, the area's main east-west drag. Finding a street address is another matter, however, for even many local residents don't fully comprehend the post office's bizarre naming and numbering system along U.S. 98.

In Fort Walton Beach, U.S. 98 is known as "Miracle Strip Parkway," with "southwest" and "southeast" addresses on the mainland and "east" addresses on Okaloosa Island.

In Destin, U.S. 98 is officially known as "Highway 98 East" from the Destin Bridge east to Airport Road, and street numbers get progressively higher as you head east from the bridge. East of Airport Road, however, the post office calls U.S. 98 the "Emerald Coast Parkway"—although locals still say a place is on "98 East." The highway also is known as the Emerald Coast Parkway in Walton County, but the street-numbering system changes completely once you pass the county line.

Adding to the confusion in Destin, "Old Highway 98 East" is a short spur from Airport Road to the western side of Henderson Beach State Park, and "Scenic Highway 98 East" parallels the real U.S. 98 along the beach from the eastern side of Henderson Beach to Sandestin.

In other words, call and ask for directions if you're not sure how to find an establishment here.

For a cab in Fort Walton Beach, call **Black and Gold Taxi** (© 850/244-7303) or **Yellow Cab** (© 850/244-3600). In Destin, call **Destin Taxi** (© 850/654-5700). Fares are based on a zone system rather than meters, with a $5 minimum. Trips within Fort Walton Beach or Destin should range from $5 to $10.

TIME   The area is in the Central Time zone, 1 hour behind Miami, Orlando, Jacksonville, and Tallahassee.

HITTING THE BEACH

DESTIN   Like an oasis in the middle of Destin's rapid development, the 208-acre **Henderson Beach State Park** ⚓⚓, east of Destin Harbor on U.S. 98, allows easy access to swimming, sunning, surf fishing, picnicking, and seabird-watching along its 1½ miles of beach. There are restrooms, outdoor showers, and surf chairs for people with disabilities. The area is open daily from 8am to sunset. Admission is $4 per vehicle with up to 8 occupants, $1 for pedestrians and cyclists. Several good restaurants are just outside the park's western boundary. The park has 60 campsites in a wooded setting. They cost $21, including electricity, and can be reserved up to 11 months in advance. Pets on leashes are allowed in the park, including the beach and campground. For camping reservations call © 800/326-3521 or go to www.reserveamerica.com. For more information, contact the park at 1700 Emerald Coast Pkwy., Destin, FL 32541 (© 850/837-7550; www.floridastateparks.org/hendersonbeach).

The **James W. Lee Park,** between Destin and Sandestin on Scenic Highway 98, has a long white-sand beach overlooked by covered picnic tables, an ice-cream parlor, and a moderately priced seafood restaurant with great views.

FORT WALTON BEACH Do your loafing on the white sands of **Okaloosa Island,** joined to the mainland by the high-rise Brooks Bridge over Santa Rosa Sound. Most resort hotels and amusement parks are grouped around the Gulfarium marine park on U.S. 98, east of the bridge. Here you'll find **The Boardwalk,** a collection of tin-roofed beachside buildings that have a games arcade for the kids, a saloon for adults, covered picnic areas, a summertime snack bar, and a seafood restaurant. Just to the east, you can use the restrooms, cold-water showers, and other free facilities at **Beasley Park,** home of the Okaloosa County Visitor Welcome Center.

Across U.S. 98, the Okaloosa portion of the **Gulf Islands National Seashore** has picnic areas and sailboats for rent on Choctawhatchee Bay, plus access to the Gulf. Admission to this part of the national seashore is free.

SOUTHERN WALTON COUNTY Sporting the finest stretch of white sand on the Gulf, **Grayton Beach State Park** ★★★, on County Road 30A, also has 356 acres of pine forests surrounding scenic Western Lake. There's a boat ramp and a campground with electric hookups on the lake. Get a leaflet at the main gate for a self-guided tour of the nature trail. Pets are not allowed anywhere in the recreation area. The area is open daily from 8am to sunset. Admission is $4 per vehicle with up to eight occupants, $1 per pedestrian or bicyclist. Campsites cost $19, including electricity. For camping reservations call ✆ **800/326-3521** or go to www.reserveamerica.com. For information, contact the park at 357 Main Park Rd., Santa Rosa Beach, FL 32459 (✆ **850/231-4210;** www.floridastateparks.org/graytonbeach).

Seaside has free parking along County Road 30A and is a good spot for a day at the beach, a stroll or bike ride around the quaint village, and a tasty meal at one of its restaurants.

AFFORDABLE OUTDOOR ACTIVITIES

BOATING & BOAT RENTALS Pontoon boats are highly popular for use on the back bays and Sunday-afternoon floating parties in East Pass. Several companies rent them, including **Adventure Pontoon Rentals** (✆ 850/837-3041), **B&J Boat Rentals** (✆ 850/243-4488), **East Pass Watersports** (✆ 850/654-4253), and **Destin Water Toys** (✆ 850/837-7755), all on Destin Harbor. Expect to pay about $80 for a half day, $125 for a full day. Destin Water Toys also has speedboats for rent ($125–$175 for 4 hr. and $175–$285 for 8 hr.).

CRUISES The *Emerald Magic* (✆ 850/837-1293; www.moodysinc.com) and the *Southern Star* (✆ 888/424-7217 or 850/837-7741; www.dolphin-sstar.com) have daily dolphin and sunset cruises June through August and by arrangement the rest of the year. The *Emerald Magic* is operated by Moody's, on U.S. 98 at Destin Harbor (see "Fishing," below), while the *Southern Star* docks in Destin at the Harbor Walk Marina, behind the Lucky Snapper Restaurant. The *Emerald Magic* charges $15 for adults, $7.50 for kids 3 to 12. The *Southern Star* costs $17 for adults, $7 for children 3 to 12, and $14 for seniors.

FISHING Billing itself as the "World's Luckiest Fishing Village," Destin has Florida's largest charter-boat fleet, with more than 140 vessels based at the marinas lining the north shore of Destin Harbor, on U.S. 98 east of the Destin Bridge. Arranging a trip is as easy as walking along the Destin Harbor waterfront, where you will find the booking booths of several agents, such as **Harborwalk Charters** (✆ **800/242-2824** or 850/837-2343; www.harborwalkfishing.com), **Pelican Charters** (✆ 850/837-2343), and **Harbor Cove Charters** (✆ 850/837-2222).

Rates for private charters range from about $440 to $1,320 per boat, depending on the length of the voyage.

A less-expensive way to try your luck is on a larger group-oriented party boat such as those operated by **Moody's,** at 194 U.S. 98 east on Destin Harbor (© 850/837-1293; www.moodysinc.com). Moody's charges $35 per person ($30 off season) for its half-day runs (morning is the best time to fish). Children 8 to 12 and nonfishing sightseers are charged half price.

You don't have to go to sea to fish from the catwalk of the 3,000-foot **Destin Bridge** over East Pass. The marinas and bait shops at Destin Harbor can provide gear, bait, and a fishing license. In Fort Walton Beach, you can cast a line off **Okaloosa Island Fishing Pier,** 1030 Miracle Strip Pkwy. E. (U.S. 98; © 850/244-1023). The pier is open 24 hours a day. Adults pay $6.50 to fish; children 12 and under pay $3.50. Observers pay $1. Bait and equipment rentals are available.

GOLF   For advance information on area courses, contact the **Emerald Coast Golf Association,** P.O. Box 304, Destin, FL 32540. Also look for *South Coast Golf Guide,* the free annual directory published in Pensacola (p. 530). Be sure to ask if your choice of accommodations offers golf packages, which can mean significant savings.

For course information online, go to www.golf.com and www.floridagolfing. com, or call the **Florida Sports Foundation** (© 850/488-8347) or **Florida Golfing** (© 866/833-2663).

On the mainland, nonresidents are welcome to play at the city-owned **Fort Walton Beach Golf Club,** on Lewis Turner Boulevard (C.R. 189) north of town (© 850/833-9530; www.fwb.org/golf). The club has two 18-hole courses—the **Pines** and the **Oaks** (© 850/833-9528)—plus a pro shop. Greens fees at both courses are about $35 year-round, including a cart.

In Destin, scenic **Indian Bayou Golf and Country Club,** off Airport Road (© 850/837-6191), has three 9-hole courses with large greens and wide fairways. They look easy, but watch out for water hazards and strategically placed hidden bunkers! Greens fees, including cart, are about $60.

In southern Walton County, **Sandestin Golf and Beach Resort** on U.S. 98 East (© 850/267-8211 for tee times) is the largest facility here (p. 546). Its 72 holes are spread over three outstanding championship courses. The Baytowne and Links courses overlook Choctawhatchee Bay. Fees for 18 holes are $65 to $125 for resort guests, $85 to $145 for nonguests.

Some of the 18 championship holes at **Emerald Bay Golf Club,** 2 miles east of the Mid-Bay Bridge on U.S. 98 (© 850/837-5197; www.emeraldbaydestin. com), run along Choctawhatchee Bay; the water adds both beauty and challenges to the otherwise wide and forgiving fairways. Greens fees are about $80 with cart; $65 in winter.

In southern Walton County, the semiprivate **Santa Rosa Golf & Beach Club,** off County Road 30A in Dune Allen Beach (© 850/267-2229; www. santarosaclub.com), offers a challenging 18-hole course through tall pines looking out to vistas of the Gulf. The club has a pro shop, a beachside restaurant, a lounge, and tennis courts. Fees are about $70 in summer, $50 off season.

In Niceville, a 20-minute drive north via the Mid-Bay Bridge, nonguests may play golf (four 9-hole courses) or tennis (21 courts) at the **Bluewater Bay Resort** (© 850/897-3241; www.bwbresort.com), which also has condominiums for rent.

Call ahead for reservations and current fees at all these clubs, and ask about afternoon and early-evening specials.

SAILING **Sailing South** (© 850/837-7245; www.sailingsouth.com), on U.S. 98 at Destin Harbor, has half-day cruises aboard the 72-foot schooner *Daniel Webster Clements*. The 2½-hour afternoon cruises stop for swimming and snorkeling virtually under the Destin Bridge; these cost $35 for adults and $20 for kids under 12. It also offers sunset cruises (same rates and length). The 54-foot schooner *Nathaniel Bowditch* (© 850/650-8787; www.bowditchsailing.com) will take you on sunset and half-day shelling excursions ($35 adults, $20 kids 12 and under).

SCUBA DIVING & SNORKELING At least a dozen dive shops are located along the beaches. Considered one of the best, **Scuba Tech Diving Charters** has two locations in Destin: at 301 U.S. 98 E. (© 850/837-2822; www.scubatech nwfl.com) and at 10004 U.S. 98 E. (© 850/837-1933), about ½ mile west of the Sandestin Beach Resort.

WATERSPORTS Hobie Cats, WaveRunners, jet boats, jet skis, and parasailing are available all along the beach. The largest selection of operators are at the marinas just east of the Destin Bridge, behind Hooter's and Fat Tuesday's pubs, including **Boogies** (© 850/654-4497) and **Destin Watertoys** (© 888/357-2608 or 850/837-7755; www.destinwatertoys.com).

EXPLORING THE AREA

Florida's Gulfarium *Kids* The country's second oldest marine park (it opened in 1955) features ongoing 25-minute shows with dolphins, California sea lions, Peruvian penguins, loggerhead turtles, sharks, sting rays, moray eels, and alligators. There are fascinating exhibits, including the Living Sea, with special windows for viewing undersea life. During one of the shows, a scuba diver explains the sea life while swimming among the various creatures. The Spotted Dolphin Encounter is a terrific program in which brave participants receive an up-close and personal hand-to-flipper encounter with two of their Pantropical Spotted dolphins, Kiwi and Daphne. A trainer will guide you through the 40-minute interactive session. If you're not satisfied with seeing a few dolphins and leaving, expect to spend about 3 hours here between all the shows and exhibits.

1010 Miracle Strip Pkwy. (U.S. 98) on Okaloosa Island. © 850/244-5169. www.gulfarium.com. Admission $17 adults, $15 seniors, $10 children 4–11, free for children 3 and under; Dolphin encounter $100. Mid-May to Labor Day daily 9am–6pm (park closes 8pm); Sept to mid-May daily 9am–4pm (park closes 6pm).

Indian Temple Mound and Museum This ceremonial mound, one of the largest ever discovered, dates from A.D. 1200. The museum showcases part of its collection of more than 6,000 ceramic artifacts from southeastern American Indian tribes, the nation's largest such collection. Exhibits depict the lifestyles of the four tribes that lived in the Choctawhatchee Bay region for 12,000 years.

139 Miracle Strip Pkwy. SE, on the mainland. © 850/833-9595. www.fwb.org/content.php?page=55. Park free admission; museum $2 adults, $1 children 6–17, free for children 5 and under. Park daily dawn–dusk. Museum Sept–May Mon–Fri 10am–4pm, Sat 9am–4pm; June–Aug Mon–Sat 9am–4:30pm, Sun 12:30–4:30pm.

U.S. Air Force Armament Museum ✿ Although this fascinating museum is not on a par with Pensacola's National Museum of Naval Aviation, you'll love it if you're into warplanes. Located on the world's largest air force base, it traces military developments from World War II through Operation Desert Storm. Reconnaissance, fighter, and bomber planes, including the SR-71 Blackbird spy plane, are on display.

100 Museum Dr., off Eglin Pkwy. (Fla. 85) at Eglin Air Force Base, 5 miles north of downtown. © 850/882-4062. Free admission. Daily 9:30am–4:30pm. Closed federal holidays.

GREAT OUTLET SHOPPING

Silver Sands Factory Stores ★★, on U.S. 98 between Destin and Sandestin (© **800/510-6255** or 850/864-9771; www.silversandsfactorystores.com), has more than 120 upscale stores such as Liz Claiborne, DKNY, J. Crew, Brooks Brothers, Hartmann luggage, Coach leather, Dooney & Burke, Bose electronics, and so on. Shops are open Monday through Saturday from 10am to 9pm (to 7pm Jan–Feb), Sunday from 10am to 6pm (noon–6pm Jan–Feb). There are electronic games for kids and a sports bar for adults.

ACCOMMODATIONS YOU CAN AFFORD

The area has a vast supply of condominiums and cottages for rent. One good-value example is Venus by the Sea condos, listed below. The visitor information offices (see the "Visitor Information" section on p. 540) will provide lists of others for rent. The largest rental agent is **Abbott Realty Services,** 3500 Emerald Coast Pkwy., Destin, FL 32541 (© **888/909-6807;** fax 850/654-2937; www.abbott-resorts.com). It publishes a magazine-size annual brochure picturing and describing its many properties throughout the area.

There are several commercial campgrounds here, but the best camping is at **Henderson Beach State Park** in Destin and at **Grayton Beach State Park** in south Walton County (see "Hitting the Beach," earlier in this chapter).

State and local governments add 9% to 11% to all hotel and campground bills.

DESTIN

A former Comfort Inn, the local **Motel 6,** 405 U.S. 98 E. (© **800/466-8356** or 850/837-0007; fax 850/837-5325; www.motel6.com), sitting across the highway from the harbor, has rooms that are generally larger than those at many other members of this cut-rate chain. There's also an outdoor swimming pool on the premises, which makes it a more attractive place to stay.

Best Western SummerPlace Inn   Located just one block from the beach, this four-story, Spanish-motif Best Western is a refreshing change from its cookie cutter siblings, offering innlike rooms and suites decorated with wildlife prints. A few suites have hot tubs in their living rooms. The more expensive Gulf-side units have balconies (those facing the bay do not). Larger units have microwave ovens and refrigerators. Doors open from an indoor pool, a whirlpool, and an exercise room to an outdoor pool, but you'll have to negotiate your way across busy U.S. 98 to reach the Gulf.

14047 Emerald Coast Pkwy. (U.S. 98, at Airport Rd.), Destin, FL 32541. © **888/232-2499** or 850/650-8003. Fax 850/650-8004. www.bestwestern.com/summerplaceinn. 72 units. Summer $119–$179; off season $49–$99. Rates include continental breakfast and local telephone calls. AE, DISC, MC, V. **Amenities:** Indoor and outdoor pools; exercise room; Jacuzzi; business center; coin-op washers and dryers. *In room:* A/C, TV, dataport, fridge, coffeemaker, hair dryer.

Worth a Splurge for Hopeless Romantics

Henderson Park Inn ★★★   This inn is absolutely stunning in an Edith Wharton, *Age of Innocence* way. At the end of Old U.S. 98 on the undeveloped eastern edge of the Henderson Beach State Park, this shingle-sided, Cape Hatteras–style bed-and-breakfast is the area's most romantic get-away-from-it-all escape (children and pets are not accepted). Individually decorated in a Victorian theme, the rooms have high ceilings, fireplaces, Queen Anne furniture, and Gulf views from private balconies. Most have Jacuzzis and some have canopy beds. The main building (16 rooms are in a separate shingle-sided structure next door) sports a beachside veranda complete with old-fashioned rocking chairs from which you can admire the glorious sunsets. Guests are treated to a Southern-style buffet breakfast and to beer and wine at the nightly before-dinner social hour in the wonderful Veranda Restaurant (reservations recommended), which opens to the wraparound porch of the main building. Guests are provided with complimentary beach umbrellas and chairs.

2700 Scenic Hwy. 98 E. (P.O. Box 30), Destin, FL 32541. (C) **800/336-4853** or 850/837-4853. Fax 850/654-0405. www.hendersonparkinn.com. 35 units. Summer $189–$334 double; off season $95–$189 double. Rates include full breakfast and evening cocktails. Packages and weekly rates available. AE, DISC, MC, V. No children or pets accepted. **Amenities:** Restaurant; bar; heated outdoor pool; Jacuzzi; limited room service; laundry service. *In room:* A/C, TV, dataport, fridge, coffeemaker, hair dryer, iron.

Worth a Splurge for Golf & Tennis Players & for Families with Children

Hilton Sandestin Beach & Golf Resort ★★ *Kids* This all-inclusive, all-suites beachside resort, housed in two adjacent towers, is the top full-service hotel here. It's nicely situated on the grounds of Sandestin Golf and Beach Resort (see the next listing) and shares its golf and tennis facilities. The spacious "junior suites" in the old wing are geared toward families, with a special area for children's bunk beds. Miniature golf, three pools, 13 tennis courts, four championship golf courses, and the stunning private beach make for a very enticing stay.

4000 Sandestin Blvd. S., Destin, FL 32541. (C) **800/367-1271** or 850/267-9500. Fax 850/267-3076. www.sandestinresort.hilton.com. 598 suites. Summer $260–$395 suite; off season $160–$335 suite. Golf and tennis packages available. AE, DC, DISC, MC, V. **Amenities:** 2 restaurants; 2 bars; indoor and outdoor pools; golf course; tennis courts; health club; spa; Jacuzzi; watersports equipment rentals; children's programs; game room; concierge; activities desk; car-rental desk; business center; shopping arcade; salon; 24-hr. room service; massage; babysitting; laundry service; coin-op washers and dryers; concierge-level rooms. *In room:* A/C, TV, dataport, minibar, coffeemaker, hair dryer, iron.

Sandestin Golf and Beach Resort ★★★ *Kids* Although it could be mistaken for yet another Stepfordized planned community, this luxurious real-estate development is one of Florida's biggest sports-oriented resorts and is the epitome of the great escape. It sprawls over 2,400 acres complete with a spectacular beach 5 miles west of Destin, plus a marina. It's notable for its 81 holes of championship golf and its tennis clinic, plus a fully equipped sports spa and health center. An array of handsomely decorated accommodations overlooks the Gulf or Choctawhatchee Bay, the golf fairways, lagoons, or a nature preserve. The hotel rooms and suites are in the Bayside Inn. They all have kitchenettes and balconies, but you'd be wise to opt for one of the much more spacious junior suites or one-, two-, and three-bedroom condominium apartments, which are in high- and midrise buildings either on the Gulf or along the manicured fairways. The privately owned condominiums are individually decorated and come with full kitchen and patio or balcony, and many have washers and dryers. Most amenities are a short walk or bike or free tram ride away, and a tunnel runs under U.S. 98 to connect Sandestin's Gulf and bay areas. The coolest, newest addition to this resort cum city is the **Village of Baytowne Wharf,** a 28-acre pedestrian village overlooking the Choctawhatchee Bay, featuring a unique collection of more than two dozen specialty merchants and charming eateries to lively nightclubs. It also features hotel and one-, two- and three-bedroom luxury accommodations surrounding the bay with rates ranging from $89 in the off season to $272 during the summer. Fantastic kids and teens programs include Jolee Island Nature Park, a mile-long trail dotted with weather-beaten, double-wide porch swings, where you can sit and watch the waters of Horseshoe Bayou lap up against the shore or catch the sunset over Choctawhatchee Bay.

If you want to stay near Sandestin Golf and Beach Resort without paying its prices, there's a modern **Sleep Inn** a mile west at 5000 Emerald Coast Pkwy. (U.S. 98; ⓒ **800/627-5337** or 850/654-7022).

9300 Emerald Coast Pkwy. W. (U.S. 98), Destin, FL 32541. ⓒ **800/277-0800** or 850/267-8000 in the U.S., or 800/933-7846 in Canada. Fax 850/267-8222. www.sandestin.com. 175 units, 620 condo apts. Summer $155–$210 double, $210–$560 condo apt; off season $85–$190 double, $105–$395 condo apt. Packages and weekly/monthly rates available. Rates include health club, bicycle, Boogie Board, canoe, and kayak use; 1-hr. tennis daily; discounts on other amenities. AE, DC, DISC, MC, V. **Amenities:** 3 restaurants; 3 bars; 9 heated outdoor pools; 4 golf courses; 18 tennis courts; spa; Jacuzzi; watersports equipment rentals; children's programs; game room; concierge; shopping arcade; salon; limited room service (hotel only); massage; babysitting; laundry service; coin-op washers and dryers. *In room:* A/C, TV, dataport, kitchen, coffeemaker, hair dryer, iron.

FORT WALTON BEACH

The managers of Venus by the Sea (see below) also run the **Sea Crest Condominiums,** located next door at 895 Santa Rosa Blvd. (ⓒ **800/476-1885** or 850/301-9600; fax 850/301-9205; www.seacrestcondos.com). The 112 units in this seven-story building aren't as spacious as those in Venus, but they're considerably more luxurious, and those on the higher floors have great views toward the west. The complex has indoor and outdoor pools (actually one pool; you can swim under a glass partition between them), and it sits next to a county park with a boardwalk leading over the dunes to the beach.

Among chain motels here is the **Hampton Inn Ft. Walton Beach,** 1112 Santa Rosa Blvd. (ⓒ **800/426-7866** or 850/301-0906; www.hamptoninnfwb.com). It's adjacent to the Radisson Beach Resort and shares its facilities (see below).

Radisson Beach Resort ⭐ *Kids*   A glass-enclosed elevator climbs a soaring, six-story lean-to atrium lobby to rooms with spectacular Gulf views from their standing-room-only balconies at this resort where you'll never be bored. An Olympic-size heated pool and lazy river raft ride, fitness center, two lighted tennis courts, a basketball court, beach volleyball, and a pirate ship-shaped playground for kids are just some of the resort's many diversions. Rooms are standard unless you book an Emerald Suite, in which case you'll never leave your bathroom because a large Jacuzzi tub sits directly in front of a floor to ceiling window overlooking the water. Beach lovers are more likely to appreciate the units in an older two-story motel building that have sitting-room patios or balconies facing the Gulf. Other units in the older building open to a lush courtyard surrounding a pool. In the atrium, a tropically adorned cafe serves breakfast, lunch, and dinner, and a bar has nightly entertainment during summer.

1110 Santa Rosa Blvd. (at U.S. 98), Fort Walton Beach, FL 32548. ⓒ **800/333-3333** or 850/243-9181. Fax 850/664-7652. www.radisson.com/ftwaltonfl. 287 units. Summer $129–$230 double; off season $69–$129 double. Packages available. AE, DC, DISC, MC, V. **Amenities:** Restaurant; 2 bars; 3 outdoor pools (1 children's); 2 lighted hard tennis courts; exercise room; watersports equipment rentals; limited room service; babysitting; laundry service. *In room:* A/C, TV, dataport, coffeemaker, hair dryer, iron.

Ramada Plaza Beach Resort ⭐   This big resort boasts the prettiest outdoor areas in northwest Florida, with waterfalls cascading over lofty rocks and a romantic grotto bar, all surrounded by thick tropical foliage. Although there is another swimming pool, a large sun deck, and a bar out by the beach, this gorgeous courtyard would have even more charm if it weren't cut off from the Gulf by a six-story block of hotel rooms. The guest rooms and the one-bedroom suites in this beachfront building are the best here, with Gulf or courtyard views from balconies or patios. The least-expensive units, in the adjacent building, overlook a parking lot. Though the decor is blasé, the hotel's views make up for that. On-site dining options include a barbecue shack out in the tropical forest. The Boardwalk beach pavilion and restaurants are next door.

1500 E. Miracle Strip Pkwy. (U.S. 98), Fort Walton Beach, FL 32548. ℂ **800/874-8962** or 850/243-9161. Fax 850/243-2391. www.ramadafwb.com. 335 units. Summer $120–$185 double, $280–$350 suite; off season $70–$195 double, $160–$270 suite. AE, DC, DISC, MC, V. **Amenities:** 3 restaurants; 3 bars; 2 outdoor pools (1 heated); exercise room; Jacuzzi; watersports equipment rentals; children's programs; game room; limited room service; coin-op washers and dryers. *In room:* A/C, TV, dataport, fridge, coffeemaker, hair dryer, iron, safe.

Venus by the Sea ⭐ *Value*   Offering considerably more space than a hotel normally would at these rates, this pleasant, three-story enclave on western Okaloosa Island was built in the 1970s and has been well maintained ever since, though the decor is still stuck in the '70s (think retirement home) and should be updated. Each of the one-, two-, and three-bedroom units has a long living/dining/kitchen room, with a rear door leading to a balcony or to a patio opening to a grassy courtyard. The beach is a short walk across the dunes, and you can stroll along the undeveloped beach at an Eglin Air Force Base auxiliary facility about 600 feet away. The same management also operates the new and much more luxurious **Sea Crest Condominiums** next door (see above), and guests here can use the indoor-outdoor pool there.

885 Santa Rosa Blvd., Fort Walton Beach, FL 32548. ℂ **800/476-1885** or 850/301-9600. Fax 850/301-9205. www.venuscondos.com. 45 units. Summer $130–$205 apt; off season $70–$100 apt. Weekly and monthly rates available. Ask for off season specials. MC, V. **Amenities:** Outdoor pool; tennis court; coin-op washers and dryers. *In room:* A/C, TV/VCR, kitchen, coffeemaker, iron.

Super-Cheap Sleeps

Marina Motel   This family-operated, self-described "fisherman's motel" may look like a shack from the outside, but it has clean, comfortable rooms and apartments directly across U.S. 98 from the magnificent public beach at Beasley Park. A low-slung, brick-fronted motel block holds most of the rooms. Other units are in two-story stucco structures near a marina whose 560-foot pier is home to charter-fishing boats. Two one-bedroom apartments at the end of the complex overlook the marina and bay. All units here have refrigerators and microwaves; 16 have full kitchens. If traffic is too busy to cross U.S. 98 to the beach (there are no nearby overpasses or traffic lights), you can sun at the motel's little bayside beach or take a dip in its roadside pool.

1345 E. Miracle Strip Pkwy. (U.S. 98), Fort Walton Beach, FL 32548. ℂ **800/237-7021** or 850/244-1129. Fax 850/243-6063. www.marinamotel.net. 38 units. Summer $69–$89 double, $115–$150 apt; off season $39–$69 double, $65–$99 apt. AE, DC, DISC, MC, V. **Amenities:** Outdoor pool; coin-op washers and dryers. *In room:* A/C, TV, kitchen (efficiencies and apts only), fridge, coffeemaker, iron.

SEASIDE

Mayberry meets Metropolitan Home here in this pastel-hued community where life seems like a dreamlike state of mind. If you decide to rent a home or a **romantic honeymoon cottage** ⭐⭐ in this quaint village, contact the **Seaside Cottage Rental Agency,** P.O. Box 4730, Seaside, FL 32459 (ℂ **800/277-8696** or 850/231-1320; fax 850/231-2293; www.seasidefl.com). The agency has several hundred cottages in its rental inventory, from one to six bedrooms. The beachside cottages are one of Florida's best getaways for newlyweds or anyone else looking for a romantic escape, though if you want a little more privacy and less action, you might want to choose Rosemary Beach (p. 549) instead.

GREAT DEALS ON DINING

Except for the strip on Okaloosa Island, a plethora of national fast-food and family chain restaurants line U.S. 98.

Tips **Luxurious Cottages & Luscious Surroundings at Rosemary Beach**

Rosemary Beach, a newer, smaller, and, I think, better, Seaside-style community, offers a collection of about 300 luxurious Pan-Caribbean-style cottages and carriage houses (studios to six-bedroom cottages), all of which are nonsmoking. This is another pedestrian-friendly community—almost everything on the 107 acres is within a 5-minute walk from the town center—and most of the homes are owned by people who live here part-time and lease to vacationers the rest of the year. The white-sand (and soft as talculm powder) beach here is ridiculously gorgeous though guests can also choose from among four pools (one indoors). Nothing on the architecturally stunning and strikingly planted property here is more than four stories, and all the homes telescope in from the beach so everyone can have a (at least partial) view of the Gulf. Other amenities include a health club, bike rental, a raquet club, a 2.3-mile fitness trail, a spa, shops, a town hall and post office, and a few very good restaurants. Cottages were individually designed and decorated, so check online for exactly what yours will have and to see pictures of each of the properties before deciding. Though they all come with full kitchens, washers/dryers, and TV/VCR, some have added amenities such as Jacuzzis or private pools. There is also a B&B on premises (rooms start at $118), and the town is building a full-service hotel. Daily rates are $153 to $968 in spring and fall, $183 to $1,062 in summer, and $143 to $812 during winter. Rosemary Beach is located at the east end of County Road 30-A (© **888/855-1551;** www.rosemarybeach.com) just 8 miles east of Seaside.

DESTIN

If you didn't catch a fish to be grilled at Fisherman's Wharf (see below), you can buy one to brag about from **Sexton's Seafood,** 602 Hwy. 98 E., opposite Destin Harbor (© **850/837-3040**). It's the best market here.

AJ's Seafood & Oyster Bar 🐟🐟 SEAFOOD   Jimmy Buffett tunes set the tone at this fun, Tiki-topped establishment on the picturesque Destin Harbor docks, where fishing boats unload their daily catches right into the kitchen. The best items here are grilled or fried fish, but raw or steamed Apalachicola oysters also headline the menu. You can sample a bit of everything with a "run of the kitchen" seafood platter. AJ's is most famous for its topside bar, Club Bimini, featuring live bands (you should have dinner elsewhere if you're not in a partying mood) and open nightly. At lunch, picnic tables on the covered dock make a fine venue with a view across the harbor. Locals love this place and you will, too.

116 Hwy. 98 E., Destin Harbor. © 850/837-1913. www.ajs-destin.com. Main courses $11–$22; sandwiches and salads $6–$9. AE, DISC, MC, V. Apr–Sept Sun–Thurs 11am–10pm, Fri–Sat 11am–midnight (bar until 4am); off season daily 11am–9pm.

Back Porch 🐟 SEAFOOD   This cedar-shingled seafood shack offers glorious beach and Gulf views from its long porch. The popular, casual restaurant originated charcoal-grilled amberjack, which you'll now see on menus throughout Florida. Other fish and seafood, as well as chicken and juicy hamburgers, also come from the coals. Monthly specials feature crab, lobster, and seasonal fish. Come early, order a rum-laden Key Lime Freeze, and enjoy the sunset. The Back Porch sits with a number of other restaurants near the western boundary of the Henderson Beach State Park and is a popular hangout for Frisbee players and sunbathers.

1740 Old Hwy. 98 E. © 850/837-2022. www.backporchseafood.com. Main courses $12–$20; sandwiches, burgers, and pastas $6.50–$9. AE, DC, DISC, MC, V. Apr–Sept daily 11am–11pm; off season daily 11am–10pm. From U.S. 98, turn toward the beach at the Hampton Inn.

Fisherman's Wharf Seafood House ★★ SEAFOOD   Go fishing, then bring your catch here and the chef will chargrill it at this atmospheric restaurant next to a charter fleet marina (the restaurant hosts most of Destin's fishing competitions). If you struck out fishing, and didn't stop by Sexton's Seafood on the way here to buy a few filets (see above), you can select from the restaurant's fresh-off-the-boat catch for grilling, broiling, frying, or blackening. Charcoal grilling is the house specialty—the triggerfish filet comes white and flaky but still moist. All main courses include a trip to the salad bar, rice pilaf, baked potato, or roasted vegetables. Although this building dates from 1996, it reminds us of an Old Florida fish camp, with rough-hewn wood walls and double-hung windows looking out to a large harborside deck, a venue during the warmer months for two bars, an oyster bar, live music, and great sunsets.

210D Hwy. 98 E., Destin Harbor. © 850/654-4766. www.fishwharf.com. Main courses $11–$21; sandwiches and burgers $6–$9; cook-your-catch $7 lunch, $10 dinner. AE, DC, DISC, MC, V. Summer daily 11am–11pm (deck bar open later); off season daily 11am–9pm.

Fudpucker's Beachside Bar and Grill ★ AMERICAN   A sprawling, 26,000 square foot complex, Fudpucker's is a beachside burger and beer joint with a twist—or, rather, many twists. For one, there's also a sushi bar. The decor is funky, with antique beer cans, mirrors and what they call "Fud Junk." The Fudburger is the menu's most popular, but an unabridged selection of everything from fried crab to Puckeroni Pizza is available for the taking. Eight different dining rooms, a kids' playground, and game rooms with air hockey and video games are nothing compared to Fudpucker's Gator Beach, the restaurant's very own alligator collection located in the pond underneath the building. Live music and a new addition, Club Key West, make this place one of the area's most popular night spots. **Fudpucker's on the Island,** 108 Santa Rosa Blvd., Fort Walton Beach (© 850/243-3833), is the original, located on Okaloosa Island.

20001 Emerald Coast Pkwy. © 850/654-4200. Reservations accepted only for hibachi tables. Main courses $12–$21. AE, DC, DISC, MC, V. Mon–Wed 11am–10pm; Thurs–Sat 11am–4am.

Super-Cheap Eats

Callahan's Island Restaurant & Deli ★ *Value* AMERICAN/DELI   The best place in the area for picnic fare, this family-operated deli offers burgers, excellent Reubens, and other made-to-order sandwiches, pastas, and nightly specials such as charcoal-grilled chicken and grilled pork chops. A long refrigerator

---

(Fun Fact Building Fences

Seaside's Urban Code requires that all homes sport white-painted wood picket fences at the street-front and path-front property lines, and that no two fences be the same on any one avenue. Explore all the fences, which range from subdued to downright wacky.

case across the rear holds a variety of top-grade cheeses, deli meats, steaks, and chops (choose your own cut, and the chef will chargrill it to order). Tables and booths are set up garden fashion, adding an outdoorsy ambience to this pleasant storefront establishment. Locals like to do lunch here. Breakfast is served only on Saturday mornings.

950 Gulf Shore Dr. (2 blocks south of U.S. 98). ℃ 850/837-6328. Main courses $8–$16; sandwiches, burgers, and salads $4–$7. DISC, MC, V. Mon–Fri 10am–9pm; Sat 8am–9pm.

Donut Hole SOUTHERN   Available around the clock, breakfasts at this popular spot highlight eggs Benedict, hot fluffy biscuits under sausage gravy, Belgian waffles, and freshly baked doughnuts. Lunch sees fresh deli sandwiches, half-pound burgers, and big salads. The rough-hewn building has booths and counter seating. Be prepared to wait on the deck, especially on weekends. Daily specials such as half a Southern fried chicken with three country-style vegetables and dessert are a bargain. There's another Donut Hole, open daily from 6am to 10pm, on U.S. 98 East in southern Walton County 2½ miles east of the Sandestin Beach Resort (℃ **850/267-3239**).

635 U.S. 98 E. ℃ 850/837-8824. Breakfast $4–$7.50; sandwiches, salads, and burgers $4.50–$7.50; main courses $6.50–$10. No credit cards. Daily 24 hr. Closed 2 weeks before Christmas.

Worth a Splurge

Copper Grill ★★ STEAK   An upscale restaurant lit by gas torches, the Copper Grill is a delicious dichotomy of swank and kitsch—check out the zebra prints inside the dining room. Each table has its own DVD player, television screen, and coffeemaker, and, to add to the distraction, there's an open pit grill in the middle of the action. Their Angus beef is top-notch, but order the steak fondue—it's absolutely to die for.

11225 Hwy. 98. ℃ 850/654-6900. Reservations recommended. Main courses $18–$35. Sun–Thurs 5:30–9:30pm; Fri–Sat 5:30–11pm.

Marina Cafe ★★★ NEW AMERICAN   Destin's finest restaurant provides a classy atmosphere with soft candlelight, subdued music, and walls of glass overlooking the harbor. The changing menu always offers nouveau preparations of seafood. Pizzas are topped with the likes of spicy cayenne rock shrimp, roasted corn, and onion marmalade, and pastas might feature fusilli with roast chicken, sun-dried tomatoes, goat cheese, broccoli, pine nuts, and an herb-and-balsamic-vinegar broth. The marine cuisine includes pan-seared redfish with a sausage crust and almond-crusted mahimahi. Try the sautéed spicy lump crab cakes with roasted pepper butter and habanero-tomato relish and my favorite, the chipotle-honey barbecued Gulf shrimp, roasted poblano, onion, and corn quesadilla, with a spicy tomato-mint salsa. Weather permitting, enjoy the outdoor deck for drinks and appetizers.

404 Hwy. 98 E., Destin Harbor. ℃ 850/837-7960. www.marinacafe.com/marina/marina.html. Reservations recommended. Main courses $15–$29; pizza and pasta $9–$17. AE, DC, DISC, MC, V. Daily 5–11pm. Closed first 3 weeks in Jan.

FORT WALTON BEACH

Caffè Italia ★★ NORTHERN ITALIAN   Nada Eckhardt is from Croatia, but she met her American husband, Jim, while working at a restaurant named Caffè Italia in northern Italy. The Eckhardts duplicated that establishment in this 1925 Sears Roebuck mail-order house tucked away on the waterfront. You can dine on the patio with a view of the sound through sprawling live oak trees (one table is set romantically under a gazebo) or dine inside, where Nada has installed floral tablecloths and photos from the old country. A limited but fine menu includes excellent pizzas; pasta dishes such as tortellini with tomatoes, chicken, and peas in Alfredo sauce; northern Italian risotto with either asparagus or smoked salmon; and meat and seafood dishes to fit the season. Don't expect to make a full meal by ordering only pasta, because meals are served in the authentic Italian fashion, with a small portion of pasta preceding the seafood or meat course. On the other hand, you can quickly fill up on the seasoned, pizza-dough bread sticks served with olive oil for dipping. The cappuccino is absolutely first-rate, as are the genuine Italian desserts.

189 Brooks St., on the mainland in the block west of Brooks Bridge. © 850/664-0035. Reservations recommended. Main courses $15–$18; pizza and pasta $8–$13. AE, DC, DISC, MC, V. Sun and Tues–Fri 11am–10pm; Sat 5–11pm. Closed Thanksgiving, Christmas.

Pandora's Restaurant & Lounge ✿ STEAKS/PRIME RIB/SEAFOOD
The front part of this unusual restaurant is a beached yacht now housing the main-deck lounge. Below is a beam-ceilinged dining room aglow with lights from copper chandeliers. Try for the private Bob Hope booth, where you can dine below two of the great comedian's golf clubs (he used to come here to raise money for a local air force widows' home). Anything from the charcoal grill is excellent, including the wonderful bacon-wrapped scallops offered as an appetizer. Several varieties of freshly caught fish are among the main-course choices, but steaks and prime rib keep the locals coming back for more. The tender beef is cut on the premises and grilled to perfection. The delicious breads and pies are homemade. There's another Pandora's in Grayton Beach at the corner of Fla. 283 and County Road 30A (© 850/231-4102).

1120B Santa Rosa Blvd. © 850/244-8669. Reservations recommended. Main courses $12–$25. AE, DISC, MC, V. Sun–Thurs 5–10pm; Fri–Sat 5–10:30pm.

Super-Cheap Eats

Big City Coffeehouse and Cafe COFFEE/PASTRIES/DELI   For a caffeine fix, an inexpensive breakfast or lunch, or afternoon tea, head to Tina and Jim Ivanchukov's bright yellow-and-purple cafe on the mainland near the Brooks Bridge. In addition to offering gourmet coffees, the owners make great salads such as herb-roasted chicken with apples, walnuts, and tarragon dressing (sold by the pound), and sandwiches served on homemade focaccia bread.

201 Miracle Strip Pkwy. SE (U.S. 98). © 850/664-0664. Sandwiches and salads $6.50–$9. MC, V. Mon–Fri 7am–7pm; Sat 8am–5pm; Sun 8am–3pm.

SEASIDE

Several cafes and sandwich shops in Seaside's Gulf-side shopping complex offer inexpensive snacks to beachgoers.

Worth a Splurge

Bud & Alley's ✿✿ SEAFOOD/STEAKS/MEDITERRANEAN   In this cracked-crab-and-champagne-loving village, Bud & Alley's features spectacular sunsets from the rooftop bar and a menu that changes frequently but always has savory surprises. The offerings feature an infusion of Basque, Italian, Louisianian, and Floridian dishes that might include seafood stew (clams, mussels, scallops, shrimp, and fish in a saffron-fresh fennel sauce) or sautéed heads-on shrimp with garlic, shallots, and cracked pepper. You can dine indoors or out, on the screened porch, or under an open-air gazebo where you'll hear the waves splashing against the white sands.

County Rd. 30A, in the beachside shops. © 850/231-5900. www.budandalleys.com. Reservations recommended. Main courses $18–$29; lunch $7.50–$23. MC, V. Apr–Sept Sun–Thurs 11:30am–3pm and 5:30–9:30pm, Fri–Sat 11:30am–3pm and 5:30–10pm; Oct–Mar Sun–Thurs 5:30–9pm, Fri–Sat 5:30–9:30pm.

DESTIN & FORT WALTON BEACH AFTER DARK

Most resorts spotlight live entertainment during the summer season, including the Radisson Beach Resort and the Ramada Plaza Beach Resort in Fort Walton Beach, and the Hilton Sandestin Beach & Golf Resort and Sandestin Golf and Beach Resort in southern Walton County (see "Accommodations You Can Afford," earlier in this chapter). It's a good idea to inquire ahead to be sure of what's scheduled, especially during the slow season October through February.

For other ideas and listings of what's happening, pick up a copy of the weekly *Walton Sun* newspaper.

DESTIN   Several Destin restaurants offer entertainment nightly during summer, on weekends in the off season. The dockside **AJ's Club Bimini,** 116 U.S. 98 E. (© 850/837-1913), has live reggae under a big thatch-roofed deck. A somewhat older, if not more sober, crowd gathers for entertainment at the big harborside deck at **Fisherman's Wharf,** on U.S. 98 East (© 850/654-4766); **The Deck,** on U.S. 98 East at the Harbor Docks restaurant, overlooking the harbor (© 850/837-2506); and **Harry T's Boat House** (© 850/654-4800), also on the harbor; and for Irish tunes nightly year-round at **McGuire's Irish Pub & Brewery** (© 850/650-0567), in the Harborwalk Shops on U.S. 98 just east of the Destin Bridge. See "Great Deals on Dining," earlier in this chapter, for details about the restaurants. The **Grande Isle Sky Bar,** above Grazti Italian Restaurant, 1771 Old Hwy. 98 (© 850/837-7475), draws the after-dinner crowd from the Back Porch and other adjacent restaurants.

Twenty-somethings are attracted to the dance club, rowdy saloon, Jimmy Buffett–style reggae bar, and sports TV and billiards parlor all under one roof at the acclaimed **Nightown,** 140 Palmetto St. (© 850/837-6448; www.nightown.com), near the harbor on the inland side of U.S. 98 East. One admission covers it all. There's live music Friday and Saturday nights and amateur boxing on Tuesdays. Nearby, **Hogs Breath Destin,** 541 Hwy. 98 E. (© 850/837-5991; www.hogs breath.com), is another lively pub with bands playing rock, blues, and jazz.

Out toward Sandestin, **Fudpucker's Beachside Bar & Grill,** 20001 Hwy. 98 E. (© 850/654-4200), opposite the Henderson Beach State Park, offers double the fun with two summertime stages. There's another Fudpucker's at 108 Santa Rosa Blvd. on Okaloosa Island in Fort Walton Beach (© 850/243-3833).

FORT WALTON BEACH   Country music and dancing fans will find a home at the **Seagull,** on Miracle Strip Parkway (U.S. 98) opposite the Gulfarium (© 850/243-3413). The generations of air force pilots who have hung out here call it the "Dirty Gull." Its main rival for the country set is the **High Tide Oyster Bar,** at Okaloosa Island off the Brooks Bridge (© 850/244-2624).

3 Panama City Beach

100 miles E of Pensacola, 100 miles SW of Tallahassee

Panama City Beach, a Spring Break mecca that was once erroneously featured as a bleak, desolate wasteland of sun and strip malls in the Ashley Judd film *Ruby in Paradise,* has long been known as the "Redneck Riviera," since it's a mecca for millions of vacationers from the bordering states of Georgia, Alabama, Mississippi, and Louisiana. It still has a seemingly unending strip of bars, amusement parks, and old-fashioned motels. But this lively and crowded destination (in season) also has luxury resorts and condominiums to go along with its 20-plus miles of sandy beaches, golf courses, fishing, boating, and fresh seafood.

Panama City Beach is the most seasonal resort in Northwest Florida, since many restaurants, attractions, and even some hotels close between October and spring break in March. Spring break is a big deal here; MTV even sets up shop in Panama City Beach for annual beach-party broadcasts.

ESSENTIALS

GETTING THERE   The commuter arms of **Delta** (© 800/221-1212), **Northwest** (© 800/225-2525), and **US Airways** (© 800/428-4322) fly into **Panama City/Bay County International Airport** (© **850/763-6751;** www.pcairport. com), on Lisenby Avenue, north of St. Andrews Boulevard, in Panama City.

Alamo (© 800/327-9633), **Avis** (© 800/331-1212), **Budget** (© 800/527-0700), **Enterprise** (© 800/325-8007), **Hertz** (© 800/654-3131), and **National** (© 800/CAR-RENT) have rental-car offices here.

Taxi fares to the beach are about $25.

The Sunset Limited service on **Amtrak** (© **800/USA-RAIL;** www.amtrak.com) stops at Chipley, 45 miles north of Panama City.

VISITOR INFORMATION   For advance information, contact the **Panama City Beach Convention & Visitors Bureau,** P.O. Box 9473, Panama City Beach, FL 32417 (© **800/722-3224** in the U.S., 800/553-1330 in Canada, or 850/233-6503; fax 850/233-5072; www.800pcbeach.com). It operates a visitor information center in the city hall complex, 17001 Panama City Beach Pkwy. (U.S. 98), at Fla. 79. The center is open daily from 8am to 5pm, closed New Year's Day, Thanksgiving, and Christmas.

GETTING AROUND   The **Bay Town Trolley** (© **850/769-0557**) runs five times a day Monday through Friday year-round along Thomas Drive and on Front Beach Road as far west as Fla. 79. Rides cost 50¢. Call for the schedule. For taxis, call **Yellow Cab** (© **850/763-4691**). Fares at the beach are $2.50 to climb aboard and $1.50 per mile, or $5 to $10 for rides within Panama City Beach.

TIME   The Panama City area is in the Central Time zone, 1 hour behind Miami, Orlando, and Tallahassee.

HITTING THE BEACH: ST. ANDREWS STATE PARK

A nearly unbroken strand of fine white sand fronts all 22 miles of Panama City Beach, but the highlight for many is **St. Andrews State Park** ⟨★★★⟩, at the east end of the beach. With more than 1,000 acres of dazzling white sand and dunes, this preserved wilderness demonstrates what the area looked like before motels and condominiums lined the beach. Lacy, golden sea oats sway in the refreshing Gulf breezes, and fragrant rosemary grows wild. Picnic areas are on the Gulf beach and the Grand Lagoon. Restrooms and open-air showers are available for beachgoers. For anglers, there are jetties and a boat ramp. A nature trail reveals wading birds and perhaps an alligator or two. And drive carefully here, for the area is home to foxes, coyotes, and a herd of deer. Overnight camping is permitted (see "Accommodations You Can Afford," below). A historic turpentine still that's on display was formerly used by lumbermen to make turpentine and rosin, both important for caulking the old wooden ships.

The park's 176 RV and tent **campsites** are among the state's most beautiful, especially the 40 situated in a pine forest right on the shores of Grand Lagoon. They are very popular, so reservations are highly recommended—and absolutely essential in summer (call © **800/326-3521** or go to the website www.reserveamerica.com). Sites cost $17 to $19 March through September. They drop to $10 to $12 October through February.

Park admission is $5 per car with two to eight occupants, $3 for single-occupant vehicles, and $1 for pedestrians and cyclists. The area is open daily from 8am to sunset. Pets are not allowed in the park. For more information or for camping reservations, contact the park at 4607 State Park Lane, Panama City, FL 32408 (© 850/233-5140; www.floridastateparks.org/standrews).

Pristine **Shell Island** 🌟🌟, a 7½-mile-long, 1-mile-wide barrier island that's accessible only by boat, sits a few hundred yards across an inlet from St. Andrews State Park. This uninhabited natural preserve is great for shelling and also fun for swimming, suntanning, or just relaxing. Visitors can bring chairs, beach gear, coolers, food, and beverages. The best way to get there is on the park's **Shell Island Shuttle** (© 800/227-0132 or 850/234-7245; www.shellislandshuttle.com), which runs every 30 minutes daily from 9am to 5pm in summer, weekends from 10am to 3pm in spring and fall. Fares are $9.50 for adults, $5.50 for children 11 and under, plus admission fees to the state recreation area (see above). A special snorkel package costs $18, including shuttle ride and equipment. Kayak rentals cost $35 a day for a single-seat boat, $45 for a double seater.

Several cruise boats go to Shell Island, including the glass-bottom *Captain Anderson III,* which cruises there from Captain Anderson's Marina, 5500 N. Lagoon Dr., at Thomas Drive (© 850/234-3435). It charges $16 for adults, $10 for kids 12 and under (Mar–Oct).

AFFORDABLE OUTDOOR ACTIVITIES

BOATING   A variety of rental boats are available at the marinas near the Thomas Drive bridge over Grand Lagoon. These include the **Captain Davis Queen Fleet,** based at Captain Anderson's Marina, 5500 N. Lagoon Dr. (© 800/874-2415, or 850/234-3435 from nearby states); the **Passport Marina,** 5325 N. Lagoon Dr. (© 850/234-5609); the **Port Lagoon Yacht Basin,** 5201 N. Lagoon Dr. (© 850/234-0142); the **Pirates Cove Marina,** 3901 Thomas Dr. (© 850/234-3939); and the **Treasure Island Marina,** 3605 Thomas Dr. (© 850/234-6533).

Many resorts and hotels provide beach toys for their guests' use. WaveRunners, jet boats, inflatables, and other equipment can be rented from **Lagoon Rentals** (© 850/234-7245).

CRUISES   You'll have your choice of numerous cruises here, from sailing to visiting the dolphins aboard noisy jet skis. The visitor information center (see above) has information about them all—and discount coupons for many.

Children get a kick out of the make-believe swashbucklers on the *Sea Dragon* (© 850/234-7400; www.piratecruise.net), an 80-foot-long replica of a pirate ship that goes on 2-hour cruises from its dock next to the Treasure Ship on Thomas Drive at Grand Lagoon. The trips cost $16, $14 for seniors, $12 for children 3 to 12, and is free for children under 3. Call for seasonal schedules and reservations.

FISHING   The least-expensive way to try your luck fishing is with **Captain Anderson's Deep Sea Fishing,** at Captain Anderson's Marina on Thomas Drive at Grand Lagoon (© 800/874-2415 or 850/234-5940; www.captandersons fishing.com/trips.html). The captain's party-boat trips last from 5 to 6 hours, with prices ranging from about $35 to $40 per person, including bait and tackle. Observers can go along for $20 less.

The more expensive charter-fishing boats depart daily from March to November from the marinas mentioned in "Boating," above.

You definitely won't get seasick casting your line from the **M. B. Miller County Pier,** 12213 Front Beach Rd. (© **850/233-3039**), or the **Dan Russell Municipal Pier,** 16101 Front Beach Rd. (© **850/233-5080**).

GOLF   **Bay Point Yacht and Country Club,** 3900 Marriott Dr., off Jan Cooley Road (© **850-235-6950;** www.baypointgolf.com), offers 36 holes of championship play, including the Bruce Devlin–designed **Lagoon Legends** ★★ course, rated as one of the country's most difficult. Both it and the Club Meadows course have clubhouses, putting greens, driving ranges, clinics, and private instruction. Greens fees with cart start at about $55 in summer and $60 in winter, depending on the day of the week.

The **Edgewater Beach Resort,** 11212 U.S. 98A (© **850/235-4044**), also has a 9-hole resort course, and its guests have access to **The Hombre,** 120 Coyote Pass, 3 miles west of the Hathaway Bridge off Panama City Beach Parkway/U.S. 98 (© **850/234-3573**), a par-72 championship course that is home to the Nike Panama City Beach Classic. Fifteen of its 18 holes have water hazards (the unforgiving 7th hole sits on an island). Greens fees are about $65 in summer, $60 in winter, including cart.

The course at the semiprivate **Holiday Golf Club,** 100 Fairway Blvd. (© **850/ 234-1800**), sports lake-lined fairways and elevated greens. Greens fees with cart are about $45 in summer, $35 in winter. You can play at night on a lighted 9-hole, par-29 executive course.

The least-expensive place to play here is the flat and forgiving **Signal Hill,** 9516 N. Thomas Dr. (© **850/234-3218**), where you'll pay about $20 to walk 18 holes in summer, $15 in winter. Add about $10 per person for a cart.

For course information online, go to www.golf.com and www.floridagolfing. com, or call the **Florida Sports Foundation** (© **850/488-8347**) or **Florida Golfing** (© **866/833-2663**).

SCUBA DIVING & SNORKELING   Although the area is too far north for extensive coral formations, more than 50 artificial reefs and shipwrecks in the Gulf waters off Panama City attract a wide variety of sea life. The largest local operator is **Hydrospace Dive Shop,** 6422 W. Hwy. 98 (© **850/234-3063;** www. hydrospace.com). Others include **Panama City Dive Center,** 4823 Thomas Dr. (© **850/235-3390;** www.pcdivecenter.com); **Emerald Coast Divers,** 5121 Thomas Dr. (© **800/945-DIVE** or 850/233-3355); and **Pete's Scuba Center,** 9007 Front Beach Rd. (© **800/401-DIVE** or 850/230-8006). These companies lead dives, teach courses, and take snorkelers to the grass flats off Shell Island.

EXPLORING THE AREA

Gulf World Marine Park *Kids*   This landscaped tropical garden and marine attraction features shows with talented dolphins, sea lions, penguins, and more. Not to be upstaged, parrots perform daily, too. Sea turtles, alligators, and other critters also call Gulf World home. Scuba demonstrations, shark feedings, and underwater shows keep the crowds entertained. The park also has special interactive programs, including trainer for a day ($175 per person), dolphin encounter ($125), and a Meet the Dolphins tour ($6). Allow about 3½ hours to see it all, more if you do one of the encounters.

15412 Front Beach Rd. (at Hill Ave.), Panama City Beach. © 850/234-5271. www.gulfworldmarinepark.com. Admission $20 adults, $14 children 5–11, free for children under 5. Summer daily 9am–4pm; off season daily 9am–2pm.

ZooWorld Zoological & Botanical Park ★ *Kids*   Sitting in a pine forest, this educational and entertaining zoo is an active participant in the Species Survival

Plan, which helps protect endangered species by employing specific breeding and housing programs. Among the 350 guests here are orangutans and other primates; lions, tigers, and leopards; and alligators and other reptiles. Also included are a walk-through aviary, a bat exhibit, and a petting zoo. The zoo's newest and most precious attraction is The Tilghman Infant Care Facility, a nursery facility that allows you to closely view the baby animals born at ZooWorld.

9008 Front Beach Rd. (near Moylan Dr.), Panama City Beach. ℂ 850/230-1243. Admission $11 adults, $6.95 children 3–11, free for children under 3. Daily 9am–5:30pm (to 4:30pm in winter).

AMUSEMENT PARKS

For that Panama City meets Coney Island vibe, there are two amusement parks at which to kill some time. A 105-foot-high roller coaster is just one of the 30 rides at the **Miracle Strip Amusement Park,** 12000 Front Beach Rd., at Alf Coleman Road (ℂ **850/234-5810;** www.miraclestrippark.com; $5.50 per person, more for rides and shows). Little ones will love the traditional carousel. Nine acres of fun include continuing live entertainment and tons of junk food. The adjoining **Shipwreck Island Water Park** (ℂ **850/234-0368;** www.shipwreckisland.com; $25 for guests over 50 in. tall, $20 for those 35–50 in., free for those under 35 in.) offers a variety of water amusements, including the 1,600-foot-long winding Lazy River for tubing and a daring 35 mph Speed Slide. The Tad Pole Hole is exclusively for young kids. Lounge chairs, umbrellas, and inner tubes are free, and lifeguards are on duty. Combination tickets are available. Both are open weekends from mid-March to Memorial Day, then daily to mid-August, and weekends from then to Labor Day weekend.

SHOPPING

The main branch of **Alvin's Island Tropical Department Store,** 12010 Front Beach Rd. (ℂ **850/234-3048;** www.alvinsisland.com), opposite the James I. Lark Sr. Visitors Information Center, is an attraction in itself. It not only sells a wide range of beach gear and apparel, but also has cages containing colorful parrots, tanks with small sharks, and an enclosure with alligators. The sharks are fed at 11am daily; the gators get theirs at 4pm in summer only. (Only in Florida— live sharks and alligators in a department store!)

ACCOMMODATIONS YOU CAN AFFORD

There are scores of motels along the beach here, ranging from small mom-and-pop operations to sizable members of national chains. The annual guide distributed by the Panama City Beach Convention & Visitors Bureau has a complete list (p. 554).

The most modern of the chain motels are the recently renovated **Howard Johnson Resort Hotel,** 9400 S. Thomas Dr. (ℂ **800/654-2000** or 850/234-6521), and the **Four Points by Sheraton,** 9600 S. Thomas Dr. (ℂ **888/625-5144** or 850/234-6511), both part of the redeveloped Boardwalk Beach Resort area, a center of beach action.

Panama City Beach also abounds with condominium complexes, such as the Edgewater Beach Resort listed below. Among the many rental agents are **Coldwell Banker Beach Rental,** 726 Thomas Dr., Panama City Beach, FL 32408 (ℂ **800/621-2462** or 850/235-4075; fax 850/233-2833; www.panamabeach rentals.com); and **Condo World,** 8815A Thomas Dr. (P.O. Box 9456), Panama City Beach, FL 32408 (ℂ **800/232-6636** in the U.S., 800/824-5411 in Canada, or 850/234-5564; fax 850/233-6725; www.condoworld.net).

The best camping is at the lovely sites in **St. Andrews State Park,** one of this area's major attractions (p. 554).

Rates at even the most expensive properties here drop precipitously during winter, when the town rolls up the sidewalks. Bay County adds 3.5% tax to all hotel and campground bills, bringing the total add-on tax (with the county's 6% sales tax) to 9.5%.

Beachcomber by the Sea ✷   Watercolors by local artist Paul Brent grace every unit in this eight-story all-suites, Spring Breaker-free (they're prohibited, really, I swear!) resort, built and opened in 1998 at the junction of Front Beach Road and Fla. 79. They also have balconies overlooking a Gulf-side swimming pool and hot tub bordered by a concrete deck accented by areas of palm trees. The well-equipped suites come in two sizes. The larger editions have living rooms with sleeper sofas and bedrooms with either king-size or two double beds. Bathrooms and kitchenettes separate the living rooms and bedrooms. The suites are similar to those at the Flamingo Motel & Tower (see below), except that here they have air conditioners in both the living rooms and the bedrooms. The smaller units are more like motel rooms, but they have microwaves. Two of the smaller units also have whirlpool tubs. There's no restaurant here but several are nearby, and complimentary continental breakfast is available in the lobby each morning.

17101 Front Beach Rd., Panama City Beach, FL 32413. © 888/886-8916 or 850/233-3600. Fax 850/233-3622. www.beachcomberbythesea.com. 96 units. Summer $109–$250; off season $39–$109. Rates include continental breakfast. Packages available. AE, DISC, MC, V. **Amenities:** Heated outdoor pool; access to nearby health club; Jacuzzi; game room; coin-op washers and dryers. *In room:* A/C, TV, dataport, kitchen, fridge, coffeemaker, hair dryer, iron.

Flamingo Motel & Tower ✷ *(Value)*   The Lancaster family takes great pride in the gorgeous tropical garden surrounding a heated swimming pool and a large sun deck overlooking the Gulf at their well-maintained motel. The brightly decorated rooms have either full kitchens or refrigerators and microwave ovens. They can sleep two to six people, some in separate bedrooms. Kitchenette rooms in a two-story motel block across the road are less appealing but will accommodate six to eight. Budget-conscious families can opt for lower-priced rooms, accommodating two to four. Next door, the seven-story Flamingo Tower contains 49 suites, all sporting living rooms with sofa beds and dining tables; bedrooms with ceiling fans and their own TVs; kitchens; and balconies overlooking the Gulf and a beachside swimming pool and hot tub. These suites have air-conditioning units in their living rooms but not in their bedrooms (the ceiling fans will come in handy during the hot, humid summer months). Some older units have shower-only bathrooms.

15525 Front Beach Rd., Panama City Beach, FL 32413. © 800/828-0400 or 850/234-2232. Fax 850/234-1292. www.flamingomotel.com. 117 units. Summer $94–$159; off season $39–$139. AE, DISC, MC, V. **Amenities:** 2 heated outdoor pools; access to nearby health club; Jacuzzi; watersports equipment rental; coin-op washers and dryers. *In room:* A/C, TV, kitchen, fridge, coffeemaker.

Worth a Splurge

Edgewater Beach Resort ✷✷ *(Kids)*   One of the Panhandle's largest condominium resorts, this sports-oriented, private, gated facility enjoys a beautiful beachfront location and 110 tropically landscaped acres. Units in five Gulf-side towers offer commanding views of the emerald Gulf and gorgeous sunsets from their private balconies. A pedestrian overpass leads across Front Beach Road to low-rise apartments and townhomes fringing ponds and the fairways of the resort's 9-hole golf course. A daytime shuttle runs around the resort to swimming pools, whirlpools, the tennis center, and the golf course (guests also get privileges at the 18-hole Hombre Golf Club, ¼ mile north). The gorgeous 11,000 square foot, Polynesian-style pool with waterfalls, islands, and a deck features live entertainment daily from 11am to 4pm.

11212 Front Beach Rd. (P.O. Box 9850), Panama City Beach, FL 32407. ℂ 800/874-8686 or 850/235-4044. Fax 850/235-6899. www.edgewaterbeachresort.com. 500 units. Summer $166–$471 condo; off season $86–$174 condo. $5-per-day, per-unit amenities fee. Weekly rates and maid service available. AE, DC, DISC, MC, V. **Amenities:** 2 restaurants; 2 bars; 11 heated outdoor pools; 9-hole golf course; 11 tennis courts; health club; Jacuzzi; watersports equipment rentals; children's programs; concierge; car-rental desk; limited room service; babysitting; coin-op washers and dryers. *In room:* A/C, TV, dataport, kitchen, coffeemaker, hair dryer, iron.

Holiday Inn SunSpree Resort ⭐

One building removed from the Edgewater Beach Resort and across the road from the Shoppes at Edgewater, this 15-story establishment is the top full-service Gulf-front hotel here. It's designed in an arch, with all rooms having balconies looking directly down on the beach, where a heated, foot-shaped, lagoon-style swimming pool and wooden sun deck are separated from the beach by a row of palms and Polynesian torches, which are lighted at night. The hotel has won architectural awards for its dramatic lobby with a waterfall and the Fountain of Wishes (the coins go to charity). The attractive, spacious guest rooms feature full-size ice-making refrigerators, microwave ovens, and two spacious vanity areas with their own lavatory sinks. Decor is dramatically different from your typical Holiday Inn and is more reminiscent of a resort in, say, the Caribbean, with its pastel colors and tile floors.

11127 Front Beach Rd., Panama City Beach, FL 32407. ℂ 800/633-0266 or 850/234-1111. Fax 850/235-1907. www.holidayinnsunspree.com. 340 units. Summer $159–$239 double; off season $75–$139 double. AE, DC, DISC, MC, V. **Amenities:** 2 restaurants; 1 bar; heated outdoor pool; exercise room; Jacuzzi; watersports equipment rentals; game room; concierge; limited room service; babysitting; laundry service; concierge-level rooms. *In room:* A/C, TV, dataport, fridge, coffeemaker, hair dryer, iron, safe.

Marriott's Bay Point Resort Village ⭐⭐ *Value*

Not only is this luxurious vacation miniworld ranked among the nation's top golf and tennis resorts, but it's an extraordinarily good value for Florida as well. Although guests pay extra for most activities, its room rates are among the top steals in the state. They would be higher if the property were beside the Gulf; instead, it's the centerpiece of a manicured real-estate development sprawling over 1,100 acres on a wildlife sanctuary bordered by St. Andrews Bay and the Grand Lagoon. Situated beside the lagoon, the luxurious, vivid-coral stucco hotel is surrounded by gardens, palm trees, oaks, and magnolias. From the glamorous three-story lobby, window walls look out to scenic water views and two swimming pools (one in its own glass-enclosed building). Furnished in dark woods, the newly renovated Marriott-esque rooms are spacious and luxurious, and all have balconies or patios. The highlights for duffers are the Lagoon Legends and the Club Meadows golf courses (see Bay Point Yacht and Country Club under "Affordable Outdoor Activities," earlier in this chapter). Watersports here are at Grand Lagoon Beach, reached by the hotel's long pier. There's also a free shuttle to the Gulf beaches from here.

4200 Marriott Dr., Panama City Beach, FL 32408. ℂ 800/874-7105 or 850/236-6000. Fax 850/236-6158. www.marriottbaypoint.com. 356 units. Summer $149–$209 double; off season $149–$159 double. Packages available. AE, DC, DISC, MC, V. From Thomas Dr., take Magnolia Beach Rd. and bear right on Dellwood Rd. to resort complex. **Amenities:** 2 restaurants; 2 bars; 3 heated outdoor pools; indoor pool; 2 golf courses; 4 tennis courts; health club; Jacuzzi; watersports equipment rental; bike rental; concierge; business center; limited room service; massage; babysitting; laundry service; coin-op washers and dryers; concierge-level rooms. *In room:* A/C, TV, dataport, fridge, coffeemaker, hair dryer, iron.

GREAT DEALS ON DINING

Except for fast-food joints, there aren't many national-chain family restaurants in Panama City Beach (you'll find those along 15th and 23rd sts. over in Panama City). One local chain worth a meal is the **Montego Bay Seafood House** (www. montegobaypcb.com), which offers a wide range of fairly inexpensive munchies, sandwiches, burgers, and seafood main courses. Branches are at the "curve" at 4920 Thomas Dr. (© **850/234-8686**) and in the Shoppes at Edgewater, Front Beach Drive at 473 Beckrich Rd. (© **850/233-6033**).

Pay attention to the restaurant hours here, because some places are closed during the winter months. Even if they're open, many will close early when business is slow. Call ahead to make sure the restaurant you want to go to is open.

Billy's Steamed Seafood Restaurant *Value* SEAFOOD   More a lively raw bar than a restaurant, Billy and Eloise Poole's casual spot has been serving the best crabs in town since 1982. These are hard-shell blue crabs prepared Maryland style: steamed with spicy Old Bay Seasoning. Unlike crab houses in Baltimore, however, Billy and Eloise remove the crab's top shell, clean out the "mustard" (intestines), and cut the crabs in two for you; all you have to do is "pick" the meat. Don't worry, they'll show you. Other steamed morsels include shrimp (also with spicy seasoning), oysters, crabs, and lobster served with corn on the cob and garlic bread. Order anything from the briny deep here, but pass over other items.

3000 Thomas Dr. (between Grand Lagoon and Magnolia Beach Rd.). © 850/235-2349. Main courses $5.50–$18; sandwiches $3.50–$5.50. AE, DISC, MC, V. Daily 11am–9pm.

Captain Anderson's Restaurant & Waterfront Seafood Market SEAFOOD ✦   Since 1953, this famous restaurant has been attracting early diners, who come to watch the fishing fleet unload the catch of the day at the busy marina on Grand Lagoon. It's so popular, in fact, that you may have to wait 2 hours for a table during the peak summer months; three bars are there to help you pass the time. The Captain's menu is noted for grilled local fish (grouper, amberjack, and yellowfin tuna), crab-stuffed jumbo shrimp, and a heaped-high seafood platter. The food isn't as interesting as at Hamilton's Seafood Restaurant & Lounge across the road (see below), but the local atmosphere makes it worth a visit while you're here.

5551 N. Lagoon Dr. (at Thomas Dr.). © 850/234-2225. www.captanderson.com. Main courses $11–$37. AE, DC, DISC, MC, V. Summer Mon–Sat 4–10pm; off season Mon–Sat 4:30–10pm. Closed Nov–Jan.

Hamilton's Seafood Restaurant & Lounge ✦ SEAFOOD   Proprietor Steve Stevens continues in the tradition of his noted Mississippi-born, restaurateur father. The attractive blond-wood and knotty-pine restaurant lies on Grand Lagoon. The grilled grouper with shrimp, scallops, and crab is a real treat. Several other dishes are locally unique to Hamilton's, such as spicy snapper étouffée and a Greek-accented shrimp Christo. Mesquite-grilled fish and steaks are also house specialties, and vegetarians can order a coal-fired vegetable kabob served over angel-hair pasta. The Lagoon Saloon makes the wait for a table pass quickly, and you can select from an extensive selection of well-chosen California and French wines.

5711 N. Lagoon Dr. (at Thomas Dr.). © 850/234-1255. www.hamiltonspcbeach.com. Main courses $13–$25. AE, DISC, MC, V. Summer daily 4–10pm; off season Mon–Thurs 5–9pm, Fri–Sat 5–9:30pm. Closed 1 week in Jan.

WORTH A SPLURGE

Canopies ✦✦ SEAFOOD/STEAKS   This area's most elegant restaurant and purveyor of its finest cuisine occupies a 1910-vintage gray clapboard house with a magnificent view of St. Andrews Bay. Dining is outside on the patio or on an enclosed veranda, and the dark, cozy bar in the old living room invites before- or after-dinner drinks. The menu changes monthly but always offers the consistently excellent creamy she-crab soup under a flaky croissant dome. Other selections could include sushi-quality yellowfin tuna in a sherry-soy sauce served over a haystack of leeks; a "trio" of tuna, salmon, and grouper with a citrus-butter sauce served with a mandarin-orange salsa and Vidalia-onion mashed potatoes; and sautéed grouper with lump crab meat in a sherry-butter sauce. Forget the crab cakes. Landlubbers can partake of award-winning beef, veal, lamb, pork, and game dishes. White-chocolate mousse is among several wonderful sweet endings.

4423 W. Hwy. 98 (1 mile east of Hathaway Bridge on U.S. 98). (C) 850/872-8444. www.canopiespc.com. Reservations recommended. Main courses $18–$26; early-bird specials $11. AE, DC, DISC, MC, V. Daily 5–10pm. Early-bird specials 5–6pm.

SPECIAL DINING EXPERIENCES

You've got to see the **Treasure Ship,** at Treasure Island Marina, 3605 S. Thomas Dr. at Grand Lagoon ((C) 850/234-8881; http://thetreasureship.com), to believe it. This amazing 2 acres of ship space claims to be the world's largest land-based Spanish galleon and a reputed replica of the three-masted sailing ships that carried loot from the New World to Spain in the 16th and 17th centuries. You can get anything from an ice-cream cone to peel-it-yourself shrimp to a sophisticated dinner in the restaurant and bar here, which are open daily from 4:30 to 10pm (and sometimes later); closed during the winter months. Call to make sure it's open when you want to go.

Lady Anderson **dinner-dance cruises** are a romantic evening escape; they're available March through October. This modern, three-deck ship boards at Captain Anderson's Marina, 5550 N. Lagoon Dr. ((C) 800/360-0510 or 850/234-5940; www.ladyanderson.com), Monday through Saturday evenings, with the cruises lasting from 7 to 10pm. Buffet dinners are featured, followed by live music for dancing Monday, Wednesday, Friday, and Saturday nights, gospel music on Tuesday and Thursday. Dinner-dance tickets cost $40 for adults, $38 for seniors, $23 for children 6 to 11, and $15 for children 2 to 5. Gospel music cruises go for $35 for adults, $33 for seniors, $23 for children 6 to 11, and $15 for children 2 to 5. Tips are included. Summertime reservations should be made well in advance.

PANAMA CITY & PANAMA CITY BEACH AFTER DARK

THE PERFORMING ARTS   The Rader family and a cast of 20 perform year-round in the **Ocean Opry Show,** 8400 Front Beach Rd., Panama City Beach ((C) 850/234-5464; www.oceanopryshow.com), the area's answer to the Grand Ole Opry. There's a show every night at 8pm during the summer, less frequently during the off season. Popcorn, hot dogs, and soft drinks are available. Admission is about $20 for adults, half price for children ages 5 through 11. Prices jump to $30 or more when stars like Kitty Welles, B. J. Thomas, and the Wilkensons are in town, usually during winter. The box office opens at 9am Monday through Saturday, and reservations are recommended but not required.

THE CLUB & BAR SCENE   The **Breakers,** 12627 Front Beach Rd. ((C) 850/234-6060), is the area's premier supper club, with unsurpassed Gulf views and music for dining and dancing. You'll swear The King has risen from the grave as "Elvis Presley" and other impersonators of **Clutch Rock 'n' Roll Cafe** perform here. The show is worth the $10 to $15 per-person cover charge. The beachfront **Harpoon Harry's Waterfront Cafe** is part of the same complex.

Romantic lounges with live entertainment are at the **Treasure Ship,** 3605 S. Thomas Dr. (© **850/234-8881**), where comedian-hypnotist Mike Harvey performs during summer in the top-floor Captain's Quarters; and at the **Boar's Head,** 17290 Front Beach Rd. (© **850/234-6628**).

The 20-something crowd likes to boogie all night at beach clubs such as **Schooners,** 5121 Gulf Dr. (© **850/235-3555**), where every table has a Gulf view; **Club La Vella,** a bikini-contest kind of place and one of Florida's largest nightclubs, also on the beach at 8813 Thomas Dr. (© **850/234-3866**); and **Sharkey's on the Gulf,** 15201 Front Beach Rd. (© **850/235-2420**). The clubs often stay open until 4am in summer while their bands play on. **Pineapple Willie's Lounge,** beachside at 9900 S. Thomas Dr. (© **850/235-0928**), is open from 11am until 2am, serving ribs basted with Jack Daniel's and spotlighting live entertainment during summer and a host of sports-TVs year-round.

4 Apalachicola ★★

65 miles E of Panama City, 80 miles W of Tallahassee

Sometimes called Florida's Last Frontier (a claim that overlooks the Everglades), **Apalachicola** makes a fascinating day trip from Panama City Beach or Tallahassee, as well as a destination in its own right. The long, gorgeous beaches on **St. George Island,** 7 miles from town, are among America's best. Justifiably famous for Apalachicola oysters, the bays and estuaries are great for fishing and boating. And if you love nature, the area is also rich in wildlife preserves.

The charming little town of Apalachicola (pop. 2,600) was a major seaport each autumn from 1827 to 1861, when plantations in Alabama and Georgia shipped tons of cotton down the Apalachicola River to the Gulf. The town had a racetrack, an opera house, and a civic center that hosted balls, socials, and gambling. The population shrank during the mosquito-infested summer months, however, when yellow fever and malaria epidemics struck. It was during one of these outbreaks that Dr. John Gorrie of Apalachicola tried to develop a method of cooling his patients' rooms. In doing so, he invented the forerunner of the air conditioner, a device that made Florida tourism possible and life a whole lot more bearable for locals during summer months.

Apalachicola has traditionally made its living primarily from the Gulf and the lagoonlike bay protected by a chain of offshore barrier islands. Today, this area produces the bulk of Florida's oyster crop, and shrimping and fishing are major industries, too. The town has also been discovered by a number of urban expatriates, who have moved here, restored old homes, and opened interesting antiques and gift shops (there aren't many towns this size where you can buy Crabtree & Evelyn products).

ESSENTIALS

GETTING THERE   The nearest airport is 65 miles to the west at Panama City Beach (p. 554). From there you'll have to rent a car or take an expensive taxi ride. The Tallahassee airport is about 85 miles to the northeast (p. 567). **Croom's Transportation** (© **888/653-8132** or 850/653-2400) has airport shuttle service between Tallahassee and Apalachicola ($105 for one passenger, $10 for each additional person).

The scenic way to drive here is via the Gulf-hugging U.S. 98 from Panama City Beach, or via U.S. 319 and U.S. 98 from Tallahassee. From I-10, take exit 142 at Marianna, then follow Fla. 71 south to Port St. Joe, and then take U.S. 98 east to Apalachicola.

VISITOR INFORMATION   The **Apalachicola Bay Chamber of Commerce,** 99 Market St., Apalachicola, FL 32320 (© **850/653-9419;** fax 850/653-8219; www.apalachicolabay.org), supplies information about the area from its office on Market Street (U.S. 98) between Avenue D and Avenue E. The chamber is open Monday through Friday from 9:30am to 5pm.

TIME   The town is in the Eastern Time zone, like Orlando, Miami, and Tallahassee (it's 1 hr. ahead of Panama City Beach and the rest of the Panhandle). *Note:* Many shops are closed on Wednesday afternoon, when Apalachicolans go fishing.

BEACHES, PARKS & WILDLIFE REFUGES

Some experts consider the 9 miles of beaches in **St. George Island State Park** ★★★ to be among America's best. This pristine 9-mile-long nature preserve occupies the eastern end of St. George Island, about 15 miles east of Apalachicola. A 4-mile-long paved road leads through the dunes to picnic areas, restrooms, showers, and a boat launch. An unpaved trail leads another 5 miles to the island's eastern end, but be careful: It's easy to get stuck in the soft sand, even in a four-wheel-drive sport-utility vehicle. From a hiking trail leading from the campground out a narrow peninsula on the bay side, you can see countless terns, snowy plovers, black skimmers, and other birds. Entry costs $3 for a vehicle with one occupant, $5 for vehicles with two to eight occupants, and $1 for pedestrians and bicyclists. Campsites cost $19. The park is open daily from 8am to sunset. Pets are allowed. For more information, contact the park at 1900 E. Gulf Beach Dr., St. George Island, FL 32328 (© **850/927-2111;** www.florida stateparks.org/stgeorgeisland).

There are no facilities whatsoever at the **St. Vincent National Wildlife Refuge,** southwest of Apalachicola and it's accessible only by boat. The U.S. Fish & Wildlife Service has left this 12,358-acre barrier island in its natural state, but visitors are welcome to walk through its pine forests, marshlands, ponds, dunes, and beaches. In addition to native species such as bald eagles and alligators, the island is home to a small herd of sambar deer from Southeast Asia. Red wolves are bred here for re-establishment in other wildlife areas. Access is by boat only. **St. Vincents Island Shuttle Service** (© **850/229-1065;** www.stvincentisland. com), at Indian Pass, 21 miles west of Apalachicola via U.S. 98 and County Roads 30A and 30B, will take you to the island in a pontoon boat. If you bring your bike, they'll drop you on one end of the island and pick you up later at the other. Call for prices and reservations, which are required.

The refuge headquarters, at the north end of Market Street in town, has exhibits of wetland flora and fauna. It's open Monday through Friday from 8am to 4:30pm. Admission is free. For more information, contact the refuge at P.O. Box 447, Apalachicola, FL 32329 (© **850/653-8808**).

The huge **Apalachicola National Forest** (p. 580) begins a few miles northeast of town. It has a host of facilities, including canoeing and mountain-bike trails.

AFFORDABLE OUTDOOR ACTIVITIES

CRUISES   Jeanni McMillan of **Journeys of St. George Island** ★ (© **850/927-3259;** www.sgislandjourneys.com) takes guests on narrated nature cruises to the barrier islands and on canoe and kayak trips in the creeks and streams of the Apalachicola River basin. She also has night hikes with blue-crab netting, shelling excursions, and fishing and scalloping trips, plus excursions tailored exclusively for children. Prices range from $25 to $75 per person. Reservations are required, so call her to find out what she's offering when you'll be in town.

Jeanni also rents canoes, kayaks, sailboats, and sailboards. She's closed January and February.

A less adventurous way to see the marshes, swamps, and shallow-water rivers is via a nature cruise with **EcoVentures, Inc.** (© 850/653-2593; www.apalachicola tours.com). It uses the *Osprey,* a 40-foot, all-weather boat that can carry up to 32 passengers. Fares are $20 for adults, $10 for children under 16. Call for schedule and reservations.

You can go afternoon or sunset sailing on the bay for hours on Captain Jerry Weber's 40-foot sloop *Wind Catcher* (© 850/653-3881). The 2½-hour voyages cost $35 for adults, $20 for children under 16, including snacks and soft drinks. Reservations are essential.

FISHING   You can't go oystering, but fishing is excellent in these waters, where trout, redfish, flounder, tarpon, shark, drum, and other fish abound. The chamber of commerce (see above) can help arrange charters on the local boats, many of which dock at the Rainbow Inn on Water Street. For guides, contact **Robinson Brothers Guide Service** (© 850/653-8896; fax 850/653-3118; www.flaredfish.com). Rates run about $300 for a half day and $400 to $600 for a full day for up to four anglers.

EXPLORING THE TOWN

Start your visit by picking up a map and a self-guided tour brochure from the chamber of commerce (see above), and then stroll around Apalachicola's waterfront, business district, and Victorian-era homes.

Along Water Street, several tin warehouses date to the town's seafaring days of the late 1800s, as does the 1840s-era **Sponge Exchange** at Commerce Street and Avenue E. A highlight of the residential area, centered around Gorrie Square at Avenue D and 6th Street, is the Greek Revival–style **Trinity Episcopal Church,** built in New York and shipped here in 1837. At the water end of 6th Street, Battery Park has a children's playground. A number of excellent art galleries and gift shops are grouped on Market Street, Avenue D, and Commerce Street.

The showpiece at the **John Gorrie Museum State Park** ⚘, Avenue D at 6th Street (© 850/653-9347; www.floridastateparks.org/johngorriemuseum), is a replica of Doctor Gorrie's cooling machine, a prototype of today's air conditioner: It really works! The park is open Thursday through Monday from 9am to 5pm; closed New Year's Day, Thanksgiving, and Christmas. Admission is $1, free for children 6 and under.

The newly renovated **Dixie Theater,** 21 Ave. E. (© 850/653-3200), a 1912 movie house, hosts live theater and maintains the original ticket booth and facades restored to their original glory.

The **Estuarine Walk,** at the north end of Market Street on the grounds of the Apalachicola National Estuarine Research Reserve (© 850/653-8063), contains aquariums full of fish and turtles, and displays of various other estuarine life. It's open Monday through Friday from 8am to 5pm. Admission is free.

ACCOMMODATIONS YOU CAN AFFORD

Built in 1997, the 42-room **Best Western Apalach Inn,** 249 Hwy. 98 W. (© 800/ 528-1234 or 850/653-9131; fax 850/653-9136; www.apalachicola.com/best western), a mile west of downtown, is the only national chain hotel here.

Apalachicola River Inn ⚘   The town's only waterfront accommodation, this two-story motel's rough-hewn exterior timbers make it look like one of the neighboring warehouses. Units in the main building all have views across a marina to Apalachicola Bay. Those on the second floor are larger and have balconies, making them preferable to the smaller downstairs units, whose doors open directly onto the marina's boardwalk. All rooms have been renovated, adding new carpeting, new windows, doors, and French Doors. Most of the upstairs rooms have shower-only bathrooms. Two rooms and a two-bedroom apartment in a building next door have whirlpool tubs.

123 Water St., Apalachicola, FL 32320. © **850/653-8139.** Fax 850/653-2018. www.apalachicolariverinn.com. 26 units. $95–$115 double; $125–$160 Jacuzzi suite; $200–$250 2-bedroom suite. AE, DC, DISC, MC, V. Pets accepted in smoking rooms ($10 nightly fee). **Amenities:** Restaurant; bar. *In room:* A/C, TV.

Coombs House Inn ★★★ The most luxurious accommodation here, this large bed-and-breakfast occupies two Victorian homes. The main house was built in 1905 by a lumber baron, and it shows: Polished black cypress paneling lines the entire central hallway and grand parlor. Each of the 10 guest rooms in the main house is tastefully decorated, with lots of Victorian reproductions. The Coombs Suite, with bay windows, a sofa, a four-poster bed, and its own whirlpool, is outstanding. The "Love Bungalow" has its own private entrance. Less grand but still impressive are eight rooms in another restored Victorian, known as the "Coombs House East," half a block away. One of these rooms has a whirlpool tub and bidet, and there's an apartment in the carriage house over there. One room in each house is equipped for guests with disabilities. A major truck route, U.S. 98, runs along the north side of both houses; request a south room to escape the periodic road noise. Guests are treated to complimentary wine receptions on weekends. The complimentary breakfast is hardly just Danish and coffee, but a home-cooked extravaganza. All rooms are smoke-free.

80 6th St., Apalachicola, FL 32320. © **850/653-9199.** Fax 850/653-2785. www.coombshouseinn.com. 18 units, all with bathroom. $79–$225 double. Rates include full breakfast. DISC, MC, V. **Amenities:** Access to nearby health club; free use of mountain bikes. *In room:* A/C, TV, dataport, fridge (3 units), hair dryer.

Gibson Inn ★★ Built in 1907 as a seaman's hotel and gorgeously restored, this cupola-topped inn is such a brilliant example of Victorian architecture that it's listed on the National Register of Historic Inns. No two guest rooms are alike (some still have the original sinks in the sleeping areas), but all are richly furnished with period reproductions. Nonguests are welcome to wander upstairs and peek into unoccupied rooms (whose doors are left open). Reservations are advised during summer and spring and fall weekends, and as much as 5 years ahead for the seafood festival in November. Grab a drink from the bar and relax in one of the high-back rockers on the old-fashioned veranda. The dining room serves excellent seafood and is open to all comers, so don't expect this to be private like a bed-and-breakfast; instead, you'll find yourself in a reborn, absolutely charming turn-of-the-20th-century hotel.

51 Ave. C, Apalachicola, FL 32320. © **850/653-2191.** Fax 850/653-3521. www.gibsoninn.com. 31 units, all with bathroom. $90–$100 double; $105–$145 suite. AE, MC, V. **Amenities:** Restaurant; bar. *In room:* A/C, TV.

SUPER-CHEAP SLEEPS

Rancho Inn On the western edge of the historic district, this older, Spanish-look motel has been spiffed up by owners Mark and Mary Lynn Rodgers, who keep it clean and well maintained. Although simple when compared to the more expensive properties here, the motel rooms are spacious and comfortable, and all have microwave ovens and fridges. Restaurants are also within walking distance.

240 Hwy. 98 W., Apalachicola, FL 32320. © **850/653-9435.** Fax 850/653-9180. www.ranchoinn.com. 32 units. $55–$150 double. AE, DISC, MC, V. Pets accepted ($6 fee). **Amenities:** Outdoor pool; bicycle rental. *In room:* A/C, TV, dataport, fridge, coffeemaker.

GREAT DEALS ON DINING

Townsfolk still plop down on the round stools at the marble-topped counter to order Coca-Colas and milkshakes at the **Old Time Soda Fountain & Lunch-eonette,** 93 Market St. (℃ **850/653-2606**). This 1950s relic was once the town drugstore. It's open Monday through Saturday from 10am to 5pm.

The Boss Oyster ✯ SEAFOOD   You've heard about the aphrodisiac proper-ties of Apalachicola oysters. Well, you can see if those properties are real at this rustic, dockside eatery, whose motto is "Shut Up and Shuck." In fact, this is one of the best places in Florida to try the bivalves raw, steamed, or under a dozen toppings ranging from capers to crab meat. They'll even steam three dozen of them and let you do the shucking. Steamed shrimp also are offered, as are deli-cious po'boy sandwiches. Most main courses come from the fryer, so consider this joint a great local experience, not fine dining. Sit at picnic tables inside, on a screened porch, or out on the dock.

125 Water St. (between aves. C and D). ℃ 850/653-9364. Main courses $17–$22; oysters $4.50–$14; sand-wiches and baskets $7–$10. AE, DC, DISC, MC, V. Apr–Sept Sun–Thurs 11:30am–10pm, Fri–Sat 11:30am–11pm; Oct–Mar Sun–Thurs 11:30am–9pm, Fri–Sat 11:30am–10pm.

Chef Eddie's Magnolia Grill ✯✯✯ CONTINENTAL/CAJUN   One of the top places to dine in Northwest Florida, Boston-bred chef-owner Eddie Cass's pleasant, homey restaurant offers nightly specials ranging from classic French rack of lamb and beef Wellington to fresh local seafood with New Orleans–style sauces. You will long remember Eddie's mahimahi Pontchartrain with cream and artichoke hearts. The snapper butter pecan and black-bean grouper are two other memorable dishes. Start with a bowl of spicy seafood gumbo, a consistent hit during the Florida Seafood Festival. No smoking inside.

99 11th St. (between aves. E and F). ℃ 850/653-8000. www.chefeddiesmagnoliagrill.com. Reservations recommended. Main courses $12–$28. MC, V. Mon–Sat 6–9:30pm.

The Owl Cafe ✯✯ SEAFOOD   Ensconced on the first floor of a two-story clapboard commercial building in the heart of downtown, this sophisticated restaurant ranks only behind Chef Eddie's Magnolia Grill as having the best cui-sine in town. Go for the nightly fresh seafood specials or opt for the terrific grouper with garlic, capers, and artichokes. Now paneled in rich wood, the walls are adorned with the works of noted local photographer Richard Bickel.

15 Ave. D (at Commerce St.). ℃ 850/653-9888. Reservations recommended. Main courses $12–$25. MC, V. Mon–Sat 11:30am–3pm and 5:30–10pm.

APALACHICOLA AFTER DARK

Nocturnal diversions are scarce in this small town, but you can catch summer-stock performances of plays like *Same Time Next Year* in the lovingly restored, 1912-vintage **Dixie Theatre,** 21 Ave. D (℃ **850/653-3200**). Tickets range from $10 to $25, depending on the show.

Locals like to have their after-work drinks in the fine old bar at the **Gibson Inn** and then hit the **Roseate Spoonbill Lounge,** in the Apalachicola River Inn (see "Accommodations You Can Afford," above), where bands play on weekend evenings.

5 Tallahassee

163 miles W of Jacksonville, 191 miles E of Pensacola, 250 miles NW of Orlando

As a University of Miami alum, I was practically taught to hate Tallahassee, just because it's the home of the Miami Hurricanes' biggest rivals—Florida State

University's Seminoles (or 'Noles as locals refer to them). Because I couldn't care less about football, I just chalked Tallahassee up to being the state capital, and, later in life, command central for that pesky 2000 election bug known as the chad. Boy, was I wrong. It's not just about football and hanging chads at all. There's tons of charm and nonvoting history here, too.

Tallahassee was selected as Florida's capital in 1823 because it was halfway between St. Augustine and Pensacola, then the state's major cities. That location puts it almost in Georgia, and, in fact, Tallahassee has more in common with Macon than with Miami. There's as much Old South ambience here as anywhere else you're likely to visit in Florida. You'll find lovingly restored 19th-century homes and buildings, including the 1845 Old Capitol. They all sit among so many towering pines and sprawling live oaks that you'll think you're in an enormous forest. The trees form virtual tunnels along Tallahassee's five official Canopy Roads, which are lined with historic plantations, ancient Native-American settlement sites and mounds, gorgeous gardens, quiet parks with picnic areas, and beautiful lakes and streams. And the nearby Apalachicola National Forest is a virtual gold mine of outdoor pursuits.

While tradition and history are important here, you'll also find the modern era, beginning with the New Capitol Building towering 22 stories over downtown. Usually sleepy Tallahassee takes on a very lively persona when the legislature is in session and when the football teams of Florida State University and Florida A&M University take to the gridiron.

If you're inclined to give your credit cards a workout, the nearby town of Havana is Florida's antiquing capital.

ESSENTIALS

GETTING THERE   AirTran (© 800/AIR-TRAN), **Delta** (© 800/221-1212), **Northwest** (© 800/225-2525), and **US Airways** (© 800/428-4322) serve **Tallahassee Regional Airport** (© **850/891-7802;** http://talgov.com/citytlh/aviation), 10 miles southwest of downtown on Southeast Capital Circle.

Alamo (© 800/327-9633), **Avis** (© 800/331-1212), **Budget** (© 800/527-0700), **Hertz** (© 800/654-3131), and **National** (© 800/CAR-RENT) have airport sites; **Dollar** (© 800/800-4000), **Enterprise** (© 800/325-8007), and **Thrifty** (© 800/367-2277) are nearby.

You can take a taxi to downtown for about $15.

Amtrak's transcontinental train the Sunset Limited stops in Tallahassee at 918½ Railroad Ave. (© **800/872-7245;** www.amtrak.com).

VISITOR INFORMATION   For information in advance of your arrival, contact the **Tallahassee Area Convention and Visitors Bureau,** 200 W. College Ave. (P.O. Box 1369), Tallahassee, FL 32302 (© **800/628-2866** or 850/413-9200; fax 850/487-4621; www.seetallahassee.com). The bureau's excellent quarterly visitor's guide has descriptions (including hours and admission fees) of just about everything going on here.

Fun Fact   **Where Slaves Were Welcome**

Built in 1838, **The First Presbyterian Church,** on Park Avenue at Adams Street, is the city's oldest church and remains an important African-American historic site since slaves were welcome to worship here without their masters' consent.

Downtown Tallahassee

ATTRACTIONS ●
Black Archives Research Center
  and Museum **13**
Florida State University
  Museum of Fine Arts **6**
Knott House Museum
  ("The House That Rhymes") **8**
Meginnis-Monroe House **7**
Museum of Florida History **11**

WHERE TO STAY ■
Cabot Lodge North **1**
Governors Inn **9**
Quality Inn & Suites **10**

WHERE TO DINE ◆
Anthony's **3**
Bahn Thai **12**
Barnacle Bill's Seafood
  Restaurant **2**
Chez Pierre **4**
Kool Beanz Café **5**

Go to the **Tallahassee Area Visitor Information Center,** 106 E. Jefferson St. across from the capitol (© **850/413-9200**), for free street and public-transportation maps, brochures, and pamphlets outlining tours of the historic districts and the Canopy Roads. The center is open Monday through Friday from 8am to 5pm, Saturday from 9am to noon.

For statewide information, a **Florida Welcome Center** is in the west foyer of the New Capitol Building (see below).

GETTING AROUND   Operated by TALTRAN, the city's public-transportation agency (© **850/891-5200;** www.state.fl.us/citytlh/taltran), the free **Old Town Trolley** is the best way to see the sights of historic downtown Tallahassee. You can get on or off at any point between Adams Street Commons, at the corner of Jefferson and Adams streets, and the Governor's Mansion (see the exact route on the "Downtown Tallahassee" map). The trolley runs Monday through Friday every 20 minutes between 7am and 6:30pm.

TALTRAN also provides city bus service from its downtown terminal at Tennessee and Adams streets ($1 adults, 50¢ kids 12 and under and seniors). Both the ticket booths there and at the Tallahassee Area Visitor Information Center have route maps and schedules.

For taxi service, call **Yellow Cab** (© **850/580-8080**) or **City Taxi** (© **850/562-4222**). Fares are $1.75 at flag fall, plus $1.50 per mile.

TIME   Tallahassee is in the Eastern Time zone, like Orlando, Miami, and Apalachicola. It's 1 hour ahead of the rest of the Panhandle.

EXPLORING THE CITY
THE CAPITOL COMPLEX

Florida's capitol complex, on South Monroe Street at Apalachee Parkway, dominates the downtown area and should be your first stop after the Tallahassee Area Visitor Information Center, just across Jefferson Street.

The **New Capitol Building** (© **850/488-6167**), a $43 million skyscraper, was built in 1977 to replace the 1845-vintage Old Capitol. State legislators meet here for at least 60 days, usually beginning in March. The chambers of the house and the senate have public viewing galleries. For a spectacular view, take the elevators to the 22nd-floor **observatory,** where, on a clear day, you can see all the way to the Gulf of Mexico. You can also view works by Florida artists while up there. The New Capitol is open Monday through Friday from 8am to 5pm.

Directly in front of the skyscraper is the strikingly white **Old Capitol** ✿ (© **850/487-1902;** www.flheritage.com/museum/sites/oldcapitol). With its majestic dome, this "Pearl of Capitol Hill" has been restored to its original beauty. An eight-room exhibit portrays Florida's political history. Turn-of-the-20th-century furnishings, cotton gins, and other artifacts are also of interest. The Old Capitol is open Monday through Friday from 9am to 4:30pm, Saturday from 10am to 4:30pm, and Sunday and holidays from noon to 4:30pm. Admission is free to the old and the new capitols.

The twin granite towers of the **Vietnam Veterans Memorial,** honoring Florida's Vietnam vets, are across Monroe Street from the Old Capitol. Next to it, facing Apalachee Parkway, the **Union Bank Museum** (© **850/561-2603**) is housed in Florida's oldest-surviving bank building. For a while, it was the Freedman's Savings and Trust Company, which served emancipated slaves. Now part of FAMU's Black Archives Research Center, it now houses a small but interesting collection of artifacts and documents reflecting black history and culture that are definitely worth a brief visit. Admission is free. Open Monday through Friday from 9am to 4pm.

The Old Town Trolley will take you to the lovely Georgian-style **Governor's Mansion,** north of the capitol at Adams and Brevard streets (© **850/488-4661**). Enhanced by a portico patterned after Andrew Jackson's columned antebellum home in Tennessee, the Hermitage, and surrounded by giant magnolia trees and landscaped lawns, the mansion is furnished with 18th- and 19th-century antiques and collectibles. Tours are given when the legislature is in session, usually beginning in March. Call for schedules and reservations.

Located adjacent to the Governor's Mansion, **The Grove** was home to Ellen Call Long, known as "The Tallahassee Girl," the first child born after Tallahassee was settled.

HISTORIC DISTRICTS
Although modern buildings have made inroads into the downtown area, Tallahassee makes an ongoing effort to preserve its historic homes and buildings.

Many of them are concentrated in three historic districts within an easy walk north of the capitol complex. The information center in the New Capitol (see "Essentials," above) distributes free brochures of walking tours that cover the three areas. Taken together, the tours are about 4 miles long and should take half a day. Most interesting is the Park Avenue District, 3 blocks north of the capitol complex, which you can see in about 1 hour.

ADAMS STREET COMMONS This 1-block-long winding brick and landscaped area along Adams Street begins on the north side of the capitol complex (it's between Jefferson St. and College Ave.) and retains an old-fashioned town-square atmosphere. Restored buildings include the Governor's Club, a 1900s Masonic lodge, and Gallie's Hall, where Florida's first five African-American college students received their Florida A&M University diplomas in 1892. Restaurants, shops, and Gallie Alley are also here. Adams Street crosses Park Avenue 3 blocks north of the capitol complex. This is a good place for lunch at one of several cafes that cater to downtown office workers.

PARK AVENUE HISTORIC DISTRICT The 7 blocks of Park Avenue between Martin Luther King Jr. Boulevard and North Meridian Street are a lovely promenade of beautiful trees, gardens, and outstanding old mansions. This broad avenue, with a shady median strip lined with moss-bearded live oaks, was originally named 200 Foot Street and then McCarty Street, but was later renamed Park Avenue to satisfy a snobbish Anglophile society matron who didn't want an Irish name imprinted on her son's wedding invitations.

Several Park Avenue historic homes are open to the public, including the **Knott House Museum,** at Calhoun Street (see "Museums, Galleries & Archaeological Sites," below). **The Columns,** at Duval Street, was built in the 1830s and is the city's oldest surviving building (it's now the home of the Tallahassee Chamber of Commerce). **The First Presbyterian Church,** at Adams Street, built in 1838, is the city's oldest church and has been an important African-American historic site since slaves were welcome to worship here without their masters' consent. **The Walker Library,** between Monroe and Calhoun streets, was one of Florida's first libraries, dating from 1903 (it's home to Springtime Tallahassee, which is the city's top special event). Just north of Park Avenue on Gadsden Street, the **Meginnis-Monroe House** contains the Lemoyne Art Gallery (see "Museums, Galleries & Archaeological Sites," below).

At Martin Luther King Jr. Boulevard, the adjacent **Old City Cemetery** and **Episcopal Cemetery** contain the graves of Prince Achille Murat, Napoleon's nephew, and Princess Catherine Murat, his wife and George Washington's grand-niece. Also buried here are two governors and numerous Confederate and Union soldiers who died at the Battle of Natural Bridge during the Civil War. The cemeteries are important to African-American history since a number of slaves and the first black Florida A&M graduates are interred here. The visitor information center in the New Capitol has a cemetery walking-tour brochure.

CALHOUN STREET HISTORIC DISTRICT   The 3 blocks of Calhoun Street between Tennessee and Georgia streets, and running east on Virginia Street to Leon High School, sport elaborate homes built by prominent citizens between 1830 and 1880. A highlight here is the **Brokaw-McDougall House,** in front of Leon High School at the eastern end of Virginia Street, which was built in 1856.

MUSEUMS, GALLERIES & ARCHAEOLOGICAL SITES

Black Archives Research Center and Museum ✿   Housed in the columned library built by Andrew Carnegie in 1908, and located on the grounds of the Florida Agricultural and Mechanical University (FAMU), this fascinating research center and museum displays one of the nation's most extensive collections of African-American artifacts, as well as such treasures as a 500-piece Ethiopian cross collection. The archives contain one of the world's largest collections on African-American history. Visitors can listen to tapes of gospel music and of elderly people reminiscing about the past. FAMU was founded in 1887, primarily as a black institution. Today it's acclaimed for its business, engineering, and pharmacy schools.

Martin Luther King Jr. Blvd. and Gamble St., on the Florida A&M University campus. ✆ 850/599-3020. www.famu.edu. Free admission. Mon–Fri 9am–4pm. Closed major holidays. Parking lot next to building.

Florida State University Museum of Fine Arts ✿   This permanent, 4,000-piece collection features 16th-century Dutch paintings, 20th-century American paintings, Japanese prints, pre-Colombian artifacts, and much more. Touring exhibits are displayed every few weeks.

250 Fine Arts Building, Copeland and Call sts. (on the FSU campus). ✆ 850/644-6836. www.mofa.fsu.edu. Free admission. Mon–Fri 9am–4pm, Sat–Sun 1pm–4pm (Sept-April) Closed on Holidays and weekends May–Aug, unless otherwise noted.

Foster Tanner Art Center   The focus in this gallery is on works by local, national, and international African-American artists, with a wide variety of paintings, sculptures, and more.

Florida A&M University (between Osceola and Gamble sts., off Martin Luther King Jr. Blvd.). ✆ 850/599-3161. www.famu.edu. Free admission. Mon–Fri 9am–5pm.

Knott House Museum ("The House That Rhymes") ✿✿   Adorned by a columned portico, this stately mansion was constructed in 1843, probably by a free black builder named George Proctor. Florida's first reading of the Emancipation Proclamation took place here in 1865. In 1928 it was purchased by politician William Knott, whose wife, Louella, wrote eccentric (read: kooky) rhymes about the house and its elegant Victorian furnishings, including the nation's largest collection of 19th-century gilt-framed mirrors, and about social, economic, and political events of the era. Attached by satin ribbons to tables, chairs, and lamps, her poems are the museum's most unusual feature. The house is in the Park Avenue Historic District and is listed in the National Register of

Historic Places. It's preserved as it looked in 1928, when the Knott family left it and all of its contents to the city (it's now administered by the Museum of Florida History). The museum gift shop carries Victorian greeting cards, paper dolls, tin toy replicas, reprints of historic newspapers, and other nostalgic items.

301 E. Park Ave. (at Calhoun St.). ✆ 850/922-2459. http://www.taltrust.org/knott.htm. Free admission. Wed–Fri 1–4pm; Sat 10am–4pm. 1-hr. tours depart on the hour.

Meginnis-Monroe House ★★ This restored 1852 antebellum home is listed on the National Register of Historic Places and is a lovely setting for fine art. The home's **Lemoyne Art Gallery** is named in honor of Jacques LeMoyne, a member of a French expedition to Florida in 1564. Commissioned to depict the natives' dwellings and map the seacoast, LeMoyne was the first European artist known to have visited North America. Exhibits here include permanent displays by local artists, traveling exhibits, sculpture, pottery, and photography—everything from the traditional to the avant-garde. The gardens, with an old-fashioned gazebo, are spectacular during the Christmas holiday season. Programs of classical music are combined with visual arts during the year; check in advance for the current schedule.

125 N. Gadsden St. (between Park Ave. and Call St.). ✆ 850/222-8800. www.lemoyne.org. Admission $1, free Sun and every day for children 12 and under. Tues–Sat 10am–5pm; Sun 1–5pm. Closed holidays.

Mission San Luís de Apalachee ★ A Spanish Franciscan mission named San Luís was set up in 1656 on this hilltop, already a principal village of the Apalachee Indians. From then until 1704, it served as the capital of a chain of Spanish missions in Northwest Florida. The mission complex included a tribal council house, a Franciscan church, a Spanish fort, and residential areas. Based on extensive archaeological and historical research, the council house and the 10-by-50-foot thatch-roofed church have been reconstructed. They are both open to the public. So is a reconstruction of the 50-by-110-foot thatch-roof mission church. Interpretive markers are located across the 60-acre site, and self-guided tour brochures are available at the visitor center. Call for a schedule of ranger-led guided tours on weekends.

2021 Mission Rd. (between W. Tennessee and Tharpe sts.). ✆ 850/487-3711. www.taltrust.org/san_luis.htm. Free admission. Tues–Sun 10am–4pm. Closed Thanksgiving and Christmas. From downtown, take Tennessee St. (U.S. 90) west to entrance on right past Ocala St.

Museum of Florida History ★ An 11-foot-tall mastodon greets you at this state history museum, where you look back 12,000 years to the first Native Americans to live in Florida (mastodons were very much alive back then). Ancient artifacts from Native American tribes are exhibited, plus such relics from Florida's past as a reconstructed steamboat and treasures from 16th- and 17th-century sunken Spanish galleons. Inquire about guided tours and special exhibits. Visitor parking is available in the garage around the corner on St. Augustine Street between Bronough and Duvall streets.

Lower level of R. A. Gray Building, 500 S. Bronough St. (at Pensacola St.). ✆ 850/245-6400. http://dhr.dos. state.fl.us/museum. Free admission (suggested donation $3 adults, $1 children). Mon–Fri 9am–4:30pm; Sat 10am–4:30pm; Sun and holidays noon–4:30pm. Closed Thanksgiving and Christmas.

A PARK & GARDEN

Maclay State Gardens ★★ In 1923, New York financier Alfred B. Maclay and his wife, Louise, began planting the floral wonderland that surrounded their winter home on Lake Hall, on Tallahassee's northeastern outskirts. After her husband's death in 1944, Louise continued his dream of an ornamental garden

---

Fun Fact **High Flying**

Florida State University's **Flying High Circus** (☎ **800/757-2146** or **850/644-6500**; www.fsu.edu/~circus) calls itself the "Greatest Collegiate Show on Earth" and that's no small boast. It's arguably the grandest college circus in the country. Look for the big top and watch rehearsals during March, then enjoy performances (juggling, hand balancing, bicycle, and trapeze) the first 2 weekends in April ($5–$12).

---

to delight the public. In 1953, the land was bequeathed to the state of Florida. The more than 300 acres of flowers feature at least 200 varieties; 28 acres are devoted exclusively to azaleas and camellias. The surrounding park offers nature trails, canoe rentals, boating, picnicking, swimming, and fishing. The high blooming season is January through April, with the peak about mid-March. Beyond the house and gardens, the state park also includes Lake Overstreet, around which wind 5½ miles of hiking, biking, and horseback-riding trails, making this a major venue for those outdoor activities.

3540 Thomasville Rd. (U.S. 319, north of I-10). ☎ **850/487-4556.** www.ssnow.com/maclay. Admission to park $4 per vehicle with up to 8 passengers, $1 for pedestrians and cyclists. May–Dec free admission to gardens; Jan–Apr $4 adults, $2 children under 12. Park open daily 8am–sunset. Gardens daily 9am–5pm. Maclay House daily 9am–5pm Jan–Apr; closed May–Dec.

TRAVELING THE CANOPY ROADS

Graced by canopies of live oaks draped with Spanish moss, the St. Augustine, Miccousukee, Meridian, Old Bainbridge, and Centerville roads are the five official Canopy Roads leading out of Tallahassee. Driving is slow on these winding, two-lane country roads (the locals only reluctantly are turning some limited sections of them into four-lane highways); some of them are canopied for as much as 20 miles. Take along a picnic lunch, since there are few places to buy a meal along these tranquil byways.

The visitor information center in the New Capitol (p. 569) provides a useful driving guide map of the Canopy Roads and Leon County's country lanes.

If you have time for only one, take **Old Bainbridge Road,** which leads to the Lake Jackson Mounds State Archaeological Site in the northwest suburbs and then on to Havana, Florida's antiquing capital (see "Shopping," below).

SHOPPING

Antiques hounds flock to the little village of **Havana** ★★, 12 miles northwest of I-10 on U.S. 27. Havana used to make its living growing shade tobacco (the outer wrapper on cigars). When that industry fizzled in the 1960s, the town went with it. Things turned around 20 years later, however, when Havana began opening art galleries and antiques, handcrafts, and collectibles shops. Today, these are housed in lovingly restored, turn-of-the-20th-century brick buildings along Havana's commercial streets. Just drive into town on Main Street (U.S. 27), turn left on 7th Avenue, find a parking place, and start browsing. You'll have plenty of company on weekends.

Bradley's Country Store, about 8 miles north of I-10 on Centerville Road (☎ **850/893-1647**; www.bradleyscountrystore.com), sells more than 80,000 pounds of homemade sausage a year, both over the counter and from mail orders. You can also buy coarse-ground grits, country-milled corn meal, hogshead cheese, liver pudding, cracklings, and specially cured hams here. This friendly store, which is on the National Register of Historic Places, is also a sightseeing attraction with self-guided tours. It's open Monday through Friday from 8am to 6pm, Saturday from 8am to 5pm.

AFFORDABLE OUTDOOR ACTIVITIES & SPECTATOR SPORTS

BIKING & IN-LINE SKATING The 16-mile **Tallahassee–St. Marks Historic Railroad Trail State Park** (© 850/922-6007; www.abfla.com/parks/ TallahasseeStMarks/tallahasseestmarks.html) is the city's most popular bike route. Constructed with the financial assistance of wealthy Panhandle cotton-plantation owners and merchants, this was Florida's oldest railroad, functioning from 1837 to 1984. Cotton and other products were transported from Tallahassee to St. Marks for shipment to other cities. In recent years, the tracks were removed and 16 miles of the historic trail were improved for joggers, hikers, bicyclists, and horseback riders. A paved parking lot is at the north entrance, on Woodville Highway (Fla. 363), just south of Southeast Capital Circle. See "Side Trips from Tallahassee," beginning on p. 577, for more about what you can see in the St. Marks area.

The **Apalachicola National Forest** also has extensive mountain-biking trails (p. 580), and there are 5½ miles of trails at **Maclay State Gardens** (see "A Park & Garden," above).

GOLF Play golf at outstanding Hilaman Park, 2737 Blair Stone Rd., where the **Hilaman Park Municipal Golf Course** features 18 holes (par 72), a driving range, racquetball and squash courts, and a swimming pool. Rental equipment is available at the club, and there's a restaurant, too (© 850/891-3935 for information and fees). Compared with most courses in Florida, greens fees are a steal: about $27 on weekdays, $32 on weekends, including cart (they're about $15 and $21, respectively, if you walk). The park also includes the recently renovated **Jake Gaither Municipal Golf Course,** at Bragg and Pasco streets (© 850/891-3942), with a 9-hole, par-35 fairway and a pro shop. Call for fees.

The leading golf course is at the **Killearn Country Club and Inn** (© 800/ 476-4101 or 850/893-2186; www.killearncc.com), which once hosted the Sprint Classic. Moss-draped oaks enhance the beautiful 27-hole championship course, which is for members with reciprocal privileges only. Call for fees.

For course information online, go to www.golf.com and www.floridagolfing. com, or call the **Florida Sports Foundation** (© 850/488-8347) or **Teebone Golfing** (© 866/833-2663).

SPECTATOR SPORTS Tallahassee succumbs to football frenzy whenever the perennially powerful Seminoles of **Florida State University (FSU)** take to the gridiron. Call © 888/378-6653 or 850/644-1830 (www.seminoles.com) well in advance for tickets. Even when the Seminoles play on the road, everything except Tallahassee's many sports bars comes to a stop while fans watch the games on TV.

The **Florida A&M University (FAMU)** Rattlers are cheered on by the school's high-stepping, world-famous Marching 100 Band. Call © 850/599-3230 or check the website at www.famu.edu/athletics for FAMU schedules and tickets.

Both FSU and FAMU have seasonal basketball, baseball, tennis, and track schedules. Call the numbers above for information.

ACCOMMODATIONS YOU CAN AFFORD

There is no high or low season here, but every hotel and motel for miles around is completely booked during FSU and FAMU football weekends from September to November, at graduation in May, and, to a far lesser degree, weekdays during the 60-day legislative session that begins in March. Reserve well in advance or you may have to stay 60 miles or more from the city. For the schedules, call FSU or FAMU (see "Spectator Sports," above).

Most hotels are concentrated in three areas: downtown Tallahassee, north of downtown along North Monroe Street at exit 199 off I-10 (where you'll find most chains), and along Apalachee Parkway east of downtown.

Tax on all hotel and campground bills is 10% in Leon County.

Cabot Lodge North *Value*   It looks like a random motel, really, but look closer. There's charm to be found here. A clapboard plantation-style house with a tin roof and a partially screened wraparound porch provides Southern country charm to distinguish this friendly motel from its nearby competitors. Guests can relax in straight-back rockers on the porch or on comfy sofas and easy chairs by a fireplace in the living room. Although the guest rooms in the two-story motel buildings out back don't hold up their end of the atmosphere factor, they're still quite satisfactory at these rates, and they give quick access to the outdoor swimming pool. Guests can also enjoy a complimentary continental breakfast buffet and evening cocktails.

2735 N. Monroe St., Tallahassee, FL 32303. © **800/223-1964** or 850/386-8880. Fax 850/386-4254. www. cabotlodge.com. 160 units. $66–$88 double. Rates include continental breakfast, evening reception, and local phone calls. AE, DC, DISC, MC, V. **Amenities:** Outdoor pool; access to nearby health club; laundry service. *In room:* A/C, TV, dataport, hair dryer (king-size bedrooms only).

Quality Inn & Suites *Value*   In contrast to most Quality Inns, this property loses some of the motel, chain-gang feel in favor of a classy, marble-lined lobby and guest rooms furnished with sofas and reclining wing chairs. A complimentary continental breakfast is served in a lounge with views of the inn's swimming pool, and guests can partake of a free wine bar Monday through Thursday evenings. A nearby restaurant will deliver food, and several fast-food and family-style restaurants are within a short walk.

2020 Apalachee Pkwy., Tallahassee, FL 32301. © **800/228-5151** or 850/877-4437. Fax 850/878-9964. www. qualityinn.com. 100 units. $79 double; $129 suite. Rates include full breakfast, evening drinks, and local phone calls. AE, DC, DISC, MC, V. **Amenities:** Outdoor pool; access to nearby health club; Jacuzzi; business center; limited room service; laundry service. *In room:* A/C, TV, dataport, fridge, coffeemaker, hair dryer, iron, safe.

WORTH A SPLURGE

Governors Inn ★★   This is the place for legislators, lobbyists, groupies, and Southern gentry to stay, an elegantly furnished inn just half a block north of the Old Capitol in the Adams Street Commons historic district. It's very old school Washington, D.C. The building was once a livery stable, and part of its original architecture has been preserved, including the impressive beams. The guest rooms are distinctive, with four-poster beds, black-oak writing desks, rock-maple armoires, and antique accouterments. Of the suites, each one named for a Florida governor, one has a whirlpool bathtub; another has a loft bedroom with wood-burning fireplace. Complimentary continental breakfast and afternoon cocktails

---

Fun Fact **Count Them Out**

Demand for hotel rooms during the weekends of Florida State University football games is so great that the high-powered lawyers representing then–Vice President Gore and then–Texas Governor George W. Bush had to vacate their rooms when the University of Florida Gators came to play the 'Noles during the 2000 presidential election dispute.

are presented in the pine-paneled Florida Room, and a restaurant across the street provides limited room service. Hang out in the bar area and eavesdrop on amusing political banter. The staff here is superfriendly and helpful.

209 S. Adams St., Tallahassee, FL 32301. (C) **800/342-7717** in Florida, or 850/681-6855. Fax 850/222-3105. www.thegovinn.com. 40 units. $149–$159 double; $169–$229 suite. Rates include continental breakfast and evening cocktails. AE, DC, DISC, MC, V. **Amenities:** Access to nearby health club; limited room service; laundry service. *In room:* A/C, TV, dataport.

GREAT DEALS ON DINING

Numerous budget-priced fast-food and family chain restaurants lie along Apalachee Parkway and North Monroe Street.

Anthony's ✿ SOUTHERN ITALIAN   Locals flock to Dick Anthony's elegantly relaxed trattoria, which supplies them with the city's best Italian cuisine. Among his specialties is *pesce Venezia,* spinach fettuccine tossed in a cream sauce with scallops, crab, and fish. Chicken piccata and chicken San Marino are also favorites, and Dick's thick, juicy steaks are always popular with beef eaters. A wall-size wine cupboard features choices from Italy and the United States by the bottle or glass. Espresso pie leads the dessert menu.

1950 Thomasville Rd., at Bradford Rd. in the Betton Place Shops. (C) **850/224-1447.** Reservations recommended. Main courses $12–$23. AE, DC, DISC, MC, V. Daily 5–9pm.

Bahn Thai THAI/CANTONESE   Lamoi (Sue) Snyder and progeny have been serving the spicy cuisine of her native Thailand at this storefront since 1979. In deference to local Southerners, who may never have sampled anything spicier than cheese grits, much of her menu is devoted to mild Cantonese-style Chinese dishes. More adventurous diners, however, flock here to order such authentic tongue-burners as *yon voon-sen,* a combination of shrimp, chicken, bean threads, onions, lemon grass, ground peanuts, and the obligatory chile peppers. Sue's specialty is her deliciously sweet, slightly gingered version of Penang curry. You can ask her to turn down the heat in her other Thai dishes. Come at lunch and sample it all from the all-you-can-eat buffet—a real bargain.

1319 S. Monroe St. (between Oakland Ave. and Harrison St.). (C) **850/224-4765.** Main courses $6–$15; lunch buffet $7; dinner buffet $11. DISC, MC, V. Mon–Thurs 11am–2:30pm and 5–10pm; Fri 11am–2:30pm and 5–10:30pm; Sat 5–10:30pm.

Barnacle Bill's Seafood Restaurant SEAFOOD   There's always plenty of action at this noisy, very casual spot, a favorite of the downtown crowd, including journalists, bureaucrats, and politicians. Freshly shucked Apalachicola oysters are the stars at the enormous tile-topped raw bar in the middle of the room, but the menu offers a mélange of seafood to please the palates of the singles, couples, and families who flock here. The cooking is simple and usually done by Florida State University students working part-time jobs. Best bets are charcoal-grilled mahimahi, tuna, amberjack, and grouper. For a smoked sensation, try the mahimahi and amberjack cured on the premises. During nice weather, guests can sit at outdoor tables under a lean-to tent. A downstairs bar serves the regular seafood items plus sushi, deli sandwiches, and salads.

1830 N. Monroe St. (north of Tharpe St.). (C) **850/385-8734.** www.barnaclebills.com. Main courses $8–$17 (most $10–$12); sandwiches and salads $5–$9. AE, DC, DISC, MC, V. Sun–Thurs 11am–11pm; Fri–Sat 11am–midnight.

Kool Beanz Cafe ★★ ECLECTIC   The coolest cafe in town, this noisy emporium of trendy cooking draws lots of patrons in their late 20s and early 30s who appreciate exciting blends of flavors. The joint is dimly lit but painted in bright pastels from the Caribbean. You'll find many island-style items on the constantly changing menu, including Jamaican jerk grouper served with black beans, rice, and a sweet tropical-fruit relish. You may want to get here early because more-inventive items like the seared but rare tuna crusted with spice and served with a terrific roasted-peanut sauce will sell out early, as will the curried lamb shank and the pork tenderloin marinated with orange molasses.

921 Thomasville Rd. (at Williams St.). © **850/224-2466.** Main courses $13–$18. AE, DISC, MC, V. Mon–Fri 11am–2:30pm and 5:30–10pm; Sat 5:30–10pm.

WORTH A SPLURGE

Chez Pierre ★★ TRADITIONAL FRENCH   You become an instant Fran-cophile in Florida at this chic restaurant in a beautifully restored 1920s brick home. French-born chef Eric Favier and his American wife and partner, Karen Cooley, offer traditional French cuisine either inside the house—where the walls are adorned with changing, for-sale works by local artists—or outside on a large deck nearly shaded by live oaks draped with Spanish moss. Opening to the deck, a bistro-style bar provides a light-fare menu between lunch and dinner. Chez Pierre offers daily specials to take advantage of fresh produce. Among the win-ners are rack of lamb, a version of Provençal-style ratatouille, and crab cakes with a luscious mustard and thyme demi-glacé. French table wines are moderately priced, and California house wines are also served. Live music regularly accom-panies dining.

1215 Thomasville Rd. (at 6th Ave.). © **850/222-0936.** www.chezpierre.com. Reservations recommended. Main courses $15–$29. AE, DC, DISC, MC, V. Mon–Sat 11am–10pm; Sun 11am–2:30pm and 6–9pm.

TALLAHASSEE AFTER DARK

Check the "Limelight" section of Friday's *Tallahassee Democrat* (www.tallahassee democrat.com) for weekend entertainment listings.

As a college town, Tallahassee has numerous pubs and nightclubs with live dance music, not to mention a multitude of sports bars. Pick up a copy of *Break* and other entertainment tabloids at **Barnacle Bill's Seafood Restaurant** or other entertainment venues.

One of the best bars in town is **Bullwinkle's Saloon,** 620 W. Tennessee St. (© **850/224-0651**), a capital institution with a laid-back vibe and even a Thirsty Moose Club in which members never pay a cover and drink free every Wednesday and Friday. For live music, **Floyd's Music Store,** 666 W. Tennessee St. (© **850/222-3506**), features local and national bands and, for the daring, a mosh pit that fills up quickly, so get there early. West Tennessee Street is where you'll find most of the happening bars in town.

The major performing-arts venue is the **Tallahassee–Leon County Civic Center,** 505 W. Pensacola St. (© **800/322-3602** or 850/222-0400; www.tlccc.org), which features a Broadway series, concerts, and sporting events including Florida State University (FSU) collegiate basketball games. Special concerts are presented by the **Tallahassee Symphony Orchestra** (www.tsolive.org) at FSU Ruby Diamond Auditorium, at College Avenue and Copeland Street (© **850/224-0461**). **The FSU Mainstage/School of Theatre,** at the Fine Arts Building on Call and Copeland streets (© **850/644-6500**), presents excel-lent productions from classic dramas to comedies.

SIDE TRIPS FROM TALLAHASSEE

The following excursions are generally on the way to Apalachicola, so if you're headed that way, plan to make a detour or two.

WAKULLA SPRINGS 🐾🐾

The world's largest and deepest freshwater spring is 15 miles south of Tallahassee in the 2,860-acre **Edward W. Ball Wakulla Springs State Park** 🐾🐾, on Fla. 267 just east of its junction with Fla. 61. Ball, a financier who administered the du Pont estate, turned the springs and the moss-draped surrounding forest into a preservation area. Divers have mapped an underwater cave system extending more than 6,000 feet back from the spring's mouth. Wakulla has been known to dispense an amazing 14,325 gallons of water per second at certain times. Mastodon bones, including those of Herman, now in Tallahassee's Museum of Florida History, were found in the caves. Also, the 1930s *Tarzan* movies starring Johnny Weissmuller were filmed here.

A free 10-minute orientation movie is offered at the park's theater at the waterfront. You can hike or bike along the nature trails, and swimming is allowed, but only in designated areas. ***Note:*** It's important to observe swimming rules here since alligators are present.

If the spring water is clear enough, 30-minute glass-bottom-boat sightseeing trips depart every 45 minutes daily, from 9:45am to 5pm during daylight savings time, 9:15am to 4:30pm the rest of the year. Even if the water is murky, you're likely to see alligators, birds, and other wildlife on 30-minute riverboat cruises, which operate during these same hours. Either boat ride costs $6 for adults, $4 for children under 13.

Entrance fees to the park are $4 per vehicle with up to eight passengers, $1 for pedestrians and bicyclists. The park is open daily from 8am to dusk.

For more information, contact the park at 550 Wakulla Springs Dr., Wakulla Springs, FL 32305 (© **850/224-5950;** fax 850/561-7251; www.floridastateparks. org/wakullasprings).

Accommodations You Can Afford

Wakulla Springs Lodge 🐾   On the shore of Wakulla Springs, this dated but charming lodge is distinctive for its magnificent Spanish architecture and ornate old-world furnishings, such as rare Spanish tiles, black-granite tables, marble floors, and ceiling beams painted with Florida scenes by a German artist (supposedly Kaiser Wilhelm's court painter). The guest rooms are simple by today's standards (you'll get a marble bathroom and phone but no TV). By all means, ask for a room in the front, so you'll have a lake view. You don't have to be a lodge guest to enjoy the warm, smoky ambience of the great lobby with its huge stone fireplace and arched windows looking onto the springs, or to enjoy reasonably priced meals featuring Southern cuisine in the lovely Ball Room (reservations recommended). The fountain (a 60-ft.-long marble drugstore-style counter for old-fashioned ice-cream sodas) provides snacks and sandwiches. The only thing missing here are signs of taxidermy—no boar, deer, or bear heads perched high on the wall anywhere.

550 Wakulla Park Dr., Wakulla Springs, FL 32305. © **850/224-5950.** Fax 850/561-7251. 27 units. $79–$99 double. AE, DISC, MC, V. **Amenities:** Restaurant. *In room:* A/C.

THE ST. MARKS AREA

Rich history lives in the area around the little village of **St. Marks,** 18 miles south of the capital at the end of both Fla. 363 and the Tallahassee–St. Marks Historic Railroad Trail State Park (p. 574).

After marching overland from Tampa Bay in 1528, the Spanish conquistador Panfilo de Narvaez and 300 men arrived at this strategic point at the confluence of the St. Marks and Wakulla Rivers near the Gulf of Mexico. Since their only avenue back to Spain was by sea, they built and launched the first ships made by Europeans in the New World. Some 11 years later, Hernando de Soto and his 600 men arrived here after following Narvaez's route from Tampa. They marked the harbor entrance by hanging banners in the trees, then moved inland. Two wooden forts were built here, one in 1679 and one in 1718, and a stone version was begun in 1739. The fort shifted among Spanish, British, and Native American hands until General Andrew Jackson took it away from the Spanish in 1819.

Parts of the old Spanish bastion wall and Confederate earthworks built during the Civil War are in the **San Marcos de Apalache Historic State Park,** reached by turning right at the end of Fla. 363 in St. Marks and following the paved road. A museum built on the foundation of the old marine hospital holds exhibits and artifacts covering the area's history. The site is open Thursday through Monday from 9am to 5pm, closed New Year's Day, Thanksgiving, and Christmas. Admission to the site is free; admission to the museum costs $1, free for children 6 and under. For more information, contact the site at 1022 DeSoto Park Dr., Tallahassee, FL 32301 (© **850/922-6007;** www.floridastate parks.org/sanmarcos).

De Soto's men marked the harbor entrance in what is now the **St. Marks Lighthouse and National Wildlife Refuge** ✦, P.O. Box 68, St. Marks, FL 32355 (© **850/925-6121**). Operated by the U.S. Fish and Wildlife Service, this 65,000-acre preserve occupies much of the coast from the Aucilla River east of St. Marks to the Ochlockonee River west of Panacea and is home to more species of birds than anyplace else in Florida except the Everglades. The visitor center is 3½ miles south of U.S. 98 on Lighthouse Road (Fla. 59); turn south off U.S. 98 at Newport, about 2 miles east of St. Marks. Stop at the center for self-guided tour maps of the roads and extensive hiking trails, some of them built atop levees running through the marshland.

The 80-foot-tall **St. Marks Lighthouse,** 8 miles south of the visitor center, was built in 1842 of limestone blocks 4 feet thick at the base. The nearby beach is also a popular crabbing spot.

Admission to the refuge is $4 per vehicle, $1 for pedestrians and bicyclists (federal Duck Stamps and National Park Service passports accepted). The refuge is open daily from sunrise to sunset, the visitor center, Monday through Friday from 8am to 4pm and Saturday and Sunday from 10am to 5pm (closed all federal holidays). Contact the refuge for information about seasonal tours and hunting.

In 1865, during the final weeks of the Civil War, federal troops landed at the lighthouse and launched a surprise attack on Tallahassee. The Confederates quickly assembled an impromptu army of wounded soldiers, old men, and boys

---

Tips A Ramshackle Riverside Lunch

Tallahasseeans love to drive or bike down to St. Marks and have a waterside lunch at **Posey's Oyster Bar,** at the end of Fla. 363 (© **850/925-6172**). Some nighttime patrons at this ramshackle wooden restaurant and bar can get rowdy, especially when country-and-western bands are playing on weekends, but it's a fine place for freshly shucked oysters or smoked mullet during the day. Be sure to walk all the way through the dining rooms to the bar beside the St. Marks River. Posey's opens daily at 10am (entrees are about $6–$11).

as young as 14. This ragtag bunch fought the Federal regulars for 5 days at what is now the **Natural Bridge Battlefield State Historic Site.** Surprisingly, the old men and boys won. As a result, Tallahassee remained the only Confederate state capital east of the Mississippi never to fall into Yankee hands. The historic site is on County Road 2192, 6 miles east of Woodville on the St. Marks River, halfway between Tallahassee and St. Marks. Follow the signs from Fla. 363 and go to the end of the pavement. It's open daily from 8am to sunset and admission is free. For more information, contact the San Marcos de Apalache Historic State Park (see above) or check www.floridastateparks.org/naturalbridge.

APALACHICOLA NATIONAL FOREST

The largest of Florida's three national forests, this huge preserve encompasses 600,000 acres stretching from Tallahassee's outskirts southward to the Gulf Coast and westward some 70 miles to the Apalachicola River. Included are a variety of woodlands, rivers, streams, lakes, and caves populated by a host of wildlife. There are picnic facilities with sheltered tables and grills, canoe and mountain-bike trails, campgrounds with tent and RV sites, and a number of other facilities, some of them especially designed for visitors with disabilities.

The **Leon Sinks Area** is closest to Tallahassee, 5½ miles south of Southeast Capital Circle on U.S. 319 near the Leon–Wakulla County line. Nature trails and boardwalks lead from one sinkhole (a lake formed when water erodes the underlying limestone) to another. The trails are open daily from 8am to 8pm.

A necessary stop before heading into this wilderness is the **Wakulla Area Ranger District,** 57 Taft Dr., Crawfordville, FL 32327 (© **850/926-3561;** fax 850/926-1904), a visitor center, which provides information about the forest and its facilities and sells topographical and canoe trail maps. The station is off U.S. 319, about 20 miles south of Tallahassee and 2 miles north of Crawfordville. It's open Monday through Thursday from 8am to 4:30pm, Friday from 8am to 4pm.

Index

FROMMER'S® COMPLETE TRAVEL GUIDES

Alaska
Alaska Cruises & Ports of Call
American Southwest
Amsterdam
Argentina & Chile
Arizona
Atlanta
Australia
Austria
Bahamas
Barcelona, Madrid & Seville
Beijing
Belgium, Holland & Luxembourg
Bermuda
Boston
Brazil
British Columbia & the Canadian Rockies
Brussels & Bruges
Budapest & the Best of Hungary
Calgary
California
Canada
Cancún, Cozumel & the Yucatán
Cape Cod, Nantucket & Martha's Vineyard
Caribbean
Caribbean Ports of Call
Carolinas & Georgia
Chicago
China
Colorado
Costa Rica
Cruises & Ports of Call
Cuba
Denmark
Denver, Boulder & Colorado Springs
England
Europe
Europe by Rail
European Cruises & Ports of Call

Florence, Tuscany & Umbria
Florida
France
Germany
Great Britain
Greece
Greek Islands
Halifax
Hawaii
Hong Kong
Honolulu, Waikiki & Oahu
India
Ireland
Italy
Jamaica
Japan
Kauai
Las Vegas
London
Los Angeles
Maryland & Delaware
Maui
Mexico
Montana & Wyoming
Montréal & Québec City
Munich & the Bavarian Alps
Nashville & Memphis
New England
Newfoundland & Labrador
New Mexico
New Orleans
New York City
New York State
New Zealand
Northern Italy
Norway
Nova Scotia, New Brunswick & Prince Edward Island
Oregon
Ottawa
Paris
Peru

Philadelphia & the Amish Country
Portugal
Prague & the Best of the Czech Republic
Provence & the Riviera
Puerto Rico
Rome
San Antonio & Austin
San Diego
San Francisco
Santa Fe, Taos & Albuquerque
Scandinavia
Scotland
Seattle
Shanghai
Sicily
Singapore & Malaysia
South Africa
South America
South Florida
South Pacific
Southeast Asia
Spain
Sweden
Switzerland
Texas
Thailand
Tokyo
Toronto
Turkey
USA
Utah
Vancouver & Victoria
Vermont, New Hampshire & Maine
Vienna & the Danube Valley
Virgin Islands
Virginia
Walt Disney World® & Orlando
Washington, D.C.
Washington State

FROMMER'S® DOLLAR-A-DAY GUIDES

Australia from $50 a Day
California from $70 a Day
England from $75 a Day
Europe from $85 a Day
Florida from $70 a Day
Hawaii from $80 a Day

Ireland from $80 a Day
Italy from $70 a Day
London from $90 a Day
New York City from $90 a Day
Paris from $90 a Day
San Francisco from $70 a Day

Washington, D.C. from $80 a Day
Portable London from $90 a Day
Portable New York City from $90 a Day
Portable Paris from $90 a Day

FROMMER'S® PORTABLE GUIDES

Acapulco, Ixtapa & Zihuatanejo
Amsterdam
Aruba
Australia's Great Barrier Reef
Bahamas
Berlin
Big Island of Hawaii
Boston
California Wine Country
Cancún
Cayman Islands
Charleston
Chicago
Disneyland®
Dominican Republic
Dublin

Florence
Frankfurt
Hong Kong
Las Vegas
Las Vegas for Non-Gamblers
London
Los Angeles
Los Cabos & Baja
Maine Coast
Maui
Miami
Nantucket & Martha's Vineyard
New Orleans
New York City
Paris

Phoenix & Scottsdale
Portland
Puerto Rico
Puerto Vallarta, Manzanillo & Guadalajara
Rio de Janeiro
San Diego
San Francisco
Savannah
Vancouver
Vancouver Island
Venice
Virgin Islands
Washington, D.C.
Whistler

FROMMER'S® NATIONAL PARK GUIDES

Algonquin Provincial Park
Banff & Jasper
Family Vacations in the National
  Parks

Grand Canyon
National Parks of the American
  West
Rocky Mountain

Yellowstone & Grand Teton
Yosemite & Sequoia/Kings
  Canyon
Zion & Bryce Canyon

FROMMER'S® MEMORABLE WALKS

Chicago
London

New York
Paris

San Francisco

FROMMER'S® WITH KIDS GUIDES

Chicago
Las Vegas
New York City

Ottawa
San Francisco
Toronto

Vancouver
Walt Disney World® & Orlando
Washington, D.C.

SUZY GERSHMAN'S BORN TO SHOP GUIDES

Born to Shop: France
Born to Shop: Hong Kong,
  Shanghai & Beijing

Born to Shop: Italy
Born to Shop: London

Born to Shop: New York
Born to Shop: Paris

FROMMER'S® IRREVERENT GUIDES

Amsterdam
Boston
Chicago
Las Vegas
London

Los Angeles
Manhattan
New Orleans
Paris
Rome

San Francisco
Seattle & Portland
Vancouver
Walt Disney World®
Washington, D.C.

FROMMER'S® BEST-LOVED DRIVING TOURS

Austria
Britain
California
France

Germany
Ireland
Italy
New England

Northern Italy
Scotland
Spain
Tuscany & Umbria

THE UNOFFICIAL GUIDES®

Beyond Disney
California with Kids
Central Italy
Chicago
Cruises
Disneyland®
England
Florida
Florida with Kids
Inside Disney

Hawaii
Las Vegas
London
Maui
Mexico's Best Beach Resorts
Mini Las Vegas
Mini Mickey
New Orleans
New York City
Paris

San Francisco
Skiing & Snowboarding in the
  West
South Florida including Miami &
  the Keys
Walt Disney World®
Walt Disney World® for
  Grown-ups
Walt Disney World® with Kids
Washington, D.C.

SPECIAL-INTEREST TITLES

Athens Past & Present
Cities Ranked & Rated
Frommer's Best Day Trips from London
Frommer's Best RV & Tent Campgrounds
  in the U.S.A.
Frommer's Caribbean Hideaways
Frommer's China: The 50 Most Memorable Trips
Frommer's Exploring America by RV
Frommer's Gay & Lesbian Europe
Frommer's NYC Free & Dirt Cheap

Frommer's Road Atlas Europe
Frommer's Road Atlas France
Frommer's Road Atlas Ireland
Frommer's Wonderful Weekends from
  New York City
The New York Times' Guide to Unforgettable
  Weekends
Retirement Places Rated
Rome Past & Present

Travel Tip: He who finds the best hotel deal has more to spend on facials involving knobbly vegetables.

Hello, the Roaming Gnome here. I've been nabbed from the garden and taken round the world. The people who took me are so terribly clever. They find the best offerings on Travelocity. For very little cha-ching. And that means I get to be pampered and exfoliated till I'm pink as a bunny's doodah.

travelocity®

1-888-TRAVELOCITY / travelocity.com / America Online Keyword: Travel

Travel Tip: Make sure there's customer service for any change of plans — involving friendly natives, for example.

One can plan and plan, but if you don't book with the right people you can't seize le moment and canoodle with the poodle named Pansy. I, for one, am all for fraternizing with the locals. Better yet, if I need to extend my stay and my gnome nappers are willing, it can all be arranged through the 800 number at, oh look, how convenient, the lovely company coat of arms.

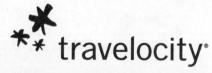